VOICES *of* IRELAND

VOICES

of IRELAND

————

MALACHY
MCCOURT

*Classic Writings
of a Rich and Rare Land*

RUNNING PRESS
PHILADELPHIA · LONDON

MAY 2 3 2003

To Thomas L. O'Halloran, Headmaster of Leamys School, Limerick, Ireland.
He exulted in the taste of textured words, and for us awestruck schoolboys, "still
the wonder grew that one small head could carry all he knew."

Library of Congress Cataloguing-in-Publication Number 2002100445

ISBN 0-7624-1336-0

Author photo courtesy of Malachy McCourt

Cover photograph: © Ryuichi Sato/Photonica

Edited by Michael Washburn

Cover and interior design by Matthew Goodman

Typography by Scribe

Texts of *Uncle Silas, Dubliners, The Ballad of Reading Gaol and Other Poems, A Modest Proposal, The Playboy of the Western World,* and *Early Poems* of W.B. Yeats courtesy of Dover Publications.

Texts by Michael Collins courtesy of CELT, History Department, University College, Cork.

This book may be ordered by mail from the publisher. Please include $2.50 for shipping and handling.

But try your bookstore first!

Running Press Book Publishers

125 South Twenty-second Street

Philadelphia, PA 19103-4399

Visit us on the web!

www.runningpress.com

CONTENTS

A Note on the Texts

The texts in this book derive from the original printed editions. We have made no attempt to modernize the usage, spelling, or punctuation of the various works, or to make them consistent with each other in these respects. In some cases, we have relied on a text published a few years after the first edition and containing few or no differences from the original. The text of *Castle Rackrent* derives from the edition published in 1903 by The Century Co. The selections from *Irish Myths and Legends* come from a reprint of an early edition of *Gods and Fighting Men: The Story of the Tuatha de Danaan and of the Fianna of Ireland, Arranged and Put Into English by Lady Gregory.* For a few of the less-known works, we have seen fit to include a modest apparatus of either footnotes or endnotes.

The Editors

INTRODUCTION

A whole introduction could be written by simply quoting the authors who star in this collection. What a varied crew they are, with hardly anything in common except they were born, they wrote, and they are all dead. Some of them are Irish, some are Anglo-Irish, some are neither but got themselves befogged in the Celtic Twilight and ended with settling down in that Island of Saints and Scholars, as we were taught in reverential school. Outside of school we referred to ourselves as an Island of Rogues and Robbers. Take your pick.

In any case, the fearless and irreverent George Bernard Shaw, another Irishman who could never settle into a normal life and ended up talking and writing all the days of his existence, wrote something about Ireland that seems to have its effect on the unwary visitor or inhabitant, to wit: Ireland, sir, is like no other place under the heavens, said he. No man has touched its sod or breathed its air without being changed for the better or the worse. It produces two kinds of men in strange profusion: Saints and Traitors!

This is a paraphrase of sorts. But it is interesting that good old George seems to have excluded women from either praise or excoriation. But come to think of it, Shaw was a vegetarian, a most un-Irish trait.

It's odd that G.B.S. didn't refer to the other profession so colorfully spread on not only Ireland's mystical landscape but on the world's, namely writers. Is there any explanation for the explosion of wordsmen and wordswomen? The spiritual soil from which they sprang is not a rich one, raped and bloodied as it was by centuries of foreign occupation by invaders with all the sensitivity of the Hun and none of his charm.

So what is it about the Irish, Ireland, and the Word? In the early days was the Word, and the Irish who can cause offense, and that can be delightful. On the other hand, smart-ass quips don't answer any questions. Someone said that the capitalist will sell the last existing piece of rope with which to hang him for robbing the poor, and it was said if the Irishman is given the choice of restraining his tendency to quip and living or uttering the quip and being hanged, he will choose the quip and leave the world and himself laughing. There was a hanging judge, a Briton of course, Lord Norbury, who suffered from gluttony and boozing, thus he sentenced thousands of Irish to be hanged for any of the two hundred offenses which could be punished by hanging because his indigestion and hangover gave him severe stomach- and headaches.

There was a diminutive Irish barrister named John Philpot Curran who constantly risked Norbury's ire. One day riding in a carriage together and passing a gibbet on which hung one of his Lordship's prisoners, Norbury remarked, "I wonder where you would be, Curran, if justice were done."

"Riding alone, m'lord," responded Curran.

For hundreds of years, the Irish were kept enclosed in a spiritual concentration camp, imprisoned behind a magisterial, somber, and imperialistic phalanx of British jackboots whose spokesmen told the world that behind them were millions of mad Irishmen who if they were unloosed into the world would inundate it with torrents of revolutionary prose, seditious song, and penetrating poetry and that all that stood between an unsuspecting civilization and the rampaging literary hordes were the guns, the cannon, the pitiful artillery and the mere might of the British Empire. They slaughtered as many of them as they could but still they came, the pagan Irish, the Catholic Irish, the atheist Irish, the Anglo-Irish, even the suborned English-Irish. They didn't have guns to turn into ploughshares and they didn't have ploughshares to turn into anything. Just words, waves of words, drowning out and overwhelming the hangman, the roar of artillery, and the rattle of musketry, and it wasn't at all bad for a world made fearful by British propaganda. It is axiomatic in the annals of colonial oppression that if the victim speaks against a regime, takes up arms for freedom, or takes up the pen in the cause, he/she is labeled a terrorist or simply a criminal. With hardly an exception all the leaders of Irish rebellions were writers and many of them simply poets. An ineluctable crowd they were, who may not have entirely believed that the pen is mightier than the sword but that it can inflict a larger array of wounds not necessarily fatal.

But the nagging question still is what births the writer and the word in this North Atlantic island of 32,000 square miles about 320 miles long and 135 miles across, which can be covered in a day and would take centuries to explore.

There were six invasions ere St. Patrick set foot on Ireland's shore as a slave. The last three being the Firbolgs, the Tuatha de Danaan, and lastly the Milesians speaking, one presumes, the Gaelic language, and then Patrick bringing Latin followed by the Vikings who brought the Norse tongue, and then with the blessings of Pope Adrian the VI (an Englishman) the Normans came bringing French with them, and finally the English bringing their dull tongue which was burnished and brightened by Irish craftspeople for many centuries to come.

A theater critic for *Time* magazine writing about Brendan Behan's play *The Hostage* said the Irish derive the greatest benefit from the English language. They court it like a beautiful woman and then make it bray with donkey laughter. They fling it at the sky like paint pots full of rainbow colors and then they make it chant a dirge of man's fate and of man's follies like a soft rain falling on the barren bog. They have paid the oppressor the supreme compliment of taking his language and turning it to sorcery. One would think the writer of that critique was a Hibernian himself. There are a half billion or so words in the English tongue, and it's likely all of them have been used by Irish writers in the colored verbal tapestries which are woven unendingly, universal in understanding and simply beautiful in their flow. In a survey of language use by the United Nations some years ago, it was discovered that the average working-class lad, American and European, used about two thousand words a year whereas the average working-class Irish lad used many times (7,000 approximately) more than his foreign counterparts.

There is not a great deal of attention or respect paid to what is generally known as proper English or indeed grammatical English. If the thought can be communicated in one word, the Irish will try to use a thousand. There is a historic perception coursing through the Irish psyche that the English, particularly the upper-class English, do not understand the English language and that the Irish were put on earth to make things clear to them. Of course there is an awareness that most upper-class Brits are Teutons and that English is a second language to them. Most people use language to communicate whereas in Ireland it was frequently used in great torrents of words to obfuscate. The average resident of that island hesitates to lie, and as a waterfall engulfs droplets Irish speech engulfs words. The English respond by treating the Hibernians as a mob of unruly children given to violent tantrums, unprovoked attacks on authority, and to singing at the most inappropriate times, such as when losing a battle. They have succeeded in reducing the Irish gift for language with the subtle propaganda that all we say and write is empty of substance. If an Englishman speaks well, he is applauded as eloquent, if the Irishman speaks well, they smile down at him patronizingly and remark that he must have kissed the Blarney Stone or that he has the "gift of the gab" which in truth is no gift as gab means idle chatter speech without substance, meaningless natter. But still they talk.

George Bernard Shaw is not included in this collection as there is no system for reducing him to manageable reading proportions. As many of the writers in this collection are of outside blood the weather conditions may affect them as they affect the native, indeed as Shaw said, "The Irish climate will stamp an immigrant more deeply and durably in two years than the English climate will in two hundred." And I suppose love of words will do wonders for a nation's literature.

Jonathan Swift might be the first Irisher to blast through the prison wall behind which the oppressor had herded the tumultuous mob. A man born in Dublin in the year 1667, and who died in the same city in the year 1745 having reached the extraordinary age for that time of 78 years, when the average citizen checked out at 47 years. He was a cantankerous man, was Swift, who loved and lost and loved and won. As Dean of the Protestant St. Patrick's Cathedral in Dublin he had access to all the seats of power. If there was happiness in the world, it seemed as if he were determined to avoid it. It's odd that his *Gulliver's Travels* has given him fame in the children's literary world as he did not like children and intended the story for grown intelligent people. Living and being a clergyman in Dublin was not the height of Swift's ambition, indeed he would have much preferred the luxury and sumptuousness of London, but as he had offended all those who had the power to make him a bishop or give him a living, there he was tied to a past that gave him no joy. Nobody really knows if he were as perverse as he would like us to think. A dour-looking man, quite tall, who rarely smiled but could keep a room rocking with laughter at his wit. He pretended to despise the poor Irish and yet gave much of his money for the relief of poverty. He said that Everyman desires to live long, but no man would be old. Looking at a dying tree once he remarked that like it he would like to die from the top down.

The poor man suffered from Meniere's disease and subsequently was afflicted with Arteriosclerosis, which combination led to him being declared to be "of unsound mind and memory" in 1742. It was in 1729, however, in a rage at the inhumanity of the conservative government's treatment of the suffering Irish peasantry that he wrote *A Modest Proposal for Preventing the Children of the Poor People of Ireland from being a Burden to Their Parents or Country and for Making Them Beneficial to Their Publick,* to give it its full title.

To say this brilliant native caused a thunderous uproar amongst the reigning murderous conservatives of the day is understating the reaction. They didn't understand satire, and the average conservative reading it today still has the same reaction. It would delight Jonathan Swift and make him chortle behind the black stone over his tomb in the cathedral on which is inscribed:

> The body of Jonathan Swift, Doctor of Sacred Theology, dean of this cathedral church is buried here, where fierce indignation can no more lacerate his heart. Go, traveler, and imitate, if you can, one who strove with all his strength to champion liberty.

It's an oddity that the Irish were so busy surviving that they had no time to sit back to take a look at their own culture and their own societal doings. Surviving is a pain in the arse to people who like to relax, talk, and rhapsodize about their own lives. So it was left to what is known as "the gentry" to chronicle Irish peasant doings. Sometimes known as The Ascendancy (which someone defined as an English Protestant on an Irish horse), these folk became fascinated by Irishness. One of them was a woman named Maria Edgeworth, who though born in England lived most of her life in Ireland. Maria dearly loved her father, a man who had four wives and fathered twenty-two children. Among other things, the young Edgeworth lady ran her father's estate, knew about bookkeeping, and collaborated with the father on a book about practical education and an essay on Irish Bulls. An Irish Bull is not an animal, it is a figure of speech which intentionally or unintentionally misleads the listener regarding the meaning of what is being mentioned but at the same time manages to give a clear picture of the message, for example: "Half of the lies our opponents tell about us are not true." My explanation of the Irish Bull is bullish itself. Anyway, Maria Edgeworth lived in County Longford where she wrote her little novel *Castle Rackrent*. It was supposedly the slide to ruin of an aristocratic family as seen through the eyes of an aging peasant. In it Maria Edgeworth captures the language and spirit of a century of rural history. It is comic and tragic and above all it contains the necessary Celtic ingredient of satire. For some reason Maria Edgeworth stopped writing for the last fifteen years of her life. Perhaps she felt she had written all she could write about her adopted land and its people.

During her lifetime, the right of people to be left alone was ably and forcefully advocated by Thomas Jefferson, and the Irish devoutly wished that this precept be observed by all nations, but now as kings arose in morning, yawning and stretching and wondering how to fill the day, it was likely they would be startled into full consciousness by the blinding thought, "Why don't I invade Ireland?" And invade they would, and to their astonishment the Irish would resist and be called all sorts of names for that resistance. And if aristocratic types such as Hamilton Rowan Lord Edward Fitzgerald or Theobald Wolfe Tone saw the justice and the need for this resistance, they were called traitors who supported terrorism. So it was in 1798 that the Irish rose up again to resist the genocidal attacks on their homeland and culture and once more were defeated even though the French gave some help. That thwarted rebellion is chronicled by the objective pen of C.H. Teeling in *The History of the Rebellion of 1798*. The executions and deaths of the participants prefigured the violence and cruelty recorded centuries later by James Stephens and Michael Collins in their respective accounts, included herein.

Clergymen and their offspring seem to produce their fair share of literature, and the not always pious and prayerful Joseph Sheridan LeFanu was the son of a Huguenot cleric, and his mother was sister to the brilliant playwright Richard B. Sheridan. LeFanu was a sociable sort of fellow, well-liked and most welcome in any society in which he cared to move. There was his wife Susan and their four children, whom he loved dearly. Having read law at Trinity College, it was not to his liking, and he became a journalist as did his contemporary Irishman Bram Stoker, whose Dracula creation keeps many of us awake at night. All literary life seems to be plagiarism in ways, so that it was said that Maria Edgeworth influenced Walter Scott, the Scottish novelist and poet, and Scott in turn influenced LeFanu. Great Scott!

LeFanu had purchased some magazines and newspapers where are serialized some occult and supernatural horror tales to great acclaim, though the literati of the day looked down on such writing, and here again we find LeFanu influencing good old Charles Dickens. Always a prolific writer was Joseph S. LeFanu, and a good life was his what with a happy family, devoted wife, and healthy children, money, satisfying work, and then down comes the divine banana skin, and you end up on your arse stunned at the suddenness and unexpectedness of it all. In the case of LeFanu it was the sudden death of his beloved wife that spun him into the downward spiral of silent despair. He became a recluse and was known as The Invisible Prince. Still he wrote, and the tales got darker and darker, and for those who advocate the beneficial qualities of green tea, a perusal of LeFanu's classic story, coincidentally called "Green Tea," might lead to a rethinking of this reputedly healthy beverage. Suicide pops up as a theme in LeFanu's work, leaving one to wonder if that were a constant in his grief-stricken life. In our selection here, *Uncle Silas*, we are drawn into a mystery by kindness and gentleness to a point where there is no turning back despite our horror and our fear. Be not afraid, for it's a beautifully written story and you will be all the better for having read it.

Once again, a comparatively little-known Irish author began writing in his particular vein before the immortal household names made their contributions to the genre. LeFanu was only a student when he began turning out supernatural tales and mysteries, before Poe and Dickens directed their efforts to the supernatural tale. Nor does he stand alone as a seminal Irish explorer of the bizarre.

A very odd bird by the name of Charles Robert Maturin, who like Swift was a clergyman, but there the resemblance ceases, burst on the Dublin literary scene with two novels, *The Fatal Revenge* (1807) and *The Milesian Chief* (1812). The man was mad for dancing no matter the time of day, and if there was no partner a chair would do as well. There was no such thing as an eccentric among the Irish well-to-do, as class and a bit of money allowed the upper classes free rein in the cuckoo department. Maturin though a cleric was fond of dressing in the latest fashions to the point of being a dandy. His mind however was not dandified, as can be seen when one reads the classic macabre tale of Melmoth the Wanderer, which limits of space have kept us from including here.

There is nothing quite like a tale of a young person on the way to a dilapidated old mansion in a carriage, and therein is a dilapidated old miserly man dying and in dread of his surroundings and of those who have been his servants for years. The usual distrust of the lower classes is exhibited here, but it's a tale which it is said might have influenced Edgar Allen Poe. A mere 42 when he died, Maturin's story still instils that fearful feeling in the reader who wants to stop reading but must go on.

Roger Casement was an Irish upper-class type who had been knighted by the monarch for exposing the horrors and brutalities of colonialism in the Congo and Peru (non-British colonies of course), but when he attempted to remove the British yoke from the neck of Ireland, they besmirched his character, saying he was, horror of horrors, a homosexual, and then tried him for treason, and they hanged him. Casement was very much influenced by a woman named Alice Stopford Green, the widow of an English historian named John R. Green. Alice had become an ardent Irish nationalist as well as taking over the finishing of her deceased husband's book *Conquest of England*, but got herself involved in a gun-running scheme which involved friend Roger Casement and other well-to-do Anglo-Irish. She stayed very much involved in Irish affairs until her death in 1929, and herein we include her *Ourselves Alone in Ulster*.

> Sticks-stones will
> break my bones
> But names will never
> hurt me.

Really? Well, let's take a look at poor Oscar Fingal O'Flahertie Willis Wilde, son of Dr. (Sir) William Wilde, a noted eye surgeon and archaeologist, and of Lady Jane Wilde, a splendid poet known as Speranza, who was also a nationalistic lady. Both parents were well and truly published and there was no doubt that Oscar would be launched into a world of his own choosing. When he began a relation-ship with the son of the Marquis of Queensbury, one Lord Alfred Douglas affectionately known as Bosie, the Marquis was not happy about this and left a card at Oscar's club on which was writ: "To Oscar Wilde posing as a sodomite for all to read."

Wilde decided to sue for slander for this name-calling, and in the course of the trial it was revealed that homosexual acts had been committed. Such a thing had never been heard of in England before, as homosexuality was unknown in the empire. Shortly after he lost his slander suit, Wilde was arrested and charged with said homosexual practices. He had been urged to flee the country, which he could, but thought he could stand trial and charm the court. Nobody found his witticisms in the courtroom to be funny, as details of his involvement with boys from the streets, tough dock workers, and many details of what was considered a saga of a sordid life emerged. He was found guilty and sentenced to two years at hard labor in Reading Gaol (pronounced jail). And there he wrote *De Profundis*, an accusatory letter to his paramour Bosie, and under the name Sebastian Melmoth published the famous jail epic. It was said he chose the name Sebastian because that lad was a Christian martyr who was riddled with arrows and the prison uniform of the day was also festooned with printed arrows. *Melmoth the Wanderer* was as we have seen written by Charles Maturin and Oscar claimed him as a grand uncle. So this brilliant poet, wit, playwright, and iconoclast died at 46 years as a result of being called a name. Repeat after me:

Each man kills the
Thing he loves.

William Butler Yeats is a name that is as well known as any film star. Willie, another Irish Protestant, was born into a lower-middle-class family in a Dublin suburb. From an early age art in all forms and the occult were his obsessions, and later on we could add the beautiful Maud Gonne (McBride) to that list. The early poems have as much to do with the other world and the nether world as the later ones were to deal with Irish nationalistic aspirations and his undying fascination with Maud Gonne, who married a romantic figure, Major John McBride, executed by the British in 1916. As Willie couldn't convince Maud Gonne to marry, so he proposed to her daughter, who it is said merely smiled and said no thank you!

There is nearly always a sense of loss or impending loss in these poems and indeed in the whole repertoire of Yeats's poetry. His search for longevity on earth took him to Switzerland for investigation of the efficacy of implanting monkey glands in humans, and his quest for immortality took him to séances and gatherings of occultists all over the earth. In one sense he was romantically attracted by the myths and fairy tales and supernatural stories of the Irish peasantry, but he was repelled by the possibility of human contact. They were by turns loud/taciturn, voluble/silent, and personal hygiene was mostly lacking, and Yeats had very sensitive nostrils. An ardent nationalist was Willie, who founded the Abbey Theater along with Lady Gregory to further the cause of Gaelic and its culture. Artists are often excused aberrant behavior because they are not considered normal human beings, but Yeats blotted his copybook when he took up with a fascist gang, the Blueshirts, led by a General O'Duffy which subscribed to the philosophies of Benito Mussolini and Adolf Hitler. It was as well perhaps he died ere he saw what these two were to wreak on the world. Someone said he outlived everything except his genius. He also outlived Joyce, Wilde, Stephens, Synge. For years his body was kept in France but was finally brought back and buried in a graveyard in Sligo under Ben Bulben, and the most famous of all epitaphs is written by himself of course on his gravestone for all to see:

> Cast a cold eye
> On life, on death.
> Horseman, pass by!

There is one author whose work is the foundation stone for all stories and legends of peasant Ireland. Much as Irish-Americans want to be descended from kings and in some cases queens, there is no denying that we were squashed by the might of the British military and with some not inconsiderable help from Irish traitors with conservative tendencies. Regardless of oppression, then, people revive and live and sing and sing again. Survivalism leads to the growth and production of many odd objects of art and artifacts in what are called primitive societies. The Irish then made things of wood, musical instruments, from goatskins they made drums and from reeds they made pipes and whistles and they wove wool into ganseys and pampooties and came up with an exuberance of language to leave the oppressor scratching his pate. Because of the strength of the oral tradition, William Carleton was able to listen and annotate carefully the wild stories of an uninhibited yet oppressed class. The destruction of the way of life of the peasantry became the fertilizer in the growth of Irish nationalism which weed-like sprang up in unexpected places. Carleton was born a Catholic and after he moved to Dublin he became a

Protestant. Life was easier for the Protestants as, though they were in a minority, they held the land and thus the power.

The land question left its permanent imprint on Carleton, who despite his gifts would die poor, much like the peasants whose eloquent voice he was. The acute inequality he saw around him would not really change for the better, for him or for anyone, during his lifetime or for many years thereafter. For all of that, William Carleton was a keen observer of rural life and customs and was not the least bit intimidated by authority as he chronicled the quite explicit doings of the country folks at various celebrations such as weddings, christenings, harvest gatherings, and wakes. With Italians the big celebration is the baptism, with the French it is marriage, and with the Irish it is the wake. The Irish Catholic generally subscribes to the notion that the dead man has gone to a more salubrious climate, so stop the mourning. Carleton documents the goings-on at wakes in his *Traits and Stories of the Irish Peasantry*. A number of them are quite sexual in nature, which ultimately led the church to step in and lay down ecclesiastical law as to what was allowed and what was banned.

But as one wake reveler said to the dead man, You shoulda been there.

James Stephens is noted for a couple or three things, and he ought to be noted for more in the public mind. It is noted that he was born in Dublin in 1882 and died in 1950. Herbert Kenny in his wonderful book *Literary Dublin* describes Stephens as a dolichocephalic lustrous-eyed gnome of a man, gentle by nature, with a great love of animals. However he did write *The Crock of Gold*, possibly the best-known piece of Irish mythology ever recorded, which was nearly destroyed by being turned into a crock of sh-t musical called *Finian's Rainbow*, but it survived. James Joyce, it is said, asked James to finish *Finnegans Wake* should anything happen to prevent him from doing it himself, something incidental to life like death. If Yeats wrote the poem that inspired the Easter Rebellion, James Stephens wrote the most graphic account of that most amazing week in the history of that blood-spattered green isle when a terrible beauty was born. It is a tale populated by adventurers on a ride as thrilling as any of the narratives that unfold in the stories and novels Stephens also penned. The grisly acts Stephens witnessed, such as the shooting of a civilian in front of a barricade the rebels had thrown up, do not detract from the nationalistic fervor of his white-knuckle account.

The most famous renaissance is the Italian one, but to the Irish literati, indeed to many non-Irish, the Celtic Revival is the one. I have often thought that to have a renaissance one must have something to renaisse from, so what did the Irish revive and from where. In any case Isabelle Augusta Persse, better known as Lady

Gregory thanks to having married Sir William Gregory, collaborated with W.B. Yeats and John Millington Synge to found the ultimate stage for Irish art and aspirations, the Abbey Theatre. Here again is a Protestant into whose blood came that syndrome which afflicts all who stay in Ireland for too long, known as More Irish Than The Irish Themselves. She learned the native language along with her son Robert, and even after he was shot down over Italy in the War to End All Wars which many Irish vigorously opposed, she never closed her mind or her purse to the cause of her beloved Abbey Theatre.

She had a bit of lisp, and as usual in Ireland there is no mercy shown to those outsiders who would become assimilated. But nobody could exceed her mastery of native idioms, customs, and beliefs, gained from her close relationship with the servants on her family's estate. When Yeats got an offer to compile a book of Irish myths and legends, he declined, saying he knew a woman who was perfect for the job. Her Ladyship smiled, endowed, contributed, and wrote her own stories and plays and left this enduring legacy of a generous-hearted and artistic woman.

If you want to know how the term playboy entered popular parlance, look no further. If the peasants in the west of Ireland had any inkling that this word would be closely associated with naked women who unfold, they would collapse in laughing glee. John Millington Synge (pronounced Sing) had gone off to France to write as he was entranced with the French Romantics. However Willie Yeats, he of a practical mind, told Synge to return to Ireland and write about what was under his nose which the man did. Now some people say the speech of the people as recorded by Synge is as overwrought as an eastern wall hanging, but it is astounding in fluidity and enveloping in its softness. This playwright wrote with obvious love and affection and yet he was as honest as could be. To quote him,

> On the stage one must have joy, one must have reality and people have grown sick of the false joy of musical comedy that has been given them in place of the rich joy found only in what is superb and wild in reality. In a good play every speech should be as fully flavored as a nut or apple and such speeches cannot be written by anyone who works among people who have shut their lips on poetry.

When *Playboy of the Western World* was presented at the Abbey Theatre in January 1907, which resulted in a riot by very proper Hibernians who insisted that words like "shift" the undergarment should not be mentioned on the stage, the play did go on for its week's run, but again when it was presented in New York another riot ensued, and again in Philadelphia.

Nobody remembers the rioters who are all dead, and the *Playboy of the Western*

World still bounds across the stages of the world. Now let me make that most fatuous of all statements.

Let me introduce someone who needs no introduction, namely James Joyce. In case you don't know, this man stood the world of literature on its noodle when he wrote *Ulysses* and invented a new form of expression with *Finnegan's Wake*. Prior to that he careered about Dublin's pubs and brothels with abandon till he took an intense dislike of the culture, the people, the church, and decided that he would depart for silence, exile, and cunning. He may have departed from Ireland, but it never left him. His companion whom he eventually married was the aptly named Nora Barnacle, with whom he had two children, Lucia and Giorgio. Like many of his contemporaries, Joyce suffered from congenital eye disease which eventually left him almost totally blind. There is hardly an Irish writer or a writer in Ireland who escapes the wrath of some entity be it the church, the government, the Association for the Preservation of Irish Chastity, the Society for the Elimination of Bad Words, and County Council, the Tourist Board, the Arch Confraternity to Preserve the Good Name of Limerick, and like Synge, Beckett, Behan, the book *Dubliners* was delayed publication because it might cause someone to sue. It was eventually published in 1914, although Joyce did not make much money on it, and indeed throughout his life he was in constant financial hot water.

Michael Collins was a mere thirty-two years of age when he was shot and killed in 1922 during the so-called civil war that broke out in Ireland after Collins had signed a treaty with the British. Prior to that he had been an expert in guerrilla warfare knocking off hundreds of enemy troops, the police, undercover agents, informers, traitors, and anyone who stood obstructing the path to Irish freedom. His spies were everywhere and his specialty was infiltrating all communication media. Some described him as a kind man devoted to duty, and others said he was a ruthless cold-blooded killer. Were he alive today and engaged in the same activities for freedom, he would of course be labeled a terrorist. Read on!

So here we have twelve people, nine men and three women, with all the men dying before the age of eighty and all three women hopping over it. There are Protestants, collapsed Catholics, heterosexuals, homosexuals, mad people and not so mad people, and the commonality is having been embraced by Ireland lovingly or otherwise. As Synge said, in Ireland for a few years more we have a popular imagination that is fiery and magnificent and tender, so that those of us who wish to write start with a chance that is not given to writers in places where the springtime of local life has been forgotten and the harvest is a memory only and the straw has been turned into bricks.

JONATHAN SWIFT

♣

(1667-1745)

By the time Jonathan Swift was born in Dublin, on November 30, 1667, his father, Jonathan Sr., had already died and his mother, Abigail, would soon leave him to return to her home in England. It was this inauspicious start in life that clearly helped shape Swift's later passions, namely the fight for the rights of the Irish, and he would ultimately be recognized as one of the most brilliant satirists in world literature.

Not much is known about the early years of Jonathan Swift. After his mother deserted Ireland for her native England, Swift stayed behind with an older sister Jane, and was raised predominantly by uncles. A nurse was apparently so fond of the young Jonathan and so reluctant to let the toddler out of her sight, that she took him with her to visit a dying relative in England. The nurse, however, did not inform any of Swift's family of her hasty voyage to Whitehaven, and it was feared Jonathan had been kidnapped. Scholars have long held that the story of this voyage at sea was in the back of Swift's mind when he wrote *Gulliver's Travels*.

Her penchant for towing babies overseas on family matters notwithstanding, the nurse was believed to have taught the young Swift to read at a very early age. But by the age of six, he was in the care of his uncle Godwin, who did his best to ensure that Swift received the highest quality education possible in Ireland, and to that end he enrolled the precocious lad in the prestigious Kilkenny Grammar School, where he stayed for eight years. In 1682, Swift enrolled himself at Trinity College in Dublin as a pensioner, and took on a highly conservative curriculum, with focus on Aristotelian logic, physics, and literature. He showed little promise outside of language and literature courses, and in 1686, he graduated from Trinity *speciali gratia*, meaning "by special favor." Swift decided to continue his studies at

Trinity in pursuit of an advanced degree, but in 1689, war broke out in Ireland, closing down the college, and he fled to Leicester to be briefly reunited with his mother.

In England, Swift ultimately gained employment with Sir William Temple at Moor Park in Surrey, tackling mostly secretarial duties. Here, Swift was given complete access to his employer's library of which he took advantage, spending an inordinate amount of his free time satisfying his intellectual curiosity. Over time, he gained more of Temple's confidence and trust and his responsibilities increased. Temple once sent him before King William III to plea for passage of a particular bill, but Swift's arguments did not prevent the King from vetoing the bill. However, the event was significant to Swift, who later admitted that it "helped to cure him of vanity."

By 1690, Swift was beginning to suffer an ailment he described as "that old vertigo" which would plague him for the rest of his life. The disease was thought to be "Meniere's Disease," an inner ear disorder which produces nausea and vertigo. Doctors believed that he would improve his condition if he returned to Ireland, and Temple procured for him a letter of recommendation to the Secretary of State. But nothing would come of it, and Swift would, the following year, return to England and resume his work with Temple. Encouraged by his employer, Swift enrolled himself in Oxford University and went on to receive his M.A. degree. He also began to write poetry in his leisure time and published his first poem in 1692. Upon reading it, Swift's distant cousin, the poet John Dryden, is said to have remarked, "Cousin Swift, you will never be a poet."

Meanwhile, Swift had taken to tutoring the eight-year-old daughter of one of Temple's sister's companion, Esther Johnson, known to Swift as "Stella." Some scholars have speculated that Swift and Stella were secretly married at some point, for they maintained an extraordinarily close and lasting relationship, and Swift's series of letters (eventually published as *The Journal to Stella*) was testament to this bond.

In 1694, Swift returned to Ireland to take holy orders, and the following year, he was ordained as a priest in the Church of Ireland. Still, he returned to Sir William Temple and wrote *The Battle of the Books* in 1697, a satire defending Temple's besieged position in a controversy over the literary merit of modern authors versus the authors of classics. Swift had also been composing *A Tale of the Tub*, a satire on the religious extremes of both Catholicism and Calvinism—a work literary scholars described as his first great piece of prose.

In 1699, Sir William Temple died and Swift, unable to find work in England, returned to Ireland, securing a position as chaplain and secretary to the Earl of Berkeley, the Lord Chief Justice of Ireland. He continued to write essays and political pamphlets, all the while hoping to return to England, but his work, *A Tale of the Tub*, though published anonymously later, was generally attributed to Swift. Queen Anne considered the work blasphemous, effectively putting a damper on any preferment ambitions Swift might have had in England.

By 1700, Swift became the Vicar of Laracor and was presented to the Prebend of Dunlavin in St. Patrick's Cathedral in Dublin. It is also around this time that he became politically active, aligning himself with the Whig party. He began traveling back and forth to England as emissary of Irish clergy, lobbying for the remission of taxes on their incomes. However, the Whig government and Queen Anne herself, who suspected Swift of being irreligious, rejected his plea. By 1710, Swift had become disenchanted with the Whig party and focused his allegiance on the Tories, becoming the editor of their newspaper, *The Examiner*. Then, in 1714, Queen Anne died and George I assumed the throne, shutting out the Tories from power, effectively removing any chance Swift had of receiving his preferment in England. It was a bitter disappointment to Swift, who would later write that he was forced to return to Ireland "to die. . . like a poisoned rat in a hole."

Several years would pass before Swift emerged from his depression and self-imposed hiatus from publishing. It is generally acknowledged that Swift's most biting satires resulted from the disappointment of his "exile" to Ireland. He became obsessed with what he perceived to be blatant inequities in English political policies directed at Ireland, namely those implemented by Sir Robert Walpole, the Whig Prime Minister, and began to publish tracts and missives on the mounting problems encountered by the Irish. Some, such as *The Drapier Letters*, an essay published in 1724 which criticized the English for attempting to debase Irish coinage, were not only satirical pieces that provoked public opinion, but instrumental agents in provoking change in English policies. Two years later, Swift would publish his best-known work, *Gulliver's Travels*, a social satire in the guise of fantasy that parodied and attacked English politics and social practices. The book was a considerable commercial success, but because of an imaginative and adventurous story that appealed significantly to children, it was and is considered one of the most misread works in English literature.

In 1729, Swift wrote and published *A Modest Proposal*, a scathing and searing satirical indictment of living conditions in Ireland. As much as he may have railed against and detested his life in Ireland, Swift was enraged by the injustice of England's control over the Irish. In *A Modest Proposal*, Swift proposes that the children of Ireland's poor be bred for consumption to eliminate the increasing number of citizens living in poverty. The plump children could be marketed to rich Englishmen, who would pay handsomely for the prestige of consuming these rare delicacies, Swift wrote. He also took absentee landlords to task, writing:

> I grant this food will be somewhat dear, and therefore very proper for landlords, who, as they have already devoured most of the parents, seem to have the best title to the children.

Swift makes an impassioned economic case for this practice, discussing long and short-term societal benefits, as well as offering the most delicious methods of stewing or roasting succulent babes. The essay was probably his most caustic and scandalous, but the deplorable and desperate nature of his "solution" to one of Ireland's largest challenges at the time elevated Swift to something of a national hero late in life.

By 1735, Swift had begun to suffer more seriously from Meniere's Disease, which was little understood at the time. In addition to the nausea and dizziness he felt, Swift's memory also began to deteriorate. Senility slowly set in until he suffered a paralytic stroke in 1738. Some have speculated that Swift suffered from dementia in his final years before he passed away in 1745. He was buried in St. Patrick's Cathedral next to Stella, who died in 1728, and on the wall next to Swift's coffin is the self-penned Latin epitaph:

> The body of Jonathan Swift, Doctor of Sacred Theology, dean of this cathedral church is buried here, where fierce indignation can no more lacerate his heart. Go, traveler, and imitate, if you can, one who strove with all his strength to champion liberty.

In addition to putting the word "Swiftian" into the English lexicon, Jonathan Swift was a champion for common sense and reason in a world he viewed as increasingly irrational.

A MODEST PROPOSAL

FOR PREVENTING THE CHILDREN OF POOR PEOPLE IN IRELAND FROM
BEING A BURTHEN TO THEIR PARENTS OR COUNTRY, AND FOR MAKING
THEM BENEFICIAL TO THE PUBLIC.

♣

It is a melancholy object to those who walk through this great town or travel in the country, when they see the streets, the roads, and cabin doors, crowded with beggars of the female sex, followed by three, four, or six children, all in rags and importuning every passenger for an alms. These mothers, instead of being able to work for their honest livelihood, are forced to employ all their time in strolling to beg sustenance for their helpless infants; who as they grow up either turn thieves for want of work, or leave their dear native country to fight for the pretender in Spain, or sell themselves to the Barbadoes.

I think it is agreed by all parties that this prodigious number of children in the arms, or on the backs, or at the heels of their mothers, and frequently of their fathers, is in the present deplorable state of the kingdom a very great additional grievance; and therefore whoever could find out a fair, cheap, and easy method of making these children sound useful members of the commonwealth, would deserve so well of the public as to have his statue set up for a preserver of the nation.

But my intention is very far from being confined to provide only for the children of professional beggars; it is of a much greater extent, and shall take in the whole number of infants at a certain age who are born of parents in effect as little able to support them as those who demand our charity in the streets.

As to my own part, having turned my thoughts for many years upon this important subject, and maturely weighed the several schemes of our projectors, I have always found them grossly mistaken in their computation. It is true, a child just dropped from its dam, may be supported by her milk for a solar year, with little other nourishment; at most not above the value of 2*s.*, which the mother may certainly get, or the value in scraps by her lawful occupation of begging; and it is exactly at one year old that I propose to provide for them in such a manner as instead of being a charge upon their parents or the parish, or wanting food and raiment for the rest of their lives, they shall on the contrary contribute to the feeding, and partly to the clothing, of many thousands.

There is likewise another great advantage in my scheme, that it will prevent those voluntary abortions, and that horrid practice of women murdering their bastard children, alas, too frequent among us! sacrificing the poor innocent babes I doubt more to avoid the expense than the shame, which would move tears and pity in the most savage and inhuman breast.

The number of souls in this kingdom being usually reckoned one million and a half, of these I calculate there may be about 200,000 couple whose wives are breeders; from whose number I subtract 30,000 couple who are able to maintain their own children, (although I apprehend there cannot be so many, under the present distresses of the kingdom;) but this being granted, there will remain 170,000 breeders. I again subtract 50,000 for those women who miscarry, or whose children die by accident or disease within the year. There only remain 120,000 children of poor parents annually born. The question therefore is, how this number shall be reared and provided for? which as I have already said under the present situation of affairs is utterly impossible by all the methods hitherto proposed. For we can neither employ them in handicraft or agriculture; we neither build houses (I mean in the country) nor cultivate land; they can very seldom pick up a livelihood by stealing, till they arrive at six years old, except where they are of towardly parts; although I confess they learn the rudiments much earlier; during which time, they can however be properly looked upon only as probationers; as I have been informed by a principal gentlemen in the county of Cavan, who protested to me that he never knew above one or two instances under the age of six, even in a part of the kingdom so renowned for the quickest proficiency in that art.

I am assured by our merchants, that a boy or a girl before twelve years old is no saleable commodity; and even when they come to this age they will not yield above 3*l.* or 3*l.* 2*s.* 6*d.* at most on the exchange; which cannot turn to account either to the parents or kingdom, the charge of nutriment and rags having been at least four times that value.

I shall now therefore humbly propose my own thoughts, which I hope will not be liable to the least objection.

I have been assured by a very knowing American of my acquaintance in London, that a young healthy child well nursed is at a year old the most delicious, nourishing, and wholesome food, whether stewed, roasted, baked, or boiled; and I make no doubt that it will equally serve in a fricasse or a ragout.

I do therefore humbly offer it to public consideration that of the 120,000 children already computed, 20,000 may be reserved for breed, whereof only one-fourth part to be males; which is more than we allow to sheep, black cattle or swine; and my reason is, that these children are seldom the fruits of marriage, a circumstance not much regarded by savages, therefore one male will be sufficient to serve four females. That the remaining 100,000 may be a year old, be offered in sale to the persons of quality and fortune through the kingdom; always advising the mother to let them suck plentifully in the last month, so as to render them plump and fat for a good table. A child will make two dishes at an entertainment for friends; and when the family dines alone, the fore or hind quarter will make a reasonable dish, and seasoned with a little pepper or salt will be very good boiled in the fourth day, especially in winter.

I have reckoned upon a medium that a child just born will weigh 12 pounds, and in a solar year, if tolerably nursed, will increase to 28 pounds.

I grant this food will be somewhat dear, and therefore very proper for landlords, who, as they have already devoured most of the parents, seem to have the best title to the children.

Infant's flesh will be in season throughout the year, but more plentifully in March, and a little before and after: for we are told by a grave author, an eminent French physician, that fish being a prolific diet, there are more children born in Roman catholic countries about nine months after Lent than at any other season; therefore, reckoning a year after Lent, the markets will be more glutted than usual, because the number of popish infants is at least three to one in this kingdom: and therefore it will have one other collateral advantage, by lessening the number of papists among us.

I have already computed the change of nursing a beggar's child (in which list I reckon all cottagers, labourers, and four-fifths of the farmers) to be about 2s. per annum, rags included; and I believe no gentleman would repine to give 10s. for the carcass of a good fat child, which as I have said will make four dishes of excellent nutritive meat, when he has only some particular friend or his own family to dine with him. Thus the squire will learn to be a good landlord, and grow popular among his tenants; the mother will have 8s. net profit, and be fit for work till she produces another child.

Those who are more thrifty (as I must confess the times require) may flay the carcass; the skin of which artificially dressed will make admirable gloves for ladies, and summer boots for fine gentlemen.

As to our city of Dublin, shambles may be appointed for this purpose in the most convenient parts of it, and butchers we may be assured will not be wanting; although I rather recommend buying the children alive than dressing them hot from the knife as we do roasting pigs.

A very worthy person, a true lover of his country and whose virtues I highly esteem, was lately pleased in discoursing on this matter to offer a refinement upon my scheme. He said that many gentlemen of this kingdom, having of late destroyed their deer, he conceived that the want of venison might well be supplied by the bodies of young lads and maidens, not exceeding 14 years of age nor under 12; so great a number of both sexes in every country being now ready to starve for want of work and service; and these to be disposed of by their parents if alive, or otherwise by their nearest relations. But with due deference to so excellent a friend and so deserving a patriot, I cannot be altogether in his sentiments; for as to the males, my American acquaintance assured me, from frequent experience, that their flesh was generally tough and lean, like that of our schoolboys by continual exercise, and their taste disagreeable; and to fatten them would not answer the charge. Then as to the females, it would I think with humble submission be a loss to the public, because they soon would become breeders themselves: and besides, it is not improbable that some scrupulous people might be apt to censure such a practice, (although indeed very unjustly,) as a little bordering upon cruelty; which, I confess, has always been with me the strongest objection against any project; how well so ever intended.

But in order to justify my friend, he confessed that his expedient was put into his head by the famous Psalmanazar, a native of the island Formosa, who came from thence to London above twenty years ago; and in conversation told my friend, that in his country when any young person happened to be put to death, the executioner sold the carcass to persons of quality as a prime dainty; and that in his time the body of a plump girl of 15, who was crucified for an attempt to poison the emperor, was sold to his imperial majesty's prime minister of state, and other great mandarins of the court, in joints from the gibbet, at 400 crowns. Neither indeed can I deny, that if the same use were made of several plump young girls in this town, who without one single groat to their fortunes cannot stir abroad without a chair, and appear at playhouse and assemblies in foreign fineries which they never will pay for, the kingdom would not be the worse.

Some persons of a desponding spirit are in great concern about that vast number of poor people, who are aged, diseased, or maimed, and I have been desired to employ my thoughts what course may be taken to ease the nation of so grievous an encumbrance. But I am not in the least pain upon that matter, because it is very well known that they are every day dying and rotting by cold and famine, and filth and vermin, as fast as can be reasonably expected. And as to the young labourers they are now in almost as hopeful a condition; they cannot get work, and consequently pine away for want of nourishment, to a degree that if at any time they are accidentally hired to common labour, they have not strength to perform it; and thus the country and themselves are happily delivered from the evils to come.

I have too long digressed and therefore shall return to my subject. I think the advantages by the proposal which I have made, are obvious and many as well as of the highest importance.

For first, as I have already observed, it would greatly lessen the number of papists, with whom we are yearly over-run, being the principal breeders of the nation as well as our most dangerous enemies; and who stay at home on purpose to deliver the kingdom to the pretender, hoping to take advantage by the absence of so many good protestants, who have chosen rather to leave their country than stay at home and pay tithes against their conscience to an episcopal curate.

Secondly, The poorer tenants will have something valuable of their own, which by law may be made liable to distress and help to pay their landlord's rent, their corn and cattle being already seized, and money a thing unknown.

Thirdly, Whereas the maintenance of 100,000 children, from two years old and upward, cannot be computed at less than 10*s.* a-piece per annum, the nation's stock will be thereby increased 50,000*l.* per annum, beside the profit of a new dish introduced to the tables of all gentlemen of fortune in the kingdom who have any refinement in taste. And the money will circulate among ourselves, the goods being entirely of our own growth and manufacture.

Fourthly, The constant breeders, beside the gain of 8*s.* sterling per annum by the sale of their children, will be rid of the charge of maintaining them after the first year.

Fifthly, This food would likewise bring great custom to taverns; where the vintners will certainly so prudent as to procure the best receipts for dressing it to perfection, and consequently have their houses frequented by all the fine gentlemen, who justly value themselves upon their knowledge in good eating: and a skillful cook, who understands how to oblige his guests, will contrive to make it as expensive as they please.

Sixthly, This would be a great inducement to marriage, which all wise nations have either encouraged by rewards or enforced by laws and penalties. It would increase the care and tenderness of mothers toward their children, when they were sure of a settlement for life to the poor babes, provided in some sort by the public, to their annual profit or expense. We should see an honest emulation among the married women, which of them could bring the fattest child to the market. Men would become as fond of their wives during the time of their pregnancy as they are now of their mares in foal, their cows in calf, their sows when they are ready to

farrow; nor offer to beat or kick them (as is too frequent a practice) for fear
of a miscarriage.

Many other advantages might be enumerated. For instance, the addition of
some thousand carcasses in our exportation of barreled beef, the propagation of
swine's flesh, and improvement in the art of making good bacon, so much wanted
among us by the great destruction of pigs, too frequent at our table; which are no
way comparable in taste or magnificence to a well-grown, fat, yearling child, which
roasted whole will make a considerable figure at a lord mayor's feast or any other
public entertainment. But this and many others I omit, being studious of brevity.

Supposing that 1000 families in this city would be constant customers for
infants' flesh, beside others who might have it at merry-meetings, particularly at
weddings and christenings, I compute that Dublin would take off annually about
20,000 carcasses; and the rest of the kingdom (where probably they will be sold
somewhat cheaper) the remaining 80,000.

I can think of no one objection that will possibly be raised against this proposal, unless it should be urged that the number of people will be thereby much lessened in the kingdom. This I freely own, and it was indeed one principal design in
offering it to the world. I desire the reader will observe, that I calculate my remedy
for this one individual kingdom of Ireland and for no other that ever was, is, or I
think ever can be upon earth. Therefore let no man talk to me of other expedients:
of taking our absentees at 5s. a pound: of using neither clothes nor household furniture except what is of our own growth and manufacture: of utterly rejecting the
materials and instruments that promote foreign luxury: of curing the expensiveness
of pride, vanity, idleness, and gaming in our women: of introducing a vein of parsi-
mony, prudence, and temperance: of learning to love our country, in the want of
which we differ even from LAPLANDERS and the inhabitants of TOPINAM-
BOO: of quitting our animosities and factions, nor acting any longer like the Jews,
who were murdering one another at the very moment their city was taken: of being
a little cautious not to sell our country and conscience for nothing: of teaching
landlords to have at least one degree of mercy toward their tenants: lastly, of putting a spirit of honesty, industry, and skill into our shopkeepers; who, if a resolution could now be taken to buy only our negative goods, would immediately unite
to cheat and exact upon us in the price, the measure, and the goodness, not could
ever yet be brought to make one fair proposal of just dealing through often and
earnestly invited to it.

Therefore I repeat, let no man talk to me of these and the like expedients, till
he has at least some glimpse of hope that there will be ever some hearty and sincere

attempt to put them in practice.

But as to myself, having been wearied out for many years with offering vain, idle, visionary thoughts, and at length utterly despairing of success I fortunately fell upon this proposal; which, as it is wholly new, so it has something solid and real, of no expense and little trouble, full in our own power and whereby we can incur no danger in disobliging ENGLAND. For this kind of commodity will not bear exportation, the flesh being of too tender a consistence to admit along continuance in salt, although perhaps I could name a country which would be glad to eat up our whole nation without it.

After all, I am not so violently bent upon my own opinion as to reject any offer proposed by wise men, which shall be found equally innocent , cheap, easy, and effectual. But before something of that kind shall be advanced in contradiction to my scheme, and offering a better, I desire the author or authors will be pleased maturely to consider two points. First, as things now stand, how they will be able to find food and raiment for 100,000 useless mouths and backs. And secondly, there being a round million of creatures in human figure throughout this kingdom, whose whole subsistence put into a common stock would leave them in debt 2,000,000*l.* sterling, adding those who are beggars by profession to the bulk of farmers, cottagers, and labourers, with the wives and children who are beggars in effect; I desire those politicians who dislike my overture, and may perhaps be so bold as to attempt an answer, that they will first ask the parents of these mortals, whether they would not at this day think it a great happiness to have been sold for food at a year old in the manner I prescribe, and thereby have avoided such a perpetual scene of misfortunes as they have since gone through by the oppression of landlords, the impossibility of paying rent without money or trade, the want of common sustenance, with neither house nor clothes to cover them from the inclemencies of the weather, and the most inevitable prospect of entailing the like or greater miseries upon their breed for ever.

I profess, in the sincerity of my heart, that I have not the least personal interest in endeavouring to promote this necessary work, having no other motive than the public good of my country, by advancing our trade, providing for infants, relieving the poor, and giving some pleasure to the rich. I have no children by which I can propose to get a single penny; the youngest being nine years old, and my wife past child-bearing.

MARIA EDGEWORTH

♣

(1767-1849)

Maria Edgeworth's first novel, *Castle Rackrent: An Hibernian Tale,* was published anonymously in 1800, but word quickly spread that Edgeworth was the author of this groundbreaking book, and over the next decade, she developed into the most celebrated and financially successful of English novelists. Admired by Jane Austen and Lord Byron, Edgeworth, despite social access to the most prominent writers of her time, was most influenced by her father, Richard Lovell Edgeworth. An eccentric, strong-willed intellectual, politician, inventor, writer and landlord, Richard was an ever-present force in Maria's life—so much so that she never left his estate once in Ireland. Whatever commercial success or critical praise she received did not compare to her father's reception of her work, and she once said, "Where would I be without my father? I should sink into that nothing from which he has raised me."

There are many critics who have pointed out that Maria was so heavily influenced by Richard, her novels suffered because of it. Overly didactic is a phrase that surfaces repeatedly in any critical discussion of Maria's work, but it would be disingenuous to assume that she was merely speaking her father's mind. In fact, one reason for her publishing *Castle Rackrent* anonymously was to avoid the scrupulous editing her father often imposed on her work. With *Castle Rackrent,* Edgeworth moved to the forefront of regional novels—a genre that inspired the greatest writers of her day, including Sir Walter Scott. The realistic dialogue of Irish peasant life and their relationships with landlords inspired King George III to remark, after reading her work, "I know something now of my Irish subjects."

Maria Edgeworth was born on New Year's Day in 1767, the second of twenty-two children fathered by Richard Lovell Edgeworth. Her mother, Anna Maria

Elers, died when Maria was six, shortly after the birth of her fifth child, and Maria's only memory of her consisted of receiving a final kiss on her deathbed. Richard would ultimately marry three more times in his life, each time bringing more children and younger and younger stepmothers into Maria's life, the last one being younger than Maria herself. But her loyalty to her father enabled her to take the role of dutiful daughter quite seriously, and she ultimately performed more than her share of parental duties for her younger siblings over the years.

As a child, however, Maria was raised in England and attended school in Derby. Richard wanted nothing more than a first-rate education for his children, especially Maria, whose talents he seemed to recognize at an early age and whom he expected to contribute something of significance to the world. Maria ultimately attended a prestigious school headed by Mrs. Davis in Upper Wimpole Street in London, and early on, Maria demonstrated story-telling talents as well as writing abilities that were recognized and encouraged by her father. Her father was extraordinarily concerned about the shortcomings of female education and was determined to see to it that Maria not be deprived of her intellectual rights. He wanted her, as he once wrote, "to have a tincture of every species of literature, and form a taste by choice and not by chance."

However, sending Maria away to school affected her in ways Richard might not have intended. She wrote stories to please her father because she was insecure and felt abandoned by him. Richard was without question, more involved with his second wife and children. The children from his first marriage were raised according to Jean-Jacques Rousseau's idealistic doctrine, but because his first son and namesake became a wanderer at sea with no clear direction in life, Richard considered the Frenchman's philosophy a failure, and with his new wife, Honora, he was determined to begin anew. Lonely and isolated from the family while away at school, Maria's stories became her only solace and she focused on themes that would please her father. Richard was so taken by her stories that he gave her additional writing exercises and assignments to stimulate her thinking, and the two grew closer because of their intellectual bond despite the fact that the relationship existed mostly through correspondence for several years.

In 1780, Honora died, and at her request, Richard married her sister Elizabeth Sneyd just eight months later. The next year, he took the family to live with him in his Irish estate, and this time he included Maria. Once in Ireland, she became an accountant for his estate and took on additional business responsibilities as well. As the oldest child, she helped to educate her younger siblings, and at fifteen, she began writing tales her father told of Irish peasantry. She became so immersed in the lives of the Irish tenants she encountered while at the estate, she could not resist including all the rich details and dialogue in her fiction for years to come. In 1791, she started writing children's stories—a genre she would never truly abandon, and for which she probably received notoriety. In her children's stories, it was apparent that she was incorporating the educational theories and practices her father had espoused, and her second book, *The Parent's Assistant; or Stories for Children,* published in 1796, was very popular in England at the end of the 18th century. Each story that appeared in the collection, such as "Forgive and Forget" and "Lazy Lawrence" had a lesson in it for children of every age, as children were encouraged to work through moral situations with their parents who read to them. Plot and character, generally abandoned in her children's stories, were elements of writing that Edgeworth would ultimately make more use of in her novels.

By 1798, Elizabeth Sneyd had passed away, and Richard married Frances Anna Beaufort (Fanny), an Anglo-Irishwoman who was younger than Maria. This appalled Maria at first, but she ultimately formed a long-lasting friendship with her new stepmother that lasted over fifty years. At thirty-one years old, Maria Edgeworth was about to witness her father and Frances bring six more children into the family. It was about this time that Maria began to write *Castle Rackrent* clandestinely, as her father considered novel writing petty and frivolous. She told him she was busy writing "tales" that fell in line with his social and educational theories, when in fact she was experimenting with a bold and unique narrative technique. She told her tales from two perspectives, the naïve and loyal Rackrent family servant, Thady, and a wizened English editor who provides the perfect counterbalance mixing humor and poignancy to the novel.

The book clearly incorporated elements of the Edgeworth family estate, criticizing absentee Anglo-Irish landlords and landed gentry and the exploitation of peasants that was prevalent in Ireland. Thady recounts four generations of Rackrents in narration that is both amusing and warm, but clearly unreliable. The "Editor" places the story in the context of a historical setting, which was Edgeworth's ironic method of stating that this kind of peasant exploitation was no longer a modern-day problem. The people of Ireland knew better, of course. *Castle Rackrent* was an immediate success upon its publication in 1800, and the public clamored for more "Irish tales" from the writer who would later be referred to as the "Irish Jane Austen" and the "female Sir Walter Scott." Yet despite the commercial success of her novel, Edgeworth was in no hurry to abandon her children's stories, though she did ultimately add her name to the title page of *Castle Rackrent's* third edition a year after its initial publication.

Richard Edgeworth decided in 1802 to take his family abroad somewhat under the guise of a literary tour for Maria, and one that was highly successful. But the main purpose was to find suitable husbands for his daughters. It was on this trip that she met an inventor and the private secretary of the King of Sweden, Abraham Niclas Clewberg-Edelcrantz, the gentleman who would court her for years. From her correspondence, it was revealed that she would have married Edelcrantz if he were willing to leave the King and relocate to Ireland, since she was apparently not willing to live in Sweden. She probably knew, too, that Edelcrantz would never live in Ireland and that he would probably be her last chance at marriage. Maria also ultimately became a close friend of Sir Walter Scott, and some biographers have suggested that they may have had an even closer relationship than she enjoyed with Edelcrantz. Marriage never materialized for Maria, however, and the strongest relationship in her life was the one she had with her father.

By 1813, Edgeworth was considered one of the most important writers in the world, rivaling only Scott who actually credited Edgeworth for inspiring his Waverley novels. She was the originator of the regional novel, inspiring Ivan Turgenev and James Fenimore Cooper alike, and William Butler Yeats declared her the first serious novelist of the Irish upper classes. Although her books were most popular in English society and even the upper classes of the United States, she was also one of the first authors to write for the middle and lower classes.

In spite of all her success as a writer, she continued to help Richard with the business of his estate, especially as his health declined in 1814. He continued to edit her work right up until his death in 1817, as well as working on his own memoirs, which he intended for Maria to finish. For many moths after his death, she could not concentrate on anything but children's stories, and it wasn't until 1820 when she finally finished her father's memoirs. Some critics, reviewing the book, took it upon themselves to criticize Richard Edgeworth, whom they viewed as an overbearing egotist who manipulated and interfered with his more talented daughter.

Following her father's death, Maria completely ran the estate and saved it from ruin. With her father no longer her literary adviser, she turned to Scott for professional guidance. Remarkably, she did not publish another work of fiction until 1834 with *Helen,* the story of a female politician. In *Helen,* she abandoned the didactic tones that had dominated her work previously, and she helped insure her prophetic reputation by putting her work at the forefront of sexual equality. Though not as critically or commercially successful as her earlier books, some critics have maintained that it was because she attempted to write a "silver fork" novel that appealed only to the upper classes. This was ironic because her last decades were spent running her father's estate and seeing to it that the famine that appeared in Ireland in the 1840s was alleviated somewhat by the family's generosity. The Edgeworths ordered large quantities of flour and rice from Boston, which they gave to the starving masses, and they barely survived themselves. In 1849, Maria Edgeworth herself died at her home in Edgeworthstown, in the arms of her dear friend and stepmother, Fanny, at the age of eighty-one. Because of her moralizing tales, future generations have not always looked kindly on her life and work, but Maria Edgeworth brought more attention to Irish affairs than any other writer of her time.

CASTLE RACKRENT

♣

Monday Morning[1]

Having, out of friendship for the family, upon whose estate, praised be Heaven! I and mine have lived rent-free time out of mind, voluntarily undertaken to publish the MEMOIRS OF THE RACKRENT FAMILY, I think it my duty to say a few words, in the first place, concerning myself. My real name is Thady Quirk, though in the family I have always been known by no other than "Honest Thady," afterward, in the time of Sir Murtagh, deceased, I remember to hear them calling me "Old Thady," and now I've come to "Poor Thady"; for I wear a long greatcoat winter and summer, which is very handy, as I never put my arms into the sleeves; they are as good as new, though come Holantide next I've had it these seven years: it holds on by a single button round my neck, cloak fashion. To look at me, you would hardly think "Poor Thady" was the father of Attorney Quirk; he is a high gentle-man, and never minds what poor Thady says, and having better than fifteen hundred a year, landed estate, looks down upon honest Thady; but I wash my hands of his doings, and as I have lived so will I die, true and loyal to the family. The family of the Rackrents is, I am proud to say, one of the most ancient in the kingdom. Everybody knows this is not the old family name, which was O'Shaughlin, related to the kings of Ireland—but that was before my time. My grandfather was driver to the great Sir Patrick O'Shaughlin, and I heard him, when I was a boy, telling how the Castle Rackrent estate came to Sir Patrick; Sir Tallyhoo Rackrent was cousin-german to him, and had a fine estate of his own, only never a gate upon it, it being his maxim that a car was the best gate. Poor gentleman! he lost a fine hunter and his life, at last, by it, all in one day's hunt. But I ought to bless that day, for the estate came straight into *the* family, upon one condition, which Sir Patrick O'Shaughlin at the time took sadly to heart, they say, but thought better of it afterwards, seeing how large a stake depended upon it: that he should, by Act of Parliament, take and bear the surname and arms of Rackrent.

Now it was that the world was to see what was *in* Sir Patrick. On coming into the estate he gave the finest entertainment ever was heard of in the country; not a man could stand after supper but Sir Patrick himself, who could sit out the best man in Ireland, let alone the three kingdoms itself.[1] He had his house, from one year's end to another, as full of company as ever it could hold, and fuller; for rather than be left out of the parties at Castle Rackrent, many gentlemen, and those men of the first consequence and landed estates in the country—such as the O'Neills of Ballynagrotty, and the Moneygawls of Mount Juliet's Town, and O'Shannons of New Town Tullyhog—made it their choice, often and often, when there was no room to be had for love nor money, in long winter nights, to sleep in the chicken-house, which Sir Patrick had fitted up for the purpose of accommodating his friends and the public in general, who honoured him with their company unexpectedly at Castle Rackrent; and this went on I can't tell you how long. The whole country rang with his praises!—Long life to him! I'm sure I love to look upon his picture, now opposite to me; though I never saw him, he must have been a portly gentleman—his neck something short, and remarkable for the largest pimple on his nose, which, by his particular desire, is still extant in his picture, said to be a striking likeness, though taken when young. He is said also to be the inventor of raspberry whisky, which is very likely, as nobody has ever appeared to dispute it with him, and as there still exists a broken punch-bowl at Castle Rackrent, in the garret, with an inscription to that effect—a great curiosity. A few days before his death he was very merry; it being his honour's birthday, he called my grandfather in—God bless him!—to drink the company's health, and filled a bumper himself, but could not carry it to his head, on account of the great shake in his hand; on this he cast his joke, saying, "What would my poor father say to me if he was to pop out of the grave, and see me now? I remember when I was a little boy, the first bumper of claret he gave me after dinner, how he praised me for carrying it so steady to my mouth. Here's my thanks to him—a bumper toast." Then he fell to singing the favourite song he learned from his father—for the last time, poor gentleman—he sung it that night as loud and as hearty as ever, with a chorus:

> He that goes to bed, and goes to bed sober,
> Falls as the leaves do, falls as the leaves do, and dies in October;
> But he that goes to bed, and goes to bed mellow,
> Lives as he ought to do, lives as he ought to do, and dies in honest fellow.

Sir Patrick died that night: just as the company rose to drink his health with three cheers, he fell down in a sort of fit, and was carried off; they sat it out, and were surprised, on inquiry in the morning, to find that it was all over with poor Sir Patrick. Never did any gentleman live and die more beloved in the country by rich and poor. His funeral was such a one as was never known before or since in the county! All the gentlemen in the three counties were at it; far and near, how they flocked! my great-grandfather said, that to see all the women, even in their red cloaks, you would have taken them for the army drawn out. Then such a fine whillaluh![1] you might have heard it to the farthest end of the county, and happy the man who could get but a sight of the hearse! But who'd have thought it? just as all was going on right, through his own town they were passing, when the body was seized for debt—a rescue was apprehended from the mob; but the heir, who attended the funeral, was against that, for fear of consequences, seeing that those villains who came to serve acted under the disguise of the law: so, to be sure, the law must take its course, and little gain had the creditors for their pains. First and foremost, they had the curses of the country: and Sir Murtagh Rackrent, the new heir, in the next place, on account of this affront to the body, refused to pay a shilling of the debts, in which he was countenanced by all the best gentlemen of property, and others of his acquaintance; Sir Murtagh alleging in all companies that he all along meant to pay his father's debts of honour, but the moment the law was taken of him, there was an end of honour to be sure. It was whispered (but none but the enemies of the family believe it) that this was all a sham seizure to get quit of the debts which he had bound himself to pay in honour.

It's a long time ago, there's no saying how it was, but this for certain, the new man did not take at all after the old gentleman; the cellars were never filled after his death, and no open house, or anything as it used to be; the tenants even were sent away without their whisky.[2] I was ashamed myself, and knew not what to say for the honour of the family; but I made the best of a bad case, and laid it all at my lady's door, for I did not like her anyhow, nor anybody else; she was of the family of the Skinflints, and a widow; it was a strange match for Sir Murtagh; the people in the country thought he demeaned himself greatly,[3] but I said nothing: I knew how it was. Sir Murtagh was a great lawyer, and looked to the great Skinflint estate; there, however, he overshot himself; for though one of the co-heiresses, he was never the better for her, for she outlived him many's the long day—he could not see that to be sure when he married her. I must say for her, she made him the best of wives, being a very notable, stirring woman, and looking close to every-thing. But I always suspected she had Scotch blood in her veins; anything else I could have looked over in her, from a regard to the family. She was a strict observ-er, for self and servants, of Lent, and all fast-days, but not holidays. One of the maids having fainted three times the last day of Lent, to keep soul and body together, we put a morsel of roast beef into her mouth, which came from Sir Murtagh's dinner, who never fasted, not he; but somehow or other it unfortunately reached my lady's ears, and the priest of the parish had a complaint made of it the next day, and the poor girl was forced, as soon as she could walk, to do penance for it, before she could get any peace or absolution, in the house or out of it. However, my lady was very charitable in her own way. She had a charity school for poor children, where they were taught to read and write gratis, and where they were kept well to spinning gratis for my lady in return; for she had always heaps of duty yarn from the tenants, and got all her household linen out of the estate from first to last; for after the spinning, the weavers on the estate took it in hand for nothing, because of the looms my lady's interest could get from the Linen Board to distribute gratis. Then there was a bleach-yard near us, and the tenant dare refuse my lady nothing, for fear of a lawsuit Sir Murtagh kept hanging over him about the watercourse. With these ways of managing, 'tis surprising how cheap my lady got things done, and how proud she was of it. Her table the same way, kept for next to nothing; duty fowls, and duty turkeys, and duty geese,[1] came as fast as we could eat 'em, for my lady kept a sharp look-out, and knew to a tub of butter everything the tenants had, all round. They knew her way, and what with fear of driving for rent and Sir Murtagh's lawsuits, they were kept in such good order, they never thought of coming near Castle Rackrent without a present of something or other—nothing too much or too little for my lady—eggs, honey, butter, meal, fish, game, grouse, and herrings, fresh or salt, all went for something. As for their young pigs, we had them, and the best bacon and hams they could make up, with all young chickens in spring; but they were a set of poor wretches, and we had nothing but misfortunes with them, always breaking and running away. This, Sir Murtagh and my lady said, was all their former landlord Sir Patrick's fault, who let 'em all get the half-year's rent into arrear; there was something in that to be sure. But Sir Murtagh was as much the contrary way; for let alone making English tenants[2] of them, every soul, he was always driving and driving, and pounding and pounding, and canting and canting,[3] and replevying and replevying, and he made a good living of trespassing cattle; there was always some tenant's pig, or horse, or cow, or calf, or goose, trespassing, which was so great a gain to Sir Murtagh, that he did not like to hear me talk of repairing fences. Then his heriots and duty-work[4] brought him in something, his turf was cut, his potatoes set and dug, his hay brought home, and, in short, all the work about his house done for nothing; for in all our leases there were strict clauses heavy with penalties, which Sir Murtagh knew well how to enforce; so many days' duty-work of man and horse, from every tenant, he was to have, and had, every year; and when a man vexed him, why, the finest day he could pitch on, when the cratur was getting in his own harvest, or thatching his cabin, Sir Murtagh made it a principle to call upon him and his horse; so he taught 'em all, is he said, to know the law of landlord and tenant. As for law, I believe no man, dead or alive, ever loved it so well as Sir Murtagh. He had once sixteen suits pending, at a time, and I never saw him so much himself: roads, lanes, bogs, wells, ponds, eel-wires, orchards, trees, tithes, vagrants, gravel-pits, sandpits, dunghills, and nuisances, everything upon the face of the earth furnished him good matter for a suit. He used to boast that he had a lawsuit for every letter in the alphabet. How I used to wonder to see Sir Murtagh in the midst of the papers in his office! Why, he could hardly turn about for them. I made bold to shrug my shoulders once in his presence, and thanked my stars I was not born a gentleman to so much toil and trouble; but Sir Murtagh took me up short with his old proverb, "Learning is better than house or land." Out of forty-nine suits which he had, he never lost one but seventeen;[1] the rest he gained with costs, double costs, treble costs sometimes; but even that did not pay. He was a very learned man in the law, and had the character of it; but how it was I can't tell, these suits that he carried cost him a power of money: in the end he sold some hundreds a year of the family estate;—but he was a very learned man in the law, and I know nothing of the matter, except having a great regard for the family; and I could not help grieving when he sent me to post up notices of the sale of the fee simple of the lands and appurtenances of Timoleague.

"I know, honest Thady," says he, to comfort me, "what I'm about better than you do; I'm only selling to get the ready money wanting to carry on my suit with spirit with the Nugents of Carrickashaughlin."

He was very sanguine about that suit with the Nugents of Carrickashaughlin. He could have gained it, they say, for certain, had it pleased Heaven to have spared him to us, and it would have been at the least a plump two thousand a year in his way; but things were ordered otherwise—for the best to be sure. He dug up a fairy-mount[2] against my advice, and had no luck afterwards. Though a learned man in the law, he was a little too incredulous in other matters. I warned him that I heard the very Banshee that my grandfather heard under Sir Patrick's window a few days before his death. But Sir Murtagh thought nothing of the Banshee, nor of his cough, with a spitting of blood, brought on, I understand, by catching cold in attending the courts, and overstraining his chest with making himself heard in one of his favourite causes. He was a great speaker with a powerful voice; but his last speech was not in the courts at all. He and my lady, though both of the same way of thinking in some things, and though she was as good a wife and great economist as you could see, and he the best of husbands, as to looking into his affairs, and making money for his family; yet I don't know how it was, they had a great deal of sparring and jarring between them. My lady had her privy purse; and she had her weed ashes,[1] and her sealing money[2] upon the signing of all the leases, with something to buy gloves besides; and, besides, again often took money from the tenants, if offered properly, to speak for them to Sir Murtagh about abatements and renewals. Now the weed ashes and the glove money fie allowed her clear perquisites; though once when he saw her in a new gown saved out of the weed ashes, he told her to my face (for he could say a sharp thing) that she should not put on her weeds before her husband's death. But in a dispute about an abatement my lady would have the last word, and Sir Murtagh grew mad[3]; I was within hearing of the door, and now I wish I had made bold to step in. He spoke so loud, the whole kitchen was out on the stairs.[4] All on a sudden he stopped, and my lady too. Something has surely happened, thought I; and so it was, for Sir Murtagh in his passion broke a blood-vessel, and all the law in the land could do nothing in that case. My lady sent for five physicians, but Sir Murtagh died, and was buried. She had a fine jointure settled upon her, and took herself away, to the great joy of the tenantry. I never said anything one way or the other whilst she was part of the family, but got up to see her go at three o'clock in the morning.

"It's a fine morning, honest Thady," says she; "goodbye to ye." And into the carriage she stepped, without a word more, good or bad, or even half-a-crown; but I made my bow, and stood to see her safe out of sight for the sake of the family.

Then we were all bustle in the house, which made me keep out of the way, for I walk slow and hate a bustle; but the house was all hurry-skurry, preparing for my new master. Sir Murtagh, I forgot to notice, had no childer; so the Rackrent estate went to his younger brother, a young dashing officer, who came amongst us before I knew for the life of me whereabouts I was, in a gig or some of them things, with another spark along with him, and led horses, and servants, and dogs, and scarce a place to put any Christian of them into; for my late lady had sent all the feather-beds off before her, and blankets and household linen, down to the very knife-cloths, on the cars to Dublin, which were all her own, lawfully paid for out of her own money. So the house was quite bare, and my young master, the moment ever he set foot in it out of his gig, thought all those things must come of themselves, I believe, for he never looked after anything at all, but harum-scarum called for everything as if we were conjurors, or he in a public-house. For my part, I could not bestir myself anyhow; I had been so much used to my late master and mistress, all was upside down with me, and the new servants in the servants' hall were quite out of my way; I had nobody to talk to, and if it had not been for my pipe and tobacco, should, I verily believe, have broke my heart for poor Sir Murtagh.

But one morning my new master caught a glimpse of me as I was looking at his horse's heels, in hopes of a word from him. "And is that old Thady?" says he, as he got into his gig: I loved him from that day to this, his voice was so like the family; and he threw me a guinea out of his waist coat-pocket, as he drew up the reins with the other hand, his horse rearing too; I thought I never set my eyes on a finer figure of a man, quite another sort from Sir Murtagh, though withal, *to me*, a family likeness. A fine life we should have led, had he stayed amongst us, God bless him! He valued a guinea as little as any man: money to him was no more than dirt, and his gentleman and groom, and all belonging to him, the same; but the sporting season over, he grew tired of the place, and having got down a great architect for the house, and an improver for the grounds, and seen their plans and elevations, he fixed a day for settling with the tenants, but went off in a whirlwind to town, just as some of them came into the yard in the morning. A circular letter came next post from the new agent, with news that the master was sailed for England, and he must remit £500 to Bath for his use before a fortnight was at an end; bad news still for the poor tenants, no change still for the better with them. Sir Kit Rackrent, my young master, left all to the agent; and though he had the spirit of a prince, and lived away to the honour of his country abroad, which I was proud to hear of, what were we the better for that at home. The agent was one of your middlemen, who grind the face of the poor, and can never bear a man with a hat upon his head: he ferreted the tenants out of their lives; not a week without a call for money, drafts upon drafts from Sir Kit; but I laid it all to the fault of the agent; for, says I, what can Sir Kit do with so much cash, and he a single man? But still it went. Rents must be all paid up to the day, and afore; no allowance for improving tenants, no consideration for those who had built upon their farms: no sooner was a lease out, but the land was advertised to the highest bidder; all the old tenants turned out, when they spent their substance in the hope and trust of a renewal from the landlord. All was now let at the highest penny to a parcel of poor wretches, who meant to run away, and did so, after taking two crops out of the ground. Then fining down the year's rent came into fashion[1]—anything for the ready penny; and with all this and presents to the agent and the driver,[2] there was no such thing as standing it. I said nothing, for I had a regard for the family; but I walked about thinking if his honour Sir Kit knew all this, it would go hard with him but he'd see us righted; not that I had anything for my own share to complain of, for the agent was always very civil to me when he came down into the country, and took a great deal of notice of my son Jason. Jason Quirk, though he be my son, I must say was a good scholar from his birth, and a very 'cute lad: I thought to make him a priest,[1] but he did better for himself; seeing how he was as good a clerk as any in the county, the agent gave him his rent accounts to copy, which he did first of all for the pleasure of obliging the gentleman, and would take no thing at all for his trouble, but was always proud to serve the family. By and by a good farm bounding us to the east fell into his honour's hands, and my son put in a proposal for it: why shouldn't he, as well as another? The proposals all went over to the master at the Bath, who knowing no more of the land than the child unborn, only having once been out a-grousing on it before he went to England; and the value of lands, as the agent informed him, failing every year in Ireland, his honour wrote over in all haste a bit of a letter, saying he left it all to the agent, and that he must let it as well as he could—to the best bidder, to be sure—and send him over £200 by return of post: with this the agent gave me a hint, and I spoke a good word for my son, and gave out in the country that nobody need bid against us. So his proposal was just the thing, and he a good tenant; and he got a promise of an abatement in the rent after the first year, for advancing the half-year's rent at signing the lease, which was wanting to complete the agent's £200 by the return of the post, with all which my master wrote back he was well satisfied. About this time we learnt from the agent, as a great secret, how the money went so fast, and the reason of the thick coming of the master's drafts: he was a little too fond of play; and Bath, they say, was no place for no young man of his for tune, where there were so many of his own countrymen, too, hunting him up and down, day and night, who had nothing to lose. At last, at Christmas, the agent wrote over to stop the drafts, for he could raise no more money on bond or mortgage, or from the tenants, or anyhow, nor had he any more to lend himself, and desired at the same time to decline the agency for the future, wishing Sir Kit his health and happiness, and the compliments of the season, for I saw the letter before ever it was sealed, when my son copied it. When the answer came there was a new turn in affairs, and the agent was turned out; and my son Jason, who had corresponded privately with his honour occasionally on business, was forthwith desired by his honour to take the accounts into his own hands, and look them over, till further orders. It was a very spirited letter to be sure: Sir Kit sent his service, and the compliments of the season, in return to the agent, and he would fight him with pleasure to-morrow, or any day, for sending him such a letter, if he was born a gentleman, which he was sorry (for both their sakes) to find (too late) he was not. Then, in a private post-script, he condescended to tell us that all would be speedily settled to his satisfaction, and we should turn over a new leaf, for he was going to be married in a fortnight to the grandest heiress in England, and had only immediate occasion at present for £200, as he would not choose to touch his lady's fortune for travelling expenses home to Castle Rackrent, where he intended to be, wind and weather permitting, early in the next month; and desired fires, and the house to be painted, and the new building to go on as fast as possible, for the reception of him and his lady before that time; with several words besides in the letter, which we could not make out because, God bless him! he wrote in such a flurry. My heart warmed to my new lady when I read this: I was almost afraid it was too good news to be true; but the girls fell to scouring, and it was well they did, for we soon saw his marriage in the paper, to a lady with I don't know how many tens of thousand pounds to her fortune: then I watched the post-office for his landing; and the news came to my son of his and the bride being in Dublin, and on the way home to Castle Rackrent. We had bonfires allover the country, expecting him down the next day, and we had his coming of age still to celebrate, which he had not time to do properly before he left the country; therefore, a great ball was expected, and great doings upon his coming, as it were, fresh to take possession of his ancestors' estate. I never shall forget the day he came home; we had waited and waited all day long till eleven o'clock at night, and I was thinking of sending the boy to lock the gates, and giving them up for that night, when there came the carriages thundering up to the great hall door. I got the first sight of the bride; for when the carriage door opened, just as she had her foot on the steps, I held the flam[1] full in her face to light her, at which she shut her eyes, but I had a full view of the rest of her, and greatly shocked I was, for by that light she was little better than a blackamoor, and seemed crippled; but that was only sitting so long in the chariot.

"You're kindly welcome to Castle Rackrent, my lady," says I (recollecting who she was). "Did your honour hear of the bonfires?"

His honour spoke never a word, nor so much as handed her up the steps—he looked to me no more like himself than nothing at all; I know I took him for the skeleton of his honour. I was not sure what to say next to one or t'other, but seeing she was a stranger in a foreign country, I thought it but right to speak cheerful to her; so I went back again to the bonfires.

"My lady," says I, as she crossed the hall, "there would have been fifty times as many; but for fear of the horses, and frightening your ladyship, Jason and I forbid them, please your honour."

With that she looked at me a little bewildered.

"Will I have a fire lighted in the state-room to-night?" was the next question I put to her, but never a word she answered; so I concluded she could not speak a word of English, and was from foreign parts. The short and the long of it was, I couldn't tell what to make of her; so I left her to herself, and went straight down to the servants' hall to learn something for certain about her. Sir Kit's own man was tired, but the groom set him a-talking at last, and we had it all out before ever I closed my eyes that night. The bride might well be a great fortune—she was a *Jewish* by all accounts, who are famous for their great riches. I had never seen any of that tribe or nation before, and could only gather that she spoke a strange kind of English of her own, that she could not abide pork or sausages, and went neither to church or mass. Mercy upon his honour's poor soul, thought I; what will become of him and his, and all of us, with his heretic blackamoor at the head of the Castle Rackrent estate? I never slept a wink all night for thinking of it; but before the servants I put my pipe in my mouth, and kept my mind to myself, for I had a great regard for the family; and after this, when strange gentlemen's servants came to the house, and would begin to talk about the bride, I took care to put the best foot foremost, and passed her for a nabob in the kitchen, which accounted for her dark complexion and everything.

The very morning after they came home, however, I saw plain enough how things were between Sir Kit and my lady, though they were walking together arm in arm after breakfast, looking at the new building and the improvements.

"Old Thady," said my master, just as he used to do, "how do you do?"

"Very well, I thank your honour's honour," said I; but I saw he was not well pleased, and my heart was in my mouth as I walked along after him.

"Is the large room damp, Thady?" said his honour.

"Oh damp, your honour! how should it be but as dry as a bone," says I, "after all the fires we have kept in it day and night? It's the barrack-room[1] your honour's talking on."

"And what is a barrack-room, pray, my dear?" were the first words I ever heard out of my lady's lips.

"No matter, my dear," said he, and went on talking to me, ashamed-like I should witness her ignorance. To be sure, to hear her talk one might have taken her for an innocent,[2] for it was, "What's this, Sir Kit? and what's that, Sir Kit?" all the way we went. To be sure, Sir Kit had enough to do to answer her.

"And what do you call that, Sir Kit?" said she; "that—that looks like a pile of black bricks, pray, Sir Kit?"

"My turf-stack, my dear," said my master, and bit his lip.

Where have you lived, my lady, all your life, not to know a turf-stack when you see it? thought I; but I said nothing. Then by and by she takes out her glass, and begins spying over the country.

"And what's all that black swamp out yonder, Sir Kit? says she.

"My bog, my dear," says he, and went on whistling.

"It's a very ugly prospect, my dear," says she.

"You don't see it, my dear," says he, "for we've planted it out; when the trees grow up in summertime—" says he.

"Where are the trees," said she, "my dear?" still looking through her glass.

"You are blind, my dear," says he; "what are these under your eyes?"

"These shrubs?" said she.

"Trees," said he.

"Maybe they are what you call trees in Ireland, my dear," said she; "but they are not a yard high, are they?"

"They were planted out but last year, my lady," says I, to soften matters between them, for I saw she was going the way to make his honour mad with her: "they are very well grown for their age, and you'll not see the bog of Allyballycarricko'shaughlin at-all-at-all through the skreen, when once the leaves come out. But, my lady, you must not quarrel with any part or parcel of Allyballycarricko'shaughlin, for you don't know how many hundred years that same bit of bog has been in the family; we would not part with the bog of Allyballycarricko'shaughlin upon no account at all; it cost the late Sir Murtagh two hundred good pounds to defend his title to it and boundaries against the O'Learys, who cut a road through it."

Now one would have thought this would have been hint enough for my lady, but she fell to laughing like one out of their right mind, and made me say the name of the bog over, for her to get it by heart, a dozen times; then she must ask me how to spell it, and what was the meaning of it in English—Sir Kit standing by whistling all the while. I verily believed she laid the corner-stone of all her future misfortunes at that very instant; but I said no more, only looked at Sir Kit.

There were no balls, no dinners, no doings; the country was all disappointed—Sir Kit's gentleman said in a whisper to me, it was all my lady's own fault, because she was so obstinate about the cross.

"What cross?" says I; "is it about her being a heretic?"

"Oh, no such matter," says he; "my master does not mind her heresies, but her diamond cross—it's worth I can't tell you how much, and she has thousands of

English pounds concealed in diamonds about her, which she as good as promised to give up to my master before he married; but now she won't part with any of them, and she must take the consequences."

Her honeymoon, at least her Irish honeymoon, was scarcely well over, when his honour one morning said to me, "Thady, buy me a pig!" and then the sausages were ordered, and here was the first open breaking-out of my lady's troubles. My lady came down herself into the kitchen to speak to the cook about the sausages, and desired never to see them more at her table. Now my master had ordered them, and my lady knew that. Tile cook took my lady's part, because she never came down into the kitchen, and was young and innocent in housekeeping, which raised her pity; besides, said she, at her own table, surely my lady should order and disorder what she pleases. But the cook soon changed her note, for my master made it a principle to have the sausages, and swore at her for a Jew herself, till he drove her fairly out of the kitchen; then, for fear of her place, and because he threatened that my lady should give her no discharge without the sausages, she gave up, and from that day forward always sausages, or bacon, or pig-meat in some shape or other, went up to table; upon which my lady shut herself up in her own room, and my master said she might stay there, with an oath: and to make sure of her, he turned the key in the door, and kept it ever after in his pocket. We none of us ever saw or heard her speak for seven years after that: he carried her dinner himself. Then his honour had a great deal of company to dine with him, and balls in the house, and was as gay and gallant, and as much himself as before he was married; and at dinner he always drank my Lady Rackrent's good health and so did the company, and he sent out always a servant with his compliments to my Lady Rackrent, and the company was drinking her ladyship's health, and begged to know if there was anything at table he might send her, and the man came back, after the sham errand, with my Lady Rackrent's compliments, and she was very much obliged to Sir Kit—she did not wish for anything, but drank the company's health. The country, to be sure, talked and wondered at my lady's being shut up, but nobody chose to interfere or ask any impertinent questions, for they knew my master was a man very apt to give a short answer himself, and likely to call a man out for it afterwards: he was a famous shot, had killed his mail before be came of age, and nobody scarce dared look at him whilst at Bath. Sir Kit's character was so well known in the country that he lived in peace and quietness ever after, and was a great favourite with the ladies, especially when in process of time, in the fifth year of her confinement, my Lady Rackrent fell ill and took entirely to her bed, and he gave out that she was now skin and bone, and could not last through tile winter. In this he had two physicians' opinions to back him (for now he called in two physicians for her), and tried all his arts to get the diamond cross from her on her death-bed, and to get her to make a will in his favour of her separate possessions; but there she was too tough for him. He used to swear at her behind her back after kneeling to her face, and call her in the presence of his gentleman his stiff-necked Israelite, though before he married her that same gentleman told me he used to call her (how he could bring it out, I don't know) "my pretty Jessica!" To be sure it must have been hard for her to guess what sort of a husband he reckoned to make her. When she was lying, to all expectation, on her deathbed of a broken heart, I could not but pity her, though she was a Jewish, and considering too it was no fault of hers to be taken with my master, so young as she was at the Bath, and so fine a gentleman as Sir Kit was when he courted her; and considering too, after all they had heard and seen of him as a husband, there were now no less than three ladies in our county talked of for his second wife, all at daggers drawn with each other, as his gentleman swore, at the balls, for Sir Kit for their partner— I could not but think them bewitched, but they all reasoned with themselves that Sir Kit would make a good husband to any Christian but a Jewish, I suppose, and especially as he was now a reformed rake; and it was not known how my lady's fortune was settled in her will, nor how the Castle Rackrent estate was all mortgaged, and bonds out against him, for he was never cured of his gaming tricks; but that was the only fault he had, God bless him!

My lady had a sort of fit, and it was given out that she was dead, by mistake: this brought things to a sad crisis for my poor master. One of the three ladies showed his letters to her brother, and claimed his promises, whilst another did the same. I don't mention names. Sir Kit, in his defence, said he would meet any man who dared to question his conduct; and as to the ladies, they must settle it amongst them who was to be his second, and his third, and his fourth, whilst his first was still alive, to his mortification and theirs. Upon this, as upon all former occasions, he had the voice of the country with him, on account of the great spirit and propriety he acted with. He met and shot the first lady's brother: the next day he called out the second, who had a wooden leg, and their place of meeting by appointment being in a new-ploughed field, the wooden-leg man stuck fast in it. Sir Kit, seeing his situation, with great candour fired his pistol over his head; upon which the seconds interposed, and convinced the parties there had been a slight misunderstanding between them: thereupon they shook hands cordially, and went home to dinner together. This gentleman, to show the world how they stood together, and by the advice of the friends of both parties, to re-establish his sister's

injured reputation, went out with Sir Kit as his second, and carried his message
next day to the last of his adversaries: I never saw him in such fine spirits as that
day be went out—sure enough he was within ames-ace of getting quit handsomely
of all his enemies; but unluckily, after hitting the toothpick out of his adversary's
finger and thumb, he received a ball in a vital part, and was brought home, in little
better than an hour after the affair, speechless on a hand-barrow to my lady. We
got the key out of his pocket the first thing we did, and my son Jason ran to
unlock the barrack-room, where my lady had been shut up for seven years, to ac
quaint her with the fatal accident. The surprise bereaved her of her senses at first,
nor would she believe but we were putting some new trick upon her, to entrap her
out of her jewels, for a great while, till Jason bethought himself of taking her to the
window, and showed her the men bringing Sir Kit up the avenue upon the hand-
barrow, which had immediately the desired effect; for directly she burst into tears,
and pulling her cross from her bosom, she kissed it with as great devotion as ever I
witnessed, and lifting up her eyes to heaven, uttered some ejaculation, which none
present heard; but I take the sense of it to be, she returned thanks for this unexpected interposition in her favour when she had least reason to expect it. My master was greatly lamented: there was no life in him when we lifted him off the barrow, so he was laid out immediately, and "waked" the same night. The country was
all in an uproar about him, and not a soul but cried shame upon his murderer,
who would have been hanged surely, if he could have been brought to his trial,
whilst the gentlemen in the country were up about it; but he very prudently withdrew himself to the Continent before the affair was made public. As for the young
lady who was the immediate cause of the fatal accident, however innocently, she
could never show her head after at the balls in the county or any place; and by the
advice of her friends and physicians, she was ordered soon after to Bath, where it
was expected, if anywhere on this side of the grave, she would meet with the recovery of her health and lost peace of mind. As a proof of his great popularity, I need
only add that there was a song made upon my master's untimely death in the
newspapers, which was in everybody's mouth, singing up and down through the
country, even down to the mountains, only three days after his unhappy exit. He
was also greatly bemoaned at the Curragh,[1] where his cattle were well known; and
all who had taken up his bets were particularly inconsolable for his loss to society.
His stud sold at the cant[2] at the greatest price ever known in the county; his
favourite horses were chiefly disposed of amongst his particular friends, who would
give any price for them for his sake; but no ready money was required by the new
heir, who wished not to displease any of the gentlemen of the neighbourhood just

upon his coming to settle amongst them; so a long credit was given where requisite, and the cash has never been gathered in from that day to this.

But to return to my lady. She got surprisingly well after my master's decease. No sooner was it known for certain that he was dead, than all the gentlemen within twenty miles of us came in a body, as it were, to set my lady at liberty, and to protest against her confinement, which they now for the first time understood was against her own consent. The ladies too were as attentive as possible, striving who should be foremost with their morning visits; and they that saw the diamonds spoke very handsomely of them, but thought it a pity they were not bestowed, if it had so pleased God, upon a lady who would have become them better. All these civilities wrought little with my lady, for she had taken an unaccountable prejudice against the country, and everything belonging to it, and was so partial to her native land, that after parting with the cook, which she did immediately upon my master's decease, I never knew her easy one instant, night or day, but when she was packing up to leave us. Had she meant to make any stay in Ireland, I stood a great chance of being a great favourite with her; for when she found I understood the weathercock, she was always finding some pretence to be talking to me, and asking me which way the wind blew, and was it likely, did I think, to continue fair for England. But when I saw she had made up her mind to spend the rest of her days upon her own income and jewels in England, I considered her quite as a foreigner, and not at all any longer as part of the family. She gave no vails to the servants at Castle Rackrent at parting, notwithstanding the old proverb of "as rich as a Jew," which she, being a Jewish, they built upon with reason. But from first to last she brought nothing but misfortunes amongst us; and if it had not been all along with her, his honour, Sir Kit, would have been now alive in all appearance. Her diamond cross was, they say, at the bottom of it all; and it was a shame for her, being his wife, not to show more duty, and to have given it up when be condescended to ask so often for such a bit of a trifle in his distresses, especially when he all along made it no secret he married for money. But we will not bestow another thought upon her. This much I thought it lay upon my conscience to say, in justice to my poor master's memory.

'Tis an ill wind that blows nobody no good: the same wind that took the Jew Lady Rackrent over to England brought over the new heir to Castle Rackrent.

Here let me pause for breath in my story, for though I had a great regard for every member of the family, yet without compare Sir Conolly, commonly called, for short, amongst his friends, Sir Condy Rackrent, was ever my great favourite, and, indeed, the most universally beloved man I had ever seen or heard of, not excepting his great ancestor Sir Patrick, to whose memory he, amongst other instances of generosity, erected a handsome marble stone in the church of Castle Rackrent, setting forth in large letters his age, birth, parentage, and many other virtues, concluding with the compliment so justly due, that "Sir Patrick Rackrent lived and died a monument of old Irish hospitality."

CONTINUATION OF THE MEMOIRS OF THE RACKRENT FAMILY

HISTORY OF SIR CONOLLY RACKRENT.

Sir Condy Rackrent, by the grace of God heir-at-law to the Castle Rackrent estate, was a remote branch of the family. Born to little or no fortune of his own, he was bred to the bar, at which, having many friends to push him and no mean natural abilities of his own, tic doubtless would in process of time, if he could have borne the drudgery of that study, have been rapidly made King's Counsel at the least; but things were disposed of otherwise, and he never went the circuit but twice, and then made no figure for want of a fee, and being unable to speak in public. He received his education chiefly in the college of Dublin, but before he came to years of discretion lived in the country, in a small but slated house within view of the end of the avenue. I remember him, bare footed and headed, running through the street of O'Shaughlin's Town, and playing at pitch-and-toss, ball, marbles, and what not, with the boys of the town, amongst whom my son Jason was a great favourite with him. As for me, he was ever my white-headed boy: often's the time, when I would call in at his father's, where I was always made welcome, he would slip down to me in the kitchen, and love to sit on my knee whilst I told him stories of the family and the blood from which he was sprung, and how he might look forward, if the then present man should die without childer, to being at the head of the Castle Rackrent estate. This was then spoke quite and clear at random to please the child, but it pleased Heaven to accomplish my prophecy afterwards, which gave him a great opinion of my judgment in business. He went to a little grammar-school with many others, and my son amongst the rest, who was in his class, and not a little useful to him in his book-learning, which he acknowledged with gratitude ever after. These rudiments of his education thus completed, he got a-horseback, to which exercise he was ever addicted, and used to gallop over the country while yet but a slip of a boy, under the care of Sir Kit's huntsman, who was very fond of him, and often lent him his gun, and took him out a-shooting under his own eye. By these means he became well acquainted and popular amongst the poor in the neighbourhood early, for there was not a cabin at which he had not stopped some morning or other, along with the huntsman, to drink a glass of burnt whisky out of an eggshell, to do him good and warm his heart and drive the cold out of his stomach. The old people always told him he was a great likeness of Sir Patrick, which made him first have an ambition to take after him, as far as his fortune should allow. He left us when of an age to enter the college, and there completed his education and nineteenth year, for as he was not born to an estate, his friends thought it incumbent on them to give him the best education which could be had for love or money, and a great deal of money consequently was spent upon him at College and Temple. He was very little altered for the worse by what he saw there of the great world, for when he came down into the country to pay us a visit, we thought him just the same man as ever—hand and glove with every one, and as far from high, though not without his own proper share of family pride, as any man ever you see. Latterly, seeing how Sir Kit and the Jewish lived together, and that there was no one between him and the Castle Rackrent estate, he neglected to apply to the law as much as was expected of him, and secretly many of the tenants and others advanced him cash upon his note of hand value received, promising bargains of leases and lawful interest, should he ever come into the estate. All this was kept a great secret for fear the present man, hearing of it, should take it into his head to take it ill of poor Condy, and so should cut him off for ever by levying a fine, and suffering a recovery to dock the entail.[1] Sir Murtagh would have been the man for that; but Sir Kit was too much taken up philandering to consider the law in this case, or any other. These practices I have mentioned to account for the state of his affairs—I mean Sir Condy's upon his coming into the Castle Rackrent estate. He could not command a penny of his first year's income, which, and keeping no accounts, and the great sight of company be did, with many other causes too numerous to mention, was the origin of his distresses. My son Jason, who was now established agent, and knew everything, explained matters out of the face to Sir Conolly, and made him sensible of his embarrassed situation. With a great nominal rent-roll, it was almost all paid away in interest; which being for convenience suffered to run on, soon doubled the principal, and Sir Condy was obliged to pass new bonds for the interest, now grown principal, and so on. Whilst this was going on, my son requiring to be paid for his trouble and many years' service in the family gratis, and Sir Condy not willing to take his affairs into his own hands, or to look them even in the face, he gave my son a bargain of some acres which fell out of lease at a reasonable rent. Jason set the land, as soon as his lease was scaled, to under-tenants, to make the rent, and got two hundred a year profit rent; which was little enough considering his long agency. He bought the land at twelve years' purchase two years afterwards, when Sir Condy was pushed for money on an execution, and was at the same time allowed for his improvements thereon. There was a sort of hunting-lodge upon the estate, convenient to my son Jason's land, which he had his eye upon about this time; and he was a little jealous of Sir Condy, who talked of setting it to a stranger who was just come into the country—Captain Moneygawl was the man. He was son and heir to the Moneygawls of Mount Juliet's Town, who had a great estate in the next county to ours; and my master was loth to disoblige the young gentleman, whose heart was set upon the Lodge; so he wrote him back that the Lodge was at his service, and if he would honour him with his company at Castle Rackrent, they could ride over together some morning and look at it before signing the lease. Accordingly, the captain came over to us, and he and Sir Condy grew the greatest friends ever you see, and were for ever out a-shooting or hunting together, and were very merry in the evenings; and Sir Condy was invited of course to Mount Juliet's Town; and the family intimacy that had been in Sir Patrick's time was now recollected, and nothing would serve Sir Condy but he must be three times a week at the least with his new friends, which grieved me, who knew, by the captain's groom and gentleman, how they talked of him at Mount Juliet's Town, making him quite, as one may say, a laughing-stock and a butt for the whole company; but they were soon cured of that by an accident that surprised 'em not a little, as it did me. There was a bit of a scrawl found upon the waiting-maid of old Mr. Moneygawl's youngest daughter, Miss Isabella, that laid open the whole; and her father, they say, was like one out of his right mind, and swore it was the last thing he ever should have thought of, when he invited my master to his house, that his daughter should think of such a match. But their talk signified not a straw, for as Miss Isabella's maid reported, her young mistress was fallen over head and ears in love with Sir Condy from the first time that ever her brother brought him into the house to dinner. The servant who waited that day behind my master's chair was the first who knew it, as he says; though it's hard to believe him, for he did not tell it till a great while afterwards; but, however, it's likely enough, as the thing turned out, that he was not far out of the way, for towards the middle of dinner, as he says, they were talking of stage-plays, having a playhouse, and being great play-actors at Mount Juliet's Town; and Miss Isabella turns short to my master, and says:

"Have you seen the play-bill, Sir Condy?"

"No, I have not," said he.

"Then more shame for you," said the captain her brother, "not to know that my sister is to play Juliet to-night, who plays it better than any woman on or off the stage in all Ireland."

"I am very happy to hear it," said Sir Condy; and there the matter dropped for the present.

But Sir Condy all this time, and a great while afterwards, was at a terrible non-plus; for he had no liking, not he, to stage-plays, nor to Miss Isabella either—to his mind, as it came out over a bowl of whisky-punch at home, his little Judy M'Quirk, who was daughter to a sister's son of mine, was worth twenty of Miss Isabella. He had seen her often when he stopped at her father's cabin to drink whisky out of the eggshell, out hunting, before he came to the estate, and, as she gave out, was under something like a promise of marriage to her. Anyhow, I could not but pity my poor master, who was so bothered between them, and he an easy-hearted man, that could not disoblige nobody—God bless him! To be sure, it was not his place to behave ungenerous to Miss Isabella, who had disobliged all her relations for his sake, as he remarked; and then she was locked up in her chamber, and forbid to think of him any more, which raised his spirit, because his family was, as he observed, as good as theirs at any rate, and the Rackrents a suitable match for the Moneygawls any day in the year; all which was true enough. But it grieved me to see that, upon the strength of all this, Sir Condy was growing more in the mind to carry off Miss Isabella to Scotland, in spite of her relations, as she desired.

"It's all over with our poor Judy!" said I, with a heavy sigh, making bold to speak to him one night when he was a little cheerful, and standing in the servants' hall all alone with me, as was often his custom.

"Not at all," said he; "I never was fonder of Judy than at this present speaking; and to prove it to you," said he and he took from my hand a halfpenny change that I had just got along with my tobacco—and to prove it to you, Thady," says he, "it's a toss-up with me which I should marry this minute, her or Mr. Moneygawl of Mount Juliet's Town's daughter—so it is."

"Oh—boo! boo!"[29] says I, making light of it, to see what he would go on to next; "your honour's joking, to be sure; there's no compare between our poor Judy and Miss Isabella, who has a great fortune, they say."

"I'm not a man to mind a fortune, nor never was," said Sir Condy, proudly, "whatever her friends may say; and to make short of it," says he, "I'm come to a determination upon the spot." With that he swore such a terrible oath as made me cross myself. "And by this book," said he, snatching up my ballad-book, mistaking it for my prayer-book, which lay in the window,—"and by this book," says he, "and by all the books that ever were shut and opened, it's come to a toss-up with me, and I'll stand or fall by the toss; and so Thady, hand me over that *pin* [30] out of the ink-horn"; and he makes a cross on the smooth side of the halfpenny; "Judy M'Quirk," says he, "her mark."

God bless him! his hand was a little unsteadied by all the whisky-punch he had taken, but it was plain to see his heart was for poor Judy. My heart was all as one as in my mouth when I saw the halfpenny up in the air, but I said nothing at all; and when it came down I was glad I had kept myself to myself, for to be sure now it was all over with poor Judy.

"Judy's out a luck," said I, striving to laugh.

"I'm out a luck," said he; and I never saw a man look so cast down: he took up the halfpenny off the flag, and walked away quite sober-like by the shock. Now, though as easy a man, you would think, as any in the wide world, there was no such thing as making him unsay one of these sort of vows, which he had learned to reverence when young, as I well remember teaching him to toss up for bog-berries on my knee. So I saw the affair was as good as settled between him and Miss Isabella, and I had no more to say but to wish her joy, which I did the week afterwards, upon her return from Scotland with my poor master.

My new lady was young, as might be supposed of a lady that had been carried off by her own consent to Scotland; but I could only see her at first through her veil, which, from bashfulness or fashion, she kept over her face.

"And am I to walk through all this crowd of people, my dearest love?" said she to Sir Condy, meaning us servants and tenants, who had gathered at the back gate.

"My dear," said Sir Condy, "there's nothing for it but to walk, or to let me carry you as far as the house, for you see the back road is too narrow for a carriage, and the great piers have tumbled down across the front approach; so there's no driving the right way, by reason of the ruins."

"Plato, thou reasonest well!" said she, or words to that effect, which I could noways understand; and again, when her foot stumbled against a broken bit of a car-wheel, she cried out, "Angels and ministers of grace defend us!" Well, thought I, to be sure, if she's no Jewish, like the last, she is a mad woman for certain, which is as bad: it would have been as welt for my poor master to have taken up with poor Judy, who is in her right mind anyhow.

She was dressed like a mad woman, moreover, more than like any one I ever saw afore or since, and I could not take my eyes off her, but still followed behind her; and her feathers on the top of her hat were broke going in at the low back door, and she pulled out her little bottle out of her pocket to smell when she found herself in the kitchen, and said, "I shall faint with the heat of this odious, odious place."

"My dear, it's only three steps across the kitchen, and there's a fine air if your veil was up," said Sir Condy; and with that threw back her veil, so that I had then a full sight of her face. She had not at all the colour of one going to faint, but a fine complexion of her own, as I then took it to be, though her maid told me after it was all put on; but even complexion and all taken in, she was no way, in point of good looks, to compare to poor Judy, and withal she had a quality toss with her; but maybe it was my over-partiality to Judy, into whose place I may say she stepped, that made me notice all this.

To do her justice, however, she was, when we came to know her better, very liberal in her housekeeping—nothing at all of the skinflint in her; she left everything to the housekeeper, and her own maid, Mrs. Jane, who went with her to Scotland; gave her the best of characters for generosity. She seldom or ever wore a thing twice the same way, Mrs. Jane told us, and was always pulling her things to pieces and giving them away, never being used, in her father's house, to think of expense in anything; and she reckoned to be sure to go on the same way at Castle Rackrent; but when I came to inquire, I learned that her father was so mad with her for running off, after his locking her up and forbidding her to think any more of Sir Condy, that he would not give her a farthing; and it was lucky for her she had a few thousands of her own, which had been left to her by a good grandmother, and these were very convenient to begin with. My master and my lady set out in great style; they had the finest coach and chariot, and horses and liveries, and cut the greatest dash in the county, returning their wedding visits; and it was immediately reported that her father had undertaken to pay all my master's debts, and of course all his tradesmen gave him a new credit, and everything went on smack smooth, and I could not but admire my lady's spirit, and was proud to see Castle Rackrent again in all its glory. My lady had a fine taste for building, and furniture, and playhouses, and she turned everything topsy-turvy, and made the barrack-room into a theatre, as she called it, and she went on as if she had a mint of money at her elbow; and to be sure I thought she knew best, especially as Sir Condy said nothing to it one way or the other. All he asked—God bless him!—was to live in peace and quietness, and have his bottle or his whisky-punch at night to himself. Now this was little enough, to be sure, for any gentleman; but my lady couldn't abide the smell of the whisky-punch.

"My dear," says he, "you liked it well enough before we were married, and why not now?"

"My dear," said she, "I never smelt it, or I assure you I should never have prevailed upon myself to marry you."

"My dear, I am sorry you did not smell it, but we can't help that now," returned my master, without putting himself in a passion, or going out of his way, but just fair and easy helped himself to another glass, and drank it off to her good health.

All this the butler told me, who was going backwards and forwards unnoticed with the jug, and hot water, and sugar, and all he thought wanting. Upon my master's swallowing the last glass of whisky-punch my lady burst into tears, calling him an ungrateful, base, barbarous wretch; and went off into a fit of hysterics, as I think Mrs. Jane called it, and my poor master was greatly frightened, this being the first thing of the kind he had seen; and he fell straight on his knees before her, and, like a good-hearted cratur as he was, ordered the whisky-punch out of the room, and bid 'em throw open all the windows, and cursed himself: and then my lady came to herself again, and when she saw him kneeling there, bid him get up, and not forswear himself any more, for that she was sure he did not love her, and never had. This we learned from Mrs. Jane, who was the only person left present at all this.

"My dear," returns my master, thinking, to be sure, of Judy, as well he might, "whoever told you so is an incendiary, and I'd have 'em turned out of the house this minute, if you'll only let me know which of them it was."

"Told me what?" said my lady, starting upright in her chair.

"Nothing at all, nothing at all," said my master, seeing he had overshot himself, and that my lady spoke at random; "but what you said just now, that I did not love you, Bella; who told you that?"

"My own sense," she said, and she put her handkerchief to her face, and leant back upon Mrs. Jane, and fell to sobbing as if her heart would break.

"Why now, Bella, this is very strange of you," said my poor master; "if nobody has told you nothing, what is it you are taking on for at this rate, and exposing yourself and me for this way?"

"Oh, say no more, say no more; every word you say kills me," cried my lady; and she ran on like one, as Mrs. Jane says, raving, "Oh, Sir Condy, Sir Condy! I that had hoped to find in you—"

"Why now, faith, this is a little too much; do, Bella, try to recollect yourself, my dear; am not I your husband, and of your own choosing, and is not that enough?"

"Oh, too much! too much!" cried my lady, wringing her bands.

"Why, my dear, come to your right senses, for the love of heaven. See, is not the whisky-punch, jug and bowl and all, gone out of the room long ago? What is it, in the wide world, you have to complain of?"

But still my lady sobbed and sobbed, and called herself the most wretched of women; and among other out-of-the-way provoking things, asked my master, was he fit company for her, and he drinking all night? This nettling him, which it was hard to do, he replied, that as to drinking all night, he was then as sober as she was herself, and that it was no matter flow much a man drank, provided it did noways affect or stagger him: that as to being fit company for her, he thought himself of a family to be fit company for any lord or lady in the land; but that he never prevented her from seeing and keeping what company she pleased, and that he bad done his best to make Castle Rackrent pleasing to her since her marriage, having always had the house full of visitors, and if her own relations were not amongst them, he said that was their own fault, and their pride's fault, of which he was sorry to find her ladyship had so unbecoming a share. So concluding, he took his candle and walked off to his room, and my lady was in her tantarums for three days after; and would have been so much longer, no doubt, but some of her friends, young ladies, and cousins, and second cousins, came to Castle Rackrent, by my poor master's express invitation, to see her, and she was in a hurry to get up, as Mrs. Jane called it, a play for them, and so got well, and was as finely dressed, and as happy to look at, as ever; and all the young ladies, who used to be in her room dressing of her, said in Mrs. Jane's hearing that my lady was the happiest bride ever they had seen, and that to be sure a love-match was the only thing for happiness, where the parties could any way afford it.

As to affording it, God knows it was little they knew of the matter; my lady's few thousands could not last for ever, especially the way she went on with them; and letters from tradesfolk came every post thick and threefold, with bills as long as my arm, of years' and years' standing. My son Jason had 'em all handed over to him, and the pressing letters were all unread by Sir Condy, who hated trouble, and could never be brought to hear talk of business, but still put it off and put it off, saying, "Settle it anyhow," or, "Bid 'em call again to-morrow," or, "Speak to me about it some other time." Now it was hard to find the right time to speak, for in the mornings he was abed, and in the evenings over his bottle, where no gentleman chooses to be disturbed. Things in a twelvemonth or so came to such a pass there was no making a shift to go on any longer, though we were all of us well enough used to live from hand to mouth at Castle Rackrent. One day, I remember, when there was a power of company, all sitting after dinner in the dusk, not to say dark, in the drawing-room, my lady having rung five times for candles, and none to go up, the housekeeper sent up the footman, who went to my mistress, and whispered behind her chair how it was.

"My lady, says he," there are no candles in the house."

"Bless me, says she;" then take a horse and gallop off as fast as you can to Carrick O'Fungus, and get some."

"And in the meantime tell them to step into the playhouse, and try if there are not some bits left," added Sir Condy, who happened to be within hearing. The man was sent up again to my lady, to let her know there was no horse to go, but one that wanted a shoe.

"Go to Sir Condy then; I know nothing at all about the horses," said my lady; "why do you plague me with these things?" How it was settled, I really forget, but to the best of my remembrance, the boy was sent down to my son Jason's to borrow candles for the night. Another time, in the winter, and on a desperate cold day, there was no turf in for the parlour and above stairs, and scarce enough for the cook in the kitchen. The little *gossoon* was sent off to the neighbours, to see and beg or borrow some, but none could he bring back with him for love or money; so, as needs must, we were forced to trouble Sir Condy—Well, and if there's no turf to be had in the town or country, why, what signifies talking any more about it; can't ye go and cut down a tree?"

"Which tree, please your honour?" I made bold to say.

"Any tree at all that's good to burn," said Sir Condy; send off smart and get one down, and the fires lighted, before my lady gets up to breakfast, or the house will be too hot to hold us."

He was always very considerate in all things about my lady, and she wanted for nothing whilst he had it to give. Well, when things were tight with them about this time, my son Jason put in a word again about the Lodge, and made a genteel offer to lay down the purchase-money, to relieve Sir Condy's distresses. Now Sir Condy had it from the best authority that there were two writs come down to the sheriff against his person, and the sheriff, as ill-luck would have it, was no friend of his, and talked how he must do his duty, and how he would do it, if it was against the first man in the country, or even his own brother, let alone one who had voted against him at the last election, as Sir Condy had done. So Sir Condy was fain to take the purchase-money of the Lodge from my son Jason to settle matters; and sure enough it was a good bargain for both parties, for my son bought the fee-simple of a good house for him and his heirs for ever, for little or nothing, and by selling of it for that same my master saved himself from a gaol. Every way it turned out fortunate for Sir Condy, for before the money was all gone there came a general election, and he being so well beloved in the county, and one of the oldest families, no one had a better right to stand candidate for the vacancy; and he was called upon by all his friends, and the whole county I may say, to declare himself against the old member, who bad little thought of a contest. My master did not relish the thoughts of a troublesome canvas, and all the ill-will he might bring upon himself by disturbing the peace of the county, besides the expense, which was no trifle; but all his friends called upon one another to subscribe, and they formed themselves into a committee, and wrote all his circular letters for him, and engaged all his agents, and did all the business unknown to him; and he was well pleased that it should be so at last, and my lady herself was very sanguine about the election; and there was open house kept night and day at Castle Rackrent, and I thought I never saw my lady look so well in her life as she did at that time. There were grand dinners, and all the gentlemen drinking success to Sir Condy till they were carried off; and then dances and balls, and the ladies all finishing with a raking pot of tea in the morning.[1] Indeed, it was well the company made it their choice to sit up all night, for there were not half beds enough for the sights of people that were in it, though there were shake-downs in the drawing-room always made up before sunrise for those that liked it. For my part, when I saw the doings that were going on, and the loads of claret that went down the throats of them that had no right to be asking for it, and the sights of meat that went up to table and never came down, besides what was carried off to one or t'other below stair, I couldn't but pity my poor master, who was to pay for all; but I said nothing, for fear of gaining myself ill-will. The day of election will come some time or other, says I to myself, and all will be over; and so it did, and a glorious day it was as any I ever had the happiness to see.

"Huzza! huzza! Sir Condy Rackrent for ever!" was the first thing I hears in the morning, and the same and nothing else all day, and not a soul sober only just when polling, enough to give their votes as became 'em, and to stand the browbeating of the lawyers, who came tight enough upon us; and many of our freeholders were knocked off, having never a freehold that they could safely swear to, and Sir Condy was not willing to have any man perjure himself for his sake, as was done on the other side, God knows; but no matter for that. Some of our friends were dumbfounded by the lawyers asking them: Had they ever been upon the ground where their freeholds lay? Now, Sir Condy being tender of the consciences of them that had not been on the ground, and so could not swear to a freehold when cross-examined by them lawyers, sent out for a couple of cleavesful of the sods of his farm of Gulteeshinnagh; and as soon as the sods came into town, he set each man upon his sod, and so then, ever after, you know, they could fairly swear they had been upon the ground. We gained the day by this piece of honesty.[1] I thought I should have died in the streets for joy when I seed my poor master chaired, and he bareheaded, and it raining as hard as it could pour; but all the crowds following him up and down, and he bowing and shaking hands with the whole town.

"Is that Sir Condy Rackrent in the chair?" says a stranger man in the crowd.

"The same," says I. "Who else should it be? God bless him!"

"And I take it, then, you belong to him?" says he. "Not at all," says I; "but I live under him, and have done so these two hundred years and upwards, me and mine."

"It's lucky for you, then," rejoins he, "that he is where he is; for was he any-where else but in the chair, this minute he'd be in a worse place; for I was sent down on purpose to put him up, and here's my order for so doing in my pocket."

It was a writ that villain the wine merchant had marked against my poor master for some hundreds of an old debt, which it was a shame to be talking of at such a time as this.

"Put it in your pocket again, and think no more of it anyways for seven years to come, my honest friend," says I; "he's a member of Parliament now, praised be God, and such as you can't touch him: and if you'll take a fool's advice, I'd have you keep out of the way this day, or you'll run a good chance of getting your deserts amongst my master's friends, unless you choose to drink his health like everybody else."

"I've no objection to that in life," said he. So we went into one of the public-houses kept open for my master; and we had a great deal of talk about this thing and that. "And how is it," says he, "your master keeps on so well upon his legs? I heard say he was off Holantide twelve-month past."

"Never was better or heartier in his life," said I.

"It's not that I'm after speaking of," said he; "but there was a great report of his being ruined."

"No matter," says I, "the sheriffs two years running were his particular friends, and the sub-sheriffs were both of them gentlemen, and were properly spoken to; and so the writs lay snug with therm, and they, as I understand by my son Jason the custom in them cases is, returned the writs as they came to them to those that sent him—much good may it do them!—with a word in Latin, that no such per-son as Sir Condy Rackrent, Bart., was to be found in those parts."

"Oh, I understand all those ways better—no offence—than you," says he, laughing, and at the same time filling his glass to my master's good health, which convinced me be was a warm friend in his heart after all, though appearances were a little suspicious or so at first. "To be sure," says he, still cutting his joke, "when a man's over head and shoulders in debt, he may live the faster for it, and the better if he goes the right way about it; or else how is it so many live on so well, as we see every day, after they are ruined?"

"How is it," says I, being a little merry at the time— "how is it but just as you see the ducks in the chicken-yard, just after their heads are cut off by the cook, running round and round faster than when alive?"

At which conceit be fell a-laughing, and remarked he had never had the happiness yet to see the chicken-yard at Castle Rackrent.

"It won't be long so, I hope," says I; "you'll be kindly welcome there, as everybody is made by my master: there is not a freer-spoken gentleman, or a better beloved, high or low, in all Ireland."

And of what passed after this I'm not sensible, for we drank Sir Condy's good health and the downfall of his enemies till we could stand no longer ourselves. And little did I think at the time, or till long after, how I was harbouring my poor master's greatest of enemies myself. This fellow had the impudence, after coming to see the chicken-yard, to get me to introduce him to my son Jason; little more than the man that never was born did I guess at his meaning by this visit: he gets him a correct list fairly drawn out from my son Jason of all my master's debts, and goes straight round to the creditors and buys them all up, which he did easy enough, seeing the half of them never expected to see their money out of Sir Condy's hands. Then, when this base-minded limb of the law, as I afterwards detected him in being, grew to be sole creditor over all, he takes him out a custodiam on all the denominations and sub-denominations, and even carton[1] and half-carton upon the estate; and not content with that, must have an execution against the master's goods and down to the furniture, though little worth, of Castle Rackrent itself. But this is a part of my story I'm not come to yet, and it's bad to be forestalling: ill news flies fast enough all the world over.

To go back to the day of the election, which I never think of but with pleasure and tears of gratitude for those good times: after the election was quite and clean over, there comes shoals of people from all parts, claiming to have obliged my master with their votes, and putting him in mind of promises which he could never remember him self to have made: one was to have a freehold for each of his four sons; another was to have a renewal of a lease; another an abatement; one came to be paid ten guineas for a pair of silver buckles sold my master on the hustings, which turned out to be no better than copper gilt; another had a long bill for oats, the half of which never went into the granary to my certain knowledge, and the other half was not fit for the cattle to touch; but the bargain was made the week before the election, and the coach and saddle-horses were got into order for the day, besides a vote fairly got by them oats; so no more reasoning on that head. But then there was no end to them that were telling Sir Condy he had engaged to make their sons excise men, or high constables, or the like; and as for them that had bills to give in for liquor, and beds, and straw, and ribands, and horses, and post-chaises for the gentlemen freeholders that came from all parts and other counties to vote for my master, and were not, to be sure, to be at any charges, there was no standing against all these; and, worse than all, the gentlemen of my master's committee, who managed all for him, and talked how they'd bring him in without costing him a penny, and subscribed by hundreds very genteelly, forgot to pay their subscriptions, and had laid out in agents' and lawyers' fees and secret service money to the Lord knows how much; and my master could never ask one of them for their subscription you are sensible, nor for the price of a fine horse he had sold one of them; so it all was left at his door. He could never, God bless him again! I say, bring himself to ask a gentleman for money, despising such sort of conversation himself; but others, who were not gentlemen born, behaved very uncivil in pressing him at this very time, and all he could do to content 'em all was to take himself out of the way as fast as possible to Dublin, where my lady had taken a house fitting for him as a member of Parliament, to attend his duty in there all the winter. I was very lonely when the whole family was gone, and all the things they had ordered to go, and forgot, sent after them by the car. There was then a great silence in Castle Rackrent, and I went moping from room to room, hearing the doors clap for want of right locks, and the wind through the broken windows, that the glazier never would come to mend, and the rain coming through the roof and best ceilings all over the house for want of the slater, whose bill was not paid, besides our having no slates or shingles for that part of the old building which was shingled and burnt when the chimney took fire, and had been open to the weather ever since. I took myself to the servants' hall in the evening to smoke my pipe as usual, but missed the bit of talk we used to have there sadly, and ever after was content to stay in the kitchen and boil my little potatoes, and put up my bed there, and every post-day I looked in the newspaper, but no news of my master in the House; he never spoke good or bad, but, as the butler wrote down word to my son Jason, was very ill-used by the Government about a place that was promised him and never given, after his supporting them against his conscience very honourably, and being greatly abused for it, which hurt him greatly, he having the name of a great patriot in the country before. The house and living in Dublin too were not to be had for nothing, and my son Jason said, "Sir Condy must soon be looking out for a new agent, for I've done my part, and can do no more. If my lady had the bank of Ireland to spend, it would go all in one winter, and Sir Condy would never gainsay her, though he does not care the rind of a lemon for her all the while."

Now I could not bear to hear Jason giving out after this manner against the family, and twenty people standing by in the street. Ever since he had lived at the Lodge of his own he looked down, howsomever, upon poor old Thady, and was grown quite a great gentleman, and had none of his relations near him; no wonder he was no kinder to poor Sir Condy than to his own kith or kin.[41] In the spring it was the villain that got the list of the debts from him brought down the custodiam, Sir Condy still attending his duty in Parliament; and I could scarcely believe my own old eyes, or the spectacles with which I read it, when I was shown my son Jason's name joined in the custodiam; but he told me it was only for form's sake, and to make things easier than if all the land was under the power of a total stranger. Well, I did not know what to think; it was hard to be talking ill of my own, and I could not but grieve for my poor master's fine estate, all torn by these vultures of the law; so I said nothing, but just looked on to see how it would all end.

It was not till the month of June that he and my lady came down to the country. My master was pleased to take me aside with him to the brewhouse that same evening, to complain to me of my son and other matters, in which he said he was confident I had neither art nor part; he said a great deal more to me, to whom he had been fond to talk ever since he was my white-headed boy before he came to the estate; and all that he said about poor Judy I can never forget, but scorn to repeat. He did not say an unkind word of my lady, but wondered, as well he might, her relations would do nothing for him or her, and they in all this great distress. He did not take anything long to heart, let it be as it would, and had no more malice or thought of the like in him than a child that can't speak; this night it was all out of his head before he went to his bed. He took his jug of whisky-punch—my lady was grown quite easy about the whisky-punch by this time, and so I did suppose all was going on right betwixt them, till I learnt the truth through Mrs. Jane, who talked over the affairs to the housekeeper, and I within hearing. The night my master came home, thinking of nothing at all but just making merry, he drank his bumper toast "to the deserts of that old curmudgeon my father-in-law, and all enemies at Mount Juliet's Town." Now my lady was no longer in the mind she formerly was, and did noways relish hearing her own friends abused in her presence, she said.

"Then why don't they show themselves your friends," said my master, "and oblige me with the loan of the money I condescended, by your advice, my dear, to ask? It's now three posts since I sent off my letter, desiring in the postscript a speedy answer by the return of the post, and no account at all from them yet."

"I expect they'll write to *me* next post," says my lady, and that was all that passed then; but it was easy from this to guess there was a coolness betwixt them, and with good cause.

The next morning, being post-day, I sent off the gossoon early to the post-office, to see was there any letter likely to set matters to rights, and he brought back one with the proper post-mark upon it, sure enough, and I had no time to examine or make any conjecture more about it, for into the servants' hall pops Mrs. Jane with a blue bandbox in her hand, quite entirely mad.

"Dear ma'am, and what's the matter?" says I.

"Matter enough," says she; "don't you see my bandbox is wet through, and my best bonnet here spoiled, besides my lady's, and all by the rain coming in through that gallery window that you might have got mended if you'd had any sense, Thady, all the time we were in town in the winter?"

"Sure, I could not get the glazier, ma'am," says

"You might have stopped it up anyhow," says she.

"So I did, ma'am, to the best of my ability; one of the panes with the old pillow-case, and the other with a piece of the old stage green curtain. Sure I was as careful as possible all the time you were away, and not a drop of rain came in at that window of all the windows in the house, all winter, ma'am, when under my care; and now the family's come home, and it's summer-time, I never thought no more about it, to be sure; but dear, it's a pity to think of your bonnet, ma'am. But here's what will please you, ma'am—a letter from Mount Juliet's Town for my lady.

With that she snatches it from me without a word more, and runs up the back stairs to my mistress; I follows with a slate to make up the window. This window was in the long passage—or gallery, as my lady gave out orders to have it called— in the gallery leading to my master's bedchamber and hers. And when I went up with the slate, the door having no lock, and the bolt spoilt, was ajar after Mrs. Jane, and, as I was busy with the window, I heard all that was saying within.

"Well, what's in your letter, Bella, my dear?" says he: "you're a long time spelling it over."

"Won't you shave this morning, Sir Condy?" says she, and put the letter into her pocket.

"I shaved the day before yesterday," said he, "my dear, and that's not what I'm thinking of now; but anything to oblige you, and to have peace and quietness, my dear"—and presently I had a glimpse of him at the cracked glass over the chimney-piece, standing up shaving himself to please my lady. But she took no notice, but went on reading her book, and Mrs. Jane doing her hair behind.

"What is it you're reading there, my dear?—phoo, I've cut myself with this razor; the man's a cheat that sold it me, but I have not paid him for it yet. What is it you're reading there? Did you hear me asking you, my dear?"

"*The Sorrows of Werter*," replies my lady, as well as I could hear.

"I think more of the sorrows of Sir Condy," says my master, joking like. "What news from Mount Juliet's Town?"

"No news," says she, "but the old story over again; my friends all reproaching me still for what I can't help now."

"Is it for marrying me?" said my master, still shaving. "What signifies, as you say, talking of that, when it can't be help'd now?"

With that she heaved a great sigh that I heard plain enough in the passage.

"And did not you use me basely, Sir Condy," says she, "not to tell me you were ruined before I married you?"

"Tell you, my dear!" said he. "Did you ever ask me one word about it? And had not you friends enough of your own, that were telling you nothing else from morning to night, if you'd have listened to them slanders?"

"No slanders, nor are my friends slanderers; and I can't bear to hear them treat-ed with disrespect as I do," says my lady, and took out her pocket-handkerchief; "they are the best of friends, and if I had taken their advice—But my father was wrong to lock me up, I own. That was the only unkind thing I can charge him with; for if he had not locked me up, I should never have had a serious thought of running away as I did."

"Well, my dear," said my master, "don't cry and make yourself uneasy about it now, when it's all over, and you have the man of your own choice, in spite of 'em all."

"I was too young, I know, to make a choice at the time you ran away with me, I'm sure," says my lady, and another sigh, which made my master, half-shaved as he was, turn round upon her in surprise.

"Why, Bell," says he, "you can't deny what you know as well as I do, that it was at your own particular desire, and that twice under Your own hand and seal expressed, that I should carry you off as I did to Scotland, and marry you there."

"Well, say no more about it, Sir Condy," said my lady, pettish-like; "I was a child then, you know."

"And as far as I know, you're little better now, my dear Bella, to be talking in this manner to your husband's face; but I won't take it ill of you, for I know it's something in that letter you put into your pocket just now that has set you against me all on a sudden, and imposed upon your understanding."

"It's not so very easy as you think it, Sir Condy, to impose upon my understanding," said my lady.

"My dear," says he, "I have, and with reason, the best opinion of your understanding of any man now breathing; and you know I have never set my own in competition with it till now, my dear Bella," says he, taking her hand from her book as kind as could be—till now, when I have the great advantage of being quite cool, and you not; so don't believe one word your friends say against your own Sir Condy, and lend me the letter out of your pocket, till I see what it is they can have to say."

"Take it then," says she; "and as you are quite cool, I hope it is a proper time to request you'll allow me to comply with the wishes of all my own friends, and return to live with my father and family, during the remainder of my wretched existence, at Mount Juliet's Town."

At this my poor master fell back a few paces, like one that had been shot.

"You're not serious, Bella," says he; "and could you find it in your heart to leave me this way in the very middle of my distresses, all alone?" But recollecting himself after his first surprise, and a moment's time for reflection, he said, with a great deal of consideration for my lady, "Well, Bella, my dear, I believe you are right; for what could you do at Castle Rackrent, and an execution against the goods coming down, and the furniture to be canted, and an auction in the house all next week? So you have my full consent to go, since that is your desire; only you must not think of my accompanying you, which I could not in honour do upon the terms I always have been, since our marriage, with your friends. Besides, I have business to transact at home; so in the meantime, if we are to have any breakfast this morning, let us go down and have it for the last time in peace and comfort, Bella."

Then as I heard my master coming to the passage door, I finished fastening up my slate against the broken pane; and when he came out I wiped down the window-seat with my wig,[42] and bade him a "good-morrow" as kindly as I could, seeing he was in trouble, though he strove and thought to hide it from me.

"This window is all racked and tattered," says I, "and it's what I'm striving to mend."

"It *is* all racked and tattered, plain enough," says he, "and never mind mending it, honest old Thady," says he; "it will do well enough for you and I, and that's all the company we shall have left in the house by and by."

"I'm sorry to see your honour so low this morning," says I; "but you'll be better after taking your breakfast."

"Step down to the servants' hall," said he, "and bring me up the pen and ink into the parlour, and get a sheet of paper from Mrs. Jane, for I have business that can't brook to be delayed; and come into the patient with the pen and ink yourself, Thady, for I must have you to witness my signing a paper I have to execute in a hurry."

Well, while I was getting of the pen and ink-horn, and the sheet of paper, I ransacked my brains to think what could be the papers my poor master could have to execute in such a hurry, he that never thought of such a thing as doing business afore breakfast in the whole course of his life, for any man living; but this was for my lady, as I afterwards found, and the more genteel of him after all her treatment.

I was just witnessing the paper that he had scrawled over, and was shaking the ink out of my pen upon the carpet, when my lady came in to breakfast, and she started as if it had been a ghost; as well she might, when she saw Sir Condy writing at this unseasonable hour.

"That will do very well, Thady," says he to me, and took the paper I had signed to, without knowing what upon the earth it might be, out of my hands, and walked, folding it up, to my lady.

"You are concerned in this, my Lady Rackrent," said he, putting it into her hands; "and I beg you'll keep this memorandum safe, and show it to your friends the first thing you do when you get home; but put it in your pocket now, my dear, and let us eat our breakfast, in God's name.

"What is all this?" said my lady, opening the paper in great curiosity.

"It's only a bit of a memorandum of what I think becomes me to do whenever I am able," says my master; "you know my situation, tied hand and foot at the present time being, but that can't last always, and when I'm dead and gone the land will be to the good, Thady, you know; and take notice it's my intention your lady should have a clear five hundred a year jointure off the estate afore any of my debts are paid."

"Oh, please your honour," says I, "I can't expect to live to see that time, being now upwards of fourscore years of age, and you a young man, and likely to continue so, by the help of God."

I was vexed to see my lady so insensible too, for alt she said was, "This is very genteel of you, Sir Condy. You need not wait any longer, Thady." So I just picked up the pen and ink that had tumbled on the floor, and heard my master finish with saying, "You behaved very genteel to me, my dear, when you threw all the little you had in Your power along with yourself into my hands; and as I don't deny but what you may have had some things to complain of,"—to be sure he was thinking then of Judy, or of the whisky-punch, one or t'other, or both,—"and as I don't deny but you may have had something to complain of, my dear, it is but fair you should have something in the form of compensation to look forward to agreeably in future; besides, it's an act of justice to myself, that none of your friends, my dear, may ever have it to say against me, I married for money, and not for love."

"That is the last thing I should ever have thought of saying of you, Sir Condy," said my lady, looking very gracious.

"Then, my dear," said Sir Condy, "we shall part as good friends as we met; so all's right."

I was greatly rejoiced to hear this, and went out of the parlour to report it all to the kitchen. The next morning my lady and Mrs. Jane set out for Mount Juliet's Town in the jaunting-car. Many wondered at my lady's choosing to go away, considering all things, upon the jaunting-car, as if it was only a party of pleasure; but they did not know till I told them that the coach was all broke in the journey down, and no other vehicle but the car to be had. Besides, my lady's friends were to send their coach to meet her at the cross-roads; so it was all done very proper.

My poor master was in great trouble after my lady left us. The execution came down, and everything at Castle Rackrent was seized by the gripers, and my son Jason, to his shame be it spoken, amongst them. I wondered, for the life of me, how he could harden himself to do it; but then he had been studying the law, and had made himself Attorney Quirk; so he brought down at once a heap of accounts upon my master's head. To cash lent, and to ditto, and to ditto, and to ditto and oats, and bills paid at the milliner's and linen-draper's, and many dresses for the fancy balls in Dublin for my lady, and all the bills to the workmen and tradesmen for the scenery of the theatre, and the chandler's and grocer's bills, and tailor's, besides butcher's and baker's, and, worse than all, the old one of that base wine merchant's, that wanted to arrest my poor master for the amount on the election day, for which amount Sir Condy afterwards passed his note of hand, bearing lawful interest from the date thereof; and the interest and compound interest was now mounted to a terrible deal on many other notes and bonds for money borrowed, and there was, besides, hush-money to the sub-sheriffs, and sheets upon sheets of old and new attorneys' bills, with heavy balances, "as per former account furnished," brought forward with interest thereon; then there was a powerful deal due to the Crown for sixteen years' arrear of quit-rent of the town-lands of Carrickashaughlin, with driver's fees, and a compliment to the receiver every year for letting the quit-rent run on to oblige Sir Condy, and Sir Kit afore him. Then there were bills for spirits and ribands at the election time, and the gentlemen of the committee's accounts unsettled, and their subscription never gathered; and there were cows to be paid for, with the smith and farrier's bills to be set against the rent of the demesne, with calf and hay money; then there was all the servants' wages, since I don't know when, coming due to them, and sums advanced for them by my son Jason for clothes, and boots, and whips, and odd moneys for sundries expended by them in journeys to town and elsewhere, and pocket-money for the master continually, and messengers and postage before his being a Parliament man. I can't myself tell you what besides; but this I know, that when the evening came on the which Sir Condy had appointed to settle all with my son Jason, and when he comes into the parlour, and sees the sight of bills and load of papers all gathered on the great dining-table for him, he puts his hands before both his eyes, and cried out, "Merciful Jasus! what is it I see before me?" Then I sets an arm-chair at the table for him, and with a deal of difficulty he sits him down, and my son Jason hands him over the pen and ink to sign to this man's bill and t'other man's bill, all which he did without making the least objections. Indeed, to give him his due, I never seen a man more fair and honest, and easy in all his dealings, from first to last, as Sir Condy, or more willing to pay every man his own as far as he was able, which is as much as any one can do.

"Well," says he, joking like with Jason, "I wish we could settle it all with a stroke of my grey goose quill. What signifies making me wade through all this ocean of papers here; can't you now, who understand drawing out an account, debtor and creditor, just sit down here at the corner of the table and get it done out for me, that I may have a clear view of the balance, which is all I need be talking about, you know?"

"Very true, Sir Condy; nobody understands business better than yourself," says Jason.

"So I've a right to do, being born and bred to the bar," says Sir Condy. "Thady, do step out and see are they bringing in the things for the punch, for we've just done all we have to do for this evening."

I goes out accordingly, and when I came back Jason was pointing to the balance, which was a terrible sight to my poor master.

"Pooh! pooh! pooh!" says he. "Here's so many noughts they dazzle my eyes, so they do, and put me in mind of all I suffered larning of my numeration table, when I was a boy at the day-school along with you, Jason—units, tens, hundreds, tens of hundreds. Is the punch ready, Thady?" says he, seeing me.

"Immediately; the boy has the jug in his hand; it's coming upstairs, please your honour, as fast as possible," says I, for I saw his honour was tired out of his life; but Jason, very short and cruel, cuts me off with —"Don't be talking of punch yet awhile; it's no time for punch yet a bit—units, tens, hundreds," goes he on, count-ing over the master's shoulder, units, tens, hundreds, thousands.

"A-a-ah! hold your hand," cries my master. "Where in this wide world am I to find hundreds, or units itself, let alone thousands?"

"The balance has been running on too long," says Jason, sticking to him as I could not have done at the time, if you'd have given both the Indies and Cork to boot; "the balance has been running on too long, and I'm distressed myself on your account, Sir Condy, for money, and the thing must be settled now on the spot, and the balance cleared off," says Jason.

"I'll thank you if you'll only show me how," says Sir Condy.

"There's but one way," says Jason, "and that's ready enough. When there's no cash, what can a gentleman do but go to the land?"

"How can you go to the land, and it under custodiam to yourself already?" says Sir Condy; "and another custodiam hanging over it? And no one at all can touch it, you know, but the custodees."

"Sure, can't you sell, though at a loss? Sure you can sell, and I've a purchaser ready for you," says Jason.

"Have you so?" says Sir Condy. "That's a great point gained. But there's a thing now beyond all, that perhaps you don't know yet, barring Thady has let you into the secret."

"Sarrah bit of a secret, or anything at all of the kind, has he learned from me these fifteen weeks come St. John's Eve," says I, "for we have scarce been upon speaking terms of late. But what is it your honour means of a secret?"

"Why, the secret of the little keepsake I gave my Lady Rackrent the morning she left us, that she might not go back empty-handed to her friends."

"My Lady Rackrent, I'm sure, has baubles and keepsakes enough, as those bills on the table will show," says Jason; "but whatever it is," says he, taking up his pen, "we must add it to the balance, for to be sure it can't be paid for."

"No, nor can't till after my decease," says Sir Condy; "that's one good thing."

Then colouring up a good deal, he tells Jason of the memorandum of the five hundred a year jointure he had settled upon my lady; at which Jason was indeed mad, and said a great deal in very high words, that it was using a gentleman who had the management of his affairs, and was, moreover, his principal creditor, extremely ill to do such a thing without consulting him, and against his knowledge and consent. To all which Sir Condy had nothing to reply, but that, upon his conscience, it was in a hurry and without a moment's thought on his part, and he was very sorry for it, but if it was to do over again he would do the same; and he appealed to me, and I was ready to give my evidence, if that would do, to the truth of all he said.

So Jason with much ado was brought to agree to a compromise.

"The purchaser that I have ready," says he, "will be much displeased, to be sure, at the encumbrance on the land, but I must see and manage him. Here's a deed ready drawn up; we have nothing to do but to put in the consideration money and our names to it."

"And how much am I going to sell?—the lands of O'Shaughlin's Town, and the lands of Gruneaghoolaghan, and the lands of Crookaghnawaturgh," says he, just reading to himself. "And—oh, murder, Jason! sure you won't put this in—the castle, stable, and appurtenances of Castle Rackrent?"

"Oh, murder!" says I, clapping my hands; "this is too bad, Jason."

"Why so?" said Jason. "When it's all, and a great deal more to the back of it, lawfully mine, was I to push for it."

"Look at him," says I, pointing to Sir Condy, who was just leaning back in his arm-chair, with his arms falling beside him like one stupefied; "is it you, Jason, that can stand in his presence, and recollect all he has been to us, and all we have been to him, and yet use him so at the last?"

"Who will you find to use him better? I ask you," said Jason; "if he can get a better purchaser, I'm content; I only offer to purchase, to make things easy, and oblige him; though I don't see what compliment I am under, if you come to that. I have never had, asked, or charged more than sixpence in the pound, receiver's fees, and where would he have got an agent for a penny less?"

"Oh, Jason! Jason! how will you stand to this in the face of the county, and all who know you?" says I; "and what will people think and say when they see you living here in Castle Rackrent, and the lawful owner turned out of the seat of his ancestors, without a cabin to put his head into, or so much as a potato to eat?"

Jason, whilst I was saying this, and a great deal more, made me signs, and winks, and frowns; but I took no heed, for I was grieved and sick at heart for my poor master, and couldn't but speak.

"Here's the punch," says Jason, for the door opened; "here's the punch!"

Hearing that, my master starts up in his chair, and recollects himself, and Jason uncorks the whisky.

"Set down the jug here," says he, making room for it beside the papers opposite to Sir Condy, but still not stirring the deed that was to make over all.

Well, I was in great hopes he had some touch of mercy about him when I saw him making the punch, and my master took a glass; but Jason put it back as he was going to fill again, saying: "No, Sir Condy, it shan't be said of me I got your signature to this deed when you were half-seas over: you know your name and handwriting in that condition would not, if brought before the courts, benefit me a straw; wherefore, let us settle all before we go deeper into the punch-bowl."

"Settle all as you will," said Sir Condy, clapping his hands to his ears; "but let me hear no more. I'm bothered to death this night."

"You've only to sign," said Jason, putting the pen to him.

"Take all, and be content," said my master. So he signed; and the man who brought in the punch witnessed it, for I was not able, but crying like a child; and besides, Jason said, which I was glad of, that I was no fit witness, being so old and doting. It was so bad with me, I could not taste a drop of the punch itself, though my master himself, God bless him! in the midst of his trouble, poured out a glass for me, and brought it up to my lips.

"Not a drop; I thank your honour's honour as much as if I took it, though." And I just set down the glass as it was, and went out, and when I got to the street door the neighbours' childer, who were playing at marbles there, seeing me in great trouble, left their play, and gathered about me to know what ailed me; and I told them all, for it was a great relief to me to speak to these poor childer, that seemed to have some natural feeling left in them; and when they were made sensible that Sir Condy was going to leave Castle Rackrent for good and all, they set up a whillaluh that could be heard to the farthest end of the street; and one—fine boy he was—that my master had given an apple to that morning, cried the loudest; but they all were the same sorry, for Sir Condy was greatly beloved amongst the childer, for letting them go a-nutting in the demesne, without saying a word to them, though my lady objected to them. The people in the town, who were the most of them standing at their doors, hearing the childer cry, would know the reason of it; and when the report was made known, the people one and all gathered in great anger against my son Jason, and terror at the notion of his coming to be landlord over them, and they cried, "No Jason! no Jason! Sir Condy! Sir Condy! Sir Condy Rackrent for ever!" And the mob grew so great and so loud, I was fright-

ened, and made my way back to the house to warn my son to make his escape, or
hide himself for fear of the consequences. Jason would not believe me till they
came all round the house, and to the windows with great shouts. Then he grew
quite pale, and asked Sir Coney what had he best do?

"I'll tell you what you had best do," said Sir Condy, who was laughing to see
his fright; "finish your glass first, then let's go to the window and show ourselves,
and I'll tell 'em—or you shall, if you please—that I'm going to the Lodge for
change of air for my health, and by my own desire, for the rest of my days."

"Do so," said Jason, who never meant it should have been so, but could not
refuse him the Lodge at this unseasonable time. Accordingly, Sir Condy threw
up the sash and explained matters, and thanked all his friends, and bid them look
in at the punch-bowl, and observe that Jason and he had been sitting over it very
good friends; so the mob was content, and he sent them out some whisky to
drink his health, and that was the last time his honour's health was ever drunk
at Castle Rackrent.

The very next day, being too proud, as he said to me, to stay an hour longer in
a house that did not belong to him, he sets off to the Lodge, and I along with him
not many hours after. And there was great bemoaning through all O'Shaughlin's
Town, which I stayed to witness, and gave my poor master a full account of when I
got to the Lodge. He was very low, and in his bed, when I got there, and complained of a great pain about his heart; but I guessed it was only trouble and all the
business, let alone vexation, he had gone through of late; and knowing the nature
of him from a boy, I took my pipe, and whilst smoking it by the chimney began
telling him how he was beloved and regretted in the county, and it did him a deal
of good to hear it.

"Your honour has a great many friends yet that you don't know of, rich and
poor, in the county," says I; "for as I was coming along the road I met two gentlemen in their own carriages, who asked after you, knowing me, and wanted to
know where you was and all about you, and even how old I was. Think of that."

Then he wakened out of his doze, and began questioning me who the gentlemen were. And the next morning it came into my head to go, unknown to anybody, with my master's compliments, round to many of the gentlemen's houses,
where he and my lady used to visit, and people that I knew were his great friends,
and would go to Cork to serve him any day in the year, and I made bold to try to
borrow a trifle of cash from them. They all treated me very civil for the most part,
and asked a great many questions very kind about my lady and Sir Condy and all
the family, and were greatly surprised to learn from me Castle Rackrent was sold,

and my master at the Lodge for health; and they all pitied him greatly, and he had their good wishes, if that would do; but money was a thing they unfortunately had not any of them at this time to spare. I had my journey for my pains, and I, not used to walking, nor supple as formerly, was greatly tired, but had the satisfaction of telling my master, when I got to the Lodge, all the civil things said by high and low.

"Thady," says he, "all you've been telling me brings a strange thought into my head. I've a notion I shall not be long for this world anyhow, and I've a great fancy to see my own funeral afore I die." I was greatly shocked, at the first speaking, to hear him speak so light about his funeral, and he to all appearance in good health; but recollecting myself, answered:

"To be sure it would be as fine a sight as one could see, I dared to say," and one I should be proud to witness," and I did not doubt his honour's would be as great a funeral as ever Sir Patrick O'Shanghlin's was, and such a one as that had never been known in the county afore or since. But I never thought he was in earnest about seeing his own funeral himself till the next day he returns to it again.

"Thady," says he, "as far as the wake¹ goes, sure I might without any great trouble have the satisfaction of seeing a bit of my own funeral."

"Well, since your honour's honour's so bent upon it says I, not willing to cross him, and he in trouble, we must see what we can do."

So he fell into a sort of sham disorder, which was easy done, as he kept his bed, and no one to see him; and I got my shister, who was an old woman very handy about the sick, and very skilful, to come up to the Lodge to nurse him; and we gave out, she knowing no better, that he was just at his latter end, and it answered beyond anything; and there was a great throng of people, men, women, and childer, and there being only two rooms at the Lodge, except what was locked up full of Jason's furniture and things, the house was soon as full and fuller than it could hold, and the heat, and smoke, and noise wonderful great; and standing amongst them that were near the bed, but not thinking at all of the dead, I was startled by the sound of my master's voice from under the greatcoats that had been thrown all at top, and I went close up, no one noticing.

"Thady," says he, "I've had enough of this; I'm smothering, and can't hear a word of all they're saying of the deceased."

"God bless you, and lie still and quiet," says I, "a bit longer, for my shister's afraid of ghosts, and would die on the spot with fright was she to see you come to life all on a sudden this way without the least preparation."

So he lays him still, though well nigh stifled, and I made all haste to tell the secret of the joke, whispering to one and t'other, and there was a great surprise, but not so great as we had laid out it would. "And aren't we to have the pipes and tobacco, after coming so far to-night?" said some; but they were all well enough pleased when his honour got up to drink with them, and sent for more spirits from a shebeen-house,[44] where they very civilly let him have it upon credit. So the night passed off very merrily, but to my mind Sir Condy was rather upon the sad order in the midst of it all, not finding there had been such a great talk about himself after his death as he had always expected to hear.

The next morning, when the house was cleared of them, and none but my shister and myself left in the kitchen with Sir Condy, one opens the door and walks in, and who should it be but Judy M'Quirk herself! I forgot to notice that she had been married long since, whilst young Captain Moneygawl lived at the Lodge, to the captain's huntsman, who after a whilst 'listed and left her, and was killed in the wars. Poor Judy fell off greatly in her good looks after her being married a year or two; and being smoke-dried in the cabin, and neglecting herself like, it was hard for Sir Condy himself to know her again till she spoke; but when she says, "It's Judy M'Quirk, please your honour; don't you remember her?"

"Oh, Judy, is it you?" says his honour. "Yes, sure, I remember you very well; but you're greatly altered, Judy."

"Sure it's time for me," says she. "And I think your honour, since I seen you last—but that's a great while ago—is altered too."

"And with reason, Judy," says Sir Condy, fetching a sort of a sigh. "But how's this, Judy?" he goes on. "I take it a little amiss of you that you were not at my wake last night."

"Ah, don't be being jealous of that," says she; "I didn't hear a sentence of your honour's wake till it was all over, or it would have gone hard with me but I would have been at it, sure; but I was forced to go ten miles up the country three days ago to a wedding of a relation of my own's, and didn't get home till after the wake was over. But," says she, "it won't be so, I hope, the next time,[45] please your honour."

"That we shall see, Judy," says his honour, "and maybe sooner than you think for, for I've been very unwell this while past, and don't reckon anyway I in long for this world."

At this Judy takes up the corner of her apron, and puts it first to one eye and then to t'other, being to all appearance in great trouble; and my shister put in her word, and bid his honour have a good heart, for she was sure it was only the gout that Sir Patrick used to have flying about him, and he ought to drink a glass or a bottle extraordinary to keep it out of his stomach; and he promised to take her advice, and sent out for more spirits immediately; and Judy made a sign to me, and I went over to the door to her, and she said, "I wonder to see Sir Condy so low: has he heard the news?"

"What news?" says I.

"Didn't ye hear it, then?" says she; "my Lady Rackrent that was is kilt[1] and lying for dead, and I don't doubt but it's all over with her by this time."

"Mercy on us all," says I; "how was it?"

"The jaunting-car it was that ran away with her," says Judy. "I was coming home that same time from Biddy M'Guggin's marriage, and a great crowd of people too upon the road, coming from the fair of Crookaghnawaturgh, and I sees a jaunting-car standing in the middle of the road, and with the two wheels off and all tattered. 'What's this?' says I. 'Didn't ye hear of it?' says they that were looking on; 'it's my Lady Rackrent's car, that was running away from her husband, and the horse took fright at a carrion that lay across the road, and so ran away with the jaunting-car, and my Lady Rackrent and her maid screaming, and the horse ran with them against a car that was coming from the fair with the boy asleep on it, and the lady's petticoat hanging out of the jaunting-car caught, and she was dragged I can't tell you how far upon the road, and it all broken up with the stones just going to be pounded, and one of the road-makers, with his sledgehammer in his hand, stops the horse at the last; but my Lady Rackrent was all kilt[1] and smashed, and they lifted her into a cabin hard by, and the maid was found after where she had been thrown in the gripe of a ditch, her cap and bonnet all full of bog water, and they say my lady can't live anyway.' Thady, pray now is it true what I'm told for sartain, that Sir Condy has made over all to your son Jason?"

"All," says I.

"All entirely?" says she again.

"All entirely," says I.

"Then," says she, "that's a great shame; but don't be telling Jason what I say."

"And what is it you say?" cries Sir Condy, leaning over betwixt us, which made Judy start greatly. "I know the time when Judy M'Quirk would never have stayed so long talking at the door and I in the house."

"Oh!" says Judy, "for shame, Sir Condy; times are altered since then, and it's my Lady Rackrent you ought to be thinking of."

"And why should I be thinking of her, that's not thinking of me now?" says Sir Condy.

"No matter for that," says Judy, very properly; "it's time you should be thinking of her, if ever you mean to do it at all, for don't you know she's lying for death?

"My Lady Rackrent!" says Sir Condy, in a surprise; "why it's but two days since we parted, as you very well know, Thady, in her full health and spirits, and she, and her maid along, with her, going to Mount Juliet's Town on her jaunting-car."

"She'll never ride no more on her jaunting-car," said Judy, "for it has been the death of her, sure enough."

"And is she dead then?" says his honour.

"As good as dead, I hear," says Judy; "but there's Thady here as just learnt the whole truth of the story as I had it, and it's fitter he or anybody else should be telling it you than I, Sir Condy: I must be going home to the childer."

But he stops her, but rather from civility in him, as I could see very plainly, than anything else, for Judy was, as his honour remarked at her first coming in, greatly changed, and little likely, as far as I could see—though she did not seem to be clear of it herself—little likely to be my Lady Rackrent now, should there be a second toss-up to be made. But I told him the whole story out of the face, just as Judy had told it to me, and he sent off a messenger with his compliments to Mount Juliet's Town that evening, to learn the truth of the report, and Judy bid the boy that was going call in at Tim M'Enerney's shop in O'Shaughlin's Town and buy her a new shawl.

"Do so," said Sir Condy, "and tell Tim to take no money from you, for I must pay him for the shawl myself." At this my shister throws me over a look, and I says nothing, but turned the tobacco in my mouth, whilst Judy began making a many words about it, and saying how she could not be beholden for shawls to any gentleman. I left her there to consult with my shister, did she think there was anything in it, and my shister thought I was blind to be asking her the question, and I thought my shister must see more into it than I did, and recollecting all past times and everything, I changed my mind, and came over to her way of thinking, and we settled it that Judy was very like to be my Lady Rackrent after all, if a vacancy should have happened.

The next day, before his honour was up, somebody comes with a double knock at the door, and I was greatly surprised to see it was my son Jason.

"Jason, is it you?" said I; "what brings you to the Lodge?" says I. "Is it my Lady Rackrent? We know that already since yesterday."

"Maybe so," says he; "but I must see Sir Condy about it."

"You can't see him yet," says I; "sure he is not awake."

"What then," says he, "can't he be wakened, and I standing at the door?"

"I'll not be disturbing his honour for you, Jason," says I; "many's the hour you've waited in your time, and been proud to do it, till his honour was at leisure to speak to you. His honour," says I, raising my voice, at which his honour wakens of his own accord, and calls to me from the room to know who it was I was speaking to. Jason made no more ceremony, but follows me into the room.

"How are you, Sir Condy?" says he; "I'm happy to see you looking so well; I came up to know how you did to-day, and to see did you want for anything at the Lodge."

"Nothing at all, Mr. Jason, I thank you," says he; for his honour had his own share of pride, and did not choose, after all that had passed, to be beholden, I suppose, to my son; "but pray take a chair and be seated, Mr. Jason."

Jason sat him down upon the chest, for chair there was none, and after he had set there some time, and a silence on all sides,

"What news is there stirring in the country, Mr. Jason Quirk?" says Sir Condy, very easy, yet high like.

"None that's news to you, Sir Condy, I hear," says Jason. "I am sorry to hear of my Lady Rackrent's accident."

"I'm much obliged to you, and so is her ladyship, I'm sure," answered Sir Condy, still stiff; and there was another sort of a silence, which seemed to lie the heaviest on my son Jason.

"Sir Condy," says he at last, seeing Sir Condy disposing himself to go to sleep again, "Sir Condy, I daresay you recollect mentioning to me the little memorandum you gave to Lady Rackrent about the £500 a year jointure."

"Very true," said Sir Condy; "it is all in my recollection."

"But if my Lady Rackrent dies, there's an end of all jointure," says Jason.

"Of course," says Sir Condy.

"But it's not a matter of certainty that my Lady Rackrent won't recover," says Jason.

"Very true, sir," says my master.

"It's a fair speculation, then, for you to consider what the chance of the jointure of those lands, when out of custodiam, will be to you."

"Just five hundred a year, I take it, without any speculation at all," said Sir Condy.

"That's supposing the life dropt, and the custodiam off, you know; begging your pardon, Sir Condy, who understands business, that is a wrong calculation."

"Very likely so," said Sir Condy; "but, Mr. Jason, if you have anything to say to me this morning about it, I'd be obliged to you to say it, for I had an indifferent night's rest last night, and wouldn't be sorry to sleep a little this morning."

"I have only three words to say, and those more of consequence to you, Sir Condy, than me. You are a little cool, I observe; but I hope you will not be offended at what I have brought here in my pocket," and he pulls out two long rolls, and showers down golden guineas upon the bed.

"What's this," said Sir Condy; "it's long since—" but his pride stops him.

"All these are your lawful property this minute, Sir Condy, if you please," said Jason.

"Not for nothing, I'm sure," said Sir Condy, and laughs a little. "Nothing for nothing, or I'm under a mistake with you, Jason."

"Oh, Sir Condy, we'll not be indulging ourselves in any unpleasant retrospects," says Jason; "it's my present intention to behave, as I'm sure you will, like a gentleman in this affair. Here's two hundred guineas, and a third I mean to add if you should think proper to make over to me all your right and title to those lands that you know of."

"I'll consider of it," said my master; and a great deal more, that I was tired listening to, was said by Jason, and all that, and the sight of the ready cash upon the bed, worked with his honour; and the short and the long of it was, Sir Condy gathered up the golden guineas, and tied them up in a handkerchief, and signed some paper Jason brought with him as usual, and there was an end of the business: Jason took himself away, and my master turned himself round and fell asleep again.

I soon found what had put Jason in such a hurry to conclude this business. The little gossoon we had sent off the day before with my master's compliments to Mount Juliet's Town, and to know how my lady did after her accident, was stopped early this morning, coming back with his answer through O'Shaughlin's Town, at Castle Rackrent, by my son Jason, and questioned of all he knew of my lady from the servant at Mount Juliet's Town; and the gossoon told him my Lady Rackrent was not expected to live over night; so Jason thought it high time to be moving to the Lodge, to make his bargain with my master about the jointure afore it should be too late, and afore the little gossoon should reach us with the news. My master was greatly vexed—that is, I may say, as much as ever I seen him—when he found how he had been taken in; but it is as some comfort to have the ready cash for immediate consumption in the house, anyway.

And when Judy came up that evening, and brought the childer to see his honour, he unties the handkerchief, and God bless him! whether it was little or much he had, 'twas all the same with him—he gives 'em all round guineas apiece.

"Hold up your head," says my shister to Judy, as Sir Condy was busy filling out a glass of punch for her eldest boy—"Hold up your head, Judy; for who knows but we may live to see you yet at the head of the Castle Rackrent estate?"

"Maybe so," says she, "but not the way you are thinking of."

I did not rightly understand which way Judy was looking when she made this speech till a while after.

"Why, Thady, you were telling me yesterday that Sir Condy had sold all entirely to Jason, and where then does all them guineas in the handkerchief come from?"

"They are the purchase-money of my lady's jointure," says I.

Judy looks a little bit puzzled at this. "A penny for your thoughts, Judy," says my shister; "hark, sure Sir Condy is drinking her health."

He was at the table in the room,[48] drinking with the exciseman and the gauger, who came up to see his honour, and we were standing over the fire in the kitchen.

"I don't much care is he drinking my health or not," says Judy; "and it is not Sir Condy I'm thinking of, with all your jokes, whatever he is of me."

"Sure you wouldn't refuse to be my Lady Rackrent, Judy, if you had the offer?" says I.

"But if I could do better!" says she.

"How better?" says I and my shister both at once.

"How better?" says she. "Why, what signifies it to be my Lady Rackrent and no castle? Sure what good is the car, and no horse to draw it?"

"And where will ye get the horse, Judy?" says I.

"Never mind that," says she; "maybe it is your own son Jason might find that."

"Jason!" says I; "don't be trusting to him, Judy. Sir Condy, as I have good reason to know, spoke well of you when Jason spoke very indifferently of you, Judy."

"No matter," says Judy; "it's often men speak the contrary just to what they think of us."

"And you the same way of them, no doubt," answered I. "Nay, don't be denying it, Judy, for I think the better of ye for it, and shouldn't be proud to call ye the daughter of a shister's son of mine, if I was to hear ye talk ungrateful, and anyway disrespectful of his honour."

"What disrespect," says she, "to say I'd rather, if it was my luck, be the wife of another man?"

"You'll have no luck, mind my words, Judy," says I; and all I remembered about my poor master's goodness in tossing up for her afore he married at all came across me, and I had a choking in my throat that hindered me to say more.

"Better luck, anyhow, Thady," says she, "than to be like some folk, following the fortunes of them that have none left."

"Oh! King of Glory!" says I, "hear the pride and ungratitude of her, and he giving his last guineas but a minute ago to her childer, and she with the fine shawl on her he made her a present of but yesterday!"

"Oh, troth, Judy, you're wrong now," says my shister, looking at the shawl.

"And was not he wrong yesterday, then," says she, "to be telling me I was greatly altered, to affront me?"

"But, Judy," says I, "what is it brings you here then at all in the mind you are in; is it to make Jason think the better of you?"

"I'll tell you no more of my secrets, Thady," says she, "nor would have told you this much, bad I taken you for such an unnatural fader as I find you are, not to wish your own son preferred to another."

"Oh, troth, you are wrong now, Thady," says my shister.

Well, I was never so put to it in my life: between these womens, and my son and my master, and all I felt and thought just now, I could not, upon my conscience, tell which was the wrong from the right. So I said not a word more, but was only glad his honour had not the luck to hear all Judy had been saying of him, for I reckoned it would have gone nigh to break his heart; not that I was of opinion he cared for her as much as she and my shister fancied, but the ungratitude of the whole from Judy might not plase him; and he could never stand the notion of not being well spoken of or beloved like behind his back. Fortunately for all parties concerned, he was so much elevated at this time, there was no danger of his understanding anything, even if it had reached his ears. There was a great horn at the Lodge, ever since my master and Captain Moneygawl was in together, that used to belong originally to the celebrated Sir Patrick, his ancestor; and his honour was fond often of telling the story that he learned from me when a child, how Sir Patrick drank the full of this horn without stopping, and this was what no other man afore or since could without drawing breath. Now Sir Condy challenged the gauger, who seemed to think little of the horn, to swallow the contents, and had it filled to the brim with punch; and the gauger said it was what he could not do for nothing, but he'd hold Sir Condy a hundred guineas he'd do it.

"Done," says my master; "I'll lay you a hundred golden guineas to a tester[49] you don't."

"Done," says the gauger; and done and done's enough between two gentlemen. The gauger was cast, and my master won the bet, and thought he'd won a hundred guineas, but by the wording it was adjudged to be only a tester that was his due by the exciseman. It was all one to him; he was as well pleased, and I was glad to see him in such spirits again.

The gauger—bad luck to him!—was the man that next proposed to my master to try himself, could he take at a draught the contents of the great horn.

"Sir Patrick's horn!" said his honour; "hand it to me: I'll hold you your own bet over again I'll swallow it."

"Done," says the gauger; "I'll lay ye anything at all you do no such thing."

"A hundred guineas to sixpence I do," says he; "bring me the handkerchief." I was loth, knowing he meant the handkerchief with the gold in it, to bring it out in such company, and his honour not very able to reckon it. "Bring me the handkerchief, then, Thady," says he, and stamps with his foot; so with that I pulls it out of my greatcoat pocket, where I had put it for safety. Oh, how it grieved me to see the guineas counting upon the table, and they the last my master had! Says Sir Condy to me, "Your hand is steadier than mine to-night, old Thady, and that's a wonder; fill you the horn for me." And so, wishing his honour success, I did; but I filled it, little thinking of what would befall him. He swallows it down, and drops like one shot. We lifts him up, and he was speechless, and quite black in the face. We put him to bed, and in a short time he wakened, raving with a fever on his brain. He was shocking either to see or hear.

"Judy! Judy! have you no touch of feeling? Won't you stay to help us nurse him?" says I to her, and she putting on her shawl to go out of the house.

"I'm frightened to see him," says she, "and wouldn't nor couldn't stay in it; and what use? He can't last till the morning." With that she ran off. There was none but my shister and myself left near him of all the many friends he had.

The fever came and went, and came and went, and lasted five days, and the sixth he was sensible for a few minutes, and said to me, knowing me very well, "I'm in a burning pain all withinside of me, Thady." I could not speak, but my shister asked him would he have this thing or t'other to do him good? "No," says he, "nothing will do me good no more," and he gave a terrible screech with the torture he was in; then again a minute's ease—brought to this by drink," says he. "Where are all the friends?—where's Judy? Gone, hey? Ay, Sir Condy has been a fool all his days," said he; and there was the last word he spoke, and died. He had but a very poor funeral after all.

If you want to know any more, I'm not very well able to tell you; but my Lady Rackrent did not die, as was expected of her, but was only disfigured in the face ever after by the fall and bruises she got; and she and Jason, immediately after my poor master's death, set about going to law about that jointure; the memorandum not being on stamped paper, some say it is worth nothing, others again it may do; others say Jason won't have the lands at any rate; many wishes it so. For my part, I'm tired wishing for anything in this world, after all I've seen in it; but I'll say nothing—it would be a folly to be getting myself ill-will in my old age. Jason did not marry, nor think of marrying Judy, as I prophesied, and I am not sorry for it: who is? As for all I have here set down from memory and hearsay of the family, there's nothing but truth in it from beginning to end. That you may depend upon, for where's the use of telling lies about the things which everybody knows as well as I do?

The Editor could have readily made the catastrophe of Sir Condy's history more dramatic and more pathetic, if he thought it allowable to varnish the plain round tale of faithful Thady. He lays it before the English reader as a specimen of manners and characters which are perhaps unknown in England. Indeed, the domestic habits of no nation in Europe were less known to the English than those of their sister country, till within these few years.

Mr. Young's picture of Ireland, in his tour through that country, was the first faithful portrait of its inhabitants. All the features in the foregoing sketch were taken from the life, and they are characteristic of that mixture of quickness, simplicity, cunning, carelessness, dissipation, disinterestedness, shrewdness, and blunder, which, in different forms and with various success, has been brought upon the stage or delineated in novels.

It is a problem of difficult solution to determine whether a union will hasten or retard the amelioration of this country. The few gentlemen of education who now reside in this country will resort to England. They are few, but they are in nothing inferior to men of the same rank in Great Britain. The best that can happen will be the introduction of British manufacturers in their places.

Did the Warwickshire militia, who were chiefly artisans, teach the Irish to drink beer? or did they learn from the Irish to drink whisky?

Glossary.

Some friends, who have seen Thady's history since it has been printed, have suggested to the Editor, that many of the terms and idiomatic phrases, with which it abounds, could not be intelligible to the English reader without further explanation. The Editor has therefore furnished the following Glossary.

Page 38. *Monday morning.*—Thady begins his memoirs of the Rackrent Family by dating *Monday morning*, because no great undertaking can be auspiciously commenced in Ireland on any morning but *Monday morning*. "Oh, please God we live till Monday morning, we'll set the slater to mend the roof of the house. On Monday morning we'll fall to, and cut the turf. On Monday morning we'll see and begin mowing. On Monday morning, please your honour, we'll begin and dig the potatoes," etc.

All the intermediate days, between the making of such speeches and the ensuing Monday, are wasted: and when Monday morning comes, it is ten to one that the business is deferred to *the next* Monday morning. The Editor knew a gentleman, who, to counteract this prejudice, made his workmen and labourers begin all new pieces of work upon a Saturday.

Page 39. *Let alone the three kingdoms itself.*—*Let alone*, in this sentence, means *put out of consideration.* The phrase, *let alone*, which is now used as the imperative of a verb, may in time become a conjunction, and may exercise the ingenuity of some future etymologist. The celebrated Horne Tooke has proved most satisfactorily, that the conjunction *but* comes from the imperative of the Anglo-Saxon verb (*beoutan*) *to be out;* also, that *if* comes from *gif,* the imperative of the Anglo-Saxon verb which signifies *to give*, etc.

Page 40. *Whillaluh.*—Ullaloo, Gol, or lamentation over the dead—

> Magnoque ululante tumultus.—VIRGIL.
>
> Ululatibus omne
>
> Implevere nemus.—OVID.

A full account of the Irish Gol, or Ullaloo, and of the Caoinan or Irish funeral song, with its first semichorus, second semichorus, full chorus of sighs and groans, together with the Irish words and music, may be found in the fourth volume of the *Transactions of the Royal Irish Academy.* For the advantage of *lazy* readers, who would rather read a page than walk a yard, and from compassion, not to say sympathy, with their infirmity, the Editor transcribes the following passages:

"The Irish have been always remarkable for their funeral lamentations; and this peculiarity has been noticed by almost every traveller who visited them; and it seems derived from their Celtic ancestors, the primæval inhabitants of this isle....

"It has been affirmed of the Irish, that to cry was more natural to them than to any other nation, and at length the Irish cry became proverbial....

"Cambrensis in the twelfth century says, the Irish then musically expressed their griefs; that is, they applied the musical art, in which they excelled all others, to the orderly celebration of funeral obsequies, by dividing the mourners into two bodies, each alternately singing their part, and the whole at times joining in full chorus... The body of the deceased, dressed in grave clothes, and ornamented with flowers, was placed on a bier, or some elevated spot. The relations and keeners (*singing mourners*) ranged themselves in two divisions, one at the head, and the other at the feet of the corpse. The bards and croteries had before prepared the funeral Caoinan. The chief bard of the head chorus began by singing the first stanza, in a low, doleful tone, which was softly accompanied by the harp: at the conclusion, the foot semichorus began the lamentation, or Ullaloo, from the final note of the preceding stanza, in which they were answered by the head semichorus; then both united in one general chorus. The chorus of the first stanza being ended, the chief bard of the foot semichorus began the second Gol or lamentation, in which be was answered by that of the head; and then, as before, both united in the general full chorus. Thus alternately were the song and choruses performed during the night. The genealogy, rank, possessions, the virtues and vices of the dead were rehearsed, and a number of interrogations were addressed to the deceased; as, Why did he die? If married, whether his wife was faithful to him, his sons dutiful, or good hunters or warriors? If a woman, whether her daughters were fair or chaste? If a young man, whether he had been crossed in love; or if the blue-eyed maids of Erin treated him with scorn?"

We are told, that formerly the feet (the metrical feet) of the Caoinan were much attended to; but on the decline of the Irish bards these feet were gradually neglected, and the Caoinan fell into a sort of slipshod metre amongst women. Each province had different Caoinans, or at least different imitations of the original. There was the Munster cry, the Ulster cry, etc. It became an extempore performance, and every set of keeners varied the melody according to their own fancy.

It is curious to observe how customs and ceremonies degenerate. The present Irish cry, or howl, cannot boast of such melody, nor is the funeral procession conducted with much dignity. The crowd of people who assemble at these funerals sometimes amounts to a thousand, often to four or five hundred. They gather as the bearers of the hearse proceed on their way, and when they pass through any village, or when they come near any houses, they begin to cry—Oh! Oh! Oh! Oh! Oh! Agh! Agh! raising their notes from the first *Oh!* to the last *Agh!* in a kind of mournful howl. This gives notice to the inhabitants of the village that *a funeral is passing*, and immediately they flock out to follow it. In the province of Munster it is a common thing for the women to follow a funeral, to join in the universal cry with all their might and main for some time, and then to turn and ask—"Arrah! who is it that's dead?—who is it we're crying for?" Even the poorest people have their own burying-places—that is, spots of ground in the churchyards where they say that their ancestors have been buried ever since the wars of Ireland; and if these burial-places are ten miles from the place where a man dies, his friends and neighbours take care to carry his corpse thither. Always one priest, often five or six priests, attend these funerals; each priest repeats a mass, for which he is paid, sometimes a shilling, sometimes half a crown, sometimes half a guinea, or a guinea, according to their circumstances, or, as they say, according to the *ability* of the deceased. After the burial of any very poor man, who has left a widow or children, the priest makes what is called *a collection* for the widow; he goes round to every person present, and each contributes sixpence or a shilling, or what they please. The reader will find in the note upon the word *Wake*, more particulars respecting the conclusion of the Irish funerals.

Certain old women, who cry particularly loud and well, are in great request, and, as a man said to the Editor, "Every one would wish and be proud to have such at his funeral, or at that of his friends." The lower Irish are wonderfully eager to attend the funerals of their friends and relations, and they make their relationships branch out to a great extent. The proof that a poor man has been well beloved during his life is his having a crowded funeral. To attend a neighbour's funeral is a cheap proof of humanity, but it does not, as some imagine, cost nothing. The time spent in attending funerals may be safely valued at half a million to the Irish nation; the Editor thinks that double that sum would not be too high an estimate. The habits of profligacy and drunkenness which are acquired at *wakes* are here put out of the question. When a labourer, a carpenter, or a smith, is not at his work, which frequently happens, ask where he is gone, and ten to one the answer is—"Oh, faith, please your honour, he couldn't do a stroke to-day, for he's gone to *the* funeral."

Even beggars, when they grow old, go about begging *for their own funerals;* that is, begging for money to buy a coffin, candles, pipes, and tobacco. For the use of the candles, pipes, and tobacco, see *Wake*.

Those who value customs in proportion to their antiquity, and nations in proportion to their adherence to ancient customs, will doubtless admire the Irish *Ullaloo*, and the Irish nation, for persevering in this usage from time immemorial. The Editor, however, has observed some alarming symptoms, which seem to prognosticate the declining taste for the Ullaloo in Ireland. In a comic theatrical entertainment, represented not long since on the Dublin stage, a chorus of old women was introduced, who set up the Irish howl round the relics of a physician, who is supposed to have fallen under the wooden sword of Harlequin. After the old women have continued their Ullaloo for a decent time, with all the necessary accompaniments of wringing their hands, wiping or rubbing their eyes with the corners of their gowns or aprons, etc., one of the mourners suddenly suspends her lamentable cries, and, turning to her neighbour, asks, "Arrah now, honey, who is it we're crying for?"

Page 40. *The tenants were sent away without their whisky.*—It is usual with some landlords to give their inferior tenants a glass of whisky when they pay their rents. Thady calls it *their* whisky; not that the whisky is actually the property of the tenants, but that it becomes their *right* after it has been often given to them. In this general mode of reasoning respecting *rights* the lower Irish are not singular, but they are peculiarly quick and tenacious in claiming these rights. "Last year your honour gave me some straw for the roof of my house and I *expect* your honour will be after doing the same this year." In this manner gifts are frequently turned into tributes. The high and low are not always dissimilar in their habits. It is said, that the Sublime Ottoman Porte is very apt to claim gifts as tributes: thus it is dangerous to send the Grand Seignor a fine horse on his birthday one year, lest on his next birthday he should expect a similar present, and should proceed to demonstrate the reasonableness of his expectations.

Page 40. *He demeaned himself greatly* —means, he lowered or disgraced himself much.

Page 41. *Duty fowls, duty turkeys, and duty geese* .—In many leases in Ireland, tenants were *formerly* bound to supply an inordinate quantity of poultry to their landlords. The Editor knew of thirty turkeys being reserved in one lease of a small farm.

Page 41. *English tenants* .—An English tenant does not mean a tenant who is an Englishman, but a tenant who pays his rent the day that it is due. It is a common prejudice in Ireland, amongst the poorer classes of people, to believe that all tenants in England pay their rents on the very day when they become due. An Irishman, when be goes to take a farm, if he wants to prove to his landlord that he is a substantial man, offers to become an *English tenant*. If a tenant disobliges his landlord by voting against him, or against his opinion, at an election, the tenant is immediately informed by the agent that he must become an *English tenant*. This threat does not imply that he is to change his language or his country, but that he must pay all the arrear of rent which he owes, and that he must thenceforward pay his rent on that day when it becomes due.

Page 41. *Canting* —does not mean talking or writing hypocritical nonsense, but selling substantially by auction.

Page 41. *Duty work.*—It was formerly common in Ireland to insert clauses in leases, binding tenants to furnish their landlords with labourers and horses for several days in the year. Much petty tyranny and oppression have resulted from this feudal custom. Whenever a poor man disobliged his landlord the agent sent to him for his duty work; and Thady does not exaggerate when he says, that the tenants were often called from their own work to do that of their landlord. Thus the very means of earning their rent were taken from them: whilst they were getting home their landlord's harvest, their own was often ruined, and yet their rents were expected to be paid as punctually as if their time had been at their own disposal. This appears the height of absurd injustice.

In Esthonia, amongst the poor Sclavonian race of peasant slaves, they pay tributes to their lords, not under the name of duty work, duty geese, duty turkeys, etc., but under the name of *righteousnesses*. The following ballad is a curious specimen of Esthonian poetry:—

> This is the cause that the country is ruined,
> And the straw of the thatch is eaten away,
> The gentry are come to live in the land—
> Chimneys between the village,
> And the proprietor upon the white floor!
> The sheep brings forth a lamb with a white forehead,
> This is paid to the lord for a *righteousness sheep*.
> The sow farrows pigs,
> They go to the spit of the lord.
> The hen lays eggs,
> They go into the lord's frying-pan.
> The cow drops a male calf,
> That goes into the lord's herd as a bull.
> The mare foals a horse foal,
> That must be for my lord's nag.
> The boor's wife has sons,
> They must go to look after my lord's poultry.

Page 42. *Out of forty-nine suits which he had, he never lost one but seventeen.*— Thady's language in this instance is a specimen of a mode of rhetoric common in Ireland. An astonishing assertion is made in the beginning of a sentence, which ceases to be in the least surprising, when you hear the qualifying explanation that follows. Thus a man who is in the last stage of staggering drunkenness will, if he can articulate, swear to you—"Upon his conscience now, and may he never stir from the spot alive if he is telling a lie, upon his conscience he has not tasted a drop of anything, good or bad, since morning at-all-at-all, but half a pint of whisky, please your honour."

Page 42. *Fairy-mounts*—Barrows. It is said that these high mounts were of great service to the natives of Ireland when Ireland was invaded by the Danes. Watch was always kept on them, and upon the approach of an enemy a fire was lighted to give notice to the next watch, and thus the intelligence was quickly communicated through the country. Some years ago, the common people believed that these barrows were inhabited by fairies, or, as they called them, by the good people. "Oh, troth, to the best of my belief, and to the best of my judgment and opinion," said an elderly man to the Editor, "it was only the old people that had nothing to do, and got together, and were telling stories about them fairies, but to the best of my judgment there's nothing in it. Only this I heard myself not very many years back from a decent kind of a man, a grazier, that, as he was coming just fair and easy (quietly) from the fair, with some cattle and sheep, that he had not sold, just at the church of ———, at an angle of the road like, he was met by a good-looking man, who asked him where he was going? And he answered, 'Oh, far enough, I must be going all night.' 'No, that you mustn't nor won't (says the man), you'll sleep with me the night, and you'll want for nothing, nor your cattle nor sheep neither, nor your beast (horse); so come along with me.' With that the grazier lit (alighted) from his horse, and it was dark night; but presently he finds himself, he does not know in the wide world how, in a fine house, and plenty of everything to eat and drink; nothing at all wanting that he could wish for or think of. And he does not mind (recollect or know) how at last he falls asleep; and in the morning he finds himself lying, not in ever a bed or a house at all, but just in the angle of the road where first he met the strange man: there he finds himself lying on his back on the grass, and all his sheep feeding as quiet is ever all round about him, and his horse the same way, and the bridle of the beast over his wrist. And I asked him what he thought of it; and from first to last he could think of nothing, but for certain sure it must have been the fairies that entertained him so well. For there was no house to see anywhere nigh hand, or any building, or barn, or place at all, but only the church and the mote (barrow). There's another odd thing enough that they tell about this same church, that if any person's corpse, that had not a right to be buried in that churchyard, went to be burying there in it, no, not all the men, women, or childer in all Ireland could get the corpse anyway into the churchyard; but as they would be trying to go into the churchyard, their feet would seem to be going backwards instead of forwards; ay, continually backwards the whole funeral would seem to go; and they would never set foot with the corpse in the churchyard. Now they say that it is the fairies do all this; but it is my opinion it is all idle talk, and people are after being wiser now."

The country people in Ireland certainly *had* great admiration mixed with reverence, if not dread, of fairies. They believed that beneath these fairy-mounts were spacious subterraneous palaces, inhabited by *the good people*, who must not on any account be disturbed. When the wind raises a little eddy of dust upon the road, the poor people believe that it is raised by the fairies, that it is a sign that they are journeying from one of the fairies' mounts to another, and they say to the fairies, or to the dust as it passes, "God speed ye, gentlemen; God speed ye." This averts any evil that *the good people* might be inclined to do them. There are innumerable stories told of the friendly and unfriendly feats of these busy fairies; some of these tales are ludicrous, and some romantic enough for poetry. It is a pity that poets should lose such convenient, though diminutive machinery. By the bye, Parnell, who showed himself so deeply skilled in faerie lore," was an Irishman; and though he has presented his fairies to the world in the ancient English dress of "Britain's isle, and Arthur's days," it is probable that his first acquaintance with them began in his native country.

Some remote origin for the most superstitious or romantic popular illusions or vulgar errors may often be discovered. In Ireland, the old churches and churchyards have been usually fixed upon as the scenes of wonders. Now antiquaries tell us, that near the ancient churches in that kingdom eaves of various constructions have from time to time been discovered, which were formerly used as granaries or magazines by the ancient inhabitants, and as places to which they retreated in time of danger. There is (p. 84 of the *R. I. A. Transactions* for 1789) a particular account of a number of these artificial caves at the west end of the church of Killossy, in the county of Kildare. Under a rising ground, in a dry sandy soil, these subterraneous dwellings were found: they have pediment roofs, and they communicate with each other by small apertures. In the Brehon laws these are mentioned, and there are fines inflicted by those laws upon persons who steal from the subterraneous granaries. All these things show that there was a real foundation for the stories which were told of the appearance of lights, and of the sounds of voices, near these places. The persons who bad property concealed there, very willingly countenanced every wonderful relation that tended to make these places objects of sacred awe or superstitious terror.

Page 43. *Weed ashes.*—By ancient usage in Ireland, all the weeds on a farm belonged to the farmer's wife, or to the wife of the squire who holds the ground in his own hands. The great demand for alkaline salts in bleaching rendered these ashes no inconsiderable perquisite.

Page 43. *Sealing money.*—Formerly it was the custom in Ireland for tenants to give the squire's lady from two to fifty guineas as a perquisite upon the sealing of their leases. The Editor not very long since knew of a baronet's lady accepting fifty guineas as sealing money, upon closing a bargain for a considerable farm.

Page 43. *Sir Murtagh grew mad*—Sir Murtagh grew angry.

Page 43. *The whole kitchen was out on the stairs*—means that all the inhabitants of the kitchen came out of the kitchen, and stood upon the stairs. These, and similar expressions, show how much the Irish are disposed to metaphor and amplification.

Page 44. *Fining down the year's rent.*—When an Irish gentleman, like Sir Kit Rackrent, has lived beyond his income, and finds himself distressed for ready money, tenants obligingly offer to take his land at a rent far below the value, and to pay him a small sum of money in hand, which they call fining down the yearly rent. The temptation of this ready cash often blinds the landlord to his future interest.

Page 44. *Driver.*—A man who is employed to drive tenants for rent; that is, to drive the cattle belonging to tenants to pound. The office of driver is by no means a sinecure.

Page 45. *I thought to make him a priest.*—It was customary amongst those of Thady's rank in Ireland, whenever they could get a little money, to send their sons abroad to St. Omer's, or to Spain, to be educated as priests. Now they are educated at Maynooth. The Editor has lately known a young lad, who began by being a post-boy, afterwards turn into a carpenter, then quit his plane and work-bench to study his *Humanities*, as he said, at the college of Maynooth; but after he had gone through his course of Humanities, he determined to be a soldier instead of a priest.

Page 46. *Flam.*—Short for flambeau.

Page 47. *Barrack-room.*—Formerly it was customary, in gentlemen's houses in Ireland, to fit up one large bedchamber with a number of beds for the reception of occasional visitors. These rooms were called Barrack-rooms.

Page 47. *An innocent*—in Ireland, means a simpleton, an idiot.

Page 51. *The Curragh*—is the Newmarket of Ireland.

Page 51. *The cant.*—The auction.

Page 54. *And so should cut him of for ever by levying a fine, and suffering a recovery to dock the entail.*—The English reader may perhaps be surprised at the extent of Thady's legal knowledge, and at the fluency with which he pours forth law-terms; but almost every poor man in Ireland, be he farmer, weaver, shopkeeper, or steward, is, besides his other occupations, occasionally a lawyer. The nature of process-es, ejectments, custodiams, injunctions, replevins, etc., is perfectly known to them, and the terms as familiar to them as to any attorney. They all love law. It is a kind of lottery, in which every man, staking his own wit or cunning against his neigh-bour's property, feels that he has little to lose, and much to gain.

"I'll have the law of you, so I will!" is the saying of an Englishman who expects justice. "I'll have you before his honour," is the threat of an Irishman who hopes for partiality. Miserable is the life of a justice of the peace in Ireland the day after a fair, especially if he resides near a small town. The multitude of the *kilt* (*kilt* does not mean *killed*, but hurt) and wounded who come before his honour with black eyes or bloody heads is astonishing: but more astonishing is the number of those who, though they are scarcely able by daily labour to procure daily food, will nev-ertheless, without the least reluctance, waste six or seven hours of the day lounging in the yard or court of a justice of the peace, waiting to make some complaint about—nothing. It is impossible to convince them that *time is money*. They do not set any value upon their own time, and they think that others estimate theirs at less than nothing. Hence they make no scruple of telling a justice of the peace a story of an hour long about a *tester* (sixpence); and if he grows impatient, they attribute it to some secret prejudice which he entertains against them.

Their method is to get a story completely by heart, and to tell it, as they call it, *out of the face*, that is, from the beginning to the end, without interruption.

"Well, my good friend, I have seen you lounging about these three hours in the yard; what is your business?"

"Please your honour, it is what I want to speak one word to your honour."

"Speak then, but be quick. What is the matter?"

"The matter, please your honour, is nothing at-all-at-all, only just about the grazing of a horse, please your honour, that this man here sold me at the fair of Gurtishannon last Shrove fair, which lay down three times with myself, please your honour, and *kilt* me; not to be telling your honour of how, no later back than yes-terday night, he lay down in the house there within, and all the childer standing round, and it was God's mercy he did not fall atop of them, or into the fire to burn himself. So please your honour, to-day I took him back to this man, which owned him, and after a great deal to do, I got the mare again I *swopped* (*exchanged*) him for; but he won't pay the grazing of the horse for the time I had him, though he promised to pay the grazing in case the horse didn't answer; and he never did a day's work, good or bad, please your honour, all the time he was with me, and I had the doctor to him five times anyhow. And so, please your honour, it is what I expect your honour will stand my friend, for I'd sooner come to your honour for justice than to any other in all Ireland. And so I brought him here before your honour, and expect your honour will make him pay me the grazing, or tell me, can I process him for it at the next assizes, please your honour?"

The defendant now turning a quid of tobacco with his tongue into some secret cavern in his mouth, begins his defence with—"Please your honour, under favour, and saving your honour's presence, there's not a word of truth in all this man has been saying from beginning to end, upon my conscience, and I wouldn't for the value of the horse itself, grazing and all, be after telling your honour a lie. For, please your honour, I have a dependence upon your honour that you'll do me justice, and not be listening to him or the like of him. Please your honour, it's what he has brought me before your honour, because he hid a spite against me about some oats I sold your honour, which he was jealous of, and a shawl his wife got at my shister's shop there without, and never paid for; so I offered to set the shawl against the grazing, and give him a receipt in full of all demands, but he wouldn't out of spite, please your honour; so he brought me before your honour, expecting your honour was mad with me for cutting down the tree in the horse park, which was none of my doing, please your honour—ill-luck to them that went and belied me to your honour behind my back! So if your honour is pleasing, I'll tell you the whole truth about the horse that be swopped against my mare out of the face. Last Shrove fair I met this man, Jemmy Duffy, please your honour, just at the corner of the road, where the bridge is broken down, that your honour is to have the presentment for this year—long life to you for it! And he was at that time coming from the fair of Gurtishannon, and I the same way. 'How are you, Jemmy?' says I. 'Very well, I thank ye kindly, Bryan,' says he; 'shall we turn back to Paddy Salmon's and take a naggin of whisky to our better acquaintance?' 'I don't care if I did, Jemmy,' says I; 'only it is what I can't take the whisky, because I'm under an oath against it for a month.' Ever since, please your honour, the day your honour met me on the road, and observed to me I could hardly stand, I had taken so much; though upon my conscience your honour wronged me greatly that same time—ill-luck to them that belied me behind my back to your honour! Well, please your honour, as I was telling you, as he was taking the whisky, and we talking of one thing or t'other, he makes me an offer to swop his mare that he couldn't sell at the fair of Gurtishannon, because nobody would be troubled with the beast, please your honour, against my horse, and to oblige him I took the mare—sorrow take her! and him along with her! She kicked me a new car, that was worth three pounds ten, to tatters the first time I ever put her into it, and I expect your honour will make him pay me the price of the car, anyhow, before I pay the grazing, which I've no right to pay at-all-at-all, only to oblige him. But I leave it all to your honour; and the whole grazing he ought to be charging for the beast is but two and eightpence halfpenny, anyhow, please your honour. So I'll abide by what your honour says, good or bad. I'll leave it all to your honour."

I'll leave *it* all to your honour—literally means, I'll leave all the trouble to your honour.

The Editor knew a justice of the peace in Ireland who had such a dread of *having it all left to his honour*, that he frequently gave the complainants the sum about which they were disputing, to make peace between them, and to get rid of the trouble of hearing their stories *out of the face*. But he was soon cured of this method of buying off disputes, by the increasing multitude of those who, out of pure regard to his honour, came "to get justice from him, because they would sooner come before him than before any man in all Ireland."

Page 62. *A raking pot of tea.*—We should observe, this custom has long since been banished from the higher orders of Irish gentry. The mysteries of a raking pot of tea, like those of the Bona Dea, are supposed to be sacred to females; but now and then it has happened that some of the male species, who were either more audacious, or more highly favoured than the rest of their sex, have been admitted by stealth to these orgies. The time when the festive ceremony begins varies according to circumstances, but it is never earlier than twelve o'clock at night; the joys of a raking pot of tea depending on its being made in secret, and at an unseasonable hour. After a ball, when the more discreet part of the company has departed to rest, a few chosen female spirits, who have footed it till they can foot it no longer, and till the sleepy notes expire under the slurring hand of the musician, retire to a bedchamber, call the favourite maid, who alone is admitted, bid her *put down the kettle*, lock the door, and amidst as much giggling and scrambling as possible, they get round a tea-table, on which all manner of things are huddled together. Then begin mutual railleries and mutual confidences amongst the young ladies, and the faint scream and the loud laugh is heard, and the romping for letters and pocket-books begins, and gentlemen are called by their surnames, or by the general name of fellows! pleasant fellows! charming fellows! odious fellows! abominable fellows! and there all prudish decorums are forgotten, and then we might be convinced how much the satirical poet was mistaken when he said—

There is no woman where there's no reserve.

The merit of the original idea of a raking pot of tea evidently belongs to the washerwoman and the laundry-maid. But why should not we have *Low life above stairs* as well as *High life below stairs?*

Page 63. *We gained the day by this piece of honesty.*—In a dispute which occurred some years ago in Ireland, between Mr. E. and Mr. M., about the boundaries of a farm, an old tenant of Mr. M.'s cut a sod from Mr. M.'s land, and inserted it in a spot prepared for its reception in Mr. E.'s land; so nicely was it inserted, that no eye could detect the junction of the grass. The old man, who was to give his evidence as to the property, stood upon the inserted sod when the *viewers* came, and swore that the ground he *then stood upon* belonged to his landlord, Mr. M.

The Editor had flattered himself that the ingenious contrivance which Thady records, and the similar subterfuge of this old Irishman, in the dispute concerning boundaries, were instances of '*cuteness* unparalleled in all but Irish story: an English friend, however, has just mortified the Editor's national vanity by an account of the following custom, which prevails in part of Shropshire. It is discreditable for women to appear abroad after the birth of their children till they have been *churched.* To avoid this reproach, and at the same time to enjoy the pleasure of gadding, whenever a woman goes abroad before she has been to church, she takes a tile from the roof of her house, and puts it upon her head: wearing this panoply all the time she pays her visits, her conscience is perfectly at ease; for she can afterwards safely declare to the clergyman, that she "has never been from under her own roof till she came to be churched."

Page 64. *Carton, and half-carton.*—Thady means cartron, and half-cartron. "According to the old record in the black book of Dublin, a *cantred* is said to contain 30 *villatas terras*, which are also called *quarters* of land (quarterons, *cartrons*); every one of which quarters must contain so much ground as will pasture 400 cows, and 17 plough-lands. A knight's fee was composed of 8 hydes, which amount to 160 acres, and that is generally deemed about a *plough-land.*"

The Editor was favoured by a learned friend with the above extract, from a MS. of Lord Totness's in the Lambeth library.

Page 77. *Wake.*—A wake in England means a festival held upon the anniversary of the saint of the parish. At these wakes, rustic games, rustic conviviality, and rustic courtship, are pursued with all the ardour and all the appetite which accompany such pleasures as occur but seldom. In Ireland a wake is a midnight meeting, held professedly for the indulgence of holy sorrow, but usually it is converted into orgies of unholy joy. When an Irish man or woman of the lower order dies, the straw which composed the bed, whether it has been contained in a bag to form a mattress, or simply spread upon the earthen floor, is immediately taken out of the house, and burned before the cabin door, the family at the same time setting up the death howl. The ears and eyes of the neighbours being thus alarmed, they flock to the house of the deceased, and by their vociferous sympathy excite and at the same time soothe the sorrows of the family.

It is curious to observe how good and bad are mingled in human institutions. In countries which were thinly inhabited, this custom prevented private attempts against the lives of individuals, and formed a kind of coroner's inquest upon the body which bad recently expired, and burning the straw upon which the sick man lay became a simple preservative against infection. At night the dead body is waked, that is to say, all the friends and neighbours; of the deceased collect in a barn or stable, where the corpse is laid upon some boards, or an unhinged door, supported upon stools, the face exposed, the rest of the body covered with a white sheet. Round the body are stuck in brass candlesticks, which have been borrowed perhaps at five miles' distance, as many candles as the poor person can beg or borrow, observing always to have an odd number. Pipes and tobacco are first distributed, and then, according to the *ability* of the deceased, cakes and ale, and sometimes whisky, are *dealt* to the company.

> Deal on, deal on, my merry men all,
>   Deal on your cakes and your wine,
> For whatever is dealt at her funeral to-day
>   Shall be dealt to-morrow at mine.

After a fit of universal sorrow, and the comfort of a universal dram, the scandal of the neighbourhood, as in higher circles, occupies the company. The young lads and lasses romp with one another, and when the fathers and mothers are at last overcome with sleep and whisky (*vino et somno*), the youth become more enterprising, and are frequently successful. It is said that more matches are made at wakes than at weddings.

Page 79. *Kilt.*—This word frequently occurs in the preceding pages, where it means not *killed,* but much *hurt.* In Ireland, not only cowards, but the brave "die many times before their death."—There *killing is no murder.*

WILLIAM CARLETON

♣

(1794-1869)

William Carleton was born on March 4, 1794 at Prillisk, Clogher, County Tyrone, one of fourteen children. His father, James Carleton, a tenant farmer, was a man blessed with an extraordinary memory. His mother, Mary Kelly, was like James a poor Catholic who struggled and could not escape the difficult life of Irish peasantry. Yet they did manage to pass on to their children, most notably William, a love of language and song and Irish folklore. These precious gifts would ultimately enable William to elevate himself from the rural poverty of a farm life, into a different poverty—one of a struggling artist and writer in Dublin. But the contrast was immeasurable.

Because the family moved frequently from farm to farm in the northern parts of Ireland, young William was educated at various "Hedge Schools" which existed during times of Penal laws where Catholics were educated clandestinely. In fact, Carleton would later write *The Hedge School*—a "sketch" that he included in his classic two-volume collection, *Traits and Stories of the Irish Peasantry.* This collection, almost immediately upon its publication in 1830, put Carleton at the forefront of Irish novelists. Despite the fact that Carleton never achieved much financial success, he was most certainly one of the most important voices in history.

William Butler Yeats, nearly sixty years after the publication of *Traits and Stories,* wrote a review of Carleton's *The Red-Haired Man's Wife,* in which he stated, "William Carleton was a great Irish historian. The history of a nation is not in parliaments and battle-fields, but in what the people say to each other on fair-days and high days and in how they farm, and quarrel, and go on pilgrimage. These things has Carleton recorded." It was indeed his realistic interpretation of Irish life and history, for better or for worse, on which Carleton built his legacy.

It was clear early in Carleton's childhood that an education would have a lasting effect on his life. While at a classical school in Donagh, he studied under a curate named Keenan from 1814 to 1816, which seemed to influence him greatly, but amusing stories of early Irish peasant education, such as the sketch, "Denis O'Shaughnessy" demonstrated Carleton's fondness for the more spontaneous elements of schooling. When he was about seventeen years old, Carleton's father died, one of "the two bitterest calamities" of his young life—the other being his love of a girl named Anne Duffy who married another man. The death of his father, however, had more dire consequences, as his family immediately began to suffer financial strain. A life in the church appeared to be William's necessary calling.

When Carleton was nineteen years old, he participated in a religious pilgrimage, which was common among former Hedge School pupils in Ireland at the time. Yet the experience (which he later wrote about in *The Lough Derg Pilgrim*) had the effect of stifling any thoughts he might have entertained of a life in the Church. In fact, the pilgrimage may well have driven him toward becoming a Protestant later in his life.

In his autobiography published years after his death in 1869, Carleton addressed his religious ambiguity, recalling a tale from his childhood where he had his fortune told by a "Scotch gypsy" who, with the help of Carleton's sister, learned that young William was preparing for a life in the church. He wrote, "I remember the words as distinctly as if I had heard them only yesterday. 'He will never be a priest,' said she, 'he will love the girls too well; but when he grows up, he will go to Dublin, and become a great man.'"

After the death of his father, Carleton's family found itself in dire financial condition and his brothers and sisters began to disperse to find work. To some extent, William remained financially dependent on his family, since he appeared not to take his proficiency in the stone-cutting trade as serious as his love of adventure and dancing. A fallout with his brother-in-law over money set him off on his travels about Ireland, where he immersed himself in the Irish country life—a love for which he would later couvey in his writing. In "Wildgoose Lodge" which appeared in *Traits and Stories of the Irish Peasantry*, Carleton wrote warmly of his travels: "there never was any man of letters who had an opportunity of knowing and describing the manners of the Irish people so thoroughly as I had. I was one of themselves, and mingled in all those sports and pastimes in which their characters are most clearly developed."

Like his father, Carleton entertained the people he surrounded himself with by telling tales, but he quickly realized that Irish folklore was not as successful as original material when it came to currying the favor of young Irish ladies. As if to make a prophet of the Scotch gypsy, who, years earlier, predicted Carleton would become a great man in Dublin, he "started out for the great city with two-and-ninepence in my pocket." Once in Dublin, Carleton lived a gypsy-like existence himself, getting by on his wits, his storytelling abilities and on handouts from new friends. He picked up work as a tutor for an evangelist's son, and then fell in love with the evangelist's niece, Jane Anderson, whom he married in 1822. Ever the dramatist, Carleton, who had lost yet another job, this time a clerkship in a Protestant Sunday school, enraged his father-in-law, who felt his daughter deserved a better fate than marriage to Carleton. Upon learning of Jane's pregnancy, her father locked her in her room, and the romantic Carleton attempted a daring rescue by scaling a garden wall at night and fighting with his wife's father and her guards. Carleton was eventually subdued and jailed for the evening, but his mother-in-law was apparently moved by Carleton's plight and arranged his release. Anderson later gave birth to the couple's child.

One of Carleton's greatest gifts as a writer was his detailed description of the subtleties of the Irish condition. He understood and was able to present realistically customs, social practices and perhaps most importantly, the language of Ireland's rural populace. He published his first book, *Father Butler; The Lough Dearg Pilgrim: Being Sketches of Irish Manners* in 1829, but followed that book the next year with *Traits and Stories of the Irish Peasantry*—a two-volume work that made him one of the most respected writers in Ireland. The book included stories that had been published in the *Christian Examiner* as well as the *Dublin Literary Gazette* and the *National Magazine,* and they were important in that they helped to eradicate some of the myths and stereotypes of Irish peasants as being inferior, clever but diabolical and clumsy with language. Carleton was a key figure in the Irish literary renaissance, and he became something of a spokesman for the country. What does it say of a country if the son of a peasant was capable of producing literature of the highest quality?

By 1845, Carleton had gone on to write a good many novels, four in that year alone. *Traits and Stories* had been popular enough to warrant several new editions. Yet he was never able to overcome his financial shortcomings. He managed his money poorly and let lapse the copyrights of his works. In fact, it was believed that he never earned more than 150 pounds per year for his writing, despite his prolific nature. He published frequently and saw his books go into several editions, yet other writers with similar sales, such as Maria Edgeworth, were able to earn almost ten times Carleton's earnings with a single book. By 1868, Carleton was still having financial difficulties, when he turned his attention to an autobiography as something of a last gasp. He was, by this point, blind and terminally ill, yet he managed to tap into his memory, much as his father did decades ago, to recall with vivid detail, events and circumstances from decades ago.

Critics have long held that Carleton's autobiography was second only to *Traits and Stories of the Irish Peasantry* as his most important work. In the autobiography, which was ultimately unfinished, Carleton recalls a life of great struggle and hardship. He colorfully described his own youth, both with heroic flair and bitter irony as a journey of the human spirit, which, although not necessarily ending in triumph, certainly had poignancy. "I have often thought that man's life is divided or separated into a series of small epics," he wrote, "not epics that are closed by happiness, however, but by pain."

Carleton died in January of 1869, and despite his literary accomplishments, he left this world every bit as poor as the rural Irish he wrote of. Such passion for the Irish peasantry did not go unnoticed; as W.B. Yeats once wrote, "The great thing about Carleton was that he always remained a peasant, hating and loving with his class. On one point he was ever consistent, was always a peasant moralist; that is the land question."

Traits And Stories
Of The Irish Peasantry

by WILLIAM CARLETON.
COMPRISING
THE PARTY FIGHT AND FUNERAL.
THE HEDGE SCHOOL.
THE STATION.
With Two Illustrations by Phiz.
LONDON: GEORGE ROUTLEDGE AND CO.,
FARRINGDON STREET.
1853.

♣

PUBLISHERS' PREFACE.

In introducing a New Edition of Carleton's "Traits and Stories" at a popular price to the public at large, the Publishers have but little to observe, as the distinguished editors of the *Quarterly* and the *Edinburgh* Reviews have passed very recently their encomiums upon the Work, describing it "as the truest and fullest picture of the Irish Peasantry that any master-hand could hope to depict, and a work that future generations alone must look to for a memorial of the inhabitants of that troubled land."

Farringdon Street,
August, 1853.

THE PARTY FIGHT AND FUNERAL.

———

[We ought, perhaps, to inform our readers that the connection between a party fight and funeral is sufficiently strong to justify the author in classing them under the title which is prefixed to this story. The one being usually the natural result of the other, is made to proceed from it, as is the custom in real life among the Irish. Such is the preface with which we deem it necessary to introduce the following sketch to those who shall honour us with a perusal.]

It has been long laid down as a universal principle, that self-preservation is the first law of nature. An Irishman, however, has nothing to do with this; he disposes of it as he does of the other laws, and washes his hands out of it altogether. But commend him to a fair, dance, funeral, or, wedding, or to any other sport where there is a likelihood of getting his head or his bones broken, and if he survive, he will remember you with a kindness peculiar to himself, to the last day of his life— will drub you from head to heel if he finds that any misfortune has kept you out of a row beyond the usual period of three months—will render the same service to any of your friends that stand in need of it—or, in short, will go to the world's end, or fifty miles farther, as he himself would say, to serve you, provided you can procure him a bit of decent fighting. Now, in truth and soberness, it is difficult to account for this propensity; especially when the task of ascertaining it is assigned to those of another country, or even to those Irishmen whose rank in life places them too far from the customs, prejudices, and domestic opinions of their native peas- antry—none of which can be properly known without mingling with them. To my own knowledge, however, it proceeds in a great measure from *education*. And here I would beg leave to point out an omission of which the several boards of education have been guilty, and which, I believe, no one but myself has yet been sufficiently acute and philosophical to ascertain, as forming a *sine qua non* in the national instruction of the lower orders of Irishmen.

The cream of the matter is this:—a species of ambition prevails in the Green Isle, not known in any other country. It is an ambition of about three miles by four in extent; or, in other words is bounded by the limits of the parish in which the subject of it may reside. It puts itself forth early in the character, and a hardy perennial it is. In my own case, its first development was noticed in the hedge- school which I attended. I had not been long there, till I was forced to declare myself either for the Caseys or the Murphys, two tiny factions, that had split the school between them. The day on which the ceremony of my declaration took place was a solemn one. After school, we all went to the bottom of a deep valley, a short distance from the school-house; up to the moment of our assembling there, I had not taken my stand under either banner: that of the Caseys was a sod of turf, stuck on the end of a broken fishing-rod—the eagle of the Murphys was a Cork- red potato, hoisted in the same manner. The turf was borne by an urchin, who afterwards distinguished himself in fairs and markets as a *builla batthah*** of the first grade, and from this circumstance he was nicknamed *Parrah Rackhan.*[†] The potato was borne by little Mickle M'Phauden Murphy, who afterwards took away Katty Bane Sheridan, without asking either her own consent or her father's. They

*Cudgel Player
[†]Paddy riot

were all then boys, it is true, but they gave a tolerable promise of that eminence which they subsequently attained.

When we arrived at the bottom of the glen, the Murphys and the Caseys, including their respective followers, ranged themselves on either side of a long line, which was drawn between the belligerent powers with the butt-end of one of the standards. Exactly on this line was I placed. The word was then put to me in full form—"Whether will you side with the dacent Caseys, or the blackguard Murphys?" "Whether will you side with the dacent Murphys, or the blackguard Caseys?" "The potato for ever!" said I, throwing up my caubeen, and running over to the Murphy standard. In the twinkling of an eye we were at it; and in a short time the deuce an eye some of us had to twinkle. A battle-royal succeeded, that lasted near half an hour, and it would probably have lasted about double the time, were it not for the appearance of the "master," who was seen by a little shrivelled *vidette,* who wanted an arm, and could take no part in the engagement. This was enough—we instantly radiated in all possible directions, so that by the time he had descended through the intricacies of the glen to the field of battle, neither victor nor vanquished was visible, except, perhaps, a straggler or two as they topped the brow of the declivity, looking back over their shoulders, to put themselves out of doubt as to their visibility by the master. They seldom looked in vain, however; for there he usually stood, shaking up his rod, silently prophetic of its application on the following day. This threat, for the most part, ended in smoke; for except he horsed about forty or fifty of us, the infliction of impartial justice was utterly out of his power.

But besides this, there never was a realm in which the evils of a divided cabinet were more visible: the truth is, the monarch himself was under the influence of female government—an influence which he felt it either contrary to his inclination, or beyond his power to throw off. "Poor Norah, long may *you reign,*" we often used to exclaim, to the visible mortification of the "master," who felt the benevolence of the wish bottomed upon an indirect want of allegiance to himself. Well, it was a *touching* scene!—how we used to stand with the waistbands of our small-clothes cautiously grasped in our hands, with a timid show of resistance, our brave red faces slobbered over with tears, as we stood naked for execution! Never was there a finer specimen of deprecation in eloquence than we then exhibited—the supplicating look right up into the master's face—the touching modulation of the whine—the additional tightness and caution with which we grasped the waistbands with one hand, when it was necessary to use the other in wiping our eyes and noses with the polished sleeve-cuff—the sincerity and vehemence with which we promised never to be guilty again, still shrewdly including the condition of present impunity, for our offence:—"this—one—time—master, if ye plaise, Sir;" and the utter hopelessness and despair which were legible in the last groan, as we grasped the "master's" leg in utter recklessness of judgment, were all perfect in their way. Reader, have you ever got a reprieve from the gallows? I beg pardon, my dear Sir; I only meant to ask, are you capable of entering into what a personage of that description might be supposed to feel, on being informed, after the knot had been neatly tied under the left ear, and the cap drawn over his eyes, that his majesty had granted him a full pardon? But you remember your own school-boy days, and that's enough.

The nice discrimination with which Norah used to time her interference was indeed surprising. God help us! limited was our experience, and shallow our little judgments, or we might with less trouble than Sir Humphry Davy deciphered the Herculaneum MSS. have known what the master meant, when with the upraised arm hung over us, his eye was fixed upon the door of the kitchen, waiting for Norah's appearance.

Long, my fair and virtuous countrywomen, I repeat it to you all, as I did to Norah—may you reign in the hearts and affections of your husbands, (but no where else,) the grace, ornaments, and happiness of their hearths and lives, you jewels, you! You are paragons of all that's good, and your feelings are highly creditable to yourselves and to humanity.

When Norah advanced, with her brawny uplifted arm, (for she was a powerful woman,) and forbidding aspect, to interpose between us and the avenging terrors of the birch, do you think that she did not reflect honour on her sex and the national character? I sink the base allusion to the *miscaum* of fresh butter, which we had placed in her hands that morning, or the dish of eggs, or of meal, which we had either begged or stolen at home, as a present for her; disclaiming, at the same time, the rascally idea of giving it from any motive beneath the most lofty-minded and disinterested generosity on our part.

Then again, never did a forbidding face shine with so winning and amicable an expression as did her's on that merciful occasion. The sun dancing an hornpipe on Easter Sunday morning, or the full moon sailing as proud as a peacock in a new halo-head-dress, was a very disrespectable sight, compared to Norah's red beaming face, shrouded in her dowd cap with long ears, that descended to her masculine and substantial neck. Owing to her influence, the whole economy of the school was good; for we were permitted to cuff one another, and do whatever we pleased, with impunity, *if* we brought the meal, eggs, or butter; except some scape-goat who was not able to accomplish this, and he generally received on his own miserable carcase what was due to us all.

Poor Jack Murray! His last words on the scaffold, for being concerned in the murder of Pierce, the gauger, were, that he got the first of his bad habits under Pat Mulligan and Norah—that he learned to steal by secreting at home, butter and meal to paste up the master's eyes to his bad conduct—and that his fondness for quarrelling arose from being permitted to head a faction at school; a most ungrateful return for the many acts of grace which the indulgence of Norah caused to be issued in his favour.

I was but a short time under Pat, when, after the general example, I had my cudgel, which I used to carry regularly to a certain furze bush within fifty perches of the "seminary," where I hid it till after "dismiss." I grant it does not look well in me to become my own panegyrist; but I can at least declare, that there were few among the Caseys able to resist the prowess of this right arm, puny as it was at the period in question. Our battles were obstinate and frequent; but as the quarrels of the two families and their relations on each side were as bitter and pugnacious in fairs and markets as ours were in school, we hit upon the plan of holding our Lilliputian engagements upon the same days on which our fathers and brothers contested. According to this plan, it very often happened that the corresponding parties were successful, and as frequently, that whilst the Caseys were well drubbed in the fair, their sons were victorious at school, and *vice versa*.

For my part, I was early trained to cudgelling, and before I reached my fourteenth year, could pronounce as sage and accurate an opinion upon the merits of a *shillelagh*, as it is called, or cudgel, as a veterinary surgeon of sixty could upon a dead ass at first sight. Our plan of preparing is this:—we sallied out to any place where there was an underwood of blackthorn or oak, and, having surveyed the premises with the eye of a connoisseur, we selected the straightest root-growing piece which we could find: for if not root-growing, we did not consider it worth cutting, knowing from experience, that a branch, how straight and fair soever it might look, would snap in the twist and tug of war. Having cut it as close to the root as possible, we then lopped off the branches, and put it up in the chimney to season. When seasoned, we took it down, and wrapping it in brown paper, well steeped in bog's lard or oil, we buried it in a horse dunghill, paying it a daily visit for the purpose of making it straight by doubling back the bends or angles across the knee, in a direction contrary to their natural tendency. Having daily repeated this until we had made it straight, and renewed the oiled wrapping paper until the staff was perfectly saturated, we then rubbed it well with a woollen cloth, containing a little black-lead and grease, to give it a polish. This was the last process, except that if we thought it too light at the top, we used to bore a hole in the lower end with a red-hot iron spindle, into which we poured melted lead, for the purpose of giving it the knock-down weight.

There were very few of Paddy Mulligan's scholars without a choice collection of them, and scarcely one who had not, before his fifteenth year, a just claim to be called the hero of a hundred fights, and the heritor of as many bumps on the cranium as would strike both Gall and Spurzheim speechless.

Now this, be it known, was, and in some districts yet is, an integral part of an Irish peasant's *education*. In the northern parts of Ireland, where the population of the Catholics on the one side, and of Protestants and Dissenters on the other, is nearly equal, I have known the respective scholars of Catholic and Protestant schools to challenge each other, and meet half-way to do battle, in vindication of their respective creeds; or for the purpose of establishing the character of their respective masters as the more learned man; for if we were to judge by the nature of the education then received, we would be led to conclude that a more commercial nation than Ireland was not on the face of the earth, it being the indispensible part of every scholar's business to become acquainted with the *three sets of Bookkeeping.*

The boy who was the handiest and the most daring with the cudgel at Paddy Mulligan's school was Denis Kelly, the son of a wealthy farmer in the neighbourhood. He was a rash, hot-tempered, good-natured lad, possessing a more than common share of this blackthorn ambition; on which account he was cherished by his relations as a boy that was likely at a future period to be able to walk over the course of the parish, in fair, market, or patron. He certainly grew up a stout, able, young fellow; and before he reached nineteen years, was unrivalled at the popular exercises of the peasantry. Shortly after that time he made his *debut* in a party-quarrel, which took place in one of the Christmas *Margamores,** and fully sustained the anticipations which were formed of him by his relations. For a year or two afterwards no quarrel was fought without him; and his prowess rose until he had gained the very pinnacle of that ambition which he had determined to reach. About this time I was separated from him, having found it necessary, in order to accomplish my objects in life, to reside with a relation in another part of the country.

The period of my absence, I believe, was about fourteen years, during which space I heard no account of him whatsoever. At length, however, that inextinguishable attachment which turns the affections and memory to the friends of our early

*Big Markets

days—to those scenes which we traversed when the heart was light and the spirits buoyant—determined me to make a visit to my native place, that I might witness the progress of time and care upon those faces that were once so familiar to me; that I might once more look upon the meadows, and valleys, and groves, and mountains where I had so often played, and to which I still found myself bound by a tie that a more enlightened view of life and nature only made stronger and more enduring. I accordingly set off, and arrived late in the evening of a December day, at a little town within a few miles of my native home. On alighting from the coach and dining, I determined to walk home, as it was a fine frosty night. The full moon hung in the blue unclouded firmament in all her lustre, and the stars shone out with that tremulous twinkling motion, so peculiarly remarkable in frost. I had been absent, I said, about fourteen years, and felt that the enjoyment of this night would form an era in the records of my memory and my feelings. I find myself indeed utterly incapable of expressing what I experienced, but those who have ever been in similar circumstances will understand what I mean. A strong spirit of practical poetry and romance was upon, me; and I thought that a common-place approach in the open day would have rendered my return to the scenes of my early life a very stale and unedifying matter.

I left the inn at seven o'clock, and as I had only five miles to walk, I would just arrive about nine, allowing myself to saunter on at the rate of two miles and a half per hour. My sensations, indeed, as I went along, were singular; and as I took a solitary road that went across the mountains, the loneliness of the walk, the deep gloom of the valleys, the towering height of the dark hills, and the pale silvery light of a sleeping lake, shining dimly in the distance below, gave me such a distinct notion of the sublime and beautiful, as I have seldom since experienced. I recommend every man who has been fourteen years absent from his native fields to return by moonlight.

Well, there is a mystery yet undiscovered in our being, for no man can know his feelings or his capacities. Many a slumbering thought, and sentiment, and association, reposes within him, of which he is utterly ignorant, and which, except he come in contact with those objects whose influence over his mind can alone call them into being, may never be awakened, or give him one moment of either pleasure or pain. There is, therefore, a great deal in the position which we hold in society, and simply in situation. I felt this on *that* night: for the tenor of my reflections was new and original, and my feelings had a warmth and freshness in them, which nothing but the situation in which I then found myself could give them. The force of association, too, was powerful; for as I advanced nearer home, the names of hills, and lakes, and mountains, that I had utterly forgotten, as I thought, were distinctly revived in my memory; and a crowd of youthful thoughts and feelings, that I imagined my intercourse with the world and the finger of time had blotted out of my being, began to crowd afresh on my fancy. The name of a townland would instantly return with its appearance; and I could now remember the history of families and individuals that had long been effaced from my recollection.

But what is even more singular is, that the superstitious terrors of my boyhood began to come over me, as formerly, whenever a spot noted for supernatural appearances met my eye. It was in vain that I exerted myself to expel them, by throwing the barrier of philosophic reasoning in their way; they still clung to me, in spite of every effort to the contrary. But the fact is, that I was, for the moment, the slave of a morbid and feverish sentiment, that left me completely at the mercy of the dark and fleeting images that passed over my fancy. I now came to a turn where the road began to slope down into the depths of a valley that ran across it. When I looked forward into the bottom, all was darkness impenetrable, for the moon-beams were thrown off by the height of the mountains that rose on each side of it. I felt an indefinite sensation of fear, because at that moment I recollected that it had been, in my younger days, notorious as the scene of an apparition, where the spirit of a murdered pedlar had never been known to permit a solitary traveller to pass without appearing to him, and walking cheek-by-jowl along with him to the next house on the way, at which spot he usually vanished. The influence of my feelings, or, I should rather say, the physical excitement of my nerves, was by no means slight, as these old traditions recurred to me; although, at the same time, my moral courage was perfectly unimpaired, so that, notwithstanding this involuntary apprehension, I felt a degree of novelty and curiosity in descending the valley: "If it appear," said I, "I shall at least satisfy myself as to the truth of apparitions."

My dress consisted of a long, dark surtout, the collar of which, as the night was keen, I had turned up about my ears, and the corners of it met round my face. In addition to this I had a black silk handkerchief tied across my mouth, to keep out the night air, so that, as my dark fur travelling cap came down over my face, there was very little of my countenance visible. I now had advanced half way into the valley, and all about me was dark and still: the moon-light was not nearer than the top of the hill which I was descending; and I often turned round to look upon it, so silvery and beautiful it appeared at a distance. Sometimes I stood for a few moments, admiring its effect, and contemplating the dark mountains as they stood out against the firmament, then kindled into magnificent grandeur by the myriads of stars that glowed in its expanse. There was perfect silence and solitude around me; and, as I stood alone in the dark chamber of the mountains, I felt the impressiveness of the situation gradually supersede my terrors. A sublime sense of religious awe descended on me; my soul kindled into a glow of solemn and elevated devotion, which gave me a more intense perception of the presence of God than I had ever before experienced. "How sacred—how awful," thought I, "is this place!—how impressive is this hour!—surely, I feel myself at the footstool of God! The voice of worship is in this deep, soul-thrilling silence, and the tongue of praise speaks, as it were, from the very solitude of the mountains!" I then thought of Him who went up into a mountain-top to pray, and felt the majesty of those admirable descriptions of the Almighty, given in the Old Testament, blend in delightful harmony with the beauty and fitness of the Christian dispensation, that brought life and immortality to light. "Here," said I, "do I feel that I am indeed immortal, and destined for scenes of a more exalted and comprehensive existence!"

I then proceeded further into the valley, completely freed from the influence of old and superstitious associations. A few perches below me, a small river crossed the road, over which was thrown a little stone bridge of rude workmanship. This bridge was the spot on which the apparition was said to appear; and as I approached it, I felt the folly of those terrors which had only a few minutes before beset me so strongly. I found my moral energies recruited, and the dark phantasms of my imagination dispelled by the light of religion, which had refreshed me with a deep sense of the Almighty presence. I accordingly walked forward, scarcely bestowing a thought upon the history of the place, and had got within a few yards of the bridge, when on resting my eye accidentally upon the little elevation formed by its rude arch, I perceived a black coffin placed at the edge of the road, exactly upon the bridge!

It may be evident to the reader, that, however satisfactory the force of philosophical reasoning might have been upon the subject of the solitude, I was too much the creature of sensation for an hour before, to look on such a startling object with firm nerves. For the first two or three minutes, therefore, I exhibited as finished a specimen of the dastardly, as could be imagined. My hair absolutely raised my cap some inches off my head; my mouth opened to an extent which I did not conceive it could possibly reach; I thought my eyes shot out from their sockets; and my fingers spread out and became stiff though powerless. The *"obstupui"* was perfectly realized in me, for, with the exception of a single groan, which I gave on first seeing the object, I found that if one word would save my life, or transport me to my own fire-side, I could not utter it. I was also rooted to the earth, as if by magic; and although instant tergiversation and flight had my most hearty concurrence, I could not move a limb, nor even raise my eye off the sepulchral-looking object which lay before me. I now felt the perspiration fall from my face in torrents, and the strokes of my heart fell audibly on my ear. I even attempted to say "God preserve me," but my tongue was dumb and powerless, and could not move. My eye was still upon the coffin, when I perceived that, from being motionless, it instantly began to swing, first in a lateral, then in a longitudinal direction, although it was perfectly evident that no human hand was nearer it than my own. At length I raised my eyes off it, for my vision was strained to an aching intensity which I thought must have occasioned my eye strings to crack. I looked instinctively about me for assistance—but all was dismal, silent, and solitary: even the moon had disappeared among a few clouds that I had not noticed in the sky.

As I stood in this state of indescribable horror, I saw the light gradually fade away from the tops of the mountains, giving the scene around me a dim and spectral ghastliness, which, to those who were never in such a situation, is altogether inconceivable.

At length I thought I heard a noise as it were, of a rushing tempest, sweeping from the hills down into the valley; but, on looking up, I could perceive nothing but the dusky desolation that brooded over the place. Still the noise continued; again I saw the coffin move: I then felt, the motion communicated to myself, and found my body borne and swung backwards and forwards, precisely according to the motion of the coffin. I again attempted to utter a cry for assistance, but could not: the motion of my body still continued, as did the approaching noise in the hills. I looked up a second time in the direction in which the valley wound off between them, but, judge of what I must have suffered, when I beheld one of the mountains moving, as it were, from its base, and tumbling down towards the spot on which I stood. In the twinkling of an eye the whole scene, hills and all, began to tremble, to vibrate and to fly round me, with a rapid, delirious motion; the stars shot back into the depths of heaven, and disappeared; the ground on which I stood began to pass from beneath my feet; a noise like the breaking of a thousand gigantic billows again burst from every direction, and I found myself instantly overwhelmed by some deadly weight, which protrasted me on the earth, and deprived me of sense and motion.

I know not how long I continued in this state; but I remember that, on opening my eyes, the first object that presented itself to me, was the sky glowing as before with ten thousand stars, and the moon walking in her unclouded brightness through the heavens. The whole circumstance then rushed back upon my mind, but with a sense of horror very much diminished; I arose, and, on looking towards the spot, perceived the coffin in the same place. I then stood, and endeavouring to collect myself, viewed it as calmly as possible; it was, however, as motionless and distinct as when I first saw it. I now began to reason upon the matter, and to consider that it was pusillanimous in me to give way to such boyish terrors. The confidence, also, which my heart, only a short time before this, had experienced in the presence and protection of the Almighty, again returned, and, along with it, a degree of religious fortitude, which invigorated my whole system. "Well," thought I, "in the name of God I shall ascertain what you are, let the consequence be what it may." I then advanced until I stood exactly over it, and raising my foot, gave it a slight kick. "Now," said I, "nothing remains but to ascertain whether it contains a dead body, or not;" but, on raising the end of it, I perceived, by its lightness, that it was empty. To investigate the cause of its being left in this solitary spot was, however, not within the compass of my philosophy, so I gave that up. On looking at it more closely, I noticed a plate, marked with the name and age of the person for whom it was intended, and on bringing my eye near the letters, I was able between fingering and reading, to make out the name of my old cudgel-fighting school-fellow, Denis Kelly.

This discovery threw a partial light upon the business; but I now remembered to have heard of individuals who had seen black, unearthly coffins, inscribed with the names of certain living persons; and that these were considered as ominous of the death of those persons. I accordingly determined to be certain that this was a real coffin; and as Denis's house was not more than mile before me, I decided on carrying it that far: "If he be dead," thought I, "it will be all right, and if not, we will see more about it." My mind, in fact, was diseased by terror. I instantly raised the coffin, and as I found a rope lying on the ground under it, I strapped it about my shoulders and proceeded: nor could I help smiling when I reflected upon the singular transition which the man of sentiment and sensation so strangely underwent;—from the sublime contemplation of the silent mountain solitude and the spangled heavens to the task of carrying a coffin! It was an adventure, however, and I was resolved to see, how it would terminate.

There was from the bridge an ascent in the road, not so gradual as that by which I descended on the other side; and as the coffin was rather heavy, I began to repent of having any thing to do with it; for I was by no means experienced in carrying coffins. The carriage of it was, indeed, altogether an irksome and unpleasant concern; for owing to my ignorance of using the rope that tied it skilfully, it was every moment sliding down my back, dragging along the stones, or bumping against my heels: besides, I saw no sufficient grounds I had for entering upon the ludicrous and odd employment of carrying another man's coffin, and was several times upon the point of washing my hands out of it altogether. But the novelty of the incident, and the mystery in which it was involved, decided me in bringing it as far as Kelly's house, which was exactly on my way home.

I had yet half a mile to go; but I thought it would be best to strap it more firmly about my body before I could start again: I therefore set it standing on its end, just at the turn of the road, until I should breathe a little, for I was rather exhausted by a trudge under it of half a mile and upwards. Whilst the coffin was in this position, I standing exactly behind it, (Kelly had been a tall man, consequently it was somewhat higher than I was) a crowd of people bearing lights, advanced round the corner; and the first object which presented itself to their vision, was the coffin in that position, whilst I was totally invisible behind it. As soon as they saw it, there was an involuntary cry of consternation from the whole crowd; at this time I had the coffin once more strapped firmly by a running knot to my shoulders, so that I could loose it whenever I pleased. On seeing the party, and hearing certain expressions which dropped from them, I knew at once that there had been some unlucky blunder in the business on their part; and I would have given a good deal to be out of the circumstances in which I then stood. I felt that I could not possibly have accounted for my situation, without bringing myself in for as respectable a portion of rank cowardice, as those who ran away from the coffin; for that it was left behind in a fit of terror, I now entertained no doubt whatever, particularly when I remembered the traditions connected with the spot in which I found it.

† *"Manim a Yea agus a wurrah!"** exclaimed one of them, "if the black man hasn't brought it up from the bridge: *dher a lorna heena,*† he did; for it was above the bridge we first seen him: jist for all the world—the Lord be about us—as Antony and me war coming out on the road at the bridge, there he was standing—a headless man, all black, widout face or eyes upon him—and then we cut acrass the fields home."

"But where is he now, Eman?" said one of them, "are you sure you seen him?"

"Seen him!" both exclaimed, "do ye think we'd take to our scrapers like two hares, only we did; arrah, bad manners to you, do you think the coffin could walk up wid itself from the bridge to this, only he brought it?—isn't that enough?"

"Thrue for yees," the rest exclaimed, "but what's to be done?"

"Why to bring the coffin home, now that we're all together," another observed; "they say he never appears to more than two at wanst, so he won't be apt to show

*My soul to God and the Virgin.
116   †By the very book.

himself now."

"Well, boys, let two of you go down to it," said one of them, "and we'll wait here till yees bring it up."

"Yes," said Eman Dhu, "do you go down, Owen, as you have the Scapular on you, and the jug of holy water in your hand, and let Billy M'Shane, here, repate the *confeethur* along wid you."

"Isn't it the same thing, Eman," replied Owen, "if I shake the holy water on you, and whoever goes wid you; sure you know that if only one dhrop of it touched you, the devil himself couldn't harm you!"

"And what needs yourself be afraid, then," retorted Eman; "and you has the Scapular on you to the back of that? Didn't you say, as you war coming out, that if it *was* the devil, you'd disparse him?"

"You had betther not be mintioning his name, you *omadhaun*," replied the other; "if I was your age, and hadn't a wife and childre on my hands, it's myself that would trust in God, and go down manfully; but the people are hen-hearted now, besides what they used to be in my time."

During this conversation, I had resolved, if possible, to keep up the delusion, until I could get myself extricated with due secrecy out of this ridiculous situation; and I was glad to find that owing to their cowardice there was some likelihood of effecting my design.

"Ned," said one of them to a little man, "go down and speak to it, as it can't harm *you.*"

"Why, sure," said Ned, with a tremor in his voice, "I can speak to it, where I am, widout going within rache of it. Boys, stay close to me: hem—In the name of—but don't you think I had betther spake to it in the Latin I sarve mass wid; it can't but answer that, for the *sowl* of it, seeing it's a blest language?"

"Very well," the rest replied; "try that, Ned; give it the best and ginteelest grammar you have, and maybe it may thrate us dacent."

Now it so happened that, in my school-boy days, I had joined, from mere frolic, a class of young fellows who were learning what is called the *"Sarvin' of Mass,"* and had impressed it so accurately on a pretty retentive memory, that I never forgot it. At length, Ned pulled out his beads, and bedewed himself most copiously with the holy water. He then shouted out, with a voice which resembled that of a man in an ague fit— *"Dom-i-n-us vo-bis-cum?"* *"Et cum spi ritu tuo,"* I replied, in a husky sepulchral tone, from behind the coffin. As soon as I uttered these words, the whole crowd ran back instinctively with affright; and Ned got so weak, that they were obliged to support him.

"Lord have marcy on us," said Ned; "boys, isn't it an awful thing to speak to a spirit: my hair is like I dunna what, it's sticking up so stiff upon my head."

"Spake to it in English, Ned," said they, "till we hear what it will say. Ax it does any thing trouble it; or whether its *sowl's* in Purgatory."

"Wouldn't it be betther," observed another, "to ax it who murdhered it—maybe it wants to discover that?"

"In the—na-me of—Go-o-d-ness," said Ned, down to me, "what are you?"

"I'm the soul," I replied, in the same voice, "of the pedlar that was murdered on the bridge below."

"And—who—was—it, Sur, wid—submission, that—murdhered—you?"

To this I made no reply.

"I say," continued Ned, "in—the—name—of—G-o-o-d-ness—who was it—that took the liberty of murdhering you, dacent man?"

"Ned Corrigan," I answered, giving his own name.

"Hem! God presarve us! Ned Corrigan!" he exclaimed. "What Ned, for there's two of them—Is it myself, or the *other* vagabone?"

"Yourself, you murderer!" I replied.

"Ho!" said Ned, getting quite stout—"Is that you, neighbour? Come, now, walk out wid yourself out of that coffin, you vagabone you, whoever you are."

"What do you mane, Ned, by spaking to it that-a-way?" the rest inquired.

"Hut," said Ned, "it's some fellow or other that's playing a thrick upon us. Sure I never knew neither act nor part of the murdher, nor or the murdherers; and you know, if it was any thing of that nature, it couldn't tell me a lie, and me a Scapularian, along wid axing it in God's name, wid Father Feasthalagh's Latin."

"Big tare-an'-ouns!" said the rest; "if we thought it was any man making fun of us, but we'd crop the ears off his head, to tache him to be joking!"

To tell the truth, when I heard this suggestion, I began to repent or my frolic; but I was determined to make another effort to finish the adventure creditably.

"Ned," said they, "throw some of the holy water on us all, and in the name of St. Pether and the Blessed Virgin, we'll go down and examine it in a body."

This they considered a good thought, and Ned was sprinkling the water about him in all directions, whilst he repeated some jargon which was completely unintelligible. They then began to approach the coffin at dead-march time, and I felt that this was the only moment in which my plan could succeed—for had I waited until they came down, all would have been discovered. As soon, therefore, as they began to move towards me, I also began, with equal solemnity, to retrograde towards *them;* so that, as the coffin was between us, it seemed to move without human means.

"Stop, for God's sake, stop," shouted Ned; "it's movin'! It has made the coffin alive; don't you see it stepping this way widout hand or foot, barring the boords!"

There was now a halt to ascertain the fact: but I still retrograded. This was sufficient—a cry of terror broke from the whole group, and, without waiting for further evidence, they set off in the direction they came from, at fall speed, Ned flinging the jug of holy water at the coffin, lest the latter should follow, or the former encumber him in his flight. Never was there so complete a discomfiture; and so eager were they to escape, that several of them came down on the stones; and I could hear them shouting with desperation, and imploring the more advanced not to leave them behind. I instantly disentangled myself from the coffin, and left it standing exactly in the middle of the road, for the next passenger to give it a lift as far as Denis Kelly's, if he felt so disposed. I lost no time in making the best of my way home; and on passing poor Denis's house, I perceived, by the bustle and noise within, that he was dead.

I had given my friends no notice of this visit; my reception was, consequently the warmer, as I was not expected. That evening was a happy one, which I shall long remember. At supper I alluded to Kelly, and received from my brother a full account, as given in the following narrative, of the circumstances which caused his death.

"I need not remind you, Toby, of our school-boy days, nor of the principles usually imbibed at such schools as that in which the two tiny factions of the Caseys and the Murphys qualified themselves—among the latter of whom you cut so distinguished a figure. You will not, therefore, be surprised to hear that those two factions are as bitter as ever; and that the boys who, at Pat Mulligan's school belaboured each other, in imitation of their brothers and fathers, continue to set the same iniquitous example to their children; so that this groundless and hereditary enmity is likely to descend to future generations—unless, indeed, the influence of a more enlightened system of education may check it. But, unhappily, there is a strong suspicion of the object proposed by such a system; so that the advantages likely to result from it to the lower orders of the people will be slow and distant."

"But, John," said I, "now that we are upon that subject, let me ask what really *is* the bone of contention between Irish factions?"

"I assure you," he replied, "I am almost as much at a loss, Toby, to give you a satisfactory answer, as if you asked me the elevation of the highest mountain on the moon; and I believe you would find equal difficulty in ascertaining the cause of their feuds from the factions themselves. I really am convinced they know not, nor, if I rightly understand them, do they much care. Their object is to fight, and the turning of a straw will at any time furnish them with sufficient grounds for that. I do not think, after all, that the enmity between them is purely personal: they do not hate each other individually; but having originally had one quarrel upon some trifling occasion, the beaten party could not bear the stigma of defeat without another trial of strength. Then, if they succeed, the *onus* of retrieving lost credit is thrown upon the party that was formerly victorious. If they fail a second time, the double triumph of their conquerors excites them to a greater determination to throw off the additional disgrace; and this species of alternation perpetuates the evil.

"These habits, however, familiarise our peasantry to acts of outrage and vio-lence—the bad passions are cultivated and nourished, until crimes, which peace-able men look upon with fear and horror, lose their real magnitude and deformity in the eyes of Irishmen. I believe this kind of undefined hatred between either par-ties or nations, is the most dangerous and fatal spirit which could pervade any por-tion of society. If you hate a man for an obvious and palpable injury, it is likely that when he cancels that injury by an act of subsequent kindness, accompanied by an exhibition of sincere sorrow, you will cease to look upon him as your enemy; but where the hatred is such that, while feeling it, you cannot, on a sober examina-tion of your heart, account for it, there is little hope that you will ever be able to stifle the enmity which you entertain against him. This, however, in politics and religion, is what is frequently designated as principle—a word on which men, pos-sessing higher and greater advantages than the poor ignorant peasantry of Ireland, pride themselves. In sects and parties, we may mark its effects among all ranks and nations. I, therefore, seldom wish, Toby, to hear a man assert that he is of this party or that, from *principle;* for I am usually inclined to suspect that he is not, in this case, influenced by *conviction.*

"Kelly was a man who, but for these scandalous proceedings among us, might have been now alive and happy. Although his temperament was warm, yet that warmth communicated itself to his good as well as to his evil qualities. In the beginning his family were not attached to any faction—and when I use the word *faction,* it is in contradistinction to the word *party*—for faction, you know, is applied to a feud or grudge between Roman Catholics exclusively. But when he was young, he ardently attached himself to the Murphys; and, having continued among them until manhood, he could not abandon them, consistently with that sense of mistaken honour which forms so prominent a feature in the character of the Irish peasantry. But although the Kellys were not *faction-men,* they were bitter *party-men,* being the ringleaders of every quarrel which took place between the Catholics and Protestants, or, I should rather say, between the Orangemen and Whiteboys.

"From the moment when Denis attached himself to the Murphys, until the day he received the beating which subsequently occasioned his death, he never withdrew from them. He was in all their battles; and in course of time, induced his relations to follow his example; so that, by general consent, they were nicknamed the 'Errigle Slashers.' Soon after you left the country, and went to reside with my uncle, Denis married a daughter of little Dick Magrath's, from the Raceroad, with whom he got a little money. She proved a kind, affectionate wife; and, to do him justice, I believe he was an excellent husband.—Shortly after his marriage his father died, and Denis succeeded him in his farm; for you know that, among the peasantry, the youngest usually gets the landed property—the elder children being obliged to provide for themselves according to their ability, as otherwise a population would multiply upon a portion of land inadequate to their support.

"It was supposed that Kelly's marriage would have been the means of producing a change in him for the better but it did not. He was, in fact, the slave of a low, vain ambition, which constantly occasioned him to have some quarrel or other on his hands; and, as he possessed great physical courage and strength, he became the champion of the parish. It was in vain that his wife used every argument to induce him to relinquish such practices; the only reply he was in the habit of making, was a good-humoured slap on the back and a laugh, saying,

"'That's it, Honor; sure and isn't that the Magraths, all over, that would let the manest spalpeen that ever chewed cheese thramp upon them, widout raising a hand in their own defence; and I don't blame you for being a coward, seeing that you have their blood in your veins—not but that there ought to be something bether in you, afther all; for it's the M'Karrons by your mother's side, that had the good dhrop of their own, in them, any how—but you're a Magrath, out and out.'

"'And, Denis,' Honor would reply. 'it would be a blessed day for the parish, if all in it were as peaceable as the same Magraths. There would be no sore heads, nor broken bones, nor fighting, nor slashing of one another in fairs and markets, when people ought to be minding their business. You're ever and always at the Magraths, bekase they don't join you agin the Caseys or the Orangemen, and more fools they'd be to make or meddle between you, having no spite agin either of them; and it would be wiser for you to be *sed* by the Magraths, and *red* your hands out of sich ways altogether. What did ever the Murphys do to serve you or any of your family, that you'd go to make a great man of yourself fighting for them? Or what did the poor Caseys do to make you go agin the honest people? Arrah, bad manners to me, if you know what you're about, or, if *sonse*,* or grace can ever come of it; and mind my words, Denis, if God hasn't sed it, you'll live to rue your folly for the same work.'

"At this Denis would laugh heartily. 'Well said, Honor *Magrath,* but not *Kelly.* Well, it's one comfort that our childher aren't likely to follow your side of the house, any way.—Come here, Lanty—come over, acushla, to your father! Lanty, ma bouchal, what 'ill you do when you grow a man?'

"'I'll buy a horse of my own to ride on, daddy.'

"'A horse, Lanty!—and so you will, ma bouchal; but that's not it—sure that's not what I mane, Lanty. What'ill you do to the Caseys?'

"'Ho, ho! the Caseys!—I'll bate the blackguards wid your blackthorn, daddy!'

"'Ha, ha, ha!—that's my stout man—my brave little sodger! *Wus dha lamh, avick!*—give me your hand, my son! Here, Nelly,' he would say to the child's eldest sister, 'give him a brave whang of bread, to make him able to bate the Caseys. Well, Lanty, who more will you leather, a-hagur?'

"'All the Orangemen—I'll kill all the Orangemen!'

"This would produce another laugh from the father, who would again kiss and shake hands with his son, for these early manifestations of his own spirit.

"'Lanty, ma bouchal,' he would say, 'thank God, you're not a *Magrath;* 'tis you that's a *Kelly,* every blessed inch of you!—and if you turn out as good a *buillagh batthah* as your father afore you, I'll be contint, avourneen!'

"'God forgive you, Denis,' the wife would reply, 'it's long before you'd think of larning him his prayers, or his catechism, or any thing that's good! Lanty, agra, come over to myself, and never heed what that man says; for, except you have some poor body's blessing, he'll bring you to no good.'

"Sometimes, however, Kelly's own natural good sense, joined with the remonstrances of his wife, prevailed for a short time, and he would withdraw himself from the connection altogether; but the force of habit and of circumstances was too strong in him, to hope that he could ever overcome it by his own firmness, for he was totally destitute of religion. The peaceable intervals of his life were, therefore, very short.

"One summer evening I was standing in my own garden, when I saw a man galloping up towards me at full speed. When he approached, I recognized him as one of the Murphy faction, and perceived that he was cut and bleeding.

"'Murphy,' said I, 'what's the matter?'

"'Hard fighting, Sir,' said he, 'is the matter. The Caseys gathered all their faction, bekase they heard that Denis Kelly has given us up, and they're sweeping the street wid us. I'm going hot foot for Kelly, Sir, for even the very name of him will turn the tide in our favour. Along wid that, I have sint in a score of the Duggans, and, if I get in Denis, plase God we'll clear the town of them!"

"He then set off, but pulled up abruptly, and said—

"'Arrah, Mr. Darcy, maybe you'd be civil enough to lind me the loan of a sword, or bagnet, or gun, or any thing that way, that would be sarviceable to a body on a pinch?'

"'Yes!' said I, 'and enable you to commit murder. No, no, Murphy: I'm sorry it's not in my power to put a final stop to such dangerous quarrels!'

"He then dashed off, and in the course of a short time, I saw him and Kelly, both on horseback, hurrying into the town in all possible baste, armed with their cudgels. The following day, I got my dog and gun, and sauntered about the hills, making a point to call upon Kelly. I found him with his head tied up, and his arm in a sling.

"'Well, Denis,' said I, 'I find you have kept your promise of giving up quarrels!'

"'And so I did, Sir,' said Denis; 'but, sure you wouldn't have me for to go desart them, when the Caseys war three to one over them. No: God be thanked, I'm not so mane as that, any how. Besides, they welted both my brothers within an inch of their lives.'

"'I think they didn't miss yourself,' said I.

"'You may well say they did not, Sir,' he replied; 'and, to tell God's thruth, they thrashed us right and left out of the town, although we rallied three times, and came in agin. At any rate, it's the first time, for the last five years, that they dare go up and down the street, calling out for the face of a Murphy, or a Kelly—for they're as bitter now agin us as agin the Murphys themselves.'

"'Well, I hope, Denis,' I observed, 'that what occurred yesterday will prevent you from entering into their quarrels in future. Indeed, I shall not give over, until I prevail on you to lead a quiet and peaceable life, as the father of a rising family ought to do.'

"'Denis,' said the wife, when I alluded to the children, looking at him with a reproachful and significant expression—'Denis, do you hear *that!*—the *father* of a family, Denis! Oh, then, God look down on that family, but it's——Musha, God bless you and yours, Sir,' said she to me, dropping that part of the subject abruptly—'it's kind of you to trouble yourself about him, at all at all; it's what them that has a betther right to do it, doesn't do.'

"'I hope,' said I, 'that Denis's own good sense will show him the folly and guilt of his conduct, and that he will not, under any circumstances, enter into their battles in future. Come, Denis, will you promise me this?'

"'If any man,' replied Denis, 'could make me do it, it's yourself, Sir, or any one of your family; but, if the priest of the parish was to go down on his two knees before me, I wouldn't give it up till we give them vagabone Caseys one glorious battherin', which, plase God, we'll do, and are well able to do, before a month of Sundays goes over us. Now, Sir, you needn't say another word,' said he, seeing me about to speak, 'for, by Him that made me, we'll do it. If any man, I say, could persuade me agin it, you could; but, if we don't pay them full interest for what we got, why, my name's not Denis Kelly—ay, sweep them like varmint out of the town, body and sleeves!'

"I saw argument would be lost on him, so I only observed that I feared it would, eventually, end badly.

"'Och, many and many's the time, Mr. Darcy,' said Honor, 'I prophesied the same thing; and if God hasn't said it, he'll be coming home a corpse to me some day or other, for he got as much bating, Sir, as would be enough to kill a horse; and to tell you God's truth, Sir, he's breeding up his childher——'

"'Honor,' said Kelly, irritated—'whatever I do, do I lave it in your power to say that I'm a bad husband; so don't *rise* me by your talk, for I don't like to be provoked. I *know* it's wrong, but what can I do? Would you have me for to show the *Garran bane** and lave them like a cowardly thraitor, now that the other faction is coming up to be their match?—no; let what will come of it, I'll never do the mane thing—death before dishonour!'

"In this manner, Kelly went on for years; sometimes, indeed, keeping quiet for a short period, but eventually drawn in, from the apprehension of being reproached with want of honour and truth to his connexion. This, truly, is an imputation which no peasant could endure; nor, were he thought capable of treachery, would his life be worth a single week's purchase. Many a time have I seen Kelly reeling home, his head and face sadly cut, the blood streaming from him, and his wife and some neighbour on each side of him—the poor woman weeping and deploring the senseless and sanguinary feuds in which her husband took so active a part.

"About three miles from this, down at the Long Ridge, where the Shannons live, dwelt a family of the M'Guigans, cousins to Denis. They were any thing but industrious, although they might have lived very independently, having held a farm on what they call an *old take,* which means a long lease taken out when the lands were cheap. It so happened, however, that, like too many of their countrymen, they

*The white Horse, i.e., be wanting in mettle.

paid little attention to the cultivation of their farm, the consequence of which neglect was, that they became embarrassed, and overburdened with arrears. Their landlord was old Sam Simmons, whose only fault to his tenants was an excess of indulgence, and a generous disposition wherever he could possibly get an opportunity,
to scatter his money about him, upon the spur of a benevolence, which it would
seem never ceased goading him to acts of the most Christian liberality and kindness. Along with these excellent qualities, he was remarkable for a most rooted
aversion to law and lawyers; for he would lose one hundred pounds rather than
recover that sum by legal proceedings, even when certain that five pounds would
effect it; but he seldom or never was known to pardon a breach of the peace.

"I have always found that an *excess* of indulgence in a landlord never fails ultimately to injure and relax the industry of the tenant; at least, this was the effect
which *his* forbearance produced on them. But the most extraordinary good-nature
has its limits, and so had his; after repeated warning, and the most unparalleled
patience on his part, he was at length compelled to determine on at once removing
them from his estate, and letting his land to some more efficient and deserving
tenant. He accordingly desired them to remove their property from the premises,
as he did not wish, he said, to leave them without the means of entering upon
another farm, if they felt so disposed. This they refused to do, adding, that they
would at least put him to the expense of ejecting them. He then gave orders to his
agent to seize; but they, in the mean time, had secreted their effects by night
among their friends and relations, sending a cow to this one, and a horse to that;
so that when the bailiff came to levy his execution, he found very little except the
empty walls. They were, however, ejected without ceremony, and driven altogether
off the farm, for which they had actually paid nothing for the three preceding
years. In the mean time the farm was advertised to be let, and several persons had
offered themselves as tenants; but what appeared very remarkable was, that the
Roman Catholics seldom came a second time to make any further inquiry about it;
or if they did, Simmons observed that they were sure to withdraw their proposals,
and ultimately decline having any thing to do with it.

"This was a circumstance which he could not properly understand; but the fact
was, that the peasantry were, to a man, members of a widely-extending system of
Whiteboyism, the secret influence of which intimidated such of their own religion
as intended to take it, and prevented them from exposing themselves to the penalty
which they knew those who should dare to occupy it must pay. In a short time,
however, the matter began to be whispered about, until it spread gradually, day
after day, through the parish, that those who already had proposed, or intended to

propose, were afraid to enter upon the land on any terms. Hitherto, it is true, these threats floated about only in the invisible form of rumour.

"The farm had been now unoccupied for about a year: party-spirit ran very high among the peasantry, and no proposals came in, or were at all likely to come. Simmons then got advertisements printed, and had them posted up in the most conspicuous parts of this and the neighbouring parishes. It was expected, however, that they would be torn down; but instead of that, there was a written notice posted up immediately under each, which ran in the following words:—

'TAKE NOTESS.

'Any man that'll dare to take the farm belonging to yellow Sam Simmons, and sitivated at the long ridge, will be flayed alive.

'MAT MIDNIGHT.

'B. N.—*It's it that was latterrally occupied by the M'Guigans.'*

"This occasioned Simmons and the other magistrates of the barony to hold a meeting, at which they subscribed to the amount of fifty pounds, as a reward for discovering the author or authors of the threatening notice; but the advertisement containing the reward, which was posted in the usual places through the parish, was torn down on the first night after it was put up. In the mean time, a man, nicknamed Vengeance—Vesey Vengeance, in consequence of his daring and fearless spirit, and his bitterness in retaliating injury—came to Simmons, and proposed for the farm. The latter candidly mentioned the circumstances of the notice, and fairly told him that he was running a personal risk in taking it.

"'Leave that to me, Sir,' said Vengeance; 'if you will set me the farm at the terms I offer, I am willing to become your tenant; and let them that posted up the notices go to old Nick, or if they annoy me, let them take care I don't send them there. I am a true-blue, Sir—a purple man—have lots of fire-arms, and plenty of stout fellows in the parish, ready and willing to back me; and, by the light-of-day! if they make or meddle with me or mine, we will hunt them in the face of the world, like so many mad dogs, out of the country: what are they but a pack of *ribles,** that would cut our throats, if they dared?'

"'I have no objection," said Simmons, 'that you should express a firm determination to defend your life, and protect your property; but I utterly condemn the spirit with which you seem to be animated. Be temperate and sober, but be firm. I will afford you every assistance and protection in my power, both as a magistrate and a landlord; but if you speak so incautiously, the result may be serious, if not fatal, to yourself.'

"'Instead of that,' said Vengeance, 'the more a man appears to be afeard, the more danger he is in, as I know by what I have seen; but, at any rate, if they injure me, I wouldn't ask better sport than taking down the ribles—the bloody-minded villains! Isn't it a purty thing, that a man darn't put one foot past the other, only as *they* wish? By the light-of-day, I'll pepper them!'

"Shortly after this, Vengeance, braving all their threats, removed to the farm, and set about its cultivation with skill and vigour. He had not been long there, however, when a notice was posted one night on his door, giving him ten days to clear off from this interdicted spot, threatening, in case of non-compliance, to make a bonfire of the house and offices, inmates included. The reply which Vengeance made to this was fearless and characteristic. He wrote another notice, which he posted on the chapel door, stating that he would not budge an inch— recommending, at the same time, such as intended paying him a nightly visit to be careful that they might not chance to go home with their heels foremost. This, indeed, was setting them completely at defiance, and would, no doubt, have been fatal to Vesey, were it not for a circumstance which I will now relate:—In a little dell below Vesey's house, lived a poor woman called Doran, a widow; she inhabited a small hut, and was principally supported by her two sons, who were servants— one to a neighbouring farmer, a Roman Catholic, and the other to Dr. Ableson, Rector of the parish. He who had been with the Rector lost his health shortly before Vengeance succeeded the M'Guigans as occupier of the land in question, and was obliged to come home to his mother. He was then confined to his bed, from which, indeed, he never rose.

"This boy had been his mother's principal support—for the other was unsettled, and paid her but little attention, being, like most of those in his situation, fond of drinking, dancing, and attending fairs. In short, he became a Ribbonman and con-sequently was obliged to attend their nightly meetings. Now it so happened that for a considerable time after the threatening notice had been posted on Vengeance's door, he received no annoyance, although the period allowed for his departure had been long past, and the purport of the paper uncomplied with. Whether this pro-ceeded from an apprehension on the part of the Ribbonmen of receiving a warmer welcome than they might wish, or whether they deferred the execution of their threat until Vengeance might be off his guard, I cannot determine; but the fact is, that some months had elapsed and Vengeance remained hitherto unmolested.

"During this interval the distress of Widow Doran had become known to the inmates of his family, and his mother—for she lived with him—used to bring down each day some nourishing food to the sick boy. In these kind offices she was very punctual; and so great was the poverty of the poor widow, and so destitute the situation of her sick son, that, in fact, the burden of their support lay principally upon Vengeance's family.

"Vengeance was a small, thin man, with fair hair, and fiery eyes; his voice was loud and shrill, his utterance rapid, and the general expression of his countenance irritable. His motions were so quick, that he rather seemed to run than walk. He was a civil, obliging neighbour, but performed his best actions with a bad grace; a firm, unflinching friend, but a bitter and implacable enemy. Upon the whole, he was generally esteemed and respected—though considered as an eccentric character, for such, indeed, he was. On hearing of Widow Doran's distress, he gave orders that a portion of each meal should be regularly sent down to her and her son; and from that period forward they were both supported principally from his table.

"In this way some months had passed, and still Vengeance was undisturbed in his farm. It often happened, however, that Doran's other son came to see his brother; and during these visits it was but natural that his mother and brother should allude to the kindness which they daily experienced from Vesey.

"One night, about twelve o'clock, a tap came to Widow Doran's door, who happened to be attending the invalid, as he was then nearly in the last stage of his illness. When she opened it, the other son entered, in an evident hurry, having the appearance of a man who felt deep and serious anxiety.

"'Mother,' said he, 'I was very uneasy entirely about Mick, and just started over to see him, although they don't know at home that I'm out, so I can't stay a crack; but I wish you would go to the door for two or three minutes, as I have something to say to *him*.'

"'Why, thin, Holy Mother!—Jack, a-hagur, is there any thing the matther, for you look as if you had seen something?'

"'Nothing worse than myself, mother,' he replied; 'nor there's nothing the matther at all—only I have a few words to say to Mick here, that's all.'

"The mother accordingly removed herself out of hearing.

"'Mick,' says the boy, 'this is a bad business—I wish to God I was clear and clane out of it.'

"'What is it;' said Mick, alarmed.

"'Murther, I'm afeard, if God doesn't turn it off of them, some how.'

"'What do you mane, man, at all?' said the invalid, raising himself, in deep emotion, on his elbow, from his poor straw bed.

"'Vengeance,' said he—'Vengeance, man—he's going to get it. I was out with the boys on Sunday evening, and *at last* it's agreed on to visit him to-morrow night. I'm sure and sartin he'll never escape, for there's more in for him than taking the farm, and daring them so often as he did—he shot two fingers off of a brother-in-law of Jem Reilly's one night that they war on for threshing him, and that's coming home to him along with the rest.'

"'In the name of God, Jack,' inquired Mick, 'what do they intend to do to him?'

"'Why,' replied Jack, 'it's agreed to put a coal in the thatch, in the first place; and although they were afeard to name what he's to get besides, I doubt they'll make a spatch-cock of *himself.* They won't meddle with any other of the family, though—but *he's down* for it.'

"'Are *you* to be one of them?' asked Mick.

"'I was the third man named,' replied the other, 'bekase, they said, I knew the place.'

"'Jack,' said his emaciated brother, with much solemnity, raising himself up in the bed—'Jack, if you have act or part in that bloody business, God in his glory you'll never see. Fly the country—cut off a finger or toe—break your arm—or do something that may prevent you from being there. Oh, my God!' he exclaimed, whilst the tears fell fast down his pale cheeks—'to go to murder the man, and lave his little family widout a head or a father over them, and his wife a widow! To burn his place, widout rhime, or rason, or offince. Jack, if you go, I'll die cursing you. I'll appear to you—I'll let you rest neither night nor day, sleeping nor waking, in bed or out of bed. I'll haunt you, till you'll curse the very day you war born.'

"Whisht, Micky,' said Jack, 'you're frightening me: I'll not go—will that satisfy you?'

"'Well, dhrop down on your two knees, there,' said Micky, 'and swear before the God that has his eye upon you this minute, that you'll have no hand in injuring him or his, while you live. If you don't do this, I'll not rest in my grave, and maybe I'll be a corpse before mornin'.'

"'Well, Micky,' said Jack, who, though wild and unthinking, was a lad whose heart and affections were good, 'it would be hard for me to refuse you that much, and you not likely to be long wid me—I will;' and he accordingly knelt down and swore solemnly, in words which his brother dictated to him, that he would not be concerned in the intended murder.

"'Now, give me your hand, Jack,' said the invalid; 'God bless you—and so he will. Jack, if I depart before I see you again, I'll die happy, That man has supported me and my mother for near the last three months, bad as you all think him. Why,

Jack, we would both be dead of hunger long ago, only for his family; and, my God! to think of such a murdhering intention makes my blood run cowld'—

"'You had better give him a hint, then,' said Jack, 'some way, or he'll be done for, as sure as you're stretched on that bed; but don't mintion names, if you wish to keep me from being murdhered for what I did. I must be off now, for I stole out of the barn;* and only that Atty Laghy's gone along wid the master to the —— fair, to help him to sell the two coults, I couldn't get over at all.'

"'Well, go home, Jack, and God bless you, and so he will, for what you did this night.'

"Jack accordingly departed, after bidding his mother and brother farewell.

"When the old woman came in, she asked her son if there was any thing wrong with his brother, but he replied that there was not.

"'Nothing at all,' said he—'but will you go up airly in the morning, plase God, and tell Vesey Johnston that I want to see him; and—that—I have a great dale to say to him.'

"'To be sure I will, Micky; but, Lord guard us, what ails you, avourneen, you look so frightened?'

"'Nothing at all, at all, mother; but will you go where I say airly to-morrow, for me?'

"'It's the first thing I'll do, God willin',' replied the mother. And the next morning Vesey was down with the invalid very early, for the old woman kept her word, and paid him a timely visit.

"'Well, Micky, my boy,' said Vengeance, as he entered the hut, 'I hope you're no worse this morning.'

"'Not worse, Sir,' replied Mick; 'nor, indeed, am I any thing better either, but much the same way. Sure it's I that knows very well that my time here is but short.'

"'Well, Mick, my boy,' said Vengeance, 'I hope you're prepared for death—and that you expect forgiveness, like a Christian. Look up, my boy, to God at once, and pitch the priests and their craft to ould Nick, where they'll all go at the long run.'

"'I blieve,' said Mick, with a faint smile, 'that you're not very fond of the priests, Mr. Johnston; but if you knew the power they possess as well as I do, you wouldn't spake of them so bad, any how.'

"'Me fond of them!' replied the other; 'why, man, they're a set of the most gluttonous, black-looking hypocrites, that ever walked on neat's leather; and ought to be hunted out of the country—hunted out of the country, by the light of day! every one of them; for they do nothing but egg up the people against the Protestants.'

*Labouring servants in Ireland, usually sleep in barns.

"'God help you, Mr. Johnston,' replied the invalid; 'I pity you from my heart for the opinion you hould about the blessed crathurs. I suppose if you were sthruck dead on the spot wid a blast from the fairies, that you think a priest couldn't cure you by one word's spaking?'

"'Cure me!' said Vengeance, with a laugh of disdain; 'by the light of day, if I caught one of them curing me, I'd give him the purtiest chase you ever saw in your life, across the hills.'

"'Don't you know,' said Mick, 'that priest Dannelly cured Bob Arthurs of the falling sickness—until he broke the vow that was laid upon him, of not going into a church, and the minute he crossed the church-door, didn't he dhrop down as bad as ever—and what could the minister do for him?'

"'And don't *you* know,' rejoined Vengeance, 'that that's all a parcel of the most lying stuff possible; lies—lies—all lies—and vagabondism. Why, Mick, you Papishes worship the priests; you think they can bring you to heaven at a word. By the light of day, they must have good sport laughing at you, when they get among one another. Why don't they teach you, and give you the Bible to read, the ribelly rascals? but they're afraid you'd know too much then.'

"'Well, Mr. Johnston,' said Mick, 'I blieve you'll never have a good opinion of them, at any rate.'

"'Ay, when the sky falls,' replied Vengeance, 'but you're now on your death-bed, and why don't you pitch them to ould Nick, and get a Bible? Get a Bible, man; there's a pair of them in my house, that's never used at all—except my mother's, and she's at it night and day. I'll send one of them down to you: turn yourself to God—to your Redeemer, that died on the mount of Jehoshaphat, or somewhere about Jerusalem, for your sins—and don't go out of the world from the hand of a rascally priest, with a band about your eyes, as if you were at blindman's-buff; for, by the light of day, you're as blind as a bat in a religious way.'

"'There's no use in sending me a Bible,' replied the invalid, 'for I can't read it: but, whatever you may think, I'm very willing to lave my salvation with my priest.'

"'Why, man,' observed Vengeance, 'I thought you were going to have sense at last, and that you sent for me to give you some spiritual consolation.'

"'No, Sir,' replied Mick; 'I have two or three words to spake to you.'

"'Come, come, Mick, now that we're on a spiritual subject, I'll hear nothing from you till I try whether it's possible to give you a true insight into religion. Stop, now, and let us lay our heads together, that we may make out something of a dacenter creed for you to believe in, than the one you profess. Tell me truth, do you believe in the priests?'

"'How?' replied Mick; 'I believe that they're holy men—but I know they can't save me widout the Redeemer, and his blessed mother.'

"'By the light above us, you're shuffling, Mick—I say you do believe in them—now don't tell me to the contrary—I say you're shuffling as fast as possible.'

"'I tould you truth, Sir,' replied Mick, 'and if you don't blieve me, I can't help it.'

"'Don't trust in the priests, Mick; that's the main point to secure your salvation.'

"Mick, who knew his prejudices against the priests, smiled faintly, and replied—

"'Why, Sir, I trust in them as bein' able to make inthercession wid God for me, that's all.'

"'They make intercession! By the stool I'm sitting on, a single word from one of them would ruin you. They, a set of ribles, to make interest for you in heaven! Didn't they rise the rebellion in Ireland? answer me that.'

"'This is a subject, Sir, we would never agree on,' replied Mick.

"'Have you the Ten Commandments?' enquired Vesey.

"'I doubt my mimory's not clear enough to have them in my mind,' said the lad, feeling keenly the imputation of ignorance, which he apprehended from Vesey's blunt observations.'

"'Vesey, however, had penetration enough to perceive his feelings, and with more delicacy than could be expected from him, immediately moved the question.

"'No matter, Mick,' said he, 'if you would give up the priests, we would get over that point; as it is, I'll give you a lift in the Commandments; and as I said awhile ago, if you take my advice I'll work up a creed for you, that you may depend upon. But now for the Commandments;—let me see.

"'First:—Thou shalt have no other gods but me. Don't you see, man, how that peppers the priests?

"'Second:—Remember that thou keep holy the Sabbath day.

"' Third:—Thou shalt not make to thyself—no—hang it no—I'm out—that's the Second—very right—Third:—Honour thy Father and thy Mother—you understand that, Mick?—It means that you are bound to—to—just so—to honour your father and your mother, poor woman.'

"'My father—God be good to him—is dead near fourteen years, Sir,' replied Mick.

"'Well, in that case, Mick, you see all that's left for you is to honour your mother—although I'm not certain of that either; the Commandments make no allowance at all for death, and in that case, why, living, or dead, the surest way is to respect and obey them—that is—if the thing wern't impossible. I wish we had blind George M'Gin here, Mick, although he's as great a rogue as ever escaped hemp, yet he'd beat the devil himself at a knotty point.'

"'His breath would be bad about a dying man,' observed Mick.

"'Ay, or a living one,' said Vesey; 'however, let us get on—we were at the Third: Fourth:—Thou shalt do no murder.'

"At the word murder, Mick started, and gave a deep groan—whilst his eyes and features assumed a great and hollow expression, resembling that of a man struck with an immediate sense of horror and affright.

"'Oh, for heaven's sake, Sir, stop there,' said Doran; 'that brings to my mind the business I had with you, Mr. Johnston.'

"'What is it about?' enquired Vengeance, in his usual eager manner.

"'Do you mind, said Mick, 'that a paper was stuck one night upon your door, threatening you, if you wouldn't lave that farm you're in?

"'I do; the blood-thirsty villians! but they knew a trick worth two of coming near me.'

"'Well,' said Mick, 'a strange man that I never seen before, come into me last night, and tould me, if I'd see you, to say that you would get a visit from the boys this night, and to take care of yourself.'

"'Give me the hand, Mick,' said Vengeance—'give me the hand: in spite of the priests, by the light of day, you're an honest fellow—This night, you say, they're to come? And what are the bloody wretches to do, Mick? But I needn't ask that, for I suppose it's to murder myself, and to burn my place.'

"'I'm afeard, Sir, you're not far from the truth,' replied Mick; 'but, Mr. Johnston, for God's sake, don't mintion my name; for, if you do, I'll get myself what they war laying out for you—be burned in my bed maybe.'

"'Never fear, Mick,' replied Vengeance; 'your name will never cross my lips.'

"'It's a great thing,' said Mick, 'that would make me turn informer; but sure, only for your kindness and the goodness of your family, the Lord spare you to one another, mightn't I be dead long ago? I couldn't have one minute's peace if you or yours came to any harm, when I could prevint it.'

"'Say no more, Mick,' said Vengeance, taking his hand again; 'I know that, leave the rest to me; but how do you find yourself, my poor fellow; you look weaker than you did, a good deal.'

"'Indeed I'm going very fast, Sir,' replied Mick; 'I know it'll soon be over with me.'

"'Hut, no, man,' said Vengeance, drawing his hand rapidly across his eyes, and clearing his voice—'not at all, don't say so: would a little broth serve you? or a bit of fresh meat?—or would you have a fancy for any thing that I could make out for you? I'll get you wine, if you think it would do you good.'

"'God reward you,' said Mick, feebly—'God reward you, and open your eyes to the truth. Is my mother likely to come in, do you think?'

"'She must be here in a few minutes,' the other replied; 'she was waiting till they'd churn, that she might bring you down a little fresh milk and butter.'

"'I wish she was wid me,' said the poor lad, 'for I'm lonely wantin' her—her voice, and the very touch of her hands goes to my heart. Mother, come to me—and let me lay my head upon your breast, agra machree, for I think it will be for the last time: we lived lonely, avourneen, wid none but ourselves—sometimes in happiness, when the nabours 'ud be kind to us—and sometimes in sorrow, when there 'ud be none to help us. It's over now, mother, and I'm lavin' you for ever?'

"Vengeance wiped his eyes—'Rouse yourself,—Mick,' said he—'rouse yourself.'

"'Who is that sitting along with you on the stool?' said Mick.

"'No one,' replied his neighbour—'but what's the matter with you, Mick?—your face is changed.'

"'Mick, however, made no reply; but after a few slight struggles, in which he attempted to call upon his mother's name, he breathed his last. When Vengeance saw that he was dead,—looked upon the cold, miserable hut in which this grateful and affectionate young man was stretched,—and then reflected on the important service he had just rendered him, he could not suppress his tears.

"After sending down some of the females to assist his poor mother in laying him out, Vengeance went among his friends and acquaintances, informing them of the intelligence he had received, without mentioning the source from which he had it. After dusk that evening, they all flocked, as privately as possible, to his house, to the number of thirty or forty, well provided with arms and ammunition. Some of them stationed themselves in the out-houses, some behind the garden hedge, and others in the dwelling-house."

When my brother had got thus far in his narrative, a tap came to the parlour-door, and immediately a stout-looking man, having the appearance of a labourer, entered the room.

"Well, Lachlin," said my brother, "what's the matter?"

"Why, Sir," said Lachlin, scratching his head, "I had a bit of a favour to ax, if it would be plasin' to you to grant it to me."

"What is that?" said my brother.

"Do you know, Sir," said he, "I haven't been at a wake—let us see—this two or three years, any how; and, if you'd have no objection, why, I'd slip up a while to Denis Kelly's; he's a distant relation of my own, Sir; and blood's thicker than wather, you know."

"I'm just glad you came in, Lachlin," said my brother; "I didn't think of you—take a chair here, and never heed the wake to-night, but sit down and tell us about the attack on Vesey Vengeance, long ago. I'll get you a tumbler of punch; and, instead of going to the wake, I will allow you to go to the funeral tomorrow."

"Ah, Sir," said Lachlin, "you know whenever the punch is consarned, I'm aisily persuaded; but not making little of your tumbler, Sir," said the shrewd fellow, "I would get two or three of them if I went to the wake."

"Well, sit down," said my brother, handing him one, "and we won't permit you to get thirsty while you're talking, at all events."

"In throth, you haven't your heart in the likes of it," said Lachlin. "Gintlemen, your healths—your health, Sir, and we're happy to see you wanst more. Why, thin, I remember you, Sir, when you were a gorsoon, passing to school wid your satchell on your back; but, I'll be bound, you're by no means as soople now as you were thin. Why, Sir," turning to my brother, "he could fly, or kick football wid the rabbits.—Well, this is raal stuff!"

"Now, Lachlin," said my brother, "give us an account of the attack you made on Vesey Vengeance's house, at the Long Ridge, when all his party were chased out of the town."

"Why, thin, Sir, I ought to be ashamed to mintion it; but you see, gintlemen, there was no getting over being connected wid them—for a man's life wouldn't be his own if he refused;—but I hope your brother's *safe*, Sir!"

"Oh, perfectly safe, Lachlin; you may rest assured he'll never mention it."

"Well, Sir," said Lachlin, addressing himself to me, "Vesey Vengeance was——."

"Lachlin," said my brother, "he knows all about Vesey; just give an account of the attack."

"The attack, Sir!—no, but the chivey we got over the mountains. Why, Sir, we met in an ould empty house, you see, that belonged to the Farrells of Ballyboulteen, that went over to America that spring. There war none wid us, you may be sure, but them that war *up;* and in all we might be about sixty or seventy. The M'Guigans, one way or another, got it up first among them, bekase they expected that Mr. Simmons would take them back when he'd find that no one else dare venthur upon their land. There war at that time two fellows down from the county Longford in their neighbourhood, of the name of Collier—although that wasn't their right name—they were here upon their keeping, for the murder of a proctor in their own part of the country. One of them was a tall, powerful fellow, with sandy hair, and red brows; the other was a slender chap, that must have been drawn into it by his brother—for he was very mild and innocent and always persuaded us agin evil. The M'Guigans brought lashings of whiskey, and made them that war to go foremost amost drunk—these war the two Colliers, some of the strangers from behind the mountains, and a son of Widdy Doran's, that knew every inch about the place, for he was bred and born jist below the house a bit. He wasn't wid us, however, in regard of his brother being *under* boord that night; but, instid of him, Tim M'Guigan went to show the way up the little glin to the house, though, for that matther, the most of us knew as well as he did—but we didn't like to be the first to put a hand to it, if we could help it.

"At any rate, we sot in Farrell's empty house, drinking whiskey, till they war all gathered, when about two dozen of their got the damp seat from the chimley, and rubbed it over their faces, making them so black, that their own relations couldn't know them. We then went across the country in little lots, of about six, or ten, or a score, and we war glad that the wake was in Widdy Doran's, seeing that, if any one would meet us, we war going to it you know, and the blackening of the faces would pass for a frolic; but there was no great danger of being met, for it was now long beyant midnight.

"Well, jintlemen, it puts me into a tremble, even at this time, to think of how little we cared about doing what we were bent upon. Them that had to manage the business war more than half drunk; and, hard fortune to me, but you would think it was to a wedding they went—some of them singing songs aginst the law—some of them quite merry, and laughing as if they had found a mare's nest. The big fellow, Collier, had a dark lanthern wid a half-burned turf in it to light the bonfire, as they said; others had guns and pistols—some of them charged, and some of them not; some had bagnets, and ould rusty swords, pitchforks, and so on. Myself had nothing in my hand but the flail I was thrashing wid that day; and to tell the thruth, the divil a step I would have gone with them, only for fraid of my health: for, as I said awhile agone, if any discovery was made afterwards, them that promised to go, and turned tail, would be marked as the informers. Neither was I so blind, but I could see that there war plenty there that would stay away if they durst.

"Well, we went on till we came to a little dark corner below the house, where we met and held a council of war upon what we should do. Collier and the other strangers from behind the mountains war to go first, and the rest war to stand round the house at a distance—he carried the lantern, a bagnet, and a horse pistol; and half-a-dozen more war to bring over bottles of straw from Vengeance's own haggard, to hould up to the thatch. It's all past and gone now—but three of the Reillys were desperate against Vesey that night, particularly one of them that he had shot about a year and a-half before—that is peppered two of the right hand fingers off of him, one night in a scuffle, as Vesey came home from an Orange-lodge. Well, all went on purty fair; we had got as far as the out-houses, where we stopped, to see if we could hear any noise; but all was quiet as you plase.

"'Now, Vengeance,' says Reilly, swearing a terrible oath out of him—'you murdering Orange villain, you're going to get your pay,' says he.

"'Ay,' says M'Guigan, 'what he often threatened to others, he'll soon meet himself, plase God—come boys,' says he, 'bring the straw and light it, and just lay it up, my darlings, nicely to the thatch here, and ye'll see what a glorious bonfire we'll have of the black Orange villain's blankets, in less than no time.'

"'Some of us could hardly stand this: 'Stop, boys,' cried one of Dan Slevin's sons—'stop, Vengeance is bad enough, but his wife and childher never offinded us—we'll not burn the place.'

"'No,' said others, spaking out when they heard any body at all having courage to do so—'it's too bad, boys, to burn the place; for if we do,' says they, 'some of the innocent may be burned before they get out from the house, or even before they waken out of their sleep.'

"'Knock at the door first,' says Slevin, 'and bring Vengeance out; let us cut the ears off of his head, and lave him.'

"'Damn him!' says another, 'let us not take the vagabone's life; it's enough to take the ears from him, and to give him a *prod* or two of a bagnet on the ribs; but don't kill him.'

"'Well, well,' says Reilly, 'let us knock at the door, and get himself and the family out,' says he; 'and then we'll see what can be done wid him.'

"'Tattheration to me; says the big Longford fellow, 'if he had served me, Reilly, as he did you, but I'd roast him in the flames of his own house,' says he.

"'I'd have *you* to know, says Slevin, 'that you have no command here, Collier. I'm captain at the present time,' says he; 'and more nor what I wish shall not be done. Go over,' says he to the black faces, 'and rap him up.'

"Accordingly, they began to knock at the door, commanding Vengeance to get up and come out to them.

"'Come, Vengeance,' says Collier, 'put on you, my good fellow, and come out till two or three of your neighbours, that wish you well, gets a sight of your purty face, you babe of grace!'

"'Who are you that wants me, at all?' says Vengeance, from within.

"'Come out first,' says Collier; 'a few friends that has a crow to pluck with you: walk out, avourneen; or if you'd rather be roasted alive, why you may stay where you are,' says he.

"'Gentlemen,' says Vengeance, 'I have never, to my knowledge, offinded any of you; and I hope you won't be so cruel as to take an industrious, hard-working man from his family, in the clouds of the night, to do him an injury. Go home, gentlemen, in the name of God, and let me and mine alone. You're all mighty dacent gentlemen, you know, and I'm determined never to make or meddle with any of you. Sure, I know right well it's purtecting me you would be, dacent gentlemen. But I don't think there's any of my neighbours there, or they wouldn't stand by and see me injured.'

"'Thrue for you, avick,' says they, giving, at the same time, a terrible pattherrara agin the door, with two or three big stones.

"'Stop, stop!' says Vengeance, 'don't break the door, and I'll open it. I know you're mercital, dacent gentlemen—I know you're merciful.'

"So the thief came and unbarred it quietly, and the next minute about a dozen of them that war within the house let slap at us. As God would have had it, the crowd didn't happen to be fornent the door, or numbers of them would have been shot, and the night was dark, too, which was in our favour. The first volley was scarcely over, when there was another slap from the out-houses; and after that, another from the gardens; and, after that, to be sure, we took to our scrapers. Several of them were badly wounded; but, as for Collier, he was shot dead, and M'Guigan was taken prisoner, with five more, on the spot. There never was such a chase as we got; and only that they thought there was more of us in it, they might have tuck most of us prisoners.

"'Fly, boys!' says M'Guigan, as soon as they fired out of the house—'we've been sould.' says he, 'but I'll die game, any how,'—and so he did, poor fellow; for although he and the other four war transported, one of them never sould the pass or stagged. Not but that they might have done it, for all that, only that there was a whisper sent to them, that if they *did,* a single sowl belonging to one of them wouldn't be left living. The M'Guigans were cousins of Denis Kelly's, that's now laid out there above.

"From the time this tuck place till after the sizes, there wasn't a stir among them, on any side; but when they war over, the boys began to prepare. Denis, heavens be his bed, was there in his glory. This was in the spring 'sizes, and the

May fair soon followed. Ah! that was the bloody sight, I'm tould—for I wasn't at it—atween the Orangemen and them. The Ribbonmen war bate, though, but not till after there was a desperate fight on both sides. I was tould that Denis Kelly that day knocked down five-and-twenty men in about three quarters of an hour; and only that long John Grimes hot him a *polthoge* on the sconce with the butt-end of the gun, it was thought the Orangemen would be beat. That blow broke his skull, and was the manes of his death. He was carried home senseless."

"Well, Lachlin," said my brother, "if you didn't see it, I did. I happened to be looking out of John Carson's upper window—for it wasn't altogether safe to contemplate it within reach of the missiles. It was certainly a dreadful and a barbarous sight. You have often observed the calm, gloomy silence that precedes a thunderstorm; and had you been there that day, you might have seen it illustrated in a scene much more awful. The thick living mass of people extended from the corner-house, nearly a quarter of a mile, at this end of the town, up to the parsonage on the other side. During the early part of the day, every kind of business was carried on in a hurry and an impatience, which denoted the little chance they knew there would be for transacting it in the evening.

"Up to the hour of four o'clock, the fair was unusually quiet, and, on the whole, presented nothing in any way remarkable; but after that hour you might observe the busy stir and hum of the mass settling down into a deep, brooding, portentous silence, that was absolutely fearful. The females with dismay and terror pictured in their faces, hurried home; and in various instances you might see mothers, and wives, and sisters, clinging about the sons, husbands, and brothers, attempting to drag them by main force from the danger which they knew impended over them. In this they seldom succeeded; for the person so urged was usually compelled to tear himself from them by superior strength.

"The pedlars, and basket-women, and such as had tables and standings erected in the streets, commenced removing them with all possible haste. The shopkeepers, and other inhabitants of the town, put up their shutters, in order to secure their windows from being shattered. Strangers, who were compelled to stop in town that night, took shelter in the inns and other houses of entertainment where they lodged so that about five-o'clock the street was completely clear, and free for action.

"Hitherto there was not a stroke—the scene became even more silent and gloomy, although the moral darkness of their ill-suppressed passions was strongly contrasted with the splendour of the sun, that poured down a tide of golden light upon the multitude. This contrast between the natural brightness of the evening, and the internal gloom of their hearts, as the beams of the sun rested upon the ever-moving crowd, would, to any man who knew the impetuosity with which the spirit of religious hatred was soon to rage among them, produce novel and singular sensations. For, after all, Toby, there is a mysterious connection between natural and moral things, which often invests both nature and sentiment with a feeling that certainly would not come home to our hearts, if such a connection did not exist. A rose-tree beside a grave will lead us from sentiment to reflection; and any other association, where a painful or melancholy thought is clothed with a garb of joy or pleasure, will strike us more deeply in proportion as the contrast is strong. On seeing the sun or moon struggling through the darkness of surrounding clouds, I confess; although you may smile, that I feel for the moment a diminution of enjoyment—something taken, as it were, from the sum of my happiness.

"Ere the quarrel commenced, you might see, a dark and hateful glare scowling from the countenances of the two parties, as they viewed and approached each other in the street—the eye was set in deadly animosity, and the face marked with an ireful paleness, occasioned at once by revenge and apprehension. Groups were silently hurrying with an eager and energetic step to their places of rendezvous, grasping their weapons more closely, or grinding their teeth in the impatience of their fury. The veterans on each side were, surrounded by their respective followers, anxious to act under their direction; and the very boys seemed to be animated with a martial spirit, much more eager than that of those who had greater experience in party quarrels.

"Jem Finigan's public-house was the head quarters and rallying point of the Ribbonmen; the Orangemen assembled in that of Joe Sherlock, the master of an Orange lodge. About six o'clock, the crowd in the street began gradually to fall off to the opposite ends of the town—the Roman Catholics towards the north and the Protestants towards the south. Carson's window, from which I was observing their motions, was exactly half way between them, so that I had a distinct view of both. At this moment I noticed Denis Kelly coming forward from the closely condensed mass formed by the Ribbonmen: he advanced with his cravat off, to the middle of the vacant space between the parties, holding a fine oak cudgel in his hand. He then stopped, and addressing the Orangemen, said,

"'Where's Vengeance and his crew now? Is there any single Orange villain among you that dare come down and meet me here, like a man? Is John Grimes there? for if he is, before we begin to take you *out of a face*—to hunt you altogether out of the town, ye Orange villains—I would be glad that he'd step down to Denis Kelly here for two or three minutes—I'll not keep him longer.'

"There was now a stir and a murmur among the Orangemen, as if a rush was about to take place towards Denis; but Grimes, whom I saw endeavouring to curb them in, left the crowd, and advanced towards him.

"At this moment an instinctive movement among both masses took place; so that when Grimes had come within a few yards of Kelly, both parties were within two or three perches of them. Kelly was standing, apparently off his guard, with one hand thrust carelessly into the breast of his waistcoat, and the cudgel in the other; but his eye was fixed calmly upon Grimes as he approached. They were both powerful, fine men—brawney, vigorous, and active: Grimes had somewhat the advantage of the other in height; he also fought with his left hand, from which circumstance he was nicknamed *Kitthouge*. He was a man of a dark, stern-looking countenance; and the tones of his voice were deep, sullen, and of appalling strength.

"As they approached each other, the windows on each side of the street were crowded; but there was not a breath to be heard in any direction, nor from either party. As for myself, my heart palpitated with anxiety. What *they* might have felt I do not know: but they must have experienced considerable apprehension; for as they were both the champions of their respective parties, and had never before met in single encounter, their characters depended on the issue of the contest.

"'Well, Grimes,' said Denis, 'sure I've often wished for this same meetin', man, betune myself and you; I have what you're goin' to get, *in* for you this long time; but you'll get it now, avick, plase God——'

"'It was not to scould I came, you popish, ribly rascal,' replied Grimes, but to give you what you're long——'

"Ere the word had been out of his mouth, however, Kelly sprung over to him; and making a feint, as if he intended to lay the stick on his ribs, he swung it past without touching him, and, bringing it round his own head like lightning, made it tell with a powerful back-stroke, right on Grimes's temple, and in an instant his own face was sprinkled with the blood which sprung from the wound. Grimes staggered forward towards his antagonist, seeing which, Kelly sprung back, and was again meeting him with full force, when Grimes, turning a little, clutched Kelly's stick in his right hand, and being left-handed himself ere the other could wrench the cudgel from him, he gave him a terrible blow upon the back part of the head, which laid Kelly in the dust.

"There was then a deafening shout from the Orange party; and Grimes stood until Kelly should be in the act of rising, ready then to give him another blow. The coolness and generalship of Kelly, however, were here very remarkable; for, when he was just getting to his feet, 'Look at your party coming down upon me!' he exclaimed to Grimes, who turned round to order them back, and, in the interim, Kelly was upon his legs.

"I was surprised at the coolness of both men; for Grimes was by no means inflated with the boisterous triumph of his party—nor did Denis get into a blind rage on being knocked down. They approached again, their eyes kindled into savage fury, tamed down into the wariness of experienced combatants; for a short time they stood eyeing each other, as if calculating upon the contingent advantages of attack or defence. This was a moment of great interest; for, as their huge and powerful frames stood out in opposition, strung and dilated by the impulse of passion and the energy of contest, no judgment, however experienced, could venture to anticipate the result of the battle, or name the person likely to be victorious. Indeed it was surprising how the natural sagacity of these men threw their attitudes and movements into scientific form and elegance. Kelly raised his cudgel, and placed it transversely in the air, between himself and his opponent; Grimes instantly placed his against it—both weapons thus forming a St. Andrew's cross—whilst the men themselves stood foot to foot, calm and collected. Nothing could be finer than their proportions, nor superior to their respective attitudes; their broad chests were in a line—their thick, well-set necks, laid a little back, as were their bodies—without, however, losing their balance—and their fierce but calm features, grimly, but placidly scowling at each other, like men who were prepared for the onset.

"At length, Kelly made an attempt to repeat his former feint, with variations; for, whereas he had sent the first blow to Grimes's right temple, he took measures now to reach the left; his action was rapid, but equally quick was the eye of his antagonist, whose cudgel was up in ready guard to meet the blow. It met it; and with such surprising power was it sent and opposed, that both cudgels, on meeting, bent across each other into curves. An involuntary huzza followed this from their respective parties—not so much on account of the skill displayed by the combatants, as in admiration of their cudgels, and of the judgment with which they must have been selected. In fact, it was the staves, rather than the men, that were praised; and certainly the former did their duty. In a moment their shillelaghs were across each other once more, and the men resumed their former attitudes; their savage determination, their kindled eyes, the blood which disfigured the face of Grimes, and begrimmed also the countenance of his antagonist into a deeper expression of ferocity, occasioned many a cowardly heart to shrink from the sight. There they stood, gory and stern, ready for the next onset; it was first made by Grimes, who tried to practise on Kelly the feint which Kelly had before practised on him. Denis, after his usual manner, caught the blow in his open hand, and clutched the staff with an intention of holding it until he might visit Grimes—now apparently unguarded—with a levelling blow; but Grimes's effort to wrest the cudgel from his grasp, drew all Kelly's strength to that quarter, and prevented him from availing himself from the other's defenceless attitude. A trial of muscular power ensued, and their enormous bodily strength was exhibited in the stiff tug for victory. Kelly's address prevailed; for while Grimes pulled against him with all his collected vigour, the former suddenly let go his hold, and the latter, having lost his balance, staggered back: lightning could not be more quick than the action of Kelly, as, with tremendous force, his cudgel rung on the unprotected head of Grimes, who fell, or rather was shot to the ground, as if some superior power had dashed him against it; and there he lay for a short time, quivering under the blow he had received.

"A peal of triumph now arose from Kelly's party; but Kelly himself, placing his arms a-kimbo, stood calmly over his enemy, awaiting his return to the conflict. For nearly five minutes he stood in this attitude, during which time. Grimes did not stir; at length, Kelly stooped a little, and peering closely into his face, exclaimed—

"'Why, then, is it acting you are? any how, I wouldn't put it past you, you cunning vagabone; 'tis lying to take breath he is—get up, man, I'd scorn to touch you till you're on your legs; not all as one, for sure it's yourself would show *me* no such forbearance. Up with you, man alive, I've none of your own thrachery in me. I'll not *rise* my cudgel till you're on your guard.'

"There was an expression of disdain mingled with a glow of honest, manly generosity on his countenance, as he spoke, which made him at once the favourite with such spectators as were not connected with either of the parties. Grimes arose; and it was evident that Kelly's generosity deepened his resentment more than the blow which had sent him so rapidly to the ground; however, he was still cool, but his brows knit, his eye flashed with double fierceness, and his complexion settled into a dark blue shade, which gave to his whole visage an expression fearfully ferocious. Kelly hailed this as the first appearance of passion; *his* brow expanded as the other approached, and a dash of confidence, if not of triumph, softened, in some degree, the sterness of his features.

"With caution they encountered again, each collected for a spring, their eyes gleaming at each other like those of tigers. Grimes made a motion as if he would have struck Kelly with his fist; and, as the latter threw up his guard against the blow, he received a stroke from Grimes's cudgel in the under part of the right arm. This had been directed at his elbow, with an intention of rendering the arm powerless; it fell short, however, yet was sufficient to relax the grasp which Kelly held of his weapon. Had Kelly been a novice, this stratagem alone would have soon vanquished him; his address, however, was fully equal to that of his antagonist. The staff dropped instantly from his grasp, but a stout thong of black polished leather, with a shining tassel at the end of it had bound it securely to his massive wrist; the cudgel, therefore, only dangled from his arm, and did not, as the other expected, fall to the ground, or put Denis to the necessity of stooping for it—Grimes's object being to have struck him in that attitude.

"A flash of indignation now shot from Kelly's eye, and with the speed of lightning, he sprung within Grimes's weapon, determined to wrest it from him. The grapple that ensued was gigantic in a moment Grimes's staff was parallel with the horizon between them, clutched in the powerful grasp of both. They stood exactly opposite, and rather close to each other; their arms sometimes stretched out stiff and at full length, again contracted, until their faces, glowing and distorted by the energy of the contest, were drawn almost together. Sometimes, the prevailing strength of one would raise the staff slowly, and with gradually developed power, up in a perpendicular position, again, the re-action of opposing strength would strain it back, and sway the weighty frame of the antagonist, crouched and set into desperate resistance, along with it; whilst the hard pebbles under their feet were crumbled into powder, and the very street itself furrowed into gravel by the shock of their opposing strength. Indeed, so well matched a pair never met in contest; their strength, their wind, their activity, and their natural science appeared to be perfectly equal.

"At length, by a tremendous effort, Kelly got the staff twisted nearly out of Grimes's hand, and a short shout, half encouraging, half indignant, came from Grimes's party. This added shame to his other passions, and threw an impulse of almost superhuman strength into him: he recovered his advantage, but nothing more; they twisted—they heaved their great frames against each other—they struggled—their action became rapid—they swayed each other this way and that—their eyes like fire—their teeth locked, and their nostrils dilated. Sometimes they twined about each other like serpents, and twirled round with such rapidity, that it was impossible to distinguish them—sometimes, when a pull of more than ordinary power took place, they seemed to cling together almost without motion, bending down until their heads nearly touched the ground, their cracking joints seeming to stretch by the effort, and the muscles of their limbs standing out from the flesh, strung into amazing tension.

"In this attitude were they, when Denis, with the eye of a hawk, spied a disadvantage in Grimes's position; he wheeled round, placed his broad shoulder against the shaggy breast of the, other, and giving him what is called an 'inside crook,' strained him, despite of every effort, until he fairly got him on his shoulder, and off the point of resistance. There was a cry of alarm from the windows, particularly from the females, as Grimes's huge body was swung over Kelly's shoulder, until it came down in a crash upon the hard gravel of the street, while Denis stood in triumph, with his enemy's staff in his hand. A loud huzza followed this from all present except the Orangemen, who stood bristling with fury and shame for the temporary defeat of their champion.

Denis again had his enemy at his mercy; but he scorned to use his advantage ungenerously; he went over, and placing the staff in his hands—for the other had got to his legs—retrograded to his place, and desired Grimes to defend himself.

"After considerable manœuvering on both sides, Denis, who appeared to be the more active of the two, got an open on his antagonist, and by a powerful blow upon Grimes's ear, sent him to the ground with amazing force. I never saw such a blow given by mortal; the end of the cudgel came exactly upon the ear, and as Grimes went down, the blood spurted out of his mouth and nostrils; he then kicked convulsively several times as he lay upon the around, and that moment I really thought he would never have breathed more.

"The shout was again raised by the Ribbonmen, who threw up their hats, and bounded from the ground with the most vehement exultation. Both parties then waited to give Grimes time to rise and renew the battle, but he appeared perfectly contented to remain where be was: for there appeared no signs of life or motion in him.

"'Have you got your *gruel,* boy?' said Kelly, going over to where he lay;—'Well, you met Denis Kelly at last, didn't you? and there you lie; but, plase God, the most of your sort will soon lie in the same state. Come, boys,' said Kelly, addressing his own party, 'now for bloody Vengeance and his crew, that thransported the M'Guigans and the Caffries, and murdered Collier. Now, boys, have at the murderers, and let us have satisfaction for all!'

"A mutual rush instantly took place; but, ere the Orangemen came down to where Grimes lay, Kelly had taken his staff, and handed it to one of his own party. It is impossible to describe the scene that ensued. The noise of the blows, the shouting, the yelling, the groans, the scalped heads, and gory visages, gave both to the eye and the ear an impression that could not easily be forgotten. The battle was obstinately maintained on both sides for nearly an hour; and with a skill of manœuvering, attack, and retreat, that was astonishing.

"Both parties arranged themselves against each other, forming something like two lines of battle, and these extended along the town, nearly from one end to the other. It was curious to remark the difference in the persons and appearances of the combatants. In the Orange line, the men were taller and of more powerful frames; but the Ribbonmen were more hardy, active, and courageous. Man to man, notwithstanding their superior bodily strength, the Orangemen could never fight the others; the former depend too much upon their fire and side-arms, but they are by no means so well trained to the use of the cudgel as their enemies. In the district where the scene of this fight is laid, the Catholics generally inhabit the mountainous part of the country, to which, when the civil feuds of worse times prevailed, they had been driven at the point of the bayonet; the Protestants and Presbyterians, on the other hand, who came in upon their possessions, occupy the richer and more fertile tracts of the land, living, of course, more wealthy, with less labour, and on better food. The characteristic features produced by these causes are such as might be expected—the Catholic being, like his soil, hardy, thin, and capable of bearing all weathers; and the Protestants, larger, softer, and more inactive.

"Their advance to the first onset was far different from a faction fight. There existed a silence here, that powerfully evinced the inextinguishable animosity with which they encountered. For some time they fought in two compact bodies, that remained unbroken so long as the chances of victory were doubtful. Men went down, and were up, and went down in all directions with uncommon rapidity; and as the weighty phalanx of Orangemen stood out against the nimble line of their mountain adversaries, the intrepid spirit of the latter, and their surprising skill and activity soon gave symptoms of a gradual superiority in the conflict. In the course of about half an hour, the Orange party began to give way in the northern end of the town; and, as their opponents pressed them warmly and with unsparing hand, the heavy mass formed by their numbers began to break, and this decomposition ran up their line, until in a short time they were thrown into utter confusion. They now fought in detached parties; but these subordinate conflicts, though shorter in duration than the shock of the general battle, were much more inhuman and destructive; for whenever any particular gang succeeded in putting their adversaries to flight they usually ran to the assistance of their friends in the nearest fight—by which means they often fought three to one. In these instances the persons inferior in number suffered such barbarities, as it would be painful to detail.

"There lived, a short distance out of the town, a man nicknamed Jemsy Boccagh, on account of his lameness—he was also sometimes called 'Hip-an'-go-constant'—who fell the first victim to party spirit. He had got arms on seeing his friends likely to be defeated, and had the hardihood to follow, with charged bayonet, a few Ribbonmen, whom he attempted to intercept, as they fled from a large number of their enemies, who had got them separated from their comrades. Boccagh ran across a field, in order to get before them on the road, and was in the act of climbing a ditch, when one of them, who carried a spade-shaft struck him a blow on the head, which put all end to his existence.

"This circumstance imparted, of course, fiercer hatred to both parties—triumph inspiring the one, a thirst for vengeance nerving the other. Kelly inflicted tremendous punishment in every direction; for scarcely a blow fell from him which did not bring a man to the ground. It absolutely resembled a military engagement, for the number of combatants amounted at least to two thousand men. In many places the street was covered with small pools and clots of blood, which flowed from those who lay insensible—while others were borne away bleeding, groaning, or staggering, having been battered into a total unconsciousness of the scene about them.

"At length the Orangemen gave way, and their enemies, yelling with madness and revenge, began to beat them with unrestrained fury. The former, finding that they could not resist the impetuous tide which burst upon them, fled back past the church, and stopped not until they had reached an elevation, on which lay two or three heaps of stones, that had been collected for the purpose of paving the streets. Here they made a stand, and commenced a vigorous discharge of them against their pursuers. This checked the latter; and the others, seeing them hesitate, and likely to retreat from the missiles, pelted them with such effect, that the tables became turned, and the Ribbonmen made a speedy flight back into the town.

"In the mean time several Orangemen had gone into Sherlock's, where a considerable number of arms had been deposited, with an intention of resorting to them in case of a defeat at the cudgels. These now came out, and met the Ribbonmen on their flight from those who were pelting them with the stones. A dreadful scene ensued. The Ribbonmen, who had the advantage in numbers, finding themselves intercepted before by those who had arms, and pursued behind by those who had recourse to the stones, fought with uncommon bravery and desperation. Kelly, who was furious, but still collected and decisive, shouted out in Irish, lest the opposite party might understand him 'Let every *two* men seize upon *one* of those who have the arms.'

"This was attempted, and effected with partial success: and I have no doubt, but the Orangemen would have been ultimately beaten and deprived of their weapons, were it not that many of them, who had got their pistols out of

Sherlock's, discharged them among their enemies, and wounded several. The Catholics could not stand this; but, wishing to retaliate as effectually as possible, lifted stones wherever they could find them, and kept up the fight at a distance, as they retreated. On both sides, wherever a solitary foe was caught straggling from the rest, he was instantly punished with a most cruel and blood-thirsty spirit.

"It was just about this time that I saw Kelly engaged with two men, whom he kept at bay with great ease—retrograding, however, as he fought, towards his own party. Grimes, who had for some time before this recovered and joined the light once more, was returning, after having pursued several of the Ribbonmen past the market-house, where he spied Kelly thus engaged. With a Volunteer gun in his hand, and furious with the degradation of his former defeat, he ran over and struck him with the butt-end of it upon the temple—and Denis fell. When the stroke was given, an involuntary cry of 'Murder—foul, foul!' burst from those who looked on from the windows; and long John Steele, Grimes's father-in-law, in indignation, raised his cudgel to knock him down for this treacherous and malignant blow;— but a person out of Neal Cassidy's backyard hurled a round stone, about six pounds in weight, at Grimes's head, that felled him to the earth, leaving him as insensible, and nearly in as dangerous a state, as Kelly—for his jaw was broken.

"By this time the Catholics had retreated out of the town, and Denis might probably have received more punishment, had those who were returning from the pursuit recognised him; but James Wilson, seeing the dangerous situation in which he lay, came out, and, with the assistance of his servant-man, brought him into his own house. When the Orangemen had driven their adversaries off the field, they commenced the most hideous yellings through the streets—got music, and played party tunes—offered any money for the face of a Papist; and any of that religion who were so unfortunate as to make their appearance, were beaten in the most relentless manner. It was precisely the same thing on the part of the Ribbonmen; if a Protestant, but above all an Orangeman, came in their way, he was sure to be treated with barbarity: for the retaliation on either side was dreadfully unjust—the innocent suffering as well as the guilty. Leaving the window, I found Kelly in a bad state below stairs.

"'What's to be done?' said I to Wilson.

"'I know not,' replied he, 'except I put him between us on my jaunting car, and drive him home.'

"This appeared decidedly the best plan we could adopt; so, after putting to the horse, we placed him on the car, sitting one on each side of him, and, in this manner, left him at his own house."

"Did you run no risk," said I, "in going among Kelly's friends, whilst they were under the influence of party feeling and exasperated passion?"

"No," said he; "we had rendered many of them acts of kindness, and had never exhibited any spirit but a *friendly* one towards them; and such individuals, but only such, *might walk through a crowd of enraged Catholics or Protestants, quite unmolested.*"

"The next morning Kelly's landlord, Sir W. R——and two magistrates, were at his house, but he lay like a log, without sense or motion. Whilst they were there, Surgeon S——e arrived, and, after examining his head, declared that the skull was fractured. During that and the following day, the house was surrounded by crowds, anxious to know his state; and nothing might be heard amongst most of them, but loud and undisguised expressions of the most ample revenge. The wife was frantic; and, on seeing me, hid her face in her hands, exclaiming,

"'Ah, Sir, I knew it would come to this; and you, too, tould him the same thing. *My* curse and *God's* curse on it for quarrelling! Will it never stop in the counthry, till they rise some time, and murdher one another out of the face!'

"As soon as the swelling in his head was reduced, Surgeon S——e performed the operation of trepanning, and thereby saved his life; but his strength and intellect were gone—and he just lingered for four months, a feeble, drivelling simpleton, until, in consequence of a cold, which produced inflammation in the brain, he died, as hundreds have died, the victim of party spirit."

Such was the account which I heard of my old school-fellow, Denis Kelly; and, indeed, when I reflected upon the nature of the education he received, I could not but admit, that the consequences were such as might naturally be expected to result from it.

The next morning a relation of Mrs. Kelly's came down to my brother, hoping that, as they wished to have as decent a funeral as possible, he would be so kind as to attend it.

"Musha, God knows, Sir," said the man, "it's poor Denis, heavens be his bed! that had the regard and reverence for every one, young and ould, of your father's family; and it's himself that would be the proud man, if he was living, to see you, Sir, riding after his coffin."

"Well," said my brother, "let Mrs. Kelly know, that I shall certainly attend, and so will my brother, here, who has come to pay me a visit.—Why, I believe, Tom, you forget him!"

"Your brother, Sir! Is it Master Toby, that used to cudgel the half of the counthry when he was at school? Gad's my life, *Masther* Toby, (I was now about thirty-six) but it's your four quarters, sure enough! Arrah, thin, Sir, who'd think it—you're grown so full and stout?—but, faix, you'd always the bone in you! Ah, Masther Toby!" said he, "he's lying cowld, this morning, that would be the happy man to lay his eyes wanst more upon you. Many an' many's the winther's evening did he spind, talking about the time when you and he were bouchals together, and of the pranks you played at school, but especially of the time you both leathered the four Grogans, and tuck the apples from them—my poor fellow!—and now to be stretched a corpse, lavin' his poor widdy and childher behind him!"

I accordingly expressed my sorrow for Denis's death, which, indeed, I sincerely regretted, for he possessed materials for an excellent character, had not all that was amiable and good in him been permitted to run wild.

As soon as my trunk and travelling-bag had been brought from the inn, where I had left them the preceding night, we got our horses, and, as we wished to show particular respect to Denis's remains, rode up, with some of our friends, to the house. When we approached, there were large crowds of the country-people before the door of his well-thatched and respectable-looking dwelling, which had three chimneys, and a set of sash-windows, clean and well glazed. On our arrival, I was soon recognised and surrounded by numbers of those to whom I had formerly been known, who received and welcomed me with a warmth of kindness and sincerity, which it would be in vain to look for among the peasantry of any other nation.

Indeed, I have uniformly observed, that when no religious or political feeling influences the heart and principles of an Irish peasants he is singularly sincere and faithful in his attachments, and has always a bias to the generous and the disinterested. To my own knowledge, circumstances frequently occur, in which the ebullition of party spirit is altogether temporary, subsiding after the cause that produced it has passed away, and leaving the kind peasant to the natural, affectionate, and generous impulses of his character. But poor Paddy, unfortunately, is as combustible a material in politics or religion, as in fighting—thinking it his duty to take the weak* side, without any other consideration, than because it is the weak side.

*A gentleman once told me an anecdote, of which he was an eye-witness. Some peasants, belonging to opposite factions, had met under peculiar circumstances; there were, however, two on one side, and four on the other—in this case, there was likely to be no fight; but, in order to balance the number, one of the more numerous party joined the weak side—"bekase, boys, it would be a burnin' shame, so it would, for four to kick two; and, except I join them, by the powers, there's no chance of there being a bit of sport, or a row, at all at all!" Accordingly, he did join them, and the result of it was, that he and his party were victorious; so honestly did he fight!

When we entered the house I was almost suffocated with the strong fumes of tobacco-smoke, snuff, and whiskey; and, as I had been an old school-fellow of Denis', my appearance was the signal for a general burst of grief among his relations, in which the more distant friends and neighbours of the deceased joined, to keep up the keening.I have often, indeed always, felt that there is something extremely touching in the Irish cry; in fact, that it breathes the very spirit of wild and natural sorrow. The Irish peasantry, whenever a death takes place, are exceedingly happy in seizing upon any contingent, circumstances that may occur, and making them subservient to the excitement of grief for the departed, or the exultation and praise of his character and virtues. My entrance was a proof of this—I had scarcely advanced to the middle of the floor, when my intimacy with the deceased, our boyish sports, and even our quarrels, were adverted to with a natural eloquence and pathos, that, in spite of my firmness, occasioned me to feel the prevailing sorrow. They spoke, or chaunted mournfully, in Irish; but the substance of what they said was as follows:—

"Oh, Denis, Denis, avourneen! you're lying low, this morning of sorrow!—lying low are you, and does not know who it is (alluding to me) that is standing over you, weeping for the days you spent together in your youth! It's yourself, *acushla agus asthore machree,* (the pulse and beloved of my heart) that would stretch out the fight hand warmly to, welcome him to the place of his birth, where you had both been so often happy about the green hills and valleys with each other! He's here now, standing over you; and it's he, of all his family, kind and respectable as they are, that was your own favourite, Denis, *avourneen dheelish!* He alone was the companion that you loved!—with no other could you be happy!—For him did you fight, when he wanted a friend in your young quarrels! and if you had a dispute with him, were not you sorry for it? Are you not now stretched in death before him, and will he not forgive you?"

All this was uttered, of course, extemporaneously, and without the least preparation. They then passed on to an enumeration of his virtues as a father, a husband, son, and brother—specified his worth as he stood related to society in general, and his kindness as a neighbour and a friend.

An occurrence now took place, which may serve in some measure, to throw light upon many of the atrocities and outrages which take place in Ireland. Before I mention it, however, I think it necessary to make a few observations relative to it I am convinced that those who are intimately acquainted with the Irish peasantry, will grant that there is not on the earth a class of people in whom the domestic affections of blood-relationship are so pure, strong, and sacred. The birth of a child will occasion a poor man to break in upon the money set apart for his landlord, in order to keep the christening among his friends and neighbours with due festivity. A marriage exhibits a spirit of joy, an exuberance of happiness and delight, to be found only in the Green Island; and the death of a member of a family is attended with a sincerity of grief, scarcely to be expected from men so much the creatures of the more mirthful feelings. In fact, their sorrow is a solecism inhumanity—at once deep and loud—mingled up, even in its greatest paroxysms, with a laughter-loving spirit. It is impossible that an Irishman, sunk in the lowest depths of affliction, could permit his grief to flow in all the sad solemnity of affliction, even for a day, without some glimpse of his natural humour throwing a faint and rapid light over the gloom within him. No: there is an amalgamation of sentiments in his mind, which, as I said before, would puzzle any philosopher to account for. Yet it would be wrong to say, though his grief has something of an unsettled and ludicrous character about it, that he is incapable of the most subtle and delicate shades of sentiment, or the deepest and most desolating intensity of sorrow. But he laughs off those heavy vapours which hang about the moral constitution of the people of other nations, giving them a morbid habit, which leaves them neither strength nor firmness to resist calamity—which they feel less keenly than an Irishman, exactly as a healthy man will feel the pangs of death with more acuteness than one who is wasted away by debility and decay. Let any man witness an emigration, and he will satisfy himself that this is true. I am convinced that Goldsmith's inimitable description of one in his "Deserted Village," was a picture drawn from actual observation. Let him observe the emigrant as he crosses the Atlantic, and he will find, although he joins the jest, and the laugh, and the song, that he will seek a silent corner or a silent hour to indulge the sorrow which he still feels for the friends, the companions, and the native fields that he has left behind him. This constitution of mind is beneficial: the Irishman seldom or never hangs himself, because he is capable of too much real feeling to permit himself to become the slave of that which is factitious. There is no void in his affections or sentiments, which a morbid and depraved sensibility could occupy; but his feelings, of what character soever they may be, are strong, because they are fresh and healthy. For this reason, I maintain, that when the domestic affections come under the influence of either grief or joy, the peasantry of no nation are capable of feeling so deeply. Even on the ordinary occasions of death, sorrow, though it alternates with mirth and cheerfulness, in a manner peculiar to themselves, lingers long in the unseen recesses of domestic life: *any hand therefore, whether by law or violence, that plants a wound* HERE, *will suffer to the death.*

When my brother and I entered the house, the body had just been put into the coffin; and it is usual after this takes place, and before it is nailed down, for the immediate relatives of the family to embrace the deceased, and take their last look and farewell to his remains. In the present instance, the children were brought over, one by one, to perform that trying and melancholy ceremony. The first was an infant on the breast, whose little innocent mouth was held down to that of its dead father; the babe smiled upon his still and solemn features, and would have played with his grave clothes, but that the murmur of unfeigned sorrow which burst from all present, occasioned it to be removed. The next was a fine little girl, of three or four years, who inquired where they were going to bring her daddy, and asked if he would not soon come back to her.

"My daddy's sleepin' a long time," said the child, "but I'll waken him till he sings me 'Peggy Slevin.' I like my daddy best, bekase I sleep wid him—and he brings me good things from the fair, he bought me this ribbon," said she, pointing to a ribbon which he had purchased for her.

The rest of the children were sensible of their loss, and truly it was a distressing scene. His eldest son and daughter, the former about fourteen, the latter about two years older lay on the coffin, kissing his lips, and were with difficulty torn away from it.

"Oh!" said the boy, "he is going from us, and night or day we will never see him or hear of him more! Oh! father—father—is that the last sight we are ever to see of your face? Why, father dear, did you die, and leave us for ever—for ever— wasn't your heart good to us, and your words kind to us—Oh! your last smile is smiled—your last kiss given—and your last kind word spoken to your childhre that you loved, and that loved you as we did. Father, core of my heart, are you gone for ever, and your voice departed? Oh! the murdherers, oh! the murdherers, the murdherers!" he exclaimed, "that killed my father; for only for them, he would be still wid us: but, by the God that's over me, if I live, night or day I will not rest, till I have blood for blood; nor do I care who hears it, nor if I was hanged the next minute."*

As these words escaped him, a deep and awful murmur of suppressed vengeance burst from his relations. At length their sorrow became too strong to be repressed; and as it was the time to take their last embrace and look of him, they came up, and after fixing their eyes on his face in deep affliction, their lips began to quiver, and their countenance became convulsed. They then burst out simultaneously into a tide of violent grief, which, after having indulged in it for some time, they checked. But the resolution of revenge was stronger than their grief, for standing

*Such were the words.

over his dead body—they repeated, almost word for word, the vow of vengeance which the son had just sworn. It was really a scene dreadfully and terribly solemn; and I could not avoid reflecting upon the mystery of nature, which can, from the deep power of domestic affection, cause to spring a determination to crime of so black a dye.—Would to God that our peasantry had a clearer sense of moral and religious duties, and were not left so much as they are to the headlong impulse of an ardent temperament, and an impetuous character; and would to God that the clergy who superintend their education and morals, had a better knowledge of human nature!

During all this time the heart-broken widow sat beyond the coffin, looking upon what passed with a stupid sense of bereavement; and when they had all performed this last ceremony, it was found necessary to tell her that the time was come for the procession of the funeral, and that they only waited for her to take, as the rest did, her last look and embrace of her husband. When she heard this, it pierced her like an arrow: she became instantly collected, and her complexion assumed a dark sallow shade of despairing anguish, which it was an affliction even to look upon. She then stooped over the coffin, and kissed him several times, after which she ceased sobbing, and lay silently with her mouth to his.

The character of a faithful wife sorrowing for a beloved husband, has that in it which compels both respect and sympathy. There was not at this moment a dry eye in the house. She still lay silent on the coffin; but, as I observed that her bosom seemed not to heave as it did a little before, I was convinced that she had become insensible. I accordingly beckoned to Kelly's brother, to whom I mentioned what I had suspected; and, on his going over to ascertain the truth, he found her as I had said. She was then brought to the air, and after some trouble recovered; but I recommended them to put her to bed, and not to subject her to any unnecessary anguish, by a custom which was really too soul-piercing to endure. This, however, was, in her opinion, the violation of an old rite, sacred to her heart and affections—she would not hear of it for an instant. Again she was helped out between her brother and brother-in-law; and, after stooping down, and doing as the other had done—

"Now," said she, "I will sit here, and keep him under my eye as long as I can—surely you won't blame me for it; you all know the kind husband he was to me, and the good right I have to be sorry for him! Oh!" she added, "is it thrue at all?—is he my own Denis, the young husband of my early—and my first love, in good arnest, dead, and going to leave me here—me, Denis, that you loved so tindherly, and our childher, that your brow was never clouded aginst? Can I believe myself,

or is it a dhrame? Denis, *avick machree! avick machree!* your hand was dreaded, and
a good right it had, for it was the manly hand, that was ever and always raised in
defence of them that wanted a friend; abroad, in the faction-fight, against the
oppressor, your name was ever feared, *acushla!*—but *at home*—AT HOME—*where
was your fellow?* Denis achra, do you know the lips that's spaking to you?——your
young bride—your heart's light—Oh! I rimimber the day you war married to me
like yesterday. Oh! avourneen, then and since wasn't the heart of your own Honor
bound up in you—yet not a word even to me. Well, agrah machree, tisn't your
fault, it's the first time you ever refused to spake to your own Honor. But you're
dead, avourneen, or it wouldn't be so—you're dead before my eyes—husband of
my heart, and all my hopes and happiness goes into the coffin and the grave along
wid you, for ever!"

All this time she was rocking herself from side to side, her complexion pale and
ghastly as could be conceived. When the coffin was about to be closed, she retired
until it was nailed down, after which she returned with her bonnet and cloak on
her, ready to accompany it to the grave. I was astonished—for I thought she could
not have walked two steps without assistance; but it was the custom, and to neglect
it, I found, would have thrown the imputation of insincerity upon her grief. While
they were preparing to bring the coffin out, I could hear the chat and conversation
of those who were standing in crowds before the door, and occasionally a loud,
vacant laugh, and sometimes a volley of them, responsive to the jokes of some rustic wit, probably the same person who acted master of the revels at the wake.

Before the coffin was finally closed, Ned Corrigan, whom I had put to flight
the preceding night, came up, and repeated the *De profundis* in very strange Latin,
over the corpse. When this was finished, he got a jug of holy water, and after dipping his thumb in it, first made the sign of the cross upon his own forehead, and
afterwards sprinkled it upon all present, giving my brother and myself an extra
compliment, supposing, probably, that we stood most in need of it. When this was
over, he sprinkled the corpse and the coffin in particular most profusely. He then
placed two pebbles from Lough Derg, and a bit of holy candle, upon the breast of
the corpse, and having said a *Pater* and *Ave,* in which he was joined by the people,
he closed the lid, and nailed it down.

"Ned," said his brother, "are his feet and toes loose?"

"Musha, but that's more than myself knows," replied Ned—"Are they, Katty?"
said he, inquiring from the sister of the deceased.

"Arrah, to be sure, avourneen!" answered Katty—"div you think we would lave
him to be tied that-a-way, when he'd be risin' out of his last bed? Wouldn't it be

too bad to have his toes tied thin, avourneen?"

The coffin was then brought out and placed upon four chairs before the door, to be keened; and, in the mean time, the friends and well-wishers of the deceased were brought into the room to get each a glass of whiskey, as a token of respect. I observed also, that such as had not seen any of Kelly's relations until then, came up, and shaking hands with them, said—"I'm sorry for your loss!" This expression of condolence was uniform, and the usual reply was—"Thank you, Mat, or Jim!" with a pluck of the skirts, accompanied by a significant nod, to follow. They then got a due share of whiskey; and it was curious, after they came out, their faces a little flushed, and their eyes watery with the strong, ardent spirits, to hear with what heartiness and alacrity they entered into Denis's praises.

When he had been keened in the street, there being no hearse, the coffin was placed upon two handspikes which were fixed across, but parallel to each other under it. These were borne by four men, one at the end of each, with the point of it crossing his body a little below his stomach; in other parts of Ireland, the coffin is borne on the shoulders, but this is more convenient and less distressing.

When we got out upon the road, the funeral was of great extent—for Kelly had been highly respected. On arriving at the *merin* which bounded the land he had owned, the coffin was laid down, and a loud and wailing *keena* took place over it. It was again raised, and the funeral proceeded in a direction which I was surprised to see it take, and it was not until an acquaintance of my brother's had explained the matter that I understood the cause of it. In Ireland when a murder is perpetrated, it is usual, as the funeral proceeds to the grave-yard, to bring the corpse to the house of him who committed the crime, and lay it down at his door, while the relations of the deceased kneel down, and, with an appalling solemnity, utter the deepest imprecations, and invoke the justice of heaven on the head of the murderer. This, however, is usually omitted if the residence of the criminal be completely out of the line of the funeral, but if it be possible, by any circuit, to approach it, this dark ceremony is never omitted. In cases where the crime is doubtful, or unjustly imputed, those who are thus visited come out, and laying their right hand upon the coffin, protest their innocence of the blood of the deceased, calling God to witness the truth of their asseverations; but, in cases where the crime is clearly proved against the murderer, the door is either closed, the ceremony repelled by violence, or the house abandoned by the inmates until the funeral passes.

The death of Kelly, however, could not be actually, or, at least, directly considered a murder, for it was probable that Grimes did not inflict the stroke with an intention of taking away his life, and, besides, Kelly survived it four months.—

Grimes's house was not more than fifteen perches from the road; and when the corpse was opposite the little bridle way that led tip to it, they laid it down for a moment, and the relations of Kelly surrounded it, offering up a short prayer, with uncovered heads. It was then borne toward the house, whilst the keening commenced in a loud and wailing cry, accompanied with clapping of hands, and every other symptom of external sorrow. But, independent of their compliance with this ceremony, as an old usage, there is little doubt that the appearance of any thing connected with the man who certainly occasioned Kelly's death, awoke a keener and more intense sorrow for his loss. The wailing was thus continued until the coffin was laid opposite Grimes's door; nor did it cease then, but, on the contrary, was renewed with louder and more bitter lamentations.

As the multitude stood compassionating the affliction of the widow and orphans, it was the most impressive and solemn spectacle that could be witnessed. The very house seemed to have a condemned look; and, as a single wintry breeze waved a tuft of long grass that grew on a seat of turf at the side of the door, it brought the vanity of human enmity before my mind with melancholy force. When the keening ceased, Kelly's wife, with her children, knelt, their faces towards the house of their enemy, and invoked, in the strong language of excited passion, the justice of heaven upon the head of the man who had left her a widow, and her children fatherless. I was anxious to know if Grimes would appear to disclaim the intention of murder; but I understood that he was at market—for it happened to be market-day.

"Come out!" said the widow—"come out, and look at the sight that's here before you! Come and view *your own work!* Lay but your hand upon the coffin, and the blood of him you murdhered will spout, before God and these Christhen people, in your guilty face! But, oh! may the Almighty God bring this home to you!*—May you never lave this life, John Grimes, till worse nor has overtaken me and mine falls upon you and yours! May our curse light upon you this day!—the curse, I say, of the widow and the orphans, that your bloody hand has made us, may it blast you! May you, and all belonging to you wither off of the 'arth! Night and day, sleeping and waking—like snow off the ditch may you melt, until your name and your place will be disremimbered, except to be cursed by them that will hear of you and your hand of murdher! Amin, we pray God this day!—and the widow and orphan's prayer will not fall to the ground while your guilty head is above? Childhre, did you all say it?"

At this moment a deep, terrific murmur, or rather ejaculation, corroborative of assent to this dreadful imprecation, pervaded the crowd in a fearful manner; their

---

*Does not this usage illustrate the proverb of the guilt being brought home to a man, when there is no doubt of his criminality?

countenances darkened, their eyes gleamed, and their scowling visages, stiffened into an expression of determined vengeance.

When these awful words were uttered, Grimes's wife and daughters approached the window in tears, sobbing, at the same time, loudly and bitterly.

"You're wrong," said the wife—"you're wrong, Widow Kelly, in saying that my husband *murdhered* him!—he did *not* murdher him; for, when you and yours were far from him, I heard John Grimes declare before the God who's to judge him, that he had no thought or intention of taking his life; he struck him in anger, and the blow did him an injury that was not intended. Don't curse him, Honor Kelly," said she—"don't curse him so fearfully; but, above all, don't curse me and my innocent childher, for we never harmed you, nor wished you ill! *But it was this party work did it!* Oh, my God!" she exclaimed, wringing her hands, in utter bitterness of spirit, "when will it be ended between friends and neighbours, that ought to live in love and kindness together, instead of fighting in this blood-thirsty manner!"

She then wept more violently, as did her daughters.

"May God give me mercy in the last day, Mrs. Kelly, as I pity from my heart and soul you and your orphans," she continued; "but don't curse us, for the love of God—for you know we should forgive our enemies, as we ourselves, that are the enemies of God, hope to be forgiven."

"May God forgive me, then, if I have wronged you or your husband," said the widow, softened by their distress; "but you know, that whether he intended his life or not, the stroke he gave him has left my childher without a father, and myself dissolate. Oh, heavens above me!" she exclaimed, in a scream of distraction and despair, "is it possible—is it thrue—that my manly husband—the best father that ever breathed the breath of life—my own Denis, is lying dead—murdhered before my eyes! Put your hands on my head, some of you—put your hands on my head, or it will go to pieces. Where are you, Denis—where are you, the strong of hand, and the tender of heart? Come to me, darling, I want you in my distress. I want comfort, Denis; and I'll take it from none but yourself, for kind was your word to me in all my afflictions!"

All present were affected; and, indeed, it was difficult to say, whether Kelly's wife or Grimes's was more to be pitied at the moment. The affliction of the latter and of her daughters was really pitiable; their sobs were loud, and the tears streamed down their cheeks like rain. When the widow's exclamations had ceased, or rather were lost in the loud cry of sorrow which were uttered by the keeners and friends of the deceased—they, too, standing somewhat apart from the rest, joined in it bitterly; and the solitary wail of Mrs. Grimes differing in character from that of those who had been trained to modulate the most profound grief into strains of a melancholy nature, was particularly wild and impressive. At all events, her Christian demeanour, joined to the sincerity of her grief, appeased the enmity of many; so true is it that a soft answer turneth away wrath. I could perceive, however, that the resentment of Kelly's male relations did not at all appear to be in any degree moderated.

The funeral again proceeded, and I remarked that whenever a strange passenger happened to meet it, he always turned back, and accompanied it for a short distance, after which he resumed his journey, it being considered unlucky to omit this usage on meeting a funeral. Denis's residence was not more than two miles from the churchyard, which was situated in the town where be had received the fatal blow. As soon as we had got on about the half of this way, the priest of the parish met us, and the funeral, after proceeding a few perches more, turned into a green field, in the corner of which stood a table with the apparatus for saying mass spread upon it.

The coffin was then laid down once more, immediately before this temporary altar; and the priest, after having robed himself, the wrong side of the vestments out, as is usual in the case of death, began to celebrate mass for the dead, the congregation all kneeling. When this was finished, the friends of the deceased approached the altar, and after some private conversation, the priest turned round, and inquired aloud—

"Who will give offerings?"

The people were acquainted with the manner in which this matter is conducted, and accordingly knew what to do. When the priest put the question, Denis's brother, who was a wealthy man, came forward, and laid down two guineas on the altar; the priest took this up, and putting it on a plate, set out among the multitude, accompanied by two or three of those who were best acquainted with the inhabitants of the parish. He thus continued putting the question, distinctly, after each man had paid; and according as the money was laid down, those who accompanied the priest pronounced the name of the person who gave it, so that all present might hear it. This is also done to enable the friends of the deceased to know not only those who show them this mark of respect, but those who neglect it, in order that they may treat them in the same manner on similar occasions. The amount of money so received is very great; for there is a kind of emulation among the people, as to who will act with most decency and spirit, that is exceedingly beneficial to the priest. In such instances the difference of religion is judiciously overlooked; for although the prayers of Protestants are declined on those occasions, yet it seems the same objection does not hold good against their money, and accordingly they pay as well as the rest. When the priest came round to where I stood, he shook hands with my brother, with whom he appeared to be on very friendly and familiar terms; he and I were then introduced to each other.

"Come," said he, with a very droll expression of countenance, shaking the plate at the same time up near my brother's nose—"Come, Mr. D'Arcy, down with your offerings, if you wish to have a friend with St. Peter when you go as far as the gates; down with your money, Sir, and you shall be remembered, depend upon it."

"Ah!" said my brother, pulling out a guinea, "I would with the greatest pleasure; but I fear this guinea is not orthodox. I'm afraid it has the heretical mark upon it."

"In that case," replied his reverence laughing heartily, "your only plan is to return it to the bosom of the church, by laying it on the plate here—it will then be *within the pale,* you know."

This reply produced a good deal of good-humour among that part of the crowd which immediately surrounded them—not excepting his nearest relations, who laughed heartily.

"Well," said my brother, as he laid it on the plate, "how many prayers will you offer up in my favour for this?"

"Leave *that* to myself," said his Reverence, looking at the *money*—"it will be before you when you go to St. Peter."

He then held the plate over to me in a droll manner; and I added another guinea to my brother's gift; for which I had the satisfaction of having my name called out so loud, that it might be heard a quarter of a mile off.

"God bless you, Sir," said the priest, "and I thank you."

"John," said I, when he left us, "I think that is a pleasant, and rather a sensible man?"

"He's as jovial a soul," replied my brother, "as ever gave birth to a jest, and he sings a right good song. Many a convivial hour have he and I spent together; but, as to being a Catholic in *their* sense—Lord help you! At all events, he is no bigot; but, on the contrary, a liberal—and, putting religion out of the question, a kind and benevolent man."

When the offerings were all collected, he returned to the altar, repeated a few additional prayers in prime style as rapid as lightning; and after hastily shaking the holy water on the crowd, the funeral moved on. It was now two o'clock, the day clear and frosty, and the sun unusually bright for the season. During mass, many were added to those who formed the funeral train at the outset; so that, when we got out upon the road, the procession appeared very large. After this, few or none joined it; for it is esteemed by no means *"dacent"* to do so *after* mass—because, in that case, the matter is ascribed to an evasion of the offerings; but those whose delay has not really been occasioned by this motive, make it a point to pay them at the grave-yard, or after the interment, and sometimes even on the following day—so jealous are the peasantry of having any degrading suspicion attached to their generosity.

The order of the funeral now was as follows:—Foremost the women—next to them the corpse, surrounded by the relations—the eldest son, in deep affliction, "led the coffin," as chief mourner, holding in his hand the corner of a sheet or piece of linen, fastened to the *mort-cloth.* After the coffin came those who were on foot, and in the rear were the equestrians. When we were a quarter of a mile from the church-yard, the funeral was met by a dozen of singing boys, belonging to a chapel choir, which the priest, who was fond of music, had some time before formed. They fell in, two by two, immediately behind the corpse, and commenced singing the *Requiem,* or Latin hymn for the dead.

The scene through which we passed at this time, though not clothed with the verdure and luxuriant beauty of summer, was, nevertheless marked by that solemn and decaying splendour which characterises a fine country, lit up by the melancholy light of a winter setting sun. It was, therefore, much more in character with the occasion. Indeed I felt it altogether beautiful; and, as the "dying day-hymn stole aloft," the dim sun-beams fell, through a vista of naked motionless trees, upon the coffin, which was borne with a slower and more funereal pace then before, in a manner that threw a solemn and visionary light upon the whole procession. This, however, was raised to something dreadfully impressive, when the long train, thus proceeding with a motion so mournful, was seen each covered with a profusion of crimson ribbons, to indicate that the corpse they bore owed his death to a deed of murder. The circumstance of the sun glancing his rays upon the coffin was not unobserved by the peasantry, who considered it as a good omen to the spirit of the departed.

As we went up the street which had been the scene of the quarrel that proved so fatal to Kelly, the coffin was again laid down on the spot where he received his death-blow; and, as was usual, the wild and melancholy *keena* was raised. My brother saw many of Grimes's friends among the spectators, but he himself was not visible. Whether Kelly's party saw them or not, we could not say; if they did, they seemed not to notice them, for no expression of revenge or indignation escaped them.

At length, we entered the last receptacle of the dead. The coffin was now placed upon the shoulders of the son and brothers of the deceased, and borne round the church-yard; whilst the priest, with his stole upon him, preceded it, reading prayers for the eternal repose of the soul. Being then laid beside the grave, a *"De profundis"* was repeated by the priest and the mass-server; after which, a portion of fresh clay, carried from the fields, was brought to his Reverence, who read a prayer over it, and consecrated it. This is a ceremony which is never omitted at the interment of a Roman Catholic. When it was over, the coffin was lowered into the grave, and the blessed clay shaken over it. The priest now took the shovel in his own hands, and threw in the three first shovelsful—one in the name of the Father, one in the name of the Son, and one in the name of the Holy Ghost. The sexton then took it, and in a short time Denis Kelly was fixed for ever in his narrow bed.

While these ceremonies were going forward, the church-yard presented a characteristic picture. Beside the usual groups who straggle through the place, to amuse themselves by reading the inscriptions on the tombs, you might see many individuals kneeling on particular graves, where some relation lay—for the benefit of whose soul they offered up their prayers, with an attachment and devotion which one cannot but admire. Sometimes all the surviving members of the family would assemble, and repeat a *Rosary* for the same purpose. Again, you might see an unhappy woman beside a newly-made grave, giving way to lamentation and sorrow for the loss of a husband, or of some beloved child. Here, you might observe the "last bed" ornamented with hoops, decked in white paper, emblematic of the virgin innocence of the individual who slept below;—there, a little board-cross informing you that "this monument was erected by a disconsolate husband to the memory of his beloved wife." But that which excited greatest curiosity was a sycamore tree, which grew in the middle of the burying ground.

It is necessary to inform the reader, that in Ireland many of the church-yards are exclusively appropriated to the interment of Roman Catholics, and, consequently, no Protestant corpse would be permitted to pollute or desecrate them. This was one of them: but it appears that, by some means or other, the body of a Protestant had been interred in it—and hear the consequence! The next morning heaven marked its disapprobation of this awful visitation by a miracle; for, ere the sun rose from the east, a full-grown sycamore had shot up out of the heretical grave, and stands there to this day, a monument at once of the profanation and its consequence. Crowds were looking at this tree, feeling a kind of awe, mingled with wonder, at the deed which drew down such a visible and lasting mark of God's displeasure. On the tomb-stones near Kelly's grave, men and women were seated, smoking tobacco to their very heart's content; for, with that profusion which char acterises the Irish in every thing, they had brought out large quantities of tobacco, whiskey, and bunches of pipes. On such occasions it is the custom for those who attend the wake or the funeral to bring a full pipe home with them; and it is expected that as often as it is used, they will remember to say, "God be merciful to the soul of him that this pipe was over."

The crowd, however, now began to disperse and the immediate friends of the deceased sent the priest, accompanied by Kelly's brother, to request that we would come in, as the last mark of respect to poor Denis's memory, and take a glass of wine and a cake.

"Come, Toby," said my brother, "we may as well go in, as it will gratify them; we need not make much delay, and we will still be at home in sufficient time for dinner."

"Certainly you will," said the priest; "for you shall both come and dine with me to-day."

"With all my heart," said my brother; "I have no objection, for I know you give it good."

When we went in, the punch was already reeking from immense white jugs, that couldn't hold less than a gallon each,

"Now," said his Reverence, very properly, "you have had a dacent and creditable funeral, and have managed every thing with great propriety; let me request, therefore, that you will not get drunk, nor permit yourselves to enter into any disputes or quarrels; but be moderate in what you take, and go home peaceably."

"Why, thin, your Reverence," replied the widow, "he's now in his grave, and, thank God, it's he that had the dacent funeral all out—ten good gallons did we put on you, astore, and it's yourself that liked the dacent thing, any how—but sure, Sir, it would shame him where he's lyin', if we disregarded him so far as to go home widout bringing in our friends, that didn't desart us in our throuble, an' thratin' them for their kindness."

While Kelly's brother was filling out all their glasses, the priest, my brother, and I, were taking a little refreshment. When the glasses were filled, the deceased's brother raised his in his hand, and said—

"Well, gintlemen," addressing us, "I hope you'll pardon me for not dhrinking your healths first; but people, you know, can't break through an ould custom, at any rate—so I give poor Denis's health, that's in his *warm* grave, and God be marciful to his sowl."*

The priest now winked at me to give them their own way; so we filled our glasses, and joined with the rest in drinking "Poor Denis's health, that's now in his

*A fact.

warm grave, and God be merciful to his soul."

When this was finished, they then drank ours, and thanked us for our kindness in attending the funeral. It was now past five o'clock; and we left them just setting into a hard bout of drinking, and rode down to his Reverence's residence.

"I saw you smile," said he, on our way, "at the blundering toast of Mat Kelly; but it would be labour in vain to attempt setting them right. What do they know about the distinctions of more refined life? Besides, I maintain, that what they said was as well calculated to express their affection, as if they had drunk honest Denis's *memory.* It is, at least, unsophisticated. But did you hear," said he, "of the apparition that was seen last night, on the mountain road above Denis's?"

"I did not *hear* of it," I replied, equivocating a little.

"Why," said he, "it is currently reported that the spirit of a murdered pedlar, which haunts the hollow of the road at Drumfurrar, chased away the two servant men as they were bringing home the coffin, and that finding it a good bit, he then got into it, and walked half a mile along the road, with the wooden surtout upon him; and, finally, that to wind up the frolic, he left it on one end half-way between the bridge and Denis's house, after putting a crowd of the countrymen to flight. I suspect some droll knave has played them a trick. I assure you, that a deputation of them, who declared that they saw the coffin move along of itself, waited upon me this morning, to know whether they ought to have put him into the coffin, or gotten another."

"Well," said my brother, in reply to him, "after dinner we will probably throw some light upon that circumstance; for I believe my brother here knows something about it."

"So, Sir," said the priest, "I perceive you have been amusing yourself at their expense?"

I seldom spent a pleasanter evening than I did with Father Molloy, (so he was called,) who was, as my brother said, a shrewd, sensible man, possessed of convivial powers of the first order. He sang us several good songs; and, to do him justice, he had an excellent voice. He regretted very much the state of party and religious feeling, which he did every thing in his power to suppress.

"But," said he, "I have little co-operation in my efforts to communicate knowledge to my flock, and implant better feelings among them. You must know," he added, "that I am no great favourite among them. On being appointed to this parish by my bishop, I found that the young man who was curate to my predecessor, had formed a party against me, thinking, by that means, eventually to get the parish himself. Accordingly, on coming here, I found the chapel doors closed on me; so that a single individual among them would not recognise me as their proper pastor. By firmness and spirit, however, I at length succeeded, after a long struggle against the influence of the curate, in gaining admission to the altar; and, by a proper representation of his conduct to the bishop, I soon made my gentleman knock under. Although beginning to gain ground in the good opinion of the people, I am by no means yet a favourite. The curate and I scarcely speak; and great number of my parishioners brand me with the epithet of the *Orange priest;* and this principally because I occasionally associate with Protestants—a habit, gentlemen, which they will find some difficulty in making me give up, as long as I can have the pleasure," said he, bowing, "of seeing such guests at my table as those with whose company I am now honoured."

It was now near nine o'clock, and my brother was beginning to relate an anecdote concerning the clergyman who had preceded Father Molloy in the parish, when a messenger from Mr. Wilson, already alluded to, came up in breathless haste, requesting the priest, for God's sake to go down into town instantly, as the Kellys and the Grimeses were engaged in a fresh quarrel.

"My God!" he exclaimed—"when will this work have an end? But, to tell you the truth, gentlemen, I apprehended it; and I fear that something still more fatal to the parties, will yet be the consequence. Mr. D'Arcy you must try—what you can do with the Grimeses, and I will manage the Kellys."

We then proceeded to the town, which was but a very short distance from the priest's house; and, on arriving, found a large crowd before the door of the house in which the Kellys had been: drinking, engaged in hard conflict. The priest was on foot, and had brought his whip with him, it being an argument, in the hands of a Roman Catholic pastor, which tells so home, that it is not to be gainsayed. Mr. Molloy and my brother now dashed in amongst them; and by remonstrance, abuse, blows, and entreaty, they with difficulty succeeded in terminating the fight. They were also assisted by Mr. Wilson and other persons, who dared not, until their appearance, run the risk of interfering between them. Wilson's servant, who had come for the priest, was still standing beside me, looking on; and, while my brother and Mr. Molloy were separating the parties, I asked him how the fray commenced.

"Why, Sir," said he, "it bein' market-day, the Grimeses chanced to be in town, and this came to the ears of the Kellys, who were drinking in Cassidy's here, till they got tipsy; some of them then broke out, and began to go up and down the street, shouting for the face of a murdhering Grimes. The Grimeses, Sir, happened at the time to be drinking with a parcel of their friends in Joe Sherlock's, and hearing the Kellys calling out for them, why, as the dhrop, Sir, was in on both sides, they were soon at it. Grimes has given one of the Kellys a great bating; but Tom M'Guigan, Kelly's cousin, a little before we came down, I'm tould, has knocked the seven senses out of him, with a pelt of a brick-bat in the stomach."

Soon after this, however, the quarrel was got under; and, in order to prevent any more bloodshed that night my brother and I got the Kellys together, and brought them as far as our residence, on their way home. As we went along, they uttered awful vows, and determinations of the deepest revenge, swearing repeatedly, that they would shoot Grimes from behind a ditch, if they could not in any other manner have his blood. They seemed highly intoxicated; and several of them were cut and abused in a dreadful manner; even the women were in such a state of excitement and alarm, that grief for the deceased was, in many instances, forgotten. Several of both sexes were singing; some laughing with triumph at the punishment they had inflicted on the enemy; others of them, softened by what they had drunk, were weeping in tones of sorrow that might be heard a couple of miles off. Among the latter were many of the men, some of whom, as they staggered along with their frieze big-coats hanging off one shoulder clapped their hands, and roared like bulls, as if they intended, by the loudness of their grief then, to compensate for their silence when sober. It was also quite ludicrous to see the men kissing each other, sometimes in this maudling sorrow, and at others when exalted into the very madness of mirth. Such as had been cut in the scuffle, on finding the blood trickle down their faces, would wipe it off—then look at it, and break out into a parenthetical volley of curses against the Grimeses; after which, they would resume their grief, hug each other in mutual sorrow, and clap their hands as before. In short, such a group could be seen no where but in Ireland.

When my brother and I had separated from them, I asked him what had become of Vengeance, and if he were still in the country.

"No," said he; "with all his courage and watchfulness, he found that his life was not safe; he, accordingly, sold off his property, and collecting all his ready cash, emigrated to America, where, I hear, he is doing well."

"God knows," I replied, "I shouldn't be surprised if one half of the population were to follow his example, for the state of society here, among the lower orders, is truly deplorable."

THE HEDGE SCHOOL.

There never was a more unfounded calumny, than that which would impute to the Irish peasantry an indifference to education. I may, on the contrary, fearlessly assert that the lower orders of no country ever manifested such a positive inclination for literary acquirements, and that, too, under circumstances strongly calculated to produce carelessness and apathy on this particular subject. Nay, I do maintain, that he who is intimately acquainted with the character of our countrymen, must acknowledge, that their zeal for book learning, not only is strong and ardent, when opportunities of scholastic education occur, but that it increases in proportion as these opportunities are rare and unattainable. The very name and nature of Hedge Schools are proof of this for what stronger point could be made out, in illustration of my position, than the fact, that, despite of obstacles, whose very idea would crush ordinary enterprize—when not even a shed could be obtained in which to assemble the children of an Irish village, the worthy pedagogue selected the first green spot on the sunny side of a quick-set-thorn hedge, which he conceived adapted for his purpose, and there, under the scorching rays of a summer sun, and in defiance of spies and statutes, carried on the work of instruction. From this circumstance the name of Hedge School originated; and, however it may be associated with the ludicrous, I maintain, that it is highly creditable to the character of the people, and an encouragement to those who wish to see them receive pure and correct educational knowledge. A Hedge School, however, in its original sense, was but a temporary establishment, being only adopted until such a schoolhouse could be erected, as was in those days deemed sufficient to hold such a number of children as were expected, at all hazards, to attend it.

The opinion, I know, which has been long entertained of Hedge Schoolmasters, was, and still is, unfavourable; but the character of these worthy and eccentric persons has been misunderstood, for the stigma attached to their want of knowledge should have rather been applied to their want of morals, because, on this latter point only were they indefensible. The fact is, that Hedge Schoolmasters were a class of men, from whom morality was not expected by the peasantry; for strange to say, one of their strongest recommendations to the good opinion of the people, as far as their literary talents and qualifications were concerned, was an inordinate love of whiskey and if to this could be added a slight touch of derangement, the character was complete.

On once asking an Irish peasant, why he sent his children to a schoolmaster who was notoriously addicted to spirituous liquors, rather than to a man of sober habits who taught in the same neighbourhood,

"Why do I sind them to Mat Meegan, is it?" he replied—"and do you think, Sir," said he, "that I'd sind them to that dry-headed dunce, Mr. Frazher, with his black coat upon him, and his caroline hat, and him wouldn't taste a glass of poteen wanst in seven years? Mat, Sir, likes it, and teaches the boys ten times betther whin he's dhrunk nor whin he's sober; and you'll never find a good tacher, Sir, but's fond of it. As for Mat. when he's *half gone,* I'd turn him agin the country for deepness in larning; for it's then he rhymes it out of him, that it would do one good to hear him."

"So," said I, "you think that a love of drinking poteen is a sign of talent in a schoolmaster."

"Ay, or in any man else, Sir," he replied. "Look at tradesmen, and 'tis always the cleverest that you'll find fond of the dhrink! If you had hard Mat and Frazher, the other evening, at it—what a hare Mat made of him; but he was just in proper tune for it, being, at the time, purty well I thank you, and did not lave him a leg to stand upon. He took him in Euclid's Ailments and Logicals, and proved in Frazher's teeth, that the candlestick before them was the church-steeple, and Frazher himself the parson; and so sign was on it, the other couldn't disprove it, but had to give in."

"Mat, then," I observed, "is the most learned man on this walk."

"Why, thin, I doubt that same, Sir," replied he, "for all he's so great in the books; for, you see, while they were ding dust at it, who comes in but mad Delany, and he attacked Mat, and, in less than no time, rubbed the consate out of *him,* as clane as *he* did out of Frazher."

"Who is Delany?" I inquired.

"He was the makings of a priest, Sir, and was in Maynooth a couple of years, but he took in the knowledge so fast, that, bedad, he got *cracked wid larnin*'—for a *dunce,* you see, never cracks wid it, in regard of the thickness of the skull: no doubt but he's too many for Mat, and can go far beyond him in the books; but then, like that, he's still brightest whin he has a sup in his head."

These are prejudices which the Irish peasantry have long entertained concerning the character of hedge schoolmasters; but, granting them to be unfounded, as they generally are, yet it is an indisputable fact, that hedge schoolmasters were as superior in literary knowledge and acquirements to the class of men who are now engaged in the general education of the people, as they were beneath them in moral and religious character.—The former part of this assertion will, I am aware, appear rather startling to many. But it is true; and one great cause why the character of Society Teachers is undervalued, in many instances, by the people, proceeds from a conviction on their parts, that they are, and must be, incapable, from the slender portion of learning they have received, of giving their children a sound and practical education.

But that we may put this subject in a clearer light, we will give a sketch of the course of instruction which was deemed necessary for a hedge schoolmaster, and, let it be contrasted with that which falls to the lot of those engaged in the conducting of schools patronized by the Education Societies of the present day.

When a poor man, about twenty or thirty years ago, understood from the schoolmaster who educated his sons, that any of them was particularly "cute at his larnin'," the ambition of the parent usually directed itself to one of three objects—he would either make him a priest, a clerk, or a schoolmaster. The determination once fixed, the boy was set apart from every kind of labour, that he might be at liberty to bestow his undivided time and talents to the objects set before him. His parents strained every nerve to furnish him with the necessary books, and always took care that his appearance and dress should be more decent than those of any other member of the family. If the church were in prospect, he was distinguished, after he had been two or three years at his Latin, by the appellation of "the young priest," an epithet to him of the greatest pride and honour; but if destined only to wield the ferula, his importance in the family, and the narrow circle of his friends, was by no means so great. If, however, the goal of his future ambition as a schoolmaster was humbler, that of his literary career was considerably extended. He usually remained at the next school in the vicinity until he supposed that he had completely drained the master of all his knowledge. This circumstance was generally discovered in the following manner:—As soon as he judged himself a match for his teacher, and possessed sufficient confidence in his own powers, he penned him a formal challenge to meet him in literary contest, either in his own school, before competent witnesses, or at the chapel-green, on the Sabbath day, before the arrival of the priest, or probably after it—for the priest himself was generally the moderator and judge upon these occasions. This challenge was generally couched in rhyme, and either sent by the hands of a common friend, or posted upon the chapel door.

These contests, as the reader perceives, were always public, and were witnessed by the peasantry with intense interest. If the master sustained a defeat, it was not so much attributed to his want of learning, as to the overwhelming talent of his opponent; nor was the success of the pupil generally followed by the expulsion of the master—for this was but the first of a series of challenges which the former proposed to undertake, ere he eventually settled himself in the exercise of his profession.

I remember being present at one of them, and a ludicrous exhibition it was. The parish priest, a red-faced, jocular little man, was president, and his curate, a scholar of six feet two inches in height, and a schoolmaster from the next parish, were judges. I will only touch upon two circumstances in their conduct, which evinced a close, instinctive knowledge of human nature in the combatants. The master would not condescend to argue off his throne—a piece of policy to which, in my opinion, he owed his victory (for he won); whereas the pupil insisted that he should meet him on equal ground, face to face, in the lower end of the room. It was evident that the latter could not divest himself of his boyish terrors as long as the other sat, as it were, in the plenitude of his former authority, contracting his brows with habitual sternness, thundering out his arguments, with a most menacing and Stentorian voice, while he thumped his desk with his shut fist, or struck it with his great rule at the end of each argument, in a manner that made the youngster put his hands behind him several times, to be certain that that portion of his dress, which is *unmentionable,* was tight upon him.

If in these encounters the young candidate for the honours of the literary sceptre was not victorious, he again resumed his studies, under his old preceptor, with renewed vigour and becoming humility; but if he put the schoolmaster down, his next object was to seek out some other teacher, whose celebrity was unclouded within his own range. With him he had a fresh encounter, and its result was similar to what I have already related. If victorious, he sought out another and more learned opponent; and if defeated, he became the pupil of his conqueror—going night about, during his sojourn at the school, with the neighbouring farmers' sons, whom he assisted in their studies, as a compensation for his support. He was called, during these peregrinations, the *Poor Scholar,* a character which secured him the esteem and hospitable attention of the peasantry, who never fail in respect to any one characterised by a zeal for learning and knowledge.

In this manner he proceeded, a literary knight-errant, filled with a chivalrous love of letters, which would have done honour to the most learned peripatetic of them all; enlarging his own powers, and making fresh acquisitions of knowledge as he went along. His contests, his defeats, and his triumphs, of course, were frequent; and his habits of thinking and reasoning must have been considerably improved, his acquaintance with classical and mathematical authors rendered more intimate, and his powers of illustration and comparison more clear and happy.

After three or four years spent in this manner, he usually returned to his native place, sent another challenge to the schoolmaster, in the capacity of a candidate for his situation, and, if successful, drove him out of the district, and established himself in his situation. The vanquished master sought a new district, sent a new challenge, in his turn, to some other teacher, and usually put him to flight in the same manner. The terms of defeat or victory, according to their application, were called *sacking* and *bogging*.

"There was a great argument entirely, Sir," said a peasant once, when speaking of these contests, "'twas at the chapel on Sunday week, betane young Tom Brady, that was a poor scholar in Munsther, and Mr. Hartigan, the schoolmaster."

"And who was victorious?" I inquired.

"Why, Sir, and maybe 'twas young Brady that didn't *sack* him clane, before the priest and all, and went nigh to *bog* the priest himself in Greek. His Reverence was only two words beyant him; but he sacked the masther, any how, and showed him in the Grammatical and Dixonary where he was wrong."

"And what is Brady's object in life?" I asked. "What does he intend to do?"

"Intend to do, is it? I'm tould nothing less nor going into Thrinity College in Dublin, and expects to bate them all there, out and out; he's first to make something they call a seizure;* and, afther making that good, he's to be a counsellor. So, Sir, you see what it is to resave good schoolin', and to have the larnin'; but, indeed, it's Brady that's the great head-piece entirely."

Unquestionably, many who received instruction in this manner have distinguished themselves in the Dublin University; and I have no hesitation in saying, that young men educated in Irish hedge-schools, as they were called, have proved themselves to be better classical scholars and mathematicians, generally speaking, than any proportionate number of those educated in our first-rate academies. The Munster masters have long been, and still are, particularly celebrated for making excellent classical and mathematical scholars.

That a great deal of ludicrous pedantry generally accompanied this knowledge is not at all surprising, when we consider the rank these worthy teachers held in life, and the stretch of inflation at which their pride was kept by the profound reverence excited by their learning among the people. It is equally true, that each of them had a stock of *crambos* ready for accidental encounter, which would have puzzled Euclid or Sir Isaac Newton himself; but even these trained their minds to habits of acuteness and investigation. When a schoolmaster of this class had established himself as a good mathematician, the predominant enjoyment of his heart and life was to write the epithet Philomath after his name; and this, whatever

*Sizar.

document he subscribed, was never omitted. If he witnessed a will, it was Timothy Fagan, Philomath; if he put his name to a promissory note, it was Tim. Fagan, Philomath; if he addressed a love-letter to his sweetheart, it was still Timothy Fagan—or whatever the name might be—Philomath; and this was always written in legible and distinct copyhand, sufficiently large to attract the observation of the reader.

It was also usual for a man who had been a pre-eminent and extraordiary schol-ar, to have the epithet Great prefixed to his name. I remember one of this descrip-tion, who was called the Great O'Brien, par excellence. In the latter years of his life he gave up teaching, and led a circulating life, going round from school to school, and remaining a week or a month alternately among his brethren. His visits were considered an honour, and raised considerably the literary character of those with whom he resided; for he spoke of dunces with the most dignified contempt, and the general impression was, that he would scorn even to avail himself of their hos-pitality. Like most of his brethern, he could not live without the poteen; and his custom was, to drink a pint of it in its native purity before he entered into any lit-erary contest, or made any display of his learning at wakes or other Irish festivities; and most certainly, however blameable the practice, and injurious to health and morals, it threw out his talents and his powers in a most surprising manner.

It was highly amusing to observe the peculiarity which the consciousness of superior knowledge impressed upon the conversation and personal appearance of this decaying race. Whatever might have been the original conformation of their physical structure, it was sure, by the force of acquired habit, to transform itself into a stiff, erect, consequential, and unbending manner, ludicrously characteristic of an inflated sense of their extraordinary knowledge, and a proud and commiser-ating contempt of the dark ignorance by which, in despite of their own light, they were surrounded. Their conversation, like their own crambos, was dark and diffi-cult to be understood; their words, truly sesquipedalian; their voice, loud and com-manding in its tones; their deportment, grave and dictatorial, but completely inde-scribable, and certainly original to the last degree, in those instances where the ready, blundering, but genuine humour of their country maintained an unyielding rivalry in their disposition, against the natural solemnity which was considered necessary to keep up the due dignity of their character.

In many of these persons, where the original humour and gaiety of the disposi-tion were known, all efforts at the grave and dignified were complete failures, and these were enjoyed by the peasantry and their own pupils, nearly with the sensa-tions which the enactment of Hamlet by Liston would necessarily produce. At all events, their education, allowing for the usual exceptions, was by no means superficial; and the reader has already received a sketch of the trials which they had to undergo, before they considered themselves qualified to enter upon the duties of their calling. Their life was, in fact, a state of literary warfare; and they felt that a mere elementary knowledge of their business would have been insufficient to carry them, with suitable credit, through the attacks to which they were exposed from travelling teachers, whose mode of establishing themselves in schools, was, as I said, by driving away the less qualified, and usurping their places. This according to the law of opinion, and the custom which prevailed, was very easily effected, for the peasantry uniformly encouraged those whom they supposed to be the most competent; as to moral or religious instruction, neither was expected from them, so that the indifference of the moral character was no bar to their success.

———

The village of Findramore was situated at the foot of a long green hill, the outline of which formed a low arch, as it rose to the eye against the horizon. This hill was studded with clumps of beeches, and sometimes enclosed as a meadow. In the month of July, when the grass on it was long, many an hour have I spent in solitary enjoyment, watching the wavy motion produced upon its pliant surface by the sunny winds, or the flight of the cloud-shadows, like gigantic phantoms, as they swept rapidly over it, whilst the murmur of the rocking trees, and the glancing of their bright leaves in the sun, produced a heartfelt pleasure, the very memory of which rises in my imagination, like some fading recollection of a brighter world.

At the foot of this hill ran a clear, deep-banked river, bounded on one side by a slip of rich, level meadow, and on the other by a kind of common for the village geese, whose white feathers, during the summer season, lay scattered over its green surface. It was also the play-ground for the boys of the village school; for there ran that part of the river, which, with very correct judgment, the urchins had selected as their bathing-place. A little slope, or watering-ground in the bank, brought them to the edge of the stream, where the bottom fell away into the fearful depths of the whirlpool, under the hanging oak on the other bank. Well do I remember the first time I ventured to swim across it, and even yet do I see, in imagination, the two bunches of water flaggons on which the inexperienced swimmers trusted themselves in the water.

About two hundred yards above this, the *boreen,** which led from the village to the main road, crossed the river, by one of those old narrow bridges, whose arches rise like round ditches across the road—an almost impassable barrier to horse and car. On parsing the bridge, in a northern direction, you found a range of low

*A little road.

thatched houses on each side of the road; and if one o'clock, the hour of dinner, drew near, you might observe columns of blue smoke curling up from a row of chimneys, some made of wicker creels plastered over with a rich coat of mud; some, of old, narrow, bottomless tubs; and others, with a greater appearance of taste, ornamented with thick, circular ropes of straw, sewed together like bees' skeps, with the peel of a brier; and many having nothing but the open vent above. But the smoke by no means escaped by its legitimate aperture, for you might observe little clouds of it bursting out of the doors and windows; the panes of the latter being mostly stopped at other times with old hats and rags, were now left entirely open for the purpose of giving it a free escape.

Before the doors, on right and left, was a series of dunghills, each with its concomitant sink of green, rotten water; and if it happened that a stout-looking woman, with watery eyes and a yellow cap, hung loosely upon her matted locks, came, with a chubby urchin on one arm, and a pot of dirty water in her hand, its unceremonious ejection in the aforesaid sink would be apt to send you up the village with your finger and thumb (for what purpose you would yourself perfectly understand) closely, but not knowingly, applied to your nostrils. But, independently of this, you would be apt to have other reasons for giving your horse, whose heels are by this time surrounded by a dozen of barking curs, and the same number of shouting urchins, a pretty sharp touch of the spurs, as well as for complaining bitterly of the odour of the atmosphere. It is no landscape without figures; and you might notice, if you are, as I suppose you to be, a man of observation, in every sink as you pass along, a "slip of a pig," stretched in the middle of the mud, the very *beau ideal* of luxury, giving occasionally a long, luxuriant grunt, highly expressive of his enjoyment; or, perhaps, an old farrower, lying in indolent repose, with half a dozen young ones justling each other for their draught, and punching her belly with their little snouts, reckless of the fumes they are creating; whilst the loud crow of the cock, as he confidently flaps his wings on his own dunghill, gives the warning note for the hour of dinner.

As you advance, you will also perceive several faces thrust out of the doors, and rather than miss a sight of you, a grotesque visage peeping by a short cut through the painless windows—or, a tattered female flying to snatch up her urchin that has been tumbling itself, heels up, in the dust of the road, lest "the gintleman's horse might ride over it;" and if you happen to look behind, you may observe a shaggy-headed youth in tattered frize, with one hand thrust indolently in his breast, standing at the door in conversation with the inmates, a broad grin of sarcastic ridicule on his face, in the act of breaking a joke or two upon yourself, or your horse; or, perhaps your jaw may be saluted with a lump of clay, just hard enough not to fall asunder as it flies, cast by some ragged gorsoon from behind a hedge, who squats himself in a ridge of corn to avoid detection.

Seated upon a hob at the door, you may observe a toil-worn man, without coat or waistcoat; his red, muscular, sun-burnt shoulder peering through the remnant of a shirt, mending his shoes with a piece of twisted flax, called a *lingel*—or, perhaps, sewing two footless stockings (*or martyeens*) to his coat, as a substitute for sleeves.

In the gardens, which are usually fringed with nettles, you will see a solitary labourer, working with that carelessness and apathy that characterise an Irishman when he labours *for himself*—leaning upon his spade to look after you, and glad of any excuse to be idle.

The houses, however, are not all such as I have described—far from it. You see, here and there, between the more humble cabins, a stout, comfortable-looking farm-house, with ornamental thatching, and well-glazed windows; adjoining to which is a hagyard, with five or six large stacks of corn, well trimmed and roped, and a fine, yellow, weather-beaten old hay-rick, half cut—not taking into account twelve or thirteen circular strata of stones, that mark out the foundations on which others had been raised. Neither is the rich swell of oaten or wheaten bread, which the good wife is baking on the griddle, unpleasant to your nostrils; nor would the bubbling of a large pot, in which you might see, should you chance to enter, a prodigious square of fat, yellow, and almost transparent bacon tumbling about, be an unpleasant object;—truly, as it hangs over a large fire, with well-swept hearth-stone, it is in good keeping with the white settle and chairs, and the dresser with noggins, wooden trenchers, and pewter dishes perfectly clean, and as well polished as a French courtier.

As you leave the village, you have, to the left, a view of the hill which I have already described, and, to the right, a level expanse of fertile country, bounded by a good view of respectable mountains, peering decently into the sky; and in a line that forms an acute angle from the point of the road where you ride, is a delightful valley, in the bottom of which shines a pretty lake; and a little beyond, on the slope of a green hill, rises a splendid house, surrounded by a park, well-wooded and stocked with deer. You have now topped the little hill above the village, and a straight line of level road, a mile long, goes forward to a country town which lies immediately behind that white church, with its spire cutting into the sky, before you. You descend on the other side, and, having advanced a few perches, look to the left, where you see a long, thatched chapel, only distinguished from a dwelling house by its want of chimneys, and a small stone cross that stands on the top of the eastern gable; behind it is a graveyard, and beside it a snug public-house, well white-washed; then, to the right, you observe a door apparently in the side of a clay bank, which rises considerably above the pavement of the road. What! you ask yourself, can this be a human habitation?—but ere you have time to answer the question, a confused buzz of voices from within reaches your ear, and the appearance of a little "gorsoon," with a red, close-cropped head and Milesian face, having in his hand a short, white stick, or the thigh bone of a horse, which you at once recognise as "the pass" of a village school, gives you the full information. He has an ink-horn, covered with leather, dangling at the button-hole (for he has long since played away the buttons) of his frize jacket—his mouth is circumscribed with a streak of ink—his pen is stuck knowingly behind his ear—his shins are dotted over with blisters, black, red, and blue—on each heel a kibe—his "leather crackers," videlicet—breeches, shrunk up upon him, and only reaching as far down as the caps of his knees. Having spied you, he places his hand over his brows, to throw back the dazzling light of the sun, and peers at you from under it, till he breaks out into a laugh, exclaiming, half to himself, and half to you,

"You a gintleman!—no, nor one of your breed never was, you procthorin' thief you!"

You are now immediately opposite the door of the seminary, when half a dozen of those seated next it notice you.

"Oh, Sir, here's a gintleman on a horse!—masther, Sir, here's a gintleman on a horse, wid boots and spurs on him, that's looking in at us,"

"Silence!" exclaims the masther; "back from the door, boys rehearse; every one of you rehearse, I say, you Bœotians, till the gintleman goes past!"

"I want to go out, if you plase, Sir."

"No, you don't, Phelim."

"I do, indeed, Sir."

"What! is it afther conthradictin' me you'd be?—don't you see the 'porter's' out, and you can't go."

"Well, 'tis Mat Meehan has it, Sir, and he's out this half hour, Sir. I can't stay in, Sir—iphfff—iphfff!"

"You want to be idling your time looking at the gintleman, Phelim."

"No indeed, Sir—iphfff!"

"Phelim, I know you of ould—go to your sate—I tell you, Phelim, you were born for the encouragement of the hemp manufacture, and you'll die promoting it."

In the mean time, the master puts his head out of the door, his body stooped to a "half bend"—a phrase, and the exact curve which it forms, I leave for the present to your own sagacity—and surveys you until you pass. That is an Irish hedge school, and the personage who follows you with his eye, a hedge schoolmaster. His name is Matthew Kavanagh; and as you seem to consider his literary establishment rather a curiosity in its kind, I will, if you be disposed to hear it, give you the history of him and his establishment, beginning, in the first place, with—

THE ABDUCTION OF MAT KAVANAGH, THE HEDGE SCHOOLMASTER.

For about three years before the period of which I write, the village of Findramore, and the parish in which it lay, were without a teacher. Mat's predecessor was a James Garraghty, a lame young man, the son of a widow, whose husband lost his life in attempting to extinguish a fire that broke out in the dwelling-house of Squire Johnston, a neighbouring magistrate. The son was a boy at the time of this disaster, and the Squire, as some compensation for the loss of his father's life in his service, had him educated at his own expense; that is to say, he gave the master who taught in the village orders to educate him gratuitously, on the condition of being horse-whipped out of the parish, if he refused. As soon as he considered himself qualified to teach, he opened a school in the village on his own account, where he taught until his death, which happened in less than a year after the commencement of his little seminary. The children usually assembled in his mother's cabin; but as she did not long survive the son, this, which was at best a very miserable residence, soon tottered to the ground. The roof and thatch were burned for firing, the mud gables fell in, and were overgrown with grass, nettles, and docks; and nothing remained but a foot or two of the little clay side-walls, which presented, when associated with the calamitous fate of their inoffensive inmates, rather a touching image of ruin upon a small scale.

Garraghty had been attentive to his little pupils, and his instructions were sufficient to give them a relish for education—a circumstance which did not escape the observation of their parents, who duly appreciated it. His death, however, deprived them of this advantage; and as school masters, under the old system, were always at a premium, it so happened, that for three years afterwards, none of that class presented himself to their acceptance. Many a trial had been made, and many a sly offer held out, as a lure to the neighbouring teachers, but they did not take; for although the country was densely inhabited, yet it was remarked that no schoolmaster ever "*thruv*" in the neighbourhood of Findramore. The place, in fact, had got a bad name. Garraghty died, it was thought, of poverty, a disease to which the Findramore schoolmasters had been always known to be subject. His predecessor, too, was hanged, along with two others, for burning the house of an "Aagint."

Then the Findramore boys were not easily dealt with, having an ugly habit of involving their unlucky teachers in those quarrels which they kept up with the Ballyscanlan boys, a fighting clan that lived at the foot of the mountains above them. These two factions, when they met, whether at fair or market, wake or wedding, could never part without carrying home on each side a dozen or two of bloody coxcombs. For these reasons, the parish of Aughindrum had for a few years been afflicted with an extraordinary dearth of knowledge; the only literary establishment which flourished in it being a parochial institution, which, however excellent in design, yet, like too many establishments of the same nature, it degenerated into a source of knowledge, morals, and education, exceedingly dry and unproductive to every person except the master, who was enabled by his honest industry to make a provision for his family absolutely surprising, when we consider the moderate nature of his ostensible income. It was, in fact, like a well dried up, to which scarcely any one ever thinks of going for water.

Such a state of things, however, could not last long. The youth of Findramore were parched for want of the dew of knowledge: and their parents and grown brethren met one Saturday evening in Barny Brady's shebeen-house, to take into consideration the best means for procuring a resident schoolmaster for the village and neighbourhood. It was a difficult point, and required great dexterity of management to enable them to devise any effectual remedy for the evil which they felt. There were present at this council, Tim Dolan, the senior of the village, and his three sons, Jem Coogan, Brian Murphy, Paddy Delany, Owen Roe O'Neil, Jack Traynor, and Andy Connell, with five or six others, whom it is not necessary to enumerate.

"Bring us in a quart, Barny," said Dolan to Brady, whom on this occasion we must designate as the host; "and let it be rale hathen."

"What do you mane, Tim?" replied the host.

"I mane," continued Dolan, "stuff that was never christened, man alive."

"Thin I'll bring you the same that Father Maguire got last night on his way home, afther anointin' cold Katty Duffy," replied Brady. "I'm sure, whatever I might be afther givin' to strangers, Tim, I'd be long sorry to give *yees* any thing but the right sort."

"That's a gay man, Barny," said Traynor; "but off wid you like shot, an' let us get it under our tooth first, an' then we'll tell you more about it.—A big rogue is the same Barny," he added, after Brady had gone to bring in the poteen, "an' never sells a dhrop that's not one whiskey and five wathers."

"But he couldn't expose it on *you,* Jack," observed Connell; "you're too ould a hand about the pot for that. Warn't you in the mountains last week?"

"Ay: but the curse of Cromwell upon the thief of a gauger, Simpson—himself and a pack o' redcoats surrounded us when we war beginnin' to *double,* and the purtiest *runnin'* that even you seen was lost; for, you see, before you could cross yourself, we had the bottoms knocked clane out of the vessels; so that the villains didn't get a hole in our coats, as they thought they would."

"I tell you," observed O'Neil, "there's a bad pill somewhere about us."

"Ay is there, Owen," replied Traynor; "and what is more, I don't think he's a hundhred miles from the place where we're sittin' in."

"Faith, maybe so, Jack," returned the other.

"I'd never give in to that," said Murphy "'Tis Barny Brady that would never turn informer—the same thing isn't in him, nor in any of his breed; there's not a man in the parish I'd thrust sooner."

"I'd jist thrust him," replied Traynor, "as far as I could throw a cow by the tail. Arrah, what's the rason that the gauger never looks next or near his place, an' it's well known that he sells poteen widout a licence, though he goes past his door wanst a week?"

"What the h—— is keepin' him at all?" inquired one of Dolan's sons.

"Look at him," said Traynor, "comin' in out of the garden; how much afeard he is! keepin' he whiskey in a phatie ridge—an' I'd kiss the book that he brought that bottle out in his pocket, instead of diggin' it up out o' the garden."

Whatever Brady's usual habits of *christening* his poteen might have been, that which he now placed before them was good. He laid the bottle on a little deal table with cross legs, and along with it a small drinking glass fixed in a bit of flat circular wood, as a substitute for the original bottom, which had been broken. They now entered upon the point in question, without further delay.

"Come, Tim," said Coogan, "you're the ouldest man, and must spake first."

"Throth, man," replied Dolan, "beggin' your pardon, I'll dhrink first—*shud-urth,* your sowl; success boys—glory to ourselves, and confusion to the Scanlan boys, any way."

"And maybe," observed Connell, "'tis we that didn't lick them well in the last fair—they're not able to meet the Findramore birds even on their own walk."

"Well, boys," said Delany, "about the masther? Our childhre will grow up like *bullockeens,* widout knowing a hap'orth; and larning, you see, is a burdyen that's asy carried."

"Ay," observed O'Neil, "as Solvester Maguire, the poet, used to say—

'Labour for larnin' before you grow ould,
For larnin' is better nor riches nor gould;
Riches an' gould they may vanquish away,
But larnin' alone it will never decay.'"

"Success, Owen! Why, you might put down the pot and warm an air to it," said Murphy.

"Well, boys, are we all safe?" asked Traynor.

"Safe!" said old Dolan. "Arrah, what are you talkin' about? Sure 'tisn't of that same spalpeen of a gauger that we'd be afraid?"

During this observation, young Dolan pressed Traynor's foot under the table, and they both went out for about five minutes.

"Father," said the son, when he and Traynor re-entered the room, "you're a wanting home."

"Who wants me, Larry, avick?" says the father.

The son immediately whispered him for a moment, when the old man instantly rose, got his hat, and after drinking another bumper of the poteen, departed.

"'Twas hardly worth while," said Delany; "the ould fellow's mettle to the back-bone, an' would never show the *garran-bane* at any rate, even if he knew all about it."

"Bad end to the syllable I'd let the same ould cook hear," said the son; "the divil thrust any man that didn't *switch the primer** for it, though he is my father; but now, boys, that the coast's clear, and all safe—where will we get a schoolmaster? Mat Kavanagh won't budge from the Scanlan boys, even if we war to put our hands undher his feet: and small blame to him, when he heads them—sure, you would not expect him to be a thraitor to his own?"

"Faith, the gorsoons is in a bad state," said Murphy, "but, boys, where will we get a man that's *up*? Why, I know 'tis betther to have any body nor be without one, but we might kill two birds wid one stone—if we could get a masther that would carry 'Articles,'† tan' swear in the boys, from time to time—an' between ourselves, if there's any danger of the hemp, we may as well lay it upon strange shoulders."

"Ay, but since Corrigan swung for the Aagint," replied Delany, "they're a little

*Take an oath.
†A copy of the Whiteboy oath and regulations.

modest in havin' act or part wid us; but the best plan is to get an advartisment wrote out, an' have it posted on the chapel door."

This hint was debated with much earnestness; but as they were really anxious to have a master—in the first place, for the simple purpose of educating their children; and in the next, for filling the situation of director and regulator of their illegal Ribbon meetings—they determined on penning an advertisement, according to the suggestion of Delany. After drinking another bottle, and amusing themselves with some further chat one of the Dolans undertook to draw up the advertisement, which ran as follows:

"ADVARTAAISMENT.

"Notes to Schoolmasthers, and to all others whom it may consarn.

"WANTED,

For the nabourbood and vircinity of the Townland of Findramore, in the Parish of Aughindrum, in the Barony of Lisnamoghry, County of Sligo, Province of Connaught, Ireland.

"TO SCHOOLMASTERS.

"Take Notes—That any Schoolmaster who understands Spellin' gramatically— Readin' and Writin', in the raal way, according to the Dixonary—Arithmatick, that is to say, the five common rules, namely, simple addition, subtraction, multiplication, and division—and addition, subtraction, multiplication, and division, of Dives's denominations. Also reduction up and down—cross multiplication of coin—the Rule of Three direck—the Rule of Three in verse—the double Rule of Three—Frackshins taught according to the vulgar and decimatin' method; and must be well practised to tache the Findramore boys how to manage the *Scuffle.*

"N. B. He must be well grounded in *that.* Practis, Discount, and Rebatin', N. B. Must be well grounded in *that* also.

"Tret and Tare—Fellowship—Allegation—Barther—Rates per Scent— Intherest—Exchange—Prophet in Loss—the Square Root—the Kibe Root— Hippothenuse—Arithmatical and Gommetrical Purgation—Compound Intherest—Loggerheadism—Questions for Exercise, and the Conendix to Algibbra. He must also know Jommithry accordin' to Grunther's scale—the Castigation of the Klipsticks—Surveying and the use of the Jacob-staff.

"N. B. Would get a good dale of Surveyin' to do in the vircinity of Findramore, particularly in *Con-acre time.* If he knew the use of the globe, it would be an accusation. He must also understand the Three Sets of Book-keeping, by single and double entry, particularly Loftus & Company of Paris, their Account of Cash and Company. And above all things, he must know how to tache the *Sarvin' of Mass in*

Latin, and be able to read Doctor Gallaher's Irish Sarmints, and explain Kolumkill's and Pastorini's Prophecies.

"N. B. If he understands *Cudgel-fencin',* it would be an accusation also—but mustn't tache us wid a staff that bends in the middle, bekase it breaks one's head across the guard. Any school master capacious and collified to instruct in the above-mintioned branches, would get a good school in the townland Findramore and its vircinity, be well fed, an' get the hoith o' good livin' among the farmers, an' would be ped—

"For Book-keepin', the three sets, a *ginny and half.*

"For Gommethry, &c. *half a ginny a quarther.*

"Arithmatic, aight and three-hapuns.

"Readin', Writin', &c. six Hogs.

"Given under our hands, this 32d of June, 1804.

"LARRY DOLAN,

"DICK DOLAN, HIS ⋈ MARK.

"JEM COOGAN, HIS ⋈ MARK.

"BRINE MURPHEY,

"PADDY DELANY, HIS ⋈ MARK.

"JACK TRAYNOR,

"ANDY CONNELL,

"OWEN ROE O'NEIL, HIS ⋈ MARK.

"N. B. *By making airly application to any of the undher-mintioned, he will hear of further particklers;* and if they find that he will shoot them, he may eypect the best o' thratement, an' be well fed among the farmers.

"N. B. Would get also a good night-school among the vircinity."

Having penned the above advertisement, it was carefully posted early the next morning on the chapel doors, with an expectation on the part of the patrons that it would not be wholly fruitless. The next week, however, passed without an application—the second also—and the third produced the same result; nor was there the slightest prospect of a schoolmaster being blown by any wind to the lovers of learning at Findramore. In the mean time, the Ballyscanlan boys took care to keep up the ill-natured prejudice which had been circulated concerning the fatality that uniformly attended such schoolmasters as settled there; and when this came to the ears of the Findramore folk, it was once more resolved that the advertisement should be again put up, with a clause containing an explanation on that point. The clause ran as follows:—

"N. B. The two last masthers that was hanged out of Findramore, that is, Mickey Corrigan, who was hanged for killing the Aagent, and Jem Garraghty, that died of a declension—Jem died in quensequence of ill health, and Mickey was hanged contrary to his own wishes; so that it wasn't either of their faults—as witness our hands this 27th of July.

"Dick Dolan, his ⋈ mark.'

This explanation, however, was as fruitless as the original advertisement; and week after week passed over without an offer from a single candidate. The "vircinity" of Findramore and its "nabourhood" seemed devoted to ignorance; and nothing remained except another effort at procuring a master by some more ingenious contrivance.

Debate after debate was, consequently, held in Barny Brady's; and, until a fresh suggestion was made by Delany, the prospect seemed as bad as ever. Delany, at length, fell upon a new plan; and it must be confessed, that it was marked in a peculiar manner by a spirit of originality and enterprise—it being nothing less than a proposal to carry off, by force or stratagem, Mat Kavanagh, who was at that time fixed in the throne of literature among the Ballyscanlan boys, quite unconscious of the honourable translation to the neighbourhood of Findramore which was intended for him. The project, when broached, was certainly a startling one, and drove most of them to a pause, before they were sufficiently collected to give an opinion on its merits.

"Nothin', boys, is asier," said Delany. "There's to be a patthern in Ballymagowan on next Sathurday—an' that's jist half way betune ourselves and the Scanlan boys. Let us musther an' go there, any how. We can keep an eye on Mat widout much trouble, an', when opportunity sarves, nick him at wanst, an' off wid him clane."

"But," said Traynor, "what would we do wid him when he'd be here? Wouldn't he cut an' run the first, opportunity?'

"How can he, ye omadhawn, if we put a manwill in our pocket, an' sware him? But we'll butther him up when he's among us; or, be me sowks, if it goes to that, force him either to settle wid ourselves, or make himself scarce in the counthry entirely."

"Divil a much force it'll take to keep him, I'm thinkin'," observed Murphy. "He'll have three times a betther school here; and if he was wanst settled, I'll engage he would take to it kindly."

"See here, boys," says Dick Dolan, in a whisper, "if that bloody villain, Brady, isn't afther standin' this quarter of an hour, strivin' to hear what we're about; but it's well we didn't bring up any thing consarnin' the other business; didn't I tell yees the desate was in 'im? Look at his shadow on the wall forninst us."

"Hould yer tongues, boys," said Traynor; "jist keep never mindin', and, be my sowks, I'll make him sup sorrow for that thrick."

"You had betther neither make nor meddle wid him," observed Delany; "jist put him out of that—but don't raise yer hand to him, or he'll sarve you as he did Jem Flanagan—put ye three or four months in the *Stone Jug*."

Traynor, however, had gone out while he was speaking, and in a few minutes dragged in Brady, whom he caught in the very act of eavesdropping.

"Jist come in, Brady," said Traynor, as he dragged him along—"walk in, man alive; sure, and sich an honest man as you are needn't be afeard of lookin' his friend in the face!—ho!—an' be my sowl, is it a spy we've got? and, I suppose would be an informer, too, if he had heard any thing to tell!"

"What's the manin' of this, boys?" exclaimed the others, feigning ignorance—"let the honest man go, Traynor. What do ye hawl him that-a-way for, ye gallis pet?"

"Honest!" replied Traynor—"how very honest he is, the desavin' villain—to be standin' at the windy there, wantin' to overhear the little harmless talk we had."

"Come, Traynor," said Brady, seizing him in his turn by the neck, "take your hands off of me, or, had fate to me, but I'll lave ye a mark."

Traynor, in his turn, had his hand twisted in Brady's cravat, which he drew tightly about his neck, until the other got nearly black in the face, "Let me go, you villain!" exclaimed Brady, "or by this blessed night that's in it, it'll be worse for you."

"Villain! is id?" replied Traynor, making a blow at him, whilst Brady snatched at a penknife which one of the others had placed on the table, after picking the tobacco out of his pipe—intending either to stab Traynor, or to cut the knot of the cravat by which he was held. The others, however, interfered, and prevented further mischief.

"Brady," said Traynor, "you'll rue this night, if ever a man did, you tracherous informin' villain. What an honest spy we have among us land a short course to you!"

"Oh, hould yer tongue, Traynor!" replied Brady: "I blieve it's best known who is both the spy and the informer. The divil a pint of poteen ever you'll run in this parish, until you clear yourself of bringing the gauger on the Traceys, bekase they tuck Mick M'Kew in preference to yourself to run it for them."

Traynor made another attempt to strike him, but was prevented. The rest now interfered; and, in the course of an hour or so, an adjustment took place.

Brady took up the tongs, and swore "by that blessed iron," that he neither heard, nor intended to hear, any thing they said, and this exculpation was followed by a fresh bottle at his own expense.

"You omadhawn," said he to Traynor, "I was ony puttin' up a dozen o' bottles into the tatch of the house, when you thought I was listenin';" and, as a proof of the truth of this, he brought them out and showed them some bottles of poteen, neatly covered up under the thatch.

Before their separation they finally planned the abduction of Kavanagh from the Patron, on the Saturday following, and after drinking another round went home to their respective dwellings.

In this speculation, however, they experienced a fresh disappointment; for, ere Saturday arrived, whether in consequence of secret intimation of their intention from Brady or some friend, or in compliance with the offer of a better situation, the fact was, that Mat Kavanagh had removed to another school, distant about eighteen miles from Findramore. But they were not to be outdone; a new plan was laid, and in the course of the next week, a dozen of the most enterprising and intrepid of the "boys," mounted each upon a good horse, went to Mat's new residence for the express purpose of securing him.

Perhaps our readers may scarcely believe, that a love of learning was so strong among the inhabitants of Findramore, as to occasion their taking such remarkable steps for establishing a schoolmaster among them; but the country was densely inhabited, the rising population exceedingly numerous, and the outcry for a schoolmaster amongst the parents of the children loud and importunate. Besides this, the illegal principles of Whiteboyism were as deeply rooted in that neighbourhood as in others; and the young men stood in need of some person who might regulate their proceedings, keep their registries, preside at and appoint their meetings, and organize, with sufficient skill and precision, not only the vast numbers who had been already enrolled as members, but who were putting forward their claims, day after day, to be admitted as such.

God knows, it is no wonder that Ireland should be as she is, and as she long has been, when we consider the fact, that those who conducted the education of her peasantry were the most active instruments in disseminating among the rising generation, such pernicious principles as those which characterise this system, so deeply rooted among the people—men, whose moral characters, were, with few exceptions, execrable—and nine-tenths of whom held situations of authority in these diabolical associations.

The fact, therefore, was, that a double motive stimulated the inhabitants of Findramore in their efforts to procure a master. The old and middle-aged heads of families were actuated by a simple wish, inseparable from Irishmen, to have their children educated; and the young men, not only by a determination to have a properly qualified person to preside at their nightly orgies, but an inclination to improve themselves in reading, writing, and arithmetic. The circumstance I am now relating is one which actually took place; and any man acquainted with the remote parts of Ireland, may have often seen bloody and obstinate quarrels among the peasantry, in vindicating a priority of claim to the local residence of a school-master among them. I could, within my own experience, relate two or three instances of this nature.

It was one Saturday night in the latter end of the month of May, that a dozen Findramore "boys," as they were called, set out upon this most singular of all liter-ary speculations, resolved, at whatever risk, to secure the person and effect the per-manent bodily presence among them of the redoubtable Mat Kavanagh. Each man was mounted on a horse, and one of them brought a spare steed for the accommo-dation of the schoolmaster. The caparison of this horse was somewhat remarkable: it consisted of a wooden straddle, such as is used by the peasantry for carrying wicker paniers or creels, which are hung upon two wooden pins, that stand up out of its sides. Under it was a straw mat, to prevent the horse's back from being stripped by the straddle. On one side of this hung a large creel, and on the other a strong sack, tied round a stone of sufficient weight to balance the empty creel. The night was warm and clear, the moon and stars all threw their mellow light from a serene, unclouded sky, and the repose of nature in the short nights of this delight-ful season, resembles that of a young virgin of sixteen—still, light, and glowing. Their way, for the most part of their journey, lay through a solitary mountain-road; and, as they did not undertake the enterprize without a good stock of poteen, their light-hearted songs and choruses awoke the echoes that slept in the mountain glens as they went along. The adventure, it is true, had as much of frolic as of seriousness in it; and merely as the means of a day's fun for the boys, it was the more eagerly entered into.

It was about midnight when they left home, and as they did not wish to arrive at the village to which they were bound, until the morning should be rather advanced, the journey was as slowly performed as possible. Every remarkable object on the way was noticed, and its history, if any particular association was connected with it, minutely detailed, whenever it happened to be known. When the sun rose, many beautiful green spots and hawthorn valleys excited, even from these unpolished and illiterate peasants, warm bursts of admiration at their fragrance and beauty. In some places, the dark flowery heath clothed the mountains to the tops, from which the grey mists, lit by a flood of light, and breaking into masses before the morning breeze, began to descend into the valleys beneath them; whilst the voice of the grouse, the bleating of sheep and lambs, the pee-weet of the wheeling lap-wing, and the song of the lark, threw life and animation over the previous stillness of the country. Sometimes a shallow river would cross the road, winding off into a valley that was overhung, on one side, by rugged precipices clothed with luxuriant heath and wild ash; whilst, on the other, it was skirted by a long sweep of greensward, skimmed by the twittering swallow, over which lay scattered numbers of sheep, cows, brood mares, and colts—many of them rising and stretching themselves ere they resumed their pasture, leaving the spots on which they lay of a deeper green. Occasionally, too, a sly-looking fox might be seen lurking about a solitary lamb, or brushing over the hills with a fat goose upon his back, retreating to his den among the inaccessible rocks, after having plundered some unsuspecting farmer.

As they advanced into the skirts of the cultivated country, they met many other beautiful spots of scenery among the upland, considerable portions of which, particularly in long sloping valleys, that faced the morning sun, were covered with hazel and brushwood, where the unceasing and simple notes of the cuckoo were incessantly plied, mingled with the more mellow and varied notes of the thrush and blackbird. Sometimes, the bright summer waterfall seemed, in the rays of the sun, like a column of light, and the springs that issued from the sides of the more distant and lofty mountains shone with a steady, dazzling brightness, on which the eye could scarcely rest. The morning, indeed, was beautiful, the fields in bloom, and every thing cheerful. As the sun rose in the heavens, nature began gradually to awaken into life and happiness; nor was the natural grandeur of a Sabbath summer morning among these piles of magnificent mountains—nor its heartfelt, but more artificial beauty in the cultivated country, lost, even upon the unphilosophical "boys" of Findramore, so true is it, that the appearance of nature will force enjoyment upon the most uncultivated heart.

When they had arrived within two miles of the little town in which Mat Kavanagh was fixed, they turned off into a deep glen, a little to the left; and, after having seated themselves under a white-thorn which grew on the banks of a rivulet, they began to devise the best immediate measures to be taken.

"Boys," said Tim Dolan, "how will we manage now with this thief of a schoolmaster, at all? Come, Jack Traynor, you that's up to still-house work—escapin' and carryin' away stills from gaugers, the bloody villains!—out wid yer spake, till we hear your opinion."

"Do ye think, boys," said Andy Connell, "that we could flatter him to come by fair mains?"

"Flatther him!" said Traynor; "and, by my sowl, if we flatther him at all, it must be by the hair of the head. No, no; let us bring him first whether he will or not, an' ax his consent afterwards!"

"I'll tell you what it is, boys," continued Connell, "I'll hould a wager, if you lave him to me, I'll bring him wid his own consint."

"No, nor sorra that you'll do, nor could do," replied Traynor; "for, along wid every thing else, he thinks he's not jist doated on by the Findramore people, being one of the Ballyscanlan tribe.—No, no, let two of us go to his place, and purtind that we have other business in the fair of Clansallagh on Monday next, and ax him in to dhrink, for he'll not refuse that, any how; then, when he's half tipsy, ax him to convoy us this far; we'll then meet you here, an' tell him some palaver or other—sit down again where we are now, and, afther making him dead dhrunk, hoise a big stone in the creel, and Mat in the sack, on the other side, wid his head out, and off wid him; and he will know neither act nor part about it, till we're at Findramore."

Having approved of this project, they pulled out each a substantial complement of stout oaten bread, which served, along with the whiskey, for breakfast. The two persons pitched on for decoying Mat were Dolan and Traynor, who accordingly set out, fall of glee at the singularity and drollness of their undertaking. It is unnecessary to detail the ingenuity with which they went about it—because, in consequence of Kavanagh's love of drink, very little ingenuity was necessary. One circumstance, however, came to light, which gave them much encouragement, and that was a discovery that Mat by no means relished his situation.

In the mean time, those who staid behind in the glen felt their patience begin to flag a little, because of the delay, made by the others, who had promised, if possible, to have the schoolmaster in the glen before two o'clock. But the fact was, that Mat, who was far less deficient in hospitality than in learning, brought them into his house, and not only treated them to plenty of whiskey, but made the wife prepare a dinner, for which he detained them, swearing, that except they stopped to partake of it, he would not convoy them to the place appointed. Evening was, therefore, tolerably far advanced, when they made their appearance at the glen, in a very equivocal state of sobriety—Mat being by far the steadiest of the three, but still considerably the worse for what he had taken. He was now welcomed by a general huzza; and on his expressing his surprise at the appearances, they pointed to their horses, telling him that they were bound for the fair of Clansallagh, for the purpose of selling them. This was the more probable, as, when a fair occurs in Ireland, it is usual for cattle-dealers, particularly horse-jockeys, to effect sales, and "show" their horses on the evening before.

Mat now sat down, and was vigorously plied with strong poteen—songs were sung, stories told, and every device resorted to that was calculated to draw out and heighten his sense of enjoyment; nor were their efforts without success; for, in the course of a short time, Mat was free from all earthly care, being incapable of either speaking or standing.

"Now, boys," said Dolan, "let us do the thing clane an' dacent. Let you, Jem Coogan, Brian Murphy, Paddy Delany, and Andy Connell, go back, and tell the wife and two childher a cock-and-a-bull story about Mat—say that he is coming to Findramore for good and all, and that'll be thruth, you know; and that he ordhered yees to bring her and them afther him; and we can come back for the furniture to-morrow."

A word was enough—they immediately set off; and the others, not wishing that Mat's wife should witness the mode of his conveyance, proceeded home, for it was now dusk. The plan succeeded admirably; and in a short time the wife and children, mounted behind the "boys" on the horses, were on the way after them to Findramore.

The reader is already aware of the plan they had adopted for translating Mat; but, as it was extremely original, I will explain it somewhat more fully. The moment the schoolmaster was intoxicated to the necessary point—that is to say, totally helpless and insensible—they opened the sack and put him in, heels foremost, tying it in such a way about his neck as might prevent his head from getting into it, thus avoiding the danger of suffocation. The sack, with Mat at full length in it, was then fixed to the pin of the straddle, so that he was in an erect posture during the whole journey. A creel was then hung at the other side, in which was placed a large stone, of sufficient weight to preserve an equilibrium; and, to prevent any accident, a droll fellow sat astride behind the straddle, amusing himself and the rest by breaking jokes upon the novelty of Mat's situation.

"Well, Mat, *ma bouchal,* how duv ye like your sitivation? I believe, for all your larnin', the Findramore boys have *sacked* you at last?"

"Ay," exclaimed another, "he *is* sacked at last, in spite of his Matthew-maticks."

"An', be my sowks," observed Traynor, "he'd be a long time goin' up a Maypowl in the state he's in—his own snail would bate him."*

*This alludes to a question in Gough's Arithmetic, which is considered difficult by hedge schoolmasters.

"Yes," said another, "but he desarves credit for travellin' from Clansallagh to Findramore, widout layin' a foot to the ground—

Wan day wid Captain Whiskey I wrastled a fall,
But faith I was no match for the captain at all—
But faith I was no match for the captain at all,
Though the landlady's measures they were damnable small.
Tooral, looral, looral, looral, lido.

Whoo—hurroo! my darlings—success to the Findramore boys! Hurroo—hurroo—the Findramore boys for ever!"

"Boys, did ever yees hear the song Mat made on Ned Mullen's fight wid Jemmy Connor's gander? Well, here it is to the tune of 'Brian O'Lynn'—

As Ned and the gander wor basting each other,
I hard a loud cry from the grey goose his mother;
I ran to assist him, wid my great speed,
Bud before I arrived the poor gander did bleed.
'Alas!' says the gander, 'I'm very ill trated,
For tracherous Mullen has me fairly defated;
Bud had you been here for to show me fair play,
I could leather his *puckan** around the lee bray.

"Bravo! Mat," addressing the insensible schoolmaster—"success, poet. Hurroo for the Findramore boys! the Bridge boys for ever!"

They then commenced, in a tone of mock gravity, to lecture him upon his future duties—detailing the advantages of his situation, and the comforts he would enjoy among them—although they might as well have addressed themselves to the stone on the other side. In this manner they got along, amusing themselves at Mat's expense, and highly elated at the success of their undertaking. About two o'clock in the morning they reached the top of the little hill above the village, when, on looking back along the level stretch of road which I have already described, they noticed their companions, with Mat's wife and children, moving briskly after them. A general huzza now took place, which, in a few minutes, was answered by two or three dozen of the young folks, who were assembled in Barny Brady's waiting for their arrival. The scene now became quite animated—cheer after cheer succeeded—jokes, laughter, and rustic wit, pointed by the spirit of Brady's poteen, flew briskly about. When Mat was unsacked, several of them came up, and, shaking him cordially by the hand, welcomed him among them. To the kindness of this reception, however, Mat was wholly insensible, having been for the greater part of the journey in a profound sleep. The boys next slipped the loop of the sack off the straddle-pin; and, carrying Mat into a farmer's house, they deposited him in a settle-bed, where he slept, unconscious of the journey he had performed, until breakfast-time on the next morning. In the mean time, the wife and children were taken care of by Mrs. Connell, who provided them with a bed, and every other comfort which they could require. The next morning, when Mat awoke, his first call was for a drink. I should have here observed, that Mrs. Kavanagh had been sent for by the good woman in whose house Mat had slept, that they might all breakfast and have a drop together, for they had already succeeded in reconciling her to the change.

"Wather!" said Mat—"a drink of wather, if it's to be had for love or money, or I'll split wid druth—I'm all in a state of conflagration; and my head—by the sowl of Newton, the inventor of fluxions, but my head is a complete illucidation of the centrifugle motion, so it is. Tundher-an'-turf! is there no wather to be had? Nancy, I say, for God's sake, quicken yourself wid the hydraulics, or the best mathematician in Ireland's gone to the abode of Euclid and Pythagoras, that first invented the multiplication table."

On cooling his burning blood with the "hydraulics," he again lay down, with the intention of composing himself for another sleep; but his eye having noticed the novelty of his situation, he once more called Nancy.

"Nancy, avourneen," he inquired, "will you be afther resolving me one single proposition—Where am I at the present spaking? Is it in the *Siminary* at home, Nancy?"

Nancy, in the mean time had been desired to answer in the affirmative, hoping that if his mind was made easy on that point, he might refresh himself easy by another hour or two's sleep, as he appeared to be not at all free from the effects of his previous intoxication.

"Why, Mat, jewel, where else would you be, a lannah, but at home? Sure, isn't here Jack, an' Biddy, ad myself, Mat, agra, along wid me. Your head isn't well, but all you want is a good rousin' sleep."

"Very well, Nancy; very well, that's enough—quite satisfacthory—*quod erat demonstrandum*. May all kinds of bad luck rest upon the Findramore boys, any way! The unlucky vagabonds—I'm the third they've done up. Nancy, off wid ye, like quicksilver, for the priest."

"The priest! Why, Mat, jewel, what puts that in your head? Sure, there's nothing wrong wid ye, only the sup o' drink you tuck yestherday."

"Go, woman," said Mat, "did you ever know me to make a wrong *calculation*? I tell you, I'm *non compos mentis* from head to heel. Head! by my sowl, Nancy, it'll soon be a *caput mortuum* wid me—I'm far gone in a disease they call an opthical delusion—the devil a thing less it is—me bein' in my own place, an' to think I'm lyin' in a settle-bed; that there is a large dresser, covered wid pewter dishes and plates; and, to crown all, the door on the wrong side of the house. Off wid ye, an' tell his Reverence that I want to be anointed, and to die in pace and charity wid all men. May the most especial kind of bad luck light down upon you, Findramore, and all that's in you, both man and baste—you have given me my gruel along wid the rest; but, thank God, you won't hang me, any how! Off, Nancy, for the priest, till I die like a Christhan, in pace and forgiveness wid the world;—all kinds of hard fortune to them! Make haste, woman, if you expect me to die like a Christhan. If they had let me alone till I'd publish to the world my Treatise upon Conic Sections—but to be cut off on my march to fame! Another drought of the hydraulics, Nancy, an' then for the priest: but see, bring Father Connell, the curate, for he understands something about Matthew-maticks; an' never heed Father Roger, for little he knows about them, not even the difference between a right line and a curve—in the page of histhory, to his everlasting disgrace, be it recorded!"

"Mat," replied Nancy, scarcely preserving her gravity, "keep yourself from talkin', an' fall asleep, then you'll be well enough."

"Is there e'er a sup at all in the house?" said. Mat; "if there is, let me get it; for there's an ould proverb, though it's a most unmathematical axiom as ever was invinted—'try a hair of the same dog that bit you;' give me a glass, Nancy, any how, an' you can go for Father Connell after. Oh, by the sowl of Isaac, that invented fluxions, what's this for?"

A general burst of laughter followed this demand and ejaculation; and Mat sat up once more in the settle, and examined the place with keener scrutiny. Nancy herself laughed heartily; and, as she banded him the full glass, entered into an explanation of the circumstances attending his translation.

Mat, at all times rather of a pliant disposition, felt rejoiced on finding that he was still compos mentis; and on hearing what took place, he could not help entering into the humour of the enterprise, at which he laughed as heartily as any of them.

"Mat," said the farmer, and half a dozen of the neighbours, "you're a happy man; there's a hundred of the boys have a school-house half built for you this same blessed sunshiny mornin', while you're lying at ase in your bed."

"By the sowl of Newton, that invinted fluxions!" replied Mat, "but I'll take revenge for the disgrace you put upon my profession, by stringing up a schoolmaster among you, and I'll hang you all! It's death to stale a four-footed animal; but what do you desarve for stalin' a Christian baste, a two-legged schoolmaster without feathers, eighteen miles, and he not to know it?"

In the course of a short time Mat was dressed, and having found benefit from the "hair of the dog that bit him," he tried another glass, which strung his nerves, or, as he himself expressed it—"they've got the raal mathematical tinsion agin." What the farmer said, however, about the school-house, had been true. Early that morning all the growing and grown young men of Findramore and its "vircinity" had assembled, selected a suitable spot, and, with merry hearts, were then busily engaged in erecting a school-house for their general accommodation.

The manner of building hedge school-houses being rather curious, I will describe it. The usual spot selected for their erection is a ditch on the road-side, in some situation where there will be as little damp as possible. From such a spot an excavation is made equal to the size of the building, so that, when this is scooped out, the back side-wall and the two gables are already formed, the banks being dug perpendicularly. The front side-wall, with a window in each side of the door, is then built of clay or green sods laid along in rows; the gables are also topped with sods, and, perhaps, a row or two laid upon the back side-wall, if it should be considered too low. Having got the erection of Mat's house thus far, they procured a scraw-spade, and repaired with a couple of dozen of cars to the next bog, from which they cut the light heathy surface in stripes the length of the roof. A scraw-spade is an instrument resembling the letter T, with an iron plate—at the lower end, considerably bent, and well adapted to the purpose for which it is intended. Whilst one party cut the scraws, another bound the couples and bauks, and a third cut as many green branches as were sufficient to wattle it. The couples, being bound, were raised—the ribs laid on—then the wattles, and afterwards the scraws.

Whilst these successive processes went forward, many others had been engaged all the morning cutting rushes; and the scraws were no sooner laid on, than half a dozen thatchers mounted the roof, and long before the evening was closed, a schoolhouse, capable of holding near a hundred children, was finished. But among the peasantry no new house is ever put up without a hearth-warming, and a dance. Accordingly the clay floor was paired—a fiddler procured—Barny Brady and his stock of poteen sent for; the young women of the village and surrounding neighbourhood attended in their best finery; dancing commenced—and it was four o'clock the next morning when the merry-makers departed, leaving Mat a new home and a hard floor, ready for the reception of his scholars.

Business now commenced. At nine o'clock the next day Mat's furniture was settled in a small cabin, given to him at a cheap rate by one of the neighbouring farmers; for, whilst the school-house was being built, two men, with horses and cars, had gone to Clansallagh, accompanied by Nancy, and removed the furniture, such as it was, to their new residence. Nor was Mat, upon the whole, displeased at what had happened; he was now fixed in a flourishing country—fertile and well cultivated: nay, the bright landscape which his school-house commanded was sufficient in itself to reconcile him to his situation. The inhabitants were in comparatively good circumstances; many of them wealthy, respectable farmers, and capable of remunerating him very decently for his literary labours; and what was equally flattering, there was a certainty of his having a numerous and well attended school, in a neighbourhood with whose inhabitants he was acquainted.

Honest, kind-hearted Paddy!—pity that you should ever feet distress or hunger!—pity that you should be compelled to seek, in another land, the hard-earned pittance by which you keep the humble cabin over the head of your chaste wife and naked children! Alas! what noble materials for composing a national character, of which humanity might be justly proud, do the lower orders of the Irish possess, if raised and cultivated by a Christian education! Pardon me, gentle reader, for this momentary ebullition; I grant I am a little dark now. I assure you, however, the tear of enthusiastic admiration, is warm on my eye-lids, when I remember the flitches of bacon, the sacks of potatoes, the bags of meal, the miscawns of butter, and the dishes of egg—not omitting crate after crate of turf, which came in such rapid succession to Mat Kavanagh, during the first week on which he opened his school. Ay, and many a bottle of stout poteen, when

> "The eye of the gauger saw it not,"

was, with a sly, good-humoured wink, handed over to Mat, or Nancy, no matter which, from under the comfortable drab jock, with velvet-covered collar, erect about the honest, ruddy face of a warm, smiling farmer; or even the tattered frize of a poor labourer—anxious to secure the attention of the "masther" to his little "*Shoneen*," whom, in the extravagance of his ambition, he destined to "wear the robes as a clargy." Let no man say, I repeat, that the Irish are not fond of education.

In the course of a month Mat's school was full to the door-posts, for, in fact, he had the parish to himself—many attending from a distance of three, four, and five miles. His merits, however, were believed to be great, and his character for learning stood high, though unjustly so: for a more superficial, and at the same time, a more presuming dunce never existed; but his character alone could secure him a good attendance; he, therefore, belied the unfavourable prejudices against the Findramore folk, which had gone abroad, and was a proof, in his own person, that the reason of the former schoolmasters' miscarriage, lay in the belief of their incapacity, which existed among the people. But Mat was one of those showy, shallow fellows, who did not lack for assurance.

The first step a hedge schoolmaster took, on establishing himself in a school, was to write out, in his best copperplate hand, a flaming advertisement, detailing, at full length, the several branches he professed himself capable of teaching. I have seen many of these—as who that is acquainted with Ireland has not?—and, beyond all doubt, if the persons that issued them were acquainted with the various heads recapitulated, they must have been buried in the most profound obscurity as no man but a walking Encyclopædia—an Admirable Crichton—could claim an intimacy with them, embracing, as they often did, the whole circle of human knowledge. 'Tis true, the vanity of the pedagogue had full scope in these advertisements, as there was none to bring him to an account, except some rival, who could only attack him on those practical subjects which were known to both. Independently of this, there was a good-natured collusion between them on these points which were beyond their knowledge, inasmuch as they were not practical but speculative, and by no means involved their character or personal interests. On the next Sunday, therefore, after Mat's establishment at Findramore, you might see a circle of the peasantry assembled at the chapel door, perusing, with suitable reverence and admiration on their faces, the following advertisement; or, perhaps, Mat himself, with a learned, consequential air, in the act of explaining it to them.

"EDUCATION.

"*Mr. Matthew Kavanagh, Philomath and Professor of the Learned Languages, begs leave to inform the Inhabitants of Findramore and its vircinity, that he Lectures on the following Branches of Education, in his Seminary at the above recited place:—*

"Spelling, Reading, Writing, and Arithmetic, upon altogether new principles, hitherto undiscovered by any excepting himself, and for which he expects a Patent from Trinity College, Dublin; or at any rate, from Squire Johnston, Esq., who paternizes many of the pupils: Book-keeping, by single and double entry—Geometry,

Trigonometry, Stereometry, Mensuration, Navigation, Gauging, Surveying, Dialling, Astronomy, Astrology, Austerity, Fluxions, Geography, ancient and modern—Maps, the Projection of the Spear—Algebra, the Use of the Globes, Natural and Moral Philosophy, Pneumatics, Optics, Dioptics, Catroptics, Hydraulics, Ærostatics, Geology, Glorification, Divinity, Mythology, Midicinality, Physic, by theory only, Metaphysics practically, Chemistry, Electricity, Galvanism, Mechanics, Antiquities, Agriculture, Ventilation, Explosion, &c.

"In Classics—Grammar, Cordery, Æsop's Fables, Erasmus' Colloquies, Cornelius Nepos, Phœdrus, Valerius Maximus, Justin, Ovid, Sallust, Virgil, Horace, Juvenal, Persius, Terence, Tully's Offices, Cicero, Manouverius Turgidus, Esculapius, Regerius, Satanus Nigrus, Quinctilian, Livy, Thomas Aquinas, Cornelius Agrippa, and Cholera Morbus.

"Greek Grammar, Greek Testament, Lucian, Homer, Sophocles, Eschylus, Thucydides, Aristophanes, Xenophon, Plato, Aristotle, Socrates, and the Works of Alexander the Great; the manners, habits, customs, usages, and meditations of the Grecians; the Greek digamma resolved, Prosody, Composition, both in prose-verse, and oratory, in English, Latin, and Greek; together with various other branches of learning and scholastic profundity—*quos enumerare longum est*—along with Irish Radically, and a small taste of Hebrew upon the Masoretic text.

"Matthew Kavanagh, Philomath."

Having posted this document upon the chapel-door, and in all the public places and cross roads of the parish, Mat considered himself as having done his duty. He now began to teach, and his school continued to increase to his heart's content, every day bringing him fresh scholars, in this manner he flourished till the beginning of winter, when those boys, who, by the poverty of their parents, had been compelled to go to service to the neighbouring farmers, flocked to him in numbers, quite voracious for knowledge. An addition was consequently built to the school-house, which was considerably too small; so that, as Christmas approached, it would be difficult to find a more numerous or merry establishment under the roof of a hedge school. But it is time to give an account of its interior.

The reader will then be pleased to picture to himself such a house as I have already described—in a line with the hedge; the eave of the back roof within a foot of the ground behind it; a large hole exactly in the middle of the "*riggin*," as a chimney; immediately under which is an excavation in the floor, burned away by a large fire of turf, loosely heaped together. This is surrounded by a circle of urchins, sitting on the bare earth, and exhibiting a series of speckled shins, all radiating towards the fire, like sausages on a *Poloni* dish. There they are—wedged as close as they can sit; one with half a thigh off his breeches—another with half an arm off his tattered coat—a third without breeches at all, wearing, as a substitute, a piece of his mother's old petticoat, pinned about his loins—a fourth, no coat—a fifth, with a cap on him, because he has got a scald, from having sat under the juice of fresh hung bacon—a sixth with a black eye—a seventh with two rags about his heels to keep his kibes clean—an eighth crying to get home, because he has got a head-ache, though it may be as well to hint, that there is a drag-hunt to start from beside his father's in the course of the day. In this ring, with his legs stretched in a most lordly manner, sits, upon a deal chair, Mat himself, with his hat on, basking in the enjoyment of unlimited authority. His dress consists of a black coat, considerably in want of repair, transferred to his shoulders through the means of a clothes-broker in the county town; a white cravat, round a large stuffing, having that part which comes in contact with the chin somewhat streaked with brown—a black waistcoat with one or two "tooth-an'-egg" metal buttons sewed on where the original had fallen off—black corduroy inexpressibles, twice dyed, and sheep's-grey stockings. In his hand is a large, broad ruler, the emblem of his power, the woful instrument of executive justice, and the signal of terror to all within his jurisdiction. In a corner below is a pile of turf, where, on entering, every boy throws his two sods, with a pitch from under his left arm. He then comes up to the master, catches his forelock with finger and thumb, and bobs down his head, by way of making him a bow and goes to his seat. Along the walls on the ground is a series of round stones, some of them capped with a straw collar or hassock, on which the boys sit; others have bosses, and many of them hobs—a light but compact kind of boggy substance found in the mountains. On these several of them sit; the greater number of them, however, have no seats whatever, but squat themselves down, without compunction, on the hard floor. Hung about, on wooden pegs driven into the walls, are the shapeless yellow "caubeens" of such as can boast the luxury of a hat, or caps made of goat or hare skin, the latter having the ears of the animal rising ludicrously over the temples, or cocked out at the sides, and the scut either before or behind, according to the taste or the humour of the wearer. The floor, which is only swept every Saturday, is strewed over with tops of quills, pens, pieces of broken slate, and tattered leaves of "Reading made Easy," or fragments of old copies. In one corner is a knot engaged at "Fox-and-geese," or the "Walls of Troy," on their slates; in another, a pair of them are "fighting bottles," which consists in striking the bottoms together, and he whose bottle breaks first, of course, loses. Behind the master is a third set, playing "heads and points"—a game of pins. Some are more industriously employed in writing their copies, which they perform seated on the ground, with their paper on a copy-board—a piece of planed deal the size of the copy, an appendage now nearly exploded—their cheek-bones laid within half an inch of the left side of the copy, and the eye set to guide the motion of the hand across, and to regulate the straightness of the lines and the forms of the letters. Others, again, of the more grown boys, are working their sums with becoming industry. In a dark corner are a pair of urchins thumping each other, their eyes steadily fixed on the master, lest he might happen to glance in that direction. Near the master himself are the larger boys, from twenty-two to fifteen—shaggy-headed slips, with loose-breasted shirts lying open about their bare chests; ragged colts, with white, dry, bristling beards upon them, that never knew a razor; strong stockings on their legs; heavy brogues, with broad, nail-paved soles; and breeches open at the knees. Nor is the establishment altogether without females; but these, in hedge schools, were too few in number to form a distinct class. They were, for the most part, the daughters of wealthy farmers, who considered it necessary to their respectability, that they should not be altogether illiterate; such a circumstance being a considerable draw back, in the opinion of an admirer, from the character of a young woman for whom he was about to propose—a draw back, too, which was always weighty in proportion to her wealth or respectability.

Having given our readers an imperfect sketch of the interior of Mat's establishment, we will now proceed, however feebly, to represent him at work—with all the machinery of the system in full operation.

"Come, boys, rehearse—(buz, buz, buz)—I'll soon be after calling up the first spelling lesson—(buz, buz, buz)—then the mathematician—bookkeepers—Latinists, and Grecians, successfully. (Buz, buz, buz)—Silence there below!—your pens. Tim Casey, isn't this a purty hour o' the day for you to come into school at; arrah, and what kept you, Tim? Walk up wid yourself here, till we have a confabulation together; you see I love to be talking to you."

"Sir, Larry Branagan, here; he's throwing spits at me out of his pen."—(Buz, buz, buz.)

"By my sowl, Larry, there's a rod in steep for you."

"Fly away, Jack—fly away, Jill; come again, Jack—"

"I had to go to Paddy Nowlan's for tobaccy, Sir, for my father." (Weeping, with his hand knowingly across his face—one eye laughing at his comrades.)

"You lie, it wasn't."

"If you call me a liar agin, I'll give you a dig in the mug."

"It's not in your jacket.'

"Isn't it?"

"Behave yourself; ha! there's the masther looking at you—ye'll get it now."

"None at all, Tim? And she's not after sinding an excuse wid you? What's that undher your arm?"

"My Gough, Sir."—(Buz, buz, buz.)

"Silence, boys. And, you blackguard Lilliputian, you, what kept you away till this?"

"One, bird pickin', two men thrashing; one bird pickin', two men thrashin'; one bird pickin'—

"Sir, they're stickin' pins in me, here."

"Who is, Briney?"

"I don't know, Sir, they're all at it."

"Boys, I'll go down to yous."

"I can't carry him, Sir, he'd be too heavy for me: let Larry Toole do it, he's stronger nor me; any way, there he's putting a corker pin in his mouth."—(Buz, buz, buz.)

"Whoo-hoo-hoo-hoo—I'll never stay away agin, Sir; indeed I won't, Sir. Oh, Sir, dear, pardon me this wan time; and if ever you cotch me doing the like agin, I'll give you lave to welt the sowl out of me."—(Buz, buz, buz.)

"Behave yourself, Barny Byrne."

"I'm not touching you."

"Yes, you are; didn't you make me blot my copy."

"Ho, by the livin', I'll pay you goin' home for this."

"Hand me the taws."

"Whoo-hoo-hoo-hoo-hoo-hoo—what'll I do, at all at all! Oh, Sir dear, Sir dear, Sir dear—hoo-hoo-hoo."

"Did she send no message good or bad, before I lay on?"

"Oh, not a word, Sir, only that my father killed a pig yesterday, and he wants you to go up to-day at dinner time."—(Buz, buz, buz.)

"It's time to get lave, it isn't, it is—it isn't, it is," &c.

"You lie, I say, your faction never was able to fight ours; didn't we lick all your dirty breed in Buillagh-battha fair?"

"Silence there."—(Buz, buz, buz.)

"Will you meet us on Sathurday, and we'll fight it out clane?"

"Ha-ha-ha! Tim, but you got a big fright, any how: whist, ma bouchal, sure I was only jokin' you; and sorry I'd be to bate your father's son, Tim. Come over, and sit beside myself at the fire here. Get up, Micky Donoghue, you big burnt-shinn'd spalpeen you, and let the dacent boy sit at the fire."

"Hullabaloo hoo-hoo-hoo—to go to give me such a welt, only for sitting at the fire, and me brought turf wid me."

"To-day, Tim?"

"Yes, Sir."

"At dinner time, is id?"

"Yes, Sir."

"Faith, the dacent strain was always in the same family."—(Buz, buz, buz.)

"Horns, horns, cock horns: oh, you up'd wid them, you lifted your fingers— that's a mark, now—hould your face, till I blacken you."

"Do you call thim two sods, Jack Lanigan? why, 'tis only one long one broke in the middle; but you must make it up to-morrow, Jack; how is your mother's tooth?—did she get it pulled out yet?"

"No, Sir."

"Well, tell her to come to me, an' I'll write a charm for it, that'll cure her— What kept you till now, Paddy Magouran?"

"Couldn't come any sooner, Sir."

"You couldn't, Sir—and why, Sir, couldn't you come any sooner, Sir?"

"See, Sir, what Andy Nowlan done to my copy."—(Buz, buz, buz.)

"Silence, I'll massacree yees, if yees don't make less noise."—(Buz, buz, buz.)

"I was down with Mrs. Kavanagh, Sir."

"You were, Paddy—an' Paddy, ma bouchal, what war you doing there, Paddy?"

"Masther, Sir, spake to Jem Kenny here; he made my nose bleed."

"Eh, Paddy?"

"I was bringin' her a layin' hen, Sir, that my mother promised her at mass on Sunday last."

"Ah, Paddy, you're a game bird, yourself, wid your layin' hens; you're as full o' mischief as an egg's full o' mate—(omnes—ha, ha, ha, ha!) Silence, boys—what are you laughin' at?—ha, ha, ha!—Paddy, can you spell Nebachodnazure for me?"

"No, Sir."

"No, nor a better scholar, Paddy, could not do that, ma bouchal; but I'll spell it for you. Silence, boys—whist, all of yees, till I spell Nebachodnazure for Paddy Magouran. Listen; and you yourself, Paddy, are one of the letthers:

A turf and a *clod* spells Nebachod—
A knife and a razure, spells Nebachodnazure—
Three pair of boots and five pair of shoes—

Spells Nebachodnazare, the king of the Jews.

"Now, Paddy, that's spelling Nebachodnazure by the science of Ventilation; but you'll never go that deep, Paddy."

"I want to go out, if you plase, Sir."

"Is that the way you ax me, you vagabone?"

"I want to go out, Sir"—(pulling down the fore lock.)

"Yes, that's something dacenter; by the sowl of Newton, that invinted fluxions, if ever you forget to make a bow again, I'll flog the enthrils out of you—wait till the pass comes in."

Then comes the spelling lesson.

"Come, boys, stand up to the spelling lesson."

"Micky, show me your book, till I look at my word. I'm fifteenth."

"Wait till I see my own."

"Why do you crush for."

"That's my place."

"No, it's not."

"Sir spake to——I'll tell the masther."

"What's the matther there?"

"Sir he won't let me into my place."

"I'm before you."

"No, you're not."

"I say, I am."

"You lie, pug-face: ha! I called you pug-face, tell now if you dare."

"Well, boys, down with your pins in the book; who's king?"

"I am, Sir."

"Who's queen?"

"Me, Sir."

"Who's prince?"

"I am prince, Sir."

"Tag rag and bob-tail, fall into your places."

"I've no pin, Sir."

"Well, down with you to the tail——now, boys."

Having gone through the spelling task, it was Mat's custom to give out six hard words selected according to his judgment—as a final test; but he did not always confine himself to that. Sometimes he could put a number of syllables arbitrarily together, forming a most heterogeneous combination of articulate sounds.

"Now, boys, here's a deep word, that'll thry yees: come, Larry, spell *me-mo-man-dran-san-ti-fi-can-du-ban-dan-ti-al-i-ty*, or *mis-an-thro-po-mor-phi-ta-ni-a-nus-mi-ca-li-a-tion;*—that's too hard for you, is it? Well, then, spell phthisic. Oh, that's physic you're spellin'. Now, Larry, do you know the difference between physic and phthisic?"

"No, Sir."

"Well, I'll expound it: phthisic, you see, manes—whisht, boys; will yees hould yer tongues there—phthisic, Larry, signifies—that is, phthisic—mind, it's not physic I'm expounding, but phthisic—boys, will yees stop yer noise there—signifies—but, Larry, it's so deep a word in larnin' that I should draw it out on a slate for you: and now I remimber, man alive, you're not far enough on yet to undherstand it: but what's physic, Larry?"

"Isn't that, Sir, what my father tuck, the day he got sick, Sir?"

"That's the very thing, Larry; it has what larned men call a medical property, and resembles little ricketty Dan Reilly there—it retrogrades. Och! och! I'm the boy that knows things——you see now how I expounded them two hard words for yees, boys—don't yees?"

"Yes, Sir," &c. &c.

"So, Larry, you haven't the larnin' for that either: but here's an 'asier one—spell me Ephabridotas (Epaphroditas)—you can't! hut! man—you're a big dunce entirely, that little shoneen Sharkey there below would *sack*. God be wid the day when I was the likes of you—it's I that was the bright gorsoon entirely—and so sign was on it, when a great larned traveller—silence, boys, till I tell yees this, [a dead silence]—from Thrinity College, all the way in Dublin, happened to meet me one day—seeing the slate and Gough, you see, undher my arm, he axes me—'Arrah, Mat,' says he, 'what are you *in?*' says he. 'Faix, I'm in my waistcoat, for one thing,' says I, off hand—silence, childhre, and don't laugh so loud—(ha, ha, ha!) So he looks closer at me: 'I see that,' says he, 'but what are you reading?' 'Nothing, at all at all,' says I; 'bad manners to the taste, as you may see, if you've your eye-sight.' 'I think,' says he, 'you'll be apt to die in your waistcoat;' and set spurs to a fine saddle mare he rid—faith he did so—thought me so cute—(*omnes*—ha, ha, ha!) Whisht, boys, whisht; isn't it a terrible thing that I can't tell yees a joke, but you split your sides laughing at it—(ha, ha, ha!)—don't laugh so loud, Barney Casey."—(ha, ha, ha!)

Barney—"I want to go out, if you plase, Sir"

"Go, avick; you'll be a good scholar yet, Barney. Faith, Barney knows whin to laugh, any how."

"Well, Larry, you can't spell Ephabridotas?—thin, here's a short weeshy one, and whoever spells it will get the pins;—spell a red rogue wid three letters. You, Micky? Dan? Jack? Natty? Alick? Andy? Pether? Jim? Tim? Pat? Rody? you? you? you? Now, boys, I'll hould ye my little Andy here, that's only beginning the *Rational Spelling Book,* bates you all; come here, Andy, alanna: now, boys, if he bates you, you must all bring him a little *miscaun* of butter between two kale blades, in the mornin', for himself; here, Andy avourneen, spell red rogue wid three letthers."

Andy—"M, a, t—Mat."

"No, no, avick, that's myself, Andy; it's red rogue, Andy—hem!—F—."

"F, o, x—fox."

"That's a man, Andy. Now, boys, mind what you owe Andy in the mornin', plase God, won't yees?"

"Yes, Sir." "Yes, Sir." "Yes, Sir." "I will, Sir.". "And I will, Sir." "And so will I, Sir." &c. &c. &c.

I know not whether the Commissioners of Education found the monitorial system of instruction in such of the old hedge schools as maintained an obstinate resistance to the innovations of modern plans. That Bell and Lancaster deserve much credit for applying and extending the principle (I speak without any reference to its merits) I do not hesitate to grant; but it is unquestionably true, that the principle was reduced to practice in Irish hedge schools long before either of these worthy gentlemen were in existence. I do not, indeed, at present remember, whether or not they claim it as a discovery, or simply as an adaptation of a practice which experience, in accidental cases, had found useful, and which they considered capable of more extensive benefit. I remember many instances, however, in which it was applied—and applied, in my opinion, though not as a permanent system, yet more judiciously than it is at present. I think it a mistake to suppose that silence, among a number of children in school, is conducive to the improvement either of health or intellect. That the chest and the lungs are benefited by giving full play to the voice, I think will not be disputed; and that a child is capable of more intense study and abstraction in the din of a school-room, than in partial silence, (if I may be permitted the word,) is a fact, which I think any rational observation would establish. There is something cheering and cheerful in the noise of friendly voices about us—it is a restraint taken off the mind, and it will run the lighter for it—it produces more excitement, and puts the intellect in a better frame for study. The obligation to silence, though it may give the master more ease, imposes a new moral duty upon the child, the sense of which must necessarily weaken his application. Let the boy speak aloud, if he pleases—that is, to a certain pitch; let his blood circulate; let the natural secretions take place, and to physical effluvia be thrown off by a free exercise of voice and limbs: but do not keep him dumb and motionless as a statue—his blood and his intellect both in a state of stagnation, and his spirit below zero. Do not send him in quest of knowledge alone, but let him have cheerful companionship on his way; for, depend upon it, that the man who expects too much either in discipline or morals from a boy, is not, in my opinion, acquainted with human nature. If an urchin titter at his own joke, or that of another—if he give him a jagg of a pin under the desk, imagine not that it will do him an injury, whatever phrenologists may say concerning the organ of destructiveness. It is an exercise to the mind, and he will return to his business with greater vigour and effect. Children are not men, nor influenced by the same motives—they do not reflect, because their capacity for reflection is imperfect; so is their reason: whereas, on the contrary, their faculties for education (excepting judgment, which strengthens my argument) are in greater vigour in youth than in manhood. The general neglect of this distinction is, I am convinced, a stumbling block in the way of youthful instruction, though it characterises all our modern systems. We should never forget that they are children; nor should we bind them by a system, whose standard is taken from the maturity of human intellect. We may bend our reason to theirs, but we cannot elevate their capacity to our own. We may produce an external appearance, sufficiently satisfactory to ourselves; but, in the mean time, it is propable that the child may be growing in hypocrisy, and settling down into the habitual practice of a fictitious character.

But another and more serious objection may be urged against the present strictness of scholastic discipline—which is, that it deprives the boy of a sense of free and independent agency. I speak this with limitations, for a master should be a monarch in his school, but by no means a tyrant; and decidedly the very worst species of tyranny is that which stretches the young mind upon the bed of too rigorous a discipline—like the despot who exacted from his subjects so many barrels of perspiration, whenever there came a long and severe frost. Do not familiarize the mind when young to the toleration of slavery, lest it prove afterwards incapable of recognising and relishing the principle of an honest and manly independence. I have known many children, on whom a rigour of discipline, affecting the mind only, (for corporal punishment is now almost exploded,) impressed a degree of timidity almost bordering on pusillanimity. Away, then, with the specious and long-winded arguments of a false and mistaken philosophy. A child will be a child, and a boy a boy, to the conclusion of the chapter. Bell or Lancaster would not relish the pap or caudle-cup three times a day: neither would an infant on the breast feel comfortable after a gorge of ox beef. Let them, therefore, put a little of the mother's milk of human kindness and consideration into their strait-laced systems.

A hedge schoolmaster was the general scribe of the parish, to whom all who wanted letters or petitions written, uniformly applied—and these were glorious opportunities for the pompous display of pedantry: the remuneration usually consisted of a bottle of whiskey.

A poor woman, for instance, informs Mat that she wishes to have a letter written to her son, who is a soldier abroad.

"An', how long is he gone, ma'am?"

"Och, thin, masther, he's from me goin' an fifteen years; an' a comrade of his was spakin' to Jim Dwyer, an' says his ridgment's lyin' in the Island of Budanages, somewhere in the back parts of Africa."

"An' is it a letther or petition you'd be afther havin' me to indite for you, ma'am?"

"Och, a letther, Sir—a letther, masther; an' may the Lord grant you all kinds of luck, good, bad, an' indifferent, both to you an' yours: an well it's known, by the same token, that it's yourself has the nice hand at the pen entirely, an' can indite a letther or pertition, that the priest o' the parish mightn't be ashamed to own to it."

"Why, thin, 'tis I that 'ud scorn to deteriorate upon the superiminence of my own execution at inditin' wid a pen in my hand: but would you feel a delectability in my superscriptionizin' the epistolary correspondency, ma'am, that I'm about to adopt?"

"Eagh? och, what am I sayin'!—*Sir*—masther—*Sir?*—the noise of the crathurs, you see, is got into my ears; and, besides, I'm a bit bothered on both sides of my head, ever since I had that weary weed."

"Silence, boys; bad manners to yees will ye be asy, you Lilliputian Bœotians—by my s——hem—upon my credit, if I go down to that corner, I'll castigate yees in dozens: I can't spake to this dacent woman, with your insuperable turbulentiality."

"Ah, avourneen, masther, but the larnin's a fine thing, any how; an' maybe 'tis yourself that hasn't the tongue in your head, an' can spake the tall, high-flown English; a wurrah, but your tongue hangs well, any how—the Lord increase it!"

"Lanty Cassidy, are you gettin' on wid yer, Stereometry? *festina, mi discipuli; vocabo Homerum, mox atque mox.* You see, ma'am I must tache thim to spike an' effectuate a translation of the larned languages sometimes."

"Arrah, masther, dear, how did you get it all into your head, at all at all?"

"Silence, boys—*tace*—'*conticuere omnes intentique ora tenebant.*' Silence, I say agin.'

"You could slip over, maybe, to Doran's, masther, do you see? You'd do it bet-ther there, I'll engage: sure an' you'd want a dhrop to steady your hand, any how.'

"Now, boys, I am goin' to indite a small taste of literal correspondency over at the public-house here; you *literati* will hear the lessons for me, boys, till afther I'm back agin; but mind, boys, *absente domino, strepuunt servi*—meditate on the philos-ophy of that; and, Mick Mahon, take your slate and put down all the names; and, upon my sou—hem—credit, I'll castigate any boy guilty of *misty manners* on my retrogadation thither;—*ergo momentote, cave ne titubes mandataque frangas.*"

"In throth, Sir, I'd be long sarry to throuble you; but he's away fifteen years, and I wouldn't thrust it to another; and the corplar that commands the ridgment would regard your hand-write and your inditin'.

"Don't, ma'am, plade the smallest tast of apology"

"Eagh?"

"I'm happy that I can sarve you, ma'am."

"Musha, long life to you, masther, for that same, any how—but it's yourself that's deep in the larnin' and the langridges; the Lord incrase yer knowledge—sure, an' we all want his blessin', you know."

THE RETURN.

"Well, boys, ye've been at it—here's swelled faces and bloody noses. What blackened your eye, Callaghan? You're a purty prime ministher, ye boxing black-guard you: I left you to keep pace among these factions, and you've kicked up a purty dust. What blackened your eye—egh?"

"I'll tell you, Sir, whin I come in, if you plase."

"Ho, you vagabones, this is the ould work of the faction between the Bradys and the Callaghans—bastin' one another; but, by my sowl, I'll baste you all through other. You don't want to go out, Callaghan. You had fine work here since; there's a dead silence now; but I'll pay you presently. Here, Duggan, go out wid Callaghan, an see that you bring him back in less than no time. It's not enough for your fathers and brothers to be at it, who have a right to fight, but you must battle betune you—have your field days itself!"

(*Duggan returns*)—"Hoo—hoo—Sir, my nose. Oh, *murdher sheery,* my nose is broked!"

"Blow your nose, you spalpeen you—where's Callaghan?"

"Oh, Sir, bad luck to him every day he rises out of his bed; he got a stone in his fist, too, that he *hot* me a pelt on the nose wid, and then made off home."

"Home, is id? Start, boys, off—chase him, lie into him—asy, curse yees, take time gettin' out: that's it—keep to him—don't wait for me: take care, you little spalpeens, or you'll brake your bones, so you will: blow the dust of this road, I can't see my way in it!"

"Oh! murdher, Jem, agra, my knee's out o' joint."

"My elbow's smashed, Paddy. Bad luck to him—the divil fly away wid him—oh! ha! ha!—oh! ha! ha! murdher—hard fortune to me, but little Mickey Geery fell, an thripped the masther, an' himself's disabled now—his black breeches split too—look at him feelin' them—oh! oh! ha! ha!—by tare-an'-outy, Callaghan will be murdhered, if they cotch him."

This was a specimen of civilization which Ireland only could furnish: nothing, indeed, could be more perfectly ludicrous than such a chase; and such scenes were by no means uncommon in hedge schools, for, wherever severe punishment was dreaded—and, in truth, most of the hedgemasters were unfeeling tyrants—the boy, if sufficiently grown to make a good race, usually broke away, and fled home at the top of his speed. The pack then were usually led on by the master, who mostly headed them himself, all in full cry, exhibiting such a scene as should be witnessed, in order to be enjoyed. The neighbours, men, women, and children, ran out to be spectators; the labourers, suspended their work to enjoy it, assembling, on such eminences as commanded a full view of the pursuit.

"Bravo, boys—success, masther; lie into him—where's your huntin'-horn, Mr. Kavanagh—he'll bate yees, if ye don't take the wind of him. Well done, Callaghan, keep up your heart, your sowl, and you'll do it asy—yer gaining on them, ma bouchal—the masther's down, you gallows clip, an' there's none but the scholars afther ye—he's safe."

"Not he; I'll hould a naggin, the poor scholar has him; don't you see he's close at his heels."

"*Done,* by my song—they'll never come up wid him; listen to their leather crackers and cord-a-roys, as their knees bang agin one another. Hark forrit, boys! hark forrit! huzzaw, you thieves, huzzaw!"

"Yer beagles is well winded, Mr. Kavanagh, an' gives good tongue."

"Well, masther, you had your chase for nothin', I see."

"Mr. Kavanagh," another would observe, "I didn't think you war so stiff in the hams, as to let the gorsoon bate you that-a-way—your wind's failin', Sir."

"The schoolmaster was abroad" then, and never was the "march of intellect" at once so rapid and unsuccessful.

During the summer season, it was the usual practice for the scholars to transfer their paper, slates, and books, to the green which lay immediately behind the school house, where they stretched themselves on the grass, and resumed their business. Mat would bring out his chair, and, placing it on the shady side of the hedge, sit with his pipe in his mouth, the contented lord of his little realm, whilst nearly a hundred and fifty scholars of all sorts and sizes, lay scattered over the grass, basking under the scorching sun in all the luxury of novelty, nakedness, and freedom. The sight was original and characteristic, and such as Mr. Brougham would have been delighted with—"The schoolmaster was abroad again."

As soon as one o'clock drew near, Mat would pull out his Ring-dial, holding it against the sun, and declare the hour.

"Now, boys, to yer dinners, and the rest to play."

"Hurroo, darlins, to play—the masther says its dinner-time!—whip-spur-an'-away-grey—hurroo—whack—hurroo!"

"Masther, Sir, my father bid me ax you home to yer dinner."

"No, he'll come to huz—come wid me if you plase, Sir."

"Sir, never heed them; my mother, Sir, has some of what you know—of the flitch I brought to Shoneen on last Aisther, Sir."

This was a subject on which the boys gave themselves great liberty, an invitation, even when, not accepted, being an indemnity for the day; it was usually followed by a battle between the claimants, and bloody noses were the issue. The master himself, after deciding to go where he was certain of getting the best dinner, generally put an end to the quarrels by a reprimand, and then gave notice to the disappointed claimants of the successive days on which he would attend at their respective houses.

"Boys, you all know my maxim; to go, for fear of any jealousies, boys, wherever I get the worst dinner; so tell me now, boys, what yer dacent mothers have all got at home for me?'

"My mother killed a fat hen yesterday, Sir, an' you'll have a lump of bacon and 'flat dutch along wid it."

"We'll have hang beef and greens, Sir."

"We tried the praties this mornin', Sir, an' we'll have new praties, and bread and butther, Sir."

"Well, it's all good, boys; but rather than show favour or affection, do you see, I'll go wid Andy, here, and take share of the hen an' bacon; but, boys, for all that, I'm fonder of the other things, you persave; and as I can't go wid you, Mat, tell your respectable mother that I'll be with her tomorrow; and with you, Larry, ma bouchal, the day afther."

If a master were a single man, he usually "went round" with the scholars each night; but there were generally a few comfortable farmers, leading men in the parish, at whose house he chiefly resided; and the children of these men were treated with the grossest and most barefaced partiality. They were altogether privileged persons, and had liberty to beat and abuse the other children of the school, who were certain of being most unmercifully flogged, if they even dared to prefer a complaint against the favourites. Indeed the instances of atrocious cruelty in hedge schools, were almost incredible, and such as, in the present enlightened time, would not be permitted. As to the state of the "poor scholar," it exceeded belief; for he was friendless and unprotected. But though legal prosecutions in those days were never resorted to, yet, according to the characteristic notions of the Irish retributive justice, certain cases occurred, in which a signal, and, at times, a fatal vengeance was executed on the person of the brutal master. Sometimes the brothers and other relatives of the mutilated child would come in a body to the school, and flog the pedagogue with his own taws, until his back was lapped in blood. Sometimes they would beat him until few symptoms of life remained.

Occasionally he would get a nocturnal notice to quit the parish in a given time, under a penalty which seldom proved a dead letter in case of non-compliance. Not unfrequently did those whom he had, when boys, treated with such barbarity, go back to him, when young men, not so much for education's sake, as for the especial purpose of retaliating upon him for his former cruelty. When cases of this nature occurred, he found himself a mere cipher in his school, never daring to practice excessive severity in their presence. Instances have come to our own knowledge, of masters, who, for their mere amusement, would go out to the next hedge, cut a large branch of furze or thorn, and having first carefully arranged the children in a row round the walls of the school, their naked legs stretched out before them, would sweep round the branch, bristling with spikes and prickles, with all his force against their limbs, until, in a few minutes, a circle of blood was visible on the ground where they sat, their legs appearing as if they had been scarified. This the master did, whenever he happened to be drank, or in a remarkably good humour. The poor children, however, were obliged to laugh loud, and enjoy it, though the tears were falling down their cheeks, in consequence of the pain he inflicted. To knock down a child with the fist, was considered nothing harsh; nor, if a boy were cut, or prostrated by a blow of a cudgel on the head, did he ever think of representing the master's cruelty to his parents. Kicking on the shins with the point of a brogue or shoe, bound round the edge of the sole with iron nails, until the bone was laid open, was a common punishment; and as for the usual slapping, horsing, and flogging, they were inflicted with a brutality that in every case richly deserved for the tyrant, not only a peculiar whipping by the hand of the common executioner, but a separation from civilized society by transportation for life. It is a fact, however, that in consequence of the general severity practised in hedge schools, excesses of punishment did not often produce retaliation against the master; these were only exceptions, isolated cases that did not affect the general character of the discipline in such schools.

Now, when we consider the total absence of all moral and religious principles in these establishments, and the positive presence of all that was wicked, cruel, and immoral, need we be surprised at the character of Ireland at this enlightened day. But her education and herself were neglected, and now behold the consequence!

I am sorry to perceive the writings of many respectable persons on Irish topics, imbued with a tinge of spurious liberality, that frequently occasions them to depart from truth. To draw the Irish character as it *is*, as the model of all that is generous, hospitable, and magnanimous, is in some degree fashionable; but although I am as warm an admirer of all that is really excellent and amiable in my countrymen as any man, yet I cannot, nor will I, extenuate their weak and indefensible points. That they possess the *elements* of a noble and exalted national character, I grant; nay, that they actually do possess such a character, under limitations, I am ready to maintain. Irishmen, setting aside their religious and political prejudices, are grateful, affectionate, honourable, faithful, generous, and even magnanimous; but, under the stimulus of religious and political feeling, they are treacherous, cruel, and inhuman—will murder, burn, and exterminate, not only without compunction, but with a satanic delight, worthy of a savage. Their education, indeed, was truly barbarous; they were trained and habituated to cruelty, revenge, and personal hatred, in their schools. Their knowledge was directed to evil purposes—disloyal principles were industriously insinuated into their minds by their teachers, every one of whom was a leader of some illegal association. The matter placed in their hands was of a most inflammatory and pernicious nature, as regarded polities: and as far as religion and morality were concerned, nothing could be more gross and superstitious than the books which circulated among them. Eulogiums on murder, robbery, and theft, were read with delight in the histories of Freney the Robber, and the Irish Rogues and Rapparees; ridicule of the Word of God, and hatred to the Protestant religion, in a book called Ward's Cantos, written in Hudibrastic verse; the downfall of the Protestant Establishment, and the exaltation of the Romish Church, in Columbkill's Prophecy, and latterly in that of Pastorini; a belief in every species of religious imposture, in the Lives of the Saints, of St. Patrick, of

St. Columbkill, of St. Teresa, St. Francis Xavier, the Holy Scapular, and several other works, disgraceful to human reason. Political and religious ballads of the vilest doggrel, miraculous legends of holy friars persecuted by Protestants, and of signal vengeance inflicted by their divine power on their persecutors, were in the mouths of the young and old, and of course, firmly fixed in their credulity.

Their weapons of controversy were drawn from the Fifty Reasons, the Doleful Fall of Andrew Sall, the Catholic Christian, the grounds of the Catholic Doctrine, a Net for the Fishers of Men, and several other publications, of the same class. The books of amusement read in these schools, including the first mentioned in this list, were, the Seven Champions of Christendom, the Seven Wise Masters and Mistresses of Rome, Don Belianis of Greece, the Royal Fairy Tales, the Arabian Nights Entertainments, Valentine and Orson, Gesta Romanorum, Dorastus and Faunia, the History of Reynard the Fox, the Chevalier Faublax; to those I may add, the Battle of Aughrim, Siege of Londonderry, History of the Young Ascanius, a name by which the Pretender was designated, and the Renowned History of the Siege of Troy; the Forty Thieves, Robin Hood's Garland, the Garden of Love and Royal Flower of Fidelity, Parimus and Parismenus; along with others, the names of which shall not appear on these pages. With this specimen of education before our eyes, is it at all extraordinary that Ireland should be as she is?

"Thady Bradly, will you come up wid your slate, till I examine you in your figures? Go out, Sir, and blow your nose first, and don't be after making a looking-glass out of the sleeve of your jacket. Now that Thady's out, I'll hould you, boys, that none of yees know how to expound his name—eh? do yees? But I needn't ax—well, 'tis Thadeus; and, maybe, that's as much as the priest that christened him knew. Boys, you see what it is to have the larnin'—to lade the life of a gintleman, and to be able to talk deeply wid the clargy! Now, I could run down any man in arguin', except a priest; and if the bishop was afther consecratin' me, I'd have more larnin' than the most of them; but you see I'm not consecrated—and—well, 'tis no matther—I only say that the more's the pity.

"Well, Thady, when did you go into subtraction?"

"The day beyond yesterday, Sir; yarra musha, sure 'twas yourself, Sir, that shet me the first sum."

"Masther, Sir, Thady Bradly stole *my* cutter—that's my cutter, Thady Bradly.'

"No it's not," (in a low voice).

"Sir, that's my cutter—an' there's three nicks in id."

"Thady, is that his cutter?"

"There's your cutter for you. Sir, I found it on the flure and didn't know who own'd it."

"You know'd very well who own'd it; didn't Dick Martin see you liftin' it off o' my slate, when I was out?"

"Well, if Dick Martin saw him, it's enough: an' 'tis Dick that's the tindher-hearted boy, an would knock you down wid a lump of a stone, if he saw you mur-therin' but a fly!"

"Well, Thady—throth Thady, I fear you'll undherstand subtraction better nor your tacher: I doubt you'll apply it to 'Practice' all your life ma bouchal, and that you'll be apt to find it 'the Rule of False' at last. Well, Thady, from one thousand pounds, no shillings and no pince, how will you subtract one pound? Put it down on your slate—this way,

$$1000 \ 00 \ 00$$
$$1 \ 00 \ 00$$

"I don't know how to shet about it, masther."

"You don't? an' how dare you tell me so, you *shingawn* you—you Cornelius Agrippa you—go to your sate and study it, or I'll—ha! be off, you"—

"Pierce Mahon, come up wid your multiplication. Pierce, multiply four hun-dred by two—put it down—that's it,

$$400$$
$$\text{By } 2$$

"Twice nought is one." (Whack, whack.) "Take that as an illustration—is that one?"

"Faith, masther, that's two, any how; but, Sir, is not wanst nought nothin'; now, masther, sure there can't be less than nothin'."

"Very good, Sir."

"If wanst nought be nothin', then twice nought must be *somethin,*' for it's dou-ble what wasnt nought is—see how I'm sthruck for nothin', an' me knows it—hoo! hoo! hoo!"

"Get out, you Esculapian; bud I'll give you somethin', by-and-by, just to make you remimber that you know *nothin'*—off wid you to your sate, you spalpeen you—to tell me that there can't be less than nothin', when it's well known that sporting Squire O'Canter is worth a thousand pounds less than nothin'."

"Paddy Doran, come up to your 'Intherest,' Well, Paddy, what's the intherest of a hundred pound, at five per cent? Boys, have manners, you thieves you.'

"Do you mane, masther, *per cent. per annum?*"

"To be sure I do—how do you state it?"

"I'll say, as a hundher pound is to one year, so is five per cent. per annum."

"Hum—why—what's the number of the sum, Paddy?"

"'Tis No. 84, Sir." (The master steals a glance at the Key to Gough.)

"I only want to look at it in the Gough, you see, Paddy—an' how dare you give me such an answer, you big-headed dunce, you—go off an' study it, you rascally Lilliputian—off wid you, and don't let me see your ugly mug till you know it."

"Now, *gintlemen,* for the Classics; and first for the Latinaarians—Larry Cassidy, come up wid your Asop. Larry, you're a year at Latin, an' I don't think you know Latin for *frize,* what your own coat is made of, Larry. But, in the first place, Larry, do you know what a man that taches Classics is called?"

"A schoolmasther, Sir." (Whack, whack, whack.)

"Take that for your ignorance—and that to the back of it—ha! that'll tache you—to call a man that taches Classics a schoolmasther, indeed! 'Tis a Profissor of Humanity itself, he is—(whack, whack, whack,)—ha! you ringleader, you; you're as bad as Dick O'Connell, that no masther in the county could get any good of, in regard that he put the whole school together by the ears, wherever he'll be, though the spalpeen wouldn't stand fight himself. Hard fortune to you! to go to put such an affront upon me, an' me a Profissor of Humanity. What's Latin for pantaloons?"

"Fem—fem—femi."

"No, it's not, Sir."

"Femora—"

"Can you do it?"

"Don't strike me, Sir; don't strike me, Sir, an' I will."

"I say, can you do it?"

"Femorali,"—(whack, whack, whack,)—"*Ah,* Sir! *ah,* Sir! 'tis femorali—*ah,* Sir! 'tis femorali—*ah,* Sir!"

"This thratement to a Profissor of Humanity—(drives him head over heels to his seat,)—Now, Sir, maybe you'll have Latin for throwsers agin or, by my sowl, if you don't, you must peel, and I'll tache you what a Profissor of Humanity is!

"Dan Shiel, you little starved-looking spalpeen, will you come up to your Illocution?—and a purty figure you cut at it, wid a voice like a penny thrumpet Dan! Well, what speech have you got now, Dan, ma bouchal. Is it 'Romans, counthrymin, and lovers?'"

"No, Shir; yarrah, didn't I *spake* that speech before? 'tis wan, masther, that I'm afther *pennen'* myself!".

"No, you didn't, you fairy; ah, Dan, little as you are, you take credit for more than ever you spoke, Dan, agrah; but, faith, the same thrick will come agin you some time or other, avick! Go and get that speech betther; I see by your face, you haven't it: of wid you, and get a patch upon your breeches, your little knees are through them, though 'tisn't by prayin' you've wore them, any how, you little hop-o'-my-thumb you, wid a voice like a rat in a thrap; and yet you'll be practisin' Illocution: off wid you, man alive! You little spitfire you, if you and your school-fellow, Dick O'Connell, had been wid the Jews whin they wanted to burn down the standin corn of the Philistius, the divil a fox they might bother their heads about, for yees both would have carried fire-brands by the hundher for them. Spake the next speech bitther—between you and Dick, you keep the school in per-petual agitation."

Sometimes the neighbouring gentry used to call into Mat's establishment, moved probably by a curiosity excited by his character, and the general conduct of the school. On one occasion Squire Johnston and an English gentleman paid him rather an unexpected visit. Mat had that morning got a new scholar, the son of a dancing tailor in the neighbourhood; and as it was reported that the son was nearly equal to the father in that accomplishment, Mat insisted on having a specimen of his skill. He was the more anxious on this point, as it would con-tribute to the amusement of a travelling schoolmaster, who had paid him rather a hostile visit, which Mat, who dreaded a literary challenge, feared might occasion him some trouble.

"Come up here, you little *sartor,* till we get a dacent view of you. You're a son of Ned Malone's—aren't you?"

"Yes, and of Mary Malone, my mother, too, Sir."

"Why thin, that's not bad, any how—what's your name?"

"Dick, Sir."

"Now, Dick, ma bouchal, isn't it true that you can dance a hornpipe?"

"Yes, Sir."

"Here, Larry Brady, take the door off the hinges, an' lay it down on the flure, till Dick Malone dances the Humours of Glynn: silence, boys, not a word; but just keep lookin' an."

"Who'll sing, Sir? for I can't be afther dancin' a step widout the music."

"Boys, which of yees 'ill sing for Dick? I say, boys, will none of yees give Dick the Harmony? Well, come, Dick, I'll sing for you myself:—

"Torral lol, lorral lol, lorral lol, lorral, lol—
Toldherol, lorral lol, lorral lol, lol," &c. &c.

"I say, Misther Kavanagh," said the strange master, "what angle does Dick's heel form in the second step of the treble, from the kibe on the left foot to the corner of the door forninst him?"

To this mathematical poser Mat made no reply, only sang the tune with redoubled loudness and strength, whilst little Dicky pounded the old crazy door with all his skill and alacrity. The "boys" were delighted.

"Bravo, Dick, that's a man—welt the flure—cut the buckle—murdher the clocks—rise upon suggaun, and sink upon gad—down the flure flat, foot about—keep one foot on the ground, and t'other never off it," saluted him from all parts of the house.

Sometimes he would receive a sly hint, in feigned voice, to call for "Devil stick the Fiddler," alluding to the master. Now a squeaking voice would chime in; by and by another, and so on, until the master's bass had a hundred and forty trebles, all in chorus to the same tune.

Just at this moment the two gentlemen entered; and, reader, you may conceive, but I cannot describe the face which Mat (who sat with his back to the door, and did not see them until they were some time in the house,) exhibited on the occasion. There he sung ore rotundo, throwing forth an astounding tide of voice; whilst little Dick, a thin, pale-faced urchin, with his head, from which the hair stood erect sunk between his hollow shoulders, was performing prodigious feats of agility.

"What's the matter? what's the matter?" said the gentlemen. "Good morning, Mr. Kavanagh?"

"——Tooral lol, lol——

Oh, good——oh, good morning——gintlemen, with extrame kindness," replied Mat, rising suddenly up, but not removing his hat, although the gentlemen instantly uncovered.

"Why, thin, gintlemen," he continued, "you have caught us in our little relaxations to-day; but—hem!—I mane to give the boys a holiday for the sake of this honest and respectable gintleman in the frize jock, who is not entirely ignorant, you persave, of litherature; and we had a small taste, gintlemen, among ourselves, of Sathurnalian licentiousness, *ut ita dicam,* in regard of—hem!—in regard of this lad here, who was dancing a hornpipe upon the door, and we, in absence of bether music, had to supply him with the harmony; but, as your honours know, gintlemen, the greatest men have bent themselves on espacial occasions."

"Make no apology, Mr. Kavanagh; it's very commendable in you to *bend* yourself by condescending to amuse your pupils."

"I beg your pardon, Squire, I can take freedoms with you; but perhaps the concomitant gintleman, your friend here, would be pleased to take my stool. Indeed, I always use a chair, but the back of it, if I may be permitted the use of a small portion of jocularity, was as frail as the fair sect: it went home yisterday to be minded. Do, Sir, condescind to be *sated.* Upon my reputation, Squire, I'm sorry that I have not accommodation for you, too, Sir; except one of these hassocks, which, in joint considheration with the length of your honour's legs, would be, I anticipate, rather low; but *you,* Sir, will honour me by taking the stool."

By considerable importunity he forced the gentleman to comply with his courtesy; but no sooner had he fixed himself upon the seat, than it overturned, and stretched him, black coat and all, across a wide concavity in the floor, nearly filled up with white ashes produced from mountain turf. In a moment he was completely white on one side, and exhibited a most laughable appearance; his hat, too, was scorched, and nearly burned on the turf coals. Squire Johnston laughed heartily, as did the other schoolmaster, whilst the Englishman completely lost his temper—swearing that so uncivilized an establishment was not between the poles.

"I solemnly supplicate upwards of fifty pardons," said Mat; "bad manners to it for a stool! but, your honour, it was my own defect of speculation, bekase, you see, it's *minus* a leg—a circumstance of which you warn't in a proper capacity to take cognation, as not being personally acquainted with it. I humbly supplicate upwards of fifty pardons."

The Englishman was now nettled, and determined to wreak his ill temper on Mat, by turning him, and his establishment into ridicule.

"Isn't this, Mister——I forget your name, Sir."

"Mat Kavanagh, at your sarvice."

"Very well, my learned friend, Mr. Mat Kavanagh, isn't this precisely what is called *a hedge school?*"

"A hedge-school!" replied Mat, highly offended; "My siminary a hedge-school! No Sir; I scorn the *cognomen, in toto.* This, Sir, is a Classical and Mathematical Siminary, under the personal superintendance of your humble servant."

"Sir," replied the other master, who till then was silent, wishing, perhaps, to sack Mat in presence of the gentleman, "it is a hedge-school; and he is no scholar, but an ignoramus, whom I'd sack in three minutes, that would be ashamed of a hedge-school."

"Ay," says Mat, changing his tone, and taking the cue from his friend, whose learning he dreaded, "it's just, for argument's sake, a hedge-school; and, what is more, I scorn to be ashamed of it."

"And do you not teach occasionally under the hedge behind the house here?"

"Granted," replied Mat; "and now, where's your *vis consequentiæ?*"

"Yes," subjoined the other, "produce your vis *consequentiæ.*"

The Englishman himself was rather at a loss for the *vis consequentiæ,* and replied, "Why don't you live, and learn, and teach like civilized beings, and not assemble like wild asses—pardon me, my friend, for the simile——at least like wild colts, in such clusters behind the ditches?"

"A clusther of wild coults!" said Mat; "that shows what you are no man of classical larnin' would use such a word."

"Permit me, Sir," replied the strange master, "to ax your honour one question—did you receive a *classical* education? Are you college-bred?"

"Yes," replied the Englishman; "I can reply to both in the affirmative. I'm a Cantabrigian."

"You're a *what?*" asked Mat.

"I am a Cantabrigian."

"Come, Sir, you must explain yourself, if you plase. I'll take my oath that's neither a classical nor a mathematical tarm."

The gentleman smiled. "I was educated in the English College of Cambridge."

"Well," says Mat, "and may be you would be as well off if you had picked up your larnin' in our own Thrinity; there's good picking in Thrinity, for gintlemen like you, that are sober and harmless about the brains, in regard of not being overly bright."

"You talk with contempt of a hedge school," replied the other master. "Did you never hear, for all so long as you war in Cambridge, of a nate little spot in Greece, called the Groves of Academus?

Inter lucos Academi quærere verum.

What was Plato himself but a hedge schoolmaster? and, with humble submission, it casts no slur on an Irish tacher to be compared to him, I think. You forget, also, Sir, that the Dhruids taught under their oaks."

"Ay," added Mat, "and the Tree of Knowledge, too. Faith, an' if that same tree was now in being, if there wouldn't be hedge schoolmasters, there would be plinty of hedge scholars, any how—particularly if the fruit was well tasted."

"I believe, Millbank, you must give in," said Squire Johnston. "I think you have got the worst of it."

"Why," said Mat, "if the gintleman's not afther bein' sacked clane, I'm not here."

"Are you a mathematician," enquired Mat's friend, determined to follow up his victory; "do you know Mensuration?"

"Come, I do know Mensuration," said the Englishman, with confidence.

"And how would you find the solid contents of *a load of thorns?*" said the other.

"Ay, or how will you consther and parse me this sintince?" said Mat——

> "Regibus et dodbus solemus stopere windous,
>
> Nos numerus sumus fruges consumere nati,
>
> Stercora flat stiro rara terra-tantaro bungo."

"Aisy, Mister Kavanagh," replied the other, "let the Cantabrigian resolve the one I propounded him first."

"And let the Cantabrigian then take up mine," said Mat: "and if he can expound it, I'll give him a dozen more to bring home in his pocket, for the Cambridge folk to crack after their dinner, along wid their nuts."

"Can you do the 'Snail?'" inquired the stranger.

"Or 'A and B on opposite sides of a wood,' without the Key?" said Mat.

"Maybe," said the stranger, who threw off the frize jock, and exhibited a muscular frame of great power, cased in an old black coat—"maybe the gintleman would like to get a small taste of the '*Scuffle.*'"

"Not at all," replied the Englishman; "divel the least curiosity I have for it—I assure you I have not. What the deuce do they mean, Johnston? I hope you have influence over them."

"Hand me down that cudgel, Jack Brady, till I show the gintleman the 'Snail' and the 'Maypole,'" said Mat.

"Never mind, my lad; never mind, Mr.——a——Mr. Kavanagh. I give up the contest, I resign you the palm, gentlemen. The hedge school has beaten Cambridge hollow."

"One poser more, before you go, Sir," said Mat—"Can you give Latin for a *game-egg* in two words?"

"Eh, a game egg? No, by my honor, I cannot—gentlemen, I yield."

"Ay, I thought so," replied Mat; "bring it home to Cam-bridge, anyhow, and let them chew their cuds upon it, you persave; and, by the sowl of Newton, it will puzzle the whole establishment, or my name's not Kavanagh."

"It will, I am convinced," replied the gentleman, eyeing the herculean frame of the strange teacher, and the substantial cudgel in Mat's hand; "it will, undoubtedly.

But who is this most miserable, naked lad here, Mr. Kavanagh?"

"Why, Sir," replied Mat, with his broad Milesian face, expanding with a forthcoming joke, "he is, Sir, in a sartin and especial particularity, a namesake of your own."

"How is that, Mr. Kevanagh?"

"My name's not Kevanagh," replied Mat, "but Kavanagh; the Irish A for ever!"

"Well, but how is the lad a namesake of mine?" said the Englishman.

"Bekase, you see, he's a *poor scholar,* Sir," replied Mat; "an' hope your honour will pardon me for the facetiousness——

Quid vetat ridentem dicere verum?

as Horace says to Mæcenas, on the first of the Sathirs?"

"There, Mr. Kavanagh, is the price of a suit of clothes for him."

"Michael, will you rise up, Sir, and make the gintleman a bow?.He has given you the price of a shoot of clothes, ma bouchal."

Michael came up with a thousand rags dangling about him; and, catching his fore-lock, bobbed down his head after the usual manner, saying—"Musha yarrah, long life to your honour every day you rise, an' the Lord grant your sowl a short stay in purgatory, wishin' ye, at the same time, a happy death afterwards!"

The gentlemen could not stand this, but laughed so heartily that the argument was fairly knocked up.

It appeared, however, that Squire Johnston did not visit Mat's school from mere curiosity.

"Mr. Kavanagh," said he, "I would be glad to have a little private conversation with you, and will thank you to walk down the road a little with this gentleman and me."

When the gentlemen and Mat had gone ten or fifteen yards from the school door, the Englishman heard himself congratulated in the following phrases:

"How do you feel afther bein' *sacked,* gintleman? The masther sacked you! You're a purty scholar! It's not you, Mr. Johnston, it's the other. You'll come to argue agin, will you? Where's your head, now? Bah! Come back till we put the soogaun* about your neck. Bah! You must go to school to Cam-bridge agin, before you can argue an Irisher! Look at the figure he cuts! Why duv ye put the one foot past the other, when ye walk, for? Bah! Dunce!!"

"Well, boys, never heed yees for that," shouted Mat; "never fear but I'll castigate yees, ye spalpeen villains, as soon as I go back. Sir," said Mat, "I supplicate upwards of fifty pardons. I assure you, Sir, I'll give them a most inordinate castiga-

The soogaun was a collar of straw which was put round the necks of the dunces, who were then placed at the door, that their disgrace might be as public as possible.

tion, for their want of respectability."

"What's the Greek for tobaccy?" they continued—"or for Larry O'Toole? or for bletherum skite? How many beans make five? What's Latin for poteen, and flummery? You a mathemathitician! could you measure a snail's horn? How does your hat stay up and nothing undher it? Will you fight Barny Farrell wid one hand tied? I'd lick you myself! What's Greek for gosther?" with many other expressions of a similar stamp.

"Sir," said Mat, "lave the justice of this in my hands. By the sowl of Newton, your own counthryman, ould Mac, I'll flog the marrow out of them."

"You have heard, Mr. Kavanagh," continued Mr. Johnston, as they went along, "of the burning of Moore's stable and horses, the night before last. The fact is, that the magistrates of the county are endeavouring to get the incendiaries, and would render a service to any person capable, either directly or indirectly of facilitating that object, or stumbling on a clew to the transaction."

"And how could I do you a sarvice in it, Sir?" inquired Mat.

"Why," replied Mr. Johnston, "from the children. If you could sift them in an indirect way, so as, without suspicion, to ascertain the absence of a brother, or so, on that particular night, I might have it in my power to serve you, Mr. Kavanagh. There will be a large reward offered to-morrow, besides."

"Oh, damn the penny of the reward ever I'd finger, even if I knew the whole conflagration," said Mat: "but lave the siftin' of the children wid myself, and if I can get any thing out of them, you'll hear from me; but your honour must keep a close mouth, or you might have occasion to lend me the money for my own funeral some o' these days. Good morning, gintlemen."

The gentlemen departed.

"May the most ornamental kind of hard fortune pursue you every day you rise, you desavin villian, that would have me turn *informer*, bekase your brother-in-law, rack-rintin' Moore's stable and horses were burnt; but I'd see you and all your breed in the flames o' hell first." Such was Mat's soliloquy as he entered the school on his return.

"Now, boys, I'm afther givin' yees to-day and to-morrow for a holy-day: to-morrow we will have our Gregory; a fine faste, plinty of poteen, and a fiddle; and you will tell your brothers and sisters to come in the evening to the dance. You must bring plinty of bacon, hung beef, and fowls, bread and cabbage—not forgetting the phaties, and sixpence a-head for the *crathur*, boys, won't yees?"

The next day, of course, was one of festivity: every boy brought, in fact, as much provender as would serve six; but the surplus gave Mat some good dinners for three months to come. This feast was always held upon St. Gregory's day, from which circumstance it had its name. The pupils were at liberty for that day to conduct themselves as they pleased: and the consequence was, that they became generally intoxicated, and were brought home in that state to their parents. If the children of two opposite parties chanced to be at the same school, they usually had a fight, of which the master was compelled to feign ignorance; for if he identified himself with either faction, his residence in the neighbourhood would be short. In other districts, where Protestant schools were in existence, a battle-royal commonly took place between the opposite establishments, in some field lying half-way between them. This has often occurred.

Every one must necessarily be acquainted with the ceremony of *barring out.* This took place at Easter and Christmas. The master was brought or sent out on some fool's errand, the door shut and barricadoed, and the pedagogue excluded, until a certain term of vacation was extorted. With this, however, the master never complied until all his efforts at forcing an entrance were found to be ineffectual; because if he succeeded in getting in, they not only had no claim to a long vacation, but were liable to be corrected. The schoolmaster had also generally the clerkship of the parish; an office, however, which in the country parts of Ireland is without any kind of salary, beyond what results from the patronage of the priest, a matter of serious moment to a teacher, who, should he incur his Reverence's displeasure, would be immediately driven out of the parish. The master, therefore, was always tyrannical and insolent to the people, in proportion as he stood high in the estimation of the priest. He was also the master of ceremonies at all wakes and funerals, and usually sat among a crowd of the village sages engaged in exhibiting his own learning and in recounting the number of his religious and literary disputations.

One day, soon after the visit of the gentlemen above mentioned, two strange men came into Mat's establishment—rather, as Mat thought, in an unceremonious manner.

"Is your name Matthew Kavanagh?" said one of them.

"That is indeed the name that's upon me", said Mat, with rather an infirm voice, whilst his face got as pale as ashes.

"Well, said the fellow, we'll jist trouble you to walk with us a bit."

"How far, with submission, are yees goin' to bring me?" said Mat.

"Do you know Johnny Short's hotel?"*

"My curse upon you, Findramore," exclaimed Mat, in a paroxism of anguish, "every day you rise! but your breath's unlucky to a schoolmasther; and it's no lie what was often said, that no schoolmasther ever thruv in you, but something ill came over him."

"Don't curse the town, man alive," said the constable, "but curse your own ignorance and folly; any way, I wouldn't stand in your coat for the wealth of the three kingdoms. You'll undoubtedly swing, unless you turn king's evidence. It's about Moore's business, Mr. Kavanagh."

"Dang the that I'd do, even if I knew any thing about it; but, God be praised for it, I can set them all at defiance—that I'm sure of. Gintlemen, innocence is a jewel."

"But Barny Brady, that keeps the sheebeen house—you know him—is of another opinion. You and some of the Findramore boys took a sup in Barny's on a sartin night?"

"Ay, did we, on many a night, and will agin, plase Providence—no harm in takin' a sup, any how—by the same token, that maybe you and yer friend here would have a drop of rale stuff, as a thrate from me?"

"I know a thrick worth two of that," said the man; "I thank ye kindly, Mr. Kavanagh."

One Tuesday morning, about six weeks after this event, the largest crowd ever remembered in that neighbourhood was assembled at Findramore. Hill, whereon had been erected a certain wooden machine, yclept—a gallows. A little after the hour of eleven o'clock, two carts were descried winding slowly down a slope in the southern side of the town and church, which I have already mentioned, as terminating the view along the level road north of the hill. As soon as they were observed, a low, suppressed ejaculation of horror ran through the crowd, painfully perceptible to the car—in the expression of ten thousand murmurs all blending into one deep groan—and to, the eye, by a simultaneous motion that ran through the crowd like an electric shock. The place of execution was surrounded by a strong detachment of military; and the carts that conveyed the convicts were also strongly guarded.

As the prisoners approached the fatal spot, which was within sight of the place where the outrage had been perpetrated, the shrieks and lamentations of their relations and acquaintances were appalling, indeed. Fathers, mothers, sisters, brothers, cousins, and all persons to the most remote degree of kindred and acquaintance-ship, were present—all excited by the alternate expression of grief and low-breathed vows of retaliation; not only relations, but all who were connected with them by the bonds of their desperate and illegal oaths. Every eye, in fact, corruscated with a wild and savage fire, that shot from under brows knit in a spirit that seemed to cry out blood, vengeance—blood, vengeance. The expression was truly awful, and what rendered it more terrific, was the writhing reflection, that numbers and were physical force unavailing against a comparatively small body of armed troops. This condensed the fiery impulse of the moment into an expression of subdued rage, that really shot like livid gleams from their visages.

At length the carts stopped under the gallows; and, after a short interval spent in devotional exercise, three of the culprits ascended the platform, who, after recommending themselves to God, and avowing their innocence, although the clearest possible evidence of guilt had been brought against them, were launched into another life, among the shrieks and groans of the multitude. The other three then ascended, two of them either declined, or had not strength to address the assembly. The third advanced to the edge of the boards—*it was Mat.* After two or three efforts to speak, in which he was unsuccessful from bodily weakness, he at length addressed them as follows:

"My friends and good people—In hopes that you may be all able to demonstrate the last proposition laid down by a dying man, I undertake to address you before I depart to that world where Euclid, De Carts, and many other larned men are gone before me. There is nothing in all philosophy more true, than that, as the multiplication-table says, 'two and two makes four;' but it is equally veracious and worthy of credit, that if you do not abnegate this system that you work the common rules of your proceedings by—if you don't become loyal men, and give up burnin' and murdherin', the solution of it will be found on the gallows. I acknowledge myself to be guilty, for not separatin' myself clane from yees; we have been all guilty, and may God forgive thim that jist now departed wid a lie in their mouth."

Here he was interrupted by a volley of execrations and curses, mingled with "stag, informer, thraithor to the thrue cause!" which, for some time, compelled him to be silent.

"You may curse," continued Mat; "but it's too late now to abscond the truth—the 'sum' of my wickedness and folly is worked out and you see the *'answer.'* God forgive me, many a young crathur I enticed into the *Ribbon* business and now it's to end in *Hemp!* Obey the law, or, if you don't, you'll find it a *lex talionis*—the construction of which is, that if a man burns or murdhers, he won't miss hanging; take warning by me—by us all; for, although I take God to witness that I was not at the perpetration of the crime that I'm to be suspinded for, yet I often connived, when I might have superseded the carrying of such intintions into effectuality. I die in pace wid all the world, save an' except the Findramore people, whom, may the maledictionary execration of a dying man follow into eternal infinity! My manuscription of conic sections—" Here an extraordinary buz commenced among the crowd, which rose gradually into a shout of wild, astounding exultation. The sheriff followed the eyes of the multitude, and perceived a horseman dashing with breathless fury up towards the scene of execution. He carried and waved a white handkerchief on the end of a rod, and made signals with his hat to stop the execution. He arrived, and brought a full pardon for Mat, and a commutation of sentence to transportation for life, for the other two. What became of Mat I know not; but in Findramore he never dared to appear, as certain death would have been the consequence of his not dying *game*. With respect to Barry Brady, who kept the shebeen, and was the principal evidence against those who were concerned in this outrage, he was compelled to enact an *ex tempore* death in less than a month afterwards; having been found dead, with a slip of paper in his mouth, inscribed— *"This is the fate of all Informers."*

THE STATION.

Our readers are to suppose the Reverend Philemy M'Guirk, parish priest of Tirneer, to be standing upon the altar of the chapel, facing the congregation, after having gone through the canon of the Mass; and having nothing more of the service to perform, than the usual prayers with which he closes the ceremony.

"Take notice, that the Stations for the following week will be bold as follows:— *"On Monday, in Jack Gallagher's, of Corraghnamoddagh.* Are you there, Jack?"

"To the fore, yer Reverence."

"Why, then, Jack, there's something ominous—something auspicious—to happen, or we wouldn't have you here; for it's very seldom that you make part or parcel of this *present* congregation; seldom are you here, Jack, it must be confessed: however, you know the old classical proverb, or if *you* don't, *I* do, which will just answer as well—*Non semper ridet Apollo*—it's not every day *Manus* kills a bullock: so, as you *are* here, be prepared for us on Monday."

"Never fear, yer Reverence, never fear; I think you ought to know that the grazin' at Corraghnamoddagh's not bad."

"To do you justice, Jack, the mutton was always good with you, only if you would get it better killed it would be an improvement."

"Very well, yer Rev'rence, I'll do it."

"On Tuesday in Peter Murtagh's of the Crooked Commons. Are you there, Peter?"

"Here, yer Reverence."

"Indeed, Peter, I might know you are here; and I wish that a great many of *my* flock would take example by you: if they did, I wouldn't be so far behind in getting in my *dues*. Well, Peter, I suppose you know that this is Michaelmas?"

"So fat, yer Reverence, that they're not able to wag; but, any way, Katty has them marked for you—two fine young crathurs, only last year's fowl, and the ducks isn't a taste behind them—she's crammin' them this month past."

"I believe you, Peter, and I would take your word for more than the condition of the geese—remember me to Katty, Peter."

"On Wednesday in Parrah More Slevin's, of Mullaghfadh. Are you there, Parrah More?"—No answer. "Parah More Slevin?"—Silence. "Parrah More Slevin, of Mullaghfadh?"—No reply. "Dan Fagan?"

"Present, Sir."

"Do you know what keeps that reprobate from mass?"

"I bleeve he's takin' advantage, Sir, of the frast, to get in his praties to-day, in respect of the bad footin', Sir, for the horses in the bog when there's not a frast. Any how, betune that and a bit of a sore head that he got, yer Reverence, on Thursday last in takin' part wid the O'Scallaghans agin the Bradys, I believe he had to stay away to-day."

"On the Sabbath day, too, without my leave! Well, tell him from me, that I'll make an example of him to the whole parish, if he doesn't attend mass better. Will the Bradys and the O'Scallaghans never be done with their quarrelling? I protest, if they don't live like Christians, I'll read them out from the altar. Will you tell Parrah More that I'll hold a station in his house on next Wednesday?"

"I will, Sir; I will, yer Reverence."

"On Thursday in Phaddy Sheemus Phaddhy's of the Esker. Are you there, Phaddy?"

"Wid the help of God, I'm here, Sir."

"Well, Phaddhy, how is yer son Briney, that's at the Latin? I hope he's coming on well at it?"

"Why, Sir, he's not more nor a year and a half at it yet, and he's got more book amost nor he can carry—he'll break me buying books for him."

"Well, that's a good sign, Phaddhy, but why don't you bring him to me till I examine him?"

"Why, never a one of me can get him to go, Sir, he's so much afeard of yer Reverence."

"Well Phaddhy, we were once modest and bashful ourselves, and I'm glad to hear that he's afraid of his *clargy;* but let him be prepared for me on Thursday, and maybe I'll let him know something he never heard before; I'll give him a

Maynooth touch."

"Do you hear that Briney," said the father, aside to the son, who knelt at his knee—"ye must give up yer hurling and idling now, you see. Thank yer Reverence, thank you, docthor."

"On Friday in Barny O'Darby's, alias *Barny Butter's.* Are you there, Barny?"

"All that's left of me is here, Sir."

"Well, Barny, how is the butter trade this season?"

"It's a little on the rise now, Sir; in a month or so I'm expecting it will be brisk enough; *Boney,* Sir, is doing that much for us any way."

"Ay, and, Barny, he'll do more than that for us: God prosper *him* at all events— I only hope the time's coming, Barny, when every one will be able to eat his own butter, and his own beef, too."

"God send it, Sir."

"Well, Barny, I didn't hear from your brother Ned these two or three months; what has become of him?"

"Ah, yer Reverence, Pentland done him up."

"What! the gauger?"

"He did, the thief; but maybe he'll sup sorrow for it, afore he's much oulder."

"And who do you think informed, Barny?"

"Oh, I only wish we knew that, Sir."

"I wish *I* knew it, and if I thought any miscreant here would become an *informer,* I'd make an example of him. Well, Barny, on Friday next; but I suppose Ned has a drop still—eh, Barny?"

"Why, Sir, we'll be apt to have something stronger nor wather, any how."

"Very well, Barny: your family was always a dacent and spirited family, I'll say that for them: but tell me, Barny, did you begin to *dam* the river yet?* I think the trouts and eels are running by this time.""The creels are made, yer Reverence, though we did not set them yet; but on Tuesday night, Sir, wid the help o' God, we'll be ready."

"You can *corn* the trouts, Barry, and the eels too; but, should you catch nothing, go to Pat Hartigan, Captain Sloethorn's game-keeper, and if you tell him it's for me, he'll drag you a batch out of the fish-pond."

---

*It is usual among the peasantry to form, about Michaelmas, small artificial cascades, called *dams,* under which they place long deep wicker creels, shaped like inverted cones, for the purpose of securing the fish that are now on their return to the large rivers, after having deposited their spawn in the higher and remoter streams. It is surprising what a number of fish, particularly of eels, are caught in this manner—sometimes from one barrel to three in the course of a single night!

"Ah! then, yer Reverence, it's 'imself that'ill do that wid a heart an' a half."

Such was the conversation which took place between the Reverend Philemy M'Guirk, and those of his parishioners in whose houses he had appointed to hold a series of stations, for the week ensuing the Sunday laid in this our account of that hitherto undescribed portion of the Romish discipline.

Now, the reader is to understand, that a station in this sense differs from a station made to any peculiar spot, remarkable for local sanctity. There a station means the performance of a pilgrimage to a certain place, under peculiar circumstances and the going through a stated number of prayers and other penitential ceremonies, for the purpose of wiping out sin in this life, or of relieving the soul of some relation from the pains of purgatory in the other; here, it simply means the coming of the parish priest and his curate to some house in the townland, on a day publicly announced from the altar for that purpose, on the preceding Sabbath.

This is done to give those who live within the district in which the station is held an opportunity of *coming to their duty,* as frequenting the ordinance of confession is emphatically called. Those who attend confession in this manner once a year, are considered *merely* to have done their duty; it is expected, however, that they should *approach the tribunal,* as it is termed, at least twice during that period, that is, at the two great feasts of Christmas and Easter. The observance or omission of this rite among Roman Catholics, establishes, in a great degree, the nature of individual character. The man who frequents his duty will seldom be pronounced a bad man, let his conduct and principles be what they may in other respects; and he who neglects it, is looked upon, by those who attend it, as in a state little short of reprobation, no matter how correct or religious he may be, either in public; or private life.

When the "giving out" of the stations was over, and a few more jests were broken by his Reverence, to which the congregation paid the tribute of a general and uproarious laugh, he turned round on his heel, and with the greatest *sang froid* resumed the performance of the mass, whilst his flock began to finger their beads with faces as grave as if nothing of the kind had occurred. When mass was finished, and the holy water sprinkled upon the people, out of a tub carried by the mass-server through the chapel for that purpose, the priest gave them a fine Latin benediction, and they dispersed.

Now, of the four individuals in whose houses the "stations" were appointed to be held, we will select *Phaddhy Sheemus Phaddhy* for our purpose; and this we do, because it was the first time in which a station was ever kept in his house, and consequently *Phaddhy* and his wife had to undergo the initiatory ceremony of entertaining Father *Philemy* and his curate, the Reverend *Con M'Coul,* at dinner.

Phaddhy Sheemus Phaddhy had been, until a short time before the period in question, a very poor man; but a little previous to that event, a brother of his, who had no children, died very rich—that is, for a farmer—and left him his property, or, at least, the greater part of it. While Phaddhy was poor, it was surprising what little notice he excited from his Reverence; in fact, I have heard him acknowledge, that during all the days of his poverty, he never got a nod of recognition or kindness from Father Philemy, although he sometimes did, he said, from Father Con, his curate, who honoured him on two occasions so far as to challenge him to a bout at throwing the shoulder-stone, and once to a leaping match, at both of which exercises Father Con, but for the superior power of Phaddhy, had been unrivalled.

"It was an unlucky day to him," said Phaddhy, "that he went to challenge me, at all, at all; for I was the only man that ever bate him, and he wasn't able to hould up his head in the parish, for many a day afther."

As soon, however, as Phaddhy became a man of substance, one would almost think that there had been a secret relationship between his good fortune and Father Philemy's memory; for, on their first meeting, afther Phaddhy's getting the property, the latter shook him most cordially by the hand—a proof that, had not his recollection been as much improved as Phaddhy's circumstances, he could by no means have remembered him; but this is a failing in the memory of many, as well as in that of Father Philemy. Phaddhy, however, *was no Donnell,* to use his own expression, and saw as far into a deal board as another man.

"And so, Phaddhy," said the priest, "how are all your family?—six you have, I think?"

"Four, yer Rev'rence, only four," said Phaddhy, winking at Tim Dillon, his neighbour, who happened to be present—"three boys an' one girl."

"Bless my soul, and so it is indeed, Phaddhy, and I ought to know it; and how is your wife Sarah?—I mean, I hope Mrs. Sheemus Phaddhy is well: by the bye, is that old complaint of her gone yet?—a pain in the stomach, I think it was, that used to trouble her—I hope in God, Phaddhy, she's getting over it, poor thing. Indeed, I remember telling her, last Easter, when she came to her duty, to eat oaten bread and butter with water-grass every morning, *fasting,* it cured myself of the same complaint."

"Why, thin, I'm very much obliged to your Rev'rence, for purscribin' for her," replied Phaddhy;—"for, sure enough, she has neither pain nor ache, at the present time, for the best rason in the world, docthor, that she'll be dead jist seven years, if

God spares yer Rev'rence an' myself till tomorrow fortnight, about five o'clock in the mornin'."

This was more than Father Philemy could stand with a good conscience, so after getting himself out of the dilemma as well as he could, he shook Phaddhy again very cordially, by the hand saying, "Well, good bye, Phaddhy, and God be good to poor Sarah's soul—I now remember her funeral, sure enough, and a dacent one it was, for indeed she was a woman that had every body's good word—and, between you and me, she made a happy death, that's as far as we can judge here; for, after all, there may be danger, Phaddhy, there may be danger, you under-stand—however, it's your own business, and your duty, too, to think of that; but I believe you're not the man that would be apt to forget her."

"Phaddhy, ye thief o' the world," said Tim Dillon, when Father Philemy was gone, "there's no comin' up to ye; how could you make sich a fool of his Rev'rence, as to tell 'im that Katty was dead, an' that you had any four childher, an' you has eleven o' them, an' the wife in good health?"

"Why, jist. Tim," replied Phaddhy, with his usual shrewdness, "to tache his Rev'rence himself to practice truth a little: if he didn't know that I got the stockin' of guineas and the Lisnaskey farm by my brother Barney's death, div ye think that he'd notish me at all at all?—not himself, avick; an' maybe he won't be afther comin' round to me for a sack of my best oats, instead of the bushel I used to give him, and houldin' a couple of stations wid me every year."

"But won't he go mad when he hears you tould him nothing but lies?"

"Not now, Tim," answered Phaddhy—"not now, thank God I'm not a poor man, an he'll keep his temper. I'll warrant you the horsewhip won't be up now, although, afore this, I wouldn't say but it might—though the poorest day I ever was, id's myself that wouldn't let a priest or friar lay a horsewhip to my back, an' that you know, Tim."

Phaddhy's sagacity, however, was correct; for, a short time after this conversa-tion, Father Philemy, when collecting his oats, gave him a call, laughed heartily at the sham account of Katty's death, examined young Briney in his Latin, who was called after his uncle—pronounced him very *cute,* and likely to become a great scholar—promised his interest with the bishop to get him into Maynooth, and left the family, after having shaken hands with, and stroked down the heads of, all the children.

When Phaddhy, on the Sunday in question, heard the public notice given of the Station about to be held in his house, notwithstanding his correct knowledge of Father Philemy's character, on which he looked with a competent portion of contempt, he felt a warmth of pride about his heart, that arose from the honour of having a station, and of entertaining the clergy in their official capacity, under his own roof, and at his own expense; that gave him, he thought, a personal consequence, which even the "stockin' of guineas" and the Lisnaskey farm were unable, of themselves, to confer upon him. He did enjoy, 'tis true, a very fair portion of happiness on succeeding to his brother's property, but this would be a triumph over the envious and ill-natured remarks which several of his neighbours and distant relations had taken the liberty of indulging in against him, on the occasion of his good fortune. He left the chapel, therefore, in good spirits, whilst Briney, on the contrary, hung a lip of more melancholy pendency than usual, in dread apprehension of the examination that he expected to be inflicted on him by his Reverence at the Station.

Before I introduce the conversation which look place between Phaddhy and Briney, as they went home, on the subject of this literary ordeal, I must observe, that there is a custom, hereditary in some Irish families, of calling fathers by their *Christian* names, instead of by the usual appellation of "father." This usage was observed, not only by Phaddhy and his son, but by all the Phaddhy's of that family, generally. Their surname was *Doran,* but in consequence of the great numbers in that part of the country who bore the same name, it was necessary, as of old, to distinguish the several branches of it by the Christian names of their fathers and grandfathers, and sometimes this distinction went as far back as the great-grandfather. For instance—Phaddhy Sheemus Phaddhy, meant Phaddhy, the son of Sheemus, the son of Phaddhy; and his son, Briney, was called, Brian Phaddhy Sheemus Phaddhy, or, *anglice,* Bernard the son of Patrick, the son of James, the son of Patrick. But the custom of children calling fathers, in a *viva voce* manner, by their Christian names, was independent of the other more general usage of the patronymic.

"Well, Briney," said Phaddhy, as the father and son returned home, cheek by jowl, from the chapel, "I suppose Father Philemy will go very deep in the Latin wid ye on Thursday; do ye think ye'll be able to answer him?"

"Why, Phaddhy," replied Briney, "how could *I* be able to answer a clargy?—doesn't he know all the languages, and I'm only in the *Fibulæ Æsiopii* yet."

"Is that Latin or Greek, Briney?"

"It's Latin, Phaddhy."

"And what's the translation of that?"

"It signifies the *Fables of Æsiopius.*"

"Bliss my sowl! and Briney did ye consther that out of yer own head?"

"Hogh! that's little of it. If ye war to hear me consther *Gallus Gallinaceus,* a dunghill cock!"

"And, Briney, are ye in Greek at all yet?"

"No, Phaddhy, I'll not be in Greek till I'm in Virgil and Horace, and thin I'll be near finished."

"And how long will it be till that, Briney?"

"Why, Phaddhy, ye know I'm only a year and a half at the Latin, and in two years more I'll be in the Greek?"

"Do ye think will ye ever be as larned as Father Philemy, Briney?"

"Don't ye know whin I'm a clargy I will; but I'm only a *lignum sacerdotis* yet, Phaddhy."

"What's *ligdum saucerdoatis,* Briney?"

"A block of a priest, Phaddy."

"Now, Briney, I suppose Father Philemy knows every thing."

"Ay, to be sure he does; all the languages that's spoken through the world, Phaddhy."

"And must all the priests know them, Briney?—how many are they?"

"Seven—sartinly, every priest must know them or how could they lay the divil, if he'd spake to them in a tongue they couldn't understand, Phaddhy?"

"Ah, I declare, Briney, I see it now; ony for that, poor Father Philip, the heavens be his bed, wouldn't be able to lay ould Warnock, that haunted Squire Sloethorn's stables."

"Is that when the two horses was stole, Phaddhy?"

"The very time, Briney; but God be thanked, Father Philip settled him to the day of judgment."

"And where did he put him, Phaddhy?"

"Why, he wanted to be put anundher the hearth-stone; but Father Philip made him walk away with himself into a thumb-bottle, and tied a stone to it, and then sent him to where he got a cooling, the thief, at the bottom of the lough behind the house."

"Well, I'll tell you what I'm thinking I'll be apt to do, Phaddhy, when I'm a clargy."

"And what is that, Briney?"

"Why, I'll——but, Phaddhy, don't be talking of this, bekase, if it should come to be known, I might get my brains knocked out by some of the heretics."

"Never fear, Briney, there's no danger of *that*—but what is it?"

"Why, I'll translate all the Protestants into asses, and then we'll get our hands

*I have no hesitation in asserting, that the bulk of the Irish peasantry really believe that the Romish priests have this power.

red of them altogether."

"Well, that flogs for cuteness, and it's a wondher the clargy* doesn't do it, and them has the power; for 'twould give us pace entirely. But, Briney, will you spake in Latin to Father Philemy, on Thursday?"

"To tell you the thruth, Phaddhy, I would rather he wouldn't examine me this bout, at all at all."

"Ay, but you know we couldn't go agin him, Briney, bekase he promised to get you into the college. Will you spake some Latin now till I hear you?"

"Hem!—*Verbum personaley cohairit cum nomnatibo numbera at parsona at numquam sera yeast at bonis moras voia.*"

"Bless my heart!—and, Briney, where's that taken from?"

"From Syntax, Phaddhy."

"And who was Shintax—do you know, Briney?"

"He was a Roman, Phaddhy, bekase there's a Latin prayer in the beginning of the book."

"Ay, was he—a priest, I'll warrant him. Well, Briney, do you mind yer Latin, and get on wid yer larnin', and whin you grow up you'll have a pair of boots, and a horse of your own (and a good broadcloth black coat, too,) to ride on, every bit as good as Father Philemy's, and maybe betther nor Father Con's."

From this point, which usually wound up these colloquies between the father and son, the conversation usually diverged into the more spacious fields of science; so that, by the time they reached home, Briney had probably given the father a learned dissertation upon the elevation of the clouds above the earth, and told him within how many thousand miles they approached it, at their nearest point of approximation.

"Katty," said Phaddhy, when he got home; "we're to have a station here on Thursday next; 'twas given out from the altar to-day by Father Philemy."

"Oh, wurrah, wurrah!" exclaimed Katty, overwhelmed at the consciousness of her own incapacity to get up a dinner in sufficient style for such guests—"wurrah, wurrah! Phaddhy, ahagur, what on the livin' earth will we do, at all at all! Why we'll never be able to manage it."

"Arrah why, Katty, woman, what do they want but their skinful to eat and dhrink, and I'm sure we're able to allow them that, any way"

"Arrah, bad manners to me, but you're enough to vex a saint—'their skinful to eat and dhrink!'—you common crathur you, to spake that-a-way of the clargy, as if it was ourselves or the labourers you war spaking of."

"Ay, and aren't we every bit as good as they are, if you go to that?—haven't we sowls to be saved as well as themselves?"

"'As good as they are?'—As good as the clargy!! *Manum a yea, agus wurrah!**—listen to what he says! Phaddhy, take care of yourself, you've got rich, now; but, for all that, take care of yourself. You had betther not bring the priest's ill-will, or his bad heart upon us. You know they never thruv that had it; and maybe it's a short time your riches might stay wid you, or maybe it's a short time you might stay wid them at any rate, God forgive you, and I hope he will, for makin' use of sich unsanctified words to your lawful clargy."

"Well, but what do you intind to do?—or, what do you think of getting for them?" inquired Phaddhy.

"Indeed, it's very little matther what I get for them, or what I'll do either—sorrow one of myself cares almost: for a man in his senses, that ought to know better, to make use of such low language about the blessed and holy crathurs, that hasn't a stain of sin about them, no more than the child unborn!"

"So *you* think?"

"So *I* think! ay, and it would be betther for you that you thought so, too; but ye don't know what's before yee yet, Phaddhy; and now take warnin' in time, and mend your life."

"Why, what do you see wrong in my life? am I a drunkard? am I lazy? did ever I neglect my business? was I ever bad to you or to the childher? didn't I always give yees yer fill to ate? and kept yees as well clad as yer neighbours that was richer? don't I go on my knees, too every night and morning?"

"That's true enough, but what signifies it all? When did ye cross a priest's foot, to go to your duty? not for the last five years, Phaddhy—not since poor Torly (God be good to him) died of the mazles, and that'ill be five years, a fortnight before Christmas."

"And what are you the betther of all yer confessions? did they ever mend yer temper, avourneen? no, indeed, Katty, but you're ten times worse tempered coming back from the priest than before ye go to him."

"Oh, Phaddhy! Phaddhy! God look down apon you this day, or any man that's in yer hardened state—I see there's no use in spaking to you, for you'll still be the ould cut."

"Ay, will I; so you may as well give up talking about it. Arrah, woman!" said Phaddhy, raising his yoice, "who does it ever make betther—show me a man now in all the neighbourhood, that's a pin-point the holier of it? Isn't there Jemmy Shields, that goes to *his duty* wanst a month, malivogues his wife and family this minute, and then claps them to a Rosary the next; but the ould boy's a thrifle to him of a fast day, afther coming from the priest. Betune ourselves, Katty, you're not much behind him."

Katty made no reply to this, but turned up her eyes, and crossed herself, at the wickedness of her unmanageable husband.

"Well, Briney," said she, turning abruptly to the son, "don't take patthern by that man, if you expect to do any good; let him be a warning to you to mind yer duty, and respect yer clargy—and prepare yerself, now that I think of it, to go to Father Philemy or Father Con on Thursday but don't be said or led by that man, for I'm sure I dunna how he intinds to face the man above when he laves this world—and to keep from his duty, and to spake of his clargy as he does!"

There are few men without their weak sides. Phaddhy, although the priests were never very much his favourites, was determined to give what he himself called a *let-out* on this occasion, simply to show his ill-natured neighbours that, notwithstanding their unfriendly remarks, he knew "what it was to be dacent," as well as his betters; and Katty seconded him in his resolution, from her profound veneration for the *clargy*.

Every preparation was accordingly entered into, and every plan adopted that could possibly be twisted into a capability of contributing to the entertainment of Fathers Philemy and Con.

One of these large round stercoraceous nosegays, that, like many other wholesome plants, make up by odour what is wanting in floral beauty, and which lay rather too *contagious,* as Phaddhy expressed it, to the door of his house, was transplanted by about half a dozen labourers, and as many barrows, in the course of a day or two, to a bed some yards distant from the spot of its first growth; because, without any reference whatsoever to the nasal sense, it was considered that it might be rather an *eye-sore* to their Reverences on approaching the door. Several concave inequalities, which constant attrition had worn in the earthen floor of the kitchen, were filled up with blue clay, brought on a car from the bank of a neighbouring river, for the purpose. The dresser, chairs, tables, pots, and pans, all underwent a rigour of discipline, as if some remarkable event was about to occur; nothing less, it must be supposed, than a complete domestic revolution, and a new state of things. Phaddhy himself cut two or three large furze bushes, and, sticking them on the end of a pitchfork, attempted to sweep down the chimney. For this purpose he mounted on the back of a chair, that he might be able to reach the top with more ease; but, in order that his footing might be firm, he made one of the servant-men sit upon the chair, to keep it steady during the operation. Unfortunately, however, it so happened that this man was needed to assist in removing a meal chest to another part of the house; this was under Katty's superintendence, who, seeing the fellow sit rather more at his ease than she thought the hurry and importance of the occasion permitted, called him, with a little of her usual sharpness and energy, to assist in removing the chest. For some reason or other, which it is not necessary to mention here, the fellow bounced from his seat, in obedience to the shrill tones of Katty, and the next moment Phaddhy (who was in a state of abstraction in the chimney, and totally unconscious of what was going forward below) made a descent decidedly contrary to the nature of that which most aspirants would be inclined to relish. A severe stun, however, was the most serious injury he received on his own part, and several round oaths, with a good drubbing, fell to the servant; but unluckily he left the furze bush behind him in the highest and narrowest part of the chimney; and were it not that an active fellow succeeded in dragging it up from the outside of the roof, the chimney ran considerable risk, as Katty said, of being choaked.

But along with the lustration which every fixture within the house was obliged to undergo, it was necessary that all the youngsters should get new clothes; and for this purpose, Jemmy Lynch, the tailor, with his two journeymen and three apprentices, were sent for in all haste, that he might fit Phaddhy and each of his six sons, in suits, from a piece of home-made frize, which Katty did not intend to break up till "towarst Christmas."

A station is no common event, and accordingly the web was cut up, and the tailor left a wedding-suit half-made, belonging to Edy Dolan, a thin old bachelor, who took it into his head to try his hand at becoming a husband ere he'd die. As soon as Jemmy and his train arrived, a door was taken off the hinges, and laid on the floor, for himself to sit upon, and a new drugget quilt was spread beside it, for his journeymen and apprentices. With nimble fingers they plied the needle and thread, and when night came, a turf was got, into which was stuck a piece of rod, pointed at one end and split at the other; the "white candle," slipped into a shaving of the fringe that was placed in the cleft end of the stick, was then lit, whilst many a pleasant story, told by Jemmy, who had been once in Dublin for six weeks, delighted the circle of lookers-on that sat around them.

At length the day previous to the important one arrived. Hitherto, all hands had contributed to make every thing in and about the house look "dacent;"— scouring, washing, sweeping, pairing, and repairing, had been all disposed of. The boys got their hair cut to the quick with the tailor's scissors; and such of the girls as were not full grown, got only that which grew on the upper part of the head taken of, by a cut somewhat resembling the clerical tonsure, so that they looked extremely wild and unsettled, with their straight locks projecting over their ears; every thing, therefore, of the less important arrangements had been gone through—but the weighty and momentons concern was as yet unsettled.

This was the feast; and alas I never was the want of experience more strongly felt than here. Katty was a bad cook, even to a proverb; and bore so indifferent a character in the country for cleanliness, that very few would undertake to eat her butter. Indeed, she was called Katty *Sallagh** on this account: however, this prejudice, whether ill or well founded, was wearing fast away, since Phaddhy had succeeded to the stocking of guineas, and the Lisnaskey farm. It might be, indeed, that her former poverty helped her neighbours to see this blemish more clearly: but the world is so seldom in the habit of judging people's qualities or failings through this medium, that the supposition is rather doubtful. Be this as it may, the arrangements for the breakfast and dinner must be made. There was plenty of bacon, and abundance of cabbages—eggs, *ad infinitum*—oaten and wheaten bread in piles—turkeys, geese, pullets, as fat as aldermen—cream as rich as Crœsus—and three gallons of poteen, one sparkle of which, as Father Philemy said in the course of the evening, would lay the hairs on St. Francis himself in his most self-negative mood, if he saw it. So far so good: every thing excellent and abundant in its way. Still the higher and more refined items—the *deliciæ epularum*—must be added. *White bread,* and tea, and sugar were yet to be got; and lump-sugar for the punch; and a tea-pot and cups and saucers to be borrowed and what else? Let me see. Yes; there was *boxty* bread to be made, to take, if they liked, with their tea; and for this purpose a number of raw-peeled potatoes was ground upon the rough side of a tin collinder, and afterwards put into a sheet, (for table-cloths they had none,) which was twisted in contrary directions by two of the stoutest men about the house, until it was shrunk up into a round hard lump in the middle, and made quite dry; it was then taken and (being mixed with a little flour, and some of Katty's questionable butter,) formed into flat cakes, and baked upon the griddle.

Well, suppose all things disposed for to-morrow's feast;—suppose Phaddhy himself to have butchered the fowl, because Katty, who was not able to bear the sight of blood, had not the heart to kill "he crathurs:" and imagine to yourself one of the servant men taking his red-hot tongs out of the fire, and squeezing a large lump of hog's lard, placed in a grisset, or *Kam,* on the hearth, to grease all their brogues; then see in your mind's eye those two fine, fresh-looking girls, slily taking their old rusty fork out of the fire, and going to a bit of three-cornered looking-glass, pasted into a board, or, perhaps, to a pail of water, there to curl up their rich-flowing locks, that had hitherto never known a curl but such as nature gave them.

On one side of the hob sit two striplings, "thryin' wan another in their cate-chise," that they may be able to answer, with some credit, tomorrow. On the other hob sits Briney, hard at his Syntax, with the *Fibulæ Æsiopii,* as he called it, placed open at a particular passage, on the seat under him, with a hope that, when Father Philemy will examine him, the book may open at his favourite fable of the *"Gallus Gallinaceus*—a dung-hill cock."* Phaddhy himself is obliged to fast this day, there being one day of his Penance yet unperformed, since the last time he was at his duty, which was, as aforesaid, about five years; and Katty, now that every thing is cleaned up and ready, kneels down in a corner to go over her beads, rocking herself in a placid silence that is only broken by an occasional malediction against the ser-vants, or the cat, when it attempts the abduction of one of the dead fowl.

The next morning the family were up before the sun, who rubbed his eyes, and swore that he must have overslept himself, on seeing such a merry column of smoke dancing over Phaddhy's chimney. A large wooden dish was placed upon the threshold of the kitchen door, filled with water, in which, with a trencher of oat-meal for soap, they successively scrubbed their faces and hands to some purpose. In a short time afterwards. Phaddhy and the sons were eased, stiff and awkward, in their new suits, with the tops of their fingers just peeping over the sleeve cuffs. The horses in the stable were turned out to the fields, being obliged to make room for their betters, that were soon expected under the reverend bodies of Father Philemy and his curate; whilst about half a bushel of oats was left in the manger, to regale them on their arrival. Little Richard Maguire was sent down to the *five-acres,* with the pigs, on purpose to keep them from about the house, they not being supposed fit company at a set-dinner. A roaring turf fire, which blazed two yards up the chimney, had been put down; on this was placed a large pot, filled with water for the tea, because they had no kettle.

By this time the morning was tolerably advanced, and the neighbours were beginning to arrive in twos and threes, to wipe out old scores. Katty had sent sev-eral of the gorsoons "to see if they could see any sight of the clargy," but hitherto their Reverences were invisible. At length, after several fruitless embassies of this description, Father Con was seen jogging along, on his easy going hack, engaged in the perusal of *his Office,* previous to his commencing the duties of the day. As soon as his approach was announced, a chair was immediately placed for him in a room off the kitchen—the parlour, such as it was, having been reserved for Father Philemy himself, as the place of greater honour. This was an arrangement, however, which went against the grain of Phaddhy, who, had he got his will, would have established Father Con in the most comfortable apartment of the house: but that old vagabond, human nature, is the same under all circumstances—or, as Katty would have (in her own phraseology) expressed it, "still the ould cut;" for even there the influence of rank and elevation was sufficient to throw merit into the shade; and the parlour-seat was allotted to Father Philemy, merely for being Parish Priest, although it was well known that he could not *"tare off"* mass in half the time that Father Con could; could not throw a sledge, or shoulder-stone, within a perch of him, nor scarcely clear a street channel, whilst the latter could jump one-and-twenty feet at a running leap. But these are rubs which men of merit must occasionally bear; and, when exposed to them, they must only rest satisfied in the consciousness of their own deserts.

From the moment that Father Con became visible, the conversation of those who were collected in Phaddhy's, dropped gradually, as he approached the house, into a silence which was only broken by an occasional short observation, made by one or two of those who were in habits of the greatest familiarity with the priest; but when they heard the noise of his horse's feet near the door, the silence became general and uninterrupted.

There can scarcely be a greater contrast in anything, than that presented by the beginning of a station-day and its close. In the morning, the faces of those who are about to confess, present an expression, in which terror, awe, guilt, and veneration, may be easily traced; but in the evening all is mirth and jollity. Before confession every man's memory is employed in running over the catalogue of crimes, as they are to be found in the prayer-books, under the ten commandments, the seven deadly sins, the *Commandments* of the Church! the four sins that cry to heaven for vengeance, and the seven sins against the Holy Ghost. How is it possible, therefore, that a man who is thus engaged in endeavouring to recollect and classify his individual offences, can possibly feel sincere sorrow, or the fear of God? According to the constitution of the human mind, it cannot be done.

It is wrong to say, that the Roman Catholic peasantry go *spontaneously* to comply with this unnatural rite: in many instances, it is true, they do; but they generally approach it with terror, and the most unequivocal reluctance; and nothing but the strange and superstitious belief, that the priests can absolve them from the guilt of their individual sins, how black and enormous soever they may be, induces them to go at all.

When Father Con arrived, Phaddhy and Katty were instantly at the door to welcome him.

"*Musha, cead milliah failtha ghud,* to our house, Father Con, avourneen!" said Katty, dropping him a low curtsey, and spreading her new, brown, quilted petticoat, as far out on each side of her as it would go—"musha, and it's you that's welcome from my heart out."

"I thank you," said honest Con, who, as he knew not her name, did not pretend to know it.

"Well, Father Con," said Phaddhy, "this is the first time you have ever come to us this away; but, plase God, it won't be the last, I hope."

"I hope not, Phaddhy," said Father Con, who, notwithstanding his simplicity of character, loved a good dinner in the very core of his heart, "I hope not, *indeed,* Phaddhy."

He then threw his eye about the premises, to see what point he might set his temper to during the remainder of the day; for it is right to inform our readers, that a priest's temper, at a station, generally rises or falls, according to the prospect of his cheer.

Here, however, a little vista, or pantry, jutting out from the kitchen, and left ostentatiously open, presented him with a view which made his very nose curl with kindness. What it contained we do not pretend to say, not having seen it ourselves; we judge, therefore, only by its effects upon his physiognomy.

"Why, Phaddhy," he says, this is a very fine house you've got over you throwing his eye again towards a wooden buttress which supported one of the rafters that was broken.

"Why then, your Riverence, it would not be a bad one", Phaddhy replied, "if it had a new roof, and new side-walls; and I intend to get both next summer, if God spares me till then."

"Then, upon my word, if it had new sidewalls, a new roof, and new gavels, too," replied Father Con, "it would certainly look a great deal the better for it;—and do you intend to get them next summer, Phaddhy?'

"If God spares me, Sir."

"Are all these fine gorsoons yours, Phaddhy?"

"Why, so Katty says, your Reverence," replied Phaddhy, with a good-humoured laugh.

"Havn't you got one of them for the Church, Phaddhy?"

"Yes, your Reverence, there's one of them that I hope will live to have the *robes* upon him. Come over, Briney, and speak to Father Con.—He's not very far in his Latin yet, Sir; but his master tells me that he hasn't the likes of him in his school for brightness—Briney, will you come over, I say; come over, sirrah, and spake to the gintleman, and him wants to shake hands wid you—come up man, what are you afeard of?—sure Father Con's not going to examine you now."

"No, no, Briney," said Father Con; "I'm not about to examine you at present."

"He's a little dashed, yer Reverence, bekase he thought you war going to put him through some of his Latin," said the father, bringing him up like a culprit to Father Con, who shook hands with him, and, after a few questions as to the books he read, and his progress, dismissed him.

"But, Father Con, wid submission," said Katty "where's Father Philemy from us?—sure, we expected him along wid you, and he wouldn't go to disappoint us?"

"Oh, you needn't fear that, Katty," replied Father Con—"he'll be here present-ly—before breakfast, I'll engage for him, at any rate; but he had a touch of a head-ache this morning, and wasn't able to rise so early as I was."

During this conversation a little crowd collected about the door of the room in which he was to hear the confessions, each struggling and fighting to get the first turn; but here, as in the more important concerns of this world, the weakest went to the wall. He now went into the room, and, taking Katty herself first, the door was closed upon them, and he gave her absolution; and thus he continued to con-fess and absolve them, one by one, until breakfast.

Whenever a station occurs in Ireland, a crowd of mendicants and other strolling impostors seldom fail to attend it; on this occasion, at least, they did not. The day, though frosty, was fine; and the door was surrounded by a train of this description, including both sexes, some sitting on stones, some on stools, with their blankets rolled up under them; and other more ostensibly devout, on their knees, hard at prayer; which, lest their piety might escape notice, our readers may be assured, they did not offer up in silence. On one side you might observe a sturdy fellow, with a pair of tattered urthins secured to his back by a sheet or blanket pinned across his breast with a long iron skewer, their heads just visible at his shoulders, munching a thick piece of wheaten bread, and the father on his knees, with a huge wooden cross in his hand, repeating his *padereens,* and occasionally throwing a jolly eye towards the door, or, through the window opposite which be knelt, into the kitchen, as often as any peculiar stir or commotion led him to suppose that break-fast, the loadstar of his devotion, was about to be produced.

Scattered about the door, were knots of these, men and women, occasionally chatting together; and when the subject of their conversation happened to be exhausted, resuming their beads until some new topic would occur, and so on alternately.

The interior of the kitchen where the neighbours were assembled, presented an appearance somewhat more decorous. Andy Lalor, the mass-server, in whom the priest had the greatest confidence, stood in a corner examining, in their catechism, those who intended to confess; and, if they were able to stand the test, he gave them a bit of twisted brown paper as a ticket, and they were received at the tribunal.

The first question the priest uniformly puts to the penitent is, "Can you repeat the *Confiteor?"* If the latter answers in the affirmative, he goes on until he comes to the words, *mea culpa, mea culpa, mea maxima culpa,* when he stops, it being improper to repeat the remainder until after he has confessed; but, if he is ignorant of the *Confiteor, the priest repeats it for him!* and he commences the rehearsal of his offences, specifically as they occurred; and not only does he reveal his individual crimes, but his very thoughts and intentions. By this wily regulation our readers may easily perceive, that the penitent is completely at the mercy of the priest—that all family feuds, quarrels, and secrets, are laid open to his eye—that the ruling passions of men's lives are held up before him, and all the weaknesses and propensities of a corrupt nature—all the unguarded avenues of the human heart and character are brought within his positive knowledge, and that too, as they exist in the young and the old, the married and the single, the male and the female. It has been often wondered at, why there is, and has been, such a deplorable prostration of reason and moral independence before the priesthood of the Church of Rome, in the persons of their followers; but, let me ask, would it not be a greater anomaly were it otherwise? How is it possible for any individual who throws open the secret corruptions and failings of his heart before the eye of a priest—who puts him in possession of all the crimes and delinquencies of his life, to stand in the confidence of a manly and erect independence before him? Is it possible that he should be able to look him in the face, or bear the force of his glance? Under these circumstances, without at all considering the influence produced by the spiritual power with which Roman Catholics believe the priests to be invested, let us not think it strange that such a melancholy debasement characterizes the laity of the Romish Church.

It was curious to remark the ludicrous expression of temporary sanctity which was apparent on the countenances of many young men and maidens who were remarkable in the neighbourbood for attending dances and wakes, but who, on the present occasion, were sobered down to a gravity which sat very awkwardly upon them; particularly in the eyes of those who knew the lightness and drollery of their characters. This, however, was observable only *before* confession; for, as soon as "the priest's blessed hand had been over them," their gloom and anxiety passed away, and the thoughtless buoyancy of their natural disposition resumed its influence over their minds. A good-humoured nod, or a sly wink, from a young man to his female acquaintance, would now be indulged in; or, perhaps, a small joke would escape, which seldom failed to produce a subdued laugh from such as *had* confessed, or an impatient rebuke from those who had *not*.

"Tim!" one would exclaim, "arn't ye ashamed or afeard to get an that-a-way, and his Reverence undher the wan roof wid ye?"

"Tim, you had betther dhrop your joking," a second would observe, "and not be putting us through other, wherein we have our offences to remimber; you have got your *job* over, and now you have nothing to trouble you."

"Indeed, it's fine behaviour," a third would say, "and you afther coming from the priest's knee; and what is more, didn't *resave* yet; but, wait till Father Con appears, and, I'll warrant, you'll be as grave as another, for all you're so stout now."

The conversation would then pass to the merits of Father Philemy and Father Con, as confessors.

"Well;" one would observe—"for my part, I'd rather go to Father Philemy, fifty times over, than wanst to Father Con, bekase he never axes questions; but whatever you like to tell him, he hears it, and forgives you at wanst."

"And so sign's an it," observed another; "he could confess more in a day, than Father Con could in a week."

"But for all that," observed Andy Lawlor, "it's still best to go to the man that puts the questions, you persave, and that won't let the turning of a straw escape him. Whin myself goes to Father Philemy, somehow or other, I totally disremember more nor wan half of what I intinded to tell him, but Father Con misses nothing, for he axes it."

When the last observation was finished, Father Con, finding that the usual hour for breakfast had arrived, came into the kitchen, to prepare for the celebration of mass. For this purpose, a table was cleared, and just in the nick of time arrived old Moll Brian, the vestment woman, or itinerant sacristan, whose usual occupation was to carry the priest's *robes* and other apparatus, from station to station. In a short time, Father Con was surpliced and robed; Andy Lawlor, whose face was charged with commensurate importance during the ceremony, *sarved* Mass, and answered the priest stoutly in Latin, although he had not the advantage of understanding that sacerdotal language. Those who had *confessed*, now *communicated;* after which, each of them took a draught of water out of a small jug, which was banded round from one to another. The ceremony then closed, and those who had partaken of the sacrament, with the exception of such as were detained for breakfast, after filling their bottles with holy water, went borne with a light heart. A little before the mass had been finished, Father Philemy arrived; but, as Phaddhy and

Katty were then preparing to *receive,* they could not at that moment give him a formal reception. As soon, however, as communion was over, the *cead milliah failtah*
was repeated, with the usual warmth, by both, and by all their immediate friends.

Breakfast was now laid in Katty's best style, and with an originality of arrangement that scorned all precedent. Two tables were placed, one after another, in the
kitchen; for the other rooms were not sufficiently large to accommodate the company. Father Philemy filled the seat of honour at the head of the table, with his
back to an immense fire. On his right hand sat Father Con; on his left, Phaddhy
himself, "to keep the *clargy* in company;" and, in due succession after them, their
friends' and neighbours, each taking precedence according to the most scrupulous
notions of respectability. Beside Father Con sat "Pether Malone," a "young collegian," who had been sent home from Maynooth to try his native air for the recovery of his health, which was declining. He arrived only a few minutes after Father
Philemy, and was a welcome reinforcement to Phaddhy, in the arduous task of sustaining the conversation with suitable credit.

With respect to the breakfast, I can only say, that it was superabundant—that
the tea was as black as bog water—that there were hen, turkey, and geese eggs—
plates of toast soaked, crust, and crumb, in butter, and lest there might be a deficiency, one of the daughters sat on a stool at the fire, with her open hand, by way
of a fire-screen, across her red, half-scorched brows, toasting another plateful, and,
to crown all, on each corner of the table was a bottle of whiskey. At the lower
board sat the youngsters, under the surveillance of Katty's sister, who presided in
that quarter. When they were commencing breakfast, "Father Philemy," said Katty,
"won't yer Rev'rence bless the mate, if ye plase?"

"If I don't do it myself," said Father Philemy, who was just after sweeping the
top off a turkey egg, "I'll get them that will.—Come," said he to the collegian,
"give us grace, Peter, you'll never learn younger."

This, however, was an unexpected blow to Peter, who knew that an English
grace would be incompatible with his "college breeding" yet was unprovided with
any in Latin. The eyes of the company were now fixed upon him, and he blushed
like scarlet on finding himself in a predicament so awkward and embarrassing.
"Aliquid, Petre, aliquid; 'de profundis'—si habes nihil aliud," said Father Philemy, feeling for his embarrassment, and giving, him a hint. This was not lost, for Peter
began, and gave them the De profundis, a Latin psalm which Roman Catholics
repeat for the relief of the souls in purgatory. They forgot, however, that there was
a person in company who considered himself as having an equal claim to the repetition of at least the one-half of it; and, accordingly, when Peter got up, and repeat-

---

*This prayer is generally repeated by two persons.

ed the first verse, Andy Lawlor got also on his legs, and repeated the response.* This staggered Peter a little, who hesitated as uncertain how to act.

"Perge, Petre, Perge," said Father Philemy, looking rather wistfully at his egg— *"Perge, stultus est et asinus quoque."* Peter and Andy proceeded until it was finished, when they resumed their seats.

The conversation during breakfast was as sprightly, as full of fun and humour as such breakfast's usually are. The priest, Phaddhy, and the young collegian had a topic of their own, whilst the rest were engaged in a kind of bye-play until the meal was finished.

"Father Philemy," said Phaddhy, in his capacity of host, "before we begin we'll all take a dhrop of what's in the bottle, if its not displasing to yer Reverence; and, sure, I know, 'tis the same that doesn't come wrong at a station, any how."

This, *more majorum,* was complied with; and the glass, as usual, went round the table, beginning with their Reverences. They had not, however, been long at breakfast, when a circumstance occurred, which, that our readers may be enabled to form an opinion upon it, renders it necessary for us to go back a little in our narrative.

In the immediate vicinity of the scene of our present sketch, lived a man named Jack Shields, who was considered by his neighbours to be a person of an amiable benevolent disposition; moral and inoffensive in his conduct, as well as upright and honest in his principles and dealings—but looked upon to be somewhat eccentric in his general manners. Shields was a man very much addicted to reading, and had entertained, for years before the period in question, rather singular opinions upon several tenets of his own church. He read both the Douay and the Protestant Bibles, in defiance of the priest; gave mass up altogether, except when he understood that the priest was to preach, and then he was punctual in his attendance. He had also abandoned confession—having often been heard to say, that he did not think his brother sinner had any power to absolve his soul from the guilt which he incurred in relation to God. "I know," he would say "*I am sure,* that *God can* forgive me; but I have not the same certainty as to the priest. God has commanded me to come to *Himself,* repenting, and has promised to pardon me; now this is enough for me, so I'll take the sure side."

When this came to the priest's ears, together with the account of his absenting himself from mass, he sent for him one day that he held a station in the neighbourhood, and Shields, with his Bible in his pocket, waited upon him without any reluctance.

"Jack," said the priest, "is all this true that I hear about you?"

"Now, doesn't yer Reverence know," replies, Jack, "that that's more than I can say till I hear it?"

"I'm told," said the priest, addressing himself to what he considered to be the root of the evil—"I'm told, Jack, that you've got a Protestant Bible under your roof."

"I have," replied Shields, "and a Catholic one to the back of that, which I suppose your Reverence didn't hear."

"I should think," said the other, "the Bible of your own church ought to be sufficient for you."

"The doctrines of our church are all just and true I suppose?" replied Jack, more skilfully than his Reverence was prepared for.

"You suppose!" replied the other; "Why, do you doubt it, Sir?"

"I'm not saying I do, your Reverence," responded Jack; "I suppose the Bible is equal to the church in soundness—I mean our own Bible."

"Undoubtedly," said the priest; "it is the written word of God."

"Well, now it's comfortable to hear your Reverence say so; because, as our church is true in all her doctrines and practices, and as our Bible is equally sound and uncorrupt, why, wid the help of God, I'll go home and examine both; and surely, as you have no fear that by doing so, I can find out any thing wrong in the church, you can't object against this."

"If you believe the church to be pure," said the priest, "what necessity is there for your entering upon such a task?"

"Why, I believe it to be so," replied the other "yet, some how, if you were to ax me why I believe this—may I never do harm, but your Reverence would puzzle me."

"Don't you believe, Sir," said Father Philemy, "whatever the church proposes for your belief?"

"I'll tell you what," replied Jack, "to make short work of it, I don't know the tythe of what the church proposes to my belief: no, nor the tythe of that again: and now, your Reverence, how can I believe what I don't know? How-an'-ever, I'm sartinly very willing that the church should give me proper instructions in what I'm to believe; but then, Docthor, on the other hand, where am I to go to look for the church?"

Father Philemy closed his eyes a little, and peered at Shields, as if he would have looked into his very spirit: "Shields," said he, dropping the subject, however, "I perceive clearly that you are verging into heresy, which is the result of your reading heretical books: you must send me that Bible—you must send me both Bibles;

and, moreover, you must mind your business, and let theology alone."

"I don't neglect my business," said the other; "and I'm very willing to send you both back; but before I do, yer Reverence must tell me—where I'm to find the church: may I never do harm, but I'm longing to have one meeting with her: some how or other, I think it would be pleasant to hear a few wards upon the subject from her own lips, that is, if one *could* stumble on her; for, although it's said she's 'visible,' not a wan of myself ever was able to lay my two living eyes upon her yet."

"Sir," says Father Philemy, "you should have better breeding than to address me, or speak of the Church in that sneering, disrespectful manner—there is more reverence due to us both."

"I declare it, your Reverence," replied Shields, "I'm in the hoith of good humour with both of you; but I've got no answer to my question. Now, suppose I want the Church, where am I to find her, Docthor?"

"Jack, the doctrines of our Church are specified and promulgated in her own councils and decrees, and they are to be found there."

"Very good, Sir; there's some satisfaction in that; I like to come to the point: and may I ask yer Reverence, how many councils there were?"

"What's that to you, Sir, how many there ere," replied Father Philemy: "it's not the number of councils you are to believe, but the doctrines contained in their decrees."

"Well, Sir, I don't object against that same, for there's rason in it; but will yer Reverence lend me the book they're in, until I run my eye over them—I'll not keep it more nor a day or two, and I'll take especial good care of it; for, to tell the truth, I think it ought to be in every body's hands."

"In the first place, Jack," replied Father Philemy, "I'll show you now the nature of *implicit* faith: the doctrines of our Church are contained in several large folio books, not one word of which you could understand, for you are not a classical scholar; you see, therefore, Jack, that it's not for an ignorant fellow like you to be turning your brain about what does not come under your line of duty; but, for all that you're bound to believe them, under pain of excommunication. These doctrines are laid down and explained by the pastors of our Church, whose duty it is to enforce them; and in case of obstinacy or unbelief, to exercise the authority which the Church has delegated to them against the refractory and disobedient."

During this cogent argument of the priest's, Shields stood with a countenance on which astonishment was very strongly depicted. "The short and the long of it is this," he replied, "that the Church won't show herself to the poor and ignorant, at all at all—to none but the priests and so we're to believe what we don't know, and what we can't know, and without having an opportunity of knowing whether its true or not. That's not fair, I think; then, in the next Place, the priest is all the Church we have to go to, whatever we want to know."

"And is not that sufficient?" said the priest.

"Yes; but how are we to know that the priest sticks to the Church, whin we can't see her rale doctrines? And agin, Docthor—how are we to know that all these doctrines are right, if we're not allowed to try and compare them with the word of God, which you grant can't be wrong? May I never sin, Docthor, but I think it's a little too hard to keep us from the Church and the word of God, both."

"Jack, my dear friend," said Father Philemy, in a softened conciliating tone, "you are bewildering yourself—indeed, you are; and I am sorry to see you in such a perplexed state of mind; but, as I said before, it is the consequence of your endeavouring to go beyond your depth, to understand more than you are bound to know. I'm sorry also to find that you neglect your duty of late, and that you are never seen at mass."

"I would rather, Sir," said Shields, "that you had brought about a meeting between me and the Church—but the truth is, that yer Reverence represints the Church."

"Ay, now, John, it's something about that; you are beginning to speak sense; I certainly stand in that capacity to every one of my parishioners, and, for that reason, they are bound to hear *me* as they would the Church."

"Yet," said Jack, with a sarcastic pertinacity that was by no means savoury to his Reverence, "the Church is *holy,* and *apostolical,* and *universal?*"

"She is," replied the priest.

"And yer Reverence represints her!" said the other. "Now, Father Philemy, do you remember the day that you held the Station in my own house?"

"I do, about Easter last," replied the priest.

"Well, *so do I,*" said Shields, without adding another word.

Father Philemy now lost his temper; for, although he fairly exposed himself to the *argumentum ad hominem,* yet he was incapable of bearing it with patience. "Shields," said he, "I have borne your sneers with too much indulgence, because I have a regard for your family, and for yourself; but I tell you now, that I insist, Sir, on your depositing *both* your Bibles in my hands—I say, I *insist* on it; and if you do not come to your duty, and attend mass as usual, I will expose you from the altar; and if that doesn't do, I'll take other measures—so look to it.

"If yer Rev'rence," replied the other, "wishes to get any good of me, *convince me*—otherwise, Sir, you needn't resort to bullying, for that's the very thing would make me stiffer; and, in respect of denouncing me from the althar—if ye did, I wouldn't stay two days in yer Church."

"I see," said the priest, "you're nothing but a headstrong fool, and it is only a loss of time, and a waste of patience to speak to you."

"I know I'm very little that's good," says Shields; "but I know yer Rev'rence has given me no satisfaction concarning the Church. Now, Sir, before I lave you——"

"And that can't be a moment too soon, you blackguard you," interrupted Father Philemy.

"I say Sir, before I lave you, let me ask, did not the son of God himself spake and prache, and address himself to the poor?—didn't he instruct them in all things necessary for them to know? didn't he command them, with his own blessed lips, to sarche the Scriptures, for that they contained eternal life? You desire me to come to my duty: did ever the Lord himself tell us, that a fellow-crathur could forgive us our sins?—or, whether did he bid us come to you, or himself? Will yer Rev'rence answer me these questions? You say, *you* can forgive me my sins, and that I ought to come to you for that purpose. My Redeemer says, that HE can and WILL forgive me my sins, if I repent and go to HIM; which am I to follow—you or the Almighty? 'Come to ME,' he says, 'all ye that labour and are heavy laden, and I will give you rest; if your sins were like scarlet, they shall be as white as snow.' Your Rev'rence stands there as the Church, and you bid me close the Word of God, and not read it. The Lord desires me to search it; and, indeed, Docthor, I'm very far from going to obey you or the Church either, before God himself, when *you* and *He* command different things. And with respect of going to mass, did Christ or his Apostles spake to the people in an unknown tongue that they did not understand? Instead of that same, didn't the Apostles get the gift of tongues, that the strange nations might understand their prayers and instructions? No; as God has promised to forgive me, I'll go to God, and, with his blessing, I'll tache my childher to do the same."

"Get out, you reprobate," replied Father Philemy, wholly losing his temper; "out with you, and don't pollute the dacent man's house with your heretical breath, you vagabone you. I'll lay my horsewhip to your back."

"Ay, that's your strongest argument," replied Jack. "That's your usual method of convincing—and a creditable one it is."

Shields then withdrew; and when he was gone, "That man's going straight to hell," observed his Reverence, "and, what is more, he'll bring his children along with him."

"The Lord be about us Father Philemy," observed those who were present, "don't prophesy sich a thing!—who would think it, and he so good and sensible a man?"

"Tom," said the priest, "after all, I believe there is but one way with him, and that's mildness—the fellow may lead but he won't drive; run after him and tell him to stop and eat his dinner with us; I suppose you'll have no objection to that, Phaddhy?"

"Is it me, yer Rev'rence?—och, och, and it's his father's son that would be welcome to a pratie and wather, if I had but that."

"Well, tell him to stop and spend the evening with us; say that I wish to have some conversation with him in a friendly way."

Shields, however, saw through this *finesse,* and was determined to disappoint his Reverence. "Tell him that I'll hear him some other time," said he, smiling. "I know that the argument his Rev'rence would bring against me might *lay me on my back,* but it couldn't convince me for all that. Didn't I give him a right bit about the station?"

"I tell ye, Jack," replied the other, "it's a big shame for ye to be getting an as ye do; you should go to yer duty and to mass like another."

"Ah, Tom," said Jack, "lave that to myself; do you think I'd do any thing that would go against my own salvation? But ye may tell him this, that, excepting he goes to drive me out of it, I'll never lave the church I'm in, bekase I believe I can be saved in it as well as in any other, although my knee I'll never bend under him, or any other man by way of confession, while I live." So saying, he pursued his way home.

When the man returned, he repeated the conversation that passed between him and Shields, not omitting a word.

"Well," said the priest, "I'm not surprised that the Church interdicts the Word of God to the laiety; for, when one of them gets it for any length of time into his hands, he becomes as cunning as a bag fox: did you only hear that fellow just now? Nothing will do him, indeed, but *conviction!*—however, he is a stiff-necked animal, and must only be allowed to take his own swing, and be damned his own way."

Shields literally kept his word; for, true to his views, he neither went to mass nor confession afterwards. In such tenets of his own church as he believed were true and scriptural, he educated and instructed his son and daughter, the only children he had. He also permitted both to attend mass, and the former to go to confession; but the daughter he would by no means allow to frequent that distressing rite.

His wife, however, who was as weak and as bigotted as the husband was firm and liberal, perpetually harrassed the daughter about the sin of neglecting confession; but the latter was intimately acquainted with the Bible, and without at all being aware of it, was considerably more attached to the Protestant, than to her own Church. For two or three years, that is, during the period in which the mere girl approximates to the full-grown woman, the mother's arguments to induce her to go to her duty were fruitless for the father had drawn by no means a favourable character of confession, and the daughter possessing a pure and modest mind, entertained a rooted aversion against it. But a little before the time of Phaddhy's Station, the mother began to exhibit symptoms of a decline, and as she never ceased pressing the former on this point, the affection which was excited in the daughter's breast by the apprehension of losing her, induced a compliance on her part, which no other circumstances could have effected—for Mary (so she was called,) possessed much of her father's good sense, firmness, and independence.

The mother having, at length, prevailed, she and Mary attended at Phaddhy's early on the morning of the station in question. As soon as they entered the house, there was an especial welcome for both, particularly for the daughter, because the peculiar principles in which Shield's had educated her, and her own firm adherence to them, were well known.

"Well, Katty, avourneen," said her mother—"blessed be the holy mother of God for it, she has come at long last; and it's well for her, ahagur, that she took my advice, I hope, for, indeed, Phaddhy," turning the discourse to him, "I won't be long with her—see how that bit of a walk up here has left me without a blast of breath in my body!"

The mother was certainly very much exhausted, and had every appearance of being in a deep and rapid decline. As she uttered these words, the daughter, who sat removed from the crowd that occupied the lower end of the house, fixed her eyes upon her, and, in an instant, her long, dark lashes were filled with tears. Mary, indeed, was a girl of uncommon personal beauty and fine figure, and, as she sat with her pocket handkerchief between her hands, and her dark eyes shining through her tears, she was certainly calculated to excite a strong interest in her favour. She wore no cap, but had a dark ribbon tied simply round her head, from which her brown clustering locks fell in thick luxuriant curls over her fair neck and shoulders. Her hair was divided before, and showed a white polished forehead that would have graced a higher station in life. It might have been easily remarked, that her attendance here was involuntary, for there was a feverish anxiety about her amounting to a visible tremor. She was wrapped in thought, and sometimes appeared so pale, that one might almost feel apprehensive of her swooning away—

at other times so flushed, that her face and neck were suffused with one glow of crimson. In this state of agitation she remained until the person who had been in with Father Con came out; her mother then said—"Mary, come now, acushla, there's nobody with Father Con: come and pluck up courage, alannah—you won't be long, and the best way for you is to get it over you, and then your mind will be aisy." Mary, however, got as pale as death, and her lips became white. She rose up, but was obliged to sit down again, until she regained more strength. In the meantime, her mother and Katty, and several other of the women then present, afforded her every assistance; as her lips were parched, she asked for a drink of water, but this she could not get.

"Mary, asthore," said the mother, "you know you couldn't get a dhrink of wather till afther you resave the sacrament.

"I wish, mother dear," said the modest girl, "my father was with me; if he was, I wouldn't be so weak, I think."

This she spoke in a very feeble voice, for all the moral instincts and delicate sensibilities of a modest disposition were up in arms against this profane violation—this daring intrusion into those recesses of the human heart, which are, and ought to be, visible only to that God to whom all things are known.

At last, by the force of flattery and persuasion, eked out with several melancholy allusions by the mother to her own state of health, Mary went in to comply with an ordinance which she felt to be revolting and indelicate in the highest degree; one which her soul detested and shrunk from, with mingled detestation and horror. On her return from the confessional, she walked up to the remote seat she had before occupied, which was instantly vacated on her approach to it; for the beauty of her person, and her modesty, commanded general admiration and respect. There was now a marked change visible in her countenance and demeanour; for although she sat as quiet as usual, there was on her complexion a flush of deeper hue than had mantled her check before; her eye, too, was lit with a spark, much more vivid than the mild and mellow light which usually shone there. Instead of appearing timid, her nerves were evidently strung to a high degree of firmness and tension, and her whole air betrayed marks of distress, indignation, and disgust. When she came out, her mother went in to confess, who was the last Father Con heard before mass. From the time Mary left Father Con, until breakfast, she was certainly suffering intensely from her own feelings and reflections; for it was with much difficulty that she suppressed the tears which started to her eyes. Indeed, it was evident that if she had been alone, she would have relieved herself very much by weeping; but an apprehension of attracting notice restrained her tears, whilst it increased her distress. This state of prolonged excitement was more than she could bear; for a short time afterwards a powerful re-action in the state of her animal spirits and nerves took place. She became deadly and fearfully pale; and after many struggles against the weight which sank down her spirits so heavily, she at length fell into a fit of strong and alarming convulsions. This was an interruption to the harmony of the breakfast, which was by no means expected. She was now removed into another room; the women, with much difficulty, succeeded in restoring her to conscious-ness, or, at least, in assisting nature to restore herself. When she found herself among none but her own sex, she gave full vent to her tears, and wept long and bitterly. She then insisted on going home to her father, a determination which no force or entreaty could prevent her from putting into execution. She accordingly departed without noticing any one in the house, and the breakfast went on gloomily enough until it was finished.

Such was the effect which the unnatural and gross act of disclosing the frailties and weaknesses of a female to a man in private, had upon the natural modesty of a young woman. To make such an act a religious ceremony, when we consider the weakness of human passion, is probably the best clue to the complacency with which the Roman Catholic priesthood bear a life of celibacy. Of Mary it is only necessary to say, that ere many years passed, she and her father both embraced the Protestant faith.

Hitherto, Father Philemy had not had time to bestow any attention on the state of Katty's larder, as he was in the habit of doing, with a view to ascertain the sever-al items contained therein for dinner. But as soon as the breakfast things were removed, and the coast clear, he took a peep into the pantry, and, after throwing his eye over its contents, sat down at the fire, making Phaddhy take a seat beside him, for the especial purpose of sounding him as to the practicability of effecting a certain design which was then snugly latent in his Reverence's fancy. The fact was, that on taking the survey of the premises aforesaid, he discovered that, although there was abundance of fowl, and fish, and bacon, and hung-beef—yet, by some unaccountable and disastrous omission, there was neither fresh mutton nor fresh beef. The priest, it must be confessed, was a man of considerable fortitude, but this was a blow for which he was scarcely prepared—particularly as a boiled leg of mut-ton was one of his fifteen favourite joints at dinner. He accordingly took two or three pinches of snuff in rapid succession, and a seat at the fire as I have said, plac-ing Phaddhy, unconscious of his design, immediately beside him.

Now, the reader knows that Phaddhy was a man possessing a considerable por-tion of dry, sarcastic humour, along with that natural quickness of penetration and shrewdness for which most of the Irish peasantry are, in a very peculiar degree, remarkable; add to this that Father Philemy, in consequence of his contemptuous bearing to him before he came in for his brother's property, stood not very high in his estimation. The priest knew this, and consequently felt that the point in question would require to be managed, on his part, with suitable address.

"Phaddhy," says his Reverence, "sit down here till we chat a little, before I commence the duties of the day. I'm happy to see that you have such a fine thriving family: how many sons and daughters have you?"

"Six sons, yer Reverence," replied Phaddhy, "and five daughters: indeed, Sir, they're as well to be seen as their neighbours, considhering all things. Poor crathurs, they get fair play* now, thank God, compared to what they used to get— God rest their poor uncle's sowl for that. Only for him, your Reverence, there would be very few inquiring this or any other day about them."

"Did he die as rich as they said, Phaddhy?" enquired his Reverence.

"Hut, Sir," replied Phaddhy, determined to take what he afterwards called a rise out of the priest; "they knew little about it—as rich as they said, Sir! no, but three times as rich, itself: but any how, he was the man that could make the money."

"I'm very happy to hear it, Phaddhy, on your account, and that of your children. God be good to him—*requiescat animus ejus in pace, per omnia secula seculorum, Amen!*—he liked a drop in his time, Phaddhy, as well as ourselves, eh?"

"*Amen, amen*—the heavens be his bed!—he did, poor man! but he had it at first cost, your Reverence, for he run it all himself in the mountains: he could afford to take it."

"Yes, Phaddhy, the heavens be his bed, I pray; no Christmas or Easter ever passed, but he was sure to send me the little keg of stuff that never saw water; but, Phaddhy, there's one thing that concerns me about him, in regard of his love of drink—I'm afraid it's a throuble to him where he is at present; and I was sorry to find that, although he died full of money, he didn't think it worth his while to leave even the price of a mass to be said for the benefit of his own soul."

"Why, sure you know, Father Philemy, that he wasn't what they call a dhrinking man: once a quarther, or so, he sartinly did take a jorum; and except at these times, he was very sober. But God look upon us both yer Reverence—or upon myself, any way; for I haven't yer excuse for dhrinking, seeing I'm no clargy; but if *he's* to suffer for his doings that-a-way, I'm afeard *we'll* have a troublesome reckoning of it."

"Hem, a-hem!—Phaddhy," replied the priest, "he has raised you and your children from poverty, at all events, and you ought to consider *that*. If there is any

*By this is meant good food and clothing.

thing in your power to contribute to the relief of his soul, you have a strong duty upon you to do it; and a number of masses, offered up devoutly, would——"

"Why, he did, Sir, raise both myself and my childre from poverty," said Phaddhy, not willing to let that point go farther—"*that* I'll always own to; and I hope in God that whatever little trouble might be upon him for the dhrop of dhrink, will be wiped off by this kindness to us."

"He hadn't even a *month's mind!!*"

"And it's not but I spoke to him about both, yer Reverence."

"And what did he say, Phaddhy?"

"'Phaddhy,' said he, 'I have been giving Father M'Guirk, one way or another, between whiskey, oats, and dues, a great deal of money every year; and now, afther I'm dead,' says he, 'isn't it an ungrateful thing of him not to offer up one mass for my sowl, except I leave him payment for it.'"

"Did he say that, Phaddhy?"

"I'm giving you his very words, yer Reverence."

"Phaddhy, I deny it; it's a big lie—he could not make use of such words, and he going to face death. I say you could not listen to them; the hair would stand on your head if he did: but God forgive him!—that's the worst I wish him. Didn't the hair stand on your head, Phaddhy, to hear him?"

"Why, then, to tell yer Reverence God's truth, I can't say it did."

"You can't say it did! and if I was in your coat, I would be ashamed to say it did not. I was always troubled about the way the fellow died, but I hadn't the slightest notion that he went off such a reprobate. I fought *his* battle and *yours* hard enough yesterday; but I knew less about him then than I do now."

"And what, wid submission, did you fight our battles about, yer Reverence?" enquired Phaddhy.

"Yesterday evening, in Parrah More Slevin's, they had him a miser, and yourself they set down as a very little better."

"Then I don't think I desarved that from Parrah More, any how, Father Philemy; I think I can show myself as dacent as Parrah More or ally of *his* faction."

"It was not Parrah More himself, or his family, that said any thing about you, Phaddhy," said the priest. "but others that were present. You must know that we were all to be *starved* here to-day."

"Oh! oh!" exclaimed Phaddhy, who was hit most palpably upon the weakest side—the very sorest spot about him, "they think bekase this is the first station that ever was held in *my* house, that you won't be thrated as you ought; bat they'll be disappointed; and I hope, for so far, that yer Reverence and yer friends had no rason to complain."

"Not in the least, Phaddhy, considering that it was a first station; and if the dinner goes as well off as the breakfast, they'll be biting their nails: but I should not wish myself that they would have it in their power to sneer or throw any slur over you about it.——Go along, Dolan," exclaimed his Reverence to a countryman who came in from the street, where those stood who were for confession, to see if he had gone to his room—"Go along, you vagrant, don't you see I'm not gone to the *tribunal* yet?——But it's no matter about that, Phaddhy, it's of other things you ought to think: when were you at your duty?"

"This morning, Sir," replied the other—"but I'd have them to understand, that had the presumption to use my name in any such manner, that I know when and where to be dacint with any mother's son of Parrah More's faction; and *that* I'll be afther whispering to them some of these mornings, plase goodness."

"Well, well, Phaddhy, don't put yourself in a passion about it, particularly so soon after having been at confession—it's not right—I told them myself, that we'd have a leg of mutton and a bottle of wine at all events, for it was what *they* had; but that's not worth talking about: when were you with the priest before, Phaddhy?"

"If I wasn't able, it would be another thing, but, as long as I'm able, I'll let them know that I have the spirit"—said Phaddhy, smarting under the imputation of niggardliness—"when was I at confession before, Father Philemy? Why, then, dear forgive me, not these five years;—and I'd surely be the first of the family that would show a mane spirit, or a want of hospitality."

"A leg of mutton is a good dish, and a bottle of wine is fit for the first man in the land!" observed his Reverence—"five years!—why, is it possible you stayed away so long, Phaddhy!—how could you expect to prosper with five years' burden of sin upon your conscience—what would it cost you——?"

"Indeed, myself's no judge, your Rev'rence, as to that; but, cost what it will, I'll get both."

"I say, Phaddhy, what trouble would it cost you to come to your duty twice a year at the very least; and, indeed, I would advise you to become a monthly communicant, Parrah More was speaking of it as to himself, and you ought to go——."

"And I will go and bring Parrah More here to his dinner, this very day, if it was only to let him see with his own eyes——."

"You ought to go once a month, if it was only to set an example to your children, and to show the neighbours bow a man of substance and respectability, and the head of a family, ought to carry himself."

"Where is the best wine, got, yer Rev'rence?"

"Alick M'Loughlin, *my nephew,* I believe, keeps the best wine and spirits in Ballyslantha.—You ought also, Phaddhy, to get a scapular, and become a scapulari-an; I wish your brother had thought of *that,* and he wouldn't have died in so hardened a state, nor neglected to make a pruvision for the benefit of his soul, as he did."

"Lave the rest to me, yer Revrence, I'll get it—Mr. M'Loughlin will give me the right Part, if he has it betune him and death."

"M'Loughlin! what are you talking about?"

"Why, what is your Rev'rence talking about?"

"The scapular," said the priest.

"But I mane the wine and the mutton," says Phaddhy.

"And is that the way you treat me, you reprobate you?" replied his Reverence, in a passion: "is that the kind of attention you're paying me, and I advising you, all this time, *for the good of your soul?* Phaddhy, I tell you, you're enough to vex me to the core—-five years!—only once at confession in five years! What do I care about your mutton and your wine!—you may get dozens of them if you wish; or, may be, it would be more like a Christian to never mind getting them, and let the neigh-bours *laugh* away. It would teach you humility, you hardened creature, and God knows you want it; for my part, I'm speaking to you about other things; but that's the way with the most of you—mention any spiritual subject that concerns your soul, and you turn a deaf car to it—here, Dolan, come in to your duty. In the meantime, you may as well tell Katty not to boil the mutton too much; it's on your knees you ought to be at your rosary, or the seven penitential psalms."

"Thrue for you, Sir," said Phaddhy; "but as to going wanst a month, I'm afeard, yer Rev'rence, if it would shorten my timper as it does Katty's, that we'd be bad company for one another; she comes home from confession, newly set, like a razor, every bit as sharp; and I'm sure that I'm within the truth when I say, there's no bearing her."

"That's because you have no relish for any thing spiritual yourself, you nager you," replied his Reverence, "or you wouldn't see her tempor in that light—but, now that I think of it, where, did you get that stuff we had at breakfast?"

"Ay, that's the sacret; but I know yet Rev'rence would like it: did Parrah More equal it? No, nor one of his faction couldn't lay his finger on such a dhrop."

"I wish you could get me a few gallons of it," said the Priest; "but let us dhrop that; I say, Phaddhy, you're too worldly and careless about your duty."

"Well, Father Philemy, there's a good time coming; I'll mend yet."

"You want it, Phaddhy."

"Would three gallons do, Sir?"

"I would rather you would give me five, Phaddhy; but go to your rosary."

"It's the penitential psalm, first, Sir," said Phaddhy, "and the rosary at night. I'll try, anyhow; and if I can make off five for you, I will."

"Thank you, Phaddhy; but I would recommend you to say the rosary *before* night."

"I believe yer Reverence is right," replied Phaddhy, looking somewhat slyly in the priest's face, "I think it's best to make sure of it now, in regard that in the evening your Reverence—do you persave?"

"Yes," said his Reverence, "you're in a better frame of mind at present, Phaddhy, being fresh from confession." So saying, his Reverence, for whom Phaddhy, with all his shrewdness in general was not a match, went into his room, that he might send home about four dozen of honest, good-humoured, thoughtless, jovial, swearing, drinking, fighting and murdering Hibernians, free from every possible stain of sin and wickedness!

"Are you all ready now?" said the priest to a crowd of country people who were standing about the kitchen door, pressing to get the "first turn" at the tribunal, which, on this occasion, consisted of a good oak chair, with his Reverence upon it.

"Why do you crush forward in that manner, you ill-bred spalpeens? Can't you stand back and behave yourselves like common Christians!—back with you, or, if you make me get my whip, I'll soon clear you from about the dacent man's door. Hagarty, why do you crush them two girls there, you great Turk you? Look at the vagabonds!—Where's my whip?" said he, running in, and coming out in a fury, when he commenced cutting about him, until they dispersed in all directions. He then returned into the house; and, after calling in about two dozen, began to catechise them as follows, still holding the whip in his hand, whilst many of those individuals, who, at a party quarrel, in fair or market, or in the more inhuman crimes of murder or nightly depredations, were as callous and hardened specimens of humanity as ever set the laws of civilized society at defiance, stood trembling before him like slaves, absolutely pale and breathless with fear.

"Come, Kelly," said he to one of them, "are you fully prepared for the two blessed sacraments of Penance and the Eucharist, that you are about to receive? Can you read, Sir?"

"Can I read, is id?—my *brother Barney* can, yer Rev'rence," replied Kelly, sensible, amid all the disadvantages around him, of the degradation of his ignorance.

"What's that to me, Sir?" said the priest, "what your brother Barney can do—can you not read yourself?—and, may be," be continued parenthetically, "your brother Barney's not much the holier for his knowledge."

"I cannot, yer Reverence," said Kelly in a tone of regret.

"I hope you have your Christian Doctrine; at all events," said the priest,—"Go on with the Confiteor."

Kelly went on— *"Confeetur Dimniportenti batchy Mary semplar virginy, batchy Mickletoe Archy Angelo batchy Johnny Bartisty, sanctris postlis—Petrum hit Paulum, omnium sanctris, et tabby, pasture quay a pixavit minus coglety ashy hony verbum et offer him smaxy quilta smaxy quilta smaxy maxin in quilta."* *

"Very well, Kelly, right enough, all except the pronouncing, which wouldn't pass muster in Maynooth, however. How many kinds of commandments are there?"

"Two, Sir."

"What are they?"

"God's and the Church's."

"Repeat God's share of them."

He then repeated the first commandment according to *his* catechism.

"Very good, Kelly, very good. Now, you must know that the heretics split that into two, for no other reason in the world only to knock our blessed images on the head; but we needn't expect them to have much conscience. Well, now, repeat the commandments of the Church."

"First—Sundays and holidays, Mass thou shalt sartinly hear;
Second—All holidays sanctificate throughout all the whole year.
Third—Lent, Ember days, and Virgils, thou shalt be sartin to fast;
Fourth—Fridays and Saturdays flesh thou shalt not good, bad, or indifferent, taste.
Fifth—In Lent and Advent, nuptial fastes gallantly forbear.
Sixth—Confess your sins, at laste once dacently and soberly every year.
Seventh—Receive your God at cofission about great Easter-day;

---

*We subjoin the original for the information of our readers:—
"Confiteor Deo Omnipotenti, beatæ Mariæ, semper Virgini, beato Michaelo Archangelo, beato Johanni Baptistæ, sanctis Apostolis, Petro et Paulo, omnibus sanctis, et tibi, pater, quia, peccavi nimis cogitatione, verbo, et opera, mea culpa, mea culpa, mea maxima culpa." Let not our readers suppose, that the above version in the mouth of a totally illiterate peasant is overcharged, for we have the advantage of remembering how we ourselves used to hear it pronounced in our early days. We will back the version in the text against Edward Irving's new language for any money.

Eighth—And to his church and his own frolicsome clargy neglect not tides to pay.

"Well," said his Reverence, "now, the great point is, do you understand them?"

"Wid the help of God I hope so, yer Rev'rence—and I have also the three thriptological vartues."

"Theological, sirrah!"

"Theojollyological vartues; the four sins that cry to heaven for vingeance; the *five* carnal vartues—prudence, justice, timptation, and solitude;* the six holy Christian gifts; the seven deadly sins; the eight grey attitudes——"

"Grey attitudes! Oh, the Bæotian!" exclaimed his Reverence: "listen to the way in which he's playing havoc among them—stop, Sir," for Kelly was going on at full speed—"stop, Sir; I tell you it's not *grey* attitudes, but *bay* attitudes—doesn't every one know the eight beatitudes?"

"The eight *bay* attitudes; the nine ways of being guilty of another's sins; the ten commandments; the twelve fruits of a Christian; the fourteen stations of the cross; the fifteen mysteries of the passion——"

"Kelly," said his Reverence, interrupting him, and heralding the joke, for so it was intended, with a hearty chuckle, "you're getting fast out of your teens, ma bouchal!" and this was, of course, honoured with a merry peal, extorted as much by an effort at softening the rigour of examination, as by the traditionary duty, which entails upon the Irish laity the necessity of laughing at a priest's jokes, without any reference at all to their quality. Nor was his Reverence's own voice the first to subside into that gravity which became the solemnity of the occasion; for, even whilst he continued the interrogatories, his eye was laughing at the conceit with which it was evident the inner man was not competent to grapple. "Well, Kelly, I can't say but you've answered very well, as far as the *repeating* of them goes: but, do you perfectly *understand* all the commandments of the church?"

"I do, Sir," replied Kelly, whose confidence kept pace with his Reverence's good humour.

"Well, what is meant by the fifth?"

"The fifth, Sir?" said the other, rather confounded—"I must begin agin, Sir, and go on till I come to it."

"Well," said the priest, "never mind that; but tell us what the eighth means?"

Kelly stared at him a second time, but was not able to advance. "First—Sundays and holidays, mass thou shalt hear;" but before he had proceeded to the second, a person who stood at his elbow began to whisper to him the proper reply, and, in

*Temperance and fortitude.

the act of doing so, received a lash of the whip across the ear for his pains.

"You blackguard you!" exclaimed Father Philemy, "take that—how dare you attempt to prompt any person that I'm examining?"

Those who stood around Kelly now fell back to a safe distance, and all was silence, terror, and trepidation once more.

"Come, Kelly, go on—the eighth?"

Kelly was still silent.

"Why, you ninny you, didn't you repeat it just now. 'Eighth—And to his church neglect not tithes to pay.' Now that I have put the words in your mouth, what does it mean?"

Kelly having thus got the cue, replied in the words of the Catechism, "To pay *tides* to the lawful *pasterns* of the church, Sir."

"*Pasterns!* oh, you ass you, pasterns! You poor, base, contemptible, crawling reptile, as if we trampled you under our hooves—oh, you! scruff of the earth! Stop, I say—it's *pastors.*"

"Pasthors of the church."

"And tell me, do you fulfil that commandment?"

"I do, Sir."

"It's a lie, Sir," replied the priest, brandishing the whip over his head, whilst Kelly, instinctively, threw up his guard to protect himself from the blow; "It's a lie, Sir," repeated his Reverence, "you don't fulfil it. What *is* the church?"

"The church is the congregation of the faithful that purfiss the true faith, and are obadient to the pope."

"And who do you pay your tithes to?"

"To the parson, Sir."

"And, you poor varmint you, is *he* obadient to the pope?"

Kelly only smiled at the want of comprehension which prevented him from seeing the thing according to the view which his Reverence took of it.

"Well, now," continued Father Philemy, "who are the lawful pastors of God's church?"

"You are, Sir, and all our own priests."

"And who ought you to pay your tithes to?"

"To you, Sir, in coorse; sure I always knew that, yer Rev'rence."

"And—what's the reason, then, you don't pay them to me instead of the parson?"

This was a puzzler to Kelly, who only knew his own side of the question. "You have me there, Sir," he replied with a grin.

"Because," said his Reverence, "the Protestants, for the present, have the law of the land on their aide, and power over you to compel the payment of tithes to themselves; but we have right, justice, and the law of God on ours; and, if every thing was in its proper place, it is not to the *parsons*, but to *us*, that you would pay them."

"Well, well, Sir," replied Kelly, who now experienced a community of feeling upon the subject with his Reverence, that instantly threw him into a familiarity of manner which he thought the point between them justified—"who knows, Sir?" said he with a knowing smile, "there's a good time coming, yer Rev'rence."

"Ay," said Father Philemy, "wait till we get once into the Big House, and if we don't turn the scales—if the Established Church doesn't, go down, why, there's no truth in Scripture. Now, Kelly, all's right but the money—have you brought your dues?"

"Here it is, Sir," said Kelly, handing him his dues for the last year.

It is to be observed here, that, according as the penitents went to be examined, or to kneel down to confess, a certain sum was exacted from each, which varied according to the arrears that might have been due to the priest. Indeed, it is not unusual for the host and hostess, on these occasions, to be refused a participation in the sacrament, until they pay this money, notwithstanding the considerable expense they are put to in entertaining not only the clergy, but a certain number of their own friends and relations.

"Well, stand aside, I'll hear you first; and now come up here, you young gentleman, that laughed so heartily a while ago at my joke—ha, ha, ha!—come up here, child."

A lad now approached him, whose face, on a first view, had something simple and thoughtless in it, but in which, on a closer inspection, might be traced, a lurking, sarcastic humour, of which his Reverence never dreamt.

"You're for confession, of course," said the priest.

"*Of coorse*," said the lad, echoing him, and laying a stress upon the word, which did not much elevate the meaning of the blind compliance in general with the rite in question.

"Oh!" exclaimed the priest, recognizing him when he approached—"you are Dan Fegan's son, and designed for the church yourself; you are a good Latinist, for I remember examining you in Erasmus about two years ago—*Quomodo se habet corpus tuum Charum ligmum sacerdotis?*"

"*Valde, Domine*," replied the lad, "*Quomodo se habet anima tua, charum exemplar sacerdotage, et fulcrum robustissimum Ecclesiæ sacrosanctæ.*"

"Very good, Harry," replied his Reverence, laughing—"stand aside; I'll hear you after Kelly."

He then called up a man with a long melancholy face, which he noticed before to have been proof against his joke, and after making two or three additional fruitless experiments upon his gravity, he commenced a cross fire of peevish interrogatories, which would have excluded him from the "tribunal" on that occasion, were it not that the man was remarkably well prepared, and answered the priest's questions very pertinently.

This over, he repaired to his room, where the work of absolution commenced; and, as there was a considerable number to be rendered sinless be fore the hour of dinner, he contrived to unsin them with an alacrity that was really surprising.

Immediately after the conversation already detailed, between his Reverence and Phaddhy, the latter sought Katty, that he might communicate to her the unlucky oversight which they had committed, in neglecting to provide fresh meat and wine. "We'll be disgraced for ever," said Phaddhy, "without either a bit of mutton or a bottle of wine for the gintlemen, and that Parrah More Slevin had both."

"And I hope," replied Katty, "that you're not so mane as to let any of that faction out-do you in *dacency*, the nagerly set! It was enough for them to bate us in the law-shoot about the horse, and not to have the laugh agin at us about this."

"Well, that same law-shoot is not over with them yet," said Phaddhy; "wait till the spring fair comes, and if I don't have a faction gathered that'll sweep them out of the town, why in name's not Phaddhy! But where is Mat till we sind him off?"

"Arrah, Phaddhy," said Katty, "wasn't it friendly of Father Philemy to give us the *hard word* about the wine and mutton?"

"Very friendly," retorted Phaddhy, who, after all, appeared to have suspected the priest—"very friendly, indeed, when it's to put a good joint before himself, and a bottle of wine in his jacket. No, no, Katty! it's not altogether for the sake of Father Philemy, but I wouldn't have the neighbours say that I was near and undacent; and, above all things, I wouldn't be worse nor the Slevins—for the same set would keep it up agin us long enough."

Our readers will admire the tact with which Father Philemy worked upon the rival feeling between the factions; but, independently of this, there is a generous hospitality in an Irish peasant which would urge him to any stratagem, were it even the disposal of his only cow, sooner than incur the imputation of a narrow, or, as he himself terms it, "an undacent" or "nagerly" spirit.

In the course of a short time, Phaddhy dispatched two messengers, one for the wine, and another for the mutton; and, that they might not have cause for any unnecessary delay, he gave them the two Reverend gentlemen's horses, ordering them to spare neither whip nor spur until they returned. This was an agreeable command to the messengers, who, as soon as they found themselves mounted, made a bet of a "trate," to be paid on arriving in the town to which they were sent, to him who should first reach a little stream that crossed the road at the entrance of it, called the "pound burn." But I must not forget to state, that they not only were mounted on the priests' horses, but took their great coats, as the day had changed, and threatened to rain. Accordingly, on getting out upon the main road they set off, whip and spur, at full speed, justling one another, and cutting each other's horses as if they had been intoxicated; and the fact is, that, owing to the liberal distribution of the bottle that morning, they were not far from it.

"Bliss us!" exclaimed the country people, as they passed, "what on airth can be the matther with Father Philemy and Father Con that they're abusing wan another at sich a rate!"

"Oh!" exclaimed another, "it's apt to be a sick call, and they're thrying to be there before the body grows cowld."

"Ay, or may be," a third conjectured, "it's to ould Magennis, that's on the point of death, and going to lave all his money behind him, and they're striving to see who'll get there first."

But their astonishment was not a whit lessened, when, in about an hour afterwards, they perceived them both return; the person who represented Father Con, having an overgrown leg of mutton slung behind his back like an Irish harp, reckless of its friction against his Reverence's coat, which it had completely saturated with grease, and the duplicate of Father Philemy with a sack over his shoulder, in the bottom of which was half a dozen of Mr. M'Laughlin's best port.

Phaddhy, in the meantime, being determined to mortify his rival Parrah More by a superior display of hospitality, waited upon that personage, and exacted a promise from him to come down and partake of the dinner—a promise which the other was not slack in fulfilling. Phaddhy's heart was now on the point of taking its rest, when it occurred to him that there yet remained one circumstance in which he might utterly eclipse his rival, and that was to ask Captain Wilson, his landlord, to meet their Reverences at dinner. He accordingly went over to him, for he only lived a few miles distant, having first communicated the thing privately to Katty, and requested that as their Reverences that day held a station in his house, and would dine there, he would have the kindness to come along with them. To this the Captain, who was intimate with both the clergymen, gave a ready compliance, and Phaddhy returned home in high spirits.

In the meantime the two priests were busy in the work of absolution; the hour of three had arrived, and they had many to shrive; but, in the course of a short time, a Reverend auxiliary made his appearance, accompanied by one of Father Philemy's nephews, who was then about to enter Maynooth. This clerical gentleman had been appointed to a parish, but owing to some circumstances which were known only in the distant part of the diocese where he had resided, he was deprived of it, and had, at the period I am writing of, no appointment in the church, though he was in full orders. If I mistake not, he incurred his bishop's displeasure by being too warm an advocate for domestic nomination, a piece of discipline, the re-establishment of which was then attempted by the junior clergymen of the diocese wherein the scene of this station is laid. Be this as it may, he came in time to assist the gentlemen in absolving those penitents (as we must call them so) who still remained unconfessed.

During all this time Katty was in the plenitude of her authority, and her sense of importance manifested itself in a manner that was by no means softened by having been that morning at her duty. Her tones were not so shrill, nor so loud as they would have been, had not their Reverences been within hearing; but what was wanting in loudness, was displayed in a firm and decided energy, that vented itself frequently in the course of the day upon the backs and heads of her sons, daughters, and servants, as they crossed her path in the impatience and bustle of her employment. It was truly ludicrous to see her, on encountering one of them in these fretful moments, give him a drive head foremost against the wall, exclaiming, as she shook her fist at him, "Ho, you may bless your stars, that they're under the roof, or it wouldn't go so asy wid you; for if goodness hasn't said it, you'll make me lose my sowl this blessed and holy day: but this is still the case—the very time I go to my duty, the devil (between us and harm) is sure to throw fifty temptations acrass me, and to help him, you must come in my way—but wait till to-morrow, and if I don't pay you for this, I'm not here."

That a station is an expensive ordinance to the peasant who is honoured by having one held in his house, no one who knows the characteristic hospitality of the Irish people can doubt. I have reason, however, to think, that since the Church of Rome and her discipline have undergone so rigorous a scrutiny by the advocates of scriptural truth, she has been much more cautious in the manner in which they have been conducted. The policy of Romanism has uniformly been, to adapt herself to the circumstances by which she may be surrounded; and as the unbecoming licentiousness, which about twenty, or even so late as fifteen years ago, trod so closely upon the heels of a ceremony which the worship of God and the administration of sacramental rites, should have in a peculiar manner solemnized, was utterly disgraceful and shocking—she felt that it was expedient, as knowledge advanced around her, to practice a greater degree of external decorum and circumspection, lest her *little ones* should be scandalized. This, however, did not render it necessary that she should effect much reformation on this point in those parts of the kingdom which are exclusively Catholic; and accordingly stations, with some exceptions in a certain diocese, go on much in the old manner, as to the expense which they occasion the people to incur, and the jolly convivial spirit which winds them up.

About four o'clock the penitents were at length all dispatched; and those who were to be detained for dinner, many of whom had not eaten any thing until then, in consequence of the necessity of receiving the Eucharist fasting, were taken aside to taste some of Phaddhy's poteen. Of course, no remorse was felt at the impiety of mingling it so soon with the sacrament they had just received, believing, as they did, the latter to contain the immaculate Deity; but, indeed, their Reverences at breakfast had set them a pretty example on that point. At length the hour of dinner arrived, and along with it the redoubtable Parrah More Slevin, Captain Wilson, and another nephew of Father Philemy's, who had come to know what detained his brother who had conducted the auxiliary priest to Phaddhy's. It is surprising, on these occasions, to think how many uncles, and nephews, and cousins, to the forty-second degree, find it needful to follow their Reverences on messages of various kinds; and it is equally surprising to observe with what exactness they drop in during the hour of dinner. Of course, any blood-relation or friend of the priest's must be received with cordiality; and consequently they do not return without solid proofs of the good-natured hospitality of poor Paddy, who feels no greater pleasure than in showing his "dacency" to any belonging to his Reverence.

I dare say it would be difficult to find a more motley and diversified company than sat down to the ungarnished fare which Katty laid before them. There were first, Fathers Philemy, Con, and the Auxiliary from the far part of the diocese; next followed Captain Wilson, Peter Malone, and Father Philemy's two nephews; after these came Phaddhy himself, Parrah More Slevin, with about two dozen more of the most remarkable and uncouth personages that could sit down to table. There were besides about a dozen of females, most of whom by this time, owing to Katty's private kindness, and a slight thirst occasioned by the long fast, were in a most independent and placid state of feeling. Father Philemy, *ex officio,* filled the chair—he was a small man, with cherub cheeks as red as roses, black twinkling eyes, and double chin; was of the fat-headed genus, and, if phrenologists be correct, must have given indications of early piety, for he was bald before his time, and had the organ of veneration standing visible on his crown; his hair, from having once been black, had become an iron-grey, and hung down behind his ears, resting on the collar of his coat according to the old school, to which, I must remark, he belonged, having been educated on the Continent. His coat had large double breasts, the lappels of which hung down loosely on each side, being the prototype of his waistcoat, whose double breasts fell downwards in the same manner—his black small-clothes had silver buckles at the knees, and the gaiters, which did not reach up so far, discovered a pair of white lamb's-wool stockings, some what retreating from their original colour.

Father Con was a tall, muscular, able-bodied young man, with an immensely broad pair of shoulders, of which he was vain; his black hair was cropped close, except a thin portion of it which was trimmed quite evenly across his eye brows; he was rather bow-limbed, and when walking looked upwards, holding out his elbows from his body, and letting the lower parts of his arms fall down, so that he went as if he carried a keg under each; his coat, though not well made, was of the best glossy broad cloth—and his long clerical boots went up about his knees like a dragoon's; there was an awkward stiffness about him, in very good keeping with a dark melancholy cast of countenance, in which, however, a man might discover an air of simplicity not to be found in the visage of his superior, Father Philemy.

The latter gentleman filled the chair, as I said, and carved the goose; on his right sat Captain Wilson; on his left, the Auxiliary—next to them Father Con, the nephews, Peter Malone, *et cetera*. To enumerate the items of the dinner is unnecessary, as our readers have a pretty accurate notion of them from what we have already said. We can only observe, that when Phaddhy saw it laid, and all the wheels of the system fairly set a-going, he looked at Parrah More with an air of triumph which he could not conceal. It is also unnecessary for us to give the conversation in full, nor, indeed, would we attempt giving any portion of it, seeing it was not very edifying, except for the purpose of showing the spirit in which a religious ceremony, looked upon by its advocates as one of particular solemnity, is too frequently closed.

The talk in the beginning was altogether confined to the clergymen and Mr. Wilson, including a few diffident contributions from "Pether Malone," and the "two nephews."

"Mr. M'Guirk," observed Captain Wilson, after the conversation had taken several turns, "I'm sure that in the course of your professional duties, Sir you must have had occasion to make many observations upon human nature, from the cir-

cumstance of seeing it in every condition and state of feeling possible; from the
baptism of the infant, until the aged man receives the last rites of your church, and
the sweet consolations of religion from your hand."

"Not a doubt of it, Phaddhy," said Father Philemy to Phaddhy, whom he had
been addressing at the time, "not a doubt of it; and I'll do every thing in my power
to get him in too, and I am told he is bright."

"Uncle," said one of the nephews, "this gentleman is speaking to you."

"And why not?" continued his Reverence, who was so closely engaged with
Phaddhy, that he did not hear even the nephew's appeal—"a bishop—and why
not? Has he not as good a chance of being a bishop as any of them? though, God
knows, it is not always merit that gets a bishoprick in any church, or I myself
might——But let that pass," said he, fixing his eyes on the bottle.

"Father Philemy," said Father Con, "Captain Wilson was addressing himself to
you in a most especial manner."

"Oh! Captain, I beg ten thousand pardons, I was engaged talking with Phaddhy
here about his son, who is a young shaving of our cloth, Sir; he is intended for the
mission.——Phaddhy, I will either examine him myself, or make Father Con,
examine him, by-and-by.——Well, Captain?"

The Captain now repeated what he had said.

"Very true, Captain, and we do see it in as many shapes as ever—Con, what do
you call him?—put on him."

"Proteus," subjoined Con, who was famous at the classics.

Father Philemy nodded for the assistance, and continued—"but as for human
nature, Captain, give it to me at a good roasting christening; or, what is better
again, at a jovial wedding between two of my own parishioners—say this pretty,
fair-haired daughter of Phaddhy Sheemus Phaddhy's here, and long Ned Slevin,
Parrah More's son there—eh, Phaddhy, will it be a match?—what do you say,
Parrah More? Upon my veracity I must bring that about."

"Why, then, yer Reverence," replied Phaddhy, who was now a little softened,
and forgot his enmity against Parrah More for the present, "unlikelier things
might happen."

"It won't be my fault," said Parrah More, "if my son Ned has no objection."

"*He* object!" replied Father Philemy, "if *I* take it in hands, let me see who'll dare
to object; doesn't the Scripture say it? and sure we can't go against the Scripture."

"By the by," said Captain Wilson, who was a dry humourist, "I am happy to be
able to infer from what you say, Father Philemy, that you are not as the clergymen
of your church are supposed to be, inimical to the Bible."

"Me an enemy to the Bible! no such thing, Sir; but, Captain, begging your pardon, we'll have nothing more about the Bible: you see we are met here, as friends and good fellows, to enjoy ourselves after the severity of our spiritual duties, and we must relax a little; we can't always carry long faces like Methodist parsons—come, Parrah More, let the Bible take a nap, and give us a song."

His Reverence was now seconded in his motion by the most of all present, and Parrah More, accordingly gave them a song. After a few songs more, the conversation went on as before.

"Now, Parrah More," said Phaddhy, "you must try *my wine;* I hope it's as good as what *you* gave his Reverence yesterday."

The words, however, had scarcely passed his lips, when Father Philemy burst out into a fit of laughter, clapping and rubbing his hands in a manner the most astonishing. "Oh, Phaddhy, Phaddhy!" shouted his Reverence, laughing heartily, "I *done* you for once—I done you, my man, cute as you thought yourself: why, you nager you, did you think to put us off with punch, and you have a stocking of hard guineas hid in a hole in the wall?"

"What does yer Rev'rence mane," said Phaddhy; "for myself can make no undherstanding out of it, at all at all?"

To this his Reverence only replied by another laugh.

"*I* gave his Reverence no wine," said Parrah More, in reply to Phaddhy's question.

"What!" said Phaddhy, "none yesterday, at the station held with you?"

"Not a bit of me ever thought of it."

"Nor no mutton?"

"Why, then, devil a morsel of mutton, Phaddhy; but we had a rib of beef."

Phaddhy now looked over to his Reverence rather sheepishly, with the smile of a man on his face who felt himself foiled. "Well, yer Reverence has *done* me, sure enough," he replied, rubbing his head—"I give it up to you, Father Philemy; but, any how, I'm glad I got it, and you're all welcome from the core of my heart. I'm only sorry I haven't as much more now to thrate you all like gintlemen; but there's some yet, and as much punch as will make all our heads come round."

Our readers must assist us with their own imaginations, and suppose the conversation to have passed very pleasantly, and the night, as well as the guests, to be somewhat *far gone.* The principal part of the conversation was borne by the three clergymen, Captain Wilson, and Phaddhy; that of the two nephews and Peter Malone ran in an under current of its own; and in the preceding part of the night, those who occupied the bottom of the table, spoke to each other rather in whispers, being too much restrained by that rustic bashfulness which ties up the tongues of those who feel that their consequence is overlooked among their superiors. According as the punch circulated, however, their diffidence began to wear off; and occasionally an odd laugh or so might be heard to break the monotony of their silence. The youngsters, too, though at first almost in a state of terror, soon commenced plucking each other; and a titter, or a suppressed burst of laughter, would break forth from one of the more waggish, who was put to a severe task in afterwards composing his countenance into sufficient gravity to escape detection, and a competent portion of chastisement the next day, for not being able to "behave himself with betther manners."

During these juvenile breaches of decorum, Katty would raise her arm in a threatening attitude, shake her head at them, and look up at the clergy, intimating more by her earnestness of gesticulation than met the ear. Several songs again went round, of which, truth to tell, Father Philemy's were by far the best; for he possessed a rich, comic expression of eye, which, added to suitable ludicrousness of gesture, and a good voice, rendered him highly arousing to the company. Father Con declined singing, as being decidedly serious, though he was often solicited.

"He!" said Father Philemy, "he's no more voice than a wool-pack; but Con's a cunning fellow. What do you think, Captain Wilson, but he pretends to be too pious to sing, and gets credit for piety—not because he is devout, but because he has a bad voice: now, Con, you can't deny it, for there's not a man in the three kingdoms knows it better than myself; you sit there with a face upon you that might go before the lamentations of Jeremiah the Prophet, when you ought to be as jovial as another."

"Well, Father Philemy," said Phaddhy, "as he won't sing, may be, wid submission, he'd examine Briney in his Latin, till his mother and I hear how he's doing at it."

"Ay, he's fond of dabbling at Latin, so he may try him—I'm sure I have no objection——: so, Captain, as I was telling you——"

"Silence there below!" said Phaddhy to those at the lower end of the table, who were now talkative enough; "will yees whisht there till Father Con hears Briney a lesson in his Latin. Where are you, Briney? come here, ma bouchal."

But Briney had absconded when he saw that the tug of war was about to commence. In a few minutes, however, the father returned, pushing the boy before him, who, in his reluctance to encounter the ordeal of examination, clung to every chair, table, and person in his way, hoping that his restiveness might induce them to postpone the examination till another occasion. The father however, was inexorable, and by main force dragged him from all his holds, and placed him beside Father Con.

"What's come over you, at all at all, you insignified *shingawn* you, to affront the gintleman in this way, and he kind enough to go for to give you an *examination?*— come now, you had betther not vex me, I tell you, but hould up your head, and spake out loud, that we can all hear you: now, Father Con, achora, you'll not be too hard upon him in the beginning, till he gets into it, for he's aisy dashed."

"Here, Briney," said Father Philemy, handing him his tumbler, "take a pull of this, and if you have any courage at all in you it will raise it;—take a good pull."

Briney hesitated.

"Why but you take the glass out of his Reverence's hand, sarrah," said the father—"what! is it without dhrinking his Reverence's health first!"

Briney gave a most melancholy nod at his Reverence, as he put the tumbler to his mouth, which he nearly emptied, notwithstanding his shyness.

"For my part," said his Reverence, looking at the almost empty tumbler, "I am pretty sure that that same chap will be able to take care of himself through life. And so, Captain,——" said he, resuming the conversation with Captain Wilson— for his notice of Briney was only parenthetical.

Father Con now took the book, which was Æsop's Fables, and, in accordance with Briney's intention, it opened exactly at the favourite fable of Gallus Gallinaceus. He was not aware, however, that Briney had kept that place open during the preceding part of the week, in order to effect this point. Father Philemy, however, was now beginning to relate another anecdote to the Captain, and the thread of his narrative twined rather ludicrously with that of the examination.

Briney, after a few hems, at length proceeded,—"*Gallus Gallinaceus,* a dunghill cock——"

"So, Captain, I was just after coming out of Widow Moylan's—it was in the Lammas fair—and a large one, by the by, it was—so, Sir, who should come up to me but Branagan. 'Well, Branagan,' said I 'how does the world go now with you?'—"

"*Gallus Gallinaceus,* a dunghill cock——"

——"Says he. 'And how is that?' says I,——"

"*Gallus Gallinaceus*——"

——"Says he, 'Hut tut, Branagan,' says I—'you're drunk.' 'That's the thing, Sir,' says Branagan, 'and I want to explain it all to your Reverence.' 'Well,' said I, 'go on.'——"

"*Gallus Gallinaceus,* a dunghill cock——"

——"Says he,——Let your *Gallus Gallinaceus* go to roost for this night, Con," said Father Philemy, who did not relish the interruption of his story; "I say, Phaddhy, send the boy to bed, and bring him down in your hand to my house on Saturday morning, and we will both examine him, but this is no time for it, and me engaged in conversation with Captain Wilson.—So, Captain——'Well, Sir,' says Branagan, and he staggering, 'I took an oath against liquor, and I want your Reverence to break it,' says he. 'What do you mean?' I enquired. 'Why, please your Reverence,' said he, 'I took an oath against liquor, as I told you, not to drink more nor a pint of whiskey in one day, and I want your Reverence to break it for me, and make it only half a pint; for I find that a pint is too much for me; by the same token, that when I get that far, your Reverence, I disremember the oath entirely.'"

The influence of the bottle now began to be felt, and the conversation absolutely blew a gale, wherein hearty laughter, good strong singing loud argument, and general good-humour blended into one uproarious peal of hilarity, accompanied by some smart flashes of wit and humour, which would not disgrace a prouder banquet. Phaddhy, in particular, melted into a spirit of the most unbounded benevolence—a spirit that would (if by any possible means he could effect it) embrace the whole human race; that is to say, he would raise them, man, woman, and child, to the same elevated state of happiness which he enjoyed himself. That, indeed, was happiness in perfection, as pure and as unadulterated as the poteen which created it. How could he be otherwise than happy?—he had succeeded to a good property, and a stocking of hard guineas, without the hard labour of acquiring them; he had the "clargy" under his roof at last, partaking of a hospitality which he felt himself well able to afford them; he had settled with his Reverence for five years' arrears of sin, all of which had been wiped out of his conscience by the blessed absolving hand of the priest; he was training up Briney for the Mission, and, though last, not least, he was——far gone in his seventh tumbler!

"Come, jinteels," said he, "spare nothing here—there's lashings of every thing; thrate yourselves dacent, and don't be saying to-morrow or next day, that ever my father's son was nagerly. Death alive, Father Con, what are you doin'? Why, then, bad manners to me if that'ill sarve, any how."

"Phaddhy," replied Father Con, "I assure you I have done my duty."

"Very well, Father Con, granting all that, it's no sin to repate a good turn, you know. Not a word I'll hear, yer Reverence—one tumbler along with myself, if it was only for ould times." He then filled Father Con's tumbler, with his own hand, in a truly liberal spirit. "Arrah Father Con, do you remember the day we had the leapin'-match, and the bout at the shoulder-stone?"

"Indeed, I'll not forget it, Phaddhy."

"And it's yourself that may say that; but I bleeve I rubbed the consate off of your Reverence—only that's betune ourselves, you persave."

"You did win the palm, Phaddhy, I'll not deny it; but you are the only man that ever bet me at either of the athletics."

"And I'll say this for yer Reverence, that you are one of the best and most able-bodied gintlemen I ever engaged with. Ah! Father Con, I'm past all that now—but no matter, here's yer Reverence's health, and a shake hands; Father Philemy, yer health, docthor: yer strange Reverence's health—Captain Wilson, not forgetting you, Sir: Mr. Pether, yours; and I hope to see you soon with the robes upon you, and to be able to prache us a good sarmon. Parrah More—*wus dha lauv** give me yer hand, you steeple you; and I hav'nt the smallest taste of objection to what Father Philemy hinted at—ye'll observe. Katty, you thief o' the world, where are you? Your health, avourneen; come here, and give us your fist, Katty: bad manners to me if I could forget you afther all;—the best crathur, your Reverence, undher the sun, except when yer Reverence puts yer comedher on her at confession, and then she's a little sharp or so, not a doubt of it: but no matther, Katty ahagur, you do it all for the best. And Father Philemy, maybe it's myself didn't put the thrick upon you in the Maragy More, about Katty's death—ha, ha, ha! Jack M'Cramer, yer health—all yer healths, and yer welcome here, if you war seven times as many. Briney, where are you, ma bouchal? Come up and shake hands wid yer father, as well as another—come up, acushla, and kiss me. Ah, Briney, my poor fellow, ye'll never be the cut of a man yer father was; but no matther, avourneen, ye'll be a bether man, I hope; and God knows you may asy be that, for Father Philemy, I'm not what I ought to be, yer Reverence; however, I may mend, and will, maybe, before a month of Sundays goes over me: but, for all that, Briney, I hope to see the day when you'll be siting an ordained priest, at my own table; if I once saw that, I could die contented—so mind yer larning, acushla, and his Reverence here will back you, and make intherest to get you into the college. Musha, God pity them crathurs at the door—aren't they gone yet? Listen to them, coughin', for fraid we'd forget them: and throth and they won't be forgot this bout, any how—Katty, avourneen, give them every one, big and little, young and ould, their skinfull—don't lave a wrinkle in them; and see, take one of them bottles—the crathurs, they're starved sitting there all night in the could—and give them a couple of glasses a-piece—it's good, yer Reverence, to have the poor body's blessing at all times; and now, as I was saying, Here's all yer healths! *and from the very veins of my heart yer welcome here.*"

*The translation follows it.

Our readers may perceive that Phaddhy

> "Was not only blest, but glorious,
> O'er a' the ills o' life victorious;"

for, like the generality of our peasantry, the native drew to the surface of his character those warm, hospitable, and benevolent virtues, which a purer system of morals and education would most certainly keep in full action, without running the risk, as in the present instance, of mixing bad habits with frank, manly, and generous qualities.

*   *   *   *   *   *   *   *   *   *

*   *   *   *   *   *   *   *   *   *

"I'll not go, Con—I tell you I'll not go, till I sing another song. Phaddhy, you're a prince—but where's the use of lighting more candles now, man, than you had in the beginning of the night? Is Captain Wilson gone? Then, peace be with him; it's a pity he wasn't on the right side, for he's not the worst of them. Phaddhy, where are you?

"Why, yer Reverence," replied Katty, "he's got a little unwell, and jist laid down his head a bit."

"Katty," said Father Con, "you had better get a couple of the men to accompany Father Philemy home; for, though the night's clear, he doesn't see his way very well in the dark—poor man, his eyesight's failing him fast."

"Then, the more's the pity, Father Con. Here, Denis, let yourself and Mat go home wid Father Philemy."

"Good night, Katty," said Father Con—"Good night: and may our blessing *sanctify* you all."

"Good night, Father Con, ahagur," replied Katty; "and for goodness' sake see that they take care of Father Philemy, for it's himself that's the blessed and holy crathur, and the pleasant gintleman, out and out."

"Good night, Katty," again repeated Father Con, as the cavalcade proceeded in a body—"Good night!" And so ended the Station.

Joseph Sheridan LeFanu

♣

(1814-1873)

Joseph Sheridan LeFanu's life had all the markings of prosperity and good fortune. He was born into a family of means, he received the finest education, and after college, he graduated with a law degree and was called to the bar. The business of journalism, however, captured his imagination, and he abandoned any career in law he might have once imagined for himself. Instead, LeFanu began to acquire newspapers in Ireland, appointing himself editor and publishing his own stories, which he ultimately serialized. Affable and social, LeFanu gained some measure of popularity around Dublin for his work, but running newspapers and a loving devotion to his wife and four children appeared to be his main passions.

Then everything changed. The sudden death of his wife deeply depressed him, and the life he'd carved for himself took a dramatic turn. LeFanu ultimately withdrew from society altogether, rarely venturing outside his house during daylight hours. All his gloom and pessimism flowed into his writing, which he worked on obsessively, and he became known as the "Invisible Prince." He wrote from midnight to dawn, and turned out some of the most prolific horror and supernatural stories of the Victorian era. His tales were wildly popular and he was a bestselling author for two decades.

Yet critical praise eluded him during his time, as the literary elite looked on horror fiction with disdain, and LeFanu's work drifted into obscurity, even though writers such as Henry James and Dorothy Sayers admitted that they were admirers. It wasn't until 1923 that the noted scholar and ghost story writer M.R. James published some of LeFanu's stories in the collection, *Madam Crowl's Ghost and Other Tales of Mystery,* rescuing the Irish writer's work from oblivion. He is best known today for his suspense story, *Uncle Silas* (1864), as well as his murder mystery, *The House by the Churchyard* (1863) and "Carmilla," a vampire story that inspired Bram

Stoker's Dracula.

Joseph Thomas Sheridan LeFanu was born in Dublin in 1814, the son of Thomas Philip LeFanu, a clergyman of Huguenot origins. On his mother's side, he was related to the noted playwright, Richard Brinsley Sheridan, and at an early age, LeFanu demonstrated a passion for language, writing poems throughout his childhood. Schooled at home initially by his father and by private tutors, LeFanu ultimately attended Trinity College in Dublin where he read law and graduated in 1837. However, it was not his wife's death much later in 1858 that sparked his interest in ghost stories. LeFanu was dabbling in supernatural fiction while still a student, and *The Purcell Papers,* a collection of supernatural stories published posthumously in 1880, were proof of his lifelong passion for mysteries. In fact, LeFanu was writing mystery stories before Edgar Allan Poe and Charles Dickens. He joined the staff of *Dublin University Magazine* in 1837, two years before being called to the Irish Bar. His first story, "The Ghost and the Bonesetter" appeared in the magazine in 1838, and he would later purchase the *Dublin University Magazine* some twenty years later and turn it into one of Europe's most talked-about magazines.

By 1840, LeFanu had begun his journalistic enterprise, buying the *Protestant Guardian* and the *Warden,* and appointing himself editor of both. He also acquired shares in three other newspapers in Ireland, including *Evening Packet* and *Dublin Evening Mail,* and it was not uncommon for him to publish his work anonymously in serialized form in any of them. It was around this time that LeFanu began seriously pursuing Susanna Bennett, the woman he would ultimately marry in 1843. Together, they had four children. LeFanu's first novel, *The Cock and Anchor* was published in 1845, and chronicled old Dublin, and literary critics noticed that Le Fanu was clearly influenced by the work of Walter Scott, the Scottish novelist and poet.

If Dickens understood the dramatic possibilities of haunted suicides, such as Nicholas Nickleby, it is generally acknowledged that it was because of his fascination with LeFanu's work. Hallucinations, ghosts, spectral monkeys and other preternatural beings, either literal or metaphorically representing an institution, often figured prominently in LeFanu's stories, driving the main characters to their demise. His classic story, "The Green Tea" is indicative of these themes. The story depicts the nightmarish world of Reverend Jennings, who is constantly being pursued by what he perceives is an evil spirit—a monkey that no one else can see. Unable to bear it any longer, Jennings slits his own throat. A doctor later concludes that Jennings simply drank too much green tea, which was responsible for opening his patient's "inner eye" on his spiritual world.

"The Green Tea" so fascinated Dickens, he included the story in his periodical *All the Year Round* in 1869. In fact, the dark world of suicide would be a common theme in LeFanu's work, and literary scholars imagined that LeFanu's constant return to the theme offered a rare peek into the soul of the author himself. In 1858, his wife Susanna died, and LeFanu retreated into a world of isolation and despair. He was notorious for staying up the entire night to write his supernatural stories, and only occasionally ventured out into the daylight, mostly to visit his newspapers.

But the years immediately following his wife's death were his most prolific, despite what can only be described as his increasingly pessimistic outlook on life. LeFanu came to despise and distrust the social scene he was, until recently, a part of. Politically, he had no taste for the course of Irish politics, and he avoided politics in all 14 of his novels. The supernatural world was where he chose to express himself, and in the years after Susanna's death, he wrote constantly, turning out *The House by the Churchyard* in 1863, followed the next year by *Uncle Silas* and *Wylder's Hand*.

In his novels, LeFanu was just as captivated by the melancholy air of Ireland that has inspired countless writers, and was equally cognizant of the its haunting scenery. The Ireland he was capable of describing in rich, visual phrases lent itself perfectly as a background to his ghost stories, with ruined, torchlit chapels and castles and moonlight hanging over an ancient Irish cemetery. LeFanu's stories touched upon several recurring themes, most prominently, those where innocent people find themselves at the mercy of the society they aspire to attain. In *The Room at the Dragon Volant,* society's vision of romance and love are the undoing of the hero. In *Uncle Silas,* the institution is none other than the family. Silas Ruthvyn is the alter ego of Austin Ruthvyn, a dark double to his own brother.

In the novel, the brother dies and his daughter Maud goes to live with her uncle Silas—a man suspected of murdering an old gambling acquaintance and framing the death to resemble suicide. Slowly LeFanu unfolds a disturbing mystery, as Maud and the reader begin to discover that the holy, kind and wise uncle is not what he appears to be. Through Maud's eyes:

> Uncle Silas was always before me; the voice so silvery for an old man; so preternaturally soft; the manners so sweet, so gentle; the aspect, smiling, suffering, spectral. It was no longer a shadow; I had now seen him in the flesh. But after all, was he more than a shadow to me? When I closed my eyes I saw him before

me still, in necromantic black, ashy with pallour on which I looked with fear and pain, a face so dazzlingly pale, and those hollow, fiery, awful eyes! It sometimes seemed as if the curtain opened, and I had seen a ghost.

Silas is another of LeFanu's self-haunted characters where suicide takes on mysterious implications. In the dark, ghostly worlds created by the "Invisible Prince" in the midnight hours, one can only imagine the personal demons the author himself must have struggled with. He spent the rest of his life a widower, and died on Feburary 7, 1873, leaving behind a rich collection of beautiful work that established LeFanu as an important Irish writer in a timeless genre.

UNCLE SILAS
A TALE OF BARTRAM-HAUGH

♣

CHAPTER I

AUSTIN RUTHYN, OF KNOWL,
AND HIS DAUGHTER

It was winter—that is, about the second week in November—and great gusts were rattling at the windows, and wailing and thundering among our tall trees and ivied chimneys—a very dark night, and a very cheerful fire blazing, a pleasant mixture of good round coal and spluttering dry wood, in a genuine old fireplace, in a sombre old room. Black wainscoting glimmered up to the ceiling, in small ebony panels; a cheerful clump of wax candles on the tea-table; many old portraits, some grim and pale, others pretty, and some very graceful and charming, hanging from the walls. Few pictures, except portraits long and short, were there. On the whole, I think you would have taken the room for our parlour. It was not like our modern notion of a drawing-room. It was a long room too, and every way capacious, but irregularly shaped.

A girl, of a little more than seventeen, looking, I believe, younger still; slight and rather tall, with a great deal of golden hair, dark grey-eyed, and with a countenance rather sensitive and melancholy, was sitting at the tea-table, in a reverie. I was that girl.

The only other person in the room—the only person in the house related to me—was my father. He was Mr. Ruthyn, of Knowl, so called in his county, but he had many other places, was of a very ancient lineage, who had refused a baronetage often, and it was said even a viscounty, being of a proud and defiant spirit, and thinking themselves higher in station and purer of blood than two-thirds of the nobility into whose ranks, it was said, they had been invited to enter. Of all this family lore I knew but little and vaguely; only what is to be gathered from the fireside talk of old retainers in the nursery.

I am sure my father loved me, and I know I loved him. With the sure instinct of childhood I apprehended his tenderness, although it was never expressed in common ways. But my father was an oddity. He had been early disappointed in Parliament, where it was his ambition to succeed. Though a clever man, he failed there, where very inferior men did extremely well. Then he went abroad, and became a connoisseur and a collector; took a part, on his return, in literary and scientific institutions, and also in the foundation and direction of some charities. But he tired of this mimic government, and gave himself up to a country life, not that of a sportsman, but rather of a student, staying sometimes at one of his places and sometimes at another, and living a secluded life.

Rather late in life he married, and his beautiful young wife died, leaving me, their only child, to his care. This bereavement, I have been told, changed him—made him more odd and taciturn than ever, and his temper also, except to me, more severe. There was also some disgrace about his younger brother—my uncle Silas—which he felt bitterly.

He was now walking up and down this spacious old room, which, extending round an angle at the far end, was very dark in that quarter. It was his wont to walk up and down thus, without speaking—an exercise which used to remind me of Chateaubriand's father in the great chamber of the Chateau de Combourg. At the far end he nearly disappeared in the gloom, and then returning emerged for a few minutes, like a portrait with a background of shadow, and then again in silence faded nearly out of view.

This monotony and silence would have been terrifying to a person less accustomed to it than I. As it was, it had its effect. I have known my father a whole day without once speaking to me. Though I loved him very much, I was also much in awe of him.

While my father paced the floor, my thoughts were employed about the events of a month before. So few things happened at Knowl out of the accustomed routine, that a very trifling occurrence was enough to set people wondering and conjecturing in that serene household. My father lived in remarkable seclusion; except for a ride, he hardly ever left the grounds of Knowl; and I don't think it happened twice in the year that a visitor sojourned among us.

There was not even that mild religious bustle which sometimes besets the wealthy and moral recluse. My father had left the Church of England for some odd sect, I forget its name, and ultimately became, I was told, a Swedenborgian. But he did not care to trouble me upon the subject. So the old carriage brought my governess, when I had one, the old housekeeper, Mrs. Rusk, and myself to the parish church every Sunday. And my father, in the view of the honest rector who shook his head over him—'a cloud without water, carried about of winds, and a wandering star to whom is reserved the blackness of darkness'—corresponded with the 'minister' of his church, and was provokingly contented with his own fertility and illumination; and Mrs. Rusk, who was a sound and bitter churchwoman, said he fancied he saw visions and talked with angels like the rest of that 'rubbitch.'

I don't know that she had any better foundation than analogy and conjecture for charging my father with supernatural pretensions; and in all points when her orthodoxy was not concerned, she loved her master and was a loyal housekeeper.

I found her one morning superintending preparations for the reception of a visitor, in the hunting-room it was called, from the pieces of tapestry that covered its walls, representing scenes *à la Wouvermans,* of falconry, and the chase, dogs, hawks, ladies, gallants, and pages. In the midst of whom Mrs. Rusk, in black silk, was rummaging drawers, counting linen, and issuing orders.

'Who is coming, Mrs. Rusk?'

Well, she only knew his name. It was a Mr. Bryerly. My papa expected him to dinner, and to stay for some days.

'I guess he's one of those creatures, dear, for I mentioned his name just to Dr. Clay (the rector), and he says there *is* a Doctor Bryerly, a great conjurer among the Swedenborg sect—and that's him, I do suppose.'

In my hazy notions of these sectaries there was mingled a suspicion of necromancy, and a weird freemasonry, that inspired something of awe and antipathy.

Mr. Bryerly arrived time enough to dress at his leisure, before dinner. He entered the drawing-room—a tall, lean man, all in ungainly black, with a white choker, with either a black wig, or black hair dressed in imitation of one, a pair of spectacles, and a dark, sharp, short visage, rubbing his large hands together, and with a short brisk nod to me, whom he plainly regarded merely as a child, he sat down before the fire, crossed his legs, and took up a magazine.

This treatment was mortifying, and I remember very well the resentment of which *he* was quite unconscious.

His stay was not very long; not one of us divined the object of his visit, and he did not prepossess us favourably. He seemed restless, as men of busy habits do in country houses, and took walks, and a drive, and read in the library, and wrote half a dozen letters.

His bed-room and dressing-room were at the side of the gallery, directly opposite to my father's, which had a sort of anteroom *en suite,* in which were some of his theological books.

The day after Mr. Bryerly's arrival, I was about to see whether my father's water caraffe and glass had been duly laid on the table in this ante-room, and in doubt whether he was there, I knocked at the door.

I suppose they were too intent on other matters to hear, but receiving no answer, I entered the room. My father was sitting in his chair, with his coat and waistcoat off, Mr. Bryerly kneeling on a stool beside him, rather facing him, his black scratch wig leaning close to my father's grizzled hair. There was a large tome of their divinity lore, I suppose, open on the table close by. The lank black figure of Mr. Bryerly stood up, and he concealed something quickly in the breast of his coat.

My father stood up also, looking paler, I think, than I ever saw him till then, and he pointed grimly to the door, and said, 'Go.'

Mr. Bryerly pushed me gently back with his hands to my shoulders, and smiled down from his dark features with an expression quite unintelligible to me.

I had recovered myself in a second, and withdrew without a word. The last thing I saw at the door was the tall, slim figure in black, and the dark, significant smile following me: and then the door was shut and locked, and the two Swedenborgians were left to their mysteries.

I remember so well the kind of shock and disgust I felt in the certainty that I had surprised them at some, perhaps, debasing incantation–a suspicion of this Mr. Bryerly, of the ill-fitting black coat, and white choker–and a sort of fear came upon me, and I fancied he was asserting some kind of mastery over my father, which very much alarmed me.

I fancied all sorts of dangers in the enigmatical smile of the lank high-priest. The image of my father, as I had seen him, it might be, confessing to this man in black, who was I knew not what, haunted me with the disagreeable uncertainties of a mind very uninstructed as to the limits of the marvellous.

I mentioned it to no one. But I was immensely relieved when the sinister visitor took his departure the morning after, and it was upon this occurrence that my mind was now employed.

Some one said that Dr. Johnson resembled a ghost, who must be spoken to before it will speak. But my father, in whatever else he may have resembled a ghost, did not in that particular; for no one but I in his household–and I very seldom dared to address him until first addressed by him. I had no notion how singular this was until I began to go out a little among friends and relations, and found no such rule in force anywhere else.

As I leaned back in my chair thinking, this phantasm of my father came, and turned, and vanished with a solemn regularity. It was a peculiar figure, strongly made, thick-set, with a face large, and very stern; he wore a loose, black velvet coat and waistcoat. It was, however, the figure of an elderly rather than an old man—though he was then past seventy—but firm, and with no sign of feebleness.

I remember the start with which, not suspecting that he was close by me, I lifted my eyes, and saw that large, rugged countenance looking fixedly on me, from less than a yard away.

After I saw him, he continued to regard me for a second or two; and then, taking one of the heavy candlesticks in his gnarled hand, he beckoned me to follow him; which, in silence and wondering, I accordingly did.

He led me across the hall, where there were lights burning, and into a lobby by the foot of the back stairs, and so into his library.

It is a long, narrow room, with two tall, slim windows at the far end, now draped in dark curtains. Dusky it was with but one candle; and he paused near the door, at the left-hand side of which stood, in those days, an old-fashioned press or cabinet of carved oak. In front of this he stopped.

He had odd, absent ways, and talked more to himself, I believe, than to all the rest of the world put together.

'She won't understand,' he whispered, looking at me enquiringly. 'No, she won't. *Will* she?'

Then there was a pause, during which he brought forth from his breast pocket a small bunch of some half-dozen keys, on one of which he looked frowningly, every now and then balancing it a little before his eyes, between his finger and thumb, as he deliberated.

I knew him too well, of course, to interpose a word.

'They are easily frightened—ay, they are. I'd better do it another way.'

And pausing, he looked in my face as he might upon a picture.

'They *are*—yes—I had better do it another way—another way; yes—and she'll not suspect—she'll not suppose.'

Then he looked steadfastly upon the key, and from it to me, suddenly lifting it up, and said abruptly, 'See, child,' and, after a second or two, '*Remember* this key.'

It was oddly shaped, and unlike others.

'Yes, sir.' I always called him 'sir.'

'It opens that,' and he tapped it sharply on the door of the cabinet. 'In the daytime it is always here,' at which word he dropped it into his pocket again. 'You see?—and at night under my pillow—you hear me?'

'Yes, sir.'

'You won't forget this cabinet—oak—next the door—on your left—you won't forget?'

'No, sir.'

'Pity she's a girl, and so young—ay, a girl, and so young—no sense—giddy. You say, you'll *remember?*'

'Yes, sir.'

'It behoves you.'

He turned round and looked full upon me, like a man who has taken a sudden resolution; and I think for a moment he had made up his mind to tell me a great deal more. But if so, he changed it again; and after another pause, he said slowly and sternly—

'You will tell nobody what I have said, under pain of my displeasure.'

'Oh! no, sir!'

'Good child!'

'*Except,*' he resumed, 'under one contingency; that is, in case I should be absent, and Dr. Bryerly—you recollect the thin gentleman, in spectacles and a black wig, who spent three days here last month—should come and enquire for the key, you understand, in my absence.'

'Yes, sir.'

So he kissed me on the forehead, and said—'Let us return.'

Which, accordingly, we did, in silence; the storm outside, like a dirge on a great organ, accompanying our flitting.

CHAPTER II

UNCLE SILAS

When we reached the drawing-room, I resumed my chair, and my father his slow and regular walk to and fro, in the great room. Perhaps it was the uproar of the wind that disturbed the ordinary tenor of his thoughts; but, whatever was the cause, certainly he was unusually talkative that night.

After an interval of nearly half an hour, he drew near again, and sat down in a high-backed arm-chair, beside the fire, and nearly opposite to me, and looked at me steadfastly for some time, as was his wont, before speaking; and said he—

'This won't do—you must have a governess.'

In cases of this kind I merely set down my book or work, as it might be, and adjusted myself to listen without speaking.

'Your French is pretty well, and your Italian; but you have no German. Your music may be pretty good—I'm no judge—but your drawing might be better— yes— I believe there are accomplished ladies—finishing governesses, they call them—who undertake more than any one teacher would have professed in my time, and do very well. She can prepare you, and next winter, then, you shall visit France and Italy, where you may be accomplished as highly as you please.'

'Thank you, sir.'

'You shall. It is nearly six months since Miss Ellerton left you—too long without a teacher.'

Then followed an interval.

'Dr. Bryerly will ask you about that key, and what it opens; you show all that to *him*, and no one else.'

'But,' I said, for I had a great terror of disobeying him in ever so minute a matter, 'you will then be absent, sir—how am I to find the key?'

He smiled on me suddenly—a bright but wintry smile—it seldom came, and was very transitory, and kindly though mysterious.

'True, child; I'm glad you are so wise; *that*, you will find, I have provided for, and you shall know exactly where to look. You have remarked how solitarily I live. You fancy, perhaps, I have not got a friend, and you are nearly right—*nearly*, but not altogether. I have a very sure friend—*one*—a friend whom I once misunderstood, but now appreciate.'

I wondered silently whether it could be Uncle Silas.

'He'll make me a call, some day soon; I'm not quite sure when. I won't tell you his name—you'll hear that soon enough, and I don't want it talked of; and I must make a little journey with him. You'll not be afraid of being left alone for a time?'

'And have you promised, sir?' I answered, with another question, my curiosity and anxiety overcoming my awe. He took my questioning very good-humouredly.

'Well—*promise?*—no, child; but I'm under condition; he's not to be denied. I must make the excursion with him the moment he calls. I have no choice; but, on the whole, I rather like it—remember, I say, I rather *like* it.'

And he smiled again, with the same meaning, that was at once stern and sad. The exact purport of these sentences remained fixed in my mind, so that even at this distance of time I am quite sure of them.

A person quite unacquainted with my father's habitually abrupt and odd way of talking, would have fancied that he was possibly a little disordered in his mind. But no such suspicion for a moment troubled me. I was quite sure that he spoke of a real person who was coming, and that his journey was something momentous; and when the visitor of whom he spoke did come, and he departed with him upon that mysterious excursion, I perfectly understood his language and his reasons for saying so much and yet so little.

You are not to suppose that all my hours were passed in the sort of conference and isolation of which I have just given you a specimen; and singular and even awful as were sometimes my *tete-a-tetes* with my father, I had grown so accustomed to his strange ways, and had so unbounded a confidence in his affection, that they never depressed or agitated me in the manner you might have supposed. I had a great deal of quite a different sort of chat with good old Mrs. Rusk, and very pleasant talks with Mary Quince, my somewhat ancient maid; and besides all this, I had now and then a visit of a week or so at the house of some one of our country neighbours, and occasionally a visitor—but this, I must own, very rarely—at Knowl.

There had come now a little pause in my father's revelations, and my fancy wandered away upon a flight of discovery. Who, I again thought, could this intending visitor be, who was to come, armed with the prerogative to make my stay-at-home father forthwith leave his household goods—his books and his child—to whom he clung, and set forth on an unknown knight-errantry? Who but Uncle Silas, I thought—that mysterious relative whom I had never seen—who was, it had in old times been very darkly hinted to me, unspeakably unfortunate or unspeakably vicious—whom I had seldom heard my father mention, and then in a hurried way, and with a pained, thoughtful look. Once only he had said anything from which I could gather my father's opinion of him, and then it was so slight and enigmatical that I might have filled in the character very nearly as I pleased.

It happened thus. One day Mrs. Rusk was in the oak-room, I being then about fourteen. She was removing a stain from a tapestry chair, and I watched the process with a childish interest. She sat down to rest herself—she had been stooping over her work—and threw her head back, for her neck was weary, and in this position she fixed her eyes on a portrait that hung before her.

It was a full-length, and represented a singularly handsome young man, dark, slender, elegant, in a costume then quite obsolete, though I believe it was seen at the beginning of this century—white leather pantaloons and top-boots, a buff waistcoat, and a chocolate-coloured coat, and the hair long and brushed back.

There was a remarkable elegance and a delicacy in the features, but also a character of resolution and ability that quite took the portrait out of the category of mere fops or fine men. When people looked at it for the first time, I have so often heard the exclamation—'What a wonderfully handsome man!' and then, 'What a clever face!' An Italian greyhound stood by him, and some slender columns and a rich drapery in the background. But though the accessories were of the luxurious sort, and the beauty, as I have said, refined, there was a masculine force in that slender oval face, and a fire in the large, shadowy eyes, which were very peculiar, and quite redeemed it from the suspicion of effeminacy.

'Is not that Uncle Silas?' said I.

'Yes, dear,' answered Mrs. Rusk, looking, with her resolute little face, quietly on the portrait.

'He must be a very handsome man, Mrs. Rusk. Don't you think so?' I continued.

'He *was,* my dear—yes; but it is forty years since that was painted—the date is there in the corner, in the shadow that comes from his foot, and forty years, I can tell you, makes a change in most of us;' and Mrs. Rusk laughed, in cynical good-humour.

There was a little pause, both still looking on the handsome man in top—boots, and I said—

'And why, Mrs. Rusk, is papa always so sad about Uncle Silas?'

'What's that, child?' said my father's voice, very near. I looked round, with a start, and flushed and faltered, receding a step from him.

'No harm, dear. You have said nothing wrong,' he said gently, observing my alarm. 'You said I was always sad, I think, about Uncle Silas. Well, I don't know how you gather that; but if I were, I will now tell you, it would not be unnatural. Your uncle is a man of great talents, great faults, and great wrongs. His talents have not availed him; his faults are long ago repented of; and his wrongs I believe he feels less than I do, but they are deep. Did she say any more, madam?' he demanded abruptly of Mrs. Rusk.

'Nothing, sir,' with a stiff little courtesy, answered Mrs. Rusk, who stood in awe of him.

'And there is no need, child,' he continued, addressing himself to me, 'that you should think more of him at present. Clear your head of Uncle Silas. One day, perhaps, you will know him—yes, very well—and understand how villains have injured him.

Then my father retired, and at the door he said—

'Mrs. Rusk, a word, if you please,' beckoning to that lady, who trotted after him to the library.

I think he then laid some injunction upon the housekeeper, which was transmitted by her to Mary Quince, for from that time forth I could never lead either to talk with me about Uncle Silas. They let me talk on, but were reserved and silent themselves, and seemed embarrassed, and Mrs. Rusk sometimes pettish and angry, when I pressed for information.

Thus curiosity was piqued; and round the slender portrait in the leather pantaloons and top—boots gathered many-coloured circles of mystery, and the handsome features seemed to smile down upon my baffled curiosity with a provoking significance.

Why is it that this form of ambition—curiosity—which entered into the temptation of our first parent, is so specially hard to resist? Knowledge is power—and power of one sort or another is the secret lust of human souls; and here is, beside the sense of exploration, the undefinable interest of a story, and above all, something forbidden, to stimulate the contumacious appetite.

CHAPTER III

A NEW FACE

I think it was about a fortnight after that conversation in which my father had expressed his opinion, and given me the mysterious charge about the old oak cabinet in his library, as already detailed, that I was one night sitting at the great drawing-room window, lost in the melancholy reveries of night, and in admiration of the moonlighted scene. I was the only occupant of the room; and the lights near the fire, at its farther end, hardly reached to the window at which I sat.

The shorn grass sloped gently downward from the windows till it met the broad
level on which stood, in clumps, or solitarily scattered, some of the noblest timber
in England. Hoar in the moonbeams stood those graceful trees casting their move-
less shadows upon the grass, and in the background crowning the undulations of
the distance, in masses, were piled those woods among which lay the solitary tomb
where the remains of my beloved mother rested.

The air was still. The silvery vapour hung serenely on the far horizon, and the
frosty stars blinked brightly. Everyone knows the effect of such a scene on a mind
already saddened. Fancies and regrets float mistily in the dream, and the scene
affects us with a strange mixture of memory and anticipation, like some sweet old
air heard in the distance. As my eyes rested on those, to me, funereal but glorious
woods, which formed the background of the picture, my thoughts recurred to my
father's mysterious intimations and the image of the approaching visitor; and the
thought of the unknown journey saddened me.

In all that concerned his religion, from very early association, there was to me
something of the unearthly and spectral.

When my dear mamma died I was not nine years old; and I remember, two
days before the funeral, there came to Knowl, where she died, a thin little man,
with large black eyes, and a very grave, dark face.

He was shut up a good deal with my dear father, who was in deep affliction;
and Mrs. Rusk used to say, 'It is rather odd to see him praying with that little
scarecrow from London, and good Mr. Clay ready at call, in the village; much
good that little black whipper-snapper will do him! '

With that little black man, on the day after the funeral, I was sent out, for some
reason, for a walk; my governess was ill, I know, and there was confusion in the
house, and I dare say the maids made as much of a holiday as they could.

I remember feeling a sort of awe of this little dark man; but I was not afraid of
him, for he was gentle, though sad—and seemed kind. He led me into the garden—the Dutch garden, we used to call it—with a balustrade, and statues at the
farther front, laid out in a carpet—pattern of brilliantly—coloured flowers. We
came down the broad flight of Caen stone steps into this, and we walked in silence
to the balustrade. The base was too high at the spot where we reached it for me to
see over; but holding my hand, he said, 'Look through that, my child. Well, you
can't; but *I* can see beyond it—shall I tell you what? I see ever so much. I see a cottage with a steep roof, that looks like gold in the sunlight; there are tall trees
throwing soft shadows round it, and flowering shrubs, I can't say what, only the
colours are beautiful, growing by the walls and windows, and two little children are

playing among the stems of the trees, and we are on our way there, and in a few minutes shall be under those trees ourselves, and talking to those little children. Yet now to me it is but a picture in my brain, and to you but a story told by me, which you believe. Come, dear; let us be going.'

So we descended the steps at the right, and side by side walked along the grass lane between tall trim walls of evergreens. The way was in deep shadow, for the sun was near the horizon; but suddenly we turned to the left, and there we stood in rich sunlight, among the many objects he had described.

'Is this your house, my little men?' he asked of the children—pretty little rosy boys—who assented; and he leaned with his open hand against the stem of one of the trees, and with a grave smile he nodded down to me, saying—

'You see now, and hear, and *feel* for yourself that both the vision and the story were quite true; but come on, my dear, we have further to go.'

And relapsing into silence we had a long ramble through the wood, the same on which I was now looking in the distance. Every now and then he made me sit down to rest, and he in a musing solemn sort of way would relate some little story, reflecting, even to my childish mind, a strange suspicion of a spiritual meaning, but different from what honest Mrs. Rusk used to expound to me from the Parables, and, somehow, startling in its very vagueness.

Thus entertained, though a little awfully, I accompanied the dark mysterious little 'whipper—snapper' through the woodland glades. We came, to me quite unexpectedly, in the deep sylvan shadows, upon the grey, pillared temple, four-fronted, with a slanting pedestal of lichen—stained steps, the lonely sepulchre in which I had the morning before seen poor mamma laid. At the sight the fountains of my grief reopened, and I cried bitterly, repeating,'Oh! mamma, mamma, little mamma!' and so went on weeping and calling wildly on the deaf and the silent. There was a stone bench some ten steps away from the tomb.

'Sit down beside me, my child,' said the grave man with the black eyes, very kindly and gently. 'Now, what do you see there?' he asked, pointing horizontally with his stick towards the centre of the opposite structure.

'Oh, *that*—that place where poor mamma is?'

'Yes, a stone wall with pillars, too high for either you or me to see over. But—'

Here he mentioned a name which I think must have been Swedenborg, from what I afterwards learnt of his tenets and revelations; I only know that it sounded to me like the name of a magician in a fairy tale; I fancied he lived in the wood which surrounded us, and I began to grow frightened as he proceeded.

'But Swedenborg sees beyond it, over, and *through* it, and has told me all that concerns us to know. He says your mamma is not there.'

'She is taken away!' I cried, starting up, and with streaming eyes, gazing on the building which, though I stamped my feet in my distraction, I was afraid to approach. 'Oh, *is* mamma taken away? Where is she? Where have they brought her to?'

I was uttering unconsciously very nearly the question with which Mary, in the grey of that wondrous morning on which she stood by the empty sepulchre, accosted the figure standing near.

'Your mamma is alive, but too far away to see or hear us; but Swedenborg, standing here, can see and hear her, and tells me all he sees, just as I told you in the garden about the little boys and the cottage, and the trees and flowers which you could not see, but believed in when *I* told you. So I can tell you now as I did then; and as we are both, I hope, walking on to the same place, just as we did to the trees and cottage, you will surely see with your own eyes how true is the description which I give you.'

I was very much frightened, for I feared that when he had done his narrative we were to walk on through the wood into that place of wonders and of shadows where the dead were visible.

He leaned his elbow on his knee, and his forehead on his hand, which shaded his downcast eyes, and in that attitude described to me a beautiful landscape, radiant with a wondrous light, in which, rejoicing, my mother moved along an airy path, ascending among mountains of fantastic height, and peaks, melting in celestial colouring into the air, and peopled with human beings translated into the same image, beauty, and splendour. And when he had ended his relation, he rose, took my hand, and smiling gently down on my pale, wondering face, he said the same words he had spoken before—

'Come, dear, let us be going.'

'Oh! no, no, *no*—not now,' I said, resisting, and very much frightened.

'Home, I mean, dear. We cannot walk to the place I have described. We can only reach it through the gate of death, to which we are all tending, young and old, with sure steps.'

'And where is the gate of death?' I asked in a sort of whisper, as we walked together, holding his hand very fast, and looking stealthily. He smiled sadly and said—

'When, sooner or later, the time comes, as Hagar's eyes were opened in the wilderness, and she beheld the fountain of water, so shall each of us see the door open before us, and enter in and be refreshed.'

For a long time after this walk I was very nervous; the more so for the awful manner in which Mrs. Rusk received my statement—with stern lips and upturned hands and eyes, and an angry expostulation: 'I do wonder at you, Mary Quince, letting the child walk into the wood with that limb of darkness. It is a mercy he did not show her the devil, or frighten her out of her senses, in that lonely place!'

Of these Swedenborgians, indeed, I know no more than I might learn from good Mrs. Rusk's very inaccurate talk. Two or three of them crossed in the course of my early life, like magic-lantern figures, the disk of my very circumscribed observation. All outside was and is darkness. I once tried to read one of their books upon the future state—heaven and hell; but I grew after a day or two so nervous that I laid it aside. It is enough for me to know that their founder either saw or fancied he saw amazing visions, which, so far from superseding, confirmed and interpreted the language of the Bible; and as dear papa accepted their ideas, I am happy in thinking that they did not conflict with the supreme authority of holy writ.

Leaning on my hand, I was now looking upon that solemn wood, white and shadowy in the moonlight, where, for a long time after that ramble with the visionary, I fancied the gate of death, hidden only by a strange glamour, and the dazzling land of ghosts, were situate; and I suppose these earlier associations gave to my reverie about my father's coming visitor a wilder and a sadder tinge.

CHAPTER IV

MADAME DE LA ROUGIERRE

On a sudden, on the grass before me, stood an odd figure—a very tall woman in grey draperies, nearly white under the moon, courtesying extraordinarily low, and rather fantastically.

I stared in something like a horror upon the large and rather hollow features which I did not know, smiling very unpleasantly on me; and the moment it was plain that I saw her, the grey woman began gobbling and cackling shrilly-I could not distinctly hear *what* through the window—and gesticulating oddly with her long hands and arms.

As she drew near the window, I flew to the fireplace, and rang the bell frantically, and seeing her still there, and fearing that she might break into the room, I flew out of the door, very much frightened, and met Branston the butler in the lobby.

'There's a woman at the window!' I gasped; 'turn her away, please.'

If I had said a man, I suppose fat Branston would have summoned and sent forward a detachment of footmen. As it was, he bowed gravely, with a—'Yes,'m—
shall,'m.'

And with an air of authority approached the window.

I don't think that he was pleasantly impressed himself by the first sight of our
visitor, for he stopped short some steps of the window, and demanded rather
sternly—

'What ye doin' there, woman?'

To this summons, her answer, which occupied a little time, was inaudible to
me. But Branston replied—

'I wasn't aware, ma'am; I heerd nothin'; if you'll go round *that* way, you'll see
the hall-door steps, and I'll speak to the master, and do as he shall order.'

The figure said something and pointed.

'Yes, that's it, and ye can't miss of the door.'

And Mr. Branston returned slowly down the long room, and halted with out-
turned pumps and a grave inclination before me, and the faintest amount of interrogation in the announcement—

'Please, 'm, she says she's the governess.'

'The governess! *What* governess?'

Branston was too well-bred to smile, and he said thoughtfully—

'P'raps, 'm, I'd best ask the master?'

To which I assented, and away strode the flat pumps of the butler to the library.

I stood breathless in the hall. Every girl at my age knows how much is involved
in such an advent. I also heard Mrs. Rusk, in a minute or two more, emerge I suppose from the study. She walked quickly, and muttered sharply to herself—an evil
trick, in which she indulged when much 'put about.' I should have been glad of a
word with her; but I fancied she was vexed, and would not have talked satisfactorily. She did not, however, come my way; merely crossing the hall with her quick,
energetic step.

Was it really the arrival of a governess? Was that apparition which had
impressed me so unpleasantly to take the command of me—to sit alone with me,
and haunt me perpetually with her sinister looks and shrilly gabble?

I was just making up my mind to go to Mary Quince, and learn something definite, when I heard my father's step approaching from the library: so I quietly re-
entered the drawing-room, but with an anxious and throbbing heart.

When he came in, as usual, he patted me on the head gently, with a kind of
smile, and then began his silent walk up and down the room. I was yearning to

question him on the point that just then engrossed me so disagreeably; but the awe in which I stood of him forbade.

After a time he stopped at the window, the curtain of which I had drawn, and the shutter partly opened, and he looked out, perhaps with associations of his own, on the scene I had been contemplating.

It was not for nearly an hour after, that my father suddenly, after his wont, in a few words, apprised me of the arrival of Madame de la Rougierre to be my governess, highly recommended and perfectly qualified. My heart sank with a sure presage of ill. I already disliked, distrusted, and feared her.

I had more than an apprehension of her temper and fear of possibly abused authority. The large-featured, smirking phantom, saluting me so oddly in the moonlight, retained ever after its peculiar and unpleasant hold upon my nerves.

'Well, Miss Maud, dear, I hope you'll like your new governess—for it's more than *I* do, just at present at least,' said Mrs. Rusk, sharply—she was awaiting me in my room. 'I hate them French-women; they're not natural, I think. I gave her her supper in my room. She eats like a wolf, she does, the great raw-boned hannimal. I wish you saw her in bed as I did. I put her next the clock-room—she'll hear the hours betimes, I'm thinking. You never saw such a sight. The great long nose and hollow cheeks of her, and oogh! such a mouth! I felt a'most like little Red Riding-Hood—I did, Miss.'

Here honest Mary Quince, who enjoyed Mrs. Rusk's satire, a weapon in which she was not herself strong, laughed outright.

'Turn down the bed, Mary. She's very agreeable—she is, just now—all newcomers is; but she did not get many compliments from me, Miss—no, I rayther think not. I wonder why honest English girls won't answer the gentry for governesses, instead of them gaping, scheming, wicked furriners? Lord forgi' me, I think they're all alike.'

Next morning I made acquaintance with Madame de la Rougierre. She was tall, masculine, a little ghastly perhaps, and draped in purple silk, with a lace cap, and great bands of black hair, too thick and black, perhaps, to correspond quite naturally with her bleached and sallow skin, her hollow jaws, and the fine but grim wrinkles traced about her brows and eyelids. She smiled, she nodded, and then for a good while she scanned me in silence with a steady cunning eye, and a stern smile.

'And how is she named—what is Mademoiselle's name?' said the tall stranger.

'*Maud*, Madame.'

'Maud!—what pretty name! Eh bien! I am very sure my dear Maud she will be very good little girl—is not so?—and I am sure I shall love you vary moche. And what 'av you been learning, Maud, my dear cheaile—music, French, German, eh?'

'Yes, a little; and I had just begun the use of the globes when my governess went away.'

I nodded towards the globes, which stood near her, as I said this.

'Oh! yes—the globes;' and she spun one of them with her great hand. 'Je vous expliquerai tout cela à fond.'

Madame da la Rougierre, I found, was always quite ready to explain everything a fond;' but somehow her 'explications,' as she termed them, were not very intelligible, and when pressed her temper woke up; so that I preferred, after a while, accepting the expositions just as they came.

Madame was on an unusually large scale, a circumstance which made some of her traits more startling, and altogether rendered her, in her strange way, more awful in the eyes of a nervous *child*, I may say, such as I was. She used to look at me for a long time sometimes, with the peculiar smile I have mentioned, and a great finger upon her lip, like the Eleusinian priestess on the vase.

She would sit, too, sometimes for an hour together, looking into the fire or out of the window, plainly seeing nothing, and with an odd, fixed look of something like triumph—very nearly a smile—on her cunning face.

She was by no means a pleasant *gouvernante* for a nervous girl of my years. Sometimes she had accesses of a sort of hilarity which frightened me still more than her graver moods, and I will describe these by-and-by.

CHAPTER V

SIGHTS AND NOISES

There is not an old house in England of which the servants and young people who live in it do not cherish some traditions of the ghostly. Knowl has its shadows, noises, and marvellous records. Rachel Ruthyn, the beauty of Queen Anne's time, who died of grief for the handsome Colonel Norbrooke, who was killed in the Low Countries, walks the house by night, in crisp and sounding silks. She is not seen, only heard. The tapping of her high-heeled shoes, the sweep and rustle of her brocades, her sighs as she pauses in the galleries, near the bed-room doors; and sometimes, on stormy nights, her sobs.

There is, beside, the 'link-man,' a lank, dark-faced, black-haired man, in a sable suit, with a link or torch in his hand. It usually only smoulders, with a deep red glow, as he visits his beat. The library is one of the rooms he sees to. Unlike 'Lady Rachel,' as the maids called her, he is seen only, never heard. His steps fall noiseless as shadows on floor and carpet. The lurid glow of his smouldering torch imperfectly lights his figure and face, and, except when much perturbed, his link never blazes. On those occasions, however, as he goes his rounds, he ever and anon whirls it round his head, and it bursts into a dismal flame. This is a fearful omen, and always portends some direful crisis or calamity. It occurs, however, only one or twice in a century.

I don't know whether Madame had heard anything of these phenomena; but she did report what very much frightened me and Mary Quince. She asked us who walked in the gallery on which her bed-room opened, making a rustling with her dress, and going down the stairs, and breathing long breaths here and there. Twice, she said, she had stood at her door in the dark, listening to these sounds, and once she called to know who it was. There was no answer, but the person plainly turned back, and hurried towards her with an unnatural speed, which made her jump within her door and shut it.

When first such tales are told, they excite the nerves of the young and the ignorant intensely. But the special effect, I have found, soon wears out, and the tale simply takes its place with the rest. So it was with Madame's narrative.

About a week after its relation, I had my experience of a similar sort. Mary Quince went down-stairs for a night-light, leaving me in bed, a candle burning in the room, and there, being tired, I fell asleep before her return. When I awoke the candle had been extinguished. But I heard a step softly approaching. I jumped up—quite forgetting the ghost, and thinking only of Mary Quince—and opened the door, expecting to see the light of her candle. Instead, all was dark, and near me I heard the fall of a bare foot on the oak floor. It was as if some one had stumbled. I said, 'Mary,' but no answer came, only a rustling of clothes and a breathing at the other side of the gallery, which passed off towards the upper staircase. I turned into my room, freezing with horror, and clapt my door. The noise wakened Mary Quince, who had returned and gone to her bed half an hour before.

About a fortnight after this, Mary Quince, a very veracious spinster, reported to me, that having got up to fix the window, which was rattling, at about four o'clock in the morning, she saw a light shining from the library window. She could swear to its being a strong light, streaming through the chinks of the shutter, and moving, as no doubt the link was waved about his head by the angry 'link-man.'

These strange occurrences helped, I think, just then to make me nervous, and prepared the way for the odd sort of ascendency which, through my sense of the mysterious and supernatural, that repulsive Frenchwoman was gradually, and it seemed without effort, establishing over me.

Some dark points of her character speedily emerged from the prismatic mist with which she had enveloped it.

Mrs. Rusk's observation about the agreeability of new-comers I found to be true; for as Madame began to lose that character, her good-humour abated very perceptibly, and she began to show gleams of another sort of temper, that was lurid and dangerous.

Notwithstanding this, she was in the habit of always having her Bible open by her, and was austerely attentive at morning and evening services, and asked my father, with great humility, to lend her some translations of Swedenborg's books, which she laid much to heart.

When we went out for our walk, if the weather were bad we generally made our promenade up and down the broad terrace in front of the windows. Sullen and malign at times she used to look, and as suddenly she would pat me on the shoulder caressingly, and smile with a grotesque benignity, asking tenderly, 'Are you fatigue, ma chère?' or 'Are you cold-a, dear Maud?'

At first these abrupt transitions puzzled me, sometimes half frightened me, savouring, I fancied, of insanity. The key, however, was accidentally supplied, and I found that these accesses of demonstrative affection were sure to supervene whenever my father's face was visible through the library windows.

I did not know well what to make of this woman, whom I feared with a vein of superstitious dread. I hated being alone with her after dusk in the school-room. She would sometimes sit for half an hour at a time, with her wide mouth drawn down at the corners, and a scowl, looking into the fire. If she saw me looking at her, she would change all this on the instant, affect a sort of languor, and lean her head upon her hand, and ultimately have recourse to her Bible. But I fancied she did not read, but pursued her own dark ruminations, for I observed that the open book might often lie for half an hour or more under her eyes and yet the leaf never turned.

I should have been glad to be assured that she prayed when on her knees, or read when that book was before her; I should have felt that she was more canny and human. As it was, those external pieties made a suspicion of a hollow contrast with realities that helped to scare me; yet it was but a suspicion—I could not be certain.

Our rector and the curate, with whom she was very gracious, and anxious about my collects and catechism, had an exalted opinion of her. In public places her affection for me was always demonstrative.

In like manner she contrived conferences with my father. She was always making excuses to consult him about my reading, and to confide in him her sufferings, as I learned, from my contumacy and temper. The fact is, I was altogether quiet and submissive. But I think she had a wish to reduce me to a state of the most abject bondage. She had designs of domination and subversion regarding the entire household, I now believe, worthy of the evil spirit I sometimes fancied her.

My father beckoned me into the study one day, and said he—

'You ought not to give poor Madame so much pain. She is one of the few persons who take an interest in you; why should she have so often to complain of your ill-temper and disobedience?—why should she be compelled to ask my permission to punish you? Don't be afraid, I won't concede that. But in so kind a person it argues much. Affection I can't command—respect and obedience I may—and I insist on your rendering *both* to Madame.'

'But sir,' I said, roused into courage by the gross injustice of the charge, 'I have always done exactly as she bid me, and never said one disrespectful word to Madame.'

'I don't think, child, *you* are the best judge of that. Go, and *amend.*' And with a displeased look he pointed to the door. My heart swelled with the sense of wrong, and as I readied the door I turned to say another word, but I could not, and only burst into tears.

'There—don't cry, little Maud—only let us do better for the future. There—there—there has been enough.'

And he kissed my forehead, and gently put me out and closed the door.

In the school-room I took courage, and with some warmth upbraided Madame.

'Wat wicked cheaile!' moaned Madame, demurely. 'Read aloud those three—yes, *those* three chapters of the Bible, my dear Maud.'

There was no special fitness in those particular chapters, and when they were ended she said in a sad tone—

'Now, dear, you must commit to memory this pretty priaire for umility of art.'

It was a long one, and in a state of profound irritation I got through the task.

Mrs. Rusk hated her. She said she stole wine and brandy whenever the opportunity offered—that she was always asking her for such stimulants and pretending pains in her stomach. Here, perhaps, there was exaggeration; but I knew it was true that I had been at different times despatched on that errand and pretext for brandy to Mrs. Rusk, who at last came to her bedside with pills and a mustard blister only, and was hated irrevocably ever after.

I felt all this was done to torture me. But a day is a long time to a child, and they forgive quickly. It was always with a sense of danger that I heard Madame say she must go and see Monsieur Ruthyn in the library, and I think a jealousy of her growing influence was an ingredient in the detestation in which honest Mrs. Rusk held her.

CHAPTER VI

A WALK IN THE WOOD

Two little pieces of by-play in which I detected her confirmed my unpleasant suspicion. From the corner of the gallery I one day saw her, when she thought I was out and all quiet, with her ear at the keyhole of papa's study, as we used to call the sitting room next his bed-room. Her eyes were turned in the direction of the stairs, from which only she apprehended surprise. Her great mouth was open, and her eyes absolutely goggled with eagerness. She was devouring all that was passing there. I drew back into the shadow with a kind of disgust and horror. She was transformed into a great gaping reptile. I felt that I could have thrown something at her; but a kind of fear made me recede again toward my room. Indignation, however, quickly returned, and I came back, treading briskly as I did so. When I reached the angle of the gallery again, Madame, I suppose, had heard me, for she was half-way down the stairs.

'Ah, my dear cheaile, I am so glad to find you, and you are dress to come out. We shall have so pleasant walk.'

At that moment the door of my father's study opened, and Mrs. Rusk, with her dark energetic face very much flushed, stepped out in high excitement.

'The Master says you may have the brandy-bottle, Madame and I'm glad to be rid of it—*I* am.'

Madame courtesied with a great smirk, that was full of intangible hate and insult.

'Better your own brandy, if drink you must!' exclaimed Mrs. Rusk. 'You may come to the store-room now, or the butler can take it.'

And off whisked Mrs. Rusk for the back staircase.

There had been no common skirmish on this occasion, but a pitched battle.

Madame had made a sort of pet of Anne Wixted, an under-chambermaid, and attached her to her interest economically by persuading me to make her presents of some old dresses and other things. Anne was such an angel!

But Mrs. Rusk, whose eyes were about her, detected Anne, with a brandy-bottle under her apron, stealing upstairs. Anne, in a panic, declared the truth. Madame had commissioned her to buy it in the town, and convey it to her bed-room. Upon this, Mrs. Rusk impounded the flask; and, with Anne beside her, rather precipitately appeared before 'the Master.' He heard, and summoned Madame. Madame was cool, frank, and fluent. The brandy was purely medicinal. She produced a document in form of a note. Doctor Somebody presented his compliments to Madame de la Rougierre, and ordered her a table-spoonful of brandy and some drops of laudanum whenever the pain of stomach returned. The flask would last a whole year, perhaps two. She claimed her medicine.

Man's estimate of woman is higher than woman's own. Perhaps in their relations to men they are generally more trustworthy—perhaps woman's is the juster, and the other an appointed illusion. I don't know; but so it is ordained.

Mrs. Rusk was recalled, and I saw, as you are aware, Madame's procedure during the interview.

It was a great battle—a great victory. Madame was in high spirits. The air was sweet—the landscape charming—I, so good—everything so beautiful! Where should we go? *this* way?

I had made a resolution to speak as little as possible to Madame, I was so incensed at the treachery I had witnessed; but such resolutions do not last long with very young people, and by the time we had reached the skirts of the wood we were talking pretty much as usual.

'I don't wish to go into the wood, Madame.'

'And for what?'

'Poor mamma is buried there.'

'Is *there* the vault?' demanded Madame eagerly.

I assented.

'My faith, curious reason; you say because poor mamma is buried there you will not approach! Why, cheaile, what would good Monsieur Ruthyn say if he heard such thing? You are surely not so unkain', and I am with you. *Allons.* Let us come—even a little part of the way.'

And so I yielded, though still reluctant.

There was a grass-grown road, which we easily reached, leading to the sombre building, and we soon arrived before it.

Madame de la Rougierre seemed rather curious. She sat down on the little bank opposite, in her most languid pose—her head leaned upon the tips of her fingers.

'How very sad—how solemn!' murmured Madame. 'What noble tomb! How triste, my dear cheaile, your visit 'ere must it be, remembering a so sweet maman. There is new inscription—is it not new?' And so, indeed, it seemed.

'I am fatigue—maybe you will read it aloud to me slowly and solemnly, my dearest Maud?'

As I approached, I happened to look, I can't tell why, suddenly, over my shoulder; I was startled, for Madame was grimacing after me with a vile derisive distortion. She pretended to be seized with a fit of coughing. But it would not do: she saw that I had detected her, and she laughed aloud.

'Come here, dear cheaile. I was just reflecting how foolish is all this thing—the tomb—the epitaph. I think I would 'av no, no epitaph. We regard them first for the oracle of the dead, and find them after only the folly of the living. So I despise. Do you think your house of Knowl down there is what you call haunt, my dear?'

'Why?' said I, flushing and growing pale again. I felt quite afraid of Madame, and confounded at the suddenness of all this.

'Because Anne Wixted she says there is ghost. How dark is this place! and so many of the Ruthyn family they are buried here—is not so? How high and thick are the trees all round! and nobody comes near.'

And Madame rolled her eyes awfully, as if she expected to see something unearthly, and, indeed, looked very like it herself.

'Come away, Madame,' I said, growing frightened, and feeling that if I were once, by any accident, to give way to the panic that was gathering round me, I should instantaneously lose all control of myself. 'Oh, come away! do, Madame—I'm frightened.'

'No, on the contrary, sit here by me. It is very odd, you will think, ma chère—un gout bizarre, vraiment!—but I love very much to be near to the dead people—in solitary place like this. I am not afraid of the dead people, nor of the ghosts. 'Av you ever see a ghost, my dear?'

'Do, Madame, *pray* speak of something else.'

'Wat little fool! But no, you are not afraid. I'av seen the ghosts myself. I saw one, for example, last night, shape like a monkey, sitting in the corner, with his arms round his knees; very wicked, old, old man his face was like, and white eyes so large.'

'Come away, Madame! you are trying to frighten me,' I said, in the childish anger which accompanies fear.

Madame laughed an ugly laugh, and said—

'Eh bien! little fool!—I will not tell the rest if you are really frightened; let us change to something else.'

'Yes, yes! oh, do—pray do.'

'Wat good man is your father!'

'Very—the kindest darling. I don't know why it is, Madame, I am so afraid of him, and never could tell him how much I love him.'

This confidential talking with Madame, strange to say, implied no confidence; it resulted from fear—it was deprecatory. I treated her as if she had human sympathies, in the hope that they might be generated somehow.

'Was there not a doctor from London with him a few months ago? Dr. Bryerly, I think they call him.'

'Yes, a Doctor Bryerly, who remained a few days. Shall we begin to walk towards home, Madame? Do, pray.'

'Immediately, cheaile; and does your father suffer much?'

'No—I think not.'

'And what then is his disease?'

'Disease! he has *no* disease. Have you heard anything about his health, Madame?' I said, anxiously.

'Oh no, ma foi—I have heard nothing; but if the doctor came, it was not because he was quite well.'

'But that doctor is a doctor in theology, I fancy, I know he is a Swedenborgian; and papa is so well, he *could* not have come as a physician.'

'I am very glad, ma chère, to hear; but still you know your father is old man to have so young cheaile as you. Oh, yes—he is old man, and so uncertain life is. 'As he made his will, my dear? Every man so rich as he, especially so old, aught to 'av made his will.'

'There is no need of haste, Madame; it is quite time enough when his health begins to fail.'

'But has he really compose no will?'

'I really don't know, Madame.'

'Ah, little rogue! you will not tell—but you are not such fool as you feign yourself. No, no; you know everything. Come, tell me all about—it is for your advantage, you know. What is in his will, and when he wrote?'

'But, Madame, I really know nothing of it. I can't say whether there is a will or not. Let us talk of something else.'

'But, cheaile, it will not kill Monsieur Ruthyn to make his will; he will not come to lie here a day sooner by cause of that; but if he make no will, you may lose a great deal of the property. Would not that be pity?'

'I really don't know anything of his will. If papa has made one, he has never spoken of it to me. I know he loves me—that is enough.'

'Ah! you are not such little goose—you do know everything, of course. Come, come, tell me, little obstinate, otherwise I will break your little finger. Tell me everything.'

'I know nothing of papa's will. You don't know, Madame, how you pain me. Do let us speak of something else.'

'You do know, and you must tell, petite dure-tête, or I will break a your leetle finger.'

With which words she seized that joint, and laughing spitefully, she twisted it suddenly back. I screamed; she continued to laugh.

'Will you tell?'

'Yes, yes! let me go,' I shrieked.

She did not release it, however, immediately, but continued her torture and discordant laughter. At last, however, she did release my finger.

'So she is going to be good cheaile, and to tell everything to her affectionate gouvernante. What do you cry for, little fool?'

'You've hurt me very much—you have broken my finger,' I sobbed.

'Rub it and blow it, and give it a kees, little fool! what cross girl! I will never play with you again—never. Let us go home.'

Madame was silent and morose all the way home. She would not answer my questions, and affected to be very lofty and offended.

This did not last very long, however, and she soon resumed her wonted ways. And she returned to the question of the will, but not so directly, and with more art.

Why should this dreadful woman's thoughts be running so continually upon my father's will? How could it concern her?

CHAPTER VII

CHURCH SCARSDALE

I think all the females of our household, except Mrs. Rusk, who was at open feud with her, and had only room for the fiercer emotions, were more or less afraid of this inauspicious foreigner.

Mrs. Rusk would say in her confidences in my room—

'Where does she come from?—is she a French or a Swiss one, or is she a Canada woman? I remember one of *them* when I was a girl, and a nice limb *she* was, too! And who did she live with? Where was her last family? Not one of us knows nothing about her, no more than a child; except, of course, the Master—I do suppose he made enquiry. She's always at hugger-mugger with Anne Wixted. I'll pack that *one* about her business, if she don't mind. Tattling and whispering eternally. It's not about her own business she's a-talking. Madame de la Rougepot, *I* call her. She *does* know how to paint up to the ninety-nines—she does, the old cat. I beg your pardon, Miss, but *that* she is—a devil, and no mistake. I found her out first by her thieving the Master's gin, that the doctor ordered him, and filling the decanter up with water—the old villain; but she'll be found out yet, she will; and all the maids is afraid on her. She's not right, they think—a witch or a ghost—I should not wonder. Catherine Jones found her in her bed asleep in the morning after she sulked with you, you know, Miss, with all her clothes on, whatever was the meaning; and I think she has frightened *you,* Miss and has you as nervous as anythink—I do,' and so forth.

It was true. I *was* nervous and growing rather more so; and I think this cynical woman perceived and intended it, and was pleased. I was always afraid of her concealing herself in my room, and emerging at night to scare me. She began sometimes to mingle in my dreams, too—always awfully; and this nourished, of course, the kind of ambiguous fear in which, in waking hours, I held her.

I dreamed one night that she led me, all the time whispering something so very fast that I could not understand her, into the library, holding a candle in her other hand above her head. We walked on tiptoe, like criminals at the dead of night, and stopped before that old oak cabinet which my father had indicated in so odd a way to me. I felt that we were about some contraband practice. There was a key in the door, which I experienced a guilty horror at turning, she whispering in the same unintelligible way, all the time, at my ear. I *did* turn it; the door opened quite softly, and within stood my father, his face white and malignant, and glaring close in mine. He cried in a terrible voice, 'Death!' Out went Madame's candle, and at the same moment, with a scream, I waked in the dark—still fancying myself in the library; and for an hour after I continued in a hysterical state.

Every little incident about Madame furnished a topic of eager discussion among the maids. More or less covertly, they nearly all hated and feared her. They fancied that she was making good her footing with 'the Master;' and that she would then oust Mrs. Rusk—perhaps usurp her place—and so make a clean sweep of them all. I fancy the honest little housekeeper did not discourage that suspicion.

About this time I recollect a pedlar—an odd, gipsified-looking man—called in at Knowl. I and Catherine Jones were in the court when he came, and set down his pack on the low balustrade beside the door.

All sorts of commodities he had—ribbons, cottons, silks, stockings, lace, and even some bad jewellry; and just as he began his display—an interesting matter in a quiet country house—Madame came upon the ground. He grinned a recognition, and hoped 'Madamasel' was well, and 'did not look to see *her* here.'

'Madamasel' thanked him. 'Yes, vary well,' and looked for the first time decidedly 'put out.'

'Wat a pretty things!' she said. 'Catherine, run and tell Mrs. Rusk. She wants scissars, and lace too—I heard her say.'

So Catherine, with a lingering look, departed; and Madame said—

'Will you, dear cheaile, be so kind to bring here my purse, I forgot on the table in my room; also, I advise you, bring *your*.'

Catherine returned with Mrs. Rusk. Here was a man who could tell them something of the old Frenchwoman, at last! Slyly they dawdled over his wares, until Madame had made her market and departed with me. But when the coveted opportunity came, the pedlar was quite impenetrable. 'He forgot everything; he did not believe as he ever saw the lady before. He called a Frenchwoman, all the world over, Madamasel—that wor the name on 'em all. He never seed her in partiklar afore, as be could bring to mind. He liked to see 'em always, 'cause they makes the young uns buy.'

This reserve and oblivion were very provoking, and neither Mrs. Rusk nor Catherine Jones spent sixpence with him;—he was a stupid fellow, or worse.

Of course Madame had tampered with him. But truth, like murder, will out some day. Tom Williams, the groom, had seen her, when alone with him, and pretending to look at his stock, with her face almost buried in his silks and Welsh linseys, talking as fast as she could all the time, and slipping *money*, he did suppose, under a piece of stuff in his box.

In the mean time, I and Madame were walking over the wide, peaty sheep-walks that lie between Knowl and Church Scarsdale. Since our visit to the mausoleum in the wood, she had not worried me so much as before. She had been, indeed, more than usually thoughtful, very little talkative, and troubled me hardly at all about French and other accomplishments. A walk was a part of our daily routine. I now carried a tiny basket in my hand, with a few sandwiches, which were to furnish our luncheon when we reached the pretty scene, about two miles away, whither we were tending.

We had started a little too late; Madame grew unwontedly fatigued and sat down to rest on a stile before we had got halfway; and there she intoned, with a dismal nasal cadence, a quaint old Bretagne ballad, about a lady with a pig's head:—

> 'This lady was neither pig nor maid,
> And so she was not of human mould;
> Not of the living nor the dead.
> Her left hand and foot were warm to touch;
> Her right as cold as a corpse's flesh!
> And she would sing like a funeral bell, with a ding-dong tune.
> The pigs were afraid, and viewed her aloof;
> And women feared her and stood afar.
> She could do without sleep for a year and a day;
> She could sleep like a corpse, for a month and more.
> No one knew flow this lady fed—
> On acorns or on flesh.
> Some say that she's one of the swine-possessed,
> That swam over the sea of Gennesaret.
> A mongrel body and demon soul.
> Some say she's the wife of the Wandering Jew,
> And broke the law for the sake of pork;
> And a swinish face for a token cloth bear,
> That her shame is now, and her punishment coming.'

And so it went on, in a gingling rigmarole. The more anxious I seemed to go on our way, the more likely was she to loiter. I therefore showed no signs of impatience, and I saw her consult her watch in the course of her ugly minstrelsy, and slyly glance, as if expecting something, in the direction of our destination.

When she had sung to her heart's content, up rose Madame, and began to walk onward silently. I saw her glance once or twice, as before, toward the village of Trillsworth, which lay in front, a little to our left, and the smoke of which hung in a film over the brow of the hill. I think she observed me, for she enquired—

'Wat is that a smoke there?'

'That is Trillsworth, Madame; there is a railway station there.'

'Oh, le chemin de fer, so near! I did not think. Where it goes?'

I told her, and silence returned.

Church Scarsdale is a very pretty and odd scene. The slightly undulating sheep-walk dips suddenly into a wide glen, in the lap of which, by a bright, winding rill, rise from the sward the ruins of a small abbey, with a few solemn trees scattered round. The crows' nests hung untenanted in the trees; the birds were foraging far away from their roosts. The very cattle had forsaken the place. It was solitude itself.

Madame drew a long breath and smiled.

'Come down, come down, cheaile—come down to the churchyard.'

As we descended the slope which shut out the surrounding world, and the scene grew more sad and lonely, Madame's spirits seemed to rise.

'See 'ow many grave-stones—one, *two* hundred. Don't you love the dead, cheaile? I will teach you to love them. You shall see me die here to-day, for half an hour, and be among them. That is what I love.'

We were by this time at the little brook's side, and the low churchyard wall with a stile, reached by a couple of stepping-stones, across the stream, immediately at the other side.

'Come, now!' cried Madame, raising her face, as if to sniff the air; 'we are close to them. You will like them soon as I. You shall see five of them. Ah, ça ira, ça ira, ça ira! Come cross quickily! I am Madame la Morgue—Mrs. Deadhouse! I will present you my friends, Monsieur Cadavre and Monsieur Squelette. Come, come, leetle mortal, let us play. Ouaah!' And she uttered a horrid yell from her enormous mouth, and pushing her wig and bonnet back, so as to show her great, bald head. She was laughing, and really looked quite mad.

'No, Madame, I will not go with you,' I said, disengaging my hand with a violent effort, receding two or three steps.

'Not enter the churchyard! Ma foi—wat mauvais goˆt! But see, we are already in shade. The sun he is setting soon—where well you remain, cheaile? I will not stay long.'

'I'll stay here,' I said, a little angrily—for I *was* angry as well as nervous; and through my fear was that indignation at her extravagances which mimicked lunacy so unpleasantly, and were, I knew, designed to frighten me.

Over the stepping-stones, pulling up her dress, she skipped with her long, lank legs, like a witch joining a Walpurgis. Over the stile she strode, and I saw her head wagging, and heard her sing some of her ill-omened rhymes, as she capered solemnly, with many a grin and courtesy, among the graves and headstones, towards the ruin.

CHAPTER VIII

THE SMOKER

Three years later I learned—in a way she probably little expected, and then did not much care about—what really occurred there. I learned even phrases and looks— for the story was related by one who had heard it told—and therefore I venture to narrate what at the moment I neither saw nor suspected. While I sat, flushed and nervous, upon a flat stone by the bank of the little stream, Madame looked over her shoulder, and perceiving that I was out of sight, she abated her pace, and turned sharply towards the ruin which lay at her left. It was her first visit, and she was merely exploring; but now, with a perfectly shrewd and businesslike air, turn- ing the corner of the building, she saw, seated upon the edge of a grave-stone, a rather fat and flashily-equipped young man, with large, light whiskers, a jerry hat, green cutaway coat with gilt buttons, and waistcoat and trousers rather striking than elegant in pattern. He was smoking a short pipe, and made a nod to Madame, without either removing it from his lips or rising, but with his brown and rather good-looking face turned up, he eyed her with something of the impu- dent and sulky expression that was habitual to it.

'Ha, Deedle, you are there! an' look so well. I am here, too, quite *d*on; but my friend, she wait outside the churchyard, byside the leetle river, for she must not think I know you—so I am come *d*on.'

'You're a quarter late, and I lost a fight by you, old girl, this morning,' said the gay man, and spat on the ground; 'and I wish you would not call me Diddle. I'll call you Granny if you do.'

'Eh bien! *Dud*, then. She is vary nice—wat you like. Slim waist, wite teeth, vary nice eyes—dark—wat you say is best—and nice leetle foot and ankle.'

Madame smiled leeringly.

Dud smoked on.

'Go on,' said Dud, with a nod of command.

'I am teach her to sing and play—she has such sweet voice!

There was another interval here.

'Well, that isn't much good. I hate women's screechin' about fairies and flowers. Hang her! there's a scarecrow as sings at Curl's Divan. Such a caterwauling upon a stage! I'd like to put my two barrels into her.'

By this time Dud's pipe was out, and he could afford to converse.

'You shall see her and decide. You will walk down the river, and pass her by.'

'That's as may be; howsoever, it would not do, nohow, to buy a pig in a poke, you know. And s'pose I shouldn't like her, arter all?'

Madame sneered, with a patois ejaculation of derision.

'Vary good! Then some one else will not be so 'ard to please—as you will soon find.'

'Some one's bin a-lookin' arter her, you mean?' said the young man, with a shrewd uneasy glance on the cunning face of the French lady.

'I mean precisely—that which I mean,' replied the lady, with a teazing pause at the break I have marked.

'Come, old 'un, none of your d—— old chaff, if you want me to stay here listening to you. Speak out, can't you? There's any chap as has bin a-lookin' arter her—is there?'

'Eh bien! I suppose some.'

'Well, you *suppose,* and *I* suppose—we may *all* suppose, I guess; but that does not make a thing be, as wasn't before; and you tell me as how the lass is kep' private up there, and will be till *you*'re done educating her—a precious good'un that is!' And he laughed a little lazily, with the ivory handle of his cane on his lip, and eyeing Madame with indolent derision.

Madame laughed, but looked rather dangerous.

'I'm only chaffin', you know, old girl. *You've* bin chaffin;— w'y shouldn't *I?* But I don't see why she can't wait a bit; and what's all the d——d hurry for? *I*'m in no hurry. I don't want a wife on my back for a while. There's no fellow marries till he's took his bit o' fun, and seen life—is there! And why should I be driving with her to fairs, or to church, or to meeting, by jingo! for they say she's a Quaker— with a babby on each knee, only to please them as will be dead and rotten when *I*'m only beginning?'

'Ah, you are such charming fellow; always the same—always sensible. So I and my friend we will walk home again, and you go see Maggie Hawkes. Good-a-by, Dud—good-a-by.'

'Quiet, you fool!—can't ye?' said the young gentleman, with the sort of grin that made his face vicious when a horse vexed him. 'Who ever said I wouldn't go look at the girl? Why, you know that's just what I come here for—don't you? Only when I think a bit, and a notion comes across me, why shouldn't I speak out? I'm not one o' them shilly-shallies. If I like the girl, I'll not be mug in and mug out about it. Only mind ye, I'll judge for myself. Is that her a-coming?

'No; it was a distant sound.'

Madame peeped round the corner. No one was approaching.

'Well, you go round that a-way, and you only look at her, you know, for she is such fool—so nairvous.'

'Oh, is that the way with her?' said Dud, knocking out the ashes of his pipe on a tombstone, and replacing the Turkish utensil in his pocket. 'Well, then, old lass, good-bye,' and he shook her hand. 'And, do ye see, don't ye come up till I pass, for I'm no hand at play-acting; an' if you called me "sir," or was coming it dignified and distant, you know, I'd be sure to laugh, a'most, and let all out. So good-bye, d'ye see, and if you want me again be sharp to time, mind.

From habit he looked about for his dogs, but he had not brought one. He had come unostentatiously by rail, travelling in a third-class carriage, for the advantage of Jack Briderly's company, and getting a world of useful wrinkles about the steeplechase that was coming off next week.

So he strode away, cutting off the heads of the nettles with his cane as he went; and Madame walked forth into the open space among the graves, where I might have seen her, had I stood up, looking with the absorbed gaze of an artist on the ruin.

In a little while, along the path, I heard the clank of a step, and the gentleman in the green cutaway coat, sucking his cane, and eyeing me with an offensive familiar sort of stare the while, passed me by, rather hesitating as he did so.

I was glad when he turned the corner in the little hollow close by, and disappeared. I stood up at once, and was reassured by a sight of Madame, not very many yards away, looking at the ruin, and apparently restored to her right mind. The last beams of the sun were by this time touching the uplands, and I was longing to recommence our walk home. I was hesitating about calling to Madame, because that lady had a certain spirit of opposition within her, and to disclose a small wish of any sort was generally, if it lay in her power, to prevent its accomplishment.

At this moment the gentleman in the green coat returned, approaching me with a slow sort of swagger.

'I say, Miss, I dropped a glove close by here. May you have seen it?'

'No, sir,' I said, drawing back a little, and looking, I dare say, both frightened and offended.

'I do think I must 'a dropped it close by your foot, Miss.'

'No, sir,' I repeated.

'No offence, Miss, but you're sure you didn't hide it?'

I was beginning to grow seriously uncomfortable.

'Don't be frightened, Miss; it's only a bit o' chaff. I'm not going to search.'

I called aloud, 'Madame, Madame!' and he whistled through his fingers, and shouted, 'Madame, Madame,' and added, 'She's as deaf as a tombstone, or she'll hear that. Gi'e her my compliments, and say I said you're a beauty, Miss and with a laugh and a leer he strode off.

Altogether this had not been a very pleasant excursion. Madame gobbled up our sandwiches, commending them every now and then to me. But I had been too much excited to have any appetite left, and very tired I was when we reached home.

'So, there is lady coming to-morrow?' said Madame, who knew everything. 'Wat is her name? I forget.'

'Lady Knollys,' I answered.

'Lady Knollys—wat odd name! She is very young—is she not?'

'Past fifty, I think.'

'Hélas! She's vary old, then. Is she rich?'

'I don't know. She has a place in Derbyshire.'

'Derbyshire—that is one of your English counties, is it not?

'Oh yes, Madame,' I answered, laughing. 'I have said it to you twice since you came;' and I gabbled through the chief towns and rivers as catalogued in my geography.

'Bah! to be sure—of course, cheaile. And is she your relation?'

'Papa's first cousin.'

'Won't you present-a me, pray?—I would so like!'

Madame had fallen into the English way of liking people with titles, as perhaps foreigners would if titles implied the sort of power they do generally with us.

'Certainly, Madame.'

'You will not forget?'

'Oh no.'

Madame reminded me twice, in the course of the evening, of my promise. She was very eager on this point. But it is a world of disappointment, influenza, and rheumatics; and next morning Madame was prostrate in her bed, and careless of all things but flannel and James's powder.

Madame was *désolée*, but she could not raise her head. She only murmured a question.

'For 'ow long time, dear, will Lady Knollys remain?'

'A very few days, I believe.'

'Hélas! 'ow onlucky! maybe to-morrow I shall be better Ouah! my ear. The laudanum, dear cheaile!'

And so our conversation for that time ended, and Madame buried her head in her old red cashmere shawl.

CHAPTER IX

MONICA KNOLLYS

Punctually Lady Knollys arrived. She was accompanied by her nephew, Captain Oakley.

They arrived a little before dinner; just in time to get to their rooms and dress. But Mary Quince enlivened my toilet with eloquent descriptions of the youthful Captain whom she had met in the gallery, on his way to his room, with the servant, and told me how he stopped to let her pass, and how 'he smiled so 'ansom.'

I was very young then, you know, and more childish even than my years; but this talk of Mary Quince's interested me, I must confess, considerably. I was painting all sort of portraits of this heroic soldier, while affecting, I am afraid, a hypocritical indifference to her narration, and I know I was very nervous and painstaking about my toilet that evening. When I went down to the drawing-room, Lady Knollys was there, talking volubly to my father as I entered—a woman not really old, but such as very young people fancy aged—energetic, bright, saucy, dressed handsomely in purple satin, with a good deal of lace, and a rich point—I know not how to call it—not a cap, a sort of head-dress—light and simple, but grand withal, over her greyish, silken hair.

Rather tall, by no means stout, on the whole a good firm figure, with something kindly in her look. She got up, quite like a young person, and coming quickly to meet me with a smile—

'My young cousin!' she cried, and kissed me on both cheeks. 'You know who I am? Your cousin Monica—Monica Knollys—and very glad, dear, to see you, though she has not set eyes on you since you were no longer than that paper-knife. Now come here to the lamp, for I must look at you. Who is she like? Let me see. Like your poor mother, I think, my dear; but you've the Aylmer nose—yes—not a bad nose either, and, come! very good eyes, upon my life—yes, certainly something of her poor mother—not a bit like you, Austin.'

My father gave her a look as near a smile as I had seen there for a long time, shrewd, cynical, but kindly too, and said he—

'So much the better, Monica, eh?'

'It was not for me to say—but you know, Austin, you always were an ugly creature. How shocked and indignant the little girl looks! You must not be vexed, you loyal little woman, with Cousin Monica for telling the truth. Papa was and will be ugly all his days. Come, Austin, dear, tell her—is not it so?'

'What! depose against myself! That's not English law, Monica.'

'Well, maybe not; but if the child won't believe her own eyes, how is she to believe me? She has long, pretty hands—you have—and very nice feet too. How old is she? '

'How old, child?' said my father to me, transferring the question.

She recurred again to my eyes.

'That is the true grey—large, deep, soft—very peculiar. Yes, dear, very pretty— long lashes, and such bright tints! You'll be in the Book of Beauty, my dear, when you come out, and have all the poet people writing verses to the tip of your nose— and a very pretty little nose it is!'

I must mention here how striking was the change in my father's spirit while talking and listening to his odd and voluble old Cousin Monica. Reflected from bygone associations, there had come a glimmer of something, not gaiety, indeed, but like an appreciation of gaiety. The gloom and inflexibility were gone, and there was an evident encouragement and enjoyment of the incessant sallies of his bustling visitor.

How morbid must have been the tendencies of his habitual solitude, I think, appeared from the evident thawing and brightening that accompanied even this transient gleam of human society. I was not a companion—more childish than most girls of my age, and trained in all his whimsical ways, never to interrupt a silence, or force his thoughts by unexpected question or remark out of their monotonous or painful channel.

I was as much surprised at the good-humour with which he submitted to his cousin's saucy talk; and, indeed, just then those black-panelled and pictured walls, and that quaint, misshapen room, seemed to have exchanged their stern and awful character for something wonderfully pleasanter to me, notwithstanding the unpleasantness of the personal criticism to which the plain-spoken lady chose to subject me.

Just at that moment Captain Oakley joined us. He was my first actual vision of that awful and distant world of fashion, of whose splendours I had already read something in the three-volumed gospel of the circulating library.

Handsome, elegant, with features almost feminine, and soft, wavy, black hair, whiskers and moustache, he was altogether such a knight as I had never beheld, or even fancied, at Knowl—a hero of another species, and from the region of the demigods. I did not then perceive that coldness of the eye, and cruel curl of the voluptuous lip—only a suspicion, yet enough to indicate the profligate man, and savouring of death unto death.

But I was young, and had not yet the direful knowledge of good and evil that comes with years; and he was so very handsome, and talked in a way that was so new to me, and was so much more charming than the well-bred converse of the humdrum county families with whom I had occasionally sojourned for a week at a time.

It came out incidentally that his leave of absence was to expire the day after to-morrow. A Lilliputian pang of disappointment followed this announcement. Already I was sorry to lose him. So soon we begin to make a property of what pleases us.

I was shy, but not awkward. I was flattered by the attention of this amusing, perhaps rather fascinating, young man of the world; and he plainly addressed himself with diligence to amuse and please me. I dare say there was more effort than I fancied in bringing his talk down to my humble level, and interesting me and making me laugh about people whom I had never heard of before, than I then suspected.

Cousin Knollys meanwhile was talking to papa. It was just the conversation that suited a man so silent as habit had made him, for her frolic fluency left him little to supply. It was totally impossible, indeed, even in our taciturn household, that conversation should ever flag while she was among us.

Cousin Knollys and I went into the drawing-room together, leaving the gentle-men—rather ill-assorted, I fear—to entertain one another for a time.

'Come here, my dear, and sit near me,' said Lady Knollys, dropping into an easy chair with an energetic little plump, 'and tell me how you and your papa get on. I can remember him quite a cheerful man once, and rather amusing—yes, indeed—and now you see what a bore he is—all by shutting himself up and nursing his whims and fancies. Are those your drawings, dear?'

'Yes, very bad, I'm afraid; but there are a few, *better,* I think in the portfolio in the cabinet in the hall.'

'They are by *no* means bad, my dear; and you play, of course?'

'Yes—that is, a little—pretty well, I hope.'

'I dare say. I must hear you by-and-by. And how does your papa amuse you? You look bewildered, dear. Well, I dare say, amusement is not a frequent word in this house. But you must not turn into a nun, or worse, into a puritan. What is he? A Fifth-Monarchy-man, or something—I forget; tell me the name, my dear.'

'Papa is a Swedenborgian, I believe.'

'Yes, yes—I forgot the horrid name—a Swedenborgian, that is it. I don't know exactly what they think, but everyone knows they are a sort of pagans, my dear. He's not making one of *you,* dear—is he?'

'I go to church every Sunday.'

'Well, that's a mercy; Swedenborgian is such an ugly name, and besides, they are all likely to be damned, my dear, and that's a serious consideration. I really wish poor Austin had hit on something else; I'd much rather have no religion, and enjoy life while I'm in it, than choose one to worry me here and bedevil me hereafter. But some people, my dear, have a taste for being miserable, and provide, like poor Austin, for its gratification in the next world as well as here. Ha, ha, ha! how grave the little woman looks! Don't you think me very wicked? You know you do; and very likely you are right. Who makes your dresses, my dear? You *are* such a figure of fun!'

'Mrs. Rusk, I think, ordered *this* dress. I and Mary Quince planned it. I thought it very nice. We all like it very well.'

There was something, I dare say, very whimsical about it, probably very absurd, judged at least by the canons of fashion, and old Cousin Monica Knollys, in whose eye the London fashions were always fresh, was palpably struck by it as if it had been some enormity against anatomy, for she certainly laughed very heartily; indeed, there were tears on her cheeks when she had done, and I am sure my aspect of wonder and dignity, as her hilarity proceeded, helped to revive her merriment again and again as it was subsiding.

'There, you mustn't be vexed with old Cousin Monica,' she cried, jumping up, and giving me a little hug, and bestowing a hearty kiss on my forehead, and a jolly little slap on my cheek. 'Always remember your cousin Monica is an outspoken, wicked old fool, who likes you, and never be offended by her nonsense. A council of three—you all sat upon it—Mrs. Rusk, you said, and Mary Quince, and your wise self, the weird sisters and Austin stepped in, as Macbeth, and said, 'What is't ye do you all made answer together, 'A something or other without a name!' Now, seriously, my dear, it is quite unpardonable in Austin—your papa, I mean—to hand you over to be robed and bedizened according to the whimsies of these wild old women—aren't they old? If they know better, it's positively *fiendish*. I'll blow him up—I will indeed, my dear. You know you're an heiress, and ought not to appear like a jack-pudding.'

'Papa intends sending me to London with Madame and Mary Quince, and going with me himself, if Doctor Bryerly says he may make the journey, and then I am to have dresses and everything.'

'Well, that is better. And who is Doctor Bryerly—is your papa ill?'

'Ill; oh no; he always seems just the same. You don't think him ill—*looking* ill, I mean?' I asked eagerly and frightened.

'No, my dear, he looks very well for his time of life; but why is Doctor What's-his-name here? Is he a physician, or a divine, or a horse-doctor? and why is his leave asked?'

'I—I really don't understand.'

'Is he a what d'ye call'em—a Swedenborgian?'

'I believe so.'

'Oh, I see; ha, ha, ha! And so poor Austin must ask leave to go up to town. Well, go he shall, whether his doctor likes it or not, for it would not do to send you there in charge of your Frenchwoman, my dear. What's her name?'

'Madame de la Rougierre.'

CHAPTER X

LADY KNOLLYS REMOVES A COVERLET

Lady Knollys pursued her enquiries.

'And why does not Madame make your dresses, my dear? I wager a guinea the woman's a milliner. Did not she engage to make your dresses?'

'I—I really don't know; I rather think not. She is my governess—a finishing governess, Mrs. Rusk says.'

'Finishing fiddle! Hoity-toity! and my lady's too grand to cut out your dresses and help to sew them? And what does she do? I venture to say she's fit to teach nothing but devilment—not that she has taught you much, my dear—yet at least. I'll see her, my dear; where is she? Come, let us visit Madame. I should so like to talk to her a little.'

'But she is ill,' I answered, and all this time I was ready to cry for vexation, thinking of my dress, which must be very absurd to elicit so much unaffected laughter from my experienced relative, and I was only longing to get away and hide myself before that handsome Captain returned.

'Ill! is she? what's the matter?'

'A cold-feverish and rheumatic, she says.'

'Oh, a cold; is she up, or in bed?'

'In her room, but not in bed.'

'I should so like to see her, my dear. It is not mere curiosity, I assure you. In fact, curiosity has nothing on earth to do with it. A governess may be a very useful or a very useless person; but she may also be about the most pernicious inmate imaginable. She may teach you a bad accent, and worse manners, and heaven knows what beside. Send the housekeeper, my dear, to tell her that I am going to see her.'

'I had better go myself, perhaps,' I said, fearing a collision between Mrs. Rusk and the bitter Frenchwoman.

'Very well, dear.'

And away I ran, not sorry somehow to escape before Captain Oakley returned.

As I went along the passage, I was thinking whether my dress could be so very ridiculous as my old cousin thought it, and trying in vain to recollect any evidence of a similar contemptuous estimate on the part of that beautiful and garrulous dandy. I could not—quite the reverse, indeed. Still I was uncomfortable and feverish—girls of my then age will easily conceive how miserable, under similar circumstances, such a misgiving would make them.

It was a long way to Madame's room. I met Mrs. Rusk bustling along the passage with a housemaid.

'How is Madame?' I asked.

'Quite well, I believe,' answered the housekeeper, drily. 'Nothing the matter that *I* know of. She eat enough for two today. I wish I could sit in my room doing nothing.'

Madame was sitting, or rather reclining, in a low arm-chair, when I entered the room, close to the fire, as was her wont, her feet extended near to the bars, and a little coffee equipage beside her. She stuffed a book hastily between her dress and the chair, and received me in a state of langour which, had it not been for Mrs. Rusk's comfortable assurances, would have frightened me.

'I hope you are better, Madame,' I said, approaching.

'Better than I deserve, my dear cheaile, sufficiently well. The people are all so good, trying me with every little thing, like a bird; here is cafe—Mrs. Rusk-a, poor woman, I try to swallow a little to please her.'

'And your cold, is it better?'

She shook her head languidly, her elbow resting on the chair, and three finger-tips supporting her forehead, and then she made a little sigh, looking down from the corners of her eyes, in an interesting dejection.

'Je sens des lassitudes in all the members—but I am quaite 'appy, and though I suffer I am console and oblige des bontés, ma chère, que vous avez tous pour moi;' and with these words she turned a languid glance of gratitude on me which dropped on the ground.

'Lady Knollys wishes very much to see you, only for a few minutes, if you could admit her.'

'Vous savez les malades see *never* visitors,' she replied with a startled sort of tartness, and a momentary energy. 'Besides, I cannot converse; je sens de temps en temps des douleurs de tete—of head, and of the ear, the right ear, it is parfois agony absolutely, and now it is here.'

And she winced and moaned, with her eyes closed and her hand pressed to the organ affected.

Simple as I was, I felt instinctively that Madame was shamming. She was overacting; her transitions were too violent, and beside she forgot that I knew how well she could speak English, and must perceive that she was heightening the interest of her helplessness by that pretty tessellation of foreign idiom. I therefore said with a kind of courage which sometimes helped me suddenly—

'Oh, Madame, don't you really think you might, without much inconvenience, see Lady Knollys for a very few minutes?'

'Cruel cheaile! you know I have a pain of the ear—which makes me 'orribly suffer at this moment, and you demand me whether I will not converse with strangers. I did not think you would be so unkain, Maud; but it is impossible, you must see —quaite impossible. I never, you *know*, refuse to take trouble when I am able—never—*never*.'

And Madame shed some tears, which always came at call, and with her hand pressed to her ear, said very faintly,

'Be so good to tell your friend how you see me, and how I suffer, and leave me, Maud, for I wish to lie down for a little, since the pain will not allow me to remain longer.'

So with a few words of comfort which could not well be refused, but I dare say betraying my suspicion that more was made of her sufferings than need be, I returned to the drawing-room.

'Captain Oakley has been here, my dear, and fancying, I suppose, that you had left us for the evening, has gone to the billiard-room, I think,' said Lady Knollys, as I entered.

That, then, accounted for the rumble and smack of balls which I had heard as I passed the door.

'I have been telling Maud how detestably she is got up.'

'Very thoughtful of you, Monica!' said my father.

'Yes, and really, Austin, it is quite clear you ought to marry you want some one to take this girl out, and look after her, and who's to do it? She's a dowdy—don't you see? Such a dust! and it *is* really such a pity; for she's a very pretty creature, and a clever woman could make her quite charming.'

My father took Cousin Monica's sallies with the most wonderful good-humour. She had always, I fancy, been a privileged person, and my father, whom we all feared, received her jolly attacks, as I fancy the grim Front-de-Bœufs of old accepted the humours and personalities of their jesters.

'Am I to accept this as an overture?' said my father to his voluble cousin.

'Yes, you may, but not for myself, Austin—I'm not worthy. Do you remember little Kitty Weadon that I wanted you to marry eight-and-twenty years ago, or more, with a hundred and twenty thousand pounds? Well, you know, she has got ever so much now, and she is really a most amiable old thing, and though *you* would not have her then, she has had her second husband since, I can tell you.'

'I'm glad I was not the first,' said my father.

'Well, they really say her wealth is absolutely immense. Her last husband, the Russian merchant, left her everything. She has not a human relation, and she is in the best set!'

'You were always a match-maker, Monica,' said my father, stopping, and putting his hand kindly on hers. 'But it won't do. No, no, Monica; we must take care of little Maud some other way.'

I was relieved. We women have all an instinctive dread of second marriages, and think that no widower is quite above or below that danger; and I remember, whenever my father, which indeed was but seldom, made a visit to town or anywhere else, it was a saying of Mrs. Rusk—

'I shan't wonder, neither need you, my dear, if he brings home a young wife with him.'

So my father, with a kind look at her, and a very tender one on me, went silently to the library, as he often did about that hour.

I could not help resenting my Cousin Knollys' officious recommendation of matrimony. Nothing I dreaded more than a stepmother. Good Mrs. Rusk and Mary Quince, in their several ways, used to enhance, by occasional anecdotes and frequent reflections, the terrors of such an intrusion. I suppose they did not wish a revolution and all its consequences at Knowl, and thought it no harm to excite my vigilance.

But it was impossible long to be vexed with Cousin Monica.

'You know, my dear, your father is an oddity,' she said. 'I don't mind him—I never did, You must not. Cracky, my dear, cracky—decidedly cracky!'

And she tapped the corner of her forehead, with a look so sly and comical, that I think I should have laughed, if the sentiment had not been so awfully irreverent.

'Well, dear, how is our friend the milliner?'

'Madame is suffering so much from pain in her ear, that she says it would be quite impossible to have the honour——'

'Honour—fiddle! I want to see what the woman's like. Pain in her ear, you say? Poor thing! Well, dear, I think I can cure that in five minutes. I have it myself, now and then. Come to my room, and we'll get the bottles.

So she lighted her candle in the lobby, and with a light and agile step she scaled the stairs, I following; and having found the remedies, we approached Madame's room together.

I think, while we were still at the end of the gallery, Madame heard and divined our approach, for her door suddenly shut, and there was a fumbling at the handle. But the bolt was out of order.

Lady Knollys tapped at the door, saying—'we'll come in, please, and see you. I've some remedies, which I'm sure will do you good.'

There was no answer; so she opened the door, and we both entered. Madame had rolled herself in the blue coverlet, and was lying on the bed, with her face buried in the pillow, and enveloped in the covering.

'Perhaps she's asleep?' said Lady Knollys, getting round to the side of the bed, and stooping over her.

Madame lay still as a mouse, Cousin Monica set down her two little vials on the table, and, stooping again over the bed, began very gently with her fingers to lift the coverlet that covered her face. Madame uttered a slumbering moan, and turned more upon her face, clasping the coverlet faster about her.

'Madame, it is Maud and Lady Knollys. We have come to relieve your ear. Pray let me see it. She can't be asleep, she's holding the clothes so fast, Do, pray, allow me to see it.'

CHAPTER XI

LADY KNOLLYS SEES THE FEATURES

Perhaps, if Madame had murmured, 'It is quite well—pray permit me to sleep,' she would have escaped an awkwardness. But having adopted the role of the exhausted slumberer, she could not consistently speak at the moment; neither would it do by main force, to hold the coverlet about her face: and so her presence of mind forsook her, and Cousin Monica drew it back, and hardly beheld the profile of the sufferer, when her good-humoured face was lined and shadowed with a dark curiosity and a surprise by no means pleasant; and she stood erect beside the bed, with her mouth firmly shut and drawn down at the corners, in a sort of recoil and perturbation, looking down upon the patient.

'So that's Madame de la Rougierre?' at length exclaimed Lady Knollys, with a very stately disdain. I think I never saw anyone look more shocked.

Madame sat up, very flushed. No wonder, for she had been wrapped so close in the coverlet. She did not look quite at Lady Knollys, but straight before her, rather downward, and very luridly.

I was very much frightened and amazed, and felt on the point of bursting into tears.

'So, Mademoiselle, you have married, it seems, since I had last the honour of seeing you? I did not recognise Mademoiselle under her new name.'

'Yes—I *am* married, Lady Knollys; I thought everyone who knew me had heard of that. Very respectably married, for a person of my rank. I shall not need long the life of a governess. There is no harm, I hope?'

'I hope not,' said Lady Knollys, drily, a little pale, and still looking with a dark sort of wonder upon the flushed face and forehead of the governess, who was looking downward, straight before her, very sulkily and disconcerted.

'I suppose you have explained everything satisfactorily to Mr. Ruthyn, in whose house I find you?' said Cousin Monica.

'Yes, certainly—everything he requires—in effect there is *nothing* to explain. I am ready to answer to any question. Let *him* demand me.'

'Very good, Mademoiselle.'

'*Madame,* if you please.'

'I forgot—*Madame*—yes. I shall apprise him of everything!'

Madame turned upon her a peaked and malign look, smiling askance with a stealthy scorn.

'For myself, I have nothing to conceal. I have always done my duty. What fine scene about nothing absolutely—what charming remedies for a sick person! Ma foi! how much oblige I am for these so amiable attentions!'

'So far as I can see, Mademoiselle—Madame, I mean—you don't stand very much in need of remedies. Your ear and head don't seem to trouble you just now. I fancy these pains may now be dismissed.'

Lady Knollys was now speaking French.

'Mi ladi has diverted my attention for a moment, but that does not prevent that! suffer frightfully. I am, of course, only poor governess, and such people per- haps ought not to have pain—at least to show when they suffer. It is permitted us to die, but not to be sick.'

'Come, Maud, my dear, let us leave the invalid to her repose and to nature. I don't think she needs my chloroform and opium at present.'

'Mi ladi is herself a physic which chases many things, and powerfully affects the ear. I would wish to sleep, notwithstanding, and can but gain that in silence, if it pleases mi ladi.'

'Come, my dear,' said Lady Knollys, without again glancing at the scowling, smiling, swarthy face in the bed; 'let us leave your instructress to her *conforto.*'

'The room smells all over of brandy, my dear—does she drink?' said Lady Knollys, as she closed the door, a little sharply.

I am sure I looked as much amazed as I felt, at an imputation which then seemed to me so entirely incredible.

'Good little simpleton!' said Cousin Monica, smiling in my face, and bestowing a little kiss on my cheek 'such a thing as a tipsy lady has never been dreamt of in your philosophy. Well, we live and learn. Let us have our tea in my room—the gentlemen, I dare say, have retired.'

I assented, of course, and we had tea very cosily by her bedroom fire.

'How long have you had that woman?' she asked suddenly, after, for her, a very long rumination.

'She came in the beginning of February—nearly ten months ago—is not it?'

'And who sent her?'

'I really don't know; papa tells me so little—he arranged it all himself, I think.'

Cousin Monica made a sound of acquiescence—her lips closed, and a nod, frowning hard at the bars.

'It *is* very odd!' she said; 'how people *can* be such fools!' Here there came a little pause. 'And what sort of person is she—do you like her?'

'Very well—that is, *pretty* well. You won't tell?—but she rather frightens me. I'm sure she does not intend it, but somehow I am very much afraid of her.'

'She does not beat you?' said Cousin Monica, with an incipient frenzy in her face that made me love her.

'Oh no! '

'Nor ill—use you in any way?'

'No.'

'Upon your honour and word, Maud?'

'No, upon my honour.'

'You know I won't tell her anything you say to me; and I only want to know, that I may put an end to it, my poor little cousin.'

'Thank you, Cousin Monica very much; but really and truly she does not ill-use me.'

'Nor threaten you, child?'

'Well *no*—no, she does not threaten.'

'And how the plague *does* she frighten you, child?'

'Well I really—I'm half ashamed to tell you—you'll laugh at me—and I don't know that she wishes to frighten me. But there is something, is not there, ghosty, you know, about her?'

'*Ghosty*—is there? well, I'm sure I don't know, but I suspect there's something devilish—I mean, she seems roguish—does not she? And I really think she has had neither cold nor pain, but has just been shamming sickness, to keep out of my way.'

I perceived plainly enough that Cousin Monica's damnatory epithet referred to some retrospective knowledge, which she was not going to disclose to me.

'You knew Madame before,' I said. 'Who is she?'

'She assures me she is Madame de la Rougierre, and, I suppose, in French phrase she so calls herself,' answered Lady Knollys, with a laugh, but uncomfortably, I thought.

'Oh, dear Cousin Monica, do tell me—is she—is she very wicked? I am so afraid of her!'

'How should I know, dear Maud? But I do remember her face, and I don't very much like her, and you may depend on it, I will speak to your father in the morning about her, and don't, darling, ask me any more about her, for I really have not very much to tell that you would care to hear, and the fact is I *won't* say any more about her—there!'

And Cousin Monica laughed, and gave me a little slap on the cheek, and then a kiss.

'Well, just tell me this—'

'Well, I *won't* tell you this, nor anything—not a word, curious little woman. The fact is, I have little to tell, and I mean to speak to your father, and he, I am sure, will do what is right; so don't ask me any more, and let us talk of something pleasanter.'

There was something indescribably winning, it seemed to me, in Cousin Monica. Old as she was, she seemed to me so girlish, compared with those slow, unexceptionable young ladies whom I had met in my few visits at the county houses. By this time my shyness was quite gone, and I was on the most intimate terms with her.

'You know a great deal about her, Cousin Monica, but you won't tell me.'

'Nothing I should like better, if I were at liberty, little rogue but you know, after all, I don't really say whether I *do* know anything about her or not, or what sort of knowledge it is. But tell me what you mean by ghosty, and all about it.'

So I recounted my experiences, to which, so far from laughing at me, she listened with very special gravity.

'Does she write and receive many letters?'

I had seen her write letters, and supposed, though I could only recollect one or two, that she received in proportion.

'Are *you* Mary Quince?' asked my lady cousin.

Mary was arranging the window-curtains, and turned, dropping a courtesy affirmatively toward her.

'You wait on my little cousin, Miss Ruthyn, don't you?'

'Yes, 'm,' said Mary, in her genteelest way.

'Does anyone sleep in her room?'

'Yes, 'm, *I*—please, my lady.'

'And no one else?'

'No, 'm—please, my lady.'

'Not even the *governess*, sometimes?'

'No, please, my lady.'

'Never, you are quite sure, my dear?' said Lady Knollys, transferring the question to me.

'Oh, no, never,' I answered.

Cousin Monica mused gravely, I fancied even anxiously, into the grate; then stirred her tea and sipped it, still looking into the same point of our cheery fire.

'I like your face, Mary Quince; I'm sure you are a good creature,' she said, suddenly turning toward her with a pleasant countenance. 'I'm very glad you have got her, dear. I wonder whether Austin has gone to his bed yet!'

'I think not. I am certain be is either in the library or in his private room— papa often reads or prays alone at night, and—and he does not like to be interrupted.'

'No, no; of course not—it will do very well in the morning.'

Lady Knollys was thinking deeply, as it seemed to me.

'And so you are afraid of goblins, my dear,' she said at last, with a faded sort of smile, turning toward me; 'well, if *I* were, I know what *I* should do—so soon as I, and good Mary Quince here, had got into my bed-chamber for the night, I should stir the fire into a good blaze, and bolt the door—do you see, Mary Quince?—bolt the door and keep a candle lighted all night. You'll be very attentive to her, Mary Quince, for I—I don't think she is very strong, and she must not grow nervous: so get to bed early, and don't leave her—alone—do you see?—and—and remember to bolt the door, Mary Quince, and I shall be sending a little Christmas-box to my cousin, and I shan't forget you. Good-night.'

And with a pleasant courtesy Mary fluttered out of the room.

CHAPTER XII

A CURIOUS CONVERSATION

We each had another cup of tea, and were silent for awhile.

'We must not talk of ghosts now. You are a superstitious little woman, you know, and you shan't be frightened.'

And now Cousin Monica grew silent again, and looking briskly around the room, like a lady in search of a subject, her eye rested on a small oval portrait, graceful, brightly tinted, in the French style, representing a pretty little boy, with rich golden hair, large soft eyes, delicate features, and a shy, peculiar expression.

'It is odd; I think I remember that pretty little sketch, very long ago. I think I was then myself a child, but that is a much older style of dress, and of wearing the hair, too, than I ever saw. I am just forty-nine now. Oh dear, yes; that is a good while before I was *born*. What a strange, pretty little boy! a mysterious little fellow. Is he quite sincere, I wonder? What rich golden hair! It is very clever—a French artist, I dare say—and who *is* that little boy?'

'I never heard. Some one a hundred years ago, I dare say. But there is a picture down-stairs I am so anxious to ask you about!'

'Oh!' murmured Lady Knollys, still gazing dreamily on the crayon.

'It is the full-length picture of Uncle Silas—I want to ask you about him.'

At mention of his name, my cousin gave me a look so sudden and odd as to amount almost to a start.

'Your uncle Silas, dear? It is very odd, I was just thinking of him;' and she laughed a little.

'Wondering whether that little boy could be he.'

And up jumped active Cousin Monica, with a candle in her hand, upon a chair, and scrutinised the border of the sketch for a name or a date.

'Maybe on the back?' said she.

And so she unhung it, and there, true enough, not on the back of the drawing, but of the frame, which was just as good, in pen-and-ink round Italian letters, hardly distinguishable now from the discoloured wood, we traced—'

Silas Aylmer Ruthyn, Ætate viii. 15 *May,* 1779.'

'It is very odd I should not have been told or remembered who it was. I think if I had *ever* been told I *should* have remembered it. I do recollect this picture, though, I am nearly certain. What a singular child's face!'

And my cousin leaned over it with a candle on each side, and her hand shading her eyes, as if seeking by aid of these fair and half-formed lineaments to read an enigma.

The childish features defied her, I suppose; their secret was unfathomable, for after a good while she raised her head, still looking at the portrait, and sighed.

'A very singular face,' she said, softly, as a person might who was looking into a coffin. 'Had not we better replace it?'

So the pretty oval, containing the fair golden hair and large eyes, the pale, unfathomable sphinx, remounted to its nail, and the *funeste* and beautiful child seemed to smile down oracularly on our conjectures.

'So is the face in the large portrait—*very* singular—more, I think, than that—handsomer too. This is a sickly child, I think; but the full-length is so manly, though so slender, and so handsome too, I always think him a hero and a mystery, and they won't tell me about him, and I can only dream and wonder.'

'He has made more people than you dream and wonder, my dear Maud. I don't know what to make of him. He is a sort of idol, you know, of your father's, and yet I don't think he helps him much. His abilities were singular; so has been his misfortune; for the rest, my dear, he is neither a hero nor a wonder. So far as I know, there are very few sublime men going about the world.'

'You really must tell me all you know about him, Cousin Monica. Now don't refuse.'

'But why should you care to hear? There is really nothing pleasant to tell.'

'That is just the reason I wish it. If it were at all pleasant, it would be quite commonplace. I like to hear of adventures, dangers, and misfortunes; and above all, I love a mystery. You know, papa will never tell me, and I dare not ask him; not that he is ever unkind, but, somehow, I am afraid; and neither Mrs. Rusk nor Mary Quince will tell me anything, although I suspect they know a good deal.'

'I don't see any good in telling you, dear, nor, to say the truth, any great harm either.'

'No—now that's *quite* true—no harm. There *can't* be, for I *must* know it all some day, you know, and better now, and from *you*, than perhaps from a stranger, and in a less favourable way.'

'Upon my word, it is a wise little woman; and really, that's not such bad sense after all.'

So we poured out another cup of tea each, and sipped it very comfortably by the fire, while Lady Knollys talked on, and her animated face helped the strange story.

'It is not very much, after all. Your uncle Silas, you know, is living?'

'Oh yes, in Derbyshire.'

'So I see you do know something of him, sly girl! but no matter. You know how very rich your father is; but Silas was the younger brother, and had little more than a thousand a year. If he had not played, and did not care to marry, it would have been quite enough—ever so much more than younger sons of dukes often have; but he was—well, a *mauvais sujet*—you know what that is. I don't want to say any ill of him—more than I really know—but he was fond of his pleasures, I suppose, like other young men, and he played, and was always losing, and your father for a long time paid great sums for him. I believe he was really a most expensive and vicious young man; and I fancy he does not deny that now, for they say he would change the past if he could.

I was looking at the pensive little boy in the oval frame—aged eight years—who was, a few springs later, 'a most expensive and vicious young man,' and was now a suffering and outcast old one, and wondering from what a small seed the hemlock or the wallflower grows, and how miscroscopic are the beginnings of the kingdom of God or of the mystery of iniquity in a human being's heart.

'Austin—your papa—was very kind to him—*very*; but then, you know, he's an oddity, dear—he *is* an oddity, though no one may have told you before—and he never forgave him for his marriage. Your father, I suppose, knew more about the lady than I did—I was young then—but there were various reports, none of them pleasant, and she was not visited and for some time there was a complete estrangement between your father and your uncle Silas; and it was made up, rather oddly, on the very occasion which some people said ought to have totally separated them. Did you ever hear anything—anything *very* remarkable—about your uncle?'

'No, never, they would not tell me, though I am sure they know. Pray go on.'

'Well Maud, as I have begun, I'll complete the story, though perhaps it might have been better untold. It was something rather shocking—indeed, *very* shocking; in fact, they insisted on suspecting him of having committed a murder.'

I stared at my cousin for some time, and then at the little boy, so refined, so beautiful, so *funeste*, in the oval frame.

'Yes, dear,' said she, her eyes following mine; 'who'd have supposed he could ever have—have fallen under so horrible a suspicion?'

'The wretches! Of course, Uncle Silas—of course, he's innocent?' I said at last.

'Of course, my dear,' said Cousin Monica, with an odd look; 'but you know there are some things as bad almost to be suspected of as to have done, and the country gentlemen chose to suspect him. They did not like him, you see. His politics vexed them; and he resented their treatment of his wife—though I really think, poor Silas, he did not care a pin about her—and he annoyed them whenever he could. Your papa, you know, is very proud of his family—*he* never had the slightest suspicion of your uncle.'

'Oh no!' I cried vehemently.

'That's right, Maud Ruthyn,' said Cousin Monica, with a sad little smile and a nod. 'And your papa was, you may suppose, very angry.'

'Of course he was,' I exclaimed.

'You have no idea, my dear, *how* angry. He directed his attorney to prosecute, by wholesale, all who had said a word affecting your uncle's character. But the lawyers were against it, and then your uncle tried to fight his way through it, but the men would not meet him. He was quite slurred. Your father went up and saw the Minister. He wanted to have him a Deputy-Lieutenant, or something, in his county. Your papa, you know, had a very great influence with the Government. Beside his county influence, he had two boroughs then. But the Minister was afraid, the feeling was so very strong. They offered him something in the Colonies, but your father would not hear of it—that would have been a banishment, you know. They would have given your father a peerage to make it up, but he would not accept it, and broke with the party. Except in that way—which, you know, was connected with the reputation of the family—I don't think, considering his great wealth, he has done very much for Silas. To say truth, however, he was very liberal before his marriage. Old Mrs. Aylmer says he made a vow *then* that Silas should never have more than five hundred a year, which he still allows him, I believe, and he permits him to live in the place. But they say it is in a very wild, neglected state.'

'You live in the same county—have you seen it lately, Cousin Monica?'

'No, not very lately,' said Cousin Monica, and began to hum an air abstractedly.

CHAPTER XIII

BEFORE AND AFTER BREAKFAST

Next morning early I visited my favourite full-length portrait in the chocolate coat and top-boots. Scanty as had been my cousin Monica's notes upon this dark and eccentric biography, they were everything to me. A soul had entered that enchanted form. Truth had passed by with her torch, and a sad light shone for a moment on that enigmatic face.

There stood the *roué*—the duellist—and, with all his faults, the hero too! In that dark large eye lurked the profound and fiery enthusiasm of his ill-starred passion. In the thin but exquisite lip I read the courage of the paladin, who would have 'fought his way,' though single-handed, against all the magnates of his county, and by ordeal of battle have purged the honour of the Ruthyns. There in that delicate half-sarcastic tracery of the nostril I detected the intellectual defiance which had politically isolated Silas Ruthyn and opposed him to the landed oligarchy of his county, whose retaliation had been a hideous slander. There, too, and on his brows and lip, I traced the patience of a cold disdain. I could now see him as he was—the prodigal, the hero, and the martyr. I stood gazing on him with a girlish interest and admiration. There was indignation, there was pity, there was hope. Some day it might come to pass that I, girl as I was, might contribute by word or deed towards the vindication of that long-suffering, gallant, and romantic prodigal. It was a flicker of the Joan of Arc inspiration, common, I fancy, to many girls. I little then imagined how profoundly and strangely involved my uncle's fate would one day become with mine.

I was interrupted by Captain Oakley's voice at the window. He was leaning on the window-sill, and looking in with a smile —the window being open, the morning sunny, and his cap lifted in his hand.

'Good-morning, Miss Ruthyn. What a charming old place! quite the setting for a romance; such timber, and this really *beautiful* house. I *do* so like these white and black houses—wonderful old things. By-the-by, you treated us very badly last night—you did, indeed; upon my word, now, it really was too bad—running away, and drinking tea with Lady Knollys—so she says. I really—I should not like to tell you how very savage I felt, particularly considering how very short my time is.'

I was a shy, but not a giggling country miss. I knew I was an heiress; I knew I was somebody. I was not the least bit in the world conceited, but I think this knowledge helped to give me a certain sense of security and self-possession, which might have been mistaken for dignity or simplicity. I am sure I looked at him with a fearless enquiry, for he answered my thoughts.

'I do really assure you, Miss Ruthyn, I am quite serious; you have no idea how very much we missed you.'

There was a little pause, and, I believe, like a fool, I lowered my eyes, and blushed.

'I—I was thinking of leaving to-day; I am so unfortunate—my leave is just out—it *is* so unlucky; but I don't quite know whether my aunt Knollys will allow me to go.'

'I?—certainly, my dear Charlie, *I* don't want you at all,' exclaimed a voice—Lady Knollys's—briskly, from an open window close by; 'what could put that in your head, dear?'

And in went my cousin's head, and the window shut down.

'She is *such* an oddity, poor dear Aunt Knollys,' murmured the young man, ever so little put out, and he laughed. 'I never know quite what she wishes, or how to please her; but she's *so* good-natured; and when she goes to town for the season—she does not, always, you know—her house is really very gay—you can't think——'

Here again he was interrupted, for the door opened, and Lady Knollys entered. 'And you know, Charles,' she continued, 'it would not do to forget your visit to Snodhurst; you wrote, you know, and you have only to-night and to-morrow. You are thinking of nothing but that moor; I heard you talking to the gamekeeper; I know he is—is not he, Maud, the brown man with great whiskers, and leggings? I'm very sorry, you know, but I really must spoil your shooting, for they do expect you at Snodhurst, Charlie; and do not you think this window a little too much for Miss Ruthyn? Maud, my dear, the air is very sharp; shut it down, Charles, and you'd better tell them to get a fly for you from the town alter luncheon. Come, dear,' she said to me. 'Was not that the breakfast bell? Why does not your papa get a gong?—it is so hard to know one bell from another.'

I saw that Captain Oakley lingered for a last look, but I did not give it, and went out smiling with Cousin Knollys, and wondering why old ladies are so uniformly disagreeable.

In the lobby she said, with an odd, goodnatured look—

'Don't allow any of his love-making, my dear. Charles Oakley has not a guinea, and an heiress would be very convenient, Of course he has his eyes about him. Charles is not by any means foolish; and I should not be at all sorry to see him well married, for I don't think he will do much good any other way; but there are degrees, and his ideas are sometimes very impertinent.'

I was an admiring reader of the *Albums*, the *Souvenirs*, the *Keepsakes*, and all that flood of Christmas-present lore which yearly irrigated England, with pretty covers and engravings; and floods of elegant twaddle—the milk, not destitute of water, on which the babes of literature were then fed. On this, my genius throve. I had a little album, enriched with many gems of original thought and observation, which I jotted down in suitable language. Lately, turning over these faded leaves of rhyme and prose, I lighted, under this day's date, upon the following sage reflection, with my name appended:—

> 'Is there not in the female heart an ineradicable jealousy, which, if it sways the passions of the young, rules also the *advice* of the *aged*? Do they not grudge to youth the sentiments (though Heaven knows how *shadowed* with sorrow) which they can *no longer inspire*, perhaps even *experience*; and does not youth, in turn, sigh over the envy which has *power to blight*?
>
> MAUD AYLMER RUTHYN.'

'He has not been making love to me,' I said rather tartly, 'and he does not seem to me at all impertinent, and I really don't care the least whether he goes or stays.'

Cousin Monica looked in my face with her old waggish smile, and laughed.

'You'll understand those London dandies better some day, dear Maud; they are very well, but they like money—not to keep, of course—but still they like it and know its value.'

At breakfast my father told Captain Oakley where he might have shooting, or if he preferred going to Dilsford, only half an hour's ride, he might have his choice of hunters, and find the dogs there that morning.

The Captain smiled archly at me, and looked at his aunt. There was a suspense. I hope I did not show how much I was interested—but it would not do. Cousin Monica was inexorable.

'Hunting, hawking, fishing, fiddle-de-dee! You know, Charlie, my dear, it is quite out of the question. He is going to Snodhurst this afternoon, and without quite a rudeness, in which I should be involved too, he really can't—you know you can't, Charles! and—and he *must* go and keep his engagement.'

So papa acquiesced with a polite regret, and hoped another time.

'Oh, leave all that to me. When you want him, only write me a note, and I'll send him or bring him if you let me. I always know where to find him—don't I, Charlie?—and we shall be only too happy.'

Aunt Monica's influence with her nephew was special, for she 'tipped' him handsomely every now and then, and he had formed for himself agreeable expectations, besides, respecting her will. I felt rather angry at his submitting to this sort of tutelage, knowing nothing of its motive; I was also disgusted by Cousin Monica's tyranny.

So soon as he had left the room, Lady Knollys, not minding me, said briskly to papa, 'Never let that young man into your house again. I found him making speeches, this morning, to little Maud here; and he really has not two pence in the world—it is amazing impudence—and you know such absurd things do happen.'

'Come, Maud, what compliments did he pay you?' asked my father.

I was vexed, and therefore spoke courageously. 'His compliments were not to me; they were all to the house,' I said, drily.

'Quite as it should be—the house, of course; it is that he's in love with,' said Cousin Knollys.

"'Twas on a widow's jointure land. The archer, Cupid, took his stand.'

'Hey! I don't quite understand,' said my father, slily.

'Tut! Austin; you forget Charlie is my nephew.'

'So I did,' said my father.

Therefore the literal widow in this case *can* have no interest in view but one, and that is yours and Maud's. I wish him well, but he shan't put my little cousin and her expectations into his empty pocket—*not* a bit of it. And *there's* another reason, Austin, why you should marry—you have no eye for these things, whereas a clever *woman* would see at a glance and prevent mischief.'

'So she would,' acquiesced my father, in his gloomy, amused way. 'Maud, you must try to be a clever woman.'

'So she will in her time, but that is not come yet; and I tell you, Austin Ruthyn, if you won't look about and marry somebody, somebody may possibly marry you.'

'You were always an oracle, Monica; but *here* I am lost in total perplexity,' said my father.

'Yes; sharks sailing round you, with keen eyes and large throats; and you have come to the age precisely when men *are* swallowed up alive like Jonah.'

'Thank you for the parallel, but you know that was not a happy union, even for the fish, and there was a separation in a few days; not that I mean to trust to that; but there's no one to throw me into the jaws of the monster, and I've no notion of jumping there; and the fact is, Monica, there's no monster at all.'

'I'm not so sure.'

'But I'm quite sure,' said my father, a little drily. 'You forget how old I am, and how long I've lived alone—I and little Maud;' and he smiled and smoothed my hair, and, I thought, sighed.

'No one is ever too old to do a foolish thing,' began Lady Knollys.

'Nor to say a foolish thing, Monica. This has gone on too long. Don't you see that little Maud here is silly enough to be frightened at your fun.'

So I was, but I could not divine how he guessed it.

'And well or ill, wisely or madly, I'll *never* marry; so put that out of your head.'

This was addressed rather to me, I think, than to Lady Knollys, who smiled a little waggishly on me, and said—

'To be sure, Maud; maybe you are right; a stepdame is a risk, and I ought to have asked you first what you thought of it; and upon my honour,' she continued merrily but kindly, observing that my eyes, I know not exactly from what feeling, filled with tears, 'I'll never again advise your papa to marry, unless you first tell me you wish it.'

This was a great deal from Lady Knollys, who had a taste for advising her friends and managing their affairs.

'I've a great respect for instinct. I believe, Austin, it is truer than reason, and yours and Maud's are both against me, though I know I have reason on my side.'

My father's brief wintry smile answered, and Cousin Monica kissed me, and said—

'I've been so long my own mistress that I sometimes forget there are such things as fear and jealousy; and are you going to your governess, Maud?'

CHAPTER XIV

ANGRY WORDS

I was going to my governess, as Lady Knollys said; and so I went. The undefinable sense of danger that smote me whenever I beheld that woman had deepened since last night's occurrence, and was taken out of the region of instinct or prepossession by the strange though slight indications of recognition and abhorrence which I had witnessed in Lady Knollys on that occasion.

The tone in which Cousin Monica had asked, 'are you going to your governess?' and the curious, grave, and anxious look that accompanied the question, disturbed me; and there was something odd and cold in the tone as if a remembrance had suddenly chilled her. The accent remained in my ear, and the sharp brooding look was fixed before me as I glided up the broad dark stairs to Madame de la

Rougierre's chamber.

She had not come down to the school-room, as the scene of my studies was called. She had decided on having a relapse, and accordingly had not made her appearance down-stairs that morning, The gallery leading to her room was dark and lonely, and I grew more nervous as I approached; I paused at the door, making up my mind to knock.

But the door opened suddenly, and, like a magic-lantern figure, presented with a snap, appeared close before my eyes the great muffled face, with the forbidding smirk, of Madame de la Rougierre.

'Wat you mean, my dear cheaile?' she inquired with a malevolent shrewdness in her eyes, and her hollow smile all the time disconcerting me more even than the suddenness of her appearance; 'wat for you approach so softly? I do not sleep, you see, but you feared, perhaps, to have the misfortune of wakening me, and so you came—is it not so?—to leesten, and looke in very gently; you want to know how I was. Vous Ítes bien aimable d'avoir pensé à moi. Bah!' she cried, suddenly bursting through her irony. 'Wy could not Lady Knollys come herself and leesten to the keyhole to make her report? Fi donc! I wat is there to conceal? Nothing. Enter, if you please. Every one they are welcome' and she flung the door wide, turned her back upon me, and, with an ejaculation which I did not understand, strode into the room.

'I did not come with any intention, Madame, to pry or to intrude—you don't think so—you *can't* think so— you can't possibly mean to insinuate anything so insulting!'

I was very angry, and my tremors had all vanished now.

'No, not for *you*, dear cheaile; I was thinking to miladi Knollys, who, without cause, is my enemy. Every one has enemy; you will learn all that so soon as you are little older, and without cause she is mine. Come, Maud, speak a the truth—was it not miladi Knollys who sent you here doucement, doucement, so quaite to my door—is it not so, little rogue?'

Madame had confronted me again, and we were now standing in the middle of her floor.

I indignantly repelled the charge, and searching me for a moment with her oddly-shaped, cunning eyes, she said—

'That is good cheaile, you speak a so direct—I like that, and am glad to hear; but, my dear Maud, that woman——'

'Lady Knollys is papa's cousin,' I interposed a little gravely.

'She does hate a me so, you av no idea. She as tryed to injure me several times, and would employ the most innocent person, unconsciously you know, my dear, to assist her malice.'

Here Madame wept a little. I had already discovered that she could shed tears whenever she pleased. I have heard of such persons, but I never met another before or since.

Madame was unusually frank—no one ever knew better when to be candid. At present I suppose she concluded that Lady Knollys would certainly relate whatever she knew concerning her before she left Knowl; and so Madame's reserves, whatever they might be, were dissolving, and she growing childlike and confiding.

'Et comment va monsieur votre père aujourd'hui?'

'Very well,' I thanked her.

'And how long miladi Knollys her visit is likely to be I could not say exactly, but for some days.'

'Eh bien, my dear cheaile, I find myself better this morning, and we must return to our lessons. Je veux m'habiller, ma chère Maud; you will wait me in the school-room.'

By this time Madame, who, though lazy, could make an effort, and was capable of getting into a sudden hurry, had placed herself before her dressing-table, and was ogling her discoloured and bony countenance in the glass.

'Wat horror! I am so pale. Quel ennui! wat bore! Ow weak av I grow in two three days!'

And she practised some plaintive, invalid glances into the mirror. But on a sudden there came a little sharp inquisitive frown as she looked over the frame of the glass, upon the terrace beneath. It was only a glance, and she sat down languidly in her arm-chair to prepare, I suppose, for the fatigues of the toilet.

'My curiosity was sufficiently aroused to induce me to ask—

'But why, Madame, do you fancy that Lady Knollys dislikes you?'

''Tis not fancy, my dear Maud. Ah ha, no! Mais c'est toute une histoire—too tedious to tell now—some time maybe—and you will learn when you are little older, the most violent hatreds often they are the most without cause. But, my dear cheaile, the hours they are running from us, and I must dress. Vite, vite! so you run away to the school-room, and I will come after.'

Madame had her dressing-case and her mysteries, and palpably stood in need of repairs; so away I went to my studies. The room which we called the school-room was partly beneath the floor of Madame's bed-chamber, and commanded the same view; so, remembering my governess's peering glance from her windows, I looked out, and saw Cousin Monica making a brisk promenade up and down the terrace-walk. Well, that was quite enough to account for it. I had grown very curious, and I resolved when our lessons were over to join her and make another attempt to discover the mystery.

As I sat over my books, I fancied I heard a movement outside the door. I suspected that Madame was listening. I waited for a time, expecting to see the door open, but she did not come; so I opened it suddenly myself, but Madame was not on the threshold nor on the lobby. I heard a rustling, however, and on the staircase over the banister I saw the folds of her silk dress as she descended.

She is going, I thought, to seek an interview with Lady Knollys. She intends to propitiate that dangerous lady; so I amused some eight or ten minutes in watching Cousin Monica's quick march and right-about face upon the parade-ground of the terrace. But no one joined her.

'She is certainly talking to papa,' was my next and more probable conjecture. Having the profoundest distrust of Madame, I was naturally extremely jealous of the confidential interviews in which deceit and malice might make their representations plausibly and without answer.

'Yes, I'll run down and see—see *papa;* she shan't tell lies behind my back, horrid woman!'

At the study-door I knocked, and forthwith entered. My father was sitting near the window, his open book before him, Madame standing at the other side of the table, her cunning eyes bathed in tears, and her pocket-handkerchief pressed to her mouth. Her eyes glittered stealthily on me for an instant: she was sobbing—*désolée,* in fact—that grim grenadier lady, and her attitude was exquisitely dejected and timid. But she was, notwithstanding, reading closely and craftily my father's face. He was not looking at her, but rather upward toward the ceiling, reflectively leaning an his hand, with an expression, not angry, but rather surly and annoyed.

'I ought to have heard of this before, Madame,' my father was saying as I came in; 'not that it would have made any difference—not the least; mind that. But it was the kind of thing that I ought to have heard, and the omission was not strictly right.'

Madame, in a shrill and lamentable key, opened her voluble reply, but was arrested by a nod from my father, who asked me if I wanted anything.

'Only—only that I was waiting in the school-room for Madame, and did not know where she was.'

'Well, she is here, you see, and will join you up-stairs in a few minutes.'

So back I went again, huffed, angry, and curious, and sat back in my chair with a clouded countenance, thinking very little about lessons.

When Madame entered, I did not lift my head or eyes.

'Good cheaile! reading,' said she, as she approached briskly and reassured.

'No,' I answered tartly; 'not good, nor a child either; I'm not reading, I've been thinking.'

'Très-bien!' she said, with an insufferable smile, 'thinking is very good also; but you look unhappy—very, poor cheaile. Take care you are not grow jealous for poor Madame talking sometime to your papa; you must not, little fool. It is only for a your good, my dear Maud, and I had no objection you should stay. '

'*You*! Madame!' I said loftily. I was very angry, and showed it through my dignity, to Madame's evident satisfaction.

'No—it was your papa, Mr. Ruthyn, who weesh to speak alone; for me I do not care; there was something I weesh to tell him. I don't care who know, but Mr. Ruthyn he is deeferent.'

I made no remark.

'Come, leetle Maud, you are not to be so cross; it will be much better you and I to be good friends together. Why should a we quarrel?—wat nonsense! Do you imagine I would anywhere undertake a the education of a young person unless I could speak with her parent?—wat folly! I would like to be your friend, however, my poor Maud, if you would allow—you and I together—wat you say?'

'People grow to be friends by liking, Madame, and liking comes of itself, not by bargain; I like every one who is kind to me.'

'And so I. You are like me in so many things, my dear Maud! Are you quaite well to-day? I think you look fateague; so I feel, too, vary tire. I think we weel put off the lessons to tomorrow. Eh? and we will come to play la grace in the garden.'

Madame was plainly in a high state of exultation. Her audience had evidently been satisfactory, and, like other people, when things went well, her soul lighted up into a sulphureous good-humour, not very genuine nor pleasant, but still it was better than other moods.

I was glad when our calisthenics were ended, and Madame had returned to her apartment, so that I had a pleasant little walk with Cousin Monica.

We women are persevering when once our curiosity is roused, but she gaily foiled mine, and, I think, had a mischievous pleasure in doing so. As we were going in to dress for dinner, however, she said, quite gravely—

'I am sorry, Maud, I allowed you to see that I have any unpleasant impressions about that governess lady. I shall be at liberty some day to explain all about it, and, indeed, it will be enough to tell your father, whom I have not been able to find all day; but really we are, perhaps, making too much of the matter, and I cannot say that I know anything against Madame that is conclusive, or—or, indeed, at all; but that there are reasons, and—you must not ask any more—no, you must not.'

That evening, while I was playing the overture to Cenerentola, for the entertainment of my cousin, there arose from the tea-table, where she and my father were sitting, a spirited and rather angry harangue from Lady Knollys' lips; I turned my eyes from the music towards the speakers; the overture swooned away with a little hesitating babble into silence, and I listened.

Their conversation had begun under cover of the music which I was making, and now they were too much engrossed to perceive its discontinuance. The first sentence I heard seized my attention; my father had closed the book he was reading, upon his finger, and was leaning back in his chair, as he used to do when at all angry; his face was a little flushed, and I knew the fierce and glassy stare which expressed pride, surprise, and wrath.

'Yes, Lady Knollys, there's an animus; I know the spirit you speak in—it does you no honour,' said my father.

'And I know the spirit *you* speak in, the spirit of *madness*,' retorted Cousin Monica, just as much in earnest.' I can't conceive how you *can* be so *demented*, Austin. What has perverted you? are you *blind*?'

'*You* are, Monica; your own unnatural prejudice—*unnatural* prejudice, blinds you. What is it all?—*nothing*. Were I to act as you say, I should be a *coward* and a traitor. I see, I *do* see, all that's real. I'm no Quixote, to draw my sword on illusions.'

'There should be no halting here. How *can* you—do you ever *think*? I wonder you can breathe. I feel as if the evil one were in the house. '

A stern, momentary frown was my father's only answer, as he looked fixedly at her.

'People need not nail up horseshoes and mark their doorstones with charms to keep the evil spirit out,' ran on Lady Knollys, who looked as pale and angry, in her way, 'but you open your door in the dark and invoke unknown danger. How can you look at that child that's — she's *not* playing,' said Knollys, abruptly stopping.

My father rose, muttering to himself, and cast a lurid glance at me, as he went in high displeasure to the door. Cousin Monica, now flushed a little, glanced also silently at me, biting the tip of her slender gold cross, and doubtful how much I had heard.

My father opened the door suddenly, which he had just closed, and looking in, said, in a calmer tone—

'Perhaps, Monica, you would come for a moment to the study; I'm sure you have none but kindly feelings towards me and little Maud, there; and I thank you for your good-will; but you must see other things more reasonably, and I think you will.'

Cousin Monica got up silently and followed him, only throwing up her eyes and hands as she did so, and I was left alone, wondering and curious more than ever.

CHAPTER XV

A WARNING

I sat still, listening and wondering, and wondering and listening; but I ought to have known that no sound could reach me where I was from my father's study. Five minutes passed and they did not return. Ten, fifteen. I drew near the fire and made myself comfortable in a great arm-chair, looking on the embers, but not seeing all the scenery and *dramatis personae* of my past life or future fortunes, in their shifting glow, as people in romances usually do; but fanciful castles and caverns in blood-red and golden glare, suggestive of dreamy fairy-land, salamanders, sunsets, and palaces of fire-kings, and all this partly shaping and partly shaped by my fancy, and leading my closing eyes and drowsy senses off into dream-land. So I nodded and dozed, and sank into a deep slumber, from which I was roused by the voice of my cousin Monica. On opening my eyes, I saw nothing but Lady Knollys' face looking steadily into mine, and expanding into a good-natured laugh as she watched the vacant and lack-lustre stare with which I returned her gaze.

'Come, dear Maud, it is late; you ought to have been in your bed an hour ago.'

Up I stood, and so soon as I had begun to hear and see aright, it struck me that Cousin Monica was more grave and subdued than I had seen her.

'Come, let us light our candles and go together.'

Holding hands, we ascended, I sleepy, she silent; and not a word was spoken until we reached my room. Mary Quince was in waiting, and tea made.

'Tell her to come back in a few minutes; I wish to say a word to you,' said Lady Knollys.

The maid accordingly withdrew.

Lady Knollys' eyes followed her till she closed the door behind her.

'I'm going in the morning.'

'So soon!'

'Yes dear; I could not stay; in fact, I should have gone tonight, but it was too late, and I leave instead in the morning.'

'I am so sorry—so *very* sorry,' I exclaimed, in honest disappointment, and the walls seemed to darken round me, and the monotony of the old routine loomed more terrible in prospect.

'So am I, dear Maud.'

' But can't you stay a little longer; *won't* you?'

'No, Maud; I'm vexed with Austin—very much vexed with your father; in short, I can't conceive anything so entirely preposterous, and dangerous, and insane as his conduct, now that his eyes are quite opened, and I must say a word to you before I go, and it is just this:—you must cease to be a mere child, you must try and be a woman, Maud: now don't be frightened or foolish, but hear me out. That woman—what does she call herself—Rougierre? I have reason to believe is—in fact, from circumstances, *must* be your enemy; you will find her very deep, daring, and unscrupulous, I venture to say, and you can't be too much on your guard. Do you quite understand me, Maud?'

'I do,' said I, with a gasp, and my eyes fixed on her with a terrified interest, as if on a warning ghost.

'You must bridle your tongue, mind, and govern your conduct, and command even your features. It is hard to practise reserve; but you must—you must be secret and vigilant. Try and be in appearance just as usual; don't quarrel; tell her nothing, if you do happen to know anything, of your father's business; be always on your guard when with her, and keep your eye upon her everywhere. Observe everything, disclose nothing—do you see?'

'Yes,' again I whispered.

'You have good, honest servants about you, and, thank God, they don't like her. But you must not repeat to them one word I am now saying to you. Servants are fond of dropping hints, and letting things ooze out in that way, and in their quarrels with her would compromise you—you understand me?'

'I do,' I sighed, with a wild stare.

'And—and, Maud, don't let her meddle with your food.'

Cousin Monica gave me a pale little nod, and looked away.

I could only stare at her; and under my breath I uttered an ejaculation of terror.

'Don't be so frightened; you must not be foolish; I only wish you to be upon your guard. I have my suspicions, but I may be quite wrong; your father thinks I am a fool; perhaps I am—perhaps not; maybe he may come to think as I do. But you must not speak to him on the subject; he's an odd man, and never did and never will act wisely, when his passions and prejudices are engaged.'

'Has she ever committed any great crime?' I asked, feeling as if I were on the point of fainting.

'No, dear Maud, I never said anything of the kind; don't be so frightened: I only said I have formed, from something I know, an ill opinion of her; and an unprincipled person, under temptation, is capable of a great deal. But no matter how wicked she may be, you may defy her, simply by assuming her to be so, and acting with caution; she is cunning and selfish, and she'll do nothing desperate. But I would give her no opportunity.'

'Oh, dear! Oh, Cousin Monica, don't leave me.'

'My dear, I *can't* stay; your papa and I—we've had a quarrel. I know I'm right, and he's wrong, and he'll come to see it soon, if he's left to himself, and then all will be right. But just now he misunderstands me, and we've not been civil to one another. I could not think of staying, and he would not allow you to come away with me for a short visit, which I wished. It won't last, though; and I do assure you, my dear Maud, I am quite happy about you now that you are quite on your guard. Just act respecting that person as if she were capable of any treachery, without showing distrust or dislike in your manner, and nothing will remain in her power; and write to me whenever you wish to hear from me, and if I can be of any real use, I don't care, I'll come: so there's a wise little woman; do as I've said, and depend upon it everything will go well, and I'll contrive before long to get that nasty creature away.'

Except a kiss and a few hurried words in the morning when she was leaving, and a pencilled farewell for papa, there was nothing more from Cousin Monica for some time.

Knowl was dark again—darker than ever. My father, gentle always to me, was now—perhaps it was contrast with his fitful return to something like the world's ways, during Lady Knollys' stay—more silent, sad, and isolated than before. Of Madame de la Rougierre I had nothing at first particular to remark. Only, reader, if you happen to be a rather nervous and very young girl, I ask you to conceive my fears and imaginings, and the kind of misery which I was suffering. Its intensity I cannot now even myself recall. But it overshadowed me perpetually—a care, an alarm. It lay down with me at night and got up with me in the morning, tinting and disturbing my dreams, and making my daily life terrible. I wonder now that I lived through the ordeal. The torment was secret and incessant, and kept my mind in unintermitting activity.

Externally things went on at Knowl for some weeks in the usual routine. Madame was, so far as her unpleasant ways were concerned, less tormenting than

before, and constantly reminded me of 'our leetle vow of friendship, you remember, dearest Maud!' and she would stand beside me, and looked from the window
with her bony arm round my waist, and my reluctant hand drawn round in hers;
and thus she would smile, and talk affectionately and even playfully; for at times
she would grow quite girlish, and smile with her great carious teeth, and begin to
quiz and babble about the young 'faylows,' and tell bragging tales of her lovers, all
of which were dreadful to me.

She was perpetually recurring, too, to the charming walk we had had together
to Church Scarsdale, and proposing a repetition of that delightful excursion,
which, you may be sure, I evaded, having by no means so agreeable a recollection
of our visit.

One day, as I was dressing to go out for a walk, in came good Mrs. Rusk, the
housekeeper, to my room.

'Miss Maud, dear, is not that too far for you? It is a long walk to Church
Scarsdale, and you are not looking very well.'

'To Church Scarsdale?' I repeated; 'I'm not going to Church Scarsdale; who said
I was going to Church Scarsdale? There is nothing I should so much dislike.'

'Well, I never!' exclaimed she. 'Why, there's old Madame's been down-stairs
with me for fruit and sandwiches, telling me you were longing to go to Church
Scarsdale—'

'It's quite untrue,' I interrupted. 'She knows I hate it.'

'She does?' said Mrs. Rusk, quietly; 'and you did not tell her nothing about the
basket? Well—if there isn't a story! Now what may she be after—what is it—what
is she driving at?'

'I can't tell, but I won't go.'

'No, of course, dear, you won't go. But you may be sure there's some scheme in
her old head. Tom Fowkes says she's bin two or three times to drink tea at Farmer
Gray's—now, could it be she's thinking to marry him?' And Mrs. Rusk sat down
and laughed heartily, ending with a crow of derision.

'To think of a young fellow like that, and his wife, poor thing, not dead a
year—maybe she's got money?'

'I don't know—I don't care—perhaps, Mrs. Rusk, you mistook Madame. I will
go down; I am going out.'

Madame had a basket in her hand. She held it quietly by her capacious skirt, at
the far side, and made no allusion to the preparation, neither to the direction in
which she proposed walking, and prattling artlessly and affectionately she marched
by my side.

Thus we reached the stile at the sheep-walk, and then I paused.

'Now, Madame, have not we gone far enough in this direction?—suppose we visit the pigeon-house in the park?'

'Wat folly! my dear a Maud—you cannot walk so far.'

'Well towards home, then.'

'And wy not a this way? We ave not walk enough, and Mr. Ruthyn he will not be pleased if you do not take proper exercise. Let us walk on by the path, and stop when you like.'

'Where do you wish to go, Madame?'

'Nowhere particular—come along; don't be fool, Maud.'

'This leads to Church Scarsdale.'

'A yes indeed! wat sweet place! here we need not a walk all the way to there.'

'I'd rather not walk outside the grounds to-day, Madame.'

'Come, Maud, you shall not be fool—wat you mean, Mademoiselle?' said the stalworth lady, growing yellow and greenish with an angry mottling, and accosting me very gruffly.

'I don't care to cross the stile, thank you, Madame. I shall remain at this side.'

'You shall do wat I tell you!' exclaimed she.

'Let go my arm, Madame, you hurt me,' I cried.

She had griped my arm very firmly in her great bony hand, and seemed preparing to drag me over by main force.

'Let me go,' I repeated shrilly, for the pain increased.

'La!' she cried with a smile of rage and a laugh, letting me go and shoving me backward at the same time, so that I had a rather dangerous tumble.

I stood up, a good deal hurt, and very angry, notwithstanding my fear of her.

'I'll ask papa if I am to be so ill-used.'

'Wat av I done?' cried Madame, laughing grimly from her hollow jaws; 'I did all I could to help you over—'ow could I prevent you to pull back and tumble if you would do so? That is the way wen you petites Mademoiselles are naughty and hurt yourself they always try to make blame other people. Tell a wat you like—you think I care?'

'Very well, Madame.'

'Are a you coming?'

'No.'

She looked steadily in my face and very wickedly. I gazed at her as with dazzled eyes—I suppose as the feathered prey do at the owl that glares on them by night. I neither moved back nor forward, but stared at her quite helplessly.

'You are nice pupil-charming young person! So polite, so obedient, so amiable! I will walk towards Church Scarsdale,' she continued, suddenly breaking through the conventionalism of her irony, and accosting me in savage accents. 'You weel stay behind if you dare. I tell you to accompany—do you hear?'

More than ever resolved against following her, I remained where I was, watching her as she marched fiercely away, swinging her basket as though in imagination knocking my head off with it.

She soon cooled, however, and looking over her shoulder, and seeing me still at the other side of the stile, she paused, and beckoned me grimly to follow her. Seeing me resolutely maintain my position, she faced about, tossed her head, like an angry beast, and seemed uncertain for a while what course to take with me.

She stamped and beckoned furiously again. I stood firm, I was very much frightened, and could not tell to what violence she might resort in her exasperation. She walked towards me with an inflamed countenance, and a slight angry wagging of the head; my heart fluttered, and I awaited the crisis in extreme trepidation. She came close, the stile only separating us, and stopped short, glaring and grinning at me like a French grenadier who has crossed bayonets, but hesitates to close.

CHAPTER XVI

DOCTOR BRYERLY LOOKS IN

What had I done to excite this ungovernable fury? We had often before had such small differences, and she had contented herself with being sarcastic, teasing, and impertinent.

'So, for future you are gouvernante and I the cheaile for you to command—is not so?—and you must direct where we shall walk, Très-bien! we shall see; Monsieur Ruthyn he shall know everything. For me I do not care—not at all—I shall be rather pleased, on the contrary. Let him decide. If I shall be responsible for the conduct and the health of Mademoiselle his daughter, it must be that I shall have authority to direct her wat she must do—it must be that she or I shall obey. I ask only witch shall command for the future—voilà tout!'

I was frightened, but resolute—I dare say I looked sullen and uncomfortable. At all events, she seemed to think she might possibly succeed by wheedling; so she tried coaxing and cajoling, and patted my cheek, and predicted that I would be 'a good cheaile,' and not 'vex poor Madame,' but do for the future 'wat she tell a me.'

She smiled her wide wet grin, smoothed my hand, and patted my cheek, and would in the excess of her conciliatory paroxysm have kissed me; but I withdrew, and she commented only with a little laugh, and a 'Foolish little thing! but you will be quite amiable just now.'

'Why, Madame,' I asked, suddenly raising my head and looking her straight in the face, 'do you wish me to walk to Church Scarsdale so particularly to-day?'

She answered my steady look with a contracted gaze and an unpleasant frown.

'Wy do I?—I do not understand a you; there is *no* particular day—wat folly! Wy I like Church Scarsdale? Well, it is such pretty place. There is all! Wat leetle fool! I suppose you think I want to keel a you and bury you in the churchyard?'

And she laughed, and it would not have been a bad laugh for a ghoul.

'Come, my dearest Maud, you are not a such fool to say, if *you* tell me me go thees a way, I weel go that; and if you say, go that a way, I weel go thees—you are rasonable leetle girl—come along—*alons donc*—we shall av soche agreeable walk— weel a you?'

But I was immovable. It was neither obstinacy nor caprice, but a profound fear that governed me. I was then afraid—yes, *afraid*. Afraid of *what?* Well, of going with Madame de la Rougierre to Church Scarsdale that day. That was all. And I believe that instinct was true.

She turned a bitter glance toward Church Scarsdale, and bit her lip. She saw that she must give it up. A shadow hung upon her drab features. A little scowl—a little sneer—wide lips compressed with a false smile, and a leaden shadow mottling all. Such was the countenance of the lady who only a minute or two before had been smiling and murmuring over the stile so amiably with her idiomatic 'blarney,' as the Irish call that kind of blandishment.

There was no mistaking the malignant disappointment that hooked and warped her features—my heart sank—a tremendous fear overpowered me. Had she intended poisoning me? What was in that basket? I looked in her dreadful face. I felt for a minute quite frantic. A feeling of rage with my father, with my Cousin Monica, for abandoning me to this dreadful rogue, took possession of me, and I cried, help-lessly wringing my hands—

'Oh! it is a shame—it is a shame—it is a shame!'

The countenance of the gouvernante relaxed. I think she in turn was frightened at my extreme agitation. It might have worked unfavourably with my father.

'Come, Maud, it is time you should try to control your temper. You shall not walk to Church Scarsdale if you do not like—I only invite. *There!* It is quite as you please, where we shall walk then? Here to the peegeon-house? I think you say. Tout bien! Remember I concede you everything. Let us go.'

We went, therefore, towards the pigeon-house, through the forest trees; I not speaking as the children in the wood did with their sinister conductor, but utterly silent and scared; she silent also, meditating, and sometimes with a sharp side-glance gauging my progress towards equanimity. Her own was rapid; for Madame was a philosopher, and speedily accommodated herself to circumstances. We had not walked a quarter of an hour when every trace of gloom had left her face, which had assumed its customary brightness, and she began to sing with a spiteful hilarity as we walked forward, and indeed seemed to be approaching one of her waggish, frolicsome moods. But her fun in these moods was solitary. The joke, whatever it was, remained in her own keeping. When we approached the ruined brick tower— in old times a pigeon-house—she grew quite frisky, and twirled her basket in the air, and capered to her own singing.

Under the shadow of the broken wall, and its ivy, she sat down with a frolic-some *plump,* and opened her basket, inviting me to partake, which I declined. I must do her justice, however, upon the suspicion of poison, which she quite disposed of by gobbling up, to her own share, everything which the basket contained.

The reader is not to suppose that Madame's cheerful demeanour indicated that I was forgiven, Nothing of the kind. One syllable more, on our walk home, she addressed not to me. And when we reached the terrace, she said—

'You will please, Maud, remain for two—three minutes in the Dutch garden, while I speak with Mr. Ruthyn in the study.'

This was spoken with a high head and an insufferable smile; and I more haughtily, but quite gravely, turned without disputing, and descended the steps to the quaint little garden she had indicated.

I was surprised and very glad to see my father there. I ran to him, and began, 'Oh! papa!' and then stopped short, adding only, 'may I speak to you now?'

He smiled kindly and gravely on me.

'Well, Maud, say your say.'

' Oh, sir, it is only this: I entreat that our walks, mine and Madame's may be confined to the grounds.'

'And why?'

'I—I'm afraid to go with her.'

'Afraid!' he repeated, looking hard at me. 'Have you lately had a letter from Lady Knollys?'

'No, papa, not for two months or more.'

There was a pause.

'And why *afraid*, Maud?'

'She brought me one day to Church Scarsdale; you know what a solitary place it is, sir; and she frightened me so that I was afraid to go with her into the church-yard. But she went and left me alone at the other side of the stream, and an impudent man passing by stopped and spoke to me, and seemed inclined to laugh at me, and altogether frightened me very much, and he did not go till Madame happened to return.'

'What kind of man—young or old?'

'A young man; he looked like a farmer's son, but very impudent, and stood there talking to me whether I would or not; and Madame did not care at all, and laughed at me for being frightened; and, indeed, I am very uncomfortable with her.'

He gave me another shrewd look, and then looked down cloudily and thought.

'You say you are uncomfortable and frightened. How is this—what causes these feelings?'

'I don't know, sir; she likes frightening me; I am afraid of her—we are all afraid of her, I think. The servants, I mean, as well as I.'

My father nodded his head contemptuously, twice or thrice, and muttered, 'A pack of fools!'

'And she was so very angry to-day with me, because I would not walk again with her to Church Scarsdale. I am very much afraid of her. I—' and quite unpremeditatedly I burst into tears.

'There, there, little Maud, you must not cry. She is here only for your good. If you are afraid—even *foolishly* afraid—it is enough. Be it as you say; your walks are henceforward confined to the grounds; I'll tell her so.'

I thanked him through my tears very earnestly.

'But, Maud, beware of prejudice; women are unjust and violent in their judgments. Your family has suffered in some of its members by such injustice. It behoves us to be careful not to practise it.'

That evening in the drawing-room my father said, in his usual abrupt way—

'About my departure, Maud: I've had a letter from London this morning, and I think I shall be called away sooner than I at first supposed, and for a little time we must manage apart from one another. Do not be alarmed. You shall not be in Madame de la Rougierre's charge, but under the care of a relation; but even so, little Maud will miss her old father, I think.'

His tone was very tender, so were his looks; he was looking down on me with a smile, and tears were in his eyes. This softening was new to me. I felt a strange thrill of surprise, delight, and love, and springing tip, I threw my arms about his neck and wept in silence. He, I think, shed tears also.

'You said a visitor was coming; some one, you mean, to go away with. Ah, yes, you love him better than me.'

'No, dear, no; but I *fear* him; and I am sorry to leave you, little Maud.'

'It won't be very long,' I pleaded.

'No, dear,' he answered with a sigh.

I was tempted almost to question him more closely on the subject, but he seemed to divine what was in my mind, for he said—

'Let us speak no more of it, but only bear in mind, Maud, what I told you about the oak cabinet, the key of which is here,' and he held it up as formerly: 'you remember what you are to do in case Doctor Bryerly should come while I am away?'

'Yes, sir.'

His manner had changed, and I had returned to my accustomed formalities.

It was only a few days later that Dr. Bryerly actually did arrive at Knowl, quite unexpectedly, except, I suppose, by my father. He was to stay only one night.

He was twice closeted in the little study up-stairs with my father, who seemed to me, even for him, unusually dejected, and Mrs. Rusk inveighing against 'them rubbitch,' as she always termed the Swedenborgians, told me 'they were making him quite shaky-like, and he would not last no time, if that lanky, lean ghost of a fellow in black was to keep prowling in and out of his room like a tame cat.'

I lay awake that night, wondering what the mystery might be that connected my father and Dr. Bryerly. There was something more than the convictions of their strange religion could account for. There was something that profoundly agitated my father.

It may not be reasonable, but so it is. The person whose presence, though we know nothing of the cause of that effect, is palpably attended with pain to anyone who is dear to us, grows odious, and I began to detest Doctor Bryerly.

It was a grey, dark morning, and in a dark pass in the gallery, near the staircase, I came full upon the ungainly Doctor, in his glossy black suit.

I think, if my mind had been less anxiously excited on the subject of his visit, or if I had not disliked him so much, I should not have found courage to accost him as I did. There was something sly, I thought, in his dark, lean face; and he looked so low, so like a Scotch artisan in his Sunday clothes, that I felt a sudden pang of indignation, at the thought that a great gentleman, like my father, should have suffered under his influence, and I stopped suddenly, instead of passing him by with a mere salutation, as he expected, 'May I ask a question, Doctor Bryerly?'

'Certainly.'

'Are you the friend whom my father expects?'

'I don't quite see.'

'The friend, I mean, with whom he is to make an expedition to some distance, I think, and for some little time?'

'No,' said the Doctor, with a shake of his head.

'And who is he?'

'I really have not a notion, Miss.'

'Why, he said that *you knew,*' I replied.

The Doctor looked honestly puzzled.

'Will he stay long away? pray tell me.'

The Doctor looked into my troubled face with inquiring and darkened eyes, like one who half reads another's meaning; and then he said a little briskly, but not sharply—

'Well, *I* don't know, I'm sure, Miss; no, indeed, you must have mistaken; there's nothing that *I* know.'

There was a little pause, and he added—

'No. He never mentioned any friend to me.' I fancied that he was made uncomfortable by my question, and wanted to hide the truth. Perhaps I was partly right.

'Oh! Doctor Bryerly, pray, *pray* who is the friend, and where is he going?'

'I do *assure* you,' he said, with a strange sort of impatience, 'I don't know; it is all nonsense.'

And he turned to go, looking, I think, annoyed and disconcerted.

A terrific suspicion crossed my brain like lightning.

'Doctor, one word,' I said, I believe, quite wildly. 'Do you—do you think his mind is at all affected?'

'Insane?' he said, looking at me with a sudden, sharp inquisitiveness, that brightened into a smile. 'Pooh, pooh! Heaven forbid! not a saner man in England.'

Then with a little nod he walked on, carrying, as I believed, notwithstanding his disclaimer, the secret with him. In the afternoon Doctor Brverly went away.

CHAPTER XVII

AN ADVENTURE

For many days after our quarrel, Madame hardly spoke to me. As for lessons, I was not much troubled with them. It was plain, too, that my father had spoken to her, for she never after that day proposed our extending our walks beyond the precincts of Knowl.

Knowl, however, was a very considerable territory, and it was possible for a much better pedestrian than I to tire herself effectually, without passing its limits. So we took occasionally long walks.

After some weeks of sullenness, during which for days at a time she hardly spoke to me, and seemed lost in dark and evil abstraction, she once more, and somewhat suddenly, recovered her spirits, and grew quite friendly. Her gaieties and friendliness were not reassuring, and in my mind presaged approaching mischief and treachery. The days were shortening to the wintry span. The edge of the red sun had already touched the horizon as Madame and I, overtaken at the warren bv his last beams, were hastening homeward.

A narrow carriage-road traverses this wild region of the park, to which a distant gate gives entrance. On descending into this unfrequented road, I was surprised to see a carriage standing there. A thin, sly postilion, with that pert, turned-up nose which the old caricaturist Woodward used to attribute to the gentlemen of Tewkesbury, was leaning on his horses, and looked hard at me as I passed. A lady who sat within looked out, with an extra-fashionable bonnet on, and also treated us to a stare. Very pink and white checks she had, very black glossy hair and bright eyes—fat, bold, and rather cross, she looked—and in her bold way she examined us curiously as we passed.

I mistook the situation. It had once happened before that an intending visitor at Knowl had entered the place by that parkroad, and lost several hours in a vain search for the house.

'Ask him, Madame, whether they want to go to the house; I dare say they have missed their way,' whispered I.

'*Eh bien* they will find again. I do not choose to talk to postboys; *allons!*'

But I asked the man as we passed, 'Do you want to reach the house?'

By this time he was at the horses' heads, buckling the harness.

'Noa,' he said in a surly tone, smiling oddly on the winkers, but, recollecting his politeness, he added, 'Noa, thankee, misses, it's what they calls a picnic; we'll be takin' the road now.'

He was smiling now on a little buckle with which he was engaged.

'Come—nonsense!' whispered Madame sharply in my ear, and she whisked me by the arm, so we crossed the little stile at the other side.

Our path lay across the warren, which undulates in little hillocks. The sun was down by this time, blue shadows were stretching round us, colder in the splendid contrast of the burnished sunset sky.

Descending over these hillocks we saw three figures a little in advance of us, not far from the path we were tracing. Two were standing smoking and chatting at intervals: one tall and slim, with a high chimney-pot, worn a little on one side, and a white great-coat buttoned up to the chin; the other shorter and stouter, with a dark-coloured wrapper. These gentlemen were facing rather our way as we came over the edge of the eminence, but turned their backs on perceiving our approach. As they did so, I remember so well each lowered his cigar suddenly with the simultaneousness of a drill. The third figure sustained the picnic character of the group, for he was repacking a hamper. He stood suddenly erect as we drew near, and a very ill-looking person he was, low-browed, square-chinned, and with a broad, broken nose. He wore gaiters, and was a little bandy, very broad, and had a closely-cropped bullet head, and deep-set little eyes. The moment I saw him, I beheld the living type of the burglars and bruisers whom I had so often beheld with a kind of scepticism in *Punch*. He stood over his hamper and scowled sharply at us for a moment; then with the point of his foot he jerked a little fur cap that lay on the ground into his hand, drew it tight over his lowering brows, and called to his companions, just as we passed him—'Hallo! mister. How's this?'

'All right,' said the tall person in the white great-coat, who, as he answered, shook his shorter companion by the arm, I thought angrily.

This shorter companion turned about. He had a muffler loose about his neck and chin. I thought he seemed shy and irresolute, and the tall man gave him a great jolt with his elbow, which made him stagger, and I fancied a little angry, for he said, as it seemed, a sulky word or two.

The gentleman in the white surtout, however, standing direct in our way, raised his hat with a mock salutation, placing his hand on his breast, and forthwith began to advance with an insolent grin and an air of tipsy frolic.

'Jist in time, ladies; five minutes more and we'd a bin off. Thankee, Mrs. Mouser, ma'am, for the honour of the meetin', and more particular for the pleasure of making your young lady's acquaintance—niece, ma'am? daughter, ma'am? granddaughter, by Jove, is it? Hallo! there, mild'n, I say, stop packin'.' This was to the ill-favoured person with the broken nose. 'Bring us a couple o' glasses and a bottle o' curaçoa; what are you fear'd on, my dear? this is Lord Lollipop, here, a reg'lar charmer, wouldn't hurt a fly, hey Lolly? Isn't he pretty, Miss? and I'm Sir Simon Sugarstick—so called after old Sir Simon, ma'am; and I'm so tall and straight, Miss, and slim—ain't I? and ever so sweet, my honey, when you come to know me, just like a sugarstick; ain't I, Lolly, boy?'

'I'm Miss Ruthyn, tell them, Madame,' I said, stamping on the ground, and very much frightened.

'Be quaite, Maud. If you are angry, they will hurt us; leave me to speak,' whispered the gouvernante.

All this time they were approaching from separate points. I glanced back, and saw the ruffianly-looking man within a yard or two, with his arm raised and one finger up, telegraphing, as it seemed, to the gentlemen in front.

'Be quaite, Maud,' whispered Madame, with an awful adjuration, which I do not care to set down. 'They are teepsy; don't seem 'fraid.'

I *was* afraid—terrified. The circle had now so narrowed that they might have placed their hands on my shoulders.

'Pray, gentlemen, wat you want? *weel* a you 'av the goodness to permit us to go on?'

I now observed for the first time, with a kind of shock, that the shorter of the two men, who prevented our advance, was the person who had accosted me so offensively at Church Scarsdale. I pulled Madame by the arm, whispering, 'Let us run.'

'Be quaite, my dear Maud,' was her only reply.

'I tell you what,' said the tall man, who had replaced his high hat more jauntily than before on the side of his head, 'We've caught you now, fair game, and we'll let you off on conditions. You must not be frightened, Miss. Upon my honour and soul, I mean no mischief; do I, Lollipop? I call him Lord Lollipop; it's only chaff, though; his name's Smith. Now, Lolly, I vote we let the prisoners go, when we just introduce them to Mrs. Smith; she's sitting in the carriage, and keeps Mr. S. here in precious good order, I promise you. There's easy terms for you, eh, and we'll have a glass o' curaçoa round, and so part friends. Is it a bargain? Come!'

'Yes, Maud, we must go—wat matter?' whispered Madame vehemently.

'You shan't,' I said, instinctively terrified.

'You'll go with Ma'am, young'un, won't you?' said Mr. Smith, as his companion called him.

Madame was holding my arm, but I snatched it from her, and would have run; the tall man, however, placed his arms round me and held me fast with an affectation of playfulness, but his grip was hard enough to hurt me a good deal. Being now thoroughly frightened, after an ineffectual struggle, during which I heard Madame say, 'You fool, Maud, weel you come with me? see wat you are doing,' I began to scream, shriek after shriek, which the man attempted to drown with loud hooting, peals of laughter, forcing his handkerchief against my mouth, while Madame continued to bawl her exhortations to 'be quaite' in my ear.

'I'll lift her, I say!' said a gruff voice behind me.

But at this instant, wild with terror, I distinctly heard other voices shouting. The men who surrounded me were instantly silent, and all looked in the direction of the sound, now very near, and I screamed with redoubled energy. The ruffian behind me thrust his great hand over my mouth.

'It is the gamekeeper,' cried Madame. '*Two* gamekeepers—we are safe—thank Heaven!' and she began to call on Dykes by name.

I only remember, feeling myself at liberty—running a few steps—seeing Dykes' white furious face—clinging to his arm, with which he was bringing his gun to a level, and saying, 'Don't fire—they'll murder us if you do.'

Madame, screaming lustily, ran up at the same moment.

'Run on to the gate and lock it—I'll be wi' ye in a minute,' cried he to the other gamekeeper; who started instantly on this mission, for the three ruffians were already in full retreat for the carriage.

Giddy—wild—fainting—still terror carried me on.

'Now, Madame Rogers—s'pose you take young Misses on—I must run and len' Bill a hand.'

'No, no; you moste not,' cried Madame. 'I am fainting myself, and more villains they may be near to us.'

But at this moment we heard a shot, and, muttering to himself and grasping his gun, Dykes ran at his utmost speed in the direction of the sound.

With many exhortations to speed, and ejaculations of alarm, Madame hurried me on toward the house, which at length we reached without further adventure.

As it happened, my father met us in the hall. He was perfectly transported with fury on hearing from Madame what had happened, and set out at once, with some of the servants, in the hope of intercepting the party at the park-gate.

Here was a new agitation; for my father did not return for nearly three hours, and I could not conjecture what might be occurring during the period of his absence. My alarm was greatly increased by the arrival in the interval of poor Bill, the under-gamekeeper, very much injured.

Seeing that he was determined to intercept their retreat, the three men had set upon him, wrested his gun, which exploded in the struggle, from him, and beat him savagely. I mention these particulars, because they convinced everybody that there was something specially determined and ferocious in the spirit of the party, and that the fracas was no mere frolic, but the result of a predetermined plan.

My father had not succeeded in overtaking them. He traced them to the Lugton Station, where they had taken the railway, and no one could tell him in what direction the carriage and posthorses had driven.

Madame was, or affected to be, very much shattered by what had occurred. Her recollection and mine, when my father questioned us closely, differed very materially respecting many details of the *personnel* of the villanous party. She was obstinate and clear; and although the gamekeeper corroborated my description of them, still my father was puzzled. Perhaps he was not sorry that some hesitation was forced upon him, because although at first he would have gone almost any length to detect the persons, on reflection he was pleased that there was not evidence to bring them into a court of justice, the publicity and annoyance of which would have been inconceivably distressing to me.

Madame was in a strange state—tempestuous in temper, talking incessantly— every now and then in floods of tears, and perpetually on her knees pouring forth torrents of thanksgiving to Heaven for our joint deliverance from the hands of those villains. Notwithstanding our community of danger and her thankfulness on my behalf, however, she broke forth into wrath and railing whenever we were alone together.

'Wat fool you were! so disobedient and obstinate; if you 'ad done wat *I* say, then we should av been quaite safe; those persons they were tipsy, and there is nothing so dangerous as to quarrel with tipsy persons; I would 'av brought you quaite safe—the lady she seem so nice and quaite, and we should 'av been safe with her— there would 'av been nothing absolutely; but instead you would scream and pooshe, and so they grow quite wild, and all the impertinence and violence follow of course; and that a poor Bill—all his beating and danger to his life it is cause entirely by you.'

And she spoke with more real virulence than that kind of upbraiding generally exhibits.

'The beast!' exclaimed Mrs. Rusk, when she, I, and Mary Quince were in my room together, 'with all her crying and praying, I'd like to know as much as she does, maybe, about them rascals. There never was sich like about the place, long as I remember it, till she came to Knowl, old witch! with them unmerciful big bones of hers, and her great bald head, grinning here, and crying there, and her nose everywhere. The old French hypocrite!'

Mary Quince threw in an observation, and I believe Mrs. Rusk rejoined, but I heard neither. For whether the housekeeper spoke with reflection or not, what she said affected me strangely. Through the smallest aperture, for a moment, I had had a peep into Pandemonium. Were not peculiarities of Madame's demeanour and advice during the adventure partly accounted for by the suggestion? Could the proposed excursion to Church Scarsdale have had any purpose of the same sort? What was proposed? How was Madame interested in it? Were such immeasurable treason and hypocrisy possible? I could not explain nor quite believe in the shapeless suspicion that with these light and bitter words of the old housekeeper had stolen so horribly into my mind.

After Mrs. Rusk was gone I awoke from my dismal abstraction with something like a moan and a shudder, with a dreadful sense of danger.

'Oh! Mary Quince,' I cried, 'do *you* think she really knew?'

'*Who,* Miss Maud?'

'Do you think Madame knew of those dreadful people? Oh, no—say you don't—you don't believe it—tell me she did not. I'm distracted, Mary Quince, I'm frightened out of my life.'

'There now, Miss Maud, dear—there now, don't take on so—why should she?—no sich a thing. Mrs. Rusk, law bless you, she's no more meaning in what she says than the child unborn.'

But I was really frightened. I was in a horrible state of uncertainty as to Madame de la Rougierre's complicity with the party who had beset us at the warren, and afterwards so murderously beat our poor gamekeeper. How was I ever to get rid of that horrible woman? How long was she to enjoy her continual opportunities of affrighting and injuring me?

'She hates me—she hates me, Mary Quince; and she will never stop until she has done me some dreadful injury. Oh! will no one relieve me—will no one take her away? Oh, papa, papa, papa! you will be sorry when it is too late.'

I was crying and wringing my hands, and turning from side to side, at my wits' ends, and honest Mary Quince in vain endeavoured to quiet and comfort me.

CHAPTER XVIII

A MIDNIGHT VISITOR

The frightful warnings of Lady Knollys haunted me too. Was there no escape from the dreadful companion whom fate had assigned me? I made up my mind again and again to speak to my father and urge her removal. In other things he indulged me; here, however, he met me drily and sternly, and it was plain that he fancied I was under my cousin Monica's influence, and also that he had secret reasons for persisting in an opposite course. Just then I had a gay, odd letter from Lady Knollys, from some country house in Shropshire. Not a word about Captain Oakley. My eye skimmed its pages in search of that charmed name. With a peevish feeling I tossed the sheet upon the table. Inwardly I thought how ill-natured and unwomanly it was.

After a time, however, I read it, and found the letter very good-natured. She had received a note from papa. He had 'had the impudence to forgive *her* for *his* impertinence.' But for my sake she meant, notwithstanding this aggravation, really to pardon him; and whenever she had a disengaged week, to accept his invitation to Knowl, from whence she was resolved to whisk me off to London, where, though I was too young to be presented at Court and come out, I might yet— besides having the best masters and a good excuse for getting rid of Medusa—see a great deal that would amuse and surprise me.

'Great news, I suppose, from Lady Knollys?' said Madame, who always knew who in the house received letters by the post, and by an intuition from whom they came.

'Two letters—you and your papa. She is quite well, I hope?'

'Quite well, thank you, Madame.'

Some fishing questions, dropped from time to time, fared no better. And as usual, when she was foiled even in a trifle, she became sullen and malignant.

That night, when my father and I were alone, he suddenly closed the book he had been reading, and said—

'I heard from Monica Knollys to-day. I always liked poor Monnie; and though she's no witch, and very wrongheaded at times, yet now and then she does say a thing that's worth weighing. Did she ever talk to you of a time, Maud, when you are to be your own mistress?'

'No,' I answered, a little puzzled, and looking straight in his rugged, kindly face.

'Well, I thought she might—she's a rattle, you know—always *was* a rattle, and that sort of people say whatever comes uppermost. But that's a subject for me, and more than once, Maud, it has puzzled me.'

He sighed.

'Come with me to the study, little Maud.'

So, he carrying a candle, we crossed the lobby, and marched together through the passage, which at night always seemed a little awesome, darkly wainscoted, uncheered by the cross-light from the hall, which was lost at the turn, leading us away from the frequented parts of the house to that misshapen and lonely room about which the traditions of the nursery and the servants' hall had had so many fearful stories to recount.

I think my father had intended making some disclosure to me on reaching this room. If so, he changed his mind, or at least postponed his intention.

He had paused before the cabinet, respecting the key of which he had given me so strict a charge, and I think he was going to explain himself more fully than he had done, But he went on, instead, to the table where his desk, always jealously locked, was placed, and having lighted the candles which stood by it, he glanced at me, and said—

'You must wait a little, Maud; I shall have something to say to you. Take this candle and amuse yourself with a book meanwhile.'

I was accustomed to obey in silence. I chose a volume of engravings, and ensconced myself in a favourite nook in which I had often passed a half-hour similarly. This was a deep recess by the fireplace, fenced on the other side by a great old escritoir, into this I drew a stool, and, with candle and book, I placed myself snugly in the narrow chamber. Every now and then I raised my eyes and saw my father either writing or ruminating, as it seemed to me, very anxiously at his desk.

Time wore on—a longer time than be had intended, and still he continued absorbed at his desk. Gradually I grew sleepy, and as I nodded, the book and room faded away, and pleasant little dreams began to gather round me, and so I went off into a deep slumber.

It must have lasted long, for when I wakened my candle had burnt out; my father, having quite forgotten me, was gone, and the room was dark and deserted. I felt cold and a little stiff, and for some seconds did not know where I was.

I had been wakened, I suppose, by a sound which I now distinctly heard, to my great terror, approaching. There was a rustling; there was a breathing. I heard a creaking upon the plank that always creaked when walked upon in the passage. I held my breath and listened, and coiled myself up in the innermost recess of my little chamber.

Sudden and sharp, a light shone in from the nearly-closed study door. It shone angularly on the ceiling like a letter L reversed. There was a pause. Then some one knocked softly at the door, which after another pause was slowly pushed open. I expected, I think, to see the dreaded figure of the linkman. I was scarcely less frightened to see that of Madame de la Rougierre. She was dressed in a sort of grey silk, which she called her Chinese silk—precisely as she had been in the daytime. In fact, I do not think she had undressed. She had no shoes on. Otherwise her toilet was deficient in nothing. Her wide mouth was grimly closed, and she stood scowling into the room with a searching and pallid scrutiny, the candle held high above her head at the full stretch of her arm.

Placed as I was in a deep recess, and in a seat hardly raised above the level of the floor, I escaped her, although it seemed to me for some seconds, as I gazed on this spectre, that our eyes actually met.

I sat without breathing or winking, staring upon the formidable image which with upstretched arm, and the sharp lights and hard shadows thrown upon her corrugated features, looked like a sorceress watching for the effect of a spell.

She was plainly listening intensely. Unconsciously she had drawn her lower lip altogether between her teeth, and I well remember what a deathlike and idiotic look the contortion gave her. My terror lest she should discover me amounted to positive agony. She rolled her eyes stealthily from corner to corner of the room, and listened with her neck awry at the door.

Then to my father's desk she went. To my great relief, her back was towards me. She stooped over it, with the candle close by; I saw her try a key—it could be nothing else—and I heard her blow through the wards to clear them.

Then, again, she listened at the door, candle in hand, and then with long tiptoe steps came back, and papa's desk in another moment was open, and Madame cautiously turning over the papers it contained.

Twice or thrice she paused, glided to the door, and listened again intently with her head near the ground, and then returned and continued her search, peeping into papers one after another, tolerably methodically, and reading some quite through.

While this felonious business was going on, I was freezing with fear lest she should accidentally look round and her eyes light on me; for I could not say what she might not do rather than have her crime discovered.

Sometimes she would read a paper twice over; sometimes a whisper no louder than the ticking of a watch, sometimes a brief chuckle under her breath, bespoke the interest with which here and there a letter or a memorandum was read.

For about half an hour, I think, this went on; but at the time it seemed to me all but interminable. On a sudden she raised her head and listened for a moment, replaced the papers deftly, closed the desk without noise, except for the tiny click of the lock, extinguished the candle, and rustled stealthily out of the room, leaving in the darkness the malign and hag-like face on which the candle had just shone still floating filmy in the dark.

Why did I remain silent and motionless while such an outrage was being committed? If, instead of being a very nervous girl, preoccupied with an undefinable terror of that wicked woman, I had possessed courage and presence of mind, I dare say I might have given an alarm, and escaped from the room without the slightest risk. But so it was; I could no more stir than the bird who, cowering under its ivy, sees the white owl sailing back and forward under its predatory cruise.

Not only during her presence, but for more than an hour after, I remained cowering in my hiding-place, and afraid to stir, lest she might either be lurking in the neighborhood, or return and surprise me.

You will not be astonished, that after a night so passed I was ill and feverish in the morning. To my horror, Madame de la Rougierre came to visit me at my bedside. Not a trace of guilty consciousness of what had passed during the night was legible in her face. She had no sign of late watching, and her toilet was exemplary.

As she sat smiling by me, full of anxious and affectionate enquiry, and smoothed the coverlet with her great felonious hand, I could quite comprehend the dreadful feeling with which the deceived husband in the 'Arabian Nights' met his ghoul wife, after his nocturnal discovery.

Ill as I was, I got up and found my father in that room which adjoined his bed-chamber. He perceived, I am sure, by my looks, that something unusual had happened. I shut the door, and came close beside his chair.

'Oh, papa, I have such a thing to tell you!' I forgot to call him 'Sir.' 'A secret; and you won't say who told you? Will you come down to the study?'

He looked hard at me, got up, and kissing my forehead, said—'Don't be frightened, Maud; I venture to say it is a mare's nest; at all events, my child, we will take care that no danger reaches you; come, child.'

And by the hand he led me to the study. When the door was shut, and we had reached the far end of the room next the window, I said, but in a low tone, and holding his arm fast—

'Oh, sir, you don't know what a dreadful person we have living with us—Madame de la Rougierre, I mean. Don't let her in if she comes; she would guess what I am telling you, and one way or another I am sure she would kill me.'

'Tut, tut, child. You *must* know that's nonsense,' he said, looking pale and stern.

'Oh no, papa. I am horribly frightened, and Lady Knollys thinks so too.'

'Ha! I dare say; one fool makes many. We all know what Monica thinks.'

'But I *saw* it, papa. She stole your key last night, and opened your desk, and read all your papers.'

'Stole my key!' said my father, staring at me perplexed, but at the same instant producing it. 'Stole it! Why here it is!'

'She unlocked your desk; she read your papers for ever so long. Open it now, and see whether they have not been stirred.'

He looked at me this time in silence, with a puzzled air; but he did unlock the desk, and lifted the papers curiously and suspiciously. As he did so he uttered a few of those inarticulate interjections which are made with closed lips, and not always intelligible; but he made no remark.

Then he placed me on a chair beside him, and sitting down himself, told me to recollect myself, and tell him distinctly all I had seen. This accordingly I did, he listening with deep attention.

'Did she remove any paper?' asked my father, at the same time making a little search, I suppose, for that which lie fancied might have been stolen.

'No; I did not see her take anything.'

'Well, you are a good girl, Maud. Act discreetly. Say nothing to anyone—not even to your cousin Monica.'

Directions which, coming from another person would have had no great weight, were spoken by my father with an earnest look and a weight of emphasis that made them irresistibly impressive, and I went away with the seal of silence upon my lips.

'Sit down, Maud, *there*. You have not been very happy with Madame de la Rougierre. It is time you were relieved. This occurrence decides it.'

He rang the bell.

'Tell Madame de la Rougierre that I request the honour of seeing her for a few minutes here.'

My father's communications to her were always equally ceremonious. In a few minutes there was a knock at the door, and the same figure, smiling, courtesying, that had scared me on the threshold last night, like the spirit of evil, presented itself.

My father rose, and Madame having at his request taken a chair opposite, look-ing, as usual in his presence, all amiability, he proceeded at once to the point.

'Madame de la Rougierre, I have to request you that you will give me the key now in your possession, which unlocks this desk of mine.'

With which termination he tapped his gold pencil-case suddenly on it.

Madame, who had expected something very different, became instantly so pale, with a dull purplish hue upon her forehead, that, especially when she had twice essayed with her white lips, in vain, to answer, I expected to see her fall in a fit.

She was not looking in his face; her eyes were fixed lower, and her mouth and cheek sucked in, with a strange distortion at one side.

She stood up suddenly, and staring straight in his face, she succeeded in saying, after twice clearing her throat—

'I cannot comprehend, Monsieur Ruthyn, unless you intend to insult me.'

'It won't do, Madame; I must have that false key, I give you the opportunity of surrendering it quietly here and now.'

'But who dares to say I possess such thing?' demanded Madame, who, having rallied from her momentary paralysis, was now fierce and voluble as I had often seen her before.

'You know, Madame, that you can rely on what I say, and I tell you that you were seen last night visiting this room, and with a key in your possession, opening this desk, and reading my letters and papers contained in it. Unless you forthwith give me that key, and any other false keys in your possession—in which case I shall rest content with dismissing you summarily—I will take a different course. You know I am a magistrate;—and and I shall have you, your boxes, and places upstairs, searched forthwith, and I will prosecute you criminally. The thing is clear; you aggravate by denying; you must give me that key, if you please, instantly, otherwise I ring this bell, and you shall see that I mean what I say.'

There was a little pause. He rose and extended his hand towards the bell-rope. Madame glided round the table, extended her hand to arrest his.

'I will do everything, Monsieur Ruthyn—whatever you wish.'

And with these words Madame de la Rougierre broke down altogether. She sobbed, she wept, she gabbled piteously, all manner of incomprehensible roulades of lamentation and entreaty; coyly, penitently, in a most interesting agitation, she produced the very key from her breast, with a string tied to it. My father was little moved by this piteous tempest. He coolly took the key and tried it in the desk, which it locked and unlocked quite freely, though the wards were complicated. He shook his head and looked her in the face.

'Pray, who made this key? It is a new one, and made expressly to pick this lock.'

But Madame was not going to tell any more than she had expressly bargained for; so she only fell once more into her old paroxysm of sorrow, self-reproach, extenuation, and entreaty.

'Well,' said my father, 'I promised that on surrendering the key you should go. It is enough. I keep my word. You shall have an hour and a half to prepare in. You must then be ready to depart. I will send your money to you by Mrs. Rusk; and if you look for another situation, you had better not refer to me. Now be so good as to leave me.'

Madame seemed to be in a strange perplexity. She bridled up, dried her eyes fiercely, and dropped a great courtesy, and then sailed away towards the door.

Before reaching it she stopped on the way, turning half round, with a peaked, pallid glance at my father, and she bit her lip viciously as she eyed him. At the door the same repulsive pantomime was repeated, as she stood for a moment with her hand upon the handle. But she changed her bearing again with a sniff, and with a look of scorn, almost heightened to a sneer, she made another very low courtesy and a disdainiul toss of her head, and so disappeared, shutting the door rather sharply behind her.

CHAPTER XIX

AU REVOIR

Mrs. Rusk was fond of assuring me that Madame 'did not like a bone in my skin.' Instinctively I knew that she bore me no good-will, although I really believe it was her wish to make me think quite the reverse. At all events I had no desire to see Madame again before her departure, especially as she had thrown upon me one momentary glance in the study, which seemed to me charged with very peculiar feelings.

You may be very sure, therefore, that I had no desire for a formal leave-taking at her departure. I took my hat and cloak, therefore, and stole out quietly.

My ramble was a sequestered one, and well screened, even at this late season, with foliage; the pathway devious among the stems of old trees, and its flooring interlaced and groined with their knotted roots. Though near the house, it was a sylvan solitude; a little brook ran darkling and glimmering through it, wild strawberries and other woodland plants strewed the ground, and the sweet notes and flutter of small birds made the shadow of the boughs cheery.

I had been fully an hour in this picturesque solitude when I heard in the distance the ring of carriage-wheels, announcing to me that Madame de la Rougierre had fairly set out upon her travels. I thanked heaven; I could have danced and sung with delight; I heaved a great sigh and looked up through the branches to the clear blue sky.

But things are oddly timed. Just at this moment I heard Madame's voice close at my ear, and her large bony hand was laid on my shoulder. We were instantly face to face—I recoiling, and for a moment speechless with fright.

In very early youth we do not appreciate the restraints which act upon malignity, or know how effectually fear protects us where conscience is wanting. Quite alone, in this solitary spot, detected and overtaken with an awful instinct by my enemy, what might not be about to happen to me at that moment?

'Frightened as usual, Maud,' she said quietly, and eyeing me with a sinister smile,' and with cause you think, no doubt. Wat 'av you done to injure poor Madame? Well, I think I know, little girl, and have quite discover the cleverness of my sweet little Maud—Eh—is not so? Petite carogne—ah, ha, ha!'

I was too much confounded to answer.

'You see, my dear cheaile,' she said, shaking her uplifted finger with a hideous archness at me, 'you could not hide what you 'av done from poor Madame. You cannot look so innocent but I can see your pretty little villany quite plain—you dear little diablesse.

'Wat I 'av done I 'av no reproach of myself for it. If I could explain, your papa would say I 'av done right, and you should thank me on your knees; but I cannot explain yet.'

She was speaking, as it were, in little paragraphs, with a momentary pause between each, to allow its meaning to impress itself.

'If I were to choose to explain, your papa he would implore me to remain. But no—I would not—notwithstanding your so cheerful house, your charming servants, your papa's amusing society, and your affectionate and sincere heart, my sweet little maraude.

'I am to go to London first, where I 'av, oh, so good friends! next I will go abroad for some time; but be sure, my sweetest Maud, wherever I may 'appen to be, I will remember you—ah, ha! Yes; *most certainly,* I will remember you.

'And although I shall not be always near, yet I shall know everything about my charming little Maud; you will not know how, but I shall indeed, *everything.* And be sure, my dearest cheaile, I will some time be able to give you the sensible proofs of my gratitude and affection—you understand.

'The carriage is waiting at the yew-tree stile, and I must go on. You did not expect to see me—here; I will appear, perhaps, as suddenly another time. It is great pleasure to us both—this opportunity to make our adieux. Farewell! my dearest little Maud. I will never cease to think of you, and of some way to recompense the kindness you 'av shown for poor Madame.'

My hand hung by my side, and she took, not it, but my thumb, and shook it, folded in her broad palm, and looking on me as she held it, as if meditating mischief. Then suddenly she said—

'You will always remember Madame, I *think,* and I will remind you of me beside; and for the present farewell, and I hope you may be as 'appy as you deserve.'

The large sinister face looked on me for a second with its latent sneer, and then, with a sharp nod and a spasmodic shake of my imprisoned thumb, she turned, and holding her dress together, and showing her great bony ankles, she strode rapidly away over the gnarled roots into the perspective of the trees, and I did not awake, as it were, until she had quite disappeared in the distance.

Events of this kind made no difference with my father; but every other face in Knowl was gladdened by the removal. My energies had returned, my spirits were come again. The sunlight was happy, the flowers innocent, the songs and flutter of the birds once more gay, and all nature delightful and rejoicing.

After the first elation of relief, now and then a filmy shadow of Madame de la Rougierre would glide across the sunlight, and the remembrance of her menace return with an unexpected pang of fear.

'Well, if *there* isn't impittens!' cried Mrs. Rusk. 'But never you trouble your head about it, Miss. Them sort's all alike—you never saw a rogue yet that was found out and didn't threaten the honest folk as he was leaving behind with all sorts; there was Martin the gamekeeper, and Jervis the footman, I mind well how hard they swore all they would not do when they was a-going, and who ever heard of them since? They always threatens that way—them sort always does, and none ever the worse—not but she would if she could, mind ye, but there it is; she can't do nothing but bite her nails and cuss us—not she—ha, ha, ha!'

So I was comforted. But Madame's evil smile, nevertheless, from time to time, would sail across my vision with a silent menace, and my spirits sank, and a Fate, draped in black, whose face I could not see, took me by the hand, and led me away, in the spirit, silently, on an awful exploration from which I would rouse myself with a start, and Madame was gone for a while.

She had, however, judged her little parting well. She contrived to leave her glamour over me, and in my dreams she troubled me.

I was, however, indescribably relieved. I wrote in high spirits to Cousin Monica; and wondered what plans my father might have formed about me, and whether we were to stay at home, or go to London, or go abroad. Of the last—the pleasantest arrangement, in some respects—I had nevertheless an occult horror. A secret conviction haunted me that were we to go abroad, we should there meet Madame, which to me was like meeting my evil genius.

I have said more than once that my father was an odd man and the reader will, by this time, have seen that there was much about him not easily understood. I often wonder whether, if he had been franker, I should have found him less odd than I supposed, or more odd still. Things that moved me profoundly did not apparently affect him at all. The departure of Madame, under the circumstances which attended it, appeared to my childish mind an event of the vastest importance. No one was indifferent to the occurrence in the house but its master. He never alluded again to Madame de la Rougierre. But whether connected with her exposure and dismissal, I could not say, there did appear to be some new care or trouble now at work in my father's mind.

'I have been thinking a great deal about you, Maud. I am anxious. I have not been so troubled for years. Why has not Monica Knollys a little more sense?'

This oracular sentence he spoke, having stopped me in the hall; and then saying, 'We shall see,' he left me as abruptly as he appeared.

Did he apprehend any danger to me from the vindictiveness of Madame?

A day or two afterwards, as I was in the Dutch garden, I saw him on the terrace steps. He beckoned to me, and came to meet me as I approached.

'You must be very solitary, little Maud; it is not good. I have written to Monica: in a matter of detail she is competent to advise; perhaps she will come here for a short visit.'

I was very glad to hear this.

'*You* are more interested than for my time *I* can be, in vindicating his character.'

'Whose character, sir?' I ventured to enquire during the pause that followed.

One trick which my father had acquired from his habits of solitude and silence was this of assuming that the context of his thoughts was legible to others, forgetting that they had not been spoken.

'Whose?—Your uncle Silas's. In the course of nature he must survive me. He will then represent the family name. Would you make some sacrifice to clear that name, Maud?'

I answered briefly; but my face, I believe, showed my enthusiasm.

He turned on me such an approving smile as you might fancy lighting up the rugged features of a pale old Rembrandt.

'I can tell you, Maud; if my life could have done it, it should not have been undone—*ubi lapsus, quid feci*. But I had almost made up my mind to change my plan, and leave all to time—*edax rerum*—to illuminate or to *consume*. But I think little Maud would like to contribute to the restitution of her family name. It may cost you something—are you willing to buy it at a sacrifice? Is there—I don't speak of fortune, that is not involved—but is there any other honourable sacrifice you would shrink from to dispel the disgrace under which our most ancient and honourable name must otherwise continue to languish?'

'Oh, none—none indeed, sir—I am delighted!'

Again I saw the Rembrandt smile.

'Well, Maud, I am sure there is *no* risk; but you are to suppose there is. Are you still willing to accept it?

Again I assented.

'You are worthy of your blood, Maud Ruthyn. It will come soon, and it won't last long. But you must not let people like Monica Knollys frighten you.'

I was lost in wonder.

'If you allow them to possess you with their follies, you had better recede in time—they may make the ordeal as terrible as hell itself. You have zeal—have you nerve?'

I thought in such a cause I had nerve for anything.

'Well, Maud, in the course of a few months—and it may be sooner—there must be a change. I have had a letter from London this morning that assures me of that. I must then leave you for a time; in my absence be faithful to the duties that will arise. To whom much is committed, of him will much be required. You shall promise me not to mention this conversation to Monica Knollys. If you are a talking girl, and cannot trust yourself, say so, and we will not ask her to come. Also, don't invite her to talk about your uncle Silas—I have reasons. Do you quite understand my conditions?'

'Yes, sir.'

'Your uncle Silas,' he said, speaking suddenly in loud and fierce tones that sounded from so old a man almost terrible, 'lies under an intolerable slander. I don't correspond with him; I don't sympathise with him; I never quite did. He has grown religious, and that's well; but there are things in which even religion should not bring a man to acquiesce; and from what I can learn, he, the person primarily affected—the cause, though the innocent cause—of this great calamity—bears it with an easy apathy which is mistaken, and liable easily to be mistaken, and such as no Ruthyn, under the circumstances, ought to exhibit. I told him what he ought to do, and offered to open my purse for the purpose but he would not, or *did* not; indeed, he *never* took my advice; he followed his own, and a foul and dismal shoal he has drifted on. It is not for his sake—why should I?—that I have longed and laboured to remove the disgraceful slur under which his ill-fortune has thrown us. He troubles himself little about it, I believe—he's meek, meeker than I. He cares less about his children than I about you, Maud; he is selfishly sunk in futurity—a feeble visionary. I am not so. I believe it to be a duty to take care of others beside myself. The character and influence of an ancient family is a peculiar heritage—sacred but destructible; and woe to him who either destroys or suffers it to perish!'

This was the longest speech I ever heard my father speak before or after. He abruptly resumed—

'Yes, we will, Maud—you and I—we'll leave one proof on record, which, fairly read, will go far to convince the world.'

He looked round, but we were alone. The garden was nearly always solitary, and few visitors ever approached the house from that side.

'I have talked too long, I believe; we are children to the last. Leave me, Maud. I think I know you better than I did, and I am pleased with you. Go, child—I'll sit here.'

If he had acquired new ideas of me, so had I of him from that interview. I had no idea till then how much passion still burned in that aged frame, nor how full of energy and fire that face, generally so stern and ashen, could appear. As I left him seated on the rustic chair, by the steps, the traces of that storm were still discernible on his features. His gathered brows, glowing eyes, and strangely hectic face, and the grim compression of his mouth, still showed the agitation which, somehow, in grey old age, shocks and alarms the young.

CHAPTER XX

AUSTIN RUTHYN SETS OUT ON HIS JOURNEY

The Rev. William Fairfield, Doctor Clay's somewhat bald curate, a mild, thin man, with a high and thin nose, who was preparing me for confirmation, came next day; and when our catechetical conference was ended, and before lunch was announced, my father sent for him to the study, where he remained until the bell rang out its summons.

'We have had some interesting—I may say *very* interesting—conversation, your papa and I, Miss Ruthyn,' said my reverend *vis-à-vis,* so soon as nature was refreshed, smiling and shining, as he leaned back in his chair, his hand upon the table, and his finger curled gently upon the stem of his wine-glass. 'It never was your privilege, I believe, to see your uncle, Mr. Silas Ruthyn, of Bartram-Haugh?'

'No—never; he leads so retired—so *very* retired a life.'

'Oh, no,—of course, no; but I was going to remark a likeness—I mean, of course, a *family* likeness—only *that* sort of thing—you understand—between him and the profile of Lady Margaret in the drawing-room—is not it Lady Margaret?— which you were so good as to show me on Wednesday last. There certainly *is* a likeness. I *think* you would agree with me, if you had the pleasure of seeing your uncle.'

'You know him, then? I have never seen him.'

'Oh dear, yes—I am happy to say, I know him very well. I have that privilege. I was for three years curate of Feltram, and I had the honour of being a pretty constant visitor at Bartram-Haugh during that, I may say, protracted period; and I think it really never has been my privilege and happiness, I may say, to enjoy the acquaintance and society of so very experienced a Christian, as my admirable friend, I may call him, Mr. Ruthyn, of Bartram-Haugh. I look upon him, I do assure you, quite in the light of a saint; not, of course, in the Popish sense, but in the very highest, you will understand me, which *our* Church allows,—a man built up in faith—full of faith—faith and grace—altogether exemplary; and I often ventured to regret, Miss Ruthyn, that Providence in its mysterious dispensations should have placed him so far apart from his brother, your respected father. His influence and opportunities would, no doubt, we may venture to hope, at least have been blessed; and, perhaps, we—my valued rector and I—might possibly have seen more of him at church, than, I deeply regret, we *have* done.' He shook his head a little, as he smiled with a sad complacency on me through his blue steel spectacles, and then sipped a little meditative sherry.

'And you saw a good deal of my uncle?'

'Well, a *good* deal, Miss Ruthyn—I may say a *good* deal—principally at his own house. His health is wretched—miserable health—a sadly afflicted man he has been, as, no doubt, you are aware. But afflictions, my dear Miss Ruthyn, as you remember Doctor Clay so well remarked on Sunday last, though birds of ill omen, yet spiritually resemble the ravens who supplied the prophet; and when they visit the faithful, come charged with nourishment for the soul.

'He is a good deal embarrassed pecuniarily, I should say,' continued the curate, who was rather a good man than a very well-bred one.' He found a difficulty—in fact it was not in his power—to subscribe generally to our little funds, and—and objects, and I used to say to him, and I really felt it, that it was more gratifying, such were his feeling and his power of expression, to be refused by him than assisted by others.'

'Did papa wish you to speak to me about my uncle?' I enquired, as a sudden thought struck me; and then I felt half ashamed of my question.

He looked surprised.

'No, Miss Ruthyn, certainly not. Oh dear, no. It was merely a conversation between Mr. Ruthyn and me. He never suggested my opening that, or indeed any other point in my interview with you, Miss Ruthyn—not the least.'

'I was not aware before that Uncle Silas was so religious.'

He smiled tranquilly, not quite up to the ceiling, but gently upward, and shook his head in pity for my previous ignorance, as he lowered his eyes—

'I don't say that there may not be some little matters in a few points of doctrine which we could, perhaps, wish otherwise. But these, you know, are speculative, and in all essentials he is Church—not in the perverted modern sense; far from it— unexceptionably Church, strictly so. Would there were more among us of the same mind that is in him! Ay, Miss Ruthyn, even in the highest places of the Church herself.'

The Rev. William Fairfield, while fighting against the Dissenters with his right hand, was, with his left, hotly engaged with the Tractarians. A good man I am sure he was, and I dare say sound in doctrine, though naturally, I think, not very wise. This conversation with him gave me new ideas about my uncle Silas. It quite agreed with what my father had said. These principles and his increasing years would necessarily quiet the turbulence of his resistance to injustice, and teach him to acquiesce in his fate.

You would have fancied that one so young as I, born to wealth so vast, and living a life of such entire seclusion, would have been exempt from care. But you have seen how troubled my life was with fear and anxiety during the residence of Madame de la Rougierre, and now there rested upon my mind a vague and awful anticipation of the trial which my father had announced, without defining it.

An 'ordeal' he called it, requiring not only zeal but nerve, which might possibly, were my courage to fail, become frightful, and even intolerable. What, and of what nature, could it be? Not designed to vindicate the fair fame of the meek and submissive old man —who, it seemed, had ceased to care for his bygone wrongs, and was looking to futurity—but the reputation of our ancient family.

Sometimes I repented my temerity in having undertaken it. I distrusted my courage. Had I not better retreat, while it was yet time? But there was shame and even difficulty in the thought. How should I appear before my father? Was it not important—had I not deliberately undertaken it—and was I not bound in conscience? Perhaps he had already taken steps in the matter which committed *him*. Besides, was I sure that, even were I free again, I would not once more devote myself to the trial, be it what it might? You perceive I had more spirit than courage. I think I had the mental attributes of courage; but then I was but a hysterical girl, and in so far neither more nor less than a coward.

No wonder I distrusted myself; no wonder also my will stood out against my timidity. It was a struggle, then; a proud, wild resolve against constitutional cowardice.

Those who have ever had cast upon them more than their strength seemed framed to bear—the weak, the aspiring, the adventurous and self-sacrificing in will, and the faltering in nerve—will understand the kind of agony which I sometimes endured.

But, again, consolation would come, and it seemed to me that I must be exaggerating my risk in the coming crisis; and certain at least, if my father believed it attended with real peril, he would never have wished to see me involved in it. But the silence under which I was bound was terrifying—double so when the danger was so shapeless and undivulged.

I was soon to understand it all—soon, too, to know all about my father's impending journey, whither, with what visitor, and why guarded from me with so awful a mystery.

That day there came a lively and goodnatured letter from Lady Knollys. She was to arrive at Knowl in two or three days' time. I thought my father would have been pleased, but he seemed apathetic and dejected.

'One does not always feel quite equal to Monica. But for you—yes, thank God. I wish she could only stay, Maud, for a month or two; I may be going then, and would be glad—provided she talks about suitable things—very glad, Maud, to leave her with you for a week or so.'

There was something, I thought, agitating my father secretly that day. He had the strange hectic flush I had observed when he grew excited in our interview in the garden about Uncle Silas. There was something painful, perhaps even terrible, in the circumstances of the journey he was about to make, and from my heart I wished the suspense were over, the annoyance past, and he returned.

That night my father bid me good-night early and went upstairs, After I had been in bed some little time, I heard his hand-bell ring. This was not usual. Shortly after I heard his man, Ridley, talking with Mrs. Rusk in the gallery. I could not be mistaken in their voices. I knew not why I was startled and excited, and had raised myself to listen on my elbow. But they were talking quietly, like persons giving or taking an ordinary direction, and not in the haste of an unusual emergency.

Then I heard the man bid Mrs. Rusk good-night and walk down the gallery to the stairs, so that I concluded he was wanted no more, and all must therefore be well. So I laid myself down again, though with a throbbing at my heart, and an ominous feeling of expectation, listening and fancying footsteps.

I was going to sleep when I heard the bell ring again; and, in a few minutes, Mrs. Rusk's energetic step passed along the gallery; and, listening intently, I heard, or fancied, my father's voice and hers in dialogue. All this was very unusual, and again I was, with a beating heart, leaning with my elbow on my pillow.

Mrs. Rusk came along the gallery in a minute or so after, and stopping at my door, began to open it gently. I was startled, and challenged my visitor with—

'Who's there?'

'It's only Rusk, Miss. Dearie me! and are you awake still?'

Is papa ill?'

'Ill! not a bit ill, thank God. Only there's a little black book as I took for your prayer-book, and brought in here; ay, here it is, sure enough, and he wants it. And then I must go down to the study, and look out this one, "C, 15;" but I can't read the name, noways; and I was afraid to ask him again; if you be so kind to read it, Miss—I suspeck my eyes is a-going.'

I read the name; and Mrs. Rusk was tolerably expert at finding out books, as she had often been employed in that way before. So she departed.

I suppose that this particular volume was hard to find, for she must have been a long time away, and I had actually fallen into a doze when I was roused in an instant by a dreadful crash and a piercing scream from Mrs. Rusk. Scream followed scream, wilder and more terror-stricken. I shrieked to Mary Quince, who was sleeping in the room with me:—'Mary, do you hear? what is it? It is something dreadful.'

The crash was so tremendous that the solid flooring even of my room trembled under it, and to me it seemed as if some heavy man had burst through the top of the window, and shook the whole house with his descent. I found myself standing at my own door, crying, 'Help, help! murder! murder!' and Mary Quince, frightened half out of her wits, by my side.

I could not think what was going on. It was plainly something most horrible, for Mrs. Rusk's screams pealed one after the other unabated, though with a muffled sound, as if the door was shut upon her; and by this time the bells of my father's room were ringing madly.

'They are trying to murder him!' I cried, and I ran along the gallery to his door, followed by Mary Quince, whose white face I shall never forget, though her entreaties only sounded like unmeaning noises in my ears.

'Here! help, help, help I cried, trying to force open the door.

'Shove it, shove it, for God's sake! he's across it,' cried Mrs. Rusk's voice from within; 'drive it in. I can't move him.'

I strained all I could at the door, but ineffectually. We heard steps approaching. The men were running to the spot, and shouting as they did so—

'Never mind; hold on a bit; here we are; all right;' and the like.

We drew back, as they came up. We were in no condition to be seen. We listened, however, at my open door.

Then came the straining and bumping at the door. Mrs. Rusk's voice subsided to a sort of wailing; the men were talking all together, and I suppose the door opened, for I heard some of the voices, on a sudden, as if in the room; and then came a strange lull, and talking in very low tones, and not much even of that.

'What is it, Mary? what *can* it be?' I ejaculated, not knowing what horror to suppose. And now, with a counterpane about my shoulders, I called loudly and imploringly, in my horror, to know what had happened.

But I heard only the subdued and eager talk of men engaged in some absorbing task, and the dull sounds of some heavy body being moved.

Mrs. Rusk came towards us looking half wild, and pale as a spectre, and putting her thin hands to my shoulders, she said 'Now, Miss Maud, darling, you must go back again; 'tisn't no place for you; you'll see all, my darling, time enough—you will. There now, there, like a dear, do get into your room.'

What was that dreadful sound? Who had entered my father's chamber? It was the visitor whom we had so long expected, with whom he was to make the unknown journey, leaving me alone. The intruder was Death!

CHAPTER XXI

ARRIVALS

My father was dead—as suddenly as if he had been murdered, One of those fearful aneurisms that lie close to the heart, showing no outward sign of giving way in a moment, had been detected a good time since by Dr. Bryerly. My father knew what must happen, and that it could not be long deferred. He feared to tell me that he was soon to die. He hinted it only in the allegory of his journey, and left in that sad enigma some words of true consolation that remained with me ever after. Under his rugged ways was hidden a wonderful tenderness. I could not believe that he was actually dead. Most people for a minute or two, in the wild tumult of such a shock, have experienced the same skepticism. I insisted that the doctor should be instantly sent for from the village.

'Well, Miss Maud, dear, I *will* send to please you, but it is all to no use. If only you saw him yourself you'd know that. Mary Quince, run you down and tell Thomas, Miss Maud desires he'll go down this minute to the village for Dr. Elweys.'

Every minute of the interval seemed to me like an hour. I don't know what I said, but I fancied that if he were not already dead, he would lose his life by the delay. I suppose I was speaking very wildly, for Mrs. Rusk said—

'My dear child, you ought to come in and see him; indeed but you should, Miss Maud. He's quite dead an hour ago. You'd wonder all the blood that's come from him—you would indeed it's soaked through the bed already.'

'Oh, don't, don't, *don't,* Mrs. Rusk.'

'Will you come in and see him, just?

'Oh, no, no, no, no!"

'Well, then, my dear, don't of course, if you don't like; there's no need. Would not you like to lie down, Miss Maud? Mary Quince, attend to her. I must go into the room for a minute or two.'

I was walking up and down the room in distraction. It was a cool night; but I did not feel it. I could only cry:—' Oh, Mary, Mary! what shall I do? Oh, Mary Quince! what shall I do?'

It seemed to me it must be near daylight by the time the Doctor arrived. I had dressed myself. I dared not go into the room where my beloved father lay.

I had gone out of my room to the gallery, where I awaited Dr. Elweys, when I saw him walking briskly after the servant, his coat buttoned up to his chin, his hat in his hand, and his bald head shining. I felt myself grow cold as ice, and colder and colder, and with a sudden sten my heart seemed to stand still.

I heard him ask the maid who stood at the door, in that low, decisive, mysterious tone which doctors cultivate—

'In *here?*'

And then, with a nod, I saw him enter.

'Would not you like to see the Doctor, Miss Maud?' asked Mary Quince.

The question roused me a little.

'Thank you, Mary; yes, I must see him.'

And so, in a few minutes, I did. He was very respectful, very sad, semi-undertakerlike, in air and countenance, but quite explicit. I heard that my dear father 'had died palpably from the rupture of some great vessel near the heart.' The disease had, no doubt, been 'long established, and is in its nature incurable.' It is 'consolatory in these cases that in the act of dissolution, which is instantaneous, there can be no suffering.' These, and a few more remarks, were all he had to offer; and having had his fee fom Mrs. Rusk, he, with a respectful melancholy, vanished.

I returned to my room, and broke into paroxysms of grief, and after an hour or more grew more tranquil.

From Mrs. Rusk I learned that he had seemed very well—better than usual, indeed—that night, and that on her return from the study with the book he required, he was noting down, after his wont, some passages which illustrated the text on which he was employing himself. He took the book, detaining her in the room, and then mounting on a chair to take down another book from a shelf, he had fallen, with the dreadful crash I had heard, dead upon the floor. He fell across the door, which caused the difficulty in opening it. Mrs. Rusk found she had not strength to force it open. No wonder she had given way to terror. I think I should have almost lost my reason.

Everyone knows the reserved aspect and the taciturn mood of the house, one of whose rooms is tenanted by that mysterious guest.

I do not know how those awful days, and more awful nights, passed over. The remembrance is repulsive. I hate to think of them. I was soon draped in the conventional black, with its heavy folds of crape. Lady Knollys came, and was very kind. She undertook the direction of all those details which were to me so inexpressibly dreadful. She wrote letters for me beside, and was really most kind and useful, and her society supported me indescribably. She was odd, but her eccentricity was leavened with strong common sense; and I have often thought since with admiration and gratitude of the tact with which she managed my grief.

There is no dealing with great sorrow as if it were under the control of our wills. It is a terrible phenomenon, whose laws we must study, and to whose conditions we must submit, if we would mitigate it. Cousin Monica talked a great deal of my father. This was easy to her, for her early recollections were full of him.

One of the terrible dislocations of our habits of mind respecting the dead is that our earthly future is robbed of them, and we thrown exclusively upon retrospect. From the long look forward they are removed, and every plan, imagination, and hope henceforth a silent and empty perspective. But in the past they are all they ever were. Now let me advise all who would comfort people in a new bereavement to talk to them, very freely, all they can, in this way of the dead. They will engage in it with interest, they will talk of their own recollections of the dead, and listen to yours, though they become sometimes pleasant, sometimes even laughable. I found it so. It robbed the calamity of something of its supernatural and horrible abruptness; it prevented that monotony of object which is to the mind what it is to the eye, and prepared the faculty for those mesmeric illusions that derange its sense.

Cousin Monica, I am sure, cheered me wonderfully. I grow to love her more and more, as I think of all her trouble, care, and kindness.

I had not forgotten my promise to dear papa about the key, concerning which he had evinced so great an anxiety. It was found in the pocket where he had desired me to remember he always kept it, except when it was placed, while he slept, under his pillow.

'And so, my dear, that wicked woman was actually found picking the lock of your poor papa's desk. I *wonder* he did not punish her—you know that is *burglary*.'

'Well, Lady Knollys, you know she is gone, and so I care no more about her— that is, I mean, I need not fear her.'

'No, my dear, but you must call me Monica—do you mind—I'm your cousin, and you call me Monica, unless you wish to vex me. No, of course, you need not be afraid of her. And she's gone. But I'm an old thing, you know, and not so ten-der-hearted as you; and I confess I should have been very glad to hear that the wicked old witch had been sent to prison and hard labour—I should. And what do you suppose she was looking for—what did she want to steal? I think I can guess— what do *you* think?'

'To read the papers; maybe to take bank-notes—I'm not sure,' I answered.

'Well, I think most likely she wanted to get at your poor papa's *will*—that's *my* idea.

'There is nothing surprising in the supposition, dear,' she resumed. 'Did not you read the curious trial at York, the other day? There is nothing so valuable to steal as a will, when a great deal of property is to be disposed of by it. Why, you would have given her ever so touch money to get it back again. Suppose you go down, dear—I'll go with you, and open the cabinet in the study.'

'I don't think I can, for I promised to give the key to Dr. Bryerly, and the meaning was that *he* only should open it.'

Cousin Monica uttered an inarticulate 'H'm!' of surprise or disapprobation.

'Has he been written to?'

'No, I do not know his address.'

'Not know his address! come, that is curious,' said Knollys, a little testily.

I could not—no one now living in the house could furnish even a conjecture. There was even a dispute as to which train he had gone by—north or south—they crossed the station at an interval of five minutes. If Dr. Bryerly had been an evil spirit, evoked by a secret incantation, there could not have been more complete darkness as to the immediate process of his approach.

'And how long do you mean to wait, my dear? No matter; at all events you may open the *desk*; you may find papers to direct you—you may find Dr. Bryerly's address—you may find, heaven knows what.'

So down we went—I assenting—and we opened the desk. How dreadful the desecration seems—all privacy abrogated—the shocking compensation for the silence of death!

Henceforward all is circumstantial evidence—all conjectural—except the *litera scripta,* and to this evidence every notebook, and every scrap of paper and private letter, must contribute—ransacked, bare in the light of day—what it can.

At the top of the desk lay two notes sealed, one to Cousin Monica, the other to me. Mine was a gentle and loving little farewell — nothing more — which opened afresh the fountains of my sorrow, and I cried and sobbed over it bitterly and long.

The other was for 'Lady Knollys.' I did not see how she received it, for I was already absorbed in mine. But in awhile she came and kissed me in her girlish, goodnatured way. Her eyes used to fill with tears at sight of my paroxysms of grief. Then she would begin, 'I remember it was a saying of his,' and so she would repeat it—something maybe wise, maybe playful, at all events consolatory—and the circumstances in which she had heard him say it, and then would follow the recollections suggested by these; and so I was stolen away half by him, and half by Cousin Monica, from my despair and lamentation.

Along with these lay a large envelope, inscribed with the words 'Directions to be complied with immediately on my death.' One of which was, 'Let the event be *forthwith* published in the *county* and principal *London* papers.' This step had been already taken. We found no record of Dr. Bryerly's address.

We made search everywhere, except in the cabinet, which I would on no account permit to be opened except, according to his direction, by Dr. Bryerly's hand. But nowhere was a will, or any document resembling one, to be found. I had now, therefore, no doubt that his will was placed in the cabinet.

In the search among my dear father's papers we found two sheafs of letters, neatly tied up and labelled—these were from my uncle Silas.

My cousin Monica looked down upon these papers with a strange smile; was it satire—was it that indescribable smile with which a mystery which covers a long reach of years is sometimes approached?

These were odd letters. If here and there occurred passages that were querulous and even abject, there were also long passages of manly and altogether noble sentiment, and the strangest rodomontade and maunderings about religion. Here and there a letter would gradually transform itself into a prayer, and end with a doxology and no signature; and some of them expressed such wild and disordered views respecting religion, as I imagine he can never have disclosed to good Mr. Fairfield, and which approached more nearly to the Swedenborg visions than to anything in the Church of England.

I read these with a solemn interest, but my cousin Monica was not similarly moved. She read them with the same smile—faint, serenely contemptuous, I thought—with which she had first looked down upon them. It was the countenance of a person who amusedly traces the working of a character that is well understood.

'Uncle Silas is very religious?' I said, not quite liking Lady Knollys' looks.

'Very,' she said, without raising her eyes or abating her old bitter smile, as she glanced over a passage in one of his letters.

'You don't think he *is*, Cousin Monica?' said I. She raised her head and looked straight at me.

'Why do you say that, Maud?'

'Because you smile incredulously, I think, over his letters.'

'Do I?' said she; 'I was not thinking—it was quite an accident. The fact is, Maud, your poor papa quite mistook me. I had no prejudice respecting him—no theory. I never knew what to think about him. I do not think Silas a product of nature, but a child of the Sphinx, and I never could understand him—that's all.'

'I always felt so too; but that was because I was left to speculation, and to glean conjectures as I might from his portrait, or anywhere. Except what you told me, I never heard more than a few sentences; poor papa did not like me to ask questions about him, and I think he ordered the servants to be silent.'

'And much the same injunction this little note lays upon me—not quite, but something like it; and I don't know the meaning of it.'

And she looked enquiringly at me.

'You are not to be *alarmed* about your uncle Silas, because your being afraid would unfit you for an *important service* which you have undertaken for your family, the nature of which I shall soon understand, and which, although it is quite *passive*, would be made very sad if *illusory fears* were allowed to *steal into your mind*.'

She was looking into the letter in poor papa's handwriting, which she had found addressed to her in his desk, and emphasised the words, I suppose, which she quoted from it.

'Have you any idea, Maud, darling, what this *service* may be?' she enquired, with a grave and anxious curiosity in her countenance.

'None, Cousin Monica; but I have thought long over my undertaking to do it, or submit to it, be it what it may; and I will keep the promise I voluntarily made, although I know what a coward I am, and often distrust my courage.'

'Well, I am not to frighten you.'

'How could you? Why should I be afraid? *Is* there anything frightful to be disclosed? Do tell me—you *must* tell me.'

'No, darling, I did not mean *that*—I don't mean that;—I could, if I would; I—I don't know exactly what I meant. But your poor papa knew him better than I—in fact, I did not know him at all—that is, ever quite understood him—which your poor papa, I see, had ample opportunities of doing.' And after a little pause, she added—'So you do not know what you are expected to do or to undergo.'

'Oh! Cousin Monica, I know you think he committed that murder,' I cried, starting up, I don't know why, and I felt that I grew deadly pale.

'I don't believe any such thing, you little fool; you must not say such horrible things, Maud,' she said, rising also, and looking both pale and angry. 'Shall we go out for a little walk? Come, lock up these papers, dear, and get your things on; and if that Dr. Bryerly does not turn up to-morrow, you must send for the Rector, good Doctor Clay, and let him make search for the will—there may be directions about many things, you know; and, my dear Maud, you are to remember that Silas is *my* cousin as well as your uncle. Come, dear, put on your hat.'

So we went out together for a little cloistered walk.

CHAPTER XXII

SOMEBODY IN THE ROOM WITH THE COFFIN

When we returned, a 'young' gentleman had arrived. We saw him in the parlour as we passed the window. It was simply a glance, but such a one as suffices to make a photograph, which we can study afterwards, at our leisure. I remember him at this moment—a man of six-and-thirty—dressed in a grey travelling suit, not over-well made; light-haired, fat-faced, and clumsy; and he looked both dull and cunning, and not at all like a gentleman.

Branston met us, announced the arrival, and handed me the stranger's credentials. My cousin and I stopped in the passage to read them.

'*That's* your uncle Silas's,' said Lady Knollys, touching one of the two letters with the tip of her finger.

'Shall we have lunch, Miss?'

'Certainly.' So Branston departed.

'Read it with me, Cousin Monica,' I said. And a very curious letter it was. It spoke as follows:—

'How can I thank my beloved niece for remembering her aged and forlorn kinsman at such a moment of anguish?'

I had written a note of a few, I dare say, incoherent words by the next post after
my dear father's death.

'It is, however, in the hour of bereavement that we most value the ties that are
broken, and yearn for the sympathy of kindred.'

Here came a little distich of French verse, of which I could only read *ciel*
and *l'amour.*

'Our quiet household here is clouded with a new sorrow. How inscrutable are
the ways of Providence! I—though a few years younger—how much the more
infirm—how shattered in energy and in mind—how mere a burden—how entirely
de trop—am spared to my sad place in a world where I can be no longer useful,
where I have but one business—prayer, but one hope—the tomb; and he—apparently so robust—the centre of so much good—so necessary to you—so necessary,
alas! to me—is taken! He is gone to his rest—for us, what remains but to bow our
heads, and murmur, "His will be done"? I trace these lines with a trembling hand,
while tears dim my old eyes. I did not think that any earthly event could have
moved me so profoundly. From the world I have long stood aloof. I once led a life
of pleasure—alas! of wickedness—as I now do one of austerity; but as I never was
rich, so my worst enemy will allow I never was avaricious. My sins, I thank my
Maker, have been of a more reducible kind, and have succumbed to the discipline
which Heaven has provided. To earth and its interests, as well as to its pleasures, I
have long been dead. For the few remaining years of my life I ask but quiet—an
exemption from the agitations and distractions of struggle and care, and I trust to
the Giver of all Good for my deliverance—well knowing, at the same time, that
whatever befalls will, under His direction, prove best. Happy shall I be, my dearest
niece, if in your most interesting and, in some respects, forlorn situation, I can be
of any use to you. My present religious adviser—of whom I ventured to ask counsel on your behalf—states that I ought to send some one to represent me at the
melancholy ceremony of reading the will which my beloved and now happy brother has, no doubt, left behind; and the idea that the experience and professional
knowledge possessed by the gentleman whom I have selected may possibly be of
use to you, my dearest niece, determines me to place him at your disposal. He is
the junior partner in the firm of Archer and Sleigh, who conduct any little business
which I may have from time to time; may I entreat your hospitality for him during
a brief stay at Knowl? I write, even for a moment, upon these small matters of
business with an effort—a painful one, but necessary. Alas! my brother! The cup of

bitterness is now full. Few and evil must the remainder of my old days be. Yet, while they last, I remain always for my beloved niece, that which all her wealth and splendour cannot purchase—a loving and faithful kinsman and friend,

SILAS RUTHYN.'

'Is not it a kind letter?' I said, while tears stood in my eyes.

'Yes,' answered Lady Knollys, drily.

'But don't you think it so, really?'

'Oh! kind, very kind,' she answered in the same tone, 'and perhaps a little cunning.'

'Cunning!—how?'

'Well, you know I'm a peevish old Tabby, and of course I scratch now and then, and see in the dark. I dare say Silas is sorry, but I don't think he is in sackcloth and ashes. He has reason to be sorry and anxious, and I say I think he is both; and you know he pities you very much, and also himself a good deal; and he wants money, and you—his beloved niece—have a great deal—and altogether it is an affectionate and prudent letter and he has sent his attorney here to make a note of the will and you are to give the gentleman his meals and lodging; and Silas, very thoughtfully, invites you to confide your difficuties and troubles to *his* solicitor. It is very kind, but not imprudent.'

'Oh, Cousin Monica, don't you think at such a moment it is hardly natural that he should form such petty schemes, even were he capable at other times of practising so low? Is it not judging him hardly? and you, you know, so little acquainted with him.'

'I told you, dear, I'm a cross old thing—and there's an end: and I really don't care two pence about him; and of the two I'd much rather he were no relation of ours.'

Now, was not this prejudice? I dare say in part it was. So, too, was my vehement predisposition in his favour. I am afraid we women are factionists; we always take a side, and nature has formed us for advocates rather than judges; and I think the function, if less dignified, is more amiable.

I sat alone at the drawing-room window, at nightfall, awaiting my cousin Monica's entrance.

Feverish and frightened I felt that night. It was a sympathy, I fancy, with the weather. The sun had set stormily. Though the air was still, the sky looked wild and storm-swept. The crowding clouds, slanting in the attitude of flight, reflected their own sacred aspect upon my spirits. My grief darkened with a wild presaging of danger, and a sense of the supernatural fell upon me. It was the saddest and most awful evening that had come since my beloved father's death.

All kinds of shapeless fears environed me in silence. For the first time, dire misgivings about the form of faith affrighted me. Who were these Swedenborgians who had got about him—no one could tell how—and held him so fast to the close of his life? Who was this bilious, bewigged, black-eyed Doctor Bryerly, whom none of us quite liked and all a little feared; who seemed to rise out of the ground, and came and went, no one knew whence or whither, exercising, as I imagined, a mysterious authority over him? Was it all good and true, or a heresy and a witchcraft? Oh, my beloved father! was it all well with you?

When Lady Knollys entered, she found me in floods of tears, walking, distractedly up and down the room. She kissed me in silence; she walked back and forward with me, and did her best to console me.

'I think, Cousin Monica, I would wish to see him once more. Shall we go up?'

'Unless you really wish it very much, I think, darling, you had better not mind it. It is happier to recollect them as they were; there's a change, you know, darling, and there is seldom any comfort in the sight.'

'But I do wish it *very* much. Oh! won't you come with me?'

And so I persuaded her, and up we went hand in hand, in the deepening twilight; and we halted at the end of the dark gallery, and I called Mrs. Rusk, growing frightened.

'Tell her to let us in, Cousin Monica,' I whispered.

'She wishes to see him, my lady—does she?' enquired Mrs. Rusk, in an undertone, and with a mysterious glance at me, as she softly fitted the key to the lock.

'Are you quite sure, Maud, dear?'

'Yes, yes.'

But when Mrs. Rusk entered bearing the candle, whose beam mixed dismally with the expiring twilight, disclosing a great black coffin standing upon trestles, near the foot of which she took her stand, gazing sternly into it, I lost heart again altogether and drew back.

'No, Mrs. Rusk, she won't; and I am very glad, dear,' she added to me. 'Come, Mrs. Rusk, come away. Yes, darling,' she continued to me, 'it is much better for you;' and she hurried me away, and down-stairs again. But the awful outlines of that large black coffin remained upon my imagination with a new and terrible sense of death.

I had no more any wish to see him. I felt a horror even of the room, and for more than an hour after a kind of despair and terror, such as I have never experienced before or since at the idea of death.

Cousin Monica had had her bed placed in my room, and Mary Quince's moved to the dressing-room adjoining it. For the first time the superstitious awe that follows death, but not immediately, visited me. The idea of seeing my father enter the room, or open the door and look in, haunted me. After Lady Knollys and I were in bed, I could not sleep. The wind sounded mournfully outside, and the small sounds, the rattlings, and strainings that responded from within, constantly startled me, and simulated the sounds of steps, of doors opening, of knockings, and so forth, rousing me with a palpitating heart as often as I fell into a doze.

At length the wind subsided, and these ambiguous noises abated, and I, fatigued, dropped into a quiet sleep. I was awakened by a sound in the gallery—which I could not define. A considerable time had passed, for the wind was now quite lulled. I sat up in my bed a good deal scared, listening breathlessly for I knew not what.

I heard a step moving stealthily along the gallery. I called my cousin Monica softly; and we both heard the door of the room in which my father's body lay unlocked, some one furtively enter, and the door shut.

'What can it be? Good Heavens, Cousin Monica, do you hear it? '

'Yes, dear; and it is two o'clock!

Everyone at Knowl was in bed at eleven. We knew very well that Mrs. Rusk was rather nervous, and would not, for worlds, go alone, and at such an hour, to the room. We called Mary Quince. We all three listened, but we heard no other sound. I set these things down here because they made so terrible an impression upon me at the time.

It ended by our peeping out, all three in a body, upon the gallery. Through each window in the perspective came its blue sheet of moonshine; but the door on which our attention was fixed was in the shade, and we thought we could discern the glare of a candle through the key-hole. While in whispers we were debating this point together, the door opened, the dusky light of a candle emerged, the shadow of a figure crossed it within, and in another moment the mysterious Doctor Bryerly—angular, ungainly, in the black cloth coat that fitted little better than a coffin—issued from the chamber, candle in hand; murmuring, I suppose, a prayer—it sounded like a farewell—stepped cautiously upon the gallery floor, shutting and locking the door upon the dead; and then having listened for a second, the saturnine figure, casting a gigantic and distorted shadow upon the ceiling and side-wall from the lowered candle, strode lightly down the long dark passage, away from us.

I can only speak for myself, and I can honestly say that I felt as much frightened as if I had just seen a sorcerer stealing from his unhallowed business. I think Cousin Monica was also affected in the same way, for she turned the key on the inside of the door when we entered. I do not think one of us believed at the moment that what we had seen was a Doctor Bryerly of flesh and blood, and yet the first thing we spoke of in the morning was Doctor Bryerly's arrival. The mind is a different organ by night and by day.

CHAPTER XXIII

I TALK WITH DOCTOR BRYERLY

Doctor Bryerly had, indeed, arrived at half-past twelve o'clock at night. His summons at the hall-door was little heard at our remote side of the old house of Knowl; and when the sleepy, half-dressed servant opened the door, the lank Doctor, in glossy black clothing, was standing alone, his portmanteau on its end upon the steps, and his vehicle disappearing in the shadows of the old trees.

In he came, sterner and sharper of aspect than usual.

'I've been expected? I'm Doctor Bryerly. Haven't I? So, let whoever is in charge of the body be called. I must visit it forthwith.'

So the Doctor sat in the back drawing-room, with a solitary candle; and Mrs. Rusk was called up, and, grumbling much and very peevish, dressed and went down, her ill-temper subsiding in a sort of fear as she approached the visitor.

'How do you do, Madam? A sad visit this. Is anyone watching in the room where the remains of your late master are laid?'

'No.'

'So much the better; it is a foolish custom. Will you please conduct me to the room? I must pray where he lies—no longer *he!* And be good enough to show me my bedroom, and so no one need wait up, and I shall find my way.'

Accompanied by the man who carried his valise, Mrs. Rusk showed him to his apartment; but he only looked in, and then glanced rapidly about to take 'the bearings' of the door.

'Thank you—yes. Now we'll proceed, here, along here? Let me see. A turn to the right and another to the left—yes. He has been dead some days. Is he yet in his coffin?'

'Yes sir; since yesterday afternoon.'

Mrs. Rusk was growing more and more afraid of this lean figure sheathed in shining black cloth, whose eyes glittered with a horrible sort of cunning, and whose long brown fingers groped before him, as if indicating the way by guess.

'But, of course, the lid's not on; you've not screwed him down, hey? '

'No, sir.'

'That's well. I must look on the face as I pray. He is in his place; I here on earth. He in the spirit; I in the flesh. The neutral ground lies there. So are carried the vibrations, and so the light of earth and heaven reflected back and forward—apaugasma, a wonderful though helpless engine, the ladder of Jacob, and behold the angels of God ascending and descending on it. Thanks, I'll take the key. Mysteries to those who *will* live altogether in houses of clay, no mystery to such as will use their eyes and read what is revealed. *This* candle, it is the longer, please; no—no need of a pair, thanks; just this, to hold in my hand. And remember, all depends upon the willing mind. Why do you look frightened? Where is your faith? Don't you know that spirits are about us at all times? Why should you fear to be near the body? The spirit is everything; the flesh profiteth nothing.'

'Yes, sir,' said Mrs. Rusk, making him a great courtesy in the threshold.

She was frightened by his eerie talk, which grew, she fancied, more voluble and energetic as they approached the corpse.

'Remember, then, that when you fancy yourself alone and wrapt in darkness, you stand, in fact, in the centre of a theatre, as wide as the starry floor of heaven, with an audience, whom no man can number, beholding you under a flood of light. Therefore, though your body be in solitude and your mortal sense in darkness, remember to walk as being in the light, surrounded with a cloud of witnesses. Thus walk; and when the hour comes, and you pass forth unprisoned from the tabernacle of the flesh, although it still has its relations and its rights'—and saying this, as he held the solitary candle aloft in the doorway, he nodded towards the coffin, whose large black form was faintly traceable against the shadows beyond—'you will rejoice; and being clothed upon with your house from on high, you will not be found naked. On the other hand, he that loveth corruption shall have enough thereof. Think upon these things. Goodnight.'

And the Swedenborgian Doctor stepped into the room, taking the candle with him, and closed the door upon the shadowy still-life there, and on his own sharp and swarthy visage, leaving Mrs. Rusk in a sort of panic in the dark alone, to find her way to her room the best way she could.

Early in the morning Mrs. Rusk came to my room to tell me that Doctor Bryerly was in the parlour, and begged to know whether I had not a message for him. I was already dressed, so, though it was dreadful seeing a stranger in my then mood, taking the key of the cabinet in my hand, I followed Mrs. Rusk downstairs.

Opening the parlour door, she stepped in, and with a little courtesy said,—

'Please, sir, the young mistress—Miss Ruthyn.'

Draped in black and very pale, tall and slight, 'the young mistress' was; and as I entered I heard a newspaper rustle, and the sound of steps approaching to meet me.

Face to face we met, near the door; and, without speaking, I made him a deep courtesy.

He took my hand, without the least indication on my part, in his hard lean grasp, and shook it kindly, but familiarly, peering with a stern sort of curiosity into my face as he continued to hold it. His ill-fitting, glossy black cloth, ungainly presence, and sharp, dark, vulpine features had in them, as I said before, the vulgarity of a Glasgow artisan in his Sabbath suit. I made an instantaneous motion to withdraw my hand, but he held it firmly.

Though there was a grim sort of familiarity, there was also decision, shrewdness, and, above all, kindness, in his dark face—a gleam on the whole of the masterly and the honest—that along with a certain paleness, betraying, I thought, restrained emotion, indicated sympathy and invited confidence.

'I hope, Miss, you are pretty well?' He pronounced 'pretty' as it is spelt. 'I have come in consequence of a solemn promise exacted more than a year since by your deceased father, the late Mr. Austin Ruthyn of Knowl, for whom I cherished a warm esteem, being knit besides with him in spiritual bonds. It has been a shock to you, Miss?'

'It has, indeed, sir.'

'I've a doctor's degree, I have—Doctor of Medicine, Miss. Like St. Luke, preacher and doctor. I was in business once, but this is better. As one footing fails, the Lord provides another. The stream of life is black and angry; how so many of us get across without drowning, I often wonder, The best way is not to look too far before—just from one stepping-stone to another; and though you may wet your feet, He won't let you drown—He has not allowed me.'

And Doctor Bryerly held up his head, and wagged it resolutely.

'You are born to this world's wealth; in its way a great blessing, though a great trial, Miss, and a great trust; but don't suppose you are destined to exemption from trouble on that account, any more than poor Emmanuel Bryerly. As the sparks fly upwards, Miss Ruthyn! Your cushioned carriage may overturn on the highroad, as I may stumble and fall upon the footpath. There are other troubles than debt and privation. Who can tell how long health may last, or when an accident may happen the brain; what mortifications may await you in your own high sphere; what unknown enemies may rise up in your path; or what slanders may asperse your name—ha, ha!' It is a wonderful equilibrium—a marvellous dispensation—ha, ha!' and he laughed with a shake of his head, I thought a little sarcastically, as if he was not sorry my money could not avail to buy immunity from the general curse.

'But what money can't do, *prayer* can—bear that in mind, Miss Ruthyn. We can all pray; and though thorns and snares, and stones of fire lie strewn in our way, we need not fear them. He will give His angels charge over us, and in their hands they will bear us up, for He hears and sees everywhere, and His angels are innumerable.'

He was now speaking gently and solemnly, and paused. But another vein of thought he had unconsciously opened in my mind, and I said—

'And had my dear papa no other medical adviser?'

He looked at me sharply, and flushed a little under his dark tint. His medical skill was, perhaps, the point on which his human vanity vaunted itself, and I dare say there was something very disparaging in my tone.

'And if he *had* no other, he might have done worse. I've had many critical cases in my hands, Miss Ruthyn. I can't charge myself with any miscarriage through ignorance. My diagnosis in Mr. Ruthyn's case has been verified by the result. But I was *not* alone; Sir Clayton Barrow saw him, and took my view; a note will reach him in London. But this, excuse me, is not to the present purpose. The late Mr. Ruthyn told me I was to receive a key from you, which would open a cabinet where he had placed his will—ha! thanks,—in his study. And, I think, as there may be directions about the funeral, it had better be read forthwith. Is there any gentleman—a relative or man of business near here, whom you would wish sent for?'

'No, none, thank you; I have confidence in you, sir.'

I think I spoke and looked frankly, for he smiled very kindly, though with closed lips.

'And you may be sure, Miss Ruthyn, your confidence shall not be disappointed.' Here was a long pause. 'But you are very young, and you must have some one by in your interest, who has some experience in business. Let me see. Is not the Rector, Dr. Clay, at hand? In the town?—very good; and Mr. Danvers, who manages the estate, *he* must come. And get Grimston—you see I know all the names—Grimston, the attorney; for though he was not employed about this will, he has been Mr. Ruthyn's solicitor a great many years: we must have Grimston; for, as I suppose you know, though it is a short will, it is a very strange one. I expostulated, but you know he was very decided when he took a view. He read it to you, eh?'

'No, sir.'

'Oh, but he told you so much as relates to you and your uncle,
'Mr. Silas Ruthyn, of Bartram-Haugh?'

'No, indeed, sir.'

'Ha! I wish he had.'

And with these words Doctor Bryerly's countenance darkened.

'Mr. Silas Ruthyn is a religious man?'

'Oh, *very*!' said I.

'You've seen a good deal of him?'

'No, I never saw him,' I answered.

'H'm? Odder and odder! But he's a good man, isn't he?'

'Very good, indeed, sir—a very religious man.'

Doctor Bryerly was watching my countenance as I spoke, with a sharp and anxious eye; and then he looked down, and read the pattern of the carpet like bad news, for a while, and looking again in my face, askance, he said—

'He was very near joining *us*—on the point. He got into correspondence with Henry Voerst, one of our best men. They call us Swedenborgians, you know; but I dare say that won't go much further, now. I suppose, Miss Ruthyn, one o'clock would be a good hour, and I am sure, under the circumstances, the gentlemen will make a point of attending.'

'Yes, Dr. Bryerly, the notes shall be sent, and my cousin, Lady Knollys, would I am sure attend with me while the will is being read—there would be no objection to her presence?'

'None in the world. I can't be quite sure who are joined with me as executors. I'm almost sorry I did not decline; but it is too late regretting. One thing you must believe Miss Ruthyn: in framing the provisions of the will I was never consulted— although I expostulated against the only very unusual one it contains when I heard it. I did so strenuously, but in vain. There was one other against which I protested—having a right to do so—with better effect. In no other way does the will in any respect owe anything to my advice or dissuasion. You will please believe this; also that I am your friend. Yes, indeed, it is my duty.'

The latter words he spoke looking down again, as it were in soliloquy; and thanking him, I withdrew.

When I reached the hall, I regretted that I had not asked him to state distinctly what arrangements the will made so nearly affecting, as it seemed, my relations with my uncle Silas, and for a moment I thought of returning and requesting an explanation. But then, I bethought me, it was not very long to wait till one o'clock—so *he,* at least, would think, I went up-stairs, therefore, to the 'school-room,' which we used at present as a sitting-room, and there I found Cousin Monica awaiting me.

'Are you quite well, dear?' asked Lady Knollys, as she came to meet and kiss me.

'Quite well, Cousin Monica.'

'No nonsense, Maud! you're as white as that handkerchief—what's the matter? Are you ill—are you frightened? Yes, you're trembling—you're terrified, child.'

'I believe I *am* afraid. There *is* something in poor papa's will about Uncle Silas—about *me*. I don't know—Doctor Bryerly says, and he seems so uncomfortable and frightened himself, I am sure it is something very bad. I am *very* much frightened—I am—I *am*. Oh, Cousin Monica! you won't leave me?'

So I threw my arms about her neck, clasping her very close, and we kissed one another, I crying like a frightened child—and indeed in experience of the world I was no more.

CHAPTER XXIV

THE OPENING OF THE WILL

Perhaps the terror with which I anticipated the hour of one, and the disclosure of the unknown undertaking to which I had bound myself, was irrational and morbid. But, honestly, I doubt it; my tendency has always been that of many other weak characters, to act impetuously, and afterwards to reproach myself for consequences which I have, perhaps, in reality, had little or no share in producing.

It was Doctor Bryerly's countenance and manner in alluding to a particular provision in my father's will that instinctively awed me. I have seen faces in a nightmare that haunted me with an indescribable horror, and yet I could not say wherein lay the fascination. And so it was with his—an omen, a menace, lurked in its sallow and dismal glance.

'You must not be so frightened, darling,' said Cousin Monica. 'It is foolish; it *is, really;* they can't cut off your head, you know: they can't really harm you in any essential way. If it involved a risk of a little money, you would not mind it; but men are such odd creatures—they measure all sacrifices by money. Doctor Bryerly would look just as you describe, if you were doomed to lose 500*l.*, and yet it would not kill you.'

A companion like Lady Knollys is reassuring; but I could not take her comfort altogether to heart, for I felt that she had no great confidence in it herself.

There was a little French clock over the mantelpiece in the school-room, which

I consulted nearly every minute. It wanted now but ten minutes of one.

'Shall we go down to the drawing-room, dear?' said Cousin Knollys, who was growing restless like me.

So down-stairs we went, pausing by mutual consent at the great window at the stair-head, which looks out on the avenue. Mr. Danvers was riding his tall, grey horse at a walk, under the wide branches toward the house, and we waited to see him get off at the door. In his turn he loitered there, for the good Rector's gig, driven by the Curate, was approaching at a smart ecclesiastical trot.

Doctor Clay got down, and shook hands with Mr. Danvers and after a word or two, away drove the Curate with that upward glance at the windows from which so few can refrain.

I watched the Rector and Mr. Danvers loitering on the steps as a patient might the gathering of surgeons who are to perform some unknown operation. They, too, glanced up at the window as they turned to enter the house, and I drew back. Cousin Monica looked at her watch.

'Four minutes only. Shall we go to the drawing-room?'

Waiting for a moment to let the gentlemen get by on the way to the study, we, accordingly, went down, and I heard the Rector talk of the dangerous state of Grindleston bridge, and wondered how he could think of such things at a time of sorrow. Everything about those few minutes of suspense remains fresh in my recollection. I remember how they loitered and came to a halt at the corner of the oak passage leading to the study, and how the Rector patted the marble head and smoothed the inflexible tresses of William Pitt, as he listened to Mr. Danvers' details about the presentment; and then, as they went on, I recollect the boisterous nose-blowing that suddenly resounded from the passage, and which I then referred, and still refer, intuitively to the Rector.

We had not been five minutes in the drawing-room when Branston entered, to say that the gentlemen I had mentioned were all assembled in the study.

'Come, dear,' said Cousin Monica; and leaning on her arm I reached the study door. I entered, followed by her. The gentlemen arrested their talk and stood up, those who were sitting, and the Rector came forward very gravely, and in low tones, and very kindly, greeted me. There was nothing emotional in this salutation, for though my father never quarrelled, yet an immense distance separated him from all his neighbours, and I do not think there lived a human being who knew him at more than perhaps a point or two of his character.

Considering how entirely he secluded himself, my father was, as many people living remember, wonderfully popular in his county. He was neighbourly in every-

thing except in seeing company and mixing in society. He had magnificent shooting, of which he was extremely liberal. He kept a pack of hounds at Dollerton,
with which all his side of the county hunted through the season. He never refused
any claim upon his purse which had the slightest show of reason. He subscribed to
every fund, social, charitable, sporting, agricultural, no matter what, provided the
honest people of his county took an interest in it, and always with a princely hand;
and although he shut himself up, no one could say that he was inaccessible, for he
devoted hours daily to answering letters, and his checque-book contributed largely
in those replies. He had taken his turn long ago as High Sheriff; so there was an
end of that claim before his oddity and shyness had quite secluded him. He refused
the Lord-Lieutenancy of his county; he declined every post of personal distinction
connected with it. He could write an able as well as a genial letter when he pleased;
and his appearances at public meetings, dinners, and so forth were made in this
epistolary fashion, and, when occasion presented, by magnificent contributions
from his purse.

If my father had been less goodnatured in the sporting relations of his vast
estates, or less magnificent in dealing with his fortune, or even if he had failed to
exhibit the intellectual force which always characterised his letters on public matters, I dare say that his oddities would have condemned him to ridicule, and possibly to dislike. But every one of the principal gentlemen of his county, whose judgment was valuable, has told me that he was a remarkably able man, and that his
failure in public life was due to his eccentricities, and in no respect to deficiency in
those peculiar mental qualities which make men feared and useful in Parliament.

I could not forbear placing on record this testimony to the high mental and the
kindly qualities of my beloved father, who might have passed for a misanthrope or
a fool. He was a man of generous nature and powerful intellect, but given up to
the oddities of a shyness which grew with years and indulgence, and became inflexible with his disappointments and affliction.

There was something even in the Rector's kind and ceremonious greeting which
oddly enough reflected the mixed feelings in which awe was not without a place,
with which his neighbours had regarded my dear father.

Having done the honours—I am sure looking woefully pale—I had time to
glance quietly at the only figure there with which I was not tolerably familiar. This
was the junior partner in the firm of Archer and Sleigh who represented my uncle
Silas—a fat and pallid man of six-and-thirty, with a sly and evil countenance, and
it has always seemed to me, that ill dispositions show more repulsively in a pale fat
face than in any other.

Doctor Bryerly, standing near the window, was talking in a low tone to Mr. Grimston, our attorney.

I heard good Dr. Clay whisper to Mr. Danvers—

'Is not that Doctor Bryerly—the person with the black—the black—it's a wig, I think—in the window, talking to Abel Grimston?'

'Yes; that's he.'

'Odd-looking person—one of the Swedenborg people, is not he?' continued the Rector.

'So I am told.'

'Yes,' said the Rector, quietly; and he crossed one gaitered leg over the other, and, with fingers interlaced, twiddled his thumbs, as he eyed the monstrous sectary under his orthodox old brows with a stern inquisitiveness. I thought he was meditating theologic battle.

But Dr. Bryerly and Mr. Grimston, still talking together, began to walk slowly from the window, and the former said in his peculiar grim tones—

'I beg pardon, Miss Ruthyn; perhaps you would be so good as to show us which of the cabinets in this room your late lamented father pointed out as that to which this key belongs.'

I indicated the oak cabinet.

'Very good, ma'am—very good,' said Doctor Bryerly, as he fumbled the key into the lock.

Cousin Monica could not forbear murmuring—

'Dear! what a brute!'

The junior partner, with his dumpy hands in his pocket, poked his fat face over Mr. Grimston's shoulder, and peered into the cabinet as the door opened.

The search was not long. A handsome white paper enclosure, neatly tied up in pink tape, and sealed with large red seals, was inscribed in my dear father's hand:— 'Will of Austin R. Ruthyn, of Knowl.' Then, in smaller characters, the date, and in the corner a note—'This will was drawn from my instructions by Gaunt, Hogg, and Hatchett, Solicitors, Great Woburn Street, London, A. R. R.'

'Let *me* have a squint at that indorsement, please, gentlemen,' half whispered the unpleasant person who represented my uncle Silas.

'*'Tisn't* an indorsement. There, look—a memorandum on an envelope,' said Abel Grimston, gruffly.

'Thanks—all right—that will do,' he responded, himself making a pencil-note of it, in a long clasp-book which he drew from his coat-pocket.

The tape was carefully cut, and the envelope removed without tearing the writing, and forth came the will, at sight of which my heart swelled and fluttered up to my lips, and then dropped down dead as it seemed into its place.

'Mr. Grimston, you will please to read it,' said Doctor Bryerly, who took the direction of the process. 'I will sit beside you, and as we go along you will be good enough to help us to understand technicalities, and give us a lift where we want it.'

'It's a short will,' said Mr. Grimston, turning over the sheets *very*—considering. Here's a codicil.'

'I did not see that,' said Doctor Bryerly.

'Dated only a month ago.'

'Oh!' said Doctor Bryerly, putting on his spectacles. Uncle Silas's ambassador, sitting close behind, had insinuated his face between Doctor Bryerly's and the reader's of the will.

'On behalf of the surviving brother of the testator,' interposed the delegate, just as Abel Grimston had cleared his voice to begin, 'I take leave to apply for a copy of this instrument. It will save a deal of trouble, if the young lady as represents the testator here has no objection.'

'You can have as many copies as you like when the will is proved,' said Mr. Grimston.

'I know that; but supposing as all's right, where's the objection?'

'Just the objection there always is to acting irregular,' replied Mr. Grimston.

'You don't object to act disobliging, it seems.'

'You can do as I told you,' replied Mr. Grimston.

'Thank you for nothing,' murmured Mr. Sleigh.

And the reading of the will proceeded, while he made elaborate notes of its contents in his capacious pocket-book.

'I, Austin Alymer Ruthyn Ruthyn, being, I thank God, of sound mind and perfect recollection,' &c, &c.; and then came a bequest of all his estates real, chattels real, copyrights, leases, chattels, money, rights, interests, reversions, powers, plate, pictures, and estates and possessions whatsoever, to four persons—Lord Ilbury, Mr. Penrose Creswell of Creswell, Sir William Aylmer, Bart., and Hans Emmanuel Bryerly, Doctor of Medicine, to have and to hold,' &c. &c. Whereupon my Cousin Monica ejaculated 'Eh?' and Doctor Bryerly interposed—

'Four trustees, ma'am. We take little but trouble—you'll see go on.'

Then it came out that all this multifarious splendour was bequeathed in trust for me, subject to a bequest of 15,000*l.* to his only brother, Silas Aylmer Ruthyn, and 3,500*l.* each to the two children of his said brother; and lest any doubt should arise by reason of his, the testator's decease as to the continuance of the arrangement by way of lease under which he enjoyed his present habitation and farm, he left him the use of the mansion-house and lands of Bartram-Haugh, in the county of Derbyshire, and of the lands of so-and-so and so-and-so, adjoining thereto, in the said county, for the term of his natural life, on payment of a rent of 5*s.* per annum, and subject to the like conditions as to waste, &c., as are expressed in the said lease.

'By your leave, may I ask is them dispositions all the devises to my client, which is his only brother, as it seems to me you've seen the will before?' enquired Mr. Sleigh.

'Nothing more, unless there is something in the codicil,' answered Dr. Bryerly. But there was no mention of him in the codicil.

Mr. Sleigh threw himself back in his chair, and sneered, with the end of his pencil between his teeth. I hope his disappointment was altogether for his client. Mr. Danvers fancied, he afterwards said, that he had probably expected legacies which might have involved litigation, or, at all events, law costs, and perhaps a stewardship; but this was very barren; and Mr. Danvers also remarked, that the man was a very low practitioner, and wondered how my uncle Silas could have commissioned such a person to represent him.

So far the will contained nothing of which my most partial friend could have complained. The codicil, too, devised only legacies to servants, and a sum of 1,000*l.*, with a few kind words, to Monica, Lady Knollys, and a further sum of 3,000*l.* to Dr. Bryerly, stating that the legatee had prevailed upon him to erase from the draft of his will a bequest to him to that amount, but that, in consideration of all the trouble devolving upon him as trustee, he made that bequest by his codicil; and with these arrangements the permanent disposition of his property was completed.

But that direction to which he and Doctor Bryerly had darkly alluded, was now to come, and certainly it was a strange one. It appointed my uncle Silas my sole guardian, with full parental authority over me until I should have reached the age of twenty-one, up to which time I was to reside under his care at Bartram-Haugh, and it directed the trustees to pay over to him yearly a sum of 2,000*l.* during the continuance of the guardianship for my suitable maintenance, education, and expenses.

You have now a sufficient outline of my father's will. The only thing I painfully felt in this arrangement was, the break-up—the dismay that accompanies the disappearance of home. Otherwise, there was something rather pleasurable in the idea. As long as I could remember, I had always cherished the same mysterious curiosity about my uncle, and the same longing to behold him. This was about to be gratified. Then there was my cousin Milicent, about my own age. My life had been so lonely, that I had acquired none of those artificial habits that induce the fine-lady nature—a second, and not always a very amiable one. She had lived a solitary life, like me. What rambles and readings we should have together! what confidences and castle-buildings! and then there was a new country and a fine old place, and the sense of interest and adventure that always accompanies change in our early youth.

There were four letters all alike with large, red seals, addressed respectively to each of the trustees named in the will. There was also one addressed to Silas Alymer Ruthyn, Esq., Bartram-Haugh Manor, &c. &c., which Mr. Sleigh offered to deliver. But Doctor Bryerly thought the post-office was the more regular channel. Uncle Silas's representative was questioning Doctor Bryerly in an under-tone.

I turned my eyes on my cousin Monica—I felt so inexpressibly relieved—expecting to see a corresponding expression in her countenance. But I was startled. She looked ghastly and angry. I stared in her face, not knowing what to think. Could the will have personally disappointed her? Such doubts, though we fancy in after-life they belong to maturity and experience only, do sometimes cross our minds in youth. But the suggestion wronged Lady Knollys, who neither expected nor wanted anything, being rich, childless, generous, and frank. It was the unexpected character of her countenance that scared me, and for a moment the shock called up corresponding moral images.

Lady Knollys, starting up, raised her head, so as to see over Mr. Sleigh's shoulder, and biting her pale lip, she cleared her voice and demanded—

'Doctor Bryerly, pray, sir, is the reading concluded?'

'Concluded? Quite. Yes, nothing more,' he answered with a nod, and continued his talk with Mr. Danvers and Abel Grimston.

'And to whom,' said Lady Knollys, with an effort, 'will the property belong, in case—in case my little cousin here should die before she comes of age?'

'Eh? Well—wouldn't it go to the heir-at-law and next of kin?' said Doctor Bryerly, turning to Abel Grimston.

'Ay—to be sure,' said the attorney, thoughtfully.

'And who is that?' pursued my cousin.

'Well, her uncle, Mr. Silas Ruthyn. He's both heir-at-law and next of kin,' pursued Abel Grimston.

'Thank you,' said Lady Knollys.

Doctor Clay came forward, bowing very low, in his standing collar and single-breasted coat, and graciously folded my hand in his soft wrinkled grasp—

'Allow me, my dear Miss Ruthyn, while expressing my regret that we are to lose you from among our little flock—though I trust but for a short, a very short time—to say how I rejoice at the particular arrangement indicated by the will we have just heard read. My curate, William Fairfield, resided for some years in the same spiritual capacity in the neighbourhood of your, I will say, admirable uncle, with occasional intercourse with whom he was favoured—may I not say blessed?— a true Christian Churchman—a Christian gentleman. Can I say more? A most happy, happy choice.' A very low bow here, with eyes nearly dosed, and a shake of the head. 'Mrs. Clay will do herself the honour of waiting upon you, to pay her respects, before you leave Knowl for your temporary sojourn in another sphere.'

So, with another deep bow—for I had become a great personage all at once—he let go my hand cautiously and delicately, as if he were setting down a curious china tea-cup. And I courtesied low to him, not knowing what to say, and then to the assembly generally, who all bowed. And Cousin Monica whispered, briskly, 'Come away,' and took my hand with a very cold and rather damp one, and led me from the room.

CHAPTER XXV

I HEAR FROM UNCLE SILAS

Without saying a word, Cousin Monica accompanied me to the school-room, and on entering she shut the door, not with a spirited clang, but quietly and determinedly.

'Well, dear,' she said, with the same pale, excited countenance, 'that certainly is a sensible and charitable arrangement. I could not have believed it possible, had I not heard it with my ears.'

'About my going to Bartram-Haugh?'

'Yes, exactly so, under Silas Ruthyn's guardianship, to spend two—*three*—of the most important years of your education and your life under that roof. Is *that*, my dear, what was in your mind when you were so alarmed about what you were to be called upon to do, or undergo?'

'No, no, indeed. I had no notion what it might be. I was afraid of something serious,' I answered.

'And, my dear Maud, did not your poor father speak to you as if it *was* something serious?' said she. And so it *is*, I can tell you, something serious, and *very* serious and I think it ought to be prevented, and I certainly *will* prevent it if I possibly can.'

I was puzzled utterly by the intensity of Lady Knollys' protest. I looked at her, expecting an explanation of her meaning; but she was silent, looking steadfastly on the jewels on her right-hand fingers, with which she was drumming a staccato march on the table, very pale, with gleaming eyes, evidently thinking deeply. I began to think she *had* a prejudice against my uncle Silas.

'He is not very rich,' I commenced.

'Who?' said Lady Knollys.

'Uncle Silas,' I replied.

'No, certainly; he's in debt,' she answered.

'But then, how very highly Doctor Clay spoke of him!' I pursued.

'Don't talk of Doctor Clay. I do think that man is the greatest goose I ever heard talk. I have no patience with such men,' she replied.

I tried to remember what particular nonsense Doctor Clay had uttered, and I could recollect nothing, unless his eulogy upon my uncle were to be classed with that sort of declamation.

'Danvers is a very proper man and a good accountant, I dare say; but he is either a very deep person, or a fool—*I* believe a fool. As for your attorney, I suppose he knows his business, and also his interest, and I have no doubt he will consult it. I begin to think the best man among them, the shrewdest and the most reliable, is that vulgar visionary in the black wig. I saw him look at you, Maud, and I liked his face, though it is abominably ugly and vulgar, and cunning, too; but I think he's a just man, and I dare say with right feelings—I'm *sure* he has.'

I was quite at a loss to divine the gist of my cousin's criticism.

'I'll have some talk with Dr. Bryerly; I feel convinced he takes my view, and we must really think what had best be done.'

'Is there anything in the will, Cousin Monica, that does not appear?' I asked, for I was growing very uneasy. 'I wish you would tell me. What view do you mean?'

'No view in particular; the view that a desolate old park, and the house of a *neglected* old man, who is very poor, and has been desperately foolish, is not the right place for you, particularly at your years. It is quite shocking, and I *will* speak to Doctor Bryerly. May I ring the bell, dear?'

'Certainly;' and I rang it.

'When does he leave Knowl?'

I could not tell. Mrs. Rusk, however, was sent for, and she could tell us that he had announced his intention of taking the night train from Drackleton, and was to leave Knowl for that station at half-past six o'clock.

'May Rusk give or send him a message from me, dear?' asked Lady Knollys.

Of course she might.

'Then please let him know that I request he will be so good as to allow me a very few minutes, just to say a word before he goes.'

'You kind cousin!' I said, placing my two hands on her shoulders, and looking earnestly in her face; 'you are anxious about me, more than you say. Won't you tell me why? I am much more unhappy, really, in ignorance, than if I understood the cause.'

'Well, dear, haven't I told you? The two or three years of your life which are to form you are destined to be passed in utter loneliness, and, I am sure, neglect. You can't estimate the disadvantage of such an arrangement. It is full of disadvantages. How it could have entered the head of poor Austin—although I should not say that, for I am sure I do understand it, —but how he could for any purpose have directed such a measure is quite inconceivable. I never heard of anything so foolish and abominable, and I will prevent it if I can.'

At that moment Mrs. Rusk announced that Doctor Bryerly would see Lady Knollys; at any time she pleased before his departure.

'It shall be this moment, then,' said the energetic lady, and up she stood, and made that hasty general adjustment before the glass, which, no matter under what circumstances, and before what sort of creature one's appearance is to be made, is a duty that every woman owes to herself. And I heard her a moment after, at the stair-head, directing Branston to let Dr. Bryerly know that she awaited him in the drawing-room.

And now she was gone, and I began to wonder and speculate. Why should my cousin Monica make all this fuss about, after all, a very natural arrangement? My uncle, whatever he might have been, was now a good man—a religious man—perhaps a little severe; and with this thought a dark streak fell across my sky.

A cruel disciplinarian! had I not read of such characters?—lock and key, bread and water, and solitude! To sit locked up all night in a dark out-of-the-way room, in a great, ghosty, old-fashioned house, with no one nearer than the other wing. What years of horror in one such night! Would not this explain my poor father's hesitation, and my cousin Monica's apparently disproportioned opposition? When an idea of terror presents itself to a young person's mind, it transfixes and fills the vision, without respect of probabilities or reason.

My uncle was now a terrible old martinet, with long Bible lessons, lectures, pages of catechism, sermons to be conned by rote, and an awful catalogue of punishments for idleness, and what would seem to him impiety. I was going, then, to a frightful isolated reformatory, where for the first time in my life I should be subjected to a rigorous and perhaps barbarous discipline.

All this was an exhalation of fancy, but it quite overcame me. I threw myself, in my solitude, on the floor, upon my knees, and prayed for deliverance—prayed that Cousin Monica might prevail with Doctor Bryerly, and both on my behalf with the Lord Chancellor, or the High Sheriff, or whoever else my proper deliverer might be; and when my cousin returned, she found me quite in an agony.

'Why, you little fool! what fancy has taken possession of you now?' she cried.

And when my new terror came to light, she actually laughed a little to reassure me, and she said—

'My dear child, your uncle Silas will never put you through your duty to your neighbour; all the time you are under his roof you'll have idleness and liberty enough, and too much, I fear. It is neglect, my dear, not discipline, that I'm afraid of.'

'I think, dear Cousin Monica, you are afraid of something more than neglect,' I said, relieved, however.

'I *am* afraid of more than neglect,' she replied promptly; 'but I hope my fears may turn out illusory, and that possibly they may be avoided. And now, for a few hours at least, let us think of something else. I rather like that Doctor Bryerly. I could not get him to say what I wanted. I don't think he's Scotch, but he is very cautious, and I am sure, though he would not say so, that he thinks of the matter exactly as I do. He says that those fine people, who are named as his co-trustees, won't take any trouble, and will leave everything to him, and I am sure he is right. So we must not quarrel with him, Maud, nor call him hard names, although he certainly is intolerably vulgar and ugly, and at times very nearly impertinent—I suppose without knowing, or indeed very much caring.'

We had a good deal to think of, and talked incessantly. There were bursts and interruptions of grief, and my kind cousin's consolations. I have often since been so lectured for giving way to grief, that I wonder at the patience exercised by her during this irksome visit. Then there was some reading of that book whose claims are always felt in the terrible days of affliction. After that we had a walk in the yew garden, that quaint little cloistered quadrangle—the most solemn, sad, and antiquated of gardens.

'And now, my dear, I must really leave you for two or three hours. I have ever so many letters to write, and my people must think I'm dead by this time.'

So till tea-time I had poor Mary Quince, with her gushes of simple prattle and her long fits of vacant silence, for my companion. And such a one, who can con over by rote the old friendly gossip about the dead, talk about their ways, and looks, and likings, without much psychologic refinement, but with a simple admiration and liking that never measured them critically, but always with faith and love, is in general about as comfortable a companion as one can find for the common moods of grief.

It is not easy to recall in calm and happy hours the sensations of an acute sorrow that is past. Nothing, by the merciful ordinance of God, is more difficult to remember than pain. One or two great agonies of that time I do remember, and they remain to testify of the rest, and convince me, though I can see it no more, how terrible all that period was.

Next day was the funeral, that appalling necessity; smuggled away in whispers, by black familiars, unresisting, the beloved one leaves home, without a farewell, to darken those doors no more; henceforward to lie outside, far away, and forsaken, through the drowsy heats of summer, through days of snow and nights of tempest, without light or warmth, without a voice near. Oh, Death, king of terrors! The body quakes and the spirit faints before thee. It is vain, with hands clasped over our eyes, to scream our reclamation; the horrible image will not be excluded. We have just the word spoken eighteen hundred years ago, and our trembling faith. And through the broken vault the gleam of the Star of Bethlehem.

I was glad in a sort of agony when it was over. So long as it remained to be done, something of the catastrophe was still suspended. Now it was all over.

The house so strangely empty. No owner—no master! I with my strange momentary liberty, bereft of that irreplaceable love, never quite prized until it is lost. Most people have experienced the dismay that underlies sorrow under such circumstances.

The apartment of the poor outcast from life is now dismantled. Beds and curtains taken down, and furniture displaced; carpets removed, windows open and doors locked; the bedroom and anteroom were henceforward, for many a day, uninhabited. Every shocking change smote my heart like a reproach.

I saw that day that Cousin Monica had been crying for the first time, I think, since her arrival at Knowl; and I loved her more for it, and felt consoled. My tears have often been arrested by the sight of another person weeping, and I never could explain why. But I believe that many persons experience the same odd reaction.

The funeral was conducted, in obedience to his brief but peremptory direction, very privately and with little expense. But of course there was an attendance, and the tenants of the Knowl estate also followed the hearse to the mausoleum, as it is called, in the park, where he was laid beside my dear mother. And so the repulsive ceremonial of that dreadful day was over. The grief remained, but there was rest from the fatigue of agitation, and a comparative calm supervened.

It was now the stormy equinoctial weather that sounds the wild dirge of autumn, and marches the winter in. I love, and always did, that grand undefinable music, threatening and bewailing, with its strange soul of liberty and desolation.

By this night's mail, as we sat listening to the storm, in the drawing-room at Knowl, there reached me a large letter with a great black seal, and a wonderfully deep-black border, like a widow's crape. I did not recognise the handwriting; but on opening the funereal missive, it proved to be from my uncle Silas, and was thus expressed:—

'MY DEAREST NIECE,—This letter will reach you, probably, on the day which consigns the mortal remains of my beloved brother, Austin, your dear father, to the earth. Sad ceremony, from taking my mournful part in which I am excluded by years, distance, and broken health. It will, I trust, at this season of desolation, be not unwelcome to remember that a substitute, imperfect—unworthy—but most affectionately zealous, for the honoured parent whom you have just lost, has been appointed, in me, your uncle, by his will. I am aware that you were present during the reading of it, but I think it will be for our mutual satisfaction that our new and more affectionate relations should be forthwith entered upon. My conscience and your safety, and I trust convenience, will thereby be consulted. You will, my dear niece, remain at Knowl, until a few simple arrangements shall have been completed for your reception at this place. I will then settle the details of your little journey to us, which shall be performed as comfortably and easily as possible. I humbly pray that this affliction may be sanctified to us all, and that in our new duties we may be supported, comforted, and directed. I need not remind you that I now stand to you *in loco parentis,* which means in the relation of father, and you will not forget that you are to remain at Knowl until you hear further from me.

'I remain, my dear niece, your most affectionate uncle and guardian,

SILAS RUTHYN.'

'P.S.—Pray present my respects to Lady Knollys, who, I understand, is sojourning at Knowl. I would observe that a lady who cherishes, I have reason to fear, unfriendly feelings against your uncle, is not the most desirable companion for his ward. But upon the express condition that I am not made the subject of your discussions—a distinction which could not conduce to your forming a just and respectful estimate of me—I do not interpose my authority to bring your intercourse to an immediate close.'

As I read this postscript, my cheek tingled as if I had received a box on the ear. Uncle Silas was as yet a stranger. The menace of authority was new and sudden, and I felt with a pang of mortification the full force of the position in which my dear father's will had placed me.

I was silent, and handed the letter to my cousin, who read it with a kind of smile until she came, as I supposed, to the postscript, when her countenance, on which my eyes were fixed, changed, and with flushed cheeks she knocked the hand that held the letter on the table before her, and exclaimed—

'Did I ever hear! Well, if this isn't impertinence! *What* an old man that is!'

There was a pause, during which Lady Knollys held her head high with a frown, and sniffed a little.

'I did not intend to talk about him, but now I *will*. I'll talk away just whatever I like; and I'll stay here just as long as you let me, Maud, and you need not be one atom afraid of him. Our intercourse to an "immediate close," indeed! I only wish he were here. He should hear something!'

And Cousin Monica drank off her entire cup of tea at one draught, and then she said, more in her own way—

'I'm better!' and drew a long breath, and then she laughed a little in a waggish defiance. 'I wish we had him here, Maud, and *would* not we give him a bit of our minds! And this before the poor will is so much as proved!'

'I am almost glad he wrote that postscript; for although I don't think he has any authority in that matter while I am under my own roof,' I said, extemporising a legal opinion, 'and, therefore, shan't obey him, it has somehow opened my eyes to my real situation.'

I sighed, I believe, very desolately, for Lady Knollys came over and kissed me very gently and affectionately.

'It really seems, Maud, as if he had a supernatural sense, and heard things through the air over fifty miles of heath and hill. You remember how, just as he was probably writing that very postscript yesterday, I was urging you to come and stay with me, and planning to move Dr. Bryerly in our favour. And so I will, Maud, and to me you *shall* come—my guest, mind—I should be so delighted; and really if Silas is under a cloud, it has been his own doing, and I don't see that it is your business to fight his battle. He can't live very long. The suspicion, whatever it is dies with him, and what could poor dear Austin prove by his will but what everybody knew quite well before—his own strong belief in Silas's innocence? What an awful storm! The room trembles. Don't you like the sound? What they used to call 'wolving' in the old organ at Dorminster!'

CHAPTER XXVI

THE STORY OF UNCLE SILAS

And so it was like the yelling of phantom hounds and hunters, and the thunder of their coursers in the air—a furious, grand and supernatural music, which in my fancy made a suitable accompaniment to the discussion of that enigmatical person—martyr—angel—demon—Uncle Silas—with whom my fate was now so strangely linked, and whom I had begun to fear.

'The storm blows from that point,' I said, indicating it with my hand and eye, although the window shutters and curtains were closed. 'I saw all the trees bend that way this evening. That way stands the great lonely wood, where my darling father and mother lie. Oh, how dreadful on nights like this, to think of them—a vault!—damp, and dark, and solitary—under the storm.'

Cousin Monica looked wistfully in the same direction, and with a short sigh she said—

'We think too much of the poor remains, and too little of the spirit which lives for ever. I am sure they are happy.' And she sighed again. 'I wish I dare hope as confidently for myself. Yes, Maud, it is sad. We are such materialists, we can't help feeling so. We forget how well it is for us that our present bodies are not to last always. They are constructed for a time and place of trouble—plainly mere temporary machines that wear out, constantly exhibiting failure and decay, and with such tremendous capacity for pain. The body lies alone, and so it ought, for it is plainly its good Creator's will; it is only the tabernacle, not the person, who is clothed upon after death, Saint Paul says, "with a house which is from heaven." So Maud, darling, although the thought will trouble us again and again, there is nothing in it; and the poor mortal body is only the cold ruin of a habitation which *they* have forsaken before we do. So this great wind, you say, is blowing toward us from the wood there. If so, Maud, it is blowing from Bartram-Haugh, too, over the trees and chimneys of that old place, and the mysterious old man, who is quite right in thinking I don't like him; and I can fancy him an old enchanter in his castle, waving his familiar spirits on the wind to fetch and carry tidings of our occupations here.'

I lifted my head and listened to the storm, dying away in the distance sometimes—sometimes swelling and pealing around and above us—and through the dark and solitude my thoughts sped away to Bartram-Haugh and Uncle Silas.

'This letter,' I said at last, 'makes me feel differently. I think he is a stern old man—is he?'

'It is twenty years, now, since I saw him,' answered Lady Knollys. 'I did not choose to visit at his house.'

'Was that before the dreadful occurrence at Bartram-Haugh?'

'Yes—before, dear. He was not a reformed rake, but only a ruined one then. Austin was very good to him. Mr. Danvers says it is quite unaccountable how Silas can have made away with the immense sums he got from his brother from time to time without benefiting himself in the least. But, my dear, he played; and trying to help a man who plays, and is unlucky—and some men are, I believe, habitually unlucky—is like trying to fill a vessel that has no bottom. I think, by-the-by, my hopeful nephew, Charles Oakley, plays. Then Silas went most unjustifiably into all manner of speculations, and your poor father had to pay everything. He lost something quite astounding in that bank that ruined so many country gentlemen—poor Sir Harry Shackleton, in Yorkshire, had to sell half his estate. But your kind father went on helping him, up to his marriage—I mean in that extravagant way which was really totally useless.'

'Has my aunt been long dead?'

'Twelve or fifteen years—more, indeed—she died before your poor mamma. She was very unhappy, and I am sure would have given her right hand she had never married Silas.'

'Did you like her?'

'No, dear; she was a coarse, vulgar woman.'

'Coarse and vulgar, and Uncle Silas's wife!' I echoed in extreme surprise, for Uncle Silas was a man of fashion—a beau in his day—and might have married women of good birth and fortune, I had no doubt, and so I expressed myself.

'Yes, dear; so he might, and poor dear Austin was very anxious he should, and would have helped him with a handsome settlement, I dare say, but he chose to marry the daughter of a Denbigh innkeeper.'

'How utterly incredible!' I exclaimed.

'Not the least incredible, dear—a kind of thing not at all so uncommon as you fancy.'

'What!—a gentleman of fashion and refinement marry a person——'

'A barmaid!—just so,' said Lady Knollys. 'I think I could count half a dozen men of fashion who, to my knowledge, have ruined themselves just in a similar way.'

'Well, at all events, it must be allowed that in this he proved himself altogether unworldly.'

'Not a bit unworldly, but very vicious,' replied Cousin Monica, with a careless little laugh. 'She was very beautiful, curiously beautiful, for a person in her station. She was very like that Lady Hamilton who was Nelson's sorceress—elegantly beautiful, but perfectly low and stupid. I believe, to do him justice, he only intended to ruin her; but she was cunning enough to insist upon marriage. Men who have never in all their lives denied themselves the indulgence of a single fancy, cost what it may, will not be baulked even by that condition if the *penchant* be only violent enough.'

I did not half understand this piece of worldly psychology, at which Lady Knollys seemed to laugh.

'Poor Silas, certainly he struggled honestly against the consequences, for he tried after the honeymoon to prove the marriage bad. But the Welsh parson and the innkeeper papa were too strong for him, and the young lady was able to hold her struggling swain fast in that respectable noose—and a pretty prize he proved!'

'And she died, poor thing, broken-hearted, I heard.'

'She died, at all events, about ten years after her marriage; but I really can't say about her heart. She certainly had enough ill-usage, I believe, to kill her; but I don't know that she had feeling enough to die of it, if it had not been that she drank: I am told that Welsh women often do. There was jealousy, of course, and brutal quarrelling, and all sorts of horrid stories. I visited at Bartram-Haugh for a year or two, though no one else would. But when that sort of thing began, of course I gave it up; it was out of the question. I don't think poor Austin ever knew how bad it was. And then came that odious business about wretched Mr. Charke. You know he—he committed suicide at Bartram.'

'I never heard about that,' I said; and we both paused, and she looked sternly at the fire, and the storm roared and ha-ha-ed till the old house shook again.

'But Uncle Silas could not help that,' I said at last.

'No, he could not help it,' she acquiesced unpleasantly.

'And Uncle Silas was'—I paused in a sort of fear.

'He was suspected by some people of having killed him'—she completed the sentence.

There was another long pause here, during which the storm outside bellowed and hooted like an angry mob roaring at the windows for a victim. An intolerable and sickening sensation overpowered me.

'But *you* did not suspect him, Cousin Knollys?' I said, trembling very much.

'No,' she answered very sharply. 'I told you so before. Of course I did not.'

There was another silence.

'I wish, Cousin Monica,' I said, drawing close to her, 'you had not said *that* about Uncle Silas being like a wizard, and sending his spirits on the wind to listen. But I'm very glad you never suspected him.' I insinuated my cold hand into hers, and looked into her face I know not with what expression. She looked down into mine with a hard, haughty stare, I thought.

'Of *course* I never suspected him; and *never* ask me *that* question again, Maud Ruthyn.'

Was it family pride, or what was it, that gleamed so fiercely from her eyes as she said this? I was frightened—I was wounded—I burst into tears.

'What is my darling crying for? I did not mean to be cross. *Was* I cross?' said this momentary phantom of a grim Lady Knollys, in an instant translated again into kind, pleasant Cousin Monica, with her arms about my neck.

'No, no, indeed—only I thought I had vexed you; and, I believe, thinking of Uncle Silas makes me nervous, and I can't help thinking of him nearly always.'

'Nor can I, although we might both easily find something better to think of. Suppose we try?' said Lady Knollys.

'But, first, I must know a little more about that Mr. Charke, and what circumstances enabled Uncle Silas's enemies to found on his death that wicked slander, which has done no one any good, and caused some persons so much misery. There is Uncle Silas, I may say, ruined by it; and we all know how it darkened the life of my dear father.'

'People will talk, my dear. Your uncle Silas had injured himself before that in the opinion of the people of his county. He was a black sheep, in fact. Very bad stories were told and believed of him. His marriage certainly was a disadvantage, you know, and the miserable scenes that went on in his disreputable house—all that predisposed people to believe ill of him.'

'How long is it since it happened?'

'Oh, a long time; I think before you were born,' answered she.

'And the injustice still lives—they have not forgotten it yet?' said I, for such a period appeared to me long enough to have consigned anything in its nature perishable to oblivion.

Lady Knollys smiled.

'Tell me, like a darling cousin, the whole story as well as you can recollect it.

Who was Mr. Charke?'

'Mr. Charke, my dear, was a gentleman on the turf—that is the phrase, I think—one of those London men, without birth or breeding, who merely in right of their vices and their money are admitted to associate with young dandies who like hounds and horses, and all that sort of thing. That set knew him very well, but of course no one else. He was at the Matlock races, and your uncle asked him to Bartram-Haugh; and the creature, Jew or Gentile, whatever he was, fancied there was more honour than, perhaps, there really was in a visit to Bartram-Haugh.'

'For the kind of person you describe, it *was,* I think, a rather unusual honour to be invited to stay in the house of a man of Uncle Ruthyn's birth.'

'Well, so it was perhaps; for though they knew him very well on the course, and would ask him to their tavern dinners, they would not, of course, admit him to the houses where ladies were. But Silas's wife was not much regarded at Bartram-Haugh. Indeed, she was very little seen, for she was every evening tipsy in her bed-room, poor woman!'

'How miserable!' I exclaimed.

'I don't think it troubled Silas very much, for she drank gin, they said, poor thing, and the expense was not much; and, on the whole, I really think he was glad she drank, for it kept her out of his way, and was likely to kill her. At this time your poor father, who was thoroughly disgusted at his marriage, had stopped the supplies, you know, and Silas was very poor, and as hungry as a hawk, and they said he pounced upon this rich London gamester, intending to win his money. I am telling you now all that was said afterwards. The races lasted I forget how many days, and Mr. Charke stayed at Bartram-Haugh all this time and for some days after. It was thought that poor Austin would pay all Silas's gambling debts, and so this wretched Mr. Charke made heavy wagers with him on the races, and they played very deep, besides, at Bartram. He and Silas used to sit up at night at cards. All these particulars, as I told you, came out afterwards, for there was an inquest, you know, and then Silas published what he called his "statement," and there was a great deal of most distressing correspondence in the newspapers.'

'And why did Mr. Charke kill himself?' I asked.

'Well, I will tell you first what all are agreed about. The second night after the races, your uncle and Mr. Charke sat up till between two and three o'clock in the morning, quite by themselves, in the parlour. Mr. Charke's servant was at the Stag's Head Inn at Feltram, and therefore could throw no light upon what occurred at night at Bartram-Haugh; but he was there at six o'clock in the morning, and very early at his master's door by his direction. He had locked it, as was his habit, upon the inside, and the key was in the lock, which turned out afterwards a very important point. On knocking he found that he could not awaken his master, because, as it appeared when the door was forced open, his master was lying dead at his bedside, not in a pool, but a perfect pond of blood, as they described it, with his throat cut.'

'How horrible!' cried I.

'So it was. Your uncle Silas was called up, and greatly shocked of course, and he did what I believe was best. He had everything left as nearly as possible in the exact state in which it had been found, and he sent his own servant forthwith for the coroner, and, being himself a justice of the peace, he took the depositions of Mr. Charke's servant while all the incidents were still fresh in his memory.'

'Could anything be more straightforward, more right and wise?' I said.

'Oh, nothing of course,' answered Lady Knollys, I thought a little drily.

CHAPTER XXVII

MORE ABOUT TOM CHARKE'S SUICIDE

So the inquest was held, and Mr. Manwaring, of Wail Forest, was the only juryman who seemed to entertain the idea during the inquiry that Mr. Charke had died by any hand but his own.

'And how *could* he fancy such a thing?' I exclaimed indignantly.

'Well, you will see the result was quite enough to justify them in saying as they did, that he died by his own hand. The window was found fastened with a screw on the inside, as it had been when the chambermaid had arranged it at nine o'clock; no one could have entered through it. Besides, it was on the third story, and the rooms are lofty, so it stood at a great height from the ground, and there was no ladder long enough to reach it. The house is built in the form of a hollow square, and Mr. Charke's room looked into the narrow courtyard within. There is but one door leading into this, and it did not show any sign of having been open for years. The door was locked upon the inside, and the key in the lock, so that nobody could have made an entrance that way either, for it was impossible, you see, to unlock the door from the outside.'

'And how could they affect to question anything so clear?' I asked.

'There did come, nevertheless, a kind of mist over the subject, which gave those who chose to talk unpleasantly an opportunity of insinuating suspicions, though they could not themselves find the clue of the mystery. In the first place, it appeared that he had gone to bed very tipsy, and that he was heard singing and noisy in his room while getting to bed—not the mood in which men make away with themselves. Then, although his own razor was found in that dreadful blood (it is shocking to have to hear all this) near his right hand, the fingers of his left were cut to the bone. Then the memorandum book in which his bets were noted was nowhere to be found. That, you know, was very odd. His keys were there attached to a chain. He wore a great deal of gold and trinkets. I saw him, wretched man, on the course. They had got off their horses. He and your uncle were walking on the course.'

'Did he look like a gentleman?' I inquired, as I dare say, other young ladies would.

'He looked like a Jew, my dear. He had a horrid brown coat with a velvet cape, curling black hair over his collar, and great whiskers, very high shoulders, and he was puffing a cigar straight up into the air. I was shocked to see Silas in such company.'

'And did his keys discover anything?' I asked.

'On opening his travelling desk and a small japanned box within it a vast deal less money was found than was expected—in fact, very little. Your uncle said that he had won some of it the night before at play, and that Charke complained to him when tipsy of having had severe losses to counterbalance his gains on the races. Besides, he had been paid but a small part of those gains. About his book it appeared that there were little notes of bets on the backs of letters, and it was said that he sometimes made no other memorandum of his wagers—but this was disputed—and among those notes there was not one referring to Silas. But, then, there was an omission of all allusion to his transactions with two other well-known gentlemen. So that was not singular.'

'No, certainly; that was quite accounted for,' said I.

'And then came the question,' continued she, 'what motive could Mr. Charke possibly have had for making away with himself.'

'But is not that very difficult to make out in many cases?' I interposed.

'It was said that he had some mysterious troubles in London, at which he used to hint. Some people said that he really was in a scrape, but others that there was no such thing, and that when he talked so he was only jesting. There was no suspicion during the inquest that your uncle Silas was involved, except those questions of Mr. Manwaring's.'

'What were they?' I asked.

'I really forget; but they greatly offended your uncle, and there was a little scene in the room. Mr. Manwaring seemed to think that some one had somehow got into the room. Through the door it could not be, nor down the chimney, for they found an iron bar across the flue, near the top in the masonry. The window looked into a courtyard no bigger than a ball-room. They went down and examined it, but, though the ground beneath was moist, they could not discover the slightest trace of a footprint. So far as they could make out, Mr. Charke had hermetically sealed himself into his room, and then cut his throat with his own razor.'

'Yes,' said I, 'for it was all secured—that is, the window and the door—upon the inside, and no sign of any attempt to get in.'

'Just so; and when the walls were searched, and, as your uncle Silas directed, the wainscoting removed, some months afterwards, when the scandal grew loudest, then it was evident that there was no concealed access to the room.'

'So the answer to all those calumnies was simply that the crime was impossible,' said I.' How dreadful that such a slander should have required an answer at all!'

'It was an unpleasant affair even then, although I cannot say that anyone supposed Silas guilty; but you know the whole thing was disreputable, that Mr. Charke was a discreditable inmate, the occurrence was horrible, and there was a glare of publicity which brought into relief the scandals of Bartram-Haugh. But in a little time it became, all on a sudden, a great deal worse.'

My cousin paused to recollect exactly.

'There were very disagreeable whispers among the sporting people in London. This person, Charke, had written two letters. Yes—two. They were published about two months after, by the villain to whom they were written; he wanted to extort money. They were first talked of a great deal among that set in town; but the moment they were published they produced a sensation in the country, and a storm of newspaper commentary. The first of these was of no great consequence, but the second was very startling, embarrassing, and even alarming.'

'What was it, Cousin Monica?' I whispered.

'I can only tell you in a general way, it is so very long since I read it; but both were written in the same kind of slang, and parts as hard to understand as a prize fight. I hope you never read those things.'

I satisfied this sudden educational alarm, and Lady Knollys proceeded.

'I am afraid you hardly hear me, the wind makes such an uproar. Well, listen. The letter said distinctly, that he, Mr. Charke, had made a very profitable visit to Bartram-Haugh, and mentioned in exact figures for how much he held your uncle Silas's I.O.U.'s, for he could not pay him. I can't say what the sum was. I only remember that it was quite frightful. It took away my breath when I read it.'

'Uncle Silas had lost it?' I asked.

'Yes, and owed it; and had given him those papers called I.O.U.'s promising to pay, which, of course, Mr. Charke had locked up with his money and the insinuation was that Silas had made away with him, to get rid of this debt, and that he had also taken a great deal of his money.

'I just recollect these points which were exactly what made the impression,' continued Lady Knollys, after a short pause; 'the letter was written in the evening of the last day of the wretched man's life, so that there had not been much time for your uncle Silas to win back his money; and he stoutly alleged that he did not owe Mr. Charke a guinea. It mentioned an enormous sum as being actually owed by Silas; and it cautioned the man, an agent, to whom he wrote, not to mention the circumstance, as Silas could only pay by getting the money from his wealthy brother, who would have the management; and he distinctly said that he had kept the matter very close at Silas's request. That, you know, was a very awkward letter, and all the worse that it was written in brutally high spirits, and not at all like a man meditating an exit from the world. You can't imagine what a sensation the publication of these letters produced. In a moment the storm was up, and certainly Silas did meet it bravely—yes, with great courage and ability, What a pity he did not early enter upon some career of ambition! Well, well, it is idle regretting. He suggested that the letters were forgeries. He alleged that Charke was in the habit of boasting, and telling enormous falsehoods about his gambling transactions, especially in his letters. He reminded the world how often men affect high animal spirits at the very moment of meditating suicide. He alluded, in a manly and graceful way, to his family and their character. He took a high and menacing tone with his adversaries, and he insisted that what they dared to insinuate against him was physically impossible.'

I asked in what form this vindication appeared.

'It was a letter, printed as a pamphlet; everybody admired its ability, ingenuity, and force, and it was written with immense rapidity.'

'Was it at all in the style of his letters?' I innocently asked.

My cousin laughed.

'Oh, dear, no! Ever since he avowed himself a religious character, he had written nothing but the most vapid and nerveless twaddle. Your poor dear father used to send his letters to me to read, and I sometimes really thought that Silas was losing his faculties; but I believe he was only trying to write in character.'

'I suppose the general feeling was in his favour?' I said.

'I don't think it was, anywhere; but in his own county it was certainly unanimously against him. There is no use in asking why; but so it was, and I think it would have been easier for him with his unaided strength to uproot the Peak than to change the convictions of the Derbyshire gentlemen. They were all against him. Of course there were predisposing causes. Your uncle published a very bitter attack upon them, describing himself as the victim of a political conspiracy: and I recollect he mentioned that from the hour of the shocking catastrophe in his house, he had forsworn the turf and all pursuits and amusements connected with it. People sneered, and said he might as well go as wait to be kicked out.'

'Were there law-suits about all this?' I asked.

'Everybody expected that there would, for there were very savage things printed on both sides, and I think, too, that the persons who thought worst of him expected that evidence would yet turn up to convict Silas of the crime they chose to impute; and so years have glided away, and many of the people who remembered the tragedy of Bartram-Haugh, and took the strongest part in the denunciation, and ostracism that followed, are dead, and no new light had been thrown upon the occurrence, and your uncle Silas remains an outcast. At first he was quite wild with rage, and would have fought the whole county, man by man, if they would have met him. But he had since changed his habits and, as he says, his aspirations altogether.'

'He has become religious.'

'The only occupation remaining to him. He owes money; he is poor; he is isolated; and he says, sick and religious. Your poor father, who was very decided and inflexible, never helped him beyond the limit he had prescribed, after Silas's *mésalliance*. He wanted to get him into Parliament, and would have paid his expenses, and made him an allowance; but either Silas had grown lazy, or he understood his position better than poor Austin, or he distrusted his powers, or possibly he really is in ill-health; but he objected his religious scruples. Your poor papa thought self-assertion possible, where an injured man has right to rely upon, but he had been very long out of the world, and the theory won't do. Nothing is harder than to get a person who has once been effectually slurred, received again. Silas, I think, was right. I don't think it was practicable.

'Dear child, how late it is!' exclaimed Lady Knollys suddenly, looking at the Louis Quatorze clock, that crowned the mantelpiece.

It was near one o'clock. The storm had a little subsided, and I took a less agitated and more confident view of Uncle Silas than I had at an earlier hour of that evening.

'And what do you think of him?' I asked.

Lady Knollys drummed on the table with her finger points as she looked into the fire.

'I don't understand metaphysics, my dear, nor witchcraft. I sometimes believe in the supernatural, and sometimes I don't. Silas Ruthyn is himself alone, and I can't define him, because I don't understand him. Perhaps other souls than human are sometimes born into the world, and clothed in flesh. It is not only about that dreadful occurrence, but nearly always throughout his life; early and late he has puzzled me. I have tried in vain to understand him. But at one time of his life I am sure he was awfully wicked—eccentric indeed in his wickedness—gay, frivolous, secret, and dangerous. At one time I think he could have made poor Austin do almost anything; but his influence vanished with his marriage, never to return again. No; I don't understand him. He always bewildered me, like a shifting face, sometimes smiling, but always sinister, in an unpleasant dream.'

CHAPTER XXVIII

I AM PERSUADED

So now at last I had heard the story of Uncle Silas's mysterious disgrace. We sat silent for a while, and I, gazing into vacancy, sent him in a chariot of triumph, chapletted, ringed, and robed through the city of imagination, crying after him, 'Innocent! innocent! martyr and crowned!' All the virtues and honesties, reason and conscience, in myriad shapes—tier above tier of human faces—from the crowded pavement, crowded windows, crowded roofs, joined in the jubilant acclamation, and trumpeters trumpeted, and drums rolled, and great organs and choirs through open cathedral gates, rolled anthems of praise and thanksgiving, and the bells rang out, and cannons sounded, and the air trembled with the roaring harmony; and Silas Ruthyn, the full-length portrait, stood in the burnished chariot, with a proud, sad, clouded face, that rejoiced not with the rejoicers, and behind him the slave, thin as a ghost, white-faced, and sneering something in his ear: while I and all the city went on crying' Innocent! innocent! martyr and crowned!' And now the reverie was ended; and there were only Lady Knollys' stern, thoughtful face, with the pale light of sarcasm on it, and the storm outside thundering and lamenting desolately.

It was very good of Cousin Monica to stay with me so long. It must have been unspeakably tiresome. And now she began to talk of business at home, and plainly to prepare for immediate flight, and my heart sank.

I know that I could not then have defined my feelings and agitations. I am not sure that I even now could. Any misgiving about Uncle Silas was, in my mind, a questioning the foundations of my faith, and in itself an impiety. And yet I am not sure that some such misgiving, faint, perhaps, and intermittent, may not have been at the bottom of my tribulation.

I was not very well. Lady Knollys had gone out for a walk. She was not easily tired, and sometimes made a long excursion. The sun was setting now, when Mary Quince brought me a letter which had just arrived by the post. My heart throbbed violently. I was afraid to break the broad black seal. It was from Uncle Silas. I ran over in toy mind all the unpleasant mandates which it might contain, to try and prepare myself for a shock. At last I opened the letter. It directed me to hold myself in readiness for the journey to Bartram-Haugh. It stated that I might bring two maids with me if I wished so many, and that his next letter would give me the details of my route, and the day of my departure for Derbyshire; and he said that I ought to make arrangements about Knowl during my absence, but that he was hardly the person properly to be consulted on that matter. Then came a prayer that he might be enabled to acquit himself of his trust to the full satisfaction of his conscience, and that I might enter upon my new relations in a spirit of prayer.

I looked round my room, so long familiar, and now so endeared by the idea of parting and change. The old house—dear, dear Knowl, how could I leave you and all your affectionate associations, and kind looks and voices, for a strange land!

With a great sigh I took Uncle Silas's letter, and went down stairs to the drawing-room. From the lobby window, where I loitered for a few moments, I looked out upon the well-known forest-trees. The sun was down. It was already twilight, and the white vapours of coming night were already filming their thinned and yellow foliage. Everything looked melancholy. How little did those who envied the young inheritrex of a princely fortune suspect the load that lay at her heart, or, bating the fear of death, how gladly at that moment she would have parted with her life!

Lady Knollys had not yet returned, and it was darkening rapidly; a mass of black clouds stood piled in the west, through the chasms of which was still reflected a pale metallic lustre.

The drawing-room was already very dark; but some streaks of this cold light fell upon a black figure, which would otherwise have been unseen, leaning beside the curtains against the window frame.

It advanced abruptly, with creaking shoes; it was Doctor Bryerly.

I was startled and surprised, not knowing how he had got there. I stood staring at him in the dusk rather awkwardly, I am afraid.

'How do you do, Miss Ruthyn?' said he, extending his hand, long, hard, and brown as a mummy's, and stooping a little so as to approach more nearly, for it was not easy to see in the imperfect light. 'You're surprised, I dare say, to see me here so soon again?'

'I did not know you had arrived. I am glad to see you, Doctor Bryerly. Nothing unpleasant, I hope, has happened?'

'No, nothing unpleasant, Miss. The will has been lodged, and we shall have probate in due course; but there has been something on my mind, and I'm come to ask you two or three questions which you had better answer very considerately. Is Miss Knollys still here?'

'Yes, but she is not returned from her walk.'

'I am glad she is here. I think she takes a sound view, and women understand one another better. As for me, it is plainly my duty to put it before you as it strikes me, and to offer all I can do in accomplishing, should you wish it, a different arrangement. You don't know your uncle, you said the other day?'

'No, I've never seen him.'

'You understand your late father's intention in making you his ward?'

'I suppose he wished to show his high opinion of my uncle's fitness for such a trust.'

'That's quite true; but the nature of the trust in this instance is extraordinary.'

'I don't understand.'

'Why, if you die before you come to the age of twenty-one, the entire of the property will go to him—do you see?—and he has the custody of your person in the meantime; you are to live in his house, under his care and authority. You see now, I think, how it is; and I did not like it when your father read the will to me, and I said so. Do *you?*'

I hesitated to speak, not sure that I quite comprehended him.

'And the more I think of it, the less I like it, Miss,' said Doctor Bryerly, in a calm, stern tone.

'Merciful Heaven! Doctor Bryerly, you can't suppose that I should not be as safe in my uncle's house as in the Lord Chancellor's?' I ejaculated, looking full in his face.

'But don't you see, Miss, it is not a fair position to put your uncle in,' replied he, after a little hesitation.

'But suppose *he* does not think so. You know, if he does, he may decline it.'

'Well that's true—but he won't. Here is his letter'—and he produced it— 'announcing officially that he means to accept the office; but I think he ought to be told it is not *delicate*, under all circumstances. You know, Miss, that your uncle, Mr. Silas Ruthyn, was talked about unpleasantly once.'

'You mean'—I began.

'I mean about the death of Mr. Charke, at Bartram-Haugh.'

'Yes, I have heard that,' I said; he was speaking with a shocking *aplomb.*

'We assume, of course, *unjustly,* but there are many who think quite differently.'

'And possibly, Doctor Bryerly, it was for that very reason that my dear papa made him my guardian.'

'There can be no doubt of that, Miss; it was to purge him of that scandal.'

'And when he has acquitted himself honourably of that trust, don't you think such a proof of confidence so honourably fulfilled must go far to silence his traducers?'

'Why, if all goes well, it may do a little; but a great deal less than you fancy. But take it that you happen to *die*, Miss, during your minority. We are all mortal, and there are three years and some months to go; how will it be then? Don't you see? just fancy how people will talk.'

'I think you know that my uncle is a religious man?' said I.

'Well, Miss, what of that?' he asked again.

'He is—he has suffered intensely,' I continued. 'He has long retired from the world; he is very religious. Ask our curate, Mr. Fairfield, if you doubt it.'

'But I am not disputing it, Miss; I'm only supposing what may happen—an accident, we'll call it small-pox, diphtheria, *that's* going very much. Three years and three months, you know, is a long time. You proceed to Bartram-Haugh, thinking you have much goods laid up for many years; but your Creator, you know, may say, "Thou fool, this day is thy soul required of thee." You go—and what pray is thought of your uncle, Mr. Silas Ruthyn, who walks in for the entire inheritance, and who has long been abused like a pickpocket, or worse, in his own county, I'm told?'

'You are a religious man, Doctor Bryerly, according to your lights?' I said.

The Swedenborgian smiled.

'Well, knowing that he is so too, and having yourself experienced the power of religion, do not you think him deserving of every confidence? Don't you think it well that he should have this opportunity of exhibiting both his own character and the reliance which my dear papa reposed on it, and that we should leave all consequences and contingencies in the hands of Heaven?'

'It appears to have been the will of Heaven hitherto,' said Doctor Bryerly—I could not see with what expression of face, but he was looking down, and drawing little diagrams with his stick on the dark carpet, and spoke in a very low tone 'that your uncle should suffer under this ill report. In countervailing the appointment of Providence, we must employ our reason, with conscientious diligence, as to the means, and if we find that they are as likely to do mischief as good, we have no right to expect a special interposition to turn our experiment into an ordeal. I think you ought to weigh it well—I am sure there are reasons against it. If you make up your mind that you would rather be placed under the care, say of Lady Knollys, I will endeavour all I can to effect it.'

'That could not be done without his consent, could it?' said I.

'No, but I don't despair of getting that—on terms, of course,' remarked he.

'I don't quite understand,' I said.

'I mean, for instance, if he were allowed to keep the allowance for your maintenance—eh?'

'I mistake my uncle Silas very much,' I said, 'if that allowance is any object whatever to him compared with the moral value of the position. If he were deprived of that, I am sure he would decline the other.'

'We might try him at all events,' said Doctor Bryerly, on whose dark sinewy features, even in this imperfect light, I thought I detected a smile.

'Perhaps,' said I, 'I appear very foolish in supposing him actuated by any but sordid motives; but he is my near relation, and I can't help it, sir.'

'That is a very serious thing, Miss Ruthyn,' he replied. 'You are very young, and cannot see it at present, as you will hereafter. He is very religious, you say, and all that, but his house is not a proper place for you. It is a solitude—its master an outcast, and it has been the repeated scene of all sorts of scandals, and of one great crime; and Lady Knollys thinks your having been domesticated there will be an injury to you all the days of your life.'

'So I do, Maud,' said Lady Knollys, who had just entered the room unperceived,—' How do you do, Doctor Bryerly?—a serious injury. You have no idea how entirely that house is condemned and avoided, and the very name of its inmates tabooed.'

'How monstrous—how cruel!' I exclaimed.

'Very unpleasant, my dear, but perfectly natural. You are to recollect that quite independently of the story of Mr. Charke, the house was talked about, and the county people had cut your uncle Silas long before that adventure was dreamed of; and as to the circumstance of your being placed in his charge by his brother, who took, from strong family feeling, a totally one-sided view of the affair from the first, having the slightest effect in restoring his position in the county, you must quite give that up, Except me, if he will allow me, and the clergyman, not a soul in the country will visit at Bartram-Haugh. They may pity you, and think the whole thing the climax of folly and cruelty; but they won't visit at Bartram, or know Silas, or have anything to do with his household.'

'They will see, at all events, what my dear papa's opinion was.'

'They know that already,' answered she, 'and it has not, and ought not to have, the slightest weight with them. There are people there who think themselves just as great as the Ruthyns, or greater; and your poor father's idea of carrying it by a demonstration was simply the dream of a man who had forgotten the world, and learned to exaggerate himself in his long seclusion. I know he was beginning him-self to hesitate; and I think if he had been spared another year that provision of his will would have been struck out.'

Doctor Bryerly nodded, and he said—

'And if he had the power to dictate *now*, would he insist on that direction? It is a mistake every way, injurious to you, his child; and should you happen to die dur-ing your sojourn under your uncle's care, it would woefully defeat the testator's object, and raise such a storm of surmise and inquiry as would awaken all England, and send the old scandal on the wing through the world again.'

'Doctor Bryerly will, I have no doubt, arrange it all. In fact, I do not think it would be very difficult to bring Silas to terms; and if you do not consent to his trying, Maud, mark my words, you will live to repent it.'

Here were two persons viewing the question from totally different points; both perfectly disinterested both in their different ways, I believe, shrewd and even wise and both honourable, urging me against it, and in a way that undefinably alarmed my imagination, as well as moved my reason. I looked from one to the other—there was a silence. By this time the candies had come, and we could see one another.

'I only wait your decision, Miss Ruthyn,' said the trustee, 'to see your uncle. If his advantage was the chief object contemplated in this arrangement, he will be the best judge whether his interest is really best consulted by it or no; and I think he will clearly see that it is *not* so, and will answer accordingly.'

'I cannot answer now—you must allow me to think it over—I will do my best. I am very much obliged, my dear Cousin Monica, you are so very good, and you too, Doctor Bryerly.'

Doctor Bryerly by this time was looking into his pocket-book, and did not acknowledge my thanks even by a nod.

'I must be in London the day after to-morrow. Bartram-Haugh is nearly sixty miles from here, and only twenty of that by rail, I find. Forty miles of posting over those Derbyshire mountains is slow work; but if you say *try*, I'll see him tomorrow morning.'

'You must say try—you *must*, my dear Maud.'

'But how can I decide in a moment? Oh, dear Cousin Monica, I am so distracted! '

'But *you* need not decide at all; the decision rests with him. Come; he is more competent than you. You *must* say yes.'

Again I looked from her to Doctor Bryerly, and from him to her again. I threw my arms about her neck, and hugging her closely to me, I cried—

'Oh, Cousin Monica, dear Cousin Monica, advise me. I am a wretched creature. You must advise me.'

I did not know till now how irresolute a character was mine.

I knew somehow by the tone of her voice that she was smiling as she answered—

'Why, dear, I have advised you; I *do* advise you;' and then she added, impetuously, 'I entreat and implore, if you really think I love you, that you will *follow* my advice. It is your duty to leave your uncle Silas, whom you believe to be more competent than you are, to decide, after full conference with Doctor Bryerly, who knows more of your poor father's views and intentions in making that appointment than either you or I.'

'Shall I say, yes?' I cried, drawing her close, and kissing her helplessly. 'Oh, tell me—tell me to say, yes.'

'Yes, of course, *yes*. She agrees, Doctor Bryerly, to your kind proposal.'

'I am to understand so?' he asked.

'Very well—yes, Doctor Bryerly,' I replied.

'You have resolved wisely and well,' said he, briskly, like a man who has got a care off his mind.

'I forgot to say, Doctor Bryerly—it was very rude—that you must stay here to-night.'

'He *can't*, my dear,' interposed Lady Knolly's; 'it is a long way.'

'He will dine. Won't you, Doctor Bryerly?'

'No; he can't. You know you can't, sir,' said my cousin, peremptorily. 'You must not worry him, my dear, with civilities he can't accept. He'll bid us good-bye this moment. Good-bye, Doctor Bryerly. You'll write immediately; don't wait till you reach town. Bid him good-bye, Maud. I'll say a word to you in the hall.'

And thus she literally hurried him out of the room, leaving me in a state of amazement and confusion, not able to review my decision—unsatisfied, but still unable to recall it.

I stood where they had left me, looking after them, I suppose, like a fool.

Lady Knollys returned in a few minutes. If I had been a little cooler I was shrewd enough to perceive that she had sent poor Doctor Bryerly away upon his travels, to find board and lodging half-way to Bartram, to remove him forthwith from my presence, and thus to make my decision—if mine it was—irrevocable.

'I applaud you, my dear,' said Cousin Knollys, in her turn embracing me heartily. 'You are a sensible little darling, and have done exactly what you ought to have done.'

'I hope I have,' I faltered.

'Hope? fiddle! stuff! the thing's as plain as a pikestaff.'

And in came Branston to say that dinner was served.

CHAPTER XXIX

HOW THE AMBASSADOR FARED

Lady Knollys, I could plainly see, when we got into the brighter lights at the dinner table, was herself a good deal excited; she was relieved and glad, and was garrulous during our meal, and told me all her early recollections of dear papa. Most of them I had heard before; but they could not be told too often.

Notwithstanding my mind sometimes wandered, *often* indeed, to the conference so unexpected, so suddenly decisive, possibly so momentous; and with a dismayed uncertainly, the question—had I done right?—was always before me.

I dare say my cousin understood my character better, perhaps, after all my honest self-study, then I do even now. Irresolute, suddenly reversing my own decisions, impetuous in action as she knew me, she feared, I am sure, a revocation of my commission to Doctor Bryerly, and thought of the countermand I might send galloping after him.

So, kind creature, she laboured to occupy my thoughts, and when one theme was exhausted found another, and had always her parry prepared as often as I directed a reflection or an enquiry to the re-opening of the question which she had taken so much pains to close.

That night I was troubled. I was already upbraiding myself. I could not sleep, and at last sat up in bed, and cried. I lamented my weakness in having assented to Doctor Bryerly's and my cousin's advice. Was I not departing from my engagement to my dear papa? Was I not consenting that my Uncle Silas should be induced to second my breach of faith by a corresponding perfidy?

Lady Knollys had done wisely in despatching Doctor Bryerly so promptly; for, most assuredly, had he been at Knowl next morning when I came down I should have recalled my commission.

That day in the study I found four papers which increased my perturbation. They were in dear papa's handwriting, and had an indorsement in these words— 'Copy of my letter addressed to —, one of the trustees named in my will! Here, then, were the contents of those four sealed letters which bad excited mine and Lady Knollys' curiosity on the agitating day on which the will was read.

It contained these words:—

'I name my oppressed and unhappy brother, Silas Ruthyn, residing at my house of Bartram-Haugh, as guardian of the person of my beloved child, to convince the world if possible, and failing that, to satisfy at least all future generations of our family, that his brother, who knew him best, had implicit confidence in him, and that he deserved it. A cowardly and preposterous slander, originating in political malice, and which would never have been whispered had he not been poor and imprudent, is best silenced by this ordeal of purification. All I possess goes to him if my child dies under age; and the custody of her person I commit meanwhile to him alone, knowing that she is as safe in his as she could have been under my own care. I rely upon your remembrance of our early friendship to make this known wherever an opportunity occurs, and also to say what your sense of justice may warrant.'

The other letters were in the same spirit. My heart sank like lead as I read them. I quaked with fear. What had I done? My father's wise and noble vindication of our dishonoured name I had presumed to frustrate. I had, like a coward, receded from my easy share in the task; and, merciful Heaven, I had broken my faith with the dead!

With these letters in my hand, white with fear, I flew like a shadow to the drawing-room where Cousin Monica was, and told her to read them. I saw by her countenance how much alarmed she was by my looks, but she said nothing, only read the letters hurriedly, and then exclaimed—

'Is this all, my dear child? I really fancied you had found a second will, and had lost everything. Why, my dearest Maud, we knew all this before. We quite understood poor dear Austin's motive. Why are you so easily disturbed?'

'Oh, Cousin Monica, I think he was right; it all seems quite reasonable now; and I—oh, what a crime!—it must be stopped.'

'My dear Maud, listen to reason. Doctor Bryerly has seen your uncle at Bartram at least two hours ago. You *can't* stop it, and why on earth should you if you could? Don't you think your uncle should be consulted?' said she.

'But he has *decided.* I have his letter speaking of it as settled and Doctor Bryerly—oh, Cousin Monica, he's gone *to tempt him.'*

'Nonsense, girl! Doctor Bryerly is a good and just man, I do believe, and has, beside, no imaginable motive to pervert either his conscience or his judgment. He's not gone to tempt him—stuff!—but to unfold the facts and invite his consideration; and I say, considering how thoughtlessly such duties are often undertaken, and how long Silas has been living in lazy solitude, shut out from the world, and unused to discuss anything, I do think it only conscientious and honourable that he should have a fair and distinct view of the matter in all its bearings submitted to him before he indolently incurs what may prove the worst danger he was ever involved in.'

So Lady Knollys argued, with feminine energy, and I must confess, with a good deal of the repetition which I have sometimes observed in logicians of my own sex, and she puzzled without satisfying me.

'I don't know why I went to that room,' I said, quite frightened; 'or why I went to that press; how it happened that these papers, which we never saw there before, were the first things to strike my eye to-day.'

'What do you mean, dear?' said Lady Knollys.

'I mean this—I think I was *brought* there, and that *there* is poor papa's appeal to me, as plain as if his hand came and wrote it upon the wall.' I nearly screamed the conclusion of this wild confession.

'You are nervous, my darling; your bad nights have worn you out. Let us go out; the air will do you good; and I do assure you that you will very soon see that we are quite right, and rejoice conscientiously that you have acted as you did.'

But I was not to be satisfied, although my first vehemence was quieted. In my prayers that night my conscience upbraided me. When I lay down in bed my nervousness returned fourfold. Everybody at all nervously excitable has suffered some time or another by the appearance of ghastly features presenting themselves in every variety of contortion, one after another, the moment the eyes are closed. This night my dear father's face troubled me—sometimes white and sharp as ivory, sometimes strangely transparent like glass, sometimes all hanging in cadaverous folds, always with the same unnatural expression of diabolical fury.

From this dreadful vision I could only escape by sitting up and staring at the light. At length, worn out, I dropped asleep, and in a dream I distinctly heard papa's voice say sharply outside the bed-curtain:—'Maud, we shall be late at Bartram-Haugh.'

And I awoke in a horror, the wall, as it seemed, still ringing with the summons, and the speaker, I fancied, standing at the other side of the curtain.

A miserable night I passed. In the morning, looking myself like a ghost, I stood in my night-dress by Lady Knollys' bed.

'I have had my warning,' I said. 'Oh, Cousin Monica, papa has been with me, and ordered me to Bartram-Haugh; and go I will.'

She stared in my face uncomfortably, and then tried to laugh the matter off; but I know she was troubled at the strange state to which agitation and suspense had reduced me.

'You're taking too much for granted, Maud,' said she; 'Silas Ruthyn, most likely, will refuse his consent, and insist on your going to Bartram-Haugh.'

'Heaven grant!' I exclaimed; 'but if he doesn't, it is all the same to me, go I will. He may turn me out, but I'll go, and try to expiate the breach of faith that I fear is so horribly wicked.'

We had several hours still to wait for the arrival of the post. For both of us the delay was a suspense; for me an almost agonising one. At length, at an unlooked-for moment, Branston did enter the room with the post-bag. There was a large letter, with the Feltram post-mark, addressed to Lady Knollys—it was Doctor Bryerly's despatch; we read it together. It was dated on the day before, and its purport was thus:—

'RESPECTED MADAM,—I this day saw Mr. Silas Ruthyn at Bartram-Haugh, and he peremptorily refuses, on any terms, to vacate the guardianship, or to consent to Miss Ruthyn's residing anywhere but under his own immediate care. As he bases his refusal, first upon a conscientious difficulty, declaring that he has no right, through fear of personal contingencies, to abdicate an office imposed in so solemn a way, and so naturally devolving on him as only brother to the deceased; and secondly upon the effect such a withdrawal, at the instance of the acting trustee, Would have upon his own character, amounting to a public self-condemnation; and as he refused to discuss these positions with me, I could make no way whatsoever with him. Finding, therefore, that his mind was quite made up, after a short time I took my leave. He mentioned that preparations for his niece's reception are being completed, and that he will send for her in a few days; so that I think it will be advisable that I should go down to Knowl, to assist Miss Ruthyn with any advice she may require before her departure, to discharge servants, get inventories made, and provide for the care of the place and grounds during her minority.

'I am, respected Madam, yours truly,

HANS E. BRYERLY.'

I can't describe to you how chapfallen and angry my cousin looked. She sniffed once or twice, and then said, rather bitterly, in a subdued tone:—

'Well, *now*, I hope you are pleased?'

'No, no, no; you *know* I'm not—grieved to the heart, my only friend, my dear Cousin Monica; but my conscience is at rest; you don't know what a sacrifice it is; I am a most unhappy creature. I feel an indescribable foreboding. I am frightened; but you won't forsake me, Cousin Monica.'

'No, darling, never,' she said, sadly.

'And you'll come and see me, won't you, as often as you can?'

'Yes, dear; that is if Silas allows me; and I'm sure he will,' she added hastily, see-ing, I suppose, my terror in my face. 'All I can do, you may be sure I will, and per-haps he will allow you to come to me, now and then, for a short visit. You know I am only six miles away—little more than half an hour's drive, and though I hate Bartram, and detest Silas—Yes, I *detest Silas*,' she repeated in reply to my surprised gaze—'I *will* call at Bartram—that is, I say, if he allows me; for, you know, I haven't been there for a quarter of a century; and though I never understood Silas, I fancy he forgives no sins, whether of omission or commission.'

I wondered what old grudge could make my cousin judge Uncle Silas always so hardly—I could not suppose it was justice. I had seen my hero indeed lately so dis-respectfully handled before my eyes, that he had, as idols will, lost something of his sacredness. But as an article of faith, I still cultivated my trust in his divinity, and dismissed every intruding doubt with an exorcism, as a suggestion of the evil one. But I wronged Lady Knollys in suspecting her of pique, or malice, or anything more than that tendency to take strong views which some persons attribute to my sex.

So, then, the little project of Cousin Monica's guardianship, which, had it been poor papa's wish, would have made me so very happy, was quite knocked on the head, to revive no more. I comforted myself, however, with her promise to re-open communications with Bartram-Haugh, and we grew resigned.

I remember, next morning, as we sat at a very late breakfast, Lady Knollys, reading a letter, suddenly made an exclamation and a little laugh, and read on with increased interest for a few minutes, and then, with another little laugh, she looked up, placing her hand, with the open letter in it, beside her tea-cup.

'You'll not guess whom I've been reading about,' said she, with her head the least thing on one side, and an arch smile.

I felt myself blushing—cheeks, forehead, even down to the tips of my fingers. I anticipated the name I was to hear. She looked very much amused. Was it possible that Captain Oakley was married?

'I really have not the least idea,' I replied, with that kind of overdone careless-ness which betrays us.

'No, I see quite plainly you have not; but you can't think how prettily you blush,' answered she, very much diverted.

'I really don't care,' I replied, with some little dignity, and blushing deeper and deeper.

'Will you make a guess?' she asked.

'I *can't* guess.'

'Well, shall I tell you?'

'Just as you please.'

'Well, I will—that is, I'll read a page of my letter, which tells it all. Do you know Georgina Fanshawe?' she asked.

'Lady Georgina? No.'

'Well, no matter; she's in Paris now, and this letter is from her, and she says—let me see the place—"Yesterday, what do you think?—quite an apparition!—you shall hear. My brother Craven yesterday insisted on my accompanying him to Le Bas' shop in that odd little antique street near the Grève; it is a wonderful old curiosity shop. I forget what they call them here. When we went into this place it was very nearly deserted, and there were so many curious things to look at all about, that for a minute or two I did not observe a tall woman, in a grey silk and a black velvet mantle, and quite a nice new Parisian bonnet. You will be *charmed*, by-the-by, with the new shape—it is only out three weeks, and is quite *indescribably* elegant, *I* think, at least. They have them, I am sure, by this time at Molnitz's, so I need say no more. And now that I am on this subject of dress, I have got your lace; and I think you will be very ungrateful if you are not *charmed* with it." Well, I need not read all that—here is the rest;' and she read—

'"But you'll ask about my mysterious *dame* in the new bonnet and velvet man-tle; she was sitting on a stool at the counter, not buying, but evidently selling a quantity of stones and trinkets which she had in a card-box, and the man was pick-ing them up one by one, and, I suppose, valuing them. I was near enough to see such a darling little pearl cross, with at least half a dozen really good pearls in it, and had begun to covet them for my set, when the lady glanced over my shoulder, and she knew me —in fact, we knew one another—and who do you think she was? Well you'll not guess in a week, and I can't wait so long; so I may as well tell you at once—she was that horrid old Mademoiselle Blassemare whom you pointed out to me at Elverston; and I never forgot her face since—nor she, it seems, mine, for she turned away very quickly, and when I next saw her, her veil was down.'"

'Did not you tell me, Maud, that you had lost your pearl cross while that dreadful Madame de la Rougierre was here?'

'Yes; but—'

'I know; but what has she to do with Mademoiselle de Blassemare, you were going to say—they are one and the same person.'

'Oh, I perceive,' answered I, with that dim sense of danger and dismay with which one hears suddenly of an enemy of whom one has lost sight for a time.

'I'll write and tell Georgie to buy that cross. I wager my life it is yours,' said Lady Knollys, firmly.

The servants, indeed, made no secret of their opinion of Madame de la Rougierre, and frankly charged her with a long list of larcenies. Even Anne Wixted, who had enjoyed her barren favour while the gouvernante was here, hinted privately that she had bartered a missing piece of lace belonging to me with a gipsy pedlar, for French gloves and an Irish poplin.

'And so surely as I find it is yours, I'll set the police in pursuit.'

'But you must not bring me into court,' said I, half amused and half alarmed.

'No occasion, my dear; Mary Quince and Mrs. Rusk can prove it perfectly.'

'And why do you dislike her so very much?' I asked.

Cousin Monica leaned back in her chair, and searched the cornice from corner to corner with upturned eyes for the reason, and at last laughed a little, amused at herself.

'Well, really, it is not easy to define, and, perhaps, it is not quite charitable; but I know I hate her, and I know, you little hypocrite, you hate her as much as I;' and we both laughed a little.

'But you must tell me all you know of her history.'

'Her history?' echoed she. 'I really know next to nothing about it; only that I used to see her sometimes about the place that Georgina mentions, and there were some unpleasant things said about her; but you know they may be all lies. The worst I *know* of her is her treatment of you, and her robbing the desk'—(Cousin Monica always called it her *robbery*—'and I think that's enough to hang her.

Suppose we go out for a walk?'

So together we went, and I resumed about Madame; but no more could I extract—perhaps there was not much more to hear.

CHAPTER XXX

ON THE ROAD

All at Knowl was indicative of the break-up that was so near at hand. Doctor Bryerly arrived according to promise. He was in a whirl of business all the time. He and Mr. Danvers conferred about the management of the estate. It was agreed that the grounds and gardens should be let, but not the house, of which Mrs. Rusk was to take the care. The gamekeeper remained in office, and some out-door servants. But the rest were to go, except Mary Quince, who was to accompany me to Bartram-Haugh as my maid.

'Don't part with Quince,' said Lady Knollys, peremptorily they'll want you, but *don't*.'

She kept harping on this point, and recurred to it half a dozen times every day.

'They'll say, you know, that she is not fit for a lady's maid, as she certainly is *not*, if it in the least signified in such a wilderness as Bartram-Haugh; but she is attached, trustworthy, and honest; and those are qualities valuable everywhere, especially in a solitude. Don't allow them to get you a wicked young French milliner in her stead.'

Sometimes she said things that jarred unpleasantly on my nerves, and left an undefined sense of danger. Such as:—

'I know she's true to you, and a good creature; but is she shrewd enough?'

Or, with an anxious look:—

'I hope Mary Quince is not easily frightened.'

Or, suddenly:—

'Can Mary Quince write, in case you were ill?'

Or,

'Can she take a message exactly?'

Or,

'Is she a person of any enterprise and resource, and cool in an emergency?'

Now, these questions did not come all in a string, as I write them down here, but at long intervals, and were followed quickly by ordinary talk; but they generally escaped from my companion after silence and gloomy thought; and though I could extract nothing more defined than these questions, yet they seemed to me to point at some possible danger contemplated in my good cousin's dismal ruminations.

Another topic that occupied my cousin's mind a good deal was obviously the larceny of my pearl cross. She made a note of the description furnished by the rec-ollection, respectively, of Mary Quince, Mrs. Rusk, and myself. I had fancied her little vision of the police was no more than the result of a momentary impulse; but really, to judge by her methodical examinations of us, I should have fancied that she had taken it up in downright earnest.

Having learned that my departure from Knowl was to be so very soon, she resolved not to leave me before the day of my journey to Bartram-Haugh; and as day after day passed by, and the hour of our leave-taking approached, she became more and more kind and affectionate. A feverish and sorrowful interval it was to me.

Of Doctor Bryerly, though staying in the house, we saw almost nothing, except for an hour or so at tea-time. He breakfasted very early, and dined solitarily, and at uncertain hours, as business permitted.

The second evening of his visit, Cousin Monica took occasion to introduce the subject of his visit to Bartram-Haugh.

'You saw him, of course?' said Lady Knollys.

'Yes, he saw me; he was not well. On hearing who I was, he asked me to go to his room, where he sat in a silk dressing-gown and slippers.'

'About business principally,' said Cousin Monica, laconically.

'That was despatched in very few words; for he was quite resolved, and placed his refusal upon grounds which it was difficult to dispute. But difficult or no, mind you, he intimated that he would hear nothing more on the subject—so that was closed.'

'Well; and what is his religion now?' inquired she, irreverently.

'We had some interesting conversation on the subject. He leans much to what we call the doctrine of correspondents. He is read rather deeply in the writings of Swedenborg, and seemed anxious to discuss some points with one who professes to be his follower. To say truth, I did not expect to find him either so well read or so deeply interested in the subject.'

'Was he angry when it was proposed that he should vacate the guardianship?'

'Not at all. Contrariwise, he said he had at first been so minded himself. His years, his habits, and something of the unfitness of the situation, the remoteness of Bartram-Haugh from good teachers, and all that, had struck him, and nearly determined him against accepting the office. But then came the views which I stated in my letter, and they governed him; and nothing could shake them, he said, or induce him to re-open the question in his own mind.'

All the time Doctor Bryerly was relating his conference with the head of the family at Bartram-Haugh my cousin commented on the narrative with a variety of little 'pishes' and sneers, which I thought showed more of vexation than contempt.

I was glad to hear all that Doctor Bryerly related. It gave me a kind of confidence; and I experienced a momentary reaction. After all, could Bartram-Haugh be more lonely than I had found Knowl? Was I not sure of the society of my Cousin Millicent, who was about my own age? Was it not quite possible that my sojourn in Derbyshire might turn out a happy though very quiet remembrance through all my after-life? Why should it not? What time or place would be happy if we gave ourselves over to dismal imaginations?

So the summons reached me from Uncle Silas. The hours at Knowl were numbered.

The evening before I departed I visited the full-length portrait of Uncle Silas, and studied it for the last time carefully, with deep interest, for many minutes; but with results vaguer than ever.

With a brother so generous and so wealthy, always ready to help him forward; with his talents; with his lithe and gorgeous beauty, the shadow of which hung on that canvas—what might he not have accomplished? whom might he not have captivated? And yet where and what was he? A poor and shunned old man, occupying a lonely house and place that did not belong to him, married to degradation, with a few years of suspected and solitary life before him, and then swift oblivion his best portion.

I gazed on the picture, to fix it well and vividly in my remembrance. I might still trace some of its outlines and tints in its living original, whom I was next day to see for the first time in my life.

So the morning came—my last for many a day at Knowl—a day of partings, a day of novelty and regrets. The travelling carriage and post horses were at the door. Cousin Monica's carriage had just carried her away to the railway. We had embraced with tears; and her kind face was still before me, and her words of comfort and promise in my ears. The early sharpness of morning was still in the air; the frosty dew still glistened on the window-panes. We had made a hasty breakfast, my share of which was a single cup of tea. The aspect of the house how strange! Uncarpeted, uninhabited, doors for the most part locked, all the servants but Mrs. Rusk and Branston departed. The drawing-room door stood open, and a charwoman was washing the bare floor. I was looking my last—for who could say how long?—on the old house, and lingered. The luggage was all up. I made Mary Quince get in first, for every delay was precious; and now the moment was come. I hugged and kissed Mrs. Rusk in the hall.

'God bless you, Miss Maud, darling. You must not fret; mind, the time won't be long going over—*no* time at all; and you'll be bringing back a fine young gentleman—who knows? as great as the Duke of Wellington, for your husband; and I'll take the best of care of everything, and the birds and the dogs, till you come back; and I'll go and see you and Mary, if you'll allow, in Derbyshire;' and so forth.

I got into the carriage, and bid Branston, who shut the door, good-bye, and kissed hands to Mrs. Rusk, who was smiling and drying her eyes and courtesying on the hall-door steps. The dogs, who had started gleefully with the carriage, were called back by Branston, and driven home, wondering and wistful, looking back with ears oddly cocked and tails dejected. My heart thanked them for their kindness, and I felt like a stranger, and very desolate.

It was a bright, clear morning. It had been settled that it was not worth the trouble changing from the carriage to the railway for sake of five-and-twenty miles, and so the entire journey of sixty miles was to be made by the post road—the pleasantest travelling, if the mind were free. The grander and more distant features of the landscape we may see well enough from the window of the railway-carriage; but it is the foreground that interests and instructs us, like a pleasant gossiping history; and *that* we had, in old days, from the post-chaise window. It was more than travelling picquet. Something of all conditions of life—luxury and misery—high spirits and low;—all sorts of costume, livery, rags, millinery; faces buxom, faces wrinkled, faces kind, faces wicked;—no end of interest and suggestion, passing in a procession silent and vivid, and all in their proper scenery. The golden corn-sheafs—the old dark-alleyed orchards, and the high streets of antique towns. There were few dreams brighter, few books so pleasant.

We drove by the dark wood—it always looked dark to me where the 'mausoleum' stands—where my dear parents both lay now. I gazed on its sombre masses not with a softened feeling, but a peculiar sense of pain, and was glad when it was quite past.

All the morning I had not shed a tear. Good Mary Quince cried at leaving Knowl; Lady Knollys' eyes were not dry as she kissed and blessed me, and promised an early visit; and the dark, lean, energetic face of the housekeeper was quivering, and her cheeks wet, as I drove away. But I, whose grief was sorest, never shed a tear. I only looked about from one familiar object to another, pale, excited, not quite apprehending my departure, and wondering at my own composure.

But when we reached the old bridge, with the tall osiers standing by the buttress, and looked back at poor Knowl—the places we love and are leaving look so fairy-like and so sad in the clear distance, and this is the finest view of the gabled old house, with its slanting meadow-lands and noble timber reposing in solemn groups—I gazed at the receding vision, and the tears came at last, and I wept in silence long after the fair picture was hidden from view by the intervening uplands.

I was relieved, and when we had made our next change of horses, and got into a country that was unknown to me, the new scenery and the sense of progress worked their accustomed effects on a young traveller who had lived a particularly secluded life, and I began to experience, on the whole, a not unpleasurable excitement.

Mary Quince and I, with the hopefulness of inexperienced travellers, began already to speculate about our proximity to Bartram-Haugh, and were sorely disappointed when we heard from the nondescript courier—more like a ostler than a servant, who sat behind in charge of us and the luggage, and represented my guardian's special care—at nearly one o'clock, that we had still forty miles to go, a considerable portion of which was across the high Derbyshire mountains, before we reached Bartram-Haugh.

The fact was, we had driven at a pace accommodated rather to the convenience of the horses than to our impatience; and finding, at the quaint little inn where we now halted, that we must wait for a nail or two in a loose shoe of one of our relay, we consulted, and being both hungry, agreed to beguile the time with an early dinner, which we enjoyed very sociably in a queer little parlour with a bow window, and commanding, with a little garden for foreground, a very pretty landscape.

Good Mary Quince, like myself, had quite dried her tears by this time, and we were both highly interested, and I a little nervous, too, about our arrival and reception at Bartram. Some time, of course, was lost in this pleasant little parlour, before we found ourselves once more pursuing our way.

The slowest part of our journey was the pull up the long mountain road, ascending zig-zag, as sailors make way against a head-wind, by tacking. I forget the name of the pretty little group of houses—it did not amount to a village buried in trees, where we got our *four* horses and two postilions, for the work was severe. I can only designate it as the place where Mary Quince and I had our tea, very comfortably, and bought some gingerbread, very curious to look upon, but quite uneatable.

The greater portion of the ascent, when we were fairly upon the mountain, was accomplished at a walk, and at some particularly steep points we had to get out and go on foot. But this to me was quite delightful. I had never scaled a mountain before, and the ferns and heath, the pure boisterous air, and above all the magnificent view of the rich country we were leaving behind, now gorgeous and misty in sunset tints, stretching in gentle undulations far beneath us, quite enchanted me.

We had just reached the summit when the sun went down. The low grounds at the other side were already lying in cold grey shadow, and I got the man who sat behind to point out as well as he could the site of Bartram-Haugh. But mist was gathering over all by this time. The filmy disk of the moon which was to light us on, so soon as twilight faded into night, hung high in air. I tried to see the sable mass of wood which he described. But it was vain, and to acquire a clear idea of the place, as of its master, I must only wait that nearer view which an hour or two more would afford me.

And now we rapidly descended the mountain side. The scenery was wilder and bolder than I was accustomed to. Our road skirted the edge of a great heathy moor. The silvery light of the moon began to glimmer, and we passed a gipsy bivouac with fires alight and caldrons hanging over them. It was the first I had seen. Two or three low tents; a couple of dark, withered crones, veritable witches; a graceful girl standing behind, gazing after us; and men in odd-shaped hats, with gaudy waistcoats and bright-coloured neck-handkerchiefs and gaitered legs, stood lazily in front. They had all a wild tawdry display of colour; and a group of alders in the rear made a background of shade for tents, fires, and figures.

I opened a front window of the chariot, and called to the postboys to stop. The groom from behind came to the window.

'Are not those gipsies?' I enquired.

'Yes, please'm, them's gipsies, sure, Miss,' he answered, glancing with that odd smile, half contemptuous, half superstitious, with which I have since often observed the peasants of Derbyshire eyeing those thievish and uncanny neighbours.

CHAPTER XXXI

BARTRAM-HAUGH

In a moment a tall, lithe girl, black-haired, black-eyed, and, as I thought, inexpressibly handsome, was smiling, with such beautiful rings of pearly teeth, at the window; and in her peculiar accent, with a suspicion of something foreign in it, proposing with many courtesies to tell the lady her fortune.

I had never seen this wild tribe of the human race before—children of mystery and liberty. Such vagabondism and beauty in the figure before me! I looked at their hovels and thought of the night, and wondered at their independence, and felt my inferiority. I could not resist. She held up her slim oriental hand.

'Yes, I'll hear my fortune,' I said, returning the sibyl's smile instinctively.

'Give me some money, Mary Quince. No, *not* that,' I said, rejecting the thrifty sixpence she tendered, for I had heard that the revelations of this weird sisterhood were bright in proportion to the kindness of their clients, and was resolved to approach Bartrant with cheerful auguries. 'That five-shilling piece,' I insisted; and honest Mary reluctantly surrendered the coin.

So the feline beauty took it, with courtesies and 'thankees,' smiling still, and hid it away as if she stole it, and looked on my open palm still smiling; and told me, to my surprise, that there was *somebody* I liked very much, and I was almost afraid she would name Captain Oakley; that he would grow very rich, and that I should marry him; that I should move about from place to place a great deal for a good while to come. That I had some enemies, who should be sometimes so near as to be in the same room with me, and yet they should not be able to hurt me. That I should see blood spilt and yet not my own, and finally be very happy and splendid, like the heroine of a fairy tale.

Did this strange, girlish charlatan see in my face some signs of shrinking when she spoke of enemies, and set me down for a coward whose weakness might be profitable? Very likely. At all events she plucked a long brass pin, with a round bead for a head, from some part of her dress, and holding the point in her fingers, and exhibiting the treasure before my eyes, she told me that I must get a charmed pin like that, which her grandmother had given to her, and she ran glibly through a story of all the magic expended on it, and told me she could not part with it; but its virtue was that you were to stick it through the blanket, and while it was there neither rat, nor cat, nor snake—and then came two more terms in the catalogue, which I suppose belonged to the gipsy dialect, and which she explained to mean, as well as I could understand, the first a malevolent spirit, and the second 'a cove to cut your throat,' could approach or hurt you.

A charm like that, she gave me to understand, I must by book or by crook obtain. She had not a second. None of her people in the camp over there possessed one. I am ashamed to confess that I actually paid her a pound for this brass pin! The purchase was partly an indication of my temperament, which could never let an opportunity pass away irrevocably without a struggle, and always apprehended. Some day or other I'll reproach myself for having neglected it!' and partly a record of the trepidations of that period of my life. At all events I had her Pin, and she my pound, and I venture to say I was the gladder of the two.

She stood on the road-side bank courtseying and smiling, the first enchantress I had encountered, and I watched the receding picture, with its patches of firelight, its dusky groups and donkey carts, white as skeletons in the moonlight, as we drove rapidly away.

They, I suppose, had a wild sneer and a merry laugh over my purchase, as they sat and ate their supper of stolen poultry, about their fire, and were duly proud of belonging to the superior race.

Mary Quince, shocked at my prodigality, hinted a remonstrance.

'It went to my heart, Miss, it did. They're such a lot, voting and old, all alike thieves and vagabonds, and many a poor body wanting.'

'Tut, Mary, never mind. Everyone has her fortune told some time in her life, and you can't have a good one without paying. I think, Mary, we must be near Bartram now.'

The road now traversed the side of a steep hill, parallel to which, along the opposite side of a winding river, rose the dark steeps of a corresponding upland, covered with forest that looked awful and dim in the deep shadow, while the moonlight rippled fitfully upon the stream beneath.

'It seems to be a beautiful country,' I said to Mary Quince, who was munching a sandwich in the corner, and thus appealed to, adjusted her bonnet, and made an inspection from *her* window, which, however, commanded nothing but the heathy slope of the hill whose side we were traversing.

'Well, Miss, I suppose it is; but there's a deal o' mountains—is not there?'

And so saying, honest Mary leaned back again, and went on with her sandwich.

We were now descending at a great pace. I knew we were coming near. I stood up as well as I could in the carriage, to see over the postilions' heads. I was eager, but frightened too; agitated as the crisis of the arrival and meeting approached. At last, a long stretch of comparatively level country below us, with masses of wood as well as I could see irregularly overspreading it, became visible as the narrow valley through which we were speeding made a sudden bend.

Down we drove, and now I did perceive a change. A great grass-grown park-wall, overtopped with mighty trees; but still on and on we came at a canter that seemed almost a gallop. The old grey park-wall flanking us at one side, and a pretty pastoral hedgerow of ash-trees, irregularly on the other.

At last the postilions began to draw bridle, and at a slight angle, the moon shining full upon them, we wheeled into a wide semicircle formed by the receding park-walls, and halted before a great fantastic iron gate, and a pair of tall fluted piers, of white stone, all grass-grown and ivy-bound, with great cornices, surmounted with shields and supporters, the Ruthyn bearings washed by the rains of Derbyshire for many a generation of Ruthyns, almost smooth by this time, and looking bleached and phantasmal, like giant sentinels, with each a hand clasped in his comrade's, to bar our passage to the enchanted castle—the florid tracery of the iron gate showing like the draperies of white robes hanging from their extended arms to the earth.

Our courier got down and shoved the great gate open, and we entered, between sombre files of magnificent forest trees, one of those very broad straight avenues whose width measures the front of the house. This was all built of white stone, resembling that of Caen, which parts of Derbyshire produce in such abundance.

So this was Bartram, and here was Uncle Silas. I was almost breathless as I approached. The bright moon shining full on the white front of the old house revealed not only its highly decorated style, its fluted pillars and doorway, rich and florid carving, and balustraded summit, but also its stained and moss-grown front. Two giant trees, overthrown at last by the recent storm, lay with their upturned roots, and their yellow foliage still flickering on the sprays that were to bloom no more, where they had fallen, at the right side of the court-yard, which, like the avenue, was studded with tufted weeds and grass.

All this gave to the aspect of Bartram a forlorn character of desertion and decay, contrasting almost awfully with the grandeur of its proportions and richness of its architecture.

There was a ruddy glow from a broad window in the second row and I thought I saw some one peep from it and disappear; at the same moment there was a furious barking of dogs, some of whom ran scampering into the court-yard from a half-closed side door; and amid their uproar, the bawling of the man in the back seat, who jumped down to drive them off, and the crack of the postilions' whips, who struck at them, we drew up before the lordly door-steps of this melancholy mansion.

Just as our attendant had his hand on the knocker the door opened, and we saw, by a not very brilliant candle-light, three figures—a shabby little old man, thin, and very much stooped, with a white cravat, and looking as if his black clothes were too large, and made for some one else, stood with his hand upon the door; a young, plump, but very pretty female figure, in unusually short petticoats, with fattish legs, and nice ankles, in boots, stood in the centre; and a dowdy maid, like an old charwoman, behind her.

The household paraded for welcome was not certainly very brilliant. Amid the riot the trunks were deliberately put down by our attendant, who kept shouting to the old man at the door, and to the dogs in turn; and the old man was talking and pointing stiffly and tremulously, but I could not hear what he said.

'Was it possible—could that mean-looking old man be Uncle Silas?'

The idea stunned me; but I almost instantly perceived that he was much too small, and I was relieved, and even grateful. It was certainly an odd mode of procedure to devote primary attention to the trunks and boxes, leaving the travellers still shut up in the carriage, of which they were by this time pretty well tired. I was not sorry for the reprieve, however: being nervous about first impressions, and willing to defer mine, I sat shyly back, peeping at the candle and moonlight picture before me, myself unseen.

'Will you tell—yes or no—is my cousin in the coach?' screamed the plump young lady, stamping her stout black boot, in a momentary lull.

Yes, I was there, sure.

'And why the puck don't you let her out, you stupe, you 'Run down, Giblets, you never do nout without driving, and let Cousin Maud out. You're very welcome to Bartram.' This greeting was screamed at an amazing pitch, and repeated before I had time to drop the window, and say 'thank you.' 'I'd a let you out myself—there's a good dog, you would na' bite Cousin' (the parenthesis was to a huge mastiff, who thrust himself beside her, by this time quite pacified)—'only I daren't go down the steps, for the governor said I shouldn't.'

The venerable person who went by the name of Giblets had by this time opened the carriage door, and our courier, or 'boots'—he looked more like the latter functionary—had lowered the steps, and in greater trepidation than I experienced when in after-days I was presented to my sovereign, I glided down, to offer myself to the greeting and inspection of the plain-spoken young lady who stood at the top of the steps to receive me.

She welcomed me with a hug and a hearty buss, as she called that salutation, on each cheek, and pulled me into the hall, and was evidently glad to see me.

'And you're tired a bit, I warrant; and who's the old 'on, who?' she asked eagerly, in a stage whisper, which made my ear numb for five minutes after. 'Oh, oh, the maid! and a precious old 'un—ha, ha, ha! But lawk! how grand she is, with her black silk, cloak and crape, and I only in twilled cotton, and rotten old Coburg for Sundays. Odds I it's a shame; but you'll be tired, you will. It's a smartish pull, they do say, from Knowl. I know a spell of it, only so far as the "Cat and Fiddle," near the Lunnon-road. Come up, will you? Would you like to come in first and talk a bit wi' the governor? Father, you know, he's a bit silly, he is, this while.' I found that the phrase meant only *bodily* infirmity. 'He took a pain o' Friday, newralgie— something or other he calls it—rheumatics it is when it takes old "Giblets" there; and he's sitting in his own room; or maybe you'd like better to come to your bed-room first, for it is dirty work travelling, they do say.'

Yes; I preferred the preliminary adjustment. Mary Quince was standing behind me; and as my voluble kinswoman talked on, we had each ample time and oppor-tunity to observe the personnel of the other; and she made no scruple of letting me perceive that she was improving it, for she stared me full in the face, taking in evi-dently feature after feature; and she felt the material of my mantle pretty carefully between her finger and thumb, and manually examined my chain and trinkets, and picked up my hand as she might a glove, to con over my rings.

I can't say, of course, exactly what impression I may have produced on her. But in my cousin Milly I saw a girl who looked younger than her years, plump, but with a slender waist, with light hair, lighter than mine, and very blue eyes, rather round; on the whole very good-looking. She had an odd swaggering walk, a toss of her head, and a saucy and imperious, but rather good-natured and honest counte-nance. She talked rather loud, with a good ringing voice, and a boisterous laugh when it came.

If *I* was behind the fashion, what would Cousin Monica have thought of her? She was arrayed, as she had stated, in black twilled cotton expressive of her afflic-tion; but it was made almost as short in the skirt as that of the prints of the Bavarian broom girls. She had white cotton stockings, and a pair of black leather boots, with leather buttons, and, for a lady, prodigiously thick soles, which remind-ed me of the navvy boots I had so often admired in *Punch*. I must add that the hands with which she assisted her scrutiny of my dress, though pretty, were very much sunburnt indeed.

'And what's *her* name?' she demanded, nodding to Mary Quince, who was gaz-ing on her awfully, with round eyes, as an inland spinster might upon a whale beheld for the first time.

Mary courtesied, and I answered.

'Mary Quince,' she repeated. 'You're welcome, Quince. What shall I call her? I've a name for all o' them. Old Giles there, is Giblets. He did not like it first, but he answers quick enough now; and Old Lucy Wyat there,' nodding toward the old woman, 'is Lucia de l'Amour.' A slightly erroneous reading of Lammermoor, for my cousin sometimes made mistakes, and was not much versed in the Italian opera. 'You know it's a play, and I call her L'Amour for shortness;' and she laughed hilariously, and I could not forbear joining; and, winking at me, she called aloud, 'L'Amour.'

To which the crone, with a high-cauled cap, resembling Mother Hubbard, responded with a courtesy and 'Yes, 'm.'

'Are all the trunks and boxes took up?'

They were.

'Well, we'll come now; and what shall I call you, Quince? Let me see.'

'According to your pleasure, Miss,' answered Mary, with dignity, and a dry courtesy.

'Why, you're as hoarse as a frog, Quince. We'll call you Quinzy for the present. That'll do. Come along, Quinzy.'

So my Cousin Milly took me under the arm, and pulled me forward; but as we ascended, she let me go, leaning back to make inspection of my attire from a new point of view.

'Hallo, cousin,' she cried, giving my dress a smack with her open hand. 'What a plague do you want of all that bustle; you'll leave it behind, lass, the first bush you jump over.'

I was a good deal astounded. I was also very near laughing, for there was a sort of importance in her plump countenance, and an indescribable grotesqueness in the fashion of her garments, which heightened the outlandishness of her talk, in a way which I cannot at all describe.

What palatial wide stairs those were which we ascended, with their prodigious carved banisters of oak, and each huge pillar on the landing-place crowned with a shield and carved heraldic supporters; florid oak panelling covered the walls. But of the house I could form no estimate, for Uncle Silas's housekeeping did not provide light for hall and passages, and we were dependent on the glimmer of a single candle; but there would be quite enough of this kind of exploration in the daylight.

So along dark oak flooring we advanced to my room, and I had now an opportunity of admiring, at my leisure, the lordly proportions of the building. Two great windows, with dark and tarnished curtains, rose half as high again as the windows of Knowl; and yet Knowl, in its own style, is a fine house. The door-frames, like the window-frames, were richly carved; the fireplace was in the same massive style, and the mantelpiece projected with a mass of very rich carving. On the whole I was surprised. I had never slept in so noble a room before.

The furniture, I must confess, was by no means on a par with the architectural pretensions of the apartment. A French bed, a piece of carpet about three yards square, a small table, two chairs, a toilet table—no wardrobe—no chest of drawers.

The furniture painted white, and of the light and diminutive kind, was particularly ill adapted to the scale and style of the apartment, one end only of which it occupied, and that but sparsely, leaving the rest of the chamber in the nakedness of a stately desolation. My cousin Milly ran away to report progress to 'the Governor,' as she termed Uncle Silas.

'Well, Miss Maud, I never did expect to see the like o' that!' exclaimed honest Mary Quince. 'Did you ever see such a young lady? She's no more like one o' the family than I am. Law bless us I and what's she dressed like? Well, well, well!' And Mary, with a rueful shake of her head, clicked her tongue pathetically to the back of her teeth, while I could not forbear laughing.

'And such a scrap o' furniture! Well, well, well!' and the same ticking of the tongue followed.

But, in a few minutes, back came Cousin Milly, and, with a barbarous sort of curiosity, assisted in unpacking my trunks, and stowing away the treasures, on which she ventured a variety of admiring criticisms, in the presses which, like cupboards, filled recesses in the walls, with great oak doors, the keys of which were in them.

As I was making my hurried toilet, she entertained me now and then with more strictly personal criticisms.

'Your hair's a shade darker than mine—it's none the better o' that though—is it? Mine's said to be the right shade. I don't know—what do you say?'

I conceded the point with a good grace.

'I wish my hands was as white though—you do lick me there but it's all gloves, and I never could abide 'em. I think I'll try though—they *are* very white, sure.'

'I wonder which is the prettiest, you or me? I don't know, I'm sure—which do *you* think?'

I laughed outright at this challenge, and she blushed a little, and for the first time seemed for a moment a little shy.

'Well, you *are* a half an inch longer than me, I think—don't you?'

I was fully an inch taller, so I had no difficulty in making the proposed admission.

'Well, you do look handsome! doesn't she, Quinzy, lass? but your frock comes down almost to your heels—it does.'

And she glanced from mine to hers, and made a little kick up with the heel of the navvy boot to assist her in measuring the comparative distance.

'Maybe mine's a thought too short?' she suggested. 'Who's there? Oh! it's you, is it?' she cried as Mother Hubbard appeared at the door. 'Come in, L'Amour—don't you know, lass, you're always welcome?'

She had come to let us know that Uncle Silas would be happy to see me whenever I was ready; and that my cousin Millicent would conduct me to the room where he awaited me.

In an instant all the comic sensations awakened by my singular cousin's eccentricities vanished and I was thrilled with awe. I was about to see in the flesh—faded, broken, aged, but still identical—that being who had been the vision and the problem of so many years of my short life.

CHAPTER XXXII

UNCLE SILAS

I thought my odd cousin was also impressed with a kind of awe, though different in degree from mine, for a shade overcast her face, and she was silent as we walked side by side along the gallery, accompanied by the crone who carried the candle which lighted us to the door of that apartment which I may call Uncle Silas's presence chamber.

Milly whispered to me as we approached—

'Mind how you make a noise; the governor's as sharp as a weasel, and nothing vexes him like that.'

She was herself toppling along on tiptoe. We paused at a door near the head of the great staircase, and L'Amour knocked timidly with her rheumatic knuckles.

A voice, clear and penetrating, from within summoned us to enter. The old woman opened the door, and the next moment I was in the presence of Uncle Silas.

At the far end of a handsome wainscoted room, near the hearth in which a low fire was burning, beside a small table on which stood four waxlights, in tall silver candlesticks, sat a singular-looking old man.

The dark wainscoting behind him, and the vastness of the room, in the remoter parts of which the light which fell strongly upon his face and figure expended itself with hardly any effect, exhibited him with the forcible and strange relief of a finely painted Dutch portrait. For some time I saw nothing but him.

A face like marble, with a fearful monumental look, and, for an old man, singularly vivid strange eyes, the singularity of which rather grew upon me as I looked; for his eyebrows were still black, though his hair descended from his temples in long locks of the purest silver and fine as silk, nearly to his shoulders.

He rose, tall and slight, a little stooped, all in black, with an ample black velvet tunic, which was rather a gown than a coat, with loose sleeves, showing his snowy shirt some way up the arm, and a pair of wrist buttons, then quite out of fashion, which glimmered aristocratically with diamonds.

I know I can't convey in words an idea of this apparition, drawn as it seemed in black and white, venerable, bloodless, fiery-eyed, with its singular look of power, and an expression so bewildering—was it derision, or anguish, or cruelty, or patience?

The wild eyes of this strange old man were fixed upon me as he rose; an habitual contraction, which in certain lights took the character of a scowl, did not relax as he advanced toward me with his thin-lipped smile. He said something in his clear, gentle, but cold voice, the import of which I was too much agitated to catch, and he took both my hands in his, welcomed me with a courtly grace which belonged to another age, and led me affectionately, with many inquiries which I only half comprehended, to a chair near his own.

'I need not introduce my daughter; she has saved me that mortification. You'll find her, I believe, good-natured and affectionate; *au reste*, I fear a very rustic Miranda, and fitted rather for the society of Caliban than of a sick old Prospero. Is it not so, Millicent?'

The old man paused sarcastically for an answer, with his eyes fixed severely on my odd cousin, who blushed and looked uneasily to me for a hint.

'I don't know who they be—neither one nor t'other.'

'Very good, my dear,' he replied, with a little mocking bow. 'You see, my dear Maud, what a Shakespearean you have got for a cousin. It's plain, however, she has made acquaintance with some of our dramatists: she has studied the role of *Miss Hoyden* so perfectly.'

It was not a reasonable peculiarity of my uncle that he resented, with a good deal of playful acrimony, my poor cousin's want of education, for which, if he were not to blame, certainly neither was she.

'You see her, poor thing, a result of all the combined disadvantages of want of refined education, refined companionship, and, I fear, naturally, of refined tastes; but a sojourn at a good French conventual school will do wonders, and I hope to manage by-and-by. In the meantime we jest at our misfortunes, and love one another, I hope, cordially.'

He extended his thin, white hand with a chilly smile towards Milly, who bounced up, and took it with a frightened look; and he repeated, holding her hand rather slightly I thought, 'Yes, I hope, very cordially,' and then turning again to me, he put it over the arm of his chair, and let it go, as a man might drop something he did not want from a carriage window.

Having made this apology for poor Milly, who was plainly bewildered, he passed on, to her and my relief, to other topics, every now and then expressing his fears that I was fatigued, and his anxiety that I should partake of some supper or tea; but these solicitudes somehow seemed to escape his remembrance almost as soon as uttered; and he maintained the conversation, which soon degenerated into a close, and to me a painful examination, respecting my dear father's illness and its symptoms, upon which I could give no information, and his habits, upon which I could.

Perhaps he fancied that there might be some family predisposition to the organic disease of which his brother died, and that his questions were directed rather to the prolonging of his own life than to the better understanding of my dear father's death.

How little was there left to this old man to make life desirable, and yet how keenly, I afterwards found, he clung to it. Have we not all of us seen those to whom life was not only *undesirable*, but positively painful—a mere series of bodily torments, yet hold to it with a desperate and pitiable tenacity—old children or young, it is all the same.

See how a sleepy child will put off the inevitable departure for bed. The little creature's eyes blink and stare, and it needs constant jogging to prevent his nodding off into the slumber which nature craves. His waking is a pain; he is quite worn out, and peevish, and stupid, and yet he implores a respite, and deprecates repose, and vows he is not sleepy, even to the moment when his mother takes him in her arms, and carries him, in a sweet slumber, to the nursery. So it is with us old children of earth and the great sleep of death, and nature our kind mother. Just so reluctantly we part with consciousness, the picture is, even to the last, so interesting; the bird in the hand, though sick and moulting, so inestimably better than all the brilliant tenants of the bush. We sit up, yawning, and blinking, and stupid, the whole scene swimming before us, and the stories and music humming off into the sound of distant winds and waters. It is not time yet; we are not fatigued; we are good for another hour still, and so protesting against bed, we falter and drop into the dreamless sleep which nature assigns to fatigue and satiety.

He then spoke a little eulogy of his brother, very polished, and, indeed, in a kind of way, eloquent. He possessed in a high degree that accomplishment, too little cultivated, I think, by the present generation, of expressing himself with perfect precision and fluency. There was, too, a good deal of slight illustrative quotation, and a sprinkling of French flowers, over his conversation, which gave to it a character at once elegant and artificial. It was all easy, light, and pointed, and being quite new to me, had a wonderful fascination.

He then told me that Bartram was the temple of liberty, that the health of a whole life was founded in a few years of youth, air, and exercise, and that accomplishments, at least, if not education, should wait upon health. Therefore, while at Bartram, I should dispose of my time quite as I pleased, and the more I plundered the garden and gipsied in the woodlands, the better.

Then he told me what a miserable invalid he was, and bow the doctors interfered with his frugal tastes. A glass of beer and a mutton chop—his ideal of a dinner—he dared not touch. They made him drink light wines, which he detested, and live upon those artificial abominations all liking for which vanishes with youth.

There stood on a side-table, in its silver coaster, a long-necked Rhenish bottle, and beside it a thin pink glass, and he quivered his fingers in a peevish way toward them.

But unless he found himself better very soon, he would take his case into his own hands, and try the dietary to which nature pointed.

He waved his fingers toward his bookcases, and told me his books were altogether at my service during my stay; but this promise ended, I must confess, disappointingly. At last, remarking that I must be fatigued, he rose, and kissed me with a solemn tenderness, placed his hand upon what I now perceived to be a large Bible, with two broad silk markers, Ted and gold, folded in it—the one, I might conjecture, indicating the place in the Old, the other in the New Testament. It stood on the small table that supported the waxlights, with a handsome cut bottle of eau-de-cologne, his gold and jewelled pencil-case, and his chased repeater, chain, and seals, beside it. There certainly were no indications of poverty in Uncle Silas's room; and he said impressively—

'Remember that book; in it your father placed his trust, in it he found his reward, in it lives my only hope; consult it, my beloved niece, day and night, as the oracle of life.'

Then he laid his thin hand on my head, and blessed me, and then kissed my forehead.

'No—a!' exclaimed Cousin Milly's lusty voice. I had quite forgotten her presence, and looked at her with a little start. She was seated on a very high old-fashioned chair; she had palpably been asleep; her round eyes were blinking and staring glassily at us; and her white legs and navvy boots were dangling in the air.

'Have you anything to remark about Noah?' enquired her father, with a polite inclination and an ironical interest.

'No—a,' she repeated in the same blunt accents; 'I didn't snore; did I? No—a.'

The old man smiled and shrugged a little at me—it was the smile of disgust.

'Good night, my dear Maud;' and turning to her, he said with a peculiar gentle sharpness, 'Had not you better wake, my dear, and try whether your cousin would like some supper?'

So he accompanied us to the door, outside which we found L'Amour's candle awaiting us.

'I'm awful afraid of the Governor, I am. Did I snore that time?'

'No, dear; at least, I did not hear it,' I said, unable to repress a smile.

'Well, if I didn't, I was awful near it,' she said, reflectively.

We found poor Mary Quince dozing over the fire; but we soon had tea and other good things, of which Milly partook with a wonderful appetite.

'I *was* in a qualm about it,' said Milly, who by this time was quite herself again. 'When he spies me a-napping, maybe he don't fetch me a prod with his pencil-case over the head. Odd I girl, it *is* sore.'

When I contrasted the refined and fluent old gentleman whom I had just left, with this amazing specimen of young ladyhood, I grew sceptical almost as to the possibility of her being his child.

I was to learn, however, how little she had, I won't say of his society, but even of his presence—that she had no domestic companion of the least pretensions to education—that she ran wild about the place—never, except in church, so much as saw a person of that rank to which she was born—and that the little she knew of reading and writing had been picked up, in desultory half-hours, from a person who did not care a pin about her manners or decorum, and perhaps rather enjoyed her grotesqueness—and that no one who was willing to take the least trouble about her was competent to make her a particle more refined than I saw her—the wonder ceased. We don't know how little is heritable, and how much simply training, until we encounter some-such spectacle as that of my poor cousin Milly.

When I lay down in my bed and reviewed the day, it seemed like a month of wonders. Uncle Silas was always before me; the voice so silvery for an old man—so preternaturally soft; the manners so sweet, so gentle; the aspect, smiling, suffering, spectral. It was no longer a shadow; I had now seen him in the flesh. But, after all, was he more than a shadow to me? When I closed my eyes I saw him before me still, in necromantic black, ashy with a pallor on which I looked with fear and pain, a face so dazzlingly pale, and those hollow, fiery, awful eyes! It sometimes seemed as if the curtain opened, and I had seen a ghost.

I had seen him; but he was still an enigma and a marvel. The living face did hot expound the past, any more than the portrait portended the future. He was still a mystery and a vision; and thinking of these things I fell asleep.

Mary Quince, who slept in the dressing-room, the door of which was close to my bed, and lay open to secure me against ghosts, called me up; and the moment I knew where I was I jumped up, and peeped eagerly from the window. It commanded the avenue and court-yard; but we were many windows removed from that over the hall-door, and immediately beneath ours lay the two giant lime trees, prostrate and uprooted, which I had observed as we drove up the night before.

I saw more clearly in the bright light of morning the signs of neglect and almost of dilapidation which had struck me as I approached. The court-yard was tufted over with grass, seldom from year to year crushed by the carriage-wheels, or trodden by the feet of visitors. This melancholy verdure thickened where the area was more remote from the centre; and under the windows, and skirting the walls to the left, was reinforced by a thick grove of nettles. The avenue was all grass-grown, except in the very centre, where a narrow track still showed the roadway. The handsome carved balustrade of the court-yard was discoloured with lichens, and in two places gapped and broken; and the air of decay was heightened by the fallen trees, among whose sprays and yellow leaves the small birds were hopping.

Before my toilet was completed, in marched my cousin Milly. We were to breakfast alone that morning, 'and so much the better,' she told me. Sometimes the Governor ordered her to breakfast with him, and 'never left off chaffing her' till his newspaper came, and 'sometimes he said such things he made her cry,' and then he only 'boshed her more,' and packed her away to her room; but she was by chalks nicer than him, talk as he might. '*Was* not she nicer? was not she? was not she?' Upon this point she was so strong and urgent that I was obliged to reply by a protest against awarding the palm of elegance between parent and child, and declaring I liked her very much, which I attested by a kiss.

'I know right well which of us you do think's the nicest, and no mistake, only you're afraid of him; and he had no business boshing me last night before you. I knew he was at it, though I couldn't twig him altogether; but wasn't he a sneak, now, wasn't he? '

This was a still more awkward question; so I kissed her again, and said she must never ask me to say of my uncle in his absence anything I could not say to his face.

At which speech she stared at me for a while, and then treated me to one of her hearty laughs, after which she seemed happier, and gradually grew into better humour with her father.

'Sometimes, when the curate calls, he has me up—for he's as religious as six, he is—and they read Bible and prays, ho—don't they? You'll have that, lass, like me, to go through; and maybe I don't hate it; oh, no!'

We breakfasted in a small room, almost a closet, off the great parlour, which was evidently quite disused. Nothing could be homelier than our equipage, or more shabby than the furniture of the little apartment. Still, somehow, I liked it. It was a total change; but one likes 'roughing it' a little at first.

CHAPTER XXXIII

THE WINDMILL WOOD

I had not time to explore this noble old house as my curiosity prompted; for Milly was in such a fuss to set out for the 'blackberry dell' that I saw little more than just so much as I necessarily traversed in making my way to and from my room.

The actual decay of the house had been prevented by my dear father; and the roof, windows, masonry, and carpentry had all been kept in repair. But short of indications of actual ruin, there are many manifestations of poverty and neglect which impress with a feeling of desolation. It was plain that not nearly a tithe of this great house was inhabited; long corridors and galleries stretched away in dust and silence, and were crossed by others, whose dark arches inspired me in the distance with an awful sort of sadness. It was plainly one of those great structures in which you might easily lose yourself, and with a pleasing terror it reminded me of that delightful old abbey in Mrs. Radcliffe's romance, among whose silent staircases, dim passages, and long suites of lordly, but forsaken chambers, begirt without by the sombre forest, the family of La Mote secured a gloomy asylum.

My cousin Milly and I, however, were bent upon an open-air ramble, and traversing several passages, she conducted me to a door which led us out upon a terrace overgrown with weeds, and by a broad flight of steps we descended to the level of the grounds beneath. Then on, over the short grass, under the noble trees, we walked; Milly in high good-humour, and talking away volubly, in her short garment, navvy boots, and a weather-beaten hat. She carried a stick in her gloveless hand. Her conversation was quite new to me, and resembled very much what I would have fancied the holiday recollections of a schoolboy; and the language in which it was sustained was sometimes so outlandish, that I was forced to laugh outright—a demonstration which she plainly did not like.

Her talk was about the great jumps she had made—how she snow—balled the chaps' in winter—how she could slide twice the length of her stick beyond 'Briddles, the cow-boy.'

With this and similar conversation she entertained me.

The grounds were delightfully wild and neglected. But we had now passed into a vast park beautifully varied with hollows and uplands, and such glorious old timber massed and scattered over its slopes and levels. Among these, we got at last into a picturesque dingle; the grey rocks peeped from among the ferns and wild flowers, and the steps of soft sward along its sides were dark in the shadows of silver-stemmed birch, and russet thorn, and oak, under which, in the vaporous night, the Erl-king and his daughter might glide on their aërial horses.

In the lap of this pleasant dell were the finest blackberry bushes, I think, I ever saw, bearing fruit quite fabulous; and plucking these, and chatting, we rambled on very pleasantly.

I had first thought of Milly's absurdities, to which, in description, I cannot do justice, simply because so many details have, by distance of time, escaped my recollection. But her ways and her talk were so indescribably grotesque that she made me again and again quiver with suppressed laughter.

But there was a pitiable and even a melancholy meaning underlying the burlesque.

This creature, with no more education than a dairy-maid, I gradually discovered had fine natural aptitudes for accomplishment—a very sweet voice, and wonderfully delicate ear, and a talent for drawing which quite threw mine into the shade. It was really astonishing.

Poor Milly, in all her life, had never read three books, and hated to think of them. One, over which she was wont to yawn and sigh, and stare fatiguedly for an hour every Sunday, by command of the Governor, was a stout volume of sermons of the earlier school of George III., and a drier collection you can't fancy. I don't think she read anything else. But she had, notwithstanding, ten times the cleverness of half the circulating library misses one meets with. Besides all this, I had a long sojourn before me at Bartram-Haugh, and I had learned from Milly, as I had heard before, what a perennial solitude it was, with a ludicrous fear of learning Milly's preposterous dialect, and turning at last into something like her. So I resolved to do all I could for her—teach her whatever I knew, if she would allow me—and gradually, if possible, effect some civilising changes in her language, and, as they term it in boarding-schools, her demeanour.

But I must pursue at present our first day's ramble in what was called Bartram

Chase. People can't go on eating blackberries always; so after a while we resumed our walk along this pretty dell, which gradually expanded into a wooded valley-level beneath and enclosed by irregular uplands, receding, as it were, in mimic bays and harbours at some points, and running out at others into broken promontories, ending in clumps of forest trees.

Just where the glen which we had been traversing expanded into this broad, but wooded valley, it was traversed by a high and close paling, which, although it looked decayed, was still very strong.

In this there was a wooden gate, rudely but strongly constructed, and at the side we were approaching stood a girl, who was leaning against the post, with one arm resting on the top of the gate.

This girl was neither tall nor short—taller than she looked at a distance; she had not a slight waist; sooty black was her hair, with a broad forehead, perpendicular but low; she had a pair of very fine, dark, lustrous eyes, and no other good feature—unless I may so call her teeth, which were very white and even. Her face was rather short, and swarthy as a gipsy's; observant and sullen too; and she did not move, only eyed us negligently from under her dark lashes as we drew near. Altogether a not unpicturesque figure, with a dusky, red petticoat of drugget, and tattered jacket of bottle-green stuff, with short sleeves, which showed her brown arms from the elbow.

'That's Pegtop's daughter,' said Milly.

'Who is Pegtop?' I asked.

'He's the miller—see, yonder it is,' and she pointed to a very pretty feature in the landscape, a windmill, crowning the summit of a hillock which rose suddenly above the level of the treetops, like an island in the centre of the valley.

'The mill not going to-day, Beauty?' bawled Milly.

'No—a, Beauty; it baint,' replied the girl, loweringly, and without stirring.

'And what's gone with the stile?' demanded Milly, aghast. 'It's tore away from the paling!'

'Well, so it be,' replied the wood nymph in the red petticoat, showing her fine teeth with a lazy grin.

'Who's a bin and done all that?' demanded Milly.

'Not you nor me, lass,' said the girl.

''Twas old Pegtop, your father, did it,' cried Milly, in rising wrath.

''Appen it wor,' she replied.

'And the gate locked.'

'That's it—the gate locked,' she repeated, sulkily, with a defiant side-glance at

Milly.

'And where's Pegtop?'

'At t'other side, somewhere; how should I know where he be?' she replied.

'Who's got the key?'

'Here it be, lass,' she answered, striking her hand on her pocket.

'And how durst you stay us here? Unlock it, huzzy, this minute!' cried Milly, with a stamp.

Her answer was a sullen smile.

'Open the gate this instant!' bawled Milly.

'Well, I *won't.*'

I expected that Milly would have flown into a frenzy at this direct defiance, but she looked instead puzzled and curious—the girl's unexpected audacity bewildered her.

'Why, you fool, I could get over the paling as soon as look at you, but I won't. What's come over you? Open the gate, I say, or I'll make you.'

'Do let her alone, dear,' I entreated, fearing a mutual assault. 'She has been ordered, may be, not to open it. Is it so, my good girl?'

'Well, thou'rt not the biggest fool o' the two,' she observed, commendatively, 'thou'st hit it, lass.'

'And who ordered you?' exclaimed Milly.

'Fayther.'

'Old Pegtop. Well, *that's* summat to laugh at it is—our servant a-shutting us out of our own grounds.'

'No servant o' yourn!'

'Come, lass, what do you mean?'

'He be old Silas's miller, and what's that to thee?'

With these words the girl made a spring on the hasp of the padlock, and then got easily over the gate.

'Can't you do that, cousin?' whispered Milly to me, with an impatient nudge. 'I *wish* you'd try.'

'No, dear—come away, Milly,' and I began to withdraw.

'Lookee, lass, 'twill be an ill day's work for thee when I tell the Governor,' said Milly, addressing the girl, who stood on a log of timber at the other side, regarding us with a sullen composure.

'We'll be over in spite o' you,' cried Milly.

'You lie!' answered she.

'And why not, huzzy?' demanded my cousin, who was less incensed at the affront than I expected. All this time I was urging Milly in vain to come away.

'Yon lass is no wild cat, like thee—that's why,' said the sturdy portress.

'If I cross, I'll give you a knock,' said Milly.

'And I'll gi' thee another,' she answered, with a vicious wag of the head.

'Come, Milly, *I'll* go if *you* don't,' I said.

'But we must not be beat,' whispered she, vehemently, catching my arm; 'and ye *shall* get over, and *see* what I will gi' her!'

'I'll *not* get over.'

'Then I'll break the door, for ye *shall* come through,' exclaimed Milly, kicking the stout paling with her ponderous boot.

'Purr it, purr it, purr it!' cried the lass in the red petticoat with a grin.

'Do you know who this lady is?' cried Milly, suddenly.

'She is a prettier lass than thou,' answered Beauty.

'She's *my* cousin Maud—Miss Ruthyn of Knowl—and she's a deal richer than the Queen; and the Governor's taking care of her; and he'll make old Pegtop bring you to reason.'

The girl eyed me with a sulky listlessness, a little inquisitively, I thought.

'See if he don't,' threatened Milly.

'You positively *must* come,' I said, drawing her away with me.

'Well, shall we come in?' cried Milly, trying a last summons.

'You'll not come in that much,' she answered, surlily, measuring an infinitesimal distance on her finger with her thumb, which she pinched against it, the gesture ending with a snap of defiance, and a smile that showed her fine teeth.

'I've a mind to shy a stone at you,' shouted Milly.

'Faire away; I'll shy wi' ye as long as ye like, lass; take heed o' yerself;' and Beauty picked up a round stone as large as a cricket ball.

With difficulty I got Milly away without an exchange of missiles, and much disgusted at my want of zeal and agility.

'Well, come along, cousin, I know an easy way by the river, when it's low,' answered Milly. 'She's a brute—is not she?'

As we receded, we saw the girl slowly wending her way towards the old thatched cottage, which showed its gable from the side of a little rugged eminence embowered in spreading trees, and dangling and twirling from its string on the end of her finger the key for which a battle had so nearly been fought.

The stream was low enough to make our flank movement round the end of the paling next it quite easy, and so we pur sued our way, and Milly's equanimity returned, and our ramble grew very pleasant again.

Our path lay by the river bank, and as we proceeded, the dwarf timber was succeeded by grander trees, which crowded closer and taller, and, at last, the scenery deepened into solemn forest, and a sudden sweep in the river revealed the beautiful ruin of a steep old bridge, with the fragments of a gate-house on the farther side.

'Oh, Milly darling!' I exclaimed, 'what a beautiful drawing this would make! I should so like to make a sketch of it.'

'So it would. *Make* a picture—*do!*—here's a stone that's pure and flat to sit upon, and you look very tired. Do make it, and I'll sit by you.'

'Yes, Milly, I *am* tired, a little, and I *will* sit down; but we must wait for another day to make the picture, for we have neither pencil nor paper. But it is much too pretty to be lost; so let us come again to-morrow.'

'To-morrow be hanged! you'll do it to-day, bury-me-wick, but you *shall*, I'm wearying to see you make a picture, and I'll fetch your conundrums out o' your drawer, for do't you shall.'

CHAPTER XXXIV

ZAMIEL

It was all vain my remonstrating. She vowed that by crossing the stepping-stones close by she could, by a short cut, reach the house, and return with my pencils and block-book in a quarter of an hour. Away then, with many a jump and fling, scampered Milly's queer white stockings and navvy boots across the irregular and precarious stepping-stones, over which I dared not follow her; so I was fain to return to the stone so 'pure and flat,' on which I sat, enjoying the grand sylvan solitude, the dark back ground and the grey bridge mid-way, so tall and slim, across whose ruins a sunbeam glimmered, and the gigantic forest trees that slumbered round, opening here and there in dusky vistas, and breaking in front into detached and solemn groups. It was the setting of a dream of romance.

It would have been the very spot in which to read a volume of German folklore, and the darkening colonnades and silent nooks of the forest seemed already haunted with the voices and shadows of those charming elves and goblins.

As I sat here enjoying the solitude and my fancies among the low branches of the wood, at my right I heard a crashing, and saw a squat broad figure in a stained and tattered military coat, and loose short trousers, one limb of which flapped about a wooden leg. He was forcing himself through. His face was rugged and wrinkled, and tanned to the tint of old oak; his eyes black, beadlike, and fierce, and a shock of sooty hair escaped from under his battered wide-awake nearly to his shoulders. This forbidding-looking person came stumping and jerking along toward me, whisking his stick now and then viciously in the air, and giving his fell of hair a short shake, like a wild bull preparing to attack.

I stood up involuntarily with a sense of fear and surprise, almost fancying I saw in that wooden-legged old soldier, the forest demon who haunted Der Freischütz.

So he approached shouting—

'Hollo! you—how came you here? Dost 'eer?'

And he drew near panting, and sometimes tugging angrily in his haste at his wooden leg, which sunk now and then deeper than was convenient in the sod. This exertion helped to anger him, and when he halted before me, his dark face smirched with smoke and dust, and the nostrils of his flat drooping nose expanded and quivered as he panted, like the gills of a fish; an angrier or uglier face it would not be easy to fancy.

'Ye'll all come when ye like, will ye? and do nout but what pleases yourselves, won't you? And who'rt thou? Dost 'eer—who *are* ye, I say; and what the deil seek ye in the woods here? Come, bestir thee!'

If his wide mouth and great tobacco-stained teeth, his scowl, and loud discordant tones were intimidating, they were also extremely irritating. The moment my spirit was roused, my courage came.

'I am Miss Ruthyn of Knowl, and Mr. Silas Ruthyn, your master, is my uncle.'

'Hoo!' he exclaimed more gently, 'an' if Silas be thy uncle thou'lt be come to live wi' him, and thou'rt she as come overnight—eh?'

I made no answer, but I believe I looked both angrily and disdainfully.

'And what make ye alone here? and how was I to know't, an' Milly not wi' ye, nor no one? But Maud or no Maud, I wouldn't let the Dooke hisself set foot inside the palin' without Silas said let him. And you may tell Silas them's the words o' Dickon Hawkes, and I'll stick to 'm—and what's more I'll tell him *myself*—I will; I'll tell him there be no use o' my striving and straining bee, day an' night and night and day, watchin' again poachers, and thieves, and gipsies, and they robbing lads, if rules won't be kep, and folk do jist as they pleases. Dang it, lass, thou'rt in luck I didn't heave a brick at thee when I saw thee first.'

'I'll complain of you to my uncle,' I replied.

'So do, and and 'appen thou'lt find thyself in the wrong box, lass; thou canst na' say I set the dogs arter thee, nor cau'd thee so much as a wry name, nor heave a stone at thee—did I? Well? and where's the complaint then?'

I simply answered, rather fiercely.

'Be good enough to leave me.'

'Well, I make no objections, mind. I'm takin' thy word—thou'rt Maud Ruthyn—'appen thou be'st and 'appen thou baint. I'm not aweer on't, but I takes thy word, and all I want to know's just this, did Meg open the gate to thee?'

I made him no answer, and to my great relief I saw Milly striding and skipping across the unequal stepping-stones.

'Hallo, Pegtop! what are you after now?' she cried, as she drew near.

'This man has been extremely impertinent. You know him, Milly?' I said.

'Why that's Pegtop Dickon. Dirty old Hawkes that never was washed. I tell you, lad, ye'll see what the Governor thinks o't—a-ha! He'll talk to you.'

'I done or said nout—not but I *should*, and there's the fack—she can't deny't; she hadn't a hard word from I; and I don't care the top o' that thistle what no one says—not I. But I tell thee, Milly, I stopped *some* o' thy pranks, and I'll stop more. Ye'll be shying no more stones at the cattle.'

'Tell your tales, and welcome, cried Milly. 'I wish I was here when you jawed cousin. If Winny was here she'd catch you by the timber toe and put you on your back!'

'Ay, she'll be a good un yet if she takes arter thee,' retorted the old man with a fierce sneer.

'Drop it, and get away wi' ye,' cried she, 'or maybe I'd call Winny to smash your timber leg for you.'

'A-ha! there's more on't. She's a sweet un. Isn't she?' he replied sardonically.

'You did not like it last Easter, when Winny broke it with a kick.'

'Twas a kick o' a horse,' he growled with a glance at me.

''Twas no such thing—'twas Winny did it—and he laid on his back for a week while carpenter made him a new one.' And Milly laughed hilariously.

'I'll fool no more wi' ye, losing my time; I won't; but mind ye, I'll speak wi' Silas.' And going away he put his hand to his crumpled wide-awake, and said to me with a surly difference 'Good evening, Miss Ruthyn—good evening, ma'am—and yell please remember, I did not mean nout to vex thee.'

And so he swaggered away, jerking and waddling over the sward, and was soon lost in the wood.

'It's well be's a little bit frightened—I never saw him so angry, I think; he is awful mad.'

'Perhaps he really is not aware how very rude he is,' I suggested.

'I hate him. We were twice as pleasant with poor Tom Driver—he never meddled with any one, and was always in liquor; Old Gin was the name he went by.

But this brute—I do hate him—he comes from Wigan, I think, and he's always spoiling sport—and he whops Meg—that's Beauty, you know, and I don't think she'd be half as bad only for him. Listen to him whistlin'.'

'I did hear whistling at some distance among the trees.'

'I declare if he isn't callin' the dogs! Climb up here, I tell ye,' and we climbed up the slanting trunk of a great walnut tree, and strained our eyes in the direction from which we expected the onset of Pegtop's vicious pack.

But it was a false alarm.

'Well, I don't think he *would* do that, after all—*hardly*, but he is a brute, sure!'

'And that dark girl who would not let us through, is his daughter, is she?'

'Yes, that's Meg—Beauty, I christened her, when I called him Beast; but I call him Pegtop now, and she's Beauty still, and that's the way o't.'

'Come, sit down now, an' make your picture,' she resumed so soon as we had dismounted from our position of security.

'I'm afraid I'm hardly in the vein. I don't think I could draw a straight line. My hand trembles.'

'I wish you could, Maud,' said Milly, with a look so wistful and entreating, that considering the excursion she had made for the pencils, I could not bear to disappoint her.

'Well, Milly, we must only try; and if we fail we can't help it. Sit you down beside me and I'll tell you why I begin with one part and not another, and you'll see how I make trees and the river, and—yes, *that* pencil, it is hard and answers for the fine light lines; but we must begin at the beginning, and learn to copy drawings before we attempt real views like this. And if you wish it, Milly, I'm resolved to teach you everything I know, which, after all, is not a great deal, and we shall have such fun making sketches of the same landscapes, and then comparing.'

And so on, Milly, quite delighted, and longing to begin her course of instruction, sat down beside me in a rapture, and hugged and kissed me so heartily that we were very near rolling together off the stone on which we were seated. Her boisterous delight and good-nature helped to restore me, and both laughing heartily together, I commenced my task.

'Dear me! who's that?' I exclaimed suddenly, as looking up from my block-book I saw the figure of a slight man in the careless morning-dress of a gentleman, crossing the ruinous bridge in our direction, with considerable caution, upon the precarious footing of the battlement, which alone offered an unbroken passage.

This was a day of apparitions! Milly recognised him instantly. The gentleman was Mr. Carysbroke. He had taken The Grange only for a year. He lived quite to himself, and was very good to the poor, and was the only gentleman, for ever so long, who had visited at Bartram, and oddly enough nowhere else. But he wanted leave to cross through the grounds, and having obtained it, had repeated his visit, partly induced, no doubt, by the fact that Bartram boasted no hospitalities, and that there was no risk of meeting the county folk there.

With a stout walking-stick in his hand, and a short shooting-coat, and a wide-awake hat in much better trim than Zamiel's, he emerged from the copse that covered the bridge, walking at a quick but easy pace.

'He'll be goin' to see old Snoddles, I guess,' said Milly, looking a little frightened and curious; for Milly, I need not say, was a bumpkin, and stood in awe of this gentleman's good-breeding, though she was as brave as a lion, and would have fought the Philistines at any odds, with the jawbone of an ass.

''Appen he won't see us,' whispered Milly, hopefully.

But he did, and raising his hat, with a cheerful smile, that showed very white teeth, he paused.

'Charming day, Miss Ruthyn.'

I raised my head suddenly as he spoke, from habit appropriating the address; it was so marked that he raised his hat respectfully to me, and then continued to Milly—

'Mr. Ruthyn, I hope, quite well? but I need hardly ask, you seem so happy. Will you kindly tell him, that I expect the book I mentioned in a day or two, and when it comes I'll either send or bring it to him immediately?'

Milly and I were standing, by this time, but she only stared at him, tongue-tied, her cheeks rather flushed, and her eyes very round, and to facilitate the dialogue, as I suppose, he said again—

'He's quite well, I hope?'

Still no response from Milly, and I, provoked, though myself a little shy, made answer—

'My uncle, Mr. Ruthyn, is very well, thank you,' and I felt that I blushed as I spoke.

'Ah, pray excuse me, may I take a great liberty? you are Miss Ruthyn, of Knowl? Will you think me very impertinent—I'm afraid you will—if I venture to introduce myself? My name is Carysbroke, and I had the honour of knowing poor Mr. Ruthyn when I was quite a little boy, and he has shown a kindness for me since, and I hope you will pardon the liberty I fear I've taken. I think my friend, Lady Knollys, too, is a relation of yours; what a charming person she is!'

'Oh, is not she? such a darling!' I said, and then blushed at my outspoken affection.

But he smiled kindly, as if he liked me for it; and he said—

'You know whatever I think, I dare not quite say that; but frankly I can quite understand it. She preserves her youth so wonderfully, and her fun and her good-nature are so entirely girlish. What a sweet view you have selected,' he continued, changing all at once. 'I've stood just at this point so often to look back at that exquisite old bridge. Do you observe—you're an artist, I see—something very peculiar in that tint of the grey, with those odd cross stains of faded red and yellow?'

'I do, indeed; I was just remarking the peculiar beauty of the colouring—was not I, Milly?'

Milly stared at me, and uttered an alarmed 'Yes,' and looked as if she had been caught in a robbery.

'Yes, and you have so very peculiar a background,' he resumed. 'It was better before the storm though; but it is very good still.'

Then a little pause, and 'Do you know this country at all?' rather suddenly.

'No, not in the least—that is, I've only had the drive to this place; but what I did see interested me very much.'

'You will be charmed with it when you know it better—the very place for an artist. I'm a wretched scribbler myself, and I carry this little book in my pocket,' and he laughed deprecatingly while he drew forth a thin fishing-book, as it looked. 'They are mere memoranda, you see. I walk so much and come unexpectedly on such pretty nooks and studies, I just try to make a note of them, but it is really more writing than sketching; my sister says it is a cipher which nobody but myself understands. However, I'll try and explain just two—because you really ought to go and see the places. Oh, no; not that,' he laughed, as accidentally the page blew over, 'that's the Cat and Fiddle, a curious little pot-house, where they gave me some very good ale one day.'

Milly at this exhibited some uneasy tokens of being about to speak, but not knowing what might be coming, I hastened to observe on the spirited little sketches to which he meant to draw my attention.

'I want to show you only the places within easy reach—a short ride or drive.'

So he proceeded to turn over two or three, in addition to the two he had at first proposed, and then another; then a little sketch just tinted, and really quite a charming little gem, of Cousin Monica's pretty gabled old house; and every subject had its little criticism, or its narrative, or adventure.

As he was about returning this little sketch-book to his pocket, still chatting to me, he suddenly recollected poor Milly, who was looking rather lowering; but she brightened a good deal as he presented it to her, with a little speech which she palpably misunderstood, for she made one of her odd courtesies, and was about, I thought, to put it into her large pocket, and accept it as a present.

'Look at the drawings, Milly, and then return it,' I whispered.

At his request I allowed him to look at my unfinished sketch of the bridge, and while he was measuring distances and proportions with his eye, Milly whispered rather angrily to me,

'And why should I?'

'Because he wants it back, and only meant to lend it to you,' whispered I.

'*Lend* it to me—and after you! Bury-me-wick if I look at a leaf of it,' she retorted in high dudgeon. 'Take it, lass; give it him yourself—I'll not,' and she popped it into my hand, and made a sulky step back.

'My cousin is very much obliged,' I said, returning the book, and smiling for her, and he took it smiling also and said 'I think if I had known how very well you draw, Miss Ruthyn, I should have hesitated about showing you my poor scrawls. But these are not my best, you know; Lady Knollys will tell you that I can really do better—a great deal better, I think.'

And then with more apologies for what he called his impertinence, he took his leave, and I felt altogether very much pleased and flattered.

He could not be more than twenty-nine or thirty, I thought, and he was decidedly handsome—that is, his eyes and teeth, and clear brown complexion were—and there was something distinguished and graceful in his figure and gesture; and altogether there was the indescribable attraction of intelligence; and I fancied—though this, of course, was a secret—that from the moment he spoke to us he felt an interest in me. I am not going to be vain. It was a *grave* interest, but still an interest, for I could see him studying my features while I was turning over his sketches, and he thought I saw nothing else. It was flattering, too, his anxiety that I should think well of his drawing, and referring me to Lady Knollys. Carysbroke—had I ever heard my dear father mention that name? I could not recollect it. But then he was habitually so silent, that his not doing so argued nothing.

CHAPTER XXXV

WE VISIT A ROOM IN THE SECOND STOREY

Mr. Carysbroke amused my fancy sufficiently to prevent my observing Milly's silence, till we had begun our return homeward.

'The Grange must be a pretty house, if that little sketch be true; is it far from this?'

''Twill be two mile.'

'Are you vexed, Milly?' I asked, for both her tone and looks were angry.

'Yes, I am vexed; and why not lass?'

'What has happened?'

'Well now, that is rich! Why, look at that fellow, Carysbroke: he took no more notice to me than a dog, and kep' talking to you all the time of his pictures, and his walks, and his people. Why, a pig's better manners than that.'

'But, Milly dear, you forget, he tried to talk to you, and you would not answer him,' I expostulated.

'And is not that just what I say—I can't talk like other folk ladies, I mean. Every one laughs at me; an' I'm dressed like a show, I am. It's a shame! I saw Polly Shives—what a lady she is, my eyes!—laughing at me in church last Sunday. I was minded to give her a bit of my mind. An' I know I'm queer. It's a shame, it is. Why should *I* be so rum? it is a shame! I don't want to be so, nor it isn't my fault.'

And poor Milly broke into a flood of tears, and stamped on the ground, and buried her face in her short frock, which she whisked up to her eyes; and an odder figure of grief I never beheld.

'And I could not make head or tail of what he was saying,' cried poor Milly through her buff cotton, with a stamp; 'and you twigged every word o't. An' why am I so? It's a shame—a shame! Oh, ho, ho! it's a shame!'

'But, my dear Milly, we were talking of *drawing*, and you have not learned yet, but you shall—I'll teach you; and then you'll understand all about it.'

'An' every one laughs at me—even you; though you try, Maud, you can scarce keep from laughing sometimes. I don't blame you, for I know I'm queer; but I can't help it; and it's a shame.'

'Well, my dear Milly, listen to me: if you allow me, I assure you, I'll teach you all the music and drawing I know. You have lived very much alone; and, as you say, ladies have a way of speaking of their own that is different from the talk of other people.'

'Yes, that they have, an' gentlemen too—like the Governor, and that Carysbroke; and a precious lingo it is—dang it—why, the devil himself could not understand it; an' I'm like a fool among you. I could 'most drown myself. It's a shame! It is—you know it is.—It's a shame!'

'But I'll teach you that lingo too, if you wish it, Milly; and you shall know everything that I know; and I'll manage to have your dresses better made.'

By this time she was looking very ruefully, but attentively, in my face, her round eyes and nose swelled, and her cheeks all wet.

'I think if they were a little longer—yours is longer, you know;' and the sentence was interrupted by a sob.

'Now, Milly, you must not be crying; if you choose you may be just as the same as any other lady—and you shall; and you will be very much admired, I can tell you, if only you will take the trouble to quite unlearn all your odd words and ways, and dress yourself like other people; and I will take care of that if you let me; and I think you are very clever, Milly; and I know you are very pretty.'

Poor Milly's blubbered face expanded into a smile in spite of herself; but she shook her head, looking down.

'Noa, noa, Maud, I fear 'twon't be.' And indeed it seemed I had proposed to myself a labour of Hercules.

But Milly was really a clever creature, could see quickly, and when her ungainly dialect was mastered, describe very pleasantly; and if only she would endure the restraint and possessed the industry requisite, I did not despair, and was resolved at least to do my part.

Poor Milly! she was really very grateful, and entered into the project of her education with great zeal, and with a strange mixture of humility and insubordination.

Milly was in favour of again attacking 'Beauty's' position on her return, and forcing a passage from this side; but I insisted on following the route by which we had arrived, and so we got round the paling by the river, and were treated to a provoking grin of defiance by 'Beauty,' who was talking across the gate to a slim young man, arrayed in fustian, and with an odd-looking cap of rabbit-skin on his head, which, on seeing us, he pulled sheepishly to the side of his face next to us, as he lounged, with his arm under his chin, on the top bar of the gate.

After our encounter of to-day, indeed, it was Miss Beauty's wont to exhibit a kind of jeering disdain in her countenance whenever we passed.

I think Milly would have engaged her again, had I not reminded her of her undertaking, and exerted my new authority.

'Look at that sneak, Pegtop, there, going up the path to the mill. He makes belief now he does not see us; but he does, though, only he's afraid we'll tell the Governor, and he thinks Governor won't give him his way with you. I hate that Pegtop: he stopped me o' riding the cows a year ago, he did.'

I thought Pegtop might have done worse. Indeed it was plain that a total reformation was needed here; and I was glad to find that poor Milly seemed herself conscious of it; and that her resolution to become more like other people of her station was not a mere spasm of mortification and jealousy, but a genuine and very zealous resolve.

I had not half seen this old house of Bartram-Haugh yet. At first, indeed, I had but an imperfect idea of its extent. There was a range of rooms along one side of the great gallery, with closed window-shutters, and the doors generally locked. Old L'Amour grew cross when we went into them, although we could see nothing; and Milly was afraid to open the windows —not that any Bluebeard revelations were apprehended, but simply because she knew that Uncle Silas's order was that things should be left undisturbed; and this boisterous spirit stood in awe of him to a degree which his gentle manners and apparent quietude rendered quite surprising.

There were in this house, what certainly did not exist at Knowl, and what I have never observed, thought they may possibly be found in other old houses—I mean, here and there, very high hatches, which we could only peep over by jumping in the air. They crossed the long corridors and great galleries; and several of them were turned across and locked, so as to intercept the passage, and interrupt our explorations.

Milly, however, knew a queer little, very steep and dark back stair, which reached the upper floor; so she and I mounted, and made a long ramble through rooms much lower and ruder in finish than the lordly chambers we had left below. These commanded various views of the beautiful though neglected grounds; but on crossing a gallery we entered suddenly a chamber, which looked into a small and dismal quadrangle, formed by the inner walls of this great house, and of course designed only by the architect to afford the needful light and air to portions of the structure.

I rubbed the window-pane with my handkerchief and looked out. The surrounding roof was steep and high. The walls looked soiled and dark. The windows lined with dust and dirt, and the window-stones were in places tufted with moss, and grass, and groundsel. An arched doorway had opened from the house into this darkened square, but it was soiled and dusty; and the damp weeds that overgrew the quadrangle drooped undisturbed against it. It was plain that human footsteps tracked it little, and I gazed into that blind and sinister area with a strange thrill and sinking.

'This is the second floor—there is the enclosed court-yard'—I, as it were, soliloquised.

'What are you afraid of, Maud? you look as ye'd seen a ghost,' exclaimed Milly, who came to the window and peeped over my shoulder.

'It reminded me suddenly, Milly, of that frightful business.'

'What business, Maud?—what a plague are ye thinking on?' demanded Milly, rather amused.

'It was in one of these rooms—maybe this—yes, it certainly was this—for see, the panelling has been pulled off the wall—that Mr. Charke killed himself.'

I was staring ruefully round the dim chamber, in whose corners the shadows of night were already gathering.

'Charke!—what about him?—who's Charke?' asked Milly.

'Why, you must have heard of him,' said I.

'Not as I'm aware on,' answered she. 'And he killed himself, did he, hanged himself, eh, or blowed his brains out?'

'He cut his throat in one of these rooms—*this* one, I'm sure—for your papa had the wainscoting stripped from the wall to ascertain whether there was any second door through which a murderer could have come; and you see these walls are stripped, and bear the marks of the woodwork that has been removed,' I answered.

'Well, that *was* awful! I don't know how they have pluck to cut their throats; if I was doing it, I'd like best to put a pistol to my head and fire, like the young gentleman did, they say, in Deadman's Hollow. But the fellows that cut their throats, they must be awful game lads, I'm thinkin', for it's a long slice, you know.'

'Don't, don't, Milly dear. Suppose we come away,' I said, for the evening was deepening rapidly into night.

'Hey and bury-me-wick, but here's the blood; don't you see a big black cloud all spread over the floor hereabout, don't ye see?' Milly was stooping over the spot, and tracing the outline of this, perhaps, imaginary mapping, in the air with her finger.

'No, Milly, you could not see it the floor is too dark, and it's all in shadow. It must be fancy and perhaps, after all, this is not the room.'

'Well—I think, I'm *sure* it *is.* Stand—just look.'

'We'll come in the morning, and if you are right we can see it better then. Come away,' I said, growing frightened.

And just as we stood up to depart, the white high-cauled cap and large sallow features of old L'Amour peeped in at the door.

'Lawk! what brings you here?' cried Milly, nearly as much startled as I at the intrusion.

'What brings *you* here, miss?' whistled L'Amour through her gums.

'We're looking where Charke cut his throat,' replied Milly.

'Charke the devil!' said the old woman, with an odd mixture of scorn and fury.

''Tisn't his room; and come ye out of it, please. Master won't like when he hears how you keep pulling Miss Maud from one room to another, all through the house, up and down.'

She was gabbling sternly enough, but dropped a low courtesy as I passed her, and with a peaked and nodding stare round the room, the old woman clapped the door sharply, and locked it.

'And who has been a talking about Charke—a pack o' lies, I warrant. I s'pose you want to frighten Miss Maud here' (another crippled courtesy) 'wi' ghosts and like nonsense.'

'You're out there: 'twas she told me; and much about it. Ghosts, indeed! I don't vally them, not I; if I did, I know who'd frighten me,' and Milly laughed.

The old woman stuffed the key in her pocket, and her wrinkled mouth pouted and receded with a grim uneasiness.

'A harmless brat, and kind she is; but wild—wild—she will be wild.'

So whispered L'Amour in my ear, during the silence that followed, nodding shakily toward Milly over the banister, and she courtesied again as we departed, and shuffled off toward Uncle Silas's room.

The Governor is queerish this evening,' said Milly, when we were seated at our tea. 'You never saw him queerish, did you?'

'You must say what you mean, more plainly, Milly. You don't mean ill, I hope?'

'Well! I don't know what it is; but he does grow very queer some times—you'd think he was dead a'most, maybe two or three days and nights together. He sits all the time like an old woman in a swound. Well, well, it is awful!'

'Is he insensible when in that state?' I asked, a good deal alarmed.

'I don't know; but it never signifies anything. It won't kill him, I do believe; but old L'Amour knows all about it. I hardly ever go into the room when he's so, only when I'm sent for; and he sometimes wakes up and takes a fancy to can for this one or that. One day he sent for Pegtop all the way to the mill; and when he came, he only stared at him for a minute or two, and ordered him out o' the room. He's like a child a'most, when he's in one o' them dazes.'

I always knew when Uncle Silas was 'queerish,' by the injunctions of old L'Amour, whistled and spluttered over the banister as we came up-stairs, to mind how we made a noise passing master's door; and by the sound of mysterious to-ings and fro-ings about his room.

I saw very little of him. He sometimes took a whim to have us breakfast with him, which lasted perhaps for a week; and then the order of our living would relapse into its old routine.

I must not forget two kind letters from Lady Knollys, who was detained away, and delighted to hear that I enjoyed my quiet life; and promised to apply, in person, to Uncle Silas, for permission to visit me.

She was to be for the Christmas at Elverston, and that was only six miles away from Bartram-Haugh, so I had the excitement of a pleasant look forward.

She also said that she would include poor Milly in her invitation; and a vision of Captain Oakley rose before me, with his handsome gaze turned in wonder on poor Milly, for whom I had begun to feel myself responsible.

CHAPTER XXXVI

AN ARRIVAL AT DEAD OF NIGHT

I have sometimes been asked why I wear an odd little turquois ring—which to the uninstructed eye appears quite valueless and altogether an unworthy companion of those jewels which flash insultingly beside it. It is a little keepsake, of which I became possessed about this time.

'Come, lass, what name shall I give you?' cried Milly, one morning, bursting into my room in a state of alarming hilarity.

'My own, Milly.'

'No, but you must have a nickname, like every one else.'

'Don't mind it, Milly.'

'Yes, but I will. Shall I call you Mrs. Bustle?'

'You shall do no such thing.'

'But you must have a name.'

'I refuse a name.'

'But I'll give you one, lass.'

'And *I* won't have it.'

'But you can't help me christening you.'

'I can decline answering.'

'But I'll make you,' said Milly, growing very red.

Perhaps there was something provoking in my tone, for I certainly was very much disgusted at Milly's relapse into barbarism.

'You can't,' I retorted quietly.

'See if I don't, and I'll give ye one twice as ugly.'

I smiled, I fear, disdainfully.

'And I think you're a minx, and a slut, and a fool,' she broke out, flushing scarlet.

I smiled in the same unchristian way.

'And I'd give ye a smack o' the cheek as soon as look at you.'

And she gave her dress a great slap, and drew near me, in her and thought myself, I dare say justly, a thousand times more to blame than Milly.

I searched in vain for her before breakfast. At that meal, however, we met, but in the presence of Uncle Silas, who, though silent and apathetic, was formidable; and we, sitting at a table disproportionably large, under the cold, strange gaze of my guardian, talked only what was inevitable, and that in low tones; for whenever Milly for a moment raised her voice, Uncle Silas would wince, place his thin white fingers quickly over his ear, and look as if a pain had pierced his brain, and then shrug and smile piteously into vacancy. When Uncle Silas, therefore, was not in the talking vein himself—and that was not often—you may suppose there was very little spoken in his presence.

When Milly, across the table, saw the ring upon my finger, she, drawing in her breath, said, 'Oh!' and, with round eyes and mouth, she looked so delighted; and she made a little motion, as if she was on the point of jumping up; and then her poor face quivered, and she bit her lip; and staring imploringly at me, her eyes filled fast with tears, which rolled down her round penitential cheeks.

I am sure I felt more penitent than she. I know I was crying and smiling, and longing to kiss her. I suppose we were very absurd; but it is well that small matters can stir the affections so profoundly at a time of life when great troubles seldom approach us.

When at length the opportunity did come, never was such a hug out of the wrestling ring as poor Milly bestowed on me, swaying me this way and that, and burying her face in my dress, and blubbering 'I was so lonely before you came, and you so good to me, and I such a devil; and I'll never call you a name, but Maud—my darling Maud.'

'You must, Milly—Mrs. Bustle. I'll be Mrs. Bustle, or anything you like. You must.' I was blubbering like Milly, and hugging my best; and, indeed, I wonder how we kept our feet.

So Milly and I were better friends than ever.

Meanwhile, the winter deepened, and we had short days and long nights, and long fireside gossipings at Bartram-Haugh. I was frightened at the frequency of the strange collapses to which Uncle Silas was subject. I did not at first mind them much, for I naturally fell into Milly's way of talking about them.

But one day, while in one of his 'queerish' states, he called for me, and I saw him, and was unspeakably scared.

In a white wrapper, he lay coiled in a great easy chair. I should have thought him dead, had I not been accompanied by old L'Amour, who knew every gradation and symptom of these strange affections.

She winked and nodded to me with a ghastly significance, and whispered—

'Don't make no noise, miss, till he talks; he'll come to for a bit, anon.'

Except that there was no sign of convulsions, the countenance was like that of an epileptic arrested in one of his contortions.

There was a frown and smirk like that of idiotcy, and a strip of white eyeball was also disclosed.

Suddenly, with a kind of chilly shudder, he opened his eyes wide, and screwed his lips together, and blinked and stared on me with a fatuised uncertainty, that gradually broke into a feeble smile.

'Ah! the girl—Austin's child. Well, dear, I'm hardly able—I'll speak to-morrow—next day—it is tic—neuralgia, or something—*torture*—tell her.'

So, huddling himself together, he lay again in his great chair, with the same inexpressible helplessness in his attitude, and gradually his face resumed its dreadful cast.

'Come away, miss: he's changed his mind; he'll not be fit to talk to you noways all day, maybe,' said the old woman, again in a whisper.

So forth we stole from the room, I unspeakably shocked. In fact, he looked as if he were dying, and so, in my agitation, I told the crone, who, forgetting the ceremony with which she usually treated me, chuckled out derisively,

'A-dying is he? Well, he be like Saint Paul—he's bin a-dying daily this many a day.'

I looked at her with a chill of horror. She did not care, I suppose, what sort of feelings she might excite, for she went on mumbling sarcastically to herself. I had paused, and overcame my reluctance to speak to her again, for I was really very much frightened.

'Do you think he is in danger? Shall we send for a doctor?' I whispered.

'Law bless ye, the doctor knows all about it, miss.' The old woman's face had a gleam of that derision which is so shocking in the features of feebleness and age.

'But it is a *fit*, it is paralytic, or something horrible—it can't be *safe* to leave him to chance or nature to get through these terrible attacks.'

'There's no fear of him, 'tisn't no fits at all, he's nout the worse o't. Jest silly a bit now and again. It's been the same a dozen year and more; and the doctor knows all about it,' answered the old woman sturdily. 'And ye'll find he'll be as mad as bedlam if ye make any stir about it.'

That night I talked the matter over with Mary Quince.

'They're very dark, miss; but I think he takes a deal too much laudlum,' said Mary.

To this hour I cannot say what was the nature of those periodical seizures. I have often spoken to medical men about them, since, but never could learn that excessive use of opium could altogether account for them. It was, I believe, certain, however, that he did use that drug in startling quantities. It was, indeed, sometimes a topic of complaint with him that his neuralgia imposed this sad necessity upon him.

The image of Uncle Silas, as I had seen him that day, troubled and affrighted my imagination, as I lay in my bed; I had slept very well since my arrival at Bartram. So much of the day was passed in the open air, and in active exercise, that this was but natural. But that night I was nervous and wakeful, and it was past two o'clock when I fancied I heard the sound of horses and carriage-wheels on the avenue.

Mary Quince was close by, and therefore I was not afraid to get up and peep from the window. My heart beat fast as I saw a post-chaise approach the court-yard. A front window was let down, and the postilion pulled up for a few seconds.

In consequence of some directions received by him, I fancied he resumed his route at a walk, and so drew up at the hall-door, on the steps of which a figure awaited his arrival. I think it was old L'Amour, but I could not be quite certain. There was a lantern on the top of the balustrade, close by the door. The chaise-lamps were lighted, for the night was rather dark.

A bag and valise, as well as I could see, were pulled from the interior by the post-boy, and a box from the top of the vehicle, and these were carried into the hall.

I was obliged to keep my check against the window-pane to command a view of the point of debarkation, and my breath upon the glass, which dimmed it again almost as fast as I wiped it away, helped to obscure my vision. But I saw a tall fig-ure, in a cloak, get down and swiftly enter the house, but whether male or female I could not discern.

My heart beat fast. I jumped at once to a conclusion. My uncle was worse—was, in fact, dying; and this was the physician, too late summoned to his bedside.

I listened for the ascent of the doctor, and his entrance at my uncle's door, which, in the stillness of the night, I thought I might easily hear, but no sound readied me. I listened so for fully five minutes, but without result. I returned to the window, but the carriage and horses had disappeared.

I was strongly tempted to wake Mary Quince, and take counsel with her, and persuade her to undertake a reconnoissance. The fact is, I was persuaded that my uncle was in extremity, and I was quite wild to know the doctor's opinion. But, after all, it would be cruel to summon the good soul from her refreshing nap. So, as I began to feel very cold, I returned to my bed, where I continued to listen and conjecture until I fell asleep.

In the morning, as was usual, before I was dressed, in came Milly.

'How is Uncle Silas?' I eagerly enquired.

'Old L'Amour says he's queerish still; but he's not so dull as yesterday,' answered she.

'Was not the doctor sent for?' I asked.

'Was he? Well, that's odd; and she said never a word o't to me,' answered she.

'I'm asking only,' said I.

'I don't know whether he came or no,' she replied; 'but what makes you take that in your head?'

'A chaise arrived here between two and three o'clock last night.'

'Hey! and who told you?' Milly seemed all on a sudden highly interested.

'I saw it, Milly; and some one, I fancy the doctor, came from it into the house.'

'Fudge, lass who'd send for the doctor? 'Twasn't he, I tell you, What was he like?' said Milly.

'I could only see clearly that he, or *she*, was tall, and wore a cloak,' I replied.

'Then 'twasn't him nor t'other I was thinking on, neither; and I'll be hanged but I think it will be Cormoran,' cried Milly, with a thoughtful rap with her knuckle on the table.

Precisely at this juncture a tapping came to the door.

'Come in,' said I.

And old L'Amour entered the room, with a courtesy.

'I came to tell Miss Quince her breakfast's ready,' said the old lady.

'Who came in the chaise, L'Amour?' demanded Milly.

'What chaise?' spluttered the beldame tartly.

The chaise that came last night, past two o'clock,' said Milly.

'That's a lie, and a damn lie I' cried the beldame. 'There worn't no chaise at the door since Miss Maud there come from Knowl.'

I stared at the audacious old menial who could utter such language.

'Yes, there was a chaise, and Cormoran, as I think, be come in it,' said Milly, who seemed accustomed to L'Amour's daring address.

'And there's another damn lie, as big as the t'other,' said the crone, her haggard and withered face flushing orange all over.

'I beg you will not use such language in my room,' I replied, very angrily. 'I *saw* the chaise at the door; your untruth signifies very little, but your impertinence here I will not permit. Should it be repeated, I will assuredly complain to my uncle.'

The old woman flushed more fiercely as I spoke, and fixed her bleared glare on me, with a compression of her mouth that amounted to a wicked grimace. She resisted her angry impulse, however, and only chuckled a little spitefully, saying,

'No offence, miss: it be a way we has in Derbyshire o' speaking our minds. No offence, miss, were meant, and none took, as I hopes,' and she made me another courtesy.

'And I forgot to tell you, Miss Milly, the master wants you this minute.'

So Milly, in mute haste, withdrew, followed closely by L'Amour.

CHAPTER XXXVII

DOCTOR BRYERLY EMERGES

When Milly joined me at breakfast, her eyes were red and swollen. She was still sniffing with that little sobbing hiccough, which betrays, even were there no other signs, recent violent weeping. She sat down quite silent.

'Is he worse, Milly?' I enquired, anxiously.

'No, nothing's wrong wi' him; he's right well,' said Milly, fiercely.

'What's the matter then, Milly dear?'

'The poisonous old witch! 'Twas just to tell the Gov'nor how I'd said 'twas Cormoran that came by the po'shay last night.'

'And who is Cormoran?' I enquired.

'Ay, there it is; I'd like to tell, and you want to hear—and I just daren't, for he'll send me off right to a French school—hang it—hang them all I—if I do.'

'And why should Uncle Silas care?' said I, a good deal surprised.

'They're a-tellin' lies.'

'Who?' said I.

'L'Amour—that's who. So soon as she made her complaint of me, the Gov'nor asked her, sharp enough, did anyone come last night, or a po'shay; and she was ready to swear there was no one. Are ye quite sure, Maud, you really did see aught, or 'appen 'twas all a dream?'

'It was no dream, Milly; so sure as you are there, I saw exactly what I told you,' I replied.

'Gov'nor won't believe it anyhow; and he's right mad wi' me; and he threatens me he'll have me off to France; I wish 'twas under the sea. I hate France—I do—like the devil. Don't you? They're always a-threatening me wi' France, if I dare say a word more about the po'shay, or—or anyone.'

I really was curious about Cormoran; but Cormoran was not to be defined to me by Milly; nor did she, in reality, know more than I respecting the arrival of the night before.

One day I was surprised to see Doctor Bryerly on the stairs. I was standing in a dark gallery as he walked across the floor of the lobby to my uncle's door, his hat on, and some papers in his hand.

He did not see me; and when he had entered Uncle Silas's door, I went down and found Milly awaiting me in the hall.

'So Doctor Bryerly is here,' I said.

'That's the thin fellow, wi' the sharp look, and the shiny black coat, that went up just now?' asked Milly.

'Yes, he's gone into your papa's room,' said I.

''Appen 'twas he come 'tother night. He may be staying here, though we see him seldom, for it's a barrack of a house—it is.'

The same thought had struck me for a moment, but was dismissed immediately. It certainly was *not* Doctor Bryerly's figure which I had seen.

So, without any new light gathered from this apparition, we went on our way, and made our little sketch of the ruined bridge. We found the gate locked as before; and, as Milly could not persuade me to climb it, we got round the paling by the river's bank.

While at our drawing, we saw the swarthy face, sooty locks, and old weather-stained red coat of Zamiel, who was glowering malignly at us from among the trunks of the forest trees, and standing motionless as a monumental figure in the side aisle of a cathedral. When we looked again he was gone.

Although it was a fine mild day for the wintry season, we yet, cloaked as we were, could not pursue so still an occupation as sketching for more than ten or fifteen minutes. As we returned, in passing a clump of trees, we heard a sudden outbreak of voices, angry and expostulatory; and saw, under the trees, the savage old Zamiel strike his daughter with his stick two great blows, one of which was across the head. 'Beauty' ran only a short distance away, while the swart old wood-demon stumped lustily after her, cursing and brandishing his cudgel.

My blood boiled. I was so shocked that for a moment I could not speak; but in a moment more I screamed—

'You brute! How dare you strike the poor girl?'

She had only run a few steps, and turned about confronting him and us, her eyes gleaming fire, her features pale and quivering to suppress a burst of weeping. Two little rivulets of blood were trickling over her temple.

'I say, fayther, look at that,' she said, with a strange tremulous smile, lifting her hand, which was smeared with blood.

Perhaps he was ashamed, and the more enraged on that account, for he growled another curse, and started afresh to reach her, whirling his stick in the air. Our voices, however, arrested him.

'My uncle shall hear of your brutality. The poor girl!'

'Strike him, Meg, if he does it again; and pitch his leg into the river to-night, when he's asleep.'

'I'd serve *you* the same;' and out came an oath. 'You'd have her lick her fayther, would ye? Look out!'

And he wagged his head with a scowl at Milly, and a flourish of his cudgel.

'Be quiet, Milly,' I whispered, for Milly was preparing for battle; and I again addressed him with the assurance that, on reaching home, I would tell my uncle how he had treated the poor girl.

''Tis you she may thank for't, a wheedling o' her to open that gate,' he snarled.

'That's a lie; we went round by the brook,' cried Milly.

I did not think proper to discuss the matter with him; and looking very angry, and, I thought, a little put out, he jerked and swayed himself out of sight. I merely repeated my promise of informing my uncle as he went, to which, over his shoulder, he bawled—

'Silas won't mind ye *that*,' snapping his horny finger and thumb.

The girl remained where she had stood, wiping the blood off roughly with the palm of her hand, and looking at it before she rubbed it on her apron.

'My poor girl,' I said, 'you must not cry. I'll speak to my uncle about you.'

But she was not crying. She raised her head, and looked at us a little askance, with a sullen contempt, I thought.

'And you must have these apples—won't you?' We had brought in our basket two or three of those splendid apples for which Bartram was famous.

I hesitated to go near her, these Hawkeses, Beauty and Pegtop, were such savages. So I rolled the apples gently along the ground to her feet.

She continued to look doggedly at us with the same expression, and kicked away the apples sullenly that approached her feet. Then, wiping her temple and forehead in her apron, without a word, she turned and walked slowly away.

'Poor thing! I'm afraid she leads a hard life. What strange, repulsive people they are!'

When we reached home, at the head of the great staircase old L'Amour was awaiting me; and with a courtesy, and very respectfully, she informed me that the Master would be happy to see me.

Could it be about my evidence as to the arrival of the mysterious chaise that he summoned me to this interview? Gentle as were his ways, there was something undefinable about Uncle Silas which inspired fear; and I should have liked few things less than meeting his gaze in the character of a culprit.

There was an uncertainty, too, as to the state in which I might find him, and a positive horror of beholding him again in the condition in which I had last seen him.

I entered the room, then, in some trepidation, but was instantly relieved. Uncle Silas was in the same health apparently, and, as nearly as I could recollect it, in precisely the same rather handsome though negligent garb in which I had first seen him.

Doctor Bryerly—what a marked and vulgar contrast, and yet, somehow, how reassuring I—sat at the table near him, and was tying up papers. His eyes watched me, I thought, with an anxious scrutiny as I approached; and I think it was not until I had saluted him that he recollected suddenly that he had not seen me before at Bartram, and stood up and greeted me in his usual abrupt and somewhat familiar way. It was vulgar and not cordial, and yet it was honest and indefinably kind.

Up rose my uncle, that strangely venerable, pale portrait, in his loose Rembrandt black velvet. How gentle, how benignant, how unearthly, and inscrutable!

'I need not say how she is. Those lilies and roses, Doctor Bryerly, speak their own beautiful praises of the air of Bartram. I almost regret that her carriage will be home so soon. I only hope it may not abridge her rambles. It positively does me good to look at her. It is the glow of flowers in winter, and the fragrance of a field which the Lord hath blessed.'

'Country air, Miss Ruthyn, is a right good kitchen to country fare. I like to see young women eat heartily. You have had some pounds of beef and mutton since I saw you last,' said Dr. Bryerly.

And this sly speech made, he scrutinised my countenance in silence rather embarrassingly.

'My system, Doctor Bryerly, as a disciple of Æsculapius you will approve—health first, accomplishment afterwards. The Continent is the best field for elegant instruction, and we must see the world a little, by-and-by, Maud; and to me, if my health be spared, there would be an unspeakable though a melancholy charm in the scenes where so many happy, though so many wayward and foolish, young days were passed; and I think I should return to these picturesque solitudes with, perhaps, an increased relish. You remember old Chaulieu's sweet lines—

> Désert, aimable solitude,
> Séjour du calme et de la paix,
> Asile o? n'entrèrent jamais
> Le tumulte et l'inquiétude.

I can't say that care and sorrow have not sometimes penetrated these sylvan fastnesses; but the tumults of the world, thank Heaven!—never.'

There was a sly scepticism, I thought, in Doctor Bryerly's sharp face; and hardly waiting for the impressive 'never,' he said—

'I forgot to ask, who is your banker?'

'Oh! Bartlet and Hall, Lombard Street,' answered Uncle Silas, dryly and shortly.

Dr. Bryerly made a note of it, with an expression of face which seemed, with a sly resolution, to say, 'You shan't come the anchorite over me.'

I saw Uncle Silas's wild and piercing eye rest suspiciously on me for a moment, as if to ascertain whether I felt the spirit of Doctor Bryerly's almost interruption; and, nearly at the same moment, stuffing his papers into his capacious coat pockets, Doctor Bryerly rose and took his leave.

When he was gone, I bethought me that now was a good opportunity of making my complaint of Dickon Hawkes. Uncle Silas having risen, I hesitated, and began,

'Uncle, may I mention an occurrence—which I witnessed?'

'Certainly, child,' he answered, fixing his eye sharply on me. I really think he fancied that the conversation was about to turn upon the phantom chaise.

So I described the scene which had shocked Milly and me, an hour or so ago, in the Windmill Wood.

'You see, my dear child, they are rough persons; their ideas are not ours; their young people must be chastised, and in a way and to a degree that we would look upon in a serious light. I've found it a bad plan interfering in strictly domestic misunderstandings, and should rather not.'

'But he struck her violently on the head, uncle, with a heavy cudgel, and she was bleeding very fast.'

'Ah?' said my uncle, dryly.

'And only that Milly and I deterred him by saying that we would certainly tell you, he would have struck her again; and I really think if he goes on treating her with so much violence and cruelty he may injure her seriously, or perhaps kill her.'

'Why, you romantic little child, people in that rank of life think absolutely nothing of a broken head,' answered Uncle Silas, in the same way.

'But is it not horrible brutality, uncle?'

'To be sure it is brutality; but then you must remember they are brutes, and it suits them,' said he.

I was disappointed. I had fancied that Uncle Silas's gentle nature would have recoiled from such an outrage with horror and indignation; and instead, here he was, the apologist of that savage ruffian, Dickon Hawkes.

'And he is always so rude and impertinent to Milly and to me,' I continued.

'Oh! impertinent to you—that's another matter. I must see to that. Nothing more, my dear child?'

'Well, there *was* nothing more.'

'He's a useful servant, Hawkes; and though his looks are not prepossessing, and his ways and language rough, yet he is a very kind father, and a most honest man—a thoroughly moral man, though severe—a very rough diamond though, and has no idea of the refinements of polite society. I venture to say he honestly believes that he has been always unexceptionably polite to you, so we must make allowances.'

And Uncle Silas smoothed my hair with his thin aged hand, and kissed my forehead.

'Yes, we must make allowances; we must be kind. What says the Book?— "Judge not, that ye be not judged." Your dear father acted upon that maxim—so noble and so awful—and I strive to do so. Alas I dear Austin, *longo intervallo*, far behind I and you are removed—my example and my help; you are gone to your rest, and I remain beneath my burden, still marching on by bleak and alpine paths, under the awful night.

O nuit, nuit douloureuse! O toi, tardive aurore!
Viens-tu? vas-tu venir? es-tu bien loin encore?

And repeating these lines of Chenier, with upturned eyes, and one hand lifted, and an indescribable expression of grief and fatigue, he sank stiffly into his chair, and remained mute, with eyes closed for some time. Then applying his scented handkerchief to them hastily, and looking very kindly at me, he said—

'Anything more, dear child?'

'Nothing, uncle, thank you, very much, only about that man, Hawkes; I dare say that he does not mean to be so uncivil as he is, but I am really afraid of him, and he makes our walks in that direction quite unpleasant.'

'I understand quite, my dear. I will see to it; and you must remember that nothing is to be allowed to vex my beloved niece and ward during her stay at Bartram—nothing that her old kinsman, Silas Ruthyn, can remedy.'

So with a tender smile, and a charge to shut the door 'perfectly, but without clapping it,' he dismissed me.

Doctor Bryerly had not slept at Bartram, but at the little inn in Feltram, and he was going direct to London, as I afterwards learned.

'Your ugly doctor's gone away in a fly,' said Milly, as we met on the stairs, she running up, I down.

On reaching the little apartment which was our sitting-room, however, I found that she was mistaken; for Doctor Bryerly, with his hat and a great pair of woollen gloves on, and an old Oxford grey surtout that showed his lank length to advantage, buttoned all the way up to his chin, had set down his black leather bag on the table, and was reading at the window a little volume which I had borrowed from my uncle's library.

It was Swedenborg's account of the other worlds, Heaven and Hell.

He closed it on his finger as I entered, and without recollecting to remove his hat, he made a step or two towards me with his splay, creaking boots. With a quick glance at the door, he said—

'Glad to see you alone for a minute—very glad.'

But his countenance, on the contrary, looked very anxious.

CHAPTER XXXVIII

A MIDNIGHT DEPARTURE

'I'm going this minute—I—I want to know'—another glance at the door—'are you really quite comfortable here?'

'Quite,' I answered promptly.

'You have only your cousin's company?' he continued, glancing at the table, which was laid for two.

'Yes; but Milly and I are very happy together.'

'That's very nice; but I think there are no teachers, you see—painters, and singers, and that sort of thing that is usual with young ladies. No teachers of that kind—of *any* kind—are there?'

'No; my uncle thinks it better I should lay in a store of health, he says.'

'I know; and the carriage and horses have not come; how soon are they expected?'

'I really can't say, and I assure you I don't much care. I think running about great fun.'

'You walk to church?'

'Yes; Uncle Silas's carriage wants a new wheel, he told me.'

'Ay, but a young woman of your rank, you know, it is not usual she should be without the use of a carriage. Have you horses to ride? '

I shook my head.

'Your uncle, you know, has a very liberal allowance for your maintenance and education.'

I remembered something in the will about it, and Mary Quince was constantly grumbling that 'he did not spend a pound a week on our board.'

I answered nothing, but looked down.

Another glance at the door from Doctor Bryerly's sharp black eyes.

'Is he kind to you?'

'Very kind—most gentle and affectionate.'

'Why doesn't he keep company with you? Does he ever dine with you, or drink tea, or talk to you? Do you see much of him?'

'He is a miserable invalid—his hours and regimen are peculiar. Indeed I wish very much you would consider his case; he is, I believe, often insensible for a long time, and his mind in a strange feeble state sometimes.'

'I dare say—worn out in his young days; and I saw that preparation of opium in his bottle—he takes too much.'

'Why do you think so, Doctor Bryerly?'

'It's made on water: the spirit interferes with the use of it beyond a certain limit. You have no idea what those fellows can swallow. Read the "Opium Eater." I knew two cases in which the quantity exceeded De Quincy's. Aha! it's new to you?' and he laughed quietly at my simplicity.

'And what do you think his complaint is?' I asked.

'Pooh! I haven't a notion; but, probably, one way or another, he has been all his days working on his nerves and his brain. These men of pleasure, who have no other pursuit, use themselves up mostly, and pay a smart price for their sins. And so he's kind and affectionate, but hands you over to your cousin and the servants. Are his people civil and obliging?'

'Well, I can't say much for them; there is a man named Hawkes, and his daughter, who are very rude, and even abusive sometimes, and say they have orders from my uncle to shut us out from a portion of the grounds; but I don't believe that, for Uncle Silas never alluded to it when I was making my complaint of them to-day.'

'From what part of the grounds is that?' asked Doctor Bryerly, sharply.

I described the situation as well as I could.

'Can we see it from this?' he asked, peeping from the window.

'Oh, no.'

Doctor Bryerly made a note in his pocket-book here, and I said—

'But I am really quite sure it was a story of Dickon's, he is such a surly, disobliging man.'

'And what sort is that old servant that came in and out of his room?'

'Oh, that is old L'Amour,' I answered, rather indirectly, and forgetting that I was using Milly's nickname.

'And is *she* civil?' he asked.

No, she certainly was not; a most disagreeable old woman, with a vein of wickedness. I thought I had heard her swearing.

'They don't seem to be a very engaging lot,' said Doctor Bryerly; 'but where there's one, there will be more. See here, I was just reading a passage,' and he opened the little volume at the place where his finger marked it, and read for me a few sentences, the purport of which I well remember, although, of course, the words have escaped me.

It was in that awful portion of the book which assumes to describe the condition of the condemned; and it said that, independently of the physical causes in that state operating to enforce community of habitation, and an isolation from superior spirits, there exist sympathies, aptitudes, and necessities which would, of themselves, induce that depraved gregariousness, and isolation too.

'And what of the rest of the servants, are they better?' he resumed.

We saw little or nothing of the others, except of old 'Giblets,' the butler, who went about like a little automaton of dry bones, poking here and there, and whispering and smiling to himself as he laid the cloth; and seeming otherwise quite unconscious of an external world.

'This room is not got up like Mr. Ruthyn's: does he talk of furnishings and making things a little smart? No! Well, I must say, I think he might!'

Here there was a little silence, and Doctor Bryerly, with his accustomed simul-

taneous glance at the door, said in low, cautious tones, very distinctly 'Have you been thinking at all over that matter again, I mean about getting your uncle to forego his guardianship? I would not mind his first refusal. You could make it worth his while, unless he—that is—unless he's very unreasonable indeed; and I think you would consult your interest, Miss Ruthyn, by doing so and, if possible, getting out
of this place.'

'But I have not thought of it at all; I am much happier here than I had at all expected, and I am very fond of my cousin Milly.'

'How long have you been here exactly?'

I told him. It was some two or three months.

'Have you seen your other cousin yet—die young gentleman?'

'No.'

'H'm! Aren't you very lonely?' he enquired.

'We see no visitors here; but that, you know, I was prepared for.'

Doctor Bryerly read the wrinkles on his splay boot intently and peevishly, and tapped the sole lightly on the ground.

'Yes, it is very lonely, and the people a bad lot. You'd be pleasanter somewhere else—with Lady Knollys, for instance, eh?'

'Well, *there* certainly. But I am very well here: really the time passes very pleasantly; and my uncle is so kind. I have only to mention anything that annoys me, and
he will see that it is remedied: he is always impressing that on me.'

'Yes, it is not a fit place for you,' said Doctor Bryerly. 'Of course, about your uncle,' he resumed, observing my surprised look, 'it is all right: but he's quite helpless, you know. At all events, *think* about it. Here's my address—Hans Emmanuel Bryerly, M. D., 17 King Street, Covent Garden, London—don't lose it, mind,' and he tore the leaf out of his note-book.

'Here's my fly at the door, and you must—you must' (he was looking at his watch)—'mind you *must* think of it seriously; and so, you see, don't let anyone see that. You'll be sure to leave it throwing about. The best way will be just to scratch it on the door of your press, inside, you know; and don't put my name—you'll remember that—only the rest of the address; and burn this. Quince is with you?'

'Yes,' I answered, glad to have a satisfactory word to say.

'Well, don't let her go; it's a bad sign if they wish it. Don't consent, mind; but just tip me a hint and you'll have me down. And any letters you get from Lady Knollys, you know, for she's very plain-spoken, you'd better burn them off-hand.

And I've stayed too long, though; mind what I say, scratch it with a pin, and bum that, and not a word to a mortal about it. Good-bye; oh, I was taking away your book.'

And so, in a fuss, with a slight shake of the hand, getting up his umbrella, his bag, and tin box, he hurried from the room; and in a minute more, I heard the sound of his vehicle as it drove away.

I looked after it with a sigh; the uneasy sensations which I had experienced respecting my sojourn at Bartram-Haugh were re-awakened.

My ugly, vulgar, true friend was disappearing beyond those gigantic lime trees which hid Bartram from the eyes of the outer world. The fly, with the doctor's valise on top, vanished, and I sighed an anxious sigh. The shadow of the over-arching trees contracted, and I felt helpless and forsaken; and glancing down the torn leaf, Doctor Bryerly's address met my eye, between my fingers.

I slipt it into my breast, and ran up-stairs stealthily, trembling lest the old woman should summon me again, at the head of the stairs, into Uncle Silas's room, where under his gaze, I fancied, I should be sure to betray myself.

But I glided unseen and safely by, entered my room, and shut my door. So listening and working, I, with my scissors' point, scratched the address where Doctor Bryerly had advised. Then, in positive terror, lest some one should even knock during the operation, I, with a match, consumed to ashes the tell-tale bit of paper.

Now, for the first time, I experienced the unpleasant sensations of having a secret to keep. I fancy the pain of this solitary liability was disproportionately acute in my case, for I was naturally very open and very nervous. I was always on the point of betraying it *apropos des bottes*—always reproaching myself for my duplicity; and in constant terror when honest Mary Quince approached the press, or good-natured Milly made her occasional survey of the wonders of my wardrobe. I would have given anything to go and point to the tiny inscription, and say:—'This is Doctor Bryerly's address in London. I scratched it with my scissors' point, taking every precaution lest anyone—you, my good friends, included—should surprise me. I have ever since kept this secret to myself, and trembled whenever your frank kind faces looked into the press. There—you at last know all about it. Can you ever forgive my deceit?'

But I could not make up my mind to reveal it; nor yet to erase the inscription, which was my alternative thought. Indeed I am a wavering, irresolute creature as ever lived, in my ordinary mood. High excitement or passion only can inspire me with decision. Under the inspiration of either, however, I am transformed, and often both prompt and brave.

'Some one left here last night, I think, Miss,' said Mary Quince, with a mysterious nod, one morning. ''Twas two o'clock, and I was bad with the toothache, and went down to get a pinch o' red pepper—leaving the candle a-light here lest you should awake. When I was coming up—as I was crossing the lobby, at the far end of the long gallery—what should I hear, but a horse snorting, and some people a-talking, short and quiet like. So I looks out o' the window; and there surely I did see two horses yoked to a shay, and a fellah a-pullin' a box up o' top; and out comes a walise and a bag; and I think it was old Wyat, please'm, that Miss Milly calls L'Amour, that stood in the doorway a-talking to the driver.'

'And who got into the chaise, Mary?' I asked.

'Well, Miss, I waited as long as I could; but the pain was bad, and me so awful cold; I gave it up at last, and came back to bed, for I could not say how much longer they might wait. And you'll find, Miss, 'twill be kep' a secret, like the shay as you saw'd, Miss, last week. I hate them dark ways, and secrets; and old Wyat—she does tell stories, don't she?—and she as ought to be partickler, seein' her time be short now, and she so old. It is awful, an old un like that telling such cram as she do.'

Milly was as curious as I, but could throw no light on this. We both agreed, however, that the departure was probably that of the person whose arrival I had accidentally witnessed. This time the chaise had drawn up at the side door, round the corner of the left side of the house; and, no doubt, driven away by the back road.

Another accident had revealed this nocturnal move. It was very provoking, however, that Mary Quince had not had resolution to wait for the appearance of the traveller. We all agreed, however, that we were to observe a strict silence, and that even to Wyat—L'Amour I had better continue to call her—Mary Quince was not to hint what she had seen. I suspect, however, that injured curiosity asserted itself, and that Mary hardly adhered to this self-denying resolve.

But cheerful wintry suns and frosty skies, long nights, and brilliant starlight, with good homely fires in our snuggery—gossipings, stories, short readings now and then, and brisk walks through the always beautiful scenery of Bartram-Haugh, and, above all, the unbroken tenor of our life, which had fallen into a serene routine, foreign to the idea of danger or misadventure, gradually quieted the qualms and misgivings which my interview with Doctor Bryerly had so powerfully resuscitated.

My cousin Monica, to my inexpressible joy, had returned to her country-house; and an active diplomacy, through the post-office, was negotiating the re-opening of friendly relations between the courts of Elverston and of Bartram.

At length, one fine day, Cousin Monica, smiling pleasantly, with her cloak and bonnet on, and her colour fresh from the shrewd air of the Derbyshire hills, stood suddenly before me in our sitting-room. Our meeting was that of two school-companions long separated. Cousin Monica was always a girl in my eyes.

What a hug it was; what a shower of kisses and ejaculations, enquiries and caresses! At last I pressed her down into a chair, and, laughing, she said—

'You have no idea what self-denial I have exercised to bring this visit about. I, who detest writing, have actually written five letters to Silas; and I don't think I said a single impertinent thing in one of them! What a wonderful little old thing your butler is! I did not know what to make of him on the steps. Is he a struldbrug, or a fairy, or only a ghost? Where on earth did your uncle pick him up? I'm sure he came in on All Hallows Fen, to answer an incantation—not your future husband, I hope—and he'll vanish some night into gray smoke, and whisk sadly up the chimney. He's the most venerable little thing I ever beheld in my life. I leaned back in the carriage and thought I should absolutely die of laughing. He's gone up to prepare your uncle for my visit; and I really am very glad, for I'm sure I shall look as young as Hebe after him. But who is this? Who are you, my dear?'

This was addressed to poor Milly, who stood at the corner of the chimney-piece, staring with her round eyes and plump cheeks in fear and wonder upon the strange lady.

'How stupid of me,' I exclaimed. 'Milly, dear, this is your cousin, Lady Knollys.'

'And so *you* are Millicent. Well, dear, I am very glad to see you.' And Cousin Monica was on her feet again in an instant, with Milly's hand very cordially in hers; and she gave her a kiss upon each cheek, and patted her head.

Milly, I must mention, was a much more presentable figure than when I first encountered her. Her dresses were at least a quarter of a yard longer. Though very rustic, therefore, she was not so barbarously grotesque, by any means.

CHAPTER XXXIX

COUSIN MONICA AND UNCLE SILAS MEET

Cousin Monica, with her hands upon Milly's shoulders, looked amusedly and kindly in her face. 'And,' said she, 'we must be very good friends—you funny creature, you and I. I'm allowed to be the most saucy old woman in Derbyshire—quite incorrigibly privileged; and nobody is ever affronted with me, so I say the most shocking things constantly.'

'I'm a bit that way, myself; and I think,' said poor Milly, making an effort, and growing very red; she quite lost her head at that point, and was incompetent to finish the sentiment she had prefaced.

'You think? Now, take my advice, and never wait to think my dear; talk first, and think afterwards, that is my way; though, indeed, I can't say I ever think at all. It is a very cowardly habit. Our cold-blooded cousin Maud, there, thinks sometimes; but it is always such a failure that I forgive her. I wonder when your little pre-Adamite butler will return. He speaks the language of the Picts and Ancient Britons, I dare say, and your father requires a little time to translate him. And, Milly dear, I am very hungry, so I won't wait for your butler, who would give me, I suppose, one of the cakes baked by King Alfred, and some Danish beer in a skull; but I'll ask you for a little of that nice bread and butter.'

With which accordingly Lady Knollys was quickly supplied; but it did not at all impede her utterance.

'Do you think, girls, you could be ready to come away with me, if Silas gives leave, in an hour or two? I should so like to take you both home with me to Elverston.'

'How delightful! you darling,' cried I, embracing and kissing her; 'for my part, I should be ready in five minutes; what do you say, Milly?'

Poor Milly's wardrobe, I am afraid, was more portable than handsome; and she looked horribly affrighted, and whispered in my ear—

'My best petticoat is away at the laundress; say in a week, Maud.'

'What does she say?' asked Lady Knollys.

'She fears she can't be ready,' I answered, dejectedly.

'There's a deal of my slops in the wash,' blurted out poor Milly, staring straight at Lady Knollys.

'In the name of wonder, what does my cousin mean,' asked Lady Knollys.

'Her things have not come home yet from the laundress,' I replied; and at this moment our wondrous old butler entered to announce to Lady Knollys that his master was ready to receive her, whenever she was disposed to favour him; and also to make polite apologies for his being compelled, by his state of health, to give her the trouble of ascending to his room.

So Cousin Monica was at the door in a moment, over her shoulder calling to us, 'Come, girls.'

'Please, not yet, my lady—you alone; and he requests the young ladies will be in the way, as he will send for them presently.'

I began to admire poor 'Giblets' as the wreck of a tolerably respectable servant.

'Very good; perhaps it is better we should kiss and be friends in private first,' said Cousin Knollys, laughing; and away she went under the guidance of the mummy.

I had an account of this *tête-à-tête* afterwards from Lady Knollys.

'When I saw him, my dear,' she said, 'I could hardly believe my eyes; such white hair—such a white face—such mad eyes—such a death-like smile. When I saw him last, his hair was dark; he dressed himself like a modern Englishman; and he really preserved a likeness to the full-length portrait at Knowl, that you fell in love with you know; but, angels and ministers of grace! such a spectre! I asked myself, is it necromancy, or is it delirium tremens that has reduced him to this? And said he, with that odious smile, that made me fancy myself half insane—

'"You see a change, Monica."

'What a sweet, gentle, insufferable voice he has! Somebody once told me about the tone of a glass flute that made some people hysterical to listen to, and I was thinking of it all the time. There was always a peculiar quality in his voice.

'"I do see a change, Silas," I said at last; "and, no doubt, so do you in me—a great change."

'"There has been time enough to work a greater than I observe in you since you last honoured me with a visit," said he.

'I think he was at his old sarcasms, and meant that I was the same impertinent minx he remembered long ago, uncorrected by time; and so I am, and he must not expect compliments from old Monica Knollys.

'"It is a long time, Silas; but that, you know, is not my fault," said I.

'"Not your fault, my dear—your instinct. We are all imitative creatures: the great people ostracised me, and the small ones followed. We are very like turkeys, we have so much good sense and so much generosity. Fortune, in a freak, wounded my head, and the whole brood were upon me, pecking and gobbling, gobbling and pecking, and you among them, dear Monica. It wasn't your fault, only your instinct, so I quite forgive you; but no wonder the peckers wear better than the pecked. You are robust; and I, what I am."

'"Now, Silas, I have not come here to quarrel. If we quarrel now, mind, we can never make it up—we are too old, so let us forget all we can, and try to forgive something; and if we can do neither, at all events let there be truce between us while I am here."

'"My personal wrongs I can quite forgive, and I do, Heaven knows, from my heart; but there are things which ought not to be forgiven. My children have been ruined by it. I may, by the mercy of Providence, be yet set right in the world, and so soon as that time comes, I will remember, and I will act; but my children—you will see that wretched girl, my daughter—education, society, all would come too late—my children have been ruined by it."

"'I have not done it; but I know what you mean," I said.

"You menace litigation whenever you have the means; but you forget that Austin placed you under promise, when he gave you the use of this house and place, never to disturb my title to Elverston. So there is my answer, if you mean that."

"'I mean what I mean," he replied, with his old smile.

"'You mean then," said I, "that for the pleasure of vexing me with litigation, you are willing to forfeit your tenure of this house and place."

"'Suppose I *did* mean precisely that, why should I forfeit anything? My beloved brother, by his will, has given me a right to the use of Bartram-Haugh for my life, and attached no absurd condition of the kind you fancy to his gift."

'Silas was in one of his vicious old moods, and liked to menace me. His vindictiveness got the better of his craft; but he knows as well as I do that he never could succeed in disturbing the title of my poor deal Harry Knollys; and I was not at all alarmed by his threats; and I told him so, as coolly as I speak to you now.

"'Well, Monica," he said, "I have weighed you in the balance, and you are not found wanting. For a moment the old man possessed me: the thought of my children, of past unkindness, and present affliction and disgrace, exasperated me, and I was mad. It was but for a moment—the galvanic spasm of a corpse. Never was breast more dead than mine to the passions and ambitions of the world. They are not for white locks like these, nor for a man who, for a week in every month, lies in the gate of death. Will you shake hands? *Here*—I *do* strike a truce; and I do forget and forgive *everything*."

'I don't know what he meant by this scene. I have no idea whether he was acting, or lost his head, or, in fact, why or how it occurred; but I am glad, darling, that, unlike myself, I was calm, and that a quarrel has not been forced upon me.'

When our turn came and we were summoned to the presence, Uncle Silas was quite as usual; but Cousin Monica's heightened colour, and the flash of her eyes, showed plainly that something exciting and angry had occurred.

Uncle Silas commented in his own vein upon the effect of Bartram air and liberty, all he had to offer; and called on me to say how I liked them. And then he called Milly to him, kissed her tenderly, smiled sadly upon her, and turning to Cousin Monica, said—

'This is my daughter Milly—oh! she has been presented to you down-stairs, hasn't she? You have, no doubt, been interested by her. As I told her cousin Maud, though I am not yet quite a Sir Tunbelly Clumsy, she is a very finished Miss Hoyden. Are you not, my poor Milly? You owe your distinction, my dear, to that line of circumvallation which has, ever since your birth, intercepted all civilisation on its way to Bartram. You are much obliged, Milly, to everybody who, whether naturally or un-naturally, turned a sod in that invisible, but impenetrable, work. For your accomplishments—rather singular than fashionable—you are indebted, in part, to your cousin, Lady Knollys. Is not she, Monica? *Thank* her, Milly.'

'This is your *truce*, Silas,' said Lady Knollys, with a quiet sharpness. 'I think, Silas Ruthyn, you want to provoke me to speak in a way before these young creatures which we should all regret.'

'So my badinage excites your temper, Monnie. Think how you would feel, then, if I had found you by the highway side, mangled by robbers, and set my foot upon your throat, and spat in your face. But—stop this. Why have I said this? simply to emphasize my forgiveness. See, girls, Lady Knollys and I, cousins long estranged, forget and forgive the past, and join hands over its buried injuries.'

'Well, *be* it so; only let us have done with ironies and covert taunts.'

And with these words their hands were joined; and Uncle Silas, after he had released hers, patted and fondled it with his, laughing icily and very low all the time.

'I wish so much, dear Monica,' he said, when this piece of silent by-play was over, 'that I could ask you to stay to-night; but absolutely I have not a bed to offer, and even if I had, I fear my suit would hardly prevail.'

Then came Lady Knollys' invitation for Milly and me. He was very much obliged; he smiled over it a great deal, meditating. I thought he was puzzled; and amid his smiles, he wild eyes scanned Cousin Monica's frank face once or twice suspiciously.

There was a difficulty—an *undefined* difficulty—about letting us go that day; but on a future one—soon—*very* soon—he would be most happy.

Well, there was an end of that little project, for to-day at least; and Cousin Monica was too well-bred to urge it beyond a certain point.

'Milly, my dear, will you put on your hat and show me the grounds about the house? May she, Silas? I should like to renew my acquaintance.'

'You'll see them sadly neglected, Monnie. A poor man's pleasure grounds must rely on Nature, and trust to her for effects. Where there is fine timber, however, and abundance of slope, and rock, and hollow, we sometimes gain in picturesqueness what we lose by neglect in luxury.'

Then, as Cousin Monica said she would cross the grounds by a path, and meet her carriage at a point to which we would accompany her, and so make her way home, she took leave of Uncle Silas; a ceremony whereat—without, I thought, much zeal at either side—a kiss took place.

'Now girls!' said Cousin Knollys, when we were fairly in motion over the grass, 'what do you say—will he let you come—yes or no? I can't say, but I think, dear,'—this to Milly—'he ought to let you see a little more of the world than appears among the glens and bushes of Bartram. Very pretty they are, like yourself; but very wild, and very little seen. Where is your brother, Milly; is not he older than you?'

'I don't know where; and he is older by six years and a bit.'

By-and-by, when Milly was gesticulating to frighten some herons by the river's bank into the air, Cousin Monica said confidentially to me—

'He has run away, I'm told—I wish I could believe it—and enlisted in a regiment going to India, perhaps the best thing for him. Did you see him here before his judicious self-banishment?'

'No.'

'Well, I suppose you have had no loss. Doctor Bryerly says from all he can learn he is a very bad young man. And now tell me, dear, *is* Silas kind to you?'

'Yes, always gentle, just as you saw him to-day; but we don't see a great deal of him—very little, in fact.'

'And how do you like your life and the people?' she asked.

'My life, very well; and the people, *pretty* well. There's an old woman we don't like, old Wyat, she is cross and mysterious and tells untruths; but I don't think she is dishonest—so Mary Quince says—and that, you know, is a point; and there is a family, father and daughter, called Hawkes, who live in the Windmill Wood, who are perfect savages, though my uncle says they don't mean it; but they are very disagreeable, rude people; and except them we see very little of the servants or other people. But there has been a mysterious visit; some one came late at night, and remained for some days, though Milly and I never saw them, and Mary Quince saw a chaise at the side-door at two o'clock at night.'

Cousin Monica was so highly interested at this that she arrested her walk and stood facing me, with her hand on my arm, questioning and listening, and lost, as it seemed, in dismal conjecture.

'It is not pleasant, you know,' I said.

'No, it is not pleasant,' said Lady Knollys, very gloomily.

And just then Milly joined us, shouting to us to look at the herons flying; so Cousin Monica did, and smiled and nodded in thanks to Milly, and was again silent and thoughtful as we walked on.

'You are to come to me, mind, both of you girls,' she said, abruptly; 'you shall. I'll manage it.'

When silence returned, and Milly ran away once more to try whether the old gray trout was visible in the still water under the bridge, Cousin Monica said to me in a low tone, looking hard at me—

'You've not seen anything to frighten you, Maud? Don't look so alarmed, dear,' she added with a little laugh, which was not very merry, however. 'I don't mean to frighten in any awful sense—in fact, I did not mean to frighten at all. I meant—I can't exactly express it—anything to vex, or make you uncomfortable; have you?'

'No, I can't say I have, except that room in which Mr. Charke was found dead.'

'Oh! you saw that, did you?—I should like to see it so much. Your bedroom is not near it?'

'Oh, no; on the floor beneath, and looking to the front. And Doctor Bryerly talked a little to me, and there seemed to be something on his mind more than he chose to tell me; so that for some time after I saw him I really was, as you say, frightened; but, except that, I really have had no cause. And what was in your mind when you asked me?'

'Well, you know, Maud, you are afraid of ghosts, banditti, and everything; and I wished to know whether you were uncomfortable, and what your particular bogle was just now—that, I assure you, was all; and I know,' she continued, suddenly changing her light tone and manner for one of pointed entreaty, 'what Doctor Bryerly said; and I *implore* of you, Maud, to think of it seriously; and when you come to me, you shall do so with the intention of remaining at Elverston.'

'Now, Cousin Monica, is this fair? You and Doctor Bryerly both talk in the same awful way to me; and I assure you, you don't know how nervous I am sometimes, and yet you won't, either of you, say what you mean. Now, Monica, dear cousin, won't you tell me?'

'You see, dear, it is so lonely; it's a strange place, and he so odd. I don't like the place, and I don't like him. I've tried, but I can't, and I think I never shall. He may be a very—what was it that good little silly curate at Knowl used to call him?—a very advanced Christian—that is it, and I hope he is; but if he is only what he used to be, his utter seclusion from society removes the only check, except personal fear—and he never had much of that—upon a very bad man. And you must know, my dear Maud, what a prize you are, and what an immense trust it is.'

Suddenly Cousin Monica stopped short, and looked at me as if she had gone too far.

'But, you know, Silas may be very good now, although he was wild and selfish in his young days. Indeed I don't know what to make of him; but I am sure when you have thought it over, you will agree with me and Doctor Bryerly, that you must not stay here.'

It was vain trying to induce my cousin to be more explicit.

'I hope to see you at Elverston in a very few days. I will shame Silas into letting you come. I don't like his reluctance.'

'But don't you think he must know that Milly would require some little outfit before her visit?'

'Well, I can't say. I hope that is all; but be it what it may, I'll *make* him let you come, and *immediately,* too.'

After she had gone, I experienced a repetition of those undefined doubts which had tortured me for some time after my conversation with Dr. Bryerly. I had truly said, however, I was well enough contented with my mode of life here, for I had been trained at Knowl to a solitude very nearly as profound.

CHAPTER XL

IN WHICH I MAKE ANOTHER COUSIN'S ACQUAINTANCE

My correspondence about this time was not very extensive. About once a fortnight a letter from honest Mrs. Rusk conveyed to me how the dogs and ponies were, in queer English, oddly spelt; some village gossip, a critique upon Doctor Clay's or the Curate's last sermon, and some severities generally upon the Dissenters' doings, with loves to Mary Quince, and all good wishes to me. Sometimes a welcome letter from cheerful Cousin Monica; and now, to vary the series, a copy of complimentary verses, without a signature, very adoring—very like Byron, I then fancied, and now, I must confess, rather vapid. Could I doubt from whom they came?

I had received, about a month after my arrival, a copy of verses in the same hand, in a plaintive ballad style, of the soldierly sort, in which the writer said, that as living his sole object was to please me, so dying I should be his latest thought; and some more poetic impieties, asking only in return that when the storm of battle had swept over, I should 'shed a tear' on seeing 'the *oak lie,* where it fell.' Of course, about this lugubrious pun, there could be no misconception. The Captain was unmistakably indicated; and I was so moved that I could no longer retain my secret; but walking with Milly that day, confided the little romance to that unsophisticated listener, under the chestnut trees. The lines were so amorously dejected, and yet so heroically redolent of blood and gunpowder, that Milly and I agreed that the writer must be on the verge of a sanguinary campaign.

It was not easy to get at Uncle Silas's 'Times' or 'Morning Post,' which we fancied would explain these horrible allusions; but Milly bethought her of a sergeant in the militia, resident in Feltram, who knew the destination and quarters of every regiment in the service; and circuitously, from this authority, we learned, to my infinite relief, that Captain Oakley's regiment had still two years to sojourn in England.

I was summoned one evening by old L'Amour, to my uncle's room. I remember his appearance that evening so well, as he lay back in his chair; the pillow; the white glare of his strange eye; his feeble, painful smile.

'You'll excuse my not rising, dear Maud, I am so miserably ill this evening.'

I expressed my respectful condolence.

'Yes, I *am* to be pitied; but pity is of no use, dear,' he murmured, peevishly. 'I sent for you to make you acquainted with your cousin, my son. Where are you Dudley?'

A figure seated in a low lounging chair, at the other side of the fire, and which till then I had not observed, at these words rose up a little slowly, like a man stiff after a day's hunting; and I beheld with a shock that held my breath, and fixed my eyes upon him in a stare, the young man whom I had encountered at Church Scarsdale, on the day of my unpleasant excursion there with Madame, and who, to the best of my belief, was also one of that ruffianly party who had so unspeakably terrified me in the warren at Knowl.

I suppose I looked very much affrighted. If I had been looking at a ghost I could not have felt much more scared and incredulous.

When I was able to turn my eyes upon my uncle he was not looking at me; but with a glimmer of that smile with which a father looks on a son whose youth and comeliness he admires, his white face was turned towards the young man, in whom I beheld nothing but the image of odious and dreadful associations.

'Come, sir,' said my uncle, we must not be too modest. Here's your cousin Maud—what do you say?'

'How are ye, Miss?' he said, with a sheepish grin.

'Miss! Come, come. Miss us, no Misses,' said my uncle; 'she is Maud, and you Dudley, or I mistake; or we shall have you calling Milly, madame. She'll not refuse you her hand, I venture to think. Come, young gentleman, speak for yourself.'

'How are ye, Maud?' he said, doing his best, and drawing near, he extended his hand. 'You're welcome to Bartram-Haugh, Miss.'

'Kiss your cousin, sir. Where's your gallantry? On my honour, I disown you,' exclaimed my uncle, with more energy than he had shown before.

With a clumsy effort, and a grin that was both sheepish and impudent, he grasped my hand and advanced his face. The imminent salute gave me strength to spring back a step or two, and he hesitated.

My uncle laughed peevishly.

'Well, well, that will do, I suppose. In my time first-cousins did not meet like strangers; but perhaps we were wrong; we are learning modesty from the Americans, and old English ways are too gross for us.'

'I have—I've seen him before—that is; and at this point I stopped.'

My uncle turned his strange glare, in a sort of scowl of enquiry, upon me.

'Oh!—hey! why this is news. You never told me. Where have you met— eh, Dudley?'

'Never saw her in my days, so far as I'm aweer on,' said the young man.

'No! Well, then, Maud, will *you* enlighten us?' said Uncle Silas, coldly.

'I *did* see that young gentleman before,' I faltered.

'Meaning *me*, ma'am?' he asked, coolly.

'Yes—certainly *you*. I *did*, uncle,' answered I.

'And where was it, my dear? Not at Knowl, I fancy. Poor dear Austin did not trouble me or mine much with his hospitalities.'

This was not a pleasant tone to take in speaking of his dead brother and bene-factor; but at the moment I was too much engaged upon the one point to observe it.

'I met'—I could not say my cousin—'I met him, uncle—your son—that young gentleman—I *saw* him, I should say, at Church Scarsdale, and afterwards with some other persons in the warren at Knowl. It was the night our gamekeeper was beaten.'

'Well, Dudley, what do you say to that?' asked Uncle Silas.

'I never *was* at them places, so help me. I don't know where they be; and I never set eyes on the young lady before, as I hope to be saved, in all my days,' said he, with a countenance so unchanged and an air so confident that I began to think I must be the dupe of one of those strange resemblances which have been known to lead to positive identification in the witness-box, afterwards proved to be utterly mistaken.

'You look so—so *uncomfortable*, Maud, at the idea of having seen him before, that I hardly wonder at the vehemence of his denial. There was plainly something disagreeable; but you see as respects him it is a total mistake. My boy was always a truth-telling fellow—you may rely implicitly on what he says. You were *not* at those places?'

'I wish I may——,' began the ingenuous youth, with increased vehemence.

'There, there—that will do; your honour and word as a gentleman—and *that* you are, though a poor one—will quite satisfy your cousin Maud. Am I right, my dear? I do assure you, as a gentleman, I never knew him to say the thing that was not.'

So Mr. Dudley Ruthyn began, not to curse, but to swear, in the prescribed form, that he had never seen me before, or the places I had named, 'since I was weaned, by——'

'That's enough—now shake hands, if you won't kiss, like cousins,' interrupted my uncle.

And very uncomfortably I did lend him my hand to shake.

'You'll want some supper, Dudley, so Maud and I will excuse your going. Good-night, my dear boy,' and he smiled and waved him from the room.

'That's as fine a young fellow, I think, as any English father can boast for his son—true, brave, and kind, and quite an Apollo. Did you observe how finely pro-portioned he is, and what exquisite features the fellow has? He's rustic and rough, as you see; but a year or two in the militia—I've a promise of a commission for him—he's too old for the line—will form and polish him. He wants nothing but manner; and I protest when he has had a little drilling of that kind, I do believe he'll be as pretty a fellow as you'd find in England.'

I listened with amazement. I could discover nothing but what was disagreeable in the horrid bumpkin, and thought such an instance of the blindness of parental partiality was hardly credible.

I looked down, dreading another direct appeal to my judgment; and Uncle Silas, I suppose, referred those downcast looks to maiden modesty, for he forbore to task mine by any new interrogatory.

Dudley Ruthyn's cool and resolute denial of ever having seen me or the places I had named, and the inflexible serenity of his countenance while doing so, did very much shake my confidence in my own identification of him. I could not be *quite* certain that the person I had seen at Church Scarsdale was the very same whom I afterwards saw at Knowl. And now, in this particular instance, after the lapse of a still longer period, could I be perfectly certain that my memory, deceived by some accidental points of resemblance, had not duped me, and wronged my cousin, Dudley Ruthyn?

I suppose my uncle had expected from me some signs of acquiesence in his splendid estimate of his cub, and was nettled at my silence. After a short interval he said—

'I've seen something of the world in my day, and I can say without a misgiving of partiality, that Dudley is the material of a perfect English gentleman. I am not blind, of course—the training must be supplied; a year or two of good models, active self-criticism, and good society. I simply say that the *material* is there.'

Here was another interval of silence.

'And now tell me, child, what these recollections of Church—Church—*what*?'

'Church Scarsdale,' I replied.

'Yes, thank you—Church Scarsdale and Knowl—are?'

So I related my stories as well as I could.

'Well, dear Maud, the adventure of Church Scarsdale is hardly so terrific as I expected,' said Uncle Silas with a cold little laugh; 'and I don't see, if he had really been the hero of it, why he should shrink from avowing it. I know I should not. And I really can't say that your pic-nic party in the grounds of Knowl has fright-ened me much more. A lady waiting in the carriage, and two or three tipsy young men. Her presence seems to me a guarantee that no mischief was meant; but champagne is the soul of frolic, and a row with the gamekeepers a natural conse-quence. It happened to me once—forty years ago, when I was a wild young buck—one of the worst rows I ever was in.'

And Uncle Silas poured some eau-de-cologne over the corner of his handker-chief, and touched his temples with it.

'If my boy had been there, I do assure you—and I know him—he would say so at once. I fancy he would rather *boast* of it. I never knew him utter an untruth. When you know him a little you'll say so.'

With these words Uncle Silas leaned back exhausted, and languidly poured some of his favourite eau-de-cologne over the palms of his hands, nodded a farewell, and, in a whisper, wished me good-night.

'Dudley's come,' whispered Milly, taking me under the arm as I entered the lobby. 'But I don't care: he never gives me nout; and he gets money from Governor, as much as he likes, and I never a sixpence. It's a shame!'

So there was no great love between the only son and only daughter of the younger line of the Ruthyns.

I was curious to learn all that Milly could tell me of this new inmate of

Bartram-Haugh; and Milly was communicative without having a great deal to relate, and what I heard from her tended to confirm my own disagreeable impressions about him. She was afraid of him. He was a 'woundy ugly customer in a wax, she could tell me.' He was the only one 'she ever knowed as had pluck to jaw the Governor.' But he was 'afeard on the Governor, too.'

His visits to Bartram-Haugh, I heard, were desultory; and this, to my relief, would probably not outlast a week or a fortnight. 'He *was* such a fashionable cove:' he was always 'a gadding about, mostly to Liverpool and Birmingham, and sometimes to Lunnun, itself.' He was 'keeping company one time with Beauty, Governor thought, and he was awfully afraid he'd a married her; but that was all bosh and nonsense; and Beauty would have none of his chaff and wheedling, for she liked Tom Brice;' and Milly thought that Dudley never 'cared a crack of a whip for her.' He used to go to the Windmill to have 'a smoke with Pegtop;' and he was a member of the Feltram Club, that met at the 'Plume O' Feathers.' He was I a rare good shot,' she heard; and 'he was before the justices for poaching, but they could make nothing of it.' And the Governor said 'it was all through spite of him—for they hate us for being better blood than they.' And 'all but the squires and those upstart folk loves Dudley, he is so handsome and gay—though he be a bit cross at home.' And, 'Governor says, he'll be a Parliament man yet, spite o' them all.'

Next morning, when our breakfast was nearly ended, Dudley tapped at the window with the end of his clay pipe—a 'churchwarden' Milly called it—just such a long curved pipe as Joe Willet is made to hold between his lips in those charming illustrations of 'Barnaby Rudge'—which we all know so well—and lifting his 'wide-awake' with a burlesque salutation, which, I suppose, would have charmed the 'Plume of Feathers,' he dropped, kicked and caught his I wide-awake,' with an agility and gravity, as he replaced it, so inexpressibly humorous, that Milly went off in a loud fit of laughter, with the ejaculation—

'Did you ever?'

It was odd how repulsively my confidence in my original identification always revived on unexpectedly seeing Dudley after an interval.

I could perceive that this piece of comic by—play was meant to make a suitable impression on me. I received it, however, with a killing gravity; and after a word or two to Milly, he lounged away, having first broken his pipe, bit by bit, into pieces, which he balanced in turn on his nose and on his chin, from which features he jerked them into his mouth, with a precision which, along with his excellent pantomime of eating them, highly excited Milly's mirth and admiration.

CHAPTER XLI

MY COUSIN DUDLEY

Greatly to my satisfaction, this engaging person did not appear again that day. But next day Milly told me that my uncle had taken him to task for the neglect with which he was treating us.

'He did pitch into him, sharp and short, and not a word from him, only sulky like; and I so frightened, I durst not look up almost; and they said a lot I could not make head or tail of; and Governor ordered me out o' the room, and glad I was to go; and so they had it out between them.'

Milly could throw no light whatsoever upon the adventures at Church Scarsdale and Knowl; and I was left still in doubt, which sometimes oscillated one way and sometimes another. But, on the whole, I could not shake off the misgivings which constantly recurred and pointed very obstinately to Dudley as the hero of those odious scenes.

Oddly enough, though, I now felt far less confident upon the point than I did at first sight. I had begun to distrust my memory, and to suspect my fancy; but of this there could be no question, that between the person so unpleasantly linked in my remembrance with those scenes, and Dudley Ruthyn, a striking, though possibly only a general resemblance did exist.

Milly was certainly right as to the gist of Uncle Silas's injunction, for we saw more of Dudley henceforward.

He was shy; he was impudent; he was awkward; he was conceited;—altogether a most intolerable bumpkin. Though he sometimes flushed and stammered, and never for a moment was at his case in my presence, yet, to my inexpressible disgust, there was a self-complacency in his manner, and a kind of triumph in his leer, which very plainly told me how satisfied he was as to the nature of the impression he was making upon me.

I would have given worlds to tell him how odious I thought him. Probably, however, he would not have believed me. Perhaps he fancied that 'ladies' affected airs of indifference and repulsion to cover their real feelings. I never looked at or spoke to him when I could avoid either, and then it was as briefly as I could. To do him justice, however, he seemed to have no liking for our society, and certainly never seemed altogether comfortable in it.

I find it hard to write quite impartially even of Dudley Ruthyn's personal appearance; but, with an effort, I confess that his features were good, and his figure not amiss, though a little fattish. He had light whiskers, light hair, and a pink complexion, and very good blue eyes. So far my uncle was right; and if he had been perfectly gentlemanlike, he really might have passed for a handsome man in the judgment of some critics.

But there was that odious mixture of *mauvaise honte* and impudence, a clumsiness, a slyness, and a consciousness in his bearing and countenance, not distinctly boorish, but *low*, which turned his good looks into an ugliness more intolerable than that of feature; and a corresponding vulgarity pervading his dress, his demeanour, and his very walk, marred whatever good points his figure possessed. If you take all this into account, with the ominous and startling misgivings constantly recurring, you will understand the mixed feelings of anger and disgust with which I received the admiration he favoured me with.

Gradually he grew less constrained in my presence, and certainly his manners were not improved by his growing ease and confidence.

He came in while Milly and I were at luncheon, jumped up, with a 'right—about face' performed in the air, sitting on the sideboard, whence grinning slyly and kicking his heels, he leered at us.

'Will you have something, Dudley?' asked Milly.

'No, lass; but I'll look at ye, and maybe drink a drop for company.'

And with these words, he took a sportsman's flask from his pocket; and helping himself to a large glass and a decanter, he compounded a glass of strong brandy-and-water, as he talked, and refreshed himself with it from time to time.

'Curate's up wi' the Governor,' he said, with a grin. 'I wanted a word wi' him; but I s'pose I'll hardly git in this hour or more; they're a praying and disputing, and a Bible-chopping, as usual. Ha, ha! But 'twon't hold much longer, old Wyat says, now that Uncle Austin's dead; there's nout to be made o' praying and that work no longer, and it don't pay of itself.'

'O fie! For shame, you sinner!' laughed Milly. 'He wasn't in a church these five years, he says, and then only to meet a young lady. Now, isn't he a sinner, Maud—isn't he?'

Dudley, grinning, looked with a languishing slyness at me, biting the edge of his wide-awake, which he held over his breast.

Dudley Ruthyn probably thought there was a manly and desperate sort of fascination in the impiety he professed.

'I wonder, Milly,' said I, 'at your laughing. How *can* you laugh?'

'You'd have me cry, would ye?' answered Milly.

'I certainly would not have you laugh,' I replied.

'I know I wish *some* one 'ud cry for me, and I know who,' said Dudley, in what he meant for a very engaging way, and he looked at me as if he thought I must feel flattered by his caring to have my tears.

Instead of crying, however, I leaned back in my chair, and began quietly to turn over the pages of Walter Scott's poems, which I and Milly were then reading in the evenings.

The tone in which this odious young man spoke of his father, his coarse mention of mine, and his low boasting of his irreligion, disgusted me more than ever with him.

'They parsons be slow coaches—awful slow. I'll have a good bit to wait, I s'pose. I should be three miles away and more by this time—drat it!' He was eyeing the legging of the foot which he held up while he spoke, as if calculating how far away that limb should have carried him by this time. 'Why can't folk do their Bible and prayers o' Sundays, and get it off their stomachs? I say, Milly lass, will ye see if Governor be done wi' the Curate? Do. I'm a losing the whole day along o' him.'

Milly jumped up, accustomed to obey her brother, and as she passed me, whispered, with a wink—

'*Money.*'

And away she went. Dudley whistled a tune, and swung his foot like a pendulum, as he followed her with his side-glance.

'I say, it is a hard case, Miss, a lad o' spirit should be kept so tight. I haven't a shilling but what comes through his fingers an' drat the tizzy he'll gi' me till he knows the reason why.'

'Perhaps,' I said, 'my uncle thinks you should earn some for yourself.'

'I'd like to know how a fella 's to earn money now-a-days. You wouldn't have a gentleman to keep a shop, I fancy. But I'll ha' a fistful jist now, and no thanks to he, Them executors, you know, owes me a deal o' money. Very honest chaps, of course; but they're cursed slow about paying, I know.'

I made no remark upon this elegant allusion to the executors of my dear father's will.

'An' I tell ye, Maud, when I git the tin, I know who I'll buy a farin' for. I do, lass.'

The odious creature drawled this with a sidelong leer, which, I suppose, he fancied quite irresistible.

I am one of those unfortunate persons who always blushed when I most wished to look indifferent; and now, to my inexpressible chagrin, with its accustomed perversity, I felt the blush mount to my cheeks, and glow even on my forehead.

I saw that he perceived this most disconcerting indication of a sentiment the very idea of which was so detestable, that, equally enraged with myself and with him, I did not know how to exhibit my contempt and indignation.

Mistaking the cause of my discomposure, Mr. Dudley Ruthyn laughed softly, with an insufferable suavity.

'And there's some'at, lass, I must have in return. Honour thy father, you know; you would not ha' me disobey the Governor? No, you wouldn't—would ye?'

I darted at him a look which I hoped would have quelled his impertinence; but I blushed most provokingly—more violently than ever.

'I'd back them eyes again' the county, I would,' he exclaimed, with a condescending enthusiasm. 'You're awful pretty, you are, Maud. I don't know what came over me t'other night when Governor told me to buss ye; but dang it, ye shan't deny me now, and I'll have a kiss, lass, in spite o' thy blushes.'

He jumped from his elevated seat on the sideboard, and came swaggering toward me, with an odious grin, and his arms extended. I started to my feet, absolutely transported with fury.

'Drat me, if she baint a-going to fight me!' he chuckled humorously.

'Come, Maud, you would not be ill-natured, sure? Arter all, it's only our duty. Governor bid us kiss, didn't he?'

'Don't—*don't*, sir. Stand back, or I'll call the servants.'

And as it was I began to scream for Milly.

'There's how it is wi' all they cattle! You never knows your own mind—ye don't,' he said, surlily. 'You make such a row about a bit o' play, Drop it, will you? There's no one a-harming you—is there? *I*'m not, for sartain.'

And, with an angry chuckle, he turned on his heel, and left the room.

I think I was perfectly right to resist, with all the vehemence of which I was capable, this attempt to assume an intimacy which, notwithstanding my uncle's opinion to the contrary, seemed to me like an outrage.

Milly found me alone—not frightened, but very angry. I had quite made up my mind to complain to my uncle, but the Curate was still with him; and, by the time he had gone, I was cooler, My awe of my uncle had returned. I fancied that he would treat the whole affair as a mere playful piece of gallantry. So, with the comfortable conviction that he had had a lesson, and would think twice before repeating his impertinence, I resolved, with Milly's approbation, to leave matters as they were.

Dudley, greatly to my comfort, was buffed with me, and hardly appeared, and was sulky and silent when he did. I lived then in the pleasant anticipation of his departure, which, Milly thought, would be very soon.

My uncle had his Bible and his consolations; but it cannot have been pleasant to this old *roué*, converted though he was—this refined man of fashion—to see his son grow up an outcast, and a Tony Lumpkin; for whatever he may have thought of his natural gifts, he must have known how mere a boor he was.

I try to recall my then impressions of my uncle's character. Grizzly and chaotic the image rises—silver head, feet of clay. I as yet knew little of him.

I began to perceive that he was what Mary Quince used to call 'dreadful particular'—I suppose a little selfish and impatient. He used to get cases of turtle from Liverpool. He drank claret and hock for his health, and ate woodcock and other light and salutary dainties for the same reason; and was petulant and vicious about the cooking of these, and the flavour and clearness of his coffee.

His conversation was easy, polished, and, with a sentimental glazing, cold; but across this artificial talk, with its French rhymes, racy phrases, and fluent eloquence, like a streak of angry light, would, at intervals, suddenly gleam some dismal thought of religion. I never could quite satisfy myself whether they were affectations or genuine, like intermittent thrills of pain.

The light of his large eyes was very peculiar. I can liken it to nothing but the sheen of intense moonlight on burnished metal. But that cannot express it. It glared white and suddenly—almost fatuous. I thought of Moore's lines whenever I looked on it:—

> Oh, ye dead! oh, ye dead! whom we know by the light you give
> From your cold gleaming eyes, though you move like men who live.

I never saw in any other eye the least glimmer of the same baleful effulgence, His fits, too—his hoverings between life and death—between intellect and insanity—a dubious, marsh-fire existence, horrible to look on!

I was puzzled even to comprehend his feelings toward his children. Sometimes it seemed to me that he was ready to lay down his soul for them; at others, he looked and spoke almost as if he hated them. He talked as if the image of death was always before him, yet he took a terrible interest in life, while seemingly dozing away the dregs of his days in sight of his coffin.

Oh! Uncle Silas, tremendous figure in the past, burning always in memory in the same awful lights; the fixed white face of scorn and anguish! It seems as if the Woman of Endor had led me to that chamber and showed me a spectre.

Dudley had not left Bartram-Haugh when a little note reached me from Lady

Knollys. It said—

'DEAREST MAUD,—I have written by this post to Silas, beseeching a loan of you and my Cousin Milly. I see no reason your uncle can possibly have for refusing me; and, therefore, I count confidently on seeing you both at Elverston to-morrow, to stay for at least a week. I have hardly a creature to meet you. I have been disappointed in several visitors; but another time we shall have a gayer house. Tell Milly—with my love—that I will not forgive her if she fails to accompany you.

'Believe me ever your affectionate cousin,

'MONICA KNOLLYS.'

Milly and I were both afraid that Uncle Silas would refuse his consent, although we could not divine any sound reason for his doing so, and there were many in favour of his improving the opportunity of allowing poor Milly to see some persons of her own sex above the rank of menials.

At about twelve o'clock my uncle sent for us, and, to our great delight, announced his consent, and wished us a very happy excursion.

CHAPTER XLII

ELVERSTON AND ITS PEOPLE

So Milly and I drove through the gabled high street of Feltram next day. We saw my gracious cousin smoking with a man like a groom, at the door of the 'Plume of Feathers.' I drew myself back as we passed, and Milly popped her head out of the window.

'I'm blessed,' said she, laughing, 'if he hadn't his thumb to his nose, and winding up his little finger, the way he does with old Wyat-L'Amour, ye know; and you may be sure he said something funny, for Jim Jolliter was laughin', with his pipe in his hand.'

'I wish I had not seen him, Milly. I feel as if it were an ill omen. He always looks so cross; and I dare say he wished us some ill,' I said.

'No, no, you don't know Dudley: if he were angry, he'd say nothing that's funny; no, he's not vexed, only shamming vexed.'

The scenery through which we passed was very pretty. The road brought us through a narrow and wooded glen. Such studies of ivied rocks and twisted roots! A little stream tinkled lonely through the hollow. Poor Milly! In her odd way she made herself companionable. I have sometimes fancied an enjoyment of natural scenery not so much a faculty as an acquirement. It is so exquisite in the instructed, so strangely absent in uneducated humanity. But certainly with Milly it was inborn and hearty; and so she could enter into my raptures, and requite them.

Then over one of those beautiful Derbyshire moors we drove, and so into a wide wooded hollow, where was our first view of Cousin Monica's pretty gabled house, beautified with that indescribable air of shelter and comfort which belongs to an old English residence, with old timber grouped round it, and something in its aspect of the quaint old times and bygone merry-makings, saying sadly, but genially, 'Come in: I bid you welcome. For two hundred years, or more, have I been the home of this beloved old family, whose generations I have seen in the cradle and in the coffin, and whose mirth and sorrows and hospitalities I remember. All their friends, like you, were welcome; and you, like them, will here enjoy the warm illusions that cheat the sad conditions of mortality; and like them you will go your way, and others succeed you, till at last I, too, shall yield to the general law of decay, and disappear.'

By this time poor Milly had grown very nervous; a state which she described in such very odd phraseology as threw me, in spite of myself—for I affected an impressive gravity in lecturing her upon her language—into a hearty fit of laughter.

I must mention, however, that in certain important points Milly was very essentially reformed. Her dress, though not very fashionable, was no longer absurd. And I had drilled her into speaking and laughing quietly; and for the rest I trusted to the indulgence which is always, I think, more honestly and easily obtained from well-bred than from under-bred people.

Cousin Monica was out when we arrived; but we found that she had arranged a double-bedded room for me and Milly, greatly to our content; and good Mary Quince was placed in the dressing-room beside us.

We had only just commenced our toilet when our hostess entered, as usual in high spirits, welcomed and kissed us both again and again. She was, indeed, in extraordinary delight, for she had anticipated some stratagem or evasion to prevent our visit; and in her usual way she spoke her mind as frankly about Uncle Silas to poor Milly as she used to do of my dear father to me.

'I did not think he would let you come without a battle; and you know if he chose to be obstinate it would not have been easy to get you out of the enchanted ground, for so it seems to be with that awful old wizard in the midst of it. I mean, Silas, your papa, my dear. Honestly, is not he very like Michael Scott?'

'I never saw him,' answered poor Milly. 'At least, that I'm aware of,' she added, perceiving us smile. 'But I do think he's a thought like old Michael Dobbs, that sells the ferrets, maybe you mean him?'

'Why, you told me, Maud, that you and Milly were reading Walter Scott's poems. Well, no matter. Michael Scott, my dear, was a dead wizard, with ever so much silvery hair, lying in his grave for ever so many years, with just life enough to scowl when they took his book; and you'll find him in the "Lay of the Last Minstrel," exactly like your papa, my dear. And my people tell me that your brother Dudley has been seen drinking and smoking about Feltram this week. How long does he remain at home? Not very long, eh? And, Maud, dear, he has not been making love to you? Well, I see; of course he has. And *apropos* of love-making, I hope that impudent creature, Charles Oakley, has not been teasing you with notes or verses.'

'Indeed but he has though,' interposed Miss Milly; a good deal to my chagrin, for I saw no particular reason for placing his verses in Cousin Monica's hands. So I confessed the two little copies of verses, with the qualification, however, that I did not know from whom they came.

'Well now, dear Maud, have not I told you fifty times over to have nothing to say to him? I've found out, my dear, he plays, and he is very much in debt. I've made a vow to pay no more for him. I've been such a fool, you have no notion; and I'm speaking, you know, against myself; it would be such a relief if he were to find a wife to support him; and he has been, I'm told, very sweet upon a rich old maid—a button-maker's sister, in Manchester.'

This arrow was well shot.

'But don't be frightened: you are richer as well as younger; and, no doubt, will have your chance first, my dear; and in the meantime, I dare say, those verses, like Falstaff's *billet-doux*, you know, are doing double duty.'

I laughed, but the button-maker was a secret trouble to me and I would have given I know not what that Captain Oakley were one of the company, that I might treat him with the refined contempt which his deserts and my dignity demanded.

Cousin Monica busied herself about Milly's toilet, and was a very useful lady's maid, chatting in her own way all the time; and, at last, tapping Milly under the chin with her finger, she said, very complacently—

'I think I have succeeded, Miss Milly; look in the glass. She really is a very pretty creature.'

And Milly blushed, and looked with a shy gratification, which made her still prettier, on the mirror.

Milly indeed was very pretty. She looked much taller now that her dresses were made of the usual length. A little plump she was, beautifully fair, with such azure eyes, and rich hair.

'The more you laugh the better, Milly, for you've got very pretty teeth—very pretty; and if you were my daughter, or if your father would become president of a college of magicians, and give you up to me, I venture to say I would place you very well; and even as it is we must try, my dear.'

So down to the drawing-room we went; and Cousin Monica entered, leading us both by the hands.

By this time the curtains were closed, and the drawing-room dependent on the pleasant glow of the fire, and the slight provisional illumination usual before dinner.

'Here are my two cousins,' began Lady Knollys: 'this is Miss Ruthyn, of Knowl, whom I take the liberty of calling Maud; and this is Miss Millicent Ruthyn, Silas's daughter, you know, whom I venture to call Milly; and they are very pretty, as you will see, when we get a little more light, and they know it very well themselves.'

And as she spoke, a frank-eyed, gentle, prettyish lady, not so tall as I, but with a very kind face, rose up from a book of prints, and, smiling, took our hands.

She was by no means young, as I then counted youth—past thirty, I suppose— and with an air that was very quiet, and friendly, and engaging. She had never been a mere fashionable woman plainly; but she had the ease and polish of the best society, and seemed to take a kindly interest both in Milly and me; and Cousin Monica called her Mary, and sometimes Polly. That was all I knew of her for the present.

So very pleasantly the time passed by till the dressing-bell rang, and we ran away to our room.

'Did I say anything very bad?' asked poor Milly, standing exactly before me, so soon as our door was shut.

'Nothing, Milly; you are doing admirably.'

'And I do look a great fool, don't I?' she demanded.

'You look extremely pretty, Milly; and not a bit like a fool.'

'I watch everything. I think I'll learn it at last; but it comes a little troublesome at first; and they do talk different from what I used—you were quite right there.'

When we returned to the drawing-room, we found the party already assembled, and chatting, evidently with spirit.

The village doctor, whose name I forget, a small man, grey, with shrewd grey eyes, sharp and mulberry nose, whose conflagration extended to his rugged cheeks, and touched his chin and forehead, was conversing, no doubt agreeably, with

Mary, as Cousin Monica called her guest.

Over my shoulder, Milly whispered—

'Mr. Carysbroke.'

And Milly was quite right: that gentleman chatting with Lady Knollys, his elbow resting on the chimney-piece, was, indeed, our acquaintance of the Windmill Wood. He instantly recognised us, and met us with his pleased and intelligent smile.

'I was just trying to describe to Lady Knollys the charming scenery of the Windmill Wood, among which I was so fortunate as to make your acquaintance, Miss Ruthyn. Even in this beautiful county I know of nothing prettier.'

Then he sketched it, as it were, with a few light but glowing words.

'What a sweet scene!' said Cousin Monica: 'only think of her never bringing me through it. She reserves it, I fancy, for her romantic adventures; and you, I know, are very benevolent, Ilbury, and all that kind of thing; but I am not quite certain that you would have walked along that narrow parapet, over a river, to visit a sick old woman, if you had not happened to see two very pretty demoiselles on the other side.'

'What an ill-natured speech! I must either forfeit my character for disinterested benevolence, so justly admired, or disavow a motive that does such infinite credit to my taste,' exclaimed Mr. Carysbroke. 'I think a charitable person would have said that a philanthropist, in prosecuting his virtuous, but perilous vocation, was unexpectedly *rewarded* by a vision of angels.'

'And with these angels loitered away the time which ought to have been devoted to good Mother Hubbard, in her fit of lumbago, and returned without having set eyes on that afflicted Christian, to amaze his worthy sister with poetic babblings about wood-nymphs and such pagan impieties,' rejoined Lady Knollys.

'Well, be just,' he replied, laughing; 'did not I go next day and see the patient? '

'Yes; next day you went by the same route—in quest of the dryads, I am afraid—and were rewarded by the spectacle of Mother Hubbard.'

'Will nobody help a humane man in difficulties?' Mr. Carysbroke appealed.

'I do believe,' said the lady whom as yet I knew only as Mary, that every word that Monica says is perfectly true.'

'And if it be so, am I not all the more in need of help? Truth is simply the most dangerous kind of defamation, and I really think I'm most cruelly persecuted.'

At this moment dinner was announced, and a meek and dapper little clergyman, with smooth pink cheeks, and tresses parted down the middle, whom I had not seen before, emerged from shadow.

This little man was assigned to Milly, Mr. Carysbroke to me, and I know not how the remaining ladies divided the doctor between them.

That dinner, the first at Elverston, I remember as a very pleasant repast. Everyone talked—it was impossible that conversation should flag where Lady Knollys was; and Mr. Carysbroke was very agreeable and amusing. At the other side of the table, the little pink curate, I was happy to see, was prattling away, with a modest fluency, in an under-tone to Milly, who was following my instructions most conscientiously, and speaking in so low a key that I could hardly hear at the opposite side one word she was saying.

That night, Cousin Monica paid us a visit, as we sat chatting by the fire in our room; and I told her—

'I have just been telling Milly what an impression she has made. The pretty little clergyman—*il en est épris*—he has evidently quite lost his heart to her. I dare say he'll preach next Sunday on some of King Solomon's wise sayings about the irresistible strength of women.'

'Yes,' said Lady Knollys, 'or maybe on the sensible text, "Whoso findeth a wife findeth a good thing, and obtaineth favour," and so forth. At all events, I may say, Milly, whoso findeth a husband such as he, findeth a tolerably good thing. He is an exemplary little creature, second son of Sir Harry Biddlepen, with a little independent income of his own, beside his church revenues of ninety pounds a year; and I don't think a more harmless and docile little husband could be found anywhere; and I think, Miss Maud, *you* seemed a good deal interested, too.'

I laughed and blushed, I suppose; and Cousin Monica, skipping after her wont to quite another matter, said in her odd frank way—

'And how has Silas been?—not cross, I hope, or very odd. There was a rumour that your brother, Dudley, had gone a soldiering to India, Milly, or somewhere; but that was all a story, for he has turned up, just as usual. And what does he mean to do with himself? He has got some money now—your poor father's will, Maud. Surely he doesn't mean to go on lounging and smoking away his life among poachers, and prize-fighters, and worse people. He ought to go to Australia, like Thomas Swain, who, they say, is making a fortune—a great fortune—and coming home again. That's what your brother Dudley should do, if he has either sense or spirit; but I suppose he won't too long abandoned to idleness and low company—and he'll not have a shilling left in a year or two. Does he know, I wonder, that his father has served a notice or something on Dr. Bryerly, telling him to pay sixteen hundred pounds of poor Austin's legacy to *him*, and saying that he has paid debts of the young man, and holds his acknowledgments to that amount? He won't have

a guinea in a year if he stays here. I'd give fifty pounds he was in Van Diemen's
Land—not that I care for the cub, Milly, any more than you do; but I really don't
see any honest business he has in England.'

Milly gaped in a total puzzle as Lady Knollys rattled on.

'You know, Milly, you must not be talking about this when you go home to
Bartram, because Silas would prevent your coming to me any more if he thought I
spoke so freely; but I can't help it: so you must promise to be more discreet than I.
And I am told that all kinds of claims are about to be pressed against him, now
that he is thought to have got some money; and he has been cutting down oak and
selling the bark, Doctor Bryerly has been told, in that Windmill Wood; and he has
kilns there for burning charcoal, and got a man from Lancashire who understands
it—Hawk, or something like that.'

'Ay, Hawkes—Dickon Hawkes; that's Pegtop, you know, Maud,' said Milly.

'Well, I dare say; but a man of very bad character, Dr. Bryerly says; and he has
written to Mr. Danvers about it—for that is what they call waste, cutting down
and selling the timber, and the oakbark, and burning the willows, and other trees
that are turned into charcoal, It is all *waste*, and Dr. Bryerly is about to put a stop
to it.'

'Has he got your carriage for you, Maud, and your horses?' asked Cousin
Monica, suddenly.

'They have not come yet, but in a few weeks, Dudley says, positively——'

Cousin Monica laughed a little and shook her head.

'Yes, Maud, the carriage and horses will always be coming in a few weeks, till
the time is over; and meanwhile the old travelling chariot and post-horses will do
very well;' and she laughed a little again.

'That's why the stile's pulled away at the paling, I suppose and Beauty—Meg
Hawkes, that is—is put there to stop us going through; for I often spied the smoke
beyond the windmill,' observed Milly.

Cousin Monica listened with interest, and nodded silently.

I was very much shocked. It seemed to me quite incredible. I think Lady
Knollys read my amazement and my exalted estimate of the heinousness of the
procedure in my face, for she said—

'You know we can't quite condemn Silas till we have heard what he has to say.
He may have done it in ignorance; or, it is just possible, he may have the right.'

'Quite true. He may have the right to cut down trees at Bartram-Haugh. At all
events, I am sure he thinks he has,' I echoed.

The fact was, that I would not avow to myself a suspicion of Uncle Silas. Any falsehood there opened an abyss beneath my feet into which I dared not look.

'And now, dear girls, good-night. You must be tired. We breakfast at a quarter past nine—not too early for you, I know.'

And so saying, she kissed us, smiling, and was gone.

I was so unpleasantly occupied, for some time after her departure, with the knaveries said to be practised among the dense cover of the Windmill Wood, that I did not immediately recollect that we had omitted to ask her any particulars about her guests.

'Who can Mary be?' asked Milly.

'Cousin Monica says she's engaged to be married, and I think I heard the Doctor call her *Lady* Mary, and I intended asking her ever so much about her; but what she told us about cutting down the trees, and all that, quite put it out of my head. We shall have time enough to-morrow, however, to ask questions. I like her very much, I know.'

'And I think,' said Milly, 'it is to Mr. Carysbroke she's to be married.'

'Do you?' said I, remembering that he had sat beside her for more than a quarter of an hour after tea in very close and low-toned conversation and have you any particular reason?' I asked.

'Well, I heard her once or twice call him "dear," and she called him his Christian name, just like Lady Knollys did Ilbury, I think—and I saw him gi' her a sly kiss as she was going up-stairs.'

I laughed.

'Well, Milly,' I said, 'I remarked something myself, I thought, like confidential relations; but if you really saw them kiss on the staircase, the question is pretty well settled.'

'Ay, lass.'

'You're not to say *lass.*'

'Well, *Maud, then.* I did see them with the comer of my eye, and my back turned, when they did not think I could spy anything, as plain as I see you now.'

I laughed again; but I felt an odd pang—something of mortification—something of regret; but I smiled very gaily, as I stood before the glass, un-making my toilet preparatory to bed.

'Maud—Maud—fickle Maud!—What, Captain Oakley already superseded I and Mr. Carysbroke—Oh! humiliation engaged.' So I smiled on, very much vexed; and being afraid lest I had listened with too apparent an interest to this impostor, I sang a verse of a gay little chanson, and tried to think of Captain Oakley, who somehow had become rather silly.

CHAPTER XLIII

NEWS AT BARTRAM GATE

Milly and I, thanks to our early Bartram hours, were first down next morning; and so soon as Cousin Monica appeared we attacked her.

'So Lady Mary is the *fiancée* of Mr. Carysbroke,' said I, very cleverly; 'and I think it was very wicked of you to try and involve me in a flirtation with him yesterday.'

'And who told you that, pray?' asked Lady Knollys, with a pleasant little laugh.

'Milly and I discovered it, simple as we stand here,' I answered.

'But you did not flirt with Mr. Carysbroke, Maud, did you?' she asked.

'No, certainly not; but that was not your doing, wicked woman, but my discretion. And—now that we know your secret, you must tell us all about her, and all about him; and in the first place, what is her name—Lady Mary what?' I demanded.

'Who would have thought you so cunning? Two country misses—two little nuns from the cloisters of Bartram! Well, I suppose I must answer. It is vain trying to hide anything from you; but how on earth did you find it out?'

'We'll tell you that presently, but you shall first tell us who she is,' I persisted.

'Well, that I will, of course, without compulsion. She is Lady Mary Carysbroke,' said Lady Knollys.

'A relation of Mr. Carysbroke's,' I asserted.

'Yes, a relation; but who told you he was Mr. Carysbroke?' asked Cousin Monica.

'Milly told me, when we saw him in the Windmill Wood.'

'And who told you, Milly?'

'It was L'Amour,' answered Milly, with her blue eyes very wide open.

'What does the child mean? L'Amour! You don't mean *love?*' exclaimed Lady Knollys, puzzled in her turn.

'I mean old Wyat; *she* told me and the Governor.'

'You're *not* to say that,' I interposed.

'You mean your father?' suggested Lady Knollys.

'Well, yes; father told her, and so I knew him.'

'What could he mean?' exclaimed Lady Knollys, laughing, as it were, in soliloquy; 'and I did not mention his name, I recollect now. He recognised you, and you him, when you came into the room yesterday; and now you must tell me how you discovered that he and Lady Mary were to be married.'

So Milly restated her evidence, and Lady Knollys laughed unaccountably heartily; and she said—

'They *will* be so confounded! but they deserve it; and, remember, *I* did not
say so.'

'Oh! we acquit you.'

'All I say is, such a deceitful, dangerous pair of girls—all things considered—I
never heard of before,' exclaimed Lady Knollys. 'There's no such thing as conspir-
ing in your presence.'

'Good morning. I hope you slept well.' She was addressing the lady and gentleman who were just entering the room from the conservatory. 'You'll hardly sleep so
well to-night, when you have learned what eyes are upon you. Here are two very
pretty detectives who have found out your secret, and entirely by your imprudence
and their own cleverness have discovered that you ale a pair of betrothed lovers,
about to ratify your vows at the hymeneal altar. I assure you I did not tell of you;
you betrayed yourselves. If you will talk in that confidential way on sofas, and call
one another stealthily by your Christian names, and actually kiss at the foot of the
stairs, while a clever detective is scaling them, apparently with her back toward
you, you must only take the consequences, and be known prematurely as the hero
and heroine of the forthcoming paragraph in the "Morning Post."'

Milly and I were horribly confounded, but Cousin Monica was resolved to
place us all upon the least formal terms possible, and I believe she had set about it
in the right way.

'And now, girls, I am going to make a counter-discovery, which, I fear, a little
conflicts with yours. This Mr. Carysbroke is Lord Ilbury, brother of this Lady
Mary; and it is all my fault for not having done my honours better; but you see
what clever match-making little creatures they are.'

'You can't think how flattered I am at being made the subject of a theory, even a
mistaken one, by Miss Ruthyn.'

And so, after our modest fit was over, Milly and I were very merry, like the rest,
and we all grew a great deal more intimate that morning.

I think altogether those were the pleasantest and happiest days of my life: gay,
intelligent, and kindly society at home; charming excursions—sometimes riding—
sometimes by carriage—to distant points of beauty in the county. Evenings varied
with Music, reading, and spirited conversation. Now and then a visitor for a day or
two, and constantly some neighbour from the town, or its dependencies, dropt in.
Of these I but remember tall old Miss Wintletop, most entertaining of rustic old

maids, with her nice lace and thick satin, and her small, kindly round face—pretty, I dare say, in other days, and now frosty, but kindly—who told us such delightful old stories of the county in her father's and grandfather's time; who knew the lineage of every family in it, and could recount all its duels and elopements; give us illustrative snatches from old election squibs, and lines from epitaphs, and tell exactly where all the old-world highway robberies had been committed: how it fared with the chief delinquents after the assizes; and, above all, where, and of what sort, the goblins and elves of the county had made themselves seen, from the phantom post-boy, who every third night crossed Windale Moor, by the old coach-road, to the fat old ghost, in mulberry velvet, who showed his great face, crutch, and ruffles, by moonlight, at the bow window of the old court-house that was taken down in 1803.

You cannot imagine what agreeable evenings we passed in this society, or how rapidly my good Cousin Milly improved in it. I remember well the intense suspense in which she and I awaited the answer from Bartram-Haugh to kind Cousin Monica's application for an extension of our leave of absence.

It came, and with it a note from Uncle Silas, which was curious, and, therefore, is printed here:—

'MY DEAR LADY KNOLLYS,—To your kind letter I say yes (that is, for another week, not a fortnight), with all my heart. I am glad to hear that my starlings chatter so pleasantly; at all events the refrain is not that of Sterne's. They can get out; and do get out; and shall get out as much as they please. I am no gaoler, and shut up nobody but myself. I have always thought that young people have too little liberty. My principle has been to make little free men and women of them from the first. In morals, altogether—in intellect, more than we allow—*self*-education is that which abides; and *it* only begins where constraint ends. Such is my theory. My practice is consistent. Let them remain for a week longer, as you say. The horses shall be at Elverston on Tuesday, the 7th. I shall be more than usually sad and solitary till their return; so pray, I selfishly entreat, do not extend their absence. You will smile, remembering how little my health will allow me to see of them, even when at home; but as Chaulieu so prettily says—I stupidly forget the words, but the sentiment is this— "although concealed by a sylvan wall of leaves, impenetrable— (he is pursuing his favourite nymphs through the alleys and intricacies of a rustic labyrinth)—yet, your songs, your prattle, and your laughter, faint and far away, inspire my fancy; and, through my ears, I see your unseen smiles, your blushes, your floating tresses, and your ivory feet; and so, though sad, am happy; though alone, in company;" —and such is my case.

'One only request, and I have done. Pray remind them of a promise made to me. The Book of Life—the fountain of life—it must be drunk of, night and morning, or their spiritual life expires.

'And now, Heaven bless and keep you, my dear cousin; and with all assurances of affection to my beloved niece and my child, believe me ever yours affectionately.

SILAS RUTHYN.'

Said Cousin Monica, with a waggish smile—

'And so, girls, you have Chaulieu and the evangelists; the French rhymester in his alley, and Silas in the valley of the shadow of death; perfect liberty, and a peremptory order to return in a week;—all illustrating one another. Poor Silas I old as he is, I don't think his religion fits him.'

I really rather liked his letter. I was struggling hard to think well of him, and Cousin Monica knew it; and I really think if I had not been by, she would often have been less severe on him.

As we were all sitting pleasantly about the breakfast table a day or two after, the sun shining on the pleasant wintry landscape, Cousin Monica suddenly exclaimed—

'I quite forgot to tell you that Charles Oakley has written to say he is coming on Wednesday. I really don't want him. Poor Charlie! I wonder how they manage those doctors' certificates. I know nothing ails him, and he'd be much better with his regiment.'

Wednesday!—how odd. Exactly the day after my departure. I tried to look perfectly unconcerned. Lady Knollys had addressed herself more to Lady Mary and Milly than to me, and nobody in particular was looking at me. Notwithstanding, with my usual perversity, I felt myself blushing with a brilliancy that may have been very becoming, but which was so intolerably provoking that I would have risen and left the room but that matters would have been so infinitely worse. I could have boxed my odious ears. I could almost have jumped from the window.

I felt that Lord Ilbury saw it. I saw Lady Mary's eyes for a moment resting gravely on my tell-tale—my lying checks—for I really had begun to think much less celestially of Captain Oakley. I was angry with Cousin Monica, who, knowing my blushing infirmity, had mentioned her nephew so suddenly while I was strapped by etiquette in my chair, with my face to the window, and two pair of most disconcerting eyes, at least, opposite. I was angry with myself—generally angry—refused more tea rather dryly, and was laconic to Lord Ilbury, all which, of course, was very cross and foolish; and afterwards, from my bed-room window, I saw Cousin Monica and Lady Mary among the flowers, under the drawing-room window, talking, as I instinctively knew, of that little incident. I was standing at the glass.

'My odious, stupid, *perjured* face,' I whispered, furiously, at the same time stamping on the floor, and giving myself quite a smart slap on the cheek. 'I *can't* go down—I'm ready to cry. I've a mind to return to Bartram. To-day; I am *always* blushing; and I wish that impudent Captain Oakley was at the bottom of the sea.'

I was, perhaps, thinking more of Lord Ilbury than I was aware; and I am sure if Captain Oakley had arrived that day, I should have treated him with most unjustifiable rudeness.

Notwithstanding this unfortunate blush, the remainder of our visit passed very happily for me. No one who has not experienced it can have an idea how intimate a small party, such as ours, will grow in a short time in a country house.

Of course, a young lady of a well-regulated mind cannot possibly care a pin about any one of the opposite sex until she is well assured that he is beginning, at least, to like her better than all the world beside; but I could not deny to myself that I was rather anxious to know more about Lord Ilbury than I actually did know.

There was a 'Peerage,' in its bright scarlet and gold uniform, corpulent and tempting, upon the little marble table in the drawing-room. I had many opportunities of consulting it, but I never could find courage to do so.

For an inexperienced person it would have been a matter of several minutes, and during those minutes what awful risk of surprise and detection. One day, all being quiet, I did venture, and actually, with a beating heart, got so far as to find out the letter 'Il,' when I heard a step outside the door, which opened a little bit, and I heard Lady Knollys, luckily arrested at the entrance, talk some sentences outside, her hand still upon the door-handle. I shut the book, as Mrs. Bluebeard might the door of the chamber of horrors at the sound of her husband's step, and skipped to a remote part of the room, where Cousin Knollys found me in a mysterious state of agitation.

On any other subject I would have questioned Cousin Monica unhesitatingly; upon this, somehow, I was dumb. I distrusted myself, and dreaded my odious habit of blushing, and knew that I should look so horribly guilty, and become so agitated and odd, that she would have reasonably concluded that I had quite lost my heart to him.

After the lesson I had received, and my narrow escape of detection in the very act, you may be sure I never trusted myself in the vicinity of that fat and cruel 'Peerage,' which possessed the secret, but would not disclose without compromising me.

In this state of tantalizing darkness and conjecture I should have departed, had not Cousin Monica quite spontaneously relieved me.

The night before our departure she sat with us in our room, chatting a little farewell gossip.

'And what do you think of Ilbury?' she asked.

'I think him clever and accomplished, and amusing; but he sometimes appears to me very melancholy—that is, for a few minutes together—and then, I fancy, with an effort, re-engages in our conversation.'

'Yes, poor Ilbury! He lost his brother only about five months since, and is only beginning to recover his spirits a little. They were very much attached, and people thought that he would have succeeded to the title, had he lived, because Ilbury is *difficile*—or a philosopher—or a *Saint Kevin*; and, in fact, has begun to be treated as a premature old bachelor.'

'What a charming person his sister, Lady Mary, is. She has made me promise to write to her,' I said, I suppose such hypocrites are we—to prove to Cousin Knollys that I did not care particularly to hear anything more about him.

'Yes, and so devoted to him. He came down here, and took The Grange, for change of scene and solitude—of all things the worst for a man in grief—a morbid whim, as he is beginning to find out; for he is very glad to stay here, and confesses that he is much better since he came. His letters are still addressed to him as Mr. Carysbroke; for he fancied if his rank were known, that the county people would have been calling upon him, and so he would have found himself soon involved in a tiresome round of dinners, and must have gone somewhere else. You saw him, Milly, at Bartram, before Maud came?'

Yes, she had, when he called there to see her father.

'He thought, as he had accepted the trusteeship, that he could hardly, residing so near, omit to visit Silas. He was very much struck and interested by him, and he has a better opinion of him—you are not angry, Milly—than some ill-natured people I could name; and he says that the cutting down of the trees will turn out to have been a mere slip. But these slips don't occur with clever men in other things; and some persons have a way of always making them in their own favour. And, to talk of other things, I suspect that you and Milly will probably see Ilbury at Bartram; for I think he likes you very much.'

You, did she mean *both* or only me?

So our pleasant visit was over. Milly's good little curate had been much thrown in her way by our deep and dangerous cousin Monica. He was most laudably steady; and his flirtation advanced upon the field of theology, where, happily, Milly's little reading had been concentrated. A mild and earnest interest in poor, pretty Milly's orthodoxy was the leading feature of his case; and I was highly amused at her references to me, when we had retired at night, upon the points which she had disputed with him, and her anxious reports of their low-toned conferences, carried on upon a sequestered ottoman, where he patted and stroked his crossed leg, as he smiled tenderly and shook his head at her questionable doctrine. Milly's reverence for her instructor, and his admiration, grew daily; and he was known among us as Milly's confessor.

He took luncheon with us on the day of our departure, and with an adroit privacy, which in a layman would have been sly, presented her, in right of his holy calling, with a little book, the binding of which was mediæval and costly, and whose letterpress dealt in a way which he commended, with some points on which she was not satisfactory; and she found on the fly-leaf this little inscription:—'Presented to Miss Millicent Ruthyn by an earnest well-wisher, 1st December 1844.' A text, very neatly penned, followed this; and the 'presentation' was made unctuously indeed, but with a blush, as well as the accustomed smile, and with eyes that were lowered.

The early crimson sun of December had gone down behind the hills before we took our seats in the carriage.

Lord Ilbury leaned with his elbow on the carriage window, looking in, and he said to me—

'I really don't know what we shall do, Miss Ruthyn; we shall all feel so lonely. For myself, I think I shall run away to Grange!

This appeared to me as nearly perfect eloquence as human lips could utter.

His hand still rested on the window, and the Rev. Sprigge Biddlepen was standing with a saddened smirk on the door steps, when the whip smacked, the horses scrambled into motion, and away we rolled down the avenue, leaving behind us the pleasantest house and hostess in the world, and trotting fleetly into darkness towards Bartram-Haugh.

We were both rather silent. Milly had her book in her lap, and I saw her every now and then try to read her 'earnest well-wisher's' little inscription, but there was not light to read by.

When we reached the great gate of Bartram-Haugh it was dark. Old Crowl, who kept the gate, I heard enjoining the postilion to make no avoidable noise at the hall-door, for the odd but startling reason that he believed my uncle 'would be dead by this time.'

Very much shocked and frightened, we stopped the carriage, and questioned the tremulous old porter.

Uncle Silas, it seemed, had been 'silly-ish' all yesterday, and could not be woke this morning,' and 'the doctor bad been here twice, being now in the house.'

'Is he better?' I asked, tremblingly.

'Not as I'm aweer on, Miss; he lay at God's mercy two hours agone; 'appen he's in heaven be this time.'

'Drive on—drive fast,' I said to the driver. 'Don't be frightened, Milly; please. Heaven we shall find all going well.'

After some delay, during which my heart sank, and I quite gave up Uncle Silas, the aged little servant-man opened the door, and trotted shakily down the steps to the carriage side.

Uncle Silas had been at death's door for hours; the question of life had trembled in the scale; but now the doctor said 'he might do.'

'Where was the doctor?'

'In master's room; he blooded him three hours agone.'

I don't think that Milly was so frightened as I. My heart beat, and I was trembling so that I could hardly get upstairs.

CHAPTER XLIV

A FRIEND ARISES

At the top of the great staircase I was glad to see the friendly face of Mary Quince, who stood, candle in hand, greeting us with many little courtesies, and a very haggard and pallid smile.

'Very welcome, Miss, hoping you are very well.'

'All well, and you are well, Mary? and oh! tell us quickly how is Uncle Silas?'

'We thought he was gone, Miss, this morning, but doing fairly now; doctor says in a trance like. I was helping old Wyat most of the day, and was there when doctor blooded him, an' he spoke at last; but he must be awful weak, he took a deal o' blood from his arm, Miss; I held the basin.'

'And be's better—decidedly better?' I asked.

'Well, he's better, doctor says; he talked some, and doctor says if he goes off asleep again, and begins a-snoring like he did before, we're to loose the bandage, and let him bleed till he comes to his self again; which, it seems to me and Wyat, is the same thing a'most as saying he's to be killed off-hand, for I don't believe he has a drop to spare, as you'll say likewise, Miss, if you'll please look in the basin.'

This was not an invitation with which I cared to comply. I thought I was going to faint. I sat on the stairs and sipped a little water, and Quince sprinkled a little in my face, and my strength returned.

Milly must have felt her father's danger more than I, for she was affectionate, and loved him from habit and relation, although he was not kind to her. But I was more nervous and more impetuous, and my feelings both stimulated and overpowered me more easily. The moment I was able to stand I said—thinking of nothing but the one idea—

'We must see him—*come*, Milly.'

I entered his sitting-room; a common 'dip' candle hanging like the tower of Pisa all to one side, with a dim, long wick, in a greasy candlestick, profaned the table of the fastidious invalid. The light was little better than darkness, and I crossed the room swiftly, still transfixed by the one idea of seeing my uncle.

His bed-room door beside the fireplace stood partly open, and I looked in.

Old Wyat, a white, high-cauled ghost, was pottering in her slippers in the shadow at the far side of the bed. The doctor, a stout little bald man, with a paunch and a big bunch of seals, stood with his back to the fireplace, which corresponded with that in the next room, eyeing his patient through the curtains of the bed with a listless sort of importance.

The head of the large four-poster rested against the opposite wall. Its foot was presented toward the fireplace; but the curtains at the side, which alone I could see from my position, were dosed.

The little doctor knew me, and thinking me, I suppose, a person of consequence, removed his hands from behind him, suffering the skirts of his coat to fall forward, and with great celerity and gravity made me a low but important bow; then choosing more particularly to make my acquaintance he further advanced, and with another reverence he introduced himself as Doctor Jolks, in a murmured diapason. He bowed me back again into my uncle's study, and the light of old Wyat's dreadful candle.

Doctor Jolks was suave and pompous. I longed for a fussy practitioner who would have got over the ground in half the time.

Coma, madam; coma. Miss Ruthyn, your uncle, I may tell you, has been in a very critical state; highly so. Coma of the most obstinate type. He would have sunk—he must have gone, in fact, had I not resorted to a very extreme remedy, and bled him freely, which happily told precisely as we could have wished. A wonderful constitution—a marvellous constitution—prodigious nervous fibre; the greatest pity in the world he won't give himself fair play. His habits, you know, are quite, I may say, destructive. We do our best—we do all we can, but if the patient won't cooperate it can't possibly end satisfactorily.'

And Jolks accompanied this with an awful shrug. 'Is there *anything*? Do you think change of air? What an awful complaint it is,' I exclaimed.

He smiled, mysteriously looking down, and shook his head undertaker-like.

'Why, we can hardly call it a *complaint*, Miss Ruthyn. I look upon it he has been poisoned—he has had, you understand me,' he pursued, observing my startled look, 'an overdose of opium; you know he takes opium habitually; he takes it in laudanum, he takes it in water, and, most dangerous of all, he takes it solid, in lozenges. I've known people take it moderately. I've known people take it to excess, *but* they all were particular as to *measure*, and *that* is exactly the point I've tried to impress upon him. The habit, of course, you understand is formed, there's no uprooting that; but he won't *measure*—he goes by the eye and by sensation, which I need not tell you, Miss Ruthyn, is going by *chance*; and opium, as no doubt you are aware, is strictly a poison; a poison, no doubt, which habit will enable you to partake of, I may say, in considerable quantities, without fatal consequences, but still a poison; and to exhibit a poison so, is, I need scarcely tell you, to trifle with death. He has been so threatened, and for a time he changes his haphazard mode of dealing with it, and then returns; he may escape—of course, that is possible— but he may any day overdo the thing. I don't think the present crisis will result seriously. I am very glad, independently of the honour of making your acquaintance, Miss Ruthyn, that you and your cousin have returned; for, however zealous, I fear the servants are deficient in intelligence; and as in the event of a recurrence of the symptoms—which, however, is not probable—I would beg to inform you of their nature, and how exactly best to deal with them.'

So upon these points he delivered us a pompous little lecture, and begged that either Milly or I would remain in the room with the patient until his return at two or three o'clock in the morning; a reappearance of the coma 'might be very bad indeed.'

Of course Milly and I did as we were directed. We sat by the fire, scarcely daring to whisper. Uncle Silas, about whom a new and dreadful suspicion began to haunt me, lay still and motionless as if he were actually dead.

'Had he attempted to poison himself?'

If he believed his position to be as desperate as Lady Knollys had described it, was this, after all, improbable? There were strange wild theories, I had been told, mixed up in his religion.

Sometimes, at an hour's interval, a sign of life would come—a moan from that tall sheeted figure in the bed—a moan and a pattering of the lips. Was it prayer—*what* was it? who could guess what thoughts were passing behind that white-fillited forehead?

I had peeped at him: a white cloth steeped in vinegar and water was folded round his head; his great eyes were closed, so were his marble lips; his figure straight, thin, and long, dressed in a white dressing-gown, looked like a corpse 'laid out' in the bed; his gaunt bandaged arm lay outside the sheet that covered his body.

With this awful image of death we kept our vigil, until poor Milly grew so sleepy that old Wyat proposed that she should take her place and watch with me.

Little as I liked the crone with the high-cauled cap, she would, at all events, keep awake, which Milly could not. And so at one o'clock this new arrangement began.

'Mr. Dudley Ruthyn is not at home?' I whispered to old Wyat.

'He went away wi' himself yesternight, to Cloperton, Miss, to see the wrestling; it was to come off this morning.'

'Was he sent for?'

'Not he.'

'And why not?'

'He would na' leave the sport for this, I'm thinking,' and the old woman grinned uglily.

'When is he to return?'

'When he wants money.'

So we grew silent, and again I thought of suicide, and of the unhappy old man, who just then whispered a sentence or two to himself with a sigh.

For the next hour he had been quite silent, and old Wyat informed me that she must go down for candles. Ours were already burnt down to the sockets.

'There's a candle in the next room,' I suggested, hating the idea of being left alone with the patient.

'Hoot! Miss. I *dare* na' set a candle but wax in his presence,' whispered the old woman, scornfully.

'I think if we were to stir the fire, and put on a little more coal, we should have a great deal of light.'

'He'll ha' the candles,' said Dame Wyat, doggedly; and she tottered from the chamber, muttering to herself; and I heard her take her candle from the next room and depart, shutting the outer door after her.

Here was I then alone, but for this unearthly companion, whom I feared inexpressibly, at two o'clock, in the vast old house of Bartram.

I stirred the fire. It was low, and would not blaze. I stood up, and, with my hand on the mantelpiece, endeavoured to think of cheerful things. But it was a struggle against wind and tide—vain; and so I drifted away into haunted regions.

Uncle Silas was perfectly still. I would not suffer myself to think of the number of dark rooms and passages which now separated me from the other living tenants of the house. I awaited with a false composure the return of old Wyat.

Over the mantelpiece was a looking-glass. At another time this might have helped to entertain my solitary moments, but now I did not like to venture a peep. A small thick Bible lay on the chimneypiece, and leaning its back against the mirror, I began to read in it with a mind as attentively directed as I could. While so engaged in turning over the leaves, I lighted upon two or three odd-looking papers, which had been folded into it. One was a broad printed thing, with names and dates written into blank spaces, and was about the size of a quarter of a yard of very broad ribbon. The others were mere scraps, with 'Dudley Ruthyn' penned in my cousin's vulgar round-hand at the foot. While I folded and replaced these, I really don't know what caused me to fancy that something was moving behind me, as I stood with my back toward the bed. I do not recollect any sound whatever; but instinctively I glanced into the mirror, and my eyes were instantly fixed by what I saw.

The figure of Uncle Silas rose up, and dressed in a long white morning gown, slid over the end of the bed, and with two or three swift noiseless steps, stood behind me, with a deathlike scowl and a simper. Preternaturally tall and thin, he stood for a moment almost touching me, with the white bandage pinned across his forehead, his bandaged arm stiffly by his side, and diving over my shoulder, with his long thin hand he snatched the Bible, and whispered over my head—'The serpent beguiled her and she did eat;' and after a momentary pause, he glided to the farthest window, and appeared to look out upon the midnight prospect.

It was cold, but he did not seem to feel it. With the same inflexible scowl and smile, he continued to look out for several minutes, and then with a great sigh, he sat down on the side of his bed, his face immovably turned towards me, with the same painful look.

It seemed to me an hour before old Wyat came back; and never was lover made happier at sight of his mistress than I to behold that withered crone.

You may be sure I did not prolong my watch. There was now plainly no risk of my uncle's relapsing into lethargy. I had a long hysterical fit of weeping when I got into my room, with honest Mary Quince by my side.

Whenever I closed my eyes, the face of Uncle Silas was before me, as I had seen it reflected in the glass. The sorceries of Bartram were enveloping me once more.

Next morning the doctor said he was quite out of danger, but very weak. Milly and I saw him; and again in our afternoon walk we saw the doctor marching under the trees in the direction of the Windmill Wood.

'Going down to see that poor girl there?' he said, when he had made his salutation, prodding with his levelled stick in the direction. 'Hawke, or Hawkes, I think.'

'Beauty's sick, Maud,' exclaimed Milly.

'*Hawkes.* She's upon my dispensary list. Yes,' said the doctor, looking into his little note-book—'Hawkes.'

'And what is her complaint?'

'Rheumatic fever.'

'Not infectious?'

'Not the least—no more, as we say, Miss Ruthyn, than a broken leg,' and he laughed obligingly.

So soon as the doctor had departed, Milly and I agreed to follow to Hawkes' cottage and enquire more particularly how she was. To say truth, I am afraid it was rather for the sake of giving our walk a purpose and a point of termination, than for any very charitable interest we might have felt in the patient.

Over the inequalities of the upland slope, clumped with trees, we reached the gabled cottage, with its neglected little farm-yard. A rheumatic old woman was the only attendant; and, having turned her ear in an attitude of attention, which induced us in gradually exalted keys to enquire how Meg was, she informed us in very loud tones that she had long lost her hearing and was perfectly deaf. And added considerately—

'When the man comes in, 'appen he'll tell ye what ye want.'

Through the door of a small room at the further end of that in which we were, we could see a portion of the narrow apartment of the patient, and hear her moans and the doctor's voice.

'We'll see him, Milly, when he comes out. Let us wait here.'

So we stood upon the door-stone awaiting him. The sounds of suffering had moved my compassion and interested us for the sick girl.

'Blest if here isn't Pegtop,' said Milly.

And the weather-stained red coat, the swarthy forbidding face and sooty locks of old Hawkes loomed in sight, as he stumped, steadying himself with his stick, over the uneven pavement of the yard. He touched his hat gruffly to me, but did not seem half to like our being where we were, for he looked surlily, and scratched his head under his wide-awake.

'Your daughter is very ill, I'm afraid,' said I.

'Ay—she'll be costin' me a handful, like her mother did,' said Pegtop.

'I hope her room is comfortable, poor thing.'

'Ay, that's it; she be comfortable enough, I warrant—more nor I. It be all Meg, and nout o' Dickon.'

'When did her illness commence?' I asked.

'Day the mare wor shod—*Saturday*. I talked a bit wi' the workus folk, but they won't gi'e nout—dang 'em—an' how be I to do't? It be all'ays hard bread wi' Silas, an' a deal harder now she' ta'en them pains. I won't stan' it much longer. Gammon! If she keeps on that way I'll just cut. See how the workus fellahs 'ill like *that*. '

'The Doctor gives his services for nothing,' I said.

'An' *does* nothin', bless him I ha, ha. No more nor that old deaf gammon there that costs me three tizzies a week, and haint worth a h'porth—no more nor Meg there, that's making all she can o' them pains. They be all a foolin' o' me, an' thinks I don't know't. Hey? *we*'ll see.'

All this time he was cutting a bit of tobacco into shreds on the window-stone.

'A workin' man be same as a hoss; if he baint cared, he can't work—'tisn't in him:' and with these words, having by this time stuffed his pipe with tobacco, he poked the deaf lady, who was pattering about with her back toward him, rather viciously with the point of his stick, and signed for a light.

'It baint in him, you can't get it out o' 'im, no more nor ye'll draw smoke out o' this,' and he raised his pipe an inch or two, with his thumb on the bowl, 'without backy and fire. 'Tisn't in it.'

'Maybe I can be of some use?' I said, thinking

'Maybe,' he rejoined.

By this time he received from the old deaf abigail a flaming roll of brown paper, and, touching his hat to me, he withdrew, lighting his pipe and sending up little white puffs, like the salute of a departing ship.

So he did not care to hear how his daughter was, and had only come here to light his pipe!

Just then the Doctor emerged.

'We have been waiting to hear how your poor patient is today?' I said.

'Very ill, indeed, and utterly neglected, I fear. If she were equal to it—but she's not—I think she ought to be removed to the hospital immediately.'

'That poor old woman is quite deaf, and the man is so surly and selfish! Could you recommend a nurse who would stay here till she's better? I will pay her with pleasure, and anything you think might be good for the poor girl.'

So this was settled on the spot. Doctor Jolks was kind, like most men of his calling, and undertook to send the nurse from Feltram with a few comforts for the patient; and he called Dickon to the yard-gate, and I suppose told him of the arrangement; and Milly and I went to the poor girl's door and asked, 'May we come in?'

There was no answer. So, with the conventional construction of silence, we entered. Her looks showed how ill she was. We adjusted her bed-clothes, and darkened the room, and did what we could for her—noting, beside, what her comfort chiefly required. She did not answer any questions. She did not thank us. I should almost have fancied that she had not perceived our presence, had I not observed her dark, sunken eyes once or twice turned up towards my face, with a dismal look of wonder and enquiry.

The girl was very ill, and we went every day to see her. Sometimes she would answer our questions—sometimes not. Thoughtful, observant, surly, she seemed; and as people like to be thanked, I sometimes wonder that we continued to throw our bread upon these ungrateful waters. Milly was specially impatient under this treatment, and protested against it, and finally refused to accompany me into poor Beauty's bed-room.

'I think, my good Meg,' said I one day, as I stood by her bed —she was now recovering with the sure reascent of youth—that you ought to thank Miss Milly.'

'I'll *not* thank her,' said Beauty, doggedly.

'Very well, Meg; I only thought I'd ask you, for I think you ought.'

As I spoke, she very gently took just the tip of my finger, which hung close to her coverlet, in her fingers, and drew it beneath, and before I was aware, burying her head in the clothes, she suddenly clasped my hand in both hers to her lips, and kissed it passionately, again and again, sobbing. I felt her tears.

I tried to withdraw my hand, but she held it with an angry pull, continuing to weep and kiss it.

'Do you wish to say anything, my poor Meg?' I asked.

'Nout, Miss,' she sobbed gently; and she continued to kiss my hand and weep. But suddenly she said, 'I won't thank Milly, for it's a' *you*; it baint her, she hadn't the thought—no, no, it's a' you, Miss. I cried hearty in the dark last night, thinkin' o' the apples, and the way I knocked them awa' wi' a put o' my foot, the day father rapped me ower the head wi' his stick; it was kind o' you and very bad o' me. I wish you'd beat me, Miss; ye're better to me than father or mother—better to me than a'; an' I wish I could die for you, Miss, for I'm not fit to look at you.'

I was surprised. I began to cry. I could have hugged poor Meg.

I did not know her history. I have never learned it since. She used to talk with the most utter self-abasement before me. It was no religious feeling—it was a kind of expression of her love and worship of me—all the more strange that she was naturally very proud. There was nothing she would not have borne from me except the slightest suspicion of her entire devotion, or that she could in the most trifling way wrong or deceive me.

I am not young now. I have had my sorrows, and with them all that wealth, virtually unlimited, can command; and through the retrospect a few bright and pure lights quiver along my life's dark stream—dark, but for them; and these are shed, not by the splendour of a splendid fortune, but by two or three of the simplest and kindest remembrances, such as the poorest and homeliest life may count up, and beside which, in the quiet hours of memory, all artificial triumphs pale, and disappear, for they are never quenched by time or distance, being founded on the affections, and so far heavenly.

CHAPTER XLV

A CHAPTER-FULL OF LOVERS

We had about this time a pleasant and quite unexpected visit from Lord Ilbury. He had come to pay his respects, understanding that my uncle Silas was sufficiently recovered to see visitors. 'And I think I'll run up-stairs first, and see him, if he admits me, and then I have ever so long a message from my sister, Mary, for you and Miss Millicent; but I had better dispose of my business first—don't you think so?—and I shall return in a few minutes.'

And as he spoke our tremulous old butler returned to say that Uncle Silas would be happy to see him. So he departed; and you can't think how pleasant our homely sitting-room looked with his coat and stick in it—guarantees of his return.

'Do you think, Milly, he is going to speak about the timber, you know, that Cousin Knollys spoke of? I do hope not.'

'So do I' said Milly. 'I wish he'd stayed a bit longer with us first, for if he does, father will sure to turn him out of doors, and we'll see no more of him.'

'Exactly, my dear Milly; and he's so pleasant and good-natured.'

'And he likes you awful well, he does.'

'I'm sure he likes us both equally, Milly; he talked a great deal to you at Elverston, and used to ask you so often to sing those two pretty Lancashire ballads,' I said; 'but you know when you were at your controversies and religious exercises in the window, with that pillar of the church, the Rev. Spriggs Biddlepen——'

'Get awa' wi' your nonsense, Maud; how could I help answering when he dodged me up and down my Testament and catechism?—an I 'most hate him, I tell you, and Cousin Knollys, you're such fools, I do. And whatever you say, the lord likes you uncommon, and well you know it, ye hussy.'

'I know no such thing; and you don't think it, *you* hussy, and I really don't care who likes me or who doesn't, except my relations; and I make the lord a present to you, if you'll have him.'

In this strain were we talking when he re-entered the room, a little sooner than we had expected to see him.

Milly, who, you are to recollect, was only in process of reformation, and still retained something of the Derbyshire dairymaid, gave me a little clandestine pinch on the arm just as he made his appearance.

'I just refused a present from her,' said odious Milly, in answer to his enquiring look, 'because I knew she could not spare it.'

The effect of all this was that I blushed one of my overpowering blushes. People told me they became me very much; I hope so, for the misfortune was frequent; and I think nature owed me that compensation.

'It places you both in a most becoming fight,' said Lord Ilbury, quite innocently. 'I really don't know which most to admire—the generosity of the offer or of the refusal.'

'Well, it *was* kind, if you but knew. I'm 'most tempted to tell him,' said Milly.

I checked her with a really angry look, and said, 'Perhaps you have not observed it; but I really think, for a sensible person, my cousin Milly here talks more nonsense than any twenty other girls.'

'A twenty-girl power! That's an immense compliment. I've the greatest respect for nonsense, I owe it so much; and I really think if nonsense were banished, the earth would grow insupportable.'

'Thank you, Lord Ilbury,' said Milly, who had grown quite easy in his company during our long visit at Elverston; 'and I tell you, Miss Maud, if you grow saucy, I'll accept your present, and what will you say then?'

'I really don't know; but just now I want to ask Lord Ilbury bow lie thinks my uncle looks; neither I nor Milly have seen him since his illness.'

'Very much weaker, I think; but he may be gaining strength. Still, as my business was not quite pleasant, I thought it better to postpone it, and if you think it would be right, I'll write to Doctor Bryerly to ask him to postpone the discussion for a little time.'

I at once assented, and thanked him; indeed, if I had had my way, the subject should never have been mentioned, I felt so hardhearted and rapacious; but Lord Ilbury explained that the trustees were constrained by the provisions of the will, and that I really had no power to release them; and I hoped that Uncle Silas also understood all this.

'And now,' said he, 'we've returned to Grange, my sister and I, and it is nearer than Elverston, so that we are really neighbours; and Mary wants Lady Knollys to fix a time she owes us a visit, you know—and you really must come at the same time; it will be so very pleasant, the same party exactly meeting in a new scene; and we have not half explored our neighbourhood; and I've got down all those Spanish engravings I told you of, and the Venetian missals, and all the rest. I think I remember very accurately the things you were most interested by, and they're all there; and really you must promise, you and Miss Millicent Ruthyn. And I forgot to mention—you know you complained that you were ill supplied with books, so Mary thought you would allow her to share her supply—they are the new books, you know—and when you have read yours, you and she can exchange.'

What girl was ever quite frank about her likings? I don't think I was more of a cheat than others; but I never could tell of myself. It is quite true that this duplicity and reserve seldom deceives. Our hypocrisies are forced upon some of our sex by the acuteness and vigilance of all in this field of enquiry; but if we are sly, we are also lynx-eyed, capital detectives, most ingenious in fitting together the bits and dovetails of a cumulative case; and in those affairs of love and liking, have a terrible exploratory instinct, and so, for the most part, when detected we are found out not only to be in love, but to be rogues moreover.

Lady Mary was very kind; but had Lady Mary of her own mere motion taken all this trouble? Was there no more energetic influence at the bottom of that welcome chest of books, which arrived only half an hour later? The circulating library of those days was not the epidemic and ubiquitous influence to which it has grown; and there were many places where it could not find you out.

Altogether that evening Bartram had acquired a peculiar beauty—a bright and mellow glow, in which even its gate-posts and wheelbarrow were interesting, and next day came a little cloud—Dudley appeared.

'You may be sure he wants money,' said Milly. 'He and father had words this morning.'

He took a chair at our luncheon, found fault with everything in his own laconic dialect, ate a good deal notwithstanding, and was sulky, and with Milly snappish. To me, on the contrary, when Milly went into the hall, he was mild and whimpering, and disposed to be confidential.

'There's the Governor says he hasn't a bob! Danged if I know how an old fellah in his bed-room muddles away money at that rate. I don't suppose he thinks I can git along without tin, and he knows them trustees won't gi'e me a tizzy till they get what they calls an opinion—dang 'em! Bryerly says he doubts it must all go under settlement. They'll settle me nicely if they do; and Governor knows all about it, and won't gi'e me a clanged brass farthin', an' me wi' bills to pay, an' lawyers dang 'em—writing letters. He knows summat o' that hisself, does Governor; and he might ha' consideration a bit for his own flesh and blood, *I* say. But he never does nout for none but hisself. I'll sell his books and his jewels next fit he takes—that's how I'll fit him.'

This amiable young man, glowering, with his elbows on the table and his fingers in his great whiskers, followed his homily, where clergymen append the blessing, with a muttered variety of very different matter.

'Now, Maud,' said he, pathetically, leaning back suddenly in his chair, with all his conscious beauty and misfortunes in his face, 'is not it hard lines?'

I thought the appeal was going to shape itself into an application for money; but it did not.

'I never know'd a reel beauty—first-chop, of course, I mean—that wasn't kind along of it, and I'm a fellah as can't git along without sympathy—that's why I say it—an' isn't it hard lines? Now, say it's hard lines—*haint* it, Maud?'

I did not know exactly what hard lines meant, but I said, I suppose it is very disagreeable.'

And with this concession, not caring to hear any more in the same vein, I rose, intending to take my departure.

'No, that's jest it. I knew ye'd say it, Maud. Ye're a kind lass—ye be—'tis in yer pretty face. I like ye awful, I do there's not a handsomer lass in Liverpool nor Lunnon itself—*no* where.'

He had seized my hand, and trying to place his arm about my waist, essayed that salute which I had so narrowly escaped on my first introduction.

'*Don't*, sir,' I exclaimed in high indignation, escaping at the same moment from his grasp.

'No offence, lass; no harm, Maud; you must not be so shy—we're cousins, you know—an' I wouldn't hurt ye, Maud, no more nor I'd knock my head off. I wouldn't.'

I did not wait to hear the rest of his tender protestations, but, without showing how nervous I was, I glided out of the room quietly, making an orderly retreat, the more meritorious as I heard him call after me persuasively—

'Come back, Maud. What are ye afeard on, lass? Come back, I say—do now; there's a good wench.'

As Milly and I were taking our walk that day, in the direction of the Windmill Wood, to which, in consequence perhaps of some secret order, we had now free access, we saw Beauty, for the first time since her illness, in the little yard, throwing grain to the poultry.

'How do you find yourself to-day, Meg? I am *very* glad to see you able to be about again; but I hope it is not too soon.'

We were standing at the barred gate of the little enclosure, and quite close to Meg, who, however, did not choose to raise her head, but, continuing to shower her grain and potato-skins among her hens and chickens, said in a low tone—

'Father baint in sight? Look jist round a bit and say if ye see him.'

But Dickon's dusky red costume was nowhere visible.

So Meg looked up, pale and thin, and with her old grave, observant eyes, and she said quietly—

''Tisn't that I'm not glad to see ye; but if father was to spy me talking friendly wi' ye, now that I'm hearty, and you havin' no more call to me, he'd be all'ays a watching and thinkin' I was tellin' o' tales, and 'appen he'd want me to worrit ye for money, Miss Maud; an' 'tisn't here he'd spend it, but in the Feltram pottusses, he would, and we want for nothin' that's good for us. But that's how 'twould be, an' he'd all'ays be a jawing and a lickin' of I; so don't mind me, Miss Maud, and 'appen I might do ye a good turn some day.'

A few days after this little interview with Meg, as Milly and I were walking briskly—for it was a clear frosty day—along the pleasant slopes of the sheep-walk, we were overtaken by Dudley Ruthyn. It was not a pleasant surprise. There was this mitigation, however: we were on foot, and he driving in a dog-cart along the track leading to the moor, with his dogs and gun. He brought his horse for a moment to a walk, and with a careless nod to me, removing his short pipe from his mouth, he said—

'Governor's callin' for ye, Milly; and he told me to send you slick home to him if I saw you, and I think he'll gi'e ye some money; but ye better take him while he's in the humour, lass, or mayhap ye'll go long without.'

And with those words, apparently intent on his game, he nodded again, and, pipe in mouth, drove at a quick trot over the slope of the hill, and disappeared.

So I agreed to await Milly's return while she ran home, and rejoined me where I was. Away she ran, in high spirits, and I wandered listlessly about in search of some convenient spot to sit down upon, for I was a little tired.

She had not been gone five minutes, when I heard a step approaching, and looking round, saw the dog-cart close by, the horse browsing on the short grass, and Dudley Ruthyn within a few paces of me.

'Ye see, Maud, I've bin thinkin' why you're so vexed wi' me, an' I thought I'd jest come back an' ask ye what I may a' done to anger ye so; there's no sin in that, I think—is there?'

'I'm not angry. I did not say so. I hope that's enough,' I said, startled; and, notwithstanding my speech, *very* angry, for I felt instinctively that Milly's despatch homeward was a mere trick, and I the dupe of this coarse stratagem.

'Well then, if ye baint angry, so much the better, Maud. I only want to know why you're afeard o' me. I never struck a man foul, much less hurt a girl, in my days; besides, Maud, I likes ye too well to hurt ye. Dang it, lass, you're my cousin, ye know, and cousins is all'ays together and lovin' like, an' none says again' it.'

'I've nothing to explain—there is nothing to explain. I've been quite friendly,' I said, hurriedly.

'*Friendly!* Well, if there baint a cram! How can ye think it friendly, Maud, when ye won't a'most shake hands wi' me? It's enough to make a fellah sware, or cry a'most. Why d'ye like aggravatin' a poor devil? Now baint ye an ill-natured little puss, Maud, an' I likin' ye so well? You're the prettiest lass in Derbyshire; there's nothin' I wouldn't do for ye.'

And he backed his declaration with an oath.

'Be so good, then, as to re-enter your dog-cart and drive away,' I replied, very much incensed.

'Now, there it is again! Ye can't speak me civil. Another fellah'd fly out, an' maybe kiss ye for spite; but I baint that sort, I'm all for coaxin' and kindness, an' ye won't let me. What *be* you drivin' at, Maud?'

'I think I've said very plainly, sir, that I wish to be alone. You've *nothing* to say, except utter nonsense, and I've heard quite enough. Once for all, I beg, sir, that you will be so good as to leave me.'

'Well, now, look here, Maud; I'll do anything you like—bum me if I don't—if you'll only jest be kind to me, like cousins should. What did I ever do to vex you?

If you think I like any lass better than you—some fellah at Elverston's bin talkin', maybe—it's nout but lies an' nonsense. Not but there's lots o' wenches likes me well enough, though I be a plain lad, and speaks my mind straight out.'

'I can't see that you are so frank, sir, as you describe; you have just played a shabby trick to bring about this absurd and most disagreeable interview.'

'And supposin' I did send that fool, Milly, out o' the way, to talk a bit wi' you here, where's the harm? Dang it, lass, ye mustn't be too hard. Didn't I say I'd do whatever ye wished?'

'And you *won't*,' said I.

'Ye mean to get along out o' this? Well, now, I will. There! No use, of course, askin' you to kiss and be friends, before I go, as cousins should. Well, don't be riled, lass, I'm not askin' it; only mind, I do like you awful, and 'appen I'll find ye in better humour another time. Good-bye, Maud; I'll make ye like me at last.'

And with these words, to my comfort, he addressed himself to his horse and pipe, and was soon honestly on his way to the moor.

CHAPTER XLVI

THE RIVALS

All the time that Dudley chose to persecute me with his odious society, I continued to walk at a brisk pace toward home, so that I had nearly reached the house when Milly met me, with a note which had arrived for me by the post, in her hand.

'Here, Milly, are more verses. He is a very persevering poet, whoever he is.' So I broke the seal; but this time it was prose. And the first words were 'Captain Oakley.'

I confess to an odd sensation as these remarkable words met my eye. It might possibly be a proposal. I did not wait to speculate, however, but read these sentences traced in the identical handwriting which had copied the lines with which I had been twice favoured.

'Captain Oakley presents his compliments to Miss Ruthyn, and trusts she will excuse his venturing to ask whether, during his short stay in Feltram, he might be permitted to pay his respects at Bartram-Haugh. He has been making a short visit to his aunt, and could not find himself so near without at least attempting to renew an acquaintance which he has never ceased to cherish in memory. If Miss Ruthyn would be so very good as to favour him with ever so short a reply to the question he ventures most respectfully to ask, her decision would reach him at the Hall Hotel, Feltram.'

'Well, he's a roundabout fellah, anyhow. Couldn't he come up and see you if he wanted to? They poeters, they do love writing long yarns—don't they?' And with this reflection, Milly took the note and read it through again.

'It's jolly polite anyhow, isn't it Maud?' said Milly, who had conned it over, and accepted it as a model composition.

I must have been, I think, naturally a rather shrewd girl; and considering how very little I had seen of the world—nothing in fact—I often wonder now at the sage conclusions at which I arrived.

Were I to answer this handsome and cunning fool according to his folly, in what position should I find myself? No doubt my reply would induce a rejoinder, and that compel another note from me, and that invite yet another from him; and however his might improve in warmth, they were sure not to abate. Was it his impertinent plan, with this show of respect and ceremony, to drag me into a clandestine correspondence? Inexperienced girl as I was, I fired at the idea of becoming his dupe, and fancying, perhaps, that there was more in merely answering his note than it would have amounted to, I said—

'That kind of thing may answer very 'well with button-makers, but ladies don't like it. What would your papa think of it if he found that I had been writing to him, and seeing him without his permission? If he wanted to see me he could have'—(I really did not know exactly what he could have done)—'he could have timed his visit to Lady Knollys differently; at all events, he has no right to place me in an embarrassing situation, and I am certain Cousin Knollys would say so; and I think his note both shabby and impertinent.'

Decision was not with me an intellectual process. When quite cool I was the most undecided of mortals, but once my feelings were excited I was prompt and bold.

'I'll give the note to Uncle Silas,' I said, quickening my pace toward home; 'he'll know what to do.'

But Milly, who, I fancy, had no objection to the little romance which the young officer proposed, told me that she could not see her father, that he was ill, and not speaking to anyone.

'And arn't ye making a plaguy row about nothin'? I lay a guinea if ye had never set eyes on Lord Ilbury you'd a told him to come, and see ye, an' welcome.'

'Don't talk like a fool, Milly. You never knew me do anything deceitful. Lord Ilbury has no more to do with it, you know very well, than the man in the moon.'

I was altogether very indignant. I did not speak another word to Milly. The proportions of the house are so great, that it is a much longer walk than you would suppose from the hall-door to Uncle Silas's room. But I did not cool all that way; and it was not till I had just reached the lobby, and saw the sour, jealous face, and high caul of old Wyat, and felt the influence of that neighbourhood, that I paused to reconsider. I fancied there was a cool consciousness of success behind all the deferential phraseology of Captain Oakley, which nettled me extremely. No; there could be no doubt. I tapped softly at the door.

'What is it *now*, Miss?' snarled the querulous old woman, with her shrivelled fingers on the door-handle.

'Can I see my uncle for a moment?'

'He's tired, and not a word from him all day long.'

'Not ill, though?'

'Awful bad in the night,' said the old crone, with a sudden savage glare in my face, as if *I* had brought it about.

'Oh! I'm very sorry. I had not heard a word of it.'

'No one does but old Wyat. There's Milly there never asks neither—his own child I '

'Weakness, or what?'

'One o' them fits. He'll slide awa' in one o' them some day, and no one but old Wyat to know nor ask word about it; that's how 'twill be.'

'Will you please hand him this note, if he is well enough to look at it, and say I am at the door?'

She took it with a peevish nod and a grunt, closing the door in my face, and in a few minutes returned—

'Come in wi' ye,' said Dame Wyat, and I appeared.

Uncle Silas, who, after his nightly horror or vision, lay extended on a sofa, with his faded yellow silk dressing-gown about him, his long white hair hanging toward the ground, and that wild and feeble smile lighting his face—a glimmer I feared to look upon—his long thin arms lay by his sides, with hands and fingers that stirred not, except when now and then, with a feeble motion, he wet his temples and forehead with eau de Cologne from a glass saucer placed beside him.

'Excellent girl! dutiful ward and niece!' murmured the oracle; 'heaven reward you—your frank dealing is your own safety and my peace. Sit you down, and say who is this Captain Oakley, when you made his acquaintance, what his age, fortune, and expectations, and who the aunt he mentions.'

Upon all these points I satisfied him as fully as I was able.

'Wyat—the white drops,' he called, in a thin, stern tone. 'I'll write a line presently. I can't see visitors, and, of course, you can't receive young captains before you've come out. Farewell! God bless you, dear.'

Wyat was dropping the 'white' restorative into a wine-glass and the room was redolent of ether. I was glad to escape. The figures and whole *mise en scène* were unearthly.

'Well, Milly,' I said, as I met her in the hall, 'your papa is going to write to him.'

I sometimes wonder whether Milly was right, and how I should have acted a few months earlier.

Next day whom should we meet in the Windmill Wood but Captain Oakley. The spot where this interesting *rencontre* occurred was near that ruinous bridge on my sketch of which I had received so many compliments. It was so great a surprise that I had not time to recollect my indignation, and, having received him very affably, I found it impossible, during our brief interview, to recover my lost altitude.

After our greetings were over, and some compliments neatly made, he said—

'I had such a curious note from Mr. Silas Ruthyn. I am sure he thinks me a very impertinent fellow, for it was really anything but inviting—extremely rude, in fact. But I could not quite see that because he does not want me to invade his bed-room—an incursion I never dreamed of—I was not to present myself to you, who had already honoured me with your acquaintance, with the sanction of those who were most interested in your welfare, and who were just as well qualified as he, I fancy, to say who were qualified for such an honour.'

'My uncle, Mr. Silas Ruthyn, you are aware, is my guardian and this is my cousin, his daughter.'

This was an opportunity of becoming a little lofty, and I improved it. He raised his hat and bowed to Milly.

'I'm afraid I've been very rude and stupid. Mr. Ruthyn, of course, has a perfect right to—to—in fact, I was not the least aware that I had the honour of so near a relation's—a—a— and what exquisite scenery you have! I think this country round Feltram particularly fine; and this Bartram-Haugh is, I venture to say, about the very most beautiful spot in this beautiful region. I do assure you I am tempted beyond measure to make Feltram and the Hall Hotel my head-quarters for at least a week. I only regret the foliage; but your trees show wonderfully, even in winter, so many of them have got that ivy about them. They say it spoils trees, but it cer-tainly beautifies them. I have just ten days' leave unexpired; I wish I could induce you to advise me how to apply them. What shall I do, Miss Ruthyn?'

'I am the worst person in the world to make plans, even for myself, I find it so troublesome. What do you say? Suppose you try Wales or Scotland, and climb up some of those fine mountains that look so well in winter?'

'I should much prefer Feltram. I so wish you would recommend *it*. What is this pretty plant?'

'We call that Maud's myrtle. She planted it, and it's very pretty when it's full in blow,' said Milly.

Our visit to Elverston had been of immense use to us both.

'Oh! planted by *you?*' he said, very softly, with a momentary corresponding glance. 'May I—ever so little—just a leaf?'

And without waiting for permission, he held a sprig of it next his waistcoat.

'Yes, it goes very prettily with those buttons. They are *very* pretty buttons; are not they, Milly? A present, a souvenir, I dare say?'

This was a terrible hit at the button-maker, and I thought he looked a little oddly at me, but my countenance was so 'bewitchingly simple' that I suppose his suspicions were allayed.

Now, it was very odd of me, I must confess, to talk in this way, and to receive all those tender allusions from a gentleman about whom I had spoken and felt so sharply only the evening before. But Bartram was abominably lonely. A civilised person was a valuable waif or stray in that region of the picturesque and the brutal; and to my lady reader especially, because she will probably be hardest upon me, I put it—can you not recollect any such folly in your own past life? Can you not in as many minutes call to mind at least six similar inconsistencies of your own practising? For my part, I really can't see the advantage of being the weaker sex if we are always to be as strong as our masculine neighbours.

There was, indeed, no revival of the little sentiment which I had once experienced. When these things once expire, I do believe they are as hard to revive as our dead lap-dogs, guinea-pigs, and parrots. It was my perfect coolness which enabled me to chat, I flatter myself, so agreeably with the refined Captain, who plainly thought me his captive, and was probably now and then thinking what was to be done to utilise that little bit of Bartram, or to beautify some other, when he should see fit to become its master, as we rambled over these wild but beautiful grounds.

It was just about then that Milly nudged me rather vehemently, and whispered 'Look there!'

I followed with mine the direction of her eyes, and saw my odious cousin, Dudley, in a flagrant pair of cross-barred peg-tops, and what Milly before her reformation used to call other 'slops' of corresponding atrocity, approaching our refined little party with great strides. I really think that Milly was very nearly ashamed of him. I certainly was. I had no apprehension, however, of the scene which was imminent.

The charming Captain mistook him probably for some rustic servant of the place, for he continued his agreeable remarks up to the very moment when Dudley, whose face was pale with anger, and whose rapid advance had not served to cool him, without recollecting to salute either Milly or me, accosted our elegant companion as follows:—

'By your leave, master, baint you summat in the wrong box here, don't you think?'

He had planted himself directly in his front, and looked unmistakably menacing.

'May I speak to him? Will you excuse me?' said the Captain blandly.

'Ow—ay, they'll excuse ye ready enough, I dessay; you're to deal wi' me though. Baint ye in the wrong box now?'

'I'm not conscious, sir, of being in a box at all,' replied the Captain, with severe disdain. 'It strikes me you are disposed to get up a row. Let us, if you please, get a little apart from the ladies it that is your purpose.'

'I mean to turn you out o' this the way ye came. If you make a row, so much the wuss for you, for I'll lick ye to fits.'

'Tell him not to fight,' whispered Milly; 'he'll a no chance wi' Dudley.'

I saw Dickon Hawkes grinning over the paling on which he leaned.

'Mr. Hawkes,' I said, drawing Milly with me toward that unpromising mediator, 'pray prevent unpleasantness and go between them.'

'An' git licked o' both sides? Rather not, Miss, thank ye,' grinned Dickon, tranquilly.

'Who are you, sir?' demanded our romantic acquaintance, with military sternness.

'I'll tell you who you are—you're Oakley, as stops at the Hall, that Governor wrote, over-night, not to dare show your nose inside the grounds. You're a half-starved cappen, come down here to look for a wife, and——'

Before Dudley could finish his sentence, Captain Oakley, than whose face no regimentals could possibly have been more scar let, at that moment, struck with his switch at Dudley's handsome features.

I don't know how it was done—by some 'devilish cantrip slight.' A smack was heard, and the Captain lay on his back on the ground, with his mouth full of blood.

'How do ye like the taste o' that?' roared Dickon, from his post of observation.

In an instant Captain Oakley was on his feet again, hatless, looking quite frantic, and striking out at Dudley, who was ducking and dipping quite coolly, and again the same horrid sound, only this time it was double, like a quick postman's knock, and Captain Oakley was on the grass again.

'Tapped his smeller, by——!' thundered Dickon, with a roar of laughter.

'Come away, Milly—I'm growing ill,' said I.

'Drop it, Dudley, I tell ye; you'll kill him,' screamed Milly.

But the devoted Captain, whose nose, and mouth, and shirt-front formed now but one great patch of blood, and who was bleeding beside over one eye, dashed at him again.

I turned away. I felt quite faint, and on the point of crying, with mere horror.

'Hammer away at his knocker,' bellowed Dickon, in a frenzy of delight.

'He'll break it now, if it ain't already,' cried Milly, alluding, as I afterwards understood, to the Captain's Grecian nose.

'Brayvo, little un!' The Captain was considerably the taller.

Another smack, and, I suppose, Captain Oakley fell once more.

'Hooray I the dinner-service again, by——' roared Dickon. 'Stick to that. Over the same ground-subsoil, I say. He han't enough yet.'

In a perfect tremor of disgust, I was making as quick a retreat as I could, and as I did, I heard Captain Oakley shriek hoarsely—

'You're a d——prizefighter; I can't box you.'

'I told ye I'd lick ye to fits,' hooted Dudley.

'But you're the son of a gentleman, and by——you shall fight me *as a* gentleman.'

A yell of hooting laughter from Dudley and Dickon followed this sally.

'Gi'e my love to the Colonel, and think o' me when ye look in the glass-won't ye? An' so you're goin' arter all; well, follow what's left o' yer nose. Ye forgot some o' yet ivories, didn't ye, on th' grass?'

These and many similar jibes followed the mangled Captain in his retreat.

CHAPTER XLVII

DOCTOR BRYERLY REAPPEARS

No one who has not experienced it can imagine the nervous disgust and horror which such a spectacle as we had been forced in part to witness leaves upon the mind of a young person of my peculiar temperament.

It affected ever after my involuntary estimate of the principal actors in it. An exhibition of such thorough inferiority, accompanied by such a shock to the feminine sense of elegance, is not forgotten by any woman. Captain Oakley had been severely beaten by a smaller man. It was pitiable, but also undignified; and Milly's anxieties about his teeth and nose, though in a certain sense horrible, had also a painful suspicion of the absurd.

People say, on the other hand, that superior prowess, even in such barbarous contests, inspires in our sex an interest akin to admiration. I can positively say in my case it was quite the reverse. Dudley Ruthyn stood lower than ever in my estimation; for though I feared him more, it was by reason of these brutal and cold-blooded associations.

After this I lived in constant apprehension of being summoned to my uncle's room, and being called on for an explanation of my meeting with Captain Oakley, which, notwithstanding my perfect innocence, looked suspicious, but no such inquisition resulted. Perhaps he did not suspect me; or, perhaps, he thought, not in his haste, all women are liars, and did not care to hear what I might say. I rather lean to the latter interpretation.

The exchequer just now, I suppose, by some means, was replenished, for next morning Dudley set off upon one of his fashionable excursions, as poor Milly thought them, to Wolverhampton. And the same day Dr. Bryerly arrived.

Milly and I, from my room window, saw him step from his vehicle to the court-yard.

A lean man, with sandy hair and whiskers, was in the chaise with him. Dr. Bryerly descended in the unchangeable black suit that always looked new and never fitted him.

The Doctor looked careworn, and older, I thought, by several years, than when I last saw him. He was not shown up to my uncle's room; on the contrary, Milly, who was more actively curious than I, ascertained that our tremulous butler informed him that my uncle was not sufficiently well for an interview. Whereupon Dr. Bryerly had pencilled a note, the reply to which was a message from Uncle

Silas, saying that he would be happy to see him in five minutes.

As Milly and I were conjecturing what it might mean, and before the five minutes had expired, Mary Quince entered.

'Wyat bid me tell you, Miss, your uncle wants you *this minute.*'

When I entered his room, Uncle Silas was seated at the table, with his desk before him. He looked up. Could anything be more dignified, suffering, and venerable?

'I sent for you, dear,' he said very gently, extending his thin, white hand, and taking mine, which he held affectionately while he spoke, 'because I desire to have no secrets, and wish you thoroughly to know all that concerns your own interests while subject to my guardianship; and I am happy to think, my beloved niece, that you requite my candour. Oh, here is the gentleman. Sit down, dear.'

Doctor Bryerly was advancing, as it seemed, to shake hands with Uncle Silas, who, however, rose with a severe and haughty air, not the least over-acted, and made him a slow, ceremonious bow. I wondered how the homely Doctor could confront so tranquilly that astounding statue of hauteur.

A faint and weary smile, rather sad than contemptuous, was the only sign he showed of feeling his repulse.

'How do *you* do, Miss?' he said, extending his hand, and greeting me after his ungallant fashion, as if it were an after thought.

'I think I may as well take a chair, sit,' said Doctor Bryerly, sitting down serenely, near the table, and crossing his ungainly legs.

My uncle bowed.

'You understand the nature of the business, sit. Do you wish Miss Ruthyn to remain?' asked Doctor Bryerly.

'I *sent* for her, sir,' replied my uncle, in a very gentle and sarcastic tone, a smile on his thin lips, and his strangely-contorted eyebrows raised for a moment contemptuously. 'This gentleman, my dear Maud, thinks proper to insinuate that I am robbing you. It surprises me a little, and, no doubt, you—I've nothing to conceal, and wished you to be present while he favours me more particularly with his views. I'm right, I think, in describing it as *robbery*, sir?'

'Why,' said Doctor Bryerly thoughtfully, for he was treating the matter as one of right, and not of feeling, 'it would be, certainly, taking that which does not belong to you, and converting it to your own use; but, at the worst, it would more resemble *thieving*, I think, than robbery.'

I saw Uncle Silas's lip, eyelid, and thin cheek quiver and shrink, as if with a thrill of tic-douloureux, as Doctor Bryerly spoke this unconsciously insulting answer. My uncle had, however, the self-command which is learned at the gaming-table. He shrugged, with a chilly, sarcastic, little laugh, and a glance at me.

'Your note says *waste*, I think, sir?'

'Yes, waste—the felling and sale of timber in the Windmill Wood, the selling of oak bark and burning of charcoal, as I'm informed,' said Bryerly, as sadly and quietly as a man might relate a piece of intelligence from the newspaper.

'Detectives? or private spies of your own?—or, perhaps, my servants, bribed with my poor brother's money? A very high-minded procedure.'

'Nothing of the kind, sir.'

My uncle sneered.

'I mean, sit, there has been no undue canvass for evidence, and the question is simply one of right; and it is our duty to see that this inexperienced young lady is not defrauded.'

'By her own uncle?'

'By anyone,' said Doctor Bryerly, with a natural impenetrability that excited my admiration.

'Of course you come armed with an opinion?' said my smiling uncle, insinuatingly.

'The case is before Mr. Serjeant Grinders. These bigwigs don't return their cases sometimes so quickly as we could wish.'

'Then you have *no* opinion?' smiled my uncle.

'My solicitor is quite clear upon it; and it seems to me there can be no question raised, but for form's sake.'

'Yes, for form's sake you take one, and in the meantime, upon a nice question of law, the surmises of a thick-headed attorney and of an ingenious apoth—I beg pardon, physician—are sufficient warrant for telling my niece and ward, in my presence, that I am defrauding her!'

My uncle leaned back in his chair, and smiled with a contemptuous patience over Doctor Bryerly's head, as he spoke.

'I don't know whether I used that expression, sir, but I am speaking merely in a technical sense. I mean to say, that, whether by mistake or otherwise, you are exercising a power which you don't lawfully possess, and that the effect of that is to impoverish the estate, and, by so much as it benefits you, to wrong this young lady.'

'I'm a technical defrauder, I see, and your manner conveys the rest. I thank my God, sit, I am a *very* different man from what I once was.' Uncle Silas was speaking in a low tone, and with extraordinary deliberation. 'I remember when I should have certainly knocked you down, sir, or *tried* it, at least, for a great deal less.'

'But seriously, sir, what *do* you propose?' asked Doctor Bryerly, sternly and a little flushed, for I think the old man was stirred within him; and though he did not raise his voice, his manner was excited.

'I propose to defend my rights, sir,' murmured Uncle Silas, very grim. 'I'm not without an opinion, though you are.'

'You seem to think, sit, that I have a pleasure in annoying you; you are quite wrong. I hate annoying anyone—constitutionally—I *hate* it; but don't you see, sir, the position I'm placed in? I wish I could please everyone, and do my duty.'

Uncle Silas bowed and smiled.

'I've brought with me the Scotch steward from Tolkingden, *your* estate, Miss, and if you let us we will visit the spot and make a note of what we observe, that is, assuming that you admit waste, and merely question our law.'

'If you please, sir, you and your Scotchman shall do *no such thing*; and, bearing in mind that I neither deny nor admit anything, you will please further never more to present yourself, under any pretext whatsoever, either in this house or on the grounds of Bartram-Haugh, during my lifetime.'

Uncle Silas rose up with the same glassy smile and scowl, in token that the interview was ended.

'Good-bye, sir,' said Doctor Bryerly, with a sad and thoughtful air, and hesitating for a moment, he said to me, 'Do you think, Miss, you could afford me a word in the hall?'

'Not a word, sit,' snarled Uncle Silas, with a white flash from his eyes.

There was a pause.

'Sit where you are, Maud.'

Another pause.

'If you have anything to say to my ward, sit, you will please to say it *here*.'

Doctor Bryerly's dark and homely face was turned on me with an expression of unspeakable compassion.

'I was going to say, that if you think of any way in which I can be of the least service, Miss, I'm ready to act, that's all mind, *any* way.'

He hesitated, looking at me with the same expression as if he had something more to say; but he only repeated—

'That's all, Miss.'

'Won't you shake hands, Doctor Bryerly, before you go? 'I said, eagerly approaching him.

Without a smile, with the same sad anxiety in his face, with his mind, as it seemed to me, on something else, and irresolute whether to speak it or be silent, he took my fingers in a very cold hand, and holding it so, and slowly shaking it, his grave and troubled glance unconsciously rested on Uncle Silas's face, while in a sad tone and absent way he said—

'Good-bye, Miss.' From before that sad gaze my uncle averted his strange eyes quickly, and looked, oddly, to the window.

In a moment more Doctor Bryerly let my hand go with a sigh, and with an abrupt little nod to me, he left the room; and I heard that dismallest of sounds, the retreating footsteps of a true friend, *lost*.

'Lead us not into temptation; if we pray so, we must not mock the eternal Majesty of Heaven by walking into temptation of our own accord.'

This oracular sentence was not uttered by my uncle until Doctor Bryerly had been gone at least five minutes.

'I've forbid him my house, Maud—first, because his perfectly unconscious insolence tries my patience nearly beyond endurance; and again, because I have heard unfavourable reports of him. On the question of right which he disputes, I am perfectly informed. I am your tenant, my dear niece; when I am gone you will learn how *scrupulous* I have been; you will see how, under the pressure of the most agonising pecuniary difficulties, the terriffic penalty of a misspent youth, I have been careful never by a hair's breadth to transgress the strict line of my legal privileges; alike, as your tenant, Maud, and as your guardian; how, amid frightful agitations, I have kept myself, by the miraculous strength and grace vouchsafed me—*pure*.

'The world,' he resumed after a short pause, 'has no faith in any man's conversion; it never forgets what he was, it never believes him anything better, it is an inexorable and stupid judge. What I was I will describe in blacker terms, and with more heartfelt detestation, than my traducers—a reckless prodigal, a godless profligate. Such I was; what I am, I am. If I had no hope beyond this world, of all men most miserable but with that hope, a sinner saved!'

Then he waxed eloquent and mystical. I think his Swedenborgian studies had crossed his notions of religion with strange lights. I never could follow him quite in these excursions into the region of symbolism. I only recollect that he talked of the deluge and the waters of Mara, and said, 'I am washed—I am sprinkled,' and then, pausing, bathed his thin temples and forehead with eau de Cologne; a process which was, perhaps, suggested by his imagery of sprinkling and so forth.

Thus refreshed, he sighed and smiled, and passed to the subject of Doctor Bryerly.

'Of Doctor Bryerly, I know that he is sly, that he loves money, was born poor, and makes nothing by his profession. But he possesses many thousand pounds, under my poor brother's will, of *your money*, and he has glided with, of course a modest "nolo episcopari," into the acting trusteeship, with all its multitudinous opportunities, of your immense property. That is not doing so badly for a visionary Swedenborgian. Such a man must prosper, But if he expected to make money of me, he is disappointed. Money, however, he will make of his trusteeship, as you will see. It is a dangerous resolution. But if he will seek the life of Dives, the worst I wish him is to find the death of Lazarus. But whether, like Lazarus, he be borne of angels into Abraham's bosom, or, like the rich man, only dies and is buried, and *the rest*, neither living nor dying do I desire his company.'

Uncle Silas here seemed suddenly overtaken by exhaustion. He leaned back with a ghastly look, and his lean features glistened with the dew of faintness. I screamed for Wyat. But he soon recovered sufficiently to smile his odd smile, and with it and his frown, nodded and waved me away.

CHAPTER XLVIII

QUESTION AND ANSWER

My uncle, after all, was not ill that day, after the strange fashion of his malady, be it what it might. Old Wyat repeated in her sour laconic way that there was 'nothing to speak of amiss with him.' But there remained with me a sense of pain and fear. Doctor Bryerly, notwithstanding my uncle's sarcastic reflections, remained, in my estimation, a true and wise friend. I had all my life been accustomed to rely upon others, and here, haunted by many unavowed and ill-defined alarms and doubts, the disappearance of an active and able friend caused my heart to sink.

Still there remained my dear Cousin Monica, and my pleasant and trusted friend, Lord Ilbury; and in less than a week arrived an invitation from Lady Mary to the Grange, for me and Milly, to meet Lady Knollys. It was accompanied, she told me, by a note from Lord Ilbury to my uncle, supporting her request; and in the afternoon I received a message to attend my uncle in his room.

'An invitation from Lady Mary Carysbroke for you and Milly to meet Monica Knollys; have you received it?' asked my uncle, so soon as I was seated. Answered in the affirmative, he continued—

'Now, Maud Ruthyn, I expect the truth from you; I have been frank, so shall you. Have you ever heard me spoken ill of by Lady Knollys?'

I was quite taken aback.

I felt my cheeks flushing. I was returning his fierce cold gaze with a stupid stare, and remained dumb.

'Yes, Maud, you *have.*'

I looked down in silence.

'I *know* it; but it is right you should answer; have you or have you not?'

I had to clear my voice twice or thrice. There was a kind of spasm in my throat.

'I am trying to recollect,' I said at last.

'*Do* recollect,' he replied imperiously.

There was a little interval of silence. I would have given the world to be, on any conditions, anywhere else in the world.

'Surely, Maud, you don't wish to deceive your guardian? Come, the question is a plain one, and I know the truth already. I ask you again—have you ever heard me spoken ill of by Lady Knollys?'

'Lady Knollys,' I said, half articulately, 'speaks very freely, and often half in jest but,' I continued, observing something menacing in his face, 'I have heard her express disapprobation of some things you have done.'

'Come, Maud,' he continued, in a stern, though still a low key, 'did she not insinuate that charge—then, I suppose, in a state of incubation, the other day presented here full-fledged, with beak and claws, by that scheming apothecary—the statement that I was defrauding you by cutting down timber upon the grounds?'

'She certainly did mention the circumstance; but she also argued that it might have been through ignorance of the extent of your rights.'

'Come, come, Maud, you must not prevaricate, girl. I *will* have it. Does she not habitually speak disparagingly of me, in your presence, and *to* you? *Answer.*'

I hung my head.

'Yes or no?'

'Well, perhaps so—yes,' I faltered, and burst into tears.

'There, don't cry; it may well shock you. Did she not, to your knowledge, say the same things in presence of my child Millicent? I know it, I repeat—there is no use in hesitating; and I command you to answer.'

Sobbing, I told the truth.

'Now sit still, while I write my reply.'

He wrote, with the scowl and smile so painful to witness, as he looked down upon the paper, and then he placed the note before me—

'Read that, my dear.'

It began—

'MY DEAR LADY KNOLLYS.—You have favoured me with a note, adding your request to that of Lord Ilbury, that I should permit my ward and my daughter to avail themselves of Lady Mary's invitation. Being perfectly cognisant of the ill-feeling you have always and unaccountably cherished toward me, and also of the terms in which you have had the delicacy and the conscience to speak of me before and to my child and my ward, I can only express my amazement at the modesty of your request, while peremptorily refusing it. And I shall conscientiously adopt effectual measures to prevent your ever again having an opportunity of endeavouring to destroy my influence and authority over my ward and my child, by direct or insinuated slander.

'Your defamed and injured kinsman,
SILAS RUTHYN.'

I was stunned; yet what could I plead against the blow that was to isolate me? I wept aloud, with my hands clasped, looking on the marble face of the old man.

Without seeming to hear, he folded and sealed his note, and then proceeded to answer Lord Ilbury.

When that note was written, he placed it likewise before me, and I read it also through. It simply referred him to Lady Knollys 'for an explanation of the unhappy circumstances which compelled him to decline an invitation which it would have made his niece and his daughter so happy to accept.'

'You see, my dear Maud, how frank I am with you,' he said, waving the open note, which I had just read, slightly before he folded it. 'I think I may ask you to reciprocate my candour.'

Dismissed from this interview, I ran to Milly, who burst into tears from sheet disappointment, so we wept and wailed together. But in my grief I think there was more reason.

I sat down to the dismal task of writing to my dear Lady Knollys. I implored her to make her peace with my uncle. I told her how frank he had been with me, and how he had shown me his sad reply to her letter. I told her of the interview to which he had himself invited me with Dr. Bryerly; how little disturbed he was by the accusation—no sign of guilt; quite the contrary, perfect confidence. I implored of her to think the best, and remembering my isolation, to accomplish a reconciliation with Uncle Silas. 'Only think,' I wrote, 'I only nineteen, and two years of solitude before me. What a separation!' No broken merchant ever signed the schedule of his bankruptcy with a heavier heart than did I this letter.

The griefs of youth are like the wounds of the gods—there is an ichor which heals the scars from which it flows: and thus Milly and I consoled ourselves, and next day enjoyed our ramble, our talk and readings, with a wonderful resignation to the inevitable.

Milly and I stood in the relation of *Lord Duberly* to *Doctor Pangloss*. I was to mend her 'cackleology,' and the occupation amused us both. I think at the bottom of our submission to destiny lurked a hope that Uncle Silas, the inexorable, would relent, or that Cousin Monica, that siren, would win and melt him to her purpose.

Whatever comfort, however, I derived from the absence of Dudley was not to be of very long duration; for one morning, as I was amusing myself alone, with a piece of worsted work, thinking, and just at that moment not unpleasantly, of many things, my cousin Dudley entered the room.

'Back again, like a bad halfpenny, ye see. And how a' ye bin ever since, lass? Purely, I warrant, be your looks. I'm jolly glad to see ye, I am; no cattle going like ye, Maud.'

'I think I must ask you to let go my hand, as I can't continue my work,' I said, very stiffly, hoping to chill his enthusiasm a little.

'Anything to pleasure ye, Maud, 'tain't in my heart to refuse ye nout. I a'bin to Wolverhampton, lass—jolly row there—and run over to Leamington; a'most broke my neck, faith, wi' a borrowed horse arter the dogs; ye would na care, Maud, if I broke my neck, would ye? Well, 'appen, jest a little,' he good-naturedly supplied, as I was silent.

'Little over a week since I left here, by George; and to me it's half the almanac like; can ye guess the reason, Maud?'

'Have you seen your sister, Milly, or your father, since your return?' I asked coldly.

'*They'll* keep, Maud, never mind 'em; it be you I want to see—it be you I wor thinkin' on a' the time. I tell ye, lass, I'm all'ays a thinkin' on ye.'

' I think you ought to go and see your father; you have been away, you say, some time. I don't think it is respectful.' I said, a little sharply.

'If ye bid me go I'd a'most go, but I could na quite; there's nout on earth I would na do for you, Maud, excep' leaving you.'

'And that,' I said, with a petulant flush, 'is the only thing on earth I would ask you to do.'

'Blessed if you baint a blushin', Maud,' he drawled, with an odious grin.

His stupidity was proof against everything.

'It is *too* bad!' I muttered, with an indignant little pat of my foot and mimic stamp.

'Well, you lasses be queer cattle; ye're angry wi' me now, cos ye think I got into mischief—ye do, Maud; ye know't, ye buxsom little fool, down there at Wolverhampton; and jest for that ye're ready to turn me off again the minute I come back; 'tisn't fair.'

'I don't *understand* you, sit; and I *beg* that you'll leave me.'

'Now, didn't I tell ye about leavin' ye, Maud? 'tis the only thing I can't compass for yet sake. I'm jest a child in yere hands, I am, ye know. I can lick a big fellah to pot as limp as a rag, by George!'—(his oaths were not really so mild)—'ye see summat o' that t'other day. Well, don't be vexed, Maud; 'twas all along o' you; ye know, I wor a bit jealous, 'appen; but anyhow I can do it; and look at me here, jest a child, I say, in yer hands.'

'I wish you'd go away. Have you nothing to do, and no one to see? Why *can't* you leave me alone, sir?'

''Cos I can't, Maud, that's jest why; and I wonder, Maud, how can you be so ill-natured, when you see me like this; how can ye?'

'I wish Milly would come,' said I peevishly, looking toward the door.

'Well, I'll tell you how it is, Maud. I may as well have it out. I like you better than any lass that ever I saw, a deal; you're nicer by chalks; there's none like ye—there isn't; and I wish you'd have me. I ha'n't much tin—father's run through a deal, he's pretty well up a tree, ye know; but though I baint so rich as some folk, I'm a better man, 'appen; and if ye'd take a tidy lad, that likes ye awful, and 'id die for your sake, why here he is.'

'What can you mean, sit?' I exclaimed, rising in indignant bewilderment.

'I mean, Maud, if ye'll marry me, you'll never ha' cause to complain; I'll never let ye want for nout, nor gi'e ye a wry word.'

'Actually a proposal!' I ejaculated, like a person speaking in a dream.

I stood with my hand on the back of a chair, staring at Dudley; and looking, I dare say, as stupefied as I felt.

'There's a good lass, ye would na deny me,' said the odious creature, with one knee on the seat of the chair behind which I was standing, and attempting to place his arm lovingly round my neck.

This effectually roused me, and starting back, I stamped upon the ground with actual fury.

'What has there ever been, sir, in my conduct, words, or looks, to warrant this unparalleled audacity? But that you are as stupid as you are impertinent, brutal, and ugly, you must, long ago, sit, have seen how I dislike you. How dare you, sir? Don't presume to obstruct me; I'm going to my uncle.'

I had never spoken so violently to mortal before.

He in turn looked a little confounded; and I passed his extended but motionless arm with a quick and angry step.

He followed me a pace or two, however, before I reached the door, looking horridly angry, but stopped, and only swore after me some of those 'wry words' which I was never to have heard. I was myself, however, too much incensed, and moving at too rapid a pace, to catch their import; and I had knocked at my uncle's door before I began to collect my thoughts.

'Come in,' replied my uncle's voice, clear, thin, and peevish.

I entered and confronted him.

'Your son, sir, has insulted me.'

He looked at me with a cold curiosity steadly for a few seconds, as I stood panting before him with flaming cheeks.

'Insulted you?' repeated he. 'Egad, you surprise me!'

The ejaculation savoured of 'the old man,' to borrow his scriptural phrase, more than anything I had heard from him before.

'*How?*' he continued; 'how has Dudley *insulted* you, my dear child? Come, you're excited; sit down; take time, and tell me all about it. I did not know that Dudley was here.'

'I—he—it *is* an insult. He knew very well—he *must* know I dislike him; and he presumed to make a proposal of marriage to me.'

'O—o—oh!' exclaimed my uncle, with a prolonged intonation which plainly said, Is that the mighty matter?

He looked at me as he leaned back with the same steady curiosity, this time smiling, which somehow frightened me, and his countenance looked to me wicked, like the face of a witch, with a guilt I could not understand.

'And that is the amount of your complaint. He made you a formal proposal of marriage!'

'Yes; he proposed for me.'

As I cooled, I began to feel just a very little disconcerted, and a suspicion was troubling me that possibly an indifferent person might think that, having no more to complain of, my language was perhaps a little exaggerated, and my demeanour a little too tempestuous.

My uncle, I dare say, saw some symptoms of this misgiving, for, smiling still, he said—

'My dear Maud, however just, you appear to me a little cruel; you don't seem to remember how much you are yourself to blame; you have one faithful friend at least, whom I advise your consulting—I mean your looking-glass. The foolish fellow is young, quite ignorant in the world's ways, He is in love—desperately enamoured.

Aimer c'est craindre, et craindre c'est souffrir.

And suffering prompts to desperate remedies. We must not be too hard on a rough but romantic young fool, who talks according to his folly and his pain.'

CHAPTER XLIX

AN APPARITION

'But, after all,' he suddenly resumed, as if a new thought had struck him, 'is it quite such folly, after all? It really strikes me, dear Maud, that the subject may be worth a second thought. No, no, you won't refuse to hear me,' he said, observing me on the point of protesting. 'I am, of course, assuming that you are fancy free. I am assuming, too, that you don't care twopence about Dudley, and even that you fancy you dislike him. You know in that pleasant play, poor Sheridan—delightful fellow!—all our fine spirits are dead—he makes Mrs. Malaprop say there is nothing like beginning with a little aversion. Now, though in matrimony, of course, that is only a joke, yet in love, believe me, it is no such thing. His own marriage with Miss Ogle, I *know*, was a case in point. She expressed a positive horror of him at their first acquaintance; and yet, I believe, she would, a few months later, have died rather than not have married him.'

I was again about to speak, but with a smile he beckoned me into silence.

'There are two or three points you must bear in mind. One of the happiest privileges of your fortune is that you may, without imprudence, marry simply for love. There are few men in England who could offer you an estate comparable with that you already possess; or, in fact, appreciably increase the splendour of your fortune. If, therefore, he were in all other respects eligible, I can't see that his poverty would be an objection to weigh for one moment. He is quite a rough diamond. He has been, like many young men of the highest rank, too much given up to athletic sports—to that society which constitutes the aristocracy of the ring and the turf, and all that kind of thing. You see, I am putting all the worst points first. But I have known so many young men in my day, after a madcap career of a few years among prizefighters, wrestlers, and jockeys—learning their slang and affecting their manners—take up and cultivate the graces and the decencies. There was poor dear Newgate, many degrees lower in that kind of frolic, who, when he grew tired of it, became one of the most elegant and accomplished men in the House of Peers. Poor Newgate, he's gone, too! I could reckon up fifty of my early friends who all began like Dudley, and all turned out, more or less, like Newgate.'

At this moment came a knock at the door, and Dudley put in his head most inopportunely for the vision of his future graces and accomplishments.

'My good fellow,' said his father, with a sharp sort of playfulness, 'I happen to be talking about my son, and should rather not be overheard; you will, therefore, choose another time for your visit.'

Dudley hesitated gruffly at the door, but another look from his father dismissed him.

'And now, my dear, you are to remember that Dudley has fine qualities—the most affectionate son in his rough way that ever father was blessed with; most admirable qualities—indomitable courage, and a high sense of honour; and lastly, that he has the Ruthyn blood—the purest blood, I maintain it, in England.'

My uncle, as he said this, drew himself up a little, unconsciously, his thin hand laid lightly over his heart with a little patting motion, and his countenance looked so strangely dignified and melancholy, that in admiring contemplation of it I lost some sentences which followed next.

'Therefore, dear, naturally anxious that my boy should not be dismissed from home—as he must be, should you persevere in rejecting his suit—I beg that you will reserve your decision to this day fortnight, when I will with much pleasure hear what you may have to say on the subject. But till then, observe me, not a word.'

That evening he and Dudley were closeted for a long time. I suspect that he lectured him on the psychology of ladies; for a bouquet was laid beside my plate every morning at breakfast, which it must have been troublesome to get, for the conservatory at Bartram was a desert. In a few days more an anonymous green parrot arrived, in a gilt cage, with a little note in a clerk's hand, addressed to 'Miss Ruthyn (of Knowl), Bartram-Haugh,' &c. It contained only 'Directions for caring green parrot,' at the close of which, *underlined*, the words appeared—'The bird's name is Maud.'

The bouquets I invariably left on the table-cloth, where I found them—the bird I insisted on Milly's keeping as her property. During the intervening fortnight Dudley never appeared, as he used sometimes to do before, at luncheon, nor looked in at the window as we were at breakfast. He contented himself with one day placing himself in my way in the hall in his shooting accoutrements, and, with a clumsy, shuffling kind of respect, and hat in hand, he said—

'I think, Miss, I must a spoke uncivil t'other day. I was so awful put about, and didn't know no more nor a child what I was saying; and I wanted to tell ye I'm sorry for it, and I beg your pardon—very humble, I do.'

I did not know what to say. I therefore said nothing, but made a grave inclination, and passed on.

Two or three times Milly and I saw him at a little distance in our walks. He never attempted to join us. Once only he passed so near that some recognition was inevitable, and he stopped and in silence lifted his hat with an awkward respect. But although he did not approach us, he was ostentatious with a kind of telegraphic civility in the distance. He opened gates, he whistled his dogs to 'heel,' he drove away cattle, and then himself withdrew. I really think he watched us occasionally to render these services, for in this distant way we encountered him decidedly oftener than we used to do before his flattering proposal of marriage.

You may be sure that we discussed, Milly and I, that occurrence pretty constantly in all sorts of moods. Limited as had been her experience of human society, she very clearly saw *now* how far below its presentable level was her hopeful brother.

The fortnight sped swiftly, as time always does when something we dislike and shrink from awaits us at its close. I never saw Uncle Silas during that period. It may seem odd to those who merely read the report of our last interview, in which his manner had been more playful and his talk more trifling than in any other, that from it I had carried away a profounder sense of fear and insecurity than from any other. It was with a foreboding of evil and an awful dejection that on a very dark day, in Milly's room, I awaited the summons which I was sure would reach me from my punctual guardian.

As I looked from the window upon the slanting rain and leaden sky, and thought of the hated interview that awaited me, I pressed my hand to my trouble heart, and murmured, 'O that I had wings like a dove I then would I flee away, and be at rest.'

Just then the prattle of the parrot struck my ear. I looked round on the wire cage, and remembered the words, 'The bird's name is Maud.'

'Poor bird!' I said, 'I dare say, Milly, it longs to get out. If it were a native of this country, would not you like to open the window, and then the door of that cruel cage, and let the poor thing fly away?'

'Master wants Miss Maud,' said Wyat's disagreeable tones, at the half-open door.

I followed in silence, with the pressure of a near alarm at my heart, like a person going to an operation.

When I entered the room, my heart beat so fast that I could hardly speak. The tall form of Uncle Silas rose before me, and I made him a faltering reverence.

He darted from under his brows a wild, fierce glance at old Wyat, and pointed to the door imperiously with his skeleton finger. The door shut, and we were alone.

'A chair?' he said, pointing to a seat.

'Thank you, uncle, I prefer standing,' I faltered.

He also stood—his white head bowed forward, the phosphoric glare of his strange eyes shone upon me from under his brows—his finger-nails just rested on the table.

'You saw the luggage corded and addressed, as it stands ready for removal in the hall?' he asked.

I had. Milly and I had read the cards which dangled from the trunk-handles and gun-case. The address was—'Mr. Dudley R. Ruthyn, Paris, *via* Dover.'

'I am old—agitated—on the eve of a decision on which much depends. Pray relieve my suspense. Is my son to leave Bartram to-day in sorrow, or to remain in joy? Pray answer quickly!'

I stammered I know not what. I was incoherent—wild, perhaps; but somehow I expressed my meaning—my unalterable decision. I thought his lips grew whiter and his eyes shone brighter as I spoke.

When I had quite made an end, he heaved a great sigh, and turning his eyes slowly to the right and the left, like a man in a helpless distraction, he whispered—

'God's will be done.'

I thought he was upon the point of fainting—a clay tint darkened the white of his face; and, seeming to forget my presence, he sat down, looking with a despairing scowl on his ashy old hand, as it lay upon the table.

I stood gazing at him, feeling almost as if I had murdered the old man—he still gazing askance, with an imbecile scowl, upon his hand.

'Shall I go, sir?' I at length found courage to whisper.

'*Go?*' he said, looking up suddenly; and it seemed to me as if a stream of cold sheet-lightning had crossed and enveloped me for a moment.

'Go?—oh!—a—yes—*yes*, Maud—go. I must see poor Dudley before his departure,' he added, as it were, in soliloquy.

Trembling lest he should revoke his permission to depart, I glided quickly and noiselessly from the room.

Old Wyat was prowling outside, with a cloth in her hand, pre- tending to dust the carved doorcase. She frowned a stare of enquiry over her shrunken arm on me, as I passed. Milly, who had been on the watch, ran and met me. We heard my uncle's voice, as I shut the door, calling Dudley. He had been waiting, probably, in the adjoining room. I hurried into my chamber, with Milly at my side, and there my agitation found relief in tears, as that of girlhood naturally does.

A little while after we saw from the window Dudley, looking, I thought, very pale, get into a vehicle, on the top of which his luggage lay, and drive away from Bartram.

I began to take comfort. His departure was an inexpressible relief. His final departure! a distant journey!

We had tea in Milly's room that night. Firelight and candles are inspiring. In that red glow I always felt and feel more safe, as well as more comfortable, than in the daylight—quite irrationally, for we know the night is the appointed day of such as love the darkness better than light, and evil walks thereby. But so it is. Perhaps the very consciousness of external danger enhances the enjoyment of the well-light-ed interior, just as the storm does that roars and hurtles over the roof.

While Milly and I were talking, very cosily, a knock came to the room-door, and, without waiting for an invitation to enter, old Wyat came in, and glowering at us, with her brown claw upon the door-handle, she said to Milly—

'Ye must leave your funnin', Miss Milly, and take your turn in your father's room.'

'Is he ill?' I asked.

She answered, addressing not me, but Milly—

'A wrought two hours in a fit arter Master Dudley went. 'Twill be the death o' him, I'm thinkin', poor old fellah. I wor sorry myself when I saw Master Dudley a going off in the moist to-day, poor fellah. There's trouble enough in the family without a' that; but 'twon't be a family long, I'm thinkin'. Nout but trouble, nout but trouble, since late changes came.'

Judging by the sour glance she threw on me as she said this, I concluded that I represented those 'late changes' to which all the sorrows of the house were referred.

I felt unhappy under the ill-will even of this odious old woman, being one of those unhappily constructed mortals who cannot be indifferent when they reason-ably ought, and always yearn after kindness, even that of the worthless. 'I must go. I wish you'd come wi' me, Maud, I'm so afraid all alone,' said Milly, imploringly.

'Certainly, Milly,' I answered, not liking it, you may be sure you shan't sit there alone.'

So together we went, old Wyat cautioning us for our lives to make no noise.

We passed through the old man's sitting-room, where that day had occurred his brief but momentous interview with me, and his parting with his only son, and entered the bed-room at the farther end.

A low fire burned in the grate. The room was in a sort of twilight. A dim lamp near the foot of the bed at the farther side was the only light burning there. Old Wyat whispered an injunction not to speak above our breaths, nor to leave the fireside unless the sick man called or showed signs of weariness. These were the directions of the doctor, who had been there.

So Milly and I sat ourselves down near the hearth, and old Wyat left us to our resources. We could hear the patient breathe; but he was quite still. In whispers we talked; but our conversation flagged. I was, after my wont, upbraiding myself for the suffering I had inflicted. After about half an hour's desultory whispering, and intervals, growing longer and longer, of silence, it was plain that Milly was falling asleep.

She strove against it, and I tried hard to keep her talking; but it would not do—sleep overcame her; and I was the only person in that ghastly room in a state of perfect consciousness.

There were associations connected with my last vigil there to make my situation very nervous and disagreeable. Had I not had so much to occupy my mind of a distinctly practical kind—Dudley's audacious suit, my uncle's questionable toleration of it, and my own conduct throughout that most disagreeable period of my existence,—I should have felt my present situation a great deal more.

As it was, I thought of my real troubles, and something of Cousin Knollys, and, I confess, a good deal of Lord Ilbury. When looking towards the door, I thought I saw a human face, about the most terrible my fancy could have called up, looking fixedly into the room. It was only a 'three-quarter,' and not the whole figure—the door hid that in a great measure, and I fancied I saw, too, a portion of the fingers. The face gazed toward the bed, and in the imperfect light looked like a livid mask, with chalky eyes.

I had so often been startled by similar apparitions formed by accidental lights and shadows disguising homely objects, that I stooped forward, expecting, though tremulously, to see this tremendous one in like manner dissolve itself into its harmless elements; and now, to my unspeakable terror, I became perfectly certain that I saw the countenance of Madame de la Rougierre.

With a cry, I started back, and shook Milly furiously from her trance.

'Look I look!' I cried. But the apparition or illusion was gone.

I clung so fast to Milly's arm, cowering behind her, that she could not rise.

'Milly! Milly! Milly! Milly!' I went on crying, like one struck with idiotcy, and unable to say anything else.

In a panic, Milly, who had seen nothing, and could conjecture nothing of the cause of my terror, jumped up, and clinging to one another, we huddled together into the corner of the room, I still crying wildly, 'Milly! Milly! Milly!' and nothing else.

'What is it—where is it—what do you see!' cried Milly, clinging to me as I did to her.

'It will come again; it will come; oh, heaven!

'What—what is it, Maud?'

'The face! the face!' I cried. 'Oh, Milly! Milly! Milly!'

We heard a step softly approaching the open door, and, in a horrible *sauve qui peut*, we rushed and stumbled together toward the light by Uncle Silas's bed. But old Wyat's voice and figure reassured us.

'Milly,' I said, so soon as, pale and very faint, I reached my apartment, no power on earth shall ever tempt me to enter that room again after dark.'

'Why, Maud dear, what, in Heaven's name, did you see?' said Milly, scarcely less terrified.

'Oh, I can't; I can't; I *can't*, Milly. Never ask me. It is haunted. The room is haunted *horribly*.'

'Was it Charke?' whispered Milly, looking over her shoulder, all aghast.

'No, no—don't ask me; a fiend in a worse shape.' I was relieved at last by a long fit of weeping; and all night good Mary Quince sat by me, and Milly slept by my side. Starting and screaming, and drugged with sal-volatile, I got through that night of supernatural terror, and saw the blessed light of heaven again.

Doctor folks, when he came to see my uncle in the morning, visited me also. He pronounced me very hysterical, made minute enquiries respecting my hours and diet, asked what I had for dinner yesterday. There was something a little comforting in his cool and confident pool-pooling of the ghost theory. The result was, a regimen which excluded tea, and imposed chocolate and porter, earlier hours, and I forget all beside; and he undertook to promise that, if I would but observe his directions, I should never see a ghost again.

CHAPTER L

MILLY'S FAREWELL

A few days' time saw me much better. Doctor Jolks was so contemptuously sturdy and positive on the point, that I began to have comfortable doubts about the reality of my ghost; and having still a horror indescribable of the illusion, if such it were, the room in which it appeared, and everything concerning it, I would neither speak, nor, so far as I could, think of it.

So, though Bartram-Haugh was gloomy as well as beautiful, and some of its associations awful, and the solitude that reigned there sometimes almost terrible, yet early hours, bracing exercise, and the fine air that predominates that region, soon restored my nerves to a healthier tone.

But it seemed to me that Bartram-Haugh was to be to me a vale of tears; or rather, in my sad pilgrimage, that valley of the shadow of death through which poor Christian fared alone and in the dark.

One day Milly ran into the parlour, pale, with wet cheeks, and, without saying a word, threw her arras about my neck, and burst into a paroxysm of weeping.

'What is it, Milly—what's the matter, dear—what is it?' I cried aghast, but returning her close embrace heartily.

'Oh! Maud—Maud darling, he's going to send me away.'

'Away, dear! *where* away? And leave me alone in this dreadful solitude, where he knows I shall die of fear and grief without you? Oh! no—no, it *must* be a mistake.'

'I'm going to France, Maud—I'm going away. Mrs. Jolks is going to London, day ar'ter to-morrow, and I'm to go wi' her; and an old French lady, he says, from the school will meet me there, and bring me the rest o' the way.'

'Oh—ho—ho—ho—ho—o—o—o!' cried poor Milly, hugging me closer still, with her head buried in my shoulder, and swaying me about like a wrestler, in her agony.

'I never wor away from home afore, except that little bit wi' you over there at Elverston; and you war wi' me then, Maud; an' I love ye—better than Bartram— better than a'; an' I think I'll die, Maud, if they take me away.'

I was just as wild in my woe as poor Milly; and it was not until we had wept together for a full hour—sometimes standing—sometimes walking up and down the room—sometimes sitting and getting up in turns to fall on one another's necks,—that Milly, plucking her handkerchief from her pocket, drew a note from it at the same time, which, as it fell upon the floor, she at once recollected to be one from Uncle Silas to me.

It was to this effect:—

'I wish to apprise my dear niece and ward of my plans. Milly proceeds to an admirable French school, as a pensionnaire, and leaves this on Thursday next. If after three months' trial she finds it in any way objectionable, she returns to us. If, on the contrary, she finds it in all respects the charming residence it has been presented to me, you, on the expiration of that period, join her there, until the temporary complication of my affairs shall have been so far adjusted as to enable me to receive you once more at Bartram. Hoping for happier days, and wishing to assure you that three months is the extreme limit of your separation from my poor Milly, I have written this, feeling alas! I unequal to seeing you at present.

'Bartram, Tuesday.

'P.S.—I can have no objection to your apprising Monica Knollys of these arrangements. You will understand, of course, not a copy of this letter, but its substance.'

Over this document, scanning it as lawyers do a new Act of Parliament, we took comfort. After all, it was limited; a separation not to exceed three months, possibly much shorter. On the whole, too, I pleased myself with thinking Uncle Silas's note, though peremptory, was kind.

Our paroxysms subsided into sadness; a close correspondence was arranged. Something of the bustle and excitement of change supervened. If it turned out to be, in truth, a 'charming residence,' how very delightful our meeting in France, with the interest of foreign scenery, ways, and faces, would be!

So Thursday arrived—a new gush of sorrow—a new brightening up—and, amid regrets and anticipations, we parted at the gate at the farther end of the Windmill Wood. Then, of course, were more good-byes, more embraces, and tearful smiles. Good Mrs. Jolks, who met us there, was in a huge fuss; I believe it was her first visit to the metropolis, and she was in proportion heated and important, and terrified about the train, so we had not many last words.

I watched poor Milly, whose head was stretched from the window, her hand waving many adieux, until the curve of the road, and the clump of old ash-trees, thick with ivy, hid Milly, carriage and all, from view. My eyes filled again with tears. I turned towards Bartram. At my side stood honest Mary Quince.

'Don't take on so, Miss; 'twon't be no time passing; three months is nothing at all,' she said, smiling kindly.

I smiled through my tears and kissed the good creature, and so side by side we re-entered the gate.

The lithe young man in fustian, whom I had seen talking with Beauty on the morning of our first encounter with that youthful Amazon, was awaiting our re-entrance with the key in his hand. He stood half behind the open wicket. One lean brown cheek, one shy eye, and his sharp upturned nose, I saw as we passed. He was treating me to a stealthy scrutiny, and seemed to shun my glance, for he shut the door quickly, and busied himself locking it, and then began stubbing up some thistles which grew close by, with the toe of his thick shoe, his back to us all the time.

It struck me that I recognised his features, and I asked Mary Quince.

'Have you seen that young man before, Quince?'

'He brings up game for your uncle, sometimes, Miss, and lends a hand in the garden, I believe.'

'Do you know his name, Mary?

'They call him Tom, I don't know what more, Miss.'

'Tom,' I called; 'please, Tom, come here for a moment.'

Tom turned about, and approached slowly. He was more civil than the Bartram people usually were, for he plucked off his shapeless cap of rabbit-skin with a clownish respect.

'Tom, what is your other name,—Tom *what*, my good man?' I asked.

'Tom Brice, ma'am.'

'Haven't I seen you before, Tom Brice?' I pursued, for my curiosity was excited, and with it much graver feelings; for there certainly *was* a resemblance in Tom's features to those of the postilion who had looked so hard at me as I passed the carriage in the warren at Knowl, on the evening of the outrage which had scared that quiet place.

''Appen you may have, ma'am,' he answered, quite coolly, looking down the buttons of his gaiters.

'Are you a good whip—do you drive well?

'I'll drive a plough wi' most lads hereabout,' answered Tom.

'Have you ever been to Knowl, Tom?

Tom gaped very innocently.

'Anan,' he said.

'Here, Tom, is half-a-crown.'

He took it readily enough.

'That be very good,' said Tom, with a nod, having glanced sharply at the coin.

I can't say whether he applied that term to the coin, or to his luck, or to my generous self.

'Now, Tom, you'll tell me, have you ever been to Knowl?'

'Maught a' bin, ma'am, but I don't mind no sich place—no.'

As Tom spoke this with great deliberation, like a man who loves truth, putting a strain upon his memory for its sake, he spun the silver coin two or three times into the air and caught it, staring at it the while, with all his might.

'Now, Tom, recollect yourself, and tell me the truth, and I'll be a friend to you. Did you ride postilion to a carriage having a lady in it, and, I think, several gentlemen, which came to the grounds of Knowl, when the party had their luncheon on the grass, and there was a—a quarrel with the gamekeepers? Try, Tom, to recollect; you shall, upon my honour, have no trouble about it, and I'll try to serve you.'

Tom was silent, while with a vacant gape he watched the spin of his half-crown twice, and then catching it with a smack in his hand, which he thrust into his pocket, he said, still looking in the same direction—

'I never rid postilion in my days, ma'am. I know nout o' sich a place, though 'appen I maught a' bin there; Knowl, ye ca't. I was ne'er out o' Derbyshire but thrice to Warwick fair wi' horses be rail, an' twice to York.'

'You're certain, Tom?'

'Sartin sure, ma'am.'

And Tom made another loutish salute, and cut the conference short by turning off the path and beginning to hollo after some trespassing cattle.

I had not felt anything like so nearly sure in this essay at identification as I had in that of Dudley. Even of Dudley's identity with the Church Scarsdale man, I had daily grown less confident; and, indeed, had it been proposed to bring it to the test of a wager, I do not think I should, in the language of sporting gentlemen, have cared to 'back' my original opinion. There was, however, a sufficient uncertainty to make me uncomfortable; and there was another uncertainty to enhance the unpleasant sense of ambiguity.

On our way back we passed the bleaching trunks and limbs of several ranks of barkless oaks lying side by side, some squared by the hatchet, perhaps sold, for there were large letters and Roman numerals traced upon them in red chalk. I sighed as I passed them by, not because it was wrongfully done, for I really rather leaned to the belief that Uncle Silas was well advised in point of law. But, alas I here lay low the grand old family decorations of Bartram-Haugh, not to be replaced for centuries to come, under whose spreading boughs the Ruthyns of three hundred years ago had hawked and hunted!

On the trunk of one of these I sat down to rest, Mary Quince meanwhile pattering about in unmeaning explorations. While thus listlessly seated, the girl Meg Hawkes, walked by, carrying a basket.

'Hish!' she said quickly, as she passed, without altering a pace or raising her eyes; 'don't ye speak nor look—fayther spies us; I'll tell ye next turn.'

'Next turn'—when was that? Well, she might be returning; and as she could not then say more than she had said, in merely passing without a pause, I concluded to wait for a short time and see what would come of it.

After a short time I looked about me a little, and I saw Dickon Hawkes— Pegtop, as poor Milly used to call him—with an axe in his hand, prowling luridly among the timber.

Observing that I saw him, he touched his hat sulkily, and by-and-by passed me, muttering to himself. He plainly could not understand what business I could have in that particular part of the Windmill Wood, and let me see it in his countenance.

His daughter did pass me again; but this time he was near, and she was silent. Her next transit occurred as he was questioning Mary Quince at some little distance; and as she passed precisely in the same way, she said—

'Don't you be alone wi' Master Dudley nowhere for the world's worth.'

The injunction was so startling that I was on the point of questioning the girl. But I recollected myself, and waited in the hope that in her future transits she might be more explicit. But one word more she did not utter, and the jealous eye of old Pegtop was so constantly upon us that I refrained.

There was vagueness and suggestion enough in the oracle to supply work for many an hour of anxious conjecture, and many a horrible vigil by night. Was I never to know peace at Bartram-Haugh?

Ten days of poor Milly's absence, and of my solitude, had already passed, when my uncle sent for me to his room.

When old Wyat stood at the door, mumbling and snarling her message, my heart died within me.

It was late—just that hour when dejected people feel their anxieties most— when the cold grey of twilight has deepened to its darkest shade, and before the cheerful candles are lighted, and the safe quiet of the night sets in.

When I entered my uncle's sitting-room—though his window-shutters were open and the wan streaks of sunset visible through them, like narrow lakes in the chasms of the dark western clouds—a pair of candles were burning; one stood upon the table by his desk, the other on the chimneypiece, before which his tall, thin figure stooped. His hand leaned on the mantelpiece, and the light from the candle just above his bowed head touched his silvery hair. He was looking, as it seemed, into the subsiding embers of the fire, and was a very statue of forsaken dejection and decay.

'Uncle!' I ventured to say, having stood for some time unperceived near his table.

'Ah, yes, Maud, my dear child—my *dear* child.'

He turned, and with the candle in his hand, smiling his silvery smile of suffering on me. He walked more feebly and stiffly, I thought, than I had ever seen him move before.

'Sit down, Maud—pray sit there.'

I took the chair he indicated.

'In my misery and my solitude, Maud, I have invoked you like a spirit, and you appear.'

With his two hands leaning on the table, he looked across at me, in a stooping attitude; he had not seated himself. I continued silent until it should be his pleasure to question or address me.

At last he said, raising himself and looking upward, with a wild adoration—his finger-tips elevated and glimmering in the faint mixed light—

'No, I thank my Creator, I am not quite forsaken.'

Another silence, during which he looked steadfastly at me, and muttered, as if thinking aloud—

My guardian angel!—my guardian angel! Maud, *you* have a heart.' He addressed me suddenly—'Listen, for a few moments, to the appeal of an old and broken-hearted man—your guardian—your uncle—your *suppliant*. I had resolved never to speak to you more on this subject. But I was wrong. It was pride that inspired me—mere pride.'

I felt myself growing pale and flushed by turns during the pause that followed.

'I'm very miserable—very nearly desperate. What remains for me—what remains? Fortune has done her worst—thrown in the dust, her wheels rolled over me; and the servile world, who follow her chariot like a mob, stamp upon the mangled wretch. All this had passed over me, and left me scarred and bloodless in this solitude. It was not my fault, Maud—I say it was no fault of mine; I have no remorse, though more regrets than I can count, and all scored with fire. As people passed by Bartram, and looked upon its neglected grounds and smokeless chimneys, they thought my plight, I dare say, about the worst a proud man could be reduced to. They could not imagine one half its misery. But this old hectic—this old epileptic—this old spectre of wrongs, calamities, and follies, had still one hope—my manly though untutored son—the last male scion of the Ruthyns. Maud, have I lost him? His fate—my fate—I may say *Milly's fate,*—we all await your sentence. He loves you, as none but the very young can love, and that once only in a life. He loves you desperately—a most affectionate nature—a Ruthyn, the best blood in England—the last man of the race; and I—if I lose him I lose all; and you will see me in my coffin, Maud, before many months. I stand before you in the attitude of a suppliant—shall I kneel?'

His eyes were fixed on me with the light of despair, his knotted hands clasped, his whole figure bowed toward me. I was inexpressibly shocked and pained.

'Oh, uncle I uncle!' I cried, and from very excitement I burst into tears.

I saw that his eyes were fixed on me with a dismal scrutiny. I think he divined the nature of my agitation; but he determined, notwithstanding, to press me while my helpless agitation continued.

'You see my suspense—you see my miserable and frightful suspense. You are kind, Maud; you love your father's memory; your pity your father's brother; you would not say no, and place a pistol at his head?'

'Oh! I must—I must—I *must* say no. Oh! spare me, uncle, for Heaven's sake. Don't question me—don't press me. I could not—I *could* not do what you ask.'

'I yield, Maud—I yield, my dear. I will *not* press you; you shall have time, your *own* time, to think. I will accept *no* answer now—no, *none*, Maud.'

He said this, raising his thin hand to silence me.

'There, Maud, enough. I have spoken, as I always do to you, frankly, perhaps too frankly; but agony and despair will speak out, and plead, even with the most obdurate and cruel.'

With these words Uncle Silas entered his bed-chamber, and shut the door, not violently, but with a resolute hand, and I thought I heard a cry.

I hastened to my own room. I threw myself on my knees, and thanked Heaven for the firmness vouchsafed me; I could not believe it to have been my own.

I was more miserable in consequence of this renewed suit on behalf of my odious cousin than I can describe. My uncle had taken such a line of importunity that it became a sort of agony to resist. I thought of the possibility of my hearing of his having made away with himself, and was every morning relieved when I heard that he was still as usual. I have often wondered since at my own firmness. In that dreadful interview with my uncle I had felt, in the whirl and horror of my mind, on the very point of submitting, just as nervous people are said to throw themselves over precipices through sheer dread of falling.

CHAPTER LI

SARAH MATILDA COMES TO LIGHT

Some time after this interview, one day as I sat, sad enough, in my room, looking listlessly from the window, with good Mary Quince, whom, whether in the house or in my melancholy rambles, I always had by my side, I was startled by the sound of a loud and shrill female voice, in violent hysterical action, gabbling with great rapidity, sobbing, and very nearly screaming in a sort of fury.

I started up, staring at the door.

'Lord bless us!' cried honest Mary Quince, with round eyes and mouth agape, staring in the same direction.

'Mary—Mary, what can it be?'

'Are they beating some one down yonder? I don't know where it comes from,' gasped Quince.

'I will—I will—I'll see her. It's her I want. Oo—hoo—hoo—hoo—oo—o— Miss Maud Ruthyn of Knowl. Miss Ruthyn of Knowl. Hoo—hoo—hoo— hoo—oo!'

'What on earth can it be?' I exclaimed, in great bewilderment and terror.

It was now plainly very near indeed, and I heard the voice of our mild and shaky butler evidently remonstrating with the distressed damsel.

'I'll see her,' she continued, pouring a torrent of vile abuse upon me, which stung me with a sudden sense of anger. What had I done to be afraid of anyone? How dared anyone in my uncle's house—in *my* house—mix my name up with her detestable scurrilities?

'For Heaven's sake, Miss, don't ye go out,' cried poor Quince; 'it's some drunken creature.'

But I was very angry, and, like a fool as I was, I threw open the door, exclaiming in a loud and haughty key—

'Here is Miss Ruthyn of Knowl. Who wants to see her?'

A pink and white young lady, with black tresses, violent, weeping, shrill, voluble, was flouncing up the last stair, and shook her dress out on the lobby; and poor old Giblets, as Milly used to call him, was following in her wake, with many small remonstrances and entreaties, perfectly unheeded.

The moment I looked at this person, it struck me that she was the identical lady whom I had seen in the carriage at Knowl Warren. The next moment I was in doubt; the next, still more so. She was decidedly thinner, and dressed by no means in such lady-like taste. Perhaps she was hardly like her at all. I began to distrust all these resemblances, and to fancy, with a shudder, that they originated, perhaps, only in my own sick brain.

On seeing me, this young lady—as it seemed to me, a good deal of the barmaid or lady's-maid species—dried her eyes fiercely, and, with a flaming countenance, called upon me peremptorily to produce her 'lawful husband.' Her loud, insolent, outrageous attack had the effect of enhancing my indignation, and I quite forget what I said to her, but I well remember that her manner became a good deal more decent, She was plainly under the impression that I wanted to appropriate her husband, or, at least, that he wanted to marry me; and she ran on at such a pace, and her harangue was so passionate, incoherent, and unintelligible, that I thought her out of her mind: she was far from it, however. I think if she had allowed me even a second for reflection, I should have hit upon her meaning. As it was, nothing could exceed my perplexity, until, plucking a soiled newspaper from her pocket, she indicated a particular paragraph, already sufficiently emphasised by double lines of red ink at its sides. It was a Lancashire paper, of about six weeks since, and very much worn and soiled for its age. I remember in particular a circular stain from the bottom of a vessel, either of coffee or brown stout. The paragraph was as follows, recording an event a year or more anterior to the date of the paper:—

'MARRIAGE—On Tuesday, August 7, 18—, at Leatherwig Church, by the Rev. Arthur Hughes, Dudley R. Ruthyn, Esq., only son and heir of Silas Ruthyn, Esq., of Bartram-Haugh, Derbyshire, to Sarah Matilda, second daughter of John Mangles, Esq., of Wiggan, in this county.'

At first I read nothing but amazement in this announcement, but in another moment I felt how completely I was relieved; and showing, I believe, my intense satisfaction in My countenance—for the young lady eyed me with considerable surprise and curiosity—I said—

'This is extremely important. You must see Mr. Silas Ruthyn this moment. I am certain he knows nothing of it. I will conduct you to him.'

'No more he does—I know that myself,' she replied, following me with a self-asserting swagger, and a great rustling of cheap silk.

As we entered, Uncle Silas looked up from his sofa, and closed his *Revue des Deux Mondes*.

'What is all this?' he enquired, drily.

'This lady has brought with her a newspaper containing an extraordinary statement which affects our family,' I answered.

Uncle Silas raised himself, and looked with a hard, narrow scrutiny at the unknown young lady.

'A libel, I suppose, in the paper?' he said, extending his hand for it.

'No, uncle—no; only a marriage,' I answered.

'Not Monica?' he said, as he took it. 'Pah, it smells all over of tobacco and beer,' he added, throwing a little can de Cologne over it.

He raised it with a mixture of curiosity and disgust, saying again 'pah,' as he did so.

He read the paragraph, and as he did his face changed from white, all over, to lead colour. He raised his eyes, and looked steadily for some seconds at the young lady, who seemed a little awed by his strange presence.

'And you are, I suppose, the young lady, Sarah Matilda *née* Mangles, mentioned in this little paragraph?' he said, in a tone you would have called a sneer, were it not that it trembled.

Sarah Matilda assented.

'My son is, I dare say, within reach. It so happens that I wrote to arrest his journey, and summon him here, some days since—some days since—some days since,' he repeated slowly, like a person whose mind has wandered far away from the theme on which he is speaking.

He had rung his bell, and old Wyat, always hovering about his rooms, entered.

'I want my son, immediately. If not in the house, send Harry to the stables; if not there, let him be followed, instantly. Brice is an active fellow, and will know where to find him. If he is in Feltram, or at a distance, let Brice take a horse, and Master Dudley can ride it back. He must be here without the loss of one moment.'

There intervened nearly a quarter of an hour, during which whenever he recollected her, Uncle Silas treated the young lady with a hyper-refined and ceremonious politeness, which appeared to make her uneasy, and even a little shy, and certainly prevented a renewal of those lamentations and invectives which he had heard faintly from the stair-head.

But for the most part Uncle Silas seemed to forget us and his book, and all that surrounded him, lying back in the corner of his sofa, his chin upon his breast, and such a fearful shade and carving on his features as made me prefer looking in any direction but his.

At length we heard the tread of Dudley's thick boots on the oak boards, and faint and muffled the sound of his voice as he cross-examined old Wyat before entering the chamber of audience.

I think he suspected quite another visitor, and had no expectation of seeing the particular young lady, who rose from her chair as he entered, in an opportune flood of tears, crying—

'Oh, Dudley, Dudley I—oh, Dudley, could you? Oh, Dudley, your own poor Sal! You could not—you would not—your lawful wife!'

This and a good deal more, with cheeks that streamed like a window-pane in a thunder-shower, spoke Sarah Matilda with all her oratory, working his arm, which she clung to, up and down all the time, like the handle of a pump. But Dudley was, manifestly, confounded and dumbfoundered. He stood for a long time gaping at his father, and stole just one sheepish glance at me; and, with red face and forehead, looked down at his boots, and then again at his father, who remained just in the attitude I have described, and with the same forbidding and dreary intensity in his strange face.

Like a quarrelsome man worried in his sleep by a noise, Dudley suddenly woke up, as it were, with a start, in a half-suppressed exasperation, and shook her off with a jerk and a muttered curse, as she whisked involuntarily into a chair, with more violence than could have been pleasant.

'Judging by your looks and demeanour, sir, I can almost anticipate your answers,' said my uncle, addressing him suddenly. 'Will you be good enough— pray, madame (parenthetically to our visitor), command yourself for a few moments. Is this young person the daughter of a Mr. Mangles, and is her name Sarah Matilda?'

'I dessay,' answered Dudley, hurriedly.

'Is she your wife?'

'Is she my wife?' repeated Dudley, ill at ease.

'Yes, sir; it is a plain question.'

All this time Sarah Matilda was perpetually breaking into talk, and with difficulty silenced by my uncle.

'Well, 'appen she says I am—does she?' replied Dudley.

'Is she your wife, sir?'

'Mayhap she so considers it, after a fashion,' he replied, with an impudent swagger, seating himself as he did so.

'What do *you* think, sir?' persisted Uncle Silas.

'I don't think nout about it,' replied Dudley, surlily.

'Is that account true?' said my uncle, handing him the paper.

'They wishes us to believe so, at any rate.'

'Answer directly, sir. We have our thoughts upon it. If it be true, it is capable of *every* proof. For expedition's sake I ask you. There is no use in prevaricating.'

'Who wants to deny it? It *is* true—there!

'*There!* I knew he would,' screamed the young woman, hysterically, with a laugh of strange joy.

'Shut up, will ye?' growled Dudley, savagely.

'Oh, Dudley, Dudley, darling I what have I done?'

'Bin and ruined me, jest—that's all.'

'Oh! no, no, no, Dudley. Ye know I wouldn't. I could not—*could* not hurt ye, Dudley. No, no, no!'

He grinned at her, and, with a sharp side-nod, said—

'Wait a bit.'

'Oh, Dudley, don't be vexed, dear. I did not mean it. I would not hurt ye for all the world. Never.'

'Well, never mind. You and yours tricked me finely; and now you've got me—that's all.'

My uncle laughed a very odd laugh.

'I knew it, of course; and upon my word, madame, you and he make a very pretty couple,' sneered Uncle Silas.

Dudley made no answer, looking, however, very savage.

And with this poor young wife, so recently wedded, the low villain had actually solicited me to marry him!

I am quite certain that my uncle was as entirely ignorant as I of Dudley's connection, and bad, therefore, no participation in this appalling wickedness.

'And I have to congratulate you, my good fellow, on having secured the affections of a very suitable and vulgar young woman.

'I baint the first o' the family as a' done the same,' retorted Dudley.

At this taunt the old man's fury for a moment overpowered him. In an instant he was on his feet, quivering from head to foot. I never saw such a countenance—like one of those demon-grotesques we see in the Gothic side-aisles and groinings—a dreadful grimace, monkey-like and insane—and his thin hand caught up his ebony stick, and shook it paralytically in the air.

'If ye touch me wi' that, I'll smash ye, by —!' shouted Dudley, furious, raising his hands and hitching his shoulder, just as I had seen him when he fought Captain Oakley.

For a moment this picture was suspended before me, and I screamed, I know not what, in my terror. But the old man, the veteran of many a scene of excitement, where men disguise their ferocity in calm tones, and varnish their fury with smiles, had not quite lost his self-command. He turned toward me and said—

'Does he know what he's saying?'

And with an icy laugh of contempt, his high, thin forehead still flushed, he sat down trembling.

'If you want to say aught, I'll hear ye. Ye may jaw me all ye like, and I'll stan' it.'

'Oh, I may speak? Thank you,' sneered Uncle Silas, glancing slowly round at me, and breaking into a cold laugh.

'Ay, I don't mind cheek, not I; but you must not go for to do that, ye know. Gammon. I won't stand a blow—I won't fro *no* one.

'Well, sir, availing myself of your permission to speak, I may remark, without offence to the young lady, that I don't happen to recollect the name Mangles among the old families of England. I presume you have chosen her chiefly for her virtues and her graces.'

Mrs. Sarah Matilda, not apprehending this compliment quite as Uncle Silas meant it, dropped a courtesy, notwithstanding her agitation, and, wiping her eyes, said, with a blubbered smile—

'You're very kind, sure.'

'I hope, for both your sakes, she has got a little money. I don't see how you are to live else. You're too lazy for a gamekeeper; and I don't think you could keep a pot-house, you are so addicted to drinking and quarrelling. The only thing I am quite clear upon is, that you and your wife must find some other abode than this. You shall depart this evening: and now, Mr. and Mrs. Dudley Ruthyn, you may quit this room, if you please.'

Uncle Silas had risen, and made them one of his old courtly bows, smiling a death-like sneer, and pointing to the door with his trembling fingers.

'Come, will ye?' said Dudley, grinding his teeth. 'You're pretty well done here.'

Not half understanding the situation, but looking woefully bewildered, she dropped a farewell courtesy at the door.

'Will ye *cut*?' barked Dudley, in a tone that made her jump and suddenly, without looking about, he strode after her from the room.

'Maud, how shall I recover this? The vulgar *villain*—the *fool*! What an abyss were we approaching! and for me the last hope gone—and for me utter, utter, irretrievable ruin.'

He was passing his fingers tremulously back and forward along the top of the mantelpiece, like a man in search of something, and continued so, looking along it, feebly and vacantly, although there was nothing there.

'I wish, uncle—you do not know how much I wish—I could be of any use to you. Maybe I can?'

He turned, and looked at me sharply.

'Maybe you can,' he echoed slowly. 'Yes, maybe you can,' he repeated more briskly. 'Let us—let us see—let us think—that d—— fellow!—my head!'

'You're not well, uncle?'

'Oh! yes, very well. We'll talk in the evening—I'll send for you.'

I found Wyat in the next room, and told her to hasten, as I thought he was ill. I hope it was not very selfish, but such had grown to be my horror of seeing him in one of his strange seizures, that I hastened from the room precipitately—partly to escape the risk of being asked to remain.

The walls of Bartram House are thick, and the recess at the doorway deep. As I closed my uncle's door, I heard Dudley's voice on the stairs. I did not wish to be seen by him or by his 'lady,' as his poor wife called herself, who was engaged in vehement dialogue with him as I emerged, and not caring either to re-enter my uncle's room, I remained quietly ensconced within the heavy door-case, in which position I overheard Dudley say with a savage snarl—

'You'll jest go back the way ye came. *I'm* not goin' wi' ye, if that's what ye be drivin' at—dang your impitins!'

'Oh! Dudley, dear, *what* have I done—what *have* I done—ye hate me so?'

'What a' ye done? ye vicious little beast, ye! You've got us turned out an' disinherited wi' yet d——d bosh, that's all; don't ye think it's enough?'

I could only hear her sobs and shrill tones in reply, for they were descending the stairs; and Mary Quince reported to me, in a horrified sort of way, that she saw him bundle her into the fly at the door, like a truss of hay into a hay-loft. And he stood with his head in at the window, scolding her, till it drove away.

'I knew he wor jawing her, poor thing! by the way he kep' waggin' his head—an' he had his fist inside, a shakin' in her face I'm sure he looked wicked enough for anything; an' she a crying like a babby, an' lookin' back, an' wavin' her wet hankicher to him—poor thing!—and she so young! 'Tis a pity. Dear me! I often think, Miss, 'tis well for me I never was married. And see how we all would like to get husbands for all that, though so few is happy together. 'Tis a queer world, and them that's single is maybe the best off after all.'

CHAPTER LII

THE PICTURE OF A WOLF

I went down that evening to the sitting-room which had been assigned to Milly and me, in search of a book—my good Mary Quince always attending me. The door was a little open, and I was startled by the light of a candle proceeding from the fireside, together with a considerable aroma of tobacco and brandy.

On my little work-table, which he had drawn beside the hearth, lay Dudley's pipe, his brandy-flask, and an empty tumbler; and he was sitting with one foot on the fender, his elbow on his knee, and his head resting in his hand, weeping. His back being a little toward the door, he did not perceive us; and we saw him rub his knuckles in his eyes, and heard the sounds of his selfish lamentation.

Mary and I stole away quietly, leaving him in possession, wondering when he was to leave the house, according to the sentence which I had heard pronounced upon him.

I was delighted to see old 'Giblets' quietly strapping his luggage in the hall, and heard from him in a whisper that he was to leave that evening by rail—he did not know whither.

About half an hour afterwards, Mary Quince, going out to reconnoitre, heard from old Wyat in the lobby that he had just started to meet the train.

Blessed be heaven for that deliverance! An evil spirit had been cast out, and the house looked lighter and happier. It was not until I sat down in the quiet of my room that the scenes and images of that agitating day began to move before my memory in orderly procession, and for the first time I appreciated, with a stunning sense of horror and a perfect rapture of thanksgiving, the value of my escape and the immensity of the danger which had threatened me. It may have been miserable weakness—I think it was. But I was young, nervous, and afflicted with a troublesome sort of conscience, which occasionally went mad, and insisted, in small things as well as great, upon sacrifices which my reason now assures me were absurd. Of Dudley I had a perfect horror; and yet had that system of solicitation, that dreadful and direct appeal to my compassion, that placing of my feeble girlhood in the seat of the arbiter of lily aged uncle's hope or despair, been long persisted in, my resistance might have been worn out—who can tell? and I self-sacrificed I just as criminals in Germany are teased, and watched, and cross-examined, year after year, incessantly, into a sort of madness; and worn out with the suspense, the iteration, the self-restraint, and insupportable fatigue, they at last cut all short, accuse themselves, and go infinitely relieved to the scaffold—you may guess, then, for me, nervous, self-diffident, and alone, how intense was the comfort of knowing that Dudley was actually married, and the harrowing importunity which had just commenced for ever silenced.

That night I saw my uncle. I pitied him, though I feared him. I was longing to tell him how anxious I was to help him, if only he could point out the way. It was in substance what I had already said, but now strongly urged. He brightened; he sat up perpendicularly in his chair with a countenance, not weak or fatuous now, but resolute and searching, and which contracted into dark thought or calculation as I talked.

I dare say I spoke confusedly enough. I was always nervous in his presence; there was, I fancy, something mesmeric in the odd sort of influence which, without effort, he exercised over in), imagination.

Sometimes this grew into a dismal panic, and Uncle Silas—polished, mild— seemed unaccountably horrible to me. Then it was no longer an accidental fascination of electro-biology. It was something more. His nature was incomprehensible by me. He was without the nobleness, without the freshness, without the softness, without the frivolities of such human nature as I had experienced, either within myself or in other persons. I instinctively felt that appeals to sympathies or feelings could no more affect him than a marble monument. He seemed to accommodate his conversation to the moral structure of others, just as spirits are said to assume the shape of mortals. There were the sensualities of the gourmet for his body, and there ended his human nature, as it seemed to me. Through that semi-transparent structure I thought I could now and then discern the light or the glare of his inner life. But I understood it not.

He never scoffed at what was good or noble—his hardest critic could not nail him to one such sentence; and yet, it seemed somehow to me that his unknown nature was a systematic blasphemy against it all. If fiend he was, he was yet something higher than the garrulous, and withal feeble, demon of Goethe. He assumed the limbs and features of our mortal nature. He shrouded his own, and was a profoundly reticent Mephistopheles. Gentle he had been to me—kindly he had nearly always spoken; but it seemed like the mild talk of one of those goblins of the desert, whom Asiatic superstition tells of, who appear in friendly shapes to stragglers from the caravan, beckon to them from afar, call them by their names, and lead them where they are found no more. Was, then, all his kindness but a phosphoric radiance covering something colder and more awful than the grave?

'It is very noble of you, Maud—it is angelic; your sympathy with a ruined and despairing old man. But I fear you will recoil. I tell you frankly that less than twenty thousand pounds will not extricate me from the quag of ruin in which I am entangled—lost!'

'Recoil! Far from it. I'll do it. There must be some way.'

'Enough, my fair young protectress—celestial enthusiast, enough. Though you do not, yet I recoil. I could not bring myself to accept this sacrifice. What signifies, even to me, my extrication? I lie a mangled wretch, with fifty mortal wounds on my crown; what avails the healing of one wound, when there are so many beyond all cure? Better to let me perish where I fall; and reserve your money for the worthier objects whom, perhaps, hereafter may avail to save.'

'But I *will* do this. I must. I cannot see you suffer with the power in my hands unemployed to help you,' I exclaimed.

'Enough, dear Maud; the will is here—enough: there is balm in your compassion and good-will. Leave me, ministering angel; for the present I cannot. If you *will*, we can talk of it again. Good-night.'

And so we parted.

The attorney from Feltram, I afterwards heard, was with him nearly all that night, trying in vain to devise by their joint ingenuity any means by which I might tie myself up. But there were none. I could not bind myself.

I was myself full of the hope of helping him. What was this sum to me, great as it seemed? Truly nothing. I could have spared it, and never felt the loss.

I took up a large quarto with coloured prints, one of the few books I had brought with me from dear old Knowl. Too much excited to hope for sleep in bed, I opened it, and turned over the leaves, my mind still full of Uncle Silas and the sum I hoped to help him with.

Unaccountably one of those coloured engravings arrested my attention. It represented the solemn solitude of a lofty forest; a girl, in Swiss costume, was flying in terror, and as she fled flinging a piece of meat behind her which she had taken from a little market-basket hanging upon her arm. Through the glade a pack of wolves were pursuing her.

The narrative told, that on her return homeward with her marketing, she had been chased by wolves, and barely escaped by flying at her utmost speed, from time to time retarding, as she did so, the pursuit, by throwing, piece by piece, the contents of her basket, in her wake, to be devoured and fought for by the famished beasts of prey.

This print had seized my imagination. I looked with a curious interest on the print: something in the disposition of the trees, their great height, and rude boughs, interlacing, and the awful shadow beneath, reminded me of a portion of the Windmill Wood where Milly and I had often rambled. Then I looked at the figure of the poor girl, flying for her life, and glancing terrified over her shoulder. Then I gazed on the gaping, murderous pack, and the hoary brute that led the van; and then I leaned back in my chair, and I thought—perhaps some latent association suggested what seemed a thing so unlikely—of a fine print in my portfolio from Vandyke's noble picture of Belisarius. Idly I traced with my pencil, as I leaned back, on an envelope that lay upon the table, this little inscription. It was mere fiddling; and, absurd as it looked, there was nothing but an honest meaning in it:— '20,000*l.* Date Obolum Belisario!' My dear father had translated the little Latin inscription for me, and I had written it down as a sort of exercise of memory; and also, perhaps, as expressive of that sort of compassion which my uncle's fall and miserable fate excited invariably in me. So I threw this queer little memorandum upon the open leaf of the book, and again the flight, the pursuit, and the bait to stay it, engaged my eye. And I heard a voice near the hearthstone, as I thought, say, in a stern whisper, 'Fly the fangs of Belisarius!'

'What's that?' said I, turning sharply to Mary Quince.

Mary rose from her work at the fireside, staring at me with that odd sort of frown that accompanies fear and curiosity.

'You spoke? Did you speak?' I said, catching her by the arm, very much frightened myself.

'No, Miss; no, dear!' answered she, plainly thinking that I was a little wrong in my head.

There could be no doubt it was a trick of the imagination, and yet to this hour I could recognise that clear stem voice among a thousand, were it to speak again.

Jaded after a night of broken sleep and much agitation, I was summoned next morning to my uncle's room.

He received me *oddly*, I thought. His manner had changed, and made an uncomfortable impression upon me. He was gentle, kind, smiling, submissive, as usual; but it seemed to me that he experienced henceforth toward me the same half-superstitious repulsion which I had always felt from him. Dream, or voice, or vision—which had done it? There seemed to be an unconscious antipathy and fear. When he thought I was not looking, his eyes were sometimes grimly fixed for a moment upon me. When I looked at him, his eyes were upon the book before him; and when he spoke, a person not heeding what he uttered would have fancied that he was reading aloud from it.

There was nothing tangible but this shrinking from the encounter of our eyes. I said he was kind as usual. He was even more so. But there was this new sign of our silently repellant natures. Dislike it could not be. He knew I longed to serve him. Was it shame? Was there not a shade of horror in it?

'I have not slept,' said he. 'For me the night has passed in thought, and the fruit of it is this—I *cannot*, Maud, accept your noble offer.'

'I am *very* sorry,' exclaimed I, in all honesty.

'I know it, my dear niece, and appreciate your goodness; but there are many reasons—none of them, I trust, ignoble—and which together render it impossible. No. It would be misunderstood—my honour shall not be impugned.'

'But, sir, that could not be; you have never proposed it. It would be all, from first to last, *my* doing.'

'True, dear Maud, but I know, alas! more of this evil and slanderous world than your happy inexperience can do. Who will receive our testimony? None—no, not one. The difficulty—the insuperable moral difficulty is this—that I should expose myself to the plausible imputation of having worked upon you, unduly, for this end; and more, that I could not hold myself quite free from blame. It is your voluntary goodness, Maud. But you are young, inexperienced; and it is, I hold it, my duty to stand between you and any dealing with your property at so unripe an age. Some people may call this Quixotic. In my mind it is an imperious mandate of conscience; and I peremptorily refuse to disobey it, although within three weeks an execution will be in this house!'

I did not quite know what an execution meant; but from two harrowing novels, with whose distresses I was familiar, I knew that it indicated some direful process of legal torture and spoilation.

'Oh, uncle!—oh, sir!—you cannot allow this to happen. What will people say of me? And—and there is poor Milly—and *everything*! Think what it will be.'

'It cannot be helped—*you* cannot help it, Maud. Listen to me. There will be an execution here, I cannot say exactly how soon, but, I think, in a little more than a fortnight. I must provide for your comfort. You must leave. I have arranged that you shall join Milly, for the present, in France, till I have time to look about me. You had better, I think, write to your cousin, Lady Knollys. She, with all her oddities, has a heart. Can you say, Maud, that I have been kind?'

'You have never been anything but kind,' I exclaimed.

'That I've been self-denying when you made me a generous offer?' he continued. 'That I now act to spare you pain? You may tell her, not as a message from me, but as a fact, that I am seriously thinking of vacating my guardianship—that I feel I have done her an injustice, and that, so soon as my mind is a little less tor-

tured, I shall endeavour to effect a reconciliation with her, and would wish ultimately to transfer the care of your person and education to her. You may say I have
no longer an interest even in vindicating my name. My son has wrecked himself by
a marriage. I forgot to tell you he stopped at Feltram, and this morning wrote to
pray a parting interview. If I grant it, it shall be the last. I shall never see him or
correspond with him more.'

The old man seemed much overcome, and held his hankerchief to his eyes.

'He and his wife are, I understand, about to emigrate; the sooner the better,' he
resumed, bitterly. 'Deeply, Maud, I regret having tolerated his suit to you, even for
a moment. Had I thought it over, as I did the whole case last night, nothing could
have induced me to permit it. But I have lived for so long like a monk in his cell,
my wants and observation limited to the narrow compass of this chamber, that my
knowledge of the world has died out with my youth and my hopes: and I did not,
as I ought to have done, consider many objections. Therefore, dear Maud, on this
one subject, I entreat, be silent; its discussion can effect nothing now. I was wrong,
and frankly ask you to forget my mistake.'

I had been on the point of writing to Lady Knollys on this odious subject,
when, happily, it was set at rest by the disclosure of yesterday; and being so, I
could have no difficulty in acceding to my uncle's request. He was conceding so
much that I could not withhold so trifling a concession in return.

'I hope Monica will continue to be kind to poor Milly after I am gone.'

Here there were a few seconds of meditation.

'Maud, you will not, I think, refuse to convey the substance of what I have just
said in a letter to Lady Knollys, and perhaps you would have no objection to let
me see it when it is written. It will prevent the possibility of its containing any
misconception of what I have just spoken: and, Maud, you won't forget to say
whether I have been kind. It would be a satisfaction to me to know that Monica
was assured that I never either teased or bullied my young ward.'

With these words he dismissed me; and forthwith I completed such a letter as
would quite embody what he had said; and in my own glowing terms, being in
high good-humour with Uncle Silas, recorded my estimate of his gentleness and
good-nature; and when I submitted it to him, he expressed his admiration of what
he was pleased to call my cleverness in so exactly conveying what he wished, and
his gratitude for the handsome terms in which I had spoken of my old guardian.

CHAPTER LIII

AN ODD PROPOSAL

As I and Mary Quince returned from our walk that day, and had entered the hall, I was surprised most disagreeably by Dudley's emerging from the vestibule at the foot of the great staircase. He was, I suppose, in his travelling costume—a rather soiled white surtout, a great coloured muffler in folds about his throat, his 'chimney-pot' on, and his fur cap sticking out from his pocket. He had just descended, I suppose, from my uncle's room. On seeing me he stepped back, and stood with his shoulders to the wall, like a mummy in a museum.

I pretended to have a few words to say to Mary before leaving the hall, in the hope that, as he seemed to wish to escape me, he would take the opportunity of getting quickly off the scene.

But he had changed his mind, it would seem, in the interval; for when I glanced in that direction again he had moved toward us, and stood in the hall with his hat in his hand. I must do him the justice to say he looked horribly dismal, sulky, and frightened.

'Ye'll gi'e me a word, Miss—only a thing I ought to say—for your good; by—, mind, it's for *your* good, Miss.'

Dudley stood a little way off, viewing me, with his hat in both hands and a 'glooming' countenance.

I detested the idea of either hearing or speaking to him; but I had no resolution to refuse, and only saying 'I can't imagine what you can wish to speak to me about,' I approached him. 'Wait there at the banister, Quince.'

There was a fragrance of alcohol about the flushed face and gaudy muffler of this odious cousin, which heightened the effect of his horribly dismal features. He was speaking, besides, a little thickly; but his manner was dejected, and he was treating me with an elaborate and discomfited respect which reassured me.

'I'm a bit up a tree, Miss,' he said shuffling his feet on the oak floor. 'I behaved a d—— fool; but I *baint* one o' they sort. I'm a fellah as 'ill fight his man, an' stan' up to 'm fair, don't ye see? An' I baint one o' they sort—no, *dang* it, I baint.'

Dudley delivered his puzzling harangue with a good deal of undertoned vehemence, and was strangely agitated. He, too, had got an unpleasant way of avoiding my eye, and glancing along the floor from corner to corner as he spoke, which gave him a very hang-dog air.

He was twisting his fingers in his great sandy whisker, and pulling it roughly enough to drag his cheek about by that savage purchase; and with his other hand he was crushing and rubbing his hat against his knee.

'The old boy above there be half crazed, I think; he don't mean half as he says thof, not he. But I'm in a bad fix anyhow—a regular sell it's been, and I can't get a tizzy out of him. So, ye see, I'm up a tree, Miss; and he sich a one, he'll make it a wuss mull if I let him. He's as sharp wi' me as one o' them lawyer chaps, dang 'em, and he's a lot of I O's and rubbitch o' mine; and Bryerly writes to me he can't gi'e me my legacy, 'cause he's got a notice from Archer and Sleigh a warnin' him not to gi'e me as much as a bob; for I signed it away to governor, he says—which I believe's a lie. I may a' signed some writing—'appen I did—when I was a bit cut one night. But that's no way to catch a gentleman, and 'twon't stand. There's justice to be had, and 'twon't *stand*, I say; and I'm not in 'is hands that way. Thof I may be a bit up the spout, too, I don't deny; only I baint agoin' the whole hog all at once. I'm none o' they sort. He'll find I baint.'

Here Mary Quince coughed demurely from the foot of the stair, to remind me that the conversation was protracted.

'I don't very well understand,' I said gravely; 'and I am now going upstairs.'

'Don't jest a minute, Miss; it's only a word, ye see. We'll be goin' t' Australia, Sary Mangles, an' me, aboard the *Seamew*, on the 5th. I'm for Liverpool to-night, and she'll meet me there, an'—an', please God Almighty, ye'll never see me more; an I'd rather gi'e ye a lift, Maud, before I go: an' I tell ye what, if ye'll just gi'e me your written promise ye'll gi'e me that twenty thousand ye were offering to gi'e the Governor, I'll take ye cleverly out o' Bartram, and put ye wi' your cousin Knollys, or anywhere ye like best.'

'Take me from Bartram—for twenty thousand pounds! Take me away from my guardian! You seem to forget, sir,' my indignation rising as I spoke, 'that I can visit my cousin, Lady Knollys, whenever I please.'

'Well, that is as it may be,' he said, with a sulky deliberation, scraping about a little bit of paper that lay on the floor with the toe of his boot.

'It is as it may be, and that is as I say, sit; and considering how you have treated me—your mean, treacherous, and infamous suit, and your cruel treason to your poor wife, I am amazed at your effrontery.'

I turned to leave him, being, in truth, in one of my passions.

'Don't ye be a flying' out,' he said peremptorily, and catching me roughly by the wrist, 'I baint a—going to vex ye. What a mouth you be, as can't see your way! Can't ye speak wi' common sense, like a woman—dang it—for once, and not keep brawling like a brat—can't ye see what I'm saying? I'll take ye out o' all this, and put ye wi' your cousin, or wheresoever you list, if ye'll gi'e me what I say.'

He was, for the first time, looking me in the face, but with contracted eyes, and a countenance very much agitated.

'Money?' said I, with a prompt disdain.

'Ay, money—twenty thousand pounds—*there*. On or off?' he replied, with an unpleasant sort of effort.

'You ask my promise for twenty thousand pounds, and you shan't have it.'

My cheeks were flaming, and I stamped on the ground as I spoke.

If he had known how to appeal to my better feelings, I am sure I should have done, perhaps not quite that, all at once at least, but something handsome, to assist him. But this application was so shabby and insolent! What could he take me for? That I should suppose his placing me with Cousin Monica constituted her my guardian? Why, he must fancy me the merest baby. There was a kind of stupid cunning in this that disgusted my good-nature and outraged my self-importance.

'You won't gi'e me that, then?' he said, looking down again, with a frown, and working his mouth and cheeks about as I could fancy a man rolling a piece of tobacco in his jaw.

'Certainly *not*, sir,' I replied.

'*Take* it, then,' he replied, still looking down, very black and discontented.

I joined Mary Quince, extremely angry. As I passed under the carved oak arch of the vestibule, I saw his figure in the deepening twilight. The picture remains in its murky halo fixed in memory. Standing where he last spoke in the centre of the hall, not looking after me, but downward, and, as well as I could see, with the countenance of a man who has lost a game, and a ruinous wager too—that is black and desperate. I did not utter a syllable on the way up. When I reached my room, I began to reconsider the interview more at my leisure. I was, such were my ruminations, to have agreed at once to his preposterous offer, and to have been driven, while he smirked and grimaced behind my back at his acquaintences, through Feltham in his dog-cart to Elverson; and then, to the indignation of my uncle, to have been delivered up to Lady Knollys' guardianship, and to have handed my driver, as I alighted, the handsome fare of 20,000*l*. It required the impudence of Tony Lumpkin, without either his fun or his shrewdness, to have conceived such a prodigious practical joke.

'Maybe you'd like a little tea, Miss?' insinuated Mary Quince.

'What impertinence!' I exclaimed, with one of my angry stamps on the floor. 'Not you, dear old Quince,' I added. 'No—no tea just now.'

And I resumed my ruminations, which soon led me to this train of thought—

'Stupid and insulting as Dudley's proposition was, it yet involved a great treason against my uncle. Should I be weak enough to be silent, may he not, wishing to forestal me, misrepresent all that has passed, so as to throw the blame altogether upon me?'

This idea seized upon me with a force which I could not withstand; and on the impulse of the moment I obtained admission to my uncle, and related exactly what had passed. When I had finished my narrative, which he listened to without once raising his eyes, my uncle cleared his throat once or twice, as if to speak. He was smiling—I thought with an effort, and with elevated brows. When I concluded, he hummed one of those sliding notes, which a less refined man might have expressed by a whistle of surprise and contempt, and again he essayed to speak, but continued silent. The fact is, he seemed to me very much disconcerted. He rose from his seat, and shuffled about the room in his slippers, I believe affecting only to be in search of something, opening and shutting two or three drawers, and turning over some books and papers; and at length, taking up some loose sheets of manuscript, he appeared to have found what he was looking for, and began to read them carelessly, with his back towards me, and with another effort to clear his voice, he said at last—

'And pray, what could the fool mean by all that?'

'I think he must have taken me for an idiot, sit,' I answered.

'Not unlikely. He has lived in a stable, among horses and ostlers; he has always seemed to me something like a centaur—that is a centaur composed not of man and horse, but of an ape and an ass.'

And upon this jibe he laughed, not coldly and sarcastically, as was his wont, but, I thought, flurriedly. And, continuing to look into his papers, he said, his back still toward me as he read—

'And he did not favour you with an exposition of his meaning, which, except in so far as it estimated his deserts at the modest sum you have named, appears to me too oracular to be interpreted without a kindred inspiration?'

And again he laughed. He was growing more like himself.

'As to your visiting your cousin, Lady Knollys, the stupid rogue had only five minutes before heard me express my wish that you should do so before leaving this. I am quite resolved you shall—that is, unless, dear Maud, you should yourself object; but, of course, we must wait for an invitation, which, I conjecture, will not be long in coming. In fact, your letter will naturally bring it about, and, I trust, open the way to a permanent residence with her. The more I think it over, the more am I convinced, dear niece, that as things are likely to turn out, my roof would be no desirable shelter for you; and that, under all circumstances, hers would. Such were my motives, Maud, in opening, through your letter, a door of reconciliation between us.'

I felt that I ought to have kissed his hand—that he had indicated precisely the future that I most desired; and yet there was within me a vague feeling, akin to suspicion—akin to dismay which chilled and overcast my soul.

'But, Maud,' he said, 'I am disquieted to think of that stupid jackanapes presuming to make you such an offer! A creditable situation truly—arriving in the dark at Elverston, under the solitary escort of that wild young man, with whom you would have fled from my guardianship; and, Maud, I tremble as I ask myself the question, would he have conducted you to Elverston at all? When you have lived as long in the world as I, you will appreciate its wickedness more justly.' Here there was a little pause.

'I know, my dear, that were he convinced of his legal marriage with that young woman,' he resumed, perceiving how startled I looked, 'such an idea, of course, would not have entered his head; but he does not believe any such thing. Contrary to fact and logic, he does honestly think that his hand is still at his disposal; and I certainly do suspect that he would have employed that excursion in endeavouring to persuade you to think as he does. Be that how it may, however, it is satisfactory to me to know that you shall never more be troubled by one word from that ill-regulated young man. I made him my adieux, such as they were, this evening; and never more shall he enter the walls of Bartram-Haugh while we two live.'

Uncle Silas replaced the papers which had ostensibly interested him so much, and returned. There was a vein which was visible near the angle of his lofty temple, and in moments of agitation stood out against the surrounding pallor in a knotted blue cord; and as he came back smiling askance, I saw this sign of inward tumult.

'We can, however, afford to despise the follies and knaveries of the world, Maud, as long as we act, as we have hitherto done, with perfect confidence in each other. Heaven bless you, dear Maud! Your report troubled me, I believe, more than it need—troubled me a good deal; but reflection assures me it is nothing. He is gone. In a few days' time he will be on the sea. I will issue my orders to-morrow morning, and he will never more, during his brief stay in England, gain admission to Bartram-Haugh. Good-night, my good niece; I thank you.'

And so I returned to Mary Quince, on the whole happier than I had left her, but still with the confused and jarring vision I could not interpret perpetually rising before me; and as, from time to time, shapeless anxieties agitated me, relieving them by appeals to Him who alone is wise and strong.

Next day brought me a goodnatured gossiping letter from dear Milly, written in compulsory French, which was, in some places, very difficult to interpret. She gave me a very pleasant account of the place, and her opinion of the girls who were inmates, and mentioned some of the nuns with high commendation. The language plainly cramped poor Milly's genius; but although there was by no means so much fun as an honest English letter would have brought me, there could be no mistake about her liking the place, and she expressed her honest longing to see me in the most affectionate terms.

This letter came enclosed in one to my uncle, from the proper authority in the convent; and as there was neither address within, nor post-mark without, I was as much in the dark as ever as to poor Milly's whereabouts.

Pencilled across the envelope of this letter, in my uncle's hand, were the words, 'Let me have your answer when sealed, and I will transmit it.—S. R.'

When, accordingly, some days later, I did place my letter to Milly in my uncle's hands, he told me the reason of his reserves on the subject.

'I thought it best, dear Maud, not to plague you with a secret, and Milly's present address is one. It will in a few weeks become the rallying-point of our diverse routes, when you shall meet her, and I join you both. Nobody, until the storm shall have blown over, must know where I am to be found, except my lawyer; and I think you would prefer ignorance to the trouble of keeping a secret on which so much may depend.'

This being reasonable, and even considerate, I acquiesced.

In that interval there reached me such a charming, gay, and affectionate letter— a very *long* letter, too—though the writer was scarcely seven miles away, from dear Cousin Monica, full of pleasant gossip, and rose-coloured and golden castles in the air, and the kindest interest in poor Milly, and the warmest affection for me.

One other incident varied that interval, if possible more pleasantly than those. It was the announcement, in a Liverpool paper, of the departure of the *Seamew*, bound for Melbourne; and among the passengers were reported 'Dudley Ruthyn, Esquire, of Bartram—H., and Mrs. D. Ruthyn.'

And now I began to breathe freely, I plainly saw the end of my probation approaching: a short excursion to France, a happy meeting with Milly, and then a delightful residence with Cousin Monica for the remainder of my nonage.

You will say then that my spirits and my serenity were quite restored. Not quite. How marvellously lie our anxieties, in filmy layers, one over the other! Take away that which has lain on the upper surface for so long—the care of cares—the only one, as it seemed to you, between your soul and the radiance of Heaven—and straight you find a new stratum there. As physical science tells us no fluid is without its skin, so does it seem with this fine medium of the soul, and these successive films of care that form upon its surface on mere contact with the upper air and light.

What was my new trouble? A very fantastic one, you will say—the illusion of a self-tormentor. It was the face of Uncle Silas which haunted me. Notwithstanding the old pale smile, there was a shrinking grimness, and the always-averted look.

Sometimes I fancied his mind was disordered. I could not account for the eerie lights and shadows that flickered on his face, except so. There was a look of shame and fear of me, amazing as that seems, in the sheen of his peaked smile.

I thought,' Perhaps he blames himself for having tolerated Dudley's suit—for having urged it on grounds of personal distress—for having altogether lowered, though under sore temptation, both himself and his office; and he thinks that he has forfeited my respect.'

Such was my analysis; but in the *coup-d'œil* of that white face that dazzled me in darkness, and haunted my daily reveries with a faded light, there was an intangible character of the insidious and the terrible.

CHAPTER LIV

IN SEARCH OF MR. CHARKE'S SKELETON

On the whole, however, I was unspeakably relieved. Dudley Ruthyn, Esq., and Mrs. D. Ruthyn, were now skimming the blue waves on the wings of the *Seamew*, and every morning widened the distance between us, which was to go on increasing until it measured a point on the antipodes. The Liverpool paper containing this golden line was carefully preserved in my room; and like the gentleman who, when much tried by the shrewish heiress whom he had married, used to retire to his closet and read over his marriage settlement, I used, when blue devils haunted me, to unfold my newspaper and read the paragraph concerning the *Seamew*.

The day I now speak of was a dismal one of sleety snow. My own room seemed to me cheerier than the lonely parlour, where I could not have had good Mary Quince so decorously.

A good fire, that kind and trusty face, the peep I had just indulged in at my favourite paragraph, and the certainty of soon seeing my dear cousin Monica, and afterwards affectionate Milly, raised my spirits.

'So,' said I, 'as old Wyat, you say, is laid up with rheumatism, and can't turn up to scold me, I think I'll run up stairs and make an exploration, and find poor Mr. Charke's skeleton in a closet.'

'Oh, law, Miss Maud, how can you say such things!' exclaimed good old Quince, lifting up her honest grey head and round eyes from her knitting.

I had grown so familiar with the frightful tradition of Mr. Charke and his suicide, that I could now afford to frighten old Quince with him.

'I am quite serious. I am going to have a ramble up-stairs and down-stairs, like goosey-goosey-gander; and if I do light upon his chamber, it is all the more interesting. I feel so like Adelaide, in the "Romance of the Forest," the book I was reading to you last night, when she commenced her delightful rambles through the interminable ruined abbey in the forest.'

'Shall I go with you, Miss?'

'No, Quince; stay there; keep a good fire, and make some tea. I suspect I shall lose heart and return very soon' and with a shawl about me, cowl fashion, over my head, I stole up-stairs.

I shall not recount with the particularity of the conscientious heroine of Mrs. Ann Radcliffe, all the suites of apartments, corridors, and lobbies, which I threaded in my ramble. It will be enough to mention that I lighted upon a door at the end of a long gallery, which, I think, ran parallel with the front of the house; it interested me because it had the air of having been very long undisturbed. There were two rusty bolts, which did not evidently belong to its original securities, and had been, though very long ago, somewhat clumsily superadded. Dusty and rusty they were, but I had no difficulty in drawing them back. There was a rusty key, I remember it well, with a crooked handle in the lock; I tried to turn it, but could not. My curiosity was piqued. I was thinking of going back and getting Mary Quince's assistance. It struck me, however, that possibly it was not locked, so I pulled the door and it opened quite easily. I did not find myself in a strangely-furnished suite of apartments, but at the entrance of a gallery, which diverged at right angles from that through which I had just passed; it was very imperfectly lighted, and ended in total darkness.

I began to think how far I had already come, and to consider whether I could retrace my steps with accuracy in case of a panic, and I had serious thoughts of returning.

The idea of Mr. Charke was growing unpleasantly sharp and menacing; and as I looked down the long space before me, losing itself among ambiguous shadows, lulled in a sinister silence, and as it were inviting my entrance like a trap, I was very near yielding to the cowardly impulse.

But I took heart of grace and determined to see a little more. I opened a side-door, and entered a large room, where were, in a corner, some rusty and cob-webbed bird-cages, but nothing more. It was a wainscoted room, but a white mildew stained the panels. I looked from the window: it commanded that dismal, weed-choked quadrangle into which I had once looked from another window. I opened a door at its farther end, and entered another chamber, not quite so large, but equally dismal, with the same prison-like look-out, not very easily discerned through the grimy panes and the sleet that was falling thickly outside. The door through which I had entered made a little accidental creak, and, with my heart at my lips, I gazed at it, expecting to see Charke, or the skeleton of which I had talked so lightly, stalk in at the half-open aperture. But I had an odd sort of courage which was always fighting against my cowardly nerves, and I walked to the door, and looking up and down the dismal passage, was reassured.

Well, one room more—just that whose deep-set door fronted me, with a melancholy frown, at the opposite end of the chamber. So to it I glided, shoved it open, advancing one step, and the great bony figure of Madame de la Rougierre was before me.

I could see nothing else.

The drowsy traveller who opens his sheets to slip into bed, and sees a scorpion coiled between them, may have experienced a shock the same in kind, but immeasurably less in degree.

She sat in a clumsy old arm-chair, with an ancient shawl about her, and her bare feet in a delft tub. She looked a thought more withered. Her wig shoved back disclosed her bald wrinkled forehead, and enhanced the ugly effect of her exaggerated features and the gaunt hollows of her face. With a sense of incredulity and terror I gazed, freezing, at this evil phantom, who returned my stare for a few seconds with a shrinking scowl, dismal and grim, as of an evil spirit detected.

The meeting, at least then and there, was as complete a surprise for her as for me. She could not tell how I might take it; but she quickly rallied, burst into a loud screeching laugh, and, with her old Walpurgis gaiety, danced some fantastic steps in her bare wet feet, tracking the floor with water, and holding out with finger and thumb, in dainty caricature, her slammakin old skirt, while she sang some of her nasal patois with an abominable hilarity and emphasis.

With a gasp, I too recovered from the fascination of the surprise. I could not speak though for some seconds, and Madame was first.

'Ah, dear Maud, what surprise! Are we not overjoy, dearest, arid cannot speak? I am full of joy—quite charmed—*ravie*—of seeing you, So are you of me, your face betray. Ah I yes, thou dear little baboon I here is poor Madame once more! Who could have imagine?'

'I thought you were in France, Madame,' I said, with a dismal effort.

'And so I was, dear Maud; I 'av just arrive. Your uncle Silas he wrote to the superioress for gouvernante to accompany a young lady—that is you, Maud—on her journey, and she send me; and so, ma chère, here is poor Madame arrive to charge herself of that affair.'

'How soon do we leave for France, Madame?' I asked.

'I do not know, but the old women—wat is her name?'

'Wyat,' I suggested.

'Oh! oui, Waiatt;—she says two, three week. And who conduct you to poor Madame's apartment, my dear Maud?' She inquired insinuatingly.

'No one, I answered promptly: 'I reached it quite accidentally, and I can't imagine why you should conceal yourself.' Something like indignation kindled in my mind as I began to wonder at the sly strategy which had been practised upon me.

'I 'av not conceal myself, Mademoiselle,' retorted the governness. 'I 'av act precisally as I 'av been ordered, Your uncle, Mr. Silas Ruthyn, he is afraid, Waiatt says, to be interrupted by his creditors, and everything must be done very quaitly. I have been commanded to avoid *me faire voir*, you know, and I must obey my employer—voilà tout!'

'And for how long have you been residing here?' I persisted, in the same resentful vein.

' 'Bout a week. It is soche triste place! I am so glad to see you, Maud! I've been so isolée, you dear leetle fool!'

'You are *not* glad, Madame; you don't love me—you never did,' I exclaimed with sudden vehemence.

'Yes, I am *very* glad; you know not, chère petite *niaise*, how I 'av desire to educate you a leetle more. Let us understand one another. You think I do not love you, Mademoiselle, because you have mentioned to your poor papa that little *dèrèglement* in his library. I have repent very often that so great indiscretion of my life. I thought to find some letters of Dr. Braierly. I think that man was trying to get your property, my dear Maud, and if I had found something I would tell you all about. But it was very great *sottise*, and you were very right to denounce me to Monsieur. Je n'ai point de rancune contre vous. No, no, none at all. On the contrary, I shall be your *gardienne tutelaire*—wat you call?—guardian angel—ah, yes, that is it. You think I speak *par dérision*; not at all. No, my dear cheaile, I do not speak *par moquerie*, unless perhaps the very least degree in the world.'

And with these words Madame laughed unpleasantly, showing the black caverns at the side of her mouth, and with a cold, steady malignity in her gaze.

'Yes,' I said; 'I know what you mean, Madame—you *hate* me.'

'Oh! wat great ogly word! I am shock I *vous me faites honte*. Poor Madame, she never hate any one she loves all her friends, and her enemies she leaves to Heaven while I am, as you see, more gay, more *joyeuse* than ever, they have not been 'appy—no, they have not been fortunate these others. Wen I return, I find always some of my enemy they 'av die, and some they have put themselves into embarrassment, or there has arrived to them some misfortune;' and Madame shrugged and laughed a little scornfully.

A kind of horror chilled my rising anger, and I was silent.

'You see, my dear Maud, it is very natural you should think I hate you. When I was with Mr. Austin Ruthyn, at Knowl, you know you did not like a me—never. But in consequence of our intimacy I confide you that which I 'av of most dear in the world, my reputation. It is always so. The pupil can *calomniate*, without been discover, the gouvernante. 'Av I not been always kind to you, Maud? Which 'av I use of violence or of sweetness the most? I am, like other persons, *jalouse de ma réputation*; and it was difficult to suffer with patience the banishment which was invoked by you, because chiefly for your good, and for an indiscretion to which I was excited by motives the most pure and laudable. It was you who spied so cleverly—eh I and denounce me to Monsieur Ruthyn? Helas! war bad world it is!'

'I do not mean to speak at all about that occurrence, Madame; I will not discuss it. I dare say what you tell me of the cause of your engagement here is true, and I suppose we must travel, as you say, in company; but you must know that the less we see of each other while in this house the better.'

'I am not so sure of that, my sweet little *béte*; your education has been neglected, or rather entirely abandoned, since you 'av arrive at this place, I am told. You must not be a *bestiole*. We must do, you and I, as we are ordered. Mr. Silas Ruthyn he will tell us.'

All this time Madame was pulling on her stockings, getting her boots on, and otherwise proceeding with her dowdy toilet. I do not know why I stood there talking to her. We often act very differently from what we would have done upon reflection. I had involved myself in a dialogue, as wiser generals than I have entangled themselves in a general action when they meant only an affair of outposts. I had grown a little angry, and would not betray the least symptom of fear, although I felt that sensation profoundly.

'My beloved father thought you so unfit a companion for me that he dismissed you at an hour's notice, and I am very sure that my uncle will think as he did; you are not a fit companion for me, and had my uncle known what had passed he would never have admitted you to this house—never!'

'Helas! *Quelle disgrace!* And you really think so, my dear Maud,' exclaimed Madame, adjusting her wig before her glass, in the comer of which I could see half of her sly, grinning face, as she ogled herself in it.

'I do, and so do you, Madame,' I replied, growing more frightened.

'It may be—we shall see; but everyone is not so cruel as you, *ma chère petite calomniatrice.*'

'You shan't call me those names,' I said, in an angry tremor. What name, dearest cheaile?'

'*Calomniatrice*—that is an insult.'

'Why, my most foolish little Maud, we may say rogue, and a thousand other little words in play which we do not say seriously.'

'You are not playing—you never play—you are angry, and you hate me,' I exclaimed, vehemently.

'Oh, fie!—wat shame! Do you not perceive, dearest cheaile, how much education you still need? You are proud, little de moiselle; you must become, on the contrary, quaite humble. Je ferai baiser le babouin à vous—ha, ha, ha! I weel make a you to kees the monkey. You are too proud, my dear cheaile.'

'I am not such a fool as I was at Knowl,' I said; 'you shall not terrify me here. I will tell my uncle the whole truth,' I said.

'Well, it may be that is the best,' she replied, with provoking coolness.

'You think I don't mean it?'

'Of course you *do,*' she replied.

'And we shall see what my uncle thinks of it.'

'We shall see, my dear,' she replied, with an air of mock contrition.

'Adieu, Madame!'

'You are going to Monsieur Ruthyn?—very good!'

I made her no answer, but more agitated than I cared to show her, I left the room. I hurried along the twilight passage, and turned into the long gallery that opened from it at right angles. I had riot gone half-a-dozen steps on my return when I heard a heavy tread and a rustling behind me.

'I am ready, my dear; I weel accompany you,' said the smirking phantom, hurrying after me.

'Very well,' was my reply; and threading our way, with a few hesitations and mistakes, we reached and descended the stairs, and in a minute more stood at my uncle's door.

My uncle looked hard and strangely at us as we entered. He looked, indeed, as if his temper was violently excited, and glared and muttered to himself for a few seconds; and treating Madame to a stare of disgust, he asked peevishly—

'Why am I disturbed, pray?'

'Miss Maud a Ruthyn, she weel explain,' replied Madame, with a great courtesy, like a boat going down in a ground swell.

'*Will* you explain, my dear?' he asked, in his coldest and most sarcastic tone.

I was agitated, and I am sure my statement was confused. I succeeded, however, in saying what I wanted.

'Why, Madame, this is a grave charge! Do you admit it, pray?'

Madame, with the coolest possible effrontery, denied it all with the most solemn asseverations, and with streaming eyes and clasped hands, conjured me melodramatically to withdraw that intolerable story, and to do her justice. I stared at her for a while astounded, and turning suddenly to my uncle, as vehemently asserted the truth of every syllable I had related.

'You hear, my dear child, you hear her deny everything; what am I to think? You must excuse the bewilderment of my old bead. Madame de la—that lady has arrived excellently recommended by the superioress of the place where dear Milly awaits you, and such persons are particular. It strikes me, my dear niece, that you must have made a mistake.'

I protested here. But he went on without seeming to hear the parenthesis—

'I know, my dear Maud, that you are quite incapable of wilfully deceiving any-one; but you are liable to be deceived like other young people. You were, no doubt, very nervous, and but half awake when you fancied you saw the occurrence you describe; and Madame de—de——'

'De la Rougierre,' I supplied.

'Yes, thank you—Madame de la Rougierre, who has arrived with excellent testimonials, strenuously denies the whole thing. Here is a conflict, my dear—in my mind a presumption of mistake. I confess I should prefer that theory to a peremptory assumption of guilt.'

I felt incredulous and amazed; it seemed as if a dream were being enacted before me. A transaction of the most serious import, which I had witnessed with my own eyes, and described with unexceptionable minuteness and consistency, is discredited by that strange and suspicious old man with an imbecile coolness. It was quite in vain my reiterating my statement, backing it with the most earnest asseverations. I was beating the air. It did not seem to reach his mind. It was all received with a simper of feeble incredulity.

He patted and smoothed my head—he laughed gently, and shook his while I insisted; and Madame protested her purity in now tranquil floods of innocent tears, and murmured mild and melancholy prayers for my enlightenment and reformation. I felt as if I should lose my reason.

'There now, dear Maud, we have heard enough; it is, I do believe, a delusion. Madame de la Rougierre will be your companion, at the utmost, for three or four weeks. Do exercise a little of your self-command and good sense—you know how I am tortured. Do not, I entreat, add to my perplexities. You may make yourself very happy with Madame if you will, I have no doubt.'

'I propose to Mademoiselle,' said Madame, drying her eyes with a gentle alacrity, 'to profit of my visit for her education. But she does not seem to weesh wat I think is so useful.'

'She threatened me with some horrid French vulgarism—*de faire baiser le babouin à moi*, whatever that means; and I know she hates me,' I replied, impetuously.

'Doucement—doucement!' said my uncle, with a smile at once amused and compassionate. 'Doucement! ma chère.'

With great hands and cunning eyes uplifted, Madame tearfully—for her tears came on short notice—again protested her absolute innocence. She had never in all her life so much as heard one so villain phrase.

'You see, my dear, you have misheard; young people never attend. You will do well to take advantage of Madame's short residence to get up your French a little, and the more you are with her the better.'

'I understand then, Mr. Ruthyn, you weesh I should resume my instructions?' asked Madame.

'Certainly; and converse all you can in French with Mademoiselle Maud. You will be glad, my dear, that I've insisted on it,' he said, turning to me, 'when you have reached France, where you will find they speak nothing else. And now, dear Maud—no, not a word more—you must leave me. Farewell, Madam!'

And he waved us out a little impatiently; and I, without one look toward Madame de la Rougierre, stunned and incensed, walked into my room and shut the door.

CHAPTER LV

THE FOOT OF HERCULES

I stood at the window—still the same leaden sky and feathery sleet before me—
trying to estimate the magnitude of the discovery I had just made Gradually a kind
of despair seized me, and I threw myself passionately on my bed, weeping aloud.

Good Mary Quince was, of course, beside me in a moment, with her pale, concerned face.

'Oh, Mary, Mary, she's come—that dreadful woman, Madame de la Rougierre,
has come to be my governess again; and Uncle Silas won't hear or believe anything
about her. It is vain talking; he is prepossessed. Was ever so unfortunate a creature
as I? Who could have fancied or feared such a thing? Oh, Mary, Mary, what am I
to do? what is to become of me? Am I never to shake off that vindictive, terrible
woman?'

Mary said all she could to console me. I was making too much of her. What
was she, after all, more than a governess?—she could not hurt me. I was not a
child no longer—she could not bully me now; and my uncle, though he might be
deceived for a while, would not be long finding her out.

Thus and soforth did good Mary Quince declaim, and at last she did impress
me a little, and I began to think that I had, perhaps, been making too much of
Madame's visit. But still imagination, that instrument and mirror of prophecy,
showed her formidable image always on its surface, with a terrible moving background of shadows.

In a few minutes there was a knock at my door, and Madame herself entered.
She was in walking costume. There had been a brief clearing of the weather, and
she proposed our making a promenade together.

On seeing Mary Quince she broke into a rapture of compliment and greeting,
and took what Mr. Richardson would have called her passive hand, and pressed it
with wonderful tenderness.

Honest Mary suffered all this somewhat reluctantly, never smiling, and, on the
contrary, looking rather ruefully at her feet.

'Weel you make a some tea? When I come back, dear Mary Quince, I 'av so
much to tell you and dear Miss Maud of all my adventures while I 'av been away;
it will make a you laugh ever so much. I was—what you theenk?—near, ever so
near to be married!' And upon this she broke into a screeching laugh, and shook
Mary Quince merrily by the shoulder.

I sullenly declined going out, or rising; and when she had gone away, I told Mary that I should confine myself to my room while Madame stayed.

But self-denying ordinances self-imposed are not always long observed by youth. Madame de la Rougierre laid herself out to be agreeable; she had no end of stories—more than half, no doubt, pure fictions—to tell, but all, in that triste place, amusing. Mary Quince began to entertain a better opinion of her. She actually helped to make beds, and tried to be in every way of use, and seemed to have quite turned over a new leaf; and so gradually she moved me, first to listen, and at last to talk.

On the whole, these terms were better than a perpetual skirmish; but, notwithstanding all her gossip and friendliness, I continued to have a profound distrust and even terror of her.

She seemed curious about the Bartram-Haugh family, and all their ways, and listened darkly when I spoke. I told her, bit by bit, the whole story of Dudley, and she used, whenever there was news of the *Seamew*, to read the paragraph for my benefit; and in poor Milly's battered little Atlas she used to trace the ship's course with a pencil, writing in, from point to point, the date at which the vessel was 'spoken' at sea. She seemed amused at the irrepressible satisfaction with which I received these minutes of his progress; and she used to calculate the distance;—on such a day he was two hundred and sixty miles, on such another five hundred; the last point was more than eight hundred—good, better, best—best of all would be those 'deleecious antipode, were he would so soon promener on his head twelve thousand mile away;' and at the conceit she would fall into screams of laughter.

Laugh as she might, however, there was substantial comfort in thinking of the boundless stretch of blue wave that rolled between me and that villainous cousin.

I was now on very odd terms with Madame. She had not relapsed into her favourite vein of oracular sarcasm and menace; she had, on the contrary, affected her good-humoured and genial vein. But I was not to be deceived by this. I carried in my heart that deep-seated fear of her which her unpleasant good-humour and gaiety never disturbed for a moment. I was very glad, therefore, when she went to Todcaster by rail, to make some purchases for the journey which we were daily expecting to commence; and happy in the opportunity of a walk, good old Mary Quince and I set forth for a little ramble.

As I wished to make some purchases in Feltram, I set out, with Mary Quince for my companion. On reaching the great gate we found it locked. The key, however, was in it, and as it required more than the strength of my hand to turn, Mary tried it. At the same moment old Crowle came out of the sombre lodge by its side, swallowing down a mouthful of his dinner in haste. No one, I believe, liked the long suspicious face of the old man, seldom shorn or washed, and furrowed with great, grimy perpendicular wrinkles. Leering fiercely at Mary, not pretending to see me, he wiped his mouth hurriedly with the back of his hand, and growled—

'Drop it.'

'Open it, please, Mr. Crowle,' said Mary, renouncing the task.

Crowle wiped his mouth as before, looking inauspicious; shuffling to the spot, and muttering to himself, he first satisfied himself that the lock was fast, and then lodged the key in his coat-pocket, and still muttering, retraced his steps.

'We want the gate open, please,' said Mary.

No answer.

'Miss Maud wants to go into the town,' she insisted.

'We wants many a thing we can't get,' he growled, stepping into his habitation.

'Please open the gate,' I said, advancing.

He half turned on his threshold, and made a dumb show of touching his hat, although he had none on.

'Can't, ma'am; without an order from maister, no one goes out here.'

'You won't allow me and my maid to pass the gate?' I said.

''Tisn't *me*, ma'am,' said he; 'but I can't break orders, and no one goes out without the master allows.'

And without awaiting further parley, he entered, shutting his hatch behind him.

So Mary and I stood, looking very foolish at one another. This was the first restraint I had experienced since Milly and I had been refused a passage through the Windmill paling. The rule, however, on which Crowle insisted I felt confident could not have been intended to apply to me. A word to Uncle Silas would set all right; and in the meantime I proposed to Mary that we should take a walk—my favourite ramble—into the Windmill Wood.

I looked toward Dickon's farmstead as we passed, thinking that Beauty might have been there. I did see the girl, who was plainly watching us. She stood in the doorway of the cottage, withdrawn into the shade, and, I fancied, anxious to escape observation. When we had passed on a little, I was confirmed in that belief by seeing her run down the footpath which led from the rear of the farmyard in the direction contrary to that in which we were moving.

'So,' I thought, 'poor Meg falls from me!'

Mary Quince and I rambled on through the wood, till we reached the windmill itself, and seeing its low arched door open, we entered the chiaro-oscuro of its circular basement. As we did so I heard a rush and the creak of a plank, and looking tip, I saw just a foot—no more—disappearing through the trap-door.

In the case of one we love or fear intensely, what feats of comparative anatomy will not the mind unconsciously perform? constructing the whole living animal from the turn of an elbow, the curl of a whisker, a segment of a hand. How instantaneous and unerring is the instinct!

'Oh, Mary, what have I seen!' I whispered, recovering from the fascination that held my gaze fast to the topmost rounds of the ladder, that disappeared in the darkness above the open door in the loft. 'Come, Mary—come away.'

At the same instant appeared the swarthy, sullen face of Dickon Hawkes in the shadow of the aperture. Having but one serviceable leg, his descent was slow and awkward, and having got his head to the level of the loft he stopped to touch his hat to me, and to hasp and lock the trap-door.

When this was done, the man again touched his hat, and looked steadily and searchingly at me for a second or so, while he got the key into his pocket.

'These fellahs stores their flour too long 'ere, ma'am. There's a deal o' trouble a-looking arter it. I'll talk wi' Silas, and settle that.'

By this time he had got upon the worn-tiled floor, and touching his hat again, he said—

'I'm a-goin' to lock the door, ma'am."

So with a start, and again whispering—

'Come, Mary—come away'—

With my arm fast in hers, we made a swift departure.

'I feel very faint, Mary,' said I. 'Come quickly. There's nobody following us?'

'No, Miss, dear. That man with the wooden leg is putting a padlock on the door.'

'Come *very* fast,' I said; and when we had got a little farther, I said, 'Look again, and see whether anyone is following.'

'No one, Miss,' answered Mary, plainly surprised. 'He's putting the key in his pocket, and standin' there a-lookin' after us.'

'Oh, Mary, did not you see it?'

'What, Miss?' asked Mary, almost stopping.

'Come on, Mary. Don't pause. They will observe us,' I whispered, hurrying her forward.

'What did you see, Miss?' repeated Mary.

'*Mr. Dudley*,' I whispered, with a terrified emphasis, not daring to turn my head as I spoke.

'Lawk, Miss!' remonstrated honest Quince, with a protracted intonation of wonder and incredulity, which plainly implied a suspicion that I was dreaming.

'Yes, Mary. When we went into that dreadful room—that dark, round place—I saw his foot on the ladder. *His* foot, Mary I can't be mistaken. *I won't be questioned.* You'll *find* I'm right. He's *here*. He never went in that ship at all. A fraud has been practised on me—it is infamous—it is terrible. I'm frightened out of my life. For heaven's sake, look back again, and tell me what you see.'

'*Nothing*, Miss,' answered Mary, in contagious whispers, 'but that wooden-legged chap, standin' hard by the door.'

'And no one with him?'

'No one, Miss.'

We got without pursuit through the gate in the paling. I drew breath so soon as we had reached the cover of the thicket near the chestnut hollow, and I began to reflect that whoever the owner of the foot might be—and I was still instinctively certain that it was no other than Dudley—concealment was plainly his object. I need not, then, be at all uneasy lest he should pursue us.

As we walked slowly and in silence along the grassy footpath, I heard a voice calling my name from behind. Mary Quince had not heard it at all, but I was quite certain.

It was repeated twice or thrice, and, looking in considerable doubt and trepidation under the hanging boughs, I saw Beauty, not ten yards away, standing among the underwood.

I remember how white the eyes and teeth of the swarthy girl looked, as with hand uplifted toward her ear, she watched us while, as it seemed, listening for more distant sounds.

Beauty beckoned eagerly to me, advancing, with looks of great fear and anxiety, two or three short steps toward me.

'*She* baint to come,' said Beauty, under her breath, so soon as I had nearly reached her, pointing without raising, her hand at Mary Quince.

'Tell her to sit on the ash-tree stump down yonder, and call ye as loud as she can if she sees any fellah a-comin' this way, an' rin ye back to me;' and she impatiently beckoned me away on her errand.

When I returned, having made this dispositions, I perceived bow pale the girl was.

'Are you ill, Meg?' I asked.

'Never ye mind. Well enough. Listen, Miss; I must tell it all in a crack, an' if she calls, rin awa' to her, and le' me to myself, for if fayther or t'other un wor to kotch me here, I think they'd kill me a'most. Hish! '

She paused a second, looking askance, in the direction where she fancied Mary Quince was. Then she resumed in a whisper—

'Now, lass, mind ye, ye'll keep what I say to yourself. You're not to tell that un nor any other for your life, mind, a word o' what I'm goin' to tell ye.'

'I'll not say a word. Go on.'

'Did ye see Dudley?'

'I think I saw him getting up the ladder.'

'In the mill? Ha! that's him. He never went beyond Todcaster. He staid in Feltram arter.'

It was my turn to look pale now. My worst conjecture was established.

CHAPTER LVI

I CONSPIRE

'That's a bad un, he is—oh, Miss, Miss Maud! It's nout that's good as keeps him an' fayther—(mind, lass, ye promised you would not tell no one)—as keeps them two a-talkin' and a-smokin' secret-like together in the mill. An' fayther don't know I found him out. They don't let me into the town, but Brice tells me, and he knows it's Dudley; and it's nout that's good, but summat very bad. An' I reckon, Miss, it's all about you. Be ye frightened, Miss Maud?'

I felt on the point of fainting, but I rallied.

'Not much, Meg. Go on, for Heaven's sake. Does Uncle Silas know he is here?'

'Well, Miss, they were with him, Brice told me, from eleven o'clock to nigh one o' Tuesday night, an' went in and come out like thieves, 'feard ye'd see 'em.'

'And how does Brice know anything bad?' I asked, with a strange freezing sensation creeping from my heels to my head and down again—I am sure deadly pale, but speaking very collectedly.

'Brice said, Miss, he saw Dudley a-cryin' and lookin' awful black, and says he to fayther, "'Tisn't in my line nohow, an' I can't;" and says fayther to he, "No one likes they soart o' things, but how can ye help it? The old boy's behind ye wi' his pitchfork, and ye canna stop." An' wi' that he bethought him o' Brice, and says he, "What be ye a-doin' there? Get ye down wi' the nags to blacksmith, do ye." An' oop gits Dudley, pullin' his hat ower his brows, an' says he, "I wish I was in the *Seamew*. I'm good for nout wi' this thing a-hangin' ower me." An' that's all as Brice heard. An' he's afeard a' fayther and Dudley awful, Dudley could lick him to pot if he crossed him, and he and fayther 'ud think nout o' havin' him afore the justices for poachin', and swearin' him into gaol."

'But why does he think it's about *me*?'

'Hish!' said Meg, who fancied she heard a sound, but all was quiet. 'I can't say—we're in danger, lass. I don't know why—but *he* does, an' so do I, an', for that matter, so do *ye*!'

'Meg, I'll leave Bartram.'

'Ye can't.'

'Can't. What do you mean, girl?'

'They won't let ye oot. The gates is all locked. They've dogs—they've blood-hounds, Brice says, Ye *can't* git oot, mind; put that oot o' your head.

'I tell ye what ye'll do. Write a bit o' a note to the lady yonder at Elverston; an' though Brice be a wild fellah, and 'appen not ower good sometimes, he likes me, an' I'll make him take it. Fayther will be grindin' at mill tomorrow. Coom ye here about one o'clock—that's if ye see the mill—sails a-turnin'—and me and Brice will meet ye here. Bring that old lass wi' ye. There's an old French un, though, that talks wi' Dudley. Mind ye, that un knows nout o' the matter. Brice be a kind lad to me, whatsoe'er he be wi' others, and I think he won't split. Now, lass, I must go. God help ye; God bless ye; an', for the world's wealth, don't ye let one o' them see ye've got ought in your head, not even that un.'

Before I could say another word, the girl had glided from me, with a wild gesture of silence, and a shake of her head.

I can't at all account for the state in which I was. There are resources both of energy and endurance in human nature which we never suspect until the tremendous voice of necessity summons them into play. Petrified with a totally new horror, but with something of the coldness and impassiveness of the trans formation, I stood, spoke, and acted—a wonder, almost a terror, to myself.

I met Madame on my return as if nothing had happened. I heard her ugly gabble, and looked at the fruits of her hour's shopping, as I might hear, and see, and talk, and smile, in a dream.

But the night was dreadful. When Mary Quince and I were alone, I locked the door. I continued walking up and down the room, with my hands clasped, looking at the inexorable floor, the walls, the ceiling, with a sort of imploring despair. I was afraid to tell my dear old Mary. The least indiscretion would be failure, and failure destruction.

I answered her perplexed solicitudes by telling her that I was not very well—that I was uneasy; but I did not fail to extract from her a promise that she would not hint to mortal, either my suspicions about Dudley, or our rencontre with Meg Hawkes.

I remember how, when, after we had got, late at night, into bed, I sat up, shivering with horror, in mine, while honest Mary's tranquil breathing told how soundly she slept. I got up, and looked from the window, expecting to see some of those wolfish dogs which they had brought to the place prowling about the courtyard. Sometimes I prayed, and felt tranquillised, and fancied that I was perhaps to have a short interval of sleep. But the serenity was delusive, and all the time my nerves were strung hysterically. Sometimes I felt quite wild, and on the point of screaming. At length that dreadful night passed away. Morning came, and a less morbid, though hardly a less terrible state of mind, Madame paid me an early visit. A thought struck me. I knew that she loved shopping, and I said, quite carelessly—

'Your yesterday's shopping tempts me, Madame, and I must get a few things before we leave for France. Suppose we go into Feltram to-day, and make my purchases, you and I?'

She looked from the corner of her cunning eye in my face without answering. I did not blench, and she said—

'Vary good. I would be vary 'appy,' and again she looked oddly at me.

'Wat hour, my dear Maud? One o'clock? I think that weel de very well, eh?'

I assented, and she grew silent.

I wonder whether I did look as careless as I tried. I do not know. Through the whole of this awful period I was, I think, supernatural; and I even now look back with wonder upon my strange self-command.

Madame, I hoped, had heard nothing of the order which prohibited my exit from the place. She would herself conduct me to Feltram, and secure, by accompanying me, my free egress.

Once in Feltram, I would assert my freedom, and manage to reach my dear cousin Knollys. Back to Bartram no power should convey me. My heart swelled and fluttered in the awful suspense of that hour.

Oh, Bartram-Haugh! how came you by those lofty walls? Which of my ancestors had begirt me with an impassable barrier in this horrible strait?

Suddenly I remembered my letter to Lady Knollys. If I were disappointed in effecting my escape through Feltram, all would depend upon it.

Having locked my door, I wrote as follows:—

Oh, my beloved cousin, as you hope for comfort in *your* hour of fear, aid me now. Dudley has returned, and is secreted somewhere about the grounds. It is a *fraud.* They all pretend to me that he is gone away in the *Seamew;* and he or they had his name published as one of the passengers. Madame de la Rougierre has appeared! She is here, and my uncle insists on making her my close companion. I am at my wits' ends. I cannot escape—the walls are a prison; and I believe the eyes of my gaolers are always upon me. Dogs are kept for pursuit—yes, *dogs*! and the gates are locked against my escape. God help me! I don't know where to look, or whom to trust. I fear my uncle more than all. I think I could bear this better if I knew what their plans are, even the worst. If ever you loved or pitied me, dear cousin, I conjure you, help me in this extremity. Take me away from this. Oh, darling, for God's sake take me away!

'Your distracted and terrified cousin, MAUD'

'Bartram-Haugh.'

I sealed this letter jealously, as if the inanimate missive would burst its cerements, and proclaim my desperate appeal through all the chambers and passages of silent Bartram.

Old Quince, greatly to cousin Monica's amusement, persisted in furnishing me with those capacious pockets which belonged to a former generation. I was glad of this old-world eccentricity now, and placed my guilty letter, that, amidst all my hypocrisies, spoke out with terrible frankness, deep in this receptacle, and having hid away the pen and ink, my accomplices, I opened the door, and resumed my careless looks, awaiting Madame's return.

'I was to demand to Mr. Ruthyn the permission to go to Feltram, and I think he will allow. He want to speak to you.'

With Madame I entered my uncle's room. He was reclining on a sofa, his back towards us, and his long white hair, as fine as spun glass, hung over the back of the couch.

'I was going to ask you, dear Maud, to execute two or three little commissions for me in Feltram.'

My dreadful letter felt lighter in my packet, and my heart beat violently.

'But I have just recollected that this is a market-day, and Feltram will be full of doubtful characters and tipsy persons, so we must wait till to-morrow; and Madame says, very kindly, that she will, as she does not so much mind, make any little purchases to-day which cannot conveniently wait.'

Madame assented with a courtesy to Uncle Silas, and a great hollow smile to me.

By this time Uncle Silas had raised himself from his reclining posture, and was sitting, gaunt and white, upon the sofa.

'News of my prodigal to-day,' he said, with a peevish smile, drawing the newspaper towards him. 'The vessel has been spoken again. How many miles away, do you suppose?'

He spoke in a plaintive key, looking at me, with hungry eyes, and a horribly smiling countenance.

'How far do you suppose Dudley is to-day?' and he laid the palm of his hand on the paragraph as he spoke. *Guess!*'

For a moment I fancied this was a theatric preparation to give point to the disclosure of Dudley's real whereabouts.

'It was a very long way. Guess!' he repeated.

So, stammering a little and pale, I performed the required hypocrisy, after which my uncle read aloud for my benefit the line or two in which were recorded the event, and the latitude and longitude of the vessel at the time, of which Madame made a note in her memory, for the purpose of making her usual tracing in poor Milly's Atlas.

I cannot say how it really was, but I fancied that Uncle Silas was all the time reading my countenance, with a grim and practised scrutiny; but nothing came of it, and we were dismissed.

Madame loved shopping, even for its own sake, but shopping with opportunities of peculation still more. She had had her luncheon, and was dressed for the excursion, she did precisely what I now most desired—she proposed to take charge of my commissions and my money; and thus entrusted, left me at liberty to keep tryst at the Chestnut Hollow.

So soon as I had seen Madame fairly off, I hurried Mary Quince, and got my things on quickly. We left the house by the side entrance, which I knew my uncle's windows did not command. Glad was I to feel a slight breeze, enough to make the mill-sails revolve; and as we got further into the grounds, and obtained a distant view of the picturesque old windmill, I felt inexpressibly relieved on seeing that it was actually working.

We were now in the Chestnut Hollow, and I sent Mary Quince to her old point of observation, which commanded a view of the path in the direction of the Windmill Wood, with her former order to call 'I've found it,' as loudly as she could, in case she should see anyone approaching.

I stopped at the point of our yesterday's meeting. I peered under the branches, and my heart beat fast as I saw Meg Hawkes awaiting me.

CHAPTER LVII

THE LETTER

'Come away, lass,' whispered Beauty, very pale; 'he's here —Tom Brice.'

And she led the way, shoving aside the leafless underwood, and we reached Tom. The slender youth, groom or poacher—he might answer for either—with his short coat and gaitered legs, was sitting on a low horizontal bough, with his shoulder against the trunk.

'*Don't* ye mind; sit ye still, lad,' said Meg, observing that he was preparing to rise, and had entangled his hat in the boughs. 'Sit ye still, and hark to the lady. He'll take it, Miss Maud, if he can; wi' na ye, lad?'

E'es, I'll take it,' he replied, holding out his hand.

'Tom Brice, you won't deceive me?'

'Noa, sure,' said Tom and Meg nearly in the same breath.

'You are an honest English lad, Tom—you would not betray me?' I was speaking imploringly.

'Noa, sure,' repeated Tom.

There was something a little unsatisfactory in the countenance of this light-haired youth, with the sharpish upturned nose. Throughout our interview he said next to nothing, and smiled lazily to himself, like a man listening to a child's solemn nonsense, and leading it on, with an amused irony, from one wise sally to another.

Thus it seemed to me that this young clown, without in the least intending to be offensive, was listening to me with a profound and lazy mockery.

I could not choose, however; and, such as he was, I must employ him or none.

'Now, Tom Brice, a great deal depends on this.'

'That's true for her, Tom Brice,' said Meg, who now and then confirmed my asseverations.

'I'll give you a pound *now*, Tom,' and I placed the coin and the letter together in his hand. 'And you are to give this letter to Lady Knollys, at Elverston; you know Elverston, don't you?'

'He does, Miss. Don't ye, lad?'

'E'es.'

'Well, do so, Tom, and I'll be good to you so long as I live.'

'D'ye hear, lad?'

'E'es,' said Tom; 'it's very good.'

'You'll take the letter, Tom?' I said, in much greater trepidation as to his answer than I showed.

'E'es, I'll take the letter,' said he, rising, and turning it about in his fingers under his eye, like a curiosity.

'Tom Brice,' I said, 'If you can't be true to me, say so; but don't take the letter except to give it to Lady Knollys, at Elverston. If you won't promise that, let me have the note back. Keep the pound; but tell me that you won't mention my having asked you to carry a letter to Elverston to anyone.'

For the first time Tom looked perfectly serious. He twiddled the corner of my letter between his finger and thumb, and wore very much the countenance of a poacher about to be committed.

'I don't want to chouce ye, Miss; but I must take care o' myself, ye see. The letters goes all through Silas's fingers to the post, and he'd know damn well this worn't among 'em. They do say he opens 'em, and reads 'em before they go; an' that's his diversion. I don't know; but I do believe that's how it be; an' if this one turned up, they'd all know it went be hand, and I'd be spotted for't.'

'But you know who I am, Tom, and I'd save you,' said I, eagerly.

'Ye'd want savin' yerself, I'm thinkin', if that feel oot,' said Tom, cynically. I don't say, though, I'll not take it—only this—I won't run my head again a wall for no one.'

'Tom,' I said, with a sudden inspiration, 'give me back the letter, and take me out of Bartram; take me to Elverston; it will be the best thing—for *you*, Tom, I mean—it will indeed—that ever befell you.'

With this clown I was pleading, as for my life; my hand was on his sleeve. I was gazing imploringly in his face.

But it would not do; Tom Brice looked amused again, swung his head a little on one side, grinning sheepishly over his shoulder on the roots of the trees beside him, as if he were striving to keep himself from an uncivil fit of laughter.

'I'll do what a wise lad may, Miss; but ye don't know they lads; they bain't that easy come over; and I won't get knocked on the head, nor sent to gaol 'appen, for no good to thee nor me. There's Meg there, she knows well enough I could na' manage that; so I won't try it, Miss, by no chance; no offence, Miss; but I'd rayther not, an' I'll just try what I can make o'this; that's all I can do for ye.'

Tom Brice, with these words, stood up, and looked uneasily in the direction of the Windmill Wood.

'Mind ye, Miss, coom what will, ye'll not tell o' me?'

'Whar 'ill ye go now, Tom?' inquired Meg, uneasily.

'Never ye mind, lass,' answered he, breaking his way through the thicket, and soon disappearing.

'E'es that 'ill be it—he'll git into the sheepwalk behind the mound. They're all down yonder; git ye back, Miss, to the hoose—be the side-door; mind ye, don't go round the corner; and I'll jest sit awhile among the bushes, and wait a good time for a start. And good-bye, Miss; and don't ye show like as if there was aught out o' common on your mind. Hish!'

There was a distant hallooing.

'That be fayther!' she whispered, with a very blank countenance, and listened with her sunburnt hand to her ear.

'Tisn't me, only Davy he'll be callin',' she said, with a great sign, and a joyless smile. 'Now git ye away i' God's name.'

So running lightly along the path, under cover of this thick wood, I recalled Mary Quince, and together we hastened back again to the house, and entered, as directed, by the side-door, which did not expose us to be seen from the Windmill Wood, and like two criminals, we stole up by the backstairs, and so though the side-gallery to my room; and there sat down to collect my wits, and try to estimate the exact effect of what had just occurred.

Madame had not returned. That was well; she always visited my room first, and everything was precisely as I had left it—a certain sign that her prying eyes and busy fingers had not been at work during my absence.

When she did appear, strange to say, it was to bring me unexpected comfort. She had in her hand a letter from my dear lady Knollys—a gleam of sunlight from the free and happy outer world entered with it. The moment of Madame left me to myself, I opened it and read as follows:—

'I am so happy, my dearest Maud, in the immediate prospect of see you. I have had a really kind letter from poor Silas—*poor* I say, for I really compassionate his situation, about which he has been, I do believe, quite frank—at least Ilbury says so, and somehow he happens to know. I have had quite an affecting, changed letter. I will tell you all when I see you. He wants me ultimately to undertake that which would afford me the most unmixed happiness—I mean the care of you, my dear girl. I only fear lest my too eager acceptance of the trust should excite that vein of opposition which is in most human beings, and induce him to think over his offer less favourably again. He says I must come to Bartram, and stay a night, and promises to lodge me comfortably; about which last I honestly do not care a pin, when the chance of a comfortable evening's gossip with you is in view. Silas explains his sad situation, and must hold himself in readiness for early flight, if he would avoid the risk of losing his personal liberty. It is a sad thing that he should have so irretrievably ruined himself, that poor Austin's liberality seems to have positively precipitated his extremity. His great anxiety is that I should see you before you leave for your short stay in France. He thinks you must leave before a fortnight. I am thinking of asking you to come over here; I know you would be just as well at Elverston as in France; but perhaps, as he seems disposed to do what we all wish, it may be safer to let him set about it in his own way. The truth is, I have so set my heart upon it that I fear to risk it by crossing him even in a trifle. He says I must fix an early day next week, and talks as if he meant to urge me to make a longer visit than he defined. I shall be only too happy. I begin, my dear Maud, to think that there is no use in trying to control events, and that things often turn out best, and most exactly to our wishes, by being left quite to themselves. I think it was Talleyrand who praised the talent of *waiting* so much. In high spirits, and with my head brimful of plans, I remain, dearest Maud, ever your affectionate cousin,

MONICA.'

Here was an inexplicable puzzle! A faint radiance of hope, however, began to overspread a landscape only a few minutes before darkened by total eclipse; but construct—what theory I might, all were inconsistent with many well-established and awful incongruities, and their wrecks lay strown over the troubled waters of the gulf into which I gazed.

Why was Madame here? Why was Dudley concealed about the place? Why was I a prisoner within the walls? What were those dangers which Meg Hawkes seemed to think so great and so imminent as to induce her to risk her lover's safety for my deliverance? All these menacing facts stood grouped together against the dark certainty that never were men more deeply interested in making away with one human being, than were Uncle Silas and Dudley in removing me.

Sometimes to these dreadful evidences I abandoned my soul. Sometimes, reading Cousin Monica's sunny letter, the sky would clear, and my terrors melt away like nightmares in the morning. I never repented, however, that I had sent my letter by Tom Brice. Escape from Bartram-Haugh was my hourly longing.

That evening Madame invited herself to tea with me. I did not object. It was better just then to be on friendly relations with everybody, if possible, even on their own terms. She was in one of her boisterous and hilarious moods, and there was a perfume of brandy.

She narrated some compliments paid her that morning in Feltram by that 'good crayature' Mrs. Litheways, the silk-mercer, and what 'ansom faylow' was her new foreman—(she intended plainly that I should 'queez' her)-and how 'I he follow' her with his eyes wherever she went. I thought, perhaps, he fancied she might pocket some of his lace or gloves. And all the time her great wicked eyes were rolling and glancing according to her ideas of fascination, and her bony face grinning and flaming with the 'strong drink' in which she delighted. She sang twaddling chansons, and being, as was her wont under such exhilarating influences, in a vapouring mood, she vowed that I should have my carriage and horses immediately.

'I weel try what I can do weeth your Uncle Silas. We are very good old friends, Mr. Ruthyn and I,' she said with a leer which I did not understand, and which yet frightened me.

I never could quite understand why these Jezebels like to insinuate the dreadful truth against themselves; but they do. Is it the spirit of feminine triumph overcoming feminine shame, and making them vaunt their fall as an evidence of bygone fascination and existing power? Need we wonder? Have not women preferred hatred to indifference, and the reputation of witchcraft, with all its penalties, to absolute insignificance? Thus, as they enjoyed the fear inspired among simple neighbours by their imagined traffic with the father of ill, did Madame, I think, relish with a cynical vainglory the suspicion of her satanic superiority.

Next morning Uncle Silas sent for me. He was seated at his table, and spoke his little French greeting, smiling as usual, pointing to a chair opposite.

'How far, I forget,' he said, carelessly laying his newspaper on the table, 'did you yesterday guess Dudley to be?'

'Eleven hundred miles I thought it was.'

'Oh yes, so it was;' and then there was an abstracted pause. 'I have been writing to Lord Ilbury, your trustee,' he resumed. I ventured to say, my dear Maud—(for having thoughts of a different arrangement for you, more suitable under my distressing circumstances, I do not wish to vacate without some expression of your estimate of my treatment of you while under my roof)—I ventured to say that you thought me kind, considerate, indulgent,—may I say so?'

I assented. What could I say?

'I said you had enjoyed our poor way of living here—our rough ways and liberty. Was I right?'

Again I assented.

'And, in fact, that you had nothing to object against your poor old uncle, except indeed his poverty, which you forgave. I think I said truth. Did I, dear Maud?'

Again I acquiesced.

All this time he was fumbling among the papers in his coat-pocket.

'That is satisfactory. So I expected you to say,' he murmured. 'I expected no less.'

On a sudden a frightful change spread across his face. He rose like a spectre with a white scowl.

'Then how do you account for that?' he shrieked in a voice of thunder, and smiting my open letter to Lady Knollys, face upward, upon the table.

I stared at my uncle, unable to speak, until I seemed to lose sight of him; but his voice, like a bell, still yelled in my ears.

'There! young hypocrite and liar! explain that farrago of slander which you bribed my servant to place in the hands of my kinswoman, Lady Knollys.'

And so on and on it went, I gazing into darkness, until the voice itself became indistinct, grew into a buzz, and hummed away into silence.

I think I must have had a fit.

When I came to myself I was drenched with water, my hair, face, neck, and dress. I did not in the least know where I was. I thought my father was ill, and spoke to him. Uncle Silas was standing near the window, looking unspeakably grim. Madame was seated beside me, and an open bottle of ether, one of Uncle Silas's restoratives, on the table before me.

'Who's that—who's ill—is anyone dead?' I cried.

At last I was relieved by long paroxysms of weeping. When I was sufficiently recovered, I was conveyed into my own room.

CHAPTER LVIII

LADY KNOLLYS' CARRIAGE

Next morning—it was Sunday—I lay on my bed in my dressing-gown, dull, apathetic, with all my limbs sore, and, as I thought, rheumatic, and feeling so ill that I did not care to speak or lift my head. My recollection of what had passed in Uncle Silas's room was utterly confused, and it seemed to me as if my poor father had been there and taken a share—I could not remember how—in the conference.

I was too exhausted and stupid to clear up this horrible muddle, and merely lay with my face toward the wall, motionless and silent, except for a great sigh every now and then.

Good Mary Quince was in the room—there was some comfort in that; but I felt quite worn out, and had rather she did not speak to me; and indeed for the time I felt absolutely indifferent as to whether I lived or died.

Cousin Monica this morning, at pleasant Elverston, all-unconscious of my sad plight, proposed to Lady Mary Carysbroke and Lord Ilbury, her guests, to drive over to church at Feltram, and then pay us a visit at Bartram-Haugh, to which they readily agreed.

Accordingly, at about two o'clock, this pleasant party of three arrived at Bartram. They walked, having left the carriage to follow when the horses were fed; and Madame de la Rougierre, who was in my uncle's room when little Giblets arrived to say that the party were in the parlour, whispered for a little with my uncle, who then said—

'Miss Maud Ruthyn has gone out to drive, but I shall be happy to see Lady Knollys here, if she will do me the favour to come upstairs and see me for a few moments; and you can mention that I am very far from well.'

Madame followed him out upon the lobby, and added, holding him by the collar, and whispering earnestly in his ear—

'Bring hair ladysheep up by the backstairs—mind, the backstairs.'

And the next moment Madame entered my room, with long tiptoe steps, and looking, Mary Quince said, as if she were going to be hanged.

On entering she looked sharply round, and being satisfied of Mary Quince's presence, she turned the key in the door, and made some affectionate enquiries about me in a whisper; and then she stole to the window and peeped out, standing back some way; after which she came to my bedside, murmured some tender sentences, drew the curtain a little, and making some little fidgety adjustments about the room; among the rest she took the key from the lock, quietly, and put it into her pocket.

This was so odd a procedure that honest Mary Quince rose stoutly from her chair, pointing to the lock, with her frank little blue eyes fixed on Madame, and she whispered—

'Won't you put the key in the lock, please?'

'Oh, certainly, Mary Queence; but it is better it shall be locked, for I think her uncle he is coming to see her, and I am sure she would be very much frightened, for he is very much displease, don't you see? and we can tell him she is not well enough, or asleep, and so he weel go away again, without any trouble.'

I heard nothing of this, which was conducted in close whispers; and Mary, although she did not give Madame credit for caring whether I was frightened or not, and suspected her motives in everything, acquiesced grudgingly, fearing lest her alleged reason might possibly be the true one.

So Madame hovered about the door, uneasily; and of what went on elsewhere during that period Lady Knollys afterwards gave me the following account—

'We were very much disappointed; but of course I was glad to see Silas, and your little hobgoblin butler led me upstairs to his room a different way, I think, from that I came before; but I don't know the house of Bartram well enough to speak positively. I only know that I was conducted quite across his bedroom, which I had not seen on my former visit, and so into his sitting-room, where I found him.

'He seemed very glad to see me, came forward smiling—I disliked his smile always—with both hands out, and shook mine with more warmth than I ever remembered in his greeting before, and said—

'"My dear, *dear* Monica, how *very* good of you—the very person I longed to see! I have been miserably ill, the sad consequence of still more miserable anxiety. Sit down, pray, for a moment."

'And he paid me some nice little French compliment in verse.

'"And where is Maud?" said I.

'"I think Maud is by this time about halfway to Elverston," said the old gentleman. "I persuaded her to take a drive, and advised a call there, which seemed to please her, so I conjecture she obeyed."

'"How *very* provoking!" cried I.

'"My poor Maud will be sadly disappointed, but you will console her by a visit—you have promised to come, and I shall try to make you comfortable. I shall be happier, Monica, with this proof of our perfect reconciliation. You won't deny me?"

'"Certainly not. I am only too glad to come," said I; "and I want to thank you, Silas."

'"For what?" said he.

'"For wishing to place Maud in my care. I am very much obliged to you."

'"I did not suggest it, I must say, Monica, with the least intention of obliging *you*," said Silas.

'I thought he was going to break into one of his ungracious moods.

'"But I *am* obliged to you—very much obliged to you, Silas; and you sha'n't refuse my thanks."

'"I am happy, at all events, Monica, in having won your good-will; we learn at last that in the affections only are our capacities for happiness; and how true is St.

Paul's preference of love—the principle that abideth! The affections, dear Monica, are eternal; and being so, celestial, divine, and consequently happy, deriving happiness, and bestowing it."

'I was always impatient of his or anybody else's metaphysics; but I controlled myself, and only said, with my customary impudence—

"'Well, dear Silas, and when do you wish me to come?"

"'The earlier the better," said he.

"'Lady Mary and Ilbury will be leaving me on Tuesday morning. I can come to you in the afternoon, if you think Tuesday a good day."

"'Thank you, dear Monica. I shall be, I trust, enlightened by that day as to my enemies' plans. It is a humiliating confession, Monica, but I am past feeling that. It is quite possible that an execution may be sent into this house tomorrow, and an end of all my schemes. It is not likely, however—hardly possible—before three weeks, my attorney tells me. I shall hear from him to-morrow morning, and then I shall ask you to name a very early day. If we are to have an unmolested fortnight certain, you shall hear, and name your own day."

'Then he asked me who had accompanied me, and lamented ever so much his not being able to go down to receive them; and he offered luncheon, with a sort of Ravenswood smile, and a shrug, and I declined, telling him that we had but a few minutes, and that my companions were walking in the grounds near the house.

'I asked whether Maud was likely to return soon?

"'Certainly not before five o'clock." He thought we should probably meet her on our way back to Elverston; but could not be certain, as she might have changed her plans.

'So then came—no more remaining to be said—a very affectionate parting. I believe all about his legal dangers was strictly true. How he could, unless that horrid woman had deceived him, with so serene a countenance tell me all those gross untruths about Maud, I can only admire.'

In the meantime, as I lay in my bed, Madame, gliding hither and thither, whispering sometimes, listening at others, I suddenly startled them both by saying—

'Whose carriage?'

'What carriage, dear?' inquired Quince, whose ears were not so sharp as mine.

Madame peeped from the window.

''Tis the physician, Doctor Jolks. He is come to see your uncle, my dear,' said Madame.

'But I hear a female voice,' I said, sitting up.

'No, my dear; there is only the doctor,' said Madame. 'He is come to your uncle. I tell you he is getting out of his carriage,' and she affected to watch the doctor's descent.

'The carriage is driving away!' I cried.

'Yes, it is draiving away,' she echoed.

But I had sprung from my bed, and was looking over her shoulder, before she perceived me.

'It is Lady Knollys!' I screamed, seizing the window-frame to force it up, and, vainly struggling to open it, I cried—

'I'm here, Cousin Monica. For God's sake, Cousin Monica—Cousin Monica!'

'You are mad, Meess—go back,' screamed Madame, exerting her superior strength to force me back.

But I saw deliverance and escape gliding away from my reach, and, strung to unnatural force by desperation, I pushed past her, and beat the window wildly with my hands, screaming—

'Save me—save me! Here, here, Monica, here! Cousin, cousin, oh! save me!'

Madame had seized my wrists, and a wild struggle was going on. A window-pane was broken, and I was shrieking to stop the carriage. The Frenchwoman looked black and haggard as a fury, as if she could have murdered me.

Nothing daunted—frantic—I screamed in my despair, seeing the carriage drive swiftly away-seeing Cousin Monica's bonnet, as she sat chatting with her *vis-à-vis*.

'Oh, oh, oh!' I shrieked, in vain and prolonged agony, as Madame, exerting her strength and matching her fury against my despair, forced me back in spite of my wild struggles, and pushed me sitting on the bed, where she held me fast, glaring in my face, and chuckling and panting over me.

I think I felt something of the despair of a lost spirit.

I remember the face of poor Mary Quince—its horror, its wonder—as she stood gaping into my face, over Madame's shoulder, and crying—

'What is it, Miss Maud? What is it, dear?' And turning fiercely on Madame, and striving to force her grasp from my wrists, 'Are you hurting the child? Let her go—let her go.'

'I *weel* let her go. War old fool are you, Mary Queence! She is mad, I think. She 'as lost hair head.'

'Oh, Mary, cry from the window. Stop the carriage!' I cried.

Mary looked out, but there was by this time, of course, nothing in sight.

'Why don't a you stop the carriage?' sneered Madame. 'Call a the coachman and the postilion. W'ere is the footman? Bah! *elle a le cerveau mal timbré.*'

'Oh, Mary, Mary, is it gone—is it gone? Is there nothing there?' cried I, rushing to the window; and turning to Madame, after a vain straining of my eyes, my face against the glass—

'Oh, cruel, cruel, wicked woman! why have you done this? What was it to you? Why do you persecute me? What good *can* you gain by my ruin?'

'Rueen! Par bleu! ma chère, you talk too fast. Did not a you see it, Mary Queence? It was the doctor's carriage, and Mrs. Jolks, and that eempudent faylow, young Jolks, staring up to the window, and Mademoiselle she come in soche shocking déshabille to show herself knocking at the window. 'Twould be very nice thing, Mary Queence, don't you think?'

I was sitting now on the bedside, crying in mere despair. I did not (are to dispute or to resist. Oh! why had rescue come so near, only to prove that it could not reach me? So I went on crying, with a clasping of my hands and turning up of my eyes, in incoherent prayer. I was not thinking of Madame, or of Mary Quince, or any other person, only babbling my anguish and despair helplessly in the ear of heaven.

'I did not think there was soche fool. Wat *enfant gaté*. My dear cheaile, wat a *can* you mean by soche strange language and conduct? War for should a you weesh to display yourself in the window in soche 'orrible déshabille to the people in the doctor's coach?'

'It was *Cousin Knollys*—Cousin Knollys. Oh, Cousin Knollys! You're gone—you're gone—you're *gone*!'

'And if it was Lady Knollys' coach, there was certainly a coachman and a footman; and whoever has the coach there was young gentlemen in it. If it was Lady Knollys' carriage it would 'av been *worse* than the doctor.'

'It is no matter—it is all over. Oh, Cousin Monica, your poor Maud—where is she to turn? Is there no help?'

That evening Madame visited me again, in one of her sedate and moral moods. She found me dejected and passive, as she had left me.

'I think, Maud, there is news; but I am not certain.'

I raised my head and looked at her wistfully.

'I think there is letter of *bad* news from the attorney in London.'

'Oh!' I said, in a tone which I am sure implied the absolute indifference of dejection.

'But, my dear Maud, if 't be so, we shall go at once, you and me, to join Meess Millicent in France. La belle France! You weel like so moche! We shall be so gay. You cannot imagine there are such naice girl there. They all love a me so moche, you will be delight.'

'How soon do we go?' I asked.

'I do not know. Bote I was to bring in a case of eau de cologne that came this evening, and he laid down a letter and say:— "The blow has descended, Madame! My niece must hold herself in readiness." I said, "For what, Monsieur?" *twice*, bote he did not answer. I am sure it is *un procès*. They 'av ruin him. Eh bien, my dear. I suppose we shall leave this triste place immediately. I am so rejoice. It appears to me *un cimetière*.'

'Yes, I should like to leave it,' I said, sitting up, with a great sigh and sunken eyes. It seemed to me that I had quite lost all sense of resentment towards Madame. A debility of feeling had supervened—the fatigue, I suppose, and prostration of the passions.

'I weel make excuse to go into his room again,' said Madame 'and I weel endeavor to learn something more from him, and I weel come back again to you in half an hour.'

She departed. But in half an hour did not return. I had a dull longing to leave Bartram-Haugh. For me, since the departure of poor Milly, it had grown like the haunt of evil spirits, and to escape on any terms from it was a blessing unspeakable.

Another half-hour passed, and another, and I grew insufferably feverish. I sent Mary Quince to the lobby to try and see Madame, who, I feared, was probably to-ing and fro-ing in and out of Uncle Silas's room.

Mary returned to tell me that she had seen old Wyat, who told her that she thought Madame had gone to her bed half an hour before.

CHAPTER LIX

A SUDDEN DEPARTURE

'Mary,' said I, 'I am miserably anxious to hear what Madame may have to tell; she knows the state I am in, and she would not like so much trouble as to look in at my door to say a word. Did you hear what she told me?'

'No, Miss Maud,' she answered, rising and drawing near.

'She thinks we are going to France immediately, and to leave this place perhaps for ever.'

'Heaven be praised for that, if it be so, Miss!' said Mary, with more energy than was common with her, 'for there is no luck about it, and I don't expect to see you ever well or happy in it.'

'You must take your candle, Mary, and make out her room, upstairs; I found it accidentally myself one evening.'

'But Wyat won't let us upstairs.'

'Don't mind her, Mary; I tell you to go. You must try. I can't sleep till we hear.'

'What direction is her room in, Miss?' asked Mary.

'Somewhere in *that* direction, Mary,' I answered, pointing. 'I cannot describe the turns; but I think you will find it if you go along the great passage to your left, on getting to the top of the stairs, till you come to the cross-galleries, and then turn to your left; and when you have passed four or perhaps five doors, you must be very near it, and I am sure she will hear if you call.'

'But will she tell me—she *is* such a rum un, Miss?' suggested Mary.

'Tell her exactly what I have said to you, and when she learns that you already know as much as I do, she may—unless, indeed, she wishes to torture me. If she won't, perhaps at least you can persuade her to come to me for a moment. Try, dear Mary; we can but fail.'

'Will you be very lonely, Miss, while I am away?' asked Mary, uneasily, as she lighted her candle.

'I can't help it, Mary. Go. I think if I heard we were going, I could almost get up and dance and sing. I can't bear this dreadful uncertainty any longer.'

'If old Wyat is outside, I'll come back and wait here a bit, till she's out o' the way,' said Mary; 'and, anyhow, I'll make all the haste I can. The drops and the sal-volatile is here, Miss, by your hand.'

And with an anxious look at me, she made her exit, softly, and did not immediately return, by which I concluded that she had found the way clear, and had gained the upper story without interruption.

This little anxiety ended, its subsidence was followed by a sense of loneliness, and with it, of vague insecurity, which increased at last to such a pitch, that I wondered at my own madness in sending my companion away; and at last my terrors so grew, that I drew back into the farthest corner of the bed, with my shoulders to the wall, and my bed-clothes huddled about me, with only a point open to peep at.

At last the door opened gently.

'Who's there?' I cried, in extremity of horror, expecting I knew not whom.

'Me, Miss,' whispered Mary Quince, to my unutterable relief; and with her candle flared, and a wild and pallid face, Mary Quince glided into the room, locking the door as she entered.

I do not know how it was, but I found myself holding Mary fast with both my hands as we stood side by side on the floor.

'Mary, you are terrified; for God's sake, what is the matter?' I cried.

'No, Miss,' said Mary, faintly, 'not much.'

'I see it in your face. What is it?'

'Let me sit down, Miss. I'll tell you what I saw; only I'm just a bit queerish.'

Mary sat down by my bed.

'Get in, Miss; you'll take cold. Get into bed, and I'll tell you. It is not much.'

I did get into bed, and gazing on Mary's frightened face, I felt a corresponding horror.

'For mercy's sake, Mary, say what it is?'

So again assuring me 'it was not much,' she gave me in a somewhat diffuse and tangled narrative the following facts:

On closing my door, she raised her candle above her head and surveyed the lobby, and seeing no one there she ascended the stairs swiftly. She passed along the great gallery to the left, and paused a moment at the cross gallery, and then recollected my directions clearly, and followed the passage to the right.

There are doors at each side, and she had forgotten to ask me at which Madame's was. She opened several. In one room she was frightened by a bat, which had very nearly put her candle out. She went on a little, paused, and began to lose heart in the dismal solitude, when on a sudden, a few doors farther on, she thought she heard Madame's voice.

She said that she knocked at the door, but receiving no answer, and hearing Madame still talking within, she opened it.

There was a candle on the chimneypiece, and another in a stable lantern near the window. Madame was conversing volubly on the hearth, with her face toward the window, the entire frame of which had been taken from its place: Dickon Hawkes, the Zamiel of the wooden leg, was supporting it with one hand, as it leaned imperfectly against the angle of the recess. There was a third figure standing, buttoned up in a surtout, with a bundle of tools under his arm, like a glazier, and, with a silent thrill of fear, she distinctly recognised the features as those of Dudley Ruthyn.

''Twas him, Miss, so sure as I sit here! Well, like that, they were as mute as mice; three pairs of eyes were on me. I don't know what made me so study like, but som'at told me I should not make as though I knew any but Madame; and so I made a courtesy, as well as I could, and I said, "Might I speak a word wi' ye, please, on the lobby?"

'Mr. Dudley was making belief be this time to look out at window, wi' his back to me, and I kept looking straight on Madame, and she said, "They're mendin' my broken glass, Mary," walking between them and me, and coming close up to me very quick; and so she marched me backward out o' the door, prating all the time.

'When we were on the lobby, she took my candle from my hand, shutting the door behind her, and she held the light a bit behind her ear; so 'twas full on my face, as she looked sharp into it; and, after a bit, she said again, in her queer lingo—there was two panes broke in her room, and men sent for to mend it.

'I was awful frightened when I saw Mr. Dudley, for I could not believe any such thing before, and I don't know how I could look her in the face as I did and not show it. I was as smooth and cool as yonder chimneypiece, and she has an awful evil eye to stan' against; but I never flinched, and I think she's puzzled, for as cunning as she is, whether I believe all she said, or knowed 'twas a pack o' stories. So I told her your message, and she said she had not heard another word since; but she did believe we had not many more days here, and would tell you if she heard tonight, when she brought his soup to your uncle, in half an hour's time.'

I asked her, as soon as I could speak, whether she was perfectly certain as to the fact that the man in the surtout was Dudley, and she made answer—

'I'd swear to him on that Bible, Miss.'

So far from any longer wishing Madame's return that night, I trembled at the idea of it. Who could tell who might enter the room with her when the door opened to admit her?

Dudley, so soon as he recovered the surprise, had turned about, evidently anxious to prevent recognition; Dickon Hawkes stood glowering at her. Both might have hope of escaping recognition in the imperfect light, for the candle on the chimneypiece was flaring in the air, and the light from the lantern fell in spots, and was confusing.

What could that ruffian, Hawkes, be doing in the house? Why was Dudley there? Could a more ominous combination be imagined? I puzzled my distracted head over all Mary Quince's details, but could make nothing of their occupation. I know of nothing so terrifying as this kind of perpetual puzzling over ominous problems.

You may imagine how the long hours of that night passed, and how my heart beat at every fancied sound outside my door.

But morning came, and with its light some reassurance. Early, Madame de la Rougierre made her appearance; she searched my eyes darkly and shrewdly, but made no allusion to Mary Quince's visit. Perhaps she expected some question from me, and, hearing none, thought it as well to leave the subject at rest.

She had merely come in to say that she had heard nothing since, but was now going to make my uncle's chocolate; and that so soon as her interview was ended she would see me again, and let me hear anything she should have gleaned.

In a little while a knock came to my door, and Mary Quince was ordered by old Wyat into my uncle's room. She returned flushed, in a huge fuss, to say that I was to be up and dressed for a journey in half an hour, and to go straight, when dressed, to my uncle's room.

It was good news; at the same time it was a shock. I was glad. I was stunned. I jumped out of bed, and set about my toilet with an energy quite new to me. Good Mary Quince was busily packing my boxes, and consulting as to what I should take with me, and what not.

Was Mary Quince to accompany me? He had not said a word on that point; and I feared from his silence she was to remain. There was comfort, however, in this—that the separation would not be for long; I felt confident of that; and I was about to join Milly, whom I loved better than I could have believed before our separation; but whatsoever the conditions might be, it was an indescribable relief to have done with Bartram-Haugh, and leave behind me its sinister lines of circuravallation, its haunted recesses, and the awful spectres that had lately appeared within its walls.

I stood too much in awe of my uncle to fail in presenting myself punctually at the close of the half-hour. I entered his sitting-room under the shadow of sour old Wyat's high-cauled cap; she closed the door behind me, and the conference commenced.

Madame de la Rougierre sat there, dressed and draped for a journey, and with a thick black lace veil on. My uncle rose, gaunt and venerable, and with a harsh and severe countenance. He did not offer his hand; he made me a kind of bow, more of repulsion than of respect, He remained in a standing position, supporting his crooked frame by his hand, which he leaned on a despatch-box; he glared on me steadily with his wild phosphoric eyes, from under the dark brows I have described to you, now corrugated in lines indescribably stern.

'You shall join my daughter at the Pension, in France. Madame de la Rougierre shall accompany you,' said my uncle, delivering his directions with the stern monotony and the measured pauses of a person dictating an important despatch to a secretary. 'Old Mrs. Quince shall follow with me, or, if alone, in a week. You shall pass to-night in London; to-morrow night you proceed thence to Dover, and cross by the mail-packet. You shall now sit down and write a letter to your cousin Monica Knollys, which I will first read and then despatch. To-morrow you shall write a note to Lady Knollys, from London, telling her how you have got over so much of your journey, and that you cannot write from Dover, as you must instantly start by the packet on reaching it; and that until my affairs are a little settled, you cannot write to her from France, as it is of high importance to my safety that no clue should exist as to our address. Intelligence, however, shall reach her through my attorneys, Archer and Sleigh, and I trust we shall soon return. You will, please, submit that latter note to Madame de la Rougierre, who has my directions to see that it contains no libels upon my character. Now, sit down.'

So, with those unpleasant words tingling in my ears, I obeyed.

'*Write*,' said he, when I was duly placed. 'You shall convey the substance of what I say in your own language. The imminent danger this morning announced of an execution—remember the word,' and he spelled it for me—'being put into this house either this afternoon or to-morrow, compels me to anticipate my plans, and despatch you for France this day. That you are starting with an attendant.' Here an uneasy movement from Madame, whose dignity was perhaps excited. 'An *attendant*,' he repeated, with a discordant emphasis;' and you can, if you please— but I don't *solicit* that justice—say that you have been as kindly treated here as my unfortunate circumstances would permit. That is all. You have just fifteen minutes to write. Begin.'

I wrote accordingly. My hysterical state had made me far less combative than I might have proved some months since, for there was much that was insulting as well as formidable in his manner. I completed my letter, however, to his satisfaction in the prescribed time; and he said, as he laid it and its envelope on the table—

'Please to remember that this lady is not your attendant only, but that she has authority to direct every detail respecting your journey, and will make all the necessary payments on the way. You will please, then, implicitly to comply with her directions. The carriage awaits you at the hall-door.'

Having thus spoken, with another grim bow, and 'I wish you a safe and pleasant journey,' he receded a step or two, and I, with an undefinable kind of melancholy, though also with a sense of relief, withdrew.

My letter, I afterwards found, reached Lady Knollys, accompanied by one from Uncle Silas, who said—'Dear Maud apprises me that she has written to tell you something of our movements. A sudden crisis in my miserable affairs compels a break-up as sudden here. Maud joins my daughter at the Pension, in France. I purposely omit the address, because I mean to reside in its vicinity until this storm shall have blown over; and as the consequences of some of my unhappy entanglements might pursue me even there, I must only for the present spare you the pain and trouble of keeping a secret. I am sure that for some little time you will excuse the girl's silence; in the meantime you shall hear of them, and perhaps circuitously, from me. Our dear Maud started this morning en route for her destination, very sorry, as am I, that she could not enjoy first a flying visit to Elverston, but in high spirits, notwithstanding, at the new life and sights before her.'

At the door my beloved old friend, Mary Quince, awaited me.

'Am I going with you, Miss Maud?'

I burst into tears and clasped her in my arms.

'I'm not,' said Mary, very sorrowfully; 'and I never was from you yet, Miss, since you wasn't the length of my arm.'

And kind old Mary began to cry with me.

'Bote you are coming in a few days, Mary Quince,' expostulated Madame. 'I wonder you are soche fool. What is two, three days? Bah I nonsense, girl.'

Another farewell to poor Mary Quince, quite bewildered at the suddenness of her bereavement. A serious and tremulous bow from our little old butler on the steps. Madame bawling through the open window to the driver to make good speed, and remember that we had but nineteen minutes to reach the station. Away we went. Old Crowle's iron *grille* rolled back before us. I looked on the receding landscape, the giant trees—the palatial, time—stained mansion. A strange conflict of feelings, sweet and bitter, rose and mingled in the reverie. Had I been too hard and suspicious with the inhabitants of that old house of my family? Was my uncle *justly* indignant? Was I ever again to know such pleasant rambles as some of those I had enjoyed with dear Millicent through the wild and beautiful woodlands I was leaving behind me? And there, with my latest glimpse of the front of Bartram-Haugh, I beheld dear old Mary Quince gazing after us. Again my tears flowed. I waved my handkerchief from the window; and now the park-wall hid all from view, and at a great pace, through the steep wooded glen, with the rocky and precipitous character of a ravine, we glided; and when the road next emerged, Bartram-Haugh was a misty mass of forest and chimneys, slope and hollow, and we within a few minutes of the station.

CHAPTER LX

THE JOURNEY

Waiting for the train, as we stood upon the platform, I looked back again toward the wooded uplands of Bartram; and far behind, the fine range of mountains, azure and soft in the distance, beyond which lay beloved old Knowl, and my lost father and mother, and the scenes of my childhood, never embittered except by the sibyl who sat beside me.

Under happier circumstances I should have been, at my then early age, quite wild with pleasurable excitement on entering London for the first time. But black Care sat by me, with her pale hand in mine: a voice of fear and warning, whose words I could not catch, was always in my ear. We drove through London, amid the glare of lamps, toward the West-end, and for a little while the sense of novelty and curiosity overcame my despondency, and I peeped eagerly from the window; while Madame, who was in high good-humour, spite of the fatigues of our long railway flight, screeched scraps of topographic information in my ear; for London was a picture-book in which she was well read.

'That is Euston Square, my dear—Russell Square. Here is Oxford Street—Haymarket. See, there is the Opera House—Hair Majesty's Theatre. See all the carriages waiting;' and so on, till we reached at length a little narrow street, which she told me was off Piccadilly, where we drew up before a private house, as it seemed to me—a family hotel—and I was glad to be at rest for the night.

Fatigued with the peculiar fatigue of railway travelling, dusty, a little chilly, with eyes aching and wearied, I ascended the stairs silently, our garrulous and bustling landlady leading the way, and telling her oft-told story of the house, its noble owner in old time, and how those fine drawing-rooms were taken every year during the Session by the Bishop of Rochet-on-Copeley, and at last into our double-bedded room.

I would fain have been alone, but I was too tired and dejected to care very much for anything.

At tea, Madame expanded in spirit, like a giant refreshed, and chattered and sang; and at last, seeing that I was nodding, advised my going to bed, while she ran across the street to see 'her dear old friend, Mademoiselle St. Eloi, who was sure to be up, and would be offended if she failed to make her ever so short a call.'

I cared little what she said, and was glad to be rid of her even for a short time, and was soon fast asleep.

I saw her, I know not how much later, poking about the room, like a figure in a dream, and taking off her things.

She had her breakfast in bed next morning, and I was, to my comfort, left to take mine in solitary possession of our sitting-room; where I began to wonder how little annoyance I had as yet suffered from her company, and began to speculate upon the chances of my making the journey with tolerable comfort.

Our hostess gave me five minutes of her valuable time. Her talk ran chiefly upon nuns and convents, and her old acquaintance with Madame; and it seemed to me that she had at one time driven a kind of trade, no doubt profitable enough, in escorting young ladies to establishments on the Continent; and although I did not then quite understand the tone in which she spoke to me, I often thought afterwards that Madame had represented me as a young person destined for the holy vocation of the veil.

When she was gone, I sat listlessly looking out of the window, and saw some chance equipages drive by, and now and then a fashionable pedestrian; and wondered if this quiet thoroughfare could really be one of the arteries so near the heart of the tumultuous capital.

I think my nervous vitality must have burnt very low just then, for I felt perfectly indifferent about all the novelty and world of wonders beyond, and should have hated to leave the dull tranquillity of my window for an excursion through the splendours of the unseen streets and palaces that surrounded me.

It was one o'clock before Madame joined me; and finding me in this dull mood, she did not press me to accompany her in her drive, no doubt well pleased to be rid of me.

After tea that evening, as we sat alone in our room, she entertained me with some very odd conversation—at the time unintelligible—but which acquired a tolerably distinct meaning from the events that followed. Two or three times that day Madame appeared to me on the point of saying something of grave import, as she scanned me with her bleak wicked stare.

It was a peculiarity of hers, that whenever she was pressed upon by an anxiety that really troubled her, her countenance did not look said or solicitous, as other people's would, but simply wicked. Her great gaunt mouth was compressed and drawn down firmly at the corners, and her eyes glared with a dismal scowl.

At last she said suddenly—

'Are you ever grateful, Maud?'

'I hope so, Madame,' I answered.

'And how do you show your gratitude? For instance, would a you do great deal for a person who would run *risque* for your sake?'

It struck me all at once that she was sounding me about poor Meg Hawkes, whose fidelity, notwithstanding the treason or cowardice of her lover, Tom Brice, I never doubted; and I grew at once wary and reserved.

'I know of no opportunity, thank Heaven, for any such service, Madame. How can anyone serve me at present, by themselves incurring danger? What do you mean?'

'Do you like, for example, to go to that French Pension? Would you not like better some other arrangement?'

'Of course there are other arrangements I should like better; but I see no use in talking of them; they are not to be,' I answered.

'What other arrangements do you mean, my dear cheaile?' enquired Madame. 'You mean, I suppose, you would like better to go to Lady Knollys?'

'My uncle does not choose it at present; and except with his consent nothing can be done!'

'He weel never consent, dear cheaile.'

'But he *has* consented—not immediately indeed, but in a short time, when his affairs are settled.'

'*Lanternes!* They will never be settle,' said Madame.

'At all events, for the present I am to go to France. Milly seems very happy, and I dare say I shall like it too. I am very glad to leave Bartram-Haugh, at all events.'

'But your uncle weel bring you back there,' said Madame, drily.

'It is doubtful whether he will ever return to Bartram himself,' I said.

'Ah!' said Madame, with a long-drawn nasal intonation, 'you theenk I hate you. You are quaite wrong, my dear Maud. I am, on the contrary, very much interested for you—I am, I assure you, dear a cheaile.'

And she laid her great hand, with joints misshapen by old chilblains, upon the back of mine. I looked up in her face. She was not smiling. On the contrary, her wide mouth was drawn down at the corners ruefully, as before, and she gazed on my face with a scowl from her abysmal eyes.

I used to think the flare of that irony which lighted her face so often immeasurably worse than any other expression she could assume; but this lack-lustre stare and dismal collapse of feature was more wicked still.

'Suppose I should bring you to Lady Knollys, and place you in her charge, what would a you do then for poor Madame?' said this dark spectre.

I was inwardly startled at these words. I looked into her unsearchable face, but could draw thence nothing but fear. Had she made the same overture only two days since, I think I would have offered her half my fortune. But circumstances were altered. I was no longer in the panic of despair. The lesson I had received from Tom Brice was fresh in my mind, and my profound distrust of her was uppermost. I saw before me only a tempter and betrayer, and said—

'Do you mean to imply, Madame, that my guardian is not to be trusted, and that I ought to make my escape from him, and that you are really willing to aid me in doing so?'

This, you see, was turning the tables upon her. I looked her steadily in the face as I spoke. She returned my gaze with a strange stare and a gape, which haunted me long after; and it seemed as we sat in utter silence that each was rather horribly fascinated by the other's gaze.

At last she shut her mouth sternly, and eyed me with a more determined and meaning scowl, and then said in a low tone—

'I believe, Maud, that you are a cunning and wicked little thing.'

'Wisdom is not cunning, Madame; nor is it wicked to ask your meaning in explicit language,' I replied.

'And so, you clever cheaile, we two sit here, playing at a game of chess, over this little table, to decide which shall destroy the other—is it not so?'

'I will not allow you to destroy me,' I retorted, with a sudden flash.

Madame stood up, and rubbed her mouth with her open hand. She looked to me like some evil being seen in a dream. I was frightened.

'You are going to hurt me!' I ejaculated, scarce knowing what I said.

'If I were, you deserve it. You are very *malicious*, ma chère: or, it may be, only very stupid.'

A knock came to the door.

'Come in,' I cried, with a glad sense of relief.

A maid entered.

'A letter, please, 'm,' she said, handing it to me.

'For *me*,' snarled Madame, snatching it.

I had seen my uncle's hand, and the Feltram post-mark.

Madame broke the seal, and read. It seemed but a word, for she turned it about after the first momentary glance, and examined the interior of the envelope, and then returned to the line she had already read.

She folded the letter again, drawing her nails in a sharp pinch along the creases, as she stared in a blank, hesitating way at me.

'You are stupid little ingrate, I am employ by Monsieur Ruthyn, and of course I am faithful to my employer. I do not want to talk to you. *There*, you may read that.'

She jerked the letter before me on the table. It contained but these words:—

Bartram-Haugh:
'*30th January, 1845.*

'DEAR MADAME,

'Be so good as to take the half-past eight o'clock train to *Dover* to-night. Beds are prepared.—Yours very truly,

SILAS RUTHYN.'

I cannot say what it was in this short advice that struck me with fear. Was it the thick line beneath the word 'Dover,' that was so uncalled for, and gave me a faint but terrible sense of something preconcerted?

I said to Madame—

'Why is "Dover" underlined?'

'I do not know, little fool, no more than you. How can I tell what is passing in your oncle's head when he make that a mark?'

'Has it not a meaning, Madame?'

'How can you talk like that?' she answered, more in her old way. 'You are either mocking of me, or you are becoming truly a fool!'

She rang the bell, called for our bill, saw our hostess; while I made a few hasty preparations in my room.

'You need not look after the trunks—they will follow us all right. Let us go, cheaile—we 'av half an hour only to reach the train.'

No one ever fussed like Madame when occasion offered. There was a cab at the door, into which she hurried me. I assumed that she would give all needful directions, and leaned back, very weary and sleepy already, though it was so early, listening to her farewell screamed from the cab-step, and seeing her black cloak flitting and flapping this way and that, like the wings of a raven disturbed over its prey.

In she got, and away we drove through a glare of lamps, and shop-windows, still open; gas everywhere, and cabs, busses, and carriages, still thundering through the streets. I was too tired and too depressed to look at those things. Madame, on the contrary, had her head out of the window till we reached the station.

'Where are the rest of the boxes?' I asked, as Madame placed me in charge of her box and my bag in the office of the terminus.

'They will follow with Boots in another cab, and will come safe with us in this train. Mind those two, we weel bring in the carriage with us.'

So into a carriage we got; in came Madame's box and my bag; Madame stood at the door, and, I think, frightened away intending passengers, by her size and shrillness.

At last the bell rang her into her place, the door clapt, the whistle sounded, and we were off.

CHAPTER LXI

OUR BED-CHAMBER

I had passed a miserable night, and, indeed, for many nights had not had my due proportion of sleep. Still I sometimes fancy that I may have swallowed something in my tea that helped to make me so irresistibly drowsy. It was a very dark night— no moon, and the stars soon hid by the gathering clouds. Madame sat silent, and ruminating in her place, with her rugs about her. I, in my corner similarly enveloped, tried to keep awake. Madame plainly thought I was asleep already, for she stole a leather flask from her pocket, and applied it to her lips, causing an aroma of brandy.

But it was vain struggling against the influence that was stealing over me, and I was soon in a profound and dreamless slumber.

Madame awoke me at last, in a huge fuss. She had got out all our things and hurried them away to a close carriage which was awaiting us. It was still dark and starless. We got along the platform, I half asleep, the porter carrying our rugs, by the glare of a pair of gas-jets in the wall, and out by a small door at the end.

I remember that Madame, contrary to her wont, gave the man some money. By the puzzling light of the carriage-lamps we got in and took our seats.

'Go on,' screamed Madame, and drew up the window with a great chuck; and we were enclosed in darkness and silence, the most favourable conditions for thought.

My sleep had not restored me as it might; I felt feverish, fatigued, and still very drowsy, though unable to sleep as I had done.

I dozed by fits and starts, and lay awake, or half-awake, sometimes, not think-ing but in a way imagining what kind of a place Dover would be; but too tired and listless to ask Madame any questions, and merely seeing the hedges, grey in the lamplight, glide backward into darkness, as I leaned back.

We turned off the main road, at right angles, and drew up.

'Get down and poosh it, it is open,' screamed Madame from the window.

A gate, I suppose, was thus passed; for when we resumed our brisk trot, Madame bawled across the carriage—

'We are now in the 'otel grounds.'

And so all again was darkness and silence, and I fell into another doze, from which, on waking, I found that we had come to a standstill, and Madame was standing on the low step of an open door, paying the driver. She, herself, pulled her box and the bag in. I was too tired to care what had become of the rest of our luggage.

I descended, glancing to the right and left, but there was nothing visible but a patch of light from the lamps on a paved ground and on the wall.

We stepped into the hall or vestibule, and Madame shut the door, and I thought I heard the key turn in it. We were in total darkness.

'Where are the lights, Madame—where are the people?' I asked, more awake than I had been.

''Tis pass three o'clock, cheaile, bote there is always light here.' She was groping at the side; and in a moment more lighted a lucifer match, and so a bedroom candle.

We were in a flagged lobby, under an archway at the right, and at the left of which opened long flagged passages, lost in darkness, a winding stair, barely wide enough to admit Madame, dragging her box, led upward under a doorway, in a corner at the right.

'Come, dear cheaile, take a your bag; don't mind the rugs, they are safe enough.'

'But where are we to go? There is no one!' I said, looking round in wonder. It certainly was a strange reception at an hotel.

'Never mind, my dear cheaile. They know me here, and I have always the same room ready when I write for it. Follow me quaitely.'

So she mounted, carrying the candle. The stair was steep, and the march long. We halted at the second landing, and entered a gaunt, grimy passage. All the way up we had not heard a single sound of life, nor seen a human being, nor so much as passed a gaslight.

'Viola! here 'tis, my dear old room. Enter, dearest Maud.'

And so I did. The room was large and lofty, but shabby and dismal. There was a tall four-post bed, with its foot beside the window, hung with dark-green curtains, of some plush or velvet texture, that looked like a dusty pall. The remaining furniture was scant and old, and a ravelled square of threadbare carpet covered a patch of floor at the bedside. The room was grim and large, and had a cold, vault-like atmosphere, as if long uninhabited; but there were cinders in the grate and under it. The imperfect light of our mutton-fat candle made all this look still more comfortless.

Madame placed the candle on the chimneypiece, locked the door, and put the key in her pocket.

'I always do so in *'otel*,' said she, with a wink at me.

And, then with a long 'ha!' expressive of fatigue and relief, she threw herself into a chair.

'So 'ere we are at last!' said she 'I'm glad. *There's* your bed, Maud. *Mine* is in the dressing-room.'

She took the candle, and I went in with her. A shabby pressbed, a chair, and table were all its furniture; it was rather a closet than a dressing-room, and had no door except that through which we had entered. So we returned, and very tired, wondering, I sat down on the side of my bed and yawned.

'I hope they will call us in time for the packet,' I said.

'Oh yes, they never fail,' she answered, looking steadfastly on her box, which she was diligently uncording.

Uninviting as was my bed, I was longing to lie down in it; and having made those ablutions which our journey rendered necessary, I at length lay down, having first religiously stuck my talismanic pin, with the head of sealing-wax, into the bolster.

Nothing escaped the restless eye of Madame.

'Wat is that, dear cheaile?' she enquired, drawing near and scrutinising the head of the gipsy charm, which showed like a little ladybird newly lighted on the sheet.

'Nothing—a charm—folly. Pray, Madame, allow me to go to sleep.'

So, with another look and a little twiddle between her finger and thumb, she seemed satisfied; but, unhappily for me, she did not seem at all sleepy. She busied herself in unpacking and displaying over the back of the chair a whole series of London purchases—silk dresses, a shawl, a sort of lace demi-coiffure then in vogue, and a variety of other articles.

The vainest and most slammakin of women—the merest slut at home, a milliner's lay figure out of doors—she had one square foot of looking-glass upon the chimneypiece, and therein tried effects, and conjured up grotesque simpers upon her sinister and weary face.

I knew that the sure way to prolong this worry was to express my uneasiness under it, so I bore it as quietly as I could; and at last fell fast asleep with the gaunt image of Madame, with a festoon of grey silk with a cerise stripe, pinched up in her finger and thumb, and smiling over her shoulder across it into the little shaving-glass that stood on the chimney.

I awoke suddenly in the morning, and sat up in my bed, having for a moment forgotten all about our travelling. A moment more, however, brought all back again.

'Are we in time, Madame?'

'For the packet?' she enquired, with one of her charming smiles, and cutting a caper on the floor. 'To be sure; you don't suppose they would forget. We have two hours yet to wait.'

'Can we see the sea from the window?'

No, dearest cheaile; you will see't time enough.

'I'd like to get up,' I said.

'Time enough, my dear Maud; you are fatigue; are you sure you feel quite well?'

'Well enough to get up; I should be better, I think, out of bed.'

'There is no hurry, you know; you need not even go by the next packet. Your uncle, he tell me, I may use my discretion.'

'Is there any water?'

'They will bring some.'

'Please, Madame, ring the bell.'

She pulled it with alacrity. I afterwards learnt that it did not ring.

'What has become of my gipsy pin?' I demanded, with an unaccountable sinking of the heart.

'Oh! the little pin with the red top? maybe it 'as fall on the ground; we weel find when you get up.'

I suspected that she had taken it merely to spite me. It would have been quite the thing she would have liked. I cannot describe to you how the loss of this little 'charm' depressed and excited me. I searched the bed; I turned over all the bed-clothes; I searched in and outside; at last I gave up.

'How odious!' I cried; 'somebody has stolen it merely to vex me.'

And, like a fool as I was, I threw myself on my face on the bed and wept, partly in anger, partly in dismay.

After a time, however, this blew over. I had a hope of recovering it. If Madame had stolen it, it would turn up yet. But in the meantime its disappearance troubled me like an omen.

'I am afraid, my dear cheaile, you are not very well. It is really very odd you should make such fuss about a pin! Nobody would believe! Do you not theenk it would be a good plan to take a your breakfast in your bed?'

She continued to urge this point for some time. At last, however, having by this time quite recovered my self-command, and resolved to preserve ostensibly fair terms with Madame, who could contribute so essentially to make me wretched during the rest of my journey, and possibly to prejudice me very seriously on my arrival, I said quietly—

'Well, Madame, I know it is very silly; but I had kept that foolish little pin so long and so carefully, that I had grown quite fond of it; but I suppose it is lost, and I must content myself, though I cannot laugh as you do. So I will get up now, and dress.'

'I think you will do well to get all the repose you can,' answered Madame; 'but as you please,' she added, observing that I was getting up.

So soon as I had got some of my things on, I said—

'Is there a pretty view from the window?'

'No,' said Madame.

I looked out and saw a dreary quadrangle of cut stone, in one side of which my window was placed. As I looked a dream rose up before me.

'This hotel,' I said, in a puzzled way. 'Is it a hotel? Why this is just like—it is the inner court of Bartram-Haugh!'

Madame clapped her large hands together, made a fantastic *chassé* on the floor, burst into a great nasal laugh like the scream of a parrot, and then said—

'Well, dearest Maud, is not clever trick?

I was so utterly confounded that I could only stare about me in stupid silence, a spectacle which renewed Madame's peals of laughter.

'We are at Bartram-Haugh!' I repeated, in utter consternation.'How was this done?'

I had no reply but shrieks of laughter, and one of those Walpurgis dances in which she excelled.

'It is a mistake—is it? *What* is it?

'All a mistake, of course. Bartram-Haugh, it is so like Dover, as all philosophers know.'

I sat down in total silence, looking out into the deep and dark enclosure, and trying to comprehend the reality and the meaning of all this.

'Well, Madame, I suppose you will be able to satisfy my uncle of your fidelity and intelligence. But to me it seems that his money has been ill-sent, and his directions anything but well observed.'

'Ah, ha! Never mind; I think he will forgive me,' laughed Madame.

Her tone frightened me. I began to think, with a vague but overpowering sense of danger, that she had acted under the Machiavellian directions of her superior.

'You have brought me back, then, by my uncle's orders?'

'Did I say so?'

'No; but what you have said can have no other meaning, though I can't believe it. And why have I been brought here? What is the object of all this duplicity and trick. I will know. It is not possible that my uncle, a gentleman and a kinsman, can be privy to so disreputable a manoeuvre.'

'First you will eat your breakfast, dear Maud next you can tell your story to your uncle, Monsieur Ruthyn and then you shall hear what he thinks of my so terrible misconduct. What nonsense, cheaile! Can you not think how many things may 'appen to change a your uncle's plans? Is he not in danger to be arrest? Bah! You are cheaile still; you cannot have intelligence more than a cheaile. Dress yourself, and I will order breakfast.'

I could not comprehend the strategy which had been practised on me. Why had I been so shamelessly deceived? If it were decided that I should remain here, for what imaginable reason had I been sent so far on my journey to France? Why had I been conveyed back with such mystery? Why was I removed to this uncomfortable and desolate room, on the same floor with the apartment in which Charke had met his death, and with no window commanding the front of the house, and no view but the deep and weed-choked court, that looked like a deserted churchyard in a city?

'I suppose I may go to my own room?' I said.

'Not to-day, my dear cheaile, for it was all disarrange when we go 'way; 'twill be ready again in two three days.'

'Where is Mary Quince?' I asked.

'Mary Quince I—she has follow us to France,' said Madame, making what in Ireland they call a bull.

'They are not sure where they will go or what will do for day or two more. I will go and get breakfast. Adieu for a moment.'

Madame was out of the door as she said this, and I thought I heard the key turn in the lock.

CHAPTER LXII

A WELL-KNOWN FACE
LOOKS IN

You who have never experienced it can have no idea how angry and frightened you become under the sinister insult of being locked into a room, as on trying the door I found I was.

The key was in the lock; I could see it through the hole. I called after Madame, I shook at the solid oak-door, beat upon it with my hands, kicked it—but all to no purpose.

I rushed into the next room, forgetting—if indeed I had observed it, that there was no door from it upon the gallery. I turned round in an angry and dismayed perplexity, and, like prisoners in romances, examined the windows.

I was shocked and affrighted on discovering in reality what they occasionally find—a series of iron bars crossing the window! They were firmly secured in the oak woodwork of the window-frame, and each window was, besides, so compactly screwed down that it could not open. This bedroom was converted into a prison. A momentary hope flashed on me—perhaps all the windows were secured alike! But it was no such thing: these gaol-like precautions were confined to the windows to which I had access.

For a few minutes I felt quite distracted; but I bethought me that I must now, if ever, control my terrors and exert whatever faculties I possessed.

I stood upon a chair and examined the oak-work. I thought I detected marks of new chiselling here and there. The screws, too, looked new; and they and the scars on the woodwork were freshly smeared over with some coloured stuff by way of disguise.

While I was making these observations, I heard the key stealthily stirred. I suspect that Madame wished to surprise me. Her approaching step, indeed, was seldom audible; she had the soft tread of the feline tribe.

I was standing in the centre of the room confronting her when she entered.

'Why did you lock the door, Madame?' I demanded.

She slipped in suddenly with an insidious smirk, and locked the door hastily.

'Hish!' whispered Madame, raising her broad palm; and then screwing in her cheeks, she made an ogle over her shoulder in the direction of the passage.

'Hish! be quaite, cheaile, weel you, and I weel tale you everything presently.'

She paused, with her car laid to the door.

'Now I can speak, ma chère; I weel tale a you there is bailiff in the house, two, three, four soche impertinent fallows! They have another as bad as themselve to make a leest of the furniture: we most keep them out of these rooms, dear Maud.'

'You left the key in the door on the outside,' I retorted;' that was not to keep them out, but me in, Madame.'

'*Deed* I leave the key in the door?' ejaculated Madame, with both hands raised, and such a genuine look of consternation as for a moment shook me.

It was the nature of this woman's deceptions that they often puzzled though they seldom convinced me.

'I re-ally think, Maud, all those so frequent changes and excite-ments they weel overturn my poor head.'

'And the windows are secured with iron bars—what are they for?' I whispered sternly, pointing with my finger at these grim securities.

'That is for more a than forty years, when Sir Phileep Aylmer was to reside here, and had this room for his children's nursery, and was afraid they should fall out.'

'But if you look you will find these bars have been put here very recently the screws and marks are quite new.'

'*Eendeed!*' ejaculated Madame, with prolonged emphasis, in precisely the same consternation. 'Why, my dear, they told a me downstairs what I have tell a you, when I ask the reason! Late a me see.'

And Madame mounted on a chair, and made her scrutiny with much curiosity, but could not agree with me as to the very recent date of the carpentry.

There is nothing, I think, so exasperating as that sort of falsehood which affects not to see what is quite palpable.

'Do you mean to say, Madame, that you really think those chisellings and screws are forty years old?'

'How can I tell, cheaile? What does signify whether it is forty or only fourteen years? Bah! we av other theeng to theenk about. Those villain men! I am glad to see bar and bolt, and lock and key, at least, to our room, to keep soche faylows out!'

At that moment a knock came to the door, and Madame's nasal 'in moment' answered promptly, and she opened the door, stealthily popping out her head.

'Oh, that is all right; go you long, no ting more, go way.'

'Who's there?' I cried.

'Hold a your tongue,' said Madame imperiously to the visitor, whose voice I fancied I recognised—'*go* way.'

Out slipped Madame again, locking the door; but this time she returned immediately, bearing a tray with breakfast.

I think she fancied that I would perhaps attempt to break away and escape; but I had no such thought at that moment. She hastily set down the tray on the floor at the threshold, locking the door as before.

My share of breakfast was a little tea; but Madame's digestion was seldom disturbed by her sympathies, and she ate voraciously. During this process there was a silence unusual in her company; but when her meal was ended she proposed a reconnaissance, professing much uncertainty as to whether my Uncle had been arrested or not.

'And in case the poor old gentleman be poot in what you call stone jug, where are *we* to go my dear Maud—to Knowl or to Elverston? You must direct.'

And so she disappeared, turning the key in the door as before. It was an old custom of hers, locking herself in her room, and leaving the key in the lock; and the habit prevailed, for she left it there again.

With a heavy heart I completed my simple toilet, wondering all the while how much of Madame's story might be false and how much, if any, true. Then I looked out upon the dingy courtyard below, in its deep damp shadow, and thought, 'How could an assassin have scaled that height in safety, and entered so noiselessly as not to awaken the slumbering gamester?' Then there were the iron bars across my window. What a fool had I been to object to that security!

I was labouring hard to reassure myself, and keep all ghastly suspicions at arm's length, But I wished that my room had been to the front of the house, with some view less dismal.

Lost in these ruminations of fear, as I stood at the window I was startled by the sound of a sharp tread on the lobby, and by the key turning in the lock of my door.

In a panic I sprang back into the corner, and stood with my eyes fixed upon the door. It opened a little, and the black head of Meg Hawkes was introduced.

'Oh, Meg!' I cried; 'thank God!'

'I guessed 'twas you, Miss Maud. I am feared, Miss.'

The miller's daughter was pale, and her eyes, I thought, were red and swollen.

'Oh, Meg! for God's sake, what is it all?'

'I darn't come in. The old un's gone down, and locked the cross-door, and left me to watch. They think I care nout about ye, no more nor themselves. I donna know all, but summat more nor her. They tell her nout, she's so gi'n to drink; they say she's not safe, an' awful quarrelsome. I hear a deal when fayther and Master Dudley be a-talkin' in the mill. They think, comin' in an' out, I don't mind; but I put one think an' t'other together. An' don't ye eat nor drink nout here, Miss; hide away this; it's black enough, but wholesome anyhow!' and she slipt a piece of a coarse loaf from under her apron. '*Hide* it mind. Drink nout but the water in the jug there—it's clean spring.'

'Oh, Meg! Oh, Meg! I know what you mean,' said I, faintly.

'Ay, Miss, I'm feared they'll try it; they'll try to make away wi' ye somehow. I'm goin' to your friends arter dark; I darn't try it no sooner. I'll git awa to Ellerston, to your lady-cousin, and I'll bring 'em back wi' me in a rin; so keep a good hairt, lass. Meg Hawkes will stan' to ye. Ye were better to me than fayther and mother, and a';' and she clasped me round the waist, and buried her head in my dress; 'an I'll gie my life for ye, darling, and if they hurt ye I'll kill myself.'

She recovered her sterner mood quickly—

'Not a word, lass,' she said, in her old tone. 'Don't ye try to git away—they'll *kill* ye—ye *can't* do't. Leave a' to me. It won't be, whatever it is, till two or three o'clock in the morning. I'll ha'e them a' here long afore; so keep a brave heart—there's a darling.'

I suppose she heard, or fancied she heard, a step approaching, for she said—'Hish!'

Her pale wild face vanished, the door shut quickly and softly, and the key turned again in the lock.

Meg, in her rude way, had spoken softly—almost under her breath; but no prophecy shrieked by the Pythoness ever thundered so madly in the ears of the hearer. I dare say that Meg fancied I was marvellously little moved by her words. I felt my gaze grow intense, and my flesh and bones literally freeze. She did not know that every word she spoke seemed to burst like a blaze in my brain. She had delivered her frightful warning, and told her story coarsely and bluntly, which, in effect, means distinctly and concisely; and, I dare say, the announcement so made, like a quick bold incision in surgery, was more tolerable than the slow imperfect mangling, which falters and recedes and equivocates with torture. Madame was long away. I sat down at the window, and tried to appreciate my dreadful situation. I was stupid—the imagery was all frightful; but I beheld it as we sometimes see horrors—heads cut off and houses burnt—in a dream, and without the corresponding emotions. It did not seem as if all this were really happening to me. I remember sitting at the window, and looking and blinking at the opposite side of the building, like a person unable but striving to see an object distinctly, and every minute pressing my hand to the side of my head and saying—

'Oh, it won't be—it won't be—Oh no!—never!—it could not be!' And in this stunned state Madame found me on her return.

But the valley of the shadow of death has its varieties of dread. The 'horror of great darkness' is disturbed by voices and illumed by sights. There are periods of incapacity and collapse, followed by paroxysms of active terror, Thus in my journey during those long hours I found it—agonies subsiding into lethargies, and these breaking again into frenzy. I sometimes wonder how I carried my reason safely through the ordeal.

Madame locked the door, and amused herself with her own business, without minding me, humming little nasal snatches of French airs, as she smirked on her silken purchases displayed in the daylight. Suddenly it struck me that it was very dark, considering how early it was. I looked at my watch; it seemed to me a great effort of concentration to understand it. Four o'clock, it said. Four o'clock! It would be dark at five—*night* in one hour!

'Madame what o'clock is it? Is it evening?' I cried with my hand to my forehead, like a person puzzled.

'Two three minutes past four. It bad five minutes to four when I came upstairs,' answered she, without interrupting her examination of a piece of darned lace which she was holding close to her eyes at the window.

'Oh, Madame! *Madame!* I'm frightened,' cried I, with a wild and piteous voice, grasping her arm, and looking up, as shipwrecked people may their last to heaven, into her inexorable eyes. Madame looked frightened too, I thought, as she stared into my face. At last she said, rather angrily, and shaking her arm loose—

'What you mean, cheaile?'

'Oh save me, Madame!—oh save me!—oh save me, Madame!' I pleaded, with the wild monotony of perfect terror, grasping and clinging to her dress, and looking up, with an agonised face, into the eyes of that shadowy Atropos.

'Save a you, indeed! Save! What *niaiserie!*

'Oh, Madame! Oh, *dear* Madame! for God's sake, only get me away—get me from this, and I'll do everything you ask me all my life—I will—*indeed*, Madame, I will! Oh save me! save me! *save* me!'

I was clinging to Madame as to my guardian angel in my agony.

'And who told you, cheaile, you are in any danger?' demanded Madame, looking down on me with a black and witch-like stare.

'I am, Madame—I am—in great danger! Oh, Madame, think of me—take pity on me I have none to help me—there is no one but God and you!'

Madame all this time viewed me with the same dismal stare, like a sorceress reading futurity in my face.

'Well, maybe you are—how can I tell? Maybe your uncle is mad—maybe you are mad. You have been my enemy always—why should I care?'

Again I burst into wild entreaty, and, clasping her fast, poured forth my supplications with the bitterness of death.

'I have no confidence in you, little Maud; you are little rogue—petite traitresse! Reflect, if you can, how you 'av always treat Madame. You 'av attempt to ruin me—you conspire with the bad domestics at Knowl to destroy me—and you expect me here to take a your part! You would never listen to me—you 'ad no mercy for me—you join to hunt me away from your house like wolf. Well, what you expect to find me now? *Bah!*'

This terrific 'Bah!' with a long nasal yell of scorn, rang in my cars like a clap of thunder.

'I say you are mad, petite insolente, to suppose I should care for you more than the poor hare it will care for the hound—more than the bird who has escape will love the oiseleur. I do not care—I ought not care. It is your turn to suffer. Lie down on your bed there, and suffer quaitely.'

CHAPTER LXIII

SPICED CLARET

I did not lie down; but I despaired. I walked round and round the room, wringing my hands in utter distraction. I threw myself at the bedside on my knees. I could not pray; I could only shiver and moan, with hands clasped, and eyes of horror turned up to heaven. I think Madame was, in her malignant way, perplexed. That some evil was intended me I am sure she was persuaded; but I dare say Meg Hawkes bad said rightly in telling me that she was not fully in their secrets.

The first paroxysm of despair subsided into another state. All at once my mind was filled with the idea of Meg Hawkes, her enterprise, and my chances of escape. There is one point at which the road to Elverston makes a short ascent: there is a sudden curve there, two great ash-trees, with a roadside stile between, at the right side, covered with ivy. Driving back and forward, I did not recollect having particularly remarked this point in the highway; but now it was before me, in the thin light of the thinnest segment of moon, and the figure of Meg Hawkes, her back toward me, always ascending towards Elverston. It was constantly the same picture—the same motion without progress—the same dreadful suspense and impatience.

I was now sitting on the side of the bed, looking wistfully across the room. When I did not see Meg Hawkes, I beheld Madame darkly eyeing first one then another point of the chamber, evidently puzzling over some problem, and in one of her most savage moods—sometimes muttering to herself, sometimes protruding, and sometimes screwing up her great mouth.

She went into her own room, where she remained, I think, nearly ten minutes, and on her return there was that in the flash of her eyes, the glow of her face, and the peculiar fragrance that surrounded her, that showed she had been partaking of her favourite restorative.

I had not moved since she left my room.

She paused about the middle of the floor, and looked at me with what I can only describe as her wild-beast stare.

'You are a very secrete family, you Ruthyns—you are so coning. I hate the coning people. By my faith, I weel see Mr. Silas Ruthyn, and ask wat he mean. I heard him tell old Wyat that Mr. Dudley is gone away to-night. He shall tell me everything, or else I weel make echec et mat aussi vrai que je vis.'

Madame's words had hardly ceased, when I was again watching Meg Hawkes on the steep road, mounting, but never reaching, the top of the acclivity, on the way to Elverston, and mentally praying that she might be brought safely there. Vain prayer of an agonised heart! Meg's journey was already frustrated: she was not to reach Elverston in time.

Madame revisited her apartment, and returned, not, I think, improved in temper. She walked about the room, hustling the scanty furniture hither and thither as she encountered it. She kicked her empty box out of her way, with a horrid crash, and a curse in French. She strode and swaggered round the room, muttering all the way, and turning the corners of her course with a furious whisk. At last, out of the door she went. I think she fancied she had not been sufficiently take into confidence as to what was intended for me.

It was now growing late, and yet no succour! I was seized, I remember, with a dreadful icy shivering.

I was listening for signals of deliverance. At every distant sound, half stifled with a palpitation, these sounds piercing my ear with a horrible and exaggerated distinctness—'Oh Meg!—Oh cousin Monica!—Oh come! Oh Heaven, have mercy!—Lord, have mercy!' I thought I heard a roaring and jangle of voices. Perhaps it came from Uncle Silas's room. It might be the tipsy violence of Madame. It might—merciful Heaven!—be the arrival of friends. I started to my feet; I listened, quivering with attention. Was it in my brain?-was it real? I was at the door, and it seemed to open of itself. Madame had forgotten to lock it; she was losing her head a little by this time. The key stood in the gallery door beyond; it too, was open. I fled wildly. There was a subsiding sound of voices in my uncle's room. I was, I know not how, on the lobby at the great stair—head outside my uncle's apartment. My hand was on the banisters, my foot on the first step, when below me and against the faint light that glimmered through the great window on the landing I saw a bulky human form ascending, and a voice said 'Hush!' I staggered back, and at that instant fancied, with a thrill of conviction, I heard Lady Knollys's voice in Uncle Silas' room.

I don't know how I entered the room; I was there like a ghost. I was frightened at my own state.

Lady Knollys was not there—no one but Madame and my guardian.

I can never forget the look that Uncle Silas fixed on me as he cowered, seemingly as appalled as I.

I think I must have looked like a phantom newly risen from the grave.

'What's that?—where do you come from?' whispered he.

'Death! death!' was my whispered answer, as I froze with terror where I stood.

'What does she mean?—what does all this mean?' said Uncle Silas, recovering wonderfully, and turning with a withering sneer on Madame, 'Do you think it right to disobey my plain directions, and let her run about the house at this hour?'

'Death! death! Oh, pray to God for you and me!' I whispered in the same dreadful tones.

My uncle stared strangely at me again; and after several horrible seconds, in which he seemed to have recovered himself, he said, sternly and coolly—

'You give too much place to your imagination, niece. Your spirits are in an odd state—you ought to have advice.'

'Oh, uncle, pity me! Oh, uncle, you are good! you're kind; you're kind when you think. You could not—you could not—could not! Oh, think of your brother that was always so good to you! He sees me here. He sees us both. Oh, save me, uncle save me I—and I'll give up everything to you. I'll pray to God to bless you—I'll never forget your goodness and mercy. But don't keep me in doubt. If I'm to go, oh, for God's sake, shoot me now!'

'You were always odd, niece; I begin to fear you are insane,' he replied, in the same stem icy tone.

'Oh, uncle—oh!—am I? Am I *mad*?'

'I hope not; but you'll conduct yourself like a sane person if you wish to enjoy the privileges of one.'

Then, with his finger pointing at me, he turned to Madame, and said, in a tone of suppressed ferocity—

'What's the meaning of this?—why is she here?'

Madame was gabbling volubly, but to me it was only a shrilly noise. My whole soul was concentrated in my uncle, the arbiter of my life, before whom I stood in the wildest agony of supplication.

That night was dreadful. The people I saw dizzily, made of smoke or shining vapour, smiling or frowning, I could have passed my hand through them. They were evil spirits.

'There's no ill intended you; by— there's none,' said my uncle, for the first time violently agitated. 'Madame told you why we've changed your room. You told her about the bailiffs, did not you?' with a stamp of fury he demanded of Madame, whose nasal roullades of talk were running on like a accompaniment all the time. She had told me indeed only a few hours since, and now it sounded to me like the echo of something heard a month ago or more.

'You can't go about the house, d—n it, with bailiffs in occupation. There now—there's the whole thing. Get to your room, Maud, and don't vex me. There's a good girl.'

He was trying to smile as he spoke these last words, and, with quavering soft tones, to quiet me; but the old scowl was there, the smile was corpse-like and contorted, and the softness of his tones was more dreadful than another man's ferocity.

'There, Madame, she'll go quite gently, and you can call if you want help. Don't let it happen again.'

'Come, Maud,' said Madame, encircling but not hurting my arm with her grip; 'let us go, my friend.'

I did go, you will wonder, as well you may—as you may wonder at the docility with which strong men walk through the press-room to the drop, and thank the people of the prison for their civility when they bid them good-bye, and facilitate the fixing of the rope and adjusting of the cap. Have you never wondered that they don't make a last battle for life with the unscrupulous energy of terror, instead of surrendering it so gently in cold blood, on a silent calculation, the arithmetic of despair?

I went upstairs with Madame like a somnambulist. I rather quickened my step as I drew near my room. I went in, and stood a phantom at the window, looking into the dark quadrangle. A thin glimmering crescent hung in the frosty sky, and all heaven was strewn with stars. Over the steep roof at the other side spread on the dark azure of the night this glorious blazonry of the unfathomable Creator. To me a dreadful scroll—inexorable eyes—the cloud of cruel witnesses looking down in freezing brightness on my prayers and agonies.

I turned about and sat down, leaning my head upon my arms. Then suddenly I sat up, as for the first time the picture of Uncle Silas's littered room, and the travelling bags and black boxes plied on the floor by his table—the desk, hat—case, umbrella, coats, rugs, and mufflers, all ready for a journey—reached my brain and suggested thought. The *mise en scène* had remained in every detail fixed upon my retina; and how I wondered—'When is he going—how soon? Is he going to carry me away and place me in a madhouse?'

'Am I—am I mad?' I began to think, 'Is this all a dream, or is it real?'

I remembered how a thin polite gentleman, with a tall grizzled head and a black

velvet waistcoat, came into the carriage on our journey, and said a few words to
me; how Madame whispered him something, and he murmured 'Oh!' very gently,
with raised eyebrows, and a glance at me, and thenceforward spoke no more to me,
only to Madame, and at the next station carried his hat and other travelling chattels into another carriage. Had she told him I was mad?

These horrid bars! Madame always with me! The direful hints that dropt from
my uncle! My own terrific sensations!—All these evidences revolved in my brain,
and presented themselves in turn like writings on a wheel of fire.

There came a knock to the door—

Oh, Meg! Was it she? No; old Wyat whispered Madame something about
her room.

So Madame re-entered, with a little silver tray and flagon in her hands, and a
glass. Nothing came from Uncle Silas in ungentlemanlike fashion.

'Drink, Maud,' said Madame, raising the cover, and evidently enjoying the fragrant steam.

I could not. I might have done so had I been able to swallow anything—for I
was too distracted to think of Meg's warning.

Madame suddenly recollected her mistake of that evening, and tried the
door; but it was duly locked. She took the key front her pocket and placed it in
her breast.

'You weel 'av these rooms to yourself, ma chère. I shall sleep downstairs
to-night.'

She poured out some of the hot claret into the glass abstractedly, and drank
it off.

''Tis very good—I drank without theenk. Bote 'tis very good. Why don't you
drink some?'

'I could not,' I repeated. And Madame boldly helped herself.

'Vary polite, certally, to Madame was it to send nothing at all for hair' (so she
pronounced 'her'); 'bote is all same thing.' And so she ran on in her tipsy vein,
which was loud and sarcastic, with a fierce laugh now and then.

Afterwards I heard that they were afraid of Madame, who was given to cross
purposes, and violent in her cups. She had been noisy and quarrelsome downstairs.
She was under the delusion that I was to be conveyed away that night to a remote
and safe place, and she was to be handsomely compensated for services and evidence to be afterwards given. She was not to be trusted, however, with the truth.
That was to be known but to three persons on earth.

I never knew, but I believe that the spiced claret which Madame drank was drugged. She was a person who could, I have been told, drink a great deal without exhibiting any change from it but an inflamed colour and furious temper. I can only state for certain what I saw, and that was, that shortly after she had finished the claret she lay down upon my bed, and, I now know, fell asleep. I then thought she was *feigning* sleep only, and that she was really watching me.

About an hour after this I suddenly heard a little *clink* in the yard beneath. I peeped out, but saw nothing. The sound was repeated, however—sometimes more frequently, sometimes at long intervals. At last, in the deep shadow next the farther wall, I thought I could discover a figure, sometimes erect, sometimes stooping and bowing toward the earth. I could see this figure only in the rudest outline mingling with the dark.

Like a thunderbolt it smote my brain. 'They are making my grave!'

After the first dreadful stun I grew quite wild, and ran up and down the room wringing my hands and gasping prayers to heaven. Then a calm stole over me— such a dreadful calm as I could fancy glide over one who floated in a boat under the shadow of the 'Traitor's Gate,' leaving life and hope and trouble behind.

Shortly after there came a very low tap at my door; then another, like a tiny post—knock. I could never understand why it was I made no answer. Had I done so, and thus shown that I was awake, it might have sealed my fate. I was standing in the middle of the floor staring at the door, which I expected to see open, and admit I knew not what troop of spectres.

CHAPTER LXIV

THE HOUR OF DEATH

It was a very still night and frosty. My candle had long burnt out. There was still a faint moonlight, which fell in a square of yellow on the floor near the window, leaving the rest of the room in what to an eye less accustomed than mine had become to that faint light would have been total darkness. Now, I am sure, I heard a soft whispering outside my door. I knew that I was in a state of siege! The crisis was come, and strange to say, I felt myself grow all at once resolute and self-possessed. It was not a subsidence, however, of the dreadful excitement, but a sudden screwing-up of my nerves to a pitch such as I cannot describe.

I suppose the people outside moved with great caution; and the perfect solidity of the floor, which had not anywhere a creaking board in it, favoured their noiseless movements. It was well for me that there were in the house three persons whom it was part of their plan to mystify respecting my fate. This alone compelled the extreme caution of their proceedings. They suspected that I had placed furniture against the door, and were afraid to force it, lest a crash, a scream, perhaps a long and shrilly struggle, might follow.

I remained for a space which I cannot pretend to estimate in the same posture, afraid to stir—afraid to move my eye from the door.

A very peculiar grating sound above my head startled me from my watch—something of the character of sawing, only more crunching, and with a faint continued rumble in it—utterly inexplicable, It sounded over that portion of the roof which was farthest from the door, toward which I now glided; and as I took my stand under cover of the projecting angle of a clumsy old press that stood close by it, I perceived the room a little darkened, and I saw a man descend and take his stand upon the window-stone. He let go a rope, which, however, was still fast round his body, and employed both his hands, with apparently some exertion, about something at the side of the window, which in a moment more, in one mass, bars and all, swung noiselessly open, admitting the frosty night-air; and the man, whom I now distinctly saw to be Dudley Ruthyn, kneeled on the sill, and stept, after a moment's listening, into the room. His foot made no sound upon the floor; his head was bare, and he wore his usual short shooting-jacket.

I cowered to the ground in my post of observation. He stood, as it seemed to me irresolutely for a moment, and then drew from his pocket an instrument which I distinctly saw against the faint moonlight. Imagine a hammer, one end of which had been beaten out into a longish tapering spike, with a handle something longer than usual. He drew stealthily to the window, and seemed to examine this hurriedly, and tested its strength with a twist or two of his hand. And then he adjusted it very carefully in his grasp, and made two or three little experimental picks with it in the air.

I remained perfectly still, with a terrible composure, crouched in my hiding-place, my teeth clenched, and prepared to struggle like a tigress for my life when discovered. I thought his next measure would be to light a match. I saw a lantern, I fancied, on the window-sill. But this was not his plan. He stole, in a groping way, which seemed strange to me, who could distinguish objects in this light, to the side of my bed, the exact position of which he evidently knew; he stooped over it. Madame was breathing in the deep respiration of heavy sleep. Suddenly but softly he laid, as it seemed to me, his left hand over her face, and nearly at the same instant there came a scrunching blow; an unnatural shriek, beginning small and swelling for two or three seconds into a yell such as are imagined in haunted houses, accompanied by a convulsive sound, as of the motion of running, and the arms drumming on the bed; and then another blow—and with a horrid gasp he recoiled a step or two, and stood perfectly still. I heard a horrible tremor quivering through the joints and curtains of the bedstead—the convulsions of tire murdered woman. It was a dreadful sound, like the shaking of a tree and rustling of leaves. Then once more he steps to the side of the bed, and I heard another of those horrid blows— and silence—and another—and more silence—and the diabolical surgery was ended. For a few seconds, I think, I was on the point of fainting; but a gentle stir outside the door, dose to my ear, startled me, and proved that there had been a watcher posted outside. There was a little tapping at the door.

'Who's that?' whispered Dudley, hoarsely.

'A friend,' answered a sweet voice.

And a key was introduced, the door quickly unlocked, and Uncle Silas entered. I saw that frail, tall, white figure, the venerable silver locks that resembled those upon the honoured head of John Wesley, and his thin white hand, the back of which hung so close to my face that I feared to breathe. I could see his fingers twitching nervously. The smell of perfumes and of ether entered the room with him.

Dudley was trembling now like a man in an ague-fit.

'Look what you made me do!' he said, maniacally.

'Steady, sir!' said the old man, close beside me.

'Yes, you damned old murderer! I've a mind to do for you.'

'There, Dudley, like a dear boy, don't give way; it's done. Right or wrong, we can't help it. You must be quiet,' said the old man, with a stem gentleness.

Dudley groaned.

'Whoever advised it, you're a gainer, Dudley,' said Uncle Silas.

Then there was a pause.

'I hope that was not heard,' said Uncle Silas.

Dudley walked to the window and stood there.

'Come, Dudley, you and Hawkes must use expedition. You know you must get that out of the way.'

'I've done too much. I won't do nout; I'll not touch it. I wish my hand was off first; I wish I was a soger. Do as ye like, you an' Hawkes. I won't go nigh it; damn ye both—and *that!*' and he hurled the hammer with all his force upon the floor.

'Come, come, be reasonable, Dudley, dear boy. There's nothing to fear but your own folly. You won't make a noise?'

'Oh, oh, my God!' said Dudley, hoarsely, and wiped his forehead with his open hand.

'There now, you'll be all well in a minute,' continued the old man.

'You said 'twouldn't hurt her. If I'd a known she'd a screeched like that I'd never a done it. 'Twas a damn lie. You're the damndest villain on earth.'

'Come, Dudley!' said the old man under his breath, but very sternly, 'make up your mind. If you don't choose to go on, it can't be helped; only it's a pity you began. For *you* it is a good deal—it does not much matter for *me*.'

'Ay, for *you!*' echoed Dudley, through his set teeth. 'The old talk!'

'Well, sir,' snarled the old man, in the same low tones, 'you should have thought of all this before. It's only taking leave of the world a year or two sooner, but a year or two's something. I'll leave you to do as you please.'

'Stop, will you? Stop here. I know it's a fixt thing now. If a fella does a thing he's damned for, you might let him talk a bit anyhow. I don't care much if I was shot.'

'There now—*there*—just stick to that, and don't run off again. There's a box and a bag here; we must change the direction, and take them away. The box has some jewels. Can you see them? I wish we had a light.'

'No, I'd rayther not; I can see well enough. I wish we were out o' this. *Here's* the box.'

'Pull it to the window,' said the old man, to my inexpressible relief advancing at last a few steps.

Coolness was given me in that dreadful moment, and I knew that all depended on my being prompt and resolute. I stood up swiftly. I often thought if I had happened to wear silk instead of the cachmere I had on that night, its rustle would have betrayed me.

I distinctly saw the tall stooping figure of my uncle, and the outline of his venerable tresses, as he stood between me and the dull light of the window, like a shape cut in card.

He was saying 'just to *there*,' and pointing with his long arm at that contracting patch of moonlight which lay squared upon the floor. The door was about a quarter open, and just as Dudley began to drag Madame's heavy box, with my jewel-case in it, across the floor from her room, inhaling a great breath—with a mental prayer for help-I glided on tiptoe from the room and found myself on the gallery floor.

I turned to my right, simply by chance, and followed a long gallery in the dark, not running-I was too fearful of making the least noise—but walking with the tip-toe—swiftness of terror. At the termination of this was a cross-gallery, one end of which—that to my left—terminated in a great window, through which the dusky night-view was visible. With the instinct of terror I chose the darker, and turned again to my right; hurrying through this long and nearly dark passage, I was terrified by a light, about thirty feet before me, emerging from the ceiling. In spotted patches this light fell through the door and sides of a stable lantern, and showed me a ladder, down which, from an open skylight I suppose for the cool night-air floated in my face, came Dickon Hawkes notwithstanding his maimed condition, with so much celerity as to leave me hardly a moment for consideration.

He sat on the last round of the ladder, and tightened the strap of his wooden leg.

At my left was a door-case open, but no door. I entered; it was a short passage about six feet long, leading perhaps to a backstair, but the door at the end was locked.

I was forced to stand in this recess, then, which afforded no shelter, while Pegtop stumped by with his lantern in his hand. I fancy he had some idea of listening to his master unperceived, for he stopped close to my hiding-place, blew out the candle, and pinched the long snuff with his horny finger and thumb.

Having listened for a few seconds, he stumped stealthily along the gallery which I had just traversed, and turned the corner in the direction of the chamber where the crime had just been committed, and the discovery was impending. I could see him against the broad window which in the daytime lighted this long passage, and the moment he had passed the corner I resumed my flight.

I descended a stair corresponding with that backstair, as I am told, up which Madame had led me only the night before. I tried the outer door. To my wild surprise it was open. In a moment I was upon the step, in the free air, and as instantaneously was seized by the arm in the grip of a man.

It was Tom Brice, who had already betrayed me, and who was now, in surtout and hat, waiting to drive the carriage with the guilty father and son from the scene of their abhorred outrage.

CHAPTER LXV

IN THE OAK PARLOUR

So it was vain: I was trapped, and all was over.

I stood before him on the step, the white moon shining on my face. I was trembling so that I wonder I could stand, my helpless hands raised towards him, and I looked up in his face. A long shuddering moan—'Oh—oh—oh!' was all I uttered.

The man, still holding my arm, looked, I thought frightened, into my white dumb face.

Suddenly he said, in a wild, fierce whisper—

'Never say another word' (I had not uttered one). 'They shan't hurt ye, Miss; git ye in; I don't care a damn!'

It was an uncouth speech. To me it was the voice of an angel. With a burst of gratitude that sounded in my own ears like a laugh, I thanked God for those blessed words.

In a moment more he had placed me in the carriage, and almost instantly we were in motion—very cautiously while crossing the court, until he had got the wheels upon the grass, and then at a rapid pace, improving his speed as the distance increased. He drove along the side of the back-approach to the house, keeping on the grass; so that our progress, though swaying like that of a ship in a swell, was very nearly as noiseless.

The gate had been left unlocked—he swung it open, and remounted the box. And we were now beyond the spell of Bartram-Haugh, thundering-Heaven be praised!—along the Queen's highway, right in the route to Elverston. It was literally a gallop. Through the chariot windows I saw Tom stand as he drove, and every now and then throw an awful glance over his shoulder. Were we pursued? Never was agony of prayer like mine, as with clasped hands and wild stare I gazed through the windows on the road, whose trees and hedges and gabled cottages were chasing one another backward at so giddy a speed.

We were now ascending that identical steep, with the giant ash-trees at the right and the stile between, which my vision of Meg Hawkes had presented all that night, when my excited eye detected a running figure within the hedge. I saw the head of some one crossing the stile in pursuit, and I heard Brice's name shrieked.

'Drive on—on—on!' I screamed.

But Brice pulled up. I was on my knees on the floor of the carriage, with clasped hands, expecting capture, when the door opened, and Meg Hawkes, pale as death, her cloak drawn over her black tresses, looked in.

'Oh!— ho,!— ho!—thank God she screamed.' Shake hands, lass. Tom, yer a good un! He's a good lad, Tom.'

'Come in, Meg—you must sit by me,' I said, recovering all at once.

Meg made no demur. 'Take my hand,' I said offering mine to her disengaged one.

'I can't, Miss—my arm's broke.'

And so it was, poor thing! She had been espied and overtaken in her errand of mercy for me, and her ruffian father had felled her with his cudgel, and then locked her into the cottage, whence, however, she had contrived to escape, and was now flying to Elverston, having tried in vain to get a hearing in Feltram, whose people had been for hours in bed.

The door being shut upon Meg, the steaming horses were instantly at a gallop again.

Tom was still watching as before, with many an anxious glance to rearward, for pursuit. Again he pulled up, and came to the window.

'Oh, what is it?' cried I.

''Bout that letter, Miss; I couldn't help. 'Twas Dickon, he found it in my pocket. That's a'.'

'Oh yes!—no matter—thank you—thank Heaven! Are we near Elverston?'

''Twill be a mile, Miss: and please'm to mind I had no finger in't.'

'Thanks—thank you—you're very good—I shall *always* thank you, Tom, as long as I live!'

At length we entered Elverston. I think I was half wild. I don't know how I got into the hall. I was in the oak-parlour, I believe, when I saw cousin Monica. I was standing, my arms extended. I could not speak; but I ran with a loud long scream into her arms. I forget a great deal after that.

CONCLUSION

Oh, my beloved cousin Monica! Thank Heaven, you are living still, and younger, I think, than I in all things but in years.

And Milly, my dear companion, she is now the happy wife of that good little clergyman, Sprigge Biddlepen. It has been in my power to be of use to them, and he shall have the next presentation to Dawling.

Meg Hawkes, proud and wayward, and the most affectionate creature on earth, was married to Tom Brice a few months after these events; and, as both wished to emigrate, I furnished them with the capital, and I am told they are likely to be rich. I hear from my kind Meg often, and she seems very happy.

My dear old friends, Mary Quince and Mrs. Rusk, are, alas! growing old, but living with me, and very happy. And after long solicitation, I persuaded Doctor Bryerly, the best and truest of ministers, with my dearest friend's concurrence, to undertake the management of the Derbyshire estates. In this I have been most fortunate. He is the very person for such a charge—so punctual, so laborious, so kind, and so shrewd.

In compliance with medical advice, cousin Monica hurried me away to the Continent, where she would never permit me to allude to the terrific scenes which remain branded so awfully on my brain. It needed no constraint. It is a sort of agony to me even now to think of them.

The plan was craftily devised. Neither old Wyat nor Giles, the butler, had a suspicion that I had returned to Bartram. Had I been put to death, the secret of my fate would have been deposited in the keeping of four persons only—the two Ruthyns, Hawkes, and ultimately Madame. My dear cousin Monica had been artfully led to believe in my departure for France, and prepared for my silence. Suspicion might not have been excited for a year after my death, and then would never, in all probability, have pointed to Bartram as the scene of the crime. The weeds would have grown over me, and I should have lain in that deep grave where the corpse of Madame de la Rougierre was unearthed in the darksome quadrangle of Bartram-Haugh.

It was more than two years after that I heard what had befallen at Bartram after my flight. Old Wyat, who went early, to Uncle Silas's room, to her surprise—for he had told her that he was that night to accompany his son, who had to meet the mailtrain to Derby at five o'clock in the morning—saw her old master lying on the sofa, much in his usual position.

'There was nout much strange about him,' old Wyat said, 'but that his scent-bottle was spilt on its side over on the table, and he dead.'

She thought he was not quite cold when she found him, and she sent the old butler for Doctor Jolks, who said he died of too much 'loddlum.'

Of my wretched uncle's religion what am I to say? Was it utter hypocrisy, or had it at any time a vein of sincerity in it? I cannot say. I don't believe that he had any heart left for religion, which is the highest form of affection, to take hold of. Perhaps he was a sceptic with misgivings about the future, but past the time for finding anything reliable in it. The devil approached the citadel of his heart by stealth, with many zigzags and parallels. The idea of marrying me to his son by fair means, then by foul, and, when that wicked chance was gone, then the design of seizing all by murder, supervened. I dare say that Uncle Silas thought for a while that he was a righteous man. He wished to have heaven and to escape hell, if there were such places. But there were other things whose existence was not speculative, of which some he coveted, and some he dreaded more, and temptation came. 'Now if any man build upon this foundation, gold, silver, precious stones, wood, hay, stubble, every man's work shall be made manifest; for the day shall declare it, because it shall be revealed by fire; and the fire shall try every man's work of what sort it is.' There comes with old age a time when the heart is no longer fusible or malleable, and must retain the form in which it has cooled down. 'He that is unjust, let him be unjust still; he which is filthy, let him be filthy still.'

Dudley had disappeared; but in one of her letters, Meg, writing from her Australian farm, says: 'There's a fella in toon as calls hisself Colbroke, wi' a good hoose o' wood, 15 foot length, and as by 'bout as silling o' the pearler o' Bartram—only lots o' rats, they do say, my lady—a bying and sellin' of goold back and forred wi' the diggin foke and the marchants. His chick and mouth be wry wi' scar o' burns or vitterel, an' no wiskers, bless you; but my Tom ee tolt him he knowed him for Master Doodley. I ant seed him; but he sade ad shute Tom soon is look at 'im, an' denide it, wi' mouthful o' curses and oaf. Tom baint right shure; if I seed un worts I'd no for sartin; but 'appen, 'twil best be let be.' This was all.

Old Hawkes stood his ground, relying on the profound cunning with which their actual proceedings had been concealed, even from the suspicions of the two inmates of the house, and on the mystery that habitually shrouded Bartram-Haugh and all its belongings from the eyes of the outer world.

Strangely enough, he fancied that I had made my escape long before the room was entered; and, even if he were arrested, there was no evidence, he was certain, to connect *him* with the murder, all knowledge of which he would stoutly deny.

There was an inquest on the body of my uncle, and Dr. Jolks was the chief witness. They found that his death was caused by an excessive dose of laudanum, accidentally administered by himself.'

It was not until nearly a year after the dreadful occurrences at Bartram that Dickon Hawkes was arrested on a very awful charge, and placed in gaol. It was an old crime, committed in Lancashire, that had found him out. After his conviction, as a last chance, he tried a disclosure of all the circumstances of the unsuspected death of the Frenchwoman. Her body was discovered buried where he indicated, in the inner court of Bartram-Haugh, and, after due legal enquiry, was interred in the churchyard of Feltram.

Thus I escaped the horrors of the witness-box, or the far worse torture of a dreadful secret.

Doctor Bryerly, shortly after Lady Knollys had described to him the manner in which Dudley entered my room, visited the house of Bartram-Haugh, and minutely examined the windows of the room in which Mr. Charke had slept on the night of his murder. One of these he found provided with powerful steel hinges, very craftily sunk and concealed in the timber of the window-frame, which was secured by an iron pin outside, and swung open on its removal. This was the room in which they had placed me, and this the contrivance by means of which the room had been entered. The problem of Mr. Charke's murder was solved.

I have penned it. I sit for a moment breathless. My hands are cold and damp. I rise with a great sigh, and look out on the sweet green landscape and pastoral hills, and see the flowers and birds and the waving boughs of glorious trees—all images of liberty and safety; and as the tremendous nightmare of my youth melts into air, I lift my eyes in boundless gratitude to the God of all comfort, whose mighty hand and outstretched arm delivered me. When I lower my eyes and unclasp my hands, my cheeks are wet with tears. A tiny voice is calling me 'Mamma!' and a beloved smiling face, with his dear father's silken brown tresses, peeps in.

'Yes, darling, our walk. Come away!'

I am Lady Ilbury, happy in the affection of a beloved and noblehearted husband. The shy useless girl you have known is now a mother—trying to be a good one; and this, the last pledge, has lived.

I am not going to tell of sorrows—how brief has been my pride of early maternity, or how beloved were those whom the Lord gave and the Lord has taken away. But sometimes as, smiling on my little boy, the tears gather in my eyes, and he wonders, I can see, why they come, I am drinking—and trembling while I smile— to think, how strong is love, how frail is life; and rejoicing while I tremble that, in the deathless love of those who mourn, the Lord of Life, who never gave a pang in vain, conveys the sweet and ennobling promise of a compensation by eternal reunion. So, through my sorrows, I have heard a voice from heaven say, 'Write, from hencefore blessed are the dead that die in the Lord!'

This world is a parable—the habitation of symbols—the phantoms of spiritual things immortal shown in material shape. May the blessed second-sight be mine— to recognise under these beautiful forms of earth the ANGELS who wear them; for I am sure we may walk with them if we will, and hear them speak!

ALICE STOPFORD GREEN

♣

(1847-1929)

In 1908, Alice Stopford Green published *The Making of Ireland and Its Undoing*, a book that English reviewers roundly criticized for alleged inaccuracies. The book, they reasoned, could not be considered a legitimate history because Green used early Irish literature as historical sources. Green, however, stood up to British revisionists and was unapologetic about her research. In a second edition, she did acknowledge certain errors with specific explanations and corrections, but the book retained its strong anti-imperialist tone, launching the Irish historian into the forefront of influential nationalists and ultimately leading to her nomination in 1922 to the first Irish Seanad.

Born in Kells in 1847 to Edward Adderley Stopford, the Archdeacon of Meath, and Anne Duke Stopford of County Sligo, Alice Stopford was one of nine children raised and educated in a fiercely evangelical setting, most often by a series of governesses. At the age of thirteen, she developed serious and threatening eye problems, which forced her to spend a year in a dark room, unable to tolerate the slightest bit of sunlight. Her condition also rendered her unable to read on her own for seven years, and these problems would continue to plague her for the rest of her life. In 1873, she moved with her family to Dublin where she developed a great curiosity toward the sciences, and she attended physics lectures there, but only in the company of another woman. Most of her education took place in the home.

The following year, after the death of her father, the family moved to London and she married John Richard Green, the noted historian, in 1877. The relationship proved to be precisely what Alice Stopford Green had hoped for. Her husband tutored her, and when he grew ill a few years later, she was able to act as both his nurse and his researcher. She proved to be adept at both, but it was in the years before the death of her husband in 1884, that Green truly immersed herself in the study of history.

Women are "immensely curious," she would later write, making them excellent historians. She had become her husband's collaborator and even went on to produce new and revised editions of his books, and it was during this work that she began to realize that she enjoyed and had a talent for writing herself.

John Richard Green left his wife financially secure upon his death, and she would spend the next 35 years of her life living in London, where she would establish herself as an historian on her own merits. She wrote her first book, *Town Life in the Fifteenth Century*, in 1894, and the more she began to study the history of Ireland, the more she began to develop her pronounced anti-imperialist views of the British conquest of Ireland. In 1908, *The Making of Ireland and Its Undoing* was published and A.S. Green's life would never be the same. The book came under violent attack, mostly by English reviewers who seized on alleged inaccuracies in Green's research, chiefly the fact that she used early Irish literature as historical sources. In her preface to the book, however, Green points out that in many cases, literature was all that survived, as conquering armies often made a ritual of destroying historical documents and artwork. "Thus the history of the Irish people has been left unrecorded," she wrote, "as though it had never been; as though indeed, according to some, the history were one of dishonour and rebuke."

The Making of Ireland and Its Undoing was a celebration of Irish culture and was Green's contribution to the Irish cultural revival, where nationalism flourished. She addressed the shame and humiliation the Irish had endured by attacking the myths that savages inhabited the island until British conquest:

> The Irish of to-day have themselves suffered by the calumny of their dead. They, alone among the nations, have been taunted with ancestors sunk in primitive disorders, incapable of development in the land they wasted. A picture of unrelieved barbarism "hateful to God" served to justify to strangers the English extirpation of Irish society; and has been used to depress the hearts of the Irish themselves. For their birthright—they have been told—they have inherited the failings of their race, and by the verdict of the ages have been proclaimed incapable of success in their own land, or of building up there an ordered society, trade, or culture, and have indeed ever proved themselves a people ready "to go headlong to the Devil" if England "seek not speedy remedy to prevent the same." Thus their energy has been lowered, and some natural pride abated. It is in the study of their history alone that Irishmen will find this pride restored, and their courage assured.

It was immediately apparent that the book was causing outrage because she strongly opposed the idea that Anglo-Normans brought civilization to Ireland when they conquered the country nearly a thousand years before, and not simply because of her historical reporting techniques. The Irish, she held, were lawmakers and law abiders long before the Norman Conquest and pointed to the documentation of a society that in fact maintained a sophisticated legal system prior to invasion. She maintained that the more significant inaccuracies continued to be perpetuated by English and Irish schools, teaching of an Irish history that was devoid of culture.

It is for this reason that Irish history cannot safely be ignored. Its study is needed to correct a series of misconceptions which have been for generations instilled into the minds of English and Irish alike, prejudices which have been the source of fatal errors.

Green viewed *The Making of Ireland and Its Undoing* as an important work, if only because it helped the world understand the Irish predicament. She continued to fight against British revisionists, but she did so with a spirit of optimism and cooperation. Cultural pride, she argued, would be to the benefit of all, when she wrote:

> This book will have served some purpose if it should call attention to the importance for Ireland of a critical study of national history corresponding to its revived study in other lands. For the true record of Ireland will be powerful to efface the prejudices, the contempt, and the despair that falsehood alone can foster; and to build up on solid foundations of fact the esteem and consideration that must form the only honourable relation between two neighboring peoples.

She followed this book with *Irish Nationality,* which was published in 1911 and cemented Green's reputation as a leading Irish Nationalist of the time. The book was tremendously influential with the new generation of Irish, especially within the literary resurgence, which was bringing profound attention to Irish culture. Her home in London became one of the most popular salons at the time, attracting the most prominent names in society, and Green was cultivating a reputation as not only an Irish Nationalist, but a humanitarian as well. She grew very interested in Africa and became a standing member of the Africa Society, but despite this work, she was still perceived as a threat to English society. She did not support the Ulster Unionist Party, which formed in 1905 and opposed any form of nationalism, which it viewed as confrontational and exclusive. In fact, her vocal non-support of the Unionist point of view resulted in her home being continually raided.

In 1913, Green wrote *A Woman's Place in the World of Letters*, where she noted that women writers and historians, like herself, had often in history been cloaked in reluctance and relegated to disguise their contributions, "a very complicated story, this story of precaution and disguise." But by 1918, she abandoned London, deciding that she was destined to return to Ireland, and she moved to 90 St. Stephen's Green in Dublin, which she quickly established as an intellectual meeting place. She wrote a pamphlet, *Ourselves Alone in Ulster*, attacking the Unionist Sir Edward Carson's policies. She was an ardent supporter of the Anglo-Irish Treaty of 1921, which so divided the nation that civil war ensued. But her support of the Treaty won her nomination to the first Irish Seanad in December 1922.

Alice Stopford Green's last major work, *A History of the Irish State to 1014,* came out in 1925, and the historian, author, activist and politician died in Dublin in 1929. Her legacy is clearly her historical work, which helped to create the surge of nationalism in Ireland during her lifetime and beyond.

OURSELVES ALONE IN ULSTER

♣

In a speech delivered on December 14, 1917, Mr. Lloyd George spoke of "a definite and clear line of action, intelligible in consciences of a certain quality"—"Ourselves first, ourselves last, ourselves all the time, and ourselves alone." "It is pretty mean," he added, "but there are in every country men built that way, and you must reckon with them in the world."

A subtle question of casuistry could be raised as to how great a number of people must be united to make this motto either a despicable or an honourable one. It would doubtless be thought very creditable in an Empire. How about a United Kingdom—a Nation—or half a Province of a nation?

This problem was decided without difficulty by north-east Ulster. The superiority of its wealth, the vigour of its creed, the self-confidence of its men—there were its sufficient credentials for a policy of "ourselves first and last, ourselves all the time." North-east Ulster had no wrongs or sufferings to proclaim to the human conscience. The only trouble was a story as old as the world, that in its proud prosperity it fell into those fearful apprehensions that haunt the way of the wealthy, driving them in every age to multiply safeguards and shelters for their riches and power. North-east Ulster required, in a changing world, that the guarantees of its commercial interests should remain unchanged. To secure this fixity of position rebellion under arms might be allowed. If an illegal form of government, as near high treason as could be, could assure material safety, the only question was how to perfect scientific organization, with sufficient finances to withstand every strain. Rebellion would be justified in one way only, by success. In the three phases of the northern movement it has preserved its character unchanged, and adhered to its first purpose.

I. The first phase of organized resistance was in response to the demand of three-fourths of Ireland for a grant of Home Rule to be enacted by the King and Parliament of the United Kingdom. In the heated controversies of 1910 the Right Hon. Thomas Andrews, P.C., Hon. Secretary of the Unionist Council, sounded his note of defiance by declaring that he, and he believed his colleagues, would rather be governed by Germany than by Patrick Ford and John Redmond and Company.[1] It was a time when the foreign policy of the Kaiser was a subject of the gravest alarm in England, and English anxieties were diligently exploited by the leaders of

Unionism in Ulster. Captain Watt, at a meeting of Londonderry Orangemen in August 1910, gave his warning to the new King just entered his inheritance: "It has been said that we want another King, William the Third. Well, take care that the present King is not to be another King James, but I ask you to give King George a chance before you come to any decision."[1] In January 1911, before the King was crowned, Captain Craig, M.P., warned England from his personal knowledge that Germany and the German Emperor would be preferred of the rules of John Redmond, Patrick Ford, and the Molly Maguires.[2] The year was one of continued excitement. The coronation in June was quickly followed by the "Agadir" alarm in July. It will be remembered that war with Germany was thought inevitable; officers were ready for their marching orders, and the fleet lay with sealed orders, waiting the signal to set sail. The close of the grave railway strike in England was determined by the extreme danger of the foreign situation, and the pressure which the Cabinet, under such perilous conditions, brought to bear on industrial magnates in England. But the Government eschewed controversy with imperialists of the northeast Ulster quality. Rebellious incitements were freely carried on by "Ourselves first and last." In August Sir Edward Carson stated that the passing of the Home Rule Bill would be resisted by force[3]—a threat of civil war. "If Home Rule were granted," said Mr. C. C. Craig, M.P., on October 17, 1911, "it would not matter a row of pins whether they were separated from Great Britain or whether they were not."[4]

From words they passed to deeds. The Ulster Unionist Council of four hundred members, representing Unionist Associations in Ulster constituencies, met under the Marquis of Londonderry in Belfast on September 25, 1911, and then resolved:[5]— (1) That it was their imperative duty to make arrangements for a Provisional Government of Ulster; and (2) That they hereby appointed a Commission which, in consultation with Sir Edward Carson, should frame and submit a constitution, for this Provisional Government. A silence of sixteen months followed; but the Council and secret Commission were not idle. An invigorated north-east Ulster declared its will to suppress all freedom of speech—even on the part of Ministers of the Crown—with regard to the government of Ireland. The Liberals had engaged the Ulster Hall in February 1912, for Mr. Winston Churchill, First Lord of the Admiralty, to address Belfast citizens on the subject of Home Rule. The Harbour Board refused to allow Mr. Churchill a reception as First Lord. The Hall, as the property of the whole body of citizens, was up to that time open for all forms of discussion, Tory, Liberal, Labour, and Nationalist, as represented by Mr. Redmond and Mr. Dillon. Now, however, the Orangemen seized the Hall, and held possession for a week before the meeting. No Nationalist, they declared, should sully the Ulster

Hall by his presence; and to cries of "Ulster will fight and Ulster will be right" the Unionists drove the Government representative to hold his meeting in a football ground, the Celtic Park.[1] By this first outrage they demonstrated to a humiliated Cabinet that Ulster Protestants could do as they liked.

With the second reading of the Home Rule Bill in April 1912, the education of north-east Ulster in rebellion became even more emphatic. The Rev. T. Walmesley spoke on August 13, of the prospect of the Sovereign coming one day for the ceremony of re-opening the Parliament of a free and reconciled Ireland,[2] "If," he declared, "our King should be there of his own free will, then I for one will feel myself justified in no longer regarding him as my King." There were excited ceremonies, at which Sir Edward Carson was presented with a blackthorn stick adorned with the Orange and Freemason colours; and with the banner under which William III had gone to victory on the Boyne.[3] Public emotion culminated on "Ulster Day," September 28, 1912, when the "Covenant" was signed by 218,206 men, and 228,991 women in Ulster—447,197 persons out of a population (counting those over 16) of 1,074,000.

The proceedings of the Ulster Unionist Council meanwhile were carried on in private. Nothing more was publicly heard of the "Special Commission" of 1911 till the third reading of the Home Rule Bill in January 1913. Then on January 31 the Council announced the passing by them of a notable resolution:[4]—"We ratify and confirm the further steps so far taken by the Special Commission, and approve of the draft resolutions and articles of the Ulster Provisional Government this day submitted to us, and appoint the members of the Special Commission to act as the Executive thereunder." The work of the Commission remained secret. No hint of the terms of the articles and resolutions was permitted to leak out. The Council was, in fact, a close corporation, the members of which were selected from classes prominent in the older fights for dominance and committed to the tradition of Ascendancy—peers, landowners, militia officers, ecclesiastics, and by degrees capitalists and employers. There was no pretence of representation as generally understood. Members were not chosen by the working-classes, nor even by public bodies over which Unionists had control, such as boards of guardians, urban councils, or the like; and in counties such as Cavan, Monaghan, and Donegal, which were strongly represented, not one of the members could have been openly elected by the people on his merits. A cynic might have suggested that it was a last bid of the aristocratic and superior classes, lay and ecclesiastical, in alliance with English Tories, to guide the people for their good. *The Times* on May 9, 1913, justified the high purpose of their aristocratic and religious mission. "The occasion has been used to strengthen the conservatism of Ulster—I do not use the word in a party sense. By disciplining the Ulster democracy, and by teaching it to look up to them as its natural leaders, the clergy and gentry are providing against the spread of Revolutionary doctrine and free thought."

So efficient and well-drilled a scheme of establishing the superior classes in control secured, in fact, the utmost sympathy among the English nobility and clergy, expressed in vast sums of money. The English upper classes recognized the wholesome influence of the "natural leaders" of Belfast, that vast industrial city where labour has been long accustomed to no representation; unless of late years when Protestant Unionist workers found themselves forced to invoke in any special distress the aid of a Catholic Nationalist member of Parliament. In north-east Ulster might be seen the model of discipline by the clergy and gentry, its natural leaders.

Loyalty to the Crown was no part of the new conservative mission, except on terms that the Crown accepted the decisions of the north-east Ulster Unionists. "If Home Rule is passed I would not care whether the British Empire went to smash or not," said the Rev. Chancellor Hobson on Easter Monday, 1913.[1] The threat of Germany was still freely used. Mr. James Chambers, M.P. for South Belfast, suggested it to his constituents on May 23, 1913.[2] "As regards the future, what if a day should come when Ireland would be clamouring for independence complete and thorough from Great Britain? ... What side would they take then? (A voice: "Germany.") He (Mr. Chambers) bound no man to his opinions. They owed to England allegiance, loyalty, and gratitude; but if England cast them off then he reserved the right as a betrayed man to say 'I shall act as I have a right to act. I shall sing no longer "God save the King"' ... He said there solemnly that the day England cast him off and despised his loyalty and allegiance, that day he would say: 'England, I will laugh at your calamity, I will mock when your fear cometh.'" *The Irish Churchman* on November 14, 1913,[3] gave prominence to a letter addressed to it: "It may not be known to the rank and file of Unionists that we have the offer of aid from a powerful Continental monarch who, if Home Rule is forced on the Protestants of Ireland, is prepared to send an army sufficient to release England of any further trouble in Ireland by attaching it to his dominion, believing, as he does, that if our King breaks his Coronation Oath by signing the Home Rule Bill he will, by so doing, have forfeited his claim to rule Ireland. And should our King sign the Home Rule Bill the Protestants of Ireland will welcome this Continental deliverer as their forefathers, under similar circumstances, did once before." "Can King George sign the Home Rule Bill?" ran an open letter to Mr. Asquith in the leading Unionist paper in Mr. Barrie's constituency in July

1913.[1] "Let him do so, and his Empire shall perish as true as God rules Heaven …
Therefore let King George sign the Home Rule Bill—he is no longer my King."
Such phrases were repeated on all sides in full security. Unionists had, and rightly,
no apprehension of blame. They have long known that public opinion in England
can never be roused to alarm or indignation by any Protestant propaganda, whatever be its purpose or the violence of its methods. An unquestioning trust has always
rewarded Orange Lodges.

Inspirited by uninterrupted success and the applause of English Tories, the
party of north-east Ulster opened a further enterprise. The Unionist Council met
on September 24, 1913, in the Ulster Hall, to decree itself the Central Authority
of the Provisional Government, and its Standing Committee of seventy-six was
declared to be the Executive Committee of the Provisional Government of Ulster.[2]
Sir Edward Carson was appointed head of the Central Authority, with a multitude
of Committees and Boards under him. There were the Executive Committee,
Military Council, Ulster Volunteer Committee, Volunteer Advisory Board,
Personnel Board, Supply Board, Medical Board, Finance and Business Committee,
Legal Committee, Education Committee, Publication and Literary Committee,
Customs and Excise Committee, Post Office Committee. Chaplains were appoint-
ed, and an Assessor. Power was given to Committees to co-opt a member or mem-
bers of the Ulster Women's Unionist Council.

No statement was made as to the powers and functions of either the central
authority or subordinate boards and committees. These, the public were told, "shall
be as defined hereafter." Sir Edward Carson was chairman of every committee and
board, the only link between them so far as outsiders knew. Not one working man
was selected in this one-sided State—no representative of Labour, Democracy, or
Liberalism. Ministers of religion might find a place by virtue of high office in
Freemason or Orange bodies. All members of the various committees were local
Unionist leaders, arbitrarily appointed without consulting popular opinion. It was
Dublin Castle over again without even the pretence of a Westminster Parliament as
the final authority.

This Provisional Government was ready to be called into full working order at
the command of Sir Edward Carson. For the present it exerted a complete authority as the organized Unionist Council. It found a home in the old City Hall of
Belfast, heavily subsidized by the Corporation. The leaders, familiar with the old
habit of the diplomatic craft by which States are led, exploited (with their allies) all
the chances of secret politics, and spent their unlimited resources with rich freedom and equal dexterity. From time to time public meetings were held to

announce the general decisions of the new Ulster Government, while the administration was skilfully carried out in camera. Fiery denunciations of the King and Parliament of England, and of all the rest of Ireland, along with the Pope, were addressed to the public. The immense funds at the disposal of the governing body made it easy to arrange exhilirating festivals and gatherings for the encouragement of the people. The State had been cemented by a sworn Covenant, and the attendant religious ceremonies emphasized the doctrine of a peculiar people, chosen by a special Deity. "O God," ran the prayer of one of the greatest Presbyterian assemblies in a chief centre of Covenanters, who had met on the great day of signing to consecrate their work, "O God, remember that Thou art not a God, like other gods."[1] The naturally militant and aggressive character of a "chosen people" was emphasized by a multitude of sermons in which, so far as we can judge from those printed in the papers, the texts were invariably taken from the warlike incitements of Old Testament warriors and prophets, while only two verses were adopted by the leading preachers from the New Testament of the Christian faith: "I am not come to send peace but a sword": "He that hath no sword let him sell his cloak and buy one." In such a temper the *Times* saw a spiritual hope. "The Covenant," it wrote on May 3, 1913, "was a mystical affirmation… Ulster seemed to enter into an offensive and defensive alliance with the Deity." Ministers of the various creeds, after long severance, found their meeting-place in a common political faith—the faith which was expressed later by the Protestant potentate who was to them the spiritual heir of the pious William of the Boyne: "The German people has in the Lord of Creation above an unconditional and avowed Ally on whom it can absolutely rely."

To complete the attributes of a self-contained State an army was needed. Unionist Clubs had long been formed throughout the country, whose members were easily ranged into corps of Volunteer soldiers. They were said to number 60,000 when reviewed by the new Ulster Provisional Government. It was now held necessary to replace Volunteers with wooden rifles and cannon by troops armed for active service with modern weapons. The creation of such an army was certainly illegal. But mere illegality was not an obstacle to stop the march of Ulster. In June 1913, a large consignment of arms was imported to Belfast as "electrical plant."[2] Sir Edward Carson already anticipated "Der Tag." "I like," he said on August 3, 1913, "to get nearer the enemy.[3] I like to see the men are preparing for what I call the Great Day." A Volunteer Force numbering according to report 100,000, or presently 200,000 men, was equipped by the Ulster Provisional Government on a very sumptuous scale, with khaki uniforms, military boots, motorcycles, rifles, machine-guns, and all other necessaries. A couple of Germans assisted in their training.[1] An indemnity fund of £1,000,000 was announced, to indemnify Volunteers for loss of life and property. Ambulances and nurses were provided.[2] Sir Edward Carson stated that to his personal knowledge "The forces of the Crown were already dividing into hostile camps."[3] Imperialist and Unionist Ulster set no limits to its defiance of the Imperial Government, encouraged by their English friends. Sir Edward Carson's lieutenant, the "Galloper" F. E. Smith, speaking in County Antrim on September 21, said if war began in Ulster "From that moment we hold ourselves absolved from all allegiance to this Government. From that moment we on our part will say to our fellows in England: 'To your tents, O Israel.' From that moment we shall stand side by side with you refusing to recognise any law."[4] Friends in England proposed by the help of Ulster to smash the Territorials, who were afterwards to play so great a part in the war. The *Observer* of November 30, 1913, "urged that all Unionist Lords Lieutenant should resign their position as heads of the County Territorial Associations," that "every Unionist should prepare to leave the Territorials"; and that "the whole of Unionist influence throughout the country ought to be used to prevent recruits from joining so long as there is the slightest threat of coercing Ulster." In defence of Protestant Unionism, Sir Edward Carson declared himself ready to break all laws.[5] He professed scorn and defiance of anything done "down in a little place called Westminster." His insolences were studied: "I saw," he declared in the Ulster Hall, "Mr. Lloyd George in his robes as Chancellor of the Exchequer, and I almost mistook him for a gentleman." Carson's followers blatantly announced their preference for a Protestant German ruler who would revive the glorious and immortal memory of an older William. Mr. Chambers, Solicitor-General for Ireland, gave it to be understood that he was in negotiation with the German Chancellor for the transfer of Ulster if necessary, owing to its resolve to be attached to a strictly Protestant Power. When he proclaimed in the high street of his constituency in Belfast, that if English George signed the bill he was for the German William, the vaunt was repeated on all sides.

An ignoble form of north-east Ulster bigotry manifested itself in a common cry that Catholics were all very well in their place as hewers of wood and drawers of water,[6] but under the Ulster Provisional Government no Catholic should be employed in Belfast. The battle in the shipyards is well remembered with its Catholic boycott and violent expulsion of the Catholic workingmen. All Catholics, in fact, fled or were withdrawn from the shipyards for many months, to protect them from the violence of the Protestant mob. Sir Edward Carson said no word in condemnation of this brutality, nor did any minister of religion, though Belfast never failed in denouncing outrages in the South and West.[1]

In fact the Government of the half-province justified the boast that it was ready to break all laws of the United Kingdom. A Royal Proclamation had in December, 1913, forbidden the importing of arms. Sir Edward Carson admitted no such control. The departure of the "Fanny" from Hamburg, in 1914, laden with arms for the new army was foreshadowed in the papers three weeks before its arrival at Larne in April 1914.[2] All the Volunteers were called out. They guarded Belfast, where a decoy-boat was sent in to mislead the police. They surrounded Larne and Bangor and shut them out from "the enemy." At the famous gun-running into the Irish harbour the Provisional Government took possession of the King's high-roads, ran telegraph wires to earth, confined the police to barracks, seized harbours, locked up officials of the customs, rounded up suspected Nationalists and locked them in a barn, and generally broke the public laws of sea and land. Admirals, generals, officials of the coast-guard, of police, of the post-office, and telegraph service, all connived at the lawless deeds. Public law was suspended. Evidently at Larne the Provisional Government not merely claimed but exercised the right to rebel. The fact was emphasized on April 29 in a speech by Major Crawford, the captain of the "Fanny" to a Unionist Club in County Down: "If they were put out of the Union ... he would infinitely prefer to change his allegiance right over to the Emperor of Germany, or any one else who had got a proper and stable government."[3]

England was startled. Her Prime Minister in Parliament formally denounced the whole proceeding at Larne, as "an unprecedented outrage."[4] The answer of the north-east Ulster Government to English tremors was unhesitating. Captain Craig, M.P., on July 9, 1914, read for the first time openly the preamble to the Constitution of the Ulster Provisional Government. The people, it stated, of the counties and places represented in the Ulster Unionist Council undertook to resist to the utmost the powers to be exercised over them by a Nationalist Government, and resolved if Home Rule was set up to ignore the Irish Parliament, and to assume and exercise all powers necessary for the government of Ulster, pending the restoration of direct Imperial government.[5] Fresh military preparations were made for the army, now said to have reached 200,000 men. Machine guns were landed, and rest stations arranged for refugees flying from the threatened civil war. A resolution was proposed by Lord Londonderry, stating that preparations would be made to resist by force and every other method decrees of any Nationalist Parliament that might be established.[6] At Larne, on July 11, Sir Edward Carson first announced the name of the late hero of the *Fanny*, expounded the lesson of Larne, lauded the organizers of the gun-running, classing himself among them, and directed the volunteers to be ready, "if not for peace with honour, for war with honour."[1] The Government was again flouted in the Belfast celebration of the glorious Twelfth of July. The black pirate flag was hoisted on the gate of the chief gun-runner, and as the procession passed in its multitudinous glory, Sir Edward Carson, called on to salute the lawless emblem, rose in his carriage laden with orange lilies, and more than once bowed low, to tumultuous cheers, amid flags of the Brethren and the "open Bibles" of wood borne aloft by the Orange Lodges in testimony of their rigid creed.[2] He led the March to Drumbeg of 70,000 men, where he boasted of the army mutiny and the Larne triumph.[3] There was a series of reviews. Among the forty reporters said to be gathered in Belfast for the display, three or four Germans watched the proceedings, and Baron von Kuhlmann, of the German Embassy, now the German Secretary for Foreign Affairs, arrived quietly, without information given to the Press as an honoured guest, to view the magnitude of the Protestant preparations for Civil War.[4] According to the boast of the Covenanting Government, the force raised to defy the Government at Westminster was so furnished and drilled as to be ready at any moment to take the field. English generals and English Press-men proclaimed aloud that the troops exceeded any army in training, appearance and equipment. Their defiant quality was shown the day after the Conference at Buckingham Palace had broken up, when on July 25 the Provisional Government of Ulster organized a parade through Belfast of 5,000 men in khaki, with bands, rifles, and machine-guns, all traffic in the streets being held up officially for the display.[5]

Sensational public shows, on however costly a scale of European advertisement, were but the decorative ornaments of methodical and hard-cut business. The English War Office, moved by some natural fears that the new "Army" might be tempted in the interests of Ulster to appropriate some of the military stores collected in certain mobilization centres, had before these events proposed to send military guards to protect their own material, and had thought it prudent to appoint General Sir Neville MacCready to Belfast as military governor in reserve, in cause the magistrates refused to perform their duty. He was received with shouts of "Butcher MacCready."[6] Cries of agonised terror resounded, "The English Government had planned a 'pogrom,'" "There was to be a massacre of Protestants." The country was blazing with excitement when the Provisional Government sprang to the rescue. It possessed unexploited resources in certain lofty connexions, and the wide-spread influences of Orange and Freemason propaganda in high circles were available to organise a secret conspiracy throughout the British Army and Navy, and even the Air Force, that they, should stand on the side of north-east

Ulster in all eventualities, and refuse to act against her. To their temporary annoyance the plot was accidently revealed early in 1914 by the notorious "Curragh mutiny,"[1] when the illegal complicity of generals and officers became known, whose military discipline had been degraded at the bidding of faction cries, and whose larger outlook had been eclipsed by the glamour of old ascendancies. The Prime Minister took charge of the War Office. But the discomfiture of the Provisional Government was only momentary. The Prime Minister returned to his usual position. Before the scientific organization and the warlike threats of the Unionist Council, the Government of the United Kingdom, over-awed and intimidated, succumbed and laid down all opposition.

II. The outbreak of war opened the second scene in the drama of the Provisional Government. The Council of the half-province, professing an undying loyalty to the Imperial Government which it had vanquished, became the Mayor of the Palace to the defeated powers of Westminster. It consented to fill the chief places of the Law, and to guide the Imperial Cabinet according to the Ulster formulae. Sir Edward Carson and Mr. F. E. Smith undertook as Attorney and Solicitor-General to deal in England with any rebellious-minded persons less successful than themselves; and Mr. Campbell and Mr. William Moore were in due time made Lord Chief Justice and Judge of the High Court in Ireland. The Higher Policy was thus proclaimed identical with the Higher Law, to the confusion of all objectors. In course of affairs Sir Edward Carson passed to the War Cabinet, the Admiralty, and finally to the political Propaganda, by which foreign nations were instructed as to what was or was not laudable "rebellion" in Ireland.[2]

All this implied no change in Sir Edward Carson's views, as north-east Ulster might see when on a visit to Ireland as Minister of the Crown, he gracefully accepted the gift of a silver model of the "Fanny."[3] Meanwhile in Belfast itself the Ulster Provisional Government was maintained in full force, and the second stage of the north-east movement was not less efficiently directed than the first. The Orange and Unionist Press maintained their policy of threats. The *Northern Whig* on August 24, reminded "three-fourths of the people of Ulster" (an amazing calculation) that if the Home Rule Bill became an Act they "must become either traitors to the Covenant which they have solemnly signed or rebels to the Crown." On the next day the *Belfast Evening Telegraph* commented on the suggestion to put the Home Rule Bill upon the Statute Book with a time reservation: "To do that would create a serious position. It would drive Ulster Loyalists into this position, that much as they desire to assist Britain's armed forces abroad at this juncture, and much as their help in that direction is needed, they would be compelled, through the Government's action, to remain here for the defence of their hearths and homes against an enemy no less deadly and embittered." The Unionist Council meanwhile undertook no recruiting for the war.[1] There was a good deal of local effort, on natural and liberal lines, where Protestants and Catholics enlisted together, and sent out men to fight and die at Silvia Bay—all this apart from any direction of Sir Edward Carson. Recruiting was in fact officially frowned on until the leader had given the word. A letter written by Captain Arthur O'Neill from the front urging men to enlist was refused by a Unionist paper, because Sir Edward Carson had made no pronouncement. In Tyrone, one who was urgent in calling for recruits was accused of "spoiling the game" before his leader had spoken. Covenanters declared that if the Home Rule Bill was signed there would not be a single man sent from Ulster to the war. Strange scenes of excitement were reported. Sir Edward Carson arrived unannounced in Belfast on September 1[2] to explain the bargain he had completed with the War Office before authorizing the use of Ulster troops. After some days of private negotiations he stated the terms on September 4, at a meeting of the Unionist Association, and afterwards at a public meeting. The Volunteers were to form a separate division, under their old officers, and to have back any of their officers who had had to mobilize. As for the fear of danger at home, he told them from 20,000 to 30,000 soldiers could hold Ulster, and the Volunteer force at home would be kept efficient to repel those who would try to invade their country.[3] At Larne he renewed this assurance: "I am proud of the men in the Ulster Volunteers—not only those who are enlisting, *but those who are staying at home*, to save us from a tyranny to which we will never submit."[4] His first promise was a division maintained as a separate and complete unit, without being attached to any other division. The second pledge was an assurance that the policy of the Ulster Provisional Government and the Covenant would suffer no slightest injury: "I promise you that I will reorganize the Volunteers, and that when you come back you will not find Home Rule in Ulster."[5] By these emphatic pledges the policy was confirmed of ourselves first, ourselves last, ourselves all the time.

The War Office kept to its pledge of a separate unit. The Ulster Volunteer Force were allowed, contrary to army rules, to retain their special cap badges, and flags worked for their use. But the essential bond of union lay in the signing of the Covenant, which was enforced on every member who joined the new division. In compelling the War Office to admit a separate and complete unit bound by a special political oath—a course unfamiliar in modern armies since Cromwell's time—Sir Edward Carson had won a notable victory for the Provisional Government of north-east Ulster. The triumph over the unity of the King's Imperial forces had indeed its natural effect on discipline, as may be illustrated by the Inniskillings, whose battalions, like the Irish Rifles, are divided between the Ulster Division and the Irish Division in the army. It was the Covenanting Inniskillings, under the protection of the Provisional Government, who felt at liberty to riot through Enniskillen trampling under foot and insulting Irish emblems. Meanwhile in Ulster no time was lost in affirming Sir Edward Carson's second pledge as to the security of the Volunteers and of the Covenanters. On the anniversary of Ulster Day, September 28, 1914, he in Belfast made clear to his followers the purpose of the Provisional Government. "What I propose to do" (that is after the war) "is to summon the Provisional Government and repeal the Home Rule Bill, and I propose in the same act to enact that it is the duty of the Volunteers to see that the Act shall never have effect in Ulster… Our Volunteers who cannot go abroad will go on with the work at home. We have plenty of guns, and we are going to keep them. We are afraid of nothing."[1]

Discipline was enforced with a stern hand. Even Mr. F. E. Smith, "the Galloper," was sternly rebuked by the *Northern Whig* for a temporary lapse, in his imperial enthusiasm, from the pure doctrine of the "natural leaders" of Ulster arrayed against "the spread of Revolutionary doctrine and free thought." He was accused of attempting to recruit for the British army without strict adherence to the tactics of Sir Edward Carson, by addressing a recruiting meeting at Liverpool along with leading Radicals. His intention was condemned by "the opinion of leading Unionists as to the impropriety of his conduct," and his apology was rejected. "We hope he will reconsider his decision, and that no other leading Unionists will be found on the platforms with Radicals."[2] Sir Edward Carson for his part refused to stand with Mr. Redmond at a recruiting meeting in Newry.[3] All necessary steps were taken to reinforce the militant Covenanters. Unionists over military age, or not inclined to join the army, were encouraged to take on Ulster Volunteer Force uniform and equipment, and fill up the ranks. While it was understood that the outgoing troops would on their return be used to enforce all the demands of the Covenanters—the more efficiently, as Sir Edward Carson explained, from actual experience and discipline in war—the home army was kept in being with its arms, ammunition, and equipment. The able head of the cycle corps was retained in Belfast in a good position, at a time when advertisements were posted for weeks at all the cinemas in Dublin and elsewhere calling for motor cyclists for the Ulster Division. When the War Office was in distress for supplies, if the Covenanters released to it some of their vast stores of khaki uniforms etc., it was at prices which were no disadvantage to themselves. By the aid of a submissive Cabinet at

Westminster all who had connived at the Larne "outrage" from generals downwards were given military promotion. As the correspondent of the *Manchester Guardian* pointed out on January 17, 1917, the Larne gun-running won as many titles, honours, and offices for its organizers and patrons as if it had been an incident in the first battle of Ypres. The major who had brought the "Fanny" into harbour was raised to the rank of Colonel, retained at the centre of action in Belfast, and made head of the Commissariat. In recognition of the unparalleled outrage not only the military but all other consenting officials were well provided for; not one was left derelict.[1] There was thus in the numerous and lucrative administrative posts at home an organization ready for future emergencies. The Protestant Primate illustrated the unity of the Ulster Volunteer Force at home and abroad, which he said could not be better described than in the words of Holy Writ: "There were some that went forth to the battle, and others that tarried with the stuff." The troops who remained at home were carefully linked with their comrades who had joined the army. Practically all the Volunteer officers had immediately obtained army commissions, without further question, as their indubitable right. The roll of honour gave not only the soldier's place in the British army, but his rank in the Ulster Volunteers. The Volunteers at home were as before commended to the good offices of the English army of the old intrigue. Their friends of the Curragh Mutiny were not forgotten, and in view of future emergencies special Christmas boxes of cigarettes, with encouraging mottoes and remembrances, were sent from Belfast to the officers and privates concerned.[2] A leading Liberal paper in England refused to allow any information of this incident lest it should be accused of breaking the "truce" which had been proclaimed—a truce which the Covenanters were so cheerfully defying. In Belfast, however, the event was widely advertised; and thus by silence abroad, and advertisement at home, Belfast enjoyed its well organized double triumph.

There was no lack meanwhile of sermons to glorify the unchanging fixity of the Provisional Government and the Covenant. The ladies of the movement were also useful in upholding the doctrine of ourselves first and last and all the time. In the Hospital War Supplies and in the supply of comforts for prisoners of war their object was to draw Ulster into a separate organization for the work of mercy from the rest of Ireland.

III. The third stage of the Provisional Government opened on May 21, 1917, with the proposal of a Convention to effect a settlement of the Irish question. "The Government have therefore decided," said the Premier, "to invite Irishmen to put forward their own proposals for the government of their country. We propose that Ireland should try her own hand at hammering out an instrument of government for her own people. The experiment has succeeded in other parts of the British Empire. It succeeded in Canada; it succeeded in South Africa. What was accomplished in South Africa, in Australia, and in Canada, I cannot help believing is achievable in Ireland…. No proposal on any side for the better government of Ireland can be shut out from discussion under the terms of reference." The only limitation was "within the Empire."[1] The Covenanters saw their isolation threatened, and hastened to assert their independent position. Sir John Lonsdale protested against any steps being taken to bring pressure on Ulster, relying on Mr. Asquith's promise that "Ulster should not be coerced," "The people of Ulster," he said, are a democratic community, and they possess in the Ulster Unionist Council" (a council of peers, capitalists, and employers) "a thoroughly representative organization. All that we—their representatives in this House—can do is to lay the government proposals before them." Mr. Asquith noted that the leader of Ulster Members of Parliament could not assent without referring to the Ulster Unionist Council (i.e. Provisional Government) for their decision. "If the Convention fails," he said "Heaven help us—I will not take that despondent, I may say, desperate view." Sir Edward Carson, then First Lord of the Admiralty, insisted on the absolute independence and authority of the Provisional Government. "Whether the Unionist Council will accept the invitation, or whether it will not, I am sure I do not know. Of one thing I am certain: no threats will have the slightest effect upon them. Whatever decision they take, and I hope they will take a wise one, I will be with them to the end."[2]

The scientific organization of north-east Ulster was equal to the strain. The new business was taken in hand by the Provisional Government with the same single eye and the same efficiency of control as ever. Having already a pledge-bound party, their first step was to create a pledge-bound British Government. They took the precaution of immediately insisting in Parliament on an open and unmistakable pledge that the half-province should not be outvoted by the whole of the rest of Ireland. The matter was carried through by Mr. Ronald McNeill and Mr. Bonar Law, both Sir Edward Carson's lieutenants in the Ulster militant campaign. On May 24, Mr. Ronald McNeill asked the Prime Minister whether his statement, that in the event of the Convention coming to a "substantial agreement," the Government would introduce legislation to give effect to such agreement, is to be taken as in any degree affecting his previous pledge that under no circumstances shall Ulster be coerced into submitting to the jurisdiction of an Irish Parliament: and Mr. Bonar Law answered that "There could not be 'substantial agreement' in the circumstance suggested by my hon. friend's question."[1] It was clearly understood that the object of question and answer was to nullify any conclusion come to by the Convention which is not agreed to by representives of Ulster, so that northeast Ulster should absolutely hold the fate of Ireland in its hands. A safe position being thus secured, Sir Edward Carson on June 11, stated in Parliament that he had presided in Belfast over a conference of 500 Covenanters and advised them to consent to the Convention.[2]

"Substantial agreement" became the fixed and mysterious phrase for all later ministerial pronouncements—vague and ominous. In the negotiations the Sinn Féinidhthe of the South naturally saw a direct menace to the freedom and dignity of the Convention, and a new pledge for the dominance of north-east Ulster, nor is it wonderful that they should refuse to enter a conference so trammelled before it was allowed to exist. On the other hand the Provisional Government, in its newly assured security, could devise methods adapted to the free position of Belfast and its dependencies. Members were selected for the Convention and a deliberative Committee of the Council was appointed, to whom they should report privately, and take their secret directions, without power themselves to vote or intimate the eventual intentions of the Council behind them. According to the *Manchester Guardian* of January 16, 1918, the Standing Committee maintained a strict control; and the *Northern Whig,* closely identified with the Council, told the Convention when it visited Belfast that whatever scheme of government it might fashion would find its way to the waste-paper basket. It is easy to understand the dangers of such a system, with its inevitable hindrances and delays to serious work, and the hopelessness of bringing the general interests of Ireland into equal discussion with the claims of "Ourselves first and last." The English government had already learned in past years that any appeal to Imperial necessities, and necessary sacrifices to meet them, has been met by the Provisional Government with its fixed interpretation of Imperial policy and obligations. The Covenanters will accept an Empire that is fashioned according to their own formulae, and pledged to protect their special privileges and industrial interests, in the manner which they themselves dictate. Otherwise in preparation for civil war they retain their own State policy, their government, their army; while beyond these they look to their continued alliance with the British army, and the spreading influence of Orange Lodges and Freemasonry in military circles.[3] While the rank and file change, the engineers of the Curragh mutiny grasp more firmly than ever supreme control of the entire army organization and policy.

Having proved their power of intimidating the government of England, north-east Ulster again showed its activity in what was thought by many to be a new unparalleled outrage, flung this time at the Convention. A demand was made for a redistribution of seats in Ireland to come into operation in case the Convention (which north-east Ulster, as it believed, had the pledged power to ruin) should fail in its task; and Sir John Lonsdale, representing in Parliament the policy of the Unionist Council, prepared a plan of redistribution, which would add strength to his party for the conflict at the end of the war. Once more the House of Commons was scandalized at the surrender of the Government.[1] But the compromise allowed to it was but a matter of details, leaving the principle untouched. Sir John Lonsdale, in virtue (according to the ominous comment of the *Times*)[2] his strong and respected views on the Irish situation," with Colonel Craig and the Mayor of Derry, as men whom the Government delighted to honour, accepted a peerage, a baronetcy, and a knighthood, and the public wait to see whether the service recognized is the breaking or the saving of the Convention. Whatever it be, their reward is secured in advance. So the Government drives the State with even keel over the turbulent waters, with Orange and Freemason destroyers on either side to mark the path of safety.

It must be noticed that nowhere in Ireland is there so stern a resistance to conscription as in Ulster. The numbers of those who enlisted in the first period of the war[3] (August 2, 1914, to January 8, 1916), when recruiting was most active, show that outside the military recruiting area of Belfast, where the figures are high, the counties of the North fell behind those of the South. In Donegal, Derry, Fermanagh, Tyrone, the percentage to population was 1.03; in Armagh, Cavan, Louth, and Monaghan, 1.1; in Antrim and Down, the very centre of "loyal" and Imperial enthusiasm 1.36. In Carlow, Kildare, and Wicklow, on the other hand, the percentage was 1.57; in King's and Queen's Counties, Longford, Meath, and Westmeath, 1.53; in Cork, 1.66; in Kilkenny, Tipperary, Waterford, and Wexford, 1.7. Only along the western coast where land disputes have of old raged, and where great tracts are being gradually reclaimed from the most extreme poverty by the Congested Districts Board, have the percentages fallen to .97 and .16. During the course of the war recruiting has generally ceased. The *Irish News*, of April 30, 1917, reported a meeting of the engineers in Belfast when an amendment was submitted calling upon the Government to apply conscription to Ireland as a means of relieving the demand upon the services of skilled artisans in England. Out of a meeting of fifteen hundred men, mostly Unionists, only eleven voted for conscription. The attitude of the farmers is said to be yet stronger. In the year 1916-17, according to the annual report of the Vice-Chancellor for the Queen's University in

Belfast, 440 men and 203 women had been enrolled—a record for the University, while the appended report of the Officers' Training Corps gives the number of cadets who have enlisted as 14. Attempts to recruit have failed from the fact that the majority of the students before entering were pledged by their fathers not to enlist. Yet in politics these people, or nine-tenths of them, are emphatic Carsonites.[1] Even now the reason is alleged that the Covenanters are needed at home to protect their women and their farms from "the enemy." Apart from the grossness of the libel on their Catholic fellow-countrymen, this argument takes no account of the 70,000 or more English troops detained to keep order in Ireland. A second reason advanced in various occupations is the fear of the employed men that their Unionist masters might if they were absent fill up their places with Nationalist working-men—a reason which implies considerable distrust of the political loyalty of the employers. These magnates in fact have been known to allege a preference for Catholic workmen, as they were not infected with Marxian Socialism, while the Protestant workmen were riddled with it; and that once Home Rule and Rome Rule were settled these Protestants would turn anti-capitalist and renounce the "natural leaders" of democracy. It is not impossible that the attitude of Ulster has had a more determining effect upon the Government in delaying conscription than that of the Southern Irishman; on whom, however, all the blame is publicly thrown.

North-east Ulster evidently remains the supreme example of the policy defined by the Prime Minister, "Ourselves first, ourselves last, ourselves all the time, and ourselves alone." It is a characteristic enlargement of the "Sinn Fein" of the rest of Ireland, words which are more truly translated "We ourselves," and carry the simple lesson that in need it is to the diligent efforts of only ourselves that we must look to mend our position. Ulster has made its own peculiar form of "Sinn Fein," and organized it scientifically. In this external organization alone lies its triumph. There is nothing novel in its aim of material success and preservation of the natural leaders of the democracy. If therefore the Provisional Government of the north lifts a voice of shocked indignation at "rebellion" by southern Sinn Fein, it can with justice only reprove it for a single reason, its inferior success in coercing the Imperial Government. The indignation of the Covenanters cannot rest on any ground of principle, since they have not only claimed but asserted the right to define their own view of imperial duties, and to break all laws and rise in civil war in defence of that view—"Belfast *contra mundum*." North-east Ulster, however, cannot expect to be the final judge in all causes for all time, and so practical a community (leaving out the Pope for the moment) will allow that regard for ourselves first, ourselves last, ourselves all the time, ourselves alone, has for its sanction but one final test—that of Success. The northerners must naturally repudiate with sincere contempt a movement less highly organized and financed than their own, and lacking all its advantages for victorious intrigues. Ulster aptitude and Ulster business instinct have materialized what south Ireland has dreamed of. Their leaders have been more methodical, and with their special privileges of position, riches, and allies, they have done better than the men of the south; why should they spare their contempt? The only danger they have to fear lies hidden in the secrets of the future. In due time it will be revealed whether a rigid present can be bound to a rigid past by ropes of steel—even by pledges and by "mystical" Covenants with an offensive and defensive alliance which shall secure an everlasting, and unchanging protection for Belfast's industrial wealth under the "God who is not as other Gods." Once again in the world's history it will be discovered how long men or provinces can live by organization, and the power to do what they will with their own; or whether the force of the spirit may not yet again break ancient moulds to reach a larger life. We shall learn, in due time, whether the ricketty shelters guaranteed by an old statecraft will stand against rising floods, and whether the bravest men are not those who advance under the open heavens to new horizons.

NOTES

p. 649 [1] Leaflet published by Ulster Liberal Association, *The Kaiser's Ulster Friends.*

p. 650 [1] *Ib.*

[2] *Ib.*

[3] *Hansard,* Vol. 29, p. 988 (Speech in House, Aug. 8, 1911).

[4] *Northern Whig,* Oct. 20, 1911.

[5] *Northern Whig,* Sept. 26, 1911.

p. 651 [1] *Northern Whig,* Feb. 7, 1912.

[2] Leaflet published by The Ulster Liberal Association, *The Kaiser's Ulster Friends,* p. 4.

[3] *Annual Register,* Sept. 1912, p. 210.

[4] *Northern Whig,* Feb. 1, 1913.

p. 652 [1] *Portadown News,* March 29, 1913.

[2] *Belfast Newsletter,* May 24, 1913.

[3] Letter signed "H.G." in *Irish Churchman,* Nov. 14, 1913.

p. 653 [1] Open letter to Mr. Asquith in *Coleraine Constitution,* July 1913.

[2] *Northern Whig,* Sept. 25, 1913.

p. 654 [1] Heard by the writer. Sir E. Carson was described at a luncheon of the Nonconformist Unionist Association in London, as the best embodiment, at that moment, of the ancient spirit of Nonconformity.— *Annual Register,* 1913, p. 206.

[2] An action was brought by Belfast gunsmiths against the port officials for detaining arms consigned to the plaintiffs at Hamburg, on Dec. 18, 1913. *Annual Register,* March 1914, p. 66. In May and June 1914, the *Northern Whig* records that two hundred and forty sacks of cartridges were found in a cargo of cement, and Mauser rifles and ammunition to the Value of £1,200 concealed in a furniture van with sides of false sheeting. They were entering into a "very extreme course," Sir E. Carson allowed later, "a course which could only be justified because we were being singled out for exceptional treatment of betrayal."—*Irish Times,* Feb. 4, 1918.

[3] "I like to get near the enemy. We are coming near them in the near future, and I like to see that men are preparing for what I call the great day."— *Northern Whig,* Aug. 4, 1913.

p. 655 [1] Leaflet published by Ulster Liberal Association, *The Kaiser's Ulster Friends,* p. 3.

[2] *Annual Register,* 1913, p. 205. *Times,* Sept. 27, 1913.

[3] *Northern Whig,* Sept. 25, 1913. In accepting office as head of the Provisional

Government, Sir E. Carson declared that Government policy would have a disastrous effect on the forces of the Crown, since he knew from his correspondence that these were already dividing into hostile camps. Speaking at Manchester he stated that since the army must obey lawful orders politicians must see that the passing of the Bill should not be enforced.—*Times,* Dec. 3, 1913; *Annual Register,* 1913, p. 249.

[4] *Northern Whig,* Sept. 21, 1913. "If I were an Ulster Protestant I would rather be ruled from Constantinople, by the Sultan of Turkey, than by a politician like Mr. Devlin." Belfast, July 12, 1912. Leaflet published by Ulster Liberal Association, *The Kaiser's Ulster Friends.*

[5] At the Women's Amalgamated Unionist and Tariff Reform Association, London, June 24, 1912 (as quoted by leaflet Ulster Liberal Association, *The Kaiser's Ulster Friends*), Sir E. Carson stated—"regarding the pronouncement of policy of the Government in relation to Ulster, he intended when he went over there to break every law that was possible. Let the Government take their own course. He was not a bit afraid of them, for a more wretched, miserable, time-serving opportunist lot never before sat in Parliament." "If it is illegal we don't mind that." —*Northern Whig,* Aug. 5, 1912.

"For his own part he knew nothing of legality or illegality. All he thought of was his Covenant. His Covenant to him was the text and the foundation of what was illegality and what was legality, and everything that was necessary to carry out his Covenant he believed in his conscience he was under Heaven entitled to do." —*Northern Whig,* July 14, 1914.

[6] See Redmond's speech, at Manchester, quoting the *Belfast Newsletter. Annual Register,* 1913, p. 234.

p. 656 [1] In July 1912. See legal proceedings following the onslaught on Catholic workingmen; *Northern Whig,* Jan. 13 and 16, 1913; and *Evening Telegraph,* Nov. 1912; April 1913. (McCotter and others v. *Evening Telegraph.*) The Catholics have not even yet been restored to Workman and Clark's in their old numbers.

[2] Sir Edward Carson's letter to the papers asked for funds in view of a "more forward movement," "the climax of all we have been aiming at," "involving action almost unprecedented,"—*Northern Whig,* March 14, 1914.

The gun-running is described in the *Irish Volunteer,* May 2, 1914, p. 9.

[3] *North Down Herald,* May 3, 1912.

[4] The words were "this grave and unprecedented outrage." The Government promised to undertake, without delay, appropriate steps to vindicate the authority of the law, and protect officers and servants of the King, and His Majesty's subjects

in the exercise of their duty, and in the enjoyment of their legal rights. It was admitted that a coast-guardsman died in the performance of his duty.—*Hansard,* Vol. 61, p. 1348.

[5] *Annual Register,* 1914, p. 152.

[6] The resolution was proposed at a meeting on July 11, the Twelfth being a Sunday. See *Northern Whig,* July 11-13, 1914.

p. 657 [1] *Northern Whig,* July 13, 1914.

[2] Not mentioned in the Press. Witnessed by the writer.

[3] He defied the Government to prosecute them and charged it with plots to arrest some of them as a sop to John Redmond and his cattle-drivers and boy-cotters, *Northern Whig,* July 14, 1914.

[4] See *Northern Whig,* March 22, 1917.

[5] Guns which had been distributed over the country were systematically collected from all parts to add to the formidable show of force. *Northern Whig,* July 27, 1914.

[6] Sir E. Carson used the words "pogrom plot" in his speech on Ulster Day 1914.—*Northern Whig* For "pogrom" to make "the red blood flow" see leading article, *Ib.,* July 27, 1914.

p. 658 [1] March 20. See *Annual Register,* 1914, p. 55-66, 69, which gives a summary and references. For questions in the House see *Hansard,* vol. 61, p. 1347.

Mr. Asquith took charge of the War Office from March 30 to August 5.

[2] Sir E. Carson was Attorney-General in the Government of 1915; First Lord of the Admiralty in the next Government of 1916.

[3] The presentation of the model of the notorious gun-running privateer of the Provisional Government was made in the Ulster Volunteer Hospital in the presence of Lady Londonderry.

p. 659 [1] A leader in the *Northern Whig* stated that there had been little recruiting in Ulster, for which the Government policy was to blame. Sept. 2, 1914.

A meeting was held in Belfast, August 1914, to consider the war problem. Sir E. Carson wrote they would show "without any bartering of conditions, that the cause of Great Britain is our cause ... and that we will make common cause, and suffer all sacrifices." Captain J. Craig stated that he, with Sir E. Carson, were arranging the best terms that could be fixed for the Volunteer Force to offer its services. They were ready to go forward at any length, "trusting in the first instance to Sir E. Carson to preserve their political heritage."—*Northern Whig,* Aug. 8, 1914. Observe Sir E. Carson's statement on Feb. 3, 1918: "Let those who talk of Ulster's unreasonableness remember this—that the distinct promise *we got from the*

Prime Minister of the day, and by the House of Commons, was that the question of Home Rule should stand over until the war was ended. *Then we got up our splendid Ulster Division."—Irish Times,* Feb. 4, 1918.

The Volunteer Force was said to number 80,000 drilled and armed men.— *Northern Whig,* Aug. 12. There was a parade of 300 who offered for foreign service, and 700 for home defence. *Ib.,* Aug. 17. Appeals were made constantly for contributions to the Prince of Wales' Fund.—*Ib.,* Aug. 14, 15, 18, 22, 28. A letter from Sir E. Carson commending the Ulster Defence Fund for "Our efforts to maintain our position in the United Kingdom" was inserted twice.—*Ib.,* Aug. 13, 25.

[2] The *Northern Whig* announced that Sir Edward Carson had arrived to offer the Ulster Unionist Association "a scheme sanctioned by the War Office, whereby the members of the Ulster Volunteer Force may be able to assist in defending their country in the present great crisis." "If the Ulster Volunteers agree to fight for the King and the Empire now, afterwards they will, if necessary, also fight for Ulster, and with this intention they must go on strengthening their organization and increasing their numbers."—*Northern Whig* Sept. 2, 1914.

[3] At the parade of the North Belfast Regiment, Sir E. Carson promised: "I and those who remain behind will take care that Ulster is no invaded province." —*Northern Whig,* Sept. 4, 5, 1914.

Sir E. Carson, in justifying his resignation from the Cabinet, laid stress on his position: "I am a Covenanter." This placed him in a dual capacity, for while trying to make out the best course the Government ought to adopt, on the other hand he would be thinking how that was to affect his Covenant and his pledges to the people of Ulster. He was enabled to remain in the Government as long is he did because "I was perfectly well aware that those with whom I had Covenants in this province would wish, above all things, that I should put aside all questions of local interest." He repudiated the idea of being "a traitor to Ulster and a breaker of my Covenant."—*Irish Times,* Feb. 4, 1918.

[4] *Northern Whig,* Sept. 8, 1914.

[5] The covenanters added the usual curses for the Pope. The outrage was on October 16, 1917. The account given in the long correspondence of Archdeacon Keown with Sir Bryan Mahon was not published till December 15, 1917. It is there stated that Catholics of Enniskillen had made a larger contribution to the fighting force of the war than all other religious denominations of the town combined.—*Irish Times,* Dec. 15, 1917.

p. 660 [1] The words of Sir Edward Carson to Unionist Council were:—"And I propose if necessary ... that their first Act shall be to repeal the Home Rule Act as regards Ulster. And I propose in the same Act to enact that it is the duty of the Volunteers to see that no Act, or no attempt at an Act, under that Bill shall ever have effect in Ulster." At a public meeting he promised that he and the other leaders would devote themselves "heart and soul to maintaining the organization intact, so that we may repel any invader who dares to come and try to interfere with us." He repeated the words: "We have got the men, we have got the guns—and we are going to keep the guns—and therefore what have we to be afraid of?"—*Northern Whig*, Sept. 29, 1914.

[2] Mr. F. E. Smith spoke at Liverpool on Sept. 21, along with Mr. T. P. O'Connor. In view of the recent co-operation of these two speakers in America, the *Northern Whig* objection is interesting.—*Northern Whig*, Sept. 17, 1914.

[3] The meeting was not held, as Sir E. Carson did not see any need for Mr. Redmond's proposal. It was commented on in the papers early in 1915.

p. 661 [1] Among numerous instances one may be given as an illustration. The "Competent Military Authority" in Belfast is Brigadier-General Hackett Pain, who before the war was Chief of the Staff of the Ulster Force, which had been illegally organized and armed with rifles from Germany for the purpose of resisting His Majesty's forces. He is now commanding the Northern District Irish command, and orders prohibiting meetings and the like are issued by him to those who, in the speeches of the Ulster leaders, were always alluded to as "the enemy whom we loathe."

[2] Seen by the writer.

p. 662 [1] These terms were fundamentally altered by the Prime Minister on Feb. 23, 1918.

[2] *Hansard*, Vol. 93, p. 2020.

p. 663 [1] *Ib.* Vol. 93, p. 2473.

[2] *Ib.* Vol. 94, p. 619.

[3] In Sir E. Carson's opinion it would be "indecent" in any wise to interfere with the "meditations" of the Convention. If by "settlement, settlement, settlement ... I am never done hearing of the word now—if by settlement people have in their minds surrender, well then there will be no settlement."—*Irish Times*, Feb. 4, 1918. See his earlier statement, "He would fight no one if they were allowed to take their own course, and keep their own taxes."—*Times*, Dec. 5. *Annual Register*, 1913, p. 251.

An Orange Military Lodge was started in the camp at Ballykinlar.

p. 664 [1] The Boundary Commission was appointed in October, 1917, while the Convention was sitting, and the Redistribution Bill passed by the Lords, Feb. 5,

1918. The *Freeman's Journal* and *Hansard* show the feeling aroused in and outside Parliament.

[2] In the announcement of New Year's Honours, 1918.

[3] The numbers enlisted are taken from official figures in the Viceroy's Report of Jan. 14, 1916. The Ulster Volunteer Division was not sent into battle till the summer of 1916.

p. 665 [1] On February 3 Sir E. Carson stated that he had always wished that conscription should be applied to Ireland. "We never asked that it should not." He himself had proposed an amendment to that effect. He added: "I am not going into the question of whether that is a possible policy now or not. The lapse of time makes great differences." In his own province he avoided the responsibility of advising conscription.—*Irish Times*, Feb. 4, 1918.

N.B.—The question of the support of English Unionism to civil war in Ireland has not been dealt with here. One quotation will illustrate the defiance to the Government, and the incitements to north-east Ulster, which English politicians did not scruple to use. We have the contribution to high statesmanship of Mr. Bonar Law on Nov. 28, 1913, in Dublin: "I have said on behalf of the party that if the Government attempt to coerce Ulster before they have received the sanction of the electors, *Ulster will do well to resist them, and we will support resistance to the end.*"

"I wonder whether you have tried to picture in your own minds what civil war means ... it is a prospect from which I shrink in horror, and for which I wish to avoid, if I can, any responsibility... But really we must try to think what the effect of bloodshed and civil war would be on our Parliamentary institutions, on the army, on the Empire as a whole. It would not mean anarchy; it would mean literally red ruin and the breaking up of law. It would produce results from which our country would not recover in the lifetime of any one of those whom I am addressing."

This was the high emprise upon which Mr. Bonar Law encouraged north-east Ulster to embark, and for which he promised them the support of his party "to the end."

The resistance which Mr. Bonar Law thus commended to Ulster Unionists will be recalled to mind by Irishmen in his own identical terms.

LADY GREGORY

♣

(1852-1932)

Isabella Augusta Gregory, or Lady Gregory, is best known for her relationship with William Butler Yeats. Together they founded the National Theater Society at the Abbey Theater in 1899, which was at the center of the Irish Literary Renaissance. She introduced and inspired Yeats and other key figures in the Irish dramatic movement, such as John Millington Synge and eventually Sean O'Casey, to develop plays for the Abbey repertory, which strongly influenced theater around the world. But Lady Gregory's prose contributions to the Irish Literary Renaissance are sometimes overlooked because of her perceived role with the National Theater Society. In fact, critics consider her the first important writer to employ realistic dialogue and dialects in local "Kiltartan" speech. These dialects were fairly new to theater and literature, but they had an enormous impact on some of the greatest writers of the 20th century, including Eugene O'Neill, who tried his own hand at dialect after seeing a touring production of the Abbey in the United States.

Aside from her contributions to the Irish dramatic movement, Lady Gregory, even before she met William Butler Yeats, was an accomplished writer and historian. She was constantly recording Irish peasant life while she was married to Sir William Gregory, and the sketches that resulted from these interviews provided her with a wealth of understanding and material that would influence her work in drama for decades to follow. So impressed with Lady Gregory's breadth of knowledge, when Yeats was asked to produce a volume on Irish folklore and myth, he professed he was too busy with his other writings. His solution was to convince the editors that Lady Gregory was more suitable to the task than anyone else, and he encouraged her to translate and interpret this ambitious project. The result was Lady Gregory's *Irish Myths and Legends,* which stands today as the most definitive book of its kind to come out of Ireland. In his preface to her work, Yeats wrote,

"Lady Gregory has discovered a speech as beautiful as that of Morris, and a living speech into the bargain. As she moved about among her people she learned to love the beautiful speech of those who think in Irish, and to understand that it is as true a dialect of English as the dialect that Burns wrote in. It is some hundreds of years old, and age gives a language authority."

Yeats went on to write, "She has already put a great mass of stories, in which the ancient heart of Ireland still lives, into a shape at once harmonious and characteristic; and without writing more than a very few sentences of her own to link together incidents or thoughts taken from different manuscripts, without adding more indeed than the story-teller must often have added to amend the hesitation of a moment. Perhaps more than all she had discovered a fitting dialect to tell them in."

Isabella Augusta Persse was born in 1852, the youngest daughter of Dudley and Frances Barry Persse, a landowning Anglo-Irish family of Roxborough, county Galway. Educated in private schools, she had a typical childhood for young girls of her ilk (educated, wealthy and Protestant), as she was cared for by largely uneducated, poor Catholics and was exposed to many servants and peasants who looked after the Persse estate. Untypical, however, was the young Isabella's reverence for folktales and "rebel" conversations she heard from the Irish help in their mysterious and lyrical language. She requested that one nurse teach her the Irish language, and her request was honored, mostly because it was deemed extraordinary for any Protestant of means to take an interest in a language and culture of the poverty-stricken laborers who served them.

As Isabella grew up, she took on the task of acting as an intermediary between her father's estate and the tenants, and because of the respect she gained from submerging herself into their culture, she proved to be a very effective social worker on their behalf. She helped educate their children, teaching them to read and write, and the knowledge she gained, due to her unparalleled access into the Irish peasant world, would stay the focus of her creative work for the remainder of her life. At the age of twenty-eight, she married a neighbor, Sir William Gregory of Coole, a much older man (he was 63 at the time) who was once the governor of Ceylon. He was a highly respected and distinguished man who frequently traveled with his wife, and Lady Gregory, as she was now known, soon found herself immersed in a world of British politics and art—a far cry from the country kitchens and fields where most of her socializing was done before. Lady Gregory, however, never abandoned the Irish peasant life, as she spent most of her married years writing about a culture she had studied with great passion. Just twelve years into their marriage,

Sir William died and left his estate in trust to her for their son. As Lady Gregory set about to complete her husband's memoirs for him, she soon discovered that she had literary talents even beyond her own expectations, and she immersed herself in the new literary movement that was sweeping through Ireland at the end of the 19th century. She learned Irish well enough that she could speak fluently with old villagers, and she began to collect old songs and ancient folklore. This helped her gain favor with the elite Irish writers of the renaissance, as Yeats and others were also collectors of Irish stories and poems, but did not know Irish well enough to understand all they had collected.

Lady Gregory had already established herself as a legitimate writer by the time she met Yeats in 1894, and their similar passions inspired them to create an Irish theater, which would ultimately become the center of some of the most important and influential drama of the 20th century. On May 8th of 1899, the Irish Literary Theatre in Dublin would put on Yeats's *The Countess Cathleen,* which became an immediate success and launched the theatre group into a worldwide spotlight. Literary scholars have recently discovered that Lady Gregory's contribution to *The Countess Cathleen* may have been far greater than even Yeats acknowledged. Notes in her handwriting have been discovered on the original manuscript, indicating that she may have actually written a significant amount of dialogue for the play. Yeats, however, never attempted to minimize Lady Gregory's contributions. In 1922, he did write that she shared substantially in the construction of all but two of his plays.

Lady Gregory was every bit as influential and collaborative with another of the Abbey's playwrights, John Millington Synge. Synge wrote *The Playboy of the Western World,* which was so controversial in its debut that riots ensued and a police presence in the theater was the only thing that kept the play from being shut down. Synge's play included language and sexual themes that enraged many Irish at the time, but were consistent with the peasant life that the group was passionate to explore. Yet one of the problems the Irish Literary Theatre faced was the fact that they did not have enough plays in their repertory to keep up with demand. Of Lady Gregory's plays, her one-acts in particular, the scholar and author Ann Saddlemyer, in her book, *In Defence of Lady Gregory, Playwright,* wrote, "Lady Gregory deserves her place in the constellation so clearly marked by her friends and fellow image-makers who worked together for art and for Ireland."

Her main responsibilities with the Abbey were administrative and financial, and she continued to find producers and new writers, including Sean O'Casey, to keep the theatre afloat and, most importantly, relevant. She also ran the estate in Coole, left by her husband, as a sanctuary for Yeats and other writers and artists, nurturing the greatest talents of the Irish Literary Renaissance. At the estate, writers such as George Bernard Shaw and Ireland's first president, Douglas Hyde, were encouraged to carve their initials on a large copper-beech tree (known as the "Autograph Tree"), which still stands today, though the Coole House has been taken down.

Lady Gregory's last years were marked to some extent by pain and struggle. In 1918, her son, Robert Gregory, a pilot in World War I, was shot down over Italy. Yeats honored the Coole Park estate, his partner, Lady Gregory and her son, Robert, in his poem, "The Wild Swans at Coole" (1919) which touches on youth, age and death in a conversational yet touching tone. The following year, the Irish Civil War broke out and aside from the physical threats she received, she saw her family home in Roxborough burn to the ground. In 1926, she discovered she had cancer, and lived out the remainder of her days in the Coole Park house, where she died in 1932.

Aside from her contributions to the Irish Literary Renaissance, the Abbey Theatre and the important historical work, *Irish Myths and Legends*, Lady Gregory's literary achievements are no doubt undervalued and pale in comparison to the generosity and unselfishness she displayed in her lifetime. Her love of Irish peasant culture was best exemplified in the passion she put into *Irish Myths and Legends*, of which Yeats wrote, "We Irish should keep these personages much in our hearts, for they lived in the places where we ride and go marketing, and sometimes they have met one another on the hills that cast their shadows upon our doors at evening. If we will but tell these stories to our children the Land will begin again to be a Holy Land, as it was before men gave their hearts to Greece and Rome and Judea."

SELECTIONS FROM
IRISH MYTHS AND LEGENDS

♣

The Fight with the Firbolgs

It was in a mist the Tuatha de Danaan, the people of the gods of Dana, or as some
called them, the Men of Dea, came through the air and the high air to Ireland.

It was from the north they came; and in the place they came from they had
four cities, where they fought their battle for learning: great Falias, and shining
Gorias, and Finias, and rich Murias that lay to the south. And in those cities they
had four wise men to teach their young men skill and knowledge and perfect wisdom: Senias in Murias, and Arias, the fair-haired poet, in Finias; and Urias of the
noble nature in Gorias; and Morias in Falias itself. And they brought from those
four cities their four treasures: a Stone of Virtue from Falias, that was called the Lia
Fail, the Stone of Destiny; and from Gorias they brought a Sword; and from Finias
a Spear of Victory; and from Murias the fourth treasure, the Cauldron that no
company ever went away from unsatisfied.

It was Nuada was king of the Tuatha de Danaan at that time, but Manannan,
son of Lir, was greater again. And of the others that were chief among them were
Ogma, brother to the king, that taught them writing, and Diancecht, that understood healing, and Neit, a god of battle, and Credenus the Craftsman, and
Goibniu the Smith. And the greatest among their women were Badb, a battle goddess, and Macha, whose mast-feeding was the heads of men killed in battle; and
the Morrigu, the Crow of Battle; and Eire and Fodla and Banba, daughters of the
Dagda, that all three gave their names to Ireland afterwards; and Eadon, the nurse
of poets; and Brigit, that was a woman of poetry, and poets worshipped her; for
her sway was very great and very noble. And she was a woman of healing along
with that, and a woman of smith's work, and it was she first made the whistle for
calling one to another through the night. And the one side of her face was ugly,
but the other side was very comely. And the meaning of her name was Breo-saighit,
a fiery arrow. And among the other women there were many shadow-forms and
great queens; but Dana, that was called the Mother of the Gods, was beyond

them all.

And the three things they put above all others were the plough and the sun and the hazel-tree, so that it was said in the time to come that Ireland was divided between those three, Coll the hazel, and Cecht the plough, and Grian the sun.

And they had a well below the sea where the nine hazels of wisdom were growing; that is, the hazels of inspiration and of the knowledge of poetry. And their leaves and their blossoms would break out in the same hour, and would fall on the well in a shower that raised a purple wave. And then the five salmon that were waiting there would eat the nuts, and their colour would come out in the red spots of their skin, and any person that would eat one of those salmon would know all wisdom and all poetry. And there were seven streams of wisdom that sprang from that well and turned back to it again, and the people of many arts have all drank from that well.

It was on the first day of Beltaine, that is called now May Day, the Tuatha de Danaan came, and it was to the north-west of Connacht they landed. But the Firbolgs, the Men of the Bag, that were in Ireland before them, and that had come from the South, saw nothing but a mist, and it lying on the hills.

Eochaid, son of Erc, was king of the Firbolgs at that time, and messengers came to him at Teamhair, and told him there was a new race of people come into Ireland, but whether from the earth or the skies or on the wind was not known, and that they had settled themselves at Magh Rein.

They thought there would be wonder on Eochaid when he heard that news; but there was no wonder on him, for a dream had come to him in the night, and when he asked his Druids the meaning of the dream, it is what they said, that it would not be long till there would be a strong enemy coming against him.

Then King Eochaid took counsel with his chief advisers, and it is what they agreed, to send a good champion of their own to see the strangers and to speak with them. So they chose out Sreng, that was a great fighting man, and he rose up and took his strong red-brown shield, and his two thick-handled spears, and his sword, and his head-covering, and his thick iron club, and he set out from Teamhair, and went on towards the place the strangers were, at Magh Rein.

But before he reached it, the watchers of the Tuatha de Danaan got sight of him, and they sent out one of their own champions, Bres, with his shield and his sword and his two spears, to meet him and to talk with him.

So the two champions went one towards the other slowly, and keeping a good watch on one another, and wondering at one another's arms, till they came near enough for talking; and then they stopped, and each put his shield before his body and struck it hard into the ground, and they looked at one another over the rim. Bres was the first to speak, and when Sreng heard it was Irish he was talking, his own tongue, he was less uneasy, and they drew nearer, and asked questions as to one another's family and race.

And after a while they put their shields away, and it was what Sreng said, that he had raised his in dread of the thin, sharp spears Bres had in his hand. And Bres said he himself was in dread of the thick-handled spears he saw with Sreng, and he asked were all the arms of the Firbolgs of the same sort. And Sreng took off the tyings of his spears to show them better, and Bres wondered at them, being so strong and so heavy, and so sharp at the sides though they had no points. And Sreng told him the name of those spears was Craisech, and that they would break through shields and crush flesh and bones, so that their thrust was death or wounds that never healed. And then he looked at the sharp, thin, hard-pointed spears that were with Bres. And in the end they made an exchange of spears, the way the fighters on each side would see the weapons the others were used to. And it is the message Bres sent to the Firbolgs, that if they would give up one half of Ireland, his people would be content to take it in peace; but if they would not give up that much, there should be a battle. And he and Sreng said to one another that whatever might happen in the future, they themselves would be friends.

Sreng went back then to Teamhair and gave the message and showed the spear; and it is what he advised his people, to share the country and not to go into battle with a people that had weapons so much better than their own. But Eochaid and his chief men consulted together, and they said in the end: "We will not give up the half of the country to these strangers; for if we do," they said, "they will soon take the whole."

Now as to the Men of Dea, when Bres went back to them, and showed them the heavy spear, and told them of the strong, fierce man he had got it from, and how sturdy he was and well armed, they thought it likely there would soon be a battle. And they went back from where they were to a better place, farther west in Connacht, and there they settled themselves, and made walls and ditches on the plain of Magh Nia, where they had the great mountain, Belgata, in their rear. And while they were moving there and putting up their walls, three queens of them, Badb and Macha and the Morrigu, went to Teamhair where the Firbolgs were making their plans. And by the power of their enchantments they brought mists and clouds of darkness over the whole place, and they sent showers of fire and of blood over the people, the way they could not see or speak with one another through the length of three days. But at the end of that time, the three Druids of the Firbolgs,

Cesarn and Gnathach and Ingnathach, broke the enchantment.

The Firbolgs gathered their men together then, and they came with their eleven battalions and took their stand at the eastern end of the plain of Magh Nia.

And Nuada, king of the Men of Dea, sent his poets to make the same offer he made before, to be content with the half of the country if it was given up to him. King Eochaid bade the poets to ask an answer of his chief men that were gathered there; and when they heard the offer they would not consent. So the messengers asked them when would they begin the battle. "We must have a delay," they said; "for we want time to put our spears and our armour in order, and to brighten our helmets and to sharpen our swords, and to have spears made like the ones you have. And as to yourselves," they said, "you will be wanting to have spears like our Craisechs made for you." So they agreed then to make a delay of a quarter of a year for preparation.

It was on a Midsummer day they began the battle. Three times nine hurlers of the Tuatha de Danaan went out against three times nine hurlers of the Firbolgs, and they were beaten, and every one of them was killed. And the king, Eochaid, sent a messenger to ask would they have the battle every day or every second day. And it is what Nuada answered that they would have it every day, but there should be just the same number of men fighting on each side. Eochaid agreed to that, but he was not well pleased, for there were more men of the Firbolgs than of the Men of Dea.

So the battle went on for four days, and there were great fears done on each side, and a great many champions came to their death. But for those that were alive at evening, the physicians on each side used to make a bath of healing, with every sort of healing plant or herb in it, the way they would be strong and sound for the next days fight.

And on the fourth day the Men of Dea got the upper hand, and the Firbolgs were driven back. And a great thirst came on Eochaid, their king, in the battle, and he went off the field looking for a drink, and three fifties of his men protecting him; but three fifties of the Tuatha de Danaan followed after them till they came to the strand that is called Traigh Eothaile, and they had a fierce fight there, and at last the King Eochaid fell, and they buried him there, and they raised a great heap of stones over his grave.

And when there were but three hundred men left of the eleven battalions of the Firbolgs, and Sreng at the head of them, Nuada offered them peace, and their choice among the five provinces of Ireland. And Sreng said they would take Connacht; and he and his people lived there and their children after them. It is of them Ferdiad came afterwards that made such a good fight against Cuchulain, and Erc, son of Cairbre, that gave him his death. And that battle, that was the first fought in Ireland by the Men of Dea, was called by some the first battle of Magh Tuireadh.

And the Tuatha de Danaan took possession of Teamhair, that was sometimes called Druim Cain, the Beautiful Ridge, and Liathdruim, the Grey Ridge, and Druim na Descan, the Ridge of the Outlook, all those names were given to Teamhair. And from that time it was above all other places, for its king was the High King over all Ireland. The king's rath lay to the north, and the Hill of the Hostages to the north-east of the High Seat, and the Green of Teamhair to the west of the Hill of the Hostages. And to the north-east, in the Hill of the Sidhe, was a well called Nemnach, and out of it there flowed a stream called Nith, and on that stream the first mill was built in Ireland.

And to the north of the Hill of the Hostages was the stone, the Lia Fail, and it used to roar under the feet of every king that would take possession of Ireland. And the Wall of the Three Whispers was near the House of the Women that had seven doors to the east, and seven doors to the west; and it is in that house the feasts of Teamhair used to be held. And there was the Great House of a Thousand Soldiers, and near it, to the south, the little Hill of the Woman Soldiers.

The Reign of Bres

But if Nuada won the battle, he lost his own arm in it, that was struck off by Sreng; and by that loss there came troubles and vexation on his people.

For it was a law with the Tuatha de Danaan that no man that was not perfect in shape should be king. And after Nuada had lost the battle he was put out of the kingship on that account.

And the king they chose in his place was Bres, that was the most beautiful of all their young men, so that if a person wanted to praise any beautiful thing, whether it was a plain, or a dun, or ale, or a flame, or a woman, or a man, or a horse, it is what he would say, "it is as beautiful as Bres." And he was the son of a woman of the Tuatha de Danaan, but who his father was no one knew but herself.

But in spite of Bres being so beautiful, his reign brought no great good luck to his people; for the Fomor, whose dwelling-place was beyond the sea, or as some say below the sea westward, began putting tribute on them, the way they would get them under their own rule.

It was a long time before that the Fomor came first to Ireland; dreadful they were to look at, and maimed, having but one foot or one hand, and they under the leadership of a giant and his mother. There never came to Ireland an army more horrible or more dreadful than that army of the Fomor. And they were friendly with the Firbolgs and content to leave Ireland to them, but there was jealously between them and the Men of Dea.

And it was a hard tax they put on them, a third part of their corn they asked, and a third part of their milk, and a third part of their children, so that there was not smoke rising from a roof in Ireland but was under tribute to them. And Bres made no stand against them, but let them get their way.

And as to Bres himself, he put a tax on every house in Ireland of the milk of hornless dun cows, or of the milk of cows of some other single colour, enough for a hundred men. And one time, to deceive him, Nechtan singed all the cows of Ireland in a fire of fern, and then he smeared them with the ashes of flax seed, the way they were all dark brown. He did that by the advice of the Druid Findgoll, son of Findemas. And another time they made three hundred cows of wood with dark brown pails in place of udders, and the pails were filled with black bog stuff. Then Bres came to look at the cows, and to see them milked before him, and Cian, father of Lugh, was there. And when they were milked it was the bog stuff that was squeezed out; and Bres took a drink of it thinking it to be milk, and he was not the better of it for a long time.

And there was another thing against Bres, he was no way open-handed, and the chief men of the Tuatha de Danaan grumbled against him, for their knives were never greased in his house, and however often they might visit him there was no smell of ale on their breath. And there was no sort of pleasure or merriment in his house, and no call for their poets, or singers, or harpers, or pipers, or horn-blowers, or jugglers, or fools. And as to the trials of strength they were used to see between their champions, the only use their strength was put to now was to be doing work for the king. Ogma himself, the shining poet, was under orders to bring firing to the palace every day for the whole army from the islands of Mod; and he so weak for want of food that the sea would sweep away two-thirds of his bundle every day. And as to the Dagda, he was put to build raths, for he was a good builder, and he made a trench round Rath Brese. And he used often to be tired at the work, and one time he nearly gave in altogether for want of food, and this is the way that happened. He used to meet in the house an idle blind man, Cridenbel his name was, that had a sharp tongue, and that coveted the Dagda's share of food, for he thought his own to be small beside it. So he said to him: "For the sake of your good name let the three best bits of your share be given to me." And the Dagda gave in to that every night; but he was the worse of it, for what the blind man called a bit would be the size of a good pig, and with his three bits he would take a full third of the whole.

But one day, as the Dagda was in the trench, he saw his son, Angus Og, coming to him. "That is a good meeting," said Angus; "but what is on you, for you have no good appearance to-day?" "There is a reason for that," said the Dagda, "for every evening, Cridenbel, the blind man, makes a demand for the three best bits of my share of food, and takes them from me." "I will give you an advice," said Angus. He put his hand in his bag then, and took out three pieces of gold and gave them to him.

"Put these pieces of gold into the three bits you will give this evening to Cridenbel," he said, "and they will be the best bits in the dish, and the gold will turn within him the way he will die."

So in the evening the Dagda did that; and no sooner had Cridenbel swallowed down the gold than he died. Some of the people said then to the king: "The Dagda has killed Cridenbel, giving him some deadly herb." The king believed that, and there was anger on him against Dagda, and he gave orders he should be put to death. But the Dagda said: "You are not giving the right judgment of a prince." And he told all that had happened, and how Cridenbel used to say, "Give me the three best bits before you, for my own share is not good to-night." "And on this night," he said, "the three pieces of gold were the best things before me, and I gave them to him, and he died."

The king gave orders then to have the body cut open. And they found the gold inside it, and they knew it was the truth the Dagda had told.

And Angus came to him again the next day, and he said: "Your work will soon be done, and when you are given your wages, take nothing they may offer you till the cattle of Ireland are brought before you, and choose out a heifer then, black and black-maned, that I will tell you the signs of."

So when the Dagda had brought his work to an end, and they asked him what reward he wanted, he did as Angus had bidden him. And that seemed folly to Bres; he thought the Dagda would have asked more than a heifer of him.

There came a day at last when a poet came to look for hospitality at the king's house, Corpre, son of Etain, poet of the Tuatha de Danaan. And it is how he was treated, he was put in a little dark narrow house where there was no fire, or furniture, or bed; and for a feast three small cakes, and they were brought to him on a little dish. When he rose up on the morrow he was no way thankful, and as he was going across the green, it is what he said: "Without food ready on a dish; without milk enough for a calf to grow on; without shelter; without light in the darkness of night; without enough to pay a story-teller; may that be the prosperity of Bres."

And from that day there was no good luck with Bres, but it is going down he was for ever after. And that was the first satire ever made in Ireland.

Now as to Nuada: after his arm being struck off, he was in his sickness for a while, and then Diancecht, the healer, made an arm of silver for him, with movement in every finger of it, and put it on him. And from that he was called Nuada Argat-lamh, of the Silver Hand, for ever after.

Now Miach, son of Diancecht, was a better hand at healing than his father, and had done many things. He met a young man, having but one eye, at Teamhair one time, and the young man said: "If you are a good physician you will put an eye in the place of the eye I lost." "I could put the eye of that cat in your lap in its place," said Miach. "I would like that well," said the young man. So Miach put the cat's eye in his head; but he would as soon have been without it after, for when he wanted to sleep and take his rest, it is then the eye would start at the squeaking of the mice, or the flight of the birds, or the movement of the rushes; and when he was wanting to watch an army or a gathering, it is then it was sure to be in a deep sleep.

And Miach was not satisfied with what his father had done to the king, and he took Nuada's own hand that had been struck off, and brought it to him and set it in its place, and he said: "Joint to joint, and sinew to sinew." Three days and three nights he was with the king; the first day he put the hand against his side, and the second day against his breast, till it was covered with skin, and the third day he put bulrushes that were blackened in the fire on it, and at the end of that time the king was healed.

But Diancecht was vexed when he saw his son doing a better cure than himself, and he threw his sword at his head, that it cut the flesh, but the lad healed the wound by means of his skill. Then Diancecht threw it a second time, that it reached the bone, but the lad was able to cure the wound. Then he struck him the third time and the fourth, till he cut out the brain, for he knew no physician could cure him after that blow; and Miach died, and he buried him.

And herbs grew up from his grave, to the number of his joints and sinews, three hundred and sixty-five. And Airmed, his sister, came and spread out her cloak and laid out the herbs in it, according to their virtue. But Diancecht saw her doing that, and he came and mixed up the herbs, so that no one knows all their right powers to this day.

Then when the Tuatha de Danaan saw Nuada was well as he was before, they gathered together to Teamhair, where Bres was, and they bade him give up the kingship, for he had held it long enough. So he had to give it up, though he was not very willing, and Nuada was put back in the kingship again.

There was great vexation on Bres then, and he searched his mind to know how could he be avenged on those that had put him out, and how he could gather an army against them; and he went to his mother, Eri, daughter of Delbaith, and bade her tell him what his race was.

"I know that well," she said; and she told him then that his father was a king of the Fomor, Elathan, son of Dalbaech, and that he came to her one time over a level sea in some great vessel that seemed to be of silver, but she could not see its shape, and he himself having the appearance of a young man with yellow hair, and his clothes sewed with gold, and five rings of gold about his neck. And she that had refused the love of all the young men of her own people, gave him her love, and she cried when he left her. And he gave her a ring from his hand, and bade her give it only to the man whose finger it would fit, and he went away then the same way as he had come.

And she brought out the ring then to Bres, and he put it round his middle finger, and it fitted him well. And they went then together to the hill where she was the time she saw the silver vessel coming, and down to the strand, and she and Bres and his people set out for the country of the Fomor.

And when they came to that country they found a great plain with many gatherings of people on it, and they went to the gathering that looked the best, and the people asked where did they come from, and they said they were come from Ireland. "Have you hounds with you?" they asked them then, for it was the custom at that time, when strangers came to a gathering to give them some friendly challenge. "We have hounds," said Bres. So the hounds were matched against one another, and the hounds of the Tuatha de Danaan were better than the hounds of the Fomor. "Have you horses for a race?" they asked then. "We have," said Bres. And the horses of the Tuatha de Danaan beat the horses of the Fomor.

Then they asked was any one among them a good hand with the sword, and they said Bres was the best. But when he put his hand to his sword, Elathan, his father, that was among them, knew the ring, and he asked who was this young man. Then his mother answered him and told the whole story, and that Bres was his own son.

There was sorrow on his father then, and he said: "What was it drove you out of the country you were king over?" And Bres said: "Nothing drove me out but my own injustice and my own hardness; I took away their treasures from the people, and their jewels, and their food itself. And there were never taxes put on them before I was their king."

"That is bad," said his father; "it is of their prosperity you had a right to think more than of your own kingship. And their good-will would be better than their curses," he said; "and what is it you are come to look for here?" "I am come to look for fighting men," said Bres, "that I may take Ireland by force." "You have no right to get it by injustice when you could not keep it by justice," said his father. "What advice have you for me then?" said Bres.

And Elathan bade him go to the chief king of the Fomor, Balor of the Evil Eye, to see what advice and what help would he give him.

The Coming of Finn

At the time Finn was born his father Cumhal, of the sons of Baiscne, Head of the Fianna of Ireland, had been killed in battle by the sons of Morna that were fighting with him for the leadership. And his mother, that was beautiful long-haired Muirne, daughter of Tadg, son of Nuada of the Tuatha de Danaan and of Ethlinn, mother of Lugh of the Long Hand, did not dare to keep him with her; and two women, Bodhmall, the woman Druid, and Liath Luachra, came and brought him away to care him.

It was to the woods of Slieve Bladhma they brought him, and they nursed him secretly, because of his fathers enemies, the sons of Morna, and they kept him there a long time.

And Muirne, his mother, took another husband that was king of Carraighe; but at the end of six years she came to see Finn, going through every lonely place till she came to the wood, and there she found the little hunting cabin, and the boy asleep in it, and she lifted him up in her arms and kissed him, and she sang a little sleepy song to him; and then she said farewell to the women, and she went away again.

And the two women went on caring him till he came to sensible years; and one day when he went out he saw a wild duck on the lake with her clutch, and he made a cast at her that cut the wings off her that she could not fly, and he brought her back to the cabin, and that was his first hunt.

And they gave him good training in running and leaping and swimming. One of them would run round a tree, and she having a thorn switch, and Finn after her with another switch, and each one trying to hit at the other; and they would leave him in a field, and hares along with him, and would bid him not to let the hares quit the field, but to keep before them whichever way they would go; and to teach him swimming they would throw him into the water and let him make his way out.

But after a while he went away with a troop of poets, to hide from the sons of Morna, and they hid him in the mountain of Crotta Cliach; but there was a robber in Leinster at that time, Fiacuil, son of Codhna, and he came where the poets were in Fidh Gaible and killed them all. But he spared the child and brought him to his own house, that was in a cold marsh. But the two women, Bodhmall and Liath, came looking for him after a while, and Fiacuil gave him up to them, and they brought him back to the same place he was before.

He grew up there, straight and strong and fair-haired and beautiful. And one day he was out in Slieve Bladhma, and the two women along with him, and they saw before them a herd of the wild deer of the mountain. "It is a pity," said the old women, "we not to be able to get a deer of those deer." "I will get one for you," said Finn; and with that he followed after them, and caught two stags of them and brought them home to the hunting cabin. And after that he used to be hunting for them every day. But at last they said to him: "It is best for you to leave us now, for the sons of Morna are watching again to kill you."

So he went away then by himself, and never stopped till he came to Magh Lifé, and there he saw young lads swimming in a lake, and they called to him to swim against them. So he went into the lake, and he beat them at swimming. "Fair he is and well shaped," they said when they saw him swimming, and it was from that time he got the name of Finn, that is, Fair. But they got to be jealous of his strength, and he went away and left them.

He went on then till he came to Loch Lein, and he took service there with the King of Finntraigh; and there was no hunter like him, and the king said: "If Cumhal had left a son, you would be that son."

He went from that king after, and he went into Carraighe, and there he took service with the king, that had taken his mother Muirne for his wife. And one day they were playing chess together, and he won seven games one after another. "Who are you at all?" said the king then. "I am a son of a countryman of the Luigne of Teamhair," said Finn. "That is not so," said the king, "but you are the son that Muirne my wife bore to Cumhal. And do not stop here any longer," he said, "that you may not be killed under my protection."

From that he went into Connacht looking for his father's brother, Crimall, son of Trenmor; and as he was going on his way he heard the crying of a lone woman. He went to her, and looked at her, and tears of blood were on her face. "Your face is red with blood, woman," he said. "I have reason for it," said she, "for my only son is after being killed by a great fighting man that came on us." And Finn followed after the big champion and fought with him and killed him. And the man he killed was the same man that had given Cumhal his first wound in the battle where he got his death, and had brought away his treasure-bag with him.

Now as to that treasure-bag, it is of a crane skin it was made, that was one time the skin of Aoife, the beautiful sweetheart of Ilbrec, son of Manannan, that was put into the shape of a crane through jealousy. And it was in Manannan's house it used to be, and there were treasures kept in it, Manannan's shirt and his knife, and the belt and the smith's hook of Goibniu, and the shears of the King of Alban, and the helmet of the King of Lochlann, and a belt of the skin of a great fish, and the bones of Asal's pig that had been brought to Ireland by the sons of Tuireann. All those treasures would be in the bag at full tide, but at the ebbing of the tide it would be empty. And it went from Manannan to Lugh, son of Ethlinn, and after that to Cumhal, that was husband to Muirne, Ethlinn's daughter.

And Finn took the bag and brought it with him till he found Crimall, that was now an old man, living in a lonely place, and some of the old men of the Fianna were with him, and used to go hunting for him. And Finn gave him the bag, and told him his whole story.

And then he said farewell to Crimall, and went on to learn poetry from Finegas, a poet that was living at the Boinn, for the poets thought it was always on the brink of water poetry was revealed to them. And he did not give him his own name, but he took the name of Deimne. Seven years, now, Finegas had stopped at the Boinn, watching the salmon, for it was in the prophecy that he would eat the salmon of knowledge that would come there, and that he would have all knowledge after. And when at the last the salmon of knowledge came, he brought it to where Finn was, and bade him to roast it, but he bade him not to eat any of it. And when Finn brought him the salmon after a while he said: "Did you eat any of it at all, boy?" "I did not," said Finn; "but I burned my thumb putting down a blister that rose on the skin, and after doing that, I put my thumb in my mouth." "What is your name, boy?" said Finegas. "Deimne," said he. "It is not, but it is Finn your name is, and it is to you and not to myself the salmon was given in the prophecy." With that he gave Finn the whole of the salmon, and from that time Finn had the knowledge that came from the nuts of the nine hazels of wisdom that grow beside the well that is below the sea.

And besides the wisdom he got then, there was a second wisdom came to him another time, and this is the way it happened. There was a well of the moon belonging to Beag, son of Buan, of the Tuatha de Danaan, and whoever would drink out of it would get wisdom, and after a second drink he would get the gift of foretelling. And the three daughters of Beag, son of Brian, had charge of the well, and they would not part with a vessel of it for anything less than red gold. And one day Finn chanced to be hunting in the rushes near the well, and the three women ran out to hinder him from coming to it, and one of them that had a vessel of the water in her hand, threw it at him to stop him, and a share of the water went into his mouth. And from that out he had all the knowledge that the water of that well could give.

And he learned the three ways of poetry; and this is the poem he made to show he had got his learning well:

"It is the month of May is the pleasant time; its face is beautiful; the blackbird sings his full song, the living wood is his holding, the cuckoos are singing and ever singing; there is a welcome before the brightness of the summer.

"Summer is lessening the rivers, the swift horses are looking for the pool; the heath spreads out its long hair, the weak white bog-down grows. A wildness comes on the heart of the deer; the sad restless sea is asleep.

"Bees with their little strength carry a load reaped from the flowers; the cattle go up muddy to the mountains; the ant has a good full feast.

"The harp of the woods is playing music; there is colour on the hills, and a haze on the full takes, and entire peace upon every sail.

"The corncrake is speaking, a loud-voiced poet; the high lonely waterfall is singing a welcome to the warm pool, the talking of the rushes has begun.

"The light swallows are darting; the loudness of music is around the hill; the fat soft mast is budding, there is grass on the trembling bogs.

"The bog is as dark as the feathers of the raven; the cuckoo makes a loud welcome; the speckled salmon is leaping; as strong is the leaping of the swift fighting man.

"The man is gaining; the girl is in her comely growing power; every wood is without fault from the top to the ground, and every wide good plain.

"It is pleasant is the colour of the time; rough winter is gone; every plentiful wood is white; summer is a joyful peace.

"A flock of birds pitches in the meadow; there are sounds in the green fields, there is in them a clear rushing stream.

"There is a hot desire on you for the racing of horses; twisted holly makes a leash for the hound; a bright spear has been shot into the earth, and the flag-flower is golden under it.

"A weak lasting little bird is singing at the top of his voice; the lark is singing clear tidings; May without fault, of beautiful colours.

"I have another story for you; the ox is lowing, the winter is creeping in, the summer is gone. High and cold the wind, low the sun, cries are about us; the sea is quarrelling.

"The ferns are reddened and their shape is hidden; the cry of the wild goose is heard; the cold has caught the wings of the birds; it is the time of ice-frost, hard, unhappy."

And after that, Finn being but a young lad yet, made himself ready and went up at Samhain time to the gathering of the High King at Teamhair. And it was the law at that gathering, no one to raise a quarrel or bring out any grudge against another through the whole of the time it lasted. And the king and his chief men, and Goll, son of Morna, that was now Head of the Fianna, and Caoilte, son of Ronan, and Conan, son of Morna, of the sharp words, were sitting at a feast in the great house of the Middle Court; and the young lad came in and took his place among them, and none of them knew who he was.

The High King looked at him then, and the horn of meetings was brought to him, and he put it into the boy's hand, and asked him who was he.

"I am Finn, son of Cumhal," he said, "son of the man that used to be head over the Fianna, and king of Ireland; and I am come now to get your friendship, and to give you my service."

"You are son of a friend, boy," said the king, "and son of a man I trusted."

Then Finn rose up and made his agreement of service and of faithfulness to the king; and the king took him by the hand and put him sitting beside his own son, and they gave themselves to drinking and to pleasure for a while.

Every year, now, at Samhain time, for nine years, there had come a man of the Tuatha de Danaan out of Sidhe Finnachaidh in the north, and had burned up Teamhair. Aillen, son of Midhna, his name was, and it is the way he used to come, playing music of the Sidhe, and all the people that heard it would fall asleep. And when they were all in their sleep, he would let a flame of fire out of his mouth, and would blow the flame till all Teamhair was burned.

The king rose up at the feast after a while, and his smooth horn in his hand, and it is what he said: "If I could find among you, men of Ireland, any man that would keep Teamhair till the break of day to-morrow without being burned by Aillen, son of Midhna, I would give him whatever inheritance is right for him to have, whether it be much or little."

But the men of Ireland made no answer, for they knew well that at the sound of the sweet pitiful music made by that comely man of the Sidhe, even women in their pains and men that were wounded would fall asleep.

It is then Finn rose up and spoke to the King of Ireland. "Who will be your sureties that you will fulfil this?" he said. "The kings of the provinces of Ireland," said the king, "and Cithruadh with his Druids." So they gave their pledges, and Finn took in hand to keep Teamhair safe till the breaking of day on the morrow.

Now there was a fighting man among the followers of the King of Ireland, Fiacha, son of Conga, that Cumhal, Finn's father, used to have a great liking for, and he said to Finn: "Well, boy," he said, "what reward would you give me if I would bring you a deadly spear, that no false cast was ever made with?" "What reward are you asking of me?" said Finn. "Whatever your right hand wins at any time, the third of it to be mine," said Fiacha, "and a third of your trust and your friendship to be mine." "I will give you that," said Finn. Then Fiacha brought him the spear, unknown to the sons of Morna or to any other person, and he said: "When you will hear the music of the Sidhe, let you strip the covering off the head of the spear and put it to your forehead, and the power of the spear will not let sleep come upon you."

Then Finn rose up before all the men of Ireland, and he made a round of the whole of Teamhair. And it was not long till he heard the sorrowful music, and he stripped the covering from the head of the spear, and he held the power of it to his forehead. And Aillen went on playing his little harp, till he had put every one in their sleep as he was used; and then he let a flame of fire out from his mouth to burn Teamhair. And Finn held up his fringed crimson cloak, against the flame, and it fell down through the air and went into the ground, bringing the four-folded cloak with it deep into the earth.

And when Aillen saw his spells were destroyed, he went back to Sidhe Finnachaidh on the top of Slieve Fuad; but Finn followed after him there, and as Aillen was going in at the door he made a cast of the spear that went through his heart. And he struck his head off then, and brought it back to Teamhair, and fixed it on a crooked pole and left it there till the rising of the sun over the heights and invers of the country.

And Aillen's mother came to where his body was lying, and there was great grief on her, and she made this complaint:

"Ochone! Aillen is fallen, chief of the Sidhe of Beinn Boirche; the slow clouds of death are come on him. Och! he was pleasant, Och! he was kind, Aillen, son of Midhna of Slieve Fuad.

"Nine times he burned Teamhair. It is a great name he was always looking for, Ochone, Ochone, Aillen!"

And at the breaking of day, the king and all the men of Ireland came out upon the lawn at Teamhair where Finn was. "King," said Finn, "there is the head of the man that burned Teamhair, and the pipe and the harp that made his music. And it is what I think," he said, "that Teamhair and all that is in it is saved."

Then they all came together into the place of counsel, and it is what they agreed, the headship of the Fianna of Ireland to be given to Finn. And the king said to Goll, son of Morna: "Well, Goll," he said, "is it your choice to quit Ireland or to put your hand in Finn's hand?" "By my word, I will give Finn my hand," said Goll.

And when the charms that used to bring good luck had done their work, the chief men of the Fianna rose up and struck their hands in Finn's hand, and Goll, son of Morna, was the first to give him his hand the way there would be less shame on the rest for doing it.

And Finn kept the headship of the Fianna until the end; and the place he lived in was Almhuin of Leinster, where the white dun was made by Nuada of the Tuatha de Danaan, that was as white as if all the lime in Ireland was put on it, and that got its name from the great herd of cattle that died fighting one time around the well, and that left their horns there, speckled horns and white.

And as to Finn himself, he was a king and a seer and a poet; a Druid and a knowledgeable man; and everything he said was sweet-sounding to his people. And a better fighting man than Finn never struck his hand into a king's hand, and whatever any one ever said of him, he was three times better. And of his justice it used to be said, that if his enemy and his son had come before him to be judged, it is a fair judgment he would have given between them. And as to his generosity it used to be said, he never denied any man as long as he had a mouth to eat with, and legs to bring away what he gave him; and he left no woman without her bride-price, and no man without his pay, and he never promised at night what he would not fulfil on the morrow, and he never promised in the day what he would not fulfil at night, and he never forsook his right-hand friend. And if he was quiet in peace he was angry in battle, and Oisin his son and Osgar his son's son followed him in that. There was a young man of Ulster came and claimed kinship with them one time, saying they were of the one blood. "If that is so," said Oisin, "it is from the men of Ulster we took the madness and the angry heart we have in battle." "That is so indeed," said Finn.

Finn's Household

And the number of the Fianna of Ireland at that time was seven score and ten chief men, every one of them having three times nine fighting men under him. And every man of them was bound to three things, to take no cattle by oppression, not to refuse any man, as to cattle or riches; no one of them to fall back before nine fighting men. And there was no man taken into the Fianna until his tribe and his kindred would give securities for him, that even if they themselves were all killed he would not look for satisfaction for their death. But if he himself would harm others, that harm was not to be avenged on his people. And there was no man taken into the Fianna till he knew the twelve books of poetry. And before any man was taken, he would be put into a deep hole in the ground up to his middle, and he having his shield and a hazel rod in his hand. And nine men would go the length of ten furrows from him and would cast their spears at him at the one time. And if he got a wound from one of them, he was not thought fit to join with the Fianna. And after that again, his hair would be fastened up, and he put to run through the woods of Ireland, and the Fianna following after him to try could they wound him, and only the length of a branch between themselves and himself when they started. And if they came up with him and wounded him, he was not let join them; of if his spears had trembled in his hand, or if a branch of a tree had undone the plaiting of his hair, or if he had cracked a dry stick under his foot, and he running. And they would not take him among them till he had made a leap over a stick the height of himself, and till he had stooped under one the height of his knee, and till he had taken a thorn out from his foot with his nail, and he running his fastest. But if he had done all these things, he was of Finn's people.

It was good wages Finn and the Fianna got at that time; in every district a townland, in every house the fostering of a pup or a whelp from Samhain to Beltaine, and a great many things along with that. But good as the pay was, the hardships and the dangers they went through for it were greater. For they had to hinder the strangers and robbers from beyond the seas, and every bad thing, from coming into Ireland. And they had hard work enough in doing that.

And besides the fighting men, Finn had with him his five Druids, the best that ever came into the west, Cainnelsciath, of the Shining Shield, one of them was, that used to bring down knowledge from the clouds in the sky before Finn, and that could foretell battles. And he had his five wonderful physicians, four of them belonging to Ireland, and one that came over the sea from the east. And he had his five high poets and his twelve musicians, that had among them Daighre, son of

Morna, and Suanach, son of Senshenn, that was Finn's teller of old stories, the sweetest that ever took a harp in his hand in Ireland or in Alban. And he had his three cup-bearers and his six door-keepers and his horn-players and the stewards of his house and his huntsman, Comhrag of the five hundred hounds, and his serving-men, that were under Garbhcronan, of the Rough Buzzing, and a great troop of others along with them.

And there were fifty of the best sewing-women in Ireland brought together in a rath on Magh Feman, under the charge of a daughter of the King of Britain, and they used to be making clothing for the Fianna through the whole of the year. And three of them, that were a king's daughters, used to be making music for the rest on a little silver harp; and there was a very great candlestick of stone in the middle of the rath, for they were not willing to kindle a fire more than three times in the year for fear the smoke and the ashes might harm the needlework.

And of all his musicians the one Finn thought most of was Cnu Deireoil, the Little Nut, that came to him from the Sidhe.

It was at Slieve-nam-ban, for hunting, Finn was the time he came to him. Sitting down he was on the turf-built grave that is there; and when he looked around him he saw a small little man about four feet in height standing on the grass. Light yellow hair he had, hanging down to his waist, and he playing music on his harp. And the music he was making had no fault in it at all, and it is much that the whole of the Fianna did not fall asleep with the sweetness of its sound. He came up then, and put his hand in Finn's hand. "Where do you come from, little one, yourself and your sweet music?" said Finn. "I am come," he said, "out of the place of the Sidhe in Slieve-nam-ban, where ale is drunk and made; and it is to be in your company for a while I am come here." "You will get good rewards from me, and riches and red gold," said Finn, "and my full friendship, for I like you well." "That is the best luck ever came to you, Finn," said all the rest of the Fianna, for they were well pleased to have him in their company. And they gave him the name of the Little Nut; and he was good in speaking, and he had so good a memory he never forgot anything he heard east or west; and there was no one but must listen to his music, and all the Fianna liked him well. And there were some said he was a son of Lugh Lamh-Fada, of the Long Hand.

And the five musicians of the Fianna were brought to him, to learn the music of the Sidhe he had brought from that other place; for there was never any music heard on earth but his was better. These were the three best things Finn ever got, Bran and Sceolan that were without fault, and the Little Nut from the House of the Sidhe in Slieve-nam-ban.

Birth of Bran

This, now is the story of the birth of Bran.

Finn's mother, Muirne, came one time to Almhuin, and she brought with her Tuiren, her sister. And Iollan Eachtach, a chief man of the Fianna of Ulster, was at Almhuin at the time, and he gave his love to Tuiren, and asked her in marriage, and brought her to his own house. But before they went, Finn made him give his word he would bring her back safe and sound if ever he asked for her, and he bade him find sureties for himself among the chief men of the Fianna. And Iollan did that, and the sureties he got were Caoilte and Goll and Lugaidh Lamha, and it was Lugaidh gave her into the hand of Iollan Eachtach.

But before Iollan made that marriage, he had a sweetheart of the Sidhe, Uchtdealb of the Fair Breast; and there came great jealousy on her when she knew he had taken a wife. And she took the appearance of Finn's woman-messenger, and she came to the house where Tuiren was, and she said: "Finn sends health and long life to you, queen, and he bids you to make a great feast; and come with me now," she said, "till I speak a few words with you, for there is hurry on me."

So Tuiren went out with her, and when they were away from the house the woman of the Sidhe took out her dark Druid rod from under her cloak and gave her a blow of it that changed her into a hound, the most beautiful that was ever seen. And then she went on, bringing the hound with her, to the house of Fergus Fionnliath, king of the harbour of Gallimh. And it is the way Fergus was, he was the most unfriendly man to dogs in the whole world, and he would not let one stop in the same house with him. But it is what Uchtdealb said to him: "Finn wishes you life and health, Fergus, and he says to you to take good care of his hound till he comes himself, and mind her well," she said, "for she is with young, and do not let her go hunting when her time is near, or Finn will be no way thankful to you." "I wonder at that message," said Fergus, "for Finn knows well there is not in the world a man has less liking for dogs than myself. But for all that," he said, "I will not refuse Finn the first time he sent a hound to me."

And when he brought the hound out to try her, she was the best he ever knew, and she never saw the wild creature she would not run down, and Fergus took a great liking for hounds from that.

And when her time came near, they did not let her go hunting any more, and she gave birth to two whelps.

And as to Finn, when he heard his mother's sister was not living with Iollan Eachtach, he called to him for the fulfilment of the pledge that was given to the

Fianna. And Iollan asked time to go looking for Tuiren, and he gave his word that if he did not find her, he would give himself up in satisfaction for her. So they agreed to that, and Iollan went to the hill where Uchtdealb was, his sweetheart of the Sidhe, and told her the way things were with him, and the promise he had made to give himself up to the Fianna. "If that is so," said she, "and if you will give me your pledge to keep me as your sweetheart to the end of your life, I will free you from that danger." So Iollan gave her his promise, and she went to the house of Fergus Fionnliath, and she brought Tuiren away and put her own shape on her again, and gave her up to Finn. And Finn gave her to Lugaidh Lamha that asked her in marriage.

And as to the two whelps, they stopped always with Finn, and the names he gave them were Bran and Sceolan.

Oisin's Mother

It happened one time Finn and his men were coming back from the hunting, a beautiful fawn started up before them, and they followed after it, men and dogs, till at last they were all tired and fell back, all but Finn himself and Bran and Sceolan. And suddenly as they were going through a valley, the fawn stopped and lay down on the smooth grass, and Bran and Sceolan came up with it, and they did not harm it at all, but went playing about it, licking its neck and its face.

There was wonder on Finn when he saw that, and he went on home to Almhuin, and the fawn followed after him playing with the hounds, and it came with them into the house at Almhuin. And when Finn was alone late that evening, a beautiful young woman having a rich dress came before him, and she told him it was she herself was the fawn he was after hunting that day. "And it is for refusing the love of Fear Doirche, the Dark Druid of the Men of Dea," she said, "I was put in this shape. And through the length of three years," she said, "I have lived the life of a wild deer in a far part of Ireland, and I am hunted like a wild deer. And a serving-man of the Dark Druid took pity on me," she said, "and he said that if I was once within the dun of the Fianna of Ireland, the Druid would have no more power over me. So I made away, and I never stopped through the whole length of a day till I came into the district of Almhuin. And I never stopped there till there was no one after me but only Bran and Sceolan, that have human wits; and I was safe with them, for they knew my nature to be like their own."

Then Finn gave her his love, and took her as his wife, and she stopped in Almhuin. And so great was his love for her, he gave up his hunting and all the things he used to take pleasure in, and gave his mind to no other thing but herself.

But at last the men of Lochlann came against Ireland, and their ships were in the bay below Beinn Edair, and they landed there.

And Finn and the battalions of the Fianna went out against them, and drove them back. And at the end of seven days Finn came back home, and he went quickly over the plain of Almhuin, thinking to see Sadbh his wife looking out from the dun, but there was no sign of her. And when he came to the dun, all his people came out to meet him, but they had a very downcast look. "Where is the flower of Almhuin, beautiful gentle Sadbh?" he asked them. And it is what they said: "While you were away fighting, your likeness, and the likeness of Bran and of Sceolan appeared before the dun, and we thought we heard the sweet call of the Dord Fiann. And Sadbh, that was so good and so beautiful, came out of the house," they said, "and she went out of the gates, and she would not listen to us, and we could not stop her." "Let me go meet my love," she said, "my husband, the father of the child that is not born." And with that she went running out towards the shadow of yourself that was before her, and that had its arms stretched out to her. But no sooner did she touch it than she gave a great cry and the shadow lifted up a hazel rod, and on the moment it was a fawn was standing on the grass. Three times she turned and made for the gate of the dun, but the two hounds the shadow had with him went after her and took her by the throat and dragged her back to him. "And by your hand of valour, Finn," they said, "we ourselves made no delay till we went out on the plain after her. But it is our grief, they had all vanished, and there was not to be seen woman, or fawn or Druid, but we could hear the quick tread of feet on the hard plain, and the howling of dogs. And if you would ask every one of us in what quarter he heard those sounds, he would tell you a different one."

When Finn heard that, he said no word at all, but he struck his breast over and over again with his shut hands. And he went then to his own inside room, and his people saw him no more for that day, or till the sun rose over Magh Lifé on the morrow.

And through the length of seven years from that time, whenever he was not out fighting against the enemies of Ireland, he went searching and ever searching in every far corner for beautiful Sadbh. And there was great trouble on him all the time, unless he might throw it off for a while in hunting or in battle. And through all that time he never brought out to any hunting but the five hounds he had most trust in, Bran and Sceolan and Lomaire and Brod and Lomluath, the way there would be no danger for Sadbh if ever he came on her track.

But after the end of seven years, Finn and some of his chief men were hunting on the sides of Beinn Gulbain and they heard a great outcry among the hounds, that were gone into some narrow place. And when they followed them there, they saw the five hounds of Finn in a ring, and they keeping back the other hounds, and in the middle of the ring was a young boy, with high looks, and he naked and having long hair. And he was no way daunted by the noise of the hounds, and did not look at them at all, but at the men that were coming up. And as soon as the fight was stopped Bran and Sceolan went up to the little lad, and whined and licked him, that any one would think they had forgotten their master. Finn and the others came up to him then, and put their hands on his head, and made much of him. And they brought him to their own hunting cabin, and he ate and drank with them, and before long he lost his wildness and was the same as themselves. And as to Bran and Sceolan, they were never tired playing about him.

And it is what Finn thought, there was some look of Sadbh in his face, and that it might be he was her son, and he kept him always beside him. And little by little when the boy had learned their talk, he told them all he could remember. He used to be with a deer he loved very much, he said, and that cared and sheltered him, and it was in a wide place they used to be, having hills and valleys and streams and woods in it, but that was shut in with high cliffs on every side, that there was no way of escape from it. And he used to be eating fruits and roots in the summer, and in the winter there was food left for him in the shelter of a cave. And a dark-looking man used to be coming to the place, and sometimes he would speak to the deer softly and gently, and sometimes with a loud angry voice. But whatever way he spoke, she would always draw away from him with the appearance of great dread on her, and the man would go away in great anger. And the last time he saw the deer, his mother, the dark man was speaking to her for a long time, from softness to anger. And at the end he struck her with a hazel rod, and with that she was forced to follow him, and she looking back all the while at the child, and crying after him that any one would pity her. And he tried hard to follow after her, and made every attempt, and cried out with grief and rage, but he had no power to move, and when he could hear his mother no more he fell on the grass and his wits went from him. And when he awoke it is on the side of the hill he was, where the hounds found him. And he searched a long time for the place where he was brought up, but he could not find it.

And the name the Fianna gave him was Oisin, and it is he was their maker of poems, and their good fighter afterwards.

The Best Men of the Fianna

And while Oisin was in his young youth, Finn had other good men along with him, and the best of them were Goll, son of Morna, and Caoilte, son of Ronan, and Lugaidh's Son.

As to Goll, that was of Connacht, he was very tall and light-haired, and some say he was the strongest of all the Fianna. Finn made a poem in praise of him one time when some stranger was asking what sort he was, saying how hardy he was and brave in battle, and as strong as a hound or as the waves, and with all that so kind and so gentle, and open-handed and sweet-voiced, and faithful to his friends.

And the chess-board he had was called the Solustairtech, the Shining Thing, and some of the chessmen were made of gold, and some of them of silver, and each one of them was as big as the fist of the biggest man of the Fianna; and after the death of Goll it was buried in Slieve Baune.

And as to Caoilte, that was a grey thin man, he was the best runner of them all. And he did a good many great deeds; a big man of the Fomor he killed one time, and he killed a five-headed giant in a wheeling door, and another time he made an end of an enchanted boar that no one else could get near, and he killed a grey stag that had got away from the Fianna through twenty-seven years. And another time he brought Finn out of Teamhair, where he was kept by force by the High King, because of some rebellion the Fianna had stirred up. And when Caoilte heard Finn had been brought away to Teamhair, he went out to avenge him. And the first he killed was Cuireach, a king of Leinster that had a great name, and he brought his head up to the hill that is above Buadhmaic. And after that he made a great rout through Ireland, bringing sorrow into every house for the sake of Finn, killing a man in every place, and killing the calves with the cows.

And every door the red wind from the east blew on, he would throw it open, and go in and destroy all before him, setting fire to the fields, and giving the wife of one man to another.

And when he came to Teamhair, he came to the palace, and took the clothes off the door-keeper, and he left his own sword that was worn thin in the king's sheath, and took the king's sword that had great power in it. And he went into the palace then in the disguise of a servant, to see how he could best free Finn.

And when evening came Caoilte held the candle at the king's feast in the great hall, and after a while the king said: "You will wonder at what I tell you, Finn, that the two eyes of Caoilte are in my candlestick." "Do not say that," said Finn, "and do not put reproach on my people although I myself am your prisoner, for as to

Caoilte," he said, "that is not the way with him, for it is a high mind he has, and he only does high deeds, and he would not stand serving with a candle for all the gold of the whole world."

After that Caoilte was serving the King of Ireland with drink, and when he was standing beside him he gave out a high sorrowful lament. "There is the smell of Caoilte's skin on that lament," said the king. And when Caoilte saw he knew him he spoke out and he said: "Tell me what way I can get freedom for my master." "There is no way to get freedom for him, but by doing one thing," said the king, "and that is a thing you can never do. If you can bring me together a couple of all the wild creatures of Ireland," he said, "I will give up your master to you then."

When Caoilte heard him say that he made no delay, but he set out from Teamhair, and went through the whole of Ireland to do that work for the sake of Finn. It is with the flocks of birds he began, though they were scattered in every part, and from them he went on to the beasts. And he gathered together two of every sort, two ravens from Fiodh da Bheann; two wild ducks from Loch na Seillein; two foxes from Slieve Cuilinn; two wild oxen from Burren; two swans from blue Dobhran; two owls from the wood of Faradhruim; two polecats from the branchy wood on the side of Druim da Raoin; the Ridge of the Victories; two gulls from the strand of Loch Leith; four woodpeckers from white Brosna; two plovers from Carraigh Dhain; two thrushes from Leith Lomard; two wrens from Dun Aoibh; two herons from Corrain Clebh; two eagles from Carraig of the stones; two hawks from Fiodh Chonnach; two sows from Loch Meilghe; two water-hens from Loch Erne; two moor-hens from Monadh Maith; two sparrow-hawks from Dubhloch; two stonechats from Magh Cuillean; two tomtits from Magh Tuallainn; two swallows from Sean Abhla; two cormorants from Ath Cliath; two wolves from Broit Cliathach; two blackbirds from the Strand of the Two Women; two roebucks from Luachair Ire; two pigeons from Ceas Chuir; two nightingales from Leiter Ruadh; two starlings from green-sided Teamhair; two rab-bits from Sith Dubh Donn; two wild pigs from Cluaidh Chuir; two cuckoos from Drom Daibh; two lapwings from Leanain na Furraich; two woodcocks from Craobh Ruadh; two hawks from the Bright Mountain; two grey mice from Luimneach; two otters from the Boinn; two larks from the Great Bog; two bats from the Cave of the Nuts; two badgers from the province of Ulster; two landrail from the banks of the Sionnan; two wagtails from Port Lairrge; two curlews from the harbour of Gallimh; two hares from Muirthemne; two deer from Sith Buidhe; two peacocks from Magh Mell; two cormorants from Ath Cliath; two eels from Duth Dur; two goldfinches from Slieve na-n Fun; two birds of slaughter from

Magh Bhuilg; two bright swallows from Granard; two redbreasts from the Great
Wood; two rock-cod from Cala Chairge; two sea-pigs from the great sea; two wrens
from Mios an Chuil; two salmon from Eas Mhic Muirne; two clean deer from
Gleann na Smoil; two cows from Magh Mor; two cats from the Cave of Cruachan;
two sheep from bright Sidhe Diobhlain; two pigs of the pigs of the son of Lir; a
ram and a crimson sheep from Innis.

And along with all these he brought ten hounds of the hounds of the Fianna,
and a horse and a mare of the beautiful horses of Manannan.

And when Caoilte had gathered all these, he brought them to the one place.
But when he tried to keep them together, they scattered here and there from him,
the raven went away southward, and that vexed him greatly, but he overtook it
again in Gleann da Bheann, beside Loch Lurcan. And then his wild duck went
away from him, and it was not easy to get it again, but he followed it through
every stream to grey Accuill till he took it by the neck and brought it back, and it
no way willing.

And indeed through the length of his life Caoilte remembered well all he went
through that time with the birds, big and little, travelling over hills and ditches and
striving to bring them with him, that he might set Finn his master free.

And when he came to Teamhair he had more to go through yet, for the king
would not let him bring them in before morning, but gave him a house having
nine doors in it to put them up in for the night. And no sooner were they put in
than they raised a loud screech all together, for a little ray of light was coming to
them through fifty openings, and they were trying to make their escape. And if
they were not easy in the house, Caoilte was not easy outside it, watching every
door till the rising of the sun on the morrow.

And when he brought out his troop, the name the people gave them was
"Caoilte's Rabble," and there was no wonder at all in that.

But all the profit the King of Ireland got from them was to see them together
for that one time. For no sooner did Finn get his freedom than the whole of
them scattered here and there, and no two of them went by the same road out
of Teamhair.

And that was one of the best things Caoilte, son of Ronan, ever did. And
another time he ran from the wave of Cliodna in the south to the wave of
Rudraige in the north. And Colla his son was a very good runner too, and one
time he ran a race backwards against the three battalions of the Fianna for a chess-
board. And he won the race, but if he did, he went backward over Beinn Edair
into the sea.

And very good hearing Caoilte had. One time he heard the King of the Luigne of Connacht at his hunting, and Blathmec that was with him said, "What is that hunt, Caoilte?" "A hunt of three packs of hounds," he said, "and three sorts of wild creatures before them. The first hunt," he said, "is after stags and large deer and the second hunt is after swift small hares, and the third is a furious hunt after heavy boars." "And what is the fourth hunt, Caoilte?" said Blathmec. "It is the hunt of heavy-sided, low-bellied badgers." And then they heard coming after the hunt the shouts of the lads and of the readiest of the men and the serving-men that were best at carrying burdens. And Blathmec went out to see the hunting, and just as Caoilte had told him, that was the way it was.

And he understood the use of herbs, and one time he met with two women that were very downhearted because their husbands had gone from them to take other wives. And Caoilte gave them Druid herbs, and they put them in the water of a bath and washed in it, and the love of their husbands came back to them, and they sent away the new wives they had taken.

And as to Lugaidh's Son, that was of Finn's blood, and another of the best men of the Fianna, he was put into Finn's arms as a child, and he was reared up by Duban's daughter, that had reared eight hundred fighting men of the Fianna, till his twelfth year, and then she gave him all he wanted of arms and of armour, and he went to Chorraig Conluain and the mountains of Slieve Bladhma, where Finn and the Fianna were at that time.

And Finn gave him a very gentle welcome, and he struck his hand in Finn's hand, and made his agreement of service with him. And he stopped through the length of a year with the Fianna, but he was someway sluggish through all that time, so that under his leading not more than nine of the Fianna got to kill so much as a boar or a deer. And along with that, he used to beat both his servants and his hounds.

And at last the three battalions of the Fianna went to where Finn was, at the Point of the Fianna on the edge of Loch Lein, and they made their complaint against Lugaidh's Son, and it is what they said: "Make your choice now, will you have us with you, or will you have Lugaidh's Son by himself."

Then Lugaidh's Son came to Finn, and Finn asked him, "What is it has put the whole of the Fianna against you?" "By my word," said the lad, "I do not know the reason, unless it might be they do not like me to be doing my feats and casting my spears among them."

Then Finn gave him an advice, and it is what he said: "If you have a mind to be a good champion, be quiet in a great man's house; be surly in the narrow pass. Do not beat your hound without a cause; do not bring a charge against your wife without having knowledge of her guilt; do not hurt a fool in fighting, for he is without his wits. Do not find fault with high-up persons; do not stand up to take part in a quarrel; have no dealings with a bad man or a foolish man. Let two-thirds of your gentleness be showed to women and to little children that are creeping on the floor, and to men of learning that make the poems, and do not be rough with the common people. Do not give your reverence to all; do not be ready to have one bed with your companions. Do not threaten or speak big words, for it is a shameful thing to speak stiffly unless you can carry it out afterwards. Do not forsake your lord so long as you live; do not give up any man that puts himself under your protection for all the treasures of the world. Do not speak against others to their lord, that is not work for a good man. Do not be a bearer of lying stories, or a tale-bearer that is always chattering. Do not be talking too much, do not find fault hastily; however brave you may be, do not raise factions against you. Do not be going to drinking-houses, or finding fault with old men; do not meddle with low people; this is right conduct I am telling you. Do not refuse to share your meat; do not have a niggard for your friend; do not force yourself on a great man or give him occasion to speak against you. Hold fast to your arms till the hard fight is well ended. Do not give up your opportunity, but with that follow after gentleness."

That was good advice Finn gave, and he was well able to do that; for it was said of him that he had all the wisdom of a little child that is busy about the house, and the mother herself not understanding what he is doing; and that is the time she has most pride in him.

And as to Lugaidh's Son, that advice stayed always with him, and he changed his ways, and after a while he got a great name among the poets of Ireland and of Alban, and whenever they would praise Finn in their poems, they would praise him as well.

And Aoife, daughter of the King of Lochlann, that was married to Mal, son of Aiel, King of Alban, heard the great praise the poets were giving to Lugaidh's Son, and she set her love on him for the sake of those stories.

And one time Mal her husband and his young men went hunting to Slievemor-Monaidh in the north of Alban. And when he was gone Aoife made a plan in her sunny house where she was, to go over to Ireland, herself and her nine foster-sisters. And they set out and went over the manes of the sea till they came to Beinn Edair, and there they landed.

And it chanced on that day there was a hunting going on, from Slieve Bladhma to Beinn Edair. And Finn was in his hunting seat, and his fosterling, brown-haired Duibruinn, beside him. And the little lad was looking about him on every side, and he saw a ship coming to the strand, and a queen with modest looks in the ship, and nine women along with her. They landed then, and they came up to where Finn was, bringing every sort of present with them, and Aoife sat down beside him. And Finn asked news of her, and she told him the whole story, and how she had given her love to Lugaidh's Son, and was come over the sea looking for him; and Finn made her welcome.

And when the hunting was over, the chief men of the Fianna came back to where Finn was, and every one asked who was the queen that was with him. And Finn told them her name, and what it was brought her to Ireland. "We welcome her that made that journey," said they all; "for there is not in Ireland or in Alban a better man than the man she is come looking for, unless Finn himself."

And as to Lugaidh's Son, it was on the far side of Slieve Bladhma he was hunting that day, and he was the last to come in. And he went into Finn's tent, and when he saw the woman beside him he questioned Finn the same as the others had done, and Finn told him the whole story. "And it is to you she is come," he said; "and here she is to you out of my hand, and all the war and the battles she brings with her; but it will not fall heavier on you," he said, "than on the rest of the Fianna."

And she was with Lugaidh's Son a month and a year without being asked for. But one day the three battalions of the Fianna were on the Hill of the Poet in Leinster, and they saw three armed battalions equal to themselves coming, against them, and they asked who was bringing them. "It is Mal, son of Aiel, is bringing them," said Finn, "to avenge his wife on the Fianna. And it is a good time they are come," he said, "when we are gathered together at the one spot."

Then the two armies went towards one another, and Mal, son of Aiel, took hold of his arms, and three times he broke through the Fianna, and every time a hundred fell by him. And in the middle of the battle he and Lugaidh's Son met, and they fought against one another with spear and sword. And whether the fight was short or long, it was Mal fell by Lugaidh's Son at the last.

And Aoife stood on a hill near by, as long as the battle lasted. And from that out she belonged to Lugaidh's Son, and was a mother of children to him.

The Quarrel With the Sons of Morna

One time when the Fianna were gone here and there hunting, Black Garraidh and Caoilte were sitting beside Finn, and they were talking of the battle where Finn's father was killed. And Finn said then to Garraidh: "Tell me now, since you were there yourself, what way was it you brought my father Cumhal to his death?" "I will tell you that since you ask me," said Garraidh; "it was my own hand and the hands of the rest of the sons of Morna that made an end of him." "That is cold friendship from my followers the sons of Morna," said Finn. "If it is cold friendship," said Garraidh, "put away the liking you are letting on to have for us, and show us the hatred you have for us all the while." "If I were to lift my hand against you now, sons of Morna," said Finn, "I would be well able for you all without the help of any man." "It was by his arts Cumhal got the upper hand of us," said Garraidh; "and when he got power over us," he said, "he banished us to every far country; a share of us he sent to Alban, and a share of us to dark Lochlann, and a share of us to bright Greece, parting us from one another; and for sixteen years we were away from Ireland, and it was no small thing to us to be without seeing one another through that time. And the first day we came back to Ireland," he said, "we killed sixteen hundred men, and no lie in it, and not a man of them but would be keened by a hundred. And we took their duns after that," he said, "and we went on till we were all around one house in Munster of the red walls. But so great was the bravery of the man in that house, that was your father, that it was easier to find him than to kill him. And we killed all that were of his race out on the hill, and then we made a quick rush at the house where Cumhal was, and every man of us made a wound on his body with his spear. And I myself was in it, and it was I gave him the first wound. And avenge it on me now, Finn, if you have a mind to," he said.

It was not long after that, Finn gave a feast at Almhuin for all his chief men, and there came to it two sons of the King of Alban, and sons of the kings of the great world. And when they were all sitting at the feast, the serving-men rose up and took drinking-horns worked by skilled men, and having shining stones in them, and they poured out strong drink for the champions; and it is then mirth rose up in their young men, and courage in their fighting men, and kindness and gentleness in their women, and knowledge and foreknowledge of their poets.

And then a crier rose up and shook a rough iron chain to silence the clowns and the common lads and idlers, and then he shook a chain of old silver to silence the high lords and chief men of the Fianna, and the learned men, and they all listened and were silent.

And Fergus of the True Lips rose up and sang before Finn the songs and the good poems of his forefathers; and Finn and Oisin and Lugaidh's Son rewarded him with every good thing. And then he went on to Goll, son of Morna, and told the fights and the destructions and the cattle-drivings and the courtings of his fathers; and it is well-pleased and high-minded the sons of Morna were, listening to that.

And Goll said then: "Where is my woman-messenger?" "I am here, King of the Fianna," said she. "Have you brought me my hand-tribute from the men of Lochlann?" "I have brought it surely," said she. And with that she rose up and laid on the floor of the hall before Goll a load of pure gold, the size of a good pig, and that would be a heavy load for a strong man. And Goll loosened the covering that was about it, and he gave Fergus a good reward from it as he was used to do; for there never was a wise, sharp-worded poet, or a sweet harp-player, or any learned man of Ireland or of Alban, but Goll would give him gold or silver or some good thing.

And when Finn saw that, he said: "How long is it, Goll, you have this rent on the men of Lochlann, and my own rent being on them always with it, and one of my own men, Ciaran son of Latharne, and ten hundred men of his household, guarding it and guarding my right of hunting?" And Goll saw there was anger on Finn, and he said: "It is a long time, Finn, I have that rent on the men of Lochlann, from the time your father put war and quarrels on me, and the King of Ireland joined with him, and I was made to quit Ireland by them. And I went into Britain," he said, "and I took the country and killed the king himself and did destruction on his people, but Cumhal put me out of it; and from that I went to Fionn-lochlann, and the king fell by me, and his household, and Cumhal put me out of it; and I went from that to the country of the Saxons, and the king and his household fell by me, and Cumhal put me out of it. But I came back then to Ireland, and I fought a battle against your father, and he fell by me there. And it was at that time I put this rent upon the men of Lochlann. And, Finn," he said, "it is not a rent of the strong hand you have put on them, but it is a tribute for having the protection of the Fianna of Ireland, and I do not lessen that. And you need not begrudge that tribute to me," he said, "for if I had more than that again, it is to you and to the men of Ireland I would give it."

There was great anger on Finn then, and he said: "You tell me, Goll," he said, "by your own story that you came from the city of Beirbhe to fight against my father, and that you killed him in the battle; and it is a bold thing you to tell that to me." "By your own hand," said Goll, "if you were to give me the same treatment your father gave me, I would pay you the same way as I paid him." "It would be hard for you to do that," said Finn, "for there are a hundred men in my household against every man there is in your household." "That was the same with your father," said Goll, "and I avenged my disgrace on him; and I would do the same on yourself if you earned it," he said.

Then Cairell of the White Skin, son of Finn, said: "It is many a man of Finn's household you have put down, Goll!" And Bald Conan when he heard that said: "I swear by my arms, Goll was never without having a hundred men in his household, every one of them able to get the better of yourself." "And is it to them you belong, crooked-speaking, bare-headed Conan?" said Cairell. "It is to them I belong, you black, feeble, nail-scratching, tough-skinned Cairell; and I will make you know it was Finn was in the wrong," said Conan.

With that Cairell rose up and gave a furious blow of his fist to Conan, and Conan took it with no great patience, but gave him back a blow in his teeth, and from that they went on to worse blows again. And the two sons of Goll rose up to help Conan, and Osgar went to the help of Cairell, and it was not long till many of the chief men of the Fianna were fighting on the one side or the other, on the side of Finn or on the side of the sons of Morna.

But then Fergus of the True Lips rose up, and the rest of the poets of the Fianna along with him, and they sang their songs and their poems to check and to quiet them. And they left off their fighting at the sound of the poets' songs, and they let their weapons fall on the floor, and the poets took them up, and made peace between the fighters; and they put bonds on Finn and on Goll to keep the peace for a while, till they could ask for a judgment from the High King of Ireland. And that was the end for that time of the little quarrel at Almhuin.

But it broke out again, one time there was a falling out between Finn and Goll as to the dividing of a pig of the pigs of Manannan. And at Daire Tardha, the Oak Wood of Bulls, in the province of Connacht, there was a great fight between Finn's men and the sons of Morna. And the sons of Morna were worsted, and fifteen of their men were killed; and they made their mind up that from that time they would set themselves against any friends of Finn or of his people. And it was Conan the Bald gave them that advice, for he was always bitter, and a maker of quarrels and of mischief in every place.

And they kept to their word, and spared no one. There was a yellow-haired queen that Finn loved, Berach Brec her name was, and she was wise and comely and worthy of any good man, and she had her house full of treasures, and never refused the asking of any. And any one that came to her house at Samhain time might stay till Beltaine, and have his choice then to go or to stay. And the sons of Morna had fostered her, and they went where she was and bade her to give up Finn and she need be in no dread of them. But she said she would not give up her kind lover to please them; and she was going away from them to her ship, and Art, son of Morna, made a cast of his spear that went through her body, that she died, and her people brought her up from the strand and buried her.

And as to Goll, he took a little hound that Finn thought a great deal of, Conbeg its name was, and he drowned it in the sea; and its body was brought up to shore by a wave afterwards, and it was buried under a little green hill by the Fianna. And Caoilte made a complaint over it, and he said how swift the little hound was after deer, or wild pigs, and how good at killing them, and that it was a pity it to have died, out on the cold green waves. And about that time, nine women of the Tuatha de Danaan came to meet with nine men of the Fianna, and the sons of Morna saw them coming and made an end of them.

And when Caoilte met with Goll, he made a cast of his spear at him that struck the golden helmet off his head and a piece of his flesh along with it. But Goll took it very proudly, and put on the helmet again and took up his weapons, and called out to his brothers that he was no way ashamed.

And Finn went looking for the sons of Morna in every place to do vengeance on them. They were doing robbery and destruction one time in Slieve Echtge, that got its name from Echtge, daughter of Nuada of the Silver Hand, and Finn and the Fianna were to the west, at Slieve Cairn in the district of Corcomruadh. And Finn was in doubt if the sons of Morna were gone southward into Munster or north into Connacht. So he sent Aedan and Cahal, two sons of the King of Ulster, and two hundred fighting men with them, into the beautiful pleasant province of Connacht, and every day they used to go looking for the sons of Morna from place to place. But after a while the three battalions of the Fianna that were in Corcomruadh saw the track of a troop of men, and they thought it to be the track of the sons of Morna; and they closed round them at night, and made an end of them all. But when the full light came on the morrow, they knew them to be their own people, that were with the King of Ulster's sons, and they gave three great heavy cries, keening the friends they had killed in mistake.

And Caoilte and Oisin went to Rath Medha and brought a great stone and put it over the king's sons, and it was called Lia an Imracail, the Stone of the Mistake. And the place where Goll brought his men the time he parted from Finn in anger got the name of Druimscarha, the Parting Hill of Heroes.

Death of Goll

And at last it chanced that Goll and Cairell, son of Finn, met with one another, and said sharp words, and they fought in the sea near the strand, and Cairell got his death by Goll. And there was great anger and great grief on Finn, seeing his son, that was so strong and comely, lying dead and grey, like a blighted branch.

And as to Goll, he went away to a cave that was in a point stretching out into the sea; and he thought to stop there till Finn's anger would have passed.

And Osgar knew where he was, and he went to see him, that had been his comrade in so many battles. But Goll thought it was as an enemy he came, and he made a cast of his spear at him, and though Osgar got no wound by it, it struck his shield and crushed it. And Finn took notice of the way the shield was, and when he knew that Goll had made a cast at Osgar there was greater anger again on him. And he sent out his men and bade them to watch every path and every gap that led to the cave where Goll was, the way they would make an end of him.

And when Goll knew Finn to be watching for his life that way, he made no attempt to escape, but stopped where he was, without food, without drink, and he blinded with the sand that was blowing into his eyes.

And his wife came to a rock where she could speak with him, and she called to him to come to her. "Come over to me," she said; "and it is a pity you to be blinded where you are, on the rocks of the waste sea, with no drink but the salt water, a man that was first in every fight. And come now to be sleeping beside me," she said; "and in place of the hard sea-water I will nourish you from my own breast, and it is I will do your healing. And the gold of your hair is my desire for ever," she said, "and do not stop withering there like an herb in the winter-time, and my heart black with grief within me."

But Goll would not leave the spot where he was for all she could say. "It is best as it is," he said, "and I never took the advice of a woman east or west, and I never will take it. And O sweet-voiced queen," he said, "what ails you to be fretting after me; and remember now your silver and your gold, and your silks and stuffs, and remember the seven hounds I gave you at Cruadh Ceirrge, and every one of them without slackness till he has killed the deer. And do not be crying tears after me, queen with the white hands," he said; "but remember your constant lover, Aodh, the son of the best woman of the world, that came out from Spain asking for you, and that I fought at Corcar-an-Deirg; and go to him now," he said, "for it is bad when a woman is in want of a good man."

And he lay down on the rocks, and at the end of twelve days he died. And his wife keened him there, and made a great lamentation for her husband that had such a great name, and that was the second best of the Fianna of Ireland.

And when Conan heard of the death of Goll his brother, there was great anger on him, and he went to Garraidh, and asked him to go with him to Finn to ask satisfaction for Goll. "I am not willing to go," said Garraidh, "since we could get no satisfaction for the great son of Morna." "Whether you have a mind to go or not, I will go," said Conan; "and I will make an end of every man I meet with, for the sake of yellow-haired Goll; I will have the life of Oisin, Finn's great son, and of Osgar and of Caoilte and of Daire of the Songs; I will have no forgiveness for them; we must show no respect for Finn, although we may die in the fight, having no help from Goll. And let us take that work in hand, and make no delay," he said; "for if Finn is there, his strength will be there, until we put him under his flag-stone."

But it is not likely Garraidh went with him, and he after speaking such foolish words.

And what happened to Conan in the end is not known. But there is a cairn of stones on a hill of Burren, near to Corcomruadh, and the people of Connacht say it is there he is buried, and that there was a stone found there one time, having on it in the old writing: "Conan the swift-footed, the bare-footed." But the Munster people say it is on their own side of Burren he is buried.

The Battle of Gabhra

Now, with one thing and another, the High King of Ireland had got to be someway bitter against Finn and the Fianna, and one time that he had a gathering of his people he spoke out to them, and he bade them to remember all the harm that had been done them through the Fianna, and all their pride, and the tribute they asked. "And as to myself," he said, "I would sooner die fighting the Fianna, if I could bring them down along with me, than live with Ireland under them the way it is now."

All his people were of the same mind, and they said they would make no delay, but would attack the Fianna and make an end of them. "And we will have good days of joy and of feasting," they said, "when once Almhuin is clear of them."

And the High King began to make plans against Finn; and he sent to all the men of Ireland to come and help him. And when all was ready, he sent and bade Osgar to come to a feast he was making at Teamhair.

And Osgar, that never was afraid before any enemy, set out for Teamhair, and three hundred of his men with him. And on the way they saw a woman of the Sidhe washing clothes at a river, and there was the colour of blood on the water where she was washing them. And Osgar said to her: "There is red on the clothes you are washing; and it is for the dead you are washing them." And the woman answered him, and it is what she said: "It is not long till the ravens will be croaking over your own head after the battle." "Is there any weakness in your eyes," said Osgar, "that a little story like that would set us crying? And do another foretelling for us now," he said, "and tell us will any man of our enemies fall by us before we ourselves are made an end of."

"There will nine hundred fall by yourself," she said; "and the High King himself will get his death-wound from you."

Osgar and his men went on then to the king's house at Teamhair, and they got good treatment, and the feast was made ready, and they were three days at pleasure and at drinking.

And on the last day of the drinking, the High King called out with a loud voice, and he asked Osgar would he make an exchange of spears with him. "Why do you ask that exchange," said Osgar, "when I myself and my spear were often with yourself in time of battle? And you would not ask it of me," he said, "if Finn and the Fianna were with me now." "I would ask it from any fighting man among you," said the king, "and for rent and tribute along with it." "Any gold or any treasure you might ask of us, we would give it to you," said Osgar, "but it is not right for you to ask my spear." There were very high words between them then, and they threatened one another, and at the last the High King said: "I will put my spear of the seven spells out through your body." "And I give my word against that," said Osgar, "I will put my spear of the nine spells between the meeting of your hair and your beard."

With that he and his men rose up and went out of Teamhair, and they stopped to rest beside a river, and there they heard the sound of a very sorrowful tune, that was like keening, played on a harp. And there was great anger on Osgar when he heard that, and he rose up and took his arms and roused his people, and they went on again to where Finn was. And there came after them a messenger from the High King, and the message he brought was this, that he never would pay tribute to the Fianna or bear with them at all from that time.

And when Finn heard that, he sent a challenge of battle, and he gathered together all the Fianna that were left to him. But as to the sons of Morna, it was to the High King of Ireland they gathered.

And it was at the hill of Gabhra the two armies met, and there were twenty men with the King of Ireland for every man that was with Finn.

And it is a very hard battle was fought that day, and there were great deeds done on both sides; and there never was a greater battle fought in Ireland than that one.

And as to Osgar, it would be hard to tell all he killed on that day; five score of the Sons of the Gael, and five score fighting men from the Country of Snow, and seven score of the Men of Green Swords that never went a step backward, and four hundred from the Country of the Lion, and five score of the sons of kings; and the shame was for the King of Ireland.

But as to Osgar himself, that began the day so swift and so strong, at the last he was like leaves on a strong wind, or like an aspen-tree that is falling. But when he saw the High King near him, he made for him like a wave breaking on the strand; and the king saw him coming, and shook his greedy spear, and made a cast of it, and it went through his body and brought him down on his right knee, and that was the first grief of the Fianna. But Osgar himself was no way daunted, but he made a cast of his spear of the nine spells that went into the High King at the meeting of the hair and the beard, and gave him his death. And when the men nearest to the High King saw that, they put the king's helmet up on a pillar, the way his people would think he was living yet. But Osgar saw it, and he lifted a thin bit of a slab-stone that was on the ground beside him, and he made a cast of it that broke the helmet where it was; and then he himself fell like a king.

And there fell in that battle the seven sons of Caoilte, and the son of the King of Lochlann that had come to give them his help, and it would be hard to count the number of the Fianna that fell in that battle.

And when it was ended, those that were left of them went looking for their dead. And Caoilte stooped down over his seven brave sons, and every living man of the Fianna stooped over his own dear friends. And it was a lasting grief to see all that were stretched in that place, but the Fianna would not have taken it to heart the way they did, but for being as they were, a beaten race.

And as to Oisin, he went looking for Osgar, and it is the way he found him, lying stretched, and resting on his left arm and his broken shield beside him, and his sword in his hand yet, and his blood about him on every side. And he put out his hand to Oisin, and Oisin took it and gave out a very hard cry. And Osgar said:

"It is glad I am to see you safe, my father." And Oisin had no answer to give him. And just then Caoilte came where they were, and he looked at Osgar. "What way are you now, my darling?" he said. "The way you would like me to be," said Osgar.

Then Caoilte searched the wound, and when he saw how the spear had torn its way through to the back, he cried out, and a cloud came over him and his strength failed him. "O Osgar," he said, "you are parted from the Fianna, and they themselves must be parted from battle from this out," he said, "and they must pay their tribute to the King of Ireland."

Then Caoilte and Oisin raised up Osgar on their shields and brought him to a smooth green hill till they would take his dress off. And there was not a handsbreadth of his white body that was without a wound.

And when the rest of the Fianna saw what way Osgar was, there was not a man of them that keened his own son or his brother, but every one of them came keening Osgar.

And after a while, at noonday, they saw Finn coming towards them, and what was left of the Sun-banner raised on a spear-shaft. All of them saluted Finn then, but he made no answer, and he came up to the hill where Osgar was. And when Osgar saw him coming he saluted him, and he said: "I have got my desire in death, Finn of the sharp arms." And Finn said: "It is worse the way you were, my son, on the day of the battle at Beinn Edair when the wild geese could swim on your breast, and it was my hand that gave you healing." "There can no healing be done for me now for ever," said Osgar, "since the King of Ireland put the spear of seven spells through my body." And Finn said: "It is a pity it was not I myself fell in sunny scarce Gabhra, and you going east and west at the head of the Fianna." "And if it was yourself fell in the battle," said Osgar, "you would not hear me keening after you; for no man ever knew any heart in me," he said, "but a heart of twisted horn, and it covered with iron. But the howling of the dogs beside me," he said, "and the keening of the old fighting men, and the crying of the women one after another, those are the things that are vexing me." And Finn said: "Child of my child, calf of my calf, white and slender, it is a pity the way you are. And my heart is starting like a deer," he said, "and I am weak after you and after the Fianna of Ireland. And misfortune has followed us," he said; "and farewell now to battles and to a great name, and farewell to taking tributes; for every good thing I ever had is gone from me now," he said.

And when Osgar heard those words he stretched out his hands, and his eyelids closed. And Finn turned away from the rest, and he cried tears down; and he never shed a tear through the whole length of his lifetime but only for Osgar and for Bran.

And all that were left of the Fianna gave three sorrowful cries after Osgar, for there was not one of the Fianna beyond him, unless it might be Finn or Oisin.

And it is many of the Fianna were left dead in Gabhra, and graves were made for them. And as to Lugaidh's Son, that was so tall a man and so good a fighter, they made a very wide grave for him, as was fitting for a king. And the whole length of the rath at Gabhra, from end to end, it is that was the grave of Osgar, son of Oisin, son of Finn.

And as to Finn himself, he never had peace or pleasure again from that day.

Death of Bran

One day Finn was hunting, and Bran went following after a fawn. And they were coming towards Finn, and the fawn called out, and it said: "If I go into the sea below I will never come back again; and if I go up into the air above me, it will not save me from Bran." For Bran would overtake the wild geese, she was that swift.

"Go out through my legs," said Finn then. So the fawn did that, and Bran followed her; and as Bran went under him, Finn squeezed his two knees on her, that she died on the moment.

And there was great grief on him after that, and he cried tears down the same as he did when Osgar died.

And some said it was Finn's mother the fawn was, and that it was to save his mother he killed Bran. But that is not likely, for his mother was beautiful Muirne, daughter of Tadg, son of Nuada of the Tuatha de Danaan, and it was never heard that she was changed into a fawn. It is more likely it was Oisin's mother was in it.

But some say Bran and Sceolan are still seen to start at night out of the thicket on the hill of Almhuin.

The Call of Oisin

One misty morning, what were left of the Fianna were gathered together to Finn, and it is sorrowful and downhearted they were after the loss of so many of their comrades.

And they went hunting near the borders of Loch Lein, where the bushes were in blossom and the birds were singing; and they were waking up the deer that were as joyful as the leaves of a tree in summer-time.

And it was not long till they saw coming towards them from the west a beautiful young woman, riding on a very fast slender white horse. A queen's crown she had on her head, and a dark cloak of silk down to the ground, having stars of red gold on it; and her eyes were blue and as clear, as the dew on the grass, and a gold ring hanging down from every golden lock of her hair; and her cheeks redder than the rose, and her skin whiter than the swan upon the wave, and her lips as sweet as honey that is mixed through red wine.

And in her hand she was holding a bridle having a golden bit, and there was a saddle worked with red gold under her. And as to the horse, he had a wide smooth cloak over him, and a silver crown on the back of his head, and he was shod with shining gold.

She came to where Finn was, and she spoke with a very kind, gentle voice, and she said: "It is long my journey was, King of the Fianna." And Finn asked who was she, and what was her country and the cause of her coming. "Niamh of the Golden Head is my name," she said; "and I have a name beyond all the women of the world, for I am the daughter of the King of the Country of the Young." "What was it brought you to me from over the sea, Queen?" said Finn then. "Is it that your husband is gone from you, or what is the trouble that is on you?" "My husband is not gone from me," she said, "for I never went yet to any man. But O King of the Fianna," she said, "I have given my love and my affection to your own son, Oisin of the strong hands." "Why did you give your love to him beyond all the troops of high princes that are under the sun?" said Finn. "It was by reason of his great name, and of the report I heard of his bravery and of his comeliness," she said. "And though there is many a king's son and high prince gave me his love, I never consented to any till I set my love on Oisin."

When Oisin heard what she was saying, there was not a limb of his body that was not in love with beautiful Niamh; and he took her hand in his hand, and he said: "A true welcome before you to this country young queen. It is you are the shining one," he said; "it is you are the nicest and the comeliest; it is you are better to me than any other woman; it is you are my star and my choice beyond the women of the entire world." "I put on you the bonds of a true hero," said Niamh then, "you to come away with me now to the Country of the Young." And it is what she said:

"It is the country is most delightful of all that are under the sun; the trees are stooping down with fruit and with leaves and with blossom.

"Honey and wine are plentiful there, and everything the eye has ever seen; no wasting will come on you with the wasting away of time; you will never see death or lessening.

"You will get feasts, playing and drinking; you will get sweet music on the strings; you will get silver and gold and many jewels.

"You will get, and no lie in it, a hundred swords; a hundred cloaks of the dearest silk; a hundred horses, the quickest in battle; a hundred willing hounds.

"You will get the royal crown of the King of the Young that he never gave to any one under the sun. It will be a shelter to you night and day in every rough fight and in every battle.

"You will get a right suit of armour; a sword, gold-hilted, apt for striking; no one that ever saw it got away alive from it.

"A hundred coats of armour and shirts of satin; a hundred cows and a hundred calves; a hundred sheep having golden fleeces; a hundred jewels that are not of this world.

"A hundred glad young girls shining like the sun, their voices sweeter than the music of birds; a hundred armed men strong in battle, apt at feats, waiting on you, if you will come with me to the Country of the Young.

"You will get everything I have said to you, and delights beyond them, that I have no leave to tell; you will get beauty, strength and power, and I myself will be with you as a wife."

And after she had made that song, Oisin said: "O pleasant golden-haired queen, you are my choice beyond the women of the world; and I will go with you willingly," he said.

And with that he kissed Finn his father and bade him farewell, and he bade farewell to the rest of the Fianna, and he went up then on the horse with Niamh.

And the horse set out gladly, and when he came to the strand he shook himself and he neighed three times, and then he made for the sea. And when Finn and the Fianna saw Oisin facing the wide sea, they gave three great sorrowful shouts. And as to Finn, he said: "It is my grief to see you going from me; and I am without a hope," he said, "ever to see you coming back to me again."

The Last of the Great Men

And indeed that was the last time Finn and Oisin and the rest of the Fianna of Ireland were gathered together, for hunting, for battle, for chess-playing, for drinking or for music; for they all wore away after that, one after another.

As to Caoilte, that was old and had lost his sons, he used to be fretting and lonesome after the old times. And one day that there was very heavy snow on the ground, he made this complaint:

"It is cold the winter is; the wind is risen; the fierce high-couraged stag rises up; it is cold the whole mountain is to-night, yet the fierce stag is calling. The deer of Slievecarn of the gatherings does not lay his side to the ground; he no less than the stag of the top of cold Echtge hears the music of the wolves.

"I, Caoilte, and brown-haired Diarmuid and pleasant light-footed Osgar, we used to be listening to the music of the wolves through the end of the cold night. It is well the brown deer sleeps with its hide to the hollow, hidden as if in the earth, through the end of the cold night.

"To-day I am in my age, and I know but a few men; I used to shake my spear bravely in the ice-cold morning. It is often I put silence on a great army that is very cold to-night."

And after a while he went into a hill of the Sidhe to be healed of his old wounds. And whether he came back from there or not is not known; and there are some that say he used to be talking with Patrick of the Bells the same time Oisin was with him. But that is not likely, or Oisin would not have made complaints about his loneliness the way he did.

But a long time after that again, there was a king of Ireland making a journey. And he and his people missed their way, and when night-time came on, they were in a dark wood, and no path before them.

And there came to them a very tall man, that was shining like a burning flame, and he took hold of the bridle of the king's horse, and led him through the wood till they came to the right road. And the King of Ireland asked him who was he, and first he said: "I am your candlestick"; and then he said: "I was with Finn one time." And the king knew it was Caoilte, son of Ronan, was in it.

And three times nine of the rest of the Fianna came out of the west one time to Teamhair. And they took notice that now they were wanting their full strength and their great name, no one took notice of them or came to speak with them at all. And when they saw that, they lay down on the side of the hill at Teamhair, and put their lips to the earth and died.

And for three days and a month and a year from the time of the destruction of the Fianna of Ireland, Loch Dearg was under mists.

And as to Finn, there are some say he died by the hand of a fisherman; but it is likely that is not true, for that would be no death for so great a man as Finn, son of Cumhal. And there are some say he never died, but is alive in some place yet.

And one time a smith made his way into a cave he saw, that had a door to it, and he made a key that opened it. And when he went in he saw a very wide place, and very big men lying on the floor. And one that was bigger than the rest was lying in the middle, and the Dord Fiann beside him; and he knew it was Finn and the Fianna were in it.

And the smith took hold of the Dord Fiann, and it is hardly he could lift it to his mouth, and he blew a very strong blast on it, and the sound it made was so great, it is much the rocks did not come down on him. And at the sound, the big men lying on the ground shook from head to foot. He gave another blast then, and they all turned on their elbows.

And great dread came on him when he saw that, and he threw down the Dord Fiann and ran from the cave and locked the door after him, and threw the key into the lake. And he heard them crying after him, "You left us worse than you found us." And the cave was not found again since that time.

But some say the day will come when the Dord Fiann will be sounded three times, and that at the sound of it the Fianna will rise up as strong and as well as ever they were. And there are some say Finn, son of Cumhal, has been on the earth now and again since the old times, in the shape of one of the heroes of Ireland.

And as to the great things he and his men did when they were together, it is well they have been kept in mind through the poets of Ireland and of Alban. And one night there were two men minding sheep in a valley, and they were saying the poems of the Fianna while they were there. And they saw two very tall shapes on the two hills on each side of the valley, and one of the tall shapes said to the other: "Do you hear that man down below? I was the second doorpost of battle at Gabhra, and that man knows all about it better than myself."

OSCAR WILDE

♣

(1854-1900)

When Oscar Wilde wrote *The Ballad of Reading Gaol* in 1897, he was a broken man. Just out of prison, the once flamboyant intellect was reduced to pathetic wanderings around Europe under the assumed name of Sebastian Melmoth. His birth name would not do in public anymore ("I had disgraced that name eternally," he wrote) and Wilde sank profoundly into a life of alcohol and promiscuous sex, abandoned by most of the friends who had clung to him in better days. He subsisted on borrowed money and the kindness of what few admirers remained in his life, but he would live less than three years after his release from Reading Gaol, succumbing to cerebral meningitis in the Hotel d'Alsace in Paris in 1900. His death was a marked contrast to the very manner in which he lived, ferociously outrageous and seemingly good-humored at every turn. The man who was well known for living beyond his means, sipped champagne on his deathbed and is alleged to have said, "Ah, well, then I suppose I shall have to die beyond my means."

Born in 1854, Oscar Wilde grew up in an Irish household where his parents, William and Lady Jane Francesa Wilde were quasi-celebrities in Dublin. William, aside from being a bit of a conversationalist, poet and social butterfly, was also a prominent eye and ear surgeon. He wrote several volumes on his specialty and was eventually knighted for his work, most significantly for single-handedly founding St. Marks Ophthalmic Hospital. Lady Jane was a noteworthy Irish revolutionary who published poetry under the pseudonym "Speranza" in the Irish weekly, *The Nation*. A self-proclaimed genius and extravagant entertainer, it was clear to everyone that Oscar was an acorn that did not fall far from the tree. William Butler Yeats would later remark, "When one listens to [Lady Wilde] and remembers that Sir William Wilde was in his day a famous raconteur, one finds it in no way wonderful that Oscar Wilde should be the most finished talker of our time." While

Oscar was a child, Speranza hosted weekly salons in the Wilde house, where artists, scientists and intellects gathered, and his mother encouraged Oscar to not only attend, but also participate in conversations. It was at Speranza's salons, scholars concede, that the young Wilde developed a talent for captivating the attentions of the social elite, as he often put himself in the position of amusing the adults with his precocious tales. At the age of nine, Wilde was sent off to the Portora Royal School, an institution comprised of mostly upper–middle–class children from parents who wanted the equivalent of an English education in Ireland. As his father gained more notoriety and wealth, the Wildes moved into an estate in Cong, County Mayo, and Oscar flirted with the life of an aristocrat. An honor student at Portora, Oscar was accepted into Trinity College in Dublin in 1871 and quickly established himself as a noted scholar, despite a bit of a reputation as a sloth. He befriended Trinity's Greek scholar, John Pentland Mahaffey, who introduced Wilde to the Greek aesthetic, as well as homosexuality, and Wilde's growth as an intellectual and artist flourished. Despite his already burgeoning reputation as one who achieved fame before accomplishing anything, Wilde went on to study at Oxford where he won the prestigious Newdigate Prize for his poem, "Ravenna," and he ultimately left the school a renowned scholar and a bright star.

In 1876, however, his father died, leaving the family little money but significant debt. Wilde moved to life in London, where his mother now resided, and she soon established another salon, this time in Chelsea. Wilde tried his hand at traditional courtships, including a romance with a beauty named Florence Balcombe, who jilted him to marry the writer, Bram Stoker, and he was forced to play the part of the broken-hearted lover, a role he admittedly enjoyed. Deciding a change of scenery would do him well, Wilde spent nearly a year on a lecture tour of America, where, when famously stopped by a customs agent, he replied, "I have nothing to declare, except my genius." But he did not think much of his time spent in the United States, except for a meeting with Walt Whitman, whose company Wilde truly seemed to enjoy. By 1884, Wilde returned to Europe and married, to the puzzlement of many of his closest friends, the beautiful but somewhat uninspired Constance Lloyd. The two arranged an opulent wedding with elaborate costumes and artists such as John Singer Sargent and James Whistler in attendance. But the domesticated life did not agree with Wilde. He became a literary editor for *Woman's World* magazine, but as his marriage slowly dissolved, Wilde left the magazine business and began writing and producing plays, such as *The Importance of Being Earnest*, *A Woman of No Importance* and *An Ideal Husband*. He also wrote his most famous work, *The Picture of Dorian Gray*, which many scholars believe is autobiographical in content. Whatever fame Wilde had before *Dorian Gray* could not compare with the attention he received toward the end of the 19th century. He began flaunting his homosexuality in public, and entered into a relationship with Lord Alfred Douglas, known to Wilde as "Bosie." Bosie's father, Marquis of Queensbury, the man who formulated the "Queensbury Rules" for boxing, was furious not only that his son was a homosexual, but that he was the object of the flamboyant Oscar Wilde's affections. He began stalking Wilde, referring to him in public as the "known sodomite," and Wilde, who seemed to relish the attention, quickly brought a libel suit against him. The civil suit would ultimately lead to Wilde's ruin, as Marquis of Queensbury and his lawyers would eventually parade a string of underaged male prostitutes to the stand, who confessed their intimacies with the Irish writer. The trial caused such a public scandal that criminal sodomy charges were soon brought against Wilde. The English justice system appeared to be giving Wilde the opportunity to flee the country, but Speranza threatened Wilde that she would disown him if he did not fight the charges. Wilde stayed to fight, but was defeated and sentenced to two years' hard labor, the end of which he served in Reading Gaol. Upon his release, Wilde suffered beyond his expectations. The drama of a public scandal behind him, he was confronted with the isolation and inhumanity of a caged existence, and the experience had a shattering effect on him. Confined to his cell, he wrote *De Profundis*, a 30,000-word letter to Bosie, effectively breaking off their relationship and reflecting on life, art and the actions that led to his incarceration. Wilde was eventually released from prison in 1898, but he never recovered from the anguish of his punishment. He attempted reconciliation with Constance, but was unable to resist the lure of absinthe and promiscuity, and briefly took up with Bosie again before eventually leaving for France. There, he lived off the generosity of admireres, writing occasionally for Parisian newspapers. But Oscar Wilde had one work left in him, and during the summer after his release, he set about to write the epic poem, *The Ballad of Reading Gaol*. With the help of his friend and literary executor, Robert Ross, the poem was originally published bearing Wilde's cell number (C.3.3.) rather than his name.

The ballad begins with an act of murder, purported to be the story of Charles Thomas Wooldridge, who killed his young wife, Laura Ellen in 1896 in a fit of jealousy. After his trial, Wooldridge was sentenced to be hanged in the Reading Prison yard, and this "death row" experience forms the basis of Wilde's poem. It was a cry of prison anguish, lamenting the inhumanity and indecency of the English penal system. Because of Wilde's celebrity, the poem focused a great deal of attention on the Dickensian conditions at Reading and other jails, and ultimately led to some prison reforms. Wilde, however, barely survived his sentence, and a series of illnesses contracted during his incarceration ultimately led to his death. Just 46 years old, Wilde died penniless in a rundown Parisian hotel, though not without his famous wit. Noticing the squalid décor at the scene of his deathbed, Wilde was said to have remarked, "I am in a duel to the death with this wallpaper, one of us has got to go."

THE BALLAD OF READING GAOL AND OTHER POEMS

♣

Hélas!

To drift with every passion till my soul
Is a stringed lute on which all winds can play,
Is it for this that I have given away
Mine ancient wisdom, and austere control?
Methinks my life is a twice-written scroll
Scrawled over on some boyish holiday
With idle songs for pipe and virelay,
Which do but mar the secret of the whole.
Surely there was a time I might have trod
The sunlit heights, and from life's dissonance
Struck one clear chord to reach the ears of God:
Is that time dead? lo! with a little rod
I did but touch the honey of romance
And must I lose a soul's inheritance?

To Milton

Milton! I think thy spirit hath passed away
From these white cliffs and high-embattled towers;
    This gorgeous fiery-coloured world of ours
Seems fallen into ashes dull and grey,
And the age changed unto a mimic play
    Wherein we waste our else too-crowded hours:

For all our pomp and pageantry and powers
We are but fit to delve the common clay,
Seeing this little isle on which we stand,
    This England, this sea-lion of the sea,
    By ignorant demagogues is held in fee,
Who love her not: Dear God! is this the land
    Which bare a triple empire in her hand
    When Cromwell spake the word Democracy!

Requiescat

Tread lightly, she is near
    Under the snow,
Speak gently, she can hear
    The daisies grow.

All her bright golden hair
    Tarnished with rust,
She that was young and fair
    Fallen to dust.

Lily-like, white as snow,
    She hardly knew
She was a woman, so
    Sweetly she grew.

Coffin-board, heavy stone,
    Lie on her breast,
I vex my heart alone,
    She is at rest.

Peace, peace, she cannot hear
    Lyre or sonnet,
All my life's buried here,
    Heap earth upon it.

                Avignon

Vita Nuova

I stood by the unvintageable sea
    Till the wet waves drenched face and hair with spray;
    The long red fires of the dying day
Burned in the west; the wind piped drearily;
And to the land the clamorous gulls did flee:
    "Alas!" I cried, "my life is full of pain,
    And who can garner fruit or golden grain
From these waste fields which travel ceaselessly!"
My nets gaped wide with many a break and flaw,
    Nathless I threw them as my final cast
    Into the sea, and waited for the end.
When lo! a sudden glory! and I saw
    The argent splendour of white limbs ascend,
    And in that joy forgot my tortured past.

Impression du Matin

The Thames nocturne of blue and gold
    Changed to a Harmony in grey:
    A barge with ochre-coloured hay
Dropt from the wharf: and chill and cold

The yellow fog came creeping down
    The bridges, till the houses' walls

Seemed changed to shadows and St. Paul's
Loomed like a bubble o'er the town.

Then suddenly arose the clang
　　Of waking life; the streets were stirred
　　With country waggons: and a bird
Flew to the glistening roofs and sang.

But one pale woman all alone,
　　The daylight kissing her wan hair,
　　Loitered beneath the gas lamps' flare,
With lips of flame and heart of stone.

Chanson

A ring of gold and a milk-white dove
　　Are goodly gifts for thee,
And a hempen rope for your own love
　　To hang upon a tree.

For you a House of Ivory,
　　(Roses are white in the rose-bower)
A narrow bed for me to lie,
　　(White, O white, is the hemlock flower)!

Myrtle and jessamine for you
　　(O the red rose is fair to see)!
For me the cypress and the rue,
　　(Finest of all is rosemary)!

For you three lovers of your hand,
　　(Green grass where a man lies dead)!
For me three paces on the sand,
　　(Plant lilies at my head)!

Impressions

1

Les Silhouettes

The sea is flecked with bars of grey,
The dull dead wind is out of tune,
And like a withered leaf the moon
Is blown across the stormy bay.

Etched clear upon the pallid sand
The black boat lies: a sailor boy
Clambers aboard in careless joy
With laughing face and gleaming hand.

And overhead the curlews cry,
Where through the dusky upland grass
The young brown-throated reapers pass,
Like silhouettes against the sky.

2

La Fuite de la Lune

Outer senses there is peace,
A dreamy peace on either hand,
Deep silence in the shadowy land,
Deep silence where the shadows cease.

Save for a cry that echoes shrill
From some lone bird disconsolate;
A corncrake calling to its mate;
The answer from the misty hill.

And suddenly the moon withdraws

Her sickle from the lightening skies,
    And to her sombre cavern flies,
Wrapped in a veil of yellow gauze.

The Grave of Keats

Rid of the world's injustice, and his pain,
He rests at last beneath God's veil of blue.
Taken from life when life and love were new
The youngest of the martyrs here is lain,
    Fair as Sebastian, and as early slain.
    No cypress shades his grave, no funeral yew,
    But gentle violets weeping with the dew
Weave on his bones an ever-blossoming chain.
O proudest heart that broke for misery!
    O sweetest lips since those of Mitylene!
    O poet-painter of our English Land!
Thy name was writ in water—it shall stand:
    And tears like mine will keep thy memory green,
As Isabella did her Basil-tree.

Rome

Ballade de Marguerite

(*Normande*)

I am weary of lying within the chase
When the knights are meeting in market-place.

Nay, go not thou to the red-roofed town
Lest the hooves of the war-horse tread thee down.

But I would not go where the Squires ride,
I would only walk by my Lady's side.

Alack! and alack! thou art overbold,
A Forester's son may not eat off gold.

Will she love me the less that my Father is seen
Each Martinmas day in a doublet green?

Perchance she is sewing at tapestrie,
Spindle and loom are not meet for thee.

Ah, if she is working the arras bright
I might ravel the threads by the fire-light.

Perchance she is hunting of the deer,
How could you follow o'er hill and mere?

Ah, if she is riding with the court,
I might run beside her and wind the morte.

Perchance she is kneeling in St. Denys,
(On her soul may our Lady have gramercy!)

Ah, if she is praying in lone chapelle,
I might swing the censer and ring the bell.

Come in, my son, for you look sae pale,
The father shall fill thee a stoup of ale.

But who are these knights in bright array?
Is it a pageant the rich folks play?

Tis the King of England from over sea,
Who has come unto visit our fair countrie.

But why does the curfew toll sae low?
And why do the mourners walk a-row?

O 't is Hugh of Amiens my sister's son
Who is lying stark, for his day is done.

Nay, nay, for I see white lilies clear,
It is no strong man who lies on the bier.

O 't is old Dame Jeannette that kept the hall,
I knew she would die at the autumn fall.

Dame Jeannette had not that gold-brown hair,
Old Jeannette was not a maiden fair.

O 't is none of our kith and none of our kin,
(Her soul may our Lady assoil from sin!)

But I hear the boy's voice chaunting sweet,
"Elle est morte, la Marguerite."

Come in, my son, and lie on the bed,
And let the dead folk bury their dead.

O mother, you know I loved her true:
O mother, hath one grave room for two?

Impression de Voyage

The sea was sapphire coloured, and the sky
　　Burned like a heated opal through the air;
　　We hoisted sail; the wind was blowing fair
For the blue lands that to the eastward lie.

From the steep prow I marked with quickening eye
    Zakynthos, every olive grove and creek,
    Ithaca's cliff, Lycaon's snowy peak,
And all the flower-strewn hills of Arcady.
The flapping of the sail against the mast,
    The ripple of the water on the side,
    The ripple of girls' laughter at the stern,
The only sounds:—when 'gan the West to burn,
    And a red sun upon the seas to ride.
    I stood upon the soil of Greece at last!

Panthea

Nay, let us walk from fire unto fire,
    From passionate pain to deadlier delight,—
I am too young to live without desire,
    Too young art thou to waste this summer night
Asking those idle questions which of old
Man sought of seer and oracle, and no reply was told.

For, sweet, to feel is better than to know,
    And wisdom is a childless heritage,
One pulse of passion—youth's first fiery glow,—
    Are worth the hoarded proverbs of the sage:
Vex not thy soul with dead philosophy,
Have we not lips to kiss with, hearts to love and eyes to see!

Dost thou not hear the murmuring nightingale,
    Like water bubbling from a silver jar,
So soft she sings the envious moon is pale,
    That high in heaven she is hung so far
She cannot hear that love-enraptured tune,—
Mark how she wreathes each horn with mist, yon late and labouring moon.

White lilies, in whose cups the gold bees dream,
    The fallen snow of petals where the breeze
Scatters the chestnut blossom, or the gleam
    Of boyish limbs in water,—are not these
Enough for thee, dost thou desire more?
Alas! the Gods will give nought else from their eternal store.

For our high Gods have sick and wearied grown
    Of all our endless sins, our vain endeavour
For wasted days of youth to make atone
    By pain or prayer or priest, and never, never,
Hearken they now to either good or ill,
But send their rain upon the just and the unjust at will.

They sit at ease, our Gods they sit at ease,
    Strewing with leaves of rose their scented wine,
They sleep, they sleep, beneath the rocking trees
    Where asphodel and yellow lotus twine,
Mourning the old glad days before they knew
What evil things the heart of man could dream, and dreaming do.

And far beneath the brazen floor they see
    Like swarming flies the crowd of little men,
The bustle of small lives, then wearily
    Back to their lotus-haunts they turn again
Kissing each others' mouths, and mix more deep
The poppy-seeded draught which brings soft purple-lidded sleep.

There all day long the golden-vestured sun,
    Their torch-bearer, stands with his torch ablaze,
And, when the gaudy web of noon is spun
    By its twelve maidens, through the crimson haze
Fresh from Endymion's arms comes forth the moon,
And the immortal Gods in toils of mortal passions swoon.

There walks Queen Juno through some dewy mead,

Her grand white feet flecked with the saffron dust
Of wind-stirred lilies, while young Ganymede
   Leaps in the hot and amber-foaming must,
His curls all tossed, as when the eagle bare
The frightened boy from Ida through the blue Ionian air.

There in the green heart of some garden close
   Queen Venus with the shepherd at her side,
Her warm soft body like the briar rose
   Which would be white yet blushes at its pride,
Laughs low for love, till jealous Salmacis
Peers through the myrtle-leaves and sighs for pain of lonely bliss.

There never does that dreary north-wind blow
   Which leaves our English forests bleak and bare,
Nor ever falls the swift white-feathered snow,
   Nor ever doth the red-toothed lightning dare
To wake them in the silver-fretted night
When we lie weeping for some sweet sad sin, some dead delight.

Alas! they know the far Lethæan spring,
   The violet-hidden waters well they know,
Where one whose feet with tired wandering
   Are faint and broken may take heart and go,
And from those dark depths cool and crystalline
Drink, and draw balm, and sleep for sleepless souls, and anodyne.

But we oppress our natures, God or Fate
   Is our enemy, we starve and feed
On vain repentance—O we are born too late!
   What balm for us in bruisèd poppy seed
Who crowd into one finite pulse of time
The joy of infinite love and the fierce pain of infinite crime.

O we are wearied of this sense of guilt,
   Wearied of pleasure's paramour despair,

Wearied of every temple we have built,
    Wearied of every right, unanswered prayer,
For man is weak; God sleeps; and heaven is high;
One fiery-coloured moment: one great love; and lo! we die.

Ah! but no ferry-man with labouring pole
    Nears his black shallop to the flowerless strand,
No little coin of bronze can bring the soul
    Over Death's river to the sunless land,
Victim and wine and vow are all in vain,
The tomb is sealed; the soldiers watch; the dead rise not again.

We are resolved into the supreme air,
    We are made one with what we touch and see,
With our heart's blood each crimson sun is fair,
    With our young lives each spring-impassioned tree
Flames into green, the wildest beasts that range
The moor our kinsmen are, all life is one, and all is change.

With beat of systole and of diastole
    One grand great life throbs through earth's giant heart,
And mighty waves of single Being roll
    From nerveless germ to man, for we are part
Of every rock and bird and beast and hill,
One with the things that prey on us, and one with what we kill.

From lower cells of waking life we pass
    To full perfection; thus the world grows old:
We who are godlike now were once a mass
    Of quivering purple flecked with bars of gold,
Unsentient or of joy or misery,
And tossed in terrible tangles of some wild and wind-swept sea.

This hot hard flame with which our bodies burn
    Will make some meadow blaze with daffodil,
Ay! and those argent breasts of thine will turn

To water-lilies; the brown fields men till
Will be more fruitful for our love to-night,
Nothing is lost in nature, all things live in Death's despite.

The boy's first kiss, the hyacinth's first bell,
   The man's last passion, and the last red spear
That from the lily leaps, the asphodel
   Which will not let its blossoms blow for fear
Of too much beauty, and the timid shame
Of the young bridegroom at his lover's eyes,—these with the same

One sacrament are consecrate, the earth
   Not we alone hath passions hymeneal,
The yellow buttercups that shake for mirth
   At daybreak know a pleasure not less real
Than we do, when in some fresh-blossoming wood,
We draw the spring into our hearts, and feel that life is good.

So when men bury us beneath the yew
   Thy crimson-stainèd mouth a rose will be,
And thy soft eyes lush bluebells dimmed with dew,
   And when the white narcissus wantonly
Kisses the wind its playmate some faint joy
Will thrill our dust, and we will be again fond maid and boy.

And thus without life's conscious torturing pain
   In some sweet flower we will feel the sun,
And from the linnet's throat will sing again,
   And as two gorgeous-mailèd snakes will run
Over our graves, or as two tigers creep
Through the hot jungle where the yellow-eyed huge lions sleep

And give them battle! How my heart leaps up
   To think of that grand living after death
In beast and bird and flower, when this cup,
   Being filled too full of spirit, bursts for breath,

And with the pale leaves of some autumn day
The soul earth's earliest conqueror becomes earth's last great prey.

O think of it! We shall inform ourselves
    Into all sensuous life, the goat-foot Faun,
The Centaur, or the merry bright-eyed Elves
    That leave their dancing rings to spite the dawn
Upon the meadows, shall not be more near
Than you and I to nature's mysteries, for we shall hear

The thrush's heart beat, and the daisies grow,
    And the wan snowdrop sighing for the sun
On sunless days in winter, we shall know
    By whom the silver gossamer is spun,
Who paints the diapered fritillaries,
On what wide wings from shivering pine to pine the eagle flies.

Ay! had we never loved at all, who knows
    If yonder daffodil had lured the bee
Into its gilded womb, or any rose
    Had hung with crimson lamps its little tree!
Methinks no leaf would ever bud in spring,
But for the lovers' lips that kiss, the poets' lips that sing.

Is the light vanished from our golden sun,
    Or is this dædal-fashioned earth less fair,
That we are nature's heritors, and one
    With every pulse of life that beats the air?
Rather new suns across the sky shall pass,
New splendour come unto the flower, new glory to the grass.

And we two lovers shall not sit afar,
    Critics of nature, but the joyous sea
Shall be our raiment, and the bearded star
    Shoot arrows at our pleasure! We shall be
Part of the mighty universal whole,

And through all aeons mix and mingle with the Kosmic Soul!

We shall be notes in that great Symphony
    Whose cadence circles through the rhythmic spheres,
And all the live World's throbbing heart shall be
    One with our heart; the stealthy creeping years
Have lost their terrors now, we shall not die,
The Universe itself shall be our Immortality.

Impression

Le Réveillon

    The sky is laced with fitful red,
    The circling mists and shadows flee,
    The dawn is rising from the sea,
Like a white lady from her bed.

    And jagged brazen arrows fall
    Athwart the feathers of the night,
    And a long wave of yellow light
Breaks silently on tower and hall,

    And spreading wide across the wold,
    Wakes into flight some fluttering bird,
    And all the chestnut tops are stirred,
And all the branches streaked with gold.

Apologia

Is it thy will that I should wax and wane,

Barter my cloth of gold for hodden grey,
And at thy pleasure weave that web of pain
    Whose brightest threads are each a wasted day?

Is it thy will—Love that I love so well—
    That my Soul's House should be a tortured spot
Wherein, like evil paramours, must dwell
    The quenchless flame, the worm that dieth not?

Nay, if it be thy will I shall endure,
    And sell ambition at the common mart,
And let dull failure be my vestiture,
    And sorrow dig its grave within my heart.

Perchance it may be better so—at least
    I have not made my heart a heart of stone,
Nor starved my boyhood of its goodly feast,
    Nor walked where Beauty is a thing unknown.

Many a man hath done so; sought to fence
    In straitened bonds the soul that should be free,
Trodden the dusty road of common sense,
    While all the forest sang of liberty,

Not marking how the spotted hawk in flight
    Passed on wide pinion through the lofty air,
To where some steep untrodden mountain height
    Caught the last tresses of the Sun God's hair.

Or how the little flower be trod upon,
    The daisy, that white-feathered shield of gold,
Followed with wistful eyes the wandering sun
    Content if once its leaves were aureoled.

But surely it is something to have been

The best belovèd for a little while,
  To have walked hand in hand with Love, and seen
    His purple wings flit once across thy smile.

Ay! though the gorgèd asp of passion feed
    On my boy's heart, yet have I burst the bars,
  Stood face to face with Beauty, known indeed
    The Love which moves the Sun and all the stars!

Silentium Amoris

As often-times the too resplendent sun
    Hurries the pallid and reluctant moon
  Back to her sombre cave, ere she hath won
    A single ballad from the nightingale,
    So doth thy Beauty make my lips to fail,
  And all my sweetest singing out of tune.

And as at dawn across the level mead
    On wings impetuous some wind will come,
  And with its too harsh kisses break the reed
    Which was its only instrument of song,
    So my too stormy passions work me wrong,
  And for excess of Love my Love is dumb.

But surely unto Thee mine eyes did show
    Why I am silent, and my lute unstrung;
  Else it were better we should part, and go,
    Thou to some lips of sweeter melody,
    And I to nurse the barren memory
  Of unkissed kisses, and songs never sung.

Tædium Vitæ

To stab my youth with desperate knives, to wear
This paltry age's gaudy livery,
To let each base hand filch my treasury,
To mesh my soul within a woman's hair,
And be mere Fortune's lackeyed groom,—I swear
I love it not! these things are less to me
Than the thin foam that frets upon the sea,
Less than the thistledown of summer air
Which hath no seed: better to stand aloof
Far from these slanderous fools who mock my life
Knowing me not, better the lowliest roof
Fit for the meanest hind to sojourn in,
Than to go back to that hoarse cave of strife
Where my white soul first kissed the mouth of sin.

ΓΛΥΚΥΠΙΚΡΟΣ ΕΡΩΣ

Sweet, I blame you not, for mine the fault was, had I not been made of
    common clay
I had climbed the higher heights unclimbed yet, seen the fuller air, the
    larger day.

From the wildness of my wasted passion I had struck a better, clearer song,
Lit some lighter light of freer freedom, battled with some Hydra-headed
wrong.

Had my lips been smitten into music by the kisses that but made them bleed,
You had walked with Bice and the angels on that verdant and enamelled
mead.

I had trod the road which Dante treading saw the suns of seven circles shine,

Ay! perchance had seen the heavens opening, as they opened to the
Florentine.

And the mighty nations would have crowned me, who am crownless now and
without name,
And some orient dawn had found me kneeling on the threshold of the House
of Fame.

I had sat within that marble circle where the oldest bard is as the young,
And the pipe is ever dropping honey, and the lyre's strings are ever strung.

Keats had lifted up his hymeneal curls from out the poppy-seeded wine,
With ambrosial mouth had kissed my forehead, clasped the hand of noble
love in mine.

And at springtide, when the apple-blossoms brush the burnished bosom of
the dove,
Two young lovers lying in an orchard would have read the story of our love.

Would have read the legend of my passion, known the bitter secret of my
heart,
Kissed as we have kissed, but never parted as we two are fated now to part.

For the crimson flower of our life is eaten by the canker-worm of truth
And no hand can gather up the fallen petals of the withered rose of youth.

Yet I am not sorry that I loved you—ah! what else had I a boy to do,
For the hungry teeth of time devour, and the silent-footed years pursue.

Rudderless, we drift athwart a tempest, and when once the storm of youth is
past,
Without lyre, without lute or chorus, Death the silent pilot comes at last.

And within the grave there is no pleasure, for the blindworm battens on the
root,

And Desire shudders into ashes, and the tree of Passion bears no fruit.

Ah! what else had I to do but love you, God's own mother was less dear to
me,
And less dear the Cytheræan rising like an argent lily from the sea.

I have made my choice, have lived my poems, and, though youth is gone in
wasted days,
I have found the lover's crown of myrtle better than the poet's crown of bays.

The Sphinx

In a dim corner of my room for longer than my fancy thinks
A beautiful and silent Sphinx has watched me through the shifting gloom.

Inviolate and immobile she does not rise she does not stir
For silver moons are naught to her and naught to her the suns that reel.

Red follows grey across the air, the waves of moonlight ebb and flow
But with the Dawn she does not go and in the nighttime she is there.

Dawn follows Dawn and Nights grow old and all the while this curious cat
Lies couching on the Chinese mat with eyes of satin rimmed with gold.

Upon the mat she lies and leers and on the tawny throat of her
Flutters the soft and silky fur or ripples to her pointed ears

Come forth, my lovely seneschal! so somnolent, so statuesque!
Come forth you exquisite grotesque! half woman and half animal!

Come forth my lovely languorous Sphinx! and put your head upon my knee!
And let me stroke your throat and see your body spotted like the Lynx!

And let me touch those curving claws of yellow ivory and grasp
The tail that like a monstrous Asp coils round your heavy velvet paws!

A thousand weary centuries are thine while I have hardly seen
Some twenty summers cast their green for Autumn's gaudy liveries.

But you can read the Hieroglyphs on the great sandstone obelisks,
And you have talked with Basilisks, and you have looked on Hippogriffs.

O tell me, were you standing by when Isis to Osiris knelt?
And did you watch the Egyptian melt her union for Antony

And drink the jewel-drunken wine and bend her head in mimic awe
To see the huge proconsul draw the salted tunny from the brine?

And did you mark the Cyprian kiss white Adon on his catafalque?
And did you follow Amenalk, the God of Heliopolis?

And did you talk with Thoth, and did you hear the moon-horned Io weep?
And know the painted kings who sleep beneath the wedge-shaped Pyramid?

Lift up your large black satin eyes which are like cushions where one sinks!
Fawn at my feet, fantastic Sphinx! and sing me all your memories!

Sing to me of the Jewish maid who wandered with the Holy Child,
And how you led them through the wild, and how they slept beneath
    your shade.

Sing to me of that odorous green eve when crouching by the marge
You heard from Adrian's gilded barge the laughter of Antinous

And lapped the stream and fed your drouth and watched with hot and
    hungry stare
The ivory body of that rare young slave with his pomegranate mouth!

Sing to me of the Labyrinth in which the two-formed bull was stalled!
Sing to me of the night you crawled across the temple's granite plinth

When through the purple corridors the screaming scarlet Ibis flew
In terror, and a horrid dew dripped from the moaning Mandragores,

And the great torpid crocodile within the tank shed slimy tears,
And tare the jewels from his ears and staggered back into the Nile,

And the priests cursed you with shrill psalms as in your claws you seized
   their snake
And crept away with it to slake your passion by the shuddering palms.

Who were your lovers? who were they who wrestled for you in the dust?
Which was the vessel of your Lust? What Leman had you, every day?

Did giant Lizards come and crouch before you on the reedy banks?
Did Gryphons with great metal flanks leap on you in your trampled couch?

Did monstrous hippopotami come sidling toward you in the mist?
Did gilt-scaled dragons writhe and twist with passion as you passed them by?

And from the brick-built Lycian tomb what horrible Chimera came
With fearful heads and fearful flame to breed new wonders from your womb?

Or had you shameful secret quests and did you harry to your home
Some Nereid coiled in amber foam with curious rock crystal breasts?

Or did you treading through the froth call to the brown Sidonian
For tidings of Leviathan, Leviathan or Behemoth?

Or did you when the sun was set climb up the cactus-covered slope
To meet your swarthy Ethiop whose body was of polished jet?

Or did you while the earthen skiffs dropped down the grey Nilotic flats

At twilight and the flickering bats flew round the temple's triple glyphs

Steal to the border of the bar and swim across the silent lake
And slink into the vault and make the Pyramid your lœpanar

Till from each black sarcophagus rose up the painted swathèd dead?
Or did you lure unto your bed the ivory-horned Tragelaphos?

Or did you love the god of flies who plagued the Hebrew and was splashed
With wine unto the waist? or Pasht, who had green beryls for her eyes?

Or that young god, the Tyrian, who was more amorous than the dove
Of Ashtaroth? or did you love the god of the Assyrian

Whose wings, like strange transparent talc, rose high above his hawk-
    faced head,
Painted with silver and with red and ribbed with rods of Oreichalch?

Or did huge Apis from his car leap down and lay before your feet
Big blossoms of the honey-sweet and honey-coloured nenuphar?

How subtle-secret is your smile! Did you love none then? Nay, I know
Great Ammon was your bedfellow! He lay with you beside the Nile!

The river-horses in the slime trumpeted when they saw him come
Odorous with Syrian galbanum and smeared with spikenard and with thyme.

He came along the river bank like some tall galley argent-sailed,
He strode across the waters, mailed in beauty, and the waters sank,

He strode across the desert sand: he reached the valley where you lay:
He waited till the dawn of day: then touched your black breasts with his
hand.

You kissed his mouth with mouths of flame: you made the hornèd god

your own:
You stood behind him on his throne: you called him by his secret name.

You whispered monstrous oracles into the caverns of his ears:
With blood of goats and blood of steers you taught him monstrous miracles.

White Ammon was your bedfellow! Your chamber was the steaming Nile!
And with your curved archaic smile you watched his passion come and go.

With Syrian oils his brows were bright: and widespread as a tent at noon
His marble limbs made pale the moon and lent the day a larger light.

His long hair was nine cubits' span and coloured like that yellow gem
Which hidden in their garment's hem the merchants bring from Kurdistan.

His face was as the must that lies upon a vat of newmade wine:
The seas could not insapphirine the perfect azure of his eyes.

His thick soft throat was white as milk and threaded with thin veins of blue:
And curious pearls like frozen dew were broidered on his flowing silk.

On pearl and porphyry pedestalled he was too bright to look upon:
For on his ivory breast there shone the wondrous ocean-emerald,

That mystic moonlit jewel which some diver of the Colchian caves
Had found beneath the blackening waves and carried to the Colchian witch.

Before his gilded galiot ran naked vine-wreathed corybants,
And lines of swaying elephants knelt down to draw his chariot,

And lines of swarthy Nubians bare up his litter as he rode
Down the great granite-paven road between the nodding peacock fans.

The merchants brought him steatite from Sidon in their painted ships:
The meanest cup that touched his lips was fashioned from a chrysolite.

The merchants brought him cedar chests of rich apparel bound with cords;
  His train was borne by Memphian lords: young kings were glad to be
  his guests.

Ten hundred shaven priests did bow to Ammon's altar day and night,
Ten hundred lamps did wave their light through Ammon's carven house—
  and now

Foul snake and speckled adder with their young ones crawl from stone
  to stone
For ruined is the house and prone the great rose-marble monolith!

Wild ass or trotting jackal comes and couches in the mouldering gates:
Wild satyrs call unto their mates across the fallen fluted drums.

And on the summit of the pile the blue-faced ape of Horuss sits
And gibbers while the fig-tree splits the pillars of the peristyle.

The god is scattered here and there: deep hidden in the windy sand
I saw his giant granite hand still clenched in impotent despair.

And many a wandering caravan of stately negroes silken-shawled,
Crossing the desert halts appalled before the neck that none can span.

And many a bearded Bedouin draws back his yellow-striped burnous
To gaze upon the Titan thews of him who was thy paladin.

Go, seek his fragments on the moor and wash them in the evening dew,
And from their pieces make anew thy mutilated paramour!

Go, seek them where they lie alone and from their broken pieces make
Thy bruisèd bedfellow! And wake mad passions in the senseless stone!

Charm his dull ear with Syrian hymns! he loved your body! oh, be kind,
Pour spikenard on his hair, and wind soft rolls of linen round his limbs!

Wind round his head the figured coins! stain with red fruits those pallid lips!
Weave purple for his shrunken hips! and purple for his barren loins!

Away to Egypt! Have no fear. Only one God has ever died.
Only one God has let His side be wounded by a soldier's spear.

But these, thy lovers, are not dead. Still by the hundred-cubit gate
Dog-faced Anubis sits in state with lotus-lilies for thy head.

Still from his chair of porphyry gaunt Memnon strains his lidless eyes
Across the empty land, and cries each yellow morning unto thee.

And Nilus with his broken horn lies in his black and oozy bed
And till thy coming will not spread his waters on the withering corn.

Your lovers are not dead, I know. They will rise up and hear your voice
And clash their cymbals and rejoice and run to kiss your mouth! And so,

Set wings upon your argosies! Set horses to your ebon car!
Back to your Nile! Or if you are grown sick of dead divinities

Follow some roving lion's spoor across the copper-coloured plain,
Reach out and hale him by the mane and bid him be your paramour!

Couch by his side upon the grass and set your white teeth in his throat
And when you hear his dying note lash your long flanks of polished brass

And take a tiger for your mate, whose amber sides are flecked with black,
And ride upon his gilded back in triumph through the Theban gate,

And toy with him in amorous jests, and when he turns, and snarls,
   and gnaws,
O smite him with your jasper claws! and bruise him with your agate breasts!

Why are you tarrying? Get hence! I weary of your sullen ways,

I weary of your steadfast gaze, your somnolent magnificence.

Your horrible and heavy breath makes the light flicker in the lamp,
And on my brow I feel the damp and dreadful dews of night and death.

Your eyes are like fantastic moons that shiver in some stagnant lake,
Your tongue is like a scarlet snake that dances to fantastic tunes,

Your pulse makes poisonous melodies, and your black throat is like the hole
Left by some torch or burning coal on Saracenic tapestries.

Away! The sulphur-coloured stars are hurrying through the Western gate!
Away! Or it may be too late to climb their silent silver cars!

See, the dawn shivers round the grey gilt-dialled towers, and the rain
Streams down each diamonded pane and blurs with tears the wannish day.

What snake-tressed fury fresh from Hell, with uncouth gestures and unclean,
Stole from the poppy-drowsy queen and led you to a student's cell?

What songless tongueless ghost of sin crept through the curtains of the night,
And saw my taper turning bright, and knocked, and bade you enter in?

Are there not others more accursed, whiter with leprosies than I?
Are Abana and Pharphar dry that you come here to slake your thirst?

Get hence, you loathsome mystery! Hideous animal, get hence!
You wake in me each bestial sense, you make me what I would not be.

You make my creed a barren sham, you wake foul dreams of sensual life,
And Atys with his blood-stained knife were better than the thing I am.

False Sphinx! False Sphinx! By reedy Styx old Charon, leaning on his oar,
Waits for my coin. Go thou before, and leave me to my crucifix,

Whose pallid burden, sick with pain, watches the world with wearied eyes,
And weeps for every soul that dies, and weeps for every soul in vain.

The Ballad of Reading Gaol

1

He did not wear his scarlet coat,
    For blood and wine are red,
And blood and wine were on his hands
    When they found him with the dead,
The poor dead woman whom he loved,
    And murdered in her bed.

He walked amongst the Trial Men
    In a suit of shabby grey;
A cricket cap was on his head,
    And his step seemed light and gay;
But I never saw a man who looked
    So wistfully at the day.

I never saw a man who looked
    With such a wistful eye
Upon that little tent of blue
    Which prisoners call the sky,
And at every drifting cloud that went
    With sails of silver by.

I walked, with other souls in pain,
    Within another ring,
And was wondering if the man had done
    A great or little thing,
When a voice behind me whispered low,

"That fellow's got to swing."

Dear Christ! the very prison walls
　　Suddenly seemed to reel,
And the sky above my head became
　　Like a casque of scorching steel;
And, though I was a soul in pain,
　　My pain I could not feel.

I only knew what hunted thought
　　Quickened his step, and why
He looked upon the garish day
　　With such a wistful eye;
The man had killed the thing he loved,
　　And so he had to die.

·

Yet each man kills the thing he loves,
　　By each let this be heard,
Some do it with a bitter look,
　　Some with a flattering word.
The coward does it with a kiss,
　　The brave man with a sword!

Some kill their love when they are young,
　　And some when they are old;
Some strangle with the hands of Lust,
　　Some with the hands of Gold:
The kindest use a knife, because
　　The dead so soon grow cold.

Some love too little, some too long,
　　Some sell, and others buy;
Some do the deed with many tears,
　　And some without a sigh:

For each man kills the thing he loves,
    Yet each man does not die.

He does not die a death of shame
    On a day of dark disgrace,
Nor have a noose about his neck,
    Nor a cloth upon his face,
Nor drop feet foremost through the floor
    Into an empty space.

He does not sit with silent men
    Who watch him night and day;
Who watch him when he tries to weep,
    And when he tries to pray;
Who watch him lest himself should rob
    The prison of its prey.

He does not wake at dawn to see
    Dread figures throng his room,
The shivering Chaplain robed in white,
    The Sheriff stern with gloom,
And the Governor all in shiny black,
    With the yellow face of Doom.

He does not rise in piteous haste
    To put on convict-clothes,
While some coarse-mouthed Doctor gloats, and notes
    Each new and nerve-twitched pose,
Fingering a watch whose little ticks
    Are like horrible hammer-blows.

He does not feel that sickening thirst
    That sands one's throat, before
The hangman with his gardener's gloves
    Comes through the padded door,
And binds one with three leathern thongs,

That the throat may thirst no more.

He does not bend his head to hear
    The Burial Office read,
Nor, while the anguish of his soul
    Tells him he is not dead,
Cross his own coffin, as he moves
    Into the hideous shed.

He does not stare upon the air
    Through a little roof of glass:
He does not pray with lips of clay
    For his agony to pass;
Nor feel upon his shuddering cheek
    The kiss of Caiaphas.

2

Six weeks the guardsman walked the yard,
    In the suit of shabby grey:
His cricket cap was on his head,
    And his step seemed light and gay,
But I never saw a man who looked
    So wistfully at the day.

I never saw a man who looked
    With such a wistful eye
Upon that little tent of blue
    Which prisoners call the sky
And at every wandering cloud that trailed
    Its ravelled fleeces by.

He did not wring his hands, as do
    Those witless men who dare
To try to rear the changeling Hope
    In the cave of black Despair:
He only looked upon the sun,

And drank the morning air.

He did not wring his hands nor weep,
    Nor did he peek or pine,
But he drank the air as though it held
    Some healthful anodyne;
With open mouth he drank the sun
    As though it had been wine!

And I and all the souls in pain,
    Who tramped the other ring,
Forgot if we ourselves had done
    A great or little thing,
And watched with gaze of dull amaze
    The man who had to swing.

For strange it was to see him pass
    With a step so light and gay,
And strange it was to see him look
    So wistfully at the day,
And strange it was to think that he
    Had such a debt to pay.

•

For oak and elm have pleasant leaves
    That in the spring-time shoot;
But grim to see is the gallows-tree,
    With its adder-bitten root,
And, green or dry, a man must die
    Before it bears its fruit!

The loftiest place is that seat of grace
    For which all worldlings try:
But who would stand in hempen band
    Upon a scaffold high,

And through a murderer's collar take
    His last look at the sky?

It is sweet to dance to violins
    When Love and Life are fair:
To dance to flutes, to dance to lutes
    Is delicate and rare:
But it is not sweet with nimble feet
    To dance upon the air!

So with curious eyes and sick surmise
    We watched him day by day,
And wondered if each one of us
    Would end the self-same way,
For none can tell to what red Hell
    His sightless soul may stray.

At last the dead man walked no more
    Amongst the Trial Men,
And I knew that he was standing up
    In the black dock's dreadful pen,
And that never would I see his face
    For weal or woe again.

Like two doomed ships that pass in storm
    We had crossed each other's way:
But we made no sign, we said no word,
    We had no word to say;
For we did not meet in the holy night,
    But in the shameful day.

A prison wall was round us both,
    Two outcast men we were:
The world had thrust us from its heart,
    And God from out His care:
And the iron gin that waits for Sin

Had caught us in its snare.

3

In Debtor's Yard the stones are hard,
    And the dripping wall is high,
So it was there he took the air
    Beneath the leaden sky,
And by each side a Warder walked,
    For fear the man might die.

Or else he sat with those who watched
    His anguish night and day;
Who watched him when he rose to weep,
    And when he crouched to pray;
Who watched him lest himself should rob
    Their scaffold of its prey.

The Governor was strong upon
    The Regulations Act:
The Doctor said that Death was but
    A scientific fact:
And twice a day the Chaplain called,
    And left a little tract.

And twice a day he smoked his pipe,
    And drank his quart of beer:
His soul was resolute, and held
    No hiding-place for fear;
He often said that he was glad
    The hangman's day was near.

But why he said so strange a thing
    No warder dared to ask:
For he to whom a watcher's doom
    Is given as his task,
Must set a lock upon his lips

And make his face a mask.

Or else he might be moved, and try
    To comfort or console:
And what should Human Pity do
    Pent up in Murderer's Hole?
What word of grace in such a place
    Could help a brother's soul?

With slouch and swing around the ring
    We trod the Fools' Parade!
We did not care: we knew we were
    The Devil's Own Brigade:
And shaven head and feet of lead
    Make a merry masquerade.

We tore the tarry rope to shreds
    With blunt and bleeding nails;
We rubbed the doors, and scrubbed the floors,
    And cleaned the shining rails:
And, rank by rank, we soaped the plank,
    And clattered with the pails.

We sewed the sacks, we broke the stones,
    We turned the dusty drill:
We banged the tins, and bawled the hymns,
    And sweated on the mill:
But in the heart of every man
    Terror was lying still.

So still it lay that every day
    Crawled like a weed-clogged wave:
And we forgot the bitter lot
    That waits for fool and knave,
Till once, as we tramped in from work,
    We passed an open grave.

With yawning mouth the yellow hole
    Gaped for a living thing;
The very mud cried out for blood
    To the thirsty asphalte ring:
And we knew that ere one dawn grew fair
    Some prisoner had to swing.

Right in we went, with soul intent
    On Death and Dread and Doom:
The hangman, with his little bag,
    Went shuffling through the gloom:
And I trembled as I groped my way
    Into my numbered tomb.

•

That night the empty corridors
    Were full of forms of Fear,
And up and down the iron town
    Stole feet we could not hear,
And through the bars that hide the stars
    White faces seemed to peer.

He lay as one who lies and dreams
    In a pleasant meadow-land,
The watchers watched him as he slept,
    And could not understand
How one could sleep so sweet a sleep
    With a hangman close at hand.

But there is no sleep when men must weep
    Who never yet have wept:
So we—the fool, the fraud, the knave—
    That endless vigil kept,
And through each brain on hands of pain
    Another's terror crept.

Alas! it is a fearful thing
    To feel another's guilt!
For, right, within, the Sword of Sin
    Pierced to its poisoned hilt,
And as molten lead were the tears we shed
    For the blood we had not spilt.

The warders with their shoes of felt
    Crept by each padlocked door,
And peeped and saw, with eyes of awe,
    Grey figures on the floor,
And wondered why men knelt to pray
    Who never prayed before.

All through the night we knelt and prayed,
    Mad mourners of a corse!
The troubled plumes of midnight shook
    The plumes upon a hearse:
And bitter wine upon a sponge
    Was the savour of Remorse.

               •

The grey cock crew, the red cock crew,
    But never came the day:
And crooked shapes of Terror crouched,
    In the corners where we lay:
And each evil sprite that walks by night
    Before us seemed to play.

They glided past, they glided fast,
    Like travellers through a mist:
They mocked the moon in a rigadoon
    Of delicate turn and twist,
And with formal pace and loathsome grace
    The phantoms kept their tryst.

With mop and mow, we saw them go,
    Slim shadows hand in hand:
About, about, in ghostly rout
    They trod a saraband
And the damned grotesques made arabesques,
    Like the wind upon the sand!

With the pirouettes of marionettes,
    They tripped on pointed tread:
But with flutes of Fear they filled the ear,
    As their grisly masque they led,
And loud they sang, and long they sang,
    For they sang to wake the dead.

"Oho!" they cried, "The world is wide,
    But fettered limbs go lame!
And once, or twice, to throw the dice
    Is a gentlemanly game,
But he does not win who plays with Sin
    In the secret House of Shame."

No things of air these antics were,
    That frolicked with such glee:
To men whose lives were held in gyves,
    And whose feet might not go free,
Ah! wounds of Christ! they were living things
    Most terrible to see.

Around, around, they waltzed and wound;
    Some wheeled in smirking pairs;
With the mincing step of a demirep
    Some sidled up the stairs:
And with subtle sneer, and fawning leer,
    Each helped us at our prayers.

The morning wind began to moan,

But still the night went on:
Through its giant loom the web of gloom
   Crept till each thread was spun:
And, as we prayed, we grew afraid
   Of the Justice of the Sun.

The moaning wind went wandering round
   The weeping prison-wall:
Till like a wheel of turning steel
   We felt the minutes crawl:
O moaning wind! what had we done
   To have such a seneschal?

At last I saw the shadowed bars,
   Like a lattice wrought in lead,
Move right across the whitewashed wall
   That faced my three-plank bed,
And I knew that somewhere in the world
   God's dreadful dawn was red.

At six o'clock we cleaned our cells,
   At seven all was still,
But the sough and swing of a mighty wing
   The prison seemed to fill,
For the Lord of Death with icy breath
   Had entered in to kill.

He did not pass in purple pomp,
   Nor ride a moon-white steed.
Three yards of cord and a sliding board
   Are all the gallows' need:
So with rope of shame the Herald came
   To do the secret deed.

We were as men who through a fen
   Of filthy darkness grope:

We did not dare to breathe a prayer,
    Or to give our anguish scope:
Something was dead in each of us,
    And what was dead was Hope.

For Man's grim justice goes its way,
    And will not swerve aside:
It slays the weak, it slays the strong,
    It has a deadly stride:
With iron heel it slays the strong,
    The monstrous parricide!

We waited for the stroke of eight:
    Each tongue was thick with thirst:
For the stroke of eight is the stroke of Fate
    That makes a man accursed,
And Fate will use a running noose
    For the best man and the worst.

We had no other thing to do,
    Save to wait for the sign to come:
So, like things of stone in a valley lone,
    Quiet we sat and dumb:
But each man's heart beat thick and quick,
    Like a madman on a drum!

With sudden shock the prison-clock
    Smote on the shivering air,
And from all the gaol rose up a wail
    Of impotent despair,
Like the sound that frightened marshes hear
    From some leper in his lair.

And as one sees most fearful things
    In the crystal of a dream,
We saw the greasy hempen rope

Hooked to the blackened beam,
And heard the prayer the hangman's snare
   Strangled into a scream.

And all the woe that moved him so
   That he gave that bitter cry,
And the wild regrets, and the bloody sweats,
   None knew so well as I:
For he who lives more lives than one
   More deaths than one must die.

4

There is no chapel on the day
   On which they hang a man:
The chaplain's heart is far too sick,
   Or his face is far too wan,
Or there is that written in his eyes
   Which none should look upon.

So they kept us close till nigh on noon,
   And then they rang the bell,
And the warders with their jingling keys
   Opened each listening cell,
And down the iron stair we tramped,
   Each from his separate Hell.

Out into God's sweet air we went,
   But not in wonted way,
For this man's face was white with fear,
   And that man's face was grey,
And I never saw sad men who looked
   So wistfully at the day.

I never saw sad men who looked
   With such a wistful eye
Upon that little tent of blue

We prisoners called the sky,
    And at every happy cloud that passed
        In such strange freedom by.

But there were those amongst us all
    Who walked with downcast head,
And knew that, had each got his due,
    They should have died instead:
He had but killed a thing that lived,
    Whilst they had killed the dead.

For he who sins a second time
    Wakes a dead soul to pain,
And draws it from its spotted shroud,
    And makes it bleed again,
And makes it bleed great gouts of blood,
    And makes it bleed in vain.

·

Like ape or clown, in monstrous garb
    With crooked arrows starred,
Silently we went round and round
    The slippery asphalte yard;
Silently we went round and round,
    And no man spoke a word.

Silently we went round and round,
    And through each hollow mind
The Memory of dreadful things
    Rushed like a dreadful wind,
And Horror stalked before each man,
    And Terror crept behind.

·

The warders strutted up and down,
  And watched their herd of brutes,
Their uniforms were spick and span,
  And they wore their Sunday suits.
But we knew the work they had been at,
  By the quicklime on their boots.

For where a grave had opened wide,
  There was no grave at all:
Only a stretch of mud and sand
  By the hideous prison-wall,
And a little heap of burning lime,
  That the man should have his pall.

For he has a pall, this wretched man,
  Such as few men can claim:
Deep down below a prison-yard,
  Naked for greater shame,
He lies, with fetters on each foot,
  Wrapt in a sheet of flame!

And all the while the burning lime
  Eats flesh and bone away,
It eats the brittle bone by night,
  And the soft flesh by day,
It eats the flesh and bone by turns,
  But it eats the heart alway.

•

For three long years they will not sow
  Or root or seedling there:
For three long years the unblessed spot
  Will sterile be and bare,
And look upon the wondering sky
  With unreproachful stare.

They think a murderer's heart would taint
  Each simple seed they sow.
It is not true! God's kindly earth
  Is kinder than men know,
And the red rose would but blow more red,
  The white rose whiter blow.

Out of his mouth a red, red rose!
  Out of his heart a white!
For who can say by what strange way
  Christ brings His will to light,
Since the barren staff the pilgrim bore
  Bloomed in the great Pope's sight?

But neither milk-white rose nor red
  May bloom in prison-air;
The shard, the pebble, and the flint,
  Are what they give us there:
For flowers have been known to heal
  A common man's despair.

So never will wine-red rose or white,
  Petal by petal, fall
On that stretch of mud and sand that lies
  By the hideous prison-wall,
To tell the men who tramp the Yard
  That God's Son died for all.

Yet though the hideous prison-wall
  Still hems him round and round,
And a spirit may not walk by night
  That is with fetters bound,
And a spirit may but weep that lies
  In such unholy ground,

He is at peace—this wretched man—

At peace, or will be soon:
There is no thing to make him mad,
   Nor does Terror walk at noon,
For the lampless Earth in which he lies
   Has neither Sun nor Moon.

They hanged him as a beast is hanged!
   They did not even toll
A requiem that might have brought
   Rest to his startled soul,
But hurriedly they took him out,
   And hid him in a hole.

The warders stripped him of his clothes,
   And gave him to the flies:
They mocked the swollen purple throat,
   And the stark and staring eyes:
And with laughter loud they heaped the shroud
   In which the convict lies.

The Chaplain would not kneel to pray
   By his dishonoured grave:
Nor mark it with that blessed Cross
   That Christ for sinners gave,
Because the man was one of those
   Whom Christ came down to save.

Yet all is well; he has but passed
   To life's his appointed bourne:
And alien tears will fill for him
   Pity's long-broken urn,
For his mourners will be outcast men,
   And outcasts always mourn.

5

I know not whether Laws be right,

Or whether Laws be wrong;
    All that we know who lie in gaol
       Is that the wall is strong;
And that each day is like a year,
       A year whose days are long.

But this I know, that every Law
       That men hath made for Man,
Since first Man took his brother's life,
       And the sad world began,
But straws the wheat and saves the chaff
       With a most evil fan.

This too I know—and wise it were
       If each could know the same—
That every prison that men build
       Is built with bricks of shame,
And bound with bars lest Christ should see
       How men their brothers maim.

With bars they blur the gracious moon,
       And blind the goodly sun;
And they do well to hide their Hell,
       For in it things are done
That Son of God nor son of Man
       Ever should look upon!

•

The vilest deeds like poison weeds,
       Bloom well in prison-air;
It is only what is good in Man
       That wastes and withers there:
Pale Anguish keeps the heavy gate,
       And the Warder is Despair.

For they starve the little frightened child
    Till it weeps both night and day:
And they scourge the weak, and flog the fool,
    And gibe the old and grey,
And some grow mad, and all grow bad,
    And none a word may say.

Each narrow cell in which we dwell
    Is a foul and dark latrine,
And the fetid breath of living Death
    Chokes up each grated screen,
And all, but Lust, is turned to dust
    In Humanity's machine.

The brackish water that we drink
    Creeps with a loathsome slime,
And the bitter bread they weigh in scales
    Is full of chalk and lime,
And Sleep will not lie down, but walks
    Wild-eyed, and cries to Time.

•

But though lean Hunger and green Thirst
    Like asp with adder fight,
We have little care of prison fare,
    For what chills and kills outright
Is that every stone one lifts by day
    Becomes one's heart by night.

With midnight always in one's heart,
    And twilight in one's cell,
We turn the crank, or tear the rope,
    Each in his separate Hell,
And the silence is more awful far
    Than the sound of a brazen bell.

And never a human voice comes near
    To speak a gentle word:
And the eye that watches through the door
    Is pitiless and hard:
And by all forgot, we rot and rot,
    With soul and body marred.

And thus we rust Life's iron chain,
    Degraded and alone:
And some men curse, and some men weep,
    And some men make no moan:
But God's eternal Laws are kind
    And break the heart of stone.

And every human heart that breaks,
    In prison-cell or yard,
Is as that broken box that gave
    Its treasure to the Lord,
And filled the unclean leper's house
    With the scent of costliest nard.

Ah! happy they whose hearts can break
    And peace of pardon win!
How else may man make straight his plan
    And cleanse his soul from Sin?
How else but through a broken heart
    May Lord Christ enter in?

•

And he of the swollen purple throat,
    And the stark and staring eyes,
Waits for the holy hands that took
    The Thief to Paradise;
And a broken and a contrite heart
    The Lord will not despise.

The man in red who reads the Law
    Gave him three weeks of life,
Three little weeks in which to heal
    His soul of his soul's strife,
And cleanse from every blot of blood
    The hand that held the knife.

And with tears of blood he cleansed the hand,
    The hand that held the steel:
For only blood can wipe out blood,
    And only tears can heal:
And the crimson stain that was of Cain
    Became Christ's snow-white seal.

6

In Reading gaol by Reading town
    There is a pit of shame,
And in it lies a wretched man
    Eaten by teeth of flame,
In a burning winding-sheet he lies,
    And his grave has got no name.

And there, till Christ call forth the dead,
    In silence let him lie:
No need to waste the foolish tear,
    Or heave the windy sigh:
The man had killed the thing he loved,
    And so he had to die.

And all men kill the thing they love,
    By all let this be heard,
Some do it with a bitter look,
    Some with a flattering word,
The coward does it with a kiss,
    The brave man with a sword!

The Harlot's House

We caught the tread of dancing feet,
We loitered down the moonlit street,
And stopped beneath the harlot's house.

Inside, above the din and fray,
We heard the loud musicians play
The "Treues Liebes Herz" of Strauss.

Like strange mechanical grotesques,
Making fantastic arabesques,
The shadows raced across the blind.

We watched the ghostly dancers spin
To sound of horn and violin,
Like black leaves wheeling in the wind.

Like wire-pulled automatons,
Slim silhouetted skeletons
Went sidling through the slow quadrille.

They took each other by the hand,
And danced a stately saraband;
Their laughter echoed thin and shrill.

Sometimes a clockwork puppet pressed
A phantom lover to her breast,
Sometimes they seemed to try to sing.

Sometimes a horrible marionette
Came out, and smoked its cigarette
Upon the steps like a live thing.

Then, turning to my love, I said,

"The dead are dancing with the dead,
The dust is whirling with the dust."

But she—she heard the violin,
And left my side, and entered in:
Love passed into the house of lust.

Then suddenly the tune went false,
The dancers wearied of the waltz,
The shadows ceased to wheel and whirl.

And down the long and silent street,
The dawn, with silver-sandalled feet,
Crept like a frightened girl.

Fantaisies Décoratives

Le Panneau

Under the rose-tree's dancing shade
   There stands a little ivory girl,
   Pulling the leaves of pink and pearl
With pale green nails of polished jade.

The red leaves fall upon the mould,
   The white leaves flutter, one by one,
   Down to a blue bowl where the sun,
Like a great dragon, writhes in gold.

The white leaves float upon the air,
   The red leaves flutter idly down,
   Some fall upon her yellow gown,
And some upon her raven hair.

She takes an amber lute and sings,
    And as she sings a silver crane
    Begins his scarlet neck to strain,
And flap his burnished metal wings.

She takes a lute of amber bright,
    And from the thicket where he lies
    Her lover, with his almond eyes,
Watches her movements in delight.

And now she gives a cry of fear,
    And tiny tears begin to start;
    A thorn has wounded with its dart
The pink-veined sea-shell of her ear.

And now she laughs a merry note:
    There has fallen a petal of the rose
    Just where the yellow satin shows
The blue-veined flower of her throat.

With pale green nails of polished jade,
    Pulling the leaves of pink and pearl,
    There stands a little ivory girl
Under the rose-tree's dancing shade.

Les Ballons

Against these turbid turquoise skies
    The light and luminous balloons
    Dip and drift like satin moons,
Drift like silken butterflies;

Reel with every windy gust,
    Rise and reel like dancing girls,
    Float like strange transparent pearls,
Fall and float like silver dust.

Now to the low leaves they cling,
   Each with coy fantastic pose,
   Each a petal of a rose
Straining at a gossamer string.

Then to the tall trees they climb,
   Like thin globes of amethyst,
   Wandering opals keeping tryst
With the rubies of the lime.

Canzonet

   I have no store
Of gryphon-guarded gold;
   Now, as before,
Bare is the shepherd's fold.
   Rubies nor pearls
Have I to gem thy throat;
   Yet woodland girls
Have loved the shepherd's note.

   Then pluck a reed
And bid me sing to thee,
   For I would feed
Thine ears with melody,
   Who art more fair
Than fairest fleur-de-lys,
   More sweet and rare
Than sweetest ambergris.

   What dost thou fear?
Young Hyacinth is slain,
   Pan is not here,
And will not come again.

No hornèd Faun
Treads down the yellow leas,
    No God at dawn
Steals through the olive trees.

    Hylas is dead,
Nor will he e'er divine
    Those little red
Rose-petalled lips of thine.
    On the high hill
No ivory dryads play,
    Silver and still
Sinks the sad autumn day

Symphony in Yellow

An omnibus across the bridge
    Crawls like a yellow butterfly,
    And, here and there, a passer-by
Shows like a little restless midge.

Big barges full of yellow hay
    Are moved against the shadowy wharf,
    And, like a yellow silken scarf,
The thick fog hangs along the quay.

The yellow leaves begin to fade
    And flutter from the Temple elms,
    And at my feet the pale green Thames
Lies like a rod of rippled jade.

In the Forest

Out of the mid-wood's twilight
    Into the meadow's dawn,
Ivory limbed and brown eyed,
    Flashes my Faun!

He skips through the copses singing,
    And his shadow dances along,
And I know not which I should follow,
    Shadow or song!

O Hunter, snare me his shadow!
    O Nightingale, catch me his strain!
Else moonstruck with music and madness
    I track him in vain!

To L. L.

Could we dig up this long-buried treasure,
    Were it worth the pleasure,
We never could learn love's song,
    We are parted too long.

Could the passionate past that is fled
    Call back its dead,
Could we live it all over again,
    Were it worth the pain!

I remember we used to meet
    By an ivied seat,
And you warbled each pretty word
    With the air of a bird;

And your voice had a quaver in it,
　　Just like a linnet,
And shook, as the blackbird's throat
　　With its last big note;

And your eyes, they were green and grey
　　Like an April day,
But lit into amethyst
　　When I stooped and kissed;

And your mouth, it would never smile
　　For a long, long while,
Then it rippled all over with laughter
　　Five minutes after.

You were always afraid of a shower,
　　Just like a flower:
I remember you started and ran
　　When the rain began.

I remember I never could catch you,
　　For no one could match you,
You had wonderful, luminous, fleet
　　Little wings to your feet.

I remember your hair—did I tie it?
　　For it always ran riot—
Like a tangled sunbeam of gold:
　　These things are old.

I remember so well the room,
　　And the lilac bloom
That beat at the dripping pane
　　In the warm June rain;

And the colour of your gown,
    It was amber-brown,
And two yellow satin bows
    From your shoulders rose.

And the handkerchief of French lace
    Which you held to your face—
Had a small tear left a stain?
    Or was it the rain?

On your hand as it waved adieu
    There were veins of blue;
In your voice as it said good-bye
    Was a petulant cry,

"You have only wasted your life."
    (Ah, that was the knife!)
When I rushed through the garden gate
    It was all too late.

Could we live it over again,
    Were it worth the pain,
Could the passionate past that is fled
    Call back its dead!

Well, if my heart must break,
    Dear love, for your sake,
It will break in music, I know,
    Poets' hearts break so.

But strange that I was not told
    That the brain can hold
In a tiny ivory cell,
    God's heaven and hell.

WILLIAM BUTLER YEATS

♣

(1865-1939)

William Butler Yeats was born on June 13, 1865, in Sandymount, Dublin, Ireland, the son of John Butler Yeats, a barrister who later became a portrait painter in the Irish Pre-Raphaelite movement. In 1867, the young Yeats moved with his family to London where they settled in Bedford Park. He was eventually enrolled in the Godolphin School in Hammersmith, London, but his father's career in art made for a precarious and unpredictable upbringing, and the Yeats household moved several times between London and Dublin over the course of Yeats's childhood.

Despite the fact that he was unable to put down roots at any one particular school, Yeats was encouraged by his father to study literature and art and ultimately, to pursue a passion he developed in his early teens for writing poetry. He attended the Metropolitan School of Art in Dublin in 1883 where he became acquainted with another student, George Russell—the poet and painter who, like Yeats, shared a fascination with the mystical and supernatural. Themes of reincarnation and the occult would preoccupy and fascinate Yeats to the end of his life, even on his deathbed when he penned his infamous epitaph.

By 1885, Yeats had begun to publish his poetry, with two short lyrics appearing in *The Dublin University Review*. Again, his father moved the family back to London in 1887, and Yeats devoted himself fully to becoming a professional writer. He also became more passionate about his interests in mysticism, joining the Esoteric Section of the Theosophical Society. In an age where science captivated the imagination of the populace, Yeats was drawn instead to the images and poetry of artists like William Blake.

The literary life of London was also a draw to Yeats, as he befriended W.E. Henley and William Morris and began to make a name for himself. In 1889 he published *The Wanderings of Oisin and Other Poems*, a sad and beautiful collection inspired by his study of Irish mythology.

> When you are old and gray and full of sleep,
> And nodding by the fire, take down this book
> And slowly read and dream of the soft look
> Your eyes had once, and of their shadows deep.
> ("When You Are Old")

That same year, Yeats met the Irish beauty Maud Gonne, an actress and patriot who would preoccupy his thoughts and become something of an obsession in his life. Yeats fell deeply in love with Gonne, who made it clear to him that she preferred men of action, not mere words, and Yeats joined the Irish national cause, no doubt in part because of his feelings for the beautiful Irish revolutionary. He even made an attempt to join the secret extremist Irish Republican Brotherhood, to no avail, however.

Despite the respect and admiration Gonne had for the young poet, she saved her love for her country and another revolutionary, John MacBride, whom she would ultimately marry. This devastated Yeats, and his poetry at the turn of the 19th century reflected the despair and longing he must have experienced at the time. "The White Birds" is one such poem inspired by what Yeats perceived as a love that might have been.

> A weariness comes from those dreamers, dew-dabbled, the lily and rose;
> Ah, dream not of them, my beloved, the flame of the meteor that goes,
> Or the flame of the blue star that lingers hung low in the fall of the dew:
> For I would we were changed to white birds on the wandering foam: I
> and you!

Before the turn of the century, Yeats had begun to focus his attention on the theater. He met a woman who would become a huge influence in his life— Augusta Lady Gregory—an Irish nationalist and widow with whom Yeats would ultimately co-found the Irish Literary Theatre, later known as the Abbey Theatre. It was a relationship that has become increasingly more complex as scholars continue to determine the true depth of their collaborative efforts in the theatre.

Lady Gregory first met Yeats in 1894, and she wrote in her diary that he was "looking every inch a poet, though I think his prose *Celtic Twilight* is the best thing he has done."

In 1900, Yeats was asked to write a collection of ancient Irish stories, but he claimed he did not have the time for the project. Lady Gregory, however, convinced a hesitant Yeats that she was up to the task, and after producing a sample of her translation skills, Yeats relented and supported her on the book, which ultimately became *Irish Myths and Legends* by Lady Gregory.

Yeats continued to focus his efforts on Maud Gonne, politics and the theatre. *Cathleen ni Houlihan* debuted in 1902 and immediately caused a political sensation in Ireland. Yeats had conceived the idea for the play, with Gonne in the role of Mother Ireland. The woman proclaims that only a blood sacrifice can save the nation, and calls the young men of Ireland to follow, promising eternal heroism and remembrance in return for their devotion. Yeats, who claimed the play was inspired by a dream, wrote the chant dialogue delivered by Gonne at the end of the play. In 1908, he wrote:

> One night I had a dream almost as distinct as a vision of a cottage where there was well-being and firelight and talk of a marriage, and into the midst of that cottage, there came an old woman in a long cloak. She was Ireland herself, that Cathleen ni Houlihan for whom so many stories have been told and for whose sake so many have gone to their death. I thought if I could write this out as a little play I could make others see my dream as I had seen it....We turned my dream into the little play *Cathleen ni Houlihan.*

The "we" Yeats wrote about included Lady Gregory, who had always been acknowledged as having helped Yeats with the peasant dialogue. But recently, scholars have uncovered evidence, namely notations on the original play's manuscript in Lady Gregory's handwriting, that seems to indicate that she, not Yeats, wrote the majority of the play. In fact, Lady Gregory's contribution on a number of Yeats's plays, including *On Baile's Strand, The Pot of Broth,* and *Deirdre,* among others, appears to be understated.

Yeats credited Lady Gregory on several occasions, and publicly, for her contributions to his theatrical writings, but for whatever reasons, never to the extent that scholars believe reflected the breadth of her collaboration.

By 1909, Yeats began to become disillusioned with the Irish politics, and perhaps began to take a more realistic vision of his obsession with Maud Gonne. The ethereal lyrics from his earlier works were replaced by sparse and direct imagery. He wrote satirically as well and even began offering up praise to the aristocracy. In

1912, Yeats met the American poet, Ezra Pound, who went to work as Yeats's secretary. Four years later, the Easter Rising of 1916 deeply affected Yeats. Just as he had been distancing himself from the revolutionaries, they had become nationalistic heroes, and Maud Gonne's husband was one of sixteen leaders who were executed. Allowing some time to pass, Yeats proposed yet again to Gonne, who declined the offer. Then the next year, perhaps in an attempt to get closer to Maud, Yeats proposed to her daughter, Iseult, to whom he had written several poems in previous years. She also rejected him. Alas, a few weeks later, Yeats proposed to Miss Georgie Hyde-Lees, who accepted, and the couple had two children together.

In 1917, Yeats published *The Wild Swans at Coole,* which was the beginning of what scholars generally regard as a period of unprecedented achievement in poetry. He would receive the Nobel Prize for Literature in 1923 at the age of 58, and scholars have long noted that some of his greatest poetry was written after he was awarded his Nobel Prize. He died in Roquebrune in Cape Martin in January of 1939. World War II prevented his body from being moved until 1948, when it was brought to Sligo and interred in a Protestant churchyard at Drumcliffe, "Under Ben Bulben," as were his wishes. His epitaph, which he wrote just a few days before his death, reads:

Cast a cold eye
On life, on death.
Horseman, pass by!

EARLY POEMS

♣

The Song of the Happy Shepherd

The woods of Arcady are dead,
And over is their antique joy;
Of old the world on dreaming fed;
Gray Truth is now her painted toy;
Yet still she turns her restless head:
But O, sick children of the world,
Of all the many changing things
In dreary dancing past us whirled,
To the cracked tune that Chronos sings,
Words alone are certain good.
Where are now the warring kings,
Word be-mockers?—By the Rood
Where are now the warring kings?
An idle word is now their glory,
By the stammering schoolboy said,
Reading some entangled story:
The kings of the old time are fled.
The wandering earth herself may be
Only a sudden flaming word,
In clanging space a moment heard,
Troubling the endless reverie.

Then nowise worship dusty deeds,
Nor seek, for this is also sooth;
To hunger fiercely after truth,
Lest all thy toiling only breeds
New dreams, new dreams; there is no truth

Saving in thine own heart. Seek, then,
No learning from the starry men,
Who follow with the optic glass
The whirling ways of stars that pass—
Seek, then, for this is also sooth,
No word of theirs—the cold star-bane
Has cloven and rent their hearts in twain,
And dead is all their human truth.
Go gather by the humming-sea
Some twisted, echo-harbouring shell,
And to its lips thy story tell,
And they thy comforters will be,
Rewarding in melodious guile,
Thy fretful words a little while,
Till they shall singing fade in ruth,
And die a pearly brotherhood;
For words alone are certain good:
Sing, then, for this is also sooth.

I must be gone: there is a grave
Where daffodil and lily wave,
And I would please the helpless faun,
Buried under the sleepy ground,
With mirthful songs before the dawn.
His shouting days with mirth were crowned;
And still I dream he treads the lawn,
Walking ghostly in the dew,
Pierced by my glad singing through,
My songs of old earth's dreamy youth:
But ah! she dreams not now; dream thou!
For fair are poppies on the brow:
Dream, dream, for this is also sooth.

The Sad Shepherd

There was a man whom Sorrow named his friend,
And he, of his high comrade Sorrow dreaming,
Went walking with slow steps along the gleaming
And humming sands, where windy surges wend:
And he called loudly to the stars to bend
From their pale thrones and comfort him, but they
Among themselves laugh on and sing alway:
And then the man whom Sorrow named his friend
Cried out, *Dim sea, hear my most piteous story!*
The sea swept on and cried her old cry still,
Rolling along in dreams from hill to hill;
He fled the persecution of her glory
And, in a far-off, gentle valley stopping,
Cried all his story to the dewdrops glistening,
But naught they heard, for they are always listening,
The dewdrops, for the sound of their own dropping.
And then the man whom Sorrow named his friend,
Sought once again the shore, and found a shell,
And thought, *I will my heavy story tell*
Till my own words, re-echoing, shall send
Their sadness through a hollow, pearly heart;
And my own tale again for me shall sing,
And my own whispering words be comforting,
And lo! my ancient burden may depart.
Then he sang softly nigh the pearly rim;
But the sad dweller by the sea-ways lone
Changed all he sang to inarticulate moan
Among her wildering whirls, forgetting him.

The Cloak, the Boat, and the Shoes

"What do you make so fair and bright?"

"I make the cloak of Sorrow:
O, lovely to see in all men's sight
Shall be the cloak of Sorrow,
In all men's sight."

"What do you build with sails for flight?"

"I build a boat for Sorrow,
O, swift on the seas all day and night
Saileth the rover Sorrow,
All day and night."

"What do you weave with wool so white?"

"I weave the shoes of Sorrow,
Soundless shall be the footfall light
In all men's ears of Sorrow,
Sudden and light."

The Indian upon God

I passed along the water's edge below the humid trees,
My spirit rocked in evening light, the rushes round my knees,
My spirit rocked in sleep and sighs; and saw the moorfowl pace
All dripping on a grassy slope, and saw them cease to chase
Each other round in circles, and heard the eldest speak:
Who holds the world between His bill and made us strong or weak
Is an undying moorfowl, and He lives beyond the sky.
The rains are from His dripping wing, the moonbeams from His eye.

I passed a little further on and heard a lotus talk:
Who made the world and ruleth it, He hangeth on a stalk,
For I am in His image made, and all this tinkling tide
Is but a sliding drop of rain between His petals wide.
A little way within the gloom a roebuck raised his eyes
Brimful of starlight, and he said: *The Stamper of the Skies,*
He is a gentle roebuck; for how else, I pray, could He
Conceive a thing so sad and soft, a gentle thing like me?
I passed a little further on and heard a peacock say:
Who made the grass and made the worms and made my feathers gay,
He is a monstrous peacock, and He waveth all the night
His languid tail above us, lit with myriad spots of light.

The Indian to His Love

The island dreams under the dawn
And great boughs drop tranquillity;
The peahens dance on a smooth lawn,
A parrot sways upon a tree,
Raging at his own image in the enamelled sea.

Here we will moor our lonely ship
And wander ever with woven hands,
Murmuring softly lip to lip,
Along the grass, along the sands,
Murmuring how far away are the unquiet lands:

How we alone of mortals are
Hid under quiet boughs apart,
While our love grows an Indian star,
A meteor of the burning heart,
One with the tide that gleams, the wings that gleam and dart,

The heavy boughs, the burnished dove

That moans and sighs a hundred days:
How when we die our shades will rove,
When eve has hushed the feathered ways,
With vapoury footsole among the water's drowsy blaze.

The Falling of the Leaves

Autumn is over the long leaves that love us,
And over the mice in the barley sheaves;
Yellow the leaves of the rowan above us,
And yellow the wet wild-strawberry leaves.

The hour of the waning of love has beset us,
And weary and worn are our sad souls now;
Let us part, ere the season of passion forget us,
With a kiss and a tear on thy drooping brow.

The Stolen Child

Where dips the rocky highland
Of Sleuth Wood in the lake,
There lies a leafy island
Where flapping herons wake
The drowsy water rats;
There we've hid our faery vats,
Full of berries,
And of reddest stolen cherries.
Come away, O human child!
To the waters and the wild
With a faery, hand in hand,
For the world's more full of weeping than you can understand.

Where the wave of moonlight glosses
The dim gray sands with light,
Far off by furthest Rosses
We foot it all the night,
Weaving olden dances,
Mingling hands and mingling glances
Till the moon has taken flight;
To and fro we leap
And chase the frothy bubbles,
While the world is full of troubles
And is anxious in its sleep.
Come away, O human child!
To the waters and the wild
With a faery, hand in hand,
For the world's more full of weeping than you can understand.

Where the wandering water gushes
From the hills above Glen-Car,
In pools among the rushes
That scarce could bathe a star,
We seek for slumbering trout
And whispering in their ears
Give them unquiet dreams;
Leaning softly out
From ferns that drop their tears
Over the young streams.
Come away, O human child!
To the waters and the wild
With a faery, hand in hand,
For the world's more full of weeping than you can understand.

Away with us he's going,
The solemn-eyed:
He'll hear no more the lowing
Of the calves on the warm hillside;
Or the kettle on the hob

Sing peace into his breast,
Or see the brown mice bob
Round and round the oatmeal-chest.
For he comes, the human child,
To the waters and the wild
With a faery, hand in hand,
From a world more full of weeping than he can understand.

To an Isle in the Water

Shy one, shy one,
Shy one of my heart,
She moves in the firelight
Pensively apart.

She carries in the dishes,
And lays them in a row.
To an isle in the water
With her would I go.

She carries in the candles,
And lights the curtained room,
Shy in the doorway
And shy in the gloom;

And shy as a rabbit,
Helpful and shy.
To an isle in the water
With her would I fly.

Down by the Salley Gardens

Down by the salley gardens my love and I did meet;
She passed the salley gardens with little snow-white feet.
She bid me take love easy, as the leaves grow on the tree;
But I, being young and foolish, with her would not agree.
In a field by the river my love and I did stand,
And on my leaning shoulder she laid her snow-white hand.
She bid me take life easy, as the grass grows on the weirs;
But I was young and foolish, and now am full of tears.

The Meditation of the Old Fisherman

You waves, though you dance by my feet like children at play,
Though you glow and you glance, though you purr and you dart;
In the Junes that were warmer than these are, the waves were more gay,
When I was a boy with never a crack in my heart.
The herring are not in the tides as they were of old;
My sorrow! for many a creak gave the creel in the cart
That carried the take to Sligo town to be sold,
When I was a boy with never a crack in my heart.

And ah, you proud maiden, you are not so fair when his oar
Is heard on the water, as they were, the proud and apart,
Who paced in the eve by the nets on the pebbly shore,
When I was a boy with never a crack in my heart.

The Lake Isle of Innisfree

I will arise and go now, and go to Innisfree,
And a small cabin build there, of clay and wattles made:
Nine bean rows will I have there, a hive for the honey bee,
And live alone in the bee-loud glade.

And I shall have some peace there, for peace comes dropping slow,
Dropping from the veils of the morning to where the cricket sings;
There midnight's all a glimmer, and noon a purple glow,
And evening full of the linnet's wings.

I will arise and go now, for always night and day
I hear lake water lapping with low sounds by the shore;
While I stand on the roadway, or on the pavements grey,
I hear it in the deep heart's core.

When You Are Old

When you are old and grey and full of sleep,
And nodding by the fire, take down this book,
And slowly read, and dream of the soft look
Your eyes had once, and of their shadows deep;

How many loved your moments of glad grace,
And loved your beauty with love false or true;
But one man loved the pilgrim soul in you,
And loved the sorrows of your changing face.

And bending down beside the glowing bars
Murmur, a little sadly, how love fled
And paced upon the mountains overhead
And hid his face amid a crowd of stars.

No Second Troy

Why should I blame her that she filled my days
With misery, or that she would of late
Have taught to ignorant men most violent ways,

Or hurled the little streets upon the great,
Had they but courage equal to desire?
What could have made her peaceful with a mind
That nobleness made simple as a fire,
With beauty like a tightened bow, a kind
That is not natural in an age like this,
Being high and solitary and most stern?
Why, what could she have done, being what she is?
Was there another Troy for her to burn?

September 1913

What need you, being come to sense,
But fumble in a greasy till
And add the halfpence to the pence
And prayer to shivering prayer, until
You have dried the marrow from the bone?
For men were born to pray and save,
Romantic Ireland's dead and gone,
It's with O'Leary in the grave.

Yet they were of a different kind,
The names that stilled your childish play,
They have gone about the world like wind,
But little time had they to pray
For whom the hangman's rope was spun,
And what, God help us, could they save?
Romantic Ireland's dead and gone,
It's with O'Leary in the grave.

Was it for this the wild geese spread
The grey wing upon every tide;
For this that all that blood was shed,
For this Edward Fitzgerald died,

And Robert Emmet and Wolfe Tone,
All that delirium of the brave?
Romantic Ireland's dead and gone,
It's with O'Leary in the grave.

Yet could we turn the years again,
And call those exiles as they were
In all their loneliness and pain,
You'd cry, 'Some woman's yellow hair
Has maddened every mother's son':
They weighed so lightly what they gave,
But let them be, they're dead and gone,
They're with O'Leary in the grave.

To a Friend Whose Work Has Come to Nothing

Now all the truth is out,
Be secret and take defeat
From any brazen throat,
For how can you compete,
Being honour bred, with one
Who, were it proved he lies,
Were neither shamed in his own
Nor in his neighbours' eyes?
Bred to a harder thing
Than Triumph, turn away
And like a laughing string
Whereon mad fingers play
Amid a place of stone,
Be secret and exult,
Because of all things known
That is most difficult.

JOHN MILLINGTON SYNGE

♣

(1871-1909)

On December 21, 1896, a twenty-five year old aspiring writer by the name of John Millington Synge met William Yeats at a hotel in Paris. Synge had been studying language and literature at the Sorbonne, and the impact of his meeting with the famed poet and dramatist changed Synge's life. Yeats encouraged Synge to leave Paris and live on the Aran Islands off the coast of Ireland. "Give up Paris," Yeats advised Synge, as he wrote in his preface to *The Well of the Saints.* "Go to the Aran Islands. Live there as if you were one of the people themselves; express a life that has never found expression."

Synge eventually heeded Yeats's advice, but only after he developed the first signs of lymphatic sarcoma (Hodgkin's Disease) and had the first of several major surgeries in Dublin. By the spring of 1898, he was well enough to begin living on the Aran Islands at regular intervals over the next four years. The study of Irish life became his own way of life, and the young artist immersed himself in the island culture. He took notes, photographed the people, and studied their dialect and speech, and in 1901, he wrote *The Aran Islands*, a series of essays, which some critics believe to be Synge's greatest artistic contribution. Apart from documenting the consciousness of the island' people and accomplishing what Yeats had encouraged him to do, namely "express a life that has never found expression," Synge also revealed his own consciousness—setting the stage for a life, albeit brief, of emotion and art. In documenting the rugged landscape of the Aran Islands and the isolation of the people there, Synge also uncovered a beautiful simplicity to their existence, and in essence, to the human condition, a theme that would resonate throughout his work for years to come.

Born outside Dublin, Ireland, on April 16, 1871, John Millington Synge was the youngest of five children raised in an upper-class Anglo-Irish family of

Protestants. Deeply religious, the Synge family had produced several Church of Ireland bishops in the 17th century, and owned property and estates in Galway and Wicklow. Synge's brother, Edward, managed several estates for the family and earned a reputation as a heartless landlord for his role in some high-profile evictions of elderly women during the Land War of 1887. To say that the family was anti-Catholic was something of an understatement, as several members worked tirelessly as Protestant missionaries who attempted to convert residents of the Aran Islands from Catholicism with an evangelical fury.

The year after Synge was born, his father died and the young boy began to experience the first of the many health problems that would plague his short life. Sickly and asthmatic, Synge was something of an outcast in his own family, which may have enabled him to escape the grip of his mother's bigotry and deeply religious hold on his siblings. Synge withdrew at an early age, finding solace in the beauty of Ireland and music, rather than share his family's religious convictions. He attended private school once he reached the age of ten, but would only attend for four more years before his health began to prohibit regular attendance. His mother, however, hired a private tutor to prepare him for Trinity College, from which he would ultimately graduate in 1892.

At Trinity, Synge had intended to study music. He had developed into a talented violin player, winning a scholarship from the Royal Irish Academy of Music, but he suffered from nervousness during performances, which prevented him from advancing. At the same time, he had begun writing poetry, and in the summer of 1894, he went to Paris to study seriously at the Sorbonne. Synge became a writer of literary criticism and supported himself by giving English lessons to students as he continued to study language.

Around this time, in 1896, he met and attempted to court Cherry Matheson, a young Protestant woman who ultimately spurned his advances because of his anti-religious views. But the year was not lost for Synge, as he was to meet Yeats in Paris shortly after his failed attempt at marrying, and the meeting profoundly affected his life and career.

After finishing *The Aran Islands,* which wasn't published until 1907, Synge began writing plays, beginning with *When the Moon Has Set*—the story of a young atheist landowner who falls in love with a nun. The play clearly demonstrated autobiographical content, most notably Synge's anti-religious convictions and a doomed romance with a fervently religious woman. The play was never performed, and although Yeats did not particularly care for it, he did recognize Synge's talent and encouraged him to go on writing.

In 1902, Synge wrote two more plays, *In the Shadow of the Glen* and *Riders to the Sea,* while living with his mother in a rented house in Wicklow. His time on the Aran Islands was still an influence in his work, but Synge stumbled upon something even more inspirational—the art of eavesdropping.

In the preface to his later play, *The Playboy of the Western World,* Synge described how he picked up the provincial dialect by listening in on conversations of his mother's servant girls downstairs "from a chink in the floor." Had they known he was eavesdropping, Synge assumed, they might not have conversed in their less proper English, and he was therefore able to get "more aid than any learning could have given me."

Over the next few years, Synge continued to write plays, which he showed to Yeats and Lady Gregory. On October 8, 1903, Synge's *In the Shadow of the Glen* became the first play to be staged by the fledgling Irish National Theatre Society that Yeats and Lady Gregory founded. The play was by no means a commercial or critical success immediately, but its controversial take on Irish life, and womanhood particularly, generated a great deal of publicity for the theatre. In 1906, while he was traveling with the Irish National Theatre Society, Synge fell in love with the actress Molly Allgood, 15 years younger than himself and barely educated. Allgood, whose stage name was Maire O'Neill, would later play the leading role of Pegeen Mike in his play, *The Playboy of the Western World,* which was first produced in 1907.

Synge struggled with draft after draft while writing this play, and because of his Hodgkin's disease, the last act took so long to finish that the play's opening had to be postponed—with Synge constantly revising and rewriting dialogue during rehearsals.

The play's story centers on Christy Mahon, who believes he has murdered his tyrannical father and receives a hero's welcome from the town's people. Pegeen Mike and the other eligible ladies in town yearn for his affections until Old Mahon, the father, shows up (with bandaged head) looking for his son. Despite another murder attempt, the two eventually reconcile their differences and the two men leave town together, abandoning the women.

The opening of *The Playboy of the Western World* was marked with violence and protest from the audience. They began booing the actors during the third act, and ultimately rioted by the end, leading to many arrests. The line from the play that triggered the most protest and clamor occurs when Christy declares that he has found Pegeen Mike the only suitable woman, and would not be attracted to "a drift of chosen females, standing in their shifts itself." Synge was referring to

County Mayo girls as "chosen females" and it was even believed that the actor, Willie Fay, who played Christy, departed from the text and substituted "Mayo girls" for "chosen females." The use of the word "shifts" was a reference to their undergarments, deemed offensive by many in the audience. The entire third act was considered by some critics at the time to be an affront to Irish peasants. Irish nationalism was at a high at the time, and many theatergoers were used to Ireland being depicted with reverence. Synge's characters cursed and spoke in "barbarous jargon" according to opening night reviews, and the play committed "libel upon Irish peasant men and, worse still upon Irish peasant girlhood."

Still, the "squalid, offensive production" drew a full house for the following performance, which grew so loud, none of the lines could be heard by the final act. The play had to be stopped several times to restore order, and Yeats himself addressed the crowd, imploring them not to interfere with the production. Lady Gregory, with the permission of Synge, who was now ill with influenza, made a few alterations to the text of the play, deleting some of the objectionable phrases, and the play was permitted to continue, despite nightly arrests and heavy police protection.

Clare and Kerry passed resolutions banning production of *The Playboy of the Western World*, but the clamor of the inappropriate language of the play soon became secondary to the offensiveness of a heroic murderer and the depictions of Irish peasantry. Though the play exceeded the limits of perceived decency and stoked the nationalistic flames of Ireland, it also established Synge as one of the most prolific playwrights of his time. Synge witnessed his play achieve renown and popularity abroad for the few years he lived beyond the infamous opening night. By early 1909, however, John Millington Synge had endured several operations on his neck to remove enlarged glands and never fully recovered. He began working on a new play, *Deirdre of the Sorrows,* despite being confined to his bed during an attempt at recovery, which exhausted him and delayed his marriage to Molly Allgood. Yeats loved the play and wrote that had Synge been able to finish it, it "would have been his masterwork." Synge requested that he and Lady Gregory complete it for him, with Allgood directing and playing Deirdre, but when he died on March 24, 1909, they decided to perform Synge's final version instead.

Although he was just reaching his prime and stride as a writer when he died, Synge continues to be regarded as the most highly esteemed playwright of the Irish literary renaissance. *The Playboy of the Western World* reached a worldwide audience, and by the 1920s, Synge's controversial play became a staple of Irish theater. The author, who once enraged an entire populace, is now credited with showcasing the character and individuality of Ireland during one of the most dynamic times in Irish history.

THE PLAYBOY OF THE WESTERN WORLD

♣

PERSONS IN THE PLAY

CHRISTOPHER MAHON
OLD MAHON *(his father, a squatter)*
MICHAEL JAMES FLAHERTY,
[CALLED MICHAEL JAMES *(a publican)*]
MARGARET FLAHERTY, CALLED PEGEEN MIKE *(his daughter)*
WIDOW QUIN *(a woman of about thirty)*
SHAWN KEOGH *(her cousin, a young farmer)*
PHILLY CULLEN AND JIMMY FARRELL *(small farmers)*
SARA TANSEY, SUSAN BRADY, AND HONOR BLAKE *(village girls)*
A BELLMAN
SOME PEASANTS

The action takes place near a village, on a wild coast of Mayo. The first Act passes on an evening of autumn, the other two Acts on the following day.

Act I

SCENE. Country public-house or shebeen, very rough and untidy. There is a sort of counter on the right with shelves, holding many bottles and jugs, just seen above it. Empty barrels stand near the counter. At back, a little to left of counter, there is a door into the open air, then, more to the left, there is a settle with shelves above it, with more jugs, and a table beneath a window. At the left there is a large open fire-place, with turf fire, and a small door into inner room. Pegeen, a wild-looking but fine girl, of about twenty, is writing at table. She is dressed in the usual peasant dress.

PEGEEN *(slowly as she writes)*. Six yards of stuff for to make a yellow gown. A pair of lace boots with lengthy heels on them and brassy eyes. A hat is suited for a wedding-day. A fine tooth comb. To be sent with three barrels of porter in Jimmy Farrell's creel cart on the evening of the coming Fair to Mister Michael James Flaherty. With the best compliments of this season. Margaret Flaherty.

SHAWN KEOGH (*a fat and fair young man comes in as she signs, looks round awkwardly, when he sees she is alone*). Where's himself?

PEGEEN (*without looking at him*). He's coming. (*She directs the letter.*) To Mister Sheamus Mulroy, Wine and Spirit Dealer, Castlebar.

SHAWN (*uneasily*). I didn't see him on the road.

PEGEEN. How would you see him (*licks stamp and puts it on letter*) and it dark night this half hour gone by?

SHAWN (*turning towards the door again*). I stood a while outside wondering would I have a right to pass on or to walk in and see you, Pegeen Mike (*comes to fire*), and I could hear the cows breathing, and sighing in the stillness of the air, and not a step moving any place from this gate to the bridge.

PEGEEN (*putting letter in envelope*). It's above at the cross-roads he is, meeting Philly Cullen; and a couple more are going along with him to Kate Cassidy's wake.

SHAWN (*looking at her blankly*). And he's going that length in the dark night?

PEGEEN (*impatiently*). He is surely, and leaving me lonesome on the scruff of the hill. (*She gets up and puts envelope on dresser, then winds clock.*) Isn't it long the nights are now, Shawn Keogh, to be leaving a poor girl with her own self counting the hours to the dawn of day?

SHAWN (*with awkward humour*). If it is, when we're wedded in a short while you'll have no call to complain, for I've little will to be walking off to wakes or weddings in the darkness of the night.

PEGEEN (*with rather scornful good humour*). You're making mighty certain, Shaneen, that I'll wed you now.

SHAWN. Aren't we after making a good bargain, the way we're only waiting these days on Father Reilly's dispensation from the bishops, or the Court of Rome.

PEGEEN (*looking at him teasingly, washing up at dresser*). It's a wonder, Shaneen, the Holy Father'd be taking notice of the likes of you; for if I was him I wouldn't bother with this place where you'll meet none but Red Linahan, has a squint in his eye, and Patcheen is lame in his heel, or the mad Mulrannies were driven from California and they lost in their wits. We're a queer lot these times to go troubling the Holy Father on his sacred seat.

SHAWN (*scandalized*). If we are, we're as good this place as another, maybe, and as good these times as we were for ever.

PEGEEN (*with scorn*). As good, is it? Where now will you meet the like of Daneen Sullivan knocked the eye from a peeler, or Marcus Quin, God rest him, got six months for maiming ewes, and he a great warrant to tell stories of holy Ireland till he'd have the old women shedding down tears about their feet. Where will you find the like of them, I'm saying?

SHAWN *(timidly)*. If you don't, it's a good job, maybe; for *(with peculiar emphasis on the words)* Father Reilly has small conceit to have that kind walking around and talking to the girls.

PEGEEN *(impatiently, throwing water from basin out of the door)*. Stop tormenting me with Father Reilly *(imitating his voice)* when I'm asking only what way I'll pass these twelve hours of dark, and not take my death with the fear.

[*Looking out of door.*]

SHAWN *(timidly)*. Would I fetch you the Widow Quin, maybe?

PEGEEN. Is it the like of that murderer? You'll not, surely.

SHAWN *(going to her, soothingly)*. Then I'm thinking himself will stop along with you when he sees you taking on, for it'll be a long night-time with great darkness, and I'm after feeling a kind of fellow above in the furzy ditch, groaning wicked like a maddening dog, the way it's good cause you have, maybe, to be fearing now.

PEGEEN *(turning on him sharply)*. What's that? Is it a man you seen?

SHAWN *(retreating)*. I couldn't see him at all; but I heard him groaning out, and breaking his heart. It should have been a young man from his words speaking.

PEGEEN *(going after him)*. And you never went near to see was he hurted or what ailed him at all?

SHAWN. I did not, Pegeen Mike. It was a dark, lonesome place to be hearing the like of him.

PEGEEN. Well, you're a daring fellow, and if they find his corpse stretched above in the dews of dawn, what'll you say then to the peelers, or the Justice of the Peace?

SHAWN *(thunderstruck)*. I wasn't thinking of that. For the love of God, Pegeen Mike, don't let on I was speaking of him. Don't tell your father and the men is coming above; for if they heard that story, they'd have great blabbing this night at the wake.

PEGEEN. I'll maybe tell them, and I'll maybe not.

SHAWN. They are coming at the door. Will you whisht, I'm saying?

PEGEEN. Whisht yourself.

[*She goes behind counter. Michael James, fat jovial publican, comes in followed by Philly Cullen, who is thin and mistrusting, and Jimmy Farrell, who is fat and amorous, about forty-five.*]

MEN *(together)*. God bless you. The blessing of God on this place.

PEGEEN. God bless you kindly.

MICHAEL *(to men who go to the counter)*. Sit down now, and take your rest. *(Crosses to Shawn at the fire.)* And how is it you are, Shawn Keogh? Are you coming over the sands to Kate Cassidy's wake?

SHAWN. I am not, Michael James. I'm going home the short cut to my bed.

PEGEEN *(speaking across the counter)*. He's right too, and have you no shame, Michael James, to be quitting off for the whole night, and leaving myself lonesome in the shop?

MICHAEL *(good-humouredly)*. Isn't it the same whether I go for the whole night or a part only? and I'm thinking it's a queer daughter you are if you'd have me crossing backward through the Stooks of the Dead Women, with a drop taken.

PEGEEN. If I am a queer daughter, its a queer father'd be leaving me lonesome these twelve hours of dark, and I piling the turf with the dogs barking, and the calves mooing, and my own teeth rattling with the fear.

JIMMY *(flatteringly)*. What is there to hurt you, and you a fine, hardy girl would knock the head of any two men in the place?

PEGEEN *(working herself up)*. Isn't there the harvest boys with their tongues red for drink, and the ten tinkers is camped in the east glen, and the thousand militia—bad cess to them!—walking idle through the land. There's lots surely to hurt me, and I won't stop alone in it, let himself do what he will.

MICHAEL. If you're that afeard, let Shawn Keogh stop along with you. It's the will of God, I'm thinking, himself should be seeing to you now.

[*They all turn on Shawn.*]

SHAWN *(in horrified confusion)*. I would and welcome, Michael James, but I'm afeard of Father Reilly; and what at all would the Holy Father and the Cardinals of Rome be saying if they heard I did the like of that?

MICHAEL *(with contempt)*. God help you! Can't you sit in by the hearth with the light lit and herself beyond in the room? You'll do that surely, for I've heard tell there's a queer fellow above, going mad or getting his death, maybe, in the gripe of the ditch, so she'd be safer this night with a person here.

SHAWN *(with plaintive despair)*. I'm afeard of Father Reilly, I'm saying. Let you not be tempting me, and we near married itself.

PHILLY *(with cold contempt)*. Lock him in the west room. He'll stay then and have no sin to be telling to the priest.

MICHAEL *(to Shawn, getting between him and the door)*. Go up now.

SHAWN *(at the top of his voice)*. Don't stop me, Michael James. Let me out of the door, I'm saying, for the love of the Almighty God. Let me out *(trying to dodge past him)*. Let me out of it, and may God grant you His indulgence in the hour of need.

MICHAEL *(loudly)*. Stop your noising, and sit down by the hearth.

[*Gives him a push and goes to counter laughing.*]

SHAWN *(turning back, wringing his hands)*. Oh, Father Reilly and the saints of God, where will I hide myself to-day? Oh, St. Joseph and St. Patrick and St. Brigid, and St. James, have mercy on me now!

[*Shawn turns round, sees door clear, and makes a rush for it.*]

MICHAEL *(catching him by the coat-tail)*. You'd be going, is it?

SHAWN *(screaming)*. Leave me go, Michael James, leave me go, you old Pagan, leave me go, or I'll get the curse of the priests on you, and of the scarlet-coated bishops of the courts of Rome.

[With a sudden movement he pulls himself out of his coat, and disappears out of the door, leaving his coat in Michael's hands.']

MICHAEL *(turning round, and holding up coat)*. Well, there's the coat of a Christian man. Oh, there's sainted glory this day in the lonesome west; and by the will of God I've got you a decent man, Pegeen, you'll have no call to be spying after if you've a score of young girls, maybe, weeding in your fields.

PEGEEN *(taking up the defence of her property)*. What right have you to be making game of a poor fellow for minding the priest, when it's your own the fault is, not paying a penny pot-boy to stand along with me and give me courage in the doing of my work?

[*She snaps the coat away from him, and goes behind counter with it.*]

MICHAEL *(taken aback)*. Where would I get a pot-boy? Would you have me send the bellman screaming in the streets of Castlebar?

SHAWN *(opening the door a chink and putting in his head, in a small voice)*. Michael James!

MICHAEL *(imitating him)*. What ails you?

SHAWN. The queer dying fellow's beyond looking over the ditch. He's come up, I'm thinking, stealing your hens. *(Looks over his shoulder.)* God help me, he's following me now *(he runs into room)*, and if he's heard what I said, he'll be having my life, and I going home lonesome in the darkness of the night.

[*For a perceptible moment they watch the door with curiosity. Someone coughs outside. Then Christy Mahon, a slight young man, comes in very tired and frightened and dirty.*]

CHRISTY *(in a small voice)*. God save all here!

MEN. God save you kindly.

CHRISTY *(going to the counter)*. I'd trouble you for a glass of porter, woman of the house.

[*He puts down coin.*]

PEGEEN (*serving him*). You're one of the tinkers, young fellow, is beyond camped in the glen?

CHRISTY. I am not; but I'm destroyed walking.

MICHAEL (*patronizingly*). Let you come up then to the fire. You're looking famished with the cold.

CHRISTY. God reward you. (*He takes up his glass and goes a little way across to the left, then stops and looks about him.*) Is it often the police do be coming into this place, master of the house?

MICHAEL. If you'd come in better hours, you'd have seen "Licensed for the sale of Beer and Spirits, to be consumed on the premises," written in white letters above the door, and what would the polis want spying on me, and not a decent house within four miles, the way every living Christian is a bona fide, saving one widow alone?

CHRISTY (*with relief*). It's a safe house, so.

[*He goes over to the fire, sighing and moaning. Then he sits down, putting his glass beside him and begins gnawing a turnip, too miserable to feel the others staring at him with curiosity.*]

MICHAEL (*going after him*). Is it yourself is fearing the polis? You're wanting, maybe?

CHRISTY. There's many wanting.

MICHAEL. Many surely, with the broken harvest and the ended wars. (*He picks up some stockings, etc., that are near the fire, and carries them away furtively.*) It should be larceny, I'm thinking?

CHRISTY (*dolefully*). I had it in my mind it was a different word and a bigger.

PEGEEN. There's a queer lad. Were you never slapped in school, young fellow, that you don't know the name of your deed?

CHRISTY (*bashfully*). I'm slow at learning, a middling scholar only.

MICHAEL. If you're a dunce itself, you'd have a right to know that larceny's robbing and stealing. Is it for the like of that you're wanting?

CHRISTY (*with a flash of family pride*). And I the son of a strong farmer (*with a sudden qualm*), God rest his soul, could have bought up the whole of your old house a while since, from the butt of his tailpocket, and not have missed the weight of it gone.

MICHAEL (*impressed*). If it's not stealing, it's maybe something big.

CHRISTY (*flattered*). Aye; it's maybe something big.

JIMMY. He's a wicked-looking young fellow. Maybe he followed after a young woman on a lonesome night.

CHRISTY *(shocked)*. Oh, the saints forbid, mister; I was all times a decent lad.

PHILLY *(turning on Jimmy)*. You're a silly man, Jimmy Farrell. He said his father was a farmer a while since, and there's himself now in a poor state. Maybe the land was grabbed from him, and he did what any decent man would do.

MICHAEL *(to Christy, mysteriously)*. Was it bailiffs?

CHRISTY. The divil a one.

MICHAEL. Agents?

CHRISTY. The divil a one.

MICHAEL. Landlords?

CHRISTY *(peevishly)*. Ah, not at all, I'm saying. You'd see the like of them stories on any little paper of a Munster town. But I'm not calling to mind any person, gentle, simple, judge or jury, did the like of me.

[*They all draw nearer with delighted curiosity.*]

PHILLY. Well, that lad's a puzzle-the-world.

JIMMY. He'd beat Dan Davies' circus, or the holy missioners making sermons on the villainy of man. Try him again, Philly.

PHILLY. Did you strike golden guineas out of solder, young fellow, or shilling coins itself?

CHRISTY. I did not, mister, not sixpence nor a farthing coin.

JIMMY. Did you marry three wives maybe? I'm told there's a sprinkling have done that among the holy Luthers of the preaching north.

CHRISTY *(shyly)*. I never married with one, let alone with a couple or three.

PHILLY. Maybe he went fighting for the Boers, the like of the man beyond, was judged to be hanged, quartered and drawn. Were you off east, young fellow, fighting bloody wars for Kruger and the freedom of the Boers?

CHRISTY. I never left my own parish till Tuesday was a week.

PEGEEN *(coming from counter)*. He's done nothing, so. *(To Christy)* If you didn't commit murder or a bad, nasty thing, or false coining, or robbery or butchery, or the like of them, there isn't anything that would be worth your troubling for to run from now. You did nothing at all.

CHRISTY *(his feelings hurt)*. That's an unkindly thing to be saying to a poor orphaned traveller, has a prison behind him, and hanging before, and hell's gap gaping below.

PEGEEN *(with a sign to the men to be quiet)*. You're only saying it. You did nothing at all. A soft lad the like of you wouldn't slit the windpipe of a screeching sow.

CHRISTY *(offended)*. You're not speaking the truth.

PEGEEN *(in mock rage)*. Not speaking the truth, is it? Would you have me knock the head of you with the butt of the broom?

CHRISTY *(twisting round on her with a sharp cry of horror)*. Don't strike me. I killed my poor father, Tuesday was a week, for doing the like of that.

PEGEEN *(with blank amazement)*. Is it killed your father?

CHRISTY *(subsiding)*. With the help of God I did surely, and that the Holy Immaculate Mother may intercede for his soul.

PHILLY *(retreating with Jimmy)*. There's a daring fellow.

JIMMY. Oh, glory be to God!

MICHAEL *(with great respect)*. That was a hanging crime, mister honey. You should have had good reason for doing the like of that.

CHRISTY *(in a very reasonable tone)*. He was a dirty man, God forgive him, and he getting old and crusty, the way I couldn't put up with him at all.

PEGEEN. And you shot him dead?

CHRISTY *(shaking his head)*. I never used weapons. I've no license, and I'm a law-fearing man.

MICHAEL. It was with a hilted knife maybe? I'm told, in the big world its bloody knives they use.

CHRISTY *(loudly, scandalized)*. Do you take me for a slaughter-boy?

PEGEEN. You never hanged him, the way Jimmy Farrell hanged his dog from the license, and had it screeching and wriggling three hours at the butt of a string, and himself swearing it was a dead dog, and the peelers swearing it had life?

CHRISTY. I did not then. I just riz the loy and let fall the edge of it on the ridge of his skull, and he went down at my feet like an empty sack, and never let a grunt or groan from him at all.

MICHAEL *(making a sign to Pegeen to fill Christy's glass)*. And what way weren't you hanged, mister? Did you bury him then?

CHRISTY *(considering)*. Aye. I buried him then. Wasn't I digging spuds in the field?

MICHAEL. And the peelers never followed after you the eleven days that you're out?

CHRISTY *(shaking his head)*. Never a one of them, and I walking forward facing hog, dog, or divil on the highway of the road.

PHILLY *(nodding wisely)*. It's only with a common week-day kind of a murderer them lads would be trusting their carcase, and that man should be a great terror when his temper's roused.

MICHAEL. He should their. *(To Christy.)* And where was it, mister honey, that you did the deed?

CHRISTY (*looking at him with suspicion*). Oh, a distant place, master of the house, a windy corner of high, distant hills.

PHILLY (*nodding with approval*). He's a close man, and he's right, surely.

PEGEEN. That'd be a lad with the sense of Solomon to have for a pot-boy, Michael James, if it's the truth you're seeking one at all.

PHILLY. The peelers is fearing him, and if you'd that lad in the house there isn't one of them would come smelling around if the dogs itself were lapping poteen from the dung-pit of the yard.

JIMMY. Bravery's a treasure in a lonesome place, and a lad would kill his father, I'm thinking, would face a foxy divil with a pitchpike on the flags of hell.

PEGEEN. It's the truth they're saying, and if I'd that lad in the house, I wouldn't be fearing the loosed kharki cutthroats, or the walking dead.

CHRISTY (*swelling with surprise and triumph*). Well, glory be to God!

MICHAEL (*with deference*). Would you think well to stop here and be pot-boy, mister honey, if we gave you good wages, and didn't destroy with the weight of work?

SHAWN (*coming forward uneasily*). That'd be a queer kind to bring into a decent quiet household with the like of Pegeen Mike.

PEGEEN (*very sharply*). Will you whisht? Who's speaking to you?

SHAWN (*retreating*). A bloody-handed murderer the like of ...

PEGEEN (*snapping at him*). Whisht I am saying; we'll take no fooling from your like at all. (*To Christy with a honeyed voice.*) And you, young fellow, you'd have a right to stop, I'm thinking, for we'd do our all and utmost to content your needs.

CHRISTY (*overcome with wonder*). And I'd be safe in this place from the searching law?

MICHAEL. You would, surely. If they're not fearing you, itself, the peelers in this place is decent droughty poor fellows, wouldn't touch a cur dog and not give warning in the dead of night.

PEGEEN (*very kindly and persuasively*). Let you stop a short while anyhow. Aren't you destroyed walking with your feet in bleeding blisters, and your whole skin needing washing like a Wicklow sheep.

CHRISTY (*looking round with satisfaction*). It's a nice room, and if it's not humbugging me you are, I'm thinking that I'll surely stay.

JIMMY (*jumps up*). Now, by the grace of God, herself will be safe this night, with a man killed his father holding danger from the door, and let you come on, Michael James, or they'll have the best stuff drunk at the wake.

MICHAEL *(going to the door with men)*. And begging your pardon, mister, what name will we call you, for we'd like to know?

CHRISTY. Christopher Mahon.

MICHAEL. Well, God bless you, Christy, and a good rest till we meet again when the sun'll be rising to the noon of day.

CHRISTY. God bless you all.

MEN. God bless you.

[*They go out except Shawn, who lingers at door.*]

SHAWN *(to Pegeen)*. Are you wanting me to stop along with you and keep you from harm?

PEGEEN *(gruffly)*. Didn't you say you were fearing Father Reilly?

SHAWN. There'd be no harm staying now, I'm thinking, and himself in it too.

PEGEEN. You wouldn't stay when there was need for you, and let you step off nimble this time when there's none.

SHAWN. Didn't I say it was Father Reilly ...

PEGEEN. Go on, then, to Father Reilly *(in a jeering tone)*, and let him put you in the holy brotherhoods, and leave that lad to me.

SHAWN. If I meet the Widow Quin ...

PEGEEN. Go on, I'm saying, and don't be waking this place with your noise. *(She hustles him out and bolts the door.)* That lad would wear the spirits from the saints of peace. *(Bustles about, then takes off her apron and pins it up in the window as a blind. Christy watching her timidly. Then she comes to him and speaks with bland good-humour.)* Let you stretch out now by the fire, young fellow. You should be destroyed travelling.

CHRISTY *(shyly again, drawing off his boots)*. I'm tired, surely, walking wild eleven days, and waking fearful in the night.

[*He holds up one of his feet, feeling his blisters, and looking at them with compassion.*]

PEGEEN *(standing beside him, watching him with delight)*. You should have had great people in your family, I'm thinking, with the little, small feet you have, and you with a kind of a quality name, the like of what you'd find on the great powers and potentates of France and Spain.

CHRISTY *(with pride)*. We were great surely, with wide and windy acres of rich Munster land.

PEGEEN. Wasn't I telling you, and you a fine, handsome young fellow with a noble brow?

CHRISTY *(with a flash of delighted surprise)*. Is it me?

PEGEEN. Aye. Did you never hear that from the young girls where you come from in the west or south?

CHRISTY *(with venom)*. I did not then. Oh, they're bloody liars in the naked parish where I grew a man.

PEGEEN. If they are itself, you've heard it these days, I'm thinking, and you walking the world telling out your story to young girls or old.

CHRISTY. I've told my story no place till this night, Pegeen Mike, and it's foolish I was here, maybe, to be talking free, but you're decent people, I'm thinking, and yourself a kindly woman, the way I wasn't fearing you at all.

PEGEEN *(filling a sack with straw)*. You've said the like of that, maybe, in every cot and cabin where you've met a young girl on your way.

CHRISTY *(going over to her, gradually raising his voice)*. I've said it nowhere till this night, I'm telling you, for I've seen none the like of you the eleven long days I am walking the world, looking over a low ditch or a high ditch on my north or my south, into stony scattered fields, or scribes of bog, where you'd see young, limber girls, and fine prancing women making laughter with the men.

PEGEEN. If you weren't destroyed travelling, you'd have as much talk and streeleen, I'm thinking, as Owen Roe O'Sullivan or the poets of the Dingle Bay, and I've heard all times it's the poets are your like, fine fiery fellows with great rages when their temper's roused.

CHRISTY *(drawing a little nearer to her)*. You've a power of rings, God bless you, and would there be any offence if I was asking are you single now?

PEGEEN. What would I want wedding so young?

CHRISTY *(with relief)*. We're alike, so.

PEGEEN *(she puts sack on settle and beats it up)*. I never killed my father. I'd be afeard to do that, except I was the like of yourself with blind rages tearing me within, for I'm thinking you should have had great tussling when the end was come.

CHRISTY *(expanding with delight at the first confidential talk he has ever had with a woman)*. We had not then. It was a hard woman was come over the hill, and if he was always a crusty kind, when he'd a hard woman setting him on, not the divil himself or his four fathers could put up with him at all.

PEGEEN *(with curiosity)*. And isn't it a great wonder that one wasn't fearing you?

CHRISTY *(very confidentially)*. Up to the day I killed my father, there wasn't a person in Ireland knew the kind I was, and I there drinking, waking, eating, sleeping, a quiet, simple poor fellow with no man giving me heed.

PEGEEN *(getting a quilt out of the cupboard and putting it on the sack)*. It was the girls were giving you heed maybe, and I'm thinking it's most conceit you'd have to be gaming with their like.

CHRISTY (*shaking his head, with simplicity*). Not the girls itself, and I won't tell you a lie. There wasn't anyone heeding me in that place saving only the dumb beasts of the field.

[*He sits down at fire.*]

PEGEEN (*with disappointment*). And I thinking you should have been living the like of a king of Norway or the Eastern world.

[*She comes and sits beside him after placing bread and mug of milk on the table.*]

CHRISTY (*laughing piteously*). The like of a king, is it? And I after toiling, moiling, digging, dodging from the dawn till dusk with never a sight of joy or sport saving only when I'd be abroad in the dark night poaching rabbits on hills, for I was a devil to poach, God forgive me, (*very naively*) and I near got six months for going with a dung fork and stabbing a fish.

PEGEEN. And it's that you'd call sport, is it, to be abroad in the darkness with yourself alone?

CHRISTY. I did, God help me, and there I'd be as happy as the sunshine of St. Martins Day, watching the light passing the north or the patches of fog, till I'd hear a rabbit starting to screech and I'd go running in the furze. Then when I'd my full share I'd come walking down where you'd see the ducks and geese stretched sleeping on the highway of the road, and before I'd pass the dunghill, I'd hear himself snoring out, a loud lonesome snore he'd be making all times, the while he was sleeping, and he a man'd be raging all times, the while he was waking, like a gaudy officer you'd hear cursing and damning and swearing oaths.

PEGEEN. Providence and Mercy, spare us all!

CHRISTY. It's that you'd say surely if you seen him and he after drinking for weeks, rising up in the red dawn, or before it maybe, and going out into the yard as naked as an ash tree in the moon of May, and shying clods against the visage of the stars till he'd put the fear of death into the banbhs and the screeching sows.

PEGEEN. I'd be well-nigh afeard of that lad myself, I'm thinking. And there was no one in it but the two of you alone?

CHRISTY. The divil a one, though he'd sons and daughters walking all great states and territories of the world, and not a one of them, to this day, but would say their seven curses on him, and they rousing up to let a cough or sneeze, maybe, in the deadness of the night.

PEGEEN (*nodding her head*). Well, you should have been a queer lot. I never cursed my father the like of that, though I'm twenty and more years of age.

CHRISTY. Then you'd have cursed mine, I'm telling you, and he a man never gave peace to any, saving when he'd get two months or three, or be locked in the asylums for battering peelers or assaulting men *(with depression)* the way it was a bitter life he led me till I did up a Tuesday and halve his skull.

PEGEEN *(putting her hand on his shoulder)*. Well, you'll have peace in this place, Christy Mahon, and none to trouble you, and it's near time a fine lad like you should have your good share of the earth.

CHRISTY. It's time surely, and I a seemly fellow with great strength in me and bravery of ...

[*Someone knocks.*]

CHRISTY *(clinging to Pegeen)*. Oh, glory! it's late for knocking, and this last while I'm in terror of the peelers, and the walking dead.

[*Knocking again.*]

PEGEEN. Who's there?

VOICE *(outside)*. Me.

PEGEEN. Who's me?

VOICE. The Widow Quin.

PEGEEN *(jumping up and giving him the bread and milk)*. Go on now with your supper, and let on to be sleepy, for if she found you were such a warrant to talk, she'd be stringing gabble till the dawn of day. *(He takes bread and sits shyly with his back to the door.)*

PEGEEN *(opening door, with temper)*. What ails you, or what is it you're wanting at this hour of the night?

WIDOW QUIN *(coming in a step and peering at Christy)*. I'm after meeting Shawn Keogh and Father Reilly below, who told me of your curiosity man, and they fearing by this time he was maybe roaring, romping on your hands with drink.

PEGEEN *(pointing to Christy)*. Look now is he roaring, and he stretched away drowsy with his supper and his mug of milk. Walk down and tell that to Father Reilly and to Shaneen Keogh.

WIDOW QUIN *(coming forward)*. I'll not see them again, for I've their word to lead that lad forward for to lodge with me.

PEGEEN *(in blank amazement)*. This night, is it?

WIDOW QUIN *(going over)*. This night. "It isn't fitting," says the priesteen, "to have his likeness lodging with an orphaned girl." *(To Christy.)* God save you, mister!

CHRISTY *(shyly)*. God save you kindly.

WIDOW QUIN *(looking at him with half-amazed curiosity)*. Well, aren't you a little smiling fellow? It should have been great and bitter torments did rouse your spirits to a deed of blood.

CHRISTY (*doubtfully*). It should, maybe.

WIDOW QUIN. It's more than "maybe" I'm saying, and it'd soften my heart to see you sitting so simple with your cup and cake, and you fitter to be saying your catechism than slaying your da.

PEGEEN (*at counter, washing glasses*). There's talking when any'd see he's fit to be holding his head high with the wonders of the world. Walk on from this, for I'll not have him tormented and he destroyed travelling since Tuesday was a week.

WIDOW QUIN (*peaceably*). We'll be walking surely when his supper's done, and you'll find we're great company, young fellow, when it's of the like of you and me you'd hear the penny poets singing in an August Fair.

CHRISTY (*innocently*). Did you kill your father?

PEGEEN (*contemptuously*). She did not. She hit himself with a worn pick, and the rusted poison did corrode his blood the way he never overed it, and died after. That was a sneaky kind of murder did win small glory with the boys itself.

[*She crosses to Christy's left.*]

WIDOW QUIN (*with good-humour*). If it didn't, maybe all knows a widow woman has buried her children and destroyed her man is a wiser comrade for a young lad than a girl, the like of you, who'd go helter-skeltering after any man would let you a wink upon the road.

PEGEEN (*breaking out into wild rage*). And you'll say that, Widow Quin, and you gasping with the rage you had racing the hill beyond to look on his face.

WIDOW QUIN (*laughing derisively*). Me, is it? Well, Father Reilly has cuteness to divide you now. (*She pulls Christy up.*) There's great temptation in a man did slay his da, and we'd best be going, young fellow; so rise up and come with me.

PEGEEN (*seizing his arm*). He'll not stir. He's pot-boy in this place, and I'll not have him stolen off and kidnabbed while himself's abroad.

WIDOW QUIN. It'd be a crazy pot-boy'd lodge him in the shebeen where he works by day, so you'd have a right to come on, young fellow, till you see my little houseen, a perch off on the rising hill.

PEGEEN. Wait till morning, Christy Mahon. Wait till you lay eyes on her leaky thatch is growing more pasture for her buck goat than her square of fields, and she without a tramp itself to keep in order her place at all.

WIDOW QUIN. When you see me contriving in my little gardens, Christy Mahon, you'll swear the Lord God formed me to be living lone, and that there isn't my match in Mayo for thatching, or mowing, or shearing a sheep.

PEGEEN (*with noisy scorn*). It's true the Lord God formed you to contrive indeed. Doesn't the world know you reared a black lamb at your own breast, so that the Lord Bishop of Connaught felt the elements of a Christian, and he eating it after in a kidney stew? Doesn't the world know you've been seen shaving the foxy skipper from France for a threepenny bit and a sop of grass tobacco would wring the liver from a mountain goat you'd meet leaping the hills?

WIDOW QUIN (*with amusement*). Do you hear her now, young fellow? Do you hear the way she'll be rating at your own self when a week is by?

PEGEEN (*to Christy*). Don't heed her. Tell her to go into her pigsty and not plague us here.

WIDOW QUIN. I'm going; but he'll come with me.

PEGEEN (*shaking him*). Are you dumb, young fellow?

CHRISTY (*timidly, to Widow Quin*). God increase you; but I'm pot-boy in this place, and it's here I'd liefer stay.

PEGEEN (*triumphantly*). Now you have heard him, and go on from this.

WIDOW QUIN (*looking round the room*). It's lonesome this hour crossing the hill, and if he won't come along with me, I'd have a right maybe to stop this night with yourselves. Let me stretch out on the settle, Pegeen Mike; and himself can lie by the hearth.

PEGEEN (*short and fiercely*). Faith, I won't. Quit off or I will send you now.

WIDOW QUIN (*gathering her shawl up*). Well, it's a terror to be aged a score. (*To Christy.*) God bless you now, young fellow, and let you be wary, or there's right torment will await you here if you go romancing with her like, and she waiting only, as they bade me say, on a sheepskin parchment to be wed with Shawn Keogh of Killakeen.

CHRISTY (*going to Pegeen as she bolts the door*). What's that she's after saying?

PEGEEN. Lies and blather, you've no call to mind. Well, isn't Shawn Keogh an impudent fellow to send up spying on me? Wait till I lay hands on him. Let him wait, I'm saying.

CHRISTY. And you're not wedding him at all?

PEGEEN. I wouldn't wed him if a bishop came walking for to join us here.

CHRISTY. That God in glory may be thanked for that.

PEGEEN. There's your bed now. I've put a quilt upon you I'm after quilting a while since with my own two hands, and you'd best stretch out now for your sleep, and may God give you a good rest till I call you in the morning when the cocks will crow.

CHRISTY (*as she goes to inner room*). May God and Mary and St. Patrick bless you and reward you, for your kindly talk. *(She shuts the door behind her. He settles his bed slowly, feeling the quilt with immense satisfaction.)* Well, it's a clean bed and soft with it, and it's great luck and company I've won me in the end of time—two fine women fighting for the likes of me—till I'm thinking this night wasn't I a foolish fellow not to kill my father in the years gone by.

CURTAIN

Act II

SCENE, as before. Brilliant morning light. Christy, looking bright and cheerful, is cleaning a girl's boots.

CHRISTY *(to himself counting jugs on dresser)*. Half a hundred beyond. Ten there. A score that's above. Eighty jugs. Six cups and a broken one. Two plates. A power of glasses. Bottles, a school-master'd be hard set to count, and enough in them, I'm thinking, to drunken all the wealth and wisdom of the County Clare. *(He puts down the boot carefully.)* There's her boots now, nice and decent for her evening use, and isn't it grand brushes she has? *(He puts them down and goes by degrees to the looking-glass.)* Well, this'd be a fine place to be my whole life talking out with swearing Christians, in place of my old dogs and cat, and I stalking around, smoking my pipe and drinking my fill, and never a day's work but drawing a cork an odd time, or wiping a glass, or rinsing out a shiny tumbler for a decent man. *(He takes the looking-glass from the wall and puts it on the back of a chair; then sits down in front of it and begins washing his face.)* Didn't I know rightly I was handsome, though it was the divil's own mirror we had beyond, would twist a squint across an angel's brow; and I'll be growing fine from this day, the way I'll have a soft lovely skin on me and won't be the like of the clumsy young fellows do be ploughing all times in the earth and dung. *(He starts.)* Is she coming again? *(He looks out.)* Stranger girls. God help me, where'll I hide myself away and my long neck naked to the world? *(He looks out.)* I'd best go to the room maybe till I'm dressed again.

[*He gathers up his coat and the looking-glass, and runs into the inner room. The door is pushed open, and Susan Brady looks in, and knocks on door.*]

SUSAN. There's nobody in it.

[*Knocks again.*]

NELLY *(pushing her in and following her, with Honor Blake and Sara Tansey)*. It'd be early for them both to be out walking the hill.

SUSAN. I'm thinking Shawn Keogh was making game of us and there's no such man in it at all.

HONOR (*pointing to straw and quilt*). Look at that. He's been sleeping there in the night. Well, it'll be a hard case if he's gone off now, the way we'll never set our eyes on a man killed his father, and we after rising early and destroying ourselves running fast on the hill.

NELLY. Are you thinking them's his boots?

SARA (*taking them up*). If they are, there should be his father's track on them. Did you never read in the papers the way murdered men do bleed and drip?

SUSAN. Is that blood there, Sara Tansey?

SARA (*smelling it*). That's bog water, I'm thinking, but it's his own they are surely, for I never seen the like of them for whity mud, and red mud, and turf on them, and the fine sands of the sea. That man's been walking, I'm telling you.

[*She goes down right, putting on one of his boots.*]

SUSAN (*going to window*). Maybe he's stolen off to Belmullet with the boots of Michael James, and you'd have a right so to follow after him, Sara Tansey, and you the one yoked the ass cart and drove ten miles to set your eyes on the man bit the yellow lady's nostril on the northern shore.

[*She looks out.*]

SARA (*running to window with one boot on*). Don't be talking, and we fooled to-day. (*Putting on other boot.*) There's a pair do fit me well, and I'll be keeping them for walking to the priest, when you'd be ashamed this place, going up winter and summer with nothing worth while to confess at all.

HONOR (*who has been listening at the door*). Whisht! there's someone inside the room. (*She pushes door a chink open.*) It's a man.

[*Sara kicks off boots and puts them where they were. They all stand in a line looking through chink.*]

SARA. I'll call him. Mister! Mister! (*He puts in his head.*) Is Pegeen within?

CHRISTY (*Coming in as meek as a mouse, with the looking-glass held behind his back*). She's above on the cnuceen, seeking the nanny goats, the way she'd have a sup of goat's milk for to colour my tea.

SARA. And asking your pardon, is it you's the man killed his father?

CHRISTY (*sidling toward the nail where the glass was hanging*). I am, God help me!

SARA (*taking eggs she has brought*). Then my thousand welcomes to you, and I've run up with a brace of duck's eggs for your food to-day. Pegeen's ducks is no use, but these are the real rich sort. Hold out your hand and you'll see it's no lie I'm telling you.

CHRISTY (*coming forward shyly, and holding out his left hand*). They're a great and weighty size.

SUSAN. And I run up with a pat of butter, for it'd be a poor thing to have you eating your spuds dry, and you after running a great way since you did destroy your da.

CHRISTY. Thank you kindly.

HONOR. And I brought you a little cut of cake, for you should have a thin stomach on you, and you that length walking the world.

NELLY. And I brought you a little laying pullet—boiled and all she is—was crushed at the fall of night by the curate's car. Feel the fat of that breast, mister.

CHRISTY. It's bursting, surely.

[*He feels it with the back of his hand, in which he holds the presents.*]

SARA. Will you pinch it? Is your right hand too sacred for to use at all? (*She slips round behind him.*) It's a glass he has. Well, I never seen to this day a man with a looking-glass held to his back. Them that kills their fathers is a vain lot surely.

[*Girls giggle.*]

CHRISTY (*smiling innocently and piling presents on glass*). I'm very thankful to you all to-day ...

WIDOW QUIN (*coming in quickly, at door*). Sara Tansey, Susan Brady, Honor Blake! What in glory has you here at this hour of day?

GIRLS (*giggling*). That's the man killed his father.

WIDOW QUIN (*coming to them*). I know well it's the man; and I'm after putting him down in the sports below for racing, leaping, pitching, a the Lord knows what.

SARA (*exuberantly*). That's right, Widow Quin. I'll bet my dowry that he'll lick the world.

WIDOW QUIN. If you will, you'd have a right to have him fresh and nourished in place of nursing a feast. (*Taking presents.*) Are you fasting or fed, young fellow?

CHRISTY. Fasting, if you please.

WIDOW QUIN (*loudly*). Well, you're the lot. Stir up now and give him his breakfast. (*To Christy.*) Come here to me (*she puts him on bench beside her while the girls make tea and get his breakfast*) and let you tell us your story before Pegeen will come, in place of grinning your ears off like the moon of May.

CHRISTY (*beginning to be pleased*). It's a long story; you'd be destroyed listening.

WIDOW QUIN. Don't be letting on to be shy, a fine, gamey, treacherous lad the like of you. Was it in your house beyond you cracked his skull?

CHRISTY *(shy but flattered)*. It was not. We were digging spuds in his cold, sloping, stony, divil's patch of a field.

WIDOW QUIN. And you went asking money of him, or making talk of getting a wife would drive him from his farm?

CHRISTY. I did not, then; but there I was, digging and digging, and "You squinting idiot," says he, "let you walk down now and tell the priest you'll wed the Widow Casey in a score of days."

WIDOW QUIN. And what kind was she?

CHRISTY *(with horror)*. A walking terror from beyond the hills, and she two score and five years, and two hundredweights and five pounds in the weighing scales, with a limping leg on her, and a blinded eye, and she a woman of noted misbehaviour with the old and young.

GIRLS *(clustering round him, serving him)*. Glory be.

WIDOW QUIN. And what did he want driving you to wed with her?

[*She takes a bit of the chicken.*]

CHRISTY *(eating with growing satisfaction)*. He was letting on I was wanting a protector from the harshness of the world, and he without a thought the whole while but how he'd have her hut to live in and her gold to drink.

WIDOW QUIN. There's maybe worse than a dry hearth and a widow woman and your glass at night. So you hit him then?

CHRISTY *(getting almost excited)*. I did not. "I won't wed her," says I, "when all know she did suckle me for six weeks when I came into the world, and she a liar this day with a tongue on her has the crows and seabirds scattered, the way they wouldn't cast a shadow on her garden with the dread of her curse."

WIDOW QUIN *(teasingly)*. That one should be right company.

SARA *(eagerly)*. Don't mind her. Did you kill him then?

CHRISTY. "She's too good for the like of you," says he, "and go on now or I'll flatten you out like a crawling beast has passed under a dray. " "You will not if I can help it," says I. "Go on," says he, "or I'll have the divil making garters of your limbs to-night." "You will not if I can help it," says I.

[*He sits up, brandishing his mug.*]

SARA. You were right surely.

CHRISTY *(impressively)*. With that the sun came out between the cloud and the hill, and it shining green in my face. "God have mercy on your soul," says he, lifting a scythe; "or on your own," says I, raising the loy.

SUSAN. That's a grand story.

HONOR. He tells it lovely.

CHRISTY (*flattered and confident, waving bone*). He gave a drive with the scythe, and I gave a lep to the east. Then I turned around with my back to the north, and I hit a blow on the ridge of his skull, laid him stretched out, and he split to the knob of his gullet.

[*He raises the chicken bone to his Adam's apple.*]

GIRLS (*together*). Well, you're a marvel! Oh, God bless you! You're the lad surely!

SUSAN. I'm thinking the Lord God sent him this road to make a second husband to the Widow Quin, and she with a great yearning to be wedded, though all dread her here. Lift him on her knee, Sara Tansey.

WIDOW QUIN. Don't tease him.

SARA (*going over to dresser and counter very quickly, and getting two glasses and porter*). You're heroes surely, and let you drink a supeen with your arms linked like the outlandish lovers in the sailor's song. (*She links their arms and gives them the glasses.*) There now. Drink a health to the wonders of the western world, the pirates, preachers, poteen-makers, with the jobbing jockies; parching peelers, and the juries fill their stomachs selling judgments of the English law.

[*Brandishing the bottle.*]

WIDOW QUIN. That's a right toast, Sara Tansey. Now Christy.

[*They drink with their arms linked, he drinking with his left hand, she with her right. As they are drinking, Pegeen Mike comes in with a milk can and stands aghast. They all spring away from Christy. He goes down left. Widow Quin remains seated.*]

PEGEEN (*angrily, to Sara*). What is it you're wanting?

SARA (*twisting her apron*). An ounce of tobacco.

PEGEEN. Have you tuppence?

SARA. I've forgotten my purse.

PEGEEN. Then you'd best be getting it and not fooling us here. (*To the Widow Quin, with more elaborate scorn.*) And what is it you're wanting, Widow Quin?

WIDOW QUIN (*insolently*). A penn'orth of starch.

PEGEEN (*breaking out*). And you without a white shift or a slint in your whole family since the drying of the flood. I've no starch for the like of you, and let you walk on now to Killamuck.

WIDOW QUIN (*turning to Christy, as she goes out with the girls*). Well, you're mighty huffy this day, Pegeen Mike, and, you young fellow, let you not forget the sports and racing when the noon is by.

[*They go out.*]

PEGEEN (*imperiously*). Fling out that rubbish and put them cups away. (*Christy tidies away in great haste.*) Shove in the bench by the wall. (*He does so.*) And hang that glass on the nail. What disturbed it at all?

CHRISTY (*very meekly*). I was making myself decent only, and this a fine country for young lovely girls.

PEGEEN (*sharply*). Whisht your talking of girls.

[*Goes to counter-right.*]

CHRISTY. Wouldn't any wish to be decent in a place ...

PEGEEN. Whisht I'm saying.

CHRISTY (*looks at her face for a moment with great misgivings, then as a last effort, takes up a loy, and goes towards her, with feigned assurance*). It was with a loy the like of that I killed my father.

PEGEEN (*still sharply*). You've told me that story six times since the dawn of day.

CHRISTY (*reproachfully*). It's a queer thing you wouldn't care to be hearing it and them girls after walking four miles to be listening to me now.

PEGEEN (*turning round astonished*). Four miles.

CHRISTY (*apologetically*). Didn't himself say there were only four bona fides living in the place?

PEGEEN. It's bona fides by the road they are, but that lot came over the river lepping the stories. It's not three perches when you go like that, and I was down this morning looking on the papers the postboy does have in his bag. (*With meaning and emphasis.*) For there was great news this day, Christopher Mahon.

[*She goes into room left.*]

CHRISTY (*suspiciously*). Is it news of my murder?

PEGEEN (*inside*). Murder, indeed.

CHRISTY (*loudly*). A murdered da?

PEGEEN (*coming in again and crossing right*). There was not, but a story filled half a page of the hanging of a man. Ah, that should be a fearful end, young fellow, and it worst of all for a man who destroyed his da, for the like of him would get small mercies, and when it's dead he is, they'd put him in a narrow grave, with cheap sacking wrapping him round, and pour down quicklime on his head, the way you'd see a woman pouring any frish-frash from a cup.

CHRISTY (*very miserably*). Oh, God help me. Are you thinking I'm safe? You were saying at the fall of night, I was shut of jeopardy and I here with yourselves.

PEGEEN (*severely*). You'll be shut of jeopardy no place if you go talking with a pack of wild girls the like of them do be walking abroad with the peelers, talking whispers at the fall of night.

CHRISTY *(with terror)*. And you're thinking they'd tell?

PEGEEN *(with mock sympathy)*. Who knows, God help you.

CHRISTY *(loudly)*. What joy would they have to bring hanging to the likes of me?

PEGEEN. It's queer joys they have, and who knows the thing they'd do, if it'd make the green stones cry itself to think of you swaying and swiggling at the butt of a rope, and you with a fine, stout neck, God bless you! the way you'd be a half an hour, in great anguish, getting your death.

CHRISTY *(getting his boots and putting them on)*. If there's that terror of them, it'd be best, maybe, I went on wandering like Esau or Cain and Abel on the sides of Neifin or the Erris plain.

PEGEEN *(beginning to play with him)*. It would, maybe, for I've heard the Circuit judges this place is a heartless crew.

CHRISTY *(bitterly)*. It's more than judges this place is a heartless crew. *(Looking up at her.)* And isn't it a poor thing to be starting again and I a lonesome fellow will be looking out on women and girls the way the needy fallen spirits do be looking on the Lord?

PEGEEN. What call have you to be that lonesome when there's poor girls walking Mayo in their thousands now?

CHRISTY *(grimly)*. It's well you know what call I have. It's well you know it's a lonesome thing to be passing small towns with the lights shining sideways when the night is down, or going in strange places with a dog noising before you and a dog noising behind, or drawn to the cities where you'd hear a voice kissing and talking deep love in every shadow of the ditch, and you passing on with an empty, hungry stomach failing from your heart.

PEGEEN. I'm thinking you're an odd man, Christy Mahon. The oddest walking fellow I ever set my eyes on to this hour to-day.

CHRISTY. What would any be but odd men and they living lonesome in the world?

PEGEEN. I'm not odd, and I'm my whole life with my father only.

CHRISTY *(with infinite admiration)*. How would a lovely handsome woman the like of you be lonesome when all men should be thronging around to hear the sweetness of your voice, and the little infant children should be pestering your steps I'm thinking, and you walking the roads.

PEGEEN. I'm hard set to know what way a coaxing fellow the like of yourself should be lonesome either.

CHRISTY. Coaxing?

PEGEEN. Would you have me think a man never talked with the girls would have the words you've spoken to-day? It's only letting on you are to be lonesome, the way you'd get around me now.

CHRISTY. I wish to God I was letting on; but I was lonesome all times, and born lonesome, I'm thinking, as the moon of dawn.

[*Going to door.*]

PEGEEN (*puzzled by his talk*). Well, it's a story I'm not understanding at all why you'd be worse than another, Christy Mahon, and you a fine lad with the great savagery to destroy your da.

CHRISTY. It's little I'm understanding myself, saving only that my heart's scalded this day, and I going off stretching out the earth between us, the way I'll not be waking near you another dawn of the year till the two of us do arise to hope or judgment with the saints of God, and now I'd best be going with my wattle in my hand, for hanging is a poor thing (*turning to go*), and it's little welcome only is left me in this house to-day.

PEGEEN (*sharply*). Christy! (*He turns round.*) Come here to me. (*He goes towards her.*) Lay down that switch and throw some sods on the fire. You're pot-boy in this place, and I'll not have you mitch off from us now.

CHRISTY. You were saying I'd be hanged if I stay.

PEGEEN (*quite kindly at last*). I'm after going down and reading the fearful crimes of Ireland for two weeks or three, and there wasn't a word of your murder. (*Getting up and going over to the counter.*) They've likely not found the body. You're safe so with ourselves.

CHRISTY (*astonished, slowly*). It's making game of me you were (*following her with fearful joy*), and I can stay so, working at your side, and I not lonesome from this mortal day.

PEGEEN. What's to hinder you from staying, except the widow woman or the young girls would inveigle you off?

CHRISTY (*with rapture*). And I'll have your words from this day filling my ears, and that look is come upon you meeting my two eyes, and I watching you loafing around in the warm sun, or rinsing your ankles when the night is come.

PEGEEN (*kindly, but a little embarrassed*). I'm thinking you'll be a loyal young lad to have working around, and if you vexed me a while since with your leaguing with the girls, I wouldn't give a thraneen for a lad hadn't a mighty spirit in him and a gamey heart.

[*Shawn Keogh runs in carrying a cleeve on his back, followed by the Widow Quin.*]

SHAWN (*to Pegeen*). I was passing below, and I seen your mountainy sheep eating cabbages in Jimmy's field. Run up or they'll be bursting surely.

PEGEEN. Oh, God mend them!

[*She puts a shawl over her head and runs out.*]

CHRISTY (*looking from one to the other. Still in high spirits*). I'd best go to her aid maybe. I'm handy with ewes.

WIDOW QUIN (*closing the door*). She can do that much, and there is Shaneen has long speeches for to tell you now

[*She sits down with an amused smile.*]

SHAWN (*taking something from his pocket and offering it to Christy*). Do you see that, mister?

CHRISTY (*looking at it*). The half of a ticket to the Western States!

SHAWN (*trembling with anxiety*). I'll give it to you and my new hat (*pulling it out of hamper*); and my breeches with the double seat (*pulling it off*); and my new coat is woven from the blackest shearings for three miles around (*giving him the coat*); I'll give you the whole of them, and my blessing, and the blessing of Father Reilly itself, maybe, if you'll quit from this and leave us in the peace we had till last night at the fall of dark.

CHRISTY (*with a new arrogance*). And for what is it you're wanting to get shut of me?

SHAWN (*looking to the Widow for help*). I'm a poor scholar with middling faculties to coin a lie, so I'll tell you the truth, Christy Mahon. I'm wedding with Pegeen beyond, and I don't think well of having a clever fearless man the like of you dwelling in her house.

CHRISTY (*almost pugnaciously*). And you'd be using bribery for to banish me?

SHAWN (*in an imploring voice*). Let you not take it badly, mister honey, isn't beyond the best place for you where you'll have golden chains and shiny coats and you riding upon hunters with the ladies of the land.

[*He makes an eager sign to the Widow Quin to come to help him.*]

WIDOW QUIN (*coming over*). It's true for him, and you'd best quit off and not have that poor girl setting her mind on you, for there's Shaneen thinks she wouldn't suit you though all is saying that she'll wed you now.

[*Christy beams with delight.*]

SHAWN (*in terrified earnest*). She wouldn't suit you, and she with the divil's own temper the way you'd be strangling one another in a score of days. (*He makes the movement of strangling with his hands.*) It's the like of me only that she's fit for, a quiet simple fellow wouldn't raise a hand upon her if she scratched itself.

WIDOW QUIN *(putting Shawn's hat on Christy)*. Fit them clothes on you anyhow, young fellow, and he'd maybe loan them to you for the sports. *(Pushing him towards inner door.)* Fit them on and you can give your answer when you have them tried.

CHRISTY *(beaming, delighted with the clothes)*. I will then. I'd like herself to see me in them tweeds and hat.

[*He goes into room and shuts the door.*]

SHAWN *(in great anxiety)*. He'd like herself to see them. He'll not leave us, Widow Quin. He's a score of divils in him the way it's well nigh certain he will wed Pegeen.

WIDOW QUIN *(jeeringly)*. It's true all girls are fond of courage and do hate the like of you.

SHAWN *(walking about in desperation)*. Oh, Widow Quin, what'll I be doing now? I'd inform again him, but he'd burst from Kilmainham and he'd be sure and certain to destroy me. If I wasn't so God-fearing, I'd near have courage to come behind him and run a pike into his side. Oh, it's a hard case to be an orphan and not to have your father that you're used to, and you'd easy kill and make yourself a hero in the sight of all. *(Coming up to her.)* Oh, Widow Quin, will you find me some contrivance when I've promised you a ewe?

WIDOW QUIN. A ewe's a small thing, but what would you give me if I did wed him and did save you so?

SHAWN *(with astonishment)*. You?

WIDOW QUIN. Aye. Would you give me the red cow you have and the mountainy ram, and the right of way across your rye path, and a load of dung at Michaelmas, and turbary upon the western hill?

SHAWN *(radiant with hope)*. I would surely, and I'd give you the wedding-ring I have, and the loan of a new suit, the way you'd have him decent on the wedding-day. I'd give you two kids for your dinner, and a gallon of poteen, and I'd call the piper on the long car to your wedding from Crossmolina or from Ballina. I'd give you ...

WIDOW QUIN. That'll do so, and let you whisht, for he's coming now again.

[*Christy comes in very natty in the new clothes. Widow Quin goes to him admiringly.*]

WIDOW QUIN. If you seen yourself now, I'm thinking you'd be too proud to speak to us at all, and it'd be a pity surely to have your like sailing from Mayo to the Western World.

CHRISTY *(as proud as a peacock)*. I'm not going. If this is a poor place itself, I'll make myself contented to be lodging here.

[*Widow Quin makes a sign to Shawn to leave them.*]

SHAWN. Well, I'm going measuring the race-course while the tide is low, so I'll leave you the garments and my blessing for the sports to-day. God bless you!

[*He wriggles out.*]

WIDOW QUIN (*admiring Christy*). Well, you're mighty spruce, young fellow. Sit down now while you're quiet till you talk with me.

CHRISTY (*swaggering*). I'm going abroad on the hillside for to seek Pegeen.

WIDOW QUIN. You'll have time and plenty for to seek Pegeen, and you heard me saying at the fall of night the two of us should be great company.

CHRISTY. From this out I'll have no want of company when all sorts is bringing me their food and clothing (*he swaggers to the door, tightening his belt*), the way they'd set their eyes upon a gallant orphan cleft his father with one blow to the breeches belt. (*He opens door, then staggers back.*) Saints of glory! Holy angels from the throne of light!

WIDOW QUIN (*going over*). What ails you?

CHRISTY. It's the walking spirit of my murdered da!

WIDOW QUIN (*looking out*). Is it that tramper?

CHRISTY (*wildly*). Where'll I hide my poor body from that ghost of hell?

[*The door is pushed open, and old Mahon appears on threshold. Christy darts in behind door.*]

WIDOW QUIN (*in great amusement*). God save you, my poor man.

MAHON (*gruffly*). Did you see a young lad passing this way in the early morning or the fall of night?

WIDOW QUIN. You're a queer kind to walk in not saluting at all.

MAHON. Did you see the young lad?

WIDOW QUIN (*stiffly*). What kind was he?

MAHON. An ugly young streeler with a murderous gob on him, and a little switch in his hand. I met a tramper seen him coming this way at the fall of night.

WIDOW QUIN. There's harvest hundreds do be passing these days for the Sligo boat. For what is it you're wanting him, my poor man?

MAHON. I want to destroy him for breaking the head on me with the clout of a loy. (*He takes off a big hat, and shows his head in a mass of bandages and plaster, with some pride.*) It was he did that, and amn't I a great wonder to think I've traced him ten days with that dent in my crown?

WIDOW QUIN (*taking his head in both hands and examining it with extreme delight*). That was a great blow. And who hit you? A robber maybe?

MAHON. It was my own son hit me, and he the divil a robber, or anything else, but a dirty, stuttering lout.

WIDOW QUIN (*letting go his skull and wiping her hands in her apron*). You'd best be wary of a mortified scalp, I think they call it, lepping around with that wound in the splendour of the sun. It was a bad blow surely, and you should have vexed him fearful to make him strike that gash in his da.

MAHON. Is it me?

WIDOW QUIN (*amusing herself*). Aye. And isn't it a great shame when the old and hardened do torment the young?

MAHON (*raging*). Torment him is it? And I after holding out with the patience of a martyred saint till there's nothing but destruction on, and I'm driven out in my old age with none to aid me.

WIDOW QUIN (*greatly amused*). It's a sacred wonder the way that wickedness will spoil a man.

MAHON. My wickedness, is it? Amn't I after saying it is himself has me destroyed, and he a liar on walls, a talker of folly, a man you'd see stretched the half of the day in the brown ferns with his belly to the sun.

WIDOW QUIN. Not working at all?

MAHON. The divil a work, or if he did itself, you'd see him raising up a haystack like the stalk of a rush, or driving our last cow till he broke her leg at the hip, and when he wasn't at that he'd be fooling over little birds he had—finches and felts—or making mugs at his own self in the bit of a glass we had hung on the wall.

WIDOW QUIN (*looking at Christy*). What way was he so foolish? It was running wild after the girls may be?

MAHON (*with a shout of derision*). Running wild, is it? If he seen a red petticoat coming swinging over the hill, he'd be off to hide in the sticks, and you'd see him shooting out his sheep's eyes between the little twigs and the leaves, and his two ears rising like a hare looking out through a gap. Girls, indeed!

WIDOW QUIN. It was drink maybe?

MAHON. And he a poor fellow would get drunk on the smell of a pint. He'd a queer rotten stomach, I'm telling you, and when I gave him three pulls from my pipe a while since, he was taken with contortions till I had to send him in the ass cart to the females' nurse.

WIDOW QUIN (*clasping her hands*). Well, I never till this day heard tell of a man the like of that!

MAHON. I'd take a mighty oath you didn't surely, and wasn't he the laughing joke of every female woman where four baronies meet, the way the girls would stop their weeding if they seen him coming the road to let a roar at him, and call him the looney of Mahon's.

WIDOW QUIN. I'd give the world and all to see the like of him. What kind was he?

MAHON. A small low fellow.

WIDOW QUIN. And dark?

MAHON. Dark and dirty.

WIDOW QUIN *(considering)*. I'm thinking I seen him.

MAHON *(eagerly)*. An ugly young blackguard.

WIDOW QUIN. A hideous, fearful villain, and the spit of you.

MAHON. What way is he fled?

WIDOW QUIN. Gone over the hills to catch a coasting steamer to the north or south.

MAHON. Could I pull up on him now?

WIDOW QUIN. If you'll cross the sands below where the tide is out, you'll be in it as soon as himself, for he had to go round ten miles by the top of the bay. *(She points to the door.)* Strike down by the head beyond and then follow on the roadway to the north and east.

[*Mahon goes abruptly.*]

WIDOW QUIN *(shouting after him)*. Let you give him a good vengeance when you come up with him, but don't put yourself in the power of the law, for it'd be a poor thing to see a judge in his black cap reading out his sentence on a civil warrior the like of you.

[*She swings the door to and looks at Christy, who is cowering in terror, for a moment, then she bursts into a laugh.*]

WIDOW QUIN. Well, you're the walking Playboy of the Western World, and that's the poor man you had divided to his breeches belt.

CHRISTY *(looking out: then, to her)*. What'll Pegeen say when she hears that story? What'll she be saying to me now?

WIDOW QUIN. She'll knock the head of you, I'm thinking, and drive you from the door. God help her to be taking you for a wonder, and you a little schemer making up the story you destroyed your da.

CHRISTY *(turning to the door, nearly speechless with rage, half to himself)*. To be letting on he was dead, and coming back to his life, and following after me like an old weazel tracing a rat, and coming in here laying desolation between my own self and the fine women of Ireland, and he a kind of carcase that you'd fling upon the sea ...

WIDOW QUIN *(more soberly)*. There's talking for a man's one only son.

CHRISTY *(breaking out)*. His one son, is it? May I meet him with one tooth and it aching, and one eye to be seeing seven and seventy divils in the twists of the road, and one old timber leg on him to limp into the scalding grave. *(Looking out.)* There he is now crossing the strands, and that the Lord God would send a high wave to wash him from the world.

WIDOW QUIN *(scandalized)*. Have you no shame? *(Putting her hand on his shoulder and turning him round.)* What ails you? Near crying, is it?

CHRISTY *(in despair and grief)*. Amn't I after seeing the love-light of the star of knowledge shining from her brow, and hearing words would put you thinking on the holy Brigid speaking to the infant saints, and now she'll be turning again, and speaking hard words to me, like an old woman with a spavindy ass she'd have, urging on a hill.

WIDOW QUIN. There's poetry talk for a girl you'd see itching and scratching, and she with a stale stink of poteen on her from selling in the shop.

CHRISTY *(impatiently)*. It's her like is fitted to be handling merchandise in the heavens above, and what'll I be doing now, I ask you, and I a kind of wonder was jilted by the heavens when a day was by.

[*There is a distant noise of girls' voices. Widow Quin looks from window and comes to him, hurriedly.*]

WIDOW QUIN. You'll be doing like myself, I'm thinking, when I did destroy my man, for I'm above many's the day, odd times in great spirits, abroad in the sunshine, darning a stocking or stitching a shift; and odd times again looking out on the schooners, hookers, trawlers is sailing the sea, and I thinking on the gallant hairy fellows are drifting beyond, and myself long years living alone.

CHRISTY *(interested)*. You're like me, so.

WIDOW QUIN. I am your like, and it's for that I'm taking a fancy to you, and I with my little houseen above where there'd be myself to tend you, and none to ask were you a murderer or what at all.

CHRISTY. And what would I be doing if I left Pegeen?

WIDOW QUIN. I've nice jobs you could be doing, gathering shells to make a whitewash for our hut within, building up a little goose-house, or stretching a new skin on an old curragh I have, and if my hut is far from all sides, it's there you'll meet the wisest old men, I tell you, at the corner of my wheel, and it's there yourself and me will have great times whispering and hugging....

VOICES *(outside, calling far away)*. Christy! Christy Mahon! Christy!

CHRISTY. Is it Pegeen Mike?

WIDOW QUIN. It's the young girls, I'm thinking, coming to bring you to the sports below, and what is it you'll have me to tell them now?

CHRISTY. Aid me for to win Pegeen. It's herself only that I'm seeking now. *(Widow Quin gets up and goes to window.)* Aid me for to win her, and I'll be asking God to stretch a hand to you in the hour of death, and lead you short cuts through the Meadows of Ease, and up the floor of Heaven to the Footstool of the Virgin's Son.

WIDOW QUIN. There's praying.

VOICES *(nearer)*. Christy! Christy Mahon!

CHRISTY *(with agitation)*. They're coming. Will you swear to aid and save me for the love of Christ?

WIDOW QUIN *(looks at him for a moment)*. If I aid you, will you swear to give me a right of way I want, and a mountainy ram, and a load of dung at Michaelmas, the time that you'll be master here?

CHRISTY. I will, by the elements and stars of night.

WIDOW QUIN. Then we'll not say a word of the old fellow, the way Pegeen won't know your story till the end of time.

CHRISTY. And if he chances to return again?

WIDOW QUIN. We'll swear he's a maniac and not your da. I could take an oath I seen him raving on the sands to-day.

[*Girls run in.*]

SUSAN. Come on to the sports below. Pegeen says you're to come.

SARA. The lepping's beginning, and we've a jockey's suit to fit upon you for the mule race on the sands below.

HONOR. Come on, will you?

CHRISTY. I will then if Pegeen's beyond.

SARA. She's in the boreen making game of Shaneen Keogh.

CHRISTY. Then I'll be going to her now.

[*He runs out followed by the girls.*]

WIDOW QUIN. Well, if the worst comes in the end of all, it'll be great game to see there's none to pity him but a widow woman, the like of me, has buried her children and destroyed her man.

[*She goes out.*]

CURTAIN

Act III

SCENE, as before. Later in the day. Jimmy comes in, slightly drunk.

JIMMY *(calls)*. Pegeen! *(Crosses to inner door.)* Pegeen Mike! *(Comes back again into the room.)* Pegeen! *(Philly comes in in the same state.)* *(To Philly.)* Did you see herself?

PHILLY. I did not; but I sent Shawn Keogh with the ass cart for to bear him home. *(Trying cupboards which are locked.)* Well, isn't he a nasty man to get into such staggers at a morning wake? and isn't herself the divil's daughter for locking, and she so fussy after that young gaffer, you might take your death with drought and none to heed you?

JIMMY. It's little wonder she'd be fussy, and he after bringing bankrupt ruin on the roulette man, and the trick-o'-the-loop man, and breaking the nose of the cockshot-man, and winning all in the sports below, racing, lepping, dancing, and the Lord knows what! He's right luck, I'm telling you.

PHILLY. If he has, he'll be rightly hobbled yet, and he not able to say ten words without making a brag of the way he killed his father, and the great blow he hit with the loy.

JIMMY. A man can't hang by his own informing, and his father should be rotten by now.

[*Old Mahon passes window slowly.*]

PHILLY. Supposing a man's digging spuds in that field with a long spade, and supposing he flings up the two halves of that skull, what'll be said then in the papers and the courts of law?

JIMMY. They'd say it was an old Dane, maybe, was drowned in the flood. *(Old Mahon comes in and sits down near door listening.)* Did you never hear tell of the skulls they have in the city of Dublin, ranged out like blue jugs in a cabin of Connaught?

PHILLY. And you believe that?

JIMMY *(pugnaciously)*. Didn't a lad see them and he after coming from harvesting in the Liverpool boat? "They have them there," says he, "making a show of the great people there was one time walking the world. White skulls and black skulls and yellow skulls, and some with full teeth, and some haven't only but one. "

PHILLY. It was no lie, maybe, for when I was a young lad there was a graveyard beyond the house with the remnants of a man who had thighs as long as your arm. He was a horrid man, I'm telling you, and there was many a fine Sunday I'd put him together for fun, and he with shiny bones, you wouldn't meet the like of these days in the cities of the world.

MAHON *(getting up)*. You wouldn't, is it? Lay your eyes on that skull, and tell me where and when there was another the like of it, is splintered only from the blow of a loy.

PHILLY. Glory be to God! And who hit you at all?

MAHON *(triumphantly)*. It was my own son hit me. Would you believe that?

JIMMY. Well, there's wonders hidden in the heart of man!

PHILLY *(suspiciously)*. And what way was it done?

MAHON *(wandering about the room)*. I'm after walking hundreds and long scores of miles, winning clean beds and the fill of my belly four times in the day, and I doing nothing but telling stories of that naked truth. *(He comes to them a little aggressively.)* Give me a supeen and I'll tell you now.

[*Widow Quin comes in and stands aghast behind him. He is facing Jimmy and Philly, who are on the left.*]

JIMMY. Ask herself beyond. She's the stuff hidden in her shawl.

WIDOW QUIN *(coming to Mahon quickly)*. You here, is it? You didn't go far at all?

MAHON. I seen the coasting steamer passing, and I got a drought upon me and a cramping leg, so I said, "The divil go along with him," and turned again. *(Looking under her shawl.)* And let you give me a supeen, for I'm destroyed travelling since Tuesday was a week.

WIDOW QUIN *(getting a glass, in a cajoling tone)*. Sit down then by the fire and take your ease for a space. You've a right to be destroyed indeed, with your walking, and fighting, and facing the sun *(giving him poteen from a stone jar she has brought in)*. There now is a drink for you, and may it be to your happiness and length of life.

MAHON *(taking glass greedily and sitting down by fire)*. God increase you!

WIDOW QUIN *(taking men to the right stealthily)*. Do you know what? That man's raving from his wound to-day, for I met him a while since telling a rambling tale of a tinker had him destroyed. Then he heard of Christy's deed, and he up and says it was his son had cracked his skull. O isn't madness a fright, for he'll go killing someone yet, and he thinking it's the man has struck him so?

JIMMY *(entirely convinced)*. It's a fright, surely. I knew a party was kicked in the head by a red mare, and he went killing horses a great while, till he eat the insides of a clock and died after.

PHILLY *(with suspicion)*. Did he see Christy?

WIDOW QUIN. He didn't. *(With a warning gesture.)* Let you not be putting him in mind of him, or you'll be likely summoned if there's murder done. *(Looking round at Mahon.)* Whisht! He's listening. Wait now till you hear me taking him easy and unravelling all. *(She goes to Mahon.)* And what way are you feeling, mister? Are you in contentment now?

MAHON *(slightly emotional from his drink)*. I'm poorly only, for it's a hard story the way I'm left to-day, when it was I did tend him from his hour of birth, and he a dunce never reached his second book, the way he'd come from school, manys the day, with his legs lamed under him, and he blackened with his beatings like a tinker's ass. It's a hard story, I'm saying, the way some do have their next and nighest raising up a hand of murder on them, and some is lonesome getting their death with lamentation in the dead of night.

WIDOW QUIN *(not knowing what to say)*. To hear you talking so quiet, who'd know you were the same fellow we seen pass to-day?

MAHON. I'm the same surely. The wrack and ruin of three score years; and it's a terror to live that length, I tell you, and to have your sons going to the dogs against you, and you wore out scolding them, and skelping them, and God knows what.

PHILLY *(to Jimmy)*. He's not raving. *(To Widow Quin.)* Will you ask him what kind was his son?

WIDOW QUIN *(to Mahon, with a peculiar look)*. Was your son that hit you a lad of one year and a score maybe, a great hand at racing and lepping and licking the world?

MAHON *(turning on her with a roar of rage)*. Didn't you hear me say he was the fool of men, the way from this out he'll know the orphan's lot with old and young making game of him and they swearing, raging, kicking at him like a mangy cur.

[*A great burst of cheering outside, some way off.*]

MAHON *(putting his hands to his ears)*. What in the name of God do they want roaring below?

WIDOW QUIN *(with the shade of a smile)*. They're cheering a young lad, the champion Playboy of the Western World.

[*More cheering.*]

MAHON *(going to window)*. It'd split my heart to hear them, and I with pulses in my brain-pan for a week gone by. Is it racing they are?

JIMMY *(looking from door)*. It is then. They are mounting him for the mule race will be run upon the sands. That's the playboy on the winkered mule.

MAHON *(puzzled)*. That lad, is it? If you said it was a fool he was, I'd have laid a mighty oath he was the likeness of my wandering son *(uneasily, putting his hand to his head)*. Faith, I'm thinking I'll go walking for to view the race.

WIDOW QUIN *(stopping him, sharply)*. You will not. You'd best take the road to Belmullet, and not be dilly-dallying in this place where there isn't a spot you could sleep.

PHILLY *(coming forward)*. Don't mind her. Mount there on the bench and you'll have a view of the whole. They're hurrying before the tide will rise, and it'd be near over if you went down the pathway through the crags below.

MAHON *(mounts on bench, Widow Quin beside him)*. That's a right view again the edge of the sea. They're coming now from the point. He's leading. Who is he at all?

WIDOW QUIN. He's the champion of the world, I tell you, and there isn't a hop'orth isn't falling lucky to his hands today.

PHILLY *(looking out, interested in the race)*. Look at that. They're pressing him now.

JIMMY. He'll win it yet.

PHILLY. Take your time, Jimmy Farrell. It's too soon to say.

WIDOW QUIN *(shouting)*. Watch him taking the gate. There's riding.

JIMMY *(cheering)*. More power to the young lad!

MAHON. He's passing the third.

JIMMY. He'll lick them yet!

WIDOW QUIN. He'd lick them if he was running races with a score itself.

MAHON. Look at the mule he has, kicking the stars.

WIDOW QUIN. There was a lep! *(Catching hold of Mahon in her excitement.)* He's fallen! He's mounted again! Faith, he's passing them all!

JIMMY. Look at him skelping her!

PHILLY. And the mountain girls hooshing him on!

JIMMY. It's the last turn! The post's cleared for them now!

MAHON. Look at the narrow place. He'll be into the bogs! *(With a yell.)* Good rider! He's through it again!

JIMMY. He's neck and neck!

MAHON. Good boy to him! Flames, but he's in!

[*Great cheering, in which all join.*]

MAHON *(with hesitation)*. What's that? They're raising him up. They're coming this way. *(With a roar of rage and astonishment.)* It's Christy! by the stars of God! I'd know his way of spitting and he astride the moon.

[*He jumps down and makes for the door, but Widow Quin catches him and pulls him back.*]

WIDOW QUIN. Stay quiet, will you. That's not your son. *(To Jimmy.)* Stop him, or you'll get a month for the abetting of manslaughter and be fined as well.

JIMMY. I'll hold him.

MAHON *(struggling)*. Let me out! Let me out, the lot of you! till I have my vengeance on his head to-day.

WIDOW QUIN *(shaking him, vehemently)*. That's not your son. That's a man is going to make a marriage with the daughter of this house, a place with fine trade, with a license, and with poteen too.

MAHON *(amazed)*. That man marrying a decent and a moneyed girl! Is it mad yous are? Is it in a crazy-house for females that I'm landed now?

WIDOW QUIN. It's mad yourself is with the blow upon your head. That lad is the wonder of the Western World.

MAHON. I seen it's my son.

WIDOW QUIN. You seen that you're mad. *(Cheering outside.)* Do you hear them cheering him in the zig-zags of the road? Aren't you after saying that your son's a fool, and how would they be cheering a true idiot born?

MAHON *(getting distressed)*. It's maybe out of reason that that man's himself. *(Cheering again.)* There's none surely will go cheering him. Oh, I'm raving with a madness that would fright the world! *(He sits down with his hand to his head.)* There was one time I seen ten scarlet divils letting on they'd cork my spirit in a gallon can; and one time I seen rats as big as badgers sucking the life blood from the butt of my lug; but I never till this day confused that dribbling idiot with a likely man. I'm destroyed surely.

WIDOW QUIN. And who'd wonder when it's your brain-pan that is gaping now?

MAHON. Then the blight of the sacred drought upon myself and him, for I never went mad to this day, and I not three weeks with the Limerick girls drinking myself silly, and parlatic from the dusk to dawn. *(To Widow Quin, suddenly.)* Is my visage astray?

WIDOW QUIN. It is then. You're a sniggering maniac, a child could see.

MAHON *(getting up more cheerfully)*. Then I'd best be going to the union beyond, and there'll be a welcome before me, I tell you *(with great pride)*, and I a terrible and fearful case, the way that there I was one time, screeching in a strait-ened waistcoat, with seven doctors writing out my sayings in a printed book. Would you believe that?

WIDOW QUIN. If you're a wonder itself, you'd best be hasty, for them lads caught a maniac one time and pelted the poor creature till he ran out, raving and foaming, and was drowned in the sea.

MAHON *(with philosophy)*. It's true mankind is the divil when your head's astray. Let me out now and I'll slip down the boreen, and not see them so.

WIDOW QUIN *(showing him out)*. That's it. Run to the right, and not a one will see.

[*He runs off.*]

PHILLY *(wisely)*. You're at some gaming, Widow Quin; but I'll walk after him and give him his dinner and a time to rest, and I'll see then if he's raving or as sane as you.

WIDOW QUIN *(annoyed)*. If you go near that lad, let you be wary of your head, I'm saying. Didn't you hear him telling he was crazed at times?

PHILLY. I heard him telling a power; and I'm thinking we'll have right sport, before night will fall.

[*He goes out.*]

JIMMY. Well, Philly's a conceited and foolish man. How could that madman have his senses and his brain-pan slit? I'll go after them and see him turn on Philly now.

[*He goes; Widow Quin hides poteen behind counter. Then hubbub outside.*]

VOICES. There you are! Good jumper! Grand lepper! Darlint boy! He's the racer! Bear him on, will you!

[*Christy comes in, in Jockey's dress, with Pegeen Mike, Sara, and other girls, and men.*]

PEGEEN *(to crowd)*. Go on now and don't destroy him and he drenching with sweat. Go along, I'm saying, and have your tug-of-warring till he's dried his skin.

CROWD. Here's his prizes! A bagpipes! A fiddle was played by a poet in the years gone by! A flat and three-thorned blackthorn would lick the scholars out of Dublin town!

CHRISTY *(taking prizes from the men)*. Thank you kindly, the lot of you. But you'd say it was little only I did this day if you'd seen me a while since striking my one single blow.

TOWN CRIER *(outside, ringing a bell)*. Take notice, last event of this day! Tug-of-warring on the green below! Come on, the lot of you! Great achievements for all Mayo men!

PEGEEN. Go on, and leave him for to rest and dry. Go on, I tell you, for he'll do no more. *(She hustles crowd out; Widow Quin following them.)*

MEN *(going)*. Come on then. Good luck for the while!

PEGEEN (*radiantly, wiping his face with her shawl*). Well, you're the lad, and you'll have great times from this out when you could win that wealth of prizes, and you sweating in the heat of noon!

CHRISTY (*looking at her with delight*). I'll have great times if I win the crowning prize I'm seeking now, and that's your promise that you'll wed me in a fortnight, when our banns is called.

PEGEEN (*backing away from him*). You've right daring to go ask me that, when all knows you'll be starting to some girl in your own townland, when your father's rotten in four months, or five.

CHRISTY (*indignantly*). Starting from you, is it? (*He follows her.*) I will not, then, and when the airs is warming in four months, or five, it's then yourself and me should be pacing Neifin in the dews of night, the times sweet smells do be rising, and you'd see a little shiny new moon, maybe, sinking on the hills.

PEGEEN (*looking at him playfully*). And it's that kind of a poacher's love you'd make, Christy Mahon, on the sides of Neifin, when the night is down?

CHRISTY. It's little you'll think if my love's a poacher's, or an earl's itself, when you'll feel my two hands stretched around you, and I squeezing kisses on your puckered lips, till I'd feel a kind of pity for the Lord God is all ages sitting lonesome in his golden chair.

PEGEEN. That'll be right fun, Christy Mahon, and any girl would walk her heart out before she'd meet a young man was your like for eloquence, or talk, at all.

CHRISTY (*encouraged*). Let you wait, to hear me talking, till we're astray in Erris, when Good Friday's by, drinking a sup from a well, and making mighty kisses with our wetted mouths, or gaming in a gap or sunshine, with yourself stretched back onto your necklace, in the flowers of the earth.

PEGEEN (*in a lower voice, moved by his tone*). I'd be nice so, is it?

CHRISTY (*with rapture*). If the mitred bishops seen you that time, they'd be the like of the holy prophets, I'm thinking, do be straining the bars of Paradise to lay eyes on the Lady Helen of Troy, and she abroad, pacing back and forward, with a nosegay in her golden shawl.

PEGEEN (*with real tenderness*). And what is it I have, Christy Mahon, to make me fitting entertainment for the like of you, that has such poet's talking, and such bravery of heart?

CHRISTY (*in a low voice*). Isn't there the light of seven heavens in your heart alone, the way you'll be an angel's lamp to me from this out, and I abroad in the darkness, spearing salmons in the Owen, or the Carrowmore?

PEGEEN. If I was your wife, I'd be along with you those nights, Christy Mahon, the way you'd see I was a great hand at coaxing bailiffs, or coining funny nick-names for the stars of night.

CHRISTY. You, is it? Taking your death in the hailstones, or in the fogs of dawn.

PEGEEN. Yourself and me would shelter easy in a narrow bush, *(with a qualm of dread)* but we're only talking, maybe, for this would be a poor, thatched place to hold a fine lad is the like of you.

CHRISTY *(putting his arm round her)*. If I wasn't a good Christian, it's on my naked knees I'd be saying my prayers and paters to every jackstraw you have roofing your head, and every stony pebble is paving the laneway to your door.

PEGEEN *(radiantly)*. If that's the truth, I'll be burning candles from this out to the miracles of God that have brought you from the south to-day, and I, with my gowns bought ready, the way that I can wed you, and not wait at all.

CHRISTY. It's miracles, and that's the truth. Me there toiling a long while, and walking a long while, not knowing at all I was drawing all times nearer to this holy day.

PEGEEN. And myself, a girl, was tempted often to go sailing the seas till I'd marry a Jew-man, with ten kegs of gold, and I not knowing at all there was the like of you drawing nearer, like the stars of God.

CHRISTY. And to think I'm long years hearing women talking that talk, to all bloody fools, and this the first time I've heard the like of your voice talking sweetly for my own delight.

PEGEEN. And to think it's me is talking sweetly, Christy Mahon, and I the fright of seven townlands for my biting tongue. Well, the heart's a wonder; and, I'm thinking, there won't be our like in Mayo, for gallant lovers, from this hour, to-day. *(Drunken singing is heard outside.)* There's my father coming from the wake, and when he's had his sleep we'll tell him, for he's peaceful then.

[*They separate.*]

MICHAEL *(singing outside)*.

The jailor and the turnkey
They quickly ran us down,
And brought us back as prisoners
Once more to Cavan town.

[*He comes in supported by Shawn.*]

There we lay bewailing
All in a prison bound....

[*He sees Christy. Goes and shakes him drunkenly by the hand, while Pegeen and Shawn talk on the left.*]

MICHAEL *(to Christy)*. The blessing of God and the holy angels on your head, young fellow. I hear tell you're after winning all in the sports below; and wasn't it a shame I didn't bear you along with me to Kate Cassidy's wake, a fine, stout lad, the like of you, for you'd never see the match of it for flows of drink, the way when we sunk her bones at noonday in her narrow grave, there were five men, aye, and six men, stretched out retching speechless on the holy stones.

CHRISTY *(uneasily, watching Pegeen)*. Is that the truth?

MICHAEL. It is then, and aren't you a louty schemer to go burying your poor father unbeknownst when you'd a right to throw him on the crupper of a Kerry mule and drive him westwards, like holy Joseph in the days gone by, the way we could have given him a decent burial, and not have him rotting beyond, and not a Christian drinking a smart drop to the glory of his soul?

CHRISTY *(gruffly)*. It's well enough he's lying, for the likes of him.

MICHAEL *(slapping him on the back)*. Well, aren't you a hardened slayer? It'll be a poor thing for the household man where you go sniffing for a female wife; and *(pointing to Shawn)* look beyond at that shy and decent Christian I have chosen for my daughter's hand, and I after getting the gilded dispensation this day for to wed them now.

CHRISTY. And you'll be wedding them this day, is it?

MICHAEL *(drawing himself up)*. Aye. Are you thinking, if I'm drunk itself, I'd leave my daughter living single with a little frisky rascal is the like of you?

PEGEEN *(breaking away from Shawn)*. Is it the truth the dispensation's come?

MICHAEL *(triumphantly)*. Father Reilly's after reading it in gallous Latin, and "It's come in the nick of time," says he; "so I'll wed them in a hurry, dreading that young gaffer who'd capsize the stars."

PEGEEN *(fiercely)*. He's missed his nick of time, for it's that lad, Christy Mahon, that I'm wedding now.

MICHAEL *(loudly with horror)*. You'd be making him a son to me, and he wet and crusted with his father's blood?

PEGEEN. Aye. Wouldn't it be a bitter thing for a girl to go marrying the like of Shaneen, and he a middling kind of a scarecrow, with no savagery or fine words in him at all?

MICHAEL *(gasping and sinking on a chair)*. Oh, aren't you a heathen daughter to go shaking the fat of my heart, and I swamped and drownded with the weight of drink? Would you have them turning on me the way that I'd be roaring to the dawn of day with the wind upon my heart? Have you not a word to aid me, Shaneen? Are you not jealous at all?

SHAWN (*in great misery*). I'd be afeard to be jealous of a man did slay his da.

PEGEEN. Well, it'd be a poor thing to go marrying your like. I'm seeing there's a world of peril for an orphan girl, and isn't it a great blessing I didn't wed you, before himself came walking from the west or south?

SHAWN. It's a queer story you'd go picking a dirty tramp up from the highways of the world.

PEGEEN (*playfully*). And you think you're a likely beau to go straying along with, the shiny Sundays of the opening year, when it's sooner on a bullock's liver you'd put a poor girl thinking than on the lily or the rose?

SHAWN. And have you no mind of my weight of passion, and the holy dispensation, and the drift of heifers I am giving, and the golden ring?

PEGEEN. I'm thinking you're too fine for the like of me, Shawn Keogh of Killakeen, and let you go off till you'd find a radiant lady with droves of bullocks on the plains of Meath, and herself bedizened in the diamond jewelleries of Pharaoh's ma. That'd be your match, Shaneen. So God save you now!

[*She retreats behind Christy.*]

SHAWN. Won't you hear me telling you ... ?

CHRISTY (*with ferocity*). Take yourself from this, young fellow, or I'll maybe add a murder to my deeds to-day.

MICHAEL (*springing up with a shriek*). Murder is it? Is it mad yous are? Would you go making murder in this place, and it piled with poteen for our drink to-night? Go on to the foreshore if it's fighting you want, where the rising tide will wash all traces from the memory of man.

[*Pushing Shawn towards Christy.*]

SHAWN (*shaking himself free, and getting behind Michael*). I'll not fight him, Michael James. I'd liefer live a bachelor, simmering in passions to the end of time, than face a lepping savage the like of him has descended from the Lord knows where. Strike him yourself, Michael James, or you'll lose my drift of heifers and my blue bull from Sneem.

MICHAEL. Is it me fight him, when it's father-slaying he's bred to now? (*Pushing Shawn.*) Go on you fool and fight him now.

SHAWN (*coming forward a little*). Will I strike him with my hand?

MICHAEL. Take the loy is on your western side.

SHAWN. I'd be afeard of the gallows if I struck him with that.

CHRISTY (*taking up the loy*). Then I'll make you face the gallows or quit off from this.

[*Shawn flies out of the door.*]

CHRISTY. Well, fine weather be after him, *(going to Michael, coaxingly)* and I'm thinking you wouldn't wish to have that quaking blackguard in your house at all. Let you give us your blessing and hear her swear her faith to me, for I'm mounted on the springtide of the stars of luck, the way it'll be good for any to have me in the house.

PEGEEN *(at the other side of Michael)*. Bless us now, for I swear to God I'll wed him, and I'll not renege.

MICHAEL *(standing up in the centre, holding on to both of them)*. It's the will of God, I'm thinking, that all should win an easy or a cruel end, and it's the will of God that ali should rear up lengthy families for the nurture of the earth. What's a single man, I ask you, eating a bit in one house and drinking a sup in another, and he with no place of his own, like an old braying jackass strayed upon the rocks? *(To Christy.)* It's many would be in dread to bring your like into their house for to end them, maybe, with a sudden end; but I'm a decent man of Ireland, and I liefer face the grave untimely and I seeing a score of grandsons growing up little gallant swearers by the name of God, than go peopling my bedside with puny weeds the like of what you'd breed, I'm thinking, out of Shaneen Keogh. *(He joins their hands.)* A daring fellow is the jewel of the world, and a man did split his father's middle with a single clout, should have the bravery of ten, so may God and Mary and St. Patrick bless you, and increase you from this mortal day.

CHRISTY AND PEGEEN. Amen, O Lord!

[*Hubbub outside.*]

[*Old Mahon rushes in, followed by all the crowd, and Widow Quin. He makes a rush at Christy, knocks him down, and begins to beat him.*]

PEGEEN *(dragging back his arm)*. Stop that, will you. Who are you at all?

MAHON. His father, God forgive me!

PEGEEN *(drawing back)*. Is it rose from the dead?

MAHON. Do you think I look so easy quenched with the tap of a loy?

[*Beats Christy again.*]

PEGEEN *(glaring at Christy)*. And it's lies you told, letting on you had him slitted, and you nothing at all.

CHRISTY *(catching Mahon's stick)*. He's not my father. He's a raving maniac would scare the world. *(Pointing to Widow Quin.)* Herself knows it is true.

CROWD. You're fooling Pegeen! The Widow Quin seen him this day, and you likely knew! You're a liar!

CHRISTY (*dumbfounded*). It's himself was a liar, lying stretched out with an open head on him, letting on he was dead.

MAHON. Weren't you off racing the hills before I got my breath with the start I had seeing you turn on me at all?

PEGEEN. And to think of the coaxing glory we had given him, and he after doing nothing but hitting a soft blow and chasing northward in a sweat of fear. Quit off from this.

CHRISTY (*piteously*). You've seen my doings this day, and let you save me from the old man; for why would you be in such a scorch of haste to spur me to destruction now?

PEGEEN. It's there your treachery is spurring me, till I'm hard set to think you're the one I'm after lacing in my heart-strings half-an-hour gone by. (*To Mahon.*) Take him on from this, for I think bad the world should see me raging for a Munster liar, and the fool of men.

MAHON. Rise up now to retribution, and come on with me.

CROWD (*jeeringly*). There's the playboy! There's the lad thought he'd rule the roost in Mayo. Slate him now, mister.

CHRISTY (*getting up in shy terror*). What is it drives you to torment me here, when I'd asked the thunders of the might of God to blast me if I ever did hurt to any saving only that one single blow.

MAHON (*loudly*). If you didn't, you're a poor good-for-nothing, and isn't it by the like of you the sins of the whole world are committed?

CHRISTY (*raising his hands*). In the name of the Almighty God ...

MAHON. Leave troubling the Lord God. Would you have him sending down droughts, and fevers, and the old hen and the cholera morbus?

CHRISTY (*to Widow Quin*). Will you come between us and protect me now?

WIDOW QUIN. I've tried a lot, God help me, and my share is done.

CHRISTY (*looking round in desperation*). And I must go back into my torment is it, or run off like a vagabond straying through the Unions with the dusts of August making mudstains in the gullet of my throat, or the winds of March blowing on me till I'd take an oath I felt them making whistles of my ribs within?

SARA. Ask Pegeen to aid you. Her like does often change.

CHRISTY. I will not then, for there's torment in the splendour of her like, and she a girl any moon of midnight would take pride to meet, facing southwards on the heaths of Keel. But what did I want crawling forward to scorch my understanding at her flaming brow?

PEGEEN (*to Mahon, vehemently, fearing she will break into tears*). Take him on from this or I'll set the young lads to destroy him here.

MAHON (*going to him, shaking his stick*). Come on now if you wouldn't have the company to see you skelped.

PEGEEN (*half laughing, through her tears*). That's it, now the world will see him pandied, and he an ugly liar was playing off the hero, and the fright of men.

CHRISTY (*to Mahon, very sharply*). Leave me go!

CROWD. That's it. Now Christy. If them two set fighting, it will lick the world.

MAHON (*making a grab at Christy*). Come here to me.

CHRISTY (*more threateningly*). Leave me go, I'm saying.

MAHON. I will maybe, when your legs is limping, and your back is blue.

CROWD. Keep it up, the two of you. I'll back the old one. Now the playboy.

CHRISTY (*in low and intense voice*). Shut your yelling, for if you're after making a mighty man of me this day by the power of a lie, you're setting me now to think if it's a poor thing to be lonesome, it's worse maybe to go mixing with the fools of earth.

[*Mahon makes a movement towards him.*]

CHRISTY (*almost shouting*). Keep off... lest I do show a blow unto the lot of you would set the guardian angels winking in the clouds above.

[*He swings round with a sudden rapid movement and picks up a loy.*]

CROWD (*half frightened, half amused*). He's going mad! Mind yourselves! Run from the idiot!

CHRISTY. If I am an idiot, I'm after hearing my voice this day saying words would raise the topknot on a poet in a merchant's town. I've won your racing, and your lepping, and ...

MAHON. Shut your gullet and come on with me.

CHRISTY. I'm going, but I'll stretch you first.

[*He runs at old Mahon with the loy, chases him out of the door, followed by crowd and Widow Quin. There is a great noise outside, then a yell, and dead silence for a moment. Christy comes in, half dazed, and goes to fire.*]

WIDOW QUIN (*coming in, hurriedly, and going to him*). They're turning again you. Come on, or you'll be hanged, indeed.

CHRISTY. I'm thinking, from this out, Pegeen'll be giving me praises the same as in the hours gone by.

WIDOW QUIN (*impatiently*). Come by the back-door. I'd think bad to have you stifled on the gallows tree.

CHRISTY (*indignantly*). I will not, then. What good'd be my life-time, if I left

Pegeen?

WIDOW QUIN. Come on, and you'll be no worse than you were last night and you with a double murder this time to be telling to the girls.

CHRISTY. I'll not leave Pegeen Mike.

WIDOW QUIN *(impatiently)*. Isn't there the match of her in every parish public, from Binghamstown unto the plain of Meath? Come on, I tell you, and I'll find you finer sweethearts at each waning moon.

CHRISTY. It's Pegeen I'm seeking only, and what'd I care if you brought me a drift of chosen females, standing in their shifts itself, maybe, from this place to the Eastern World?

SARA *(runs in, pulling off one of her petticoats)*. They're going to hang him. *(Holding out petticoat and shawl.)* Fit these upon him, and let him run off to the east.

WIDOW QUIN. He's raving now; but we'll fit them on him, and I'll take him, in the ferry, to the Achill boat.

CHRISTY *(struggling feebly)*. Leave me go, will you? when I'm thinking of my luck to-day, for she will wed me surely, and I a proven hero in the end of all.

[*They try to fasten petticoat round him.*]

WIDOW QUIN. Take his left hand, and we'll pull him now. Come on, young fellow.

CHRISTY *(suddenly starting up)*. You'll be taking me from her? You're jealous, is it, of her wedding me? Go on from this.

[*He snatches up a stool, and threatens them with it.*]

WIDOW QUIN *(going)*. It's in the mad-house they should put him, not in jail, at all. We'll go by the back-door, to call the doctor, and we'll save him so.

[*She goes out, with Sara, through inner room. Men crowd in the doorway. Christy sits down again by the fire.*]

MICHAEL *(in a terrified whisper)*. Is the old lad killed surely?

PHILLY. I'm after feeling the last gasps quitting his heart.

[*They peer in at Christy.*]

MICHAEL *(with a rope)*. Look at the way he is. Twist a hangman's knot on it, and slip it over his head, while he's not minding at all.

PHILLY. Let you take it, Shaneen. You're the soberest of all that's here.

SHAWN. Is it me to go near him, and he the wickedest and worst with me? Let you take it, Pegeen Mike.

PEGEEN. Come on, so.

[*She goes forward with the others, and they drop the double hitch over his head.*]

CHRISTY. What ails you?

SHAWN *(triumphantly, as they pull the rope tight on his arms).* Come on to the peelers, till they stretch you now.

CHRISTY. Me!

MICHAEL. If we took pity on you, the Lord God would, maybe, bring us ruin from the law to-day, so you'd best come easy, for hanging is an easy and a speedy end.

CHRISTY. I'll not stir. *(To Pegeen.)* And what is it you'll say to me, and I after doing it this time in the face of all?

PEGEEN. I'll say, a strange man is a marvel, with his mighty talk; but what's a squabble in your back-yard, and the blow of a loy, have taught me that there's a great gap between a gallous story and a dirty deed. *(To Men.)* Take him on from this, or the lot of us will be likely put on trial for his deed to-day.

CHRISTY *(with horror in his voice).* And it's yourself will send me off, to have a horny-fingered hangman hitching his bloody slip-knots at the butt of my car.

MEN *(pulling rope).* Come on, will you?

[*He is pulled down on the floor.*]

CHRISTY *(twisting his legs round the table).* Cut the rope, Pegeen, and I'll quit the lot of you, and live from this out, like the madmen of Keel, eating muck and green weeds, on the faces of the cliffs.

PEGEEN. And leave us to hang, is it, for a saucy liar, the like of you? *(To Men.)* Take him on, out from this.

SHAWN. Pull a twist on his neck, and squeeze him so.

PHILLY. Twist yourself. Sure he cannot hurt you, if you keep your distance from his teeth alone.

SHAWN. I'm afeard of him. *(To Pegeen.)* Lift a lighted sod, will you, and scorch his leg.

PEGEEN *(blowing the fire, with a bellows).* Leave go now, young fellow, or I'll scorch your shins.

CHRISTY. You're blowing for to torture me. *(His voice rising and growing stronger.)* That's your kind, is it? Then let the lot of you be wary, for, if I've to face the gallows, I'll have a gay march down, I tell you, and shed the blood of some of you before I die.

SHAWN *(in terror).* Keep a good hold, Philly. Be wary, for the love of God. For I'm thinking he would liefest wreak his pains on me.

CHRISTY *(almost gaily).* If I do lay my hands on you, it's the way you'll be at the fall of night, hanging as a scarecrow for the fowls of hell. Ah, you'll have a gallous jaunt I'm saying, coaching out through Limbo with my father's ghost.

SHAWN *(to Pegeen)*. Make haste, will you? Oh, isn't he a holy terror, and isn't it true for Father Reilly, that all drink's a curse that has the lot of you so shaky and uncertain now?

CHRISTY. If I can wring a neck among you, I'll have a royal judgment looking on the trembling jury in the courts of law. And won't there be crying out in Mayo the day I'm stretched upon the rope with ladies in their silks and satins snivelling in their lacy kerchiefs, and they rhyming songs and ballads on the terror of my fate?

[*He squirms round on the floor and bites Shawn's leg.*]

SHAWN *(shrieking)*. My leg's bit on me. He's the like of a mad dog, I'm thinking, the way that I will surely die.

CHRISTY *(delighted with himself)*. You will then, the way you can shake out hell's flags of welcome for my coming in two weeks or three, for I'm thinking Satan hasn't many have killed their da in Kerry, and in Mayo too.

[*Old Mahon comes in behind on all fours and looks on unnoticed.*]

MEN *(to Pegeen)*. Bring the sod, will you?

PEGEEN *(Coming over)*. God help him so. *(Burns his leg.)*

CHRISTY *(kicking and screaming)*. O, glory be to God!

[*He kicks loose from the table, and they all drag him towards the door.*]

JIMMY *(seeing old Mahon)*. Will you look what's come in?

[*They all drop Christy and run left.*]

CHRISTY *(scrambling on his knees face to face with old Mahon)*. Are you coming to be killed a third time, or what ails you now?

MAHON. For what is it they have you tied?

CHRISTY. They're taking me to the peelers to have me hanged for slaying you.

MICHAEL *(apologetically)*. It is the will of God that all should guard their little cabins from the treachery of law, and what would my daughter be doing if I was ruined or was hanged itself?

MAHON *(grimly, loosening Christy)*. It's little I care if you put a bag on her back, and went picking cockles till the hour of death; but my son and myself will be going our own way, and we'll have great times from this out telling stories of the villainy of Mayo, and the fools is here. *(To Christy, who is freed.)* Come on now.

CHRISTY. Go with you, is it? I will then, like a gallant captain with his heathen slave. Go on now and I'll see you from this day stewing my oatmeal and washing my spuds, for I'm master of all fights from now. *(Pushing Mahon.)* Go on, I'm saying.

MAHON. Is it me?

CHRISTY. Not a word out of you. Go on from this.

MAHON *(walking out and looking back at Christy over his shoulder)*. Glory be to God! *(With a broad smile.)* I am crazy again!

[*Goes.*]

CHRISTY. Ten thousand blessings upon all that's here, for you've turned me a likely gaffer in the end of all, the way I'll go romancing through a romping lifetime from this hour to the dawning of the judgment day.

[*He goes out.*]

MICHAEL. By the will of God, we'll have peace now for our drinks. Will you draw the porter, Pegeen?

SHAWN *(going up to her)*. It's a miracle Father Reilly can wed us in the end of all, and we'll have none to trouble us when his vicious bite is healed.

PEGEEN *(hitting him a box on the ear)*. Quit my sight. *(Putting her shawl over her head and breaking out into wild lamentations.)* Oh my grief, I've lost him surely. I've lost the only Playboy of the Western World.

CURTAIN

JAMES JOYCE

(1882-1941)

At just twenty-three years of age, James Joyce, in 1905, sent some short stories to George Russell, the editor of the agricultural newspaper, *The Irish Homestead*, hoping to see them published. Referred to as the "pig's paper," since crop and cattle prices were listed within its pages, Russell was interested in publishing stories that reflected the life of Irish people and was offering payment of one pound per story. Joyce submitted a dozen stories, three of which appeared in the farmer's newspaper before Russell began to realize he had a problem on his hands. Some of the stories chronicled crucial adolescent episodes of life in Dublin and were considered sexually provocative for the times. The social issues addressed by the young author, Russell concluded, were too confrontational for his "pig's paper" and better left for other literary outlets.

Joyce would take the twelve stories he sent to Russell, and eventually add three more, to the publisher Grant Richards, hoping Richards would see fit to publish them as a collection. In a letter to Richards in 1906, Joyce wrote:

> My intention was to write a chapter of the moral history of my country and I chose Dublin for the scene because that city seemed to me the center of paralysis. I have tried to present it to the indifferent public under four of its aspects: childhood, adolescence, maturity and public life. The stories are arranged in this order. I have written it for the most part in a style of scrupulous meanness and with the conviction that he is a very bold man who dares to alter in the presentment, still more to deform, whatever he has seen and heard.

After a series of starts and stops, where Richards was concerned with certain passages he found objectionable, particularly in the stories "Two Gallants" and "Grace," the collection was finally published in 1914 as *Dubliners*. The city of

Dublin that Joyce described in his stories was a city spiraling toward ruin and decay, and his depiction of the people was not always flattering. He did not romanticize the poverty prevalent in the city, and he was critical of the Catholic Church as well as the political leadership. Yet there is significance in why the collection is called *Dubliners* and not *Dublin*. "Joyce had ambivalent feelings about the people," according to Michael Barsanti, a Joyce scholar at the Rosenbach Museum and Library in Philadelphia, which is home to the original manuscript of Joyce's *Ulysses*. "The stories reflect his courage in criticizing the people of his town."

In a letter to Richards before the publication of *Dubliners*, Joyce made it clear why his often-harsh descriptions of the people of Dublin were necessary. "It is not my fault that the odour of ashpits and old weeds and offal hangs round my stories," he wrote. "I seriously believe that you will retard the course of civilization in Ireland by preventing the Irish people from having one good look at themselves in my nicely polished looking-glass."

Not surprisingly, many Irish did not appreciate the genius of James Joyce at the time *Dubliners* came out. The work was initially received as insulting to the people of Dublin, and not long after the book was released, Joyce would ultimately exile himself from Ireland and never return. From Zurich, Switzerland, he would soon establish himself as the most influential novelist of the 20th century, but his relationship with his native country would be strained, to say the least.

Born in Rathgar, a suburb of Dublin, on February 2, 1882, James Augustine Aloysius Joyce was raised in an upper-middle class environment in a family of merchants. With a bloodline that connected him to Irish nobility, Joyce's father John was an Irish Catholic patriot whose complex character works his way into two of Joyce's most prolific novels, *A Portrait of the Artist as a Young Man* and *Ulysses*. However, Joyce's father is every bit as prevalent in *Dubliners*, as John Joyce struggled with alcoholism and unemployment, as well as the family's finances. While the young Joyce was sent away to the prestigious Clongowes Wood College, a highly regarded Jesuit institution in preparation for what his parents hoped would be a life serving the Catholic Church, his father continued to plunge the family further and further down the social ladder. Clongowes Wood College also figures prominently in *A Portrait of the Artist as a Young Man*, and was instrumental in setting the wheels of disillusionment with Catholicism in motion for Joyce.

He soon enrolled at Dublin University College, where he studied language and philosophy, and he became increasingly critical of the political and religious structure of Ireland. In 1902, the twenty-year-old Joyce left Dublin for Paris, with the purported intent of studying medicine there, but instead he took up work as a journalist and teacher and existed in dire financial conditions for a year when he received a telegram informing him that his mother, Mary Jane Murray, was near death. Joyce returned to Dublin where many scholars believe his final denouncement of Catholicism occurred.

Some accounts have him refusing to kneel at his mother's deathbed, a symbolic gesture that is more likely myth than fact.

Joyce remained in Dublin for a while after his mother's death, then set off for Austria-Hungary and Italy with a chambermaid by the name of Nora Barnacle, a woman he would marry in 1931. The two lived in Trieste, where Nora gave birth to Joyce's son, Giorgio in 1905, but the family existed in near poverty while Joyce attempted to write. A collection of poems he'd been writing since his college days finallyappeared as *Chamber Music* in 1907, and it was in Trieste that Joyce wrote most of *Dubliners*, with which he would journey to Ireland in 1909 hoping to see it published. Once in Dublin, he attempted to run a cinema, but this enterprise failed, and he returned to Trieste, penniless and still without a publisher for his collection of short stories.

By 1914, Joyce now had a daughter, Lucia (born in 1907), and *Dubliners* finally came out in London. Ironically, the accomplishment of this collection was eclipsed, in part because of the delay in finding a publisher. So detailed were the characters in his stories that printers worried about libel. They saw words such as "bloody" and it was shocking to them at the time. In 1915, *A Portrait of the Artist as a Young Man* was released as a single volume, and the semi-autobiographical depiction of Stephen Dedalus and the experimental stream-of-consciousness narrative style attracted more attention than his more simply devised *Dubliners*. Yet the style and narration in *Dubliners* is powerful and every bit as meticulous.

Stories such as "Araby," "The Sisters" and "The Dead" are as rich as any stories written in the English language, and are not merely studied because of their readability in relation to Joyce's later works.

"Joyce felt that the Irish were too focused on their past and not attentive to their lives in the present," Barsanti says. "He was unrelenting in his details of Irish life. There are no insignificant details in *Dubliners*. He used a lot of symbolism and the book is meant to be read that way."

Indeed, religious artifacts and rusty bicycles take on significant meaning in many of the stories, and Joyce dwells on themes of stagnation and paralysis as characteristics not only confined to the city of Dublin, but of its inhabitants themselves. Following the publication of *Dubliners* and *Portrait*, Joyce, encouraged by

Ezra Pound, began writing *Ulysses*, the novel that would immediately lead to Joyce being declared a literary genius.

Despite living abroad, in self-imposed exile, in cities such as Trieste, Paris and Zurich, the novel is every bit as detailed in its depiction of Dublin as *Dubliners* itself, even though Joyce was already becoming blind from the effects of glaucoma. Halfway through writing *Ulysses*, Joyce endured the first of nearly a dozen eye operations. At one point, Joyce was so disappointed with the book that he tossed the manuscript into the fire, but Nora immediately retrieved it before it burned.

Ulysses was, upon publication, banned in both Britain and the United States because of obscenity issues, and it would be more than a dozen years before the novel was legalized. Still, Joyce's literary career was far from in peril as he spent the time writing *Finnegan's Wake*, his most complex novel by far, and one deemed so experimental and modern, Joyce invented his own language. Were it not for his detailed explanatory notes, which were ultimately recovered, it would probably have been impossible to read. The novel, published in 1939, was a critical failure, and what literary prestige he had built following the release of *Ulysses* began to fade after *Finnegan's Wake*.

Two years after the publication of *Finnegan's Wake*, Joyce died in Zurich at the age of 58. It wasn't until after his death that his literary genius became fully appreciated again, and his rich body of work continues to be studied with enthusiasm and wonder. "The only demand I make of my reader," Joyce once said in an interview, "is that he should devote his whole life to reading my works."

Indeed, the city of Dublin has commercially embraced James Joyce, despite the city's initial reaction to the publication of *Dubliners* in 1914.

Initially, Joyce's widow Nora did not want any of her husband's manuscripts held in any Irish museums because she felt that Ireland did not understand his work. But with the 1993 issue of an Irish ten-pound note featuring the portrait of James Joyce, it was clear that time had healed many wounds.

"Physically, many parts of the city have been preserved simply because Joyce mentions them in his work," says Barsanti. "So his effect on the city is real."

DUBLINERS

♣

The Sisters

There was no hope for him this time: it was the third stroke. Night after night I had passed the house (it was vacation time) and studied the lighted square of window: and night after night I had found it lighted in the same way, faintly and evenly. If he was dead, I thought, I would see the reflection of candles on the darkened blind for I knew that two candles must be set at the head of a corpse. He had often said to me: "I am not long for this world," and I had thought his words idle. Now I knew they were true. Every night as I gazed up at the window I said softly to myself the word *paralysis*. It had always sounded strangely in my ears, like the word *gnomon* in the Euclid and the word *simony* in the Catechism. But now it sounded to me like the name of some maleficent and sinful being. It filled me with fear, and yet I longed to be nearer to it and to look upon its deadly work.

Old Cotter was sitting at the fire, smoking, when I came downstairs to supper. While my aunt was ladling out my stirabout he said, as if returning to some former remark of his:

"No, I wouldn't say he was exactly … but there was something queer … there was something uncanny about him. I'll tell you my opinion …"

He began to puff at his pipe, no doubt arranging his opinion in his mind. Tiresome old fool! When we knew him first he used to be rather interesting, talking of faints and worms; but I soon grew tired of him and his endless stories about the distillery.

"I have my own theory about it," he said. "I think it was one of those … peculiar cases … But it's hard to say…"

He began to puff again at his pipe without giving us his theory. My uncle saw me staring and said to me:

"Well, so your old friend is gone, you'll be sorry to hear."

"Who?" said I.

"Father Flynn."

"Is he dead?"

"Mr. Cotter here has just told us. He was passing by the house."

I knew that I was under observation so I continued eating as if the news had not interested me. My uncle explained to old Cotter.

"The youngster and he were great friends. The old chap taught him a great deal, mind you; and they say he had a great wish for him."

"God have mercy on his soul," said my aunt piously.

Old Cotter looked at me for a while. I felt that his little beady black eyes were examining me but I would not satisfy him by looking up from my plate. He returned to his pipe and finally spat rudely into the grate.

"I wouldn't like children of mine," he said, "to have too much to say to a man like that."

"How do you mean, Mr. Cotter?" asked my aunt.

"What I mean is," said old Cotter, "it's bad for children. My idea is: let a young lad run about and play with young lads of his own age and not be ... Am I right, Jack?"

"That's my principle, too," said my uncle. "Let him learn to box his corner. That's what I'm always saying to that Rosicrucian there: take exercise. Why, when I was a nipper every morning of my life I had a cold bath, winter and summer. And that's what stands to me now. Education is all very fine and large ... Mr. Cotter might take a pick of that leg of mutton," he added to my aunt.

"No, no, not for me," said old Cotter.

My aunt brought the dish from the safe and put it on the table.

"But why do you think it's not good for children, Mr. Cotter?" she asked.

"It's bad for children," said old Cotter, "because their minds are so impressionable. When children see things like that, you know, it has an effect ..."

I crammed my mouth with stirabout for fear I might give utterance to my anger. Tiresome old red-nosed imbecile!

It was late when I fell asleep. Though I was angry with old Cotter for alluding to me as a child, I puzzled my head to extract meaning from his unfinished sentences. In the dark of my room I imagined that I saw again the heavy grey face of the paralytic. I drew the blankets over my head and tried to think of Christmas. But the grey face still followed me. It murmured; and I understood that it desired to confess something. I felt my soul receding into some pleasant and vicious region; and there again I found it waiting for me. It began to confess to me in a murmuring voice and I wondered why it smiled continually and why the lips were so moist with spittle. But then I remembered that it had died of paralysis and I felt that I too was smiling feebly as if to absolve the simoniac of his sin.

The next morning after breakfast I went down to look at the little house in

Great Britain Street. It was an unassuming shop, registered under the vague name of *Drapery*. The drapery consisted mainly of children's bootees and umbrellas; and on ordinary days a notice used to hang in the window, saying: *Umbrellas Re-covered.* No notice was visible now for the shutters were up. A crape bouquet was tied to the door-knocker with ribbon. Two poor women and a telegram boy were reading the card pinned on the crape. I also approached and read:

July 1st, 1895
The Rev. James Flynn (formerly of S. Catherine's Church,
Meath Street), aged sixty-five years.
R. I. P.

The reading of the card persuaded me that he was dead and I was disturbed to find myself at check. Had he not been dead I would have gone into the little dark room behind the shop to find him sitting in his am-chair by the fire, nearly smothered in his great-coat. Perhaps my aunt would have given me a packet of High Toast for him and this present would have roused him from his stupefied doze. It was always I who emptied the packet into his black snuff-box for his hands trembled too much to allow him to do this without spilling half the snuff about the floor. Even as he raised his large trembling hand to his nose little clouds of smoke dribbled through his fingers over the front of his coat. It may have been these constant showers of snuff which gave his ancient priestly garments their green faded look for the red handkerchief, blackened, as it always was, with the snuff-stains of a week, with which he tried to brush away the fallen grains, was quite inefficacious.

I wished to go in and look at him but I had not the courage to knock. I walked away slowly along the sunny side of the street, reading all the theatrical advertisements in the shop-windows as I went. I found it strange that neither I nor the day seemed in a mourning mood and I felt even annoyed at discovering in myself a sensation of freedom as if I had been freed from something by his death. I wondered at this for, as my uncle had said the night before, he had taught me a great deal. He had studied in the Irish college in Rome and he had taught me to pronounce Latin properly. He had told me stories about the catacombs and about Napoleon Bonaparte, and he had explained to me the meaning of the different ceremonies of the Mass and of the different vestments worn by the priest. Sometimes he had amused himself by putting difficult questions to me, asking me what one should do in certain circumstances or whether such and such sins were mortal or venial or only imperfections. His questions showed me how complex and mysterious were certain institutions of the Church which I had always regarded as the simplest acts. The duties of the priest towards the Eucharist and towards the secrecy of the confessional seemed so grave to me that I wondered how anybody bad ever found in himself the courage to undertake them; and I was not surprised when he told me that the fathers of the Church had written books as thick as the *Post Office Directory* and as closely printed as the law notices in the newspaper, elucidating all these intricate questions. Often when I thought of this I could make no answer or only a very foolish and halting one upon which he used to smile and nod his head twice or thrice. Sometimes he used to put me through the responses of the Mass which he had made me learn by heart; and, as I pattered, he used to smile pensively and nod his head, now and then pushing huge pinches of snuff up each nostril alternately. When he smiled he used to uncover his big discoloured teeth and let his tongue lie upon his lower lip—a habit which had made me feel uneasy in the beginning of our acquaintance before I knew him well.

As I walked along in the sun I remembered old Cotter's words and tried to remember what had happened afterwards in the dream. I remembered that I had noticed long velvet curtains and a swinging lamp of antique fashion. I felt that I had been very far away, in some land where the customs were strange—in Persia, I thought … But I could not remember the end of the dream.

In the evening my aunt took me with her to visit the house of mourning. It was after sunset; but the windowpanes of the houses that looked to the west reflected the tawny gold of a great bank of clouds. Nannie received us in the hall; and, as it would have been unseemly to have shouted at her, my aunt shook hands with her for all. The old woman pointed upwards interrogatively and, on my aunt's nodding, proceeded to toil up the narrow staircase before us, her bowed head being scarcely above the level of the banister-rail. At the first landing she stopped and beckoned us forward encouragingly towards the open door of the dead-room. My aunt went in and the old woman, seeing that I hesitated to enter, began to beckon to me again repeatedly with her hand.

I went in on tiptoe. The room through the lace end of the blind was suffused with dusky golden light amid which the candles looked like pale thin flames. He had been coffined. Nannie gave the lead and we three knelt down at the foot of the bed. I pretended to pray but I could not gather my thoughts because the old woman's mutterings distracted me. I noticed how clumsily her skirt was hooked at the back and how the heels of her cloth boots were trodden down all to one side. The fancy came to me that the old priest was smiling as he lay there in his coffin.

But no. When we rose and went up to the head of the bed I saw that he was not smiling. There he lay, solemn and copious, vested as for the altar, his large hands loosely retaining a chalice. His face was very truculent, grey and massive, with black cavernous nostrils and circled by a scanty white fur. There was a heavy odour in the room—the flowers.

We crossed ourselves and came away. In the little room downstairs we found Eliza seated in his arm-chair in state. I groped my way towards my usual chair in the corner while Nannie went to the sideboard and brought out a decanter of sherry and some wine-glasses. She set these on the table and invited us to take a little glass of wine. Then, at her sister's bidding, she poured out the sherry into the glasses and passed them to us. She pressed me to take some cream crackers also but I declined because I thought I would make too much noise eating them. She seemed to be somewhat disappointed at my refusal and went over quietly to the sofa where she sat down behind her sister. No one spoke: we all gazed at the empty fireplace.

My aunt waited until Eliza sighed and then said:

"Ah, well, he's gone to a better world."

Eliza sighed again and bowed her head in assent. My aunt fingered the stem of her wine-glass before sipping a little.

"Did he … peacefully?" she asked.

"Oh, quite peacefully, ma'am," said Eliza. "You couldn't tell when the breath went out of him. He had a beautiful death, God be praised."

"And everything … ?"

"Father O'Rourke was in with him a Tuesday and anointed him and prepared him and all."

"He knew then?"

"He was quite resigned."

"He looks quite resigned," said my aunt.

"That's what the woman we had in to wash him said. She said he just looked as if he was asleep, he looked that peaceful and resigned. No one would think he'd make such I beautiful corpse."

"Yes, indeed," said my aunt.

She sipped a little more from her glass, and said:

"Well, Miss Flynn, at any rate it must be a great comfort for you to know that you did all you could for him. You were both very kind to him, I must say."

Eliza smoothed her dress over her knees.

"Ah, poor James!" she said. "God knows we done all we could, as poor as we are—we wouldn't see him want anything while he was in it."

Nannie had leaned her head against the sofa-pillow and seemed about to fall asleep.

"There's poor Nannie," said Eliza, looking at her, "she's wore out. All the work we had, she and me, getting in the woman to wash him and then laying him out and then the coffin and then arranging about the Mass in the chapel. Only for Father O'Rourke I don't know what we'd done at all. It was him brought us all them flowers and them two candlesticks out of the chapel and wrote out the notice for the *Freeman's General* and took charge of all the papers for the cemetery and poor James's insurance."

"Wasn't that good of him?" said my aunt.

Eliza closed her eyes and shook her head slowly.

"Ah, there's no friends like the old friends," she said, "when all is said and done, no friends that a body can trust."

"Indeed, that's true," said my aunt. "And I'm sure now that he's gone to his eternal reward he won't forget you and all your kindness to him."

"Ah, poor James!" said Eliza. "He was no great trouble to us. You wouldn't hear him in the house any more than now. Still, I know he's gone and all to that …"

"It's when it's all over that you'll miss him," said my aunt.

"I know that," said Eliza. "I won't be bringing him in his cup of beef-tea any more, nor you, ma'am, sending him his snuff. Ah, poor James!"

She stopped, as if she were communing with the past and then said shrewdly:

"Mind you, I noticed there was something queer coming over him latterly. Whenever I'd bring in his soup to him there I'd find him with his breviary fallen to the floor, lying back in the chair and his mouth open."

She laid a finger against her nose and frowned: then she continued:

"But still and all he kept on saying that before the summer was over he'd go out for a drive one fine day just to see the old house again where we were all born down in Irishtown and take me and Nannie with him. If we could only get one of them new-fangled carriages that makes no noise that Father O'Rourke told him about, them with the rheumatic wheels, for the day cheap, he said, at Johnny Rush's over the way there and drive out the three of us together of a Sunday evening. He had his mind set on that … Poor James!"

"The Lord have mercy on his soul!" said my aunt.

Eliza took out her handkerchief and wiped her eyes with it. Then she put it back again in her pocket and gazed into the empty grate for some time without speaking.

"He was too scrupulous always," she said. "The duties of the priesthood was too much for him. And then his life was, you might say, crossed."

"Yes," said my aunt. "He was a disappointed man. You could see that."

A silence took possession of the little room and, under cover of it, I approached the table and tasted my sherry and then returned quietly to my chair in the corner. Eliza seemed to have fallen into a deep revery. We waited respectfully for her to break the silence: and after a long pause she said slowly:

"It was that chalice he broke … That was the beginning of it. Of course, they say it was all right, that it contained nothing, I mean. But still … They say it was the boy's fault. But poor James was so nervous. God be merciful to him!"

"And was that it?" said my aunt. "I heard something …"

Eliza nodded.

"That affected his mind," she said. "After that he began to mope by himself, talking to no one and wandering about by himself. So one night he was wanted for to go on a call and they couldn't find him anywhere. They looked high up and low down; and still they couldn't see a sight of him anywhere. So then the clerk suggested to try the chapel. So then they got the keys and opened the chapel and the clerk and Father O'Rourke and another priest that was there brought in a light for to look for him… And what do you think but there he was, sitting up by himself in the dark in his confession-box, wide-awake and laughing-like softly to himself?"

She stopped suddenly as if to listen. I too listened; but there was no sound in the house: and I knew that the old priest was lying still in his coffin as we had seen him, solemn and truculent in death, an idle chalice on his breast.

Eliza resumed:

"Wide-awake and laughing-like to himself … So then, of course, when they saw that, that made them think that there was something gone wrong with him …"

An Encounter

It was Joe Dillon who introduced the Wild West to us. Joe had a little library made up of old numbers of *The Union Jack, Pluck* and *The Halfpenny Marvel.* Every evening after school we met in his back garden and arranged Indian battles. He and his fat young brother Leo, the idler, held the loft of the stable while we tried to carry it by storm; or we fought a pitched battle on the grass. But, however well we fought, we never won siege or battle and all our bouts ended with Joe Dillon's war dance of victory. His parents went to eight-o'clock mass every morning in Gardiner Street and the peaceful odour of Mrs. Dillon was prevalent in the hall of the house. But he played too fiercely for us who were younger and more timid. He looked like some kind of an Indian when he capered round the garden, an old tea-cosy on his head, beating a tin with his fist and yelling:

"Ya! yaka, yaka, yaka!"

Everyone was incredulous when it was reported that he had a vocation for the priesthood. Nevertheless it was true.

A spirit of unruliness diffused itself among us and, under its influence differences of culture and constitution were waived. We banded ourselves together, some boldly, some in jest and some almost in fear: and of the number of these latter, the reluctant Indians who were afraid to seem studious or lacking in robustness, I was one. The adventures related in the literature of the Wild West were remote from my nature but, at least, they opened doors of escape. I liked better some American detective stories which were traversed from time to time by unkempt fierce and beautiful girls. Though there was nothing wrong in these stories and though their intention was sometimes literary they were circulated secretly at school. One day when Father Butler was hearing the four pages of Roman History clumsy Leo Dillon was discovered with a copy of *The Halfpenny Marvel*.

"This page or this page? This page? Now, Dillon, up! '*Hardly had the day*' ... Go on! What day? '*Hardly had the day dawned*' ...Have you studied it? What have you there in your pocket?"

Everyone's heart palpitated as Leo Dillon handed up the paper and everyone assumed an innocent face. Father Butler turned over the pages, frowning.

"What is this rubbish?" he said. "*The Apache Chief!* Is this what you read instead of studying your Roman History? Let me not find any more of this wretched stuff in this college. The man who wrote it, I suppose, was some wretched fellow who writes these things for a drink. I'm surprised at boys like you, educated, reading such stuff. I could understand it if you were ... National School boys. Now, Dillon, I advise you strongly, get at your work or ..."

This rebuke during the sober hours of school paled much of the glory of the Wild West for me and the confused puffy face of Leo Dillon awakened one of my consciences. But when the restraining influence of the school was at a distance I began to hunger again for wild sensations, for the escape which those chronicles of disorder alone seemed to offer me. The mimic warfare of the evening became at last as wearisome to me as the routine of school in the morning because I wanted real adventures to happen to myself. But real adventures, I reflected, do not happen to people who remain at home: they must be sought abroad.

The summer holidays were near at hand when I made up my mind to break out of the weariness of school-life for one day at least. With Leo Dillon and a boy named Mahony I planned a day's miching. Each of us saved up sixpence. We were to meet at ten in the morning on the Canal Bridge. Mahony's big sister was to write an excuse for him and Leo Dillon was to tell his brother to say he was sick. We arranged to go along the Wharf Road until we came to the ships, then to cross in the ferryboat and walk out to see the Pigeon House. Leo Dillon was afraid we might meet Father Butler or someone out of the college; but Mahony asked, very sensibly, what would Father Butler be doing out at the Pigeon House. We were reassured: and I brought the first stage of the plot to an end by collecting sixpence from the other two, at the same time showing them my own sixpence. When we were making the last arrangements on the eve we were all vaguely excited. We shook hands, laughing, and Mahony said:

"Till to-morrow, mates!"

That night I slept badly. In the morning I was first-comer to the bridge as I lived nearest. I hid my books in the long grass near the ashpit at the end of the garden where nobody ever came and hurried along the canal bank. It was a mild sunny morning in the first week of June. I sat up on the coping of the bridge admiring my frail canvas shoes which I had diligently pipeclayed overnight and watching the docile horses pulling a tramload of business people up the hill. All the branches of the tall trees which lined the mall were gay with little light green leaves and the sunlight slanted through them on to the water. The granite stone of the bridge was beginning to be warm and I began to pat it with my hands in time to an air in my head. I was very happy.

When I had been sitting there for five or ten minutes I saw Mahony's grey suit approaching. He came up the hill, smiling, and clambered up beside me on the bridge. While we were waiting he brought out the catapult which bulged from his inner pocket and explained some improvements which he had made in it. I asked him why he had brought it and he told me he had brought it to have some gas with the birds. Mahony used slang freely, and spoke of Father Butler as Old Bunser. We waited on for a quarter of an hour more but still there was no sign of Leo Dillon. Mahony, at last, jumped down and said:

"Come along. I knew Fatty'd funk it."

"And his sixpence … ?" I said.

"That's forfeit," said Mahony. "And so much the better for us—a bob and a tanner instead of a bob."

We walked along the North Strand Road till we came to the Vitriol Works and then turned to the right along the Wharf Road. Mahony began to play the Indian as soon as we were out of public sight. He chased a crowd of ragged girls, brandishing his unloaded catapult and, when two ragged boys began, out of chivalry, to fling stones at us, he proposed that we should charge them. I objected that the boys were too small, and so we walked on, the ragged troop screaming after us; "*Swaddlers! Swaddlers!*" thinking that we were Protestants because Mahony, who was dark-complexioned, wore the silver badge of a cricket club in his cap. When we came to the Smoothing Iron we arranged a siege; but it was a failure because you must have at least three. We revenged ourselves on Leo Dillon by saying what a funk he was and guessing how many he would get at three o'clock from Mr. Ryan.

We came then near the river. We spent a long time walking about the noisy streets flanked by high stone walls, watching the working of cranes and engines and often being shouted at for our immobility by the drivers of groaning carts. It was noon when we reached the quays and, as all the labourers seemed to be eating their lunches, we bought two big currant buns and sat down to eat them on some metal piping beside the river. We pleased ourselves with the spectacle of Dublin's commerce—the barges signalled from far away by their curls of woolly smoke, the brown fishing fleet beyond Ringsend, the big white sailing-vessel which was being discharged on the opposite quay. Mahony said it would be right skit to run away to sea on one of those big ships and even I, looking at the high masts, saw, or imagined, the geography which had been scantily dosed to me at school gradually taking substance under my eyes. School and home seemed to recede from us and their influences upon us seemed to wane.

We crossed the Liffey in the ferryboat, paying our toll to be transported in the company of two labourers and a little Jew with a bag. We were serious to the point of solemnity, but once during the short voyage our eyes met and we laughed. When we landed we watched the discharging of the graceful three-master which we had observed from the other quay. Some bystander said that she was a Norwegian vessel. I went to the stem and tried to decipher the legend upon it but, failing to do so, I came back and examined the foreign sailors to see had any of them green eyes for I had some confused notion … The sailors' eyes were blue and grey and even black. The only sailor whose eyes could have been called green was a tall man who amused the crowd on the quay by calling out cheerfully every time the planks fell:

"All right! All right!"

When we were tired of this sight we wandered slowly into Ringsend. The day had grown sultry, and in the windows of the grocers' shops musty biscuits lay bleaching. We bought some biscuits and chocolate which we ate sedulously as we wandered through the squalid streets where the families of the fishermen live. We could find no dairy and so we went into a huckster's shop and bought a bottle of raspberry lemonade each. Refreshed by this, Mahony chased a cat down a lane, but the cat escaped into a wide field. We both felt rather tired and when we reached the field we made at once for a sloping bank over the ridge of which we could see the Dodder.

It was too late and we were too tired to carry out our project of visiting the Pigeon House. We had to be home before four o'clock lest our adventure should be discovered. Mahony looked regretfully at his catapult and I had to suggest going home by train before he regained any cheerfulness. The sun went in behind some clouds and left us to our jaded thoughts and the crumbs of our provisions.

There was nobody but ourselves in the field. When we had lain on the bank for some time without speaking I saw a man approaching from the far end of the field. I watched him lazily as I chewed one of those green stems on which girls tell fortunes. He came along by the bank slowly. He walked with one hand upon his hip and in the other hand he held a stick with which he tapped the turf lightly. He was shabbily dressed in a suit of greenish-black and wore what we used to call a jerry hat with a high crown. He seemed to be fairly old for his moustache was ashengrey. When he passed at our feet he glanced up at us quickly and then continued his way. We followed him with our eyes and saw that when he had gone on for perhaps fifty paces he turned about and began to retrace his steps. He walked towards us very slowly, always tapping the ground with his stick, so slowly that I thought he was looking for something in the grass.

He stopped when he came level with us and bade us good-day. We answered him and he sat down beside us on the slope slowly and with great care. He began to talk of the weather, saying that it would be a very hot summer and adding that the seasons had changed greatly since he was a boy—a long time ago. He said that the happiest time of one's life was undoubtedly one's schoolboy days and that he would give anything to be young again. While he expressed these sentiments which bored us a little we kept silent. Then he began to talk of school and of books. He asked us whether we had read the poetry of Thomas Moore or the works of Sir Walter Scott and Lord Lytton. I pretended that I had read every book he mentioned so that in the end he said:

"Ah, I can see you are a bookworm like myself. Now," he added, pointing to Mahony who was regarding us with open eyes, "he is different; he goes in for games."

He said he had all Sir Walter Scott's works and all Lord Lytton's works at home and never tired of reading them. "Of course," he said, "there were some of Lord Lytton's works which boys couldn't read." Mahony asked why couldn't boys read them—a question which agitated and pained me because I was afraid the man would think I was as stupid as Mahony. The man, however, only smiled. I saw that he had great gaps in his mouth between his yellow teeth. Then he asked us which of us had the most sweethearts. Mahony mentioned lightly that he had three totties. The man asked me how many I had. I answered that I had none. He did not believe me and said he was sure I must have one. I was silent.

"Tell us," said Mahony pertly to the man, "how many have you yourself?"

The man smiled as before and said that when he was our age he had lots of sweethearts.

"Every boy," he said, "has a little sweetheart."

His attitude on this point struck me as strangely liberal in a man of his age. In my heart I thought that what he said about boys and sweethearts was reasonable. But I disliked the words in his mouth and I wondered why he shivered once or twice as if he feared something or felt a sudden chill. As he proceeded I noticed that his accent was good. He began to speak to us about girls, saying what nice soft hair they had and how soft their hands were and how all girls were not so good as they seemed to be if one only knew. There was nothing he liked, he said, so much as looking at a nice young girl, at her nice white hands and her beautiful soft hair. He gave me the impression that he was repeating something which he had learned by heart or that, magnetised by some words of his own speech, his mind was slowly circling round and round in the same orbit. At times he spoke as if he were simply alluding to some fact that everybody knew, and at times he lowered his voice and spoke mysteriously as if he were telling us something secret which he did not wish others to overhear. He repeated his phrases over and over again, varying them and surrounding them with his monotonous voice. I continued to gaze towards the foot of the slope, listening to him.

After a long while his monologue paused. He stood up slowly, saying that he had to leave us for a minute or so, a few minutes, and, without changing the direction of my gaze, I saw him walking slowly away from us towards the near end of the field. We remained silent when he had gone. After a silence of a few minutes I heard Mahony exclaim:

"I say! Look what he's doing!"

As I neither answered nor raised my eyes Mahony exclaimed again:

"I say ... He's a queer old josser!"

"In case he asks us for our names," I said, "let you be Murphy and I'll be Smith."

We said nothing further to each other. I was still considering whether I would go away or not when the man came back and sat down beside us again. Hardly had he sat down when Mahony, catching sight of the cat which had escaped him, sprang up and pursued her across the field. The man and I watched the chase. The cat escaped once more and Mahony began to throw stones at the wall she had escaladed. Desisting from this, he began to wander about the far end of the field, aimlessly.

After an interval the man spoke to me. He said that my friend was a very rough boy and asked did he get whipped often at school. I was going to reply indignantly that we were not National School boys to be *whipped*, as he called it; but I remained silent. He began to speak on the subject of chastising boys. His mind, as if magnetised again by his speech, seemed to circle slowly round and round its new centre. He said that when boys were that kind they ought to be whipped and well whipped. When a boy was tough and unruly there was nothing would do him any good but a good sound whipping. A slap on the hand or a box on the ear was no good: what he wanted was to get a nice warm whipping. I was surprised at this sentiment and involuntarily glanced up at his face. As I did so I met the gaze of a pair of bottle-green eyes peering at me from under a twitching forehead. I turned my eyes away again.

The man continued his monologue. He seemed to have forgotten his recent liberalism. He said that if ever he found a boy talking to girls or having a girl for a sweetheart he would whip him and whip him; and that would teach him not to be talking to girls. And if a boy had a girl for a sweetheart and told lies about it then he would give him such a whipping as no boy ever got in this world. He said that there was nothing in this world he would like so well as that. He described to me how he would whip such a boy as if he were unfolding some elaborate mystery. He would love that, he said, better than anything in this world; and his voice, as he led me monotonously through the mystery, grew almost affectionate and seemed to plead with me that I should understand him.

I waited till his monologue paused again. Then I stood up abruptly. Lest I should betray my agitation I delayed a few moments pretending to fix my shoe properly and then, saying that I was obliged to go, I bade him good-day. I went up the slope calmly but my heart was beating quickly with fear that he would seize me by the ankles. When I reached the top of the slope I turned round and, without looking at him, called loudly across the field:

"Murphy!"

My voice had an accent of forced bravery in it and I was ashamed of my paltry stratagem. I had to call the name again before Mahony saw me and hallooed in answer. How my heart beat as he came running across the field to me! He ran as if to bring me aid. And I was penitent; for in my heart I had always despised him a little.

Araby

North Richmond Street, being blind, was a quiet street except at the hour when the Christian Brothers' School set the boys free. An uninhabited house of two storeys stood at the blind end, detached from its neighbours in a square ground. The other houses of the street, conscious of decent lives within them, gazed at one another with brown imperturbable faces.

The former tenant of our house, a priest, had died in the back drawing-room. Air, musty from having been long enclosed, hung in all the rooms, and the waste room behind the kitchen was littered with old useless papers. Among these I found a few paper-covered books, the pages of which were curled and damp: *The Abbot*, by Walter Scott, *The Devout Communicant* and *The Memoirs of Vidocq*. I liked the last best because its leaves were yellow. The wild garden behind the house contained a central apple-tree and a few straggling bushes under one of which I found the late tenant's rusty bicycle-pump. He had been a very charitable priest; in his will he had left all his money to institutions and the furniture of his house to his sister.

When the short days of winter came dusk fell before we had well eaten our dinners. When we met in the street the houses had grown sombre. The space of sky above us was the colour of ever-changing violet and towards it the lamps of the street lifted their feeble lanterns. The cold air stung us and we played till our bodies glowed. Our shouts echoed in the silent street. The career of our play brought us through the dark muddy lanes behind the houses where we ran the gauntlet of the rough tribe, from the cottages, to the back doors of the dark dripping gardens where odours arose from the ashpits, to the dark odorous stables where a coachman smoothed and combed the horse or shook music from the buckled harness. When we returned to the street light from the kitchen windows had filled the areas. If my uncle was seen turning the corner we hid in the shadow until we had seen him safely housed. Or if Mangan's sister came out on the doorstep to call her brother in to his tea we watched her from our shadow peer up and down the street. We waited to see whether she would remain or go in and, if she remained, we left our shadow and walked up to Mangan's steps resignedly. She was waiting for us, her figure defined by the light from the half-opened door. Her brother always teased her before he obeyed and I stood by the railings looking at her. Her dress swung as she moved her body and the soft rope of her hair tossed from side to side.

Every morning I lay on the floor in the front parlour watching her door. The blind was pulled down to within an inch of the sash so that I could not be seen. When she came out on the doorstep my heart leaped. I ran to the hall, seized my books and followed her. I kept her brown figure always in my eye and, when we came near the point at which our ways diverged, I quickened my pace and passed her. This happened morning after morning. I had never spoken to her, except for a few casual words, and yet her name was like a summons to all my foolish blood.

Her image accompanied me even in places the most hostile to romance. On Saturday evenings when my aunt went marketing I had to go to carry some of the parcels. We walked through the flaring streets, jostled by drunken men and bargaining women, amid the curses of labourers, the shrill litanies of shop-boys who stood on guard by the barrels of pigs' cheeks, the nasal chanting of street-singers, who sang a *come-all-you* about O'Donovan Rossa, or a ballad about the troubles in our native land. These noises converged in a single sensation of life for me: I imagined that I bore my chalice safely through a throng of foes. Her name sprang to my lips at moments in strange prayers and praises which I myself did not understand. My eyes were often full of tears (I could not tell why) and at times a flood from my heart seemed to pour itself out into my bosom. I thought little of the future. I did not know whether I would ever speak to her or not or, if I spoke to her, how I could tell her of my confused adoration. But my body was like a harp and her words and gestures were like fingers running upon the wires.

One evening I went into the back drawing-room in which the priest had died. It was a dark rainy evening and there was no sound in the house. Through one of the broken panes I heard the rain impinge upon the earth, the fine incessant needles of water playing in the sodden beds. Some distant lamp or lighted window gleamed below me. I was thankful that I could see so little. All my senses seemed to desire to veil themselves and, feeling that I was about to slip from them, I pressed the palms of my hands together until they trembled, murmuring: *"O love! O love!"* many times.

At last she spoke to me. When she addressed the first words to me I was so confused that I did not know what to answer. She asked me was I going to *Araby*. I forgot whether I answered yes or no. It would be a splendid bazaar, she said, she would love to go.

"And why can't you?" I asked.

While she spoke she turned a silver bracelet round and round her wrist. She could not go, she said, because there would be a retreat that week in her convent.

Her brother and two other boys were fighting for their caps and I was alone at the railings. She held one of the spikes, bowing her head towards me. The light from the lamp opposite our door caught the white curve of her neck, lit up her hair that rested there and, falling, lit up the hand upon the railing. It fell over one side of her dress and caught the white border of a petticoat, just visible as she stood at ease.

"It's well for you," she said.

"If I go," I said. "I will bring you something."

What innumerable follies laid waste my waking and sleeping thoughts after that evening! I wished to annihilate the tedious intervening days. I chafed against the work of school. At night in my bedroom and by day in the classroom her image came between me and the page I strove to read. The syllables of the word *Araby* were called to me through the silence in which my soul luxuriated and cast an Eastern enchantment over me. I asked for leave to go to the bazaar on Saturday night. My aunt was surprised and hoped it was not some Freemason affair. I answered few questions in class. I watched my master's face pass from amiability to sternness; he hoped I was not beginning to idle. I could not call my wandering thoughts together. I had hardly any patience with the serious work of life which, now that it stood between me and my desire, seemed to me child's play, ugly monotonous child's play.

On Saturday morning I reminded my uncle that I wished to go to the bazaar in the evening. He was fussing at the hallstand, looking for the hatbrush, and answered me curtly:

"Yes, boy, I know."

As he was in the hall I could not go into the front parlour and lie at the window. I left the house in bad humour and walked slowly towards the school. The air was pitilessly raw and already my heart misgave me.

When I came home to dinner my uncle had not yet been home. Still it was early. I sat staring at the clock for some time and, when its ticking began to irritate me, I left the room. I mounted the staircase and gained the upper part of the house. The high cold empty gloomy rooms liberated me and I went from room to room singing. From the front window I saw my companions playing below in the street. Their cries reached me weakened and indistinct and, leaning my forehead against the cool glass, I looked over at the dark house where she lived. I may have stood them for an hour, seeing nothing but the brown-clad figure cast by my imagination, touched discreetly by the lamplight at the curved neck, at the hand upon the railings and at the border below the dress.

When I came downstairs again I found Mrs. Mercer sitting at the fire. She was an old garrulous woman, a pawnbroker's widow, who collected used stamps for some pious purpose. I had to endure the gossip of the tea-table. The meal was prolonged beyond an hour and still my uncle did not come. Mrs. Mercer stood up to go: she was sorry she couldn't wait any longer, but it was after eight o'clock and she did not like to be out late, as the night air was bad for her. When she had gone I began to walk up and down the room, clenching my fists. My aunt said:

"I'm afraid you may put off your bazaar for this night of Our Lord."

At nine o'clock I heard my uncle's latchkey in the hall-door. I heard him talking to himself and heard the hallstand rocking when it had received the weight of his overcoat. I could interpret these signs. When he was midway through his dinner I asked him to give me the money to go to the bazaar. He had forgotten.

"The people are in bed and after their first sleep now," he said.

I did not smile. My aunt said to him energetically:

"Can't you give him the money and let him go? You've kept him late enough as it is."

My uncle said he was very sorry he had forgotten. He said he believed in the old saying: "All work and no play makes Jack a dull boy." He asked me where I was going and, when I had told him a second time he asked me did I know *The Arab's Farewell to his Steed*. When I left the kitchen he was about to recite the opening lines of the piece to my aunt.

I held a florin tightly in my hand as I strode down Buckingham Street towards the station. The sight of the streets thronged with buyers and glaring with gas recalled to me the purpose of my journey. I took my seat in a third-class carriage of a deserted train. After an intolerable delay the train moved out of the station slowly. It crept onward among ruinous houses and over the twinkling river. At Westland Row Station a crowd of people pressed to the carriage doors; but the porters moved them back, saying that it was a special train for the bazaar. I remained alone in the bare carriage. In a few minutes the train drew up beside an improvised wooden platform. I passed out on to the road and saw by the lighted dial of a clock that it was ten minutes to ten. In front of me was a large building which displayed the magical name.

I could not find any sixpenny entrance and, fearing that the bazaar would be closed, I passed in quickly through a turnstile, handing a shilling to a weary -looking man. I found myself in a big hall girdled at half its height by a gallery. Nearly all the stalls were closed and the greater part of the hall was in darkness. I recognised a silence like that which pervades a church after a service. I walked into the centre of the bazaar timidly. A few people were gathered about the stalls which were still open. Before a curtain, over which the words *Café Chantant* were written in coloured lamps, two men were counting money on a salver. I listened to the fall of the coins.

Remembering with difficulty why I had come I went over to one of the stalls and examined porcelain vases and flowered tea-sets. At the door of the stall a young lady was talking and laughing with two young gentlemen. I remarked their English accents and listened vaguely to their conversation.

"O, I never said such a thing!"

"O, but you did!"

"O, but I didn't!"

"Didn't she say that?"

"Yes. I heard her."

"O, there's a ... fib!"

Observing me the young lady came over and asked me did I wish to buy anything. The tone of her voice was not encouraging; she seemed to have spoken to me out of a sense of duty. I looked humbly at the great jars that stood like eastern guards at either side of the dark entrance to the stall and murmured:

"No, thank you."

The young lady changed the position of one of the vases and went back to the two young men. They began to talk of the same subject. Once or twice the young lady glanced at me over her shoulder.

I lingered before her stall, though I knew my stay was useless, to make my interest in her wares seem the more real. Then I turned away slowly and walked down the middle of the bazaar. I allowed the two pennies to fall against the sixpence in my pocket. I heard a voice call from one end of the gallery that the light was out. The upper part of the hall was now completely dark.

Gazing up into the darkness I saw myself as a creature driven and derided by vanity; and my eyes burned with anguish and anger.

Eveline

She sat at the window watching the evening invade the avenue. Her head was leaned against the window curtains and in her nostrils was the odour of dusty cretonne. She was tired.

Few people passed. The man out of the last house passed on his way home; she heard his footsteps clacking along the concrete pavement and afterwards crunching on the cinder path before the new red houses. One time there used to be a field there in which they used to play every evening with other people's children. Then a man from Belfast bought the field and built houses in it—not like their little brown houses but bright brick houses with shining roofs. The children of the avenue used to play together in that field—the Devines, the Waters, the Dunns, little Keogh the cripple, she and her brothers and sisters. Ernest, however, never played: he was too grown up. Her father used often to hunt them in out of the field with his blackthorn stick; but usually little Keogh used to keep nix and call out when he saw her father coming. Still they seemed to have been rather happy then. Her father was not so bad then; and besides, her mother was alive. That was a long time ago; she and her brothers and sisters were all grown up; her mother was dead. Tizzie Dunn was dead, too, and the Waters had gone back to England. Everything changes. Now she was going to go away like the others, to leave her home.

Home! She looked round the room, reviewing all its familiar objects which she had dusted once a week for so many years, wondering where on earth all the dust came from. Perhaps she would never see again those familiar objects from which she had never dreamed of being divided. And yet during all those years she had never found out the name of the priest whose yellowing photograph hung on the wall above the broken harmonium beside the coloured print of the promises made to Blessed Margaret Mary Alacoque. He had been a school friend of her father. Whenever he showed the photograph to a visitor her father used to pass it with a casual word:

"He is in Melbourne now."

She had consented to go away, to leave her home. Was that wise? She tried to weigh each side of the question. In her home anyway she had shelter and food; she had those whom she had known all her life about her. Of course she had to work hard, both in the house and at business. What would they say of her in the Stores when they found out that she had run away with a fellow? Say she was a fool, perhaps; and her place would be filled up by advertisement. Miss Gavan would be glad. She had always had an edge on her, especially whenever there were people listening.

"Miss Hill, don't you see these ladies are waiting?"

"Look lively, Miss Hill, please."

She would not cry many tears at leaving the Stores.

But in her new home, in a distant unknown country, it would not be like that. Then she would be married—she, Eveline. People would treat her with respect then. She would not be treated as her mother had been. Even now, though she was over nineteen, she sometimes felt herself in danger of her father's violence. She knew it was that that had given her the palpitations. When they were growing up he had never gone for her, like he used to go for Harry and Ernest, because she was a girl; but latterly he had begun to threaten her and say what he would do to her only for her dead mother's sake. And now she had nobody to protect her. Ernest was dead and Harry, who was in the church decorating business, was nearly always down somewhere in the country. Besides, the invariable squabble for money on Saturday nights had begun to weary her unspeakably. She always gave her entire wages—seven shillings—and Harry always sent up what he could but the trouble was to get any money from her father. He said she used to squander the money, that she had no head, that he wasn't going to give her his hard-earned money to throw about the streets, and much more, for he was usually fairly bad on Saturday night. In the end he would give her the money and ask her had she any intention of buying Sunday's dinner. Then she had to rush out as quickly as she could and do her marketing, holding her black leather purse tightly in her hand as she elbowed her way through the crowds and returning home late under her load of provisions. She had hard work to keep the house together and to see that the two young children who had been left to her charge went to school regularly and got their meals regularly. It was hard work—a hard life—but now that she was about to leave it she did not find it a wholly undesirable life.

She was about to explore another life with Frank. Frank was very kind, manly, open-hearted. She was to go away with him by the night-boat to be his wife and to live with him in Buenos Ayres where he had a home waiting for her. How well she remembered the first time she had seen him; he was lodging in a house on the main road where she used to visit. It seemed a few weeks ago. He was standing at the gate, his peaked cap pushed back on his head and his hair tumbled forward over a face of bronze. Then they had come to know each other. He used to meet her outside the Stores every evening and see her home. He took her to see *The Bohemian Girl* and she felt elated as she sat in an unaccustomed part of the theatre with him. He was awfully fond of music and sang a little. People knew that they were courting and, when he sang about the lass that loves a sailor, she always felt pleasantly confused. He used to call her Poppens out of fun. First of all it had been an excitement for her to have a fellow and then she had begun to like him. He had tales of distant countries. He had started as a deck boy at a pound a month on a ship of the Allan Line going out to Canada. He told her the names of the ships he had been on and the names of the different services. He had sailed through the

Straits of Magellan and he told her stories of the terrible Patagonians. He had fallen on his feet in Buenos Ayres, he said, and had come over to the old country just for a holiday. Of course, her father had found out the affair and had forbidden her to have anything to say to him.

"I know these sailor chaps," he said.

One day he had quarrelled with Frank and after that she had to meet her lover secretly.

The evening deepened in the avenue. The white of two letters in her lap grew indistinct. One was to Harry; the other was to her father. Ernest had been her favourite but she liked Harry too. Her father was becoming old lately, she noticed; he would miss her. Sometimes he could be very nice. Not long before, when she had been laid up for a day, he had read her out a ghost story and made toast for her at the fire. Another day, when their mother was alive, they had all gone for a picnic to the Hill of Howth. She remembered her father putting on her mother's bonnet to make the children laugh.

Her time was running out but she continued to sit by the window, leaning her head against the window curtain, inhaling the odour of dusty cretonne. Down far in the avenue she could hear a street organ playing. She knew the air. Strange that it should come that very night to remind her of the promise to her mother, her promise to keep the home together as long as she could. She remembered the last night of her mother's illness; she was again in the close dark room at the other side of the hall and outside she heard a melancholy air of Italy. The organ-player had been ordered to go away and given sixpence. She remembered her father strutting back into the sickroom saying:

"Damned Italians! Coming over here!"

As she mused the pitiful vision of her mother's life laid its spell on the very quick of her being—that life of commonplace sacrifices closing in final craziness. She trembled as she heard again her mother's voice saying constantly with foolish insistence:

"Derevaun Seraun! Derevaun Seraun!"

She stood up in a sudden impulse of terror. Escape! She must escape! Frank would save her. He would give her life, perhaps love, too. But she wanted to live. Why should she be unhappy? She had a right to happiness. Frank would take her in his arms, fold her in his arms. He would save her.

.   .   .   .

She stood among the swaying crowd in the station at the North Wall. He held her hand and she knew that he was speaking to her, saying something about the passage over and over again. The station was full of soldiers with brown baggages. Through the wide doors of the sheds she caught a glimpse of the black mass of the boat, lying in beside the quay wall, with illumined portholes. She answered nothing. She felt her cheek pale and cold and, out of a maze of distress, she prayed to God to direct her, to show her what was her duty. The boat blew a long mournful whistle into the mist. If she went, to-morrow she would be on the sea with Frank, steaming towards Buenos Ayres. Their passage had been booked. Could she still draw back after all he had done for her? Her distress awoke a nausea in her body and she kept moving her lips in silent fervent prayer.

A bell clanged upon her heart. She felt him seize her hand:

"Come!"

All the seas of the world tumbled about her heart. He was drawing her into them: he would drown her. She gripped with both hands at the iron railing.

"Come!"

No! No! No! It was impossible. Her hands clutched the iron in frenzy. Amid the seas she sent a cry of anguish!

"Eveline! Evvy!"

He rushed beyond the barrier and called to her to follow. He was shouted at to go on but he still called to her. She set her white face to him, passive, like a helpless animal. Her eyes gave him no sign of love or farewell or recognition.

After the Race

The cars came scudding in towards Dublin, running evenly like pellets in the groove of the Naas Road. At the crest of the hill at Inchicore sightseers had gathered in clumps to watch the cars careering homeward and through this channel of poverty and inaction the Continent sped its wealth and industry. Now and again the clumps of people raised the cheer of the gratefully oppressed. Their sympathy, however, was for the blue cars—the cars of their friends, the French.

The French, moreover, were virtual victors. Their team had finished solidly; they had been placed second and third and the driver of the winning German car was reported a Belgian. Each blue car, therefore, received a double measure of welcome as it topped the crest of the hill and each cheer of welcome was acknowledged with smiles and nods by those in the car. In one of these trimly built cars was a party of four young men whose spirits seemed to be at present well above the level of successful Gallicism: in fact, these four young men were almost hilarious. They were Charles Ségouin, the owner of the car; André Rivière, a young electrician of Canadian birth; a huge Hungarian named Villona and a neatly groomed young man named Doyle. Ségouin was in good humour because he had unexpectedly received some orders in advance (he was about to start a motor establishment in Paris) and Rivière was in good humour because he was to be appointed manager of the establishment; these two young men (who were cousins) were also in good humour because of the success of the French cars. Villona was in good humour because he had had a very satisfactory luncheon; and besides he was an optimist by nature. The fourth member of the party, however, was too excited to be genuinely happy.

He was about twenty-six years of age, with a soft, light brown moustache and rather innocent-looking grey eyes. His father, who had begun life as an advanced Nationalist, had modified his views early. He had made his money as a butcher in Kingstown and by opening shops in Dublin and in the suburbs he had made his money many times over. He had also been fortunate enough to secure some of the police contracts and in the end he had become rich enough to be alluded to in the Dublin newspapers as a merchant prince. He had sent his son to England to be educated in a big Catholic college and had afterwards sent him to Dublin University to study law. Jimmy did not study very earnestly and took to bad courses for a while. He had money and he was popular; and he divided his time curiously between musical and motoring circles. Then he had been sent for a term to Cambridge to see a little life. His father, remonstrative, but covertly proud of the excess, had paid his bills and brought him home. It was at Cambridge that he had met Ségouin. They were not much more than acquaintances as yet but Jimmy found great pleasure in the society of one who had seen so much of the world and was reputed to own some of the biggest hotels in France. Such a person (as his father agreed) was well worth knowing, even if he had not been the charming companion he was. Villona was entertaining also—a brilliant pianist—but, unfortunately, very poor.

The car ran on merrily with its cargo of hilarious youth. The two cousins sat on the front seat; Jimmy and his Hungarian friend sat behind. Decidedly Villona was in excellent spirits; he kept up a deep bass hum of melody for miles of the road. The Frenchmen flung their laughter and light words over their shoulders and often Jimmy had to strain forward to catch the quick phrase. This was not altogether pleasant for him, as he had nearly always to make a deft guess at the meaning and shout back a suitable answer in the face of a high wind. Besides Villona's humming would confuse anybody; the noise of the car, too.

Rapid motion through space elates one; so does notoriety; so does the possession of money. These were three good reasons for Jimmy's excitement. He had been seen by many of his friends that day in the company of these continentals. At the control Ségouin had presented him to one of the French competitors and, in answer to his confused murmur of compliment, the swarthy face of the driver had disclosed a line of shining white teeth. It was pleasant after that honour to return to the profane world of spectators amid nudges and significant looks. Then as to money—he had a great sum under his control. Ségouin, perhaps, would not think it a great sum but Jimmy who, in spite of temporary errors, was at heart the inheritor of solid instincts knew well with what difficulty it had been got together. This knowledge had previously kept his bills within the limits of reasonable recklessness and, if he had been so conscious of the labour latent in money when there had been question merely of some freak of the higher intelligence, how much more so now when he was about to stake the greater part of his substance! It was a serious thing for him.

Of course, the investment was a good one and Ségouin had managed to give the impression that it was by a favour of friendship the mite of Irish money was to be included in the capital of the concern. Jimmy had a respect for his father's shrewdness in business matters and in this case it had been his father who had first suggested the investment; money to be made in the motor business, pots of money. Moreover Ségouin had the unmistakable air of wealth. Jimmy set out to translate into days' work that lordly car in which he sat. How smoothly it ran. In what style they had come careering along the country roads! The journey laid a magical finger on the genuine pulse of life and gallantly the machinery of human nerves strove to answer the bounding courses of the swift blue animal.

They drove down Dame Street. The street was busy with unusual traffic, loud with the horns of motorists and the gongs of impatient tram-drivers. Near the Bank Ségouin drew up and Jimmy and his friend alighted. A little knot of people collected on the footpath to pay homage to the snorting motor. The party was to dine together that evening in Ségouin's hotel and, meanwhile, Jimmy and his friend, who was staying with him, were to go home to dress. The car steered out slowly for Grafton Street while the two young men pushed their way through the knot of gazers. They walked northward with a curious feeling of disappointment in the exercise, while the city hung its pale globes of light above them in a haze of summer evening.

In Jimmy's house this dinner had been pronounced an occasion. A certain pride mingled with his parents' trepidation, a certain eagerness, also, to play fast and loose for the names of great foreign cities have at least this virtue. Jimmy, too, looked very well when he was dressed and, as he stood in the hall giving a last equation to the bows of his dress tie, his father may have felt even commercially satisfied at having secured for his son qualities often unpurchaseable. His father, therefore, was unusually friendly with Villona and his manner expressed a real respect for foreign accomplishments; but this subtlety of his host was probably lost upon the Hungarian, who was beginning to have a sharp desire for his dinner.

The dinner was excellent, exquisite. Ségouin, Jimmy decided, had a very refined taste. The party was increased by a young Englishman named Routh whom Jimmy had seen with Ségouin at Cambridge. The young men supped in a snug room lit by electric candle lamps. They talked volubly and with little reserve. Jimmy, whose imagination was kindling, conceived the lively youth of the Frenchmen twined elegantly upon the firm framework of the Englishman's manner. A graceful image of his, he thought, and a just one. He admired the dexterity with which their host directed the conversation. The five young men had various tastes and their tongues had been loosened. Villona, with immense respect, began to discover to the mildly surprised Englishman the beauties of the English madrigal, deploring the loss of old instruments. Rivière, not wholly ingenuously, undertook to explain to Jimmy the triumph of the French mechanicians. The resonant voice of the Hungarian was about to prevail in ridicule of the spurious lutes of the romantic painters when Ségouin shepherded his party into politics. Here was congenial ground for all. Jimmy, under generous influences, felt the buried zeal of his father wake to life within him: he aroused the torpid Routh at last. The room grew doubly hot and Ségouin's task grew harder each moment: there was even danger of personal spite. The alert host at an opportunity lifted his glass to Humanity and, when the toast had been drunk, he threw open a window significantly.

That night the city wore the mask of a capital. The five young men strolled along Stephen's Green in a faint cloud of aromatic smoke. They talked loudly and gaily and their cloaks dangled from their shoulders. The people made way for them. At the corner of Grafton Street a short fat man was putting two handsome ladies on a car in charge of another fat man. The car drove off and the short fat man caught sight of the party.

"André."

"It's Farley!"

A torrent of talk followed. Farley was an American. No one knew very well what the talk was about. Villona and Rivière were the noisiest, but all the men were excited. They got up on a car, squeezing themselves together amid much laughter. They drove by the crowd, blended now into soft colours, to a music of merry bells. They took the train at Westland Row and in a few seconds, as it seemed to Jimmy, they were walking out of Kingstown Station. The ticket-collector saluted Jimmy; he was an old man:

"Fine night, Sir!"

It was a serene summer night; the harbour lay like a darkened mirror at their feet. They proceeded towards it with linked arms, singing *Cadet Roussel* in chorus, stamping their feet at every:

"*Ho! Ho! Hohé, vraiment!*"

They got into a rowboat at the slip and made out for the American's yacht. There was to be supper, music, cards. Villona said with conviction:

"It is beautiful!"

There was a yacht piano in the cabin. Villona played a waltz for Farley and Rivière, Farley acting as cavalier and Rivière as lady. Then an impromptu square dance, the men devising original figures. What merriment! Jimmy took his part with a will: this was seeing life, at least. Then Farley got out of breath and cried "*Stop!*" A man brought in a light supper, and the young men sat down to it for form's sake. They drank, however: it was Bohemian. They drank Ireland, England, France, Hungary, the United States of America. Jimmy made a speech, a long speech, Villona saying: "*Hear! Hear!*" whenever there was a pause. There was a great clapping of hands when he sat down. It must have been a good speech. Farley clapped him on the back and laughed loudly. What jovial fellows! What good company they were!

Cards! cards! The table was cleared. Villona returned quietly to his piano and played voluntaries for them. The other men played game after game, flinging themselves boldly into the adventure. They drank the health of the Queen of Hearts and of the Queen of Diamonds. Jimmy felt obscurely the lack of an audience: the wit was flashing. Play ran very high and paper began to pass. Jimmy did not know exactly who was winning but he knew that he was losing. But it was his own fault for he frequently mistook his cards and the other men had to calculate his I.O.U.'s for him. They were devils of fellows but he wished they would stop: it was getting late. Someone gave the toast of the yacht *The Belle of Newport* and then someone proposed one great game for a finish.

The piano had stopped; Villona must have gone up on deck. It was a terrible game. They stopped just before the end of it to drink for luck. Jimmy understood that the game lay between Routh and Ségouin. What excitement! Jimmy was excited too; he would lose, of course. How much had he written away? The men rose to their feet to play the last tricks, talking and gesticulating. Routh won. The cabin shook with the young men's cheering and the cards were bundled together. They began then to gather in what they had won. Farley and Jimmy were the heaviest losers.

He knew that he would regret in the morning but at present he was glad of the rest, glad of the dark stupor that would cover up his folly. He leaned his elbows on the table and rested his head between his hands, counting the beats of his temples. The cabin door opened and he saw the Hungarian standing in a shaft of grey light:

"Daybreak, gentlemen!"

Two Gallants

The grey warm evening of August had descended upon the city and a mild warm air, a memory of summer, circulated in the streets. The streets, shuttered for the repose of Sunday, swarmed with a gaily coloured crowd. Like illumined pearls the lamps shone from the summits of their tall poles upon the living texture below which, changing shape and hue unceasingly, sent up into the warm grey evening air an unchanging, unceasing murmur.

Two young men came down the hill of Rutland Square. One of them was just bringing a long monologue to a close. The other, who walked on the verge of the path and was at times obliged to step on to the road, owing to his companion's rudeness, wore an amused listening face. He was squat and ruddy. A yachting cap was shoved far back from his forehead and the narrative to which he listened made constant waves of expression break forth over his face from the corners of his nose and eyes and mouth. Little jets of wheezing laughter followed one another out of his convulsed body. His eyes, twinkling with cunning enjoyment, glanced at every moment towards his companion's face. Once or twice he rearranged the light waterproof which he had slung over one shoulder in toreador fashion. His breeches, his white rubber shoes and his jauntily slung waterproof expressed youth. But his figure fell into rotundity at the waist, his hair was scant and grey and his face, when the waves of expression had passed over it, had a ravaged look.

When he was quite sure that the narrative had ended he laughed noiselessly for fully half a minute. Then he said:

"Well! ... That takes the biscuit!"

His voice seemed winnowed of vigour; and to enforce his words he added with humour:

"That takes the solitary, unique, and, if I may so call it, *recherché* biscuit!"

He became serious and silent when he had said this. His tongue was tired for he had been talking all the afternoon in a public-house in Dorset Street. Most people considered Lenehan a leech but, in spite of this reputation, his adroitness and eloquence had always prevented his friends from forming any general policy against him. He had a brave manner of coming up to a party of them in a bar and of holding himself nimbly at the borders of the company until he was included in a round. He was a sporting vagrant armed with a vast stock of stories, limericks and riddles. He was insensitive to all kinds of discourtesy. No one knew how he achieved the stern task of living, but his name was vaguely associated with racing tissues.

"And where did you pick her up, Corley?" he asked.

Corly ran his tongue swiftly along his upper lip.

"One night, man," he said, "I was going along Dame Street and I spotted a fine tart under Waterhouse's clock and said good-night, you know. So we went for a walk round by the canal and she told me she was a slavey in a house in Baggot Street. I put my arm round her and squeezed her a bit that night. Then next Sunday, man, I met her by appointment. We went out to Donnybrook and I brought her into a field there. She told me she used to go with a dairyman ... It was fine, man. Cigarettes every night she'd bring me and paying the tram out and back. And one night she brought me two bloody fine cigars—O, the real cheese, you know, that the old fellow used to smoke ... I was afraid, man, she'd get in the family way. But she's up to the dodge."

"Maybe she thinks you'll marry her," said Lenehan.

"I told her I was out of a job," said Corley. "I told her I was in Pim's. She doesn't know my name. I was too hairy to tell her that. But she thinks I'm a bit of class, you know."

Lenehan laughed again, noiselessly.

"Of all the good ones ever I heard," he said, "that emphatically takes the biscuit."

Corley's stride acknowledged the compliment. The swing of his burly body made his friend execute a few light skips from the path to the roadway and back again. Corley was the son of an inspector of police and he had inherited his father's frame and gait. He walked with his hands by his sides, holding himself erect and swaying his head from side to side. His head was large, globular and oily; it sweated in all weathers; and his large round hat, set upon it sideways, looked like a bulb which had grown out of another. He always stared straight before him as if he were on parade and, when he wished to gaze after someone in the street, it was necessary for him to move his body from the hips. At present he was about town. Whenever any job was vacant a friend was always ready to give him the hard word. He was often to be seen walking with policemen in plain clothes, talking earnestly. He knew the inner side of all affairs and was fond of delivering final judgments. He spoke without listening to the speech of his companions. His conversation was mainly about himself: what he had said to such a person and what such a person had said to him and what he had said to settle the matter. When he reported these dialogues he aspirated the first letter of his name after the manner of Florentines.

Lenehan offered his friend a cigarette. As the two young men walked on through the crowd Corley occasionally turned to smile at some of the passing girls but Lenehan's gaze was fixed on the large faint moon circled with a double halo. He watched earnestly the passing of the grey web of twilight across its face. At length he said:

"Well ... tell me, Corley, I suppose you'll be able to pull it off all right, eh?"

Corley closed one eye expressively as an answer.

"Is she game for that?" asked Lenehan dubiously. "You can never know women."

"She's all right," said Corley. "I know the way to get around her, man. She's a bit gone on me."

"You're what I call a gay Lothario," said Lenehan. "And the proper kind of a Lothario, too!"

A shade of mockery relieved the servility of his manner. To save himself he had the habit of leaving his flattery open to the interpretation of raillery. But Corley had not a subtle mind.

"There's nothing to touch a good slavey," he affirmed. "Take my tip for it."

"By one who has tried them all," said Lenehan.

"First I used to go with girls, you know," said Corley, unbosoming; "girls off the South Circular. I used to take them out, man, on the train somewhere and pay the tram or take them to a band or a play at the theatre or buy them chocolate and sweets or something that way. I used to spend money on them right enough," he added, in a convincing tone, as if he was conscious of being disbelieved.

But Lenehan could well believe it; he nodded gravely.

"I know that game," he said, "and it's a mug's game."

"And damn the thing I ever got out of it," said Corley.

"Ditto here," said Lenehan.

"Only off of one of them," said Corley.

He moistened his upper lip by running his tongue along it. The recollection brightened his eyes. He too gazed at the pale disc of the moon, now nearly veiled, and seemed to meditate.

"She was ... a bit of all right," he said regretfully.

He was silent again. Then he added:

"She's on the turf now. I saw her driving down Earl Street one night with two fellows with her on a car."

"I suppose that's your doing," said Lenehan.

"There was others at her before me," said Corley philosophically.

This time Lenehan was inclined to disbelieve. He shook his head to and fro and smiled.

"You know you can't kid me, Corley," he said.

"Honest to God!" said Corley. "Didn't she tell me herself?"

Lenehan made a tragic gesture.

"Base betrayer!" he said.

As they passed along the railings of Trinity College, Lenehan skipped out into the road and peered up at the clock.

"Twenty after," he said.

"Time enough," said Corley. "She'll be there all right. I always let her wait a bit."

Lenehan laughed quietly.

"Ecod! Corley, you know how to take them," he said.

"I'm up to all their little tricks," Corley confessed.

"But tell me," said Lenehan again, "are you sure you can bring it off all right? You know it's a ticklish job. They're damn close on that point. Eh? ... What?"

His bright, small eyes searched his companion's face for reassurance. Corley swung his head to and fro as if to toss aside an insistent insect, and his brows gathered.

"I'll pull it off," he said. "Leave it to me, can't you?"

Lenehan said no more. He did not wish to ruffle his friend's temper, to be sent to the devil and told that his advice was not wanted. A little tact was necessary. But Corley's brow was soon smooth again. His thoughts were running another way.

"She's a fine decent tart," he said, with appreciation; "that's what she is."

They walked along Nassau Street and then turned into Kildare Street. Not far from the porch of the club a harpist stood in the roadway, playing to a little ring of listeners. He plucked at the wires heedlessly, glancing quickly from time to time at the face of each new-corner and from time to time, wearily also, at the sky. His harp, too, heedless that her coverings had fallen about her knees, seemed weary alike of the eyes of strangers and of her master's hands. One hand played in the bass the melody of *Silent, O Moyle*, while the other hand careered in the treble after each group of notes. The notes of the air sounded deep and full.

The two young men walked up the street without speaking, the mournful music following them. When they reached Stephen's Green they crossed the road. Here the noise of trams, the lights and the crowd released them from their silence.

"There she is!" said Corley.

At the corner of Hume Street a young woman was standing. She wore a blue dress and a white sailor hat. She stood on the curbstone, swinging a sunshade in one hand. Lenehan grew lively.

"Let's have a look at her, Corley," he said.

Corley glanced sideways at his friend and an unpleasant grin appeared on his face.

"Are you trying to get inside me?" he asked.

"Damn it!" said Lenehan boldly, "I don't want an introduction. All I want is to have a look at her. I'm not going to eat her."

"O ... A look at her?" said Corley, more amiably. "Well ... I'll tell you what. I'll go over and talk to her and you can pass by."

"Right!" said Lenehan.

Corley had already thrown one leg over the chains when Lenehan called out:

"And after? Where will we meet?"

"Half ten," answered Corley, bringing over his other leg.

"Where?"

"Corner of Merrion Street. We'll be coming back."

"Work it all right now," said Lenehan in farewell.

Corley did not answer. He sauntered across the road swaying his head from side to side. His bulk, his easy pace, and the solid sound of his boots had something of the conqueror in them. He approached the young woman and, without saluting, began at once to converse with her. She swung her umbrella more quickly and executed half turns on her heels. Once or twice when he spoke to her at close quarters she laughed and bent her head.

Lenehan observed them for a few minutes. Then he walked rapidly along beside the chains at some distance and crossed the road obliquely. As he approached Hume Street corner he found the air heavily scented and his eyes made a swift anxious scrutiny of the young woman's appearance. She had her Sunday finery on. Her blue serge skirt was held at the waist by a belt of black leather. The great silver buckle of her belt seemed to depress the centre of her body, catching the light stuff of her white blouse like a clip. She wore a short black jacket with mother-of-pearl

buttons and a ragged black boa. The ends of her tulle collarette had been carefully
disordered and a big bunch of red flowers was pinned in her bosom stems upwards.
Lenehan's eyes noted approvingly her stout short muscular body. Frank rude health
glowed in her face, on her fat red cheeks and in her unabashed blue eyes. Her features were blunt. She had broad nostrils, a straggling mouth which lay open in a
contented leer, and two projecting front teeth. As he passed Lenehan took off his
cap and, after about ten seconds, Corley returned a salute to the air. This he did by
raising his hand vaguely and pensively changing the angle of position of his hat.

Lenehan walked as far as the Shelbourne Hotel where he halted and waited.
After waiting for a little time he saw them coming towards him and, when they
turned to the right, he followed them, stepping lightly in his white shoes, down
one side of Merrion Square. As he walked on slowly, timing his pace to theirs, he
watched Corley's head which turned at every moment towards the young woman's
face like a big ball revolving on a pivot. He kept the pair in view until he had seen
them climbing the stairs of the Donnybrook tram; then he turned about and went
back the way he had come.

Now that he was alone his face looked older. His gaiety seemed to forsake him
and, as he came by the railings of the Duke's Lawn, he allowed his hand to run
along them. The air which the harpist had played began to control his movements.
His softly padded feet played the melody while his fingers swept a scale of variations idly along the railings after each group of notes.

He walked listlessly round Stephen's Green and then down Grafton Street.
Though his eyes took note of many elements of the crowd through which he
passed they did so morosely. He found trivial all that was meant to charm him and
did not answer the glances which invited him to be bold. He knew that he would
have to speak a great deal, to invent and to amuse, and his brain and throat were
too dry for such a task. The problem of how he could pass the hours till he met
Corley again troubled him a little. He could think of no way of passing them but
to keep on walking. He turned to the left when he came to the corner of Rutland
Square and felt more at ease in the dark quiet street, the sombre look of which
suited his mood. He paused at !ast before the window of a poor-looking shop over
which the words *Refreshment Bar* were printed in white letters. On the glass of the
window were two flying inscriptions: *Ginger Beer* and *Ginger Ale*. A cut ham was
exposed on a great blue dish while near it on a plate lay a segment of very light
plum-pudding. He eyed this food earnestly for some time and then, after glancing
warily up and down the street, went into the shop quickly.

He was hungry for, except some biscuits which he had asked two grudging curates to bring him, he had eaten nothing since breakfast-time. He sat down at an uncovered wooden table opposite two work-girls and a mechanic. A slatternly girl waited on him.

"How much is a plate of peas?" he asked.

"Three halfpence, sir," said the girl.

"Bring me a plate of peas," he said, "and a bottle of ginger beer."

He spoke roughly in order to belie his air of gentility for his entry had been followed by a pause of talk. His face was heated. To appear natural he pushed his cap back on his head and planted his elbows on the table. The mechanic and the two work-girls examined him point by point before resuming their conversation in a subdued voice. The girl brought him a plate of grocer's hot peas, seasoned with pepper and vinegar, a fork and his ginger beer. He ate his food greedily and found it so good that he made a note of the shop mentally. When he had eaten all the peas he sipped his ginger beer and sat for some time thinking of Corley's adventure. In his imagination he beheld the pair of lovers walking along some dark road; he heard Corley's voice in deep energetic gallantries and saw again the leer of the young woman's mouth. This vision made him feel keenly his own poverty of purse and spirit. He was tired of knocking about, of pulling the devil by the tail, of shifts and intrigues. He would be thirty-one in November. Would he never get a good job? Would he never have a home of his own? He thought how pleasant it would be to have a warm fire to sit by and a good dinner to sit down to. He had walked the streets long enough with friends and with girls. He knew what those friends were worth: he knew the girls too. Experience had embittered his heart against the world. But all hope had not left him. He felt better after having eaten than he had felt before, less weary of his life, less vanquished in spirit. He might yet be able to settle down in some snug corner and live happily if he could only come across some good simple-minded girl with a little of the ready.

He paid twopence halfpenny to the slatternly girl and went out of the shop to begin his wandering again. He went into Capel Street and walked along towards the City Hall. Then he turned into Dame Street. At the corner of George's Street he met two friends of his and stopped to converse with them. He was glad that he could rest from all his walking. His friends asked him had he seen Corley and what was the latest. He replied that he had spent the day with Corley. His friends talked very little. They looked vacantly after some figures in the crowd and sometimes made a critical remark. One said that he had seen Mac an hour before in Westmoreland Street. At this Lenehan said that he had been with Mac the night before in Egan's. The young man who had seen Mac in Westmoreland Street asked was it true that Mac had won a bit over a billiard match. Lenehan did not know: he said that Holohan had stood them drinks in Egan's.

He left his friends at a quarter to ten and went up George's Street. He turned to the left at the City Markets and walked on into Grafton Street. The crowd of girls and young men had thinned and on his way up the street he heard many groups and couples bidding one another good-night. He went as far as the clock of the College of Surgeons: it was on the stroke of ten. He set off briskly along the northern side of the Green hurrying for fear Corley should return too soon. When he reached the corner of Merrion Street he took his stand in the shadow of a lamp and brought out one of the cigarettes which he had reserved and lit it. He leaned against the lamp-post and kept his gaze fixed on the part from which he expected to see Corley and the young woman return.

His mind became active again. He wondered had Corley managed it successfully. He wondered if he had asked her yet or if he would leave it to the last. He suffered all the pangs and thrills of his friend's situation as well as those of his own. But the memory of Corley's slowly revolving head calmed him somewhat: he was sure Corley would pull it off all right. All at once the idea struck him that perhaps Corley had seen her home by another way and given him the slip. His eyes searched the street: there was no sign of them. Yet it was surely half-an-hour since he had seen the clock of the College of Surgeons. Would Corley do a thing like that? He lit his last cigarette and began to smoke it nervously. He strained his eyes as each train stopped at the far corner of the square. They must have gone home by another way. The paper of his cigarette broke and he flung it into the road with a curse.

Suddenly he saw them coming towards him. He started with delight and keeping close to his lamp-post tried to read the result in their walk. They were walking quickly, the young woman taking quick short steps, while Corley kept beside her with his long stride. They did not seem to be speaking. An intimation of the result pricked him like the point of a sharp instrument. He knew Corley would fail; he knew it was no go.

They turned down Baggot Street and he followed them at once, taking the other footpath. When they stopped he stopped too. They talked for a few moments and then the young woman went down the steps into the area of a house. Corley remained standing at the edge of the path, a little distance from the front steps. Some minutes passed. Then the hall-door was opened slowly and cautiously. A woman came running down the front steps and coughed. Corley turned and went towards her. His broad figure hid hers from view for a few seconds and then she reappeared running up the steps. The door closed on her and Corley began to walk swiftly towards Stephen's Green.

Lenehan hurried on in the same direction. Some drops of light rain fell. He took them as a warning and, glancing back towards the house which the young woman had entered to see that he was not observed, he ran eagerly across the road. Anxiety and his swift run made him pant. He called out:

"Hallo, Corley!"

Corley turned his head to see who had called him, and then continued walking as before. Lenehan ran after him, settling the waterproof on his shoulders with one hand.

"Hallo, Corley!" he cried again.

He came level with his friend and looked keenly in his face. He could see nothing there.

"Well?" he said. "Did it come off?"

They had reached the corner of Ely Place. Still without answering Corley swerved to the left and went up the side street. His features were composed in stern calm. Lenehan kept up with his friend, breathing uneasily. He was baffled and a note of menace pierced through his voice.

"Can't you tell us?" he said. "Did you try her?"

Corley halted at the first lamp and stared grimly before him. Then with a grave gesture he extended a hand towards the light and, smiling, opened it slowly to the gaze of his disciple. A small gold coin shone in the palm.

The Boarding House

Mrs. Mooney was a butcher's daughter. She was a woman who was quite able to keep things to herself: a determined woman. She had married her father's foreman and opened a butcher's shop near Spring Gardens. But as soon as his father-in-law was dead Mr. Mooney began to go to the devil. He drank, plundered the till, ran headlong into debt. It was no use making him take the pledge: he was sure to break out again a few days after. By fighting his wife in the presence of customers and by buying bad meat he ruined his business. One night he went for his wife with the cleaver and she had to sleep in a neighbour's house.

After that they lived apart. She went to the priest and got a separation from him with care of the children. She would give him neither money nor food nor house-room; and so he was obliged to enlist himself as a sheriff's man. He was a shabby stooped little drunkard with a white face and a white moustache and white eyebrows, pencilled above his little eyes, which were pink-veined and raw; and all day long he sat in the bailiff's room, waiting to be put on a job. Mrs. Mooney, who had taken what remained of her money out of the butcher business and set up a boarding house in Hardwicke Street, was a big imposing woman. Her house had a floating population made up of tourists from Liverpool and the Isle of Man and, occasionally, *artistes* from the music halls. Its resident population was made up of clerks from the city. She governed the house cunningly and firmly, knew when to give credit, when to be stern and when to let things pass. All the resident young men spoke of her as *The Madam.*

Mrs. Mooney's young men paid fifteen shillings a week for board and lodgings (beer or stout at dinner excluded). They shared in common tastes and occupations and for this reason they were very chummy with one another. They discussed with one another the chances, of favourites and outsiders. Jack Mooney, the Madam's son, who was clerk to a commission agent in Fleet Street, had the reputation of being a hard case. He was fond of using soldiers' obscenities: usually he came home in the small hours. When he met his friends he had always a good one to tell them and he was always sure to be on to a good thing—that is to say, a likely horse or a likely *artiste.* He was also handy with the mits and sang comic songs. On Sunday nights there would often be a reunion in Mrs. Mooney's front drawing-room. The music-hall *artistes* would oblige; and Sheridan played waltzes and polkas and vamped accompaniments. Polly Mooney, the Madam's daughter, would also sing. She sang:

> I'm a … naughty girl
> You needn't sham:
> You know I am

Polly was a slim girl of nineteen; she had light soft hair and a small full mouth. Her eyes, which were grey with a shade of green through them, had a habit of glancing upwards when she spoke with anyone, which made her look like a little perverse madonna. Mrs. Mooney had first sent her daughter to be a typist in a corn-factor's office but, as a disreputable sheriff's man used to come every other day to the office, asking to be allowed to say a word to his daughter, she had taken her daughter home again and set her to do housework. As Polly was very lively the intention was to give her the run of the young men. Besides, young men like to feel that there is a young woman not very far away. Polly, of course, flirted with the young men but Mrs. Mooney, who was a shrewd judge, knew that the young men were only passing the time away: none of them meant business. Things went on so for a long time and Mrs. Mooney began to think of sending Polly back to type-writing when she noticed that something was going on between Polly and one of the young men. She watched the pair and kept her own counsel.

Polly knew that she was being watched, but still her mother's persistent silence could not be misunderstood. There had been no open complicity between mother and daughter, no open understanding but, though people in the house began to talk of the affair, still Mrs. Mooney did not intervene. Polly began to grow a little strange in her manner and the young man was evidently perturbed. At last, when she judged it to be the right moment, Mrs. Mooney intervened. She dealt with moral problems as a cleaver deals with meat: and in this case she had made up her mind.

It was a bright Sunday morning of early summer, promising heat, but with a fresh breeze blowing. All the windows of the boarding house were open and the lace curtains ballooned gently towards the street beneath the raised sashes. The belfry of George's Church sent out constant peals and worshippers, singly or in groups, traversed the little circus before the church, revealing their purpose by their self-contained demeanour no less than by the little volumes in their gloved hands. Breakfast was over in the boarding house and the table of the breakfast-room was covered with plates on which lay yellow streaks of eggs with morsels of bacon-fat and bacon-rind. Mrs. Mooney sat in the straw arm-chair and watched the servant Mary remove the breakfast things. She made Mary collect the crusts and pieces of broken bread to help to make Tuesday's bread-pudding. When the table was cleared, the broken bread collected, the sugar and butter safe under lock and key, she began to reconstruct the interview which she had had the night before with Polly. Things were as she had suspected: she had been frank in her questions and Polly had been frank in her answers. Both had been somewhat awkward, of course. She had been made awkward by her not wishing to receive the news in too cavalier a fashion or to seem to have connived and Polly had been made awkward not merely because allusions of that kind always made her awkward but also because she did not wish it to be thought that in her wise innocence she had divined the intention behind her mother's tolerance.

Mrs. Mooney glanced instinctively at the little gilt clock on the mantelpiece as soon as she had become aware through her revery that the bells of George's Church had stopped ringing. It was seventeen minutes past eleven: she would have lots of time to have the matter out with Mr. Doran and then catch short twelve at Marlborough Street. She was sure she would win. To begin with she had all the weight of social opinion on her side: she was an outraged mother. She had allowed him to live beneath her roof, assuming that he was a man of honour, and he had simply abused her hospitality. He was thirty-four or thirty-five years of age, so that youth could not be pleaded as his excuse; nor could ignorance be his excuse since he was a man who had seen something of the world. He had simply taken advantage of Polly's youth and inexperience: that was evident. The question was: What reparation would he make?

There must be reparation made in such cases. It is all very well for the man: he can go his ways as if nothing had happened, having had his moment of pleasure, but the girl has to bear the brunt. Some mothers would be content to patch up such an affair for a sum of money; she had known cases of it. But she would not do so. For her only one reparation could make up for the loss of her daughter's honour: marriage.

She counted all her cards again before sending Mary up to Mr. Doran's room to say that she wished to speak with him. She felt sure she would win. He was a serious young man, not rakish or loud-voiced like the others. If it had been Mr. Sheridan or Mr. Meade or Bantam Lyons her task would have been much harder. She did not think he would face publicity. All the lodgers in the house knew something of the affair; details had been invented by some. Besides, he had been employed for thirteen years in a great Catholic wine-merchant's office and publicity would mean for him, perhaps, the loss of his job. Whereas if he agreed all might be well. She knew he had a good screw for one thing and she suspected he had a bit of stuff put by.

Nearly the half-hour! She stood up and surveyed herself in the pier-glass. The decisive expression of her great florid face satisfied her and she thought of some mothers she knew who could not get their daughters off their hands.

Mr. Doran was very anxious indeed this Sunday morning. He had made two attempts to shave but his hand had been so unsteady that he had been obliged to desist. Three days' reddish beard fringed his jaws and every two or three minutes a mist gathered on his glasses so that he had to take them off and polish them with his pocket-handkerchief. The recollection of his confession of the night before was a cause of acute pain to him; the priest had drawn out every ridiculous detail of the affair and in the end had so magnified his sin that he was almost thankful at being afforded a loophole of reparation. The ham was done. What could he do now but marry her or run away? He could not brazen it out. The affair would be sure to be talked of and his employer would be certain to hear of it. Dublin is such a small city: everyone knows everyone else's business. He felt his heart leap warmly in his throat as he heard in his excited imagination old Mr. Leonard calling out in his rasping voice: "Send Mr. Doran here, please."

All his long years of service gone for nothing! All his industry and diligence thrown away! As a young man he had sown his wild oats, of course; he had boasted of his free-thinking and denied the existence of God to his companions in public-houses. But that was all passed and done with … nearly. He still bought a copy of *Reynold's Newspaper* every week but he attended to his religious duties and for nine-tenths of the year lived a regular life. He had money enough to settle down on; it was not that. But the family would look down on her. First of all there was her disreputable father and then her mother's boarding house was beginning to get a certain fame. He had a notion that he was being had. He could imagine his friends talking of the affair and laughing. She was a little vulgar; sometimes she said "I seen" and "if I had've known." But what would grammar matter if he really loved her? He could not make up his mind whether to like her or despise her for what she had done. Of course he had done it too. His instinct urged him to remain free, not to marry. Once you are married you are done for, it said.

While he was sitting helplessly on the side of the bed in shirt and trousers she tapped lightly at his door and entered. She told him all, that she had made a clean breast of it to her mother and that her mother would speak with him that morning. She cried and threw her arms round his neck, saying:

"O Bob! Bob! What am I to do? What am I to do at all?"

She would put an end to herself, she said.

He comforted her feebly, telling her not to cry, that it would be all right, never fear. He felt against his shirt the agitation of her bosom.

It was not altogether his fault that it had happened. He remembered well, with the curious patient memory of the celibate, the first casual caresses her dress, her breath, her fingers had given him. Then late one night as he was undressing for bed she had tapped at his door, timidly. She wanted to relight her candle at his for hers had been blown out by a gust. It was her bath night. She wore a loose open combing-jacket of printed flannel. Her white instep shone in the opening of her furry slippers and the blood glowed warmly behind her perfumed skin. From her hands and wrists too as she lit and steadied her candle a faint perfume arose.

On nights when he came in very late it was she who warmed up his dinner. He scarcely knew what he was eating feeling her beside him alone, at night, in the sleeping house. And her thoughtfulness! If the night was anyway cold or wet or windy there was sure to be a little tumbler of punch ready for him. Perhaps they could be happy together …

They used to go upstairs together on tiptoe, each with a candle, and on the third landing exchange reluctant goodnights. They used to kiss. He remembered well her eyes, the touch of her hand and his delirium …

But delirium passes. He echoed her phrase, applying it to himself: *"What am I to do?"* The instinct of the celibate warned him to hold back. But the sin was there; even his sense of honour told him that reparation must be made for such a sin.

While he was sitting with her on the side of the bed Mary came to the door and said that the missus wanted to see him in the parlour. He stood up to put on his coat and waistcoat, more helpless than ever. When he was dressed he went over to her to comfort her. It would be all right, never fear. He left her crying on the bed and moaning softly: *"O my God!"*

Going down the stairs his glasses became so dimmed with moisture that he had to take them off and polish them. He longed to ascend through the roof and fly away to another country where he would never hear again of his trouble, and yet a force pushed him downstairs step by step. The implacable faces of his employer and of the Madam stared upon his discomfiture. On the last flight of stairs he passed Jack Mooney who was coming up from the pantry nursing two bottles of *Bass*. They saluted coldly; and the lover's eyes rested for a second or two on a thick bulldog face and a pair of thick short arms. When he reached the foot of the stair-case he glanced up and saw Jack regarding him from the door of the return-room.

Suddenly he remembered the night when one of the music-hall *artistes*, a little blond Londoner, had made a rather free allusion to Polly. The reunion had been almost broken up on account of Jack's violence. Everyone tried to quiet him. The music-hall *artiste*, a little paler than usual, kept smiling and saying that there was no harm meant: but Jack kept shouting at him that if any fellow tried that sort of a game on with his sister he'd bloody well put his teeth down his throat, so he would.

Polly sat for a little time on the side of the bed, crying. Then she dried her eyes and went over to the looking-glass. She dipped the end of the towel in the water-jug and refreshed her eyes with the cool water. She looked at herself in profile and readjusted a hairpin above her ear. Then she went back to the bed again and sat at the foot. She regarded the pillows for a long time and the sight of them awakened in her mind secret, amiable memories. She rested the nape of her neck against the cool iron bed-rail and fell into a revery. There was no longer any perturbation visible on her face.

She waited on patiently, almost cheerfully, without alarm, her memories gradually giving place to hopes and visions of the future. Her hopes and visions were so intricate that she no longer saw the white pillows on which her gaze was fixed or remembered that she was waiting for anything.

At last she heard her mother calling. She started to her feet and ran to the banisters.

"Polly! Polly!"

"Yes, mamma?"

"Come down, dear. Mr. Doran wants to speak to you."

Then she remembered what she had been waiting for.

A Little Cloud

Eight years before he had seen his friend off at the North Wall and wished him godspeed. Gallaher had got on. You could tell that at once by his travelled air, his well-cut tweed suit, and fearless accent. Few fellows had talents like his and fewer still could remain unspoiled by such success. Gallaher's heart was in the right place and he had deserved to win. It was something to have a friend like that.

Little Chandler's thoughts ever since lunch-time had been of his meeting with Gallaher, of Gallaher's invitation and of the great city London where Gallaher lived. He was called Little Chandler because, though he was but slightly under the average stature, he gave one the idea of being a little man. His hands were white and small, his frame was fragile, his voice was quiet and his manners were refined. He took the greatest care of his fair silken hair and moustache and used perfume discreetly on his handkerchief. The half-moons of his nails were perfect and when he smiled you caught a glimpse of a row of childish white teeth.

As he sat at his desk in the King's Inns he thought what changes those eight years had brought. The friend whom he had known under a shabby and necessitous guise had become a brilliant figure on the London Press. He turned often from his tiresome writing to gaze out of the office window. The glow of a late autumn sunset covered the grass plots and walks. It cast a shower of kindly golden dust on the untidy nurses and decrepit old men who drowsed on the benches; it flickered upon all the moving figures—on the children who ran screaming along the gravel paths and on everyone who passed through the gardens. He watched the scene and thought of life; and (as always happened when he thought of life) he became sad. A gentle melancholy took possession of him. He felt how useless it was to struggle against fortune, this being the burden of wisdom which the ages had bequeathed to him.

He remembered the books of poetry upon his shelves at home. He had bought them in his bachelor days and many an evening, as he sat in the little room off the hall, he had been tempted to take one down from the bookshelf and read out something to his wife. But shyness had always held him back; and so the books had remained on their shelves. At times he repeated lines to himself and this consoled him.

When his hour had struck he stood up and took leave of his desk and of his fellow-clerks punctiliously. He emerged from under the feudal arch of the King's Inns, a neat modest figure, and walked swiftly down Henrietta Street. The golden sunset was waning and the air had grown sharp. A horde of grimy children populated the street. They stood or ran in the roadway or crawled up the steps before the gaping doors or squatted like mice upon the thresholds. Little Chandler gave them no thought. He picked his way deftly through all that minute vermin-like life and under the shadow of the gaunt spectral mansions in which the old nobility of Dublin had roystered. No memory of the past touched him, for his mind was full of a present joy.

He had never been in Corless's but he knew the value of the name. He knew that people went there after the theatre to eat oysters and drink liqueurs; and he had heard that the waiters there spoke French and German. Walking swiftly by at night he had seen cabs drawn up before the door and richly dressed ladies, escorted by cavaliers, alight and enter quickly. They wore noisy dresses and many wraps. Their faces were powdered and they caught up their dresses, when they touched earth, like alarmed Atalantas. He had always passed without turning his head to look. It was his habit to walk swiftly in the street even by day and whenever he found himself in the city late at night he hurried on his way apprehensively and excitedly. Sometimes, however, he courted the causes of his fear. He chose the darkest and narrowest streets and, as he walked boldly forward, the silence that was spread about his footsteps troubled him, the wandering, silent figures troubled him; and at times a sound of low fugitive laughter made him tremble like a leaf.

He turned to the right towards Capel Street. Ignatius Gallaher on the London Press! Who would have thought it possible eight years before? Still, now that he reviewed the past, Little Chandler could remember many signs of future greatness in his friend. People used to say that Ignatius Gallaher was wild. Of course, he did mix with a rakish set of fellows at that time, drank freely and borrowed money on all sides. In the end he had got mixed up in some shady affair, some money transaction: at least, that was one version of his flight. But nobody denied him talent. There was always a certain … something in Ignatius Gallaher that impressed you in spite of yourself. Even when he was out at elbows and at his wits' end for money he kept up a bold face. Little Chandler remembered (and the remembrance brought a slight flush of pride to his cheek) one of Ignatius Gallaher's sayings when he was in a tight corner:

"Half time now, boys," he used to say light-heartedly. "Where's my considering cap?"

That was Ignatius Gallaher all out; and, damn it, you couldn't but admire him for it.

Little Chandler quickened his pace. For the first time in his life he felt himself superior to the people he passed. For the first time his soul revolted against the dull inelegance of Capel Street. There was no doubt about it: if you wanted to succeed you had to go away. You could do nothing in Dublin. As he crossed Grattan Bridge he looked down the river towards the lower quays and pitied the poor stunted houses. They seemed to him a band of tramps, huddled together along the river-banks, their old coats covered with dust and soot, stupefied by the panorama of sunset and waiting for the first chill of night to bid them arise, shake themselves and begone. He wondered whether he could write a poem to express his idea. Perhaps Gallaher might be able to get it into some London paper for him. Could he write something original? He was not sure what idea he wished to express but the thought that a poetic moment had touched him took life within him like an infant hope. He stepped onward bravely.

Every step brought him nearer to London, farther from his own sober inartistic life. A light began to tremble on the horizon of his mind. He was not so old—thirty-two. His temperament might be said to be just at the point of maturity. There were so many different moods and impressions that he wished to express in verse. He felt them within him. He tried to weigh his soul to see if it was a poet's soul. Melancholy was the dominant note of his temperament, he thought, but it was a melancholy tempered by recurrences of faith and resignation and simple joy. If he could give expression to it in a book of poems perhaps men would listen. He would never be popular: he saw that. He could not sway the crowd but he might appeal to a little circle of kindred minds. The English critics, perhaps, would recognise him as one of the Celtic school by reason of the melancholy tone of his poems; besides that, he would put in allusions. He began to invent sentences and phrases from the notice which his book would get. "*Mr. Chandler has the gift of easy and graceful verse.*" ... "*A wistful sadness pervades these poems.*" ... "*The Celtic note.*" It was a pity his name was not more Irish-looking. Perhaps it would be better to insert his mother's name before the surname: Thomas Malone Chandler, or better still: T. Malone Chandler. He would speak to Gallaher about it.

He pursued his revery so ardently that he passed his street and had to turn back. As he came near Corless's his former agitation began to overmaster him and he halted before the door in indecision. Finally he opened the door and entered.

The light and noise of the bar held him at the doorway for a few moments. He looked about him, but his sight was confused by the shining of many red and green wine-glasses. The bar seemed to him to be full of people and he felt that the people were observing him curiously. He glanced quickly to right and left (frowning slightly to make his errand appear serious), but when his sight cleared a little he saw that nobody had turned to look at him: and there, sure enough, was Ignatius Gallaher leaning with his back against the counter and his feet planted far apart.

"Hallo, Tommy, old hero, here you are! What is it to be? What will you have? I'm taking whisky: better stuff than we get across the water. Soda? Lithia? No mineral? I'm the same. Spoils the flavour … Here, garçon, bring us two halves of malt whisky, like a good fellow … Well, and how have you been pulling along since I saw you last? Dear God, how old we're getting! Do you see any signs of aging in me-eh, what? A little grey and thin on the top—what?"

Ignatius Gallaher took off his hat and displayed a large closely cropped head. His face was heavy, pale and clean-shaven. His eyes, which were of bluish slate-colour, relieved his unhealthy pallor and shone out plainly above the vivid orange tie he wore. Between these rival features the lips appeared very long and shapeless and colourless. He bent his head and felt with two sympathetic fingers the thin hair at the crown. Little Chandler shook his head as a denial. Ignatius Gallaher put on his hat again.

"It pulls you down," he said, "Press life. Always hurry and scurry, looking for copy and sometimes not finding it: and then, always to have something new in your stuff. Damn proofs and printers, I say, for a few days. I'm deuced glad, I can tell you, to get back to the old country. Does a fellow good, a bit of a holiday. I feel a ton better since I landed again in dear dirty Dublin … Here you are, Tommy. Water? Say when."

Little Chandler allowed his whisky to be very much diluted.

"You don't know what's good for you, my boy," said Ignatius Gallaher. "I drink mine neat."

"I drink very little as a rule," said Little Chandler modestly. "An odd half-one or so when I meet any of the old crowd: that's all."

"Ah, well," said Ignatius Gallaher, cheerfully, "here's to us and to old times and old acquaintance."

They clinked glasses and drank the toast.

"I met some of the old gang to-day," said Ignatius Gallaher. "O'Hara seems to be in a bad way. What's he doing?"

"Nothing," said Little Chandler. "He's gone to the dogs."

"But Hogan has a good sit, hasn't he?"

"Yes; he's in the Land Commission."

"I met him one night in London and he seemed to be very flush … Poor O'Hara! Boose, I suppose?"

"Other things, too," said Little Chandler shortly.

Ignatius Gallaher laughed.

"Tommy," he said, "I see you haven't changed an atom. You're the very same serious person that used to lecture me on Sunday mornings when I had a sore head and a fur on my tongue. You'd want to knock about a bit in the world. Have you never been anywhere even for a trip?"

"I've been to the Isle of Man," said Little Chandler.

Ignatius Gallaher laughed.

"The Isle of Man!" he said. "Go to London or Paris: Paris, for choice. That'd do you good."

"Have you seen Paris?"

"I should think I have! I've knocked about there a little."

"And is it really so beautiful as they say?" asked Little Chandler.

He sipped a little of his drink while Ignatius Gallaher finished his boldly.

"Beautiful?" said Ignatius Gallaher, pausing on the word and on the flavour of his drink. "It's not so beautiful, you know. Of course, it is beautiful … But it's the life of Paris; that's the thing. Ah, there's no city like Paris for gaiety, movement, excitement …"

Little Chandler finished his whisky and, after some trouble, succeeded in catching the barman's eye. He ordered the same again.

"I've been to the Moulin Rouge," Ignatius Gallaher continued when the barman had removed their glasses, "and I've been to all the Bohemian cafés. Hot stuff! Not for a pious chap like you, Tommy."

Little Chandler said nothing until the barman returned with two glasses: then he touched his friend's glass lightly and reciprocated the former toast. He was beginning to feel somewhat disillusioned. Gallaher's accent and way of expressing himself did not please him. There was something vulgar in his friend which he had not observed before. But perhaps it was only the result of living in London amid the bustle and competition of the Press. The old personal charm was still there under this new gaudy manner. And, after all, Gallaher had lived, he had seen the world. Little Chandler looked at his friend enviously.

"Everything in Paris is gay," said Ignatius Gallaher. "They believe in enjoying life—and don't you think they're right? If you want to enjoy yourself properly you must go to Paris. And, mind you, they've a great feeling for the Irish there. When they heard I was from Ireland they were ready to eat me, man."

Little Chandler took four or five sips from his glass.

"Tell me," he said, "is it true that Paris is so … immoral as they say?"

Ignatius Gallaher made a catholic gesture with his right arm.

"Every place is immoral," he said. "Of course you do find spicy bits in Paris. Go to one of the students' balls, for instance. That's lively, if you like, when the *cocottes* begin to let themselves loose. You know what they are, I suppose?"

"I've heard of them," said Little Chandler.

Ignatius Gallaher drank off his whisky and shook his head.

"Ah," he said, "you may say what you like. There's no woman like the Parisienne—for style, for go."

"Then it is an immoral city," said Little Chandler, with timid insistence—"I mean, compared with London or Dublin?"

"London!" said Ignatius Gallaher. "It's six of one and half-a-dozen of the other. You ask Hogan, my boy. I showed him a bit about London when he was over there. He'd open your eye … I say, Tommy, don't make punch of that whisky: liquor up."

"No, really …"

"O, come on, another one won't do you any harm. What is it? The same again, I suppose?"

"Well … all right."

"François, the same again … Will you smoke, Tommy?"

Ignatius Gallaher produced his cigar-case. The two friends lit their cigars and puffed at them in silence until their drinks were served.

"I'll tell you my opinion," said Ignatius Gallaher, emerging after some time from the clouds of smoke in which he had taken refuge, "it's a rum world. Talk of immorality! I've heard of cases—what am I saying?—I've known them: cases of … immorality …"

Ignatius Gallaher puffed thoughtfully at his cigar and then, in a calm historian's tone, he proceeded to sketch for his friend some pictures of the corruption which was rife abroad. He summarised the vices of many capitals and seemed inclined to award the palm to Berlin. Some things he could not vouch for (his friends had told him), but of others he had had personal experience. He spared neither rank nor caste. He revealed many of the secrets of religious houses on the Continent and described some of the practices which were fashionable in high society and ended by telling, with details, a story about an English duchess—a story which he knew to be true. Little Chandler was astonished.

"Ah, well," said Ignatius Gallaher, "here we are in old jog-along Dublin where nothing is known of such things."

"How dull you must find it," said Little Chandler, "after all the other places you've seen!"

"Well," said Ignatius Gallaher, "it's a relaxation to come over here, you know. And, after all, it's the old country, as they say, isn't it? You can't help having a certain feeling for it. That's human nature ... But tell me something about yourself. Hogan told me you had ... tasted the joys of connubial bliss. Two years ago, wasn't it?"

Little Chandler blushed and smiled.

"Yes," he said. "I was married last May twelve months."

"I hope it's not too late in the day to offer my best wishes," said Ignatius Gallaher. "I didn't know your address or I'd have done so at the time."

He extended his hand, which Little Chandler took.

"Well, Tommy," he said, "I wish you and yours every joy in life, old chap, and tons of money, and may you never die till I shoot you. And that's the wish of a sincere friend, an old friend. You know that?"

"I know that," said Little Chandler.

"Any youngsters?" said Ignatius Gallaher.

Little Chandler blushed again.

"We have one child," he said.

"Son or daughter?"

"A little boy."

Ignatius Gallaher slapped his friend sonorously on the back.

"Bravo," he said, "I wouldn't doubt you, Tommy."

Little Chandler smiled, looked confusedly at his glass and bit his lower lip with three childishly white front teeth.

"I hope you'll spend an evening with us," he said, "before you go back. My wife will be delighted to meet you. We can have a little music and—"

"Thanks awfully, old chap," said Ignatius Gallaher, "I'm sorry we didn't meet earlier. But I must leave to-morrow night."

"To-night, perhaps ... ?"

"I'm awfully sorry, old man. You see I'm over here with another fellow, clever young chap he is too, and we arranged to go to a little card-party. Only for that …"

"O, in that case …"

"But who knows?" said Ignatius Gallaher considerately. "Next year I may take a little skip over here now that I've broken the ice. It's only a pleasure deferred."

"Very well," said Little Chandler, "the next time you come we must have an evening together. That's agreed now, isn't it?"

"Yes, that's agreed," said Ignatius Gallaher. "Next year if I come, *parole d'honneur.*"

"And to clinch the bargain," said Little Chandler, "we'll just have one more now."

Ignatius Gallaher took out a large gold watch and looked at it.

"Is it to be the last?" he said. "Because you know, I have an a.p."

"O, yes, positively," said Little Chandler.

"Very well, then," said Ignatius Gallaher, "let us have another one as a *deoc an doruis*—that's good vernacular for a small whisky, I believe."

Little Chandler ordered the drinks. The blush which had risen to his face a few moments before was establishing itself. A trifle made him blush at any time: and now he felt warm and excited. Three small whiskies had gone to his head and Gallaher's strong cigar had confused his mind, for he was a delicate and abstinent person. The adventure of meeting Gallaher after eight years, of finding himself with Gallaher in Corless's surrounded by lights and noise, of listening to Gallaher's stories and of sharing for a brief space Gallaher's vagrant and triumphant life, upset the equipoise of his sensitive nature. He felt acutely the contrast between his own life and his friend's, and it seemed to him unjust. Gallaher was his inferior in birth and education. He was sure that he could do something better than his friend had ever done, or could ever do, something higher than mere tawdry journalism if he only got the chance. What was it that stood in his way? His unfortunate timidity! He wished to vindicate himself in some way, to assert his manhood. He saw behind Gallaher's refusal of his invitation. Gallaher was only patronising him by his friendliness just as he was patronising Ireland by his visit.

The barman brought their drinks. Little Chandler pushed one glass towards his friend and took up the other boldly.

"Who knows?" he said, as they lifted their glasses. "When you come next year I may have the pleasure of wishing long life and happiness to Mr. and Mrs. Ignatius Gallaher."

Ignatius Gallaher in the act of drinking closed one eye expressively over the rim of his glass. When he had drunk he smacked his lips decisively, set down his glass and said:

"No blooming fear of that, my boy. I'm going to have my fling first and see a bit of life and the world before I put my head in the sack—if I ever do."

"Some day you will," said Little Chandler calmly.

Ignatius Gallaher turned his orange tie and slate-blue eyes full upon his friend. "You think so?" he said.

"You'll put your head in the sack," repeated Little Chandler stoutly, "like every-one else if you can find the girl."

He had slightly emphasised his tone and he was aware that he had betrayed himself; but, though the colour had heightened in his cheek, he did not flinch from his friend's gaze. Ignatius Gallaher watched him for a few moments and then said:

"If ever it occurs, you may bet your bottom dollar there'll be no mooning and spooning about it. I mean to marry money. She'll have a good fat account at the bank or she won't do for me."

Little Chandler shook his head.

"Why, man alive," said Ignatius Gallaher, vehemently, "do you know what it is? I've only to say the word and to-morrow I can have the woman and the cash. You don't believe it? Well, I know it. There are hundreds—what am I saying?—thou-sands of rich Germans and Jews, rotten with money, that'd only be too glad … You wait a while, my boy. See if I don't play my cards properly. When I go about a thing I mean business, I tell you. You just wait."

He tossed his glass to his mouth, finished his drink and laughed loudly. Then he looked thoughtfully before him and said in a calmer tone:

"But I'm in no hurry. They can wait. I don't fancy tying myself up to one woman, you know."

He imitated with his mouth the act of tasting and made a wry face.

"Must get a bit stale, I should think," he said.

·　　·　　·　　·　　·　　·　　·　　·　　·

Little Chandler sat in the room off the hall, holding a child in his arms. To save money they kept no servant but Annie's young sister Monica came for an hour or so in the morning and an hour or so in the evening to help. But Monica had gone home long ago. It was a quarter to nine. Little Chandler had come home late for tea and, moreover, he had forgotten to bring Annie home the parcel of coffee from Bewley's. Of course she was in a bad humour and gave him short answers. She said she would do without any tea but when it came near the time at which the shop at the corner closed she decided to go out herself for a quarter of a pound of tea and two pounds of sugar. She put the sleeping child deftly in his arms and said:

"Here. Don't waken him."

A little lamp with a white china shade stood upon the table and its light fell over a photograph which was enclosed in a frame of crumpled horn. It was Annie's photograph. Little Chandler looked at it, pausing at the thin tight lips. She wore the pale blue summer blouse which he had brought her home as a present one Saturday. It had cost him ten and elevenpence; but what an agony of nervousness it had cost him! How he had suffered that day, waiting at the shop door until the shop was empty, standing at the counter and trying to appear at his ease while the girl piled ladies' blouses before him, paying at the desk and forgetting to take up the odd penny of his change, being called back by the cashier, and finally, striving to hide his blushes as he left the shop by examining the parcel to see if it was securely tied. When he brought the blouse home Annie kissed him and said it was very pretty and stylish; but when she heard the price she threw the blouse on the table and said it was a regular swindle to charge ten and elevenpence for it. At first she wanted to take it back but when she tried it on she was delighted with it, especially with the make of the sleeves, and kissed him and said he was very good to think of her.

Hm! ...

He looked coldly into the eyes of the photograph and they answered coldly. Certainly they were pretty and the face itself was pretty. But he found something mean in it. Why was it so unconscious and ladylike? The composure of the eyes irritated him. They repelled him and defied him: there was no passion in them, no rapture. He thought of what Gallaher had said about rich Jewesses. Those dark Oriental eyes, he thought, how full they are of passion, of voluptuous longing! ... Why had he married the eyes in the photograph?

He caught himself up at the question and glanced nervously round the room. He found something mean in the pretty furniture which he had bought for his house on the hire system. Annie had chosen it herself and it reminded him of her. It too was prim and pretty. A dull resentment against his life awoke within him. Could he not escape from his little house? Was it too late for him to try to live bravely like Gallaher? Could he go to London? There was the furniture still to be paid for. If he could only write a book and get it published, that might open the way for him.

A volume of Byron's poems lay before him on the table. He opened it cautiously with his left hand lest he should waken the child and began to read the first poem in the book:

> *Hushed are the winds and still the evening gloom,*
> *Not e'en a Zephyr wanders through the grove,*
> *Whilst I return to view my Margaret's tomb*
> *And scatter flowers on the dust I love.*

He paused. He felt the rhythm of the verse about him in the room. How melancholy it was! Could he, too, write like that, express the melancholy of his soul in verse? There were so many things he wanted to describe: his sensation of a few hours before on Grattan Bridge, for example. If he could get back again into that mood …

The child awoke and began to cry. He turned from the page and tried to hush it: but it would not be hushed. He began to rock it to and fro in his arms but its wailing cry grew keener. He rocked it faster while his eyes began to read the second stanza:

> *Within this narrow cell reclines her clay,*
> *That clay where once …*

It was useless. He couldn't read. He couldn't do anything. The wailing of the child pierced the drum of his ear. It was useless, useless! He was a prisoner for life. His arms trembled with anger and suddenly bending to the child's face he shouted:

"Stop!"

The child stopped for an instant, had a spasm of fright and began to scream. He jumped up from his chair and walked hastily up and down the room with the child in his arms. It began to sob piteously, losing its breath for four or five seconds, and then bursting out anew. The thin walls of the room echoed the sound. He tried to soothe it but it sobbed more convulsively. He looked at the contracted and quivering face of the child and began to be alarmed. He counted seven sobs without a break between them and caught the child to his breast in fright. If it died! …

The door was burst open and a young woman ran in, panting.

"What is it? What is it?" she cried.

The child, hearing its mother's voice, broke out into a paroxysm of sobbing.

"It's nothing, Annie … it's nothing … He began to cry …"

She flung her parcels on the floor and snatched the child from him.

"What have you done to him?" she cried, glaring into his face.

Little Chandler sustained for one moment the gaze of her eyes and his heart closed together as he met the hatred in them. He began to stammer:

"It's nothing…. He…. he began to cry…. I couldn't…. I didn't do anything … What?"

Giving no heed to him she began to walk up and down the room, clasping the child tightly in her arms and murmuring:

"My little man! My little mannie! Was 'ou frightened, love? … There now, love! There now! … Lambabaun! Mamma's little lamb of the world! … There now!"

Little Chandler felt his checks suffused with shame and he stood back out of the lamplight. He listened while the paroxysm of the child's sobbing grew less and less; and tears of remorse started to his eyes.

Counterparts

The bell rang furiously and, when Miss Parker went to the tube, a furious voice called out in a piercing North of Ireland accent:

"Send Farrington here!"

Miss Parker returned to her machine, saying to a man who was writing at a desk:

"Mr. Alleyne wants you upstairs."

The man muttered *"Blast him!"* under his breath and pushed back his chair to stand up. When he stood up he was tall and of great bulk. He had a hanging face, dark wine-coloured, with fair eyebrows and moustache: his eyes bulged forward slightly and the whites of them were dirty. He lifted up the counter and, passing by the clients, went out of the office with a heavy step.

He went heavily upstairs until he came to the second landing, where a door bore a brass plate with the inscription *Mr. Alleyne*. Here he halted, puffing with labour and vexation, and knocked. The shrill voice cried:

"Come in!"

The man entered Mr. Alleyne's room. Simultaneously Mr. Alleyne, a little man wearing gold-rimmed glasses on a clean-shaven face, shot his head up over a pile of documents. The head itself was so pink and hairless it seemed like a large egg reposing on the papers. Mr. Alleyne did not lose a moment:

"Farrington? What is the meaning of this? Why have I always to complain of you? May I ask you why you haven't made a copy of that contract between Bodley and Kirwan? I told you it must be ready by four o'clock."

"But Mr. Shelley said, sir—"

"*Mr. Shelley said, sir* …. Kindly attend to what I say and not to what *Mr. Shelley says, sir*. You have always some excuse or another for shirking work. Let me tell you that if the contract is not copied before this evening I'll lay the matter before Mr. Crosbie .... Do you hear me now?"

"Yes, sir."

"Do you hear me now? ... Ay and another little matter! I might as well be talking to the wall as talking to you. Understand once for all that you get a half an hour for your lunch and not an hour and a half. How many courses do you want, I'd like to know ... Do you mind me now?"

"Yes, sir."

Mr. Alleyne bent his head again upon his pile of papers. The man stared fixedly at the polished skull which directed the affairs of Crosbie & Alleyne, gauging its fragility. A spasm of rage gripped his throat for a few moments and then passed, leaving after it a sharp sensation of thirst. The man recognised the sensation and felt that he must have a good night's drinking. The middle of the month was passed and, if he could get the copy done in time, Mr. Alleyne might give him an order on the cashier. He stood still, gazing fixedly at the head upon the pile of papers. Suddenly Mr. Alleyne began to upset all the papers, searching for something. Then, as if he had been unaware of the man's presence till that moment, he shot up his head again, saying:

"Eh? Are you going to stand there all day? Upon my word, Farrington, you take things easy!"

"I was waiting to see ..."

"Very good, you needn't wait to see. Go downstairs and do your work."

The man walked heavily towards the door and, as he went out of the room, he heard Mr. Alleyne cry after him that if the contract was not copied by evening Mr. Crosbie would hear of the matter.

He returned to his desk in the lower office and counted the sheets which remained to be copied. He took up his pen and dipped it in the ink but he continued to stare stupidly at the last words he had written: *In no case shall the said Bernard Bodley be* ... The evening was failing and in a few minutes they would be lighting the gas: then he could write. He felt that he must slake the thirst in his throat. He stood up from his desk and, lifting the counter as before, passed out of the office. As he was passing out the chief clerk looked at him inquiringly.

"It's all right, Mr. Shelley," said the man, pointing with his finger to indicate the objective of his journey.

The chief clerk glanced at the hat-rack, but, seeing the row complete, offered no remark. As soon as he was on the landing the man pulled a shepherd's plaid cap out of his pocket, put it on his head and ran quickly down the rickety stairs. From the street door he walked on furtively on the inner side of the path towards the corner and all at once dived into a doorway. He was now safe in the dark snug of O'Neill's shop, and, filling up the little window that looked into the bar with his inflamed face, the colour of dark wine or dark meat, he called out:

"Here, Pat, give us a g.p., like a good fellow."

The curate brought him a glass of plain porter. The man drank it at a gulp and asked for a caraway seed. He put his penny on the counter and, leaving the curate to grope for it in the gloom, retreated out of the snug as furtively as he had entered it.

Darkness, accompanied by a thick fog, was gaining upon the dusk of February and the lamps in Eustace Street had been lit. The man went up by the houses until he reached the door of the office, wondering whether he could finish his copy in time. On the stairs a moist pungent odour of perfumes saluted his nose: evidently Miss Delacour had come while he was out in O'Neill's. He crammed his cap back again into his pocket and re-entered the office, assuming an air of absent-mindedness.

"Mr. Alleyne has been calling for you," said the chief clerk severely. "Where were you?"

The man glanced at the two clients who were standing at the counter as if to intimate that their presence prevented him from answering. As the clients were both male the chief clerk allowed himself a laugh.

"I know that game," he said. "Five times in one day is a little bit ... Well, you better look sharp and get a copy of our correspondence in the Delacour case for Mr. Alleyne."

This address in the presence of the public, his run upstairs and the porter he had gulped down so hastily confused the man and, as he sat down at his desk to get what was required, he realised how hopeless was the task of finishing his copy of the contract before half past five. The dark damp night was coming and he longed to spend it in the bar, drinking with his friends amid the glare of gas and the clatter of glasses. He got out the Delacour correspondence and passed out of the office. He hoped Mr. Alleyne would not discover that the last two letters were missing.

The moist pungent perfume lay all the way up to Mr. Alleyne's room. Miss Delacour was a middle-aged woman of Jewish appearance. Mr. Alleyne was said to be sweet on her or on her money. She came to the office often and stayed a long time when she came. She was sitting beside his desk now in an aroma of perfumes, smoothing the handle of her umbrella and nodding the great black feather in her hat. Mr. Alleyne had swivelled his chair round to face her and thrown his right foot jauntily upon his left knee. The man put the correspondence on the desk and bowed respectfully but neither Mr. Alleyne nor Miss Delacour took any notice of his bow. Mr. Alleyne tapped a finger on the correspondence and then flicked it towards him as if to say: "*That's all right: you can go.*"

The man returned to the lower office and sat down again at his desk. He stared intently at the incomplete phrase: *In no case shall the said Bernard Bodley be ...* and thought how strange it was that the last three words began with the same letter. The chief clerk began to hurry Miss Parker, saying she would never have the letters typed in time for post. The man listened to the clicking of the machine for a few minutes and then set to work to finish his copy. But his head was not clear and his mind wandered away to the glare and rattle of the public-house. It was a night for hot punches. He struggled on with his copy, but when the clock struck five he had still fourteen pages to write. Blast it! He couldn't finish it in time. He longed to execrate aloud, to bring his fist down on something violently. He was so enraged that he wrote *Bernard Bernard* instead of *Bernard Bodley* and had to begin again on a clean sheet.

He felt strong enough to clear out the whole office single-handed. His body ached to do something, to rush out and revel in violence. All the indignities of his life enraged him ... Could he ask the cashier privately for an advance? No, the cashier was no good, no damn good: he wouldn't give an advance ... He knew where he would meet the boys: Leonard and O'Halloran and Nosey Flynn. The barometer of his emotional nature was set for a spell of riot.

His imagination had so abstracted him that his name was called twice before he answered. Mr. Alleyne and Miss Delacour were standing outside the counter and all the clerks had turned round in anticipation of something. The man got up from his desk. Mr. Alleyne began a tirade of abuse, saying that two letters were missing. The man answered that he knew nothing about them, that he had made a faithful copy. The tirade continued: it was so bitter and violent that the man could hardly restrain his fist from descending upon the head of the manikin before him:

"I know nothing about any other two letters," he said stupidly.

"*You—know— nothing.* Of course you know nothing," said Mr. Alleyne. "Tell me," he added, glancing first for approval to the lady beside him, "do you take me for a fool? Do you think me an utter fool?"

The man glanced from the lady's face to the little egg-shaped head and back again; and, almost before he was aware of it, his tongue had found a felicitous moment:

"I don't think, sir," he said, "that that's a fair question to put to me."

There was a pause in the very breathing of the clerks. Everyone was astounded (the author of the witticism no less than his neighbours) and Miss Delacour, who was a stout amiable person, began to smile broadly. Mr. Alleyne flushed to the hue of a wild rose and his mouth twitched with a dwarf's passion. He shook his fist in the man's face till it seemed to vibrate like the knob of some electric machine:

"You impertinent ruffian! You impertinent ruffian! I'll make short work of you! Wait till you see! You'll apologise to me for your impertinence or you'll quit the office instanter! You'll quit this, I'm telling you, or you'll apologise to me!"

•　　•　　•　　•　　•　　•　　•　　•　　•

He stood in a doorway opposite the office watching to see if the cashier would come out alone. All the clerks passed out and finally the cashier came out with the chief clerk. It was no use trying to say a word to him when he was with the chief clerk. The man felt that his position was bad enough. He had been obliged to offer an abject apology to Mr. Alleyne for his impertinence but he knew what a hornet's nest the office would be for him. He could remember the way in which Mr. Alleyne had hounded little Peake out of the office in order to make room for his own nephew. He felt savage and thirsty and revengeful, annoyed with himself and with everyone else. Mr. Alleyne would never give him an hour's rest; his life would be a hell to him. He had made a proper fool of himself this time. Could he not keep his tongue in his cheek? But they had never pulled together from the first, he and Mr. Alleyne, ever since the day Mr. Alleyne had overheard him mimicking his North of Ireland accent to amuse Higgins and Miss Parker: that had been the beginning of it. He might have tried Higgins for the money, but sure Higgins never had anything for himself. A man with two establishments to keep up, of course he couldn't …

He felt his great body again aching for the comfort of the public-house. The fog had begun to chill him and he wondered could he touch Pat in O'Neill's. He could not touch him for more than a bob—and a bob was no use. Yet he must get money somewhere or other: he had spent his last penny for the g.p. and soon it would be too late for getting money anywhere. Suddenly, as he was fingering his watch-chain, he thought of Terry Kelly's pawn-office in Fleet Street. That was the dart! Why didn't he think of it sooner?

He went through the narrow alley of Temple Bar quickly, muttering to himself that they could all go to hell because he was going to have a good night of it. The clerk in Terry Kelly's said *A crown!* but the consignor held out for six shillings; and in the end the six shillings was allowed him literally. He came out of the pawn-office joyfully, making a little cylinder of the coins between his thumb and fingers. In Westmoreland Street the footpaths were crowded with young men and women returning from business and ragged urchins ran here and there yelling out the names of the evening editions. The man passed through the crowd, looking on the spectacle generally with proud satisfaction and staring masterfully at the office-girls. His head was full of the noises of tram-gongs and swishing trolleys and his nose already sniffed the curling fumes of punch. As he walked on he preconsidered the terms in which he would narrate the incident to the boys:

"So, I just looked at him—coolly, you know, and looked at her. Then I looked back at him again—taking my time, you know. 'I don't think that that's a fair question to put to me,' says I."

Nosey Flynn was sitting up in his usual corner of Davy Byrne's and, when he heard the story, he stood Farrington a half-one, saying it was as smart a thing as ever he heard. Farrington stood a drink in his turn. After a while O'Halloran and Paddy Leonard came in and the story was repeated to them. O'Halloran stood tailors of malt, hot, all round and told the story of the retort he had made to the chief clerk when he was in Callan's of Fowne's Street; but, as the retort was after the manner of the liberal shepherds in the eclogues, he had to admit that it was not as clever as Farrington's retort. At this Farrington told the boys to polish off that and have another.

Just as they were naming their poisons who should come in but Higgins! Of course he had to join in with the others. The men asked him to give his version of it, and he did so with great vivacity for the sight of five small hot whiskies was very exhilarating. Everyone roared laughing when he showed the way in which Mr. Alleyne shook his fist in Farrington's face. Then he imitated Farrington, saying, *"And here was my nabs, as cool as you please,"* while Farrington looked at the company out of his heavy dirty eyes, smiling and at times drawing forth stray drops of liquor from his moustache with the aid of his lower lip.

When that round was over there was a pause. O'Halloran had money but neither of the other two seemed to have any; so the whole party left the shop somewhat regretfully. At the corner of Duke Street Higgins and Nosey Flynn bevelled off to the left while the other three turned back towards the city. Rain was drizzling down on the cold streets and, when they reached the Ballast Office, Farrington suggested the Scotch House. The bar was full of men and loud with the noise of tongues and glasses. The three men pushed past the whining match-sellers at the door and formed a little party at the corner of the counter. They began to exchange stories. Leonard introduced them to a young fellow named Weathers who was performing at the Tivoli as an acrobat and knockabout *artiste*. Farrington stood a drink all round. Weathers said he would take a small Irish and Apollinaris. Farrington, who had definite notions of what was what, asked the boys would they have an Apollinaris too; but the boys told Tim to make theirs hot. The talk became theatrical. O'Halloran stood a round and then Farrington stood another round, Weathers protesting that the hospitality was too Irish. He promised to get them in behind the scenes and introduce them to some nice girls. O'Halloran said that he and Leonard would go, but that Farrington wouldn't go because he was a married man; and Farrington's heavy dirty eyes leered at the company in token that he understood he was being chaffed. Weathers made them all have just one little tincture at his expense and promised to meet them later on at Mulligan's in Poolbeg Street.

When the Scotch House closed they went round to Mulligan's. They went into the parlour at the back and O'Halloran ordered small hot specials all round. They were all beginning to feel mellow. Farrington was just standing another round when Weathers came back. Much to Farrington's relief he drank a glass of bitter this time. Funds were getting low but they had enough to keep them going. Presently two young women with big hats and a young man in a check suit came in and sat at a table close by. Weathers saluted them and told the company that they were out of the Tivoli. Farrington's eyes wandered at every moment in the direction of one of the young women. There was something striking in her appearance. An immense scarf of peacock-blue muslin was wound round her hat and knotted in a great bow under her chin; and she wore bright yellow gloves, reaching to the elbow. Farrington gazed admiringly at the plump arm which she moved very often and with much grace; and when, after a little time, she answered his gaze he admired still more her large dark brown eyes. The oblique staring expression in them fascinated him. She glanced at him once or twice and, when the party was leaving the room, she brushed against his chair and said "O, pardon!" in a London accent. He watched her leave the room in the hope that she would look back at him, but he was disappointed. He cursed his want of money and cursed all the rounds he had stood, particularly all the whiskies and Apollinaris which he had stood to Weathers. If there was one thing that he hated it was a sponge. He was so angry that he lost count of the conversation of his friends.

When Paddy Leonard called him he found that they were talking about feats of strength. Weathers was showing his biceps muscle to the company and boasting so much that the other two had called on Farrington to uphold the national honour. Farrington pulled up his sleeve accordingly and showed his biceps muscle to the company. The two arms were examined and compared and finally it was agreed to have a trial of strength. The table was cleared and the two men rested their elbows on it clasping hands. When Paddy Leonard said "Go!" each was to try to bring down the other's hand on to the table. Farrington looked very serious and determined.

The trial began. After about thirty seconds Weathers brought his opponent's hand slowly down on to the table. Farrington's dark wine-coloured face flushed darker still with anger and humiliation at having been defeated by such a stripling.

"You're not to put the weight of your body behind it. Play fair," he said.

"Who's not playing fair?" said the other.

"Come on again. The two best out of three."

The trial began again. The veins stood out on Farrington's forehead, and the pallor of Weathers' complexion changed to peony. Their hands and arms trembled under the stress. After a long struggle Weathers again brought his opponent's hand slowly on to the table. There was a murmur of applause from the spectators. The curate, who was standing beside the table, nodded his red head towards the victor and said with stupid familiarity:

"Ah! that's the knack!"

"What the hell do you know about it?" said Farrington fiercely, turning on the man. "What do you put in your gab for?"

"Sh, sh!" said O'Halloran, observing the violent expression of Farrington's face. "Pony up, boys. We'll have just one little smahan more and then we'll be off."

A very sullen-faced man stood at the corner of O'Connell Bridge waiting for the little Sandymount tram to take him home. He was full of smouldering anger and revengefulness. He felt humiliated and discontented; he did not even feel drunk; and he had only twopence in his pocket. He cursed every thing. He had done for himself in the office, pawned his watch, spent all his money; and he had not even got drunk. He began to feel thirsty again and he longed to be back again in the hot reeking public-house. He had lost his reputation as a strong man, having been defeated twice by a mere boy. His heart swelled with fury and, when he thought of the woman in the big hat who had brushed against him and said *Pardon!* his fury nearly choked him.

His tram let him down at Shelbourne Road and he steered his great body along in the shadow of the wall of the barracks. He loathed returning to his home. When he went in by the side-door he found the kitchen empty and the kitchen fire nearly out. He bawled upstairs:

"Ada! Ada!"

His wife was a little sharp-faced woman who bullied her husband when he was sober and was bullied by him when he was drunk. They had five children. A little boy came running down the stairs.

"Who is that?" said the man, peering through the darkness.

"Me, pa."

"Who are you? Charlie?"

"No, pa. Tom."

"Where's your mother?"

"She's out at the chapel."

"That's right … Did she think of leaving any dinner for me?"

"Yes, pa. I—"

"Light the lamp. What do you mean by having the place in darkness? Are the other children in bed?"

The man sat down heavily on one of the chairs while the little boy lit the lamp. He began to mimic his son's flat accent, saying half to himself: "*At the chapel. At the chapel, if you please!*" When the lamp was lit he banged his fist on the table and shouted:

"What's for my dinner?"

"I'm going … to cook it, pa," said the little boy.

The man jumped up furiously and pointed to the fire.

"On that fire! You let the fire out! By God, I'll teach you to do that again!"

He took a step to the door and seized the walking-stick which was standing behind it.

"I'll teach you to let the fire out!" he said, rolling up his sleeve in order to give his arm free play.

The little boy cried, "O, pa!" and ran whimpering round the table, but the man followed him and caught him by the coat. The little boy looked about him wildly but, seeing no way of escape, fell upon his knees.

"Now, you'll let the fire out the next time!" said the man, striking at him vigorously with the stick. "Take that, you little whelp!"

The boy uttered a squeal of pain as the stick cut his thigh. He clasped his hands together in the air and his voice shook with fright.

"O, pa!" he cried. "Don't beat me, pa! And I'll … I'll say a *Hail Mary* for you … I'll say a *Hail Mary* for you, pa, if you don't beat me … I'll say a *Hail Mary* …"

Clay

The matron had given her leave to go out as soon as the women's tea was over and Maria looked forward to her evening out. The kitchen was spick and span: the cook said you could see yourself in the big copper boilers. The fire was nice and bright and on one of the side-tables were four very big barmbracks. These barmbracks seemed uncut; but if you went closer you would see that they had been cut into long thick even slices and were ready to be handed round at tea. Maria had cut them herself.

Maria was a very, very small person indeed but she had a very long nose and a very long chin. She talked a little through her nose, always soothingly: "Yes, my dear," and "No, my dear." She was always sent for when the women quarrelled over their tubs and always succeeded in making peace. One day the matron had said to her:

"Maria, you are a veritable peace-maker!"

And the sub-matron and two of the Board ladies had heard the compliment. And Ginger Mooney was always saying what she wouldn't do to the dummy who had charge of the irons if it wasn't for Maria. Everyone was so fond of Maria.

The women would have their tea at six o'clock and she would be able to get away before seven. From Ballsbridge to the Pillar, twenty minutes; from the Pillar to Drumcondra, twenty minutes; and twenty minutes to buy the things. She would be there before eight. She took out her purse with the silver clasps and read again the words *A Present from Belfast.* She was very fond of that purse because Joe had brought it to her five years before when he and Alphy had gone to Belfast on a Whit-Monday trip. In the purse were two half-crowns and some coppers. She would have five shillings clear after paying tram fare. What a nice evening they would have, all the children singing! Only she hoped that Joe wouldn't come in drunk. He was so different when he took any drink.

Often he had wanted her to go and live with them; but she would have felt herself in the way (though Joe's wife was ever so nice with her) and she had become accustomed to the life of the laundry. Joe was a good fellow. She had nursed him and Alphy too; and Joe used often say:

"Mamma is mamma but Maria is my proper mother."

After the break-up at home the boys had got her that position in the *Dublin by Lamplight* laundry, and she liked it. She used to have such a bad opinion of Protestants but now she thought they were very nice people, a little quiet and serious, but still very nice people to live with. Then she had her plants in the conservatory and she liked looking after them. She had lovely ferns and wax-plants and, whenever anyone came to visit her, she always gave the visitor one or two slips from her conservatory. There was one thing she didn't like and that was the tracts on the walls: but the matron was such a nice person to deal with, so genteel.

When the cook told her everything was ready she went into the women's room and began to pull the big bell. In a few minutes the women began to come in by twos and threes, wiping their steaming hands in their petticoats and pulling down the sleeves of their blouses over their red steaming arms. They settled down before their huge mugs which the cook and the dummy filled up with hot tea, already mixed with milk and sugar in huge tin cans. Maria superintended the distribution of the barmbrack and saw that every woman got her four slices. There was a great deal of laughing and joking during the meal. Lizzie Fleming said Maria was sure to get the ring and, though Fleming had said that for so many Hallow Eves, Maria had to laugh and say she didn't want any ring or man either; and when she laughed her grey-green eyes sparkled with disappointed shyness and the tip of her nose nearly met the tip of her chin. Then Ginger Mooney lifted up her mug of tea and proposed Maria's health while all the other women clattered with their mugs on the table, and said she was sorry she hadn't a sup of porter to drink it in. And Maria laughed again till the tip of her nose nearly met the tip of her chin and till her minute body nearly shook itself asunder because she knew that Mooney meant well though, of course, she had the notions of a common woman.

But wasn't Maria glad when the women had finished their tea and the cook and the dummy had begun to clear away the tea-things! She went into her little bedroom and, remembering that the next morning was a mass morning, changed the hand of the alarm from seven to six. Then she took off her working skirt and her house-boots and laid her best skirt out on the bed and her tiny dress-boots beside the foot of the bed. She changed her blouse too and, as she stood before the mirror, she thought of how she used to dress for mass on Sunday morning when she was a young girl; and she looked with quaint affection at the diminutive body which she had so often adorned. In spite of its years she found it a nice tidy little body.

When she got outside the streets were shining with rain and she was glad of her old brown waterproof. The tram was full and she had to sit on the little stool at the end of the car, facing all the people, with her toes barely touching the floor. She arranged in her mind all she was going to do and thought how much better it was to be independent and to have your own money in your pocket. She hoped they would have a nice evening. She was sure they would but she could not help thinking what a pity it was Alphy and Joe were not speaking. They were always falling out now but when they were boys together they used to be the best of friends: but such was life.

She got out of her tram at the Pillar and ferreted her way quickly among the crowds. She went into Downes's cake-shop but the shop was so full of people that it was a long time before she could get herself attended to. She bought a dozen of mixed penny cakes, and at last came out of the shop laden with a big bag. Then she thought what else would she buy: she wanted to buy something really nice. They would be sure to have plenty of apples and nuts. It was hard to know what to buy and all she could think of was cake. She decided to buy some plumcake but Downes's plumcake had not enough almond icing on top of it so she went over to a shop in Henry Street. Here she was a long time in suiting herself and the stylish young lady behind the counter, who was evidently a little annoyed by her, asked her was it wedding-cake she wanted to buy. That made Maria blush and smile at the young lady; but the young lady took it all very seriously and finally cut a thick slice of plumcake, parcelled it up and said:

"Two-and-four, please."

She thought she would have to stand in the Drumcondra tram because none of the young men seemed to notice her but an elderly gentleman made room for her. He was a stout gentleman and he wore a brown hard hat; he had a square red face and a greyish moustache. Maria thought he was a colonel-looking gentleman and she reflected how much more polite he was than the young men who simply stared straight before them. The gentleman began to chat with her about Hallow Eve and the rainy weather. He supposed the bag was full of good things for the little ones and said it was only right that the youngsters should enjoy themselves while they were young. Maria agreed with him and favoured him with demure nods and hems. He was very nice with her, and when she was getting out at the Canal Bridge she thanked him and bowed, and he bowed to her and raised his hat and smiled agreeably; and while she was going up along the terrace, bending her tiny head under the rain, she thought how easy it was to know a gentleman even when he has a drop taken.

Everybody said: "*O, here's Maria!*" when she came to Joe's house. Joe was there, having come home from business, and all the children had their Sunday dresses on. There were two big girls in from next door and games were going on. Maria gave the bag of cakes to the eldest boy, Alphy, to divide and Mrs. Donnelly said it was too good of her to bring such a big bag of cakes and made all the children say:

"Thanks, Maria."

But Maria said she had brought something special for papa and mamma, something they would be sure to like, and she began to look for her plumcake. She tried in Downes's bag and then in the pockets of her waterproof and then on the hall-stand but nowhere could she find it. Then she asked all the children had any of them eaten it—by mistake, of course—but the children all said no and looked as if they did not like to eat cakes if they were to be accused of stealing. Everybody had a solution for the mystery and Mrs. Donnelly said it was plain that Maria had left it behind her in the tram. Maria, remembering how confused the gentleman with the greyish moustache had made her, coloured with shame and vexation and disappointment. At the thought of the failure of her little surprise and of the two and fourpence she had thrown away for nothing she nearly cried outright.

But Joe said it didn't matter and made her sit down by the fire. He was very nice with her. He told her all that went on in his office, repeating for her a smart answer which he had made to the manager. Maria did not understand why Joe laughed so much over the answer he had made but she said that the manager must have been a very overbearing person to deal with. Joe said he wasn't so bad when you knew how to take him, that he was a decent sort so long as you didn't rub him the wrong way. Mrs. Donnelly played the piano for the children and they danced and sang. Then the two next-door girls handed round the nuts. Nobody could find the nutcrackers and Joe was nearly getting cross over it and asked how did they expect Maria to crack nuts without a nutcracker. But Maria said she didn't like nuts and that they weren't to bother about her. Then Joe asked would she take a bottle of stout and Mrs. Donnelly said there was port wine too in the house if she would prefer that. Maria said she would rather they didn't ask her to take anything: but Joe insisted.

So Maria let him have his way and they sat by the fire talking over old times and Maria thought she would put in a good word for Alphy. But Joe cried that God might strike him stone dead if ever he spoke a word to his brother again and Maria said she was sorry she had mentioned the matter. Mrs. Donnelly told her husband it was a great shame for him to speak that way of his own flesh and blood but Joe said that Alphy was no brother of his and there was nearly being a row on the head of it. But Joe said he would not lose his temper on account of the night it was and asked his wife to open some more stout. The two next-door girls had arranged some Hallow Eve games and soon everything was merry again. Maria was delighted to see the children so merry and Joe and his wife in such good spirits. The next-door girls put some saucers on the table and then led the children up to the table, blindfold. One got the prayer-book and the other three got the water;

and when one of the next-door girls got the ring Mrs. Donnelly shook her finger at the blushing girl as much as to say: *O, I know all about it!* They insisted then on blindfolding Maria and leading her up to the table to see what she would get; and, while they were putting on the bandage, Maria laughed and laughed again till the tip of her nose nearly met the tip of her chin.

They led her up to the table amid laughing and joking and she put her hand out in the air as she was told to do. She moved her hand about here and there in the air and descended on one of the saucers. She felt a soft wet substance with her fingers and was surprised that nobody spoke or took off her bandage. There was a pause for a few seconds; and then a great deal of scuffling and whispering. Somebody said something about the garden, and at last Mrs. Donnelly said something very cross to one of the next-door girls and told her to throw it out at once: that was no play. Maria understood that it was wrong that time and so she had to do it over again: and this time she got the prayer-book.

After that Mrs. Donnelly played Miss McCloud's Reel for the children and Joe made Maria take a glass of wine. Soon they were all quite merry again and Mrs. Donnelly said Maria would enter a convent before the year was out because she had got the prayer-book. Maria had never seen Joe so nice to her as he was that night, so full of pleasant talk and reminiscences. She said they were all very good to her.

At last the children grew tired and sleepy and Joe asked Maria would she not sing some little song before she went, one of the old songs. Mrs. Donnelly said "*Do, please, Maria!*" and so Maria had to get up and stand beside the piano. Mrs. Donnelly bade the children be quiet and listen to Maria's song. Then she played the prelude and said "*Now, Maria!*" and Maria, blushing very much, began to sing in a tiny quavering voice. She sang *I Dreamt that I Dwelt*, and when she came to the second verse she sang again:

> I dreamt that I dwelt in marble halls
>   With vassals and serfs at my side
> And of all who assembled within those walls
>   That I was the hope and the pride.
> I had riches too great to count, could boast
>   Of a high ancestral name,
> But I also dreamt, which pleased me most,
>   That you loved me still the same.

But no one tried to show her her mistake; and when she had ended her song Joe was very much moved. He said that there was no time like the long ago and no music for him like poor old Balfe, whatever other people might say; and his eyes filled up so much with tears that he could not find what he was looking for and in the end he had to ask his wife to tell him where the corkscrew was.

A Painful Case

Mr. James Duffy lived in Chapelizod because he wished to live as far as possible from the city of which he was a citizen and because he found all the other suburbs of Dublin mean, modern and pretentious. He lived in an old sombre house and from his windows he could look into the disused distillery or upwards along the shallow river on which Dublin is built. The lofty walls of his uncarpeted room were free from pictures. He had himself bought every article of furniture in the room: a black iron bedstead, an iron washstand, four cane chairs, a clothes-rack, a coal-scuttle, a fender and irons and a square table on which lay a double desk. A bookcase had been made in an alcove by means of shelves of white wood. The bed was clothed with white bed-clothes and a black and scarlet rug covered the foot. A little hand-mirror hung above the washstand and during the day a white-shaded lamp stood as the sole ornament of the mantelpiece. The books on the white wooden shelves were arranged from below upwards according to bulk. A complete Wordsworth stood at one end of the lowest shelf and a copy of the *Maynooth Catechism*, sewn into the cloth cover of a notebook, stood at one end of the top shelf. Writing materials were always on the desk. In the desk lay a manuscript translation of Hauptmann's *Michael Kramer*, the stage directions of which were written in purple ink, and a little sheaf of papers held together by a brass pin. In these sheets a sentence was inscribed from time to time and, in an ironical moment, the headline of an advertisement for *Bile Beans* had been pasted on to the first sheet. On lifting the lid of the desk a faint fragrance escaped—the fragrance of new cedarwood pencils or of a bottle of gum or of an overripe apple which might have been left there and forgotten.

Mr. Duffy abhorred anything which betokened physical or mental disorder. A mediaeval doctor would have called him saturnine. His face, which carried the entire tale of his years, was of the brown tint of Dublin streets. On his long and rather large head grew dry black hair and a tawny moustache did not quite cover an unamiable mouth. His cheekbones also gave his face a harsh character; but there was no harshness in the eyes which, looking at the world from under their tawny eyebrows, gave the impression of a man ever alert to greet a redeeming instinct in others but often disappointed. He lived at a little distance from his body, regarding his own acts with doubtful side-glances. He had an odd autobiographical habit which led him to compose in his mind from time to time a short sentence about himself containing a subject in the third person and a predicate in the past tense. He never gave alms to beggars and walked firmly, carrying a stout hazel.

He had been for many years cashier of a private bank in Baggot Street. Every morning he came in from Chapelizod by tram. At midday he went to Dan Burke's and took his lunch—a bottle of lager beer and a small trayful of arrowroot biscuits. At four o'clock he was set free. He dined in an eating-house in George's Street where he felt himself safe from the society of Dublin's gilded youth and where there was a certain plain honesty in the bill of fare. His evenings were spent either before his landlady's piano or roaming about the outskirts of the city. His liking for Mozart's music brought him sometimes to an opera or a concert: these were the only dissipations of his life.

He had neither companions nor friends, church nor creed. He lived his spiritual life without any communion with others, visiting his relatives at Christmas and escorting them to the cemetery when they died. He performed these two social duties for old dignity's sake but conceded nothing further to the conventions which regulate the civic life. He allowed himself to think that in certain circumstances he would rob his bank but, as these circumstances never arose, his life rolled out evenly—an adventureless tale.

One evening he found himself sitting beside two ladies in the Rotunda. The house, thinly peopled and silent, gave distressing prophecy of failure. The lady who sat next him looked round at the deserted house once or twice and then said:

"What a pity there is such a poor house to-night! It's so hard on people to have to sing to empty benches."

He took the remark as an invitation to talk. He was surprised that she seemed so little awkward. While they talked he tried to fix her permanently in his memory. When he learned that the young girl beside her was her daughter he judged her to be a year or so younger than himself. Her face, which must have been handsome, had remained intelligent. It was an oval face with strongly marked features. The eyes were very dark blue and steady. Their gaze began with a defiant note but was confused by what seemed a deliberate swoon of the pupil into the iris, revealing for an instant a temperament of great sensibility. The pupil reasserted itself quickly, this half-disclosed nature fell again under the reign of prudence, and her astrakhan jacket, moulding a bosom of a certain fulness, struck the note of defiance more definitely.

He met her again a few weeks afterwards at a concert in Earlsfort Terrace and seized the moments when her daughter's attention was diverted to become intimate. She alluded once or twice to her husband but her tone was not such as to make the allusion a warning. Her name was Mrs. Sinico. Her husband's great-great-grandfather had come from Leghorn. Her husband was captain of a mercantile boat plying between Dublin and Holland; and they had one child.

Meeting her a third time by accident he found courage to make an appointment. She came. This was the first of many meetings; they met always in the evening and chose the most quiet quarters for their walks together. Mr. Duffy, however, had a distaste for underhand ways and, finding that they were compelled to meet stealthily, he forced her to ask him to her house. Captain Sinico encouraged his visits, thinking that his daughter's hand was in question. He had dismissed his wife so sincerely from his gallery of pleasures that he did not suspect that anyone else would take an interest in her. As the husband was often away and the daughter out giving music lessons Mr. Duffy had many opportunities of enjoying the lady's society. Neither he nor she had had any such adventure before and neither was conscious of any incongruity. Little by little he entangled his thoughts with hers. He lent her books, provided her with ideas, shared his intellectual life with her. She listened to all.

Sometimes in return for his theories she gave out some fact of her own life. With almost maternal solicitude she urged him to let his nature open to the full: she became his confessor. He told her that for some time he had assisted at the meetings of an Irish Socialist Party where he had felt himself a unique figure amidst a score of sober workmen in a garret lit by an inefficient oil-lamp. When the party had divided into three sections, each under its own leader and in its own garret, he had discontinued his attendances. The workmen's discussions, he said, were too timorous; the interest they took in the question of wages was inordinate. He felt that they were hard-featured realists and that they resented an exactitude which was the product of a leisure not within their reach. No social revolution, he told her, would be likely to strike Dublin for some centuries.

She asked him why did he not write out his thoughts. For what, he asked her, with careful scorn. To compete with phrasemongers, incapable of thinking consecutively for sixty seconds? To submit himself to the criticisms of an obtuse middle class which entrusted its morality to policemen and its fine arts to impresarios?

He went often to her little cottage outside Dublin; often they spent their evenings alone. Little by little, as their thoughts entangled, they spoke of subjects less remote. Her companionship was like a warm soil about an exotic. Many times she allowed the dark to fall upon them, refraining from lighting the lamp. The dark discreet room, their isolation, the music that still vibrated in their ears united them. This union exalted him, wore away the tough edges of his character, emotionalised his mental life. Sometimes he caught himself listening to the sound of his own voice. He thought that in her eyes he would ascend to an angelical stature; and, as he attached the fervent nature of his companion more and more closely to him, he heard the strange impersonal voice which he recognised as his own, insisting on the soul's incurable loneliness. We cannot give ourselves, it said: we are our own. The end of these discourses was that one night during which she had shown every sign of unusual excitement, Mrs. Sinico caught up his hand passionately and pressed it to her cheek.

Mr. Duffy was very much surprised. Her interpretation of his words disillusioned him. He did not visit her for a week; then he wrote to her asking her to meet him. As he did not wish their last interview to be troubled by the influence of their ruined confessional they met in a little cake-shop near the Parkgate. It was cold autumn weather but in spite of the cold they wandered up and down the roads of the Park for nearly three hours. They agreed to break off their intercourse: every bond, he said, is a bond to sorrow. When they came out of the Park they walked in silence towards the tram; but here she began to tremble so violently that, fearing another collapse on her part, he bade her good-bye quickly and left her. A few days later he received a parcel containing his books and music.

Four years passed. Mr. Duffy returned to his even way of life. His room still bore witness of the orderliness of his mind. Some new pieces of music encumbered the music-stand in the lower room and on his shelves stood two volumes by Nietzsche: *Thus Spoke Zarathustra* and *The Gay Science*. He wrote seldom in the sheaf of papers which lay in his desk. One of his sentences, written two months after his last interview with Mrs. Sinico, read: Love between man and man is impossible because there must not be sexual intercourse and friendship between man and woman is impossible because there must be sexual intercourse. He kept away from concerts lest he should meet her. His father died; the junior partner of the bank retired. And still every morning he went into the city by tram and every evening walked home from the city after having dined moderately in George's Street and read the evening paper for dessert.

One evening as he was about to put a morsel of corned beef and cabbage into his mouth his hand stopped. His eyes fixed themselves on a paragraph in the evening paper which he had propped against the water-carafe. He replaced the morsel of food on his plate and read the paragraph attentively. Then he drank a glass of water, pushed his plate to one side, doubled the paper down before him between his elbows and read the paragraph over and over again. The cabbage began to deposit a cold white grease on his plate. The girl came over to him to ask was his dinner not properly cooked. He said it was very good and ate a few mouthfuls of it with difficulty. Then he paid his bill and went out.

He walked along quickly through the November twilight, his stout hazel stick striking the ground regularly, the fringe of the buff *Mail* peeping out of a side-pocket of his tight reefer overcoat. On the lonely road which leads from the Parkgate to Chapelizod he slackened his pace. His stick struck the ground less emphatically and his breath, issuing irregularly, almost with a sighing sound, condensed in the wintry air. When he reached his house he went up at once to his bedroom and, taking the paper from his pocket, read the paragraph again by the failing light of the window. He read it not aloud, but moving his lips as a priest does when he reads the prayers *Secreto*. This was the paragraph:

DEATH OF A LADY AT SYDNEY PARADE
A PAINFUL CASE

To-day at the City of Dublin Hospital the Deputy Coroner (in the absence of Mr. Leverett) held an inquest on the body of Mrs. Emily Sinico, aged forty-three years, who was killed at Sydney Parade Station yesterday evening. The evidence showed that the deceased lady, while attempting to cross the line, was knocked down by the engine of the ten o'clock slow train from Kingstown, thereby sustaining injuries of the head and right side which led to her death.

James Lennon, driver of the engine, stated that he had been in the employment of the railway company for fifteen years. On hearing the guard's whistle he set the train in motion and a second or two afterwards brought it to rest in response to loud cries. The train was going slowly.

P. Dunne, railway porter, stated that as the train was about to start he observed a woman attempting to cross the lines. He ran towards her and shouted, but, before he could reach her, she was caught by the buffer of the engine and fell to the ground.

A juror. "You saw the lady fall?"

Witness. "Yes."

Police Sergeant Croly deposed that when he arrived he found the deceased lying on the platform apparently dead. He had the body taken to the waiting-room pending the arrival of the ambulance.

Constable 57E corroborated.

Dr. Halpin, assistant house surgeon of the City of Dublin Hospital, stated that the deceased had two lower ribs fractured and had sustained severe contusions of the right shoulder. The right side of the head had been injured in the fall. The injuries were not sufficient to have caused death in a normal person. Death, in his opinion, had been probably due to shock and sudden failure of the heart's action.

Mr. H. B. Patterson Finlay, on behalf of the railway company, expressed his deep regret at the accident. The company had always taken every precaution to prevent people crossing the lines except by the bridges, both by placing notices in every station and by the use of patent spring gates at level crossings. The deceased had been in the habit of crossing the lines late at night from platform to platform and, in view of certain other circumstances of the case, he did not think the railway officials were to blame.

Captain Sinico, of Leoville, Sydney Parade, husband of the deceased, also gave evidence. He stated that the deceased was his wife. He was not in Dublin at the time of the accident as he had arrived only that morning from Rotterdam. They had been married for twenty-two years and had lived happily until about two years ago when his wife began to be rather intemperate in her habits.

Miss Mary Sinico said that of late her mother had been in the habit of going out at night to buy spirits. She, witness, had often tried to reason with her mother and had induced her to join a League. She was not at home until an hour after the accident.

The jury returned a verdict in accordance with the medical evidence and exonerated Lennon from all blame.

The Deputy Coroner said it was a most painful case, and expressed great sympathy with Captain Sinico and his daughter. He urged on the railway company to take strong measures to prevent the possibility of similar accidents in the future. No blame attached to anyone.

•　•　•　•　•　•　•　•　•

Mr. Duffy raised his eyes from the paper and gazed out of his window on the cheerless evening landscape. The river lay quiet beside the empty distillery and from time to time a light appeared in some house on the Lucan road. What an end! The whole narrative of her death revolted him and it revolted him to think that he had ever spoken to her of what he held sacred. The threadbare phrases, the inane expressions of sympathy, the cautious words of a reporter won over to conceal the details of a commonplace vulgar death attacked his stomach. Not merely had she degraded herself; she had degraded him. He saw the squalid tract of her vice, miserable and malodorous. His soul's companion! He thought of the hobbling wretches whom he had seen carrying cans and bottles to be filled by the barman. Just God, what an end! Evidently she had been unfit to live, without any strength of purpose, an easy prey to habits, one of the wrecks on which civilisation has been reared. But that she could have sunk so low! Was it possible he had deceived himself so utterly about her? He remembered her outburst of that night and interpreted it in a harsher sense than he had ever done. He had no difficulty now in approving of the course he had taken.

As the light failed and his memory began to wander he thought her hand touched his. The shock which had first attacked his stomach was now attacking his nerves. He put on his overcoat and hat quickly and went out. The cold air met him on the threshold; it crept into the sleeves of his coat. When he came to the public-house at Chapelizod Bridge he went in and ordered a hot punch.

The proprietor served him obsequiously but did not venture to talk. There were five or six working-men in the shop discussing the value of a gentleman's estate in County Kildare. They drank at intervals from their huge pint tumblers and smoked, spitting often on the floor and sometimes dragging the sawdust over their spits with their heavy boots. Mr. Duffy sat on his stool and gazed at them, without seeing or hearing them. After a while they went out and he called for another punch. He sat a long time over it. The shop was very quiet. The proprietor sprawled on the counter reading the *Herald* and yawning. Now and again a tram was heard swishing along the lonely road outside.

As he sat there, living over his life with her and evoking alternately the two images in which he now conceived her, he realised that she was dead, that she had ceased to exist, that she had become a memory. He began to feel ill at case. He asked himself what else could he have done. He could not have carried on a comedy of deception with her; he could not have lived with her openly. He had done what seemed to him best. How was he to blame? Now that she was gone he understood how lonely her life must have been, sitting night after night alone in that room. His life would be lonely too until he, too, died, ceased to exist, became a memory—if anyone remembered him.

It was after nine o'clock when he left the shop. The night was cold and gloomy. He entered the Park by the first gate and walked along under the gaunt trees. He walked through the bleak alleys where they had walked four years before. She seemed to be near him in the darkness. At moments he seemed to feel her voice touch his ear, her hand touch his. He stood still to listen. Why had he withheld life from her? Why had he sentenced her to death? He felt his moral nature falling to pieces.

When he gained the crest of the Magazine Hill he halted and looked along the river towards Dublin, the lights of which burned redly and hospitably in the cold night. He looked down the slope and, at the base, in the shadow of the wall of the Park, he saw some human figures lying. Those venal and furtive loves filled him with despair. He gnawed the rectitude of his life; he felt that he had been outcast from life's feast. One human being had seemed to love him and he had denied her life and happiness: he had sentenced her to ignominy, a death of shame. He knew that the prostrate creatures down by the wall were watching him and wished him gone. No one wanted him; he was outcast from life's feast. He turned his eyes to the grey gleaming river, winding along towards Dublin. Beyond the river he saw a goods train winding out of Kingsbridge Station, like a worm with a fiery head winding through the darkness, obstinately and laboriously. It passed slowly out of sight; but still he heard in his ears the laborious drone of the engine reiterating the syllables of her name.

He turned back the way he had come, the rhythm of the engine pounding in his ears. He began to doubt the reality of what memory told him. He halted under a tree and allowed the rhythm to die away. He could not feel her near him in the darkness nor her voice touch his ear. He waited for some minutes listening. He could hear nothing: the night was perfectly silent. He listened again: perfectly silent. He felt that he was alone.

Ivy Day in the Committee Room

Old Jack raked the cinders together with a piece of cardboard and spread them judiciously over the whitening dome of coals. When the dome was thinly covered his face lapsed into darkness but, as he set himself to fan the fire again, his crouching shadow ascended the opposite wall and his face slowly re-emerged into light. It was an old man's face, very bony and hairy. The moist blue eyes blinked at the fire and the moist mouth fell open at times, munching once or twice mechanically when it closed. When the cinders had caught he laid the piece of cardboard against the wall, sighed and said:

"That's better now, Mr. O'Connor,"

Mr. O'Connor, a grey-haired young man, whose face was disfigured by many blotches and pimples, had just brought the tobacco for a cigarette into a shapely cylinder but when spoken to he undid his handiwork meditatively. Then he began to roll the tobacco again meditatively and after a moment's thought decided to lick the paper.

"Did Mr. Tierney say when he'd be back?" he asked in a husky falsetto.

"He didn't say."

Mr. O'Connor put his cigarette into his mouth and began to search his pockets. He took out a pack of thin pasteboard cards.

"I'll get you a match," said the old man.

"Never mind, this'll do," said Mr. O'Connor.

He selected one of the cards and read what was printed on it:

MUNICIPAL ELECTIONS

Royal Exchange Ward

Mr. Richard J. Tierney, P.L.G., respectfully solicits the favour of your vote and influence at the coming election in the Royal Exchange Ward.

Mr. O'Connor had been engaged by Tierney's agent to canvass one part of the ward but, as the weather was inclement and his boots let in the wet, he spent a great part of the day sitting by the fire in the Committee Room in Wicklow Street with Jack, the old caretaker. They had been sitting thus since the short day had grown dark. It was the sixth of October, dismal and cold out of doors.

Mr. O'Connor tore a strip off the card and, lighting it, lit his cigarette. As he did so the flame lit up a leaf of dark glossy ivy in the lapel of his coat. The old man watched him attentively and then, taking up the piece of cardboard again, began to fan the fire slowly while his companion smoked.

"Ah, yes," he said, continuing, "it's hard to know what way to bring up children. Now who'd think he'd turn out like that! I sent him to the Christian Brothers and I done what I could for him, and there he goes boosing about. I tried to make him someway decent."

He replaced the cardboard wearily.

"Only I'm an old man now I'd change his tune for him. I'd take the stick to his back and beat him while I could stand over him—as I done many a time before. The mother, you know, she cocks him up with this and that ..."

"That's what ruins children," said Mr. O'Connor.

"To be sure it is," said the old man. "And little thanks you get for it, only impudence. He takes th'upper hand of me whenever he sees I've a sup taken. What's the world coming to when sons speaks that way to their fathers?"

"What age is he?" said Mr. O'Connor.

"Nineteen," said the old man.

"Why don't you put him to something?"

"Sure, amn't I never done at the drunken bowsy ever since he left school? 'I won't keep you,' I says. 'You must get a job for yourself.' But, sure, it's worse whenever he gets a job; he drinks it all."

Mr. O'Connor shook his head in sympathy, and the old man fell silent, gazing into the fire. Someone opened the door of the room and called out:

"Hello! Is this a Freemason's meeting?"

"Who's that?" said the old man.

"What are you doing in the dark?" asked a voice.

"Is that you, Hynes?" asked Mr. O'Connor.

"Yes. What are you doing in the dark?" said Mr. Hynes, advancing into the light of the fire.

He was a tall, slender young man with a light brown moustache. Imminent little drops of rain hung at the brim of his hat and the collar of his jacket-coat was turned up.

"Well, Mat," he said to Mr. O'Connor, "how goes it?"

Mr. O'Connor shook his head. The old man left the hearth, and after stumbling about the room returned with two candlesticks which he thrust one after the other into the fire and carried to the table. A denuded room came into view and the fire lost all its cheerful colour. The walls of the room were bare except for a copy of an election address. In the middle of the room was a small table on which papers were heaped.

Mr. Hynes leaned against the mantelpiece and asked:

"Has he paid you yet?"

"Not yet," said Mr. O'Connor. "I hope to God he'll not leave us in the lurch to-night."

Mr. Hynes laughed.

"O, he'll pay you. Never fear," he said.

"I hope he'll look smart about it if he means business," said Mr. O'Connor.

"What do you think, Jack?" said Mr. Hynes satirically to the old man.

The old man returned to his seat by the fire, saying:

"It isn't but he has it, anyway. Not like the other tinker."

"What other tinker?" said Mr. Hynes.

"Colgan," said the old man scornfully.

"Is it because Colgan's a working-man you say that? What's the difference between a good honest bricklayer and a publican—eh? Hasn't the working-man as good a right to be in the Corporation as anyone else—ay, and a better right than those shoneens that are always hat in hand before any fellow with a handle to his name? Isn't that so, Mat?" said Mr. Hynes, addressing Mr. O'Connor.

"I think you're right," said Mr. O'Connor.

"One man is a plain honest man with no hunker-sliding about him. He goes in to represent the labour classes. This fellow you're working for only wants to get some job or other."

"Of course, the working-classes should be represented," said the old man.

"The working-man," said Mr. Hynes, "gets all kicks and no halfpence. But it's labour produces everything. The working-man is not looking for fat jobs for his sons and nephews and cousins. The working-man is not going to drag the honour of Dublin in the mud to please a German monarch."

"How's that?" said the old man.

"Don't you know they want to present an address of welcome to Edward Rex if he comes here next year? What do we want kowtowing to a foreign king?"

"Our man won't vote for the address," said Mr. O'Connor. "He goes in on the Nationalist ticket."

"Won't he?" said Mr. Hynes. "Wait till you see whether he will or not. I know him. Is it Tricky Dicky Tierney?"

"By God! perhaps you're right, Joe," said Mr. O'Connor. "Anyway, I wish he'd turn up with the spondulics."

The three men fell silent. The old man began to rake more cinders together. Mr. Hynes took off his hat, shook it and then turned down the collar of his coat, displaying, as he did so, an ivy leaf in the lapel.

"If this man was alive," he said, pointing to the leaf, "we'd have no talk of an address of welcome."

"That's true," said Mr. O'Connor.

"Musha, God be with them times!" said the old man. "There was some life in it then."

The room was silent again. Then a bustling little man with a snuffling nose and very cold ears pushed in the door. He walked over quickly to the fire, rubbing his hands as if he intended to produce a spark from them.

"No money, boys," he said.

"Sit down here, Mr. Henchy," said the old man, offering him his chair.

"O, don't stir, Jack, don't stir," said Mr. Henchy.

He nodded curtly to Mr. Hynes and sat down on the chair which the old man vacated.

"Did you serve Aungier Street?" he asked Mr. O'Connor.

"Yes," said Mr. O'Connor, beginning to search his pockets for memoranda.

"Did you call on Grimes?"

"I did."

"Well? How does he stand?"

"He wouldn't promise. He said: 'I won't tell anyone what way I'm going to vote.' But I think he'll be all right."

"Why so?"

"He asked me who the nominators were; and I told him. I mentioned Father Burke's name. I think it'll be all right."

Mr. Henchy began to snuffle and to rub his hands over the fire at a terrific speed. Then he said:

"For the love of God, Jack, bring us a bit of coal. There must be some left."

The old man went out of the room.

"It's no go," said Mr. Henchy, shaking his head. "I asked the little shoeboy, but he said: 'O, now, Mr. Henchy, when I see the work going on properly I won't forget you, you may be sure.' Mean little tinker! 'Usha, how could he be anything else?"

"What did I tell you, Mat?" said Mr. Hynes. "Tricky Dicky Tierney."

"O, he's as tricky as they make 'em," said Mr. Henchy. "He hasn't got those little pigs' eyes for nothing. Blast his soul! Couldn't he pay up like a man instead of: 'O, now, Mr. Henchy, I must speak to Mr. Fanning … I've spent a lot of money'? Mean little schoolboy of hell! I suppose he forgets the time his little old father kept the hand-me-down shop in Mary's Lane."

"But is that a fact?" asked Mr. O'Connor.

"God, yes," said Mr. Henchy. "Did you never hear that? And the men used to go in on Sunday morning before the houses were open to buy a waistcoat or a trousers—moya! But Tricky Dicky's little old father always had a tricky little black bottle up in a corner. Do you mind now? That's that. That's where he first saw the light."

The old man returned with a few lumps of coal which he placed here and there on the fire.

"That's a nice how-do-you-do," said Mr. O'Connor. "How does he expect us to work for him if he won't stump up?"

"I can't help it," said Mr. Henchy. "I expect to find the bailiffs in the hall when I go home."

Mr. Hynes laughed and, shoving himself away from the mantelpiece with the aid of his shoulders, made ready to leave.

"It'll be all right when King Eddie comes," he said. "Well, boys, I'm off for the present. See you later. 'Bye, 'bye."

He went out of the room slowly. Neither Mr. Henchy nor the old man said anything, but, just as the door was closing, Mr. O'Connor, who had been staring moodily into the fire, called out suddenly:

"'Bye, Joe."

Mr. Henchy waited a few moments and then nodded in the direction of the door.

"Tell me," he said across the fire, "what brings our friend in here? What does he want?"

"'Usha, poor Joe!" said Mr. O'Connor, throwing the end of his cigarette into the fire, "he's hard up, like the rest of us."

Mr. Henchy snuffled vigorously and spat so copiously that he nearly put out the fire, which uttered a hissing protest.

"To tell you my private and candid opinion," he said, "I think he's a man from the other camp. He's a spy of Colgan's, if you ask me. 'Just go round and try and find out how they're getting on. They won't suspect you.' Do you twig?"

"Ah, Poor Joe is a decent skin," said Mr. O'Connor.

"His father was a decent, respectable man," Mr. Henchy admitted. "Poor old Larry Hynes! Many a good turn he did in his day! But I'm greatly afraid our friend is not nineteen carat. Damn it, I can understand a fellow being hard up, but what I can't understand is a fellow sponging. Couldn't he have some spark of manhood about him?"

"He doesn't get a warm welcome from me when he comes," said the old man. "Let him work for his own side and not come spying around here."

"I don't know," said Mr. O'Connor dubiously, as he took out cigarette papers and tobacco. "I think Joe Hynes is a straight man. He's a clever chap, too, with the pen. Do you remember that thing he wrote ... ?"

"Some of these hillsiders and fenians are a bit too clever if you ask me," said Mr. Henchy. "Do you know what my private and candid opinion is about some of those little jokers? I believe half of them are in the pay of the Castle."

"There's no knowing," said the old man.

"O, but I know it for a fact," said Mr. Henchy. "They're Castle hacks ... I don't say Hynes ... No, damn it, I think he's a stroke above that ... But there's a certain little nobleman with a cock-eye—you know the patriot I'm alluding to?"

Mr. O'Connor nodded.

"There's a lineal descendant of Major Sirr for you if you like! O, the heart's blood of a patriot! That's a fellow now that'd sell his country for fourpence—ay— and go down on his bended knees and thank the Almighty Christ he had a country to sell."

There was a knock at the door.

"Come in!" said Mr. Henchy.

A person resembling a poor clergyman or a poor actor appeared in the doorway. His black clothes were tightly buttoned on his short body and it was impossible to say whether he wore a clergyman's collar or a layman's, because the collar of his shabby frock-coat, the uncovered buttons of which reflected the candlelight, was turned up about his neck. He wore a round hat of hard black felt. His face, shining with raindrops, had the appearance of damp yellow cheese save where two rosy spots indicated the cheekbones. He opened his very long mouth suddenly to express disappointment and at the same time opened wide his very bright blue eyes to express pleasure and surprise.

"O, Father Keon!" said Mr. Henchy, jumping up from his chair. "Is that you? Come in!"

"O, no, no, no!" said Father Keon quickly, pursing his lips as if he were address-ing a child.

"Won't you come in and sit down?"

"No, no, no!" said Father Keon, speaking in a discreet, indulgent, velvety voice. "Don't let me disturb you now! I'm just looking for Mr. Fanning..."

"He's round at the Black Eagle," said Mr. Henchy. "But won't you come in and sit down a minute?"

"No, no, thank you. It was just a little business matter," said Father Keon. "Thank you, indeed."

He retreated from the doorway and Mr. Henchy, seizing one of the candlesticks, went to the door to light him downstairs.

"O, don't trouble, I beg!"

"No, but the stairs is so dark."

"No, no, I can see... Thank you, indeed."

"Are you right now?"

"All right, thanks... Thanks."

Mr. Henchy returned with the candlestick and put it on the table. He sat down again at the fire. There was silence for a few moments.

"Tell me, John," said Mr. O'Connor, lighting his cigarette with another paste-board card.

"Hm?"

"What is he exactly?"

"Ask me an easier one," said Mr. Henchy.

"Fanning and himself seem to me very thick. They're often in Kavanagh's together. Is he a priest at all?"

"'Mmmyes, I believe so ... I think he's what you call a black sheep. We haven't many of them, thank God! but we have a few ... He's an unfortunate man of some kind ..."

"And how does he knock it out?" asked Mr. O'Connor.

"That's another mystery."

"Is he attached to any chapel or church or institution or—"

"No," said Mr. Henchy, "I think he's travelling on his own account ... God forgive me," he added, "I thought he was the dozen of stout."

"Is there any chance of a drink itself?" asked Mr. O'Connor.

"I'm dry too," said the old man.

"I asked that little shoeboy three times," said Mr. Henchy, "would he send up a dozen of stout. I asked him again now, but he was leaning on the counter in his shirt-sleeves having a deep goster with Alderman Cowley."

"Why didn't you remind him?" said Mr. O'Connor.

"Well, I couldn't go over while he was talking to Alderman Cowley. I just waited till I caught his eye, and said: 'About that little matter I was speaking to you about ...' 'That'll be all right, Mr. H.,' he said. Yerra, sure the little hop-o'-my-thumb has forgotten all about it."

"There's some deal on in that quarter," said Mr. O'Connor thoughtfully. "I saw the three of them hard at it yesterday at Suffolk Street corner."

"I think I know the little game they're at," said Mr. Henchy. "You must owe the City Fathers money nowadays if you want to be made Lord Mayor. Then they'll make you Lord Mayor. By God! I'm thinking seriously of becoming a City Father myself. What do you think? Would I do for the job?"

Mr. O'Connor laughed.

"So far as owing money goes ..."

"Driving out of the Mansion House," said Mr. Henchy, "in all my vermin, with Jack here standing up behind me in a powdered wig—eh?"

"And make me your private secretary, John."

"Yes. And I'll make Father Keon my private chaplain. We'll have a family party."

"Faith, Mr. Henchy," said the old man, "you'd keep up better style than some of them. I was talking one day to old Keegan, the porter. 'And how do you like your new master, Pat?' says I to him. 'You haven't much entertaining now,' says I. 'Entertaining!' says he. 'He'd live on the smell of an oil-rag.' And do you know what he told me? Now, I declare to God, I didn't believe him."

"What?" said Mr. Henchy and Mr. O'Connor.

"He told me: 'What do you think of a Lord Mayor of Dublin sending out for a pound of chops for his dinner? How's that for high living?' says he. 'Wisha! wisha,' says I. 'A pound of chops,' says he, 'coming into the Mansion House.' 'Wisha!' says I, 'what kind of people is going at all now?'"

At this point there was a knock at the door, and a boy put in his head.

"What is it?" said the old man.

"From the *Black Eagle*," said the boy, walking in sideways and depositing a basket on the floor with a noise of shaken bottles.

The old man helped the boy to transfer the bottles from the basket to the table and counted the full tally. After the transfer the boy put his basket on his arm and asked:

"Any bottles?"

"What bottles?" said the old man.

"Won't you let us drink them first?" said Mr. Henchy.

"I was told to ask for bottles."

"Come back to-morrow," said the old man.

"Here, boy!" said Mr. Henchy, "will you run over to O'Farrell's and ask him to lend us a corkscrew—for Mr. Henchy, say. Tell him we won't keep it a minute. Leave the basket there."

The boy went out and Mr. Henchy began to rub his hands cheerfully, saying:

"Ah, well, he's not so bad after all. He's as good as his word, anyhow."

"There's no tumblers," said the old man.

"O, don't let that trouble you, Jack," said Mr. Henchy. "Many's the good man before now drank out of the bottle."

"Anyway, it's better than nothing," said Mr. O'Connor.

"He's not a bad sort," said Mr. Henchy, "only Fanning has such a loan of him. He means well, you know, in his own tinpot way."

The boy came back with the corkscrew. The old man opened three bottles and was handing back the corkscrew when Mr. Henchy said to the boy:

"Would you like a drink, boy?"

"If you please, sir," said the boy.

The old man opened another bottle grudgingly, and handed it to the boy.

"What age are you?" he asked.

"Seventeen," said the boy.

As the old man said nothing further, the boy took the bottle, said: "Here's my best respects, sir" to Mr. Henchy, drank the contents, put the bottle back on the table and wiped his mouth with his sleeve. Then he took up the corkscrew and went out of the door sideways, muttering some form of salutation.

"That's the way it begins," said the old man.

"The thin edge of the wedge," said Mr. Henchy.

The old man distributed the three bottles which he had opened and the men drank from them simultaneously. After having drunk each placed his bottle on the mantelpiece within hand's reach and drew in a long breath of satisfaction.

"Well, I did a good day's work to-day," said Mr. Henchy, after a pause.

"That so, John?"

"Yes. I got him one or two sure things in Dawson Street, Crofton and myself. Between ourselves, you know, Crofton (he's a decent chap, of course), but he's not worth a damn as a canvasser. He hasn't a word to throw to a dog. He stands and looks at the people while I do the talking."

Here two men entered the room. One of them was a very fat man, whose blue serge clothes seemed to be in danger of falling from his sloping figure. He had a big face which resembled a young ox's face in expression, staring blue eyes and a grizzled moustache. The other man, who was much younger and frailer, had a thin, clean-shaven face. He wore a very high double collar and a wide-brimmed bowler hat.

"Hello, Crofton!" said Mr. Henchy to the fat man. "Talk of the devil ..."

"Where did the boose come from?" asked the young man. "Did the cow calve?"

"O, of course, Lyons spots the drink first thing!" said Mr. O'Connor, laughing.

"Is that the way you chaps canvass," said Mr. Lyons, "and Crofton and I out in the cold and rain looking for votes?"

"Why, blast your soul," said Mr. Henchy, "I'd get more votes in five minutes than you two'd get in a week."

"Open two bottles of stout, Jack," said Mr. O'Connor.

"How can I?" said the old man, "when there's no corkscrew?"

"Wait now, wait now!" said Mr. Henchy, getting up quickly. "Did you ever see this little trick?"

He took two bottles from the table and, carrying them to the fire, put

them on the hob. Then he sat down again by the fire and took another drink from his bottle. Mr. Lyons sat on the edge of the table, pushed his hat towards the nape of his neck and began to swing his legs.

"Which is my bottle?" he asked.

"This, lad," said Mr. Henchy.

Mr. Crofton sat down on a box and looked fixedly at the other bottle on the hob. He was silent for two reasons. The first reason, sufficient in itself, was that he had nothing to say; the second reason was that he considered his companions beneath him. He had been a canvasser for Wilkins, the Conservative, but when the Conservatives had withdrawn their man and, choosing the lesser of two evils, given their support to the Nationalist candidate, he had been engaged to work for Mr. Tierney.

In a few minutes an apologetic *Pok!* was heard as the cork flew out of Mr. Lyons' bottle. Mr. Lyons jumped off the table, went to the fire, took his bottle and carried it back to the table.

"I was just telling them, Crofton," said Mr. Henchy, "that we got a good few votes to-day."

"Who did you get?" asked Mr. Lyons.

"Well, I got Parkes for one, and I got Atkinson for two, and I got Ward of Dawson Street. Fine old chap he is, too regular old toff, old Conservative! 'But isn't your candidate a Nationalist?' said he. 'He's a respectable man,' said I. 'He's in favour of whatever will benefit this country. He's a big ratepayer,' I said. 'He has extensive house property in the city and three places of business and isn't it to his own advantage to keep down the rates? He's a prominent and respected citizen,' said I, 'and a Poor Law Guardian, and he doesn't belong to any party, good, bad, or indifferent.' That's the way to talk to 'em."

"And what about the address to the King?" said Mr. Lyons, after drinking and smacking his lips.

"Listen to me," said Mr. Henchy. "What we want in this country, as I said to old Ward, is capital. The King's coming here will mean an influx of money into this country. The citizens of Dublin will benefit by it. Look at all the factories down by the quays there, idle! Look at all the money there is in the country if we only worked the old industries, the mills, the ship-building yards and factories. It's capital we want."

"But look here, John," said Mr. O'Connor. "Why should we welcome the King of England? Didn't Parnell himself …"

"Parnell," said Mr. Henchy, "is dead. Now, here's the way I look at it. Here's this chap come to the throne after his old mother keeping him out of it till the man was grey. He's a man of the world, and he means well by us. He's a jolly fine decent fellow, if you ask me, and no damn nonsense about him. He just says to himself: 'the old one never went to see these wild Irish. By Christ, I'll go myself and see what they're like.' And are we going to insult the man when he comes over here on a friendly visit? Eh? Isn't that right, Crofton?"

Mr. Crofton nodded his head.

"But after all now," said Mr. Lyons argumentatively, "King Edward's life, you know, is not the very ..."

"Let bygones be bygones," said Mr. Henchy. "I admire the man personally. He's just an ordinary knockabout like you and me. He's fond of his glass of grog and he's a bit of a rake, perhaps, and he's a good sportsman. Damn it, can't we Irish play fair?"

"That's all very fine," said Mr. Lyons. "But look at the case of Parnell now."

"In the name of God," said Mr. Henchy, "where's the analogy between the two cases?"

"What I mean," said Mr. Lyons, "is we have our ideals. Why, now, would we welcome a man like that? Do you think now after what he did Parnell was a fit man to lead us? And why, then, would we do it for Edward the Seventh?"

"This is Parnell's anniversary," said Mr. O'Connor, "and don't let us stir up any bad blood. We all respect him now that he's dead and gone—even the Conservatives," he added, turning to Mr. Crofton.

Pok! The tardy cork flew out of Mr. Crofton's bottle. Mr. Crofton got up from his box and went to the fire. As he returned with his capture he said in a deep voice:

"Our side of the house respects him, because he was a gentleman."

"Right you are, Crofton!" said Mr. Henchy fiercely. "He was the only man that could keep that bag of cats in order. 'Down, ye dogs! Lie down, ye curs!' That's the way he treated them. Come in, Joe! Come in!" he called out, catching sight of Mr. Hynes in the doorway.

Mr. Hynes came in slowly.

"Open another bottle of stout, Jack," said Mr. Henchy. "O, I forgot there's no corkscrew! Here, show me one here and I'll put it at the fire."

The old man handed him another bottle and he placed it on the hob.

"Sit down, Joe," said Mr. O'Connor, "we're just talking about the Chief."

"Ay, ay!" said Mr. Henchy.

Mr. Hynes sat on the side of the table near Mr. Lyons but said nothing.

"There's one of them, anyhow," said Mr. Henchy, "that didn't renege him. By God, I'll say for you, Joe! No, by God, you stuck to him like a man!"

"O, Joe," said Mr. O'Connor suddenly. "Give us that thing you wrote—do you remember? Have you got it on you?"

"O, ay!" said Mr. Henchy. "Give us that. Did you ever hear that, Crofton? Listen to this now: splendid thing."

"Go on," said Mr. O'Connor. "Fire away, Joe."

Mr. Hynes did not seem to remember at once the piece to which they were alluding, but, after reflecting a while, he said:

"O, that thing is it … Sure, that's old now."

"Out with it, man!" said Mr. O'Connor.

"'Sh, 'sh," said Mr. Henchy. "Now, Joe!"

Mr. Hynes hesitated a little longer. Then amid the silence he took off his hat, laid it on the table and stood up. He seemed to be rehearsing the piece in his mind. After a rather long pause he announced:

THE DEATH OF PARNELL
6th October, 1891

He cleared his throat once or twice and then began to recite

> He is dead. Our Uncrowned King is dead.
>   O, Erin, mourn with grief and woe
> For he lies dead whom the fell gang
>   Of modern hypocrites laid low.
>
> He lies slain by the coward hounds
>   He raised to glory from the mire;
> And Erin's hopes and Erin's dreams
>   Perish upon her monarch's pyre.
>
> In palace, cabin or in cot
>   The Irish heart where'er it be
> Is bowed with woe—for he is gone
>   Who would have wrought her destiny.

He would have had his Erin famed,
   The green flag gloriously unfurled,
Her statesmen, bards and warriors raised
   Before the nations of the World.

He dreamed (alas, 'twas but a dream!)
   Of Liberty: but as he strove
To clutch that idol, treachery
   Sundered him from the thing he loved.

Shame on the coward, caitiff hands
   That smote their Lord or with a kiss
Betrayed him to the rabble-rout
   Of fawning priests—no friends of his.

May everlasting shame consume
   The memory of those who tried
To befoul and smear the exalted name
   Of one who spurned them in his pride.

He fell as fall the mighty ones,
   Nobly undaunted to the last,
And death has now united him
   With Erin's heroes of the past.

No sound of strife disturb his sleep!
   Calmly he rests: no human pain
Or high ambition spurs him now
   The peaks of glory to attain.

They had their way: they laid him low.
   But Erin, list, his spirit may
Rise, like the Phoenix from the flames,
   When breaks the dawning of the day,

The day that brings us Freedom's reign.
>And on that day may Erin well
Pledge in the cup she lifts to Joy
>One grief—the memory of Parnell.

Mr. Hynes sat down again on the table. When he had finished his recitation there was a silence and then a burst of clapping: even Mr. Lyons clapped. The applause continued for a little time. When it had ceased all the auditors drank from their bottles in silence.

Pok! The cork flew out of Mr. Hynes' bottle, but Mr. Hynes remained sitting flushed and bareheaded on the table. He did not seem to have heard the invitation.

"Good man, Joe!" said Mr. O'Connor, taking out his cigarette papers and pouch the better to hide his emotion.

"What do you think of that, Crofton?" cried Mr. Henchy. "Isn't that fine? What?"

Mr. Crofton said that it was a very fine piece of writing.

A Mother

Mr. Holohan, assistant secretary of the *Eire Abu* Society, had been walking up and down Dublin for nearly a month, with his hands and pockets full of dirty pieces of paper, arranging about the series of concerts. He had a game leg and for this his friends called him Hoppy Holohan. He walked up and down constantly, stood by the hour at street corners arguing the point and made notes; but in the end it was Mrs. Kearney who arranged everything.

Miss Devlin had become Mrs. Kearney out of spite. She had been educated in a high-class convent, where she had learned French and music. As she was naturally pale and unbending in manner she made few friends at school. When she came to the age of marriage she was sent out to many houses, where her playing and ivory manners were much admired. She sat amid the chilly circle of her accomplishments, waiting for some suitor to brave it and offer her a brilliant life. But the young men whom she met were ordinary and she gave them no encouragement, trying to console her romantic desires by eating a great deal of Turkish Delight in secret. However, when she drew near the limit and her friends began to loosen their tongues about her, she silenced them by marrying Mr. Kearney, who was a bootmaker on Ormond Quay.

He was much older than she. His conversation, which was serious, took place at intervals in his great brown beard. After the first year of married life, Mrs. Kearney perceived that such a man would wear better than a romantic person, but she never put her own romantic ideas away. He was sober, thrifty and pious; he went to the altar every first Friday, sometimes with her, oftener by himself. But she never weakened in her religion and was a good wife to him. At some party in a strange house when she lifted her eyebrow ever so slightly he stood up to take his leave and, when his cough troubled him, she put the eider-down quilt over his feet and made a strong rum punch. For his part, he was a model father. By paying a small sum every week into a society, he ensured for both his daughters a dowry of one hundred pounds each when they came to the age of twenty-four. He sent the older daughter, Kathleen, to a good convent, where she learned French and music, and afterward paid her fees at the Academy. Every year in the month of July Mrs. Kearney found occasion to say to some friend:

"My good man is packing us off to Skerries for a few weeks."

If it was not Skerries it was Howth or Greystones.

When the Irish Revival began to be appreciable Mrs. Kearney determined to take advantage of her daughter's name and brought an Irish teacher to the house. Kathleen and her sister sent Irish picture postcards to their friends and these friends sent back other Irish picture postcards. On special Sundays, when Mr. Kearney went with his family to the pro-cathedral, a little crowd of people would assemble after mass at the corner of Cathedral Street. They were all friends of the Kearneys—musical friends or Nationalist friends; and, when they had played every little counter of gossip, they shook hands with one another all together, laughing at the crossing of so many hands, and said good-bye to one another in Irish. Soon the name of Miss Kathleen Kearney began to be heard often on people's lips. People said that she was very clever at music and a very nice girl and, moreover, that she was a believer in the language movement. Mrs. Kearney was well content at this. Therefore she was not surprised when one day Mr. Holohan came to her and proposed that her daughter should be the accompanist at a series of four grand concerts which his Society was going to give in the Antient Concert Rooms. She brought him into the drawing room, made him sit down and brought out the decanter and the silver biscuit-barrel. She entered heart and soul into the details of the enterprise, advised and dissuaded: and finally a contract was drawn up by which Kathleen was to receive eight guineas for her services as accompanist at the four grand concerts.

As Mr. Holohan was a novice in such delicate matters as the wording of bills and the disposing of items for a programme, Mrs. Kearney helped him. She had tact. She knew what *artistes* should go into capitals and what *artistes* should go into small type. She knew that the first tenor would not like to come on after Mr. Meade's comic turn. To keep the audience continually diverted she slipped the doubtful items in between the old favourites. Mr. Holohan called to see her every day to have her advice on some point. She was invariably friendly and advising— homely, in fact. She pushed the decanter towards him, saying:

"Now, help yourself, Mr. Holohan!"

And while he was helping himself she said:

"Don't be afraid! Don't be afraid of it!"

Everything went on smoothly. Mrs. Kearney bought some lovely blush-pink charmeuse in Brown Thomas's to let into the front of Kathleen's dress. It cost a pretty penny; but there are occasions when a little expense is justifiable. She took a dozen of two-shilling tickets for the final concert and sent them to those friends who could not be trusted to come otherwise. She forgot nothing, and, thanks to her, everything that was to be done was done.

The concerts were to be on Wednesday, Thursday, Friday and Saturday. When Mrs. Kearney arrived with her daughter at the Antient Concert Rooms on Wednesday night she did not like the look of things. A few young men, wearing bright blue badges in their coats, stood idle in the vestibule; none of them wore evening dress. She passed by with her daughter and a quick glance through the open door of the hall showed her the cause of the stewards' idleness. At first she wondered had she mistaken the hour. No, it was twenty minutes to eight.

In the dressing-room behind the stage she was introduced to the secretary of the Society, Mr. Fitzpatrick. She smiled and shook his hand. He was a little man, with a white, vacant face. She noticed that he wore his soft brown hat carelessly on the side of his head and that his accent was flat. He held a programme in his hand, and, while he was talking to her, he chewed one end of it into a moist pulp. He seemed to bear disappointments lightly. Mr. Holohan came into the dressing-room every few minutes with reports from the box-office. The *artistes* talked among themselves nervously, glanced from time to time at the mirror and rolled and unrolled their music. When it was nearly half-past eight, the few people in the hall began to express their desire to be entertained. Mr. Fitzpatrick came in, smiled vacantly at the room, and said:

"Well now, ladies and gentlemen. I suppose we'd better open the ball."

Mrs. Kearney rewarded his very flat final syllable with a quick stare of contempt, and then said to her daughter encouragingly:

"Are you ready, dear?"

When she had an opportunity, she called Mr. Holohan aside and asked him to tell her what it meant. Mr. Holohan did not know what it meant. He said that the committee had made a mistake in arranging for four concerts: four was too many.

"And the *artistes!*" said Mrs. Kearney. "Of course they are doing their best, but really they are not good."

Mr. Holohan admitted that the *artistes* were no good but the committee, he said, had decided to let the first three concerts go as they pleased and reserve all the talent for Saturday night. Mrs. Kearney said nothing, but, as the mediocre items followed one another on the platform and the few people in the hall grew fewer and fewer, she began to regret that she had put herself to any expense for such a concert. There was something she didn't like in the look of things and Mr. Fitzpatrick's vacant smile irritated her very much. However, she said nothing and waited to see how it would end. The concert expired shortly before ten, and everyone went home quickly.

The concert on Thursday night was better attended, but Mrs. Kearney saw at once that the house was filled with paper. The audience behaved indecorously, as if the concert were an informal dress rehearsal. Mr. Fitzpatrick seemed to enjoy himself: he was quite unconscious that Mrs. Kearney was taking angry note of his conduct. He stood at the edge of the screen, from time to time jutting out his head and exchanging a laugh with two friends in the corner of the balcony. In the course of the evening, Mrs. Kearney learned that the Friday concert was to be abandoned and that the committee was going to move heaven and earth to secure a bumper house on Saturday night. When she heard this, she sought out Mr. Holohan. She buttonholed him as he was limping out quickly with a glass of lemonade for a young lady and asked him was it true. Yes, it was true.

"But, of course, that doesn't alter the contract," she said. "The contract was for four concerts."

Mr. Holohan seemed to be in a hurry; he advised her to speak to Mr. Fitzpatrick. Mrs. Kearney was now beginning to be alarmed. She called Mr. Fitzpatrick away from his screen and told him that her daughter had signed for four concerts and that, of course, according to the terms of the contract, she should receive the sum originally stipulated for, whether the society gave the four concerts or not. Mr. Fitzpatrick, who did not catch the point at issue very quickly, seemed unable to resolve the difficulty and said that he would bring the matter before the committee. Mrs. Kearney's anger began to flutter in her cheek and she had all she could do to keep from asking:

"And who is the *Cometty* pray?"

But she knew that it would not be ladylike to do that: so she was silent.

Little boys were sent out into the principal streets of Dublin early on Friday morning with bundles of handbills. Special puffs appeared in all the evening papers, reminding the music-loving public of the treat which was in store for it on the following evening. Mrs. Kearney was somewhat reassured, but she thought well to tell her husband part of her suspicions. He listened carefully and said that perhaps it would be better if he went with her on Saturday night. She agreed. She respected her husband in the same way as she respected the General Post Office, as something large, secure and fixed; and though she knew the small number of his talents she appreciated his abstract value as a male. She was glad that he had suggested coming with her. She thought her plans over.

The night of the grand concert came. Mrs. Kearney, with her husband and daughter, arrived at the Antient Concert Rooms three-quarters of an hour before the time at which the concert was to begin. By ill luck it was a rainy evening. Mrs. Kearney placed her daughter's clothes and music in charge of her husband and went all over the building looking for Mr. Holohan or Mr. Fitzpatrick. She could find neither. She asked the stewards was any member of the committee in the hall and, after a great deal of trouble, a steward brought out a little woman named Miss Beirne to whom Mrs. Kearney explained that she wanted to see one of the secretaries. Miss Beirne expected them any minute and asked could she do anything. Mrs. Kearney looked searchingly at the oldish face which was screwed into an expression of trustfulness and enthusiasm and answered:

"No, thank you!"

The little woman hoped they would have a good house. She looked out at the rain until the melancholy of the wet street effaced all the trustfulness and enthusiasm from her twisted features. Then she gave a little sigh and said:

"Ah, well! We did our best, the dear knows."

Mrs. Kearney had to go back to the dressing-room.

The *artistes* were arriving. The bass and the second tenor had already come. The bass, Mr. Duggan, was a slender young man with a scattered black moustache. He was the son of a hall porter in an office in the city and, as a boy, he had sung prolonged bass notes in the resounding hall. From this humble state he had raised himself until he had become a first-rate *artiste*. He had appeared in grand opera. One night, when an operatic *artiste* had fallen ill, he had undertaken the part of the king in the opera of *Maritana* at the Queen's Theatre. He sang his music with great feeling and volume and was warmly welcomed by the gallery; but, unfortunately, he marred the good impression by wiping his nose in his gloved hand once or twice out of thoughtlessness. He was unassuming and spoke little. He said *yous* so softly that it passed unnoticed and he never drank anything stronger than milk for his voice's sake. Mr. Bell, the second tenor, was a fair-haired little man who competed every year for prizes at the Feis Ceoil. On his fourth trial he had been awarded a bronze medal. He was extremely nervous and extremely jealous of other tenors and he covered his nervous jealousy with an ebullient friendliness. It was his humour to have people know what an ordeal a concert was to him. Therefore when he saw Mr. Duggan he went over to him and asked:

"Are you in it too?"

"Yes," said Mr. Duggan.

Mr. Bell laughed at his fellow-sufferer, held out his hand and said:

"Shake!"

Mrs. Kearney passed by these two young men and went to the edge of the screen to view the house. The seats were being filled up rapidly and a pleasant noise circulated in the auditorium. She came back and spoke to her husband privately. Their conversation was evidently about Kathleen for they both glanced at her often as she stood chatting to one of her Nationalist friends, Miss Healy, the contralto. An unknown solitary woman with a pale face walked through the room. The women followed with keen eyes the faded blue dress which was stretched upon a meagre body. Someone said that she was Madam Glynn, the soprano.

"I wonder where did they dig her up," said Kathleen to Miss Healy. "I'm sure I never heard of her."

Miss Healy had to smile. Mr. Holohan limped into the dressing-room at that moment and the two young ladies asked him who was the unknown woman. Mr. Holohan said that she was Madam Glynn from London. Madam Glynn took her stand in a corner of the room, holding a roll of music stiffly before her and from time to time changing the direction of her startled gaze. The shadow took her faded dress into shelter but fell revengefully into the little cup behind her collar-bone. The noise of the hall became more audible. The first tenor and the baritone arrived together. They were both well dressed, stout and complacent and they brought a breath of opulence among the company.

Mrs. Kearney brought her daughter over to them, and talked to them amiably. She wanted to be on good terms with them but, while she strove to be polite, her eyes followed Mr. Holohan in his limping and devious courses. As soon as she could she excused herself and went out after him.

"Mr. Holohan, I want to speak to you for a moment," she said.

They went down to a discreet part of the corridor. Mrs. Kearney asked him when was her daughter going to be paid. Mr. Holohan said that Mr. Fitzpatrick had charge of that. Mrs. Kearney said that she didn't know anything about Mr. Fitzpatrick. Her daughter had signed a contract for eight guineas and she would have to be paid. Mr. Holohan said that it wasn't his business.

"Why isn't it your business?" asked Mrs. Kearney. "Didn't you yourself bring her the contract? Anyway, if it's not your business it's my business and I mean to see to it."

"You'd better speak to Mr. Fitzpatrick," said Mr. Holohan distantly.

"I don't know anything about Mr. Fitzpatrick," repeated Mrs. Kearney. "I have my contract, and I intend to see that it is carried out."

When she came back to the dressing-room her cheeks were slightly suffused. The room was lively. Two men in outdoor dress had taken possession of the fireplace and were chatting familiarly with Miss Healy and the baritone. They were the *Freeman* man and Mr. O'Madden Burke. The *Freeman* man had come in to say that he could not wait for the concert as he had to report the lecture which an American priest was giving in the Mansion House. He said they were to leave the report for him at the *Freeman* office and he would see that it went in. He was a grey-haired man, with a plausible voice and careful manners. He held an extinguished cigar in his hand and the aroma of cigar smoke floated near him. He had not intended to stay a moment because concerts and *artistes* bored him considerably but he remained leaning against the mantelpiece. Miss Healy stood in front of him, talking and laughing. He was old enough to suspect one reason for her politeness but young enough in spirit to turn the moment to account. The warmth, fragrance and colour of her body appealed to his senses. He was pleasantly conscious that the bosom which he saw rise and fall slowly beneath him rose and fell at that moment for him, that the laughter and fragrance and wilful glances were his tribute. When he could stay no longer he took leave of her regretfully.

"O'Madden Burke will write the notice," he explained to Mr. Holohan, "and I'll see it in."

"Thank you very much, Mr. Hendrick," said Mr. Holohan. "You'll see it in, I know. Now, won't you have a little something before you go?"

"I don't mind," said Mr. Hendrick.

The two men went along some tortuous passages and up a dark staircase and came to a secluded room where one of the stewards was uncorking bottles for a few gentlemen. One of these gentlemen was Mr. O'Madden Burke, who had found out the room by instinct. He was a suave, elderly man who balanced his imposing body, when at rest, upon a large silk umbrella. His magniloquent western name was the moral umbrella upon which he balanced the fine problem of his finances. He was widely respected.

While Mr. Holohan was entertaining the *Freeman* man Mrs. Kearney was speaking so animatedly to her husband that he had to ask her to lower her voice. The conversation of the others in the dressing-room had become strained. Mr. Bell, the first item, stood ready with his music but the accompanist made no sign. Evidently something was wrong. Mr. Kearney looked straight before him, stroking his beard, while Mrs. Kearney spoke into Kathleen's ear with subdued emphasis. From the hall came sounds of encouragement, clapping and stamping of feet. The first tenor and the baritone and Miss Healy stood together, waiting tranquilly, but Mr. Bell's nerves were greatly agitated because he was afraid the audience would think that he had come late.

Mr. Holohan and Mr. O'Madden Burke came into the room. In a moment Mr. Holohan perceived the hush. He went over to Mrs. Kearney and spoke with her earnestly. While they were speaking the noise in the hall grew louder. Mr. Holohan became very red and excited. He spoke volubly, but Mrs. Kearney said curtly at intervals:

"She won't go on. She must get her eight guineas."

Mr. Holohan pointed desperately towards the hall where the audience was clapping and stamping. He appealed to Mr. Kearney and to Kathleen. But Mr. Kearney continued to stroke his beard and Kathleen looked down, moving the point of her new shoe: it was not her fault. Mrs. Kearney repeated:

"She won't go on without her money."

After a swift struggle of tongues Mr. Holohan hobbled out in haste. The room was silent. When the strain of the silence had become somewhat painful Miss Healy said to the baritone:

"Have you seen Mrs. Pat Campbell this week?"

The baritone had not seen her but he had been told that she was very fine. The conversation went no further. The first tenor bent his head and began to count the links of the gold chain which was extended across his waist, smiling and humming random notes to observe the effect on the frontal sinus. From time to time everyone glanced at Mrs. Kearney.

The noise in the auditorium had risen to a clamour when Mr. Fitzpatrick burst into the room, followed by Mr. Holohan, who was panting. The clapping and stamping in the hall were punctuated by whistling. Mr. Fitzpatrick held a few bank-notes in his hand. He counted out four into Mrs. Kearney's hand and said she would get the other half at the interval. Mrs. Kearney said:

"This is four shillings short."

But Kathleen gathered in her skirt and said: "*Now Mr. Bell,*" to the first item, who was shaking like an aspen. The singer and the accompanist went out together. The noise in the hall died away. There was a pause of a few seconds: and then the piano was heard.

The first part of the concert was very successful except for Madam Glynn's item. The poor lady sang *Killarney* in a bodiless gasping voice, with all the old-fashioned mannerisms of intonation and pronunciation which she believed lent elegance to her singing. She looked as if she had been resurrected from an old stage-wardrobe and the cheaper parts of the hall made fun of her high wailing notes. The first tenor and the contralto, however, brought down the house. Kathleen played a selection of Irish airs which was generously applauded. The first part closed with a stirring patriotic recitation delivered by a young lady who arranged amateur theatricals. It was deservedly applauded; and, when it was ended, the men went out for the interval, content.

All this time the dressing-room was a hive of excitement. In one corner were Mr. Holohan, Mr. Fitzpatrick, Miss Beirne, two of the stewards, the baritone, the bass, and Mr. O'Madden Burke. Mr. O'Madden Burke said it was the most scandalous exhibition he had ever witnessed. Miss Kathleen Kearney's musical career was ended in Dublin after that, he said. The baritone was asked what did he think of Mrs. Kearney's conduct. He did not like to say anything. He had been paid his money and wished to be at peace with men. However, he said that Mrs. Kearney might have taken the *artistes* into consideration. The stewards and the secretaries debated hotly as to what should be done when the interval came.

"I agree with Miss Beirne," said Mr. O'Madden Burke. "Pay her nothing."

In another corner of the room were Mrs. Kearney and her husband, Mr. Bell, Miss Healy and the young lady who had to recite the patriotic piece. Mrs. Kearney said that the committee had treated her scandalously. She had spared neither trouble nor expense and this was how she was repaid.

They thought they had only a girl to deal with and that, therefore, they could ride roughshod over her. But she would show them their mistake. They wouldn't have dared to have treated her like that if she had been a man. But she would see that her daughter got her rights: she wouldn't be fooled. If they didn't pay her to the last farthing she would make Dublin ring. Of course she was sorry for the sake of the *artistes*. But what else could she do? She appealed to the second tenor, who said he thought she had not been well treated. Then she appealed to Miss Healy. Miss Healy wanted to join the other group but she did not like to do so because she was a great friend of Kathleen's and the Kearneys had often invited her to their house.

As soon as the first part was ended Mr. Fitzpatrick and Mr. Holohan went over to Mrs. Kearney and told her that the other four guineas would be paid after the committee meeting on the following Tuesday and that, in case her daughter did not play for the second part, the committee would consider the contract broken and would pay nothing.

"I haven't seen any committee," said Mrs. Kearney angrily. "My daughter has her contract. She will get four pounds eight into her hand or a foot she won't put on that platform."

"I'm surprised at you, Mrs. Kearney," said Mr. Holohan. "I never thought you would treat us this way."

"And what way did you treat me?" asked Mrs. Kearney.

Her face was inundated with an angry colour and she looked as if she would attack someone with her hands.

"I'm asking for my rights," she said.

"You might have some sense of decency," said Mr. Holohan.

"Might I, indeed? … And when I ask when my daughter is going to get paid I can't get a civil answer."

She tossed her head and assumed a haughty voice:

"You must speak to the secretary. It's not my business. I'm a great fellow fol-the-diddle-I-do."

"I thought you were a lady," said Mr. Holohan, walking away from her abruptly.

After that Mrs. Kearney's conduct was condemned on all hands: everyone approved of what the committee had done. She stood at the door, haggard with rage, arguing with her husband and daughter, gesticulating with them. She waited until it was time for the second part to begin in the hope that the secretaries would approach her. But Miss Healy had kindly consented to play one or two accompaniments. Mrs. Kearney had to stand aside to allow the baritone and his accompanist to pass up to the platform. She stood still for an instant like an angry stone image and, when the first notes of the song struck her ear, she caught up her daughter's cloak and said to her husband:

"Get a cab!"

He went out at once. Mrs. Kearney wrapped the cloak round her daughter and followed him. As she passed through the doorway she stopped and glared into Mr. Holohan's face.

"I'm not done with you yet," she said.

"But I'm done with you," said Mr. Holohan.

Kathleen followed her mother meekly. Mr. Holohan began to pace up and down the room, in order to cool himself for he felt his skin on fire.

"That's a nice lady!" he said. "O, she's a nice lady!"

"You did the proper thing, Holohan," said Mr. O'Madden Burke, poised upon his umbrella in approval.

Grace

Two gentlemen who were in the lavatory at the time tried to lift him up: but he was quite helpless. He lay curled up at the foot of the stairs down which he had fallen. They succeeded in turning him over. His hat had rolled a few yards away and his clothes were smeared with the filth and ooze of the floor on which he had lain, face downwards. His eyes were closed and he breathed with a grunting noise. A thin stream of blood trickled from the corner of his mouth.

These two gentlemen and one of the curates carried him up the stairs and laid him down again on the floor of the bar. In two minutes he was surrounded by a ring of men. The manager of the bar asked everyone who he was and who was with him. No one knew who he was but one of the curates said he had served the gentleman with a small rum.

"Was he by himself?" asked the manager.

"No, sir. There was two gentlemen with him."

"And where are they?"

No one knew; a voice said:

"Give him air. He's fainted."

The ring of onlookers distended and closed again elastically. A dark medal of blood had formed itself near the man's head on the tessellated floor. The manager, alarmed by the grey pallor of the man's face, sent for a policeman.

His collar was unfastened and his necktie undone. He opened his eyes for an instant, sighed and closed them again. One of the gentlemen who had carried him upstairs held a dinged silk hat in his hand. The manager asked repeatedly did no one know who the injured man was or where had his friends gone. The door of the bar opened and an immense constable entered. A crowd which had followed him down the laneway collected outside the door, struggling to look in through the glass panels.

The manager at once began to narrate what he knew. The constable, a young man with thick immobile features, listened. He moved his head slowly to right and left and from the manager to the person on the floor, as if he feared to be the victim of some delusion. Then he drew off his glove, produced a small book from his waist, licked the lead of his pencil and made ready to indite. He asked in a suspicious provincial accent:

"Who is the man? What's his name and address?"

A young man in a cycling-suit cleared his way through the ring of bystanders. He knelt down promptly beside the injured man and called for water. The constable knelt down also to help. The young man washed the blood from the injured man's mouth and then called for some brandy. The constable repeated the order in an authoritative voice until a curate came running with the glass. The brandy was forced down the man's throat. In a few seconds he opened his eyes and looked about him. He looked at the circle of faces and then, understanding, strove to rise to his feet.

"You're all right now?" asked the young man in the cycling-suit.

"Sha, 's nothing," said the injured man, trying to stand up.

He was helped to his feet. The manager said something about a hospital and some of the bystanders gave advice. The battered silk hat was placed on the man's head. The constable asked:

"Where do you live?"

The man, without answering, began to twirl the ends of his moustache. He made light of his accident. It was nothing, he said: only a little accident. He spoke very thickly.

"Where do you live?" repeated the constable.

The man said they were to get a cab for him. While the point was being debated a tall agile gentleman of fair complexion, wearing a long yellow ulster, came from the far end of the bar. Seeing the spectacle, he called out:

"Hallo, Tom, old man! What's the trouble?"

"Sha, 's nothing," said the man.

The new-comer surveyed the deplorable figure before him and then turned to the constable, saying:

"It's all right, constable. I'll see him home."

The constable touched his helmet and answered:

"All right, Mr. Power!"

"Come now, Tom," said Mr. Power, taking his friend by the arm. "No bones broken. What? Can you walk?"

The young man in the cycling-suit took the man by the other arm and the crowd divided.

"How did you get yourself into this mess?" asked Mr. Power.

"The gentleman fell down the stairs," said the young man.

"I' 'ery 'uch o'liged to you, sir," said the injured man.

"Not at all."

"'an't we have a little … ?"

"Not now. Not now."

The three men left the bar and the crowd sifted through the doors into the laneway. The manager brought the constable to the stairs to inspect the scene of the accident. They agreed that the gentleman must have missed his footing. The customers returned to the counter and a curate set about removing the traces of blood from the floor.

When they came out into Grafton Street, Mr. Power whistled for an outsider. The injured man said again as well as he could:

"I 'ery 'uch o'liged to you, sir. I hope we'll 'eet again. 'y na'e is Kernan."

The shock and the incipient pain had partly sobered him.

"Don't mention it," said the young man.

They shook hands. Mr. Kernan was hoisted on to the car and, while Mr. Power was giving directions to the carman, he expressed his gratitude to the young man and regretted that they could not have a little drink together.

"Another time," said the young man.

The car drove off towards Westmoreland Street. As it passed the Ballast Office the clock showed half-past nine. A keen east wind hit them, blowing from the mouth of the river. Mr. Kernan was huddled together with cold. His friend asked him to tell how the accident had happened.

"I 'an't, 'an," he answered, "'y 'ongue is hurt."

"Show."

The other leaned over the well of the car and peered into Mr. Kernan's mouth but he could not see. He struck a match and, sheltering it in the shell of his hands, peered again into the mouth which Mr. Kernan opened obediently. The swaying movement of the car brought the match to and from the opened mouth. The lower teeth and gums were covered with clotted blood and a minute piece of the tongue seemed to have been bitten off. The match was blown out.

"That's ugly," said Mr. Power.

"Sha, 's nothing," said Mr. Kernan, closing his mouth and pulling the collar of his filthy coat across his neck.

Mr. Kernan was a commercial traveller of the old school which believed in the dignity of its calling. He had never been seen in the city without a silk hat of some decency and a pair of gaiters. By grace of these two articles of clothing, he said, a man could always pass muster. He carried on the tradition of his Napoleon, the great Blackwhite, whose memory he evoked at times by legend and mimicry. Modern business methods had spared him only so far as to allow him a little office in Crowe Street, on the window blind of which was written the name of his firm with the address—London, E.C. On the mantelpiece of this little office a little leaden battalion of canisters was drawn up and on the table before the window stood four or five china bowls which were usually half full of a black liquid. From these bowls Mr. Kernan tasted tea. He took a mouthful, drew it up, saturated his palate with it and then spat it forth into the grate. Then he paused to judge.

Mr. Power, a much younger man, was employed in the Royal Irish Constabulary Office in Dublin Castle. The arc of his social rise intersected the arc of his friend's decline, but Mr. Kernan's decline was mitigated by the fact that certain of those friends who had known him at his highest point of success still esteemed him as a character. Mr. Power was one of these friends. His inexplicable debts were a byword in his circle; he was a debonair young man.

The car halted before a small house on the Glasnevin road and Mr. Kernan was helped into the house. His wife put him to bed, while Mr. Power sat downstairs in the kitchen asking the children where they went to school and what book they were in. The children—two girls and a boy, conscious of their father's helplessness and of their mother's absence, began some horseplay with him. He was surprised at their manners and at their accents, and his brow grew thoughtful. After a while Mrs. Kernan entered the kitchen, exclaiming:

"Such a sight! O, he'll do for himself one day and that's the holy alls of it. He's been drinking since Friday."

Mr. Power was careful to explain to her that he was not responsible, that he had come on the scene by the merest accident. Mrs. Kernan, remembering Mr. Power's good offices during domestic quarrels, as well as many small, but opportune loans, said:

"O, you needn't tell me that, Mr. Power. I know you're a friend of his, not like some of the others he does be with. They're all right so long as he has money in his pocket to keep him out from his wife and family. Nice friends! Who was he with to-night, I'd like to know?"

Mr. Power shook his head but said nothing.

"I'm so sorry," she continued, "that I've nothing in the house to offer you. But if you wait a minute I'll send round to Fogarty's, at the corner."

Mr. Power stood up.

"We were waiting for him to come home with the money. He never seems to think he has a home at all."

"O, now, Mrs. Kernan," said Mr. Power, "we'll make him turn over a new leaf. I'll talk to Martin. He's the man. We'll come here one of these nights and talk it over."

She saw him to the door. The carman was stamping up and down the footpath, and swinging his arms to warm himself.

"It's very kind of you to bring him home," she said.

"Not at all," said Mr. Power.

He got up on the car. As it drove off he raised his hat to her gaily.

"We'll make a new man of him," he said. "Good-night, Mrs. Kernan."

·   ·   ·   ·   ·   ·   ·   ·

Mrs. Kernan's puzzled eyes watched the car till it was out of sight. Then she withdrew them, went into the house and emptied her husband's pockets.

She was an active, practical woman of middle age. Not long before she had celebrated her silver wedding and renewed her intimacy with her husband by waltzing with him to Mr. Power's accompaniment. In her days of courtship, Mr. Kernan had seemed to her a not ungallant figure: and she still hurried to the chapel door whenever a wedding was reported and, seeing the bridal pair, recalled with vivid pleasure how she had passed out of the Star of the Sea Church in Sandymount, leaning on the arm of a jovial well-fed man, who was dressed smartly in a frock-coat and lavender trousers and carried a silk hat gracefully balanced upon his other arm. After three weeks she had found a wife's life irksome and, later on, when she was beginning to find it unbearable, she had become a mother. The part of mother presented to her no insuperable difficulties and for twenty-five years she had kept house shrewdly for her husband. Her two eldest sons were launched. One was in a draper's shop in Glasgow and the other was clerk to a tea-merchant in Belfast. They were good sons, wrote regularly and sometimes sent home money. The other children were still at school.

Mr. Kernan sent a letter to his office next day and remained in bed. She made beef-tea for him and scolded him roundly. She accepted his frequent intemperance as part of the climate, healed him dutifully whenever he was sick and always tried to make him eat a breakfast. There were worse husbands. He had never been violent since the boys had grown up, and she knew that he would walk to the end of Thomas Street and back again to book even a small order.

Two nights after, his friends came to see him. She brought them up to his bed-room, the air of which was impregnated with a personal odour, and gave them chairs at the fire. Mr. Kernan's tongue, the occasional stinging pain of which had made him somewhat irritable during the day, became more polite. He sat propped up in the bed by pillows and the little colour in his puffy cheeks made them resemble warm cinders. He apologised to his guests for the disorder of the room, but at the same time looked at them a little proudly with a veteran's pride.

He was quite unconscious that he was the victim of a plot which his friends, Mr. Cunningham, Mr. M'Coy and Mr. Power had disclosed to Mrs. Kernan in the parlour. The idea had been Mr. Power's, but its development was entrusted to Mr. Cunningham. Mr. Kernan came of Protestant stock and, though he had been converted to the Catholic faith at the time of his marriage, he had not been in the pale of the Church for twenty years. He was fond, moreover, of giving side-thrusts at Catholicism.

Mr. Cunningham was the very man for such a case. He was an elder colleague of Mr. Power. His own domestic life was not very happy. People had great sympathy with him, for it was known that he had married an unpresentable woman who was an incurable drunkard. He had set up house for her six times; and each time she had pawned the furniture on him.

Everyone had respect for poor Martin Cunningham. He was a thoroughly sensible man, influential and intelligent. His blade of human knowledge, natural astuteness particularised by long association with cases in the police courts, had been tempered by brief immersions in the waters of general philosophy. He was well informed. His friends bowed to his opinions and considered that his face was like Shakespeare's.

When the plot had been disclosed to her, Mrs. Kernan had said:

"I leave it all in your hands, Mr. Cunningham."

After a quarter of a century of married life, she had very few illusions left. Religion for her was a habit, and she suspected that a man of her husband's age would not change greatly before death. She was tempted to see a curious appropriateness in his accident and, but that she did not wish to seem bloody-minded, she would have told the gentlemen that Mr. Kernan's tongue would not suffer by being shortened. However, Mr. Cunningham was a capable man; and religion was religion. The scheme might do good and, at least, it could do no harm. Her beliefs were not extravagant. She believed steadily in the Sacred Heart as the most generally useful of all Catholic devotions and approved of the sacraments. Her faith was bounded by her kitchen, but, if she was put to it, she could believe also in the banshee and in the Holy Ghost.

The gentlemen began to talk of the accident. Mr. Cunningham said that he had once known a similar case. A man of seventy had bitten off a piece of his tongue during an epileptic fit and the tongue had filled in again, so that no one could see a trace of the bite.

"Well, I'm not seventy," said the invalid.

"God forbid," said Mr. Cunningham.

"It doesn't pain you now?" asked Mr. M'Coy.

Mr. M'Coy had been at one time a tenor of some reputation. His wife, who had been a soprano, still taught young children to play the piano at low terms. His line of life had not been the shortest distance between two points and for short periods he had been driven to live by his wits. He had been a clerk in the Midland Railway, a canvasser for advertisements for *The Irish Times* and for *The Freeman's Journal*, a town traveller for a coal firm on commission, a private inquiry agent, a clerk in the office of the Sub-Sheriff, and he had recently become secretary to the City Coroner. His new office made him professionally interested in Mr. Kernan's case.

"Pain? Not much," answered Mr. Kernan. "But it's so sickening. I feel as if I wanted to retch off."

"That's the boose," said Mr. Cunningham firmly.

"No," said Mr. Kernan. "I think I caught cold on the car. There's something keeps coming into my throat, phlegm or—"

"Mucus," said Mr. M'Coy.

"It keeps coming like from down in my throat; sickening thing."

"Yes, yes," said Mr. M'Coy, "that's the thorax."

He looked at Mr. Cunningham and Mr. Power at the same time with an air of challenge. Mr. Cunningham nodded his head rapidly and Mr. Power said:

"Ah, well, all's well that ends well."

"I'm very much obliged to you, old man," said the invalid.

Mr. Power waved his hand.

"Those other two fellows I was with—"

"Who were you with?" asked Mr. Cunningham.

"A chap. I don't know his name. Damn it now, what's his name? Little chap with sandy hair ..."

"And who else?"

"Harford."

"Hm," said Mr. Cunningham.

When Mr. Cunningham made that remark, people were silent. It was known that the speaker had secret sources of information. In this case the monosyllable had a moral intention. Mr. Harford sometimes formed one of a little detachment which left the city shortly after noon on Sunday with the purpose of arriving as soon as possible at some public-house on the outskirts of the city where its members duly qualified themselves as bonafide travellers. But his fellow-travellers had never consented to overlook his origin. He had begun life as an obscure financier by lending small sums of money to workmen at usurious interest. Later on he had become the partner of a very fat, short gentleman, Mr. Goldberg, in the Liffey Loan Bank. Though he had never embraced more than the Jewish ethical code, his fellow-Catholics, whenever they had smarted in person or by proxy under his exactions, spoke of him bitterly as an Irish Jew and an illiterate, and saw divine disapproval of usury made manifest through the person of his idiot son. At other times they remembered his good points.

"I wonder where did he go to," said Mr. Kernan.

He wished the details of the incident to remain vague. He wished his friends to think there had been some mistake, that Mr. Harford and he had missed each other. His friends, who knew quite well Mr. Harford's manners in drinking were silent. Mr. Power said again:

"All's well that ends well."

Mr. Kernan changed the subject at once.

"That was a decent young chap, that medical fellow," he said. "Only for him—"

"O, only for him," said Mr. Power, "it might have been a cause of seven days, without the option of a fine."

"Yes, yes," said Mr. Kernan, trying to remember. "I remember now there was a policeman. Decent young fellow, he seemed. How did it happen at all?"

"It happened that you were peloothered, Tom," said Mr. Cunningham gravely.

"True bill," said Mr. Kernan, equally gravely.

"I suppose you squared the constable, Jack," said Mr. M'Coy.

Mr. Power did not relish the use of his Christian name. He was not straight-laced, but he could not forget that Mr. M'Coy had recently made a crusade in search of valises and portmanteaus to enable Mrs. M'Coy to fulfil imaginary engagements in the country. More than he resented the fact that he had been victimised he resented such low playing of the game. He answered the question, therefore, as if Mr. Kernan had asked it.

The narrative made Mr. Kernan indignant. He was keenly conscious of his citizenship, wished to live with his city on terms mutually honourable and resented any affront put upon him by those whom he called country bumpkins.

"Is this what we pay rates for?" he asked. "To feed and clothe these ignorant bostooms ... and they're nothing else."

Mr. Cunningham laughed. He was a Castle official only during office hours.

"How could they be anything else, Tom?" he said.

He assumed a thick, provincial accent and said in a tone of command:

"65, catch your cabbage!"

Everyone laughed. Mr. M'Coy, who wanted to enter the conversation by any door, pretended that he had never heard the story. Mr. Cunningham said:

"It is supposed—they say, you know—to take place in the depot where they get these thundering big country fellows, omadhauns, you know, to drill. The sergeant makes them stand in a row against the wall and hold up their plates."

He illustrated the story by grotesque gestures.

"At dinner, you know. Then he has a bloody big bowl of cabbage before him on the table and a bloody big spoon like a shovel. He takes up a wad of cabbage on the spoon and pegs it across the room and the poor devils have to try and catch it on their plates: *65, catch your cabbage.*"

Everyone laughed again: but Mr. Kernan was somewhat indignant still. He talked of writing a letter to the papers.

"These yahoos coming up here," he said, "think they can boss the people. I needn't tell you, Martin, what kind of men they are."

Mr. Cunningham gave a qualified assent.

"It's like everything else in this world," he said. "You get some bad ones and you get some good ones."

"O yes, you get some good ones, I admit," said Mr. Kernan, satisfied.

"It's better to have nothing to say to them," said Mr. M'Coy. "That's my opinion!"

Mrs. Kernan entered the room and, placing a tray on the table, said:

"Help yourselves, gentlemen."

Mr. Power stood up to officiate, offering her his chair. She declined it, saying she was ironing downstairs, and, after having exchanged a nod with Mr. Cunningham behind Mr. Power's back, prepared to leave the room. Her husband called out to her:

"And have you nothing for me, duckie?"

"O you! The back of my hand to you!" said Mrs. Kernan tartly.

Her husband called after her:

"Nothing for poor little hubby!"

He assumed such a comical face and voice that the distribution of the bottles of stout took place amid general merriment.

The gentlemen drank from their glasses, set the glasses again on the table and paused. Then Mr. Cunningham turned towards Mr. Power and said casually:

"On Thursday night, you said, Jack?"

"Thursday, yes," said Mr. Power.

"Righto!" said Mr. Cunningham promptly.

"We can meet in M'Auley's," said Mr. M'Coy. "That'll be the most convenient place."

"But we mustn't be late," said Mr. Power earnestly, "because it is sure to be crammed to the doors."

"We can meet at half-seven," said Mr. M'Coy.

"Righto!" said Mr. Cunningham.

"Half-seven at M'Auley's be it!"

There was a short silence. Mr. Kernan waited to see whether he would be taken into his friends' confidence. Then he asked:

"What's in the wind?"

"O, it's nothing," said Mr. Cunningham. "It's only a little matter that we're arranging about for Thursday."

"The opera, is it?" said Mr. Kernan.

"No, no," said Mr. Cunningham in an evasive tone, "it's just a little … spiritual matter."

"O," said Mr. Kernan.

There was silence again. Then Mr. Power said, point blank:

"To tell you the truth, Tom, we're going to make a retreat."

"Yes, that's it," said Mr. Cunningham, "Jack and I and M'Coy here—we're all going to wash the pot."

He uttered the metaphor with a certain homely energy and, encouraged by his own voice, proceeded:

"You see, we may as well all admit we're a nice collection of scoundrels, one and all. I say, one and all," he added with gruff charity and turning to Mr. Power. "Own up now!"

"I own up," said Mr. Power.

"And I own up," said Mr. M'Coy.

"So we're going to wash the pot together," said Mr. Cunningham.

A thought seemed to strike him. He turned suddenly to the invalid and said:

"D'ye know what, Tom, has just occurred to me? You might join in and we'd have a four-handed reel."

"Good idea," said Mr. Power. "The four of us together."

Mr. Kernan was silent. The proposal conveyed very little meaning to his mind, but, understanding that some spiritual agencies were about to concern themselves on his behalf, he thought he owed it to his dignity to show a stiff neck. He took no part in the conversation for a long while, but listened, with an air of calm enmity, while his friends discussed the Jesuits.

"I haven't such a bad opinion of the Jesuits," he said, intervening at length. "They're an educated order. I believe they mean well, too."

"They're the grandest order in the Church, Tom," said Mr. Cunningham, with enthusiasm. "The General of the Jesuits stands next to the Pope."

"There's no mistake about it," said Mr. M'Coy, "if you want a thing well done and no flies about, you go to a Jesuit. They're the boyos have influence. I'll tell you a case in point …"

"The Jesuits are a fine body of men," said Mr. Power.

"It's a curious thing," said Mr. Cunningham, "about the Jesuit Order. Every other order of the Church had to be reformed at some time or other but the Jesuit Order was never once reformed. It never fell away."

"Is that so?" asked Mr. M'Coy.

"That's a fact," said Mr. Cunningham. "That's history."

"Look at their church, too," said Mr. Power. "Look at the congregation they have."

"The Jesuits cater for the upper classes," said Mr. M'Coy.

"Of course," said Mr. Power.

"Yes," said Mr. Kernan. "That's why I have a feeling for them. It's some of those secular priests, ignorant, bumptious—"

"They're all good men," said Mr. Cunningham, "each in his own way. The Irish priesthood is honoured all the world over."

"O yes," said Mr. Power.

"Not like some of the other priesthoods on the continent," said Mr. M'Coy, "unworthy of the name."

"Perhaps you're right," said Mr. Kernan, relenting.

"Of course I'm right," said Mr. Cunningham. "I haven't been in the world all this time and seen most sides of it without being a judge of character."

The gentlemen drank again, one following another's example. Mr. Kernan seemed to be weighing something in his mind. He was impressed. He had a high opinion of Mr. Cunningham as a judge of character and as a reader of faces. He asked for particulars.

"O, it's just a retreat, you know," said Mr. Cunningham. "Father Purdon is giving it. It's for business men, you know."

"He won't be too hard on us, Tom," said Mr. Power persuasively.

"Father Purdon? Father Purdon?" said the invalid.

"O, you must know him, Tom," said Mr. Cunningham stoutly. "Fine, jolly fellow! He's a man of the world like ourselves."

"Ah, … yes. I think I know him. Rather red face; tall."

"That's the man."

"And tell me, Martin … Is he a good preacher?"

"Mmmno … It's not exactly a sermon, you know. It's just a kind of a friendly talk, you know, in a common-sense way."

Mr. Kernan deliberated. Mr. M'Coy said:

"Father Tom Burke, that was the boy!"

"O, Father Tom Burke," said Mr. Cunningham, "that was a born orator. Did you ever hear him, Tom?"

"Did I ever hear him!" said the invalid, nettled. "Rather! I heard him…"

"And yet they say he wasn't much of a theologian," said Mr. Cunningham.

"Is that so?" said Mr. M'Coy.

"O, of course, nothing wrong, you know. Only sometimes, they say, he didn't preach what was quite orthodox."

"Ah! … he was a splendid man," said Mr. M'Coy.

"I heard him once," Mr. Kernan continued. "I forget the subject of his discourse now. Crofton and I were in the back of the … pit, you know … the—"

"The body," said Mr. Cunningham.

"Yes, in the back near the door. I forget now what … O yes, it was on the Pope, the late Pope. I remember it well. Upon my word it was magnificent, the style of the oratory. And his voice! God! hadn't he a voice! *The Prisoner of the Vatican*, he called him. I remember Crofton saying to me when we came out—"

"But he's an Orangeman, Crofton, isn't he?" said Mr. Power.

"'Course he is," said Mr. Kernan, "and a damned decent Orangeman, too. We went into Butler's in Moore Street—faith, I was genuinely moved, tell you the God's truth—and I remember well his very words. *Kernan*, he said, *we worship at different altars*, he said, *but our belief is the same*. Struck me as very well put."

"There's a good deal in that," said Mr. Power. "There used always be crowds of Protestants in the chapel when Father Tom was preaching."

"There's not much difference between us," said Mr. M'Coy. "We both believe in—"

He hesitated for a moment.

" ... in the Redeemer. Only they don't believe in the Pope and in the mother of God."

"But, of course," said Mr. Cunningham quietly and effectively, "our religion is *the* religion, the old, original faith."

"Not a doubt of it," said Mr. Kernan warmly.

Mrs. Kernan came to the door of the bedroom and announced:

"Here's a visitor for you!"

"Who is it?"

"Mr. Fogarty."

"O, come in! come in!"

A pale, oval face came forward into the light. The arch of its fair trailing moustache was repeated in the fair eyebrows looped above pleasantly astonished eyes. Mr. Fogarty was a modest grocer. He had failed in business in a licensed house in the city because his financial condition had constrained him to tie himself to second-class distillers and brewers. He had opened a small shop on Glasnevin Road where, he flattered himself, his manners would ingratiate him with the housewives of the district. He bore himself with a certain grace, complimented little children and spoke with a neat enunciation. He was not without culture.

Mr. Fogarty brought a gift with him, a half-pint of special whisky. He inquired politely for Mr. Kernan, placed his gift on the table and sat down with the company on equal terms. Mr. Kernan appreciated the gift all the more since he was aware that there was a small account for groceries unsettled between him and Mr. Fogarty. He said:

"I wouldn't doubt you, old man. Open that, Jack, will you?"

Mr. Power again officiated. Glasses were rinsed and five small measures of whisky were poured out. This new influence enlivened the conversation. Mr. Fogarty, sitting on a small area of the chair, was specially interested.

"Pope Leo XIII.," said Mr. Cunningham, "was one of the lights of the age. His great idea, you know, was the union of the Latin and Greek Churches. That was the aim of his life."

"I often heard he was one of the most intellectual men in Europe," said Mr. Power. "I mean, apart from his being Pope."

"So he was," said Mr. Cunningham, "if not the most so. His motto, you know, as Pope, was *Lux upon Lux—Light upon Light.*"

"No, no," said Mr. Fogarty eagerly. "I think you're wrong there. It was *Lux in*

Tenebris, I think—*Light in Darkness.*"

"O yes," said Mr. M'Coy, "*Tenebrae.*"

"Allow me," said Mr. Cunningham positively, "it was *Lux upon Lux.* And Pius IX. his predecessor's motto was *Crux upon Crux*—that is, *Cross upon Cross*—to show the difference between their two pontificates."

The inference was allowed. Mr. Cunningham continued.

"Pope Leo, you know. was a great scholar and a poet."

"He had a strong face," said Mr. Kernan.

"Yes," said Mr. Cunningham. "He wrote Latin poetry."

"Is that so?" said Mr. Fogarty.

Mr. M'Coy tasted his whisky contentedly and shook his head with a double intention, saying:

"That's no joke, I can tell you."

"We didn't learn that, Tom," said Mr. Power, following Mr. M'Coy's example, "when we went to the penny-a-week school."

"There was many a good man went to the penny-a-week school with a sod of turf under his oxter," said Mr. Kernan sententiously. "The old system was the best: plain honest education. None of your modern trumpery ..."

"Quite right," said Mr. Power.

"No superfluities," said Mr. Fogarty.

He enunciated the word and then drank gravely.

"I remember reading," said Mr. Cunningham, "that one of Pope Leo's poems was on the invention of the photograph—in Latin, of course."

"On the photograph!" exclaimed Mr. Kernan.

"Yes," said Mr. Cunningham.

He also drank from his glass.

"Well, you know," said Mr. M'Coy, "isn't the photograph wonderful when you come to think of it?"

"O, of course," said Mr. Power, "great minds can see things."

"As the poet says: *Great minds are very near to madness*," said Mr. Fogarty.

Mr. Kernan seemed to be troubled in mind. He made an effort to recall the Protestant theology on some thorny points and in the end addressed Mr. Cunningham.

"Tell me, Martin," he said. "Weren't some of the popes—of course, not our present man, or his predecessor, but some of the old popes—not exactly ... you know ... up to the knocker?"

There was a silence. Mr. Cunningham said:

"O, of course, there were some bad lots … But the astonishing thing is this. Not one of them, not the biggest drunkard, not the most … out-and-out ruffian, not one of them ever preached *ex cathedra* a word of false doctrine. Now isn't that an astonishing thing?"

"That is," said Mr. Kernan.

"Yes, because when the Pope speaks *ex cathedra*," Mr. Fogarty explained, "he is infallible."

"Yes," said Mr. Cunningham.

"O, I know about the infallibility of the Pope. I remember I was younger then… Or was it that—?"

Mr. Fogarty interrupted. He took up the bottle and helped the others to a little more. Mr. M'Coy, seeing that there was not enough to go round, pleaded that he had not finished his first measure. The others accepted under protest. The light music of whisky falling into glasses made an agreeable interlude.

"What's that you were saying, Tom?" asked Mr. M'Coy.

"Papal infallibility," said Mr. Cunningham, "that was the greatest scene in the whole history of the Church."

"How was that, Martin?" asked Mr. Power.

Mr. Cunningham held up two thick fingers.

"In the sacred college, you know, of cardinals and archbishops and bishops there were two men who held out against it while the others were all for it. The whole conclave except these two was unanimous. No! They wouldn't have it!"

"Ha!" said Mr. M'Coy.

"And they were a German cardinal by the name of Dolling … or Dowling … or—"

"Dowling was no German, and that's a sure five," said Mr. Power, laughing.

"Well, this great German cardinal, whatever his name was, was one; and the other was John MacHale."

"What?" cried Mr. Kernan. "Is it John of Tuam?"

"Are you sure of that now?" asked Mr. Fogarty dubiously. "I thought it was some Italian or American."

"John of Tuam," repeated Mr. Cunningham, "was the man."

He drank and the other gentlemen followed his lead. Then he resumed:

"There they were at it, all the cardinals and bishops and archbishops from all the ends of the earth and these two fighting dog and devil until at last the Pope himself stood up and declared infallibility a dogma of the Church *ex cathedra*. On the very moment John MacHale, who had been arguing and arguing against it, stood up and shouted out with the voice of a lion: '*Credo!*'"

"*I believe!*" said Mr. Fogarty.

"*Credo!*" said Mr. Cunningham. "That showed the faith he had. He submitted the moment the Pope spoke."

"And what about Dowling?" asked Mr. M'Coy.

"The German cardinal wouldn't submit. He left the church."

Mr. Cunningham's words had built up the vast image of the church in the minds of his hearers. His deep, raucous voice had thrilled them as it uttered the word of belief and submission. When Mrs. Kernan came into the room, drying her hands, she came into a solemn company. She did not disturb the silence, but leaned over the rail at the foot of the bed.

"I once saw John MacHale," said Mr. Kernan, "and I'll never forget it as long as I live."

He turned towards his wife to be confirmed.

"I often told you that?"

Mrs. Kernan nodded.

"It was at the unveiling of Sir John Gray's statue. Edmund Dwyer Gray was speaking, blathering away, and here was this old fellow, crabbed-looking old chap, looking at him from under his bushy eyebrows."

Mr. Kernan knitted his brows and, lowering his head like an angry bull, glared at his wife.

"God!" he exclaimed, resuming his natural face, "I never saw such an eye in a man's head. It was as much as to say: *I have you properly taped, my lad.* He had an eye like a hawk."

"None of the Grays was any good," said Mr. Power.

There was a pause again. Mr. Power turned to Mrs. Kernan and said with abrupt joviality:

"Well, Mrs. Kernan, we're going to make your man here a good holy pious and God-fearing Roman Catholic."

He swept his arm round the company inclusively.

"We're all going to make a retreat together and confess our sins—and God knows we want it badly."

"I don't mind," said Mr. Kernan, smiling a little nervously.

Mrs. Kernan thought it would be wiser to conceal her satisfaction. So she said:

"I pity the poor priest that has to listen to your tale!"

Mr. Kernan's expression changed.

"If he doesn't like it," he said bluntly, "he can ... do the other thing. I'll just tell him my little tale of woe. I'm not such a bad fellow—"

Mr. Cunningham intervened promptly.

"We'll all renounce the devil," he said, "together, not forgetting his works and pomps."

"Get behind me, Satan!" said Mr. Fogarty, laughing and looking at the others.

Mr. Power said nothing. He felt completely out-generalled. But a pleased expression flickered across his face.

"All we have to do," said Mr. Cunningham, "is to stand up with lighted candles in our hands and renew our baptismal vows."

"O, don't forget the candle, Tom," said Mr. M'Coy, "whatever you do."

"What?" said Mr. Kernan. "Must I have a candle?"

"O yes," said Mr. Cunningham.

"No, damn it all," said Mr. Kernan sensibly, "I draw the line there. I'll do the job right enough. I'll do the retreat business and confession, and … all that business. But … no candles! No, damn it all, I bar the candles!"

He shook his head with farcical gravity.

"Listen to that!" said his wife.

"I bar the candles," said Mr. Kernan, conscious of having created an effect on his audience and continuing to shake his head to and fro. "I bar the magic-lantern business."

Everyone laughed heartily.

"There's a nice Catholic for you!" said his wife.

"No candles!" repeated Mr. Kernan obdurately. "That's off!"

　　•　　•　　•　　•　　•　　•　　•　　•

The transept of the Jesuit Church in Gardiner Street was almost full; and still at every moment gentlemen entered from the side door and, directed by the lay-brother, walked on tiptoe along the aisles until they found seating accommodation. The gentlemen were all well dressed and orderly. The light of the lamps of the church fell upon an assembly of black clothes and white collars, relieved here and there by tweeds, on dark mottled pillars of green marble and on lugubrious canvases. The gentlemen sat in the benches, having hitched their trousers slightly above their knees and laid their hats in security. They sat well back and gazed formally at the distant speck of red light which was suspended before the high altar.

In one of the benches near the pulpit sat Mr. Cunningham and Mr. Kernan. In the bench behind sat Mr. M'Coy alone: and in the bench behind him sat Mr. Power and Mr. Fogarty. Mr. M'Coy had tried unsuccessfully to find a place in the bench with the others, and, when the party had settled down in the form of a quincunx, he had tried unsuccessfully to make comic remarks. As these had not been well received, he had desisted. Even he was sensible of the decorous atmosphere and even he began to respond to the religious stimulus. In a whisper, Mr. Cunningham drew Mr. Kernan's attention to Mr. Harford, the moneylender, who sat some distance off, and to Mr. Fanning, the registration agent and mayor maker of the city, who was sitting immediately under the pulpit beside one of the newly elected councillors of the ward. To the right sat old Michael Grimes, the owner of three pawnbroker's shops, and Dan Hogan's nephew, who was up for the job in the Town Clerk's office. Farther in front sat Mr. Hendrick, the chief reporter of *The Freeman's Journal,* and poor O'Carroll, an old friend of Mr. Kernan's, who had been at one time a considerable commercial figure. Gradually, as he recognised familiar faces, Mr. Kernan began to feel more at home. His hat, which had been rehabilitated by his wife, rested upon his knees. Once or twice he pulled down his cuffs with one hand while he held the brim of his hat lightly, but firmly, with the other hand.

A powerful-looking figure, the upper part of which was draped with a white surplice, was observed to be struggling up into the pulpit. Simultaneously the congregation unsettled, produced handkerchiefs and knelt upon them with care. Mr. Kernan followed the general example. The priest's figure now stood upright in the pulpit, two-thirds of its bulk, crowned by a massive red face, appearing above the balustrade.

Father Purdon knelt down, turned towards the red speck of light and, covering his face with his hands, prayed. After an interval, he uncovered his face and rose. The congregation rose also and settled again on its benches. Mr. Kernan restored his hat to its original position on his knee and presented an attentive face to the preacher. The preacher turned back each wide sleeve of his surplice with an elaborate large gesture and slowly surveyed the array of faces. Then he said:

"For the children of this world are wiser in their generation than the children of light. Wherefore make unto yourselves friends out of the mammon of iniquity so that when you die they may receive you into everlasting dwellings."

Father Purdon developed the text with resonant assurance. It was one of the most difficult texts in all the Scriptures, he said, to interpret properly. It was a text which might seem to the casual observer at variance with the lofty morality elsewhere preached by Jesus Christ. But, he told his hearers, the text had seemed to him specially adapted for the guidance of those whose lot it was to lead the life of the world and who yet wished to lead that life not in the manner of worldlings. It was a text for business men and professional men. Jesus Christ, with His divine understanding of every cranny of our human nature, understood that all men were not called to the religious life, that by far the vast majority were forced to live in the world, and, to a certain extent, for the world: and in this sentence He designed to give them a word of counsel, setting before them as exemplars in the religious life those very worshippers of Mammon who were of all men the least solicitous in matters religious.

He told his hearers that he was there that evening for no terrifying, no extravagant purpose; but as a man of the world speaking to his fellow-men. He came to speak to business men and he would speak to them in a businesslike way. If he might use the metaphor, he said, he was their spiritual accountant; and he wished each and every one of his hearers to open his books, the books of his spiritual life, and see if they tallied accurately with conscience.

Jesus Christ was not a hard taskmaster. He understood our little failings, understood the weakness of our poor fallen nature, understood the temptations of this life. We might have had, we all had from time to time, our temptations: we might have, we all had, our failings. But one thing only, he said, he would ask of his hearers. And that was: to be straight and manly with God. If their accounts tallied in every point to say:

"Well, I have verified my accounts. I find all well."

But if, as might happen, there were some discrepancies, to admit the truth, to be frank and say like a man:

"Well, I have looked into my accounts. I find this wrong and this wrong. But, with God's grace, I will rectify this and this. I will set right my accounts."

The Dead

Lily, the caretaker's daughter, was literally run off her feet. Hardly had she brought one gentleman into the little pantry behind the office on the ground floor and helped him off with his overcoat than the wheezy halldoor bell clanged again and she had to scamper along the bare hallway to let in another guest. It was well for her she had not to attend to the ladies also. But Miss Kate and Miss Julia had thought of that and had converted the bathroom upstairs into a ladies' dressing-room. Miss Kate and Miss Julia were there, gossiping and laughing and fussing, walking after each other to the head of the stairs, peering down over the banisters and calling down to Lily to ask her who had come.

It was always a great affair, the Misses Morkan's annual dance. Everybody who knew them came to it, members of the family, old friends of the family, the members of Julia's choir, any of Kate's pupils that were grown up enough, and even some of Mary Jane's pupils too. Never once had it fallen flat. For years and years it had gone off in splendid style, as long as anyone could remember; ever since Kate and Julia, after the death of their brother Pat, had left the house in Stoney Batter and taken Mary Jane, their only niece, to live with them in the dark, gaunt house on Usher's Island, the upper part of which they had rented from Mr. Fulham, the corn-factor on the ground floor. That was a good thirty years ago if it was a day. Mary Jane, who was then a little girl in short clothes, was now the main prop of the household, for she had the organ in Haddington Road. She had been through the Academy and gave a pupils' concert every year in the upper room of the Antient Concert Rooms. Many of her pupils belonged to the better-class families on the Kingstown and Dalkey line. Old as they were her aunts also did their share. Julia, though she was quite grey was still the leading soprano in Adam and Eve's, and Kate, being too feeble to go about much, gave music lessons to beginners on the old square piano in the back room. Lily, the caretaker's daughter, did house-maid's work for them. Though their life was modest, they believed in eating well; the best of everything: diamond-bone sirloins, three-shilling tea and the best bot-tled stout. But Lily seldom made a mistake in the orders, so that she got on well with her three mistresses. They were fussy, that was all. But the only thing they would not stand was back answers.

Of course, they had good reason to be fussy on such a night. And then it was long after ten o'clock and yet there was no sign of Gabriel and his wife. Besides they were dreadfully afraid that Freddy Malins might turn up screwed. They would not wish for worlds that any of Mary Jane's pupils should see him under the influ-ence; and when he was like that it was sometimes very hard to manage him. Freddy Malins always came late, but they wondered what could be keeping Gabriel: and that was what brought them every two minutes to the banisters to ask Lily had Gabriel or Freddy come.

"O, Mr. Conroy," said Lily to Gabriel when she opened the door for him, "Miss Kate and Miss Julia thought you were never coming. Good-night, Mrs. Conroy."

"I'll engage they did," said Gabriel, "but they forget that my wife here takes three mortal hours to dress herself."

He stood on the mat, scraping the snow from his goloshes, while Lily led his wife to the foot of the stairs and called out:

"Miss Kate, here's Mrs. Conroy."

Kate and Julia came toddling down the dark stairs at once. Both of them kissed Gabriel's wife, said she must be perished alive, and asked was Gabriel with her.

"Here I am as right as the mail, Aunt Kate! Go on up. I'll follow," called out Gabriel from the dark.

He continued scraping his feet vigorously while the three women went upstairs, laughing, to the ladies' dressing-room. A light fringe of snow lay like a cape on the shoulders of his overcoat and like toecaps on the toes of his goloshes; and, as the buttons of his overcoat slipped with a squeaking noise through the snow-stiffened frieze, a cold, fragrant air from out-of-doors escaped from crevices and folds.

"Is it snowing again, Mr. Conroy?" asked Lily.

She had preceded him into the pantry to help him off with his overcoat. Gabriel smiled at the three syllables she had given his surname and glanced at her. She was a slim, growing girl, pale in complexion and with hay-coloured hair. The gas in the pantry made her look still paler. Gabriel had known her when she was a child and used to sit on the lowest step nursing a rag doll.

"Yes, Lily," he answered, "and I think we're in for a night of it."

He looked up at the pantry ceiling, which was shaking with the stamping and shuffling of feet on the floor above, listened for a moment to the piano and then glanced at the girl, who was folding his overcoat carefully at the end of a shelf.

"Tell me, Lily," he said in a friendly tone, "do you still go to school?"

"O no, sir," she answered. "I'm done schooling this year and more."

"O, then," said Gabriel gaily, "I suppose we'll be going to your wedding one of these fine days with your young man, eh?"

The girl glanced back at him over her shoulder and said with great bitterness:

"The men that is now is only all palaver and what they can get out of you."

Gabriel coloured, as if he felt he had made a mistake and, without looking at her, kicked off his goloshes and flicked actively with his muffler at his patent-leather shoes.

He was a stout, tallish young man. The high colour of his cheeks pushed upwards even to his forehead, where it scattered itself in a few formless patches of pale red; and on his hairless face there scintillated restlessly the polished lenses and the bright gilt rims of the glasses which screened his delicate and restless eyes. His glossy black hair was parted in the middle and brushed in a long curve behind his ears where it curled slightly beneath the groove left by his hat.

When he had flicked lustre into his shoes he stood up and pulled his waistcoat down more tightly on his plump body. Then he took a coin rapidly from his pocket.

"O Lily," he said, thrusting it into her hands, "it's Christmas-time, isn't it? Just … here's a little …"

He walked rapidly towards the door.

"O no, sir!" cried the girl, following him. "Really, sir, I wouldn't take it."

"Christmas-time! Christmas-time!" said Gabriel, almost trotting to the stairs and waving his hand to her in deprecation.

The girl, seeing that he had gained the stairs, called out after him:

"Well, thank you, sir."

He waited outside the drawing-room door until the waltz should finish, listening to the skirts that swept against it and to the shuffling of feet. He was still discomposed by the girl's bitter and sudden retort. It had cast a gloom over him which he tried to dispel by arranging his cuffs and the bows of his tie. He then took from his waistcoat pocket a little paper and glanced at the headings he had made for his speech. He was undecided about the lines from Robert Browning, for he feared they would be above the heads of his hearers. Some quotation that they would recognise from Shakespeare or from the Melodies would be better. The indelicate clacking of the men's heels and the shuffling of their soles reminded him that their grade of culture differed from his. He would only make himself ridiculous by quoting poetry to them which they could not understand. They would think that he was airing his superior education. He would fail with them just as he had failed with the girl in the pantry. He had taken up a wrong tone. His whole speech was a mistake from first to last, an utter failure.

Just then his aunts and his wife came out of the ladies' dressing-room. His aunts were two small, plainly dressed old women. Aunt Julia was an inch or so the taller. Her hair, drawn low over the tops of her ears, was grey; and grey also, with darker shadows, was her large flaccid face. Though she was stout in build and stood erect, her slow eyes and parted lips gave her the appearance of a woman who did not know where she was or where she was going. Aunt Kate was more vivacious. Her face, healthier than her sister's, was all puckers and creases, like a shrivelled red apple, and her hair, braided in the same old-fashioned way, had not lost its ripe nut colour.

They both kissed Gabriel frankly. He was their favourite nephew, the son of their dead elder sister, Ellen, who had married T. J. Conroy of the Port and Docks.

"Gretta tells me you're not going to take a cab back to Monkstown tonight, Gabriel," said Aunt Kate.

"No," said Gabriel, turning to his wife, "we had quite enough of that last year, hadn't we? Don't you remember, Aunt Kate, what a cold Gretta got out of it? Cab windows rattling all the way, and the east wind blowing in after we passed Merrion. Very jolly it was. Gretta caught a dreadful cold."

Aunt Kate frowned severely and nodded her head at every word.

"Quite right, Gabriel, quite right," she said. "You can't be too careful."

"But as for Gretta there," said Gabriel, "she'd walk home in the snow if she were let."

Mrs. Conroy laughed.

"Don't mind him, Aunt Kate," she said. "He's really an awful bother, what with green shades for Tom's eyes at night and making him do the dumb-bells, and forcing Eva to eat the stirabout. The poor child! And she simply hates the sight of it! … O, but you'll never guess what he makes me wear now!"

She broke out into a peal of laughter and glanced at her husband, whose admiring and happy eyes had been wandering from her dress to her face and hair. The two aunts laughed heartily, too, for Gabriel's solicitude was a standing joke with them.

"Goloshes!" said Mrs. Conroy. "That's the latest. Whenever it's wet underfoot I must put on my goloshes. Tonight even, he wanted me to put them on, but I wouldn't. The next thing he'll buy me will be a diving suit."

Gabriel laughed nervously and patted his tie reassuringly, while Aunt Kate nearly doubled herself, so heartily did she enjoy the joke. The smile soon faded from Aunt Julia's face and her mirthless eyes were directed towards her nephew's face. After a pause she asked:

"And what are goloshes, Gabriel?"

"Goloshes, Julia!" exclaimed her sister. "Goodness me, don't you know what goloshes are? You wear them over your … over your boots, Gretta, isn't it?"

"Yes," said Mrs. Conroy. "Guttapercha things. We both have a pair now. Gabriel says everyone wears them on the continent."

"O, on the continent," murmured Aunt Julia, nodding her head slowly.

Gabriel knitted his brows and said, as if he were slightly angered:

"It's nothing very wonderful, but Gretta thinks it very funny because she says the word reminds her of Christy Minstrels."

"But tell me, Gabriel," said Aunt Kate, with brisk tact. "Of course, you've seen about the room. Gretta was saying …"

"O, the room is all right," replied Gabriel. "I've taken one in the Gresham."

"To be sure," said Aunt Kate, "by far the best thing to do. And the children, Gretta, you're not anxious about them?"

"O, for one night," said Mrs. Conroy. "Besides, Bessie will look after them."

"To be sure," said Aunt Kate again. "What a comfort it is to have a girl like that, one you can depend on! There's that Lily, I'm sure I don't know what has come over her lately. She's not the girl she was at all."

Gabriel was about to ask his aunt some questions on this point, but she broke off suddenly to gaze after her sister, who had wandered down the stairs and was craning her neck over the banisters.

"Now, I ask you," she said almost testily, "where is Julia going? Julia! Julia! Where are you going?"

Julia, who had gone halfway down one flight, came back and announced blandly:

"Here's Freddy."

At the same moment a clapping of hands and a final flourish of the pianist told that the waltz had ended. The drawing-room door was opened from within and some couples came out. Aunt Kate drew Gabriel aside hurriedly and whispered into his ear:

"Slip down, Gabriel, like a good fellow and see if he's all right, and don't let him up if he's screwed. I'm sure he's screwed. I'm sure he is."

Gabriel went to the stairs and listened over the banisters. He could hear two persons talking in the pantry. Then he recognised Freddy Malins' laugh. He went down the stairs noisily.

"It's such a relief," said Aunt Kate to Mrs. Conroy, "that Gabriel is here. I always feel easier in my mind when he's here ... Julia, there's Miss Daly and Miss Power will take some refreshment. Thanks for your beautiful waltz, Miss Daly. It made lovely time."

A tall wizen-faced man, with a stiff grizzled moustache and swarthy skin, who was passing out with his partner, said:

"And may we have some refreshment, too, Miss Morkan?"

"Julia," said Aunt Kate summarily, "and here's Mr. Browne and Miss Furlong. Take them in, Julia; with Miss Daly and Miss Power."

"I'm the man for the ladies," said Mr. Browne, pursing his lips until his moustache bristled and smiling in all his wrinkles. "You know, Miss Morkan, the reason they are so fond of me is—"

He did not finish his sentence, but, seeing that Aunt Kate was out of earshot, at once led the three young ladies into the back room. The middle of the room was occupied by two square tables placed end to end, and on these Aunt Julia and the caretaker were straightening and smoothing a large cloth. On the sideboard were arrayed dishes and plates, and glasses and bundles of knives and forks and spoons. The top of the closed square piano served also as a sideboard for viands and sweets. At a smaller sideboard in one corner two young men were standing, drinking hop-bitters.

Mr. Browne led his charges thither and invited them all, in jest, to some ladies' punch, hot, strong and sweet. As they said they never took anything strong, he opened three bottles of lemonade for them. Then he asked one of the young men to move aside, and, taking hold of the decanter, filled out for himself a goodly measure of whisky. The young men eyed him respectfully while he took a trial sip.

"God help me," he said, smiling, "it's the doctor's orders."

His wizened face broke into a broader smile, and the three young ladies laughed in musical echo to his pleasantry, swaying their bodies to and fro, with nervous jerks of their shoulders. The boldest said:

"O, now, Mr. Browne, I'm sure the doctor never ordered anything of the kind."

Mr. Browne took another sip of his whisky and said, with sidling mimicry:

"Well, you see, I'm like the famous Mrs. Cassidy, who is reported to have said: 'Now, Mary Grimes, if I don't take it, make me take it, for I feel I want it.'"

His hot face had leaned forward a little too confidentially and he had assumed a very low Dublin accent so that the young ladies, with one instinct, received his speech in silence. Miss Furlong, who was one of Mary Jane's pupils, asked Miss Daly, what was the name of the pretty waltz she had played; and Mr. Browne, seeing that he was ignored, turned promptly to the two young men who were more appreciative.

A red-faced young woman, dressed in pansy, came into the room, excitedly clapping her hands and crying:

"Quadrilles! Quadrilles!"

Close on her heels came Aunt Kate, crying:

"Two gentlemen and three ladies, Mary Jane!"

"O, here's Mr. Bergin and Mr. Kerrigan," said Mary Jane. "Mr. Kerrigan, will you take Miss Power? Miss Furlong, may I get you a partner, Mr. Bergin. O, that'll just do now."

"Three ladies, Mary Jane," said Aunt Kate.

The two young gentlemen asked the ladies if they might have the pleasure, and Mary Jane turned to Miss Daly.

"O, Miss Daly, you're really awfully good, after playing for the last two dances, but really we're so short of ladies to-night."

"I don't mind in the least, Miss Morkan."

But I've a nice partner for you, Mr. Bartell D'Arcy, the tenor. I'll get him to sing later on. All Dublin is raving about him."

"Lovely voice, lovely voice!" said Aunt Kate.

As the piano had twice begun the prelude to the first figure Mary Jane led her recruits quickly from the room. They had hardly gone when Aunt Julia wandered slowly into the room, looking behind her at something.

"What is the matter, Julia?" asked Aunt Kate anxiously. "Who is it?"

Julia, who was carrying in a column of table-napkins, turned to her sister and said, simply, as if the question had surprised her:

"It's only Freddy, Kate, and Gabriel with him."

In fact right behind her Gabriel could be seen piloting Freddy Malins across the landing. The latter, a young man of about forty, was of Gabriel's size and build, with very round shoulders. His face was fleshy and pallid, touched with colour only at the thick hanging lobes of his ears and at the wide wings of his nose. He had coarse features, a blunt nose, a convex and receding brow, tumid and protruded lips. His heavy-lidded eyes and the disorder of his scanty hair made him look sleepy. He was laughing heartily in a high key at a story which he had been telling Gabriel on the stairs and at the same time rubbing the knuckles of his left fist backwards and forwards into his left eye.

"Good-evening, Freddy," said Aunt Julia.

Freddy Malins bade the Misses Morkan good-evening in what seemed an off-hand fashion by reason of the habitual catch in his voice and then, seeing that Mr. Browne was grinning at him from the sideboard, crossed the room on rather shaky legs and began to repeat in an undertone the story he had just told to Gabriel.

"He's not so bad, is he?" said Aunt Kate to Gabriel.

Gabriel's brows were dark but he raised them quickly and answered:

"O, no, hardly noticeable."

"Now, isn't he a terrible fellow!" she said. "And his poor mother made him take the pledge on New Year's Eve. But come on, Gabriel, into the drawing-room."

Before leaving the room with Gabriel she signalled to Mr. Browne by frowning and shaking her forefinger in warning to and fro. Mr. Browne nodded in answer and, when she had gone, said to Freddy Malins:

"Now, then, Teddy, I'm going to fill you out a good glass of lemonade just to buck you up."

Freddy Malins, who was nearing the climax of his story, waved the offer aside impatiently but Mr. Browne, having first called Freddy Malins' attention to a disarray in his dress, filled out and handed him a full glass of lemonade. Freddy Malins' left hand accepted the glass mechanically, his right hand being engaged in the mechanical readjustment of his dress. Mr. Browne, whose face was once more wrinkling with mirth, poured out for himself a glass of whisky while Freddy

Malins exploded, before he had well reached the climax of his story, in a kink of high-pitched bronchitic laughter and, setting down his untasted and overflowing glass, began to rub the knuckles of his left fist backwards and forwards into his left eye, repeating words of his last phrase as well as his fit of laughter would allow him.

•   •   •   •   •   •   •   •

Gabriel could not listen while Mary Jane was playing her Academy piece, full of runs and difficult passages, to the hushed drawing-room. He liked music but the piece she was playing had no melody for him and he doubted whether it had any melody for the other listeners, though they had begged Mary Jane to play something. Four young men, who had come from the refreshment-room to stand in the doorway at the sound of the piano, had gone away quietly in couples after a few minutes. The only persons who seemed to follow the music were Mary Jane herself, her hands racing along the key-board or lifted from it at the pauses like those of a priestess in momentary imprecation, and Aunt Kate standing at her elbow to turn the page.

Gabriel's eyes, irritated by the floor, which glittered with beeswax under the heavy chandelier, wandered to the wall above the piano. A picture of the balcony scene in *Romeo and Juliet* hung there and beside it was a picture of the two murdered princes in the Tower which Aunt Julia had worked in red, blue and brown wools when she was a girl. Probably in the school they had gone to as girls that kind of work had been taught for one year. His mother had worked for him as a birthday present a waistcoat of purple tabinet, with little foxes' heads upon it, lined with brown satin and having round mulberry buttons. It was strange that his mother had had no musical talent though Aunt Kate used to call her the brains carrier of the Morkan family. Both she and Julia had always seemed a little proud of their serious and matronly sister. Her photograph stood before the pier-glass. She held an open book on her knees and was pointing out something in it to Constantine who, dressed in a man-o'-war suit, lay at her feet. It was she who had chosen the names of her sons for she was very sensible of the dignity of family life. Thanks to her, Constantine was now senior curate in Balbriggan and, thanks to her, Gabriel himself had taken his degree in the Royal University. A shadow passed over his face as he remembered her sullen opposition to his marriage. Some slighting phrases she had used still rankled in his memory; she had once spoken of Gretta as being country cute and that was not true of Gretta at all. It was Gretta who had nursed her during all her last long illness in their house at Monkstown.

He knew that Mary Jane must be near the end of her piece for she was playing again the opening melody with runs of scales after every bar and while he waited for the end the resentment died down in his heart. The piece ended with a trill of octaves in the treble and a final deep octave in the bass. Great applause greeted Mary Jane as, blushing and rolling up her music nervously, she escaped from the room. The most vigorous clapping came from the four young men in the doorway who had gone away to the refreshment-room at the beginning of the piece but had come back when the piano had stopped.

Lancers were arranged. Gabriel found himself partnered with Miss Ivors. She was a frank-mannered talkative young lady, with a freckled face and prominent brown eyes. She did not wear a low-cut bodice and the large brooch which was fixed in the front of her collar bore on it an Irish device and motto.

When they had taken their places she said abruptly:

"I have a crow to pluck with you."

"With me?" said Gabriel.

She nodded her head gravely.

"What is it?" asked Gabriel, smiling at her solemn manner.

"Who is G. C.?" answered Miss Ivors, turning her eyes upon him.

Gabriel coloured and was about to knit his brows, as if he did not understand, when she said bluntly:

"O, innocent Amy! I have found out that you write for *The Daily Express*. Now, aren't you ashamed of yourself?"

"Why should I be ashamed of myself?" asked Gabriel, blinking his eyes and trying to smile.

"Well, I'm ashamed of you," said Miss Ivors frankly. "To say you'd write for a paper like that. I didn't think you were a West Briton."

A look of perplexity appeared on Gabriel's face. It was true that he wrote a literary column every Wednesday in *The Daily Express*, for which he was paid fifteen shillings. But that did not make him a West Briton surely. The books he received for review were almost more welcome than the paltry cheque. He loved to feel the covers and turn over the pages of newly printed books. Nearly every day when his teaching in the college was ended he used to wander down the quays to the second-hand booksellers, to Hickey's on Bachelor's Walk, to Webb's or Massey's on Aston's Quay, or to O'Clohissey's in the by-street. He did not know how to meet her charge. He wanted to say that literature was above politics. But they were friends of many years' standing and their careers had been parallel, first at the University and then as teachers: he could not risk a grandiose phrase with her. He continued blinking his eyes and trying to smile and murmured lamely that he saw nothing political in writing reviews of books.

When their turn to cross had come he was still perplexed and inattentive. Miss Ivors promptly took his hand in a warm grasp and said in a soft friendly tone:

"Of course, I was only joking. Come, we cross now."

When they were together again she spoke of the University question and Gabriel felt more at ease. A friend of hers had shown her his review of Browning's poems. That was how she had found out the secret: but she liked the review immensely. Then she said suddenly:

"O, Mr. Conroy, will you come for an excursion to the Aran Isles this summer? We're going to stay there a whole month. It will be splendid out in the Atlantic. You ought to come. Mr. Clancy is coming, and Mr. Kilkelly and Kathleen Kearney. It would be splendid for Gretta too if she'd come. She's from Connacht, isn't she?"

"Her people are," said Gabriel shortly.

"But you will come, won't you?" said Miss Ivors, laying her warm hand eagerly on his arm.

"The fact is," said Gabriel, "I have just arranged to go—"

"Go where?" asked Miss Ivors.

"Well, you know, every year I go for a cycling tour with some fellows and so—"

"But where?" asked Miss Ivors.

"Well, we usually go to France or Belgium or perhaps Germany," said Gabriel awkwardly.

"And why do you go to France and Belgium," said Miss Ivors, "instead of visiting your own land?"

"Well," said Gabriel, "it's partly to keep in touch with the languages and partly for a change."

"And haven't you your own language to keep in touch with—Irish?" asked Miss Ivors.

"Well," said Gabriel, "if it comes to that, you know, Irish is not my language."

Their neighbours had turned to listen to the cross-examination. Gabriel glanced right and left nervously and tried to keep his good humour under the ordeal which was making a blush invade his forehead.

"And haven't you your own land to visit," continued Miss Ivors, "that you know nothing of, your own people, and your own country?"

"O, to tell you the truth," retorted Gabriel suddenly, "I'm sick of my own country, sick of it!"

"Why?" asked Miss Ivors.

Gabriel did not answer for his retort had heated him.

"Why?" repeated Miss Ivors.

They had to go visiting together and, as he had not answered her, Miss Ivors said warmly:

"Of course, you've no answer."

Gabriel tried to cover his agitation by taking part in the dance with great energy. He avoided her eyes for he had seen a sour expression on her face. But when they met in the long chain he was surprised to feel his hand firmly pressed. She looked at him from under her brows for a moment quizzically until he smiled. Then, just as the chain was about to start again, she stood on tiptoe and whispered into his ear:

"West Briton!"

When the lancers were over Gabriel went away to a remote corner of the room where Freddy Malins' mother was sitting. She was a stout feeble old woman with white hair. Her voice had a catch in it like her son's and she stuttered slightly. She had been told that Freddy had come and that he was nearly all right. Gabriel asked her whether she had had a good crossing. She lived with her married daughter in Glasgow and came to Dublin on a visit once a year. She answered placidly that she had had a beautiful crossing and that the captain had been most attentive to her. She spoke also of the beautiful house her daughter kept in Glasgow, and of all the friends they had there. While her tongue rambled on Gabriel tried to banish from his mind all memory of the unpleasant incident with Miss Ivors. Of course the girl or woman, or whatever she was, was an enthusiast but there was a time for all things. Perhaps he ought not to have answered her like that. But she had no right to call him a West Briton before people, even in joke. She had tried to make him ridiculous before people, heckling him and staring at him with her rabbit's eyes.

He saw his wife making her way towards him through the waltzing couples. When she reached him she said into his ear:

"Gabriel, Aunt Kate wants to know won't you carve the goose as usual. Miss Daly will carve the ham and I'll do the pudding."

"All right," said Gabriel.

"She's sending in the younger ones first as soon as this waltz is over so that we'll have the table to ourselves."

"Were you dancing?" asked Gabriel.

"Of course I was. Didn't you see me? What row had you with Molly Ivors?"

"No row. Why? Did she say so?"

"Something like that. I'm trying to get that Mr. D'Arcy to sing. He's full of conceit, I think."

"There was no row," said Gabriel moodily, "only she wanted me to go for a trip to the west of Ireland and I said I wouldn't."

His wife clasped her hands excitedly and gave a little jump.

"O, do go, Gabriel," she cried. "I'd love to see Galway again."

"You can go if you like," said Gabriel coldly.

She looked at him for a moment, then turned to Mrs. Malins and said:

"There's a nice husband for you, Mrs. Malins."

While she was threading her way back across the room Mrs. Malins, without adverting to the interruption, went on to tell Gabriel what beautiful places there were in Scotland and beautiful scenery. Her son-in-law brought them every year to the lakes and they used to go fishing. Her son-in-law was a splendid fisher. One day he caught a beautiful big fish and the man in the hotel cooked it for their dinner.

Gabriel hardly heard what she said. Now that supper was coming near he began to think again about his speech and about the quotation. When he saw Freddy Malins coming across the room to visit his mother Gabriel left the chair free for him and retired into the embrasure of the window. The room had already cleared and from the back room came the clatter of plates and knives. Those who still remained in the drawing-room seemed tired of dancing and were conversing quietly in little groups. Gabriel's warm trembling fingers tapped the cold pane of the window. How cool it must be outside! How pleasant it would be to walk out alone, first along by the river and then through the park! The snow would be lying on the branches of the trees and forming a bright cap on the top of the Wellington Monument. How much more pleasant it would be there than at the supper-table!

He ran over the headings of his speech: Irish hospitality, sad memories, the Three Graces, Paris, the quotation from Browning. He repeated to himself a phrase he had written in his review: "One feels that one is listening to a thought-tormented music." Miss Ivors had praised the review. Was she sincere? Had she really any life of her own behind all her propagandism? There had never been any ill-feeling between them until that night. It unnerved him to think that she would be at the supper-table, looking up at him while he spoke with her critical quizzing eyes. Perhaps she would not be sorry to see him fail in his speech. An idea came into his mind and gave him courage. He would say, alluding to Aunt Kate and Aunt Julia: "Ladies and Gentlemen, the generation which is now on the wane among us may have had its faults but for my part I think it had certain qualities of hospitality, of humour, of humanity, which the new and very serious and hypereducated generation that is growing up around us seems to me to lack." Very good: that was one for Miss Ivors. What did he care that his aunts were only two ignorant old women?

A murmur in the room attracted his attention. Mr. Browne was advancing from the door, gallantly escorting Aunt Julia, who leaned upon his arm, smiling and hanging her head. An irregular musketry of applause escorted her also as far as the piano and then, as Mary Jane seated herself on the stool, and Aunt Julia, no longer smiling, half turned so as to pitch her voice fairly into the room, gradually ceased. Gabriel recognised the prelude. It was that of an old song of Aunt Julia's—*Arrayed for the Bridal.* Her voice, strong and clear in tone, attacked with great spirit the runs which embellish the air and though she sang very rapidly she did not miss even the smallest of the grace notes. To follow the voice, without looking at the singer's face, was to feel and share the excitement of swift and secure flight. Gabriel applauded loudly with all the others at the close of the song and loud applause was born in from the invisible supper-table. It sounded so genuine that a little colour straggled into Aunt Julia's face as she bent to replace in the music-stand the old leather-bound song-book that had her initials on the cover. Freddy Malins, who had listened with his head perched sideways to hear her better, was still applauding when everyone else had ceased and talking animatedly to his mother who nodded her head gravely and slowly in acquiescence. At last, when he could clap no more, he stood up suddenly and hurried across the room to Aunt Julia whose hand he seized and held in both his hands, shaking it when words failed him or the catch in his voice proved too much for him.

"I was just telling my mother," he said, "I never heard you sing so well, never. No, I never heard your voice so good as it is to-night. Now! Would you believe that now? That's the truth. Upon my word and honour that's the truth. I never heard your voice sound so fresh and so ... so clear and fresh, never."

Aunt Julia smiled broadly and murmured something about compliments as she released her hand from his grasp. Mr. Browne extended his open hand towards her and said to those who were near him in the manner of a showman introducing a prodigy to an audience:

"Miss Julia Morkan, my latest discovery!"

He was laughing very heartily at this himself when Freddy Malins turned to him and said:

"Well, Browne, if you're serious you might make a worse discovery. All I can say is I never heard her sing half so well as long as I am coming here. And that's the honest truth."

"Neither did I," said Mr. Browne. "I think her voice has greatly improved."

Aunt Julia shrugged her shoulders and said with meek pride:

"Thirty years ago I hadn't a bad voice as voices go."

"I often told Julia," said Aunt Kate emphatically, "that she was simply thrown away in that choir. But she never would be said by me."

She turned as if to appeal to the good sense of the others against a refractory child while Aunt Julia gazed in front of her, a vague smile of reminiscence playing on her face.

"No," continued Aunt Kate, "she wouldn't be said or led by anyone, slaving there in that choir night and day, night and day. Six o'clock on Christmas morning! And all for what?"

"Well, isn't it for the honour of God, Aunt Kate?" asked Mary Jane, twisting round on the piano-stool and smiling.

Aunt Kate turned fiercely on her niece and said:

"I know all about the honour of God, Mary Jane, but I think it's not at all honourable for the pope to turn out the women out of the choirs that have slaved there all their lives and put little whipper-snappers of boys over their heads. I suppose it is for the good of the Church if the pope does it. But it's not just, Mary Jane, and it's not right."

She had worked herself into a passion and would have continued in defence of her sister for it was a sore subject with her but Mary Jane, seeing that all the dancers had come back, intervened pacifically:

"Now, Aunt Kate, you're giving scandal to Mr. Browne who is of the other persuasion."

Aunt Kate turned to Mr. Browne, who was grinning at this allusion to his religion, and said hastily:

"O, I don't question the pope's being right. I'm only a stupid old woman and I wouldn't presume to do such a thing. But there's such a thing as common everyday politeness and gratitude. And if I were in Julia's place I'd tell that Father Healy straight up to his face …"

"And besides, Aunt Kate," said Mary Jane, "we really are all hungry and when we are hungry we are all very quarrelsome."

"And when we are thirsty we are also quarrelsome," added Mr. Browne.

"So that we had better go to supper," said Mary Jane, "and finish the discussion afterwards."

On the landing outside the drawing-room Gabriel found his wife and Mary Jane trying to persuade Miss Ivors to stay for supper. But Miss Ivors, who had put on her hat and was buttoning her cloak, would not stay. She did not feel in the least hungry and she had already overstayed her time.

"But only for ten minutes, Molly," said Mrs. Conroy. "That won't delay you."

"To take a pick itself," said Mary Jane, "after all your dancing."

"I really couldn't," said Miss Ivors.

"I am afraid you didn't enjoy yourself at all," said Mary Jane hopelessly.

"Ever so much, I assure you," said Miss Ivors, "but you really must let me run off now."

"But how can you get home?" asked Mrs. Conroy.

"O, it's only two steps up the quay."

Gabriel hesitated a moment and said:

"If you will allow me, Miss Ivors, I'll see you home if you are really obliged to go."

But Miss Ivors broke away from them.

"I won't hear of it," she cried. "For goodness' sake go in to your suppers and don't mind me. I'm quite well able to take care of myself."

"Well, you're the comical girl, Molly," said Mrs. Conroy frankly.

"*Beannacht libh*," cried Miss Ivors, with a laugh, as she ran down the staircase.

Mary Jane gazed after her, a moody puzzled expression on her face, while Mrs. Conroy leaned over the banisters to listen for the hall-door. Gabriel asked himself was he the cause of her abrupt departure. But she did not seem to be in ill humour: she had gone away laughing. He stared blankly down the staircase.

At the moment Aunt Kate came toddling out of the supper-room, almost wringing her hands in despair.

"Where is Gabriel?" she cried. "Where on earth is Gabriel? There's everyone waiting in there, stage to let, and nobody to carve the goose!"

"Here I am, Aunt Kate!" cried Gabriel, with sudden animation, "ready to carve a flock of geese, if necessary."

A fat brown goose lay at one end of the table and at the other end, on a bed of creased paper strewn with sprigs of parsley, lay a great ham, stripped of its outer skin and peppered over with crust crumbs, a neat paper frill round its shin and beside this was a round of spiced beef. Between these rival ends ran parallel lines of side-dishes: two little minsters of jelly, red and yellow; a shallow dish full of blocks of blancmange and red jam, a large green leaf-shaped dish with a stalk-shaped handle, on which lay bunches of purple raisins and peeled almonds, a companion dish on which lay a solid rectangle of Smyrna figs, a dish of custard topped with grated nutmeg, a small bowl full of chocolates and sweets wrapped in gold and silver papers and a glass vase in which stood some tall celery stalks. In the centre of the table there stood, as sentries to a fruit-stand which upheld a pyramid of oranges and American apples, two squat old-fashioned decanters of cut glass, one containing port and the other dark sherry. On the closed square piano a pudding in a huge yellow dish lay in waiting and behind it were three squads of bottles of stout and ale and minerals, drawn up according to the colours of their uniforms, the first two black, with brown and red labels, the third and smallest squad white, with transverse green sashes.

Gabriel took his seat boldly at the head of the table and, having looked to the edge of the carver, plunged his fork firmly into the goose. He felt quite at ease now for he was an expert carver and liked nothing better than to find himself at the head of a well-laden table.

"Miss Furlong, what shall I send you?" he asked. "A wing or a slice of the breast?"

"Just a small slice of the breast."

"Miss Higgins, what for you?"

"O, anything at all, Mr. Conroy."

While Gabriel and Miss Daly exchanged plates of goose and plates of ham and spiced beef Lily went from guest to guest with a dish of hot floury potatoes wrapped in a white napkin. This was Mary Jane's idea and she had also suggested apple sauce for the goose but Aunt Kate had said that plain roast goose without any apple sauce had always been good enough for her and she hoped she might never eat worse. Mary Jane waited on her pupils and saw that they got the best slices and Aunt Kate and Aunt Julia opened and carried across from the piano bottles of stout and ale for the gentlemen and bottles of minerals for the ladies. There was a great deal of confusion and laughter and noise, the noise of orders and counter-orders, of knives and forks, of corks and glass-stoppers. Gabriel began to carve second helpings as soon as he had finished the first round without serving himself. Everyone protested loudly so that he compromised by taking a long draught of stout for he had found the carving hot work. Mary Jane settled down quietly to her supper but Aunt Kate and Aunt Julia were still toddling round the table, walking on each other's heels, getting in each other's way and giving each other unheeded orders. Mr. Browne begged of them to sit down and eat their suppers and so did Gabriel but they said there was time enough, so that, at last, Freddy Malins stood up and, capturing Aunt Kate, plumped her down on her chair amid general laughter.

When everyone had been well served Gabriel said, smiling:

"Now, if anyone wants a little more of what vulgar people call stuffing let him or her speak."

A chorus of voices invited him to begin his own supper and Lily came forward with three potatoes which she had reserved for him.

"Very well," said Gabriel amiably, as he took another preparatory draught, "kindly forget my existence, ladies and gentlemen, for a few minutes."

He set to his supper and took no part in the conversation with which the table covered Lily's removal of the plates. The subject of talk was the opera company which was then at the Theatre Royal. Mr. Bartell D'Arcy, the tenor, a dark-complexioned young man with a smart moustache, praised very highly the leading contralto of the company but Miss Furlong thought she had a rather vulgar style of production. Freddy Malins said there was a negro chieftain singing in the second part of the Gaiety pantomime who had one of the finest tenor voices he had ever heard.

"Have you heard him?" he asked Mr. Bartell D'Arcy across the table.

"No," answered Mr. Bartell D'Arcy carelessly.

"Because," Freddy Malins explained, "now I'd be curious to hear your opinion of him. I think he has a grand voice."

"It takes Teddy to find out the really good things," said Mr. Browne familiarly to the table.

"And why couldn't he have a voice too?" asked Freddy Malins sharply. "Is it because he's only a black?"

Nobody answered this question and Mary Jane led the table back to the legitimate opera. One of her pupils had given her a pass for *Mignon*. Of course it was very fine, she said, but it made her think of poor Georgina Burns. Mr. Browne could go back farther still, to the old Italian companies that used to come to Dublin—Tietjens, Ilma de Murzka, Campanini, the great Trebelli Giuglini, Ravelli, Aramburo. Those were the days, he said, when there was something like singing to be heard in Dublin. He told too of how the top gallery of the old Royal used to be packed night after night, of how one night an Italian tenor had sung five encores to *Let Me Like a Soldier Fall*, introducing a high C every time, and of how the gallery boys would sometimes in their enthusiasm unyoke the horses from the carriage of some great *prima donna* and pull her themselves through the streets to her hotel. Why did they never play the grand old operas now, he asked, *Dinorah*, *Lucrezia Borgia?* Because they could not get the voices to sing them: that was why."

"O, well," said Mr. Bartell D'Arcy, "I presume there are as good singers to-day as there were then."

"Where are they?" asked Mr. Browne defiantly.

"In London, Paris, Milan," said Mr. Bartell D'Arcy warmly. "I suppose Caruso, for example, is quite as good, if not better than any of the men you have mentioned."

"Maybe so," said Mr. Browne. "But I may tell you I doubt it strongly."

"O, I'd give anything to hear Caruso sing," said Mary Jane.

"For me," said Aunt Kate, who had been picking a bone, "there was only one tenor. To please me, I mean. But I suppose none of you ever heard of him."

"Who was he, Miss Morkan?" asked Mr. Bartell D'Arcy politely.

"His name," said Aunt Kate, "was Parkinson. I heard him when he was in his prime and I think he had then the purest tenor voice that was ever put into a man's throat."

"Strange," said Mr. Bartell D'Arcy. "I never even heard of him."

"Yes, yes, Miss Morkan is right," said Mr. Browne. "I remember hearing of old Parkinson but he's too far back for me."

"A beautiful, pure, sweet, mellow English tenor," said Aunt Kate with enthusiasm.

Gabriel having finished, the huge pudding was transferred to the table. The clatter of forks and spoons began again. Gabriel's wife served out spoonfuls of the pudding and passed the plates down the table. Midway down they were held up by Mary Jane, who replenished them with raspberry or orange jelly or with blanc-mange and jam. The pudding was of Aunt Julia's making and she received praises for it from all quarters. She herself said that it was not quite brown enough.

"Well, I hope, Miss Morkan," said Mr. Browne, "that I'm brown enough for you because, you know, I'm all brown."

All the gentlemen, except Gabriel, ate some of the pudding out of compliment to Aunt Julia. As Gabriel never ate sweets the celery had been left for him. Freddy Malins also took a stalk of celery and ate it with his pudding. He had been told that celery was a capital thing for the blood and he was just then under doctor's care. Mrs. Malins, who had been silent all through the supper, said that her son was going down to Mount Melleray in a week or so. The table then spoke of Mount Melleray, how bracing the air was down there, how hospitable the monks were and how they never asked for a penny-piece from their guests.

"And do you mean to say," asked Mr. Browne incredulously, "that a chap can go down there and put up there as if it were a hotel and live on the fat of the land and then come away without paying anything?"

"O, most people give some donation to the monastery when they leave," said Mary Jane.

"I wish we had an institution like that in our Church," said Mr. Browne candidly.

He was astonished to hear that the monks never spoke, got up at two in the morning and slept in their coffins. He asked what they did it for.

"That's the rule of the order," said Aunt Kate firmly.

"Yes, but why?" asked Mr. Browne.

Aunt Kate repeated that it was the rule, that was all. Mr. Browne still seemed not to understand. Freddy Malins explained to him, as best he could, that the monks were trying to make up for the sins committed by all the sinners in the outside world. The explanation was not very clear for Mr. Browne grinned and said:

"I like that idea very much but wouldn't a comfortable spring bed do them as well as a coffin?"

"The coffin," said Mary Jane, "is to remind them of their last end."

As the subject had grown lugubrious it was buried in a silence of the table during which Mrs. Malins could be heard saying to her neighbour in an indistinct undertone:

"They are very good men, the monks, very pious men."

The raisins and almonds and figs and apples and oranges and chocolates and sweets were now passed about the table and Aunt Julia invited all the guests to have either port or sherry. At first Mr. Bartell D'Arcy refused to take either but one of his neighbours nudged him and whispered something to him upon which he allowed his glass to be filled. Gradually as the last glasses were being filled the conversation ceased. A pause followed, broken only by the noise of the wine and by unsettlings of chairs. The Misses Morkan, all three, looked down at the tablecloth. Someone coughed once or twice and then a few gentlemen patted the table gently as a signal for silence. The silence came and Gabriel pushed back his chair and stood up.

The patting at once grew louder in encouragement and then ceased altogether. Gabriel leaned his ten trembling fingers on the tablecloth and smiled nervously at the company. Meeting a row of upturned faces he raised his eyes to the chandelier. The piano was playing a waltz tune and he could hear the skirts sweeping against the drawing-room door. People, perhaps, were standing in the snow on the quay outside, gazing up at the lighted windows and listening to the waltz music. The air was pure there. In the distance lay the park where the trees were weighted with snow. The Wellington Monument wore a gleaming cap of snow that flashed westward over the white field of Fifteen Acres.

He began:

"Ladies and Gentlemen.

"It has fallen to my lot this evening, as in years past, to perform a very pleasing task but a task for which I am afraid my poor powers as a speaker are all too inadequate."

"No, no!" said Mr. Browne.

"But, however that may be, I can only ask you to-night to take the will for the deed and to lend me your attention for a few moments while I endeavour to express to you in words what my feelings are on this occasion.

"Ladies and Gentlemen, it is not the first time that we have gathered together under this hospitable roof, around this hospitable board. It is not the first time that we have been the recipients—or perhaps, I had better say, the victims—of the hospitality of certain good ladies."

He made a circle in the air with his arm and paused. Everyone laughed or smiled at Aunt Kate and Aunt Julia and Mary Jane who all turned crimson with pleasure. Gabriel went on more boldly:

"I feel more strongly with every recurring year that our country has no tradition which does it so much honour and which it should guard so jealously as that of its hospitality. It is a tradition that is unique as far as my experience goes (and I have visited not a few places abroad) among the modern nations. Some would say, perhaps, that with us it is rather a failing than anything to be boasted of. But granted even that, it is, to my mind, a princely failing, and one that I trust will long be cultivated among us. Of one thing, at least, I am sure. As long as this one roof shelters the good ladies aforesaid—and I wish from my heart it may do so for many and many a long year to come—the tradition of genuine warm-hearted courteous Irish hospitality, which our forefathers have handed down to us and which we in turn must hand down to our descendants, is still alive among us."

A hearty murmur of assent ran round the table. It shot through Gabriel's mind that Miss Ivors was not there and that she had gone away discourteously: and he said with confidence in himself:

"Ladies and Gentlemen.

"A new generation is growing up in our midst, a generation actuated by new ideas and new principles. It is serious and enthusiastic for these new ideas and its enthusiasm, even when it is misdirected, is, I believe, in the main sincere. But we are living in a sceptical and, if I may use the phrase, a thought-tormented age: and sometimes I fear that this new generation, educated or hypereducated as it is, will lack those qualities of humanity, of hospitality, of kindly humour which belonged to an older day. Listening tonight to the names of all those great singers of the past it seemed to me, I must confess, that we were living in a less spacious age. Those days might, without exaggeration, be called spacious days: and if they are gone beyond recall let us hope, at least, that in gatherings such as this we shall still speak of them with pride and affection, still cherish in our hearts the memory of those dead and gone great ones whose fame the world will not willingly let die."

"Hear, hear!" said Mr. Browne loudly.

"But yet," continued Gabriel, his voice falling into a softer inflection, "there are always in gatherings such as this sadder thoughts that will recur to our minds: thoughts of the past, of youth, of changes, of absent faces that we miss here to-night. Our path through life is strewn with many such sad memories: and were we to brood upon them always we could not find the heart to go on bravely with our work among the living. We have all of us living duties and living affections which claim, and rightly claim, our strenuous endeavours.

"Therefore, I will not linger on the past. I will not let any gloomy moralising intrude upon us here to-night. Here we are gathered together for a brief moment from the bustle and rush of our everyday routine. We are met here as friends, in the spirit of good-fellowship, as colleagues, also to a certain extent, in the true spirit of *camaraderie*, and as the guests of—what shall I call them?—the Three Graces of the Dublin musical world."

The table burst into applause and laughter at this allusion. Aunt Julia vainly asked each of her neighbours in turn to tell her what Gabriel had said.

"He says we are the Three Graces, Aunt Julia," said Mary Jane.

Aunt Julia did not understand but she looked up, smiling, at Gabriel, who continued in the same vein:

"Ladies and Gentlemen.

"I will not attempt to play to-night the part that Paris played on another occasion. I will not attempt to choose between them. The task would be an invidious one and one beyond my poor powers. For when I view them in turn, whether it be our chief hostess herself, whose good heart, whose too good heart, has become a byword with all who know her, or her sister, who seems to be gifted with perennial youth and whose singing must have been a surprise and a revelation to us all to-night, or, last but not least, when I consider our youngest hostess, talented, cheerful, hard-working and the best of nieces, I confess, Ladies and Gentlemen, that I do not know to which of them I should award the prize."

Gabriel glanced down at his aunts and, seeing the large smile on Aunt Julia's face and the tears which had risen to Aunt Kate's eyes, hastened to his close. He raised his glass of port gallantly, while every member of the company fingered a glass expectantly, and said loudly:

"Let us toast them all three together. Let us drink to their health, wealth, long life, happiness and prosperity and may they long continue to hold the proud and self-won position which they hold in their profession and the position of honour and affection which they hold in our hearts."

All the guests stood up, glass in hand, and turning towards the three seated ladies, sang in unison, with Mr. Browne as leader:

> For they are jolly gay fellows,
> For they are jolly gay fellows,
> For they are jolly gay fellows,
> Which nobody can deny.

Aunt Kate was making frank use of her handkerchief and even Aunt Julia seemed moved. Freddy Malins beat time with his pudding-fork and the singers turned towards one another, as if in melodious conference, while they sang with emphasis:

> Unless he tells a lie,
> Unless he tells a lie.

Then, turning once more towards their hostesses, they sang:

> For they are jolly gay fellows,
> For they are jolly gay fellows,
> For they are jolly gay fellows,
> Which nobody can deny.

The acclamation which followed was taken up beyond the door of the supper-room by many of the other guests and renewed time after time, Freddy Malins acting as officer with his fork on high.

    •   •   •   •   •   •   •   •

The piercing morning air came into the hall where they were standing so that Aunt Kate said:

"Close the door, somebody. Mrs. Malins will get her death of cold."

"Browne is out there, Aunt Kate," said Mary Jane.

"Browne is everywhere," said Aunt Kate, lowering her voice.

Mary Jane laughed at her tone.

"Really," she said archly, "he is very attentive."

"He has been laid on here like the gas," said Aunt Kate in the same tone, "all during the Christmas."

She laughed herself this time good-humouredly and then added quickly:

"But tell him to come in, Mary Jane, and close the door. I hope to goodness he didn't hear me."

At that moment the hall-door was opened and Mr. Browne came in from the doorstep, laughing as if his heart would break. He was dressed in a long green overcoat with mock astrakhan cuffs and collar and wore on his head an oval fur cap. He pointed down the snow-covered quay from where the sound of shrill pro-longed whistling was borne in.

"Teddy will have all the cabs in Dublin out," he said.

Gabriel advanced from the little pantry behind the office, struggling into his overcoat and, looking round the hall, said:

"Gretta not down yet?"

"She's getting on her things, Gabriel," said Aunt Kate.

"Who's playing up there?" asked Gabriel.

"Nobody. They're all gone."

"O no, Aunt Kate," said Mary Jane. "Bartell D'Arcy and Miss O'Callaghan aren't gone yet."

"Someone is fooling at the piano anyhow," said Gabriel.

Mary Jane glanced at Gabriel and Mr. Browne and said with a shiver:

"It makes me feel cold to look at you two gentlemen muffled up like that. I wouldn't like to face your journey home at this hour."

"I'd like nothing better this minute," said Mr. Browne stoutly, "than a rattling fine walk in the country or a fast drive with a good spanking goer between the shafts."

"We used to have a very good horse and trap at home," said Aunt Julia sadly.

"The never-to-be-forgotten Johnny," said Mary Jane, laughing.

Aunt Kate and Gabriel laughed too.

"Why, what was wonderful about Johnny?" asked Mr. Browne.

"The late lamented Patrick Morkan, our grandfather, that is," explained Gabriel, "commonly known in his later years as the old gentleman, was a glue-boiler."

"O, now, Gabriel," said Aunt Kate. laughing, "he had a starch mill."

"Well, glue or starch," said Gabriel, "the old gentleman had a horse by the name of Johnny. And Johnny used to work in the old gentleman's mill, walking round and round in order to drive the mill. That was all very well; but now comes the tragic part about Johnny. One fine day the old gentleman thought he'd like to drive out with the quality to a military review in the park."

"The Lord have mercy on his soul," said Aunt Kate compassionately.

"Amen," said Gabriel. "So the old gentleman, as I said, harnessed Johnny and put on his very best tall hat and his very best stock collar and drove out in grand style from his ancestral mansion somewhere near Back Lane, I think."

Everyone laughed, even Mrs. Malins, at Gabriel's manner and Aunt Kate said:

"O, now, Gabriel, he didn't live in Back Lane, really. Only the mill was there."

"Out from the mansion of his forefathers," continued Gabriel, "he drove with Johnny. And everything went on beautifully until Johnny came in sight of King Billy's statue: and whether he fell in love with the horse King Billy sits on or whether he thought he was back again in the mill, anyhow, he began to walk round the statue."

Gabriel paced in a circle round the hall in his goloshes amid the laughter of the others.

"Round and round he went," said Gabriel, "and the old gentleman, who was a very pompous old gentleman, was highly indignant. 'Go on, sir! What do you mean, sir? Johnny! Johnny! Most extraordinary conduct. Can't understand the horse!'"

The peals of laughter which followed Gabriel's imitation of the incident was interrupted by a resounding knock at the hall-door. Mary Jane ran to open it and let in Freddy Malins. Freddy Malins, with his hat well back on his head and his shoulders humped with cold, was puffing and steaming after his exertions.

"I could only get one cab," he said.

"O, we'll find another along the quay," said Gabriel.

"Yes," said Aunt Kate. "Better not keep Mrs. Malins standing in the draught."

Mrs. Malins was helped down the front steps by her son and Mr. Browne and, after many manoeuvres, hoisted into the cab. Freddy Malins clambered in after her and spent a long time settling her on the seat, Mr. Browne helping him with advice. At last she was settled comfortably and Freddy Malins invited Mr. Browne into the cab. There was a good deal of confused talk, and then Mr. Browne got into the cab. The cabman settled his rug over his knees, and bent down for the address. The confusion grew greater and the cabman was directed differently by Freddy Malins and Mr. Browne, each of whom had his head out through a window of the cab. The difficulty was to know where to drop Mr. Browne along the route, and Aunt Kate, Aunt Julia and Mary Jane helped the discussion from the doorstep with cross-directions and contradictions and abundance of laughter. As for Freddy Malins he was speechless with laughter. He popped his head in and out of the window every moment to the great danger of his hat, and told his mother how the discussion was progressing, till at last Mr. Browne shouted to the bewildered cabman above the din of everybody's laughter:

"Do you know Trinity College?"

"Yes, sir," said the cabman.

"Well, drive bang up against Trinity College gates," said Mr. Browne, "and then we'll tell you where to go. You understand now?"

"Yes, sir," said the cabman.

"Make like a bird for Trinity College."

"Right, sir," said the cabman.

The house was whipped up and the cab rattled off along the quay amid a chorus of laughter and adieus.

Gabriel had not gone to the door with the others. He was in a dark part of the hall gazing up the staircase. A woman was standing near the top of the first flight, in the shadow also. He could not see her face but he could see the terra-cotta and salmon-pink panels of her skirt which the shadow made appear black and white. It was his wife. She was leaning on the banisters, listening to something. Gabriel was surprised at her stillness and strained his ear to listen also. But he could hear little save the noise of laughter and dispute on the front steps, a few chords struck on the piano and a few notes of a man's voice singing.

He stood still in the gloom of the hall, trying to catch the air that the voice was singing and gazing up at his wife. There was grace and mystery in her attitude as if she were a symbol of something. He asked himself what is a woman standing on the stairs in the shadow, listening to distant music, a symbol of. If he were a painter he would paint her in that attitude. Her blue felt hat would show off the bronze of her hair against the darkness and the dark panels of her skirt would show off the light ones. *Distant Music* he would call the picture if he were a painter.

The hall-door was closed; and Aunt Kate, Aunt Julia and Mary Jane came down the hall, still laughing.

"Well, isn't Freddy terrible?" said Mary Jane. "He's really terrible."

Gabriel said nothing but pointed up the stairs towards where his wife was standing. Now that the hall-door was closed the voice and the piano could be heard more clearly. Gabriel held up his hand for them to be silent. The song seemed to be in the old Irish tonality and the singer seemed uncertain both of his words and of his voice. The voice, made plaintive by distance and by the singer's hoarseness, faintly illuminated the cadence of the air with words expressing grief:

> O, the rain falls on my heavy locks
> And the dew wets my skin,
> My babe lies cold ...

"O," exclaimed Mary Jane. "It's Bartell D'Arcy singing and he wouldn't sing all the night. O, I'll get him to sing a song before he goes."

"O, do, Mary Jane," said Aunt Kate.

Mary Jane brushed past the others and ran to the staircase, but before she reached it the singing stopped and the piano was closed abruptly.

"O, what a pity!" she cried. "Is he coming down, Gretta?"

Gabriel heard his wife answer yes and saw her come down towards them. A few steps behind her were Mr. Bartell D'Arcy and Miss O'Callaghan.

"O, Mr. D'Arcy," cried Mary Jane, "it's downright mean of you to break off like that when we were all in raptures listening to you."

"I have been at him all the evening," said Miss O'Callaghan, "and Mrs. Conroy, too, and he told us he had a dreadful cold and couldn't sing."

"O, Mr. D'Arcy," said Aunt Kate, "now that was a great fib to tell."

"Can't you see that I'm as hoarse as a crow?" said Mr. D'Arcy roughly.

He went into the pantry hastily and put on his overcoat. The others, taken aback by his rude speech, could find nothing to say. Aunt Kate wrinkled her brows and made signs to the others to drop the subject. Mr. D'Arcy stood swathing his neck carefully and frowning.

"It's the weather," said Aunt Julia, after a pause.

"Yes, everybody has colds," said Aunt Kate readily, "everybody."

"They say," said Mary Jane, "we haven't had snow like it for thirty years; and I read this morning in the newspapers that the snow is general all over Ireland."

"I love the look of snow," said Aunt Julia sadly.

"So do I," said Miss O'Callaghan. "I think Christmas is never really Christmas unless we have the snow on the ground."

"But poor Mr. D'Arcy doesn't like the snow," said Aunt Kate, smiling.

Mr. D'Arcy came from the pantry, fully swathed and buttoned, and in a repentant tone told them the history of his cold. Everyone gave him advice and said it was a great pity and urged him to be very careful of his throat in the night air. Gabriel watched his wife, who did not join in the conversation. She was standing right under the dusty fanlight and the flame of the gas lit up the rich bronze of her hair, which he had seen her drying at the fire a few days before. She was in the same attitude and seemed unaware of the talk about her. At last she turned towards them and Gabriel saw that there was colour on her cheeks and that her eyes were shining. A sudden tide of joy went leaping out of his heart.

"Mr. D'Arcy," she said, "what is the name of that song you were singing?"

"It's called *The Lass of Aughrim*," said Mr. D'Arcy, "but I couldn't remember it properly. Why? Do you know it?"

"*The Lass of Aughrim*," she repeated. "I couldn't think of the name."

"It's a very nice air," said Mary Jane. "I'm sorry you were not in voice to-night."

"Now, Mary Jane," said Aunt Kate, "don't annoy Mr. D'Arcy. I won't have him annoyed."

Seeing that all were ready to start she shepherded them to the door, where good-night was said:

"Well, good-night, Aunt Kate, and thanks for the pleasant evening."

"Good-night, Gabriel. Good-night. Gretta!"

"Good-night, Aunt Kate, and thanks ever so much. Good-night, Aunt Julia."

"O, good-night, Gretta, I didn't see you."

"Good-night, Mr. D'Arcy. Good-night, Miss O'Callaghan."

"Good-night, Miss Morkan."

"Good-night, again."

"Good-night, all. Safe home."

"Good-night. Good-night."

The morning was still dark. A dull, yellow light brooded over the houses and the river; and the sky seemed to be descending. It was slushy underfoot; and only streaks and patches of snow lay on the roofs, on the parapets of the quay and on the area railings. The lamps were still burning redly in the murky air and, across the river, the palace of the Four Courts stood out menacingly against the heavy sky.

She was walking on before him with Mr. Bartell D'Arcy, her shoes in a brown parcel tucked under one arm and her hands holding her skirt up from the slush. She had no longer any grace of attitude, but Gabriel's eyes were still bright with happiness. The blood went bounding along his veins; and the thoughts went rioting through his brain, proud, joyful, tender, valorous.

She was walking on before him so lightly and so erect that he longed to run after her noiselessly, catch her by the shoulders and say something foolish and affectionate into her ear. She seemed to him so frail that he longed to defend her against something and then to be alone with her. Moments of their secret life together burst like stars upon his memory. A heliotrope envelope was lying beside his breakfast-cup and he was caressing it with his hand. Birds were twittering in the ivy and the sunny web of the curtain was shimmering along the floor: he could not eat for happiness. They were standing on the crowded platform and he was placing a ticket inside the warm palm of her glove. He was standing with her in the cold, looking in through a grated window at a man making bottles in a roaring furnace. It was very cold. Her face, fragrant in the cold air, was quite close to his: and suddenly he called out to the man at the furnace:

"Is the fire hot, sir?"

But the man could not hear with the noise of the furnace. It was just as well. He might have answered rudely.

A wave of yet more tender joy escaped from his heart and went coursing in warm flood along his arteries. Like the tender fire of stars moments of their life together, that no one knew of or would ever know of, broke upon and illuminated his memory. He longed to recall to her those moments, to make her forget the years of their dull existence together and remember only their moments of ecstasy. For the years, he felt, had not quenched his soul or hers. Their children, his writing, her household cares had not quenched all their souls' tender fire. In one letter that he had written to her then he had said: "Why is it that words like these seem to me so dull and cold? Is it because there is no word tender enough to be your name?"

Like distant music these words that he had written years before were borne towards him from the past. He longed to be alone with her. When the others had gone away, when he and she were in the room in the hotel, then they would be alone together. He would call her softly:

"Gretta!"

Perhaps she would not hear at once: she would be undressing. Then something in his voice would strike her. She would turn and took at him ...

At the corner of Winetavern Street they met a cab. He was glad of its rattling noise as it saved him from conversation. She was looking out of the window and seemed tired. The others spoke only a few words, pointing out some building or street. The horse galloped along wearily under the murky morning sky, dragging his old rattling box after his heels, and Gabriel was again in a cab with her, galloping to catch the boat, galloping to their honeymoon.

As the cab drove across O'Connell Bridge Miss O'Callaghan said:

"They say you never cross O'Connell Bridge without seeing a white horse."

"I see a white man this time," said Gabriel.

"Where?" asked Mr. Bartell D'Arcy.

Gabriel pointed to the statue, on which lay patches of snow. Then he nodded familiarly to it and waved his hand.

"Good-night, Dan," he said gaily.

When the cab drew up before the hotel, Gabriel jumped out and, in spite of Mr. Bartell D'Arcy's protest, paid the driver. He gave the man a shilling over his fare. The man saluted and said:

"A prosperous New Year to you, sir."

"The same to you," said Gabriel cordially.

She leaned for a moment on his arm in getting out of the cab and while standing at the curbstone, bidding the others good-night. She leaned lightly on his arm, as lightly as when she had danced with him a few hours before. He had felt proud and happy then, happy that she was his, proud of her grace and wifely carriage. But now, after the kindling again of so many memories, the first touch of her body, musical and strange and perfumed, sent through him a keen pang of lust. Under cover of her silence he pressed her arm closely to his side; and, as they stood at the hotel door, he felt that they had escaped from their lives and duties, escaped from home and friends and run away together with wild and radiant hearts to a new adventure.

An old man was dozing in a great hooded chair in the hall. He lit a candle in the office and went before them to the stairs. They followed him in silence, their feet falling in soft thuds on the thickly carpeted stairs. She mounted the stairs behind the porter, her head bowed in the ascent, her frail shoulders curved as with a burden, her skirt girt tightly about her. He could have flung his arms about her hips and held her still, for his arms were trembling with desire to seize her and only the stress of his nails against the palms of his hands held the wild impulse of his body in check. The porter halted on the stairs to settle his guttering candle. They halted, too, on the steps below him. In the silence Gabriel could hear the falling of the molten wax into the tray and the thumping of his own heart against his ribs.

The porter led them along a corridor and opened a door. Then he set his unstable candle down on a toilet-table and asked at what hour they were to be called in the morning.

"Eight," said Gabriel.

The porter pointed to the tap of the electric-light and began a muttered apology, but Gabriel cut him short.

"We don't want any light. We have light enough from the street. And I say," he added, pointing to the candle, "you might remove that handsome article, like a good man."

The porter took up his candle again, but slowly, for he was surprised by such a novel idea. Then he mumbled good-night and went out. Gabriel shot the lock to.

A ghastly light from the street lamp lay in a long shaft from one window to the door. Gabriel threw his overcoat and hat on a couch and crossed the room towards the window. He looked down into the street in order that his emotion might calm a little. Then he turned and leaned against a chest of drawers with his back to the light. She had taken off her hat and cloak and was standing before a large swinging mirror, unhooking her waist. Gabriel paused for a few moments, watching her, and then said:

"Gretta!"

She turned away from the mirror slowly and walked along the shaft of light towards him. Her face looked so serious and weary that the words would not pass Gabriel's lips. No, it was not the moment yet.

"You looked tired," he said.

"I am a little," she answered.

"You don't feel ill or weak?"

"No, tired: that's all."

She went on to the window and stood there, looking out. Gabriel waited again and then, fearing that diffidence was about to conquer him, he said abruptly:

"By the way, Gretta!"

"What is it?"

"You know that poor fellow Malins?" he said quickly.

"Yes. What about him?"

"Well, poor fellow, he's a decent sort of chap, after all," continued Gabriel in a false voice. "He gave me back that sovereign I lent him, and I didn't expect it, really. It's a pity he wouldn't keep away from that Browne, because he's not a bad fellow, really."

He was trembling now with annoyance. Why did she seem so abstracted? He did not know how he could begin. Was she annoyed, too, about something? If she would only turn to him or come to him of her own accord! To take her as she was would be brutal. No, he must see some ardour in her eyes first. He longed to be master of her strange mood.

"When did you lend him the pound?" she asked, after a pause.

Gabriel strove to restrain himself from breaking out into brutal language about the sottish Malins and his pound. He longed to cry to her from his soul, to crush her body against his, to overmaster her. But he said:

"O, at Christmas, when he opened that little Christmas-card shop in Henry Street."

He was in such a fever of rage and desire that he did not hear her come from the window. She stood before him for an instant, looking at him strangely. Then, suddenly raising herself on tiptoe and resting her hands lightly on his shoulders, she kissed him.

"You are a very generous person, Gabriel," she said.

Gabriel, trembling with delight at her sudden kiss and at the quaintness of her phrase, put his hands on her hair and began smoothing it back, scarcely touching it with his fingers. The washing had made it fine and brilliant. His heart was brimming over with happiness. Just when he was wishing for it she had come to him of her own accord. Perhaps her thoughts had been running with his. Perhaps she had felt the impetuous desire that was in him, and then the yielding mood had come upon her. Now that she had fallen to him so easily, he wondered why he had been so diffident.

He stood, holding her head between his hands. Then, slipping one arm swiftly about her body and drawing her towards him, he said softly:

"Gretta, dear, what are you thinking about?"

She did not answer nor yield wholly to his arm. He said again, softly:

"Tell me what it is, Gretta. I think I know what is the matter. Do I know?"

She did not answer at once. Then she said in an outburst of tears:

"O, I am thinking about that song, *The Lass of Aughrim.*"

She broke loose from him and ran to the bed and, throwing her arms across the bed-rail, hid her face. Gabriel stood stock-still for a moment in astonishment and then followed her. As he passed in the way of the cheval-glass he caught sight of himself in full length, his broad, well-filled shirtfront, the face whose expression always puzzled him when he saw it in a mirror, and his glimmering gilt-rimmed eyeglasses. He halted a few paces from her and said:

"What about the song? Why does that make you cry?"

She raised her head from her arms and dried her eyes with the back of her hand like a child. A kinder note than he had intended went into his voice.

"Why, Gretta?" he asked.

"I am thinking about a person long ago who used to sing that song."

"And who was the person long ago?" asked Gabriel, smiling.

"It was a person I used to know in Galway when I was living with my grandmother," she said.

The smile passed away from Gabriel's face. A dull anger began to gather again

at the back of his mind and the dull fires of his lust began to glow angrily
in his veins.

"Someone you were in love with?" he asked ironically.

"It was a young boy I used to know," she answered, "named Michael Furey. He
used to sing that song, *The Lass of Aughrim*. He was very delicate."

Gabriel was silent. He did not wish her to think that he was interested in this
delicate boy.

"I can see him so plainly," she said, after a moment. "Such eyes as he had: big,
dark eyes! And such an expression in them—an expression!"

"O, then, you were in love with him?" said Gabriel.

"I used to go out walking with him," she said, "when I was in Galway."

A thought flew across Gabriel's mind.

"Perhaps that was why you wanted to go to Galway with that Ivors girl?" he
said coldly.

She looked at him and asked in surprise:

"What for?"

Her eyes made Gabriel feel awkward. He shrugged his shoulders and said:

"How do I know? To see him, perhaps."

She looked away from him along the shaft of light towards the window
in silence.

"He is dead," she said at length. "He died when he was only seventeen. Isn't it a
terrible thing to die so young as that?"

"What was he?" asked Gabriel, still ironically.

"He was in the gasworks," she said.

Gabriel felt humiliated by the failure of his irony and by the evocation of this
figure from the dead, a boy in the gasworks. While he had been full of memories
of their secret life together, full of tenderness and joy and desire, she had been
comparing him in her mind with another. A shameful consciousness of his own
person assailed him. He saw himself as a ludicrous figure, acting as a pennyboy for
his aunts, a nervous, well-meaning sentimentalist, orating to vulgarians and idealis-
ing his own clownish lusts, the pitiable fatuous fellow he had caught a glimpse of
in the mirror. Instinctively he turned his back more to the light lest she might see
the shame that burned upon his forehead.

He tried to keep up his tone of cold interrogation, but his voice when he spoke
was humble and indifferent.

"I suppose you were in love with this Michael Furey, Gretta," he said.

"I was great with him at that time," she said.

Her voice was veiled and sad. Gabriel, feeling now how vain it would be to try to lead her whither he had purposed, caressed one of her hands and said, also sadly:

"And what did he die of so young, Gretta? Consumption, was it?"

"I think he died for me," she answered.

A vague terror seized Gabriel at this answer, as if, at that hour when he had hoped to triumph, some impalpable and vindictive being was coming against him, gathering forces against him in its vague world. But he shook himself free of it with an effort of reason and continued to caress her hand. He did not question her again, for he felt that she would tell him of herself. Her hand was warm and moist: it did not respond to his touch, but he continued to caress it just as he had caressed her first letter to him that spring morning.

"It was in the winter," she said, "about the beginning of the winter when I was going to leave my grandmother's and come up here to the convent. And he was ill at the time in his lodgings in Galway and wouldn't be let out, and his people in Oughterard were written to. He was in decline, they said, or something like that. I never knew rightly."

She paused for a moment and sighed.

"Poor fellow," she said. "He was very fond of me and he was such a gentle boy. We used to go out together, walking, you know, Gabriel, like the way they do in the country. He was going to study singing only for his health. He had a very good voice, poor Michael Furey."

"Well; and then?" asked Gabriel.

"And then when it came to the time for me to leave Galway and come up to the convent he was much worse and I wouldn't be let see him so I wrote him a letter saying I was going up to Dublin and would be back in the summer, and hoping he would be better then."

She paused for a moment to get her voice under control, and then went on:

"Then the night before I left, I was in my grandmother's house in Nuns' Island, packing up, and I heard gravel thrown up against the window. The window was so wet I couldn't see, so I ran downstairs as I was and slipped out the back into the garden and there was the poor fellow at the end of the garden, shivering."

"And did you not tell him to go back?" asked Gabriel.

"I implored of him to go home at once and told him he would get his death in the rain. But he said he did not want to live. I can see his eyes as well as well! He was standing at the end of the wall where there was a tree."

"And did he go home?" asked Gabriel.

"Yes, he went home. And when I was only a week in the convent he died and he was buried in Oughterard, where his people came from. O, the day I heard that, that he was dead!"

She stopped, choking with sobs, and, overcome by emotion, flung herself face downward on the bed, sobbing in the quilt. Gabriel held her hand for a moment longer, irresolutely, and then, shy of intruding on her grief, let it fall gently and walked quietly to the window.

She was fast asleep.

Gabriel, leaning on his elbow, looked for a few moments unresentfully on her tangled hair and half-open mouth, listening to her deep-drawn breath. So she had had that romance in her life: a man had died for her sake. It hardly pained him now to think how poor a part he, her husband, had played in her life. He watched her while she slept, as though he and she had never lived together as man and wife. His curious eyes rested long upon her face and on her hair: and, as he thought of what she must have been then, in that time of her first girlish beauty, a strange, friendly pity for her entered his soul. He did not like to say even to himself that her face was no longer beautiful, but he knew that it was no longer the face for which Michael Furey had braved death.

Perhaps she had not told him all the story. His eyes moved to the chair over which she had thrown some of her clothes. A petticoat string dangled to the floor. One boot stood upright, its limp upper fallen down: the fellow of it lay upon its side. He wondered at his riot of emotions of an hour before. From what had it proceeded? From his aunt's supper, from his own foolish speech, from the wine and dancing, the merry-making when saying good-night in the hall, the pleasure of the walk along the river in the snow. Poor Aunt Julia! She, too, would soon be a shade with the shade of Patrick Morkan and his horse. He had caught that haggard look upon her face for a moment when she was singing *Arrayed for the Bridal.* Soon, per-haps, he would be sitting in that same drawing-room, dressed in black, his silk hat on his knees. The blinds would be drawn down and Aunt Kate would be sitting beside him, crying and blowing her nose and telling him how Julia had died. He would cast about in his mind for some words that might console her, and would find only lame and useless ones. Yes, yes: that would happen very soon.

The air of the room chilled his shoulders. He stretched himself cautiously along under the sheets and lay down beside his wife. One by one, they were all becoming shades. Better pass boldly into that other world, in the full glory of some passion, than fade and wither dismally with age. He thought of how she who lay beside him had locked in her heart for so many years that image of her lover's eyes when he had told her that he did not wish to live.

Generous tears filled Gabriel's eyes. He had never felt like that himself towards any woman, but he knew that such a feeling must be love. The tears gathered more thickly in his eyes and in the partial darkness he imagined he saw the form of a young man standing under a dripping tree. Other forms were near. His soul had approached that region where dwell the vast hosts of the dead. He was conscious of, but could not apprehend, their wayward and flickering existence. His own identity was fading out into a grey impalpable world: the solid world itself, which these dead had one time reared and lived in, was dissolving and dwindling.

A few light taps upon the pane made him turn to the window. It had begun to snow again. He watched sleepily the flakes, silver and dark, falling obliquely against the lamplight. The time had come for him to set out on his journey westward. Yes, the newspapers were right: snow was general all over Ireland. It was falling on every part of the dark central plain, on the treeless hills, falling softly upon the Bog of Allen and, farther westward, softly falling into the dark mutinous Shannon waves. It was falling, too, upon every part of the lonely churchyard on the hill where Michael Furey lay buried. It lay thickly drifted on the crooked crosses and headstones, on the spears of the little gate, on the barren thorns. His soul swooned slowly as he heard the snow falling faintly through the universe and faintly falling, like the descent of their last end, upon all the living and the dead.

JAMES STEPHENS

♣

(1882-1950)

The truth is, James Stephens is not well known outside of Ireland and within Ireland, he is familiar mostly as a name on the school curriculum, generally listed as a minor contributor to the Irish literary revival. An examination of his literary career makes it abundantly clear that Stephens was a poet at heart. His short stories and novels are remarkable in their lack of structure, as characters seemingly wander in and out, have their say, then disappear, and sometimes we never hear from them again.

Stephens was fond of characters who weaved fantastical tales of adventure and journey, rich with metaphor and allegory, and because he was known as a great conversationalist himself, Stephens could not help incorporating his own love of storytelling into at least one character in every story.

With his novel, *The Crock of Gold*, an allegorical fantasy published in 1913, Stephens won the Polignac Prize, given by the Academic Committee of the Royal Society of Literature to a young writer of promise. He made an attempt to live the literary life in Paris, but despite the accolades and positive reviews of his work, he was unable to achieve any financial security, and in 1915, he returned to Dublin to assume a post as registrar at the National Gallery of Ireland. One afternoon on Easter Monday in 1916, Stephens watched in horror as rebel troops, in a botched attempt at casting off British rule, threw up a barricade that ultimately led to a civilian being shot right before him. The event unnerved and distracted him so much that he felt compelled to write *The Insurrection in Dublin*, a superb eyewitness account of the rising, considered by many a classic piece of reportage. Stephens not only reported on the incident and the historic week that followed, but he dramatically put the event into political and social context, ultimately producing what many term the definitive account of one of the most momentous events in Irish history. Perhaps, many say, it took a writer of Stephens's caliber and vision to provide the definitive account of the insurrection.

While Stephens may have reported accurately and without exaggeration in *The Insurrection in Dublin*, the same cannot be said, unfortunately, for his own life's story.

Even his date of birth is open to interpretation, as the writer claimed to be born on February 2, 1882, the birthday of James Joyce, who apparently was pleased to share it with the eccentric Irishman. Any biographical inquiries into his early life drew often his stock quotation, "My life began when I started writing," as Stephens preferred to shroud his origins in mystery.

Yet more persistent biographers were able to discover that Stephens was registered as a boarder at the Meath Protestant Industrial School for impoverished or homeless boys between the ages of six and sixteen. Stephens, however, would never admit to this and preferred to provide more elaborate and fantastic stories of his childhood. Most common was the story of his life as a circus performer, traveling about Ireland as a gypsy, sleeping in parks and fighting with swans in ponds for scraps of stale bread. Whores with hearts of gold were also prevalent in his tales of youth, as Stephens often claimed to be saved from starvation by society's castaways.

Charismatic and endearing, Stephens was every bit as visually interesting as he was loquacious. Barely five feet tall with a large head and elfish features, he cultivated a mysterious appearance that lent an air of intrigue to his self-described reputation as the leprechaun of literature in Ireland. Yet despite this invention, there was little argument that Stephens did indeed grow up without the niceties that his education and oratory powers would imply. There seemed to be some merit to his claims of being malnourished as a child and into adulthood, and he once wrote to Lewis Chase, "I have been a hungry man, many, many times." And while stories of a youth spent in a traveling circus may too have been fantasy, Stephens had once been a member of a gymnastic team which won the Irish Shield in 1901, and he was never reluctant to demonstrate his strength and agility in public feats of acrobatic prowess.

In 1896, Stephens is on record as taking employment as a junior clerk in a solicitor's office in Dublin. He would spend the better part of two decades in similar positions, a necessity he deplored, while he struggled to launch his writing career. "I would sooner be a corpse than a clerk."

By 1907, Stephens had begun contributing to *Sinn Fein*, a newspaper run by Arthur Griffith, and the writer and publisher AE (George Russell) quickly took notice. He took Stephens under his wing, introducing him to the now thriving Dublin literary scene, where he was welcomed. William Butler Yeats considered him among the giants of the legendary Dublin conversationalists, and his prestige as a writer was such that Joyce once referred to him as "my rival, the latest Irish genius." It was believed the remark was made with some sarcasm on the part of Joyce initially, but the two became good friends, and Joyce would later entrust Stephens with the task of completing *Finnegan's Wake*, had Joyce been unable to complete the novel because of his diminishing health. AE encouraged Stephens to become involved with Sinn Fein politically, and he also began attending classes at the Gaelic League, setting the wheels in motion for his own involvement in the cultural revolution behind the Irish liberation movement. It was also around this time that Stephens began a relationship with Millicent Kavanagh, a married woman who was estranged from her husband. Kavanagh (whom Stephens referred to as "Cynthia") gave birth to the couple's son, James Naoise in 1909, and the two would eventually marry in 1919, once her estranged husband had died.

The year 1909 also gave birth to Stephens's first book of poetry, *Insurrections,* which presented vivid and bleak sketches of the slums of Dublin. Stephens described a world at night on the streets of Dublin, where characters were ravenous in their search for food, in scenes so richly detailed that it was impossible to believe that the author had not experienced such trauma himself. But it wasn't until 1912, when Stephens turned out two novels and a second volume of poems, that he could leave the clerical jobs he so deplored and finally live the writing life he desired. *The Charwoman's Daughter* and *The Crock of Gold* were commercially successful for Stephens, but it is the latter novel on which his reputation rests almost entirely today. Partly allegorical, human frailties and themes of rebirth are comically presented in a tale that William Butler Yeats, presenting Stephens with the Polignac Prize, proclaimed to be proof that the city of Dublin had "begun to live with deeper life." Yeats also said that *The Crock of Gold* was "a phantasmagoria of eloquent people who have an infinite leisure for discussion." Little did the great Irish poet know the truth, for Stephens had to borrow money to travel to London to claim the prize. Stephens made light of this financial predicament in a personal letter, stating: "On the day before I was notified of the prize I made the discovery that my total wealth invisable [*sic*] and moveable goods was, item, one wife, two babies, two cats and fifteen shillings."

The following year found Stephens moving to Paris, where he wrote *Here Are Ladies,* a collection of short stories, and his third novel, *The Demi-Gods,* in the cafés. However, by 1915, with France at war and himself in need of a stable income, Stephens had to return to Dublin in August, where he assumed a post at the National Gallery of Ireland, and eventually stumbled into the events that would lead to his writing *The Insurrection in Dublin.*

Once Stephens returned to Dublin, he continued to write novels of Irish sages and imaginary universes, using the colorful language and narrative dexterity he vividly displayed before *The Insurrection in Dublin.* Yet in 1925, he moved his family permanently to London where he immersed himself again in the literary culture. Although he continued to write, most notably *Etched in Moonlight* (1928), a collection of short stories, Stephens again stumbled onto a path which would change his life. He began a career as a broadcaster for the BBC, where he was finally able to demonstrate his remarkable skills as a conversationalist. He became a popular host who would often recite his own poetry as well as tell stories of his friendships with Joyce, Yeats and AE back in Dublin. He also traveled to America regularly, where he filled lecture halls, regaling audiences with tales and reminiscences.

Following World War II, Stephens's health began to decline, and he gave his final broadcast on June 11, 1950. He sorely missed the literary scene he left behind in Dublin, and he would die in London just six months later. As generous as his contemporaries were with praise for Stephens's work, perhaps no one described his vision more eloquently than his friend, Stephen MacKenna, when he wrote in 1923: "Novel, story, hero-tale, poem, the pages sing and shine: caprice and tenderness, subtle generosities underlain by painful brutalities, extraordinary force with a winning innocence; it is seeing a power like that of a savage, a song and dance as of a child, the loving tolerance of a mystic discerning in all things, noble or trifling or ugly, always some trace of some god."

THE INSURRECTION IN DUBLIN

♣

CHAPTER I.

MONDAY.

This has taken everyone by surprise. It is possible, that, with the exception of their Staff, it has taken the Volunteers themselves by surprise; but, to-day, our peaceful city is no longer peaceful; guns are sounding, or rolling and crackling from different directions, and, although rarely, the rattle of machine guns can be heard also.

Two days ago war seemed very far away—so far, that I have covenanted with myself to learn the alphabet of music. Toni Bodkin had promised to present me with a musical instrument called a dulcimer—I persist in thinking that this is a species of guitar, although I am assured that it is a number of small metal plates which are struck with sticks, and I confess that this description of its function prejudices me more than a little against it. There is no reason why I should think dubiously of such an instrument, but I do not relish the idea of procuring music with a stick. With this dulcimer I shall be able to tap out our Irish melodies when I am abroad, and transport myself to Ireland for a few minutes, or a few bars.

In preparation for this present I had through Saturday and Sunday been learning the notes of the Scale. The notes and spaces on the lines did not trouble me much, but those above and below the line seemed ingenious and complicated to a degree that frightened me.

On Saturday I got the *Irish Times*, and found in it a long article by Bernard Shaw (reprinted from the *New York Times*). One reads things written by Shaw. Why one does read them I do not know exactly, except that it is a habit we got into years ago, and we read an article by Shaw just as we put on our boots in the morning—that is, without thinking about it, and without any idea of reward.

His article angered me exceedingly. It was called "Irish Nonsense talked in Ireland." It was written (as is almost all of his journalistic work) with that *bonhomie* which he has cultivated—it is his mannerism—and which is essentially hypocritical and untrue. *Bonhomie!* It is that man-of-the-world attitude, that shop attitude, that between-you-and-me-for-are-we-not-equal-and-cultured attitude, which

is the tone of a card-sharper or a trick-of-the-loop man. That was the tone of
Shaw's article. I wrote an open letter to him which I sent to the *New Age*, because I
doubted that the Dublin papers would print it if I sent it to them, and I knew that
the Irish people who read the other papers had never heard of Shaw, except as a
trademark under which very good Limerick bacon is sold, and that they would not
be interested in the opinions of a person named Shaw on any subject not relevant
to bacon. I struck out of my letter a good many harsh things which I said of him,
and hoped he would reply to it in order that I could furnish these acidities to him
in a second letter.

That was Saturday.

On Sunday I had to go to my office, as the Director was absent in London, and
there I applied myself to the notes and spaces below the stave, but relinquished the
exercise, convinced that these mysteries were unattainable by man, while the
knowledge that above the stave there were others and not less complex, stayed
mournfully with me.

I returned home, and as novels (perhaps it is only for the duration of the war)
do not now interest me I read for some time in Madame Blavatsky's "Secret
Doctrine," which book interests me profoundly. George Russell was out of town or
I would have gone round to his house in the evening to tell him what I thought
about Shaw, and to listen to his own much finer ideas on that as on every other
subject. I went to bed.

On the morning following I awoke into full insurrection and bloody war, but I
did not know anything about it. It was Bank Holiday, but for employments such as
mine there are not any holidays, so I went to my office at the usual hour, and after
transacting what business was necessary I bent myself to the notes above and below
the stave, and marvelled anew at the ingenuity of man. Peace was in the building,
and if any of the attendants had knowledge or rumour of war they did not mention it to me.

At one o'clock I went to lunch. Passing the corner of Merrion Row I saw two
small groups of people. These people were regarding steadfastly in the direction of
St. Stephen's Green Park, and they spoke occasionally to one another with that
detached confidence which proved they were mutually unknown. I also, but without approaching them, stared in the direction of the Green. I saw nothing but the
narrow street which widened to the Park. Some few people were standing in tentative attitudes, and all looking in the one direction. As I turned from them home-
wards I received an impression of silence and expectation and excitement.

On the way home I noticed that many silent people were standing in their doorways—an unusual thing in Dublin outside of the back streets. The glance of a Dublin man or woman conveys generally a criticism of one's personal appearance, and is a little hostile to the passer. The look of each person as I passed was steadfast, and contained an enquiry instead of a criticism. I felt faintly uneasy, but withdrew my mind to a meditation which I had covenanted with myself to perform daily, and passed to my house.

There I was told that there had been a great deal of rifle firing all the morning, and we concluded that the Military recruits or Volunteer detachments were practising that arm. My return to business was by the way I had already come. At the corner of Merrion Row I found the same silent groups, who were still looking in the direction of the Green, and addressing each other occasionally with the detached confidence of strangers. Suddenly, and on the spur of the moment, I addressed one of these silent gazers.

"Has there been an accident?" said I.

I indicated the people standing about.

"What's all this for?"

He was a sleepy, rough-looking man about 40 years of age, with a blunt red moustache, and the distant eyes which one sees in sailors. He looked at me, stared at me as at a person from a different country. He grew wakeful and vivid.

"Don't you know," said he.

And then he saw that I did not know.

"The Sinn Feiners have seized the City this morning."

"Oh!" said I.

He continued with the savage earnestness of one who has amazement in his mouth:

"They seized the City at eleven o'clock this morning. The Green there is full of them. They have captured the Castle. They have taken the Post Office."

"My God!" said I, staring at him, and instantly I turned and went running towards the Green.

In a few seconds I banished astonishment and began to walk. As I drew near the Green rifle fire began like sharply-cracking whips. It was from the further side. I saw that the Gates were closed and men were standing inside with guns on their shoulders. I passed a house, the windows of which were smashed in. As I went by a man in civilian clothes slipped through the Park gates, which instantly closed behind him. He ran towards me, and I halted. He was carrying two small packets in his hand. He passed me hurriedly, and, placing his leg inside the broken window of the house behind me, he disappeared. Almost immediately another man in civilian clothes appeared from the broken window of another house. He also had something (I don't know what) in his hand. He ran urgently towards the gates, which opened, admitted him, and closed again.

In the centre of this side of the Park a rough barricade of carts and motor cars had been sketched. It was still full of gaps. Behind it was a halted tram, and along the vistas of the Green one saw other trams derelict, untenanted.

I came to the barricade. As I reached it and stood by the Shelbourne Hotel, which it faced, a loud cry came from the Park. The gates opened and three men ran out. Two of them held rifles with fixed bayonets. The third gripped a heavy revolver in his fist. They ran towards a motor car which had just turned the corner, and halted it. The men with bayonets took position instantly on either side of the car. The man with the revolver saluted, and I heard him begging the occupants to pardon him, and directing them to dismount. A man and woman got down. They were again saluted and requested to go to the sidewalk. They did so.

NOTE—As I pen these words rifle shot is cracking from three different directions and continually. Three minutes ago there were two discharges from heavy guns. These are the first heavy guns used in the Insurrection, 25th April.

The man crossed and stood by me. He was very tall and thin, middle-aged, with a shaven, wasted face. "I want to get down to Armagh to-day," he said to no one in particular. The loose bluish skin under his eyes was twitching. The Volunteers directed the chauffeur to drive to the barricade and lodge his car in a particular position there. He did it awkwardly, and after three attempts he succeeded in pleasing them. He was a big, brown-faced man, whose knees were rather high for the seat he was in, and they jerked with the speed and persistence of something moved with a powerful spring. His face was composed and fully under command, although his legs were not. He locked the car into the barricade, and then, being a man accustomed to be commanded, he awaited an order to descend. When the order came he walked directly to his master, still preserving all the solemnity of his features. These two men did not address a word to each other, but their drilled and expressionless eyes were loud with surprise and fear and rage. They went into the Hotel.

I spoke to the man with the revolver. He was no more than a boy, not more certainly than twenty years of age, short in stature, with close curling red hair and blue eyes—a kindly-looking lad. The strap of his sombrero had torn loose on one side, and except while he held it in his teeth it flapped about his chin. His face was sunburnt and grimy with dust and sweat.

This young man did not appear to me to be acting from his reason. He was doing his work from a determination implanted previously, days, weeks perhaps, on his imagination. His mind was—where? It was not with his body. And continually his eyes went searching widely, looking for spaces, searching hastily the clouds, the vistas of the streets, looking for something that did not hinder him, looking away for a moment from the immediacies and rigours which were impressed where his mind had been.

When I spoke he looked at me, and I know that for some seconds he did not see me, said:—

"What is the meaning of all this? What has happened?"

He replied collectedly enough in speech, but with that ramble and errancy clouding his eyes.

"We have taken the City. We are expecting an attack from the military at any moment, and those people," he indicated knots of men, women and children clustered towards the end of the Green, "won't go home for me. We have the Post Office, and the Railways, and the Castle. We have all the City. We have everything."

(Some men and two women drew behind me to listen.)

"This morning," said he, "the police rushed us. One ran at me to take my revolver. I fired but I missed him, and I hit a——"

"You have far too much talk," said a voice to the young man.

I turned a few steps away, and glancing back saw that he was staring after me, but I know that he did not see me—he was looking at turmoil, and blood, and at figures that ran towards him and ran away—a world in motion and he in the centre of it astonished.

The men with him did not utter a sound. They were both older. One, indeed, a short, sturdy man, had a heavy white moustache. He was quite collected, and took no notice of the skies, or the spaces. He saw a man in rubbers placing his hand on a motor bicycle in the barricade, and called to him instantly:

"Let that alone."

The motorist did not at once remove his hand, whereupon the white-moustached man gripped his gun in both hands and ran violently towards him. He ran directly to him, body to body, and, as he was short and the motorist was very tall, stared fixedly up in his face. He roared up at his face in a mighty voice.

"Are you deaf? Are you deaf? Move back!"

The motorist moved away, pursued by an eye as steady and savage as the point of the bayonet that was level with it.

Another motor car came round the Ely Place corner of the Green and wobbled at the sight of the barricade. The three men who had returned to the gates roared "Halt," but the driver made a tentative effort to turn his wheel. A great shout of many voices came then, and the three men ran to him.

"Drive to the barricade," came the order.

The driver turned his wheel a point further towards escape, and instantly one of the men clapped a gun to the wheel and blew the tyre open. Some words were exchanged, and then a shout:

"Drive it on the rim, drive it."

The tone was very menacing, and the motorist turned his car slowly to the barricade and placed it in.

For an hour I tramped the City, seeing everywhere these knots of watchful strangers speaking together in low tones, and it sank into my mind that what I had heard was true, and that the City was in insurrection. It had been promised for so long, and had been threatened for so long. Now it was here. I had seen it in the Green, others had seen it in other parts—the same men clad in dark green and equipped with rifle, bayonet, and bandolier, the same silent activity. The police had disappeared from the streets. At that hour I did not see one policeman, nor did I see one for many days, and men said that several of them had been shot earlier in the morning; that an officer had been shot on Portobello Bridge, that many soldiers had been killed, and that a good many civilians were dead also.

Around me as I walked the rumour of war and death was in the air. Continually and from every direction rifles were crackling and rolling; sometimes there was only one shot, again it would be a roll of firing crested with single, short explosions, and sinking again to whip-like snaps and whip-like echoes; then for a moment silence, and then again the guns leaped in the air.

The rumour of positions, bridges, public places, railway stations, Government offices, having been seized was persistent, and was not denied by any voice.

I met some few people I knew. P. H., T. M., who said: "Well!" and thrust their eyes into me as though they were rummaging me for information.

But there were not very many people in the streets. The greater part of the population were away on Bank Holiday, and did not know anything of this business. Many of them would not know anything until they found they had to walk home from Kingstown, Dalkey, Howth, or wherever they were.

I returned to my office, decided that I would close it for the day. The men were very relieved when I came in, and were more relieved when I ordered the gong to be sounded. There were some few people in the place, and they were soon put out. The outer gates were locked, and the great door, but I kept the men on duty until the evening. We were the last public institution open; all the others had been closed for hours.

I went upstairs and sat down, but had barely reached the chair before I stood up again, and began to pace my room, to and fro, to and fro; amazed, expectant, inquiet; turning my ear to the shots, and my mind to speculations that began in the middle, and were chased from there by others before they had taken one thought forward. But then I took myself resolutely and sat me down, and I pencilled out exercises above the stave, and under the stave; and discovered suddenly that I was again marching the floor, to and fro, to and fro, with thoughts bursting about my head as though they were fired on me from concealed batteries.

At five o'clock I left. I met Miss P., all of whose rumours coincided with those I had gathered. She was in exceeding good humour and interested. Leaving her I met Cy—, and we turned together up to the Green. As we proceeded, the sound of firing grew more distinct, but when we reached the Green it died away again. We stood a little below the Shelbourne Hotel, looking at the barricade and into the Park. We could see nothing. Not a Volunteer was in sight. The Green seemed a desert. There were only the trees to be seen, and through them small green vistas of sward.

Just then a man stepped on the footpath and walked directly to the barricade. He stopped and gripped the shafts of a lorry lodged near the centre. At that instant the Park exploded into life and sound; from nowhere armed men appeared at the railings, and they all shouted at the man:

"Put down that lorry. Let out and go away. Let out at once."

These were the cries. The man did not let out. He halted with the shafts in his hand, and looked towards the vociferous pailings. Then, and very slowly, he began to draw the lorry out of the barricade. The shouts came to him again, very loud, very threatening, but he did not attend to them.

"He is the man that owns the lorry," said a voice beside me.

Dead silence fell on the people around while the man slowly drew his cart down by the footpath. Then three shots rang out in succession. At the distance he could not be missed, and it was obvious they were trying to frighten him. He dropped the shafts, and instead of going away he walked over to the Volunteers.

"He has a nerve," said another voice behind me.

The man walked directly towards the Volunteers, who, to the number of about ten, were lining the railings. He walked slowly, bent a little forward, with one hand raised and one finger up as though he were going to make a speech. Ten guns were pointing at him, and a voice repeated many times:

"Go and put back that lorry or you are a dead man. Go before I count four. One, two, three, four——"

A rifle spat at him, and in two undulating movements the man sank on himself and sagged to the ground.

I ran to him with some others, while a woman screamed unmeaningly, all on one strident note. The man was picked up and carried to a hospital beside the Arts Club. There was a hole in the top of his bead, and one does not know how ugly blood can look until it has been seen clotted in hair. As the poor man was being carried in, a woman plumped to her knees in the road and began not to scream but to screetch.

At that moment the Volunteers were hated. The men by whom I was and who were lifting the body, roared into the railings: —

"We'll be coming back for you, damn you."

From the railings there came no reply, and in an instant the place was again desert and silent, and the little green vistas were slumbering among the trees.

No one seemed able to estimate the number of men inside the Green, and through the day no considerable body of men had been seen, only those who held the gates, and the small parties of threes and fours who arrested motors and carts for their barricades. Among these were some who were only infants—one boy seemed about twelve years of age. He was strutting the centre of the road with a large revolver in his small fist. A motor car came by him containing three men, and in the shortest of time he had the car lodged in his barricade, and dismissed its stupified occupants with a wave of his armed hand.

The knots were increasing about the streets, for now the Bank Holiday people began to wander back from places that were not distant, and to them it had all to be explained anew. Free movement was possible everywhere in the City, but the constant crackle of rifles restricted somewhat that freedom. Up to one o'clock at night belated travellers were straggling into the City, and curious people were wandering from group to group still trying to gather information.

I remained awake until four o'clock in the morning. Every five minutes a rifle cracked somewhere, but about a quarter to twelve sharp volleying came from the direction of Portobello Bridge, and died away after some time. The windows of my flat listen out towards the Green, and obliquely towards Sackville Street. In another quarter of an hour there were volleys from Stephen's Green direction, and this continued with intensity for about twenty-five minutes. Then it fell into a sputter of fire and ceased.

I went to bed about four o'clock convinced that the Green had been rushed by the military and captured, and that the rising was at an end.

That was the first day of the insurrection.

CHAPTER II.

TUESDAY.

A sultry, lowering day, and dusk skies fat with rain.

I left for my office, believing that the insurrection was at an end. At a corner I asked a man was it all finished. He said it was not, and that, if anything, it was worse.

On this day the rumours began, and I think it will be many a year before the rumours cease. The *Irish Times* published an editorial which contained nothing but an official Proclamation that evily-disposed persons had disturbed the peace, and that the situation was well in hand. The news stated in three lines that there was a Sinn Fein rising in Dublin, and that the rest of the country was quiet.

No English or country papers came. There was no delivery or collection of letters. All the shops in the City were shut. There was no traffic of any kind in the streets. There was no way of gathering any kind of information, and rumour gave all the news.

It seemed that the Military and the Government had been taken unawares. It was Bank Holiday, and many military officers had gone to the races, or were away on leave, and prominent members of the Irish Government had gone to England on Sunday.

It appeared that everything claimed on the previous day was true, and that the City of Dublin was entirely in the hands of the Volunteers. They had taken and sacked Jacob's Biscuit Factory, and had converted it into a fort which they held. They had the Post Office, and were building barricades around it ten feet high of sandbags, cases, wire entanglements. They had pushed out all the windows and sandbagged them to half their height, while cart-loads of food, vegetables and ammunition were going in continually. They had dug trenches and were laying siege to one of the city barracks.

It was current that intercourse between Germany and Ireland had been frequent chiefly by means of submarines, which came up near the coast and landed machine guns, rifles and ammunition. It was believed also that the whole country had risen, and that many strong places and cities were in the hands of the Volunteers. Cork Barracks was said to be taken while the officers were away at the Curragh races, that the men without officers were disorganised, and the place easily captured.

It was said that Germans, thousands strong, had landed, and that many Irish Americans with German officers had arrived also with full military equipment.

On the previous day the Volunteers had proclaimed the Irish Republic. This ceremony was conducted from the Mansion House steps, and the manifesto was said to have been read by Pearse, of St. Enda's. The Republican and Volunteer flag was hoisted on the Mansion House. The latter consisted of vertical colours of green, white and orange. Kerry wireless station was reported captured, and news of the Republic flashed abroad. These rumours were flying in the street.

It was also reported that two transports had come in the night and had landed from England about 8,000 soldiers. An attack reported on the Post Office by a troop of lancers who were received with fire and repulsed. It is foolish to send cavalry into street war.

In connection with this lancer charge at the Post Office it is said that the people, and especially the women, sided with the soldiers, and that the Volunteers were assailed by these women with bricks, bottles, sticks, to cries of:

"Would you be hurting the poor men?"

There were other angry ladies who threatened Volunteers, addressing to them this petrifying query:

"Would you be hurting the poor horses?"

Indeed, the best people in the world live in Dublin.

The lancers retreated to the bottom of Sackville Street, where they remained for some time in the centre of a crowd who were carressing their horses. It may have seemed to them a rather curious kind of insurrection—that is, if they were strangers to Ireland.

In the Post Office neighbourhood the Volunteers had some difficulty in dealing with the people who surged about them while they were preparing the barricade, and hindered them to some little extent. One of the Volunteers was particularly noticeable. He held a lady's umbrella in his hand, and whenever some person became particularly annoying he would leap the barricade and chase his man half a street, hitting him over the head with the umbrella. It was said that the wonder of the world was not that Ireland was at war, but that after many hours the umbrella was still unbroken. A Volunteer night attack on the Quays was spoken of, whereat the military were said to have been taken by surprise and six carts of their ammunition captured. This was probably untrue. Also, that the Volunteers had blown up the Arsenal in the Phoenix Park.

There had been looting in the night about Sackville Street, and it was current that the Volunteers had shot twenty of the looters.

The shops attacked were mainly haber-dashers, shoe shops, and sweet shops. Very many sweet shops were raided, and until the end of the rising sweet shops were the favourite mark of the looters. There is something comical in this looting of sweet shops—something almost innocent and child-like.

Possibly most of the looters are children who are having the sole gorge of their lives. They have tasted sweetstuffs they had never toothed before, and will never taste again in this life, and until they die the insurrection of 1916 will have a sweet savour for them.

I went to the Green. At the corner of Merrion Row a horse was lying on the footpath surrounded by blood. He bore two bullet wounds, but the blood came from his throat which had been cut.

Inside the Green railings four bodies could be seen lying on the ground. They were dead Volunteers.

The rain was falling now persistently, and persistently from the Green and from the Shelbourne Hotel snipers were exchanging bullets. Some distance beyond the Shelbourne I saw another Volunteer stretched out on a seat just within the railings. He was not dead, for, now and again, his hand moved feebly in a gesture for aid; the hand was completely red with blood. His face could not be seen. He was just a limp mass, upon which the rain beat pitilessly, and he was sodden and shapeless, and most miserable to see. His companions could not draw him in for the spot was covered by the snipers from the Shelbourne. Bystanders stated that several attempts had already been made to rescue him, but that he would have to remain there until the fall of night.

From Trinity College windows and roof there was also sniping, but the Shelbourne Hotel riflemen must have seriously troubled the Volunteers in the Green.

As I went back I stayed a while in front of the hotel to count the shots that had struck the windows. There were fourteen shots through the ground windows. The holes were clean through, each surrounded by a star—the bullets went through but did not crack the glass. There were three places in which the windows had holes half a foot to a foot wide and high. Here many rifles must have fired at the one moment. It must have been as awkward inside the Shelbourne Hotel as it was inside the Green.

A lady who lived in Baggot Street said she had been up all night, and, with her neighbours, had supplied tea and bread to the soldiers who were lining the street. The officer to whom she spoke had made two or three attacks to draw fire and estimate the Volunteers' positions, numbers, &c., and he told her that he considered there were 3,000 well-armed Volunteers in the Green, and as he had only 1,000 soldiers, he could not afford to deliver a real attack, and was merely containing them.

Amiens Street station reported recaptured by the military; other stations are said to be still in the Volunteers' possession.

The story goes that about twelve o'clock on Monday an English officer had marched into the Post Office and demanded two penny stamps from the amazed Volunteers who were inside. He thought their uniforms were postal uniforms. They brought him in, and he is probably still trying to get a perspective on the occurrence. They had as prisoners in the Post Office a certain number of soldiers, and rumour had it that these men accommodated themselves quickly to duress, and were busily engaged peeling potatoes for the meal which they would partake of later on with the Volunteers.

Earlier in the day I met a wild individual who spat rumour as though his mouth were a machine gun or a linotype machine. He believed everything he heard; and everything he heard became as by magic favourable to his hopes, which were violently anti-English. One unfavourable rumour was instantly crushed by him with three stories which were favourable and triumphantly so. He said the Germans had landed in three places. One of these landings alone consisted of fifteen thousand men. The other landings probably beat that figure. The whole City of Cork was in the hands of the Volunteers, and, to that extent, might be said to be peaceful. German warships had defeated the English, and their transports were speeding from every side. The whole country was up, and the garrison was outnumbered by one hundred to one. These Dublin barracks which had not been taken were now besieged and on the point of surrender.

I think this man created and winged every rumour that flew in Dublin, and he was the sole individual whom I heard definitely taking a side. He left me, and, looking back, I saw him pouring his news into the ear of a gaping stranger whom he had arrested for the purpose. I almost went back to hear would he tell the same tale or would he elaborate it into a new thing, for I am interested in the art of story-telling.

At eleven o'clock the rain ceased, and to it succeeded a beautiful night, gusty with wind, and packed with sailing clouds and stars. We were expecting visitors this night, but the sound of guns may have warned most people away. Three only came, and with them we listened from my window to the guns at the Green challenging and replying to each other, and to where, further away, the Trinity snipers were crackling, and beyond again to the sounds of war from Sackville Street. The firing was fairly heavy, and often the short rattle of machine guns could be heard.

One of the stories told was that the Volunteers had taken the South Dublin Union Workhouse, occupied it, and trenched the grounds. They were heavily attacked by the military, who, at a loss of 150 men, took the place. The tale went that towards the close the officer in command offered them terms of surrender, but the Volunteers replied that they were not there to surrender. They were there to be killed. The garrison consisted of fifty men, and the story said that fifty men were killed.

CHAPTER III.

WEDNESDAY.

It was three o'clock before I got to sleep last night, and during the hours machine guns and rifle firing had been continuous.

This morning the sun is shining brilliantly, and the movement in the streets possesses more of animation than it has done. The movement ends always in a knot of people, and folk go from group to group vainly seeking information, and quite content if the rumour they presently gather differs even a little from the one they have just communicated.

The first statement I heard was that the Green had been taken by the military; the second that it had been re-taken; the third that it had not been taken at all. The facts at last emerged that the Green had not been occupied by the soldiers, but that the Volunteers had retreated from it into a house which commanded it. This was found to be the College of Surgeons, and from the windows and roof of this College they were sniping. A machine gun was mounted on the roof; other machine guns, however, opposed them from the roofs of the Shelbourne Hotel, the United Service Club, and the Alexandra Club. Thus a triangular duel opened between these positions across the trees of the Park.

Through the railings of the Green some rifles and bandoliers could be seen lying on the ground, as also the deserted trenches and snipers' holes. Small boys bolted in to see these sights and bolted out again with bullets quickening their feet. Small boys do not believe that people will really kill them, but small boys were killed.

The dead horse was still lying stiff and lamentable on the footpath.

This morning a gunboat came up the Liffey and helped to bombard Liberty

Hall. The Hall is breeched and useless. Rumour says that it was empty at the time, and that Connolly with his men had marched long before to the Post Office and the Green. The same source of information relates that three thousand Volunteers came from Belfast on an excursion train and that they marched into the Post Office.

On this day only one of my men came in. He said that he had gone on the roof and had been shot at, consequently that the Volunteers held some of the covering houses. I went to the roof and remained there for half an hour. There were no shots, but the firing from the direction of Sackville Street was continuous and at times exceedingly heavy.

To-day the *Irish Times* was published. It contained a new military proclamation, and a statement that the country was peaceful, and told that in Sackville Street some houses were burned to the ground.

On the outside railings a bill proclaiming Martial Law was posted.

Into the newspaper statement that peace reigned in the country one was inclined to read more of disquietude than of truth, and one said is the country so extraordinarily peaceful that it can be dismissed in three lines. There is too much peace or too much reticence, but it will be some time before we hear from outside of Dublin.

Meanwhile the sun was shining. It was a delightful day, and the streets outside and around the areas of fire were animated and, even gay. In the streets of Dublin there were no morose faces to be seen. Almost everyone was smiling and attentive, and a democratic feeling was abroad, to which our City is very much a stranger; for while in private we are a sociable and talkative people we have no street manners or public ease whatever. Every person spoke to every other person, and men and women mixed and talked without constraint.

Was the City for or against the Volunteers? Was it for the Volunteers, and yet against the rising? It is considered now (writing a day or two afterwards) that Dublin was entirely against the Volunteers, but on the day of which I write no such certainty could be put forward. There was a singular reticence on the subject. Men met and talked volubly, but they said nothing that indicated a personal desire or belief. They asked for and exchanged the latest news, or, rather, rumour, and while expressions were frequent of astonishment at the suddenness and completeness of the occurrence, no expression of opinion for or against was anywhere formulated.

Sometimes a man said, "They will be beaten of course," and, as he prophesied, the neighbour might surmise if he did so with a sad heart or a merry one, but they knew nothing and asked nothing of his views, and themselves advanced no flag.

This was among the men.

The women were less guarded, or, perhaps, knew they had less to fear. Most of the female opinion I heard was not alone unfavourable but actively and viciously hostile to the rising. This was noticeable among the best dressed class of our population; the worst dressed, indeed the female dregs of Dublin life, expressed a like antagonism, and almost in similar language. The view expressed was—

"I hope every man of them will be shot."

And—

"They ought to be all shot."

Shooting, indeed, was proceeding everywhere. During daylight, at least, the sound is not sinister nor depressing, and the thought that perhaps a life had exploded with that crack is not depressing either.

In the last two years of world-war our ideas on death have undergone a change. It is not now the furtive thing that crawled into your bed and which you fought with pillboxes and medicine bottles. It has become again a rider of the wind whom you may go coursing with through the fields and open places. All the morbidity is gone, and the sickness, and what remains to Death is now health and excitement. So Dublin laughed at the noise of its own bombardment, and made no moan about its dead—in the sunlight. Afterwards—in the rooms, when the night fell, and instead of silence that mechanical barking of the maxims and the whistle and screams of the rifles, the solemn roar of the heavier guns, and the red glare covering the sky. It is possible that in the night Dublin did not laugh, and that she was gay in the sunlight for no other reason than that the night was past.

On this day fighting was incessant at Mount Street Bridge. A party of Volunteers had seized three houses covering the bridge and converted these into forts. It is reported that military casualties at this point were very heavy. The Volunteers are said also to hold the South Dublin Union. The soldiers have seized Guinness's Brewery, while their opponents have seized another brewery in the neighbourhood, and between these two there is a continual fusilade.

Fighting is brisk about Ringsend and along the Canal. Dame Street was said to be held in many places by the Volunteers. I went down Dame Street, but saw no Volunteers, and did not observe any sniping from the houses. Further, as Dame Street is entirely commanded by the roofs and windows of Trinity College, it is unlikely that they should be here.

It was curious to observe this, at other times, so animated street, broad and deserted, with at the corners of side streets small knots of people watching. Seen from behind, Grattan's Statue in College Green seemed almost alive, and he had the air of addressing warnings and reproaches to Trinity College.

The Proclamation issued to-day warns all people to remain within doors until five o'clock in the morning, and after seven o'clock at night.

It is still early. There is no news of any kind, and the rumours begin to catch quickly on each other and to cancel one another out. Dublin is entirely cut off from England, and from the outside world. It is, just as entirely cut off from the rest of Ireland; no news of any kind filters in to us. We are land-locked and sea-locked, but, as yet, it does not much matter.

Meantime the belief grows that the Volunteers may be able to hold out much longer than had been imagined. The idea at first among the people had been that the insurrection would be ended the morning after it had began. But to-day, the insurrection having lasted three days, people are ready to conceive that it may last for ever. There is almost a feeling of gratitude towards the Volunteers because they are holding out for a little while, for had they been beaten the first or second day the City would have been humiliated to the soul.

People say: "Of course, they will be beaten." The statement is almost a query, and they continue, "but they are putting up a decent fight." For being beaten does not greatly matter in Ireland, but not fighting does matter. "They went forth always to the battle; and they always fell." Indeed, the history of the Irish race is in that phrase.

The firing from the roofs of Trinity College became violent. I crossed Dame Street some distance up, struck down the Quays, and went along these until I reached the Ballast Office. Further than this it was not possible to go, for a step beyond the Ballast Office would have brought one into the unending stream of lead that was pouring from Trinity and other places. I was looking on O'Connell Bridge and Sackville Street, and the house facing me was Kelly's—a red-brick fishing tackle shop, one half of which was on the Quay and the other half in Sackville Street. This house was being bombarded.

I counted the report of six different machine guns which played on it. Rifles innumerable and from every sort of place were potting its windows, and at intervals of about half a minute the shells from a heavy gun lobbed in through its windows or thumped mightily against its walls.

For three hours that bombardment continued, and the walls stood in a cloud of red dust and smoke. Rifle and machine gun bullets pattered over every inch of it, and, unfailingly the heavy gun pounded its shells through the windows.

One's heart melted at the idea that human beings were crouching inside that volcano of death, and I said to myself, "Not even a fly can be alive in that house."

No head showed at any window, no rifle cracked from window or roof in reply. The house was dumb, lifeless, and I thought every one of those men are dead.

It was then, and quite suddenly, that the possibilities of street fighting flashed on me, and I knew there was no person in the house, and said to myself, "They have smashed through the walls with a hatchet and are sitting in the next house, or they have long ago climbed out by the skylight and are on a roof half a block away." Then the thought came to me—they have and hold the entire of Sackville Street down to the Post Office. Later on this proved to be the case, and I knew at this moment that Sackville Street was doomed.

I continued to watch the bombardment, but no longer with the anguish which had before torn me. Near by there were four men, and a few yards away, clustered in a laneway, there were a dozen others. An agitated girl was striding from the farther group to the one in which I was, and she addressed the men in the most obscene language which I have ever heard. She addressed them man by man, and she continued to speak and cry and scream at them with all that obstinate, angry patience of which only a woman is capable.

She cursed us all. She called down diseases on every human being in the world excepting only the men who were being bombarded. She demanded of the folk in the laneway that they should march at least into the roadway and prove that they were proud men and were not afraid of bullets. She had been herself into the danger zone. Had stood herself in the track of the guns, and had there cursed her fill for half an hour, and she desired that the men should do at least what she had done.

This girl was quite young—about nineteen years of age—and was dressed in the customary shawl and apron of her class. Her face was rather pretty, or it had that pretty slenderness and softness of outline which belong to youth. But every sentence she spoke contained half a dozen indecent words. Alas, it was only that her vocabulary was not equal to her emotions, and she did not know how to be emphatic without being obscene—it is the cause of most of the meaningless swearing one hears every day. She spoke to me for a minute, and her eyes were as soft as those of a kitten and her language was as gentle as her eyes. She wanted a match to light a cigarette, but I had none, and said that I also wanted one. In a few minutes she brought me a match, and then she recommenced her tireless weaving of six vile words into hundreds of stupid sentences.

About five o'clock the guns eased off of Kelly's.

To inexperienced eyes they did not seem to have done very much damage, but afterwards, one found that although the walls were standing and apparently solid there was no inside to the house. From roof to basement the building was bare as a dog kennel. There were no floors inside, there was nothing there but blank space; and on the ground within was the tumble and rubbish that had been roof and floors and furniture. Everything inside was smashed and pulverised into scrap and dust, and the only objects that had consistency and their ancient shape were the bricks that fell when the shells struck them.

Rifle shots had begun to strike the house on the further side of the street, a jewellers' shop called Hopkins & Hopkins. The impact of these balls on the bricks was louder than the sound of the shot which immediately succeeded, and each bullet that struck brought down a shower of fine red dust from the walls. Perhaps thirty or forty shots in all were fired at Hopkins', and then, except for an odd crack, firing ceased.

During all this time there had been no reply from the Volunteers, and I thought they must be husbanding their ammunition, and so must be short of it, and that it would be only a matter of a few days before the end. All this, I said to myself, will be finished in a few days, and they will be finished; life here will recommence exactly where it left off, and except for some newly-filled graves, all will be as it had been until they become a tradition and enter the imagination of their race.

I spoke to several of the people about me, and found the same willingness to exchange news that I had found elsewhere in the City, and the same reticences as regarded their private opinions. Two of them, indeed, and they were the only two I met with during the insurrection, expressed, although in measured terms, admiration for the Volunteers, and while they did not side with them they did not say anything against them. One was a labouring man, the other a gentleman. The remark of the latter was:

"I am an Irishman, and (pointing to the shells that were bursting through the windows in front of us) I hate to see that being done to other Irishmen."

He had come from some part of the country to spend the Easter Holidays in Dublin, and was unable to leave town again.

The labouring man—he was about fifty-six years of age—spoke very quietly and collectedly about the insurrection. He was a type with whom I had come very little in contact, and I was surprised to find how simple and good his speech was, and how calm his ideas. He thought labour was in this movement to a greater extent than was imagined. I mentioned that Liberty Hall had been blown up, and that the garrison had either surrendered or been killed. He replied that a gunboat had that morning come up the river and had blown Liberty Hall into smash, but, he added, there were no men in it. All the Labour Volunteers had marched with Connolly into the Post Office.

He said the Labour Volunteers might possibly number about one thousand men, but that it would be quite safe to say eight hundred, and he held that the Labour Volunteers, or the Citizens' Army, as they called themselves, had always been careful not to reveal their numbers. They had always announced that they possessed about two hundred and fifty men, and had never paraded any more than that number at any one time. Workingmen, he continued, knew that the men who marched were always different men.

The police knew it, too, but they thought that the Citizen's Army was the *most deserted-from force* in the world.

The men, however, were not deserters—you don't, he said, desert a man like Connolly, and they were merely taking their turn at being drilled and disciplined. They were raised against the police who, in the big strike of two years ago, had acted towards them with unparalleled savagery, and the men had determined that the police would never again find them thus disorganised.

This man believed that every member of the Citizens' Army had marched with their leader.

"The men, I know," said he, "would not be afraid of anything, and," he continued, "they are in the Post Office now."

"What chance have they"

"None," he replied, "and they never said they had, and they never thought they would have any."

"How long do you think they'll be able to hold out?"

He nodded towards the house that had been bombarded by heavy guns.

"That will root them out of it quick enough," was his reply.

"I'm going home," said he then, "the people will be wondering if I'm dead or alive," and he walked away from that sad street, as I did myself a few minutes afterwards.

CHAPTER IV.

THURSDAY.

Again, the rumours greeted one. This place had fallen and had not fallen. Such a position had been captured by the soldiers; recaptured by the Volunteers, and had not been attacked at all. But certainly fighting was proceeding. Up Mount Street, the rifle volleys were continuous, and the coming and going of ambulance cars from that direction, were continuous also. Some spoke of pitched battles on the bridge, and said that as yet the advantage lay with the Volunteers.

At 11.30 there came the sound of heavy guns firing in the direction of Sackville Street. I went on the roof, and remained there for some time. From this height the sounds could be heard plainly. There was sustained firing along the whole central line of the City, from the Green down to Trinity College, and from thence to Sackville Street, and the report of the various types of arm could be easily distinguished. There were rifles, machine guns and very heavy cannon. There was another sound which I could not put a name to, something that coughed out over all the other sounds, a short, sharp bark, or rather a short noise something like the popping of a tremendous cork.

I met D. H. His chief emotion is one of astonishment at the organizing powers displayed by the Volunteers. We have exchanged rumours, and found that our equipment in this direction is almost identical. He says Sheehy Skeffington has been killed. That he was arrested in a house wherein arms were found, and was shot out of hand.

I hope this is another rumour, for, so far as my knowledge of him goes, he was not with the Volunteers, and it is said that he was antagonistic to the forcible methods for which the Volunteers stood. But the tale of his death is so persistent that one is inclined to believe it.

He was the most absurdly courageous man I have ever met with or heard of. He has been in every trouble that has touched Ireland these ten years back, and he has always been in on the generous side, therefore, and naturally, on the side that was unpopular and weak. It would seem indeed that a cause had only to be weak to gain his sympathy, and his sympathy never stayed at home. There are so many good people who "sympathise" with this or that cause, and, having given that measure of their emotion, they give no more of it or of anything else. But he rushed instantly to the street, a large stone, the lift of a footpath, the base of a statue, any place and every place was for him a pulpit; and, in the teeth of whatever oppression or disaster or power, he said his say.

There are multitudes of men in Dublin of all classes and creeds who can boast that they kicked Sheehy Skeffington, or that they struck him on the head with walking sticks and umbrellas, or that they smashed their fists into his face, and jumped on him when he fell. It is by no means an exaggeration to say that these things were done to him, and it is true that he bore ill-will to no man, and that he accepted blows, and indignities and ridicule with the pathetic candour of a child who is disguised as a man, and whose disguise cannot come off. His tongue, his pen, his body, all that he had and hoped for were at the immediate service of whoever was bewildered or oppressed. He has been shot. Other men have been shot, but they faced the guns knowing that they faced justice, however stern and oppressive; and that what they had engaged to confront was before them. He had no such thought to soothe from his mind anger or unforgiveness. He who was a pacifist was compelled to revolt to his last breath, and on the instruments of his end he must have looked as on murderers. I am sure that to the end he railed against oppression, and that he fell marvelling that the world can truly be as it is. With his death there passed away a brave man and a clean soul.

Later on this day I met Mrs. Sheehy Skeffington in the street. She confirmed the rumour that her husband had been arrested on the previous day, but further than that she had no news. So far as I know the sole crime of which her husband had been guilty was that he called for a meeting of the citizens to enrol special constables and prevent looting.

Among the rumours it was stated with every accent of certitude that Madame Markievicz had been captured in George's Street, and taken to the Castle. It was also current that Sir Roger Casement had been captured at sea and had already been shot in the Tower of London. The names of several Volunteer Leaders are mentioned as being dead. But the surmise that steals timidly from one mouth flies boldly as a certitude from every mouth that repeats it, and truth itself would now be listened to with only a gossip's ear, but no person would believe a word of it.

This night also was calm and beautiful, but this night was the most sinister and woeful of those that have passed. The sound of artillery, of rifles, machine guns, grenades, did not cease even for a moment. From my window I saw a red flare that crept to the sky, and stole over it and remained there glaring; the smoke reached from the ground to the clouds, and I could see great red sparks go soaring to enormous heights; while always, in the calm air, hour after hour there was the buzzing and rattling and thudding of guns, and, but for the guns, silence.

It is in a dead silence this Insurrection is being fought, and one imagines what must be the feeling of these men, young for the most part, and unused to violence, who are submitting silently to the crash and flame and explosion by which they are surrounded.

CHAPTER V.

FRIDAY.

This morning there are no newspapers, no bread, no milk, no news. The sun is shining, and the streets are lively but discreet. All people continue to talk to one another without distinction of class, but nobody knows what any person thinks.

It is a little singular the number of people who are smiling. I fancy they were listening to the guns last night, and they are smiling this morning because the darkness is past, and because the sun is shining, and because they can move their limbs in space, and may talk without having to sink their voices to a whisper. Guns do not sound so bad in the day as they do at night, and no person can feel lonely while the sun shines.

The men are smiling, but the women laugh, and their laughter does not displease, for whatever women do in whatever circumstances appears to have a rightness of its own.

It seems right that they should scream en danger to themselves is imminent, and it seems right that they should laugh when danger only threatens others.

It is rumoured this morning that Sackville Street has been burned out and levelled to the ground. It is said that the end is in sight; and, it is said, that matters are, if anything rather worse than better. That the Volunteers have sallied from some of their strongholds and entrenched themselves, and that in one place alone (the South Lotts) they have seven machine guns. That when the houses which they held became untenable they rushed out and seized other houses, and that, pursuing these tactics, there seemed no reason to believe that the Insurrection would ever come to an end. That the streets are filled with Volunteers in plain clothes, but having revolvers in their pockets. That the streets are filled with soldiers equally revolvers and plain clothed, and that the least one says on any subject the less one would have to answer for.

The feeling that I tapped was definitely Anti-Volunteer, but the number of people who would speak was few, and one regarded the noncommital folk who were so smiling and polite, and so prepared to talk, with much curiosity, seeking to read in their eyes, in their bearing, even in the cut of their clothes what might be the secret movements and cogitations of their minds.

I received the impression that numbers of them did not care a rap what way it went; and that others had ceased to be mental creatures and were merely machines for registering the sensations of the time.

None of these people were prepared for Insurrection. The thing had been sprung on them so suddenly that they were unable to take sides, and their feeling of detachment was still so complete that they would have betted on the business as if it had been a horse race or a dog fight.

Many English troops have been landed each night, and it is believed that there are more than sixty thousand soldiers in Dublin alone, and that they are supplied with every offensive contrivance which military art has invented.

Merrion Square is strongly held by the soldiers. They are posted along both sides of the road at intervals of about twenty paces, and their guns are continually barking up at the roofs which surround them in the great square. It is said that these roofs are held by the Volunteers from Mount Street Bridge to the Square, and that they hold in like manner wide stretches of the City.

They appear to have mapped out the roofs with all the thoroughness that had hitherto been expended on the roads, and upon these roofs they are so mobile and crafty and so much at home that the work of the soldiers will be exceedingly difficult as well as dangerous.

Still, and notwithstanding, men can only take to the roofs for a short time. Up there, there can be no means of transport, and their ammunition, as well as their food, will very soon be used up. It is the beginning of the end, and the fact that they have to take to the roofs, even though that be in their programme, means that they are finished.

From the roof there comes the sound of machine guns. Looking towards Sackville Street one picks out easily Nelson's Pillar, which towers slenderly over all the buildings of the neighbourhood. It is wreathed in smoke. Another towering building was the D.B.C. Café. Its Chinese-like pagoda was a landmark easily to be found, but to-day I could not find it. It was not there, and I knew that, even if all Sackville Street was not burned down, as rumour insisted, this great Café had certainly been curtailed by its roof and might, perhaps, have been completely burned.

On the gravel paths I found pieces of charred and burnt paper. These scraps must have been blown remarkably high to have crossed all the roofs that lie between Sackville Street and Merrion Square.

At eleven o'clock there is continuous firing, and snipers firing from the direction of Mount Street, and in every direction of the City these sounds are being duplicated.

In Camden Street the sniping and casualties are said to have been very heavy. One man saw two Volunteers taken from a house by the soldiers. They were placed kneeling in the centre of the road, and within one minute of their capture they were dead.

Simultaneously there fell several of the firing party.

An officer in this part had his brains blown into the roadway. a young girl ran into the road, picked up his cap and scraped the brains into it. She covered this poor debris with a little straw, and carried the hat piously to the nearest hospital in order that the brains might be buried with their owner.

The continuation of her story was less gloomy although it affected the teller equally.

"There is not," said she, "a cat or a dog left alive in Camden Street. They are lying stiff out in the road and up on the roofs. There's lots of women will be sorry for this war," said she, "and their pets killed on them."

In many parts of the City hunger began to be troublesome. A girl told me that her family, and another that had taken refuge with them, had eaten nothing for three days. On this day her father managed to get two loaves of bread somewhere, and he brought these home.

"When," said the girl, "my father came in with the bread the whole fourteen of us ran at him, and in a minute we were all ashamed for the loaves were gone to the last crumb, and we were all as hungry as we had been before he came in. The poor man," said she, "did not even get a bit for himself." She held that the poor people were against the Volunteers.

The Volunteers still hold Jacob's Biscuit Factory. It is rumoured that a priest visited them and counselled surrender, and they replied that they did not go there to surrender but to be killed. They asked him to give them absolution, and the story continues that he refused to do so—but this is not (in its latter part) a story that can easily be credited. The Adelaide Hospital is close to this factory, and it is possible that the proximity of the hospital, delays or hinders military operations against the factory.

Rifle volleys are continuous about Merrion Square, and prolonged machine gun firing can be heard also.

During the night the firing was heavy from almost every direction; and in the direction of Sackville Street a red glare told again of fire.

It is hard to get to bed these nights. It is hard even to sit down, for the moment one does sit down one stands immediately up again resuming that ridiculous ship's march from the window to the wall and back. I am foot weary as I have never been before in my life, but I cannot say that I am excited. No person in Dublin is excited, but there exists a state of tension and expectancy which is mentally more exasperating than any excitement could be. The absence of news is largely responsible for this. We do not know what has happened, what is happening, or what is going to happen, and the reversion to barbarism (for barbarism is largely a lack of news) disturbs us.

Each night we have got to bed at last murmuring, "I wonder will it be all over tomorrow," and this night the like question accompanied us.

CHAPTER VI.

SATURDAY.

This morning also there has been no bread, no milk, no meat, no newspapers, but the sun is shining. It is astonishing that, thus early in the Spring, the weather should be so beautiful.

It is stated freely that the Post Office has been taken, and just as freely it is averred that it has not been taken. The approaches to Merrion Square are held by the military, and I was not permitted to go to my office. As I came to this point shots were fired at a motor car which had not stopped on being challenged. Bystanders said it was Sir Horace Plunkett's car, and that he had been shot. Later we found that Sir Horace was not hurt, but that his nephew who drove the car had been severely wounded.

At this hour the rumour of the fall of Verdun was persistent. Later on it was denied, as was denied the companion rumour of the relief of Kut. Saw R. who had spent three days and the whole of his money in getting home from County Clare. He had heard that Mrs. Sheehy Skeffington's house was raided, and that two dead bodies had been taken out of it. Saw Miss P. who seemed sad. I do not know what her politics are, but I think that the word "kindness" might be used to cover all her activities. She has a heart of gold, and the courage of many lions. I then met Mr. Commissioner Bailey who said the Volunteers had sent a deputation, and that terms of surrender were being discussed. I hope this is true, and I hope mercy will be shown to the men. Nobody believes there will be any mercy shown, and it is freely reported that they are shot in the street, or are taken to the nearest barracks and shot there. The belief grows that no person who is now in the Insurrection will be alive when the Insurrection is ended.

That is as it will be. But these days the thought of death does not strike on the mind with any severity, and, should the European war continue much longer, the fear of death will entirely depart from man, as it has departed many times in history. With that great deterrent gone our rulers will be gravely at a loss in dealing with strikers and other such discontented people. Possibly they will have to resurrect the long-buried idea of torture.

The people in the streets are laughing and chatting. Indeed, there is gaiety in the air as well as sunshine, and no person seems to care that men are being shot every other minute, or bayoneted, or blown into scraps or burned into cinders. These things are happening, nevertheless, but much of their importance has vanished.

I met a man at the Green who was drawing a plan on the back of an envelope. The problem was how his questioner was to get from where he was standing to a street lying at the other side of the river, and the plan as drawn insisted that to cover this quarter of an hour's distance he must set out on a pilgrimage of more than twenty miles. Another young boy was standing near embracing a large ham. He had been trying for three days to convey his ham to a house near the Gresham Hotel where his sister lived. He had almost given up hope, and he hearkened intelligently to the idea that he should himself eat the ham and so get rid of it.

The rifle fire was persistent all day, but, saving in certain localities, it was not heavy. Occasionally the machine guns rapped in. There was no sound of heavy artillery.

The rumour grows that the Post Office has been evacuated, and that the Volunteers are at large and spreading everywhere across the roofs. The rumour grows also that terms of surrender are being discussed, and that Sackville Street has been levelled to the ground.

At half-past seven in the evening calm is almost complete. The sound of a rifle shot being only heard at long intervals.

I got to bed this night earlier than usual. At two o'clock I left the window from which a red flare is yet visible in the direction of Sackville Street, The morning will tell if the Insurrection is finished or not, but at this hour all is not over. Shots are ringing all around and down my street, and the vicious crackling of these rifles grows at times into regular volleys.

CHAPTER VII.

SUNDAY.

The Insurrection has not ceased.

There is much rifle fire, but no sound from the machine guns or the eighteen pounders and trench mortars.

From the window of my kitchen the flag of the Republic can be seen flying afar. This is the flag that flies over Jacob's Biscuit Factory, and I will know that the Insurrection has ended as soon as I see this flag pulled down.

When I went out there were few people in the streets. I met D. H., and, together, we passed up the Green. The Republican flag was still flying over the College of Surgeons. We tried to get down Grafton Street (where broken windows and two gaping interiors told of the recent visit of looters), but a little down this street we were waved back by armed sentries. We then cut away by the Gaiety Theatre into Mercer's Street, where immense lines of poor people were drawn up waiting for the opening of the local bakery. We got into George's Street, thinking to turn down Dame Street and get from thence near enough to Sackville Street to see if the rumours about its destruction were true, but here also we were halted by the military, and had to retrace our steps.

There was no news of any kind to be gathered from the people we talked to, nor had they even any rumours.

This was the first day I had been able to get even a short distance outside of my own quarter, and it seemed that the people of my quarter were more able in the manufacture of news or more imaginative than were the people who live in other parts of the city. We had no sooner struck into home parts than we found news. We were told that two of the Volunteer leaders had been shot. These were Pearse and Connolly. The latter was reported as lying in the Castle Hospital with a fractured thigh. Pearse was cited as dead with two hundred of his men, following their sally from the Post Office. The machine guns had caught them as they left, and none of them remained alive. The news seemed afterwards to be true except that instead of Pearse it was The O'Rahilly who had been killed. Pearse died later and with less excitement.

A man who had seen an English newspaper said that the Kut force had surrendered to the Turk, but that Verdun had not fallen to the Germans. The rumour was current also that a great naval battle had been fought whereat the German fleet had been totally destroyed with loss to the English of eighteen warships. It was said that among the captured Volunteers there had been a large body of Germans, but nobody believed it; and this rumour was inevitably followed by the tale that there were one hundred German submarines lying in the Stephen's Green pond.

At half-past two I met Mr. Commissioner Bailey, who told me that it was all over, and that the Volunteers were surrendering everywhere in the city. A motor car with two military officers, and two Volunteer leaders had driven to the College of Surgeons and been admitted. After a short interval Madame Marckievicz marched out of the College at the head of about 100 men, and they had given up their arms; the motor car with the Volunteer leaders was driving to other strongholds, and it was expected that before nightfall the capitulations would be complete.

I started home, and on the way I met a man whom I had encountered some days previously, and from whom rumours had sprung as though he wove them from his entrails, as a spider weaves his web. He was no less provided on this occasion, and it was curious to listen to his tale of English defeats on every front. He announced the invasion of England in six different quarters, the total destruction of the English fleet, and the landing of immense German armies on the West coast of Ireland. He made these things up in his head. Then he repeated them to himself in a loud voice, and became somehow persuaded that they had been told to him by a well-informed stranger, and then he believed them and told them to everybody he met. Amongst other things Spain had declared war on our behalf, the Chilian Navy was hastening to our relief. For a pin he would have sent France flying westward all forgetful of her own war. A singular man truly, and as I do think the only thoroughly happy person in our city.

It is half-past three o'clock, and from my window the Republican flag can still be seen flying over Jacob's factory. There is occasional shooting, but the city as a whole is quiet. At a quarter to five o'clock a heavy gun boomed once. Ten minutes later there was heavy machine gun firing and much rifle shooting. In another ten minutes the flag at Jacob's was hauled down.

During the remainder of the night sniping and military replies were incessant, particularly in my street.

The raids have begun in private houses. Count Plunkett's house was entered by the military who remained there for a very long time. Passing home about two minutes after Proclamation hour I was pursued for the whole of Fitzwilliam Square by bullets. They buzzed into the roadway beside me, and the sound as they whistled near was curious. The sound is something like that made by a very swift saw, and one gets the impression that as well as being very swift they are very heavy.

Snipers are undoubtedly on the roofs opposite my house, and they are not asleep on these roofs. Possibly it is difficult to communicate with these isolated bands the news of their companions' surrender, but it is likely they will learn, by the diminution of fire in other quarters that their work is over.

In the morning on looking from my window I saw four policemen marching into the street. They were the first I had seen for a week. Soon now the military tale will finish, the police story will commence, the political story will recommence, and, perhaps, the weeks that follow this one will sow the seed of more hatred than so many centuries will be able to uproot again, for although Irish people do not greatly fear the military they fear the police, and they have very good reason to do so.

CHAPTER VIII

THE INSURRECTION IS OVER.

The Insurrection is over, and it is worth asking what has happened, how it has happened, and why it happened?

The first question is easily answered. The finest part of our city has been blown to smithereens, and burned into ashes. Soldiers amongst us who have served abroad say that the ruin of this quarter is more complete than any thing they have seen at Ypres, than anything they have seen anywhere in France or Flanders. A great number of our men and women and children, Volunteers and civilians confounded alike, are dead, and some fifty thousand men who have been moved with military equipment to our land are now being removed therefrom. The English nation has been disorganised no more than as they were. affected by the transport of these men and material. That is what happened, and it is all that happened.

How it happened is another matter, and one which, perhaps, will not be made clear for years. All we know in Dublin is that our city burst into a kind of spontaneous war; that we lived through it during one singular week, and that it faded away and disappeared almost as swiftly as it had come. The men who knew about it are, with two exceptions, dead, and these two exceptions are in gaol, and likely to remain there long enough. (Since writing one of these men has been shot.)

Why it happened is a question that may be answered more particularly. It happened because the leader of the Irish Party misrepresented his people in the English House of Parliament. On the day of the declaration of war between England and Germany he took the Irish case, weighty with eight centuries of history and tradition, and he threw it out of the window. He pledged Ireland to a particular course of action, and he had no authority to give this pledge and he had no guarantee that it would be met. The ramshackle intelligence of his party and his own emotional nature betrayed him and us and England. He swore Ireland to loyalty as if he had Ireland in his pocket, and could answer for her. Ireland has never been disloyal to England, not even at this epoch, because she has never been loyal to England, and the profession of her National faith has been unwavering, has been known to every English person alive, and has been clamant to all the world beside.

Is it that he wanted to be cheered? He could very easily have stated Ireland's case truthfully, and have proclaimed a benevolent neutrality (if he cared to use the grandiloquent words) on the part of this country. He would have gotten his cheers, he would in a few months have gotten Home Rule in return for Irish soldiers. He would have received politically whatever England could have safely given him. But, alas, these carefulnesses did not chime with his emotional moment. They were not magnificent enough for one who felt that he was talking not to Ireland or to England, but to the whole gaping and eager earth, and so he pledged his country's credit so deeply that he did not leave her even one National rag to cover herself with.

After a lie truth bursts out, and it is no longer the radiant and serene goddess we knew or hoped for—it is a disease, it is a moral syphilis and will ravage until the body in which it can dwell has been purged. Mr. Redmond told the lie and he is answerable to England for the violence she had to be guilty of, and to Ireland for the desolation to which we have had to submit. Without his lie there had been no Insurrection; without it there had been at this moment, and for a year past, an end to the "Irish question." Ireland must in ages gone have been guilty of abominable crimes or she could not at this juncture have been afflicted with a John Redmond.

He is the immediate cause of this our latest Insurrection—the word is big, much too big for the deed, and we should call it row, or riot, or squabble, in order to draw the fact down to its dimensions, but the ultimate blame for the trouble between the two countries does not fall against Ireland.

The fault lies with England, and in these days while an effort is being made (interrupted, it is true, by cannon) to found a better understanding between the two nations it is well that England should recognize what she has done to Ireland, and should try at least to atone for it. The situation can be explained almost in a phrase. We are a little country and you, a huge country, have persistently beaten us. We are a poor country and you, the richest country in the world, have persistently robbed us. That is the historical fact, and whatever national or political necessities are opposed in reply, it is true that you have never given Ireland any reason to love you, and you cannot claim her affection without hypocrisy or stupidity.

You think our people can only be tenacious in hate—it is a lie. Our historical memory is truly tenacious, but during the long and miserable tale of our relations you have never given us one generosity to remember you by, and you must not claim our affection or our devotion until you are worthy of them. We are a good people; almost we are the only Christian people left in the world, nor has any nation shown such forbearance towards their persecutor as we have always shown to you. No nation has forgiven its enemies as we have forgiven you, time after time down the miserable generations, the continuity of our forgiveness only equalled by the continuity of your ill-treatment. Between our two countries you have kept and protected a screen of traders and politicians who are just as truly your enemies as they are ours. In the end they will do most harm to you for we are by this vaccinated against misery but you are not, and the "loyalists" who sell their own country for a shilling will sell another country for a penny when the opportunity comes and safety with it.

Meanwhile do not always hasten your presents to us out of a gun. You have done it so often that your guns begin to bore us, and you have now an opportunity which may never occur again to make us your friends. There is no bitterness in Ireland against you on account of this war, and the lack of ill-feeling amongst us is entirely due to the more than admirable behaviour of the soldiers whom you sent over here. A peace that will last for ever can be made with Ireland if you wish to make it, but you must take her hand at once, for in a few months' time she will not open it to you; the old, bad relations will re-commence, the rancor will be born and grow, and another memory will be stored away in Ireland's capacious and retentive brain.

CHAPTER IX.

THE VOLUNTEERS.

There is much talk of the extraordinary organising powers displayed in the insurrection, but in truth there was nothing extraordinary in it. The real essence and singularity of the rising exists in its simplicity, and, saving for the courage which carried it out, the word extraordinary is misplaced in this context.

The tactics of the Volunteers as they began to emerge were reduced to the very skeleton of "strategy." It was only that they seized certain central and strategical districts, garrisoned those and held them until they were put out of them. Once in their forts there was no further egress by the doors, and for purpose of entry and sortie they used the skylights and the roofs. On the roofs they had plenty of cover, and this cover conferred on them a mobility which was their chief asset, and which alone enabled them to protract the rebellion beyond the first day.

This was the entire of their home plan, and there is no doubt that they had studied Dublin roofs and means of inter-communication by roofs with the closest care. Further than that I do not think they had organised anything. But this was only the primary plan, and, unless they were entirely mad, there must have been a sequel to it which did not materialise, and which would have materialised but that the English Fleet blocked the way.

There is no doubt that they expected the country to rise with them, and they must have known what their own numbers were, and what chance they had of making a protracted resistance. The word "resistance" is the keyword of the rising, and the plan of holding out must have been rounded off with a date. At that date something else was to have happened which would relieve them.

There is not much else that could happen except the landing of German troops in Ireland or in England. It would have been, I think, immaterial to them where these were landed, but the reasoning seems to point to the fact that they expected and had arranged for such a landing, although on this point there is as yet no evidence.

The logic of this is so simple, so plausible, that it might be accepted without further examination, and yet further examination is necessary, for in a country like Ireland logic and plausibility are more often wrong than right. It may just as easily be that except for furnishing some arms and ammunition Germany was not in the rising at all, and this I prefer to believe. It had been current long before the rising that the Volunteers knew they could not seriously embarass England, and that their sole aim was to make such a row in Ireland that the Irish question would take the status of an international one, and on the discussion of terms of peace in the European war the claims of Ireland would have to be considered by the whole Council of Europe and the world.

That is, in my opinion, the metaphysic behind the rising. It is quite likely that they hoped for German aid, possibly some thousands of men, who would enable them, to prolong the row, but I do not believe they expected German armies, nor do I think they would have welcomed these with any cordiality.

In this insurrection there are two things which are singular in the history of Irish risings. One is that there were no informers, or there were no informers among the chiefs. I did hear people say in the streets that two days before the rising they knew it was to come; they invariably added that they had not believed the news, and had laughed at it. A priest said the same thing in my hearing, and it may be that the rumour was widely spread, and that, everybody, including the authorities, looked upon it as a joke.

The other singularity of the rising is the amazing silence in which it was fought. Nothing spoke but the guns; and the Volunteers on the one side and the soldiers on the other potted each other and died in whispers; it might have been said that both sides feared the Germans would hear them and take advantage of their preoccupation.

There is a third reason given for the rebellion, and it also is divorced from foreign plots. It is said, and the belief in Dublin was widespread, that the Government intended to raid the Volunteers and seize their arms. One remembers to-day the paper which Alderman Kelly read to the Dublin Corporation, and which purported to be State Instructions that the Military and Police should raid the Volunteers, and seize their arms and leaders. The Volunteers had sworn they would not permit their arms to be taken from them. A list of the places to be raided was given, and the news created something of a sensation in Ireland when it was published that evening. The Press, by instruction apparently, repudiated this document, but the Volunteers, with most of the public, believed it to be true, and it is more than likely that the rebellion took place in order to forestall the Government.

This is also an explanation of the rebellion, and is just as good a one as any other. It is the explanation which I believe to be the true one.

All the talk of German invasion and the landing of German troops in Ireland is so much nonsense in view of the fact that England is master of the seas, and that from a week before the war down to this date she has been the undisputed monarch of those ridges. During this war there will be no landing of troops in either England or Ireland unless Germany in the meantime can solve the problem of submarine transport. It is a problem which will be solved some day, for every problem can be solved, but it will hardly be during the progress of this war. The men at the head of the Volunteers were not geniuses, neither were they fools, and the difficulty of acquiring military aid from Germany must have seemed as insurmountable to them as it does to the Germans themselves. They rose because they felt that they had to do so, or be driven like sheep into the nearest police barracks, and be laughed at by the whole of Ireland as cowards and braggarts.

It would be interesting to know why, on the eve of the insurrection, Professor MacNeill resigned the presidency of the Volunteers. The story of treachery which was heard in the streets is not the true one, for men of his type are not traitors, and this statement may be dismissed without further comment or notice. One is left to imagine what can have happened during the conference which is said to have preceded the rising, and which ended with the resignation of Professor MacNeill.

This is my view, or my imagining, of what occurred. The conference was called because the various leaders felt that a hostile movement was projected by the Government, and that the times were exceedingly black for them. Neither Mr.

Birrell nor Sir Mathew Nathan had any desire that there should be a conflict in Ireland during the war. This cannot be doubted. From such a conflict there might follow all kinds of political repercussions; but although the Government favoured the policy of *laissez faire*, there was a powerful military and political party in Ireland whose whole effort was towards the disarming and punishment of the Volunteers—particularly I should say the punishment of the Volunteers. I believe, or rather I imagine, that Professor MacNeill was approached at the instance of Mr. Birrell or Sir Mathew Nathan and assured that the Government did not meditate any move against his men, and that so long as his Volunteers remained quiet they would not be molested by the authorities. I would say that Professor MacNeill gave and accepted the necessary assurances, and that when he informed his conference of what had occurred, and found that they did not believe faith would be kept with them, he resigned in the despairing hope that his action might turn them from a purpose which he considered lunatic, or, at least, by restraining a number of his followers from rising, he might limit the tale of men who would be uselessly killed.

He was not alone in his vote against a rising. The O'Rahilly and some others are reputed to have voted with him, but when insurrection was decided on, the O'Rahilly marched with his men, and surely a gallant man could not have done otherwise.

When the story of what occurred is authoritatively written (it may be written) I think that this will be found to be the truth of the matter, and that German intrigue and German money counted for so little in the insurrection as to be negligible.

CHAPTER X

SOME OF THE LEADERS

Meanwhile the insurrection, like all its historical forerunners, has been quelled in blood. It sounds rhetorical to say so, but it was not quelled in peasoup or tisane. While it lasted the fighting was very determined, and it is easily, I think, the most considerable of Irish rebellions.

The country was not with it, for be it remembered that a whole army of Irishmen, possibly three hundred thousand of our race, are fighting with England instead of against her. In Dublin alone there is scarcely a poor home in which a father, a brother, or a son is not serving in one of the many fronts which England is defending. Had the country risen, and fought as stubbornly as the Volunteers did, no troops could have beaten them—well that is a wild statement, the heavy guns could always beat them—but from whatever angle Irish people consider this affair it must appear to them tragic and lamentable beyond expression, but not mean and not unheroic.

It was hard enough that our men in the English armies should be slain for causes which no amount of explanation will ever render less foreign to us, or even intelligible; but that our men who were left should be killed in Ireland fighting against the same England that their brothers are fighting for ties the question into such knots of contradiction as we may give up trying to unravel. We can only think—this has happened—and let it unhappen itself as best it may.

We say that the time always finds the man, and by it we mean: that when a responsibility is toward there will be found some shoulder to bend for the yoke which all others shrink from. It is not always nor often the great ones of the earth who undertake these burdens—it is usually the good folk, that gentle hierarchy who swear allegiance to mournfulness and the under dog, as others dedicate themselves to mutton chops and the easy nymph. It is not my intention to idealise any of the men who were concerned in this rebellion. Their country will, some few years hence, do that as adequately as she has done it for those who went before them.

Those of the leaders whom I knew were not great men, nor brilliant—that is they were more scholars than thinkers, and more thinkers than men of action; and I believe that in no capacity could they have attained to what is called eminence, nor do I consider they coveted any such public distinction as is Doted in that word.

But in my definition they were good men—men, that is, who willed no evil, and whose movements of body or brain were unselfish and healthy. No person living is the worse off for having known Thomas MacDonagh, and I, at least, have never heard MacDonagh speak unkindly or even harshly of anything that lived. It has been said of him that his lyrics were epical; in a measure it is true, and it is true in the same measure that his death was epical. He was the first of the leaders who was tried and shot. It was not easy for him to die leaving behind two young children and a young wife, and the thought that his last moment must have been tormented by their memory is very painful. We are all fatalists when we strike against power, and I hope he put care from him as the soldiers marched him out.

The O'Rahilly also I knew, but not intimately, and I can only speak of a good humour, a courtesy, and an energy that never failed. He was a man of unceasing

ideas and unceasing speech, and laughter accompanied every sound made
by his lips.

Plunkett and Pearse I knew also, but not intimately. Young Plunkett, as he was
always called, would never strike one as a militant person. He, like Pearse and
MacDonagh, wrote verse, and it was no better nor worse than theirs were. He had
an appetite for quaint and difficult knowledge. He studied Egyptian and Sanscrit,
and distant curious matter of that sort, and was interested in inventions and the
theatre. He was tried and sentenced and shot.

As to Pearse, I do not know how to place him, nor what to say of him. If
there was an idealist among the men concerned in this insurrection it was he, and
if there was any person in the world less fitted to head an insurrection it was he
also. I never could "touch" or sense in him the qualities which other men spoke of,
and which made him military commandant of the rising. None of these men were
magnetic in the sense that Mr. Larkin is magnetic, and I would have said that
Pearse was less magnetic than any of the others. Yet it was to him and around
him they clung.

Men must find some centre either of power or action or intellect about which
they may group themselves, and I think that Pearse became the leader because his
temperament was more profoundly emotional than any of the others. He was emotional not in a flighty, but in a serious way, and one felt more that he suffered than
that he enjoyed.

He had a power; men who came into intimate contact with him began to act
differently to their own desires and interests. His schoolmasters did not always
receive their salaries with regularity. The reason that he did not pay them was the
simple one that he had no money. Given by another man this explanation would
be uneconomic, but from him it was so logical that even a child could comprehend
it. These masters did not always leave him. They remained, marvelling perhaps,
and accepting, even with stupefaction, the theory that children must be taught, but
that no such urgency is due towards the payment of wages. One of his boys said
there was no fun in telling lies to Mr. Pearse, for, however outrageous the lie, he
always believed it. He built and renovated and improved his school because the
results were good for his scholars, and somehow he found builders to undertake
these forlorn hopes.

It was not, I think, that he "put his trust in God," but that when something
had to be done he did it, and entirely disregarded logic or economics or force. He
said—such a thing has to be done and so far as one man can do it I will do it, and
he bowed straightaway to the task.

It is mournful to think of men like these having to take charge of bloody and desolate work, and one can imagine them say, "Oh! cursed spite," as they accepted responsibility.

CHAPTER XI.

LABOUR AND THE INSURRECTION.

No person in Ireland seems to have exact information about the Volunteers, their aims, or their numbers. We know the names of the leaders now. They were recited to us with the tale of their execution; and with the declaration of a Republic we learned something of their aim, but the estimate of their number runs through the figures ten, thirty, and fifty thousand. The first figure is undoubtedly too slender, the last excessive, and something between fifteen and twenty thousand for all Ireland would be a reasonable guess.

Of these, the Citizen Army or Labour side of the Volunteers, would not number more than one thousand men, and it is with difficulty such a figure could be arrived at. Yet it is freely argued, and the theory will grow, that the causes of this latest insurrection should be sought among the labour problems of Dublin rather than in any national or patriotic sentiment, and this theory is buttressed by all the agile facts which such a theory would be furnished with.

It is an interesting view, but in my opinion it is an erroneous one.

That Dublin labour was in the Volunteer movement to the strength of, perhaps, two hundred men, may be true—it is possible there were more, but it is unlikely that a greater number, or, as many, of the Citizen Army marched when the order came. The overwhelming bulk of Volunteers were actuated by the patriotic ideal which is the heritage and the burden of almost every Irishman born out of the Unionist circle, and their connection with labour was much more manual than mental.

This view of the importance of labour to the Volunteers is held by two distinct and opposed classes.

Just as there are some who find the explanation of life in a sexual formula, so there is a class to whom the economic idea is very dear, and beneath every human activity they will discover the shock of wages and profit. It is truly there, but it pulls no more than its weight, and in Irish life the part played by labour has not yet been a weighty one, although on every view it is an important one. The labour idea in Ireland has not arrived. It is in process of "becoming," and when labour problems are mentioned in this country a party does not come to the mind, but two men only—they are Mr. Larkin and James Connolly, and they are each in their way exceptional and curious men.

There is another class who implicate labour, and they do so because it enables them to urge that as well as being grasping and nihilistic, Irish labour is disloyal and treacherous.

The truth is that labour in Ireland has not yet succeeded in organising any-thing—not even discontent. It is not self-conscious to any extent, and, outside of Dublin, it scarcely appears to exist. The national imagination is not free to deal with any other subject than that of freedom, and part of the policy of our 11 masters is to see that we be kept busy with politics instead of social ideas. From their standpoint the policy is admirable, and up to the present it has thoroughly succeeded.

One does not hear from the lips of the Irish workingman, even in Dublin, any of the affirmations and rejections which have long since become the commonplaces of his comrades in other lands. But on the subject of Irish freedom his views are instantly forthcoming, and his desires are explicit, and, to a degree, informed. This latter subject they understand and have fabricated an entire language to express it, but the other they do not understand nor cherish, and they are not prepared to die for it.

It is possibly true that before any movement can attain to really national proportions there must be, as well as the intellectual ideal which gives it utterance and a frame, a sense of economic misfortune to give it weight, and when these fuse the combination may well be irresistible. The organised labour discontent in Ireland, in Dublin, was not considerable enough to impose its aims or its colours on the Volunteers, and it is the labour ideal which merges and disappears in the national one. The reputation of all the leaders of the insurrection, not excepting Connolly, is that they were intensely patriotic Irishmen, and also, but this time with the exception of Connolly, that they were not particularly interested in the problems of labour.

The great strike of two years ago remained undoubtedly as a bitter and lasting memory with Dublin labour—perhaps, even, it was not so much a memory as a hatred. Still, it was not hatred of England which was evoked at that time, nor can the stress of their conflict be traced to an English source. It was hatred of local traders, and, particularly, hatred of the local police, and the local powers and tri-bunals, which were arrayed against them.

One can without trouble discover reasons why they should go on strike again, but by no reasoning can I understand why they should go into rebellion against England, unless it was that they were patriots first and trade unionists a very long way afterwards.

I do not believe that this combination of the ideal and the practical was consummated in the Dublin insurrection, but I do believe that the first step towards the formation of such a party has now been taken, and that if, years hence, there should be further trouble in Ireland such trouble will not be so easily dealt with as this one has been.

It may be that further trouble will not arise, for the co-operative movement, which is growing slowly but steadily in Ireland, may arrange our economic question, and, incidentally, our national question also—that is if the English people do not decide that the latter ought to be settled at once.

James Connolly had his heart in both the national and the economic camp, but he was a great-hearted man, and could afford to extend his affections where others could only dissipate them.

There can be no doubt that his powers of orderly thinking were of great service to the Volunteers, for while Mr. Larkin was the magnetic centre of the Irish labour movement, Connolly was its brains. He has been sentenced to death for his part in the insurrection, and for two days now he has been dead.

He had been severely wounded in the fighting, and was tended, one does not doubt with great care, until he regained enough strength to stand up and be shot down again.

Others are dead also. I was not acquainted with them, and with Connolly I was not more than acquainted. I had met him twice many months ago, but other people were present each time, and he scarcely uttered a word on either of these occasions. I was told that he was by nature silent. He was a man who can be ill-spared in Ireland, but labour, throughout the world, may mourn for him also.

A doctor who attended on him during his last hours says that Connolly received the sentence of his death quietly. He was to be shot on the morning following the sentence. This gentleman said to him:

"Connolly, when you stand up to be shot, will you say a prayer for me?"

Connolly replied:

"I will."

His visitor continued:

"Will you say a prayer for the men who are shooting you?"

"I will," said Connolly, "and I will say a prayer for every good man in the world who is doing his duty."

He was a steadfast man in all that he undertook. We may be sure he steadfastly kept that promise. He would pray for others, who had not time to pray for himself, as he had worked for others during the years when he might have worked for himself.

CHAPTER XII.

THE IRISH QUESTIONS.

There is truly an Irish question. There are two Irish questions, and the most important of them is not that which appears in our newspapers and in our political propaganda.

The first is international, and can be stated shortly. It is the desire of Ireland to assume control of her national life. With this desire the English people have professed to be in accord, and it is at any rate so thoroughly understood that nothing further need be made of it in these pages.

The other Irish question is different, and less simply described. The difficulty about it is that it cannot be approached until the question of Ireland's freedom has by some means been settled, for this ideal of freedom has captured the imagination of the race. It rides Ireland like a nightmare, thwarting or preventing all civilising or cultural work in this country, and it is not too much to say that Ireland cannot even begin to live until that obsession and fever has come to an end, and her imagination has been set free to do the work which imagination alone can do— Imagination is intelligent kindness—we have sore need of it.

The second question might plausibly be called a religious one. It has been so called, and, for it is less troublesome to accept an idea than to question it, the statement has been accepted as truth—but it is untrue, and it is deeply and villainously untrue. No lie in Irish life has been so persistent and so mischievous as this one, and no political lie has ever been so ingeniously, and malevolently exploited.

There is no religious intolerance in Ireland except that which is political. I am not a member of the Catholic Church, and am not inclined to be the advocate of a religious system which my mentality dislikes, but I have never found real intolerance among my fellow-countrymen of that religion. I have found it among Protestants. I will limit that statement, too. I have found it among some Protestants. But outside of the North of Ireland there is no religious question, and in the North it is fundamentally more political than religious.

All thinking is a fining down of one's ideas, and thus far we have come to the statement of Ireland's second question. It is not Catholic or Nationalist, nor have I said that it is entirely Protestant and Unionist, but it is on the extreme wing of this latter party that responsibility must be laid. It is difficult, even for an Irishman living in Ireland, to come on the real political fact which underlies Irish Protestant politics, and which fact has consistently opposed and baffled every attempt made by either England or Ireland to come to terms. There is such a fact, and clustered around it is a body of men whose hatred of their country is persistent and deadly and unexplained.

One may make broad generalisations on the apparent situation and endeavour to solve it by those. We may say that loyalty to England is the true centre of their action. I will believe it, but only to a point. Loyalty to England does not inevitably include this active hatred, this blindness, this withering of all sympathy for the people among whom one is born, and among whom one has lived in peace, for they have lived in peace amongst us. We may say that it is due to the idea of privilege and the desire for power. Again, I will accept it up to a point—but these are cultural obsessions, and they cease to act when the breaking-point is reached.

I know of only two mental states which are utterly without bowels or conscience. These are cowardice and greed. Is it to a synthesis of these states that this more than mortal enmity may be traced? What do they fear, and what is it they covet? What can they redoubt in a country which is practically crimeless, or covet in a land that is almost as bare as a mutton bone? They have mesmerised themselves, these men, and have imagined into our quiet air brigands and thugs and titans, with all the other notabilities of a tale for children.

I do not think that this either will tell the tale, but I do think there is a story to be told—I imagine an esoteric wing to the Unionist Party. I imagine that Party includes a secret organisation—they may be Orangemen, they may be Masons, and, if there be such, I would dearly like to know what the metaphysic of their position is, and how they square it with any idea of humanity or social life. Meantime, all this is surmise, and I, as a novelist, have a notoriously flighty imagination, and am content to leave it at that.

But this secondary Irish question is not so terrible as it appears. It is terrible now, it would not be terrible if Ireland had national independence.

The great protection against a lie is—not to believe it; and Ireland, in this instance, has that protection. The claims made by the Unionist Wing do not rely solely on the religious base. They use all the arguments. It is, according to them, unsafe to live in Ireland. (Let us leave this insurrection of a week out of the question.) Life is not safe in Ireland. Property shivers in terror of daily or nightly appropriation. Other, undefined, but even more woeful glooms and creeps, wriggle stealthily abroad.

These things are not regarded in Ireland, and, in truth, they are not meat for Irish consumption. Irish judges are presented with white gloves with a regularity which may even be annoying to them, and were it not for political trouble they would be unable to look their salaries in the face. The Irish Bar almost weep in chorus at the words "Land Act," and stare, not dumbly, on destitution. These tales are meant for England and are sent there. They will cease to be exported when there is no market for them, and these men will perhaps end by becoming patriotic and social when they learn that they do not really command the Big Battalions. But Ireland has no protection against them while England can be thrilled by their nonsense, and while she is willing to pound Ireland to a jelly on their appeal. Her only assistance against them is freedom.

There are certain simplicities upon which all life is based, a man finds that he is hungry and the knowledge enables him to go to work for the rest of his life. A man makes the discovery (it has been a discovery to many) that he is an Irishman, and the knowledge simplifies all his subsequent political action. There is this comfort about being an Irishman, you can be entirely Irish, and claim thus to be as complete as a pebble or a star. But no Irish person can hope to be more than a muletto Englishman, and if that be an ambition and an end it is not an heroic one.

But there is an Ulster difficulty, and no amount of burking it will solve it. It is too generally conceived among Nationalists that the attitude of Ulster towards Ireland is rooted in ignorance and bigotry. Allow that both of these bad parts are included in the Northern outlook, they do not explain the Ulster standpoint; and nothing can explain the attitude of official Ireland *vis-a-vis* with Ulster.

What has the Irish Party ever done to allay Northern prejudice, or bring the discontented section into line with the rest of Ireland? The answer is pathetically complete. They have done nothing. Or, if they have done anything, it was only that which would set every Northerner grinding his teeth in anger. At a time when Orangeism was dying they raised and marshalled the Hibernians, and we have the Ulsterman's answer to the Hibernians in the situation by which we are confronted to-day. The Party had even a little statesmanship among them they would for the past ten years have marched up and down the North explaining and mollifying and courting the Black Northerner. But, like good Irishmen, they could not tear themselves away from England, and they paraded that country where parade was not so urgent, and they made orations there until the mere accent of an Irishman must make Englishmen wail for very boredom.

Some of that parade might have gladdened the eyes of the Belfast citizens; a few of those orations might have assisted the men of Derry to comprehend that, for the good of our common land, Home Rule and the unity of a nation was necessary if only to rid the country of these blatherers.

Let the Party explain why, among their political duties, they neglected the duty of placating Ulster in their proper persons. Why, in short, they boycotted Ulster and permitted political and religious and racial antagonism to grow inside of Ireland unchecked by any word from them upon that ground. Were they afraid "nuts" would be thrown at them? Whatever they dreaded, they gave Ulster the widest of wide berths, and wherever else they were visible and audible, they were silent and unseen in that part of Ireland.

The Ulster grievance is ostensibly religious; but safeguards on this count are so easily created and applied that this issue might almost be left out of account. The real difficulty is economic, and it is a tangled one. But unless profit and loss are immediately discernible the soul of man is not easily stirred by an accountant's tale, and therefore the religious banner has been waved for our kinsfolk of Ulster, and under the sacred emblem they are fighting for what some people call mammon, but which may be in truth just plain bread and butter.

Before we can talk of Ireland a nation we must make her one. A nation, politically speaking, is an aggregation of people whose interests are identical; and the interests of Ulster with the rest of Ireland rather than being identical are antagonistic. It is England orders and pays for the Belfast ships, and it is to Britain or under the goodwill of the British power that Ulster conducts her huge woollen trade. Economically the rest of Ireland scarcely exists for Ulster, and whoever insists on regarding the Northern question from an ideal plane is wasting his own time and the time of everyone who listens to him. The safeguards which Ulster will demand, should events absolutely force her to it, may sound political or religious, they will be found essentially economic, and the root of them all will be a watertight friendship with England, and anything that smells, however distantly, of hatred for England will be a true menace to Ulster. We must swallow England if Ulster is to swallow us, and until that fact becomes apparent to Ireland the Ulster problem cannot even be confronted, let alone solved.

The words Sinn Fein mean "Ourselves," and it is of ourselves I write in this chapter. More urgent than any political emancipation is the drawing together of men of good will in the endeavour to assist their necessitous land. Our eyes must be withdrawn from the ends of the earth and fixed on that which is around us and which we can touch. No politician will talk to us of Ireland if by any trick he can avoid the subject. His tale is still of Westminster and Chimborazo and the Mountains of the Moon. Irishmen must begin to think for themselves and of themselves, instead of expending energy on causes too distant to be assisted or hindered by them. I believe that our human material is as good as will be found in the world. No better, perhaps, but not worse. And I believe that all but local politics are unfruitful and soul-destroying. We have an island that is called little. It is more than twenty times too spacious for our needs, and we will not have explored the last of it in our children's lifetime. We have more problems to resolve in our towns and cities than many generations of minds will get tired of striving with. Here is the world, and all that perplexes or delights the world is here also. Nothing is lost. Not even brave men. They have been used. From this day the great adventure opens for Ireland. The Volunteers are dead, and the call is now for volunteers.

MICHAEL COLLINS

(1890-1922)

In the summer of 1922, Michael Collins, the charismatic leader of the Irish Republican Army, was on the run. The British had put a price on his head, but sketches and descriptions of him were so vague, Collins often appeared at check points himself, chatting amiably with British soldiers. By mid-August, the IRA had split allegiances, and Civil War was raging in Ireland. Collins was attempting to negotiate an end to the war and despite being ill with a stomach virus, he left on a trip to visit troops near his home county of Cork. His supporters urged him not to go, but Collins was defiant. "They wouldn't shoot me in my own county," he said. Collins visited his men and held high hopes of ending the fighting, but on his way back from Cork, his convoy was ambushed at Beal na mBlath (the mouth of flowers) and he died instantly from a gunshot to the head.

Thousands lined the streets of Dublin for his funeral, and his body lay in state for three days, as countless Irish paid their respects. Forty-four years later, Eamon de Valera, the American-born President of the Republic of Ireland and opponent of Collins during the Civil War, described Ireland's affinity for the legend of the affable leader. Said de Valera, "It's my considered opinion that in the fullness of time, history will record the greatness of Collins and it will be recorded at my expense."

Michael Collins was an Irish revolutionary whose legend and reputation has blossomed over time, just as de Valera predicted in 1966. Enigmatic and mysterious, even the circumstances of Collins's death were never fully understood, as some historians have claimed his own men may have killed him. What is clear is that Collins was a leader who always felt he was acting in the best interests of his country.

Collins was born in Sam's Cross, a small hamlet in County Cork in 1890, and the youngest of eight children. His father, Michael Collins Sr., a farmer, was 75 years old when his namesake son was born, and died just six years later. Legend has it that he urged his grieving family on his deathbed to take care of his youngest son, predicting that "One day he'll be a great man. He'll do great work for Ireland."

Collins attended national school at Lisavaird and demonstrated, at an early age, a love for reading, especially Irish nationalist writings, such as the works of the Irish poet and nationalist, Thomas Davis. At Lisavaird, the schoolmaster, Denis Lyons, was involved with the Irish Republican Brotherhood, an organization dedicated to liberating Ireland from British occupation by any means necessary. It was at Lisavaird that Collins's nationalistic pride was cultivated, and at the age of 15, he traveled to London to work at the British Postal Service. He would stay for nine years. In London, Collins pursued his athletic interests, joining the Gaelic Athletic League. But it was another organization that truly captured his interests, and Collins joined the Irish Republican Brotherhood and became its first secretary. There, he learned that preparations were being made for a rising back in Ireland and by 1916, Collins wanted to be home and involved.

On April 24, IRB soldiers and Irish Volunteers rebelled against British rule, and Collins assisted a group that occupied the General Post Office in Dublin, in what is known as the Easter Rising. The Irish people were, for the most part, fairly lukewarm about supporting such an insurgency. In the ongoing war on the continent, Irish soldiers had fought alongside the British, but passions quickly changed once British soldiers were dispatched to put down the Easter Rising, and immediately began shelling the streets of Dublin, injuring hundreds of civilians, and sixteen rebels were executed. Nearly two thousand Irishmen ended up in British detainment camps, including Collins, but less than a year later, Americans helped arrange their release.

Following the Easter Rising, support for anti-British groups, such as the Irish Volunteers and Sinn Fein began to rise, and Collins, now freed from prison, was touted as a potential leader. He was elected secretary of the National Aid Association, which assisted down-on-their-luck Volunteers, and within the next two years, he would assume a command role in the Irish Republican Brotherhood. England became alarmed, special forces were dispatched to the Ireland, known as the Black and Tans because of their uniform colors. They joined with some British Secret Service operatives, redirected to Ireland from Egypt (the Cairo Gang) and immediately the violence on both sides intensified.

Collins, already on the run, had assembled spies in the British military, and had twelve British secret service agents assassinated on November 21, 1920. Retribution was swift and merciless, as Black and Tan the English Auxiliary

Division stormed into Dublin's Croke Park that same day and indiscriminately shot 12 people at an afternoon Gaelic football game. The day became known as "Bloody Sunday" and Ireland would never be the same.

The War of Independence continued, while Black and Tans conducted raids throughout Dublin, and "Where is Michael Collins?" became a familiar cry. The ease with which Collins was able to avoid detection, all the while mounting counter-raids of his own, caused British Prime Minister Lloyd George to wonder, "Where was Michael Collins during the Great War? He'd have been worth a dozen brass-hats [British Generals]!"

By 1921, however, both sides had reached an impasse. The IRA was not going to defeat the British military, and yet showed no signs of going away. British public opinion was moving closer to opposing official policy toward Ireland, and Sinn Fein was actually gaining support internationally. The doors for negotiation were slowly opening.

Initially, Collins was reluctant, frequently reminding anyone who would listen that he was a soldier, not a politician. But Eamon de Valera refused to negotiate with the British, instead dispatching Collins and Arthur Griffith. The two Irishmen were no match for Lloyd George, who set the terms for the treaty and proposed giving limited sovereignty to a large part of Ireland. Six counties, however, would remain under direct British rule and become known as Northern Ireland. The proposed treaty put Collins in a difficult position. He knew it would not be acceptable in Dublin, but he felt it would be a step toward Irish independence and was preferable to an escalated war—one in which he was convinced the IRA would not fare well. Writing to a friend about signing the treaty, Collins said prophetically, "Think, what have I got for Ireland? Something she has wanted these past seven hundred years. Will anyone be satisfied at the bargain, will anyone? I tell you this, early this morning I signed my death warrant, I thought at the time, how incredible, how fantastic, a bullet may well have done the job six years ago. These signatures are the first real step for Ireland. If people would only remember that, the first real step."

The Anglo-Irish treaty passed the unofficial Irish parliament narrowly, and the immediate result was a divided Ireland, geographically, politically and religiously. Some suspected that Lloyd George outmaneuvered Collins to such an extent that he effectively forced the Irish to fight each other rather than the British. Ireland split into pro-Treaty and anti-Treaty forces as de Valera resigned and Collins was elected Chairman of the Provisional Government, which now took over evacuated British posts. Collins had also recently become engaged to a Longford woman by the name of Kitty Kiernan, and the two exchanged hundreds of letters during his courtship "on the run."

However, Civil War was in the air, and die-hard Republicans simply did not accept any treaty short of England out of Ireland. Six months after the peace treaty, violence broke out, especially in Belfast, where the Catholic population suffered the brunt of the attacks. Collins made every effort to avoid a war, but once it began he took command of the Free State forces. He rallied to the defense of Catholics in the North with violence, but in effect, he violated Treaty terms, thus legitimizing armed resistance in the South. Fighting broke out in Dublin and a ten-month civil war was underway in Ireland.

The strain of the Treaty and its effects was too much for Arthur Griffith, and he died of a stroke on August 12, 1922. Eight days later, Collins left on his fated mission to visit his troops in Cork. At about eight o'clock on August 22nd, his convoy came under ambush and one man died—Michael Collins. In six short years, he had ascended to the highest political ranks in Ireland, and positioned his country for freedom from British rule. Upon news of his death, Army Chief of Staff Richard Mulcahy issued a statement to his army that seemed to embody the appeal and importance of Michael Collins to Ireland. He wrote, "Stand calmly by your posts. Bend bravely and undaunted to your work. Let no cruel act of reprisal blemish your bright honour. Every dark hour that Michael Collins met since 1916 seemed but to steel that bright strength of his and temper his gay bravery. You are left each inheritors of that strength."

Notes by General Michael Collins

August, 1922

After a national struggle sustained through many centuries, we have today in Ireland a native Government deriving its authority solely from the Irish people, and acknowledged by England and the other nations of the world.

Through those centuries—through hopes and through disappointments—the Irish people have struggled to get rid of a foreign Power which was preventing them from exercising their simple right to live and to govern themselves as they pleased—which tried to destroy our nationality, our institutions, which tried to abolish our customs and blot out our civilization,—all that made us Irish, all that united us as a nation.

But Irish nationality survived. It did not perish when native government was destroyed, and a foreign military despotism was set up. And for this reason, that it was not made by the old native government and it could not be destroyed by the foreign usurping government. It was the national spirit which created the old native government, and not the native government which created the national spirit. And nothing that the foreign government could do could destroy the national spirit.

But though it survived, the soul of the nation drooped and weakened. Without the protection of a native government we were exposed to the poison of foreign ways. The national character was infected and the life of the nation was endangered. We had armed risings and political agitation. We were not strong enough to put out the foreign Power until the national consciousness was fully re-awakened. This was why the Gaelic Movement and Sinn Féin were necessary for our last successful effort. Success came with the inspiration which the new national movement gave to our military and political effort. The Gaelic spirit working through the *Dàil* and the Army was irresistible.

In this light we must look at the present situation.

The new spirit of self-reliance and our splendid unity, and an international situation which we were able to use to our advantage, enabled our generation to make the greatest and most successful national effort in our history.

The right of Ireland as a nation under arms to decide its own destiny was acknowledged. We were invited to a Peace Conference. With the authority of Ireland's elected representatives negotiations were entered into between the two belligerent nations in order to find a basis of peace.

During the war we had gathered strength by the justice of our cause, and by the way in which we had carried on the struggle. We had organised our own government, and had made the most of our military resources. The united nation showed not only endurance and courage but a humanity which was in marked contrast with the conduct of the enemy. All this gave us a moral strength in the negotiations of which we took full advantage.

But in any sane view our military resources were terribly slender in the face of those of the British Empire which had just emerged victorious from the world war. It was obvious what would have been involved in a renewal of armed conflict on a scale which we had never met before. And it was obvious what we should have lost in strength if the support of the world which had hitherto been on our side had been alienated, if Ireland had rejected terms which most nations would have regarded as terms we could honourably accept.

We had not an easy task.

We were faced with a critical military situation over against an enemy of infinitely greater potential strength. We had to face the pride and prejudice of a powerful nation which had claimed for centuries to hold Ireland as a province. We had to face all the traditions, and political experience, and strength of the British nation. And on our flank we had a section of our own people who had identified their outlook and interests with those of Britain.

It may be claimed that we did not fail in our task. We got the substance of freedom, as has already been made real before our eyes by the withdrawal of the British power.

And the people approved. And they were anxious to use the freedom secured. The national instinct was sound—that the essence of our struggle was to secure freedom to order our own life, without attaching undue importance to the formulas under which that freedom would be expressed. The people knew that our government could and would be moulded by the nation itself according to its needs. The nation would make the government, not the government the nation.

But on the return of Ireland's representatives from London, Mr. de Valera, who was then leader of the nation, condemned the Treaty in a public statement, while supporting similar proposals for peace which he described as differing 'only by a shadow'.

But he, and all the Deputies, joined in discussing and voting on the Treaty, and after full discussion and expressions of opinion from all parts of the country, the Treaty was approved.

And Mr. de Valera declared that there was a constitutional way of solving our differences. He expressed his readiness to accept the decision of the people. He resigned office, and a Provisional Government was formed to act with Dáil Éireann.

Two duties faced that Government:

To take over the Executive from the English, and to maintain public order during the transition from foreign to native government; and

To give shape in a constitution to the freedom secured.

If the Government had been allowed to carry out these duties no difficulty would have arisen with England, who carried out her part by evacuating her army and her administration. No trouble would have arisen among our own people. And the general trend of development, and the undoubted advantages of unity, would have brought the North-East quietly into union with the rest of the country, as soon as a stable national government had been established into which they could have come with confidence.

Mr. de Valera, and those who supported him in the Dáil, were asked to take part in the interim government, without prejudice to their principles, and their right to oppose the ratification of the Treaty at the elections.

They were asked to help in keeping an orderly united nation with the greatest possible strength over against England, exercising the greatest possible peaceful pressure towards the union of all Ireland, and with the greatest amount of credit for us in the eyes of the world, and with the greatest advantage to the nation itself in having a strong united government to start the departments of State, and to deal with the urgent problems of housing, land, hunger, and unemployment.

They did not find it possible to accept this offer of patriotic service.

Another offer was then made.

If they would not join in the work of transition, would they not co-operate in preserving order to allow that transition peacefully to take place? Would they not co-operate in keeping the army united, free from political bias, so as to preserve its strength for the proper purpose of defending the country in the exercise of its rights?

This also was refused.

It must be remembered that the country was emerging from a revolutionary struggle. And, as was to be expected, some of our people were in a state of excitement, and it was obviously the duty of all leaders to direct the thoughts of the people away from violence and into the steady channels of peace and obedience to authority. No one could have been blind to the course things were bound to take if this duty were neglected.

It was neglected, and events took their course.

Our ideal of nationality was distorted in hair-splitting over the meaning of sovereignty and other foreign words, under advice from minds dominated by English ideas of nationality; and, led away, some soon got out of control and betook themselves to the very methods we had learned to detest in the English and had united to drive out of the country.

By the time the *Árd Fheis* met the drift had become apparent. And the feeling in favour of keeping the national forces united was so strong that a belated agreement was arrived at. In return for a postponement of the elections, the Anti-Treaty Party pledged themselves to allow the work of the Provisional Government to proceed.

What came of that pledge?

Attempts to stampede meetings by revolver shootings, to wreck trains, the suppression of free speech, of the liberty of the Press, terrorisation and sabotage of a kind that we were familiar with a year ago. And with what object; With the sole object of preventing the people from expressing their will, and of making the government of Ireland by the representatives of the people as impossible as the English Government was made impossible by the united forces a year ago.

The policy of the Anti-Treaty Party had now become clear—to prevent the people's will from being carried out because it differed from their own, to create trouble in order to break up the only possible national government, and to destroy the Treaty with utter recklessness as to the consequences.

A section of the army, in an attempt at a military despotism, seized public buildings, took possession of the Chief Courts of Law of the Nation, dislocating private and national business, reinforced the Belfast Boycott which had been discontinued by the people's government, and commandeered public and private funds, and the property of the people.

Met by this reckless and wrecking opposition, and yet unwilling to use force against our own countrymen, we made attempt after attempt at conciliation.

We appealed to the soldiers to avoid strife, to let the old feelings of brotherhood and solidarity continue.

We met and made advances over and over again to the politicians, standing out alone on the one fundamental point on which we owed an unquestioned duty to the people—that we must maintain for them the position of freedom they had secured. We could get no guarantee that we would be allowed to carry out that duty.

The country was face to face with disaster, economic ruin, and the imminent danger of the loss of the position we had won by the national effort. If order could not be maintained, if no National Government was to be allowed to function, a vacuum would be created, into which the English would be necessarily drawn back. To allow that to happen would have been the greatest betrayal of the Irish people, whose one wish was to take and to secure and to make use of the freedom which had been won.

Seeing the trend of events, soldiers from both sides met to try and reach an understanding, on the basis that the people were admittedly in favour of the Treaty, that the only legitimate government could be one based on the people's will and that the practicable course was to keep the peace, and to make use of the position we had secured.

Those honourable efforts were defeated by the politicians. But at the eleventh hour an agreement was reached between Mr. de Valera and myself for which I have been severely criticised.

It was said that I gave away too much, that I went too far to meet them, that I had exceeded my powers in making a pact which, to some extent, interfered with the people's right to make a free and full choice at the elections.

It was a last effort on our part to avoid strife, to prevent the use of force by Irishmen against Irishmen. We refrained from opposing the Anti-Treaty Party at the elections. We stood aside from political conflict, so that, so far as we were concerned, our opponents might retain the full number of seats which they had held in the previous *Dáil.* And I undertook, with the approval of the Government, that they should hold four out of the nine offices in the new Ministry. They calculated that in this way they would have the same position in the new *Dáil* as in the old. But their calculations were upset by the people themselves, and they then dropped all pretence of representing the people, and turned definitely against them.

The Irregular Forces in the Four Courts continued in their mutinous attitude. They openly defied the newly expressed will of the people. On the pretext of enforcing a boycott of Belfast goods, they raided and looted a Dublin garage, and when the leader of the raid was arrested by the National Forces, they retaliated by the seizure of one of the principal officers of the National Army.

Such a challenge left two courses open to the National Government: either to betray its trust and surrender to the mutineers, or to fulfil its duty and carry out the work entrusted to it by the people.

The Government did its duty. Having given them one last opportunity to accept the situation, to obey the people's will, when the offer was rejected the Government took the necessary measures to protect the rights and property of the people and to disperse the armed bands which had outlawed themselves and were preying upon the nation.

Unbelievers had said that there was not, and had never been, an Irish Nation capable of harmonious, orderly development. That it was not the foreign invader but the character of the Irish themselves which throughout history had made of our country a scene of strife.

We knew this to be a libel. Our historians had shown our nationality as existing from legendary ages, and through centuries of foreign oppression.

What made Ireland a nation was a common way of life, which no military force, no political change could destroy. Our strength lay in a common ideal of how a people should live, bound together by mutual ties, and by a devotion to Ireland which shrank from no individual sacrifice. This consciousness of unity carried us to success in our last great struggle.

In that spirit we fought and won. The old fighting spirit was as strong as ever, but it had gained a fresh strength in discipline in our generation. Every county sent its boys whose unrecorded deeds were done in the spirit of Cuchulain at the Ford.

But the fight was not for one section of the nation against another, but for Ireland against the foreign oppressor. We fought for that for which alone fighting is really justified—for national freedom, for the right of the whole people to live as a nation.

And we fought in a way we had never fought before, and Ireland won a victory she had never won before.

The foreign Power was withdrawn. The civil administration passed into the hands of the elected representatives of the people. The fight with the English enemy was ended. The function of our armed forces was changed. Their duty now was to preserve the freedom won—to enable the people to use it, to realise that for which they had fought—a free, prosperous, self-governing Gaelic Ireland.

Differences as to political ideals such as remained or might develop amongst us—these were not a matter for the army, these were not a matter for force, for violence.

Under the democratic system which was being established by the representatives of the people—the freest and most democratic system yet devised—the rights of every minority were secured, and the fullest opportunity was open for every section of opinion to express and advocate its views by appeal to reason and patriotic sentiment.

In these circumstances, the only way in which individual views could be rightly put forward by patriotic Irishmen was by peaceful argument and appeal. The time had come when the best policy for Ireland could be promoted in ways which would keep the nation united—strong against the outside world, and settling its own differences peacefully at home.

To allow such a situation to develop successfully required only common sense and patriotism in the political leaders. No one denied that the new Government had the support of the people.

Of all forms of government a democracy allows the greatest freedom—the greatest possibilities for the good of all. But such a government, like all governments, must be recognised and obeyed.

The first duty of the new Government was to maintain public order, security of life, personal liberty, and property.

The duty of the leaders was to secure free discussion of public policy, and to get all parties to recognise that, while they differed, they were fellow-citizens of one free State. It should have been the political glory of Ireland to show that our differences of opinion could express themselves so as to promote, and not to destroy, the national life.

The army had to recognise that they were the servants and not the masters of the people—that their function was not to impose their will on the people but to secure to the people the right to express their own will and to order their lives accordingly.

All this might indeed appear obvious to all patriotic persons.

But with the removal of the pressure of the English enemy, the spirit of order, and unity, and devotion to Ireland as a whole was suddenly weakened in some directions. The readiness to fight remained after the occasion for fighting was gone. Some lost grasp of the ideal for which they had fought and magnified personal differences into a conflict of principles.

The road was clear for us to march forward, peaceful and united, to achieve our goal and the revival of our Gaelic civilization. The peace and order necessary for that progress was rudely broken. The united forward movement was held up by an outbreak of anarchic violence.

The nation which had kept the old heroic temper, but had learnt to govern it so that violence should be directed against the national enemy, and its differences should be matters of friendly rivalry, found itself faced with a small minority determined to break up the national unity and to destroy the government in which the nation had just shown its confidence.

They claimed to be fighting for the nation. That might be possible if there were any enemies of the nation opposing them. There are not. Resolved to fight, they are fighting, not against an enemy, but against their own nation. Blind to facts, and false to ideals, they are making war on the Irish people.

To conceal this truth they claim to be opposing the National Government which they declare to be a usurpation. In view of the elections this is absurd enough. No one can deny that the present Government rests on the will of the people, the sole authority for any government. And what was the usurpation they complained of? Simply that the Government refused to allow authority to be wrested from it by an armed minority. If it is not right for a National Government to keep public order, to prevent murder, arson, and brigandage, what are the duties of a government?

But it is not the fact that they have directed their fight against the National Government and the National Army. It was against the Irish people themselves that they directed their operations.

The anti-national character of their campaign became clear when we saw them pursuing exactly the same course as the English Black and Tans. They robbed and destroyed, not merely for the sake of loot, and from a criminal instinct to destroy (though in any candid view of their operations these elements must be seen to have been present) but on a plan, and for a definite purpose. Just as the English claimed that they were directing their attack against a 'murder gang', so the irregulars claim that they are making war on a 'usurping' government.

But, in reality, the operations and the motives in both cases were, and are, something quite different—namely, the persecution and terrorism of the unarmed population, and the attempt by economic destruction, famine, and violence, to 'make an appropriate hell' in Ireland, in the hope of breaking up the organised National Government and undermining the loyalty of the people. And of what is it all the inevitable outcome? Of the course to which the unthinking enthusiasm of some was directed when they were told repeatedly that it might be necessary to turn their arms against their brothers and to wade through Irish blood.

But the true nature of the whole movement has now demonstrated itself so that no one can doubt it. A tree is known by its fruits—we have seen the fruits. The Irish people will be confirmed in its conviction that those fruits are deadly. They will have no sympathy with anarchy and violence.

The Irish people know that true Irish nationality does not express itself in these ways. They know it is the Government, and not those who call themselves Republicans, who are upholding the national ideal.

The tactics of disruption and disorder were anti-national in paralysing the energies which were needed for building up the new Ireland.

Worse still, their violence and the passions it aroused have broken up the united concentration on the revival of our language and of our Irish life.

Worst of all, their action has been a crime against the nation in this—that the anarchy and ruin they were bringing about was undermining the confidence of the nation in itself. So far as it succeeded it was proving that our enemies were right, that we were incapable of self-government. When left to ourselves in freedom we could show nothing of the native civilization we had claimed as our own.

The Black and Tans with all their foreign brutality were unable to make of Ireland 'an appropriate hell'. The irregulars brought their country to the brink of a real hell, the black pit in which our country's name and credit would have sunk, in which our existence as a distinct nation, *our belief in ourselves as a nation* might have perished for ever. If they had succeeded in destroying the National Government, and reducing the country to anarchy, the greatest evil would have been, not that the English would have come back, that would indeed have been terrible enough, *but that they would have been welcomed back, that they would have come not as enemies, but as the only protectors who could bring order and peace.*

For hundreds of years we had preserved our national hopes. We were on the point of achieving them, but when the real test came the national consciousness lapsed in the minds of some whom the nation had trusted. The wrong done was not merely to the material prospects of the nation *but to its soul.*

The calamity was unnecessary. There lies the wrong to the nation. A simple acceptance of the people's will! That was all that was asked of them. What principle could such an acceptance have violated?

All further measures necessary will be taken to maintain peace and order.

We have to face realities.

There is no British Government any longer in Ireland. It is gone. It is no longer the enemy. We have now a native government, constitutionally elected, and it is the duty of every Irish man and woman to obey it. Anyone who fails to obey it is an enemy of the people and must expect to be treated as such.

We have to learn that attitudes and actions which were justifiable when directed against an alien administration, holding its position by force, are wholly unjustifiable against a native government which exists only to carry out the people's will, and which can be changed the moment it ceases to do so.

We have to learn that freedom imposes responsibilities.

This parliament is now the controlling body. With the unification of the administration it will be clothed with full authority. Through the parliament the people have the right, and the power, to get the constitution, the legislation, and the economic and educational arrangements they desire. The courts of law, which are now our own courts, will be reorganised to make them national in character, and the people will be able to go to them with confidence of receiving justice.

That being so, the Government believes it will have the whole force of public opinion behind it in dealing sternly with all unlawful acts of every kind, no matter under what name of political or patriotic, or any other policy that may be carried out.

The National Army, and the new Irish Police Force, acting in obedience to the Administration, will defend the freedom and rights of the Nation, and will put down crime of whatever nature, sectarian, agrarian or confiscatory.

In the special circumstances I have had to stress the Government's determination to establish the foundations of the state, to preserve the very life of the Nation. But a policy of development is engaging the attention of all departments, and will shortly be made known.

We have a difficult task before us. We have taken over an alien and cumbersome administration. We have to begin the upbuilding of the nation with foreign tools. But before we can scrap them we must first forge fresh Gaelic ones to take their place, and must temper their steel.

But if we will all work together in a mutually helpful spirit, recognising that we all seek the same end, the good of Ireland, the difficulties will disappear.

The Irish Nation is the whole people, of every class, creed, and outlook. We recognise no distinction. It will be our aim to weld all our people nationally together who have hitherto been divided in political and social and economic outlook.

Labour will be free to take its rightful place as an element in the life of the nation. In Ireland more than in any other country lies the hope of the rational adjustment of the rights and interests of all sections, and the new government starts with the resolve that Irish Labour shall be free to play the part which belongs to it in helping to shape our industrial and commercial future.

The freedom, strength, and greatness of the nation will be measured by the independence, economic well-being, physical strength and intellectual greatness of the people.

A new page of Irish history is beginning.

We have a rich and fertile country—a sturdy and intelligent people. With peace, security and union, no one can foresee the limits of greatness and well-being to which our country may not aspire.

But it is not only within our country that we have a new outlook. Ireland has now a recognised international status. Not only as an equal nation in association with the British nations, but as a member of the wider group forming the League of Nations. As a member of these groups, Ireland's representatives will have a voice in international affairs, and will use that voice to promote harmony and peaceful intercourse among all friendly nations.

In this way Ireland will be able to play a part in the new world movement, and to play that part in accordance with the old Irish tradition of an independent distinctive Irish nation, at harmony, and in close trading, cultural, and social relations, with all other friendly nations.

In this sense our outlook is new. But our national aim remains the same—a free, united Irish nation and united Irish race all over the world, bent on achieving the common aim of Ireland's prosperity and good name.

Underlying the change of outlook there is this continuity of outlook.

For 700 years the united effort has been to get the English out of Ireland. For this end, peaceful internal development had to be left neglected, and the various interests which would have had distinct aims had to sink all diversity and unite in the effort of resistance, and the ejection of the English power.

This particular united effort is now at an end. But it is to be followed by a new united effort for the actual achievement of the common goal. The negative work of expelling the English power is done. The positive work of building a Gaelic Ireland in the vacuum left has now to be undertaken.

This requires not merely unity, but diversity in unity. Each Irish interest, each phase of Irish life, industrial, commercial, cultural, social, must find expression and have a voice in the development of the country, partly by the government, and partly by co-operation and individual effort.

But they must express themselves and use their influence, not in hostility to one another, but in co-operation. And in furthering their special aims, they must do so in the light of the common ideal—a united, distinctive Irish nationality.

And there must be, to reach this ideal, and particularly so at this moment, allegiance to and support of the National Government, democratically elected. At least to the extent of assisting it to restore and maintain peace and public order, rights of life and property according to law, freedom for all individuals, parties, and creeds, to express themselves lawfully.

This is why we claim that the measures to restore order which we have taken are not repressive. They are seen to be carrying the liberative movement to completion, clearing away the débris in order to lay firm and solid the foundations on which to build the new Ireland.

Those who are restoring order, not those who tried to destroy it, are the preservers of Irish nationality. Fidelity to the real Ireland lies in uniting to build up a real Ireland in conformity with our ideal, and not in disruption and destruction as a sacrifice to the false gods of foreign-made political formulas.

The ideal is no good unless it lights our present path. Otherwise it is but a vain sentiment, or misleading will-o'-the-wisp. We can all be faithful to what is our national ideal—the Ireland of poetic tradition, and the future Ireland which will one day be—the best of what our country was, and can be again, and the perfect freedom in which it alone can be the best.

It is because this ideal is not a fact now, that we must be faithful to it, and our faithfulness to it consists in making it a fact so far as we can in ourselves and in our day.

Accepting the freedom which we have here and now is to recognise facts and is to be faithful to the national ideal as taking the best practical means to achieve as much as we can of the ideal at the moment. We grasp the substance of freedom, and are true to Ireland in using that freedom to make an actual Ireland as near to the ideal one as possible. We have not got, and cannot get now at the moment, (certainly cannot get without sacrificing the hope of things more important and essential for our true ideal)—the political Republic. If we had got it, we should not necessarily be much further forward towards our true goal—a Gaelic Ireland.

We must be true to facts if we would achieve anything in this life. We must be true to our ideal, if we would achieve anything worthy. The Ireland to which we are true, to which we are devoted and faithful, is the ideal Ireland, which means there is always something more to strive for. The true devotion lies not in melodramatic defiance or self-sacrifice for something falsely said to exist, or for mere words and formalities, which are empty, and which might be but the house newly swept and garnished to which seven worse devils entered in. It is the steady, earnest effort in face of actual possibilities towards the solid achievement of our hopes and visions, the laying of stone upon stone of a building which is actual and in accordance with the ideal pattern.

In this way, what we can do in our time, being done in faithfulness to the traditions of the past, and to the vision of the future, becomes significant and glorified beyond what it is if looked at as only the day's momentary partial work.

This is where our Irish temperament, tenacity of the past, its vivid sense of past and future greatness, readiness for personal sacrifice, belief and pride in our race, can play an unique part, if it can stand out in its intellectual and moral strength, and shake off the weaknesses which long generations of subjection and inaction have imposed upon it.

Let the nation show its true and best character: use its courage, tenacity, clear swift intellect, its pride in the service of the national ideal as our reason directs us.

'Advance and use our liberties'

In my opinion the Truce of July, 1921, could have been secured in December, 1920, at the time His Grace Archbishop Clune endeavoured to mediate, but the opportunity was lost through the too precipitate action of certain of our public men and public bodies.

The actions taken indicated an over-keen desire for peace, and although terms of Truce were virtually agreed upon, they were abandoned because the British leaders thought those actions indicated weakness, and they consequently decided to insist upon surrender of our arms. The result was the continuance of the struggle. British aggression went on unabated and our defence was kept up to the best of our ability.

I am not aware of any negotiations that preceded the Truce of July. I do know there was much visiting by well-meaning, but unauthorised persons. So far, however, as my knowledge goes, these did not have any effect on the communication from Mr. Lloyd George to President de Valera which opened up the period of correspondence between the two Governments and the subsequent negotiations in London. If there were any official conversations prior to the Lloyd George Letter, they took place entirely without my knowledge.

It has been variously stated that the Treaty was signed under duress.

I did not sign the Treaty under duress, except in the sense that the position as between Ireland and England, historically, and because of superior forces on the part of England, has always been one of duress.

The element of duress was present when we agreed to the Truce, because our simple right would have been to beat the English out of Ireland. There was an element of duress in going to London to negotiate. But there was not, and could not have been, any personal duress.

The threat of 'immediate and terrible war' did not matter overmuch to me. The position appeared to be then exactly as it appears now. The British would not, I think, have declared terrible and immediate war upon us.

They had three courses of action open to them. First, to dissolve the parliaments and put their proposals before the country; second, to resume the war by courting openly and covertly breakages of the Truce (these breakages of the Truce might easily have come from either side); thirdly, to blockade Ireland, and at the same time encourage spasmodic internal conflict.

The first course of action seemed to me to be the most likely, and, as a result of a political win on our side either No. 2 or No. 3 would have been very easily managed by the British. A political reverse would have been more damaging to us than either 2 or 3.

The threat of immediate and terrible war was probably bluff. The immediate tactics would surely have been to put the offer of July 20, which the British considered a very good offer, before the country, and, if rejected, they would have very little difficulty in carrying their own people into a war against Ireland.

Another thing I believe is that on resumption of hostilities the British would have been anxious to fight with us on the basis of belligerent rights. In such circumstances, I doubt if we would have been able to carry on a conflict with the success which had previously attended our efforts. I scarcely think that our resources would have been equal to bearing belligerent rights and responsibilities.

I am not impressed by the talk of duress, nor by threats of a declaration of immediate and terrible war. Britain has not made a declaration of war upon Egypt, neither has she made a declaration of war upon India. But is the conflict less terrible because of the absence of such declaration?

We must not be misled by words and phrases. Unquestionably the alternative to the Treaty, sooner or later, was war, and if the Irish Nation had accepted that, I should have gladly accepted it. The opponents of the Treaty have declared over and over again that the alternative to the Treaty was not war.

In my judgement, this was misleading the Irish Nation. The decision of the Irish Nation should not be given on a false basis. That was, and is, my own attitude, and if indeed, it be true, as the antagonists of the Treaty say, that the alternative to the Treaty was not war, where, then, is the heroism? Where, then, is the necessity for the future sacrifices that have been talked of so freely?

To me it would have been a criminal act to refuse to allow the Irish Nation to give its opinion as to whether it would accept this settlement or resume hostilities. That, I maintain, is a democratic stand. It has always been the stand of public representatives who are alive to their responsibilities.

The Irish struggle has always been for freedom—freedom from English occupation, from English interference, from English domination—not for freedom with any particular label attached to it.

What we fought for at any particular time was the greatest measure of freedom obtainable at that time, and it depended upon our strength whether the claim was greater than at another time or lesser than at another time.

When the national situation was very bad we lay inert; when it improved a little we looked for Repeal of the Union; when it receded again we looked for Home Rule under varying trade names; when it went still worse we spoke of some form of devolution. When our strength became greater our aim became higher, and we strove for a greater measure of freedom under the name of a Republic. But it was freedom we sought for, not the name of the form of government we should adopt when we got our freedom.

When I supported the approval of the Treaty at the meeting of D il Éireann I said it gave us freedom—not the ultimate freedom which all nations hope for and struggle for, but freedom to achieve that end. And I was, and am now, fully alive to the implications of that statement.

Under the Treaty Ireland is about to become a fully constituted nation. The whole of Ireland, as one nation, is to compose the Irish Free State, whose parliament will have power to make laws for the peace, order, and good government of Ireland, with an executive responsible to that parliament.

This is the whole basis of the Treaty. It is the bedrock from which our status springs, and any later Act of the British Parliament derives its force from the Treaty only. We have got the present position by virtue of the Treaty, and any forthcoming Act of the British Legislature will, likewise, be by virtue of the Treaty.

It is not the definition of any status which would secure to us that status, but our power to make secure, and to increase what we have gained; yet, obtaining by the Treaty the constitutional status of Canada, and that status being one of freedom and equality, we are free to take advantage of that status, and we shall set up our Constitution on independent Irish lines. And no conditions mentioned afterwards in the Treaty can affect or detract from the powers which the mention of that status in the Treaty gives us, especially when it has been proved, has been made good, by the withdrawal out of Ireland of English authority of every kind.

In fact England has renounced all right to govern Ireland, and the withdrawal of her forces is the proof of this. With the evacuation secured by the Treaty has come the end of British rule in Ireland. No foreigner will be able to intervene between our Government and our people. Not a single British soldier, nor a single British official, will ever step again upon our shores, except as guests of a free people.

Our Government will have complete control of our army, our schools, and our trade. Our soldiers, our judges, our ministers will be the soldiers, judges, and ministers of the Irish Free State. We can send our own ambassadors to Washington, to Paris, to the Vatican; we can have our own representatives on the League of Nations (if we wish).

It was freedom we fought for—freedom from British interference and domination. Let us ask ourselves these few questions: Are the English going? To what extent are they going? If the Treaty is put into operation will they, for all practical purposes, be gone?

The answer to the first question is to be seen in the evacuation that is proceeding apace. We claimed that the Treaty would secure this evacuation. The claim is being fulfilled. The Auxiliaries are practically gone. The regular British military forces are rapidly following them. The answer to the second and third questions is that they remain for negligible purposes in that the extent to which they remain is negligible.

We shall have complete freedom for all our purposes. We shall be rid completely of British interference and British rule. We can establish in its place our own rule, and exactly what kind of rule we like. We can restore our Gaelic life in exactly what form we like. We can keep what we have gained and make it secure and strong. The little we have not yet gained we can go ahead and gain.

All other questions are really questions of arrangement, in which our voice shall be the deciding voice. Any names, any formulas, any figureheads, representing England's wish to conceal the extent of her departure, to keep some pretence of her power over us, which is now gone, will be but names, formulas, figureheads. England exercised her power over us simply by the presence of her forces—military forces, police forces, legal, and social forces.

Is it seriously to be suggested that in the new order, some functionary, no matter what we may call him, will serve the purpose of all these forces, or, apart from him, the particular interpretation of the words of a document?

The British Government could only be maintained by the presence of British forces. Once these are gone the British Government can no longer arrange the form our National Government and our National life will take, nor can they set any limits to either. If we wish to make our nation a free and a great and a good nation we can do so now. But we cannot do it if we are to fight among ourselves as to whether it is to be called *Saorstàt* or *Poblacht*.

Whatever the name or the political phraseology, we cannot restore Ireland without a great united effort.

Any difficulty now in making a noble Irish-Ireland will lie in our people themselves and in the hundreds of years of anglicisation to which we have been subjected. The task before us, having got rid of the British, is to get rid of the British influences—to de-anglicise ourselves; for there are many among us who still cling to English ways, and any thoughtlessness, any carelessness, will tend to keep things on the old lines—the inevitable danger of the proximity of the two nations.

Can any restriction or limitation in the Treaty prevent us making our nation great and potent? Can the presence of a representative of the British Crown, depending on us for his resources, prevent us from doing that? Can the words of a document as to what our status is prevent us from doing that? One thing only can prevent us—disunion among ourselves.

Can we not concentrate and unite, not on the negative, but on the positive, task of making a real Ireland distinct from Britain—a nation of our own?

The only way to get rid of British contamination and the evils of corrupt materialism is to secure a united Ireland intent on democratic ways, to make our free Ireland a fact, and not to keep it for ever in dreamland as something that will never come true, and which has no practical effect or reality except as giving rise to everlasting fighting and destruction, which seem almost to have become ends in themselves in the mind of some—some who appear to be unheeding and unmindful of what the real end is.

Ireland is one—perhaps the only—country in Europe which has now living hopes for a better civilization. We have a great opportunity. Much is within our grasp. Who can lay a finger on our liberties?

If any power menaces our liberties, we are in a stronger position than before to repel the aggressor. That position will grow stronger with each year of freedom if we will all unite for the aims we have in common.

Let us advance and use these liberties to make Ireland a shining light in a dark world, to reconstruct our ancient civilization on modern lines, to avoid the errors, the miseries, the dangers, into which other nations, with their false civilizations, have fallen.

In taking the Treaty we are not going in for the flesh-pots of the British Empire—not unless we wish to. It is futile to suppose that all these tendencies would disappear under freedom by some other name, or that the government of an externally associated nation, or of a Republic, any more than a Free State, would be able to suppress them, and to force Gaelicism upon the nation.

Whatever form of free government we had, it would be the Government of the Irish Nation. All the other elements, old Unionists, Home Rulers, Devolutionists, would have to be allowed freedom and self- expression. The only way to build the nation solid and Irish is to effect these elements in a friendly national way—by attraction, not by compulsion, making them feel themselves welcomed into the Irish Nation, in which they can join and become absorbed, as long ago the Geraldines and the de Burgos became absorbed.

The Treaty is already vindicating itself. The English Die-hards said to Mr. Lloyd George and his Cabinet: 'You have surrendered'. Our own Die-hards said to us: 'You have surrendered'. There is a simple test. Those who are left in possession of the battlefield have won.

Alternative To The Treaty

Ireland 'A Mother Country'

Document No. 2 Analysed

The main difference between the Treaty and the alternative proposals put forward by Mr. de Valera (known as Document No. 2) is that one is signed by the Plenipotentiaries of both nations and has been approved by the representatives of both nations; the other is not signed.

In my belief it would not be signed in its present form; not, indeed, that it contains much that is not in the Treaty, nor that it contains much that England objects to, but simply that in its construction it is too loose. Undoubtedly, in the application of its details we should constantly have been faced with conflicting interpretations leading to inevitable discordance.

It was claimed for the document by its sponsors that it would be approved by the English people; that, on the other hand, England never kept a Treaty, nor would she keep the present Treaty. The inference, of course, is that England would keep a Treaty which she had not signed but would not keep a Treaty which she had signed. The document was not drafted by Mr. de Valera. There is little difficulty in guessing the author. Dominionism tinges every line. No Irishman who understands the tradition and the history of Ireland would think or write of his country's aspirations in the terms used in this document. In the official laudation given it by the organ of its supporters the following occurs:

"Clauses 3 and 4 must be read together. What they mean is this, that the association in matters of common concern shall be a free one, not binding Ireland to submit to the decisions either of the British alone or of a majority of the States of the Commonwealth of which Britain is one."

"It is on that footing that an Irish representative would attend meetings of the body known as the Imperial Conference, consisting of Dominion Premiers and British Cabinet Ministers to discuss and co-operate in matters of common concern. That is the footing on which the Commonwealth States act together now, and the words within quotation marks at the end of Clause 4 are taken from what is known as the Constitutional Resolution passed at the Imperial Conference of 1917.

"It will be seen that the Commonwealth States, including Britain are bound to consultation and no more. They are free to take action 'as their several Governments may determine'—a partnership based on individual freedom. Ireland would be in the same position."

Thus, Ireland is by our own free offer, under this document, represented at the Imperial Conference. Our status is taken from a Constitutional Resolution passed at an Imperial Conference. The outlook of the author of the document is bounded entirely by the horizon of the British Empire.

This is not my stand, and at a Conference in London with the British representatives I made it quite clear that Ireland was A Mother Country, with the duties and responsibilities and feelings and devotions of a mother country.

This simple statement had more effect on the British delegates than all the arguments about Dominion status, or all the arguments basing the claim of our historic nation on any new-found idea. Irish nationhood springs from the Irish people, not from any comparison with any other nation, not from any equality—inherent or acquired—with any other nation.

Clause 1 of the document, which states:

'That the legislative, executive and judicial authority of Ireland shall be derived solely from the people of Ireland', is a declaration of rights more suitable to form the basis of the Constitution of a free nation than to be incorporated in a Treaty of Peace between two nations that had been at war.

The opponents of the Treaty were most insistent on the argument that it was Britain (by passing the Treaty through her parliament) who conferred on us the Rights and Powers of the Treaty. But we definitely stipulate for a like British acquiescence in Document No. 2.

That is clear from the clause asking for ratification by the British Parliament. British ratification is a legal thing. It is no worse in one case than in the other. It is no better either. But surely no one recognises any right in Britain to agree or to disagree with that fundamental principle of freedom which concerns the people of Ireland alone.

In fact, the Treaty secures this position. Under the Treaty the English will no longer have any legislative, executive, or judicial authority in Ireland.

All such authority will be vested in the Parliament of Ireland, which alone will have power to make laws for the peace, order, and good government of Ireland.

Clauses 2, 3 and 4 of the document are all a loose paraphrase of the Treaty, dangerous and misleading in their looseness. They read:

> 'That for purposes of common concern Ireland shall be associated with the States of the British Commonwealth, viz., the Kingdom of Great Britain, the Dominion of Canada, the Commonwealth of Australia, the Dominion of New Zealand, and the Union of South Africa'.

> 'That while voting as an associate, the rights, status, and privileges of Ireland shall be in no respect less than those enjoyed by any of the component States of the British Commonwealth'.

> 'That the matters of common concern shall include Defence, Peace and War, Political Treaties, and all matters now treated as of common concern amongst the States of the British Commonwealth, and that in these matters there shall be between Ireland and the States of the British Commonwealth such concerted action, founded on consultation, as the several Governments may determine'.

Under these clauses Ireland would be committed to an association so vague that it might afford grounds for claims by Britain which might give her an opportunity to press for control in Irish affairs as common concerns, and to use, or to threaten to use, force. The Irish people could not have been asked, and would not have agreed, to commit themselves to anything so vague.

Clause 4 does not mend the matter; it makes it worse, as common concern may include anything else besides the things named. In fact, it is common knowledge that there are many common concerns in the inter-dealings between the various States of the Commonwealth.

This is a very vital point. We know that there are many things which the States of the British Commonwealth can afford to regard as common concerns which we could not afford so to regard. This is where we must be careful to protect ourselves as best we can against the disadvantages of geographical propinquity This is where we had to find some form of association which would safeguard us, as far as we could be safeguarded, in somewhat the same degree as the 3,000 miles of ocean safeguards Canada.

And it is obvious that the 'association with the British Commonwealth' mentioned in the British Prime Minister's invitation, which was accepted by Mr. de Valera on behalf of Dáil Éireann, meant association of a different kind from that of mere alliance of isolated nations, and now to suggest otherwise is not straightforward.

The question was of an association which would be honourable to Ireland, which would give us full freedom to manage our own affairs, and prevent interference by Britain; which would give the maximum security that this freedom would be observed (and we may be trusted to see that it is so observed), and which would be acceptable to Ireland as recognising her nationhood.

We negotiated from the standpoint of an independent sovereign nation, with a view to finding means of being honourably associated with the British group of nations in a way in which we were not associated with them before the negotiations.

The link which binds that group is a link which binds free nations in a voluntary association. This is what we obtained in the Treaty—-freedom within our nation, freedom of association without.

The external association mentioned in Document No. 2 has neither the honesty of complete isolation (a questionable advantage in these days of warring nationalities when it is not too easy for a small nation to stand rigidly alone) nor the strength of free partnership satisfying the different partners. Such external association was not practical politics.

Actually in this regard the terms of the Treaty are less objectionable than the formulas of the document. Restrictions in the Treaty there unquestionably are.

Restrictions in Document No. 2 equally unquestionably there are. *But the Treaty will be operative, and the restrictions must gradually tend to disappear as we go on more and more strongly solidifying and establishing ourselves as a free nation.*

Clause 5. 'That in virtue of this association of Ireland with the States of the British Commonwealth citizens of Ireland in any of these States shall not be subject to any disabilities which a citizen of one of the component States of the British Commonwealth would not be subject to, and reciprocally for citizens of these States in Ireland' is unintelligible, and does not meet the Irish wish to have some sentimental and racial ties with all the children of our race. The expression common citizenship in the Treaty is not ideal, but it is less indefinite, and it does not attempt to confine Ireland's mother claims to the States of the British Commonwealth.

Clause 6. 'That for purposes of association, Ireland shall recognise his Britannic Majesty as head of association' gives the recognition of the British Crown—a recognition which is as precise as any given in the Treaty.

It was after discussion of this clause that Mr. de Valera's alternative oath was produced. That oath, which has already been published, was incorporated in a document submitted to the British by the Irish delegation. It reads as follows: 'I do swear to bear true faith and allegiance to the Constitution of Ireland and to the Treaty of Association of Ireland with the British Commonwealth of Nations, and to recognise the King of Great Britain as head of the Associated States'. It was explained at the Dáil debate by one of the foremost anti-Treatyites that the King of Great Britain could be regarded as a managing director, the explanation being that in these modern days industrial concerns were amalgamating and entering into agreements, etc.

The King of Great Britain would then occupy the same relative position towards the Associated States as a managing director occupied towards associated businesses. Whereupon it was very wisely pointed out by a journalist who was listening to the debate that a managing director is one who manages and directs. After all, whatever we may say of royal prerogatives, or anything of that kind, no modern democratic nation is managed and directed by one ruler.

Plain people will not be impressed by this managing director nonsense. Plain people will see no difference between these oaths.

We must always rely upon our own strength to keep the freedom we have obtained and to make it secure. And the constitutional status of Canada, defined in the Treaty, gives us stronger assurance of our immunity from interference by Britain than the indefinite clauses in Document No. 2.

These clauses have nothing effective to back them. They have practically all the disadvantages of the Treaty. It is too uncertain to have our future relationship based on ifs and unless and terms like 'so far as our resources permit'. These attempts at improvement are nothing but dangerous friction spots which it is the interest of Ireland to avoid.

Much has been said by the opponents of the Treaty about 'buttressing up the British Empire'. All these defence clauses in Document No. 2 are open to exactly the same attack. Under these clauses we could not assist an Indian or Egyptian craft that happened to get into Irish waters. These countries are at war with Britain, and we should be bound by our proffered agreement to help Britain.

Under the Treaty we should have a representative on the League of Nations (if we approved of a League of Nations), and that representative would have a real power to prevent aggression against Egypt and India.

To deal with Clauses 7 and 10 together, these clauses have reference to the matter of defence, and to the ordinary observer there is little difference between them and the clauses of the Treaty covering the same subject.

The Treaty secures that the harbours at certain ports can be used only for purposes of common defence, and not for any purpose of interfering with Irish freedom (and, again, we may be trusted to ensure that this shall be so).

There is one other thing under these clauses that I should like to explain from my own knowledge of how the matter arose. The British representatives made it quite clear to us that the British people could not, or would not, for the sake of their own safety, allow any Irish Government to build submarines. Document No. 2 concedes this British claim fully. Britain does not mind if we build a dreadnought or two, a battleship or two. One submarine would be a greater menace to her than these. Document No. 2, therefore, gives way to her on the only point that really matters. Such a concession to British necessity, real or supposed, is nothing but dishonesty. Let us agree, if need be, that we shall not build submarines; but don't let us pretend that we are doing it from any motive other than the real motive.

The remaining clauses seem nothing but a repetition of the clauses of the Treaty, with only such slight verbal alterations as no one but a factionist looking for means of making mischief would have thought it worth while to have risked wrecking the Treaty for.

It is fair criticism that the Treaty contains obsolete phraseology no longer suited to the status of freedom and equality of the States of the British Commonwealth and out of touch with the realities of our freedom. But phraseology does not alter the fact of our freedom, and we have the right and will exercise the right, to use a form of words to secure an interpretation more in accordance with the facts.

As an improvement on the Treaty Document No. 2 is not honest. It may be more dictatorial in language. It does not contain in principle a 'greater reconciliation with Irish national aspirations'. It merely attaches a fresh label to the same parcel, or, rather, a label written, on purpose, illegibly in the hope of making belief that the parcel is other than it is.

THE PROOF OF SUCCESS

What the Rising of 1916 Did

Disunion Danger

Ireland is an ancient nation which from earliest times had a distinct civilization. What made Ireland what she was was her people living within the whole island as a separate and distinct community, or nation, by virtue of a common system of law and culture and traditions and ways of life and not depending upon any particular political constitutions. While this lasted strangers who came were absorbed, and the national ways were not interfered with, and were such, by their attractiveness, as to enable strangers to become Irish easily and thoroughly.

Then came English interference, and her policy of robbery and exploitation, and when she had conquered us sufficiently she began to carry out her policy—to use us to feed and enrich herself. But having a complete nationhood of our own, which Britain had to acknowledge or to trample out of existence, and having a social system which suited us, and which gave our people security in all their rights and privileges, England found the execution of her policy, though helped by our geographical propinquity, a less easy task in Ireland than in her colonies, where there was no separate nationhood and no difference of social polity.

England's idea was to make Ireland an English province. For her purposes Irish civilization was to be completely blotted out. The Gael was to go. Our lands were to be confiscated and given to aliens. Our industries were to be effectively destroyed. Everything that tended to remind us of the past, everything that tended to retain our Irish outlook, everything that helped to keep us a distinct people, everything that tended to keep alive in us our memories of our Gaelic civilization and of our Irish nationality, freedom, and prosperity, was to be obliterated.

Her method even then was to divide and rule, setting chief against chief, as later she set religion against religion.

This policy could not succeed while we had a land system by which men's rights in the land were secure and impregnable. By means of wholesale commandeering the land was taken from the people, and the feudal system of tenure, a system admirably suited for the purpose of enslavement, was imposed. The free men of Ireland, whose rights had been rooted in the soil, became the tenants, the serfs, of the usurpers, and were completely at the mercy of their new masters, the landlords, who joined with the enemy in the policy of robbing, exploiting, and exterminating the Irish people.

When England had succeeded in uprooting the old Irish system of land tenure under which everyone securely enjoyed land to cultivate and common rights of grazing, she had taken the biggest step in our subjection. It was only in so far as it attempted to reverse that subjection that the land campaign of the Davitt period was justified.

Some historian has yet to take up this aspect of the land struggle and discover a national spirit seeking to manifest itself in apparently strange ways. Were it not for this the killing of landlords would have been murder. The people undoubtedly regarded it in this way. The landlords were the agents who had taken away the liberties of the common folk, and the common folk hit at the agent whom they recognised as the common enemy.

They took first things first. They did the job which was immediately to their hands. In our generation we have no longer to shoot landlords, for landlords as they were known have mostly gone. In the same way we hope that the next generation will have no necessity to shoot an enemy, for the enemy will have gone.

In furtherance of the same policy the suppression of our industries was also necessary if Britain's desire was to be realised. It was doubly necessary. Our manufacturers competed too successfully with hers, and it was to be our privilege to exist, not as an industrial people, but for the purpose of providing England with an abundance of food.

The destruction of our democratic Gaelic social system, the discouragement, the prohibition of all enterprise, leaving us only a slave life on the land, and the imposition upon us of an alien language, alien laws, alien ideas, made our subjugation complete. Our economic subjection was necessary that we might serve Britain's purposes. Our spiritual subjection was no less necessary that we might learn to forget our former national and economic freedom and acquiesce and grow passive in our servitude.

And we learned our lesson. We forgot our freedom. We forgot our language. We forgot our own native Irish ways. We forgot our Irish love and veneration for things of the mind and character, our pride in learning, in the arts for which we had been famous, in military skill, in athletic prowess, in all which had been our glory from the days of Cormac MacArt and St. Patrick and before them.

We became the degraded and feeble imitators of our tyrants. English fashions, English material tastes and customs were introduced by the landlord class or adopted by them, and by a natural process they came to be associated in the minds of our people with gentility. The outward sign of a rise in the social scale became the extent to which we cast off everything which distinguished us as Irish and the success with which we imitated the enemy who despised us.

And slavery still exists.

To-day in Ireland, although through improved economic conditions, which have been world-wide and in which it was not possible altogether to prevent us sharing, helped by a better living on the land, bought very dearly by the purchase back again of a great part of our country from those who had never any right to it, we have been lifted out of the worst slough of destitution; although we have been turning our eyes towards the light of liberty and learning to lift our heads again as Irish men and Irish women with a land of our own, and with traditions and hopes of which no nation need feel ashamed, yet still from east to west, from north to south, we are soaked, saturated, and stupefied with the English outlook.

Only slowly, laboriously, do we turn in our chains and struggle to free ourselves from the degrading lie that what is English is necessarily respectable, and what is Irish, low and mean. Even at this moment when our daily papers and our weekly papers are writing of our newly-won freedom and rejoicing over our national hopes, they continue to announce in their leading columns the movements of English society and the births and marriages of upper-class English nonentities.

But by the completeness with which England converted us into hewers of wood and drawers of water, she in the end defeated her own purpose.

Feebly resisting at the moments when we were less completely crushed, when a brief interval came between the long periods of starvation, when we had a moment in which we could reflect upon our condition, we gradually awoke to the cause of our miseries, and we grew to learn if we would be economically free we must be nationally free, and if we would be spiritually free we must be nationally free.

The coming and the presence of the English had deprived us of life and liberty. Their ways were not our ways. Their interests and their purposes meant our destruction. We must turn back again the wheels of that infamous machine which was destroying us. We must get the English out of Ireland.

Our efforts at first were naturally timid, and they were often futile because we were too much concerned with the political side—confused in this by the example of England where nationality was always expressed that way, and was principally a matter of political organisation.

Repeal of the Union was little more than a cry gaining what real strength it had from the more vigorous hostility of the Young Ireland movement, which revived our old literature, which recovered Irish history, and spread a new spirit. That spirit was not wholly martial, but what Irishman will say to-day that it was not benefi-cial, even so?

The Fenians came and once and for all raised the banner of Ireland's freedom, with a definite military policy which, though unsuccessful at the time, had its full effect in bringing before men's minds the real road to Irish salvation.

The Fenian idea left a torch behind it with which Tom Clarke and Seàn MacDermott kindled the fires of Easter Week, and, though seemingly quenched, these were soon blazing brightly again at Solohead, at Clonfin, at Macroom, at Dublin, at many a place in Clare, in Mayo, and Monaghan, and Donegal during the recent struggle.

After the Fenians, years of death again, while famine raged over the land, till Parnell emerged to struggle for independence under the name of Home Rule which, though accompanied by the social and economic revolt of Davitt's national land policy, was bringing us back again to the dangerous idea of seeking freedom by means of some form of political weapon.

The weakness inherent in Parnell's policy was obviated by his intense personal hostility to the English. He never forgot the end in the means. But it lost that sav-ing protection when it fell into the hands of those who succeeded him and who, in the lotus-like atmosphere of the Westminster Parliament, forgot the national spirit and lost touch with the minds and feelings of their countrymen.

The collapse came when in the hands of weaker men the national effort became concentrated at the foreign parliament on English political lines. The methods adopted by the parliamentarians, the forum they had chosen, made their crum-bling an easy matter, and from the English point of view it greatly helped division in their ranks, and with division came the inevitable dissipation of energy.

We would have an identical situation to-day had we chosen the same methods and fought on the same battlefield for the last five years. In that parliamentary period, however, the people at home were growing in national consciousness and in strength and courage. The Gaelic revival and the learning of our national tongue were teaching a new national self-respect. We recalled the immortal tales of our ancient heroes, and we began to look to a future in which we could have a proud, free, distinct nation worthy of the past.

We learned that what we wanted was not a political form of Home Rule or any other kind or form of Home Rule, but a revival of Gaelic life and ways. Economic thought and study showed us that the poverty which afflicted us came from the presence of the English and their control over us; had come from landlordism and the drain of English taxation, the neglect of Irish resources, and the obstruction to

Irish industries by the domination of the English Parliament. And we saw that we must manage these things for ourselves.

And, besides the hope of material emancipation, we grew to think of love of our land, and all that it had given us and had still to give us, and what we could make of it when it was our own once more. And we became filled with a patriotic fervour before which, when the time came, force would prove impotent. The expression of this new hope and new courage manifested itself in the Easter Week Rising.

The leaven of the old Fenianism had been at work in our midst. Tom Clarke, a member of the old Fenian Brotherhood, came out from jail after sixteen years' penal servitude to take up the work where he had left it off.

Seàn MacDermott, tramping through Ireland, preached the Fenian gospel of a freedom which must be fought for, enrolled recruits, and, by his pure patriotism and lovable unselfish character, inspired all with whom he came in contact to emulate him and to be worthy of his teaching.

Our army was in existence again. It was not brought into being, as is wrongfully supposed, by the example of Carson's recruiting in North-East Ulster. It needed no such example. It was already in being—the old Irish Republican Brotherhood in fuller force.

But England's manufactured resistance in the North-East enabled our soldiers to come out into the open, with the advantage in 1916 of a Rising starting unexpectedly from the streets instead of from underground. England was unable or unwilling to interfere with her own Orange instruments, and she did not dare, therefore, to suppress ours.

Armed resistance was the indispensable factor in our struggle for freedom. It was never possible for us to be militarily strong, but we could be strong enough to make England uncomfortable (and strong enough to make England too uncomfortable). While she explains the futility of force (by others) it is the only argument she listens to. For ourselves it had that practical advantage, but it was above all other things the expression of our separate nationhood.

Unless we were willing to fight for our Nation, even without any certainty of success, we acquiesced in the doctrine of our national identity with England. It embodied, too, for us the spirit of sacrifice, the maintenance of the ideal, the courage to die for it, so that military efforts were made in nearly every generation. It was a protest, too, against our anglicisation and demoralisation, a challenge of spirit against material power, and as such bore fruit.

The Rising of 1916 was the fruit.

It appeared at the time of the surrender to have failed, but that valiant effort and the martyrdoms which followed it finally awoke the sleeping spirit of Ireland.

It carried into the hearts of the people the flame which had been burning in those who had the vision to see the pit into which we were sinking deeper and deeper and who believed that a conflagration was necessary to reveal to their countrymen the road to national death upon which we were blindly treading.

The banner of Ireland's freedom had been raised and was carried forward. During the Rising the leaders of Easter Week 'declared a Republic'. But not as a fact. We knew it was not a fact. It was a wonderful gesture—throwing down the gauntlet of defiance to the enemy, expressing to ourselves the complete freedom we aimed at, and for that reason was an inspiration to us.

If the impossible had happened, and the Rising had succeeded, and the English had surrendered and evacuated the country, we would then have been free, and we could then have adopted the republican form of government, or any other form we wished. But the Rising did not succeed as a military venture. And if it had succeeded it would have been the surrender and the evacuation which would have been the proof of our success, not the name for, nor the form of, the government we would have chosen. If we had still a descendant of our Irish Kings left, we would be as free, under a limited monarchy, with the British gone, as under a Republic.

The form of our government is our domestic Irish concern. It does not affect the fact of our national freedom. Our national freedom depends upon the extent to which we reverse the history of the last 700 years, the extent to which we get rid of the enemy and get rid of his control over our material and spiritual life.

FOUR HISTORIC YEARS

The Story of 1914–1918

How Ireland Made her Case Clear

The period from 1914 to 1918 is an important one in the struggle for Irish freedom. It was a transition period. It saw a wholesome and necessary departure from the ideas and methods which had been held and adopted for a generation, and it is a period which is misread by a great many of our people, even by some who helped that departure, and who helped to win the success we have achieved.

The real importance of the Rising of 1916 did not become apparent until 1918. It is not correct to say now that the assertion of the republican principle which was stated by the leaders of the Rising was upheld as the national policy without a break. The declaration of a Republic was really in advance of national thought, and it was only after a period of two years' propaganda that we were actually able to get solidarity on the idea.

The European War, which began in 1914, is now generally recognised to have been a war between two rival empires, an old one and a new, the new becoming such a successful rival of the old, commercially and militarily, that the world-stage was, or was thought to be, not large enough for both.

Germany spoke frankly of her need for expansion, and for new fields of enterprise for her surplus population. England, who likes to fight under a high-sounding title, got her opportunity in the invasion of Belgium. She was entering the war 'in defence of the freedom of small nationalities'.

America at first looked on, but she accepted the motive in good faith, and she ultimately joined in as the champion of the weak against the strong. She concentrated attention upon the principle of self-determination and the reign of law based upon the consent of the governed.

'Shall', asked President Wilson, 'the military power of any nation, or group of nations, be suffered to determine the fortunes of peoples over whom they have no right to rule except the right of force?'

But the most flagrant instance of the violation of this principle did not seem to strike the imagination of President Wilson, and he led the American nation—peopled so largely by Irish men and women who had fled from British oppression—into the battle and to the side of that nation which for hundreds of years had determined the fortunes of the Irish people against their wish, and had ruled them, and was still ruling them, by no other right than the right of force.

There were created by the Allied Powers half-a-dozen new Republics as a demonstration of adherence to these principles. At the same time, England's military subjection of Ireland continued. And Ireland was a nation with claims as strong as, or stronger than, those of the other small nations.

This subjugation constituted a mockery of those principles, yet the expression of them before the world as principles for which great nations were willing to pour out their blood and treasure gave us the opportunity to raise again our flag of freedom and to call the attention of the world to the denial of our claim.

We were not pro-German during the war any more than we were pro-Bulgarian, pro-Turk, or anti-French. We were anti-British, pursuing our age-long policy against the common enemy. Not only was this our policy, but it was the policy that any weak nation would have pursued in the same circumstances. We were a weak nation kept in subjection by a stronger one, and we formed and adopted our policy in light of this fact. We remembered that England's difficulty was Ireland's opportunity, and we took advantage of her engagement elsewhere to make a bid for freedom.

The odds between us were for the moment a little less unequal. Our hostility to England was the common factor between Germany and ourselves. We made common cause with France when France was fighting. We made common cause with Spain when Spain was fighting England. We made common cause with the Dutch when the Dutch were fighting England.

It so happened that on this occasion England had put a weapon into our hands against herself. The observation of the world was focused upon the mighty European War. We could call attention to the difference between England's principles as expounded to the world and her practice as against ourselves. We were put into the position of being able to force her to recognise our freedom or to oppress us for proclaiming that simple right.

Our position was our old position. Our aim was our old aim. Our intention was simply to secure liberation from the English occupation and that which it involved.

The Rising expressed our right to freedom. It expressed our determination to have the same liberty of choice in regard to our own destinies as was conceded to Poland or Czecho-Slovakia, or any other of the nations that were emerging as a result of the new doctrines being preached. The Republic which was declared at the Rising of Easter Week, 1916, was Ireland's expression of the freedom she aspired to. It was our way of saying that we wished to challenge Britain's right to dominate us.

Ireland wished to make it clear that she stood for a form of freedom equal to that of any other nation. Other nations claimed freedom, and their claims were conceded. Ireland's claim was no less strong than the claim of any nation. We had as good a right to recognition as Poland has. The position we adopted expressed our repudiation of the British government.

The British form of government was monarchical. In order to express clearly our desire to depart from all British forms, we declared a Republic. We repudiated the British form of government, not because it was monarchical, but because it was British. We would have repudiated the claim of a British Republic to rule over us as definitely as we repudiated the claim of the British monarchy.

Our claim was to govern ourselves, and the expression of the form of government was an answer to the British lie that Ireland was a domestic question. It was a gesture to the world that there could be no confusion about. It was an emphasis of our separate nationhood and a declaration that our ultimate goal was and would continue to be complete independence.

It expressed our departure from the policy of parliamentary strategy at Westminster. That policy had failed, as it was bound to fail. It had two evils involved in it. While claiming rightly to be a distinct nation, we had been acquiescing by our actions in the convenient British doctrine that we were a British province and an integral part of the United Kingdom—an acquiescence which gave Mr. Lloyd George the opportunity to question our right to freedom because for over a hundred years, he said, we had sent representatives to Westminster, and soldiers to fight in every British war.

And it had the evil effect of causing our people to look to England for any ameliorative government, and even for the gift of an instalment of freedom, and away from their own country, from themselves, who alone could give to themselves these things. So we sank more and more into subjection during this period, and it was only by a great educational effort that our national consciousness was re-awakened.

We were to learn that freedom was to be secured by travelling along a different road; that instead of it being possible for the English to bestow freedom upon us as a gift (or by means of any Treaty signed or unsigned) that it was their presence alone which denied it to us, and we must make that presence uncomfortable for them, and that the only question between us and them was the terms on which they would clear out and cease their interference with us.

But we started along the new road, the only one that could lead to freedom, at first with faltering steps, half doubtingly looking back at the old paths which had become familiar, where we knew the milestones at which we had been able to shift the burden from one shoulder to another.

The Easter Week Rising pointed out the road. But after that declaration of a Republic and all that it meant of repudiation of Britain, we lapsed into the old way, or took but uncertain steps upon the new one.

When the first by-election after the Rising took place in North Roscommon in 1917, so much had the Republic of Easter Week been forgotten and so little had its teachings yet penetrated to the minds of the people, that, though the candidate was Count Plunkett, whose son had been martyred after the Rising, he was returned only on the ground of his opposition to the Irish Party candidate.

Abstention from attendance at the British Parliament was the indispensable factor in the republican ideal—the repudiation of foreign government. But it was only after his election that the Count declared his intention not to go to Westminster, and the announcement was not received very enthusiastically by some of the most energetic of his supporters. They had returned a man, it was said, 'who did not intend to represent them anywhere'. Not only the people, but even some who had been engaged in the Rising hardly grasped the new teaching.

This election and others which followed were not won on the policy of upholding a Republic, but on the challenge it made to the old Irish Party.

There was at this stage no unity of opinion on the policy of abstention among the various elements which formed the opposition, which were joined together only on opposition to the Redmondites. At what was known as the Plunkett Convention an effort was made to get all the parts of the opposition united on such a policy but the divergence of opinion was so great that, to avoid a split, it was declared that there should be no greater union than a loose co-operation.

The North Roscommon and the South Longford elections were fought on the basis of this agreement, and there was no definite united policy until the merging of all the sectional organisations with Sinn Féin which occurred just prior to the great Àrd-Fheis of 1917.

At the South Longford election Mr. Joe McGuinness, who was then still in penal servitude, was elected on the cry: 'Put him in to get him out'. Abstention was put forward, but was so little upheld that he was returned with a majority of only 27.

At the East Clare election, though Mr. de Valera put forward the abstentionist policy and was elected by a large majority, he issued no election address, and at the three elections which followed in South Armagh, Waterford, and East Tyrone, the abstentionists were defeated.

But the people were becoming educated, and the union of all the various sects and leagues in the big organisation of Sinn Féin, as we have seen, defined the national policy as definitely abstentionist.

The Republic of Easter Week had not lived on, as is supposed, supported afresh at each election, and endorsed finally in the General Election of 1918. But the people grew to put their trust in the new policy, and to believe that the men who stood for it would do their best for Ireland, and at the General Election of 1918, fought on the principle of self-determination, they put them in power.

COLLAPSE OF THE TERROR

British Rule's Last Stages

What the Elections Meant

We have seen how in ancient Ireland the people were themselves the guardians of their land, doing all for themselves according to their own laws and customs, as interpreted by the Brehons, which gave them security, prosperity, and national greatness, and how this was upset by the English determination to blot out Irish ways, when came poverty, demoralisation and a false respect for English standards and habits.

The English power to do this rested on military occupation and on economic control. It had the added advantage of social influence operating upon a people weakened and demoralised by the state of dependence into which the English occupation had brought them.

Military resistance was attempted. Parliamentary strategy was tried. The attempts did not succeed. They failed because they did not go to the root of the question.

The real cure had to be started—that the people should recover belief in their own ways and ideas and put them into practice. Secret societies were formed and organised. The Land League came into existence. The Gaelic League came. Sinn Féin grew and developed. All these societies did much. But the effort had to be broadened into a national movement to become irresistible. It became irresistible in the Republican movement when it was backed by sufficient military force to prevent the English forces from suppressing the national revival.

The challenge of Easter Week and its sacrifices increased the growing national self-belief. All these things made a resistance against which the English, with their superior forces, pitted themselves in vain.

Ireland's story from 1918 to 1921 may be summed up as the story of a struggle between our determination to govern ourselves and to get rid of British government and the British determination to prevent us from doing either. It was a struggle between two rival Governments, the one an Irish Government resting on the will of the people and the other an alien Government depending for its existence upon military force—the one gathering more and more authority, the other steadily losing ground and growing ever more desperate and unscrupulous.

All the history of the three years must be read in the light of that fact.

Ireland had never acquiesced in government by England. Gone for ever were policies which were a tacit admission that a foreign Government could bestow freedom, or a measure of freedom, upon a nation which had never surrendered its national claim.

We could take our freedom. We would set up a Government of our own and defend it. We would take the government out of the hands of the foreigner, who had no right to it, and who could exercise it only by force.

A war was being waged by England and her Allies in defence, it was said, of the freedom of small nationalities, to establish in such nations 'the reign of law based upon the consent of the governed'. We, too, proposed to establish in Ireland 'the reign of law based upon the consent of the governed'.

At the General Election of 1918 the Irish Parliamentary Party was repudiated by the Irish people by a majority of over 70 per cent. And they gave authority to their representatives to establish a National Government. The National Government was set up in face of great difficulties. Dáil Éireann came into being. British law was gradually superseded. Sinn Féin Courts were set up. Commissions were appointed to investigate and report upon the national resources of the country with a view to industrial revival. Land courts were established which settled long-standing disputes. Volunteer police were enrolled. (They were real police, to protect life and property, not military police and police spies to act with an enemy in attacks upon both.) A loan of £400,000 was raised. The local governing bodies of the country were directed, inspected, and controlled by Dáil Éireann. We established a bank to finance societies which wished to acquire land.

But these facts must be concealed.

At first the British were content to ridicule the new Government. Then, growing alarmed at its increasing authority, attempts were made to check its activities by wholesale political arrests.

The final phase of the struggle had begun.

In the first two years all violence was the work of the British armed forces who in their efforts at suppression murdered fifteen Irishmen and wounded nearly 400 men, women, and children. Meetings were broken up everywhere. National newspapers were suppressed. Over 1,000 men and women were arrested for political offences, usually of the most trivial nature. Seventy-seven of the national leaders were deported.

No police were killed during these two years. The only disorder and bloodshed were the work of the British forces.

These forces were kept here or sent here by the British Government to harass the development of Irish self-government. They were intended to break up the national organisation. They were intended to goad the people into armed resistance. Then they would have the excuse which they hoped for. Then they could use wholesale violence, and end up by the suppression of the national movement.

But they did not succeed.

In the municipal elections in January, 1920, the people answered afresh. In the rural elections in May and June, 1920, the people repeated their answer. The people supported their leaders and their policy by even larger majorities than the majorities given by the election in November, 1918.

The British Government now decided that a greater effort was needed. The moment had come for a final desperate campaign.

The leading London newspaper, *The Times*, declared in a leading article of November 1st, 1920, that it was 'now generally admitted' that a deliberate policy of violence had been 'conceived and sanctioned in advance by an influential section of the Cabinet'.

But to admit such a policy was impossible. It was necessary to conceal the real object of the Reign of Terror, for the destruction of the national movement, which was about to begin.

First, the ground had to be prepared. In August, 1920, a law was passed 'to restore law and order in Ireland'. This law in reality abolished all law in Ireland, and left the lives and property of the people defenceless before the British forces. It facilitated and protected—and was designed to facilitate and protect—those forces in the task they were about to undertake. Coroners' inquests were prohibited, so that no inquiry could be made into the acts of violence contemplated. National newspapers, that could not be trusted to conceal the facts and to publish only supplied information, were suppressed. Newspaper correspondents were threatened.

The ground prepared, special instruments had to be selected. 'It is', said the *London Times*, 'common knowledge that the Black and Tans were recruited from ex-soldiers for a rough and dangerous task'. This 'rough and dangerous task', which had been 'conceived and sanctioned' by the British Cabinet, was to be carried out under three headings. Certain leading men, and Irish Army officers, were to be murdered, their names being entered on a list 'for definite clearance'. All who worked for or supported the national movement were to be imprisoned, and the general population was to be terrorised into submission. A special newspaper, *The Weekly Summary*, was circulated amongst the Crownage to encourage them in their 'rough and dangerous task'. As an indication of its intention it invited them in an early number 'to make an appropriate hell' in Ireland.

Excuses, for the purpose of concealment, had to be invented. The public had to be prepared for the coming campaign. Mr. Lloyd George in a speech in Carnarvon, October 7, 1920, spoke of the Irish Republican Army as 'a real murder gang'. We began to hear of 'steps necessary to put down a murderous conspiracy'. 'We have got murder by the throat', said Mr. Lloyd George.

The murders were the legitimate acts of self-defence which had been forced upon the Irish people by English aggression. After two years of forbearance, we had begun to defend ourselves and the life of our nation. We did not initiate the war, nor were we allowed to select the battleground. When the British Government, as far as lay in its power, deprived the Irish people of arms, and employed every means to prevent them securing arms, and made it a criminal (in large areas a capital) offence to carry arms, and, at the same time, began and carried out a brutal and murderous campaign against them and against their National Government, they deprived themselves of any excuse for their violence and of any cause of complaint against the Irish people for the means they took for their protection.

For all the acts of violence committed in Ireland from 1916 to 1921 England, and England alone, is responsible. She willed the conflict and fixed the form it was to take.

On the Irish side it took the form of disarming the attackers. We took their arms and attacked their strongholds. We organised our army and met the armed patrols and military expeditions which were sent against us in the only possible way. We met them by an organised and bold guerilla warfare.

But this was not enough. If we were to stand up against the powerful military organisation arrayed against us something more was necessary than a guerilla war in which small bands of our warriors, aided by their knowledge of the country, attacked the larger forces of the enemy and reduced their numbers. England could always reinforce her army. She could replace every soldier that she lost.

But there were others indispensable for her purposes which were not so easily replaced. To paralyse the British machine it was necessary to strike at individuals. Without her spies England was helpless. It was only by means of their accumulated and accumulating knowledge that the British machine could operate.

Without their police throughout the country, how could they find the men they wanted? Without their criminal agents in the capital, how could they carry out that removal of the leaders that they considered essential for their victory? Spies are not so ready to step into the shoes of their departed confederates as are soldiers to fill up the front line in honourable battle. And even when the new spy stepped into the shoes of the old one, he could not step into the old one's knowledge.

The most potent of these spies were Irishmen enlisted in the British service and drawn from the small farmer and labourer class. Well might every Irishman at present ask himself if we were doing a wrong thing in getting rid of the system which was responsible for bringing these men into the ranks of the opponents of their own race.

We struck at individuals, and by so doing we cut their lines of communication and we shook their morale. And we conducted the conflict, difficult as it was, with the unequal terms imposed by the enemy, as far as possible, according to the rules of war. Only the British Government were attacked. Prisoners of war were treated honourably and considerately, and were released after they had been disarmed.

On the English side they waged a sort of war, but did not respect the laws and usages of war. When our soldiers fell into their hands they were murderers, to be dealt with by the bullet or the rope of the hangman. They were dealt with mostly by the bullet. Strangely enough, when it became law that prisoners attempting to escape should be shot, a considerable larger number of our prisoners attempted to escape than when the greatest penalty to be expected was recapture.

The fact was that when the men whose names were upon the list were identified at once, they were shot at once. When they were identified during a raid, they were taken away and shot while attempting to escape. Or they were brought to Dublin Castle or other place of detention and questioned under torture, and on refusing to give information were murdered because they revolted, seized arms, and attacked their guards.

For these murders no members of the British forces were brought to justice. The perpetrators were but enforcing the law—restoring law and order in Ireland...".

No matter how damaging the evidence, the prisoners were invariably acquitted. Necessarily so. They were but carrying out the duties which they had been specially hired at a very high rate of pay to execute.

To excuse the terrible campaign, the world began to hear of reprisals, the natural outbreaks of the rank and file, A campaign which could no longer be concealed had to be excused—a campaign in which sons were murdered before the eyes of their mothers—in which fathers were threatened with death and done to death because they would not tell the whereabouts of their sons—in which men were made to crawl along the streets, and were taken and stripped and flogged, and sent back naked to their homes—in which towns and villages and homes were burned, and women and children left shivering in the fields.

Excuses were necessary for such deeds, and we began to hear of some hitting back by the gallant men who are doing their duty in Ireland. The London Westminster Gazette of October 27, 1920, published a message from their own correspondent at Cork which gives an instance of the way in which these gallant men performed their duty: 'A motor lorry of uniformed men, with blackened faces, arrived in Lixane from the Ballybunion district. Before entering the village they pulled up at the house of a farmer named Patrick McElligott. His two sons were pulled outside the door in night attire in a downpour of rain, cruelly beaten with the butt ends of rifles and kicked. The party then proceeded to the house of a young man named Stephen Grady, where they broke in the door. Grady escaped in his night attire through the back window. Searchlights were turned on him, but he made good his escape through the fields. His assistant, named Nolan, was knocked unconscious on the floor with a rifle, and subsequently brought outside the door almost nude and a tub of water poured over him. The party then broke into the room where Miss Grady and her mother were sleeping, pulled Miss Grady out on the road and cut her hair'.

The account tells of the burning of the creamery and of further escapades of the gallant men on their return through the village.

An instance symbolic of the fight, of the devotion and self-sacrifice on the one side, and the brutish insensibility on the other, was the murder on October 25, 1920, of young Willie Gleeson, of Finaghy, Co. Tipperary. Officers of the British Army Intelligence Staff raided the house of his father, looking for another of his sons. Hearing his father threatened with death if he would not (or could not) disclose where his son was, Willie came from his bed and offered himself in place of his father. The offer was accepted, and he was taken out into the yard and shot dead.

On the same night the same party (presumably) murdered Michael Ryan, of Curraghduff, Co. Tipperary, in the presence of his sister. Ryan was lying ill in bed with pneumonia and the sister described the scene in which one officer held a candle over the bed to give better light to his comrade in carrying out the deed.

Such reprisals could not be explained as a severe hitting back, and a new excuse was forthcoming. They were suggested as a just retribution falling upon murderers.

Mr. Lloyd George was 'firmly convinced that the men who are suffering in Ireland are the men who are engaged in a murderous conspiracy'. At the London Guildhall he announced that the police were 'getting the right men'. As it became more and more difficult to conceal the truth the plea of unpremeditation was dropped, and the violence was explained as legitimate acts of self-defence.

But when the Terror, growing evermore violent, and, consequently, ever more ineffective, failed to break the spirit of the Irish people—failed as it was bound to fail—concealment was no longer possible, and the true explanation was blurted out when Mr. Lloyd George and Mr. Bonar Law declared that their acts were necessary to destroy the authority of the Irish National Government which 'has all the symbols and all the realities of government'.

When such a moment had been reached, there was only one course left open for the British Prime Minister—to invite the Irish leaders, the murderers, and heads of the murder gang to discuss with him terms of peace. The invitation was: 'To discuss terms of peace—to ascertain how the association of Ireland with the community of nations known as the British Empire may best be reconciled with Irish national aspirations'. We all accepted that invitation.

PARTITION ACT'S FAILURE

Unity as a Means to Full Freedom

While the Terror in Ireland was at its height the British Cabinet passed the Government of Ireland Act, 1920, better known as the Partition Act. It is not quite clear what was in the minds of the British Prime Minister and his Cabinet in passing this measure. Nobody representing any Irish constituency voted for it in the British Parliament.

Nationalist Ireland took advantage of its election machinery only to repudiate the Act and to secure a fresh mandate from the people. Otherwise the Act was completely ignored by us. In the Six Counties almost one-fourth of the candidates were returned in non-recognition of the Act, while Sir James Craig himself said, they (he and his friends) accepted the parliament conferred upon them by the Act only as 'a great sacrifice'.

The Act was probably intended for propaganda purposes. It might do to allay world criticism—to draw attention away from British violence for a month or two longer. At the end of that period Ireland would, it was hoped, have been terrorised into submission. That desired end gained, a chastened nation would accept the crumb of freedom offered by the Act. Britain, with her idea of the principles of self-determination satisfied, would be able to present a bold front again before the world.

There was, probably, too, an understanding with the Orange leaders. The act entrenched them (or appeared to) within the Six Counties. No doubt, both the

British and Orange leaders had it in mind that if a bigger settlement had ultimately to be made with Ireland, a position was secured from which they could bargain.

In any settlement the North-East was to be let down gently by the British Government. Pampered for so long they had learned to dictate to and to bully the nation to which they professed to be loyal. They must be treated with tact in regard to any change of British policy towards Ireland.

They had been very useful. When the Partition Act failed to achieve what was expected of it, and when the Terror failed, a real settlement with Ireland became inevitable. The North-East was now no longer useful to prevent Irish freedom, but she could be useful in another way. She could buttress Britain's determination that, while agreeing to our freedom, Ireland must remain associated with the British group of nations. Britain's reason for insisting upon this association is that she believes it necessary for her own national safety.

Were Britain to go to that, her maximum, it could be represented to us that the North-East would never acquiesce in more. It could be represented to them that in such a settlement they would be preserving that which they professed to have at heart, the sentimental tie with the Empire to which they were supposed to be attached.

North-East Ulster had been created and maintained not for her own advantage, but to uphold Britain's policy. Everything was done to divide the Irish people and to keep them apart. If we could be made to believe we were the enemies of each other, the real enemy would be overlooked. In this policy Britain has been completely successful. She petted a minority into becoming her agents with the double advantage of maintaining her policy and keeping us divided.

Long ago, setting chief against chief served its purpose in providing the necessary excuse for declaring our lands forfeited. Plantations by Britain's agents followed. The free men of Ireland became serfs on the lands of their fathers. Ireland, by these means, was converted into a British beef farm, and when by force of change and circumstances these means became outworn the good results were continued by setting religion against religion and then worker against worker.

If we were to be kept in subjection we must be kept apart. One creed, the creed of the minority, was selected to be used for the purpose of division and domination. 'A Protestant garrison was in possession of the land, magistracy, and power of the country, holding that property under the tenure of British power and supremacy, and ready at every instant to crush the rising of the conquered'. Manufactures had become discouraged and destroyed throughout the greater part of Ireland. This was the outcome of British jealousy, and was in accordance with Britain's settled policy towards Ireland.

A revival took place during Grattan's Parliament, partly owing to the war conditions prevailing, but also due to the protection given to industry by the Parliament. The good effect lived on for a little (only for a little) after the Union. A deep depression took place in agriculture at the beginning of the nineteenth century, and agriculture had become the sole industry of the Catholic population. This gave the opportunity to point to the supposed superior qualities of the Protestant industrial worker and to prejudice him still further against his Catholic countrymen.

But North-East Ulster had not flourished and could not flourish under a policy devised for English purposes. It has resulted only in a general decline in prosperity throughout the whole country, only in an uneconomic distribution of the disappearing wealth, only, by contrast, in an appearance of prosperity in one section of the people as compared with the other. The population of Ulster has decreased by one-third since the 'forties. It is true that the population of Belfast has increased in the last two generations, but the two counties of Antrim and Down, in which Belfast is situated, contain to-day fewer people than before the Famine of 1846-8. Emigration has steadily increased. The number of emigrants from Down and Antrim, including Belfast, has in the last ten years more than doubled that of the preceding ten years.

If there has been any gain in wealth in North-East Ulster as compared with the rest of Ireland, it is obvious that the wealth has not percolated through to the workers for their weal. They, too, like their poor countrymen in Connemara, have to seek better economic conditions in America and other countries.

Capitalism has come, not only to serve Britain's purpose by keeping the people divided, but, by setting worker against worker, it has profited by exploiting both. It works on religious prejudices. It represents to the Protestant workman any attempt by the Catholic workman to get improved conditions as the cloak for some insidious political game.

Such a policy—the policy of divide and rule, and the opportunity it gives for private economic oppression—could bring nothing but evil and hardship to the whole of Ireland.

If Britain had not maintained her interference and carried out her policy the planters would have become absorbed in the old Irish way. Protestant and Catholic would have learned to live side by side in amity and co-operation. Freedom would have come long ago. Prosperity would have come with it. Ireland would have taken her rightful place in the world, the place due to her by her natural advantages, the place due to her by the unique character of her people.

Who will not say that from Britain's policy it is the North-East which has suffered most? She has lost economically and spiritually. She has suffered in reputation by allowing herself to be used for anti-national purposes. She might have gained real wealth as a sturdy and independent section of the population. She exchanged it for a false ascendancy over her countrymen, which has brought her nothing but dishonour. A large portion of her fair province has lost all its native distinctiveness. It has become merely an inferior Lancashire. Who would visit Belfast or Lisburn or Lurgan to see the Irish people at home? That is the unhappy fate of the North-East. It is neither English nor Irish.

But what of the future? The North-East is about to get back into the pages of Irish history. Being no longer useful to prevent Irish freedom, forces of persuasion and pressure are embodied in the Treaty of Peace, which has been signed by the Irish and British Plenipotentiaries, to induce North-East Ulster to join in a united Ireland.

If they join in, the Six Counties will certainly have a generous measure of local autonomy. If they stay out, the decision of the Boundary Commission, arranged for in Clause 12, would be certain to deprive Ulster of Fermanagh and Tyrone.

Shorn of those counties, she would shrink into insignificance. The burdens and financial restrictions of the Partition Act will remain on North-East Ulster if she decides to stay out. No lightening of these burdens or restrictions can be effected by the English Parliament without the consent of Ireland. Thus, union is certain. The only question for North-East Ulster is—How soon?

And that how soon may depend largely upon us, upon ourselves of Nationalist Ireland. What if the Orangemen were to get new allies in place of the departing British?

The opposition of Mr. de Valera and his followers to the Treaty is already prejudicing the chances of unity. As the division in our own ranks has become more apparent, the attitude of Sir James Craig has hardened. The organised ruffianism of the North-East has broken out afresh. British troops have been hurried to Ulster. The evacuation has been suspended.

So long as there are British troops in Ireland so long will the Orangemen hold out. While they can look to Britain they will not turn towards the South. They are not giving up their ascendancy without a struggle. Any Irishman who creates and supports division amongst us is standing in the way of a united Ireland. While the Treaty is threatened the British will remain. While the British remain the North-East will keep apart. Just as the evil British policy of divide and rule is about to end for ever, we are threatened with a new division, jeopardising the hopes of Irish rule.

No geographical barrier could have succeeded in dividing Ireland. The four or six counties are not counties of Great Britain; they are counties of Ireland. While Britain governed Ireland the North-East could remain apart, she giving allegiance where we gave revolt. Once England surrenders her right to govern us (as she has done under the Treaty) she surrenders her power to divide us. With the British gone the incentive to division is gone.

The fact of union is too strong to be interfered with without the presence of the foreigner bent on dividing us. With the British gone the Orangeman loses that support which alone made him strong enough to keep his position of domination and isolation. Without British support he becomes what he is, one of a minority in the Irish Nation. His rights are the same as those of every Irishman, but he has no rights other than those.

But Britain leaves behind a formidable legacy in the partition of view. That is there and it has to be dealt with. It is for us, to whom union is an article of our national faith, to deal with it.

Once the British are gone, I believe we can win our countrymen to allegiance to our common country. Let us convince them of our good will towards them. The first way of doing this is unity among ourselves.

We have the task before us to impregnate our northern countrymen with the national outlook. We have a million Protestant Irishmen to convert out of our small population of four-and-a-half millions. Is not that incentive enough to cause us to join together to win a far greater victory than ever we got against the British? If we could have won that victory, there would have been no enemy to vanquish.

The tendency of the sentiment in the North-East, when not interfered with, was national, and in favour of freedom and unity. In that lies our hope.

It is this serious internal problem which argues for the attainment of the final steps of freedom by evolution rather than by force—to give time to the North-East to learn to revolve in the Irish orbit and to get out of the orbit of Great Britain— in fact, internal association with Ireland, external association with Great Britain.

In acquiescing in a peace which involved some postponement of the fulfilment of our national sentiment, by agreeing to some association of our Irish nation with the British nations, we went a long way towards meeting the sentiment of the North-East in its supposed attachment to Great Britain. With such association Britain will have no ground (nor power) for interference, and the North-East no genuine cause for complaint.

Had we been able to establish a Republic at once (we are all now agreed that

that was not possible), we would have had to use our resources to coerce North-East Ulster into submission. Will anyone contend that such coercion, if it had succeeded, would have had the lasting effects which conversion on our side and acquiescence on theirs will produce?

The North-East has to be nationalised. Union must come first, unity first as a means to full freedom. Our freedom then will be built on the unshakable foundation of a united people, united in every way, in economic co-operation, and in national outlook.

I have emphasised our desire for national unity above all things. I have stated our desire to win the North-East for Ireland. We mean to do our best in a peaceful way, and if we fail the fault will not be ours.

The freedom we have secured may unquestionably be incomplete. But it is the nearest approach to an absolutely independent and unified Ireland which we can achieve amongst ourselves at the present moment. It certainly gives us the best foothold for final progress.

Let us not waste our energies brooding over *the more we might have got.* Let us look upon *what we have got.* It is a measure of freedom with which we can make an actual, living Ireland when left to our selves. Let us realise that the free Ireland obtained by the Treaty is the greatest common measure of freedom obtainable now, and the most pregnant for future development.

The freedom we have got gives us scope for all that we can achieve by the most strenuous united effort of the present generation to rebuild Ireland.

Can we not all join together to save the Irish ideal—freedom and unity—and to make it a reality?

WHY BRITAIN SOUGHT IRISH PEACE

Her Failure to Subjugate Us

Making of Treaty

Peace with Ireland, or a good case for further, and what would undoubtedly have been more intensive, war, had become a necessity to the British Cabinet. Politicians of both the great historic parties in Britain had become united in the conviction that it was essential for the British to put themselves right with the world. Referring to the peace offer which Mr. Lloyd George, on behalf of his Cabinet and Parliament, had made to Mr. de Valera in July, 1921 (an offer which was not acceptable to the Irish people) Mr. Churchill said on September 24th at Dundee: 'This offer is put forward, not as the offer of a party government confronted by a formidable opposition and anxious to bargain for the Irish vote, but with the united sanction of both the historic parties in the State, and, indeed, all parties. It is a national offer'.

Yes. It was a national offer, representing the necessity of the British to clean their Irish slate. The Premiers of the Free Nations of the British Commonwealth were in England fresh from their people. They were able to express the views of their people. The Washington Conference was looming ahead. Mr. Lloyd George's Cabinet had its economic difficulties at home. Their relationships with foreign countries were growing increasingly unhappy, the recovery of world opinion was becoming—in fact, had become—indispensable. Ireland must be disposed of by means of a generous peace. If Ireland refused that settlement, we could be shown to be irreconcilables. Then, Britain would again have a free hand for whatever further actions were necessary 'to restore law and order' in a country that would not accept the responsibility of doing so for itself.

This movement by the British Cabinet did not indicate any real change of heart on the part of Britain towards Ireland. Any stirrings of conscience were felt only by a minority. This minority was largely the same minority that had been opposed to Britain's intervention in the European War. They were the peaceful group of the English people that is averse from bloodshed on principle, no matter for what purpose, or by whom, carried out. They were opposed to the killing we had to do in self-defence quite as much as they were opposed to the aggressive killing of our people by the various British agents sent here. These pacifists were almost without any political power and had very little popular support.

Peace had become necessary. It was not because Britain repented in the very middle of her Black and Tan terror. It was not because she could not subjugate us before world conscience was awakened and was able to make itself felt. 'The progress of the coercive attempts made by the Government have proved in a high degree disappointing', said Lord Birkenhead, frankly, in the British House of Lords on August 10.

What was the position on each side? Right was on our side. World sympathy was on our side (passive sympathy, largely). We had shown a mettle that was a fair indication of what we could do again if freedom were denied us. We were united; we had taken out of the hands of the enemy a good deal of government. We knew it would be no easy matter for him to recover his lost ground in that regard. We had prevented the enemy so far from defeating us.

We had not, however, succeeded in getting the government entirely into our hands, and we had not succeeded in beating the British out of Ireland, militarily.

We had unquestionably seriously interfered with their government, and we had prevented them from conquering us. That was the sum of our achievement.

We had reached in July last the high-water mark of what we could do in the way of economic and military resistance.

The British had a bad case. World sympathy was not with them. They had been oppressing us with murderous violence. At the same time they preached elsewhere the new world doctrine of government by consent of the governed. They, too, had reached their high-water mark. They had the power, the force, the armament, to re-conquer us, but they hesitated to exercise that power without getting a world mandate. But, though they had failed in their present attempt, their troops were still in possession of our island. At the time of the Truce they were, in fact, drafting additional and huge levies into Ireland. We had recognised our inability to beat the British out of Ireland, and we recognised what that inability meant. Writing in the weekly called *The Republic of Ireland* on 21st February last, Mr. Barton, a former member of the *Dáil* Cabinet, stated, that, before the Truce of July 11th it 'had become plain that it was physically impossible to secure Ireland's ideal of a completely isolated Republic otherwise than by driving the overwhelmingly superior British forces out of the country'.

We also recognised facts in regard to North-East Ulster. We clearly recognised that our national view was not shared by the majority in the four north-eastern counties. We knew that the majority had refused to give allegiance to an Irish Republic.

Before we entered the Conference we realised these facts among ourselves. We had abandoned, for the time being, the hope of achieving the ideal of independence under the Republican form.

It is clear, that the British on their side knew that unless we obtained a real, substantial freedom we would resist to the end at no matter what cost. But they also knew that they could make a generous settlement with us. They knew equally well that an offer of such a settlement would disarm the world criticism which could no longer be ignored. They knew they could do these two major things and still preserve the nations of the British Commonwealth from violent disruption.

The British believed (and still believe) that they need not, and could not, acquiesce in secession by us, that they need not, and could not, acquiesce in the establishment of a Republican government so close to their own shores. This would be regarded by them as a challenge—a defiance which would be a danger to the very safety of England herself. It would be presented in this light to the people of England. It would be represented as a disruption of the British Empire and would form a headline for other places. South Africa would be the first to follow our example and Britain's security and prestige would be gone. The British spokesmen believed they dared not agree to such a forcible breaking away. It would show not only their Empire to be intolerable, but themselves feeble and futile.

Looking forward through the operation of world forces to the development of freedom, it is certain that at some time acquiescence in the ultimate separation of the units will come. The American colonies of Britain got their freedom by a successful war. Canada, South Africa, and the other States of the British Commonwealth are approaching the same end by peaceful growth. In this Britain acquiesces. Separation by peaceful stages of evolution does not expose her and does not endanger her.

In judging the merits, in examining the details, of the peace we brought back these factors must be taken into consideration.

Before accepting the invitation sent by Mr. Lloyd George, on behalf of his Cabinet, to a Conference, we endeavoured to get an unfettered basis for that Conference. We did not succeed. It is true we reasserted our claim that our Plenipotentiaries could only enter such a Conference as the spokesmen of an independent Sovereign State. It is equally true that this claim was tacitly admitted by Britain in inviting us to negotiate at all, but the final phase was that we accepted the invitation 'to ascertain how the association of Ireland with the group of nations known as the British Commonwealth may best be reconciled with Irish national aspirations'.

The invitation opened up the questions, What is the position of the nations forming the British Commonwealth, and how could our national aspirations best be reconciled with associations with those nations? Legally and obsoletely the nations of the Commonwealth are in a position of subservience to Britain. Constitutionally they occupy to-day a position of freedom and of equality with their mother country.

Sir Robert Borden, in the Peace Treaty debate in the Canadian House on September 2nd, 1919, claimed for Canada a 'complete sovereignty'. This claim has never been challenged by Britain. It has, in fact, been allowed by Mr. Bonar Law. General Smuts, in a debate on the same subject in the Union House on September 10th, 1919, said: 'We have secured a position of absolute equality and freedom, not only among the other States of the Empire, but among the other nations of the world'.

In other words, the former dependent Dominions of the British Commonwealth are now free and secure in their freedom.

That position of freedom, and of freedom from interference, we have secured in the Treaty. The Irish Plenipotentiaries forced from the British Plenipotentiaries the admission that our status in association with the British nations would be the constitutional status of Canada. The definition of that status is the bedrock of the Treaty. It is the recognition of our right to freedom, and a freedom which shall not be challenged.

No arrangements afterwards mentioned in the Treaty, mutual arrangements agreed upon between our nation and the British nation, can interfere with or derogate from the position which the mention of that status gives us.

The Treaty is but the expression of the terms upon which the British were willing to evacuate—the written recognition of the freedom which such evacuation in itself secures.

We got in the Treaty the strongest guarantees of freedom and security that we could have got on paper, the strongest guarantees that we could have got in a Treaty between Great Britain and ourselves. The most realistic demonstration of the amount of real practical freedom acquired was the evacuation of the British troops and the demobilisation of the military police force. In place of the British troops we have our own army. In place of the Royal Irish Constabulary we are organising our own Civic Guard—our own People's Police Force.

These things are the things of substance; these things are the safe and genuine proof that the status secured by the Treaty is what we claim it to be. They are the plainest definition of our independence; they are the clearest recognition of our national rights. They give us the surest power to maintain both our independence and rights.

It is the evacuation by the British which gives us our freedom. The Treaty is the guarantee that that freedom shall not be violated. The States of the British Commonwealth have the advantage over us of distance. They have the security which that distance gives. They have their freedom. Whatever their nominal position in relation to Britain may be, they can maintain their freedom aided by their distance.

We have not the advantage of distance. Our nearness would be a disadvantage to us under whatever form, and in whatever circumstances, we had obtained our freedom (in case of a feeling of hostility between the two countries, the nearness is, of course, more than a disadvantage to us—it is a standing danger). It was the task of the Plenipotentiaries to overcome this geographical condition in so far as any written arrangement could overcome it.

We succeeded in securing a written recognition of our status. The Treaty clauses covering this constitute a pledge that we shall be as safe from interference as Canada is safe owing to the fact of her four thousand miles of geographical separation.

Our immunity can never be challenged without challenging the immunity of Canada. Having the same constitutional status as Canada, a violation of our freedom would be a challenge to the freedom of Canada. It gives a security which we ought not lightly to despise. No such security would have been reached by the external association aimed at in Document No. 2.

The Treaty is the signed agreement between Britain and ourselves. It is the recognition of our freedom by Britain, and it is the assurance that, having withdrawn her troops, Britain will not again attempt to interfere with that freedom. The free nations of the Commonwealth are witnesses to Britain's signature.

The occupation of our ports for defensive purposes might appear to be a challenge to our security. It is not. The naval facilities are granted by us to Britain, and are accepted by her in the Treaty as by one independent nation from another by international agreement. For any purpose of interference with us these facilities cannot be used.

At the best, these facilities are, the British say, necessary for the protection of the arteries of their economic and commercial life. At the worst, they are but the expression of the fact that we are at present militarily weaker. Negotiations, therefore treaties, are the expressions of adjustments, of agreements, between two nations as to the terms on which one side will acquiesce in the proposals of the other.

The arrangement provided in the Treaty in regard to North-East Ulster is also but a matter of agreement between ourselves and Britain. It is an agreement by us that we will deal with the difficulty created by Britain. It is an assurance that we will give the North-East certain facilities to enable them to take their place willingly in the Irish Nation.

The maligned Treaty Oath was a further admission wrung from Britain of the real relationship between the British nations. Canada and South Africa continue to swear allegiance to King George, his heirs, successors, etc. They give an oath in keeping with their obsolete position of independence, but out of keeping with their actual position of freedom. Mr. de Valera's alternative oath recognised the

King of England as head of the Association—a head inferring subordinates. The Treaty Oath, however, expresses faithfulness only as symbolical of that association, and is, therefore, really a declaration that each party will be faithful to the compact.

The Irish Plenipotentiaries have been described as 'incompetent amateurs'. They were, it is said, cajoled and tricked by the wily and experienced British Prime Minister. By means of the fight we put up in the war, by means of the fight we put up in the negotiations, we got the British to evacuate our country. Not only to evacuate it militarily, but to evacuate it socially and economically as well. In addition, we got from the British a signed undertaking to respect the freedom which these evacuations give us.

We acquiesced, in return, to be associated with the British Commonwealth of Nations for certain international purposes. We granted to Britain certain naval facilities.

There is the bargain. It is for the Irish and for our friends the world over to judge whether the 'incompetent amateurs' who formed the Irish delegation of Plenipotentiaries forgot their country in making it. If our national aspirations could only have been expressed by the full Republican ideal, then they were not, and never could be, reconciled with what was understood by 'association with the group of nations known as the British Empire'.

By accepting that invitation we agreed, however some may now deceive themselves and attempt to deceive others, that we would acquiesce in some association. In return for that acquiescence we expected something tangible—evacuation, abandonment of British aggression. If we had been martially victorious over Britain there would have been no question of such acquiescence.

Now, if that is so, and it is so, the surrender of some national sentiment was for the time unavoidable. The British Empire, the British Commonwealth, or the British League of Free Nations—it does not matter what name you call it—is what it is. It is what it is, with all its trappings of feudalism, its symbols of monarchy, its feudal phraseology, its obsolete oaths of allegiance, its King a figurehead having no individual power as King, maintaining the unhealthy atmosphere of mediaeval subservience translated into modern snobbery. All this is doubly offensive to us, offensive to our Gaelic instincts of social equality which recognises only an aristocracy of the mind, and offensive from the memories of hundreds of years of tyranny carried out in the name of the British King.

Those who could not, or who would not, look these facts in the face blame us now, and more than blame us. They find fault with us that, in agreeing to some kind of association of our nation with the British nations, we were not able, by the touch of a magic wand, to get rid of all the language of Empire. That is not a fair attitude. We like that language no more, perhaps less, than do those who wish to make us responsible for its preservation. It is Britain's affair, not ours, that she cares to preserve these prevarications.

Let us look to what we have undoubtedly gained and not to what we might have gained. Let us see how the maximum value can be realised from that gain. If we would only put away dreams, and face realities, nearly all the things that count we have now for our country.

What we want is that Ireland shall be Ireland in spirit as well as in name. It is not any verbiage about sovereignty which can assure our power to shape our destinies. It is to grasp everything which is of benefit to us, to manage these things for ourselves, to get rid of the unIrish atmosphere and influence, to make our government and restore our national life on the lines which suit our national character and our national requirements best. It is now only fratricidal strife which can prevent us from making the Gaelic Ireland which is our goal.

The test of the Government we want is whether it conforms with Irish tradition and national character? Whether it will suit us and enable us to live socially and prosper? Whether we can achieve something which our old free Irish democratic life would have developed into?

We have shaken off the foreign domination which prevented us from living our own life in our own way. We are now free to do this. It depends on ourselves alone whether we can do it.

DISTINCTIVE CULTURE

Ancient Irish Civilization

Glories of the Past

It was not only by the British armed occupation that Ireland was subdued. It was by means of the destruction, after great effort, of our Gaelic civilization. This destruction brought upon us the loss almost of nationality itself. For the last 100 years or more Ireland has been a nation in little more than in name.

Britain wanted us for her own economic ends, as well as to satisfy her love of conquest. It was found, however, that Ireland was not an easy country to conquer, nor to use for the purposes for which conquests are made. We had a native culture. We had a social system of our own. We had an economic organisation. We had a code of laws which fitted us.

These were such in their beauty, their honesty, their recognition of right and justice, and in their strength, that foreigners coming to our island brought with them nothing of like attractiveness to replace them. These foreigners accepted Irish civilization, forgot their own, and eagerly became absorbed into the Irish race. Ireland, unlike Britain, had never become a part of the Roman Empire. Even if the Romans had invaded Ireland, and had been able to get a foothold, it is not probable that they would have succeeded in imposing their form of government. At that time our native civilization had become well advanced. It had advanced far past the primitive social state of the Britons and of other of the North European peoples.

And it had, through its democratic basis, which would have been strengthened and adapted as time went on, a health and permanence which would have enabled it to withstand the rivalry of the autocratic government of Rome, which always had in it the seeds of decay.

The Romans invaded Britain and imposed their government till it was destroyed by fresh invaders. And the history of England, unlike the history of Ireland, was one in which each new invasion altered the social polity of the people. Foreigners were not absorbed as in Ireland. England was affected by every fresh incursion, and English civilization to-day is the reflection of such changes.

The Roman armies did not come to Ireland. But Ireland was known to the merchants of the Empire, who brought with them not only commerce but art and culture. Ireland took from them what was of advantage, and our civilization went on growing in strength and harmony. It grew more and more to fit the Irish people, and became the expression of them. It could never have been destroyed except by deliberate uprooting aided by military violence.

The Irish social and economic system was democratic. It was simple and harmonious. The people had security in their rights, and just law. And, suited to them, their economic life progressed smoothly. Our people had leisure for the things in which they took delight. They had leisure for the cultivation of the mind, by the study of art, literature, and the traditions. They developed character and bodily strength by acquiring skill in military exercise and in the national games.

The pertinacity of Irish civilization was due to the democratic basis of its economic system, and the aristocracy of its culture.

It was the reverse of Roman civilization in which the State was held together by a central authority, controlling and defending it, the people being left to themselves in all social and intellectual matters. Highly organised, Roman civilization was powerful, especially for subduing and dominating other races, for a time. But not being rooted in the interests and respect of the people themselves, it could not survive.

Gaelic civilization was quite different. The people of the whole nation were united, not by material forces, but by spiritual ones. Their unity was not of any military solidarity. It came from sharing the same traditions. It came from honouring the same heroes, from inheriting the same literature, from willing obedience to the same law, the law which was their own law and reverenced by them.

They never exalted a central authority. Economically they were divided up into a number of larger and smaller units. Spiritually and socially they were one people.

Each community was independent and complete within its own boundaries. The land belonged to the people. It was held for the people by the Chief of the Clan. He was their trustee. He secured his position by the will of the people only. His successor was elected by the people.

The privileges and duties of the chiefs, doctors, lawyers, bards, were the same throughout the country. The schools were linked together in a national system. The bards and historians travelled from one community to another. The schools for the study of law, medicine, history, military skill, belonged to the whole nation, and were frequented by those who were chosen by each community to be their scholars.

The love of learning and of military skill was the tradition of the whole people. They honoured not kings nor chiefs as kings and chiefs, but their heroes and their great men. Their men of high learning ranked with the kings and sat beside them in equality at the high table.

It was customary for all the people to assemble together on fixed occasions to hear the law expounded and the old heroic tales recited. The people themselves contributed. They competed with each other in the games. These assemblies were the expression of our Irish civilization and one of the means by which it was preserved.

Thus Ireland was a country made up of a large number of economically independent units. But in the things of the mind and spirit the nation was one.

This democratic social polity, with the exaltation of the things of the mind and character, are the essence of ancient Irish civilization, and must provide the keynote for the new.

It suited our character and genius. While we were able to preserve it no outside enemy had any power against us. While it survived our subjection was impossible. But our invaders learned its strength and set out to destroy it.

English civilization, while it may suit the English people, could only be alien to us. It is English civilization, fashioned out of their history. For us it is a misfit. It is a garment, not something within us. We are mean, clumsy, and ungraceful, wearing it. It exposes all our defects while giving us no scope to display our good qualities. Our external and internal life has become the expression of its unfitness. The Gaelic soul of the Irish people still lives. In itself it is indestructible. But its qualities are hidden, besmirched, by that which has been imposed upon us, just as the fine, splendid surface of Ireland is besmirched by our towns and villages—hideous medleys of contemptible dwellings and mean shops and squalid public-houses, not as they should be in material fitness, the beautiful human expressions of what our God-given country is.

It is only in the remote corners of Ireland in the South and West and North-West that any trace of the old Irish civilization is met with now. To those places the social side of anglicisation was never able very easily to penetrate. To-day it is only in those places that any native beauty and grace in Irish life survive. And these are the poorest parts of our country!

In the island of Achill, impoverished as the people are, hard as their lives are, difficult as the struggle for existence is, the outward aspect is a pageant. One may see processions of young women riding down on the island ponies to collect sand from the seashore, or gathering in the turf, dressed in their shawls and in their brilliantly-coloured skirts made of material spun, woven, and dyed, by themselves, as it has been spun, woven, and dyed, for over a thousand years. Their cottages also are little changed. They remain simple and picturesque. It is only in such places that one gets a glimpse of what Ireland may become again, when the beauty may be something more than a pageant, will be the outward sign of a prosperous and happy Gaelic life.

Our internal life too has become the expression of the misfit of English civilization. With all their natural intelligence, the horizon of many of our people has become bounded by the daily newspaper, the public-house, and the racecourse. English civilization made us into the stage Irishman, hardly a caricature.

They destroyed our language, all but destroyed it, and in giving us their own they cursed us so that we have become its slaves. Its words seem with us almost an end in themselves, and not as they should be, the medium for expressing our thoughts.

We have now won the first victory. We have secured the departure of the enemy who imposed upon us that by which we were debased, and by means of which he kept us in subjection. We only succeeded after we had begun to get back our Irish ways, after we had made a serious effort to speak our own language, after we had striven again to govern ourselves. We can only keep out the enemy, and all other enemies, by completing that task.

We are now free in name. The extent to which we become free in fact and secure our freedom will be the extent to which we become Gaels again. It is a hard task. The machine of the British armed force, which tried to crush us, we could see with our physical eyes. We could touch it. We could put our physical strength against it. We could see their agents in uniform and under arms. We could see their tanks and armoured cars.

But the spiritual machine which has been mutilating us, destroying our customs, and our independent life, is not so easy to discern. We have to seek it out with the eyes of our mind. We have to put against it the whole weight of our united spiritual strength. And it has become so familiar, how are we to recognise it?

We cannot, perhaps. But we can do something else. We can replace it. We can fill our minds with Gaelic ideas, and our lives with Gaelic customs, until there is no room for any other.

It is not any international association of our nation with the British nations which is going to hinder us in that task. It lies in our own hands. Upon us will rest the praise or blame of the real freedom we make for ourselves or the absence of it.

The survival of some connection with our former enemy, since it has no power to chain us, should act as a useful irritant. It should be a continual reminder of how near we came to being, indeed, a British nation. No one now has any power to make us that but ourselves alone.

We have to build up a new civilization on the foundations of the old. And it is not the leaders of the Irish people who can do it for the people. They can but point the way. They can but do their best to establish a reign of justice and of law and order which will enable the people to do it for themselves.

It is not to political leaders our people must look, but to themselves. Leaders are but individuals, and individuals are imperfect, liable to error and weakness. The strength of the nation will be the strength of the spirit of the whole people. We must have a political, economic, and social system in accordance with our national character.

It must be a system in which our material, intellectual, and spiritual needs and tastes will find expression and satisfaction. We shall then grow to be in ourselves and in what we produce, and in the villages, towns, and cities in which we live, and in our homes, an expression of the light which is within us, as now we are in nearly all those things an indication of the darkness which has enveloped us for so long.

Economically we must be democratic, as in the past. The right of all the people must be secure. The people must become again 'the guardians of their law and of their land'. Each must be free to reap the full reward of his labour. Monopoly must not be allowed to deprive anyone of that right.

Neither, through the existence of monopoly, must capital be allowed to be an evil. It must not be allowed to draw away all the fruits of labour to itself. It must fulfil its proper function of being the means by which are brought forth fresh and fuller fruits for the benefit of all.

With real democracy in our economic life, country districts would become again living centres. The people would again be co-operating in industry, and co-operating and competing in pleasure and in culture. Our countrysides would cease to be the torpid deserts they are now, giving the means of existence and nothing more.

Our Government must be democratic in more than in name. It must be the expression of the people's wishes. It must carry out for them all, and only, what is needed to be done for the people as a whole. It must not interfere with what the people can do for themselves in their own centres. We must not have State Departments headed by a politician whose only qualification is that he has climbed to a certain rung in the political ladder.

The biggest task will be the restoration of the language. How can we express our most subtle thoughts and finest feelings in a foreign tongue? Irish will scarcely be our language in this generation, not even perhaps in the next. But until we have it again on our tongues and in our minds we are not free, and we will produce no immortal literature.

Our music and our art and literature must be in the lives of the people themselves, not as in England, the luxury of the few. England has produced some historians, many great poets, and a few great artists, but they are the treasures of the cultured minority and have no place in the lives of the main body of the English people.

Our poets and artists will be inspired in the stimulating air of freedom to be something more than the mere producers of verse and painters of pictures. They will teach us, by their vision, the noble race we may become, expressed in their poetry and their pictures. They will inspire us to live as Irish men and Irish women should. They have to show us the way, and the people will then in their turn become the inspiration of the poets and artists of the future Gaelic Ireland.

Our civilization will be glorious or the reverse, according to the character of the people. And the work we produce will be the expression of what we are. Our external life has become the expression of all we have been deprived of—something shapeless, ugly, without native life. But the spark of native life is still there and can be fanned into flame.

What we have before us is the great work of building up our nation. No soft road—a hard road, but inspiring and exalting. Irish art and Irish customs must be revived, and must be carried out by the people themselves, helped by a central Government, not controlled and managed by it; helped by departments of music, art, national painting, etc., with local centres connected with them.

The commercialising of these things—art, literature, music, the drama—as is done in other countries, must be discouraged. Everybody being able to contribute, we would have a skilled audience, criticising and appreciating, and not only, as in England, paying for seats to hear famous performers, but for real appreciative enjoyment and education.

Our national education must provide a balance of the competing elements—the real education of the faculties, and storing the mind with the best thoughts of the great men of our own and other nations. And there must be education by special training for trades and professions for the purpose of scientific eminence in medicine, law, agriculture, and commerce.

And, as fit habitations for healthy minds, we must have healthy bodies. We shall have these by becoming again skilled in military prowess and skilled in our Gaelic games, which develop strength and nerve and muscle. They teach us resource, courage, and co-operation. These games provide for our civil life those qualities of ingenuity and daring which military training teaches for the purposes of war.

Our army, if it exists for honourable purposes only, will draw to it honourable men. It will call to it the best men of our race—men of skill and culture. It will not be recruited as so many modern armies are, from those who are industrially useless.

This will certainly be so, for our army will only exist for the defence of our liberties, and of our people in the exercise of their liberties. An Irish army can never be used for the ignoble purpose of invasion, subjugation, and exploitation.

But it is not only upon our army that our security will depend. It will depend more upon the extent to which we make ourselves invulnerable by having a civilization which is indestructible. That civilization will only be indestructible by being enthroned in the lives of the people, and having its foundation resting on right, honesty, and justice.

Our army will be but secondary in maintaining our security. Its strength will be but the strength of real resistance—the extent to which we build up within ourselves what can never be invaded and what can never be destroyed—the extent to which we make strong the spirit of the Irish Nation.

We are a small nation. Our military strength in proportion to the mighty armaments of modern nations can never be considerable. Our strength as a nation will depend upon our economic freedom, and upon our moral and intellectual force. In these we can become a shining light in the world.

BUILDING UP IRELAND

Resources to be Developed

Mr. de Valera, in a speech he made on February 19, warned the people of Ireland against a life of ease, against living practically 'the life of the beasts', which, he fears, they may be tempted to do in Ireland under the Free State.

The chance that materialism will take possession of the Irish people is no more likely in a free Ireland under the Free State than it would be in a free Ireland under a Republican or any other form of government. It is in the hands of the Irish people themselves.

In the ancient days of Gaelic civilization the people were prosperous and they were not materialists. They were one of the most spiritual and one of the most intellectual peoples in Europe. When Ireland was swept by destitution and famine the spirit of the Irish people came most nearly to extinction. It was with the improved economic conditions of the last twenty years or more that it has reawakened. The insistent needs of the body more adequately satisfied, the people regained desire once more to reach out to the higher things in which the spirit finds its satisfaction. What we hope for in the new Ireland is to have such material welfare as will give the Irish spirit that freedom. We want such widely diffused prosperity that the Irish people will not be crushed by destitution into living practically 'the lives of the beasts'.

They were so crushed during the British occupation that they were described as being 'without the comforts of an English sow'. Neither must they be obliged, owing to unsound economic conditions, to spend all their powers of both mind and body in an effort to satisfy the bodily needs alone. The uses of wealth are to provide good health, comfort, moderate luxury, and to give the freedom which comes from the possession of these things.

Our object in building up the country economically must not be lost sight of. That object is not to be able to boast of enormous wealth or of a great volume of trade, for their own sake. It is not to see our country covered with smoking chimneys and factories. It is not to show a great national balance-sheet, nor to point to a people producing wealth with the self-obliteration of a hive of bees.

The real riches of the Irish nation will be the men and women of the Irish nation, the extent to which they are rich in body and mind and character.

What we want is the opportunity for everyone to be able to produce sufficient wealth to ensure these advantages for themselves. That such wealth can be produced in Ireland there can be no doubt: 'For the island is so endowed with so many dowries of nature, considering the fruitfulness of the soil, the ports, the rivers, the fishings, and especially the race and generation of men, valiant, hard, and active, as it is not easy to find such a confluence of commodities'. Such was the impression made upon a visitor who came long ago to our island. We have now the opportunities to make our land indeed fruitful, to work up our natural resources, to bring prosperity for all our people.

If our national economy is put on a sound footing from the beginning it will, in the new Ireland, be possible for our people to provide themselves with the ordinary requirements of decent living. It will be possible for each to have sufficient food, a good home in which to live in fair comfort and contentment. We shall be able to give our children bodily and mental health; and our people will be able to secure themselves against the inevitable times of sickness and old age.

That must be our object. What we must aim at is the building up of a sound economic life in which great discrepancies cannot occur. We must not have the destitution of poverty at one end, and at the other an excess of riches in the possession of a few individuals, beyond what they can spend with satisfaction and justification.

Millionaires can spend their surplus wealth bestowing libraries broadcast upon the world. But who will say that the benefits accruing could compare with those arising from a condition of things in which the people themselves everywhere, in the city, town, and village, were prosperous enough to buy their own books and to put together their own local libraries in which they could take a personal interest and acquire knowledge in proportion to that interest?

The growing wealth of Ireland will, we hope, be diffused through all our people, all sharing in the growing prosperity, each receiving according to what each contributes in the making of that prosperity, so that the weal of all is assured.

How are we to increase the wealth of Ireland and ensure that all producing it shall share in it? That is the question which will be engaging the minds of our people, and will engage the attention of the new Government.

The keynote to the economic revival must be development of Irish resources by Irish capital for the benefit of the Irish consumer in such a way that the people have steady work at just remuneration and their own share of control.

How are we to develop Irish resources? The earth is our bountiful mother. Upon free access to it depends not only agriculture, but all other trades and industries. Land must be freely available. Agriculture, our main industry, must be improved and developed. Our existing industries must be given opportunities to expand. Conditions must be created which will make it possible for new ones to arise. Means of transit must be extended and cheapened. Our harbours must be developed. Our water-power must be utilised; our mineral resources must be exploited.

Foreign trade must be stimulated by making facilities for the transport and marketing of Irish goods abroad and foreign goods in Ireland. Investors must be urged and encouraged to invest Irish capital in Irish concerns. Taxation, where it hinders, must be adjusted, and must be imposed where the burden will fall lightest and can best be borne, and where it will encourage rather than discourage industry.

We have now in Ireland, owing to the restrictions put upon emigration during the European war, a larger population of young men and women than we have had for a great many years. For their own sake and to maintain the strength of the nation room must and can be found for them.

Agriculture is, and is likely to continue to be, our chief source of wealth. If room is to be found for our growing population, land must be freely available. Land is not freely available in Ireland. Thousands of acres of the best land lie idle or are occupied as ranches or form part of extensive private estates.

Side by side with this condition there are thousands of our people who are unable to get land on which to keep a cow or even to provide themselves and their families with vegetables.

If the ranches can be broken up, if we can get the land back again into the hands of our people, there will be plenty of employment and a great increase in the national wealth.

If land could be obtained more cheaply in town and country the housing problem would not present so acute a problem. There are large areas unoccupied in towns and cities as well as in country districts. When the Convention sat in 1917 it was found that in urban areas alone, 67,000 houses were urgently needed. The figure must at the present moment be considerably higher. To ease the immediate situation, the Provisional Government has announced a grant to enable a considerable number of houses to be built. This grant, although seemingly large, is simply a recognition of the existence of the problem.

For those who intend to engage in agriculture we require specialised education. Agriculture is in these days a highly technical industry. We have the experiences of countries like Holland, Germany, Denmark to guide us. Scientific methods of farming and stock-raising must be introduced. We must have the study of specialised chemistry to aid us, as it does our foreign competitors in the countries I have named. We must establish industries arising directly out of agriculture, industries for the utilisation of the by-products of the land—bones, bristles, hides for the production of soda, glue, and other valuable substances.

With plenty of land available at an economic rent or price such industries can be established throughout the country districts, opening up new opportunities for employment.

Up to the sixteenth century Ireland possessed a colonial trade equal to England's. It was destroyed by the jealousy of English ship-owners and manufacturers, and, by means of the Navigation Laws, England swept Ireland's commerce off the seas. It is true that these Navigation Laws were afterwards removed. But the removal found the Irish capital which might have restored our ruined commerce drained away from the country by the absence of opportunities for utilising it, or by absentee landlordism, or in other ways. The development of industry in the new Ireland should be on lines which exclude monopoly profits. The product of industry would thus be left sufficiently free to supply good wages to those employed in it. The system should be on co-operative lines rather than on the old commercial capitalistic lines of the huge joint stock companies. At the same time I think we shall safely avoid State Socialism, which has nothing to commend it in a country like Ireland, and, in any case, is monopoly of another kind.

Given favourable conditions, there is a successful future for dressed meat industries on the lines of the huge co-operative industry started in Wexford; while there are many opportunities for the extension of dairying and cheese-making.

The industries we possess are nearly all capable of expansion. We can improve and extend all the following:

Brewing and distilling.

Manufacture of tobacco.

Woollen and linen industry.

Manufacture of hosiery and underclothing.

Rope and twine industry.

Manufacture of boots and shoes, saddlery, and all kinds of leather articles.

Production of hardware and agricultural machinery.

Production and curing of fish.

Of manufactured articles £48,000,000 worth are imported into Ireland yearly. A large part of these could be produced more economically at home. If land were procurable abundantly and cheaply it would be necessary also that capital should be forthcoming to get suitable sites for factories, a more easily obtained supply of power, an improvement, increase, and cheapening of the means of transport.

There are facilities for producing an enormous variety of products both for the home and foreign markets, if factories could be established. These should, as far as possible, be dispersed about the country instead of being concentrated in a few areas. This disposal will not only have the effect of avoiding congestion, but will incidentally improve the status and earnings of the country population and will enlarge their horizon.

I am not advocating the establishment of an industrial system as other countries know industrialism. If we are to survive as a distinct and free nation, industrial development must be on the general lines I am following. Whatever our solution of the question may be, we all realise that the industrial *status quo* is imperfect. However we may differ in outlook, politically or socially, it is recognised that one of the most pressing needs—if not the most pressing—is the question of labour in relation to industry, and it is consequently vitally necessary for the development of our resources that the position of employers and employees should rest on the best possible foundation.

And with this question of labour and industry is interwoven the question of land. It is no less important to have our foundations secure here. In the development of Ireland the land question presents itself under four main headings:

1) The completion of purchase of tenanted lands;

2) The extension and increase of powers of purchase of untenanted lands;

3) The question of congestion in rural districts;

4) The utilisation of lands unoccupied or withheld in urban areas.

For the purpose of such development Ireland has three great natural resources. Our coal deposits are by no means inconsiderable. The bogs of Ireland are estimated as having 500,000 million tons of peat fuel. Water-power is concentrated in her 237 rivers and 180 lakes. The huge Lough Corrib system could be utilised, for instance, to work the granite in the neighbourhood of Galway. In the opinion of experts, reporting to the Committee on the Water-Power Resources of Ireland, from the Irish lakes and rivers a total of 500,000 h.p. is capable of being developed.

The magnitude of this is more readily seen if it is appreciated that to raise this power in steam would require 7,500,000 tons of coal. With the present price of coal it should be a commercial proposition to develop our water-power as against steam, even though it did not take the place of steam-power entirely.

Schemes have been worked out to utilise the water-power of the Shannon, the Erne, the Bann, and the Liffey. It is probable that the Liffey and the Bann, being closely connected with industrial centres, can be dealt with at once. With unified control and direction, various sources of water-power could be arranged in large stations for centralised industries, and the energy could be redistributed to provide light and heat for the neighbouring towns and villages.

That the advantages of our water-power are not lost on some of the keenest minds of the day is shown by the following extract from a speech made by Lord Northcliffe on St. Patrick's Day, 1917: "The growth of the population of Great Britain has been largely due to manufactures based on the great asset, black coal. Ireland has none of the coal which has made England rich, but she possesses in her mighty rivers white coal of which millions of horse-power are being lost to Ireland every year ... I can see in the future very plainly prosperous cities, old and new, fed by the greatest river in the United Kingdom—the Shannon. I should like to read recent experts' reports on the Moy, the Suir, and the Lee."

The development of this white power will also enable the means of communication and transport by rail and road to be cheapened and extended. And there is an urgent need for cheap transit. Railway rates and shipping rates are so high that, to take one example, the cost of transit is prohibitive to the Irish fish trade.

While the Irish seas are teeming with fish, we have the Dublin market depending upon the English market for its supplies. The export of Irish fish is decreasing, and the fishing industry is neither the source of remuneration it should be to those engaged in it, nor the source of profit it could be to the country. To facilitate the transport of agricultural produce and commodities generally, a complete system of ways of communication must be established. The extension and unifying of our railways, linking up ocean ports and fishing harbours with the interior, is essential. This system will be worked in connection with our inland waterways, and will be supplemented by a motor-lorry service on our roads—and these also must be greatly improved.

Our harbours must be developed. Ireland occupies a unique geographical position. She is the stepping-stone between the Old World and the New. She should, therefore, become a great exchange mart between Europe and America. With Galway harbour improved and developed so as to receive American liners, passengers could land in Europe one or two days earlier than by disembarking at Liverpool.

The port and docks of Dublin are already making arrangements for a great increase in the volume of trade which is expected with the establishment of an Irish Government in Dublin. They are improving the port. They have schemes for providing deep water berthage for the largest ships afloat.

Soon the port of Dublin will be fitted in every way to receive and deal with all the trade which may be expected with our growing prosperity. The Board is also reclaiming land at the mouth of the Liffey, and soon some sixty acres will be available as a building site. This land is splendidly situated for commercial purposes.

It will be important to create efficient machinery for the economic marketing of Irish goods. A first step in this direction is the establishment of a clearing house in Dublin or the most convenient centre. It would form a link between a network of channels throughout Ireland through which goods could be transmitted, connecting with another network reaching out to all our markets abroad. It would examine and take delivery of goods going out and coming in, dealing with the financial business for both sides.

Such a concern would require capital and able and experienced management. With such, its success should be assured. It would be invaluable in helping our home and foreign trade. And with improved means of transit in Ireland, and an increase in the number of direct shipping routes, facilities would be in existence to make it operate successfully. It is not difficult to see the advantages of such a house. On the one hand it would be closely associated in location and business working with a central railway station where the important trunk lines converged, and on the other conveniently situated in relation to the National Customs House.

The mineral resources of Ireland have never been properly tapped. An Irish Government will not neglect this important source of wealth. The development of mines and minerals will be on national lines, and under national direction. This will prevent the monopoly by private individuals of what are purely national resources belonging to all the people of the nation. The profits from all these national enterprises—the working of mines, development of water-power, etc.—

will belong to the nation for the advantage of the whole nation. But Irish men and women as private individuals must do their share to increase the prosperity of the country. Business cannot succeed without capital. Millions of Irish money are lying idle in banks. The deposits in Irish joint stock banks increased in the aggregate by £7,318,000 during the half-year ended December 31, 1921. At that date the total of deposits and cash balances in the Irish banks was £194,391,000, to which in addition there was a sum of almost £14,000,000 in the Post Office Savings Bank. If Irish money were invested in Irish industries, to assist existing ones, and to finance new enterprises, there would be an enormous development of Irish commerce.

The Irish people have a large amount of capital invested abroad. With scope for our energies, with restoration of confidence, the inevitable tendency will be towards return of this capital to Ireland. It will then flow in its proper channel. It will be used for opening up new and promising fields in this country. Ireland will provide splendid opportunities for the investment of Irish capital, and it is for the Irish people to take advantage of these opportunities.

If they do not, investors and exploiters from outside will come in to reap the rich profits which are to be made. And, what is worse still, they will bring with them all the evils that we want to avoid in the new Ireland.

We shall hope to see in Ireland industrial conciliation and arbitration taking the place of strikes, and the workers sharing in the ownership and management of businesses. A prosperous Ireland will mean a united Ireland. With equitable taxation and flourishing trade our North-East countrymen will need no persuasion to come in and share in the healthy economic life of the country.

FREEDOM WITHIN OUR GRASP

For Ourselves to Achieve It

Work of Gaelic League and *Sinn Féin*

The freedom which has been won is the fruit of the national efforts of this generation and of preceding ones, and to judge the merits of that fruit it is necessary to recall those efforts. It is necessary to look back, and to see each one arising out of each loss which the nation sustained.

We see them working along their separate but converging lines—some mere trickling streams, others broad tributaries, but all which had sufficient strength and right direction reaching, becoming merged in, and swelling the volume of the river which flows on to freedom.

Up to the Union English interference in Ireland had succeeded only in its military and economic oppression. The national spirit survived. The country had been disarmed after the Treaty of Limerick. The land of Ireland had been confiscated. Native industry and commerce were attacked and had been crippled or destroyed, but Gaelic nationality lived on. The people spoke their own language, preserved their Gaelic customs and ways of life, and remained united in their common traditions. They had no inducement to look outside their own country, and entrenched behind their language and their national traditions, they kept their social life intact. Ireland was still the Ireland of the wholly distinctive Irish people.

The efforts of resistance made by the nation were the expressions of what had been robbed from the nation. There were military uprisings to resist some new oppression, but these were also the unconscious protests of a nation's right to defend itself by force of arms. There were also peaceful attempts to recover economic, or political, or religious freedom through the Parliament in Dublin.

With the Union came upheaval. The scene of government was transferred to England. The garrison which was becoming Gaelicised towards the end of the eighteenth century, turned away from Ireland with the destruction of the Dublin Parliament, and made London their Capital.

With Catholic Emancipation and the right to have representatives of the Irish people to sit in the foreign parliament, the national spirit was at last invaded. People began to look abroad. The anglicisation of Ireland had begun.

The English language became the language of education and fashion. It penetrated slowly at first. It was aided by the National Schools. In those schools it was the only medium of education for a people who were still Gaelic-speaking.

Side by side with this peaceful penetration, the Irish language decayed, and when the people had adopted a new language and had come to look to England for Government, they learned to see in English customs and English culture the models upon which to fashion their own.

The gifts wrung for Ireland (always wrung by agitation more or less violent in Ireland itself, and never as a result of the oratory of the Irish representatives in the British Parliament), Catholic Emancipation, Land Acts, Local Government, where not actually destructive in themselves of the Gaelic social economic system, helped in the denationalisation process.

These things undoubtedly brought ameliorative changes, but the people got into the habit of looking to a foreign authority, and they inevitably came to lose their self-respect, their self-reliance, and their national strength.

The system made them forget to look to themselves, and taught them to turn their backs upon their own country. We became the beggars of the rich neighbours who had robbed us. We lost reverence for our own nation, and we came very near to losing our national identity.

O'Connell was the product of the Ireland which arose out of this perversion. Prompted by the Young Irelanders, and urged on by the zeal of the people, stirred for the moment to national consciousness by the teaching of Davis, he talked of national liberty, but he did nothing to win it. He was a follower and not a leader of the people. He feared any movement of a revolutionary nature. Himself a Gaelic speaker, he adopted the English language, so little did he understand the strength to the nation of its own native language. His aim was little more than to see the Irish people a free Catholic community.

He would have Ireland merely a prosperous province of Britain with no national distinctiveness. Generally speaking, he acquiesced in a situation which was bringing upon the Irish nation spiritual decay.

The Young Irelanders, of whom Thomas Davis was the inspiration, were the real leaders.

They saw and felt more deeply and aimed more truly. Davis spoke to the soul of the sleeping nation—drunk with the waters of forgetfulness. He sought to unite the whole people. He fought against sectarianism and all the other causes which divided them.

He saw that unless we were Gaels we were not a nation. When he thought of the nation he thought of the men and women of the nation. He knew that unless they were free, Ireland could not be free, and to fill them again with pride in their nation he sang to them of the old splendour of Ireland, of their heroes, of their language, of the strength of unity, of the glory of noble strife, of the beauties of the land, of the delights and richness of the Gaelic life.

'A nationality founded in the hearts and intelligence of the people,' he said, 'would bid defiance to the arms of the foe and guile of the traitor. The first step to nationality is the open and deliberate recognition of it by the people themselves. Once the Irish people declare the disconnection of themselves, their feelings, and interests from the men, feelings, and interests of England, they are in march for freedom'.

That was the true National Gospel. 'Educate that you may be free', he said. 'It was only by baptism at the fount of Gaelicism that we would get the strength and ardour to fit us for freedom'.

The spirit of Davis breathed again in those who succeeded to his teaching, and who, directed by that inspiration, kept the footsteps of the nation on the right road for the march to freedom.

The Union was accompanied by both economic and national decay, and the movements of the nineteenth century were the outcome of those two evils.

But one was more a political than a national movement, unconscious of, or indifferent to, the fact that the nation was rapidly dying. Its policy was to concentrate on England and agitate for measures of reform and political emancipation. It was pleading to the spoilers for a portion of the spoils they had robbed from us.

But those who had succeeded to the teachings of Davis saw that if we continued to turn to England the nation would become extinct. We were tacitly accepting England's denial of our nationhood so useful for her propaganda purposes. We were selling our birthright for a mess of pottage.

They saw that the nation could only be preserved and freedom won by the Irish people themselves. We needed to become strong within our nation individually as the self-respecting, self-reliant men and women of the Irish nation; otherwise, we would never get into the 'march for freedom'.

The new movements were distinct, yet harmonious. They were all built on the same foundation—the necessity for national freedom. They all taught that the people must look to themselves for economic prosperity, and must turn to national culture as a means to national freedom.

They reached out to every phase of the people's lives, educating to make them free. No means were too slight to use for that purpose. The Gaelic Athletic Association reminded Irish boys that they were Gaels. It provided and restored national games as an alternative to the slavish adoption of English sport.

The Gaelic League restored the language to its place in the reverence of the people. It revived Gaelic culture. While being non-political, it was by its very nature intensely national. Within its folds were nurtured the men and women who were to win for Ireland the power to achieve national freedom. Irish history will recognise in the birth of the Gaelic League in 1893 the most important event of the nineteenth century. I may go further and say, not only the nineteenth century, but in the whole history of our nation. It checked the peaceful penetration and once and for all turned the minds of the Irish people back to their own country. It did more than any other movement to restore the national pride, honour, and self-respect. Through the medium of the language it linked the people with the past and led them to look to a future which would be a noble continuation of it.

The *Sinn Féin* movement was both economic and national, meeting, therefore, the two evils produced by the Union. Inspired by Arthur Griffith and William Rooney, it grew to wield enormous educational and spiritual power. It organised the country. It promoted what came to be known as the 'Irish-Ireland Policy'. It preached the recreation of Ireland built upon the Gael. It penetrated into Belfast and North-East Ulster, and was doing encouraging educational work, and was making the national revival general when the World War broke out in 1914.

If that work could have been completed, the freedom which has been won would have been completed. Until Ireland can speak to the world with a united distinctive voice, we shall not have earned, and shall not get, that full freedom in all its completeness which nations, that are nations, can never rest until they have achieved.

The *Sinn Féin* movement was not militant, but the militant movement existed within it, and by its side. It had for its advocates the two mightiest figures that have appeared in the whole present movement—Tom Clarke and Se n MacDermott.

The two movements worked in perfect harmony.

Rooney preached language and liberty. He inspired all whom he met with national pride and courage. 'Tell the world bravely what we seek', he said. 'We must be men if we mean to win'. He believed that liberty could not be won unless we were fit and willing to win it, and were ready to suffer and die for it.

He interpreted the national ideal as 'an Irish State governed by Irishmen for the benefit of the Irish people'. He sought to impregnate the whole people with 'a Gaelic-speaking Nationality'. 'Only then could we win freedom and be worthy of it; freedom—individual and national freedom—of the fullest and broadest character; freedom to think and act as it best beseems; national freedom to stand equally with the rest of the world'. He aimed at weaving Gaelicism into the whole fabric of our national life. He wished to have Gaelic songs sung by the children in the schools. He advocated the boycotting of English goods, always with an eye to the spiritual effect. 'We shall need to turn our towns into something more than mere huxters' shops, and as a natural consequence wells of anglicisation poisoning every section of our people'.

Only by developing our own resources, by linking up our life with the past, and adopting the civilization which was stopped by the Union could we become Gaels again, and help to win our nation back. As long as we were Gaels, he said, the influence of the foreigner was negligible in Ireland. Unless we were Gaels we had no claim to occupy a definite or distinct place in the world's life.

'We most decidedly do believe that this nation has a right to direct its own destinies. We do most heartily concede that men bred and native of the soil are the best judges of what is good for this land. We are believers in an Irish nation using its own tongue, flying its own flag, defending its own coasts, and using its own discretion when dealing with the outside world. But this we most certainly believe can never come as the gift of any parliament, British or otherwise; it can only be won by the strong right arm and grim resolve of men'. 'Neglect no weapon,' he urged, 'which the necessities and difficulties of the enemy force him to abandon to us, and make each concession a stepping-stone to further things'.

Rooney spoke as a prophet. He prepared the way and foresaw the victory, and he helped his nation to rise, and, by developing its soul, to get ready for victory.

A good tree brings forth good fruit—a barren one produces nothing. The policy represented by O'Connell, Isaac Butt, and John Redmond ended in impotence.

The freedom which Ireland has achieved was dreamed of by Wolfe Tone, was foreseen by Thomas Davis, and their efforts were broadened out until they took into their embrace all the true national movements by the 'grim resolve' of William Rooney, supported later by the 'strong right arm' of the Volunteers.

All the streams—economic, political, spiritual, cultural, and militant—met together in the struggle of 1916–21 which has ended in a Peace, in which the Treaty of Limerick is wiped out by the departure of the British armed forces, and the establishment of an Irish Army in their place. In which the Union is wiped out by the establishment of a free native Parliament which will be erected on a Constitution expressing the will of the Irish people.

With the Union came national enslavement. With the termination of the Union goes national enslavement, if we will. Freedom from any outside enemy is now ours, and nobody but ourselves can prevent us achieving it.

We are free now to get back and to keep all that was taken from us. We have no choice but to turn our eyes again to Ireland. The most completely anglicised person in Ireland will look to Britain in vain. Ireland is about to revolve once again on her own axis.

We shall no longer have anyone but ourselves to blame if we fail to use the freedom we have won to achieve full freedom. We are now on the natural and inevitable road to complete the work of Davis and Rooney, to restore our native tongue, to get back our history, to take up again and complete the education of our countrymen in the North-East in the national ideal, to renew our strength and

refresh ourselves in our own Irish civilization, to become again the Irish men and
Irish women of the distinctive Irish nation, to make real the freedom which Davis
sang of, which Rooney worked for, which Tom Clarke and Se n MacDermott and
their comrades fought and died for.

The British have given up their claim to dominate us. They have no longer any
power to prevent us making real our freedom. The complete fulfilment of our full
national freedom can, however, only be won when we are fit and willing to win it.

Can we claim that we are yet fit and willing? Is not our country still filled with
men and women who are unfit and unwilling? Are we all yet educated to be free?
Has not the greater number of us still the speech of the foreigner on our tongues?
Are not even we, who are proudly calling ourselves Gaels, little more than imitation Englishmen?

But we are free to remedy these things. Complete liberty—what it stands
for in our Gaelic imagination—cannot be got until we have impregnated the
whole of our people with the Gaelic desire. Only then shall we be worthy of the
fullest freedom.

The bold outline of freedom has been drawn by the glorious efforts of the last
five years; only the details remain to be filled in. Will not those who co-operated in
the conception and work of the masterpiece help with the finishing touches? Can
we not see that the little we have not yet gained is the expression of the falling
short of our fitness for freedom? When we make ourselves fit we shall be free. If we
could accept that truth we would be inspired again with the same fervour and
devotion by our own 'grim resolve' within the nation to complete the work which
is so nearly done.